INDEX TO AMERICAN REFERENCE BOOKS ANNUAL

1990-1994

A Cumulative Index to Subjects, Authors, and Titles

INDEX TO
AMERICAN REFERENCE BOOKS ANNUAL

1990-1994
A Cumulative Index to Subjects, Authors, and Titles

COMPILED BY ANNA GRACE PATTERSON
ASSISTED BY D. A. ROTHSCHILD

1994
LIBRARIES UNLIMITED, INC.
Englewood, Colorado

Copyright © 1994 Libraries Unlimited, Inc.
All Rights Reserved
Printed in the United States of America

No part of this publication may be reproduced, stored in a retrieval system, or transmitted, in any form or by any means, electronic, mechanical, photocopying, recording, or otherwise, without the prior written permission of the publisher.

LIBRARIES UNLIMITED. INC.
P.O. Box 6633
Englewood, CO 80155-6633
1-800-237-6124

LC 75-120328   ISBN 1-56308-272-1   ISSN 0192-6969

TABLE OF CONTENTS

Preface vii

AUTHORS AND TITLES 1

SUBJECTS 127

PREFACE

American Reference Books Annual (ARBA) is well established as a comprehensive source of reviews for all types of reference books published or distributed in the United States and Canada. The 25 annual volumes of ARBA, which began in 1970, contain more than 43,400 reviews of reference books. These titles include books on almost any topic in a variety of reference formats (e.g., almanacs, bibliographies, catalogs, dictionaries, encyclopedias, handbooks, indexes).

Access to each annual volume is provided through that volume's indexes of authors, titles, and subjects. Offering comprehensive access to authors, titles, and subjects, the cumulative index brings together five years of ARBA. Joseph Sprug prepared the first five-year volume, *Index to American Reference Books Annual 1970-1974*; Christine Gehrt-Wynar, *Index to American Reference Books Annual 1975-1979*; Ruth Blackmore, *Index to American Reference Books Annual 1980-1984*; and Anna Grace Patterson, *Index to American Reference Books Annual 1985-1989*. Although all the index volumes have contained author, title, and subject indexes, some variations in style and organization showing the unique hand of each volume's individual compiler exist among the volumes.

This five-year cumulation, *Index to American Reference Books Annual 1990-1994*, provides author, title, and subject access to all reviews in ARBA from 1990 to 1994. The cumulative index merges five years of information on published reference materials that have appeared in ARBA. Each entry in ARBA presents full bibliographic information, an evaluative review, and citations to professional journals containing other published reviews. The index is more than a location device; it is also a critical tool for the scholar, librarian, and reader seeking to tap ARBA's wealth of information.

This volume of the cumulative index covers 9,284 books reviewed during the 1990-1994 period. The author/title index provides access through author entries (e.g., Hunt, Gladys, 94n383) and through a title entry (e.g., Read for your life, 94n383). In order to offer a reasonable-sized book, short titles and abbreviated words within titles are used.

AUTHORS AND TITLES

The author/title index is arranged alphabetically word by word (when a word is abbreviated, it is filed as if it were spelled out). Multiple volumes of the same title are arranged numerically. Books with the same title published in different years are arranged chronologically. Acronyms are filed alphabetically as they appear. Numerals appear as if they were spelled out.

Author entries in the 1990-1994 index contain author's name with year and entry number.

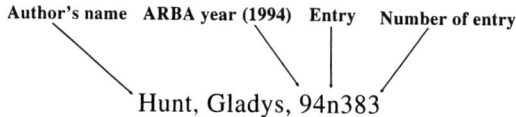

Hunt, Gladys, 94n383

Authors/editors/compilers appear in the index as their names are shown on the title page; therefore, if authors have written books under their full names, initials, or parts of both, they will appear under all forms in the index.

> Smith, J. L.
> Smith, John
> Smith, John L.

All single, joint, and corporate authors are individually indexed.

Titles appear in a shortened form in title entries. Ordinarily, subtitles are deleted. Usually, abbreviated words are filed as if they were spelled out. Entries show title, year of ARBA, and entry number.

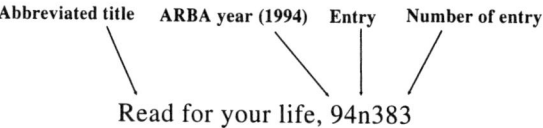

Read for your life, 94n383

SUBJECTS

The subject index, with a few variations, uses terms that are based upon the 12th edition of *Library of Congress Subject Headings*. This format allows easy access to titles from different years of ARBA. The subject terms are arranged alphabetically and ignore punctuation; therefore, one may find the following alphabetical arrangement:

> EUROPE
> EUROPE, EASTERN
> EUROPE—HISTORY
> EUROPE—POLITICS & GOVERNMENT

Each of these entries will have titles with year and entry number appearing beneath them:

> EUROPE
> Adult educ in continental Europe, 94n391
> Consumer Europe 1991, 92n173
> Slavic studies, 94n131

Cross-references, both *see* and *see also*, facilitate use of the index.

ACKNOWLEDGMENTS

Although many people have been involved in the preparation of this index, special appreciation goes to D. A. Rothschild for her work in compiling the author/title portion of this index and her assistance in data entry, David Porter for developing the computer program, Stephen Haenel for his technical advice, Pamela J. Getchell for her typesetting, and Bohdan S. Wynar for his encouragement and advice. Comments or suggestions for improvement of this index are encouraged.

Anna Grace Patterson

Author/Title Index

Reference is to year and entry number.

A. J. Lohwater's Russian-English dict of the mathematical scis, 2d ed, 91n1795
A. M. Klein: an annot bibliog, 94n1278
A Matter of Fact, staff of, 94n1851
A to Z of the Middle East, 92n118
A to zoo, 3d ed, 90n1082
A to zoo, 4th ed, 94n1176
AAAS hndbk 1989-90, 90n1435
AAAS hndbk 1993/94, 94n1579
AACJC membership dir 1989, 90n321
AACJC membership dir 1992, 93n359
AACR2 decisions & rule interpretations, 5th ed, 93n639
AALL annual meetings: an annot index of the recordings, 91n591
AARP Pharmacy Serv prescription drug hndbk, 2d ed, 93n1660
Aaseng, Nathan, 92n1454
Abate, Frank R., 92n425, 94n1084
ABC for bk collectors, 94n1026
ABC of stage lighting, 94n1475
ABCs of worship, 93n1423
Abel, Dean, 94n1662
Abel, Ernest L., 90n1689, 91n1692
ABMS compendium of certified medical specialists 1990-91, 91n1667
ABMS compendium suppl., 1991, 92n1665
Aboriginal religions in Austral., 92n1411
Aboriginal self-govt in Canada, 92n374
Aboriginality, 91n1038
Abortion: a ref hndbk, 93n851
Abortion & family planning bibliog for 1989-90, 93n850
Abortion debate in the US and Canada, 92n805
Abortion in the US, 92n1669
Abortion in the US, 1992 suppl, 94n1840
Aboussafy, David, 93n852
Abraham, Thomas, 93n1310
Abrams, A. Jay, 91n853
Abrams, Margaret Ann, 91n853
Abramson, Marcia, 90n781
Abreu, Maria Isabel, 90n1208
Abridged DDC & relative index, 12th ed, 91n617
Abromowitz, Jennifer, 92n851
Absalom! Absalom! a concordance to the novel, 91n1162
Abstracts in human-computer interaction, v.1: issue 2, June 1990, 92n1704
Abstracts of active projects FY 1990, 91n1671
Abu-Irmaileh, B. E., 92n1547
Aby, Stephen H., 92n266
Academic American ency, 90n45, 93n57
Academic laboratory chemical hazards gdbk, 92n1728
Academic Press dict of sci & tech, 93n1444
Academic yr abroad, 93n392
Academic yr abroad 1989/90, 90n345
Academy of Sciences MPR, 92n96
Acadiensis index, 1971-91, 93n526
Accardi, Bernard, 93n1301
ACCC dir of Canadian colleges & insts, 93n362
Access Canada 1990, 91n104
Access Nippon '92 business hndbk, 94n241
Access register 1988, 90n553
Access to ...
    art, 90n957
    UK higher educ, 93n380
    US govt info, 91n46
ACCIS gd to UN info sources on health, 94n1811
Accountants' index, 37th suppl, 91n169
Accounting research dir, 2d ed, 90n197
Accredited insts of postsecondary educ, 1990-91, 92n290
Accredited insts of postsecondary educ, programs, candidates, 1992-93, 94n347
Accrocco, Joseph O., 92n1772
ACEI Bibliography of Books for Children Committee, 1989, 90n1078
Acid rain: a bibliog of Canadian fed & provincial govt docs, 92n1769
Acid rain abstracts annual 1988, 90n1796
Ackelson, Richard W., 93n1265
Ackerman, Robert J., 91n880
ACM gd to computing lit 1988, 91n1720
Acocella, Nicholas, 94n831
ACRL dir of curriculum materials centers 1990, 92n291
ACRL univ lib stats 1988-89, 91n656
Acronym bk: acronyms in aerospace & defense, 91n675
Acronyms, initialisms & abbrevs dict 1992, v.1, 93n1
Acrosport, 94n817
Action art, 94n1039
Action gd to govt grants, loans, & giveaways, 94n895
Active figures of the trade union & working class movement of Russia, Ukraine, Bielorussia, & Kazakhstan, 94n262
Activist's almanac, 94n865
Ada lang vocabulary, 93n1677
Adamczyk, Alice J., 90n1314
Adamec, Christine, 93n866
Adamec, Ludwig W., 93n121
Adams, Barbara K., 92n1140
Adams, Cassandra, 92n1600
Adams, Janelle P., 90n330, 90n331
Adams, Jerome R., 92n108
Adams, Jon-K, 90n712
Adams, K. Gary, 90n1238
Adams, Mark, 91n92
Adams, Ramon F., 90n471
Adams, Raymond J., Jr., 93n1539
Adams, Robert W., 90n58, 92n242
Adams, Russ, 91n1612
Aday, Ron H., 90n782
Address bk for Germanic genealogy, 4th ed, 93n454
Ade, Robin, 90n772
Adele Wiseman: an annot bibliog, 94n1277
Adelman, Elizabeth Fagan, 94n421
Adelman, George, 91n1639
Adey, Robert, 93n1150
Adler, Larry, 93n830
Administrative sci quarterly cum index 1956-85, 90n265
Admirals of the new steel navy, 91n691
Adolescent pregnancy & parenthood, 91n894
Adoption choices, 93n869
Adoption dir, 90n799
Adoption lit for children & young adults, 93n868
Adoption resource gd, 2d ed, 92n822
Adrian, J., 90n1454
Adrian, M., 90n819

Adrienne, 92n1066
Adrienne's dict: English/French, 92n1066
Adult basic educ collection, 91n352
Adult basic educ English as a 2d lang collection, 92n329
Adult educ in continental Europe: 1986-88, 91n377
Adult educ in continental Europe: 1989-91, 94n391
Adult learner's gd to alternative & external degree programs, 94n393
Advanced research methodology, 92n73
Advances in ...
　librarianship, v.15, 93n627
　lib admin & org, v.7, 90n587
　lib admin & org, v.8, 90n588
　lib automation & networking, v.3, 90n616
　serials mgmt, v.3, 91n615
Adventure vacations, 92n433
Adventurers afloat, 90n1822
Adventuring in Austral., 91n466
Adventuring in B.C., 93n503
Adventuring in E Africa, 91n465
Adventuring in N.Z., 94n482
Adventuring in the Caribbean, 91n476
Adventuring with bks, 9th ed, 90n1075
Adventuring with bks, 10th ed, 94n1173
Adversary system, 91n568
Advertising ratios & budgets, 94n287
Advisory Committee for the Coordination of Information Systems (ACCIS), 94n788
Advisory Committee for the Co-ordination of Information Systems (ACCIS), 92n736
Adweek agency dir 1992, 92n238
Aerial atlas of ancient Crete, 94n529
Aerospace tech centres, 90n1579
Affairs in order, 92n817
Affordable housing, 90n967
Afghanistan, 93n122
Africa, 92n474
Africa: a gd to ref material, 94n94
Africa, rev ed, 90n104
Africa south of the Sahara 1990, 91n90
Africa south of the Sahara 1993, 94n91
Africa today, 1990 rev. ed, 91n437
African American biogs, 93n423
African American ency, 94n402
African American generals, 94n685
African American: social & economic conditions, 94n405
African American women, 94n960
African American writers, 92n1156
African archaeology, 94n488
African birds of prey, 92n1571
African bk world & pr, 4th ed, 90n642
African heritage of American English, 94n1081
African music, 93n1241
African names, 94n443
African pol facts since 1945, 2d ed, 92n704
African socio-economic indicators 1989, 94n92
African states & rulers, 90n503
African studies companion, 91n93
African studies thesaurus, 94n629
African theology, 94n1508
African women: a general bibliog, 1976-85, 90n850
African-American community studies from N America, 92n346
African-American traditions in song, sermon, tale, & dance, 1600s-1920, 92n874
Afro-American sources in Va., 91n391
Afro-Spanish American author 2: the 1980s, 91n1245
AFVA evaluations 1991, 93n395
Age of maturity, 1929-41, 90n1069
Agenda world: Jan 1991, worldwide ed, 92n239
AGI data sheets, 3d ed, 91n1781
Aging & sensory change, 90n781
Aging with style & savvy, 91n843
Agnes Moorehead: a bio-bibliog, 94n1413
Agos, Letitia, 90n1741
Agricultural research centres, 9th ed, 90n1446

Agricultural sftwr dir 1990, 91n1475
Agriculture dict, 93n1468
Agur, Anne M. R., 92n1646
AHE vendor dir for acquisitions librarians, 90n595
Ahlstrom, Trudy, 91n1488
Ahmed, Saleem, 90n1485
Ahtna Athabaskan dict, 92n1063
AIDS, 92n1677
AIDS: abstracts of the psychological & behavioral lit 1983-89, 2d ed, 91n1687
AIDS: abstracts of the psychological & behavioral lit 1983-91, 3d ed, 93n1650
AIDS & women, 92n1680
AIDS bibliog for 1981-86, 90n1680
AIDS crisis in America, 94n1852
AIDS dir, 94n1850
AIDS dissidents, 94n1856
AIDS funding, 93n1653
AIDS info sourcebk 1991-92, 92n1678
AIDS 1988 pt.2, 90n1679
AIDS: 1,000 full-text statistical abstracts from the A Matter of Fact database, 1984-92, 94n1851
AIIM speakers dir 1992-93, 93n1668
Aiken, S. G., 91n1531
Aiki News ency of aikido, 93n838
Aiki News 1994 dojo finder, 94n854
Aimiller, Kurt, 91n965
Air almanac 1990, 91n1816
Air pollution control, 90n1792
Air wars & aircraft, 91n685
Air-conditioning glossary, 91n1635
Aircraft carriers of the US navy, 2d ed, 90n670
Airline safety, 92n1793
Aissing, Alena, 92n1086
Aitken, Barbara B., 91n514
Akins, Imogene, 90n700, 94n743
Al Jolson: a bio-discography, 94n1365
ALA survey of librarian salaries 1993, 94n613
ALA yrbk of lib & info servs, v.14, 90n589
ALA yrbk of lib & info servs, v.15, 91n610
Aladdin/Imperial labels, 92n1299
Alain, J. M., 92n755
Alali, A. Odasuo, 92n883
Alaska place names, 4th ed, 92n426
Alaska wilderness milepost 1989, 90n439
Alaskan histl docs since 1867, 90n97
Albala, Elie, 94n1890
Albala, Leila, 91n188, 93n227
Albanian-English dict, 94n1109
Albert, George, 90n1277, 91n1311
Albert Roussel: a bio-bibliog, 90n1242
Alberta bibliog, 93n135
Albinski, Nan Bowman, 94n123
Albrecht, Gerhard, 94n706
Albright, Ronald G., 90n1624
Album of sci, 90n1421
Alchemy in Europe, 91n1763
Alcock, Harry, 91n603
Alcohol/drug abuse dict & ency, 90n821
Alcohol-related issues in the Latino population 1980-90, 94n915
Alcorn, Marianne Sidorski, 93n596
Alden Nowlan papers, 94n1276
Alderson, A. D., 94n1135
Alderton, David, 92n1560, 93n1536, 94n1704, 94n1705
Aldighieri, Ann Marie, 92n1777
Aldiss, Margaret, 93n1154
Alec Wilder: a bio-bibliog, 94n1324
Alessandro & Domenico Scarlatti: a gd to research, 94n1334
Alessandro Stradella (1639-1682): a thematic cat of his compositions, 92n1263
Alexander, Fran, 93n680
Alexander, Harriet Semmes, 90n1063
Alexander, Patrick H., 90n1407
Alexander, Robert J., 93n777
Alexander, Sharon, 94n1179

Alexander Tcherepnin: a bio-bibliog, 90n1239
Alford, B. W. E., 94n263
Alford, John A., 94n1253
Alfred Glossbrenner's master gd to free sftwr for IBMs & compatible computers, 90n1729
Alfred Hitchcock: a gd to refs & resources, 94n1450
Algeo, Adele S., 93n1064
Algeo, John, 93n1064
Alger, Mark S. M., 90n1751
Ali, Sheikh R., 90n672, 93n781
Alibert, Eric, 92n1524
Alice Faye: a bio-bibliog, 91n1360
Alice Walker: an annot bibliog 1968-86, 90n1157
Alilunas-Rodgers, Kristine, 94n122
ALISE Library & info sci educ statl report 1991, 92n576
Alkin, Marvin C., 93n331
Alkire, Leland G., Jr., 93n86
All about tropical fish, 4th ed, 90n1551
All music gd, 94n1314
All that the rain promises & more, 92n1542
Allaby, Ailsa, 92n1730
Allaby, Michael, 90n1791, 92n1730, 93n1529
Allan, Barbara, 90n1661
Allard, Denise M., 91n977
Allardice, Pamela, 92n1319
Allcock, John B., 94n722
Allen, Anne, 91n772
Allen, Beverly J., 92n1335
Allen, Bill, 91n140
Allen County Public Library Foundation, staff of, 90n397, 90n398
Allen County Public Library Genealogy Department, staff of, 90n397, 90n398, 92n394, 94n438
Allen, Geoffrey, 91n1774
Allen, Gerald R., 92n1577
Allen, Hayward, 94n413
Allen, R. E., 91n1048
Allen, Rebecca S., 92n373
Allen, Richard, 91n1260
Allen, Robert, 92n1017
Allen, Thomas B., 93n556
Allied Artists checklist, 94n1445
Allin, Craig W., 91n452
All-in-one business contactbk 1990, 91n136
Allis, James B., 93n1393
Allison, A. F., 91n1440
Allison, Sonia, 92n1483
Alliums, 94n1653
Allott, Angela M., 94n633
Allstate Motor Club RV park & campground dir 1990, 91n809
Allswang, John M., 93n793
Almanac of ...
    American pols 1990, 91n725
    American pols 1994, 94n746
    American presidents from 1789 to the present, 93n519
    British pols, 4th ed, 92n717
    bus & industrial financial ratios, 1990 ed, 91n233
    Canadian pols, 93n764
    consumer markets 1990-91, 90n222
    famous people, 4th ed, 90n28
    higher educ 1989-90, 90n332
    higher educ 1992, 93n355
    modern terrorism, 92n557
    renewable energy, 94n1983
    sci & tech, 91n1466
    the Bible, 93n1435
    the canning, freezing, preserving industries 1990-91, 92n1478
    the Christian world, 93n1415
    the 50 states, 1992 ed, 93n909
    transatlantic pols 1991-92, 92n675
    US seapower 1989, 91n690
Almeder, Robert F., 94n1495
Almond, Joseph P., Sr., 92n1599
Almquist, Sharon G., 94n1351
Alopecia, 91n1691
Alphabetical list of titles of fed statues, 92n550

Alpine wildflowers of the Rocky Mountains, 91n1525
ALSA swimmer's gd, 1993 ed, 94n861
Alston, Jon P., 94n222
Alston, R. C., 92n1189
Altbach, Philip G., 90n683, 91n341, 93n381
Alternative dir of nongovtl orgs in S Asia, rev. ed, 91n39
Alternative dispute resolution for the community, 91n565
Alternative dispute resolution sourcebk, 1993-94 ed, 94n579
Alternative health care resources, 94n1843
Alternative pr index, Jan-Mar 1991, v.23, no.1, 92n53
Alternative pr pubs of children's bks, 3d ed, 90n637
Alternative pubns, 91n672
Altham, Elizabeth, 90n402
Altman, Roberta, 92n1780, 94n1858
Alun Hoddinott: a bio-bibliog, 94n1322
Alvarez, Ruth M., 92n1179
Alves, Michael J., 91n314
Alvey, Christine E., 94n630
Alyson almanac, 90n812
Alzheimer's disease: abstracts of the psychological & behavioral lit, 91n1689
Alzheimer's, stroke, & 29 other neurological disorders sourcebk, 94n1862
Ambrose, Paul V., 92n942
Ambry, Margaret, 93n906, 94n283, 94n927
Ambry, Margaret K., 90n222, 92n171
America & the Indochina wars, 1945-90, 93n733
America in space, 92n1594
America votes 19, 92n696
America votes 20, 94n756
American & Canadian doctoral dissertations & master's theses on Africa, 1974-87, 91n91
American animated films: the silent era, 1897-1929, 91n1365
American Antiquarian Society, staff of, 94n657
American architects, 90n970
American art dir 1989-90, 90n958
American art dir 1991-92, 92n983
American artists' materials, v.2, 93n1027
American artists: signatures & monograms, 1800-1989, 91n1018
American Association for the Advancement of Science, Office of Communications, 90n1433
American Association of Individual Investors, 90n211
American automobile collections & museums, 94n2026
American Banker's banking factbk 1991, 93n236
American battle monuments, 91n680
American best sellers, 90n1130
American bibliog of Slavic & E European studies for 1990, 94n130
American big businesses dir, 1993 ed, 94n161
American bk publishing record annual cum 1988, 90n11
American bk publishing record cum 1989, 91n8
American bk publishing record cum 1991, 93n26
American bk trade dir 1990-91, 91n660
American bk trade dir 1991-92, 92n631
American bk trade dir 1993-94, 94n661
American capitols, 92n997
American Chamber of Commerce in Italy dir 1992, 94n268
American Civil Liberties Union: an annot bibliog, 94n550
American college president, 1636-1989, 92n271
American comic strip collections, 1884-1939, 91n1035
American communes 1860-1960, 91n851
American communes to 1860, 91n848
American constitution, 92n524
American Consultants League, 90n199
American Consultants League dir 1989, 90n199
American cultural leaders from colonial times to the present, 94n976
American defense annual, 1990-91, 92n652
American dir of organized labor, 93n306
American drama criticism, suppl.2 to the 2d ed, 90n1129
American drama criticism, suppl.3 to the 2d ed, 93n1168
American drama 1918-60, 93n1380
American educators' ency, 93n330
American electricians' hndbk, 12th ed, 93n1587
American ethnic lits, 94n1225
American evangelicalism, 92n1408

American export register 1992, 93n318
American farm crisis, 90n1441
American field serv archives of WW I, 1914-17, 90n657
American forecaster almanac 1990, 90n228
American foreign policy index, v.1, no.1, 94n759
American garden gdbk West, 90n1470
American graphic design, 94n1059
American Heritage college dict, 3d ed, 94n1075
American Heritage dict, 2d college ed, 93n1055
American Heritage Dictionary, editors of, 90n1032
American Heritage dict of the English lang, 3d ed, 93n1056
American Heritage Dictionaries, editors of, 94n1095
American Heritage illus hist of the US, 90n494
American higher educ, 94n323
American hist: a bibliographic review, v.4, 91n480
American hist for children & young adults, 91n487
American homelessness, 91n850
American Horticultural Society, 93n1487
American Horticultural Society ency of garden plants, 90n1467
American Horticultural Society ency of gardening, 94n1617
American humanities index for 1987, v.13, 90n885
American humanities index for 1991, v.17, 93n945
American imprints on art through 1865, 91n1003
American Indian: a multimedia ency, 94n414
American Indian ghost dance, 1870 & 1890, 92n372
American Indian lits, 92n1149
American Indian ref bks for children & young adults, 92n370
American Indian resource materials in the W hist collections, Univ of Okla., 92n364
American Indian women, 92n358
American intelligence, 1775-1990, 93n785
American Jewish Committee, 90n377
American Jewish yr bk 1989, 90n377
American Jewish yr bk 1992, 93n439
American journalism hist, 90n904
American law dict, 92n535
American leaders 1789-1991, 92n680
American legislative leaders, 1850-1910, 90n692
American Lib Assn best of the best for children, 94n1163
American Library Association Reference Books Bulletin Editorial Board, 94n3
American lib dir 1989-90, 90n582
American lib dir 1990-91, 91n607
American lib dir 1992-93, 93n623
American lib dir 1993-94, 94n610
American lib hist, 90n580
American literary biographers: 1st series, 92n1154
American literary biographers, 2d series, 93n50
American literary mags, 93n1163
American lobbyists dir 1990, 91n742
American mag journalists, 1850-1900, 90n906
American mag journalists, 1900-60: 1st series, 91n963
American manufacturers dir, 1993 ed, 94n212
American masses & requiems, 92n1302
American mass-market mags, 91n63
American Medical Assn ency of medicine, 91n1657
American Medical Assn manual of style, 8th ed, 90n895
American men & women of sci 1989-90, 90n1420
American men & women of sci 1992-93, 93n1438
American military cemeteries, 93n706
American musical theatre: a chronicle, 2d ed, 93n1385
American musicologists 1890-1945, 90n1217
American natl election studies data sourcebk, 1952-86, 91n751
American nursing, v.2, 93n1659
American orchestral music, 94n1347
American originals, 90n54
American peace movement, 93n791
American peace writers, editors, & pers, 92n752
American photographers, 90n942
American playwrights since 1945, 90n1366
American poetry index, v.4, 90n1159
American poets since WW II, 3d series, 93n1186
American pol leaders from colonial times to the present, 92n681
American pol movies, 91n1377
American pol prints 1766-1876, 93n735

American presidents, 7th ed, 91n496
American presidents: an annotated bibliog, 91n481
American profile—opinions & behavior, 1972-89, 92n79
American public opinion index 1989, 92n72
American regional cookery index, 90n1462
American Revolution 1775-1783: an ency, 94n503
American sacred music imprints 1698-1810, 91n1291
American salaries & wages survey, 92n223
American salaries & wages survey, 2d ed, 94n282
American shortline railway gd, 4th ed, 92n1799
American short-story writers, 1880-1910, 90n1133
American short-story writers, 1910-45: 1st series, 91n1156
American short-story writers, 1910-45: 2d series, 92n1164
American small city profiles, 94n941
American social leaders, 94n78
American stats index 1988, 90n837
American studies, 91n485
American suburbs, 94n946
American synagogue hist, 90n379
American theater & drama research, 92n1385
American theatre hist, 93n1381
American univs & colleges, 14th ed, 93n363
American West, 90n103
American wholesalers & distrs dir, 93n245
American wills & admins in the Prerogative Court of Canterbury, 1610-1857, 90n389
American Wind Symphony commissioning project, 93n1284
American women & the US armed forces, 93n707
American women artists past & present, v.2, 90n865
American women civil rights activists, 94n592
American women in sport, 1887-1987, 90n758
American women playwrights, 1900-30, 93n1167
American women playwrights 1964-89, 94n1228
American women sculptors, 92n1005
American women songwriters, 94n1325
American women writers on Vietnam, 91n1145
American women's fiction 1790-1870, 91n1155
American women's mags, 90n880
American writers, suppl.3, 92n1151
American-Jewish media dir, 1989, 90n890
Americanos, P. J., 92n1547
Americans in Paris, 1900-30, 90n472
America's black colleges, 94n330
America's elderly, 90n790
America's fed jobs, 92n216
America's labor leaders, 90n261
America's lowest cost colleges, 92n296
America's natl battlefield parks, 92n445
America's new fndns 1992, 93n870
America's phone bk 1989-90, 91n137
America's secret recreation areas, 94n476
America's top military careers, 94n690
America's top rated cities, 1992 ed, 94n943
America's top 300 jobs, 91n241, 94n276
Ameringer, Charles D., 94n720
Ames, Charlotte A., 91n311
Ames, Kenneth L., 91n978
AMI, v.9, issue 1, 91n968
Amick, Irene, 92n198
Ammann, Daniel, 93n1067
Ammer, Christine, 90n651, 90n1675
Ammerman, Robert T., 94n1845
Ammirato, Philip V., 91n1517
Ammon, Bette D., 93n1140, 94n1182
Ammon, Harry, 92n452
Amnesty Intl: the 1993 report on human rights around the world, 94n591
Among the Periodicals Committee, 1989, 90n1078
Amphibians & reptiles in Kans., 3d ed, 94n1749
Amphibians & reptiles of La., 90n1566
Amphibians & reptiles of the W Indies, 93n1579
Amusement park gd, 92n774
Anabolic steroids & sports, 93n1666
Anaesthesia A-Z, 94n1874
Analogy bk of related words, 92n1057

Anarchist thinkers & thought, 93n778
Anastas, Walter, 93n980
Anastazievsky, Walter, 93n981
Anatomy of a house, 92n995
Anaya, Alison, 90n321
ANC & black workers in S Africa, 1912-92, 94n103
Ancestry's concise genealogical dict, 90n384
Ancestry's red bk, 90n387
Ancestry's red bk, rev ed, 93n455
Ancient & shining ones, 94n1392
Ancient America, 92n472
Ancient Egypt, 91n542
Ancient Greece, 91n540
Ancient Rome, 91n539
Anderson, Bruce N., 91n189
Anderson, Dorothy, 90n896
Anderson, Erland, 94n1266
Anderson, Ewan A., 94n794
Anderson, James, 91n1296
Anderson, James D., 92n1186, 93n1187
Anderson, James M., 93n506
Anderson, John R., 93n1650
Anderson, Kenneth N., 92n1658
Anderson, Lois E., 92n1658
Anderson, Patricia, 92n817
Anderson, Patricia J., 93n689
Anderson, Vicki, 92n1115, 94n1196
Anderson's dir of criminal justice educ 1991, 92n538
Andonian, Cathleen Culotta, 90n1204
Andrew, Geoff, 91n1386
Andrew Jackson: a bibliog, 92n458
Andrew Johnson: a bibliog, 94n495
Andrews, Alice C., 94n321
Andrews, Deborah, 92n20
Andrews, Jean, 93n1522
Andrews, Joyce, 90n1048
Andrews, Phyllis, 90n818
Andrews, Robert, 90n81, 94n1689
Andreyeva, Victoria, 94n1128
Andriot, Donna, 91n896, 92n422, 94n55
Andriot, Jay, 91n896
Andriot, Laurie, 91n896
Ang mahalaga sa buhay, 93n1102
Angeles, Peter A., 94n1496
Angelo, Joseph A., Jr., 93n805
Anglo-American trade dir 1993, 94n264
Anglo-Irish lit, 91n1239
Angola, 94n96
Angus Wilson: a bibliog 1947-87, 90n1189
Animal anatomy on file, 91n1509
Animal health yrbk 1990, 92n1509
Animal life, 94n1685
Animal production: quarterly stats 1—1991, 92n1469
Animals around the world, 93n1530
Animated TV specials, 91n974
Ann Petry: a bio-bibliog, 94n1237
Ann Sothern: a bio-bibliog, 91n1352
Anna Freud: a gd to research, 91n790
Annals of the Metropolitan Opera, 91n1295
Anne Baxter: a bio-bibliog, 93n1318
Anne Bradstreet: a ref gd, 91n1157
Annotated bibliog for teaching conflict resolution in schools, 2d ed, 91n290
Annotated bibliog of ...
   aboriginal-controlled justice programs in Canada, 93n569
   Canadian demography 1983-89, 91n906
   criticism on Andre Gide 1973-88, 92n1233
   faculty status in lib & info sci, 93n634
   Latin American sport, 91n801
   natl sources of adult educ stats, 91n353
   N American doctoral disserations on old English lang & lit, 90n1165
   Puerto Rican bibliogs, 91n122
   S American English, 91n1065
   the official langs of Canada, 94n1068
   the Peshitta of the O.T., 90n1387
Annotated bibliog on rodent research in Latin America, 1960-85, 90n1556
Annotated bibliogs of mineral deposits in Europe, pt.2, 92n1743
Annotated checklist of the birds of Tenn., 91n1568
Annotated critical bibliog of ...
   Alfred, Lord Tennyson, 90n1186
   Augustan poetry, 91n1223
   James Joyce, 91n1240
   Joseph Conrad, 93n1207
   Langland, 92n1204
   Thomas Hardy, 90n1179
   William Morris, 92n1207
Annotated index of medieval women, 93n933
Annotated index to the commentary on John Gower's Confessio Amantis, 91n1208
Annotated list of Ont. lepidoptera, 93n1550
Annotations for the selected works of William Makepeace Thackeray, 91n1219
Annual & biennial exhibition record of the Whitney Museum of American Art 1918-89, 92n977
Annual bibliog of modern art, 1990, 93n1015
Annual dir of world leaders 1988-89, 90n681
Annual exhibition record of ...
   the Art Inst of Chicago 1888-1950, 92n978
   the Natl Academy of Design 1901-50, 91n1021
   the Pa. Academy of the Fine Arts, v.2, 91n1008
   the Pa. Academy of the Fine Arts, v.3, 91n1009
Annual obituary 1986, 90n29
Annual obituary 1990, 92n20
Annual register 1988, 90n704
Annual register 1991, 93n725
Annual register of grant support 1989, 90n802
Annual register of grant support, 26th ed, 94n888
Annual review of ...
   info sci & tech, v.25, 92n569
   info sci & tech, v.26, 93n628
   info sci & tech, v.27, 94n614
Annual stats of medical school libs in the US & Canada 1987-88, 91n654
Anshel, Mark H., 92n771
Ansley, Kenneth J., 91n641
Antarctica: an ency, 92n92
Anthologies of music, 2d ed, 94n1319
Anthony Milner: a bio-bibliog, 90n1253
Anthropological lit: an index to per articles & essays, v.2, nos.1-2, 91n381
Anthropology in use, 93n417
Anthropology of aging, 92n813
Anthropology of war, 90n647
Antiquarian cats of musical interest, 90n1225
Antiquarian, specialty, & used bk sellers 1993, 94n662
Antiquing in England, 91n979
Antisemitism: an annot bibliog, v.2, 92n377
Antonarakis, Stylianos E., 91n1679, 93n1624
Antonin Dvorak on records, 93n1262
Antonio Gardano: Venetian music printer 1538-69, 90n1214
Anzovin, Steven, 90n706
APA membership register, 1991, 93n802
Apartheid: a selective annotated bibliog, 1979-87, 91n842
Apel, Willi, 91n1264
Appalachian authors, 91n1146
Appel, Marsha C., 90n964, 94n1050
Appel, Robert, 91n1303
Appleby, Amy, 91n872
Appleton, Barbara, 94n471
Appleton, Richard, 94n471
Applied & decorative arts, 2d ed, 94n1022
Applied sci & tech index [CD-ROM], 93n1457
Applied sci & tech index 1990, 92n1468
Appropriate word, 91n1079
Apresjan, Yuri D., 93n1092
Apseloff, Marilyn Fain, 90n1076
Aquaculture sourcebk, 94n1594

Aquila, Richard, 90n1291
Aramaic bibliog, pt.1, 94n1071
Arbena, Joseph L., 91n801
Archaeological gd to Mexico's Yucatan peninsula, 94n481
Archaeology hndbk, 93n507
Archambault, Ariane, 90n1018, 93n1101, 94n1114
Architect's detail lib, 91n1032
Architect's hndbk of marble, granite, & stone, 91n1024
Architectural detailing for commercial construction, 92n994
Archives accessions annual 1988, 91n26
Archives & mss repositories in the USSR: Ukraine & Moldavia, 90n523
Archives of data-processing hist, 91n1731
Arctic, 90n115
Ardagh, John, 93n143
Arden, Heather M., 94n1282
Arden, Lorraine, 90n961
Arden, Lynie, 93n308
Are you at risk?, 92n1675
Arends, J. C., 94n1649
Arestis, Philip, 93n177
Argentina, 93n152
Argillaceous rock atlas, 92n1737
Argyle, Christopher, 92n504, 93n551
Arias, Enrique Alberto, 90n1239
Arizona game birds, 90n1529
Arizona legal research gd, 93n596
Arkansas made, v.1, 92n919
Arkansas made, v.2, 92n920
Arkansas mammals, rev ed, 91n1597
Arkin, Frieda, 91n1496
Arlen, Shelley, 92n1132
Armenian American almanac, 2d ed, 91n386
Armenian genocide, 93n530
Armenian yellow pages 1991, 92n342
Armenians: a colossal bibliographic gd to bks published in the English lang, 94n129
Armenians & Iran, 92n496
Armitage, Allan M., 94n1623
Armitage, Susan, 93n941
Arms control & disarmament, defense & military, intl security, & peace, 90n673
Arms control, disarmament, & military security dict, 90n675
Armstrong, C. J., 92n589, 92n1716, 92n1717
Armstrong, Julia I., 91n1037
Armstrong, Mary Willems, 91n1387
Armstrong, Richard B., 91n1387
Armstrong, Robert D., 93n678
Armstrong, Robert H., 91n1557, 93n1528
Army dict & desk ref, 93n717
Arndt, Thomas, 94n1690
Arnold, Ben, 94n1305
Arnold, Guy, 92n101, 92n653
Arnold, Peter, 90n759, 90n770
Arnold, Tim, 93n1523
Aronoff, Craig E., 93n178
Arora, David, 92n1542
Arora, Renu, 92n1529
Arozena, Steven, 94n647
Arpan, Jeffrey S., 94n213
ARRL hndbk for radio amateurs 1993, 94n1015
Art & architecture in Canada, 92n967
Art & architecture thesaurus, 91n618
Art & architecture thesaurus, suppl.1, 93n635
Art diary intl 1990, 92n987
Art, Henry, 94n1994
Art index, 93n1030
Art index, Nov 89-Oct 90, 92n992
Art mktg sourcebk, 94n1045
Art of black American women, 94n1046
Art of the piano, 91n1287
Art on screen, 93n1016
Art price index intl '94, 94n1049
Art world dir: arts review yrbk 1993, 94n1044
Artello, Mary Ann, 94n1809

Arthur Symons: a bibliog, 92n1212
Arthurian dict, 91n1184
Artibise, Alan F. J., 92n97
Artificial intelligence abstracts annual 1988, 90n1704
Artificial intelligence abstracts annual 1991, 94n1888
Artificial intelligence & instruction, 91n1716
Artificial intelligence dict, 92n1703
Artificial intelligence vocabulary, 90n1706
Artigau, Jean-Pierre, 92n1566
Artisthelp, 91n877
Artists as illustrators, 90n959
Artists in Mich., 1900-76, 90n947
Artists in quotation, 90n966
Artist's market, 1991, 91n1017
Artists' monograms & indiscernible signatures, 92n984
Artists of the Pacific Northwest, 94n1042
Artists of the page, 93n1022
Arts & entertainment fads, 91n1338
ArtSpeak, 92n988
A's & B's of academic scholarships, 12th ed, 90n330
A's & B's of academic scholarships, 16th ed, 94n363
Asante, Molefi K., 92n343
Ascione, Michele, 93n1761
Asdell's patterns of mammalian reproduction, 94n1731
Ash, Irene, 90n1752, 93n1709, 93n1710, 94n1932, 94n1942
Ash, Lee, 94n656
Ash, Michael, 90n1752, 93n1709, 93n1710, 94n1932, 94n1942
Ashe, traditional religion & healing in sub-Saharan Africa & the Diaspora, 91n1409
Ashford, Nigel, 92n727
Ashley dict, 90n1040
Ashworth, William, 92n1773
Asia & the Pacific, 92n93
Asia 1992 yrbk, 94n106
Asia today, rev ed, 92n412
Asian American lit, 90n1122
Asian American media ref gd, 2d ed, 92n910
Asian American studies, 90n474
Asian Americans info dir, 93n421
Asian finance dir, 1990 ed, 91n209
Asian markets, 2d ed, 92n240
Asia-Pacific/Africa-Middle East petroleum dir, 1993, 94n1971
Asimov, Isaac, 90n1440, 91n1755, 93n549
Asimov's chronology of the world, 93n549
ASM engineered materials ref bk, 90n1598
ASM hndbk, v.3, 91n1792
ASM hndbk, v.18, 93n1604
ASM International, Editorial Staff, 90n1598
ASM International Handbook Committee, 93n1604
ASM materials engineering dict, 91n1793
Aspen dict of health care admin, 90n1612
Assassination of John F. Kennedy, 94n494
Assistance & benefits info dir, 93n887
Associate degree nursing educ, 92n1687
Associated Pr world atlas, 90n405
Association for Library Service to Children, 93n1128
Association of American univ prs dir 1988-89, 90n633
Association of American univ prs dir 1990-91, 92n632
Associations Canada 1991, 92n44
Associations Canada 1992, 93n65
Associations yellow bk, v.2, no.1, 93n319
Aster, Sidney, 92n709
Asthma resources dir, 91n1690
ASTM, 92n1614, 94n1578
Astronomer's sourcebk, 93n1701
Astronomy & astrophysics ency, 93n1704
Athearn, Robert G., 90n494
Atherton, Derek P., 93n1674
Athey, Raymond, 93n1494
Atiya, Aziz S., 92n1414
Atkins, Beryl T., 94n1113
Atkins, P. J., 91n111
Atkins, Robert, 92n988
Atkins, Stephen E., 90n673, 94n585
Atkins, Thomas V., 90n597

Atkinson, Janet I., 90n99
Atkinson, Michael, 92n909
Atlantic Canadian imprints, 1801-20, 92n13
Atlantic Canadian lit in English, 92n1227
Atlas florae Europaeae, 90n1494
Atlas of ...
   Alta. lakes, 92n410
   American higher educ, 94n321
   American Indian affairs, 92n375
   American sport, 94n819
   Ark., 90n98
   breeding birds in Pa., 94n1694
   breeding birds of Mich., 93n1539
   British overseas expansion, 92n487
   British social & economic hist since c. 1700, 90n151
   cats of the world, 91n1576
   China, 91n438
   Columbus & the great discoveries, 91n427
   communism, 92n733
   conures, 94n1690
   discus of the world, 92n1575
   disease distributions, 90n1634
   dog breeds of the world, 91n1580, 94n1710
   endangered animals, 94n1686
   endangered places, 94n1987
   environmental issues, 90n1788
   human anatomy, 90n1635
   intl migration, 94n428
   legendary places, 91n1332
   livebearers of the world, 94n1721
   medieval Jewish hist, 93n440
   Mexico, 90n145
   modern Jewish hist, 91n404
   Nfld. & Lab., 93n473
   N American exploration, 94n444
   opaque & ore minerals in their assns, 92n1740
   Pa., 91n430
   parrots of the world, 92n1560
   quails, 93n1536
   snakes of the world, 92n1586
   social issues, 92n76
   S America, 93n484
   SE Asia, 90n418
   sponge morphology, 92n1584
   the Arab world, 92n115
   the Bible lands, rev ed, 91n1421
   the Crusades, 92n498
   the great caves of the world, 91n833
   the Middle East, 90n416
   the natural world, 92n1557
   the 1990 census, 94n931
   the Third World, 2d ed, 94n459
   the world, 2d ed, 94n446
   the world economy, 92n141
   the world with geophysical boundaries, 92n407
   20th century world hist, 92n497
   US environmental issues, 92n1765
   wintering N American birds, 90n1542
   world affairs, 9th ed, 93n720
   world cultures, 90n361
   world issues, 90n408
   world pol flashpoints, 94n794
Atomic bomb, 94n710
A-to-Z of women's sexuality, rev ed, 93n884
At-risk youth, 91n310
Atta-ur-Rahman, 92n1723
Aubrey, Bryan, 92n1218
Aubrey, James R., 93n1208
Audio dict, 2d ed, 92n1608
Audio video review digest, 90n918
Audiocassette & CD finder, 3d ed, 94n374
Audiovisual resources in primatology, Wis. Regional Primate Research Center, 94n1732
Audouze, Jean, 90n1743
Audubon Society ency of N American birds, 93n1537

Augarde, Tony, 92n68
Auger, C. P., 93n587
Augustine's De Civitate Dei: an annot bibliog of modern criticism, 1960-90, 93n1416
Aulestia, Gorka, 90n1036
Aumack, Sheryl, 92n1351
AUSMAP atlas of Austral., 94n455
Austin Clarke: a ref gd, 94n1293
Austin, David L., 92n1259
Australian bks in print 1989, 90n23
Australian bks in print by subject 1989, 90n24
Australian concise Oxford dict, 94n1096
Australian gd to miniature roses, 91n1502
Australian literary criticism, 1945-88, 90n1191
Australian natl dict, 90n1027
Australian pers in print 1989, 90n25
Australian pers in print 1991, 93n81
Australian plant name index, 94n1648
Australian plants identified, 92n1528
Australian ref dict, 93n131
Australian reptiles & frogs, 91n1602
Australian words & their origins, 91n1075
Australia's native forests, 91n1494
Austrian fiction writers, 1875-1913, 90n1192
Author a month (for dimes), 94n1188
Author biogs master index, 3d ed, 90n1073
Author profile collection, 93n1138
Authors & artists for ...
   young adults, v.1, 90n1091
   young adults, v.2, 90n1092
   young adults, v.6, 92n1126
Authors: critical & biographical refs, 2d ed, 94n1145
Author's gd to social work jls, 3d ed, 94n912
Authors of bks for young people, 3d ed, 91n1117
Auto dict, 94n2021
Auto museum dir USA suppl with Canadian museums, 90n1815
Automation ency, 4th ed, 90n1577
AV market place 1990, 91n969
AV market place 1992, 93n991
Avallone, Susan, 91n1372, 91n1373, 91n1374, 93n1368
Avalos, Francisco, 91n557
Avalos, Francisco A., 93n563
Aviation/space dict, 7th ed, 91n1607
Awards almanac 1991, 91n313
Awards almanac 1992, 93n871
Awards, honors, & prizes, 8th ed, 90n56
Awards, honors, & prizes, 9th ed, 93n66
Award-winning bks for children & young adults, 91n1110
Award-winning bks for children & young adults 1990-91, 94n1166
Aware traveler's dir, 1991 ed, 92n430
Awesome almanac—Ill., 94n84
Awesome almanac—Ind., 94n86
Awesome almanac—Mich., 94n87
Awesome almanac—Minn., 94n85
Awesome almanac—Wis., 94n83
AWP official gd to writing programs, 6th ed, 94n993
Axelrod, Alan, 94n1993
Axelrod, Herbert, 90n1549
Axelrod, Herbert R., 90n1548, 92n1575, 93n1553, 93n1554, 94n1711
Axelrod, Natalie, 94n1806
Axtell, B. L., 93n1464
Ayala, Marta Stiefel, 94n600
Ayala, Reynaldo, 94n600
Ayer, A. J., 94n1499
Ayers, Jerry B., 91n289
Ayn Rand: 1st descriptive bibliog, 92n1180
Ayto, John, 92n1022, 92n1480
A-Z gd to tracing ancestors in Britain, 3d ed, 90n393
A-Z gd to tracing ancestors in Britain, 4th ed, 93n461
A-Z of ...
   horse diseases & health problems, 91n1511
   opera, 92n1290
   sailing terms, 93n842
   snake keeping, 92n1589

A-Z of ... *(continued)*
   UK brands, 2d ed, 92n236
   UK mktg data, 4th ed, 92n237
   women's sexuality, 91n1661
Azevedo, Mario, 93n116

B western actors ency, 90n1341
B&T link module 2, world ed, 93n27
Babcock, Barbara A., 90n867
Baby name countdown, 91n421
Bach English-title index, 94n1331
Bach, Jean, 92n935
Bachkatov, Nina, 94n525
Bachmann, E. Theodore, 90n1410
Bachmann, Mercia Brenne, 90n1410
Bachmann, Thomas, 90n639
Back Stage hndbk for performing artists, 90n1364
Back Stage theater gd, 93n1389
Back Stage: TV, film & tape production dir, 1989 ed, 90n915
Backgrounds to Restoration & 18th-century English lit, 90n1167
Backhaus, Balbir, 93n1520
Backscheider, Paula R., 90n1170
Backus, Karen, 90n1620, 93n421, 93n1632, 94n1807
Bacon, Josephine, 91n431
Bacon's Information, Inc., 94n1003, 94n1004, 94n1014
Bacon's media calendar dir 1993, 94n1003
Bacon's newspaper/mag dir 1993, 94n1004
Bacon's publicity checker 1991, 92n899
Bacon's radio/TV dir 1993, 94n1014
Bader, Gershom, 90n1413
Badler, Mitchell M., 93n1693
Baechler, Lea, 92n1151, 92n1156, 92n1158
Baer, Beverly, 90n70, 91n50, 93n1145, 94n59
Baer, D. Richard, 94n1439
Baer, E. Kristina, 93n1046
Baer, George W., 92n735
Bagust, Harold, 94n1618
Bahat, Dan, 91n439
Bahm, Archie J., 91n1406, 94n1498
Bailey, Don V., 91n852
Bailey, Frankie Y., 93n1151
Bailey, Jill, 90n1518
Bailey, Leigh, 94n2003
Bailey, Nancy Gisbrecht, 91n1265
Bailey, Walter B., 91n1265
Bailey, William G., 90n472, 90n567, 91n41, 91n1338
Bain, Alan, 91n1447
Bain, Robert, 94n1222
Baines, Anthony, 94n1338
Bains, William, 94n1790
Bair, Alicia, 90n1359
Bair, Frank, 94n723
Bair, Frank E., 91n1693, 93n1722, 94n1862, 94n1947
Baker, Brian L., 94n566
Baker, Daniel B., 91n724, 93n730, 94n463
Baker, Darrell, 92n1331
Baker ency of the Bible, 90n1394
Baker, Hugh, 94n1792
Baker, J. H., 91n583
Baker, Jennifer, 93n738
Baker, Mark Allen, 92n925
Baker, Melvin, 91n515
Baker, Michael J., 92n241
Baker, Paul, 93n1268
Baker, Sylva, 91n1553
Baker, William, 90n1149
Baker's biographical dict of musicians, 8th ed, 93n1244
Balachandran, M., 91n897, 94n934
Balachandran, S., 91n897, 94n934
Balanchine, George, 90n1315
Balay, Robert, 93n12
Baldauf, Gretchen S., 91n370
Balder, A. P., 93n466
Balderston, Daniel, 93n1225

Baldick, Chris, 91n1099
Baldrige, Letitia, 91n1335
Baldwin, Gordon, 92n957
Bales, Jack, 91n1172
Bali, Mrinal, 92n1590
Ball field gd to diseases of greenhouse ornamentals, 93n1499
Ball pest & disease manual, 94n1624
Ballad scholarship, 90n1284
Balliet, Conrad A., 92n1238
Ballparks of N America, 90n765
Ballplayers, 91n825
Balmer, Randall, 94n1533
Balouet, Jean-Christophe, 92n1524
Balski, Grzegorz, 93n1348
Baltsan, Hayim, 93n1087
Balz, Horst, 91n1423, 93n1426, 94n1528
Banfield, James, 90n1573, 90n1800, 91n238
Bangs, Richard, 92n433
Banham, Martin, 90n1362, 94n1471
Banister, David, 90n842
Banja, Judith Rogers, 92n1131
Banjo on record, 94n1336
Bank, David, 92n55
Banking in the US, 92n183
Banking terminology, 3d ed, 91n210
Banks, Arthur S., 91n722
Banks, Erma Davis, 90n1157
Bannock, Graham, 94n159
Bantam illus world atlas, 91n422
Baquedano, Luis, 91n740
Barabas, Gabor, 91n970
Barabas, SuzAnne, 91n970
Baraga, Frederic, 94n1124
Barale, Michele Aina, 91n1238
Barba, Eugenio, 92n1374
Barbara Pym: a ref gd, 93n1209
Barbare, Richard, 90n440
Barber, John F., 92n1168
Barbour, Roger W., 90n1567, 91n1601
Barer, Burl, 94n1249
Baretta-Bekker, J. G., 94n1744
Barger, Ralph L., 91n1820
Barhydt, Frances Bartlett, 94n1580
Bariaud, Pierre, 93n1725
Barker, Gayle, 92n434
Barker, Keith, 93n7
Barker, Nicolas, 94n1026
Barker-Benfield, G. J., 93n932
Barlow, Diane, 93n917
Barlow, Richard G., 94n986
Barman, Jean, 94n924, 94n925
Barnard, Stephen, 90n1294
Barnavi, Eli, 94n424
Barnes, Carollynn M., 91n145, 91n146
Barnes, Dorothy L., 93n620
Barnett, Le Roy, 93n1778
Barnett, Lynn, 94n325, 94n371
Barney, Gerald O., 92n672
Barnhart, Clarence L., 90n1020, 90n1024, 91n1059, 92n1020
Barnhart, David K., 92n1058
Barnhart, Robert K., 91n1059, 92n1020
Barnouw, Erik, 90n887
Barnsley, Roland, 90n1466
Baron, John H., 94n1306
Bar-On, Ray, 90n430
Baron, Robert C., 90n495
Baron, Salo Wittmayer, 94n427
Barone, Michael, 91n725, 94n746
Baroque music: a research & info gd, 94n1306
Barquez, Ruben M., 91n1596
Barr, Catherine, 93n629, 94n615
Barr, Raymond, 90n1662
Barraclough, Geoffrey, 94n530
Barranger, Milly S., 91n924, 93n1315
Barrett, Jacqueline K., 94n48, 94n969

Barrett, Thomas M., 93n1487
Barrette, Bill, 90n951
Barron, Janet, 91n1223
Barron, Neil, 91n1137, 91n1138, 92n1136
Barron, Sarah, 94n1634
Barron's best buys in college educ, 2d ed, 93n364
Barron's compact gd to colleges, 7th ed, 92n298
Barron's Educational Series, College Division, 90n322, 92n298, 92n312, 93n365
Barron's Educational Series, Inc., editors of, 94n32
Barron's gd to ...
    financing a medical school educ, 91n1673
    graduate bus schools, 8th ed, 94n168
    law schools, 9th ed, 92n539
    medical & dental schools, 4th ed, 90n1656
Barron's jr fact finder, 90n46
Barron's new student's concise ency, 2d ed, 94n32
Barron's profiles of American colleges, 16th ed, 90n322
Barron's profiles of American colleges, 19th ed, 93n365
Barron's 300 best buys in college educ, 91n321
Barron's top 50, 93n366
Barry, Ken, 92n257
Barstow, Barbara, 90n1077
Bartel, Pauline, 94n1452
Bartelt, Chuck, 91n1345
Barth, Else M., 93n1392
Bartke, Wolfgang, 92n21, 92n707
Bartlett, John, 93n89
Bartlette, Reginald J., 93n1292
Barton, Barbara J., 91n1497
Bartz, Bettina, 92n623
Barzun, Jacques, 91n1132
Basart, Ann P., 90n1237
Basch, Rebecca A., 90n335
Baseball: a comp bibliog, suppl.1, 94n837
Baseball America's 1990 almanac, 91n817
Baseball America's 1990 dir, 91n818
Baseball autograph hndbk, 92n925
Baseball card dealer dir, 1990, 92n926
Baseball chronology, 92n780
Baseball ency, 7th ed, 90n764
Baseball ency, 9th ed, 94n830
Baseball ency update, 1989, 91n819
Baseball file, 93n825
Baseball gd, 1991 ed, 92n776
Baseball in the movies, 93n1351
Baseball nicknames, 93n826
Baseball quotations, 92n784
Baseball vacations, 92n782
Baseballistics, 91n827
Baseball's benchmark boxscores, 91n821
Baseball's greatest quotations, 92n783
BASELINE, editors of, 92n1352
Basford, Terry K., 91n785
Basic bus lib, 2d ed, 90n158
Basic classical & operatic recordings collection on CD for libs, 91n1294
Basic gd to online info systems for health care professionals, 90n1624
Basic gd to pesticides, 94n2009
Basic Japanese-English dict, 90n1049
Basic lib skills, 3d ed, 94n620
Basic musical lib, "P" series, 1-1000, 92n1295
Basketball abstract 1989-90, 91n829
Basketball biogs, 92n788
Basketball resource gd, 2d ed, 91n831
Baskin, Ellen, 94n1438
Baskin, Rosemary, 93n1481
Basque-English dict, 90n1036
Bassan, Fernande, 90n1042
Bassett, Charles, 92n685
Bassett, Jan, 94n516
Bassett, John E., 93n1173
Bassey, E. J., 92n792
Basta, Margo McLoone, 94n2

Basta, Nicholas, 91n242, 92n299
Bataille, Gretchen M., 92n358, 94n956
Bateman, Graham, 90n1516
Bates, G. W., 93n1524
Bates, Robert L., 92n1739
Bats of Tex., 92n1583
Batschelet, Margaret W., 91n1454
Batsford ency of embroidery techniques, 92n947
Batson, Judy G., 90n1171
Batten, Donna, 90n694, 92n566, 94n747
Batten, L. A., 92n1561
Battenfeld, Robert L., 93n1179
Battered wives, 90n577
Battie, David, 92n933
Battistella, Graziano, 92n339
Battle bk, 94n695
Battle chronicles of the Civil War, 91n501
Battle, Ed, 93n1053
Battle of Antietam & the Md. campaign of 1862, 91n482
Battle of Jutland, 93n693
Battles & battlescenes of WW II, 90n655
Battles of Coral Sea & Midway, 1942, 93n695
Battley, Nick, 92n168
Bauer, Hans, 93n1117
Baughman, Judith S., 91n1161, 92n1162, 94n1229
Baur, Tassilo, 90n1331, 94n1454
Bausell, R. Barker, 92n73
Bavishi, Vinod B., 93n263
Baxter, Angus, 90n388, 93n456
Baxter, Colin F., 94n531
Baxter, Craig, 90n117
Baxter, Herbert, 94n1639
Baxter, Pam M., 93n804, 94n805
Baxter, R. E., 94n159
Bayeux tapestry, 2d ed, 91n1005
Bayless, Bernie J., 92n60
Baytelman, Pola, 94n1320
Bazar, Beth, 90n707
BBC Monitoring, 92n80
BBC World Service, 93n542
BBC World Service glossary of current affairs, 92n80
BBC World Service Gulf Crisis chronology, 93n542
Beach, Barbara, 90n70, 91n50
Beach, Edward L., 90n668
Beach, Sally, 91n140
Beacham, Walton, 90n690
Beacham's gd to key lobbyists, 90n690
Beacon bk of quotations by women, 94n972
Beacon: college & career planning on CD-ROM, 94n349
Beacon college project dir, 94n325
Beahm, George, 90n1148
Beal, Peter, 94n1245
Beam, Amy L., 92n431
Beam's dir of intl tourist events 1991, 92n431
Bean, Lowell John, 91n400, 92n359
Bear, John, 90n323, 92n300, 94n350, 94n351, 94n1153
Beard, Charles A., 91n490
Beard, Henry, 94n1101
Beard, J. S., 92n1527
Beard, William, 91n490
Bear's gd to earning college degrees non-traditionally, 94n350
Bear's gd to earning non-traditional college degrees, 10th ed, 90n323
Beatles: a bio-bibliog, 91n1327
Beatles album file & complete discography, rev ed, 90n1296
Beatles: the ultimate recording gd, 94n1380
Beaty, H. Wayne, 91n1613, 94n1777
Beaty, Wayne, 93n1590
Beaubien, Charles A., 94n740
Beauchamp, Edward R., 90n306
Beauregard, Estelle, 91n243, 93n905
Beavers, Randell A., 94n1691
Bechhoefer, Ina S., 90n296
Bechky, Allen, 91n465
Beck, Warren A., 90n466

Becker, Charlotte B., 93n1395
Becker, Lawrence C., 93n1395
Beckson, Karl, 92n1212
Bedford, Denise, 91n656
Bedford, Frances, 94n1335
Bedford, Susan, 92n835
Bedi, Joyce E., 91n1614
Bedini, Silvio A., 92n415
Bedurftig, Friedemann, 92n493
Bee, Patricia McColl, 91n67
Beebe, Jon P., 91n1282
Beeching, Cyril Leslie, 90n1000, 91n1051
Beecroft, K. A., 91n614, 94n636
Beede, Benjamin R., 91n676
Beeler, Duane, 90n1001
Beentje, Henk, 93n1516
Beer, Colin, 90n1478
Beer, Richard L., 92n514
Beere, Carole A., 92n831
Beers, Henry Putney, 90n464
Beginning French bilingual dict, 2d ed, 90n1044
Beginning Italian bilingual dict, 2d ed, 90n1047
Beginning Spanish bilingual dict, 2d ed, 90n1058
Behind the covers, v.2, 90n1087
Behrens, David W., 93n1573
Behzad, Marion S., 93n863
Beinart, Haim, 93n440
Beintema, William J., 92n515
Beirne, Piers, 93n602
Beit-Hallahmi, Benjamin, 94n1529
Bejermi, John, 90n716, 93n763
Belanger, Sandra E., 91n933
Belkin, Gary S., 94n1095
Bell, Albert A., Jr., 93n1393
Bell, David S., 91n758
Bell, Judith, 94n1324
Bell, Maureen, 91n1183
Bell, Peter R., 93n1498
Bell, Robert E., 90n1302, 92n1320
Bellack, Alan S., 94n812
Bellinger, Peter, 93n1561
Benagh, Jim, 91n811
Bencin, Richard L., 90n273
Bencini, Marina Carcea, 93n1478
Bender, Arnold E., 92n1481
Bender, Todd K., 90n1145, 90n1146, 90n1181, 91n1565
Bendick, Jeanne, 91n1793
Bendiner, Elmer, 92n1651
Bendiner, Jessica, 92n1651
Benecke, Josephine, 90n953
Benedetto, Robert, 92n1412, 94n1520
Benedict, Audrey DeLella, 92n444
Benedictine Monks of St. Augustine's Abbey, Ramsgate, 91n1438
Benefits of exercise, 92n792
Benet's reader's ency of American lit, 92n1155
Benewick, Robert, 94n715
Benitz, William E., 90n1698
Beniukh, Ksana, 93n1094, 94n1130
Beniukh, Oleg, 93n1094, 94n1130
Benjamin Britten discography, 92n1270
Benjamin, Ludy T., Jr., 90n752
Benjamin, Ruth, 94n1309
Benjamin Tabart's juvenile lib, 92n1119
Bennett, Alison, 91n636
Bennett, George, 94n140
Bennett, George John, 93n146
Bennett, Gillian, 94n1383
Bennett, Gordon F., 91n1590
Bennett, James R., 93n951
Bennett, Joy, 90n1193, 90n1370, 93n1177, 94n1270
Bennett, Linda A., 94n395
Bennett, Pramila Ramgulam, 93n146, 94n140
Bennett, Stephen J., 94n1906
Bennett, Swannee, 92n919, 92n920
Benoit, France, 91n96

Bensen, Clark H., 94n741
Benser, Caroline Cepin, 92n1260
Benson, Eugene, 91n1400
Benson, Evelyn, 94n1129
Benson, K. Blair, 91n1615, 93n1588
Benson, Larry D., 94n1250
Benson, Margie, 94n83
Benson, Michael, 90n765
Benson, Morton, 91n1092, 91n1093, 93n463, 94n1129
Benstock, Bernard, 90n1173, 91n1196
Bentley, Elizabeth Petty, 91n584, 92n385, 92n386, 94n431
Bentley, Jeanie Huntley, 90n947
Bentley, Nicolas, 90n1177
Bentley, William K., 93n603
Benton, Michael, 94n1959
Benton, Rita, 91n1251
Benyuch, Ksana, 92n1087
Benyuch, Oleg, 92n1087, 93n1082
Benyus, Janine M., 90n1512, 91n1547, 91n1548
Beowulf scholarship, 94n1263
Bercuson, David J., 94n517
Berg, Donna Lee, 94n1097
Bergan, Ronald, 90n1348
Bergano's register of intl importers 1992/93, 93n256
Berger, Arthur S., 92n761
Berger, Gilda, 91n881
Berger, James L., 93n396
Berger, Joyce, 92n761
Berger, Melvin, 91n881
Berger, Michael A., 90n775
Berger, Sidney E., 91n1191, 93n690
Bergeron, Barbara, 91n1345
Berkman, Robert I., 91n47
Berko, Robert L, 90n223
Berkowitz, Luci, 91n1123
Berle, Gustav, 92n136, 93n200
Berleant-Schiller, Riva, 93n156
Berlin, Howard M., 91n171
Berlin, Irving N., 92n1673
Berlin, Kern, Rodgers, Hart, & Hammerstein, 91n1309
Berman, Barbara L., 93n949
Berman, F., 92n1666
Bernard E. Harkness seedlist hndbk, 2d ed, 94n1625
Bernard Malamud: a descriptive bibliog, 92n1177
Bernard Shaw: a gd to research, 93n1216
Bernard, Yolande, 90n574, 90n954, 91n288
Berndt, Thomas, 94n691
Berner, Mark S., 93n1661
Berney, K. A., 94n1467
Berney, Mary F., 91n289
Bernhard, Judith, 94n315
Bernstein, Jake, 93n201
Bernstein, Joanne E., 90n738
Bernstein, Peter W., 94n302
Berry, Dorothea M., 92n267
Berry, Fred, 92n1535
Berry, Liba, 90n591
Berryman-Fink, Cynthia, 90n266
Bertelli, Domenick M., 91n1491
Besher, Alexander, 92n137
Besserman, Lawrence, 90n1175
Bessette, Peg, 93n822
Best bks for ...
    children, 4th ed, 91n1111
    jr high readers, 92n1116
    public libs, 94n647
    sr high readers, 92n1117
Best doctors in America 1992-93, 93n1644
Best dollar values in American colleges, 91n322
Best festivals of N America, 3d ed, 91n1344
Best: high/low bks for reluctant readers, 91n367
Best in children's bks, 93n1134
Best lawyers in America 1989-90, 90n550
Best lawyers in America 1993-94, 94n562
Best nonfranchise bus opportunities, 94n199

Best of ...
  Bkfinder, 93n1123
  Children's Choices, 90n1084
  health, 91n1643
  shareware: IBM PC utilities, 91n1739
Best pet name bk ever, 91n1575
Best rated CDs 1992: jazz, popular, etc., 93n1275
Best rated CDs: classical 1992, 94n1344
Best, Reba A., 94n1892
Best ref bks 1986-90, 93n8
Best sci & tech ref bks for young people, 92n1452
Best videos for children & young adults, 92n617
Best yrs of their lives, 94n926
Bestsellers 89, 90n579
Bettelheim, Judith, 94n1399
Better Bus Bureau A-Z buying gd, 92n172
Better community cat, 91n847
Better Homes & Gardens complete gd to food & cooking, 92n1482
Better said & clearly written, 91n933
Betty Grable: a bio-bibliog, 94n1408
Beum, Robert, 92n1197
Beusterien, Pat, 92n217
Bever, Michael B., 94n1794
Bevington, John C., 91n1774
Beyer, Gerry W., 94n555
Beyerly, Elizabeth, 92n516
Beyond picture bks, 90n1077
BFI film & TV hndbk 1993, 94n1455
BG Chemie, 92n1729
Bhatnagar, K. P., 90n1587, 93n1723
Bhattacharya, S. K., 90n1587, 93n1723
Bhattacharyys, Narenda Nath, 92n1403
Bhojwani, Sant S., 92n1529
Bhushan, Bharat, 92n1621, 94n1692
Biagi, Adele, 92n1081
Biagini, Mary K., 91n1128
Bial, Linda LaPuma, 92n602
Bial, Raymond, 92n602
Bianchi, Suzan, 91n104
Bianco, David P., 94n800
Bible & modern literary criticism, 93n1432
Bible: cultural atlas for young people, 94n1546
Biblical law bibliog, 92n1445
BiblioData fulltext sources online, 90n1725
Bibliographia Malebranchiana, 94n1485
Bibliographic gd to ...
  art & architecture 1990, 92n963
  black studies 1990, 92n344
  bus & economics 1990, 92n121
  Caribbean mass communications, 94n990
  computer sci 1991, 94n1893
  conference pubns 1990, 92n3
  dance 1989, 91n1346
  dance 1991, 94n1422
  E Asian studies 1991, 94n107
  educ 1991, 94n303
  educl research, 3d ed, 92n267
  govt pubns—foreign: 1990, 92n47
  govt pubns—US: 1990, 92n48
  Latin American studies 1991, 94n141
  law 1990, 92n517
  maps & atlases 1990, 92n413
  microform pubns 1991, 94n1921
  Middle Eastern studies 1990, 93n159
  music 1990, 92n1248
  N American hist 1990, 92n453
  Soviet & E European studies 1990, 92n103
  tech 1990, 92n1450
  the comparative study of ethics, 92n1389
  the environment 1991, 94n1988
  the hist of computing, computers, & the info processing industry, 91n1721
  theatre arts 1990, 92n1375
Bibliographic index 1990, 92n4
Bibliographic style manual, 91n954

Bibliographical Center of the Institute of Contemporary Jewry, the Hebrew University of Jerusalem, 91n408
Bibliographical companion, 90n630
Bibliographical gd to African-American women writers, 94n1223
Bibliographies for African studies 1970-86, 90n106
Bibliographies in hist, 90n528
Bibliographies of studies in Victorian lit for the 10 yrs 1975-84, 92n1188
Bibliography & index of ...
  English verse, 1476-1558, 90n1166
  English verse in ms 1501-58, 94n1267
  geology, 1988, 90n1763
  geology, v.53, no.9, 90n1764
Bibliography for training in child & adolescent mental health, 92n1673
Bibliography, 1988-90, 93n1482
Bibliography of ...
  American lit, v.8, 91n1144
  American lit, v.9, 93n1162
  arms control verification, 91n712
  Bali, 93n123
  bibliogs of the langs of the world, v.1, 92n1006
  bioethics, v.15, 90n1611
  bks for children, 90n1078
  Canadiana published in Great Britain, 1519-1763, 91n517
  Christian worship, 91n1437
  Commonwealth law reports, 92n518
  contemporary American fiction, 1945-88, 90n1131
  cookery bks published in Britain 1875-1914, 90n1453
  Cuban mass communications, 94n991
  eds, translations, & commentary on Xenophon's Socratic writings, 90n1373
  English-lang works on the Babi & Baha'i faiths 1844-1985, 92n1447
  finance, 92n182
  genealogy & local hist pers with union list of major US collections, 91n412
  geographic thought, 91n443
  Greek N.T. mss, 90n1388
  histl economics to 1980, 92n123
  Indian law per articles published 1980-90, 2d ed, 94n547
  info tech, 90n613
  Latin American & Caribbean bibliogs: annual report, 1989-90, 92n109
  Latin American & Caribbean bibliogs, 1985-89: social scis & humanities, 94n145
  law & economics, 93n564
  mktg research methods, 3d ed, 91n262
  medical & biomedical biog, 91n1654
  military name lists from pre-1675 to 1900, 91n413
  miniature bks (1470-1965), 91n7
  modern Icelandic lit in translation, suppl., 1971-80, 92n1236
  native N Americans on disc, 94n415
  N.B. geology (1839-1988), 91n1783
  New Orleans imprints 1764-1864, 90n629
  new religious movements in primal societies, v.3, 91n1411
  new religious movements in primal societies, v.4, 92n1400
  new religious movements in primal societies, v.5, 92n1401
  new religious movements in primal societies, v.6, 94n1505
  N.Y. state communities, rev ed, 90n101
  N.Y. state communities, 3d ed, 91n88
  N Manitoba, 92n99
  Ont. hist 1976-1986, 90n511
  philosophy in Canada, 90n1372
  salon criticism in Paris from the ancien regime to the Restoration, 1699-1827, 93n1018
  salon criticism in Paris from the July Monarchy to the Second Republic, 1831-51, 93n1019
  Salvation Army lit in English, 90n1406
  seniors & the family research 1980-91, 93n852
  Slavic mythology, 90n1305
  Sun Yat-sen in China's Republican Revolution, 1885-1925, 93n521
  the Amarna period & its aftermath, 92n501

Bibliography of ... *(continued)*
   the Blackfoot, 90n368
   the communist intl (1919-79), v.1, 92n729
   the Holocaust Memorial Resource & Educ Center of central Fla., 92n479
   the mss of Patrick Branwell Bronte, 94n1247
   the nature & role of the holy spirit in 20th-century writings, 94n1534
   Ukrainian lit in English & French, 91n1248
   women & lit, 90n849
   writings by & about women in photography 1850-1950, 92n959
Bibliography on ...
   antisemitism, 91n409
   computational molecular biology, 94n1634
   educ in dvlpmnt & social change in sub-Saharan Africa, 91n291
   foreign & comparative law, 90n542
   Holocaust lit: suppl, 91n519
   Holocaust lit: suppl. v.2, 94n532
   old-growth forests in B.C., 92n1501
   temples of the ancient Near East & Mediterranean world, 93n1402
Bibliography Standards Committee of the Rare Books and Manuscript Section (ACRL/ALA), 92n580
Bibliometrics: an annot bibliog, 1970-90, 94n623
Bibliotecas Para La Gente Reference Committee, 90n367
Bibliotheca lexicologiae medii aevi, 90n990
Bibliotheca Trinitariorum, v.1, 90n1391
Bibliotheca Trinitariorum, v.2, 90n1392
Biblograf, S.A., editors of, 90n1059
Bicentennial concordance, 94n580
Bickers, Kenneth N., 93n745
Bickford, Angelina, 90n1061
Bickford, Sam, 90n1061
Bicknell, Peter, 92n447
Bicyclist's sourcebk, 92n791
Bidd, Donald W., 93n1342
Bieber's dict of ...
   legal abbrevs, 3d ed, 90n538
   legal abbrevs, 4th ed, 94n543
   legal citations, 3d ed, 90n543
   legal citations, 4th ed, 94n544
Biedermann, Hans, 94n979
Biegel, David E., 90n815
Bien, Andrea Ansell, 91n1021, 92n977, 92n978, 92n979
Biennial exhibition record of the Corcoran Gallery of Art 1907-67, 92n979
Biesel, David B., 92n775
Big band almanac, rev ed, 90n1290
Big bk of adventure travel, 91n455
Big footnotes, 90n1300
Big gay bk, 93n886
Big outside, rev ed, 94n1678
Big powers & the German question, 1941-90, 93n538
Big screen bk, 94n1435
Biggins, Alan, 93n152
Bignoniaceae—pt.2 (tribe tecomeae), 94n1637
Bilingual dict of dental terms: Spanish-English, 91n1683
Billboard bk of ...
   American singing groups, 94n1359
   gold & platinum records, 91n1301
   no.1 country hits, 92n1303
   no.1 hits, rev ed, 90n1292
   no.1 hits, 3d ed, 94n1360
   1-hit wonders, 91n1324
   top 40 albums, 92n1293
Billboard 1990 music & video yrbk, 92n1294
Billboard top 1000 singles 1955-90, 93n1282
Billboard's hottest hot 100 hits, 93n1276
Billiard industry source bk, 1992/1993 ed, 94n857
Billips, Connie, 93n1316
Billips, Connie J., 91n1349
Billman, Larry, 94n1408
Billy, Christopher, 90n169, 90n187, 90n188, 90n268
Billy, Christopher M., 90n267

Binary stars, 94n1929
Bindocci, Cynthia Gay, 94n948
Bing, Stanley, 91n131
Bingham, Don, 94n1024
Bingham, Joan, 94n1024
Binns, Margaret, 94n102
Binns, Tony, 94n102
Biographical dict & analysis of China's party leadership 1922-88, 92n707
Biographical dict of ...
   actors, actresses, musicians, dancers, managers & other stage personnel in London, 1660-1800, v.13, 92n1378
   actors, actresses, musicians, dancers, managers & other stage personnel in London, 1660-1800, v.14, 92n1379
   African-American, Holiness-Pentecostals 1880-1990, 91n1439
   American journalism, 90n905
   American sports: basketball & other indoor sports, 90n769
   American sports, 1989-92 suppl, 93n817
   American sports: outdoor sports, 90n757
   Canadian Jewry 1909-14, 94n410
   contemporary Catholic American writing, 90n1125
   dissenting economists, 93n177
   English women writers 1580-1720, 91n1183
   French pol leaders since 1870, 91n758
   geography, 94n465
   Hispanic lit in the US, 90n1124
   Indians of the Americas, 93n430
   life peers, 93n462
   mathematicians, 93n1736
   medicine, 92n1651
   Russian/Soviet composers, 91n1275
   Sask. artists: women artists, 92n969
   scenographers, 92n1380
   the board of governors of the Fed Reserve, 93n240
   the British Colonial Serv 1939-66, 92n713
   the extreme right since 1890, 92n732
   the Middle East, 93n161
   the Soviet Union 1917-88, 90n39
   women artists in Europe & America since 1850, 91n1007
Biographical dir of ...
   natl librarians, 90n581
   100 leading Soviet officials, 92n715
   the governors of the US 1983-88, 90n483
   the US executive branch, 1774-1989, 91n731
Biographical index to American sci, 91n1469
Biographical index to children's & young adult authors & illustrators, 93n1144
Biographies for birdwatchers, 90n1541
Biographies of ...
   American women, 91n920
   creative artists, 92n877
   scientists for sci-tech libs, 93n1440
Biography: an annot bibliog, 94n16
Biography & genealogy master index 1991, 92n392
Biography & genealogy master index [CD-ROM], 94n436
Biography index: Sept 1990-Aug 1991, 93n33
Biography index [CD-ROM], 93n34
Biography today, v.1, issue 1, 93n35
Biography today, 1992 annual cum, 94n11
Biolexicon, 92n1514
Biological & agricultural index [CD-ROM], 93n1458
Biological & agricultural index, v.75, no.6, 91n1470
Biomedical & social aspects of alcohol use, 92n1631
Biondi, Joann, 94n475
Biosystematic monograph of the genus Cucumis (Cucurbitaceae), 94n1638
Biotechnology & the research enterprise, 90n1443
Biotechnology from A to Z, 94n1790
Biotechnology gd Japan 1990-91, 91n223
Biotechnology Japan, 90n233
Biotechnology sourcebk, 90n1595
Bird atlas, 94n1702
Bird blow flies in N America, 91n1590
Bird, Christiane, 92n1306
Bird, Richard, 90n1508

Birding by ear, 91n1574
Birds alternative names, 93n1544
Birds in ...
    jeopardy, 93n1541
    Kans., 90n1544
    Kans., v.2, 93n1546
Birds of ...
    Africa, v.3, 90n1528
    Ill., 91n1558
    Japan, 93n1538
    Malheur Natl Wildlife Refuge, Oreg., 92n1564
    N America: W region, 90n1530
    Ohio, 91n1559
    Pakistan, v.1, 92n1568
    the Blue Ridge Mountains, 93n1545
    the central Rockies, 92n1572
    the lower Colorado River Valley, 92n1569
    the Middle East & N Africa, 90n1538
    Tikal, 94n1691
    Toronto & vicinity, 92n1565
Birds: the aerial hunters, 90n1517
Birds: the plant- & seed-eaters, 90n1518
Birds: the waterbirds, 90n1519
Birkenhead, Frederick Edwin Smith, Earl of, 93n604
Birkhead, Tim, 93n1540
Birnbach, Lisa, 91n323
Birnbaum, Max, 92n293
Birnes, William J., 90n1715, 90n1719, 90n1721, 90n1722, 90n1726
Birney, Alice L., 90n1064
Birosik, Patti Jean, 91n1321
Birthday bk, 92n1131
Bishop, Arthur, 93n697
Bishop, Cynthia, 93n1462
Bishop, Edward L., 94n1154
Bishop, Lloyd, 94n306
Bisk, Nathan M., 91n980
Biskupic, Joan, 93n588
Bissell, Christopher, 93n1451
Bitter, Gary G., 93n1678
Bixler, Frances, 93n1184
Biz words, 91n131
Bjarkman, Peter C., 92n778, 92n779
Bjorling, Joel, 93n806
Bjorner, Susan N., 93n975
Bjorner, Susanne, 94n1005
Black action films, 90n1344
Black adolescence, 91n892
Black Africa: a comparative hndbk, 2d ed, 90n105
Black African lit in English, 1982-86, 90n1190
Black aged in the US, 2d ed, 90n783
Black American women in lit, 90n858
Black American women in Olympic track & field, 93n843
Black American women novelists, 91n1149
Black Americans: a statl sourcebk, 92n345
Black Americans info dir, 91n392
Black Americans info dir 1994-95, 94n407
Black artist in America, 93n1033
Black arts annual 1987/88, 90n962
Black arts annual 1989/90, 93n1026
Black authors, 92n1148
Black authors & illustrators of children's bks, 2d ed, 93n1139
Black bk publishers in the US, 93n679
Black children & American institutions, 90n833
Black dance, 90n1314
Black, Donald V., 91n1648
Black elected officials, 20th ed, 94n733
Black experience in children's bks 1989, 90n1079
Black females in the US, 90n741
Black, Henry Campbell, 92n529
Black, Hester, 90n632
Black, J. L., 91n105
Black lit criticism, 93n1115
Black males in the US, 90n740
Black Olympian medalists, 92n769

Black 100, 94n406
Black resource gd, 1990-91 ed, 91n387
Black resource gd, 10th ed, 93n422
Black, Richard, 94n96
Black scientists, 93n1443
Black, Sharon, 91n619, 91n976
Black theatre & performance, 91n1398
Black women in America, 94n965
Black women in TV, 92n855
Black writers, 90n1068
Blackburn, G. Meredith III, 90n1096
Blackburn, Graham, 93n1610
Blackburn, Thomas C., 91n395
Blackfoot dict of stems, roots, & affixes, 92n1064
Blackham, Richard, 91n1293
Blacks in film & TV, 91n1355
Blacks in sci & medicine, 92n351
Black's law dict, 6th ed, 92n529
Black's medical dict, 36th ed, 91n1659
Black's medical dict, 37th ed, 93n1629
Black's vet dict, 16th ed, 90n1476
Black's vet dict, 17th ed, 93n1490
Blackwelder, Richard E., 92n1213
Blackwell companion to the enlightenment, 93n555
Blackwell dict of ...
    cognitive psychology, 93n798
    historians, 90n530
    Judaica, 94n1554
    20th-century social thought, 94n73
Blackwell ency of industrial archaeology, 94n484
Blackwell ency of the American Revolution, 92n470
Blackwell gd to blues records, 91n1314
Blackwell gd to recorded jazz, 92n1307
Blades, Joe, 93n1334
Blain, Virginia, 92n1095
Blair, D. M., 91n1783
Blair, John, 91n1323
Blair, Karen J., 90n848
Blake, Bernard, 91n709, 91n710
Blake, Robert, 90n536, 91n13
Blake set to music, 91n1252
Blakemore, Harold, 90n141, 94n142
Blakeslee, Carolyn, 90n961
Blanc, F. L., 94n1725
Blanchet, Jean, 90n954
Blanck, Jacob, 91n1144
Blanco, Richard L., 94n503
Blank, Denise, 94n3
Blank, Jacob, 93n1162
Blankenship, Frank J., 91n287
Blanpain, Roger, 94n252
Blashfield, Jean F., 94n84, 94n85
Blasi, Anthony J., 92n1397
Blatherwick, Francis John, 93n36
Blatherwick, John, 91n1817
Blaug, Mark, 90n161
Blaugher, Michael, 93n1779
Blaustein, Albert P., 94n580
Bleaney, C. H., 93n166
Blechman, Elaine A., 90n1663
Bleiberg, German, 94n1289
Bleiler, Everett F., 92n1143
Bleiler, Richard J., 92n1143
Blenz-Clucas, Beth, 92n325
Blessing, Patrick J., 93n437
Blevins, Winfred, 94n1088
Blick, George L., 91n1605
Blinderman, Charles, 92n1514
Bloch, Heinz P., 90n1585
Block, Eleanor S., 92n884
Block, Walter, 90n165
Blocksma, Mary, 91n1794
Blom, Eric, 90n1229
Bloom, Adrian, 94n1626
Bloom, Alan, 94n1626

Bloom, Ken, 92n467
Bloomberg, Marty, 92n477
Bloomfield, Elizabeth, 90n510, 91n150, 92n423
Bloomfield, G. T., 91n150, 92n423
Blooms of Bressingham garden plants, 94n1626
Bloomsbury gd to women's lit, 93n942
Bloomsbury group, 91n1181
Bloomsbury iconography, 91n1019
Blouin, Glen, 93n1515
Blue, Anthony Dias, 94n1605
Blues: a bibliographic gd, 90n1287
Blum, Annette, 94n1507
Blum, Eleanor, 92n885
Blum, Laurie, 91n211, 91n324, 92n292, 94n326, 94n327, 94n328, 94n329
Blumberg, Herbert H., 93n789
Blumenthal, Richard A., 92n301
Blumhofer, Edith L., 91n1434
Blunt, Wilfrid, 92n1540
Blyth, Alan, 90n1266
BNA Library Staff, 93n582, 94n748
BNA's dir of state & fed courts, judges, & clerks, 4th ed, 93n582
BNA's dir of state administrative codes & registers, 94n748
BNA's 1993 source bk on collective bargaining & employee relations, 94n277
Board, Marian, 91n1809
Boarding school gd, 90n320
Boarding schools dir 1991, 92n283
Boas, R. P., 91n1795
Bob Brant's best of Macintosh shareware, 94n1913
Bob Dorian's classic movies, 92n1360
Bob Dylan: a bio-bibliog, 94n1379
Bobb, F. Scott, 90n114
Bodart, Joni Richards, 94n1164
Bodian, Nat G., 90n644, 91n273
Bodian's publishing desk ref, 90n644
Bodiwala, G. G., 94n1825
Body atlas, 94n1819
Boehm, David A., 91n811
Boemer, Marilyn Lawrence, 91n971
Boger, Karl, 90n200
Bogle, Donald, 90n962, 93n1026
Bohemian register, 92n1147
Bohlander, Richard, 94n1803
Bohlander, Richard E., 93n486
Bohlen, H. David, 91n1558
Bohlin, Roy M., 91n354
Bohlke, James E., 94n1713
Boia, Lucian, 91n548, 92n502
Boivin, Michelle, 92n559
Bojnansky, V., 93n1495
Bold, Alan, 91n474
Bolger, Dorita F., 91n1412
Bollard, John K., 94n1084
Bollig, Laura E., 93n827, 93n831
Bologna, Gregory L., 90n703, 92n134
Bolton, H. Philip, 93n1210
Bolwell, Christine, 90n1692
Bond buyer 1990 yrbk, 91n172
Bond, Christopher E., 92n154
Bond, Cynthia D., 92n1150
Bond, James, 94n1693
Bond, Mary E., 90n125
Bond, Robert E., 92n154
Bongard, David L., 93n698
Bonin, Jean M., 94n1318
Bonnefoy, Yves, 92n1321
Bonner, Thomas Jr., 90n1202
Book industry trends 1991, 92n642
Book of ...
　　card games, 90n770
　　Daniel: an annot bibliog, 94n1536
　　European forecasts, 93n282
　　forest & thicket, 93n1518
　　goddesses & heroines, rev ed, 91n1334
　　Irish names, 90n400
　　lists for regulated hazardous substances 1993, 94n2010
　　military blunders, 92n659
　　1000 plays, 90n1100
　　roots, 90n1001
　　saints, 6th ed, 91n1438
　　the states, v.28, 1990-91 ed, 91n743
　　the states, v.29, 94n721
　　women, 93n935
　　women's firsts, 94n970
Book Reports & Library Talk dir of sources, 93n666
Book review digest, 86th annual cum, 92n54
Book review digest [CD-ROM], 93n76
Book review index 1988, 90n70
Book review index, 1991 cum, 94n59
Book trade in Canada with who's where, 1989/90, 91n671
BookGuide 1991, 92n927
Booklist's gd to the yr's best bks, 1992 ed, 93n9
Bookman's gd to ...
　　Americana, 10th ed, 92n459
　　hunting, shooting, angling, & related subjects, 92n799
　　the Indians of the Americas, 90n369
Bookman's price index, v.38, 91n981
Bookman's price index, v.46, 94n1025
Bookpeople: a 1st album, 91n651
Bookpeople: a multicultural album, 93n1142
Books & articles on S.C. hist, 2d ed, 93n510
Books & mags: a gd to publishing & bkselling courses in the US, 93n681
Books & pers online, v.2, no.1, 90n154
Books & pers online, 1992 ed, 93n187
Books & pers online, 94n44
Books & plays in films 1896-1915, 93n1344
Books by African-American authors & illustrators for children & young adults, 92n1122
Books for ...
　　new adult readers, 4th ed, 90n356
　　the teen age 1990, 91n362
　　you, 11th ed, 94n1165
Books in print 1989-90, 90n12
Books in print 1989-90: subject gd, 90n13
Books in print 1990-91, 91n9
Books in print 1991-92, 92n14, 93n29
Books in print 1993-94, 94n7
Books in print of the UN system, 94n788
Books in print plus, 94n8
Books in print plus with bk reviews plus, 93n28
Books in series 1985-89: cum 1985-88, 90n14
Books in Spanish for children & young adults, series 5, 90n1085
Books in Spanish for children & young adults, series 6, 94n1180
Books kids will sit still for, 2d ed, 92n627
Books of the fairs, 93n1306
Books out-of-print 1984-88, 90n15
Books to help children cope with separation & loss, v.3, 90n738
Books to read aloud with children through age 8, 91n363
Books without bias: through Indian eyes, 90n373
Boon, William, 92n1530
Boone, Jean, 90n289
Boone, Louis E., 93n218
Boos, Florence, 90n849
Bopp, Richard E., 92n604
Borck, Jim Springer, 92n871
Borden murders, 93n605
Border & territorial disputes, 3d ed, 94n722
BorderLine, 90n476
Bordman, Gerald, 93n1385, 94n1480
Borg, Ed, 90n1327
Borgatta, Edgar F., 93n847
Borgese, Elisabeth Mann, 92n1744
Boris Karloff: a bio-bibliog, 94n1409
Borklund, C. W., 92n654
Born to power, 94n155
Borne, Pierre, 93n1674
Bornschier, Volker, 90n838
Boross, P. A., 93n1482

Borowski, E. J., 93n1739
Bortin, Virginia, 94n1321
Borton, Terry, 90n53
Borwein, J. M., 93n1739
Borwein, Jonathan, 91n1796
Borwein, Peter, 91n1796
Borzvalka, I., 94n1123
BOSC dir, 1990 ed, 91n348
Boschung, Herbert T., 94n1714
Bosco, Dominick, 90n1699
Bosmajian, Haig A., 91n957
Bosnich, Victor W., 93n746
Bosoni, Anthony J., 94n557, 94n910
Bosse, David, 94n491, 94n492
Boston Art Club: exhibition record 1873-1909, 92n976
Boswell, Jeanetta, 90n1136
Boswellian studies, 3d ed, 93n1231
Boswell's literary art, 93n1232
Boswick, Storm, 93n382
Bosworth, C. E., 94n150, 94n151
Botanical Latin, 4th ed, 94n1641
Botermans, Jack, 90n771
Bothmer, A. James, 92n1641
Botswana, 94n99
Bottas, Bernice, 90n289
Botterweck, G. Johannes, 91n1424
Bottle, R. T., 94n1931
Bottomore, Tom, 94n73
Boucher, Wayne I., 93n1394
Bouckaert, Boudewijn, 93n564
Boudon, Raymond, 91n841
Boughn, Michael, 94n1234
Boulanger, Norman, 90n1368
Boulanger, Norman C., 94n1470
Boultbee, Paul G., 93n157
Bourguina, Anna, 90n522
Bourke, D. O'D, 93n1465
Bourquin, David Ray, 92n1449
Bourricaud, Francois, 91n841
Bousquet, Yves, 93n1560
Boustani, Rafic, 92n115
Bowden, Betsy, 90n991
Bowden, Edwin T., 90n1144
Bowden, Henry Warner, 94n1509
Bowen, Kelley, 94n723
Bowen, Thomas, 94n723
Bowers, Carolyn J., 92n35
Bowers, Peter M., 91n700
Bowers, Q. David, 93n1002
Bowes, D. R., 91n1782
Bowker annual lib & bk trade almanac 1989-90, 90n590
Bowker annual lib & bk trade almanac 1990-91, 91n611
Bowker annual lib & bk trade almanac, 37th ed, 93n629
Bowker annual lib & bk trade almanac, 38th ed, 94n615
Bowker's bk trade fax & phone dir 1989, 90n634
Bowker's complete video dir 1992, 93n989
Bowker's law bks & serials in print 1991, 93n565
Bowles, Edna, 91n723
Bowles, Garrett H., 90n1240
Bowman, J. Wilson, 94n330
Bowring, Richard, 94n113
Boyce, Charles, 92n1209
Boyce, David, 92n1383
Boyd, Andrew, 93n720
Boyd, Margaret A., 91n991
Boyden, Donald P., 91n61
Boyer, Richard, 91n908
Boyer, Trevor, 91n1560
Boylan, Henry, 90n38
Boylan, James C., 91n1710, 91n1711, 94n1867, 94n1868, 94n1869, 94n1870
Boyle, Kathleen Nelson, 94n869
Brace, Edward R., 94n1838
Bracken, James K., 91n1096, 92n884, 92n1094
Bracken, Susan, 92n98
Brackley, Peter, 90n1775
Bradford, James C., 91n691
Bradley: a research bibliog, 92n1390
Bradley, Fern Marshall, 93n1489, 94n1619
Bradney, Gail, 90n1334
Bradnock, Robert, 93n502
Bradnock, Roma, 93n502
Bradshaw, Peter, 94n110
Brady, George S., 92n1617
Bragonier, Reginald Jr., 91n1081
Braigen, Mila, 92n1468
Brailow, David, 94n1243
Braiman-Lipson, Judy, 90n229
Bramwell, Martyn, 90n1517, 90n1523
Brandrup, J., 91n1773
Brands & their cos, 8th ed, 91n259
Brands & their cos 1992, 93n188
Brandt, Bruce E., 94n1255
Brannan, Deborah, 93n585
Brannen, Noah S., 92n1082
Brant, Bob, 94n1913
Branyan-Broadbent, Brenda, 91n298, 92n327
Brass bibliog, 91n1283
Brauning, Daniel W., 94n1694
Braunstein, Janet, 94n299
Brawer, Moshe, 90n416, 93n484
Brazil in ref bks, 1965-89, 93n153
Brazil, Mark A., 93n1538
Brazil, Mary Jo, 92n806
Brazilian lit, 91n1243
Breaking down the walls, 93n568
Breaking through technical jargon, 91n1725
Brealey, Richard, 92n182
Brebner and Co., 91n162
Breem, Wallace, 92n518
Breen, Jon L., 94n1206
Bregman, Robert, 94n1369
Brelin, Christa, 93n373
Bremser, Martha, 94n1423
Brennan, Richard P., 93n1445
Brennan, Shawn, 92n566, 93n235, 94n968
Brennan, Shawn M., 90n694
Brennan, Stephen J., 91n831
Brenner, Donald J., 91n659, 91n673
Brenner, Robert C., 91n673
Brereton, Mary M., 94n621
Breslauer, S. Daniel, 94n1555
Breslin, J. Edward, 91n68
Bretherick, L., 92n1724
Bretherick's hndbk of reactive chemical hazards, 4th ed, 92n1724
Breuer, Hans-Peter, 91n1198
Brewer, Annie M., 93n990
Brewer, Donald E., 93n990
Brewer, Richard, 93n1539
Brewer's bk of myth & legend, 94n1391
Brewer's dict of names, 94n440
Brewer's dict of 20th-century phrase & fable, 93n1294
Bricault, Giselle C., 92n133
Brickell, Christopher, 90n1467, 94n1617
Bricker's intl dir 1989, 90n268
Bricker's intl dir, 24th ed, 94n225
Bricker's short-term executive programs, 90n169
Brickman, William W., 93n383
Bridson, Gavin D. R., 92n1513
Briggs, Asa, 93n38
Briggs, Shirley A., 94n2009
Briggs, Virginia L., 94n271
Briggs, Ward W., 91n1124
Bright, Charles D., 94n698
Bright, Donald E., 94n1722
Bright, William, 93n1050, 94n470
Brimble, Raymond J., 93n267
Brimsek, Tobi A., 90n623
Bringhurst, Robert, 94n675
Brinkle, Lydle, 91n473, 91n475

Brinkman, David, 92n1593
Brisco, Paula, 93n1633
Briscoe, James R., 91n1266
Brisebois, Madeleine, 92n326
Britain in the Middle East 1921-56, 91n125
Britain 1990, 91n112
Britain votes 4, 90n719
Britannica bk of the yr, 1991, 92n42
British architectural bks & writers 1556-1785, 92n996
British archives, 2d ed, 90n507
British biographical index, 92n55
British broadside ballads of the 16th century, 92n1220
British Computer Society Schools Committee, 90n1714
British dirs, 90n133
British electorate, 1963-87, 93n772
British English for American readers, 93n1068
British foreign policy 1918-45, rev ed, 92n709
British histl facts, 1688-1760, 90n506
British hit albums, 5th ed, 94n1362
British librarianship & info work 1986-90, v.2, 94n633
British lib dir, 90n607
British Library of Political and Economic Science, 92n147
British literary bibliog, 1970-79, 94n1244
British literary publishing houses, 1881-1965, 93n689
British mystery & thriller writers since 1940, 1st series, 91n1196
British mystery writers, 1920-39, 90n1173
British naval hist since 1815, 91n527
British pharmacopoeia 1993, 94n1876
British physiologists 1885-1914, 92n1653
British printmakers 1855-1955, 94n1057
British prose writers, 1660-1800, 2d series, 92n1194
British radio & TV pioneers, 94n1012
British Romantic novelists, 1789-1832, 93n1196
British Romantic poets, 1789-1832, 1st series, 92n1219
British Romantic prose writers, 1789-1832, 2d series, 93n1193
British sci fiction, 93n1204
British theatre yrbk 1989, 90n1361
British trademarks of the 1920s & 30s, 90n981
British women writers, 90n864
British words on tape 1991, 92n906
British writers, suppl.2, 93n1191
British/American lang dict, 93n1069
Britton, Allen Perdue, 91n1291
Britton, Donald M., 90n1490
Britton, Jane, 91n1218
Broadcast communications dict, 3d ed, 90n914
Broadcasting & cable market place 1992, 93n992
Broadcasting in the UK, 2d ed, 94n1013
Broadening views, 1968-88, 91n1152
Broadhead, Susan H., 93n112
Broadway: an encyclopedic gd to the hist, people & places of Times Square, 92n467
Broadway's prize-winning musicals, 94n1465
Brockway, Sandi, 94n74
Broderick, Barbara, 91n297
Broderick, Mick, 93n1349
Brodie, Edmund D., Jr., 90n1563
Brogan, Martha L., 92n607
Brogan, T. V. F., 90n1117, 94n1302
Bromley, David W., 94n633
Bromley, Debra J., 93n1388
Bronson, Fred, 90n1292, 93n1276, 94n1360
Brook, J. M., 91n1101
Brooke, Michael, 93n1540
Brooklin Public Library Business Library Staff, 93n202
Brooks, Barbera, 90n1468
Brooks, Tim, 90n916
Brooks-Gunn, Jeanne, 92n843
Brosman, Catharine Savage, 90n1203, 92n1233, 94n1283
Brosse, Jacques, 93n1403
Brower, Keith H., 91n1241
Brown, Angela, 92n200
Brown, Anthony E., 93n1231
Brown, Archie, 92n22
Brown, Ashley, 91n1306

Brown, Barbara E., 94n246
Brown, Catherine, 94n19
Brown, Catherine L., 90n843, 91n443
Brown, Charles N., 90n1112
Brown, Claud L., 91n1542
Brown, David E., 90n1529
Brown, Denis, 93n1285
Brown, Elsa Barkley, 94n965
Brown, Enid, 94n149
Brown, Fred, 90n1690
Brown, Gary, 94n1733
Brown, Jonathan, 93n1270
Brown, Julie, 92n419
Brown, Kenneth, 90n562
Brown, Kenneth O., 93n1398
Brown, Lawrence D., 90n197
Brown, Les, 93n986
Brown, Lesley, 94n1099
Brown, Linda, 93n333
Brown, Muriel W., 93n1120
Brown, Peter Lancaster, 91n1756
Brown, Philip J., 90n1720
Brown Publishing Network, 93n346, 93n347
Brown, Robert, 92n419
Brown, Russell K., 90n649
Brown, Wendy E., 94n1891
Browne, Edward T., Jr., 93n1494
Browne, Glenn J., 91n12
Browne, Kevin O., 91n12
Browne, Ray B., 91n12
Browne, Steven E., 93n1345
Browne, William P., 91n1476
Brownell, Kelly D., 90n1663
Browning, James A., 94n88
Browning, Larry M., 94n710
Brownrigg, Ronald, 94n1537
Brown's dir of instructional programs, 1992: K-8, 93n346
Brown's dir of instructional programs, 1992: 7-12, 93n347
Brownson, Ann L., 91n735, 91n737, 94n734, 94n735, 94n736
Brownstone, David, 92n23, 92n842, 94n920, 94n1996
Brownstone, David M., 90n238, 90n375, 90n1459, 90n1625, 91n553
Bruccoli, Aryln, 94n1243
Bruccoli, Matthew J., 90n1126, 91n1161, 92n1162
Bruce, Kimball W., 94n751
Bruce, Thomas R., 92n544
Bruhn, John G., 91n1688
Brunas, John, 92n1358
Brunas, Michael, 92n1358
Brundle, C. Richard, 93n1605
Brune, Lester H., 92n743, 93n733
Brunei, 90n118
Brunel, Pierre, 94n1155
Bruno, Frank J., 90n743, 94n807
Bruntjen, Scott, 92n18, 92n19, 93n32, 94n10
Brus, Eric, 91n1466, 94n1983
Brush up your Shakespeare!, 91n1213
Bryan, George B., 92n1376, 93n1317
Bryan, John E., 91n1498
Bryant, Brian R., 93n333
Bryer, Jackson R., 91n1153
Bryson, Bill, 93n968
Brzezinski, Mary Jo, 94n272
Buchanan, Thomas M., 90n1552
Buchmann-Moller, Frank, 91n1315
Buck, Carl Darling, 90n1030
Buck, Claire, 93n942
Buckingham, J., 90n1753
Buckingham, Peter H., 91n728
Buckland, John, 92n798
Buczacki, Stefan, 90n1500
Buddhist America, 90n1400
Budnick, Carol, 92n577
Buehrer, Beverley Bare, 91n1350, 91n1376, 94n1409
Buendia, Laurent, 91n605

Buenker, John D., 90n490
Buff, Sheila, 91n190
Buhle, Mari Jo, 91n763
Buhle, Paul, 91n763
Building construction cost data 1991, 92n192
Building construction illus, 2d ed, 92n1600
Building lib collections on aging, 92n806
Building the ref collection, 94n619
Building trades dict, 90n1588
Building your biblical studies lib, 90n1397
Bukowski, Leonard, 94n1369
Bulbs, 91n1498
Bulfinch pocket dict of art terms, 3d ed, 93n1023
Bull, C. Neil, 94n887
Bull, Edith, 90n1530
Bull, John, 90n1530
Bullock, Joyce, 94n801
Bullough, Vern L., 93n882, 93n1659
Bullwinkle, Davis A., 90n850, 90n851, 90n852
Bultman, Scott, 94n1314
Bunch, Bryan, 90n1422, 93n1455
Bunson, Margaret, 92n506
Burack, Sylvia K., 91n944, 94n999
Burchill, Mary D., 90n561
Burek, Deborah M., 91n37, 91n38, 93n245
Burels, Ned, 94n407
Burger, Barbara Lewis, 92n450
Burgess, Mary A., 94n432
Burgess, Michael, 90n598, 93n1155, 94n432, 94n1238
Burgess, Patricia, 90n29
Burgess, Scott Alan, 91n1158, 92n1173
Burgess, Stanley M., 90n1407
Burgess, Warren E., 90n1549, 92n1575, 93n1554
Burgis, Nina, 90n1177
Burke, Arthur Meredyth, 92n387
Burke, Georganne, 93n583
Burke, John Gordon, 90n1461, 92n66
Burke, Patricia D., 92n835
Burke, Patrick D., 90n674
Burkett, Nancy H., 94n657
Burma, 93n124
Burma: a study gd, 90n119
Burne, Jerome, 91n499
Burnell, Richard S., 94n634
Burnett, David, 91n1006
Burnim, Kalman A., 92n1378, 92n1379
Burns, Grant, 90n967, 94n709
Burns, Richard D., 92n454
Burns, Richard Dean, 93n733, 94n797
Buro Scientia, 90n1592
Burr, Brooks M., 92n1576
Burr, John R., 94n1482
Burrell, C. Colson, 94n1620
Burs under the saddle, 90n471
Burt, Eugene C., 90n945, 91n1022
Burton, Maurice, 90n1515, 91n1555
Burton, Robert, 90n1515, 91n1555
Burton, Rosemary, 94n464
Burton, William C., 93n574
Burwell dir of info brokers 1992, 93n654
Burwell, Helen P., 90n583, 93n654
Buschman, Isabel, 92n948
Bushell, Chris, 91n1825
Bushnell, Brooks, 94n1453
Business & legal CD-ROMS in print 1993, 94n175
Business & the environment, 93n249
Business connexions 1992, 93n228
Business info desk ref, 92n140
Business info: how to find it, how to use it, 2d ed, 93n209
Business info sourcebk, 93n200
Business jls of the US, 92n152
Business Library Staff, Brooklyn Public Library, 90n183
Business One Irwin bus & investment almanac, 1992, 93n220
Business One Irwin investor's hndbk 1993, 94n187
Business online: a Canadian gd, 91n155

Business online: the professional's gd, 91n161
Business orgs, agencies, & pubs dir, 6th ed, 93n190
Business pers index: Aug 1990-July 1991, 93n215
Business pers index [CD-ROM], 93n216
Business rankings annual, 1989, 90n183
Business rankings annual, 1992, 93n202
Business sftwr dir 1990/91, 91n138
Business Week, editors of, 94n169
Business Week's gd to the best bus schools, 91n139
Business Week's gd to the best executive educ programs, 94n169
Business who's who of Austral., 22d ed, 90n162
Bustros, Gabriel M., 92n119
Butcher, Judith, 94n1000
Butler, Brian, 94n204
Butler, Deborah A., 91n1145
Butler, Edgar W., 90n145
Butler, Kurt, 91n1674
Butler, Marian, 92n11, 92n12
Butler, Penny, 93n205
Butorin, Pavel, 91n108
Butterflies & moths, 93n1547
Butterflies through binoculars, 94n1703
Butterfly bk, 93n1551
Butterworth, Neil, 91n1267
Butterworth, Rod R., 93n1098
Butterworths law dir 1993, 94n558
Buttlar, Lois J., 90n298
Buttolph, Ken, 92n1800, 92n1801
Button in ear, 90n926
Buttress, F. A., 93n2
Buyer's gd to American wines, 2d ed, 94n1605
Buying gd issue, 1989, 90n224
Buyouts: dir of LBO financing sources, 1990 ed, 91n173
Buyouts: dir of M & A intermediaries, 1990 ed, 91n174
Buzzworm magazine, editors of, 93n1765
By Jove!, 94n1396
Byelorussian-English, English-Byelorussian dict with complete phonetics, 93n1079
Byerman, Keith, 90n1157
Byrge, Duane, 92n1359
Byrne, Art, 92n24
Byrne, John A., 91n139, 94n169
Byrne, W. J., 93n575
Bzowski, Frances Diodato, 93n1167

C. S. Lewis: a ref gd 1972-88, 94n1254
Cabell, David W. E., 94n663
Cabell's dir of publ opportunities in educ, 3d ed, 94n663
Cable, Greg, 93n1655
Cacti: the illus dict, 92n1551
CAD rating gd, 2d ed, 92n1709
CAD/CAM abstracts annual 1988, 90n1707
CAD/CAM abstracts annual 1991, 93n1690
Cadogan, Gerald, 94n529
Cadrin, Carmen, 92n1501
Caelli, William, 93n315, 94n1900
Cagle, William R., 91n1482
Cahalan, James M., 94n1291
Cahn, Robert W., 90n1599, 94n1795
Cahuilla landscape, 92n359
Caire, William, 91n1591
Calantone, Roger J., 91n260
Calder, William M. III, 91n1124
Calderini, Simonetta, 94n101
Caldwell, Ronald J., 92n478, 94n1521
Caldwell, Sandra M., 94n1521
Calendar of literary facts, 92n1100
Calenzani, Lucio, 91n1024
Calhoun, David, 91n1468
Calhoun, Milburn, 93n110
Calhoun, Randall, 94n1236
California: an environmental atlas & gd, 92n1789
California & Hawaii publishing market place, 91n661
California environmental dir, 5th ed, 94n2007

California Indians, 92n361
California Indians: primary resources, rev ed, 91n400
California initiatives & referendums 1912-90, 93n793
California legal hist mss in the Huntington Lib, 90n554
California museum dir, 2d ed, 92n63
California water resources dir, 2d ed, 92n1757
California wine winners 1989, 91n1488
California's great chardonnays, 92n1496
California's wild heritage, 91n1551
Calinger, Betty J., 92n1462
Calinger, Ronald S., 94n718
Callender, John Hancock, 91n1025
Calloway, Colin G., 92n360
Calvert, Peter, 93n774
Cambodian-English English-Cambodian dict, 91n1082
Cambridge air & space dict, 92n1591
Cambridge atlas of astronomy, 2d ed, 90n1743
Cambridge biographical dict, 92n25
Cambridge dict of Australian places, 94n471
Cambridge ency, 94n33
Cambridge ency of ...
    China, 2d ed, 93n125
    human evolution, 94n394
    India, Pakistan, Bangladesh, Sri Lanka, Nepal, Bhutan & the Maldives, 91n99
    Japan, 94n113
    Latin America & the Caribbean, 94n142
    ornithology, 93n1540
    space, 92n1592
Cambridge gd to ...
    American theatre, 94n1479
    the historic places of Britain & Ireland, 90n458
    the museums of Europe, 92n62
    theatre, updated ed, 94n1471
    world theatre, 90n1362
Cambridge hndbk of contemporary China, 92n94
Cambridge Market Intelligence, 94n223
Cambridge ritualists, 92n1132
Cameron, Lucille W., 90n264
Cameron, Myra, 94n1826
Camp Dresser & McKee, Inc., 91n1807
Camp, Norman M., 90n739
Camp, Roderic A., 93n775
Camp, Roderic Ai, 94n12
Camp, Wesley D., 91n69
Campano, Frederick W., 94n726
Campbell, Alta, 92n145, 93n208, 94n172
Campbell, Elizabeth, 92n1501
Campbell, George L., 92n1012
Campbell, Jonathan A., 90n1564
Campbell, Karlyn Kohrs, 94n957
Campbell, Malcolm, 93n832, 93n833
Campbell, Margaret, 90n1259
Campbell, R. D., 92n1792
Campbell, Robert Jean, 90n1672
Campbell, Thomas J., 91n1790
Campion, Dowland & the lutenist songwriters, 90n1222
Campus-free college degrees, 4th ed, 90n340
Campus-free college degrees, 5th ed, 93n378
Camus, Josephine, 92n1531
Can you name that team?, 92n775
Canada, 94n127
Canada: a reader's gd, 93n19
Canada & intl peace & security, 91n773
Canada Employment & Immigration Com, Career Info Directorate, 90n339
Canada legal dir 1990, 91n573
Canada legal dir 1992, 93n583
Canada media dir, 91n938
Canada tax cases: index & citator, 94n581
Canada votes 1935-88, 91n756
Canada's army in WW II, 94n702
Canadia oil industry dir, 1991, 92n1756
Canadian almanac & dir 1991, 92n98
Canadian architecture collection, 94n1053

Canadian Assn of Law Libs dir, 94n649
Canadian bk review annual 1988, 90n4
Canadian bk review annual 1990, 93n10
Canadian bks in print 1991: author & title index, 92n11
Canadian bks in print 1991: subject index, 92n12
Canadian bus & economics, 3d ed, 94n246
Canadian bus in the Pacific Rim, 94n251
Canadian children's dict, 92n1043
Canadian dict of bus & economics, 94n247
Canadian dirs 1790-1987, 90n125
Canadian Educ Assn hdnbk 1991, 92n276
Canadian environmental dir 1991, 92n1777
Canadian feminist per index, 1972-85, 92n868
Canadian feminist thesaurus, 91n620
Canadian fisheries & ocean industries dir, 3d ed, 91n224
Canadian global almanac 1993, 94n1
Canadian Health Libs Assn dir 1990-91, 92n613
Canadian hospital dir, v.38, Sept 90, 91n1645
Canadian human rights yrbk 1989-90, 92n559
Canadian illus news, Montreal 1869-83, 90n909
Canadian ISBN publs' dir 1990, 92n633
Canadian law dict, 2d ed, 92n537
Canadian law symposia index, 93n598
Canadian legal sftwr dir 1991, 92n540
Canadian lib hndbk, 94n617
Canadian lib yrbk, 4th ed, 90n591
Canadian lit index: cum index to 1986 pubs, 93n1218
Canadian lit index: cum index to 1987 pubs, 93n1219
Canadian markets 1990, 91n903
Canadian master tax gd, 1992, 93n229
Canadian media list 1992/93, 93n952
Canadian Medical Assn gd to prescription & over-the-counter drugs, 93n1661
Canadian medical device dir, 93n1642
Canadian mines hndbk 1989-90, 90n239
Canadian obituary record, 90n37
Canadian obituary record 1991, 94n18
Canadian Oxford intermediate atlas, 94n457
Canadian Oxford school atlas, 6th ed, 94n456
Canadian parliamentary gd, spring 1990, 91n755
Canadian parliamentary hndbk, 1988 ed, 90n716
Canadian parliamentary hndbk, 93n763
Canadian Payments Association, 91n212
Canadian Payments Assn dir 1990, 91n212
Canadian peace dir, 90n717
Canadian per index, v.43, 92n56
Canadian photo market, 92n962
Canadian picture dict, 92n1044
Canadian poets: vital facts, 90n1198
Canadian primary dict, 92n1045
Canadian public admin: bibliog, suppl. 5, 92n755
Canadian quaternary vocabulary, 94n1943
Canadian small business hndbk, 2d ed, 92n151
Canadian spelling dict, 7th ed, 94n1102
Canadian studies: foreign pubs & theses, 4th ed, 93n134
Canadian studies on Hungarians: a bibliog. Suppl., 94n408
Canadian who's who 1990, 92n26
Canadian Women's Indexing Group, 91n620, 92n868
Canadian women's movement, 1960-90, 94n966
Canadian world almanac & bk of facts 1991, 92n1
Canadian writers & their works: cum index, fiction series, 94n1271
Canadian writers & their works: cum index, poetry series, 94n1272
Canadian writers & their works: fiction series, 90n1194
Canadian writers & their works: poetry series, 90n1195
Canadian writer's market, 9th ed, 91n956
Canadian writers, 1920-59, 2d series, 91n1227
Canadian yrbk of intl law, v.27, 92n547
Canavan, Diane D., 93n402
Canby, Courtlandt, 90n505, 91n478
Cancer dict, 94n1858
Cancer sourcebk, v.1, 91n1693
Cancer therapy, 94n1860
Canine lexicon, 94n1706
Canned art: clip art for the Macintosh, 91n1034
Canning, Nancy, 93n1253

Cannon, John, 90n530
CANSCAIP companion, 92n875
Cantatas of J. S. Bach, 90n1256
Canter, Laurence A., 93n589
Cantor, George, 92n440, 94n416
Cantrell, Karen, 90n811
Capital source, fall 1989, 90n94
Caplan, Usher, 94n1278
Cappiello, Frank, 90n201, 92n155
Captain John Smith: a ref gd, 92n455
Capula, Massimo, 91n1603
Car bk, 1991 ed, 92n1796
Carande, Robert J., 94n1894
Caraway, Georgia Kemp, 90n893, 92n893
Carcinogenically active chemicals, 92n1682
Cardinale, Susan, 91n1182
Career advancement for women in the fed serv, 94n270
Career Associates, 93n309
Career connection, rev ed, 93n410
Career discovery ency, 91n371, 94n384
Career gd to America's top industries, 94n278
Career index, 91n370
Career opportunities for bilinguals & multilinguals, 92n1015
Career training sourcebk, 94n388
Careers & educl opportunities, 90n360
Caregiving of older adults, 94n867
Carey, Patrick W., 94n1525
Cargill, Patrick, 91n1730
Caribbean 1975-80, 94n143
Caribbean women novelists, 94n1301
Caring for kids with special needs, 94n918
Carl, Joachim, 91n1499
Carl Maria von Weber: a gd to research, 91n1274
Carlen, Claudia, 92n1409, 92n1419
Carlin, Margaret F., 92n318
Carlisle, Richard, 91n75
Carlson, Eric G., 93n377
Carlson, Rhonda, 91n630
Carman, John, 92n1389
Carmichael, Suzanne, 91n992
Carnegie lib in Ill., 92n602
Carnegie Library of Pittsburgh Science and Technology Department, 94n1584
Carner, Gary, 91n1316
Carnevale, Diane, 92n924
Caroline drama, 2d ed, 93n1202
Carolinian-English dict, 93n1080
Carothers, Diane Foxhill, 92n907
Carpenter, Allan, 90n100, 91n502, 92n84, 93n918
Carpenter, Charles C., 90n1565
Carpenter, Clive, 93n4
Carpenter, Joel A., 91n1434
Carpenter, John, 90n1696
Carpenter, Lisa, 93n957
Carpenter, Sue, 94n472
Carper, James C., 90n1377
Carper, Joyce, 92n513
Carper, N. Gordon, 92n513
Carpovich, Eugene A., 90n1429
Carpovich, Vera V., 90n1429
Carr, Dawson W., 94n1061
Carr, Donald D., 91n1786
Carr, Jennifer L., 93n281
Carr, John C., 92n268
Carradice, Ian, 91n983
Carrera, Michael A., 93n883
Carrier, Jeffrey L., 91n1351, 92n1337
Carroll, Bob, 91n828
Carroll, Frances Laverne, 90n581, 93n1122
Carroll, Mark, 90n487
Carruth, Gordon, 94n504
Carruth, Gorton, 94n1189
Carskadon, Mary A., 94n808
Carson, Anne, 93n923
Carstensen, Richard, 93n1528

Carter, April, 91n537
Carter, Craig, 91n820, 94n838
Carter, David, 93n1547
Carter, John, 94n1026
Carter, Margaret L., 91n1139
Carter, Pat, 91n993
Carter, Sarah, 91n912
Carter, Susanne, 93n1169, 94n1219
Caruba, Alan, 92n889
Carvajal, Manuel J., 94n143
Carver, Craig M., 92n1023
Cary Grant: a bio-bibliog, 91n1350
Cary, Tristram, 93n1246
Casada, James A., 91n444
Cash Box black contemporary album charts, 1975-87, 90n1277
Cash Box country album charts, 1964-88, 91n1311
Cash for college, 94n360
Cashman, Norine, 91n1012
Cashmore, E. Ellis, 90n363
Caskey, Jefferson D., 91n1146
Cass, James, 92n293
Cassel, Jeris F., 94n1483
Cassell bk of proverbs, 93n1295
Cassell careers ency, 13th ed, 94n385
Cassell, Carol, 90n813
Cassell concise English dict, 90n995
Cassell concise English dict, new ed, 94n1098
Cassell dict of literary & lang terms, 94n980
Cassell ency dict, 92n37
Cassell everyday phrases, new ed, 92n1024
Cassell food dict, 92n1483
Cassell pocket English dict, 92n1016
Cassell spelling dict, 92n1055
Cassels, Alan, 92n710
Cassiday, Bruce, 94n1207
Cassidy, Daniel J., 91n314, 94n331, 94n332, 94n333
Cassidy, Frederic G., 93n1062
Cassin, Barbara, 92n1672
Cassutt, Michael, 94n1755
Castagno, John, 90n959, 91n1018, 92n984, 92n985
Castello-Cortes, Ian, 93n172
Castillo-Speed, Lillian, 94n971
Castle, Lance, 92n1130
Castleman, Harry, 91n972
Caswell, Lucy Shelton, 90n908
Catala, Rafael, 92n1186, 93n1187
Catalog of ...
    Calif. state grants assistance 1989, 90n803
    catalogs 2, 91n195
    dicts, word bks, & philological texts, 1440-1900, 94n1074
    1st eds, 92n928
    govt inventions available for licensing 1989, 91n225
    pre-1900 vocal mss in the music lib, Univ of Calif. at Berkeley, 90n1263
    prenatally diagnosed conditions, 2d ed, 93n1654
    teratogenic agents, 6th ed, 90n1638
    teratogenic agents, 7th ed, 93n1628
    the diptera of the Australasian & oceanian regions, 91n1588
    the German-Americana collection, Univ of Cincinnati, 91n393
    the musical works of William Billings, 92n1268
    types of Coleoptera in the Canadian Natl Collection of Insects, suppl.3, 94n1728
Cataloger's gd to MARC coding & tagging for AV material, 94n627
Cataloging computer files, 94n628
Cataloging serv bulletin, no.1-52, 92n578
Catalogue of ...
    Arabic mss, fascicule 5, 90n520
    audio & video collections of Holocaust testimony, 2d ed, 93n528
    Canadian catalogues, 2d ed, 91n188
    Canadian catalogues, 3d ed, 93n227
    crime, rev ed, 91n1132
    18th-century symphonies, 90n1275
    English Bible translations, 93n1427

Catalogue of ... *(continued)*
  European sculpture in the Ashmolean Museum 1540 to the present day, 94n1067
  films & videos in the British Medical Assn lib, 94n1824
  freshwater & marine fishes of Ala., 94n1714
  healthy food, 91n1491
  medieval & renaissance mss in the Beinecke Rare Bk & Mss Lib, Yale Univ, v.3, 94n30
  mosses of Austral. & its external territories, 91n1540
  palaearctic diptera, v.7, 93n1567
  the 15th-century printed bks in the Harvard Univ Lib, v.1, 92n36
  the 15th-century printed bks in the Harvard Univ Lib, v.2, 94n31
  the Bertram R. Davis "Robert Southey" collection, 91n1218
  the Erasmus collection in the City Lib of Rotterdam, 92n1394
  the letters, tapes & photographs in the Irving Layton collection, 94n1270
  the mss in the Irving Layton collection, 90n1193
  the pre-1500 W ms bks at the Newberry Lib, 91n551
Catalogue raisonne of the graphic work of Richard Florsheim, 90n980
Catastrophes & disasters, 94n469
Catch phrases, cliches & idioms, 92n1039
Catchpole, Catherine, 93n1329
Catchpole, Terry, 93n1329
Cate, George Allan, 90n881
Cates, Jo A., 91n958
Cathey, H. Marc, 91n1503
Catholic lifetime reading plan, 90n1403
Catholic school educ in the US, 93n348
Cats, 94n1704
Cat's pajamas: a fabulous fictionary of familiar phrases, 90n1015
Catsberg, C. M. E., 91n1490
Catterall, Peter, 93n144
Cattle: a hndbk to the breeds of the world, 93n1491
Caughey, Bruce, 90n441
Caughman, Jennifer T., 93n67
Caughman, Jennifer Trzyna, 92n63, 94n2007
Cavanagh, Donna Tozzi, 94n199
Cavendish, Richard, 94n464
Cavinato, Joseph L., 91n1814
Cayne, Bernard S., 90n1437
Cayton, Mary Kupiec, 94n505
CCCC bibliog of composition & rhetoric 1987, 91n1043
CCH Tax Law editors, 92n263, 92n265
CD review digest annual 1990: classical, v.4, 92n1288
CD review digest annual 1990: jazz, popular, etc., 92n1308
CD-ROM buyer's gd & hndbk, 3d ed, 94n1917
CD-ROM dir 1990, 91n1747
CD-ROM dir 1992, 93n1691
CD-ROM finder, 1993 ed, 94n1918
CD-ROM for librarians & educators, 94n1920
CD-ROM info products: an evaluative gd & dir, 92n1716
CD-ROM info products: the evaluative gd, 92n1717
CD-ROM market place 1991, 92n1718
CD-ROM 1992, 94n645
CD-ROM per index, 93n82
CD-ROM research collections, 93n660
CD-ROM reviews 1987-90, 93n659
CD-ROM tech for info managers, 91n633
CD-ROMS in print 1991, 92n1719
CD-ROMS in print [CD-ROM], 93n1692
CD-ROMs in print 1993, 94n1919
Cecil, Nancy L., 94n1179
Cecil, Nancy Lee, 94n1178
Celebrity Services International, Inc., 91n14
Celebrity sources, 91n20
Cella, Catherine, 94n1426
Celluloid wars, 94n1451
Cember, Richard P., 94n1948
Cencig, Didier, 93n132
Censorship & Hollywood's Hispanic image, 94n1448
Census snapshot for all US places, 1990, 94n928

Center for International Financial Analysis & Research, Inc., 90n220, 90n221
Center for Research Libs hndbk, 92n608
Center for the Utilization of Federal Technology, National Technical Information Service, 91n225, 91n1463, 91n1465
Central African Republic, 94n97
Central heating: glossary, 92n1623
Central Intelligence Agency, 93n105
Central Pacific campaign, 1943-44, 91n677
Centre de Terminologie de Bruxelles, Institute Libre Marie Haps, 93n323
Centre for Canadian Studies, staff of, 92n6
Century of ...
  emblems, 91n669
  population growth, 90n834
  Pullman cars, v.2, 91n1820
Ceramics & glass: intl auctions from Jan 1st to Dec 31st, 92n974
Cerf, Christopher, 94n1101
Cevasco, G. A., 91n1222, 94n981
Chadbourne, Janice H., 92n976
Chadwick, Bruce A., 93n867
Chafetz, Morris, 92n839
Chai, Alan, 94n172
Chalcraft, Anthony, 93n20, 93n21
Chaliand, Gerard, 91n714, 94n712
Chalif, Edward L., 90n1535
Challenge of euthanasia, 91n852
Chalmers, Lex, 91n445
Chalmin, Philippe, 94n188
Chamber music: an intl gd to works & their instrumentation, 94n1349
Chamberlain, Bobby J., 93n1091
Chamberlain, Greg, 90n730, 92n723
Chamberlin, William J., 93n1427
Chambers biology dict, 90n1477
Chambers concise dict, 93n1057
Chambers concise dict of scientists, 91n1460
Chambers concise ency of film & TV, 93n1346
Chambers dict of pol biog, 93n721
Chambers dict of synonyms & antonyms, 90n1031
Chambers earth scis dict, 93n1720
Chambers English dict, 7th ed, 90n996
Chambers film quotes, 93n1374
Chambers, Frances, 90n144
Chambers nuclear energy & radiation dict, 93n1742
Chambers thesaurus, 90n997
Champion, Larry S., 94n1256
Chan, Julie S., 92n540
Chandler, David G., 90n655, 94n521
Chandler, Ralph C., 92n530
Chandler, Richard J., 90n1531
Chandna, Krishna, 94n597
Chang, Kai, 91n1626
Chang, Sidney H., 93n521
Changing wilderness values,1930-90, 92n1767
Channeling: a bibliographic exploration, 93n806
Channell, David F., 90n1572
Chant, Christopher, 93n700
Chaplin, Charles C. G., 94n1713
Chapman, Arthur D., 94n1648
Chapman, Charles F., 90n1655
Chapman, Karen J., 90n274
Chapman, Mike, 91n840
Chapman, Robert L., 93n1075
Chappell, Duncan, 91n594
Chappell, Pat, 92n1802
Character trademarks, 92n256
Characters from young adult lit, 93n1143
Characters in 19th century lit, 94n1157
Characters in 20th-century lit, 91n1103
Charitable orgs of the US 1992-92, 93n878
Charlemagne Tower collection of American colonial laws, 92n519
Charles A. Beard's the presidents in American hist, rev. ed, 91n490
Charles Darwin's marginalia, v.1, 92n1525
Charles James Fox 1749-1806: a bibliog, 93n773

Charles, Jill, 90n1358, 90n1359, 90n1360, 93n1387, 93n1388, 93n1390
Charles Press hndbk of current medical abbrevs, 3d ed, 93n1622
Charles Szladits' gd to foreign legal materials: German, 2d ed, 91n563
Charlie Chan at the movies, 90n1339
Charlie Parker discography, 94n1369
Charlton, James, 91n593, 92n780
Charny, Israel W., 92n560
Charron, Andrew, 91n1260
Charters, Alexander N., 90n357
Chartres: sources & literary interpretation, 90n969
Charts, graphics & stats index 1988-91, 93n916
Charuest, Michel, 93n905
Chase, A. R., 93n1499
Chase's annual events 1990, 91n2
Chatfield, Mary, 94n156
Chaucer & the Bible, 90n1175
Chaucer name dict, 90n1176
Chaucer's general prologue to the Canterbury Tales, 91n1201
Chaucer's Knight's Tale: an annot bibliog 1900-85, 92n1199
Chaudhuri, Brahma, 91n546
Chave, E. H., 91n1599
Cheatham, Annie, 90n313, 91n290
Checkland, Sydney, 91n129
Checklist of ...
    American imprints 1830-39: author index, 90n20
    American imprints 1830-39: title index, 90n21
    American imprints for 1840, 92n18
    American imprints for 1841, 92n19
    American imprints for 1842, 93n32
    American imprints for 1843, 94n10
    beetles of Canada & Alaska, 93n1560
    Canadian copyright deposits in the British Museum 1895-1923, v.3, pt.2, 90n40
    Canadian copyright deposits in the British Museum 1895-1923, v.4, 90n41
    Canadian copyright deposits in the British Museum 1895-1923, v.5, 90n42
    Melville reviews, 93n1178
    the Newberry Lib's printed bks in sci, medicine, tech, & the pseudoscis ca. 1460-1750, 94n1558
    women writers 1801-1900, 92n1189
Chef's bk of formulas, yields, & sizes, 92n1499
Chelekis, George, 94n895
Chemical engineering bibliog (1967-88), 91n1610
Chemical exposure & human health, 94n1861
Chemical hazard communication gdbk, 2d ed, 94n2018
Chemical lit 1700-1860, 90n1749
Chemical research faculties 1988, 90n1755
Chemical structure sftwr for personal computers, 90n1756
Chemical tradename dict, 94n1932
Chemist's ready ref hndbk, 91n1777
Chen, C. H., 94n1774
Chen, Ching-chih, 91n1745, 91n1746
Chen, Janey, 94n1110
Chen, Zhenghua, 91n1518
Chenery, Hollis, 91n151
Cheney, Walter J., 93n853
Cheng, Peter P., 91n98
Cheremisinoff, N. P., 90n1586
Cheremisinoff, Nicholas P., 90n1757, 92n1612
Cheremisinoff, Paul N., 90n1792, 90n1793, 90n1794, 92n1774
Chernofsky, Ellen, 93n441
Cherovsky, Erwin, 92n541
Cherry, Virginia R., 93n794
Chess: an annot bibliog 1969-88, 92n790
Chess ency, 92n789
Chester Himes: an annot primary & secondary bibliog, 94n1235
Cheung, King-Kok, 90n1122
Chevalier, Tracy, 90n1088, 92n1244, 94n1144
Chevrefils, Marlys, 91n1223
Chevrolet restoration dir, 91n1826
Cheynet, Bertrand, 91n1762
Chiappinelli, John A., 91n173, 91n174

Chiarmonte, Paula, 91n928
Chicago manual of style, 14th ed, 94n1001
Chicana studies index, 94n971
Chicano anthology index, 92n353
Chicano writers, 90n1123
CHID search ref gd, June 1990, 91n1638
CHID word list, June 1990, 91n1639
Chielens, Edward E., 93n1163
Child abuse & neglect, 91n602
Child apprentices in America from Christ's Hospital, London 1617-1778, 91n415
Child care, 91n893
Child care crisis, 94n923
Child Study Children's Book Committee at Bank Street College, 91n363
Child welfare stat bk 1993, 94n922
Childcraft dict, 90n1016
Childcraft: the how & why lib, 90n47, 93n58
Childers, Roberta, 92n1757, 93n1773, 94n2007
CHILDES/BIB: an annot bibliog of child lang & lang disorders, 92n269
Childhood lead poisoning prevention, 91n1697
Childhood symptoms, 94n1838
Children & adjustment to divorce, 91n861
Children of ...
    alcoholics: a bibliog & resource gd, 4th ed, 91n880
    alcoholics: a sourcebk, 92n840
    Nuggets, 91n1328
Children's animal atlas, 93n1531
Children's atlas of ...
    exploration, 94n452
    people & places, 94n454
    world hist, 90n527
Children's bk awards intl, 94n1195
Children's Book Council, 94n1191
Children's bk illus & design, 94n1062
Children's bk review index, v.14, 91n50
Children's bk review index, v.16, 93n1145
Children's bks: awards & prizes, 1992 ed, 94n1191
Children's bks in print 1989-90, 90n16
Children's bks in print 1991-92, 92n16
Children's bks in print 1993, 94n9
Children's bks of the yr, 1990 ed, 91n1108
Children's Britannica, 92n38
Children's cat, 16th ed, 92n610
Children's fiction sourcebk, 93n1125
Children's hour: radio progs for children 1929-56, 91n971
Children's lit review, v.16, 90n1090
Children's lit review, v.25, 93n1141
Children's media market place, 3d ed, 90n621
Children's ref plus, 93n11
Children's servs in the American public lib, 91n645
Children's space atlas, 93n1703
Children's writer's & illustrator's market, 1989, 90n897
Children's writer's & illustrator's market, 1992, 93n957
Children's writer's word bk, 94n996
Childwise cat, rev ed, 91n191
Childwise cat, 3d ed, 94n921
Chile, 90n141
Chilvers, Ian, 92n981, 94n1198
China business dir 1992, 93n278
China leading cos, 94n242
China statistical abstract 1989, 90n120
China trade & price stats 1988, 90n184
Chinery, Michael, 90n1546
Chinese Academy of Social Sciences, 90n121
Chinese drama, 92n1228
Chinese-English dict of enigmatic folk similes, 92n1317
Chinese-English dict of the Wu dialect, 93n1081
Ching, Francis D. K., 92n1600
Chiri, Alfredo U., 94n1895
Chironis, Nicholas P., 92n1622
Chiropractic college admissions & curriculum dir, 1988-89, 90n1659
Chitin sourcebk, 91n1764

Chittick, Kathryn, 90n1178
Choi, Patricia E., 93n249
Choice annual cum index, v.28, 92n57
Choices, v.2, 92n330
Choose a Christian college, 3d ed, 94n334
Choosing bks for children, rev. ed, 91n1120
Choral music in print master index 1991, 92n1285
Choral music of Latin America, 93n1267
Choral music reviews index 2, 1986-88, 91n1290
Chorus in opera, 94n1353
Chorzempa, Rosemary A., 94n433
Chris & Tilde Stuart's field gd to the mammals of S Africa, 90n1558
Chrissanthaki, Thana, 90n195
Christian communication, 90n886
Christian resource dir, 90n1383
Christian writer's manual of style, 90n900
Christianity in China, 90n1411
Christiansen, Kenneth, 93n1561
Christianson, Grant T., 92n1781, 94n2011
Christienne, Charles, 90n660
Christine de Pizan: a bibliog, 2d ed, 91n1233
Christner, Anne M., 92n836
Christo, Doris, 91n655
Christo prints & objects 1963-87, 90n953
Christopher Columbus ency, 92n415
Christopher Marlowe in the 80s, 94n1255
Chronicle career index, 93n405
Chronicle financial aid gd for 1991-92 school yr, 93n367
Chronicle 4-yr college databk, 1988-89, 90n333
Chronicle 4-yr college databk for 1991-92 school yr, 93n368
Chronicle of ...
    America, 91n498
    the 1st World War, v.1, 92n504
    the 1st World War, v.2, 93n551
    the world, 91n499
    W fashion, 93n1010
Chronicle of Higher Education, editors of, 90n332, 93n355
Chronicle 2-yr college databk, 1988-89, 90n334
Chronicle 2-yr college databk for 1991-92 school yr, 93n369
Chronicle vocational school manual for 1991-92 school yr, 93n406
Chronological annot bibliog of order stats, v.3, 92n846
Chronological annot bibliog of order stats, v.4, 93n902
Chronological atlas of WW II, 90n646
Chronological hist of US foreign relations, v.3, 92n743
Chronologies in old world archaeology, 3d ed, 94n485
Chronology & fact bk of the UN 1941-91, 94n792
Chronology & index of the 2d World War, 1938-45, 91n552
Chronology of ...
    African-American hist, 92n347
    conflict & resolution, 1945-85, 90n650
    Irish hist since 1500, 92n494
    Islamic hist 570-1000 CE, 90n519
    music in the Florentine theater 1751-1800, 94n1311
Chua, Romulo L., 93n1102
Chuguev, Vladimir, 90n39
Church & social action, 91n1412
Church symbolism, 2d ed, 94n1048
Churchill Livingstone's medical word gd, 92n1654
Churchill's illus medical dict, 90n1640
Cianciolo, Patricia J., 91n1109
Cibbarelli, Pamela R., 91n631, 94n644
Cichlids of North & Central America, 94n1712
Cichonski, Thomas, 94n740
Cichonski, Thomas J., 94n2017
Cieslik, Jurgen, 90n926
Cieslik, Marianne, 90n926
CIFAR's global co hndbk, 1992 ed, 93n263
Cigler, Allan J., 91n1476
Cinema sequels & remakes, 1903-87, 90n1353
Cinema sheet music, 93n1272
Cinematic vampires, 93n1353
Cinematographers, production designers, costume designers & film editors gd, 2d ed, 91n1372
Cinematographers, production designers, costume designers & film editors gd, 3d ed, 93n1371
Cinnamon, Deborah, 92n217
CIRCA Reference, staff of, 92n83
CIS 4-yr cum index, 1987-90, 93n758
CIS index to ...
    unpublished US house of representatives committee hearings 1833-1936, 92n700
    unpublished US house of representatives committee hearings 1937-46, 92n701
    US executive branch docs, 1789-1909, pt.1, 92n699
Citations & allusions to Jewish scripture in early Christian & Jewish writings through 180 CE, 93n1429
Cities & churches, 94n1502
Cities & towns in American hist, 90n847
City & state dirs in print 1990-91, 90n844
City Lights bks, 94n1220
Civardi, Anne, 90n1017
Civil rights movement, 94n595
Civil War, 90n496
Civil War battlefield gd, 91n508
Civil War maps, 2d ed, 90n648
Civil War newspaper maps: a cartobibliography of the N daily pr, 94n492
Civil War newspaper maps: a histl atlas, 94n491
Claghorn, Charles E., 90n663, 92n461
Claiborne, Robert, 90n1007, 91n1053
Claire Shaeffer's fabric sewing gd, 91n995
Clancy, Laurie, 91n1269
Clancy, Paul, 94n730
Clandestine erotic fiction in English 1800-1930, 94n1204
Clansky, Kenneth B., 90n1761
Clapham, Christopher, 92n1751
Clardy, Andrea Fleck, 92n900
Clarence L. Barnhart, 90n1021
Clark, Audrey N., 92n418
Clark, Bernadine, 93n682
Clark Blaise papers, 92n1223
Clark, Burton R., 93n358
Clark, Gladys L. H., 94n1468
Clark, Gregory R., 92n475
Clark, Janice, 90n1550
Clark, Jerome, 91n797, 91n1451, 93n807, 94n813
Clark, John O. E., 92n1029, 92n1038, 92n1056
Clark, Judith Freeman, 90n576
Clark, Murtie June, 93n457, 93n459
Clark, Robin E., 90n576
Clarke, Donald, 91n1307
Clarke, Norman F., 91n802
Clarke, Oz, 92n1484
Clarkson, Christopher, 94n29
Classic Bible study lib for today, 90n1398
Classic cult fiction, 93n1149
Classical & medieval lit criticism, v.6, 92n1133
Classical & medieval lit criticism, v.7, 92n1134
Classical ballet technique, 91n1348
Classical epic: an annot bibliog, 92n1135
Classical Greek & Roman drama, 91n1125
Classical guitar music in print, 90n1261
Classical music discographies, 1976-88, 90n1268
Classical reproducing piano roll, 91n1289
Classical scholarship, 91n1124
Claude Debussy: a gd to research, 91n1266
Claude, Louise, 92n1623
Claudio Monteverdi: a gd to research, 90n1238
Claudio, Virginia S., 92n1485
Claudy, Nicholas H., 92n1736
Clauser, Henry R., 92n1617
Clay today, 91n1040
Clayman, Charles B., 91n1657
Clayton Eshleman: a descriptive bibliog, 90n1139
CLE research gd, v.2, 94n583
Cleanth Brooks: an annot bibliog, 91n1159
Clearinghouse dir 1991-92, 92n566
Cleaver, Joanne, 93n78

Clegg, Michael B., 94n438
Clegg, Michael Barren, 91n412
Clement, Russell T., 92n968
Clemente, Rebecca, 91n354
Clements, Bonnie L., 93n850, 93n888
Clements, Patricia, 92n1095
Clergy malpractice, 92n515
Cleveland herbal, botanical, & horticultural collections, 93n1493
Cleveland Public Library, 92n1315
Clever, Glenn, 94n1275
Clewis, Beth, 93n1525
Cliff, Andrew, 94n1854
Cliff, Andrew D., 90n1634
Clifford, Denis, 90n556
Clifford, Donald H., 91n558
Clifford, J. Candace, 93n1788
Clifford Odets: a research & production sourcebk, 92n1377
Clifford Odets: an annot bibliog 1935-89, 91n1154
Clifton, Chas S., 94n1530
Climatic atlas of Mich., 92n1733
Climatic atlas of the Indian Ocean, pt.3, 91n1799
Climatological atlas of snowfall & snow depth for the NE US and SE Canada, 94n1948
Cline, Cheryl, 90n853
Cline, David, 90n1691
Cline, Ruth K. J., 91n859
Clinician's hndbk, 3d ed, 94n1847
Clinician's thesaurus, rev ed, 91n794
Clinton, Catherine, 93n932
Clinton, Helen H., 90n912
Clinton, John, 90n1622
Clockworks, 94n974
Clodfelter, Micheal, 94n692
Close, Arthur C., 90n703, 92n134, 93n744
Clough, Katherine, 94n1650
Clout, Hugh, 93n534
Cloutier, Guy, 94n582
Cloyd, Iris, 91n388
Clute, John, 94n1211
Clutton, E. H., 91n1474
Clyde, Laurel A., 94n906
CMG Information Services, 90n327, 93n361, 94n339
Coad, Brian W., 93n1555
Coastal & maritime archaeology, 92n449
Cobb, David A., 91n447
Coborn, John, 92n1586
Cocaine, 90n1695
Cocchiarelli, Joseph J., 93n1350
Cochran, Moncrieff, 94n919
Cochrane, Hamilton E., 93n1232
Cockrill, Pauline, 92n936
(Code) bk area code dir, rev ed, 90n1734
Codes of professional responsibility, 2d ed, 91n156
Codex alimentarius, v.1, 93n1479
Codex alimentarius, 2d ed, v.6, 94n1606
Codex alimentarius, v.8, 94n1607
Codignola, Luca, 93n1424
Cody, William J., 90n1490
Coe, Malcolm, 93n1516
Coffey, Timothy, 94n1651
Coffin, Tristram Potter, 93n1297
Coffman, Steve, 92n605, 94n639
Cogar, William B., 90n664
COGEL blue bk, 9th ed, 94n801
Cogeneration & small power production manual, 3d ed, 92n1606
Cogger, Harold G., 93n1575, 94n1748
Coggins, John, 94n783
Coggins, R. J., 91n1425
Coghlan, Ronan, 90n400, 93n1190
Cohen, Beth Genya, 90n325
Cohen, Hennig, 93n1297
Cohen, I. B., 90n1421
Cohen, Jay S., 90n1470
Cohen, Mark N., 91n181
Cohen, Marvin H., 90n1814

Cohen, Norman S., 91n481
Cohen, Ralph, 90n1066
Cohen, Richard M., 91n823, 92n787, 92n795
Cohen, Susan Sarah, 92n377
Cohen, William A., 91n152
Cohn, Mary, 93n747
Cohn-Sherbok, Dan, 93n1405, 94n1554
Coin atlas, 91n983
Coin World almanac, 6th ed, 91n982
Coin World, staff of, 91n982
Colaneri, John, 90n1047
Colangelo, Nicholas, 92n284
Colby, Vineta, 92n1099
Cold war chronology, 94n795
Cold war 1945-91, 94n537
Coldham, Peter Wilson, 90n389, 91n415, 91n416, 93n452, 94n430
Coldwell, Ruth, 91n472
Cole, Deborah, 90n969
Cole, Don, 93n180
Cole, Lee S., 90n1805
Cole, Sylvia, 92n878
Cole, W. Owen, 91n1452
Cole, William A., 90n1749
Coleman, Carrie C., 92n542
Coleman, Charles D., 91n163
Coleman, Edwin J., 94n45
Coleman, J. Gordon, 92n612
Coleman, J. Gordon, Jr., 93n672
Coleman, James R., 91n776
Coleman, Kathleen, 94n1284
Coletta, Paolo E., 90n665
Colette: an annot primary & secondary bibliog, 94n1285
Coley, Lemuel B., 91n1160
Colin, Patrick I, 90n1560
Collar, N. J., 94n1695
Collected papers on sports medicine research, 1982-87, 90n1687
Collectibles market gd & price index, 8th ed, 92n924
Collection agency dir, 2d ed, 93n237
Collection evaluation in academic libs, 93n677
Collection of definitions in fed statutes, 90n545
Collection of dicts & related works illustrating the dvlpmnt of the English dict, 91n1045
Collective bargaining in higher educ & the professions, bibliog no.20, 94n269
Collector's bkshelf, 92n929
Colledge, J. J., 91n692
Colleen Dewhurst: a bio-bibliog, 94n1411
College & Research Libs & College & Research Libs News: index for vs.41-50 (1980-89), 92n628
College admissions, 94n324
College admissions data hndbk 1989-90, 90n335
College admissions data hndbk 1992-93, 93n370
College admissions index of majors & sports 1989-90, 90n336
College admissions index of majors & sports 1992-93, 93n379
College Board gd to ...
    high schools, 91n307
    jobs & career planning, 91n372
    150 popular college majors, 94n352
College check mate, 3d ed, 90n331
College cost bk 1991, 91n325
College costs & financial aid hndbk 1994, 94n353
College degrees by mail, 92n300, 94n351
College Division, Barron's Educational Series, 90n337
College hndbk for transfer students 1991, 91n326
College hndbk for transfer students 1994, 94n354
College hndbk foreign student suppl. 1992, 92n302
College hndbk 1991, 91n327
College hndbk 1994, 94n355
College majors, 91n334
College majors & careers, rev ed, 94n362
College media dir 1989, 90n891
College names of the games, 90n761
College price bk 1990, 91n338
College Research Group of Concord, Massachusetts, 91n320, 91n322, 91n337

College Staff of Rugg's Recommendations, 94n364
College style sheet, 3d ed, 93n959
Collier, David, 92n643
Collier, Laurie, 94n1187
Collier, Linda P., 90n202, 92n214
Collier, Simon, 94n142
Collier's ency, 92n39
Collier's rules for desktop design & typography, 92n643
Collinge, N. E., 91n1042
Collings, Rex, 94n1106
Collingwood, Donna, 94n994
Collins, David N., 93n139
Collins field gd to the birds of Galapagos, 91n1561
Collins German-English, English-German dict unabridged, 2d ed, 94n1115
Collins, Joseph T., 92n1587, 93n1577, 94n1749
Collins, N. Mark, 92n1764, 93n1484
Collins, Pamela, 93n1255
Collins, Robert A., 90n1111, 93n1158
Collins, Robert O., 92n473
Collins Shubun English-Japanese dict, 94n1118
Collins Spanish-English, English-Spanish dict, 94n1132
Collins Spanish-English, English-Spanish dict, 2d ed, 90n1056
Collins Spanish-English, English-Spanish dict unabridged, 3d ed, 94n1133
Collins Spanish-English/English-Spanish dict, 3d ed, 93n1100
Collins, Vickie L, 92n324
Collins, William P., 92n1447
Collins-Robert French-English, English-French dict, 2d ed, 94n1113
Colombia, 92n110
Colombo, John Robert, 90n126, 93n90, 94n1
Colonial & 19th century, 90n1162
Colonial British Caribbean newspapers, 91n962
Color atlas of galaxies, 90n1748
Color compendium, 91n1011
Colorado birds, 94n1689
Colorado bk gd, 93n683
Colorado flora: E slope, 91n1524
Colorado gd, 90n441
Colorado place names, 94n470
Columbia checklist, 92n1350
Columbia dict of European pol hist since 1914, 93n529
Columbia dict of pol biog, 92n670
Columbia gd to standard American English, 94n1085
Columbia Granger's dict of poetry quotations, 93n1235
Columbia Granger's gd to poetry anthologies, 92n1243
Columbia Granger's index to poetry, 9th ed, 91n1250
Columbia Univ College of Physicians & Surgeons complete home gd to mental health, 94n1846
Columbine fax dir, 91n140
Columbus: an annot gd to the scholarship on his life & writings, 1750-1988, 92n457
Columbus dict, 92n512
Columbus' dict, 93n517
Columbus docs, 94n533
Colwell, Richard, 93n1252
Comaromi, John P., 90n599, 91n617
Comay, Joan, 94n1538
Combat arms: modern attack aircraft, 91n686
Combat arms: modern helicopters, 91n687
Combat arms: modern spyplanes, 91n688
Combat pistols, 91n986
Combinatory vocabulary of CAD/CAM in mechanical engineering, 94n1916
Combined membership list 1989-90, 90n1770
Combined membership list 1992-93, 93n1737
Combs, James, 91n1377
Combs, Richard E., 94n1145
Comecon data 1988, 91n153
Comecon data 1990, 93n907
Comic art collection cat, 94n1405
Comic-bk superstars, 94n1407
Coming to terms with acting, 94n1434
Commemorative coins of the US, 93n1002

Commentary on the medical writings of Rudolf Virchow, 92n1650
Commenting & commentaries, rev ed, 90n1393
Committee for a New England Bibliography, 91n483, 91n484
Committee of Volunteers, 94n611
Committee on History of Law in California of the State Bar in California, 90n554
Committee on the Elementary School Booklist of the National Council of Teachers of English, 90n1075
Committee on the Junior High and Middle School Booklist of the National Council of Teachers of English, 94n648, 92n1123
Committee on the Senior High School Booklist of the National Council of Teachers of English, 94n1165
Committees in the US Congress 1947-92, v.1, 94n741
Commodities price locator, 90n274
Commodity prices, 2d ed, 92n159
Commodity review & outlook 1990-91, 93n1466
Common & botanical names of weeds in Canada, 1992 ed, 93n1511
Common abbrevs in clinical medicine, 90n1633
Common, I. F. B., 92n1578
Common legumes of the Great Plains, 90n1504
Common names of N American butterflies, 93n1548
Common stock newspaper abbrevs & trading symbols, 90n213
Common stock newspaper abbrevs & trading symbols, suppl.1, 92n160
Common-sense gd to American colleges 1991-92, 92n310
Commonwealth yrbk 1991, 92n100
Communication & the mass media, 92n884
Communication serials, 1992/1993 ed, 93n982
Communications standard dict, 2d ed, 90n889
Communist & Marxist parties of the world, 2d ed, 92n728
Community, technical, & jr colleges statistical yrbk, 1990 ed, 91n328
Community, technical, & jr colleges statistical yrbk, 1992 ed, 94n356
Compact dict of doctrinal words, 90n1396
Compact gd to colleges, 6th ed, 90n337
Compact topical Bible, 92n1441
Companies & their brands 1992, 93n189
Companies that care, 93n312
Companion to ...
    aesthetics, 94n1492
    Irish hist 1603-1921, 93n539
    literary myths, heroes & archetypes, 94n1155
    Scottish hist from the Reformation to the present, 91n533
    the English civil wars, 92n484
    the Industrial Revolution, 91n159
    the medieval theatre, 90n1369
    the physical scis, 90n1436
    20th-century German lit, 93n1223
Comparative adult educ, 90n357
Comparative criminology, 93n602
Comparative gd to American colleges, 15th ed, 92n293
Comparative world data, 90n838
Compendium of ...
    American railroad radio frequencies, 12th ed, 94n2028
    food additive specifications, addendum 1, 94n1608
    pulp & paper training & research insts, 94n1614
    the Confederate armies: Ala., 93n711
    the Confederate armies: Fla. & Ark., 93n712
    the Confederate armies: N.C., 93n713
    the Confederate armies: Tenn., 93n714
    the Confederate armies: Va., 93n715
    the world's langs, 92n1012
Compilation of ASTM standard definitions, 7th ed, 92n1613
Compilation of state & fed privacy laws, 1992 ed, 94n577
Compleat Mozart, 92n1280
Complete actors' TV credits, 1948-88, v.1, 2d ed, 91n1392
Complete actors' TV credits, 1948-88, v.2, 2d ed, 91n1393
Complete & easy gd to social security & medicare, 10th ed, 94n220
Complete beverage dict, 94n1601
Complete biblical lib, 92n1422

Complete bk of ...
    emigrants 1661-99, 91n416
    emigrants 1700-50, 93n452
    emigrants 1751-76, 94n430
    herbs, spices & condiments, 91n1492
    home environmental hazards, 92n1780
    parrots, 90n1539
    spices, 92n1497
    the Olympics, 1992 ed, 93n841
    US presidents, 2d ed, 91n492
    US presidents, 3d ed, 93n514
Complete college financing gd, 2d ed, 93n371
Complete concordance to Gottfried Von Strassburg's Tristan, 94n1200
Complete concordance to Wolfram Von Eschenbach's Parzival, 91n1234
Complete custodial hndbk, 90n1606
Complete dict of furniture, rev ed, 92n955
Complete dir for people with disabilities, 1992, 93n862
Complete dir for people with learning disabilities, 1993/94, 94n372
Complete dir of large print bks & serials 1992, 93n30
Complete dir to prime time network TV shows 1946-present, 4th ed, 90n916
Complete dog bk, 18th ed, 93n1552
Complete drug ref, 1992 ed, 93n1662
Complete ency of hockey, 4th ed, 94n852
Complete gd for occupational exploration, 1993 ed, 94n387
Complete gd to ...
    closed-end funds, 90n201
    closed-end funds, 2d ed, 92n155
    life in Fla., 92n442
    medical tests, 90n1667
    prescription & non-prescription drugs, 94n1877
    special interest videos, 1991 ed, 92n1344
    symptoms, illness & surgery for people over 50, 94n1839
    Washington internships, 2d ed, 92n695
Complete golfer's cat, 91n836
Complete Gone with the Wind sourcebk, 94n1452
Complete hndbk of natural healing, 93n1648
Complete illus gd to everything sold in garden centers (except the plants), 91n1500
Complete illus gd to everything sold in hdwr stores, 90n1609
Complete James Bond movie ency, 92n1354
Complete Medicare hndbk, 91n1651
Complete medicinal herbal, 94n1666
Complete metalsmith, rev ed, 93n1008
Complete operas of Richard Strauss, 90n1271
Complete rhyming dict revised, 92n1054
Complete secretary's hndbk, 7th ed, 94n300
Complete vegetable gardener's sourcebk, rev ed, 91n1505
Completely illus atlas of reptiles & amphibians for the terrarium, 90n1569
Composite materials hndbk, 2d ed, 93n1606
Composites: an insider's gd to corporate America's activities, 91n154
Comprehensive bibliog of American constitutional & legal hist, suppl., 1980-87, 92n521
Comprehensive bibliog of English-Canadian short stories 1950-83, 90n1199
Comprehensive dict of instrumentation & control, 90n1576
Comprehensive dict of measurement & control, 2d ed, 93n1607
Comprehensive electrocardiology, 90n1685
Comprehensive glossary of psychiatry & psychology, 93n1649
Comprehensive gd to the hazardous properties of chemical substances, 94n2015
Comprehensive polymer sci, 91n1774
Comprehensive US silver dollar ency, 93n1003
Compressed Russian, 93n1097
Compton, Rae, 90n931
Compton's ency, 90n48
Compton's ency & fact-index, 94n34
Computer acronyms & abbrevs, 94n1890
Computer catalogs, 93n1673
Computer dict, 3d ed, 93n1681
Computer dict, 4th ed, 94n1904

Computer engineering hndbk, 94n1774
Computer glossary, 4th ed, 91n1723
Computer glossary, 5th ed, 93n1676
Computer graphics hndbk: geometry & mathematics, 91n1797
Computer health hazards, 92n1710
Computer industry 1993 almanac, 94n1909
Computer law & sftwr protection, 94n1892
Computer mediated communication, 93n345
Computer News for Physicians dir of medical office computer system vendors, 91n1670
Computer pers currently received in the LC, 2d ed, 90n1718
Computer professional's quick ref, 93n1685
Computer publishers & pubs, 1988-89 ed, 90n1716
Computer publishers & pubs, 1992-93 ed, 93n684
Computer sci abbrevs & acronyms, 1990 ed, 91n1719
Computer type, 92n645
Computer-based simulations in educ & training, 94n381
Computer-readable databases, 5th ed, 90n1717
Computing info dir, 7th ed, 91n1733
Computing info dir, 10th ed, 94n1908
Comte, Fernand, 93n1302
Conant, Roger, 92n1587, 93n1577
Conard, Elverne C., 90n1504
Concise AACR2, 1988 rev, 90n600
Concise American Heritage Larousse Spanish dict, 90n1057
Concise Columbia dict of quotations, 90n81
Concise Columbia ency, 2d ed, 90n49
Concise dict of ...
    American biog, 4th ed, 92n32
    biology, new ed, 92n1515
    business, 92n124
    chemistry, new ed, 92n1725
    Greek, Roman, Norse, & Egyptian mythology, 93n1303
    Indian philosophy, 90n1375
    law, 2d ed, 91n572
    mgmt, 93n317
    math, 92n1751
    military biog, 93n699
    natl bibliog, 94n13
    psychology, 2d ed, 91n792
    religion, 94n1512
Concise earth bk world atlas, 91n423
Concise earth facts, 91n424
Concise earth hist, 92n420
Concise ency biochemistry, 2d ed, 90n1481
Concise ency of ...
    Austral., 2d ed, 90n124
    biological & biomedical measurement systems, 93n1635
    building & construction materials, 91n1631
    composite materials, 91n1628
    info processing in systems & orgs, 91n1727
    Islam, 91n1448
    magnetic & superconducting materials, 93n1591
    materials characterizations, 94n1795
    materials economics, policy & mgmt, 94n1794
    medical & dental materials, 92n1662
    mineral resources, 91n1786
    modelling & simulation, 93n1674
    polymer processing & applications, 93n1582
    polymer sci & engineering, 92n1596
    semiconducting materials & related techs, 93n1592
    sftwr engineering, 94n1775
    special educ, 92n320
    traffic & transportation systems, 93n1613
    wood & wood-based materials, 91n1495
Concise English-Hungarian dict, 14th ed, 92n1075
Concise glossary of contemporary literary theory, 93n1112
Concise Hungarian-English dict, 92n1076
Concise illus dict of sci & tech, 94n1567
Concise intl ency of robotics, 91n1748
Concise Oxford companion to classical lit, 94n1198
Concise Oxford companion to the theatre, 94n1472
Concise Oxford dict of ...
    art & artists, 92n981

Concise Oxford dict of ... *(continued)*
    current English, 8th ed, 91n1048
    earth scis, 92n1730
    geography, 93n489
    literary terms, 91n1099
    proverbs, 2d ed, 93n1296
    zoology, 93n1529
Concise sci dict, 2d ed, 92n1455
Concise vet dict, 90n1473
Concordance of The Hymnal 1982, 90n1264
Concordance of The Pilgrim Hymnal, 90n1265
Concordance to ...
    Hemingway's In Our Time, 91n1163
    Henry James's The Awkward Age, 90n1145
    Henry James's The Spoils of Poynton, 90n1146
    Henry James's What Maisie Knew, 91n1165
    Herman Melville's Mardi, 92n1178
    Middle English metrical romances, 90n1174
    the complete poems of E. E. Cummings, 90n1135
    the minor poetry of Edward Taylor (1642?-1729), 93n1181
    the novels of Virginia Woolf, 92n1216
    the poetry of Edgar Allan Poe, 90n1152
    the sermons of Gerard Manley Hopkins, 90n1181
    The Towneley Plays, 91n1192
    the works of Jorge Luis Borges (1899-1986), Argentine author, 94n1299
    Thomas Paine's Common Sense & The American Crisis, 90n712
Concrete poetry, 90n1120
Condensed [congressional] dir, 92n686
Condensed ency of surfactants, 90n1752
Condon, Robert J., 92n768, 93n815
Conductor's repertory of chamber music, 94n1350
Cone, Robert J., 92n1699
Confidence woman, 93n936
Conflict & culture, rev ed, 93n419
Congleton, Robert J., 94n1483
Congregate care by county, 90n786
Congress A to Z, 2d ed, 94n728
Congress & defense 1990, 91n749
Congress & law-making, 2d ed, 90n705
Congress & the nation, v.7, 91n744
Congress dict, 94n730
Congressional & gubernatorial primaries 1991-92, 94n754
Congressional Quarterly almanac, v.45, 92n694
Congressional Quarterly's American congressional dict, 94n729
Congressional Quarterly's gd to ...
    Congress, 4th ed, 93n747
    the presidency, 91n745
    US Supreme Court, 2d ed, 91n746
Congressional Quarterly's pols in America 1990, 90n691
Congressional Quarterly's pols in America 1994, 94n749
Congressional roll call 1989, 91n747
Congressional staff dir/1, 1990, 91n735
Congressional staff dir/1, 1993, 94n734
Congressional voting gd: a 10 yr compilation, 4th ed, 93n746
Congressional yellow bk, spring 1990, v.16, no.1, 91n736
Coniferous trees, 92n1555
Conkel, Donald, 94n1712
Conn, Joey, 90n1673
Connery, Thomas B., 93n976
Connoisseur's gd to Ireland, 90n460
Connolly, Thomas, 93n519
Connors, Martin, 91n280, 93n840
Conoley, Jane Close, 90n751, 92n760, 93n803
Conolly, L. W., 91n1400
Conquest, John, 91n930
Conrad, J. David, 90n1806
Conservation atlas of tropical forests: Africa, 93n1484
Conservation atlas of tropical forests: Asia & the Pacific, 92n1764
Conservation dir 1991, 92n1788
Considine, Douglas M., 90n1430
Consoli, Joseph P., 93n1224
Consolidated index to the Canadian yrbk of intl law v.1-25, 91n590
Consolidated treaties & intl agreements, 93n756

Consortium for Research on Black Adolescence, 91n892
Constitutional glossary, 94n553
Constitutional law dict, v.1, 92n530
Construction glossary, 2d ed, 94n1773
Construction index, v.2, no.3, 90n978
Construction tech info sources, 93n1586
Consultants & consulting orgs dir 1989, 90n170
Consultants & consulting orgs dir 1991, 92n128
Consultants ref gd, 91n256
Consumer E Europe 1992, 93n283
Consumer Europe 1991, 92n173
Consumer gd computer buying gd, new ed, 90n225
Consumer Guide, editors of, 90n1668
Consumer health & nutrition index, v.8, no.1, 93n1614
Consumer health info source bk, 3d ed, 91n1680
Consumer Japan 1990, 91n261
Consumer mags of the British Isles, 94n267
Consumer power, 92n171
Consumer product & manufacturer ratings 1961-90, 94n214
Consumer Reports Books, editors of, 90n227, 90n229, 91n1342, 93n1334, 93n1481, 93n1611, 93n1784, 93n1786
Consumer Reports 1992 buying gd issue, 93n234
Consumer sourcebk 1992-93, 93n235
Consumer Spain 1991, 92n175
Consumer's dict of household, yard & office chemicals, 93n1754
Consumer's gd to ...
    aging, 94n875
    free medical info by phone & by mail, 94n1844
    medical lingo, 93n1633
    social security benefits including medicare, 12th ed, 90n223
    tests in print, 2d ed, 93n333
Consumers' gd to product grades & terms, 94n201
Consumer's index to product evaluations & info sources, 1990 annual, 92n174
Contemporary American bus leaders, 91n128
Contemporary American slang, 92n1041
Contemporary artists, 3d ed, 90n948
Contemporary atlas of the US, 92n409
Contemporary authors, v.133, 93n1108
Contemporary authors, v.134, 93n1109
Contemporary authors bibliographical series, v.3, 90n1128
Contemporary authors cumulative index, 92n1111
Contemporary authors: new revision series, v.32, 92n1096
Contemporary black biog, v.1, 93n426
Contemporary bks reflecting Canada's cultural diversity, 94n409
Contemporary Britain: an annual review 1992, 93n144
Contemporary Canadian & US women of letters, 94n1138
Contemporary Canadian childhood & youth, 94n924
Contemporary Canadian pols, 90n718
Contemporary composers, 93n1255
Contemporary critical theory, 94n1140
Contemporary designers, 2d ed, 92n921
Contemporary dramatists, 5th ed, 94n1467
Contemporary entrepreneurs, 93n178
Contemporary fiction writers of the South, 94n1222
Contemporary gay American novelists, 94n1224
Contemporary heroes & heroines, 91n12
Contemporary heroes & heroines, bk 2, 93n45
Contemporary Irish dramatists, 90n1205
Contemporary Latin American fiction, 91n1241
Contemporary legend, 94n1383
Contemporary lesbian writers of the US, 94n1226
Contemporary literary criticism, v.63, 92n1104
Contemporary literary criticism annual cum title index for 1991, 92n1105
Contemporary literary criticism: yrbk 1987, 90n1070
Contemporary masterworks, 93n1028
Contemporary musicians, 90n1221
Contemporary musicians, v.6, 93n1245
Contemporary novelists, 5th ed, 92n1191
Contemporary poets, 5th ed, 92n1244
Contemporary printed lit of the English counter-reformation between 1558 & 1640, v.1, 91n1440
Contemporary religions: a world gd, 94n1516
Contemporary sci fiction, fantasy, & horror poetry, 90n1109

Contemporary Spanish American poets, 93n1228
Contemporary theatre, film, & TV, v.7, 90n1311
Contemporary theatre, film, & TV, v.9, 93n1324
Contemporary world writers, 2d ed, 94n1144
Contemporary writers, 1960 to the present, 93n1192
Contento, William G., 90n1112, 92n1142
Contests for students, 92n289
Continental actress, 91n1395
Contribution to lit of Orcadian writer George Mackay Brown, 93n1206
Control of the media in the US, 93n951
Controvich, James T., 91n677
Conversion experience in America, 93n1418
Conversion tables: LC-Dewey, Dewey-LC, 94n630
Conway, D. J., 94n1392
Conway, McKinley, 92n1735
Conzen, Michael P., 94n461
Coogan, Michael D., 94n1545
Cook, Barrie, 91n983
Cook, Charles, 93n835
Cook, Chris, 90n506, 90n679, 90n723, 92n704, 93n559, 93n719, 93n766, 94n766
Cook, Jean G., 91n615
Cook, Ralph T., 94n1220
Cook, Samantha, 94n1430
Cooke, Jean, 91n36, 94n39
Cooke, Jennifer, 92n251
Cookerly, J. Richard, 90n750
Cooking A to Z, 90n1455
Cook's index, 90n1461
Cooksource, 91n1489
Cooley, Laurel, 92n4
Coombes, Allen J., 94n1669
Co-op source dir: spring 1993, 94n288
Cooper, Alison, 90n171
Cooper, B. Lee, 91n1302, 92n1310
Cooper, Brian E., 91n389
Cooper, Bruce E., 92n1579, 94n1724
Cooper, Carolynne, 91n882
Cooper, David E., 94n1492
Cooper, J. C., 94n1391
Cooper, Jeremy, 92n520
Cooper, Martin J., 92n1636
Cooper, Thomas W., 90n910
Cooperative learning, 92n272
Cooperative/credit union dict & ref, 91n134
Cooperman, Robert, 91n1154
Cooter, Roger, 90n754
Coover, James, 90n1224, 90n1225
Copeland, Sandra K., 90n932
Coppa, Frank J., 91n532
Copsey, David N., 90n1700
Coptic ency, 92n1414
Copy-editing, 3d ed, 94n1000
Copyediting: a practical gd, 2d ed, 91n949
Copyright bk, 4th ed, 94n637
Copyright dir 1990-91, 91n629
Copyright Information Services, staff of, 91n629
Corals of Austral. & the Indo-Pacific, 94n1747
Corbeil, Jean-Claude, 90n1018, 90n1037, 93n1077, 93n1101, 94n1114
Corbella, Enrico, 91n1024
Corbet, G. B., 92n1581, 94n1734
Corbett, James M., 93n603
Corbin, John, 91n637
Corbishley, Mike, 91n539, 91n541
Corbitt, Robert, 94n1999
Corbitt, Robert A., 91n1620
Corbridge, Stuart, 94n157
Corcoran, John, 94n855
Cordasco, Francesco, 91n777, 91n1640, 92n1647
Cordell, Helen, 93n127
Cordier, Mary Hurlbut, 90n1080
Core collection in nursing & the allied health scis, 91n1705
Core list of bks & jls in educ, 92n270

Corey, D. Steven, 92n965
Corey, Melinda, 91n1396
Corinne T. Netzer ency of food values, 93n1476
Coriolanus: an annotated bibliog, 90n1183
Corish, Patrick J., 93n1582
Corke, Bettina, 90n140
Corkill, David, 91n120
Cormier, Chantal, 94n1943
Cormier, Ramona, 91n1407
Cormorants, darters, & pelicans of the world, 94n1698
Cornelison, Pam, 94n512
Cornell, Alan, 93n1085
Cornell, Charles R., 93n33
Corning, Howard McKinley, 91n503
Cornish, Rory T., 94n775
Cornucopia, 92n1549
Coronel, R. E., 92n1475
Corporate 500, 9th ed, 92n823
Corporate 1000, winter 1988-89, 90n173
Corporate dir 1989, 90n172
Corporate dir of US public cos 1993, 94n178
Corporate eponymy, 93n184
Corporate finance sourcebk 1991, 93n238
Corporate fndn profiles, 7th ed, 94n900
Corporate giving dir 1993, 94n163
Corporate giving yellow pages 1993, 94n162
Corporate mags of the US, 93n217
Corporate museums, galleries, & visitor centers, 92n129
Corporate tech dir 1992, 93n246
Corporate trendtrac 1988, 90n196
Corporate yellow bk, v.8, no.3, 93n191
CorpTech, 93n303
Corpus almanac & Canadian sourcebk, 1989, 90n127
Corpus almanac & Canadian sourcebk, 1993, 94n125
Corrigan, Patricia, 92n1582
Corrosion & corrosion protection hndbk, 2d ed, 90n1602
Cortada, James W., 91n1721, 91n1731
Corten, Irina H., 93n1095
Cortes, Eladio, 94n1296
Cortese, Delia, 94n101
Cortright, Sandy, 91n1554
Cosentino, Peter, 92n949
Cossolotto, Matthew, 92n675
Costa, Marie, 93n851
Costa, Paul T., Jr., 91n1689
Costa Rica, 93n154
Cotten, Lee, 90n1293
Cotterell, Arthur, 91n1333
Cottingham, John, 94n1493
Couch, Gordon, 91n470
Coughlin, Bill, 94n200
Coughlin, Roberta M., 92n1503
Couliano, Ioan P., 93n1409
Council for American Private Education (CAPE) Schools, 90n317
Countdown 2000, v.2, 94n789
Counting bks are more than numbers, 91n1115
Countries of the world & their leaders yrbk 1989, 91n84
Countries of the world & their leaders yrbk 1993, 94n723
County & city extra, 1992, 93n908
County courthouse bk, 91n584
Couper, Heather, 93n1700
Courage children's illus world atlas, 91n425
Courage in the air, 93n697
Courbon, Paul, 91n833
Court reporting computer compatible machine shorthand dict, 90n289
Courtright, Gordon, 90n1482
Courvoisier's bk of the best, 94n472
Cousins, Jill, 93n203
Coutts, Brian E., 92n500
Coutts, Mary Carrington, 94n1835
Couture, Bruno, 92n193
Cover story index 1960-89, 91n964
Cover story index 1960-91, 94n1006
Cover story index: 1992 suppl, 94n1007

Covert culture sourcebk, 94n76
Covert, Nadine, 91n999, 93n1016
Covington, Michael, 90n1710, 93n1675
Covington, Paula H., 93n148
Cowan, Thomas, 90n814
Cowboy & gunfighter collectibles, 90n923
Cowden, Robert H., 90n1258, 94n1352
Cowdery, William, 92n1280
Cowell, Mark, 92n1654
Cowie, Leonard W., 91n522, 93n771
Cowie, Peter, 92n1373
Cox, Andrew, 93n767
Cox, Greg, 94n1212
Cox, J. Randolph, 90n1142, 91n1197
Cox, James C., 94n1937
Cox, John, 92n590
Cox, Michael, 90n1597
Cox, Richard, 92n446
Cox, Richard William, 93n814
Coyle, Jean M., 90n854, 93n854
Coyle, Martin, 93n1116
CPA world dir of old age, 90n787
CQ's Political Staff, 94n749
CQ's state fact finder, 94n750
Cracking Eastern Europe, 94n261
Cracking the Pacific Rim, 94n243
Crafts index for young people, 93n1005
Crafts supply sourcebk, 91n991
Cragg, Dan, 90n656, 93n704
Craggs, Stewart, 94n1323
Craggs, Stewart R., 91n1268, 91n1269, 92n1261, 94n1322
Craig, Bruce D., 91n1624
Craig, Doris, 92n1039
Craig, F. W. S., 90n719
Craig, Raymond A., 93n1181
Craig, Robert D., 90n1303, 94n120
Craighead's intl bus, travel, & relocation gd to 71 countries 1992-93, 93n264
Crain, Thomas E., 91n141
Craker, Lyle E., 91n1534
Cralle, Trevor, 92n802
Cramp, Stanley, 90n1537
Crampton, Luke, 91n1325, 92n1313
Crampton, Norman, 94n942
Crandell, George W., 91n1168
Crane, David, 94n247
Crane, Nancy B., 94n1002
Crash of rhinoceroses, 94n1106
Craven, Wesley Frank, 93n356
Crawford, L. Ann, 94n677
Crawford, Mary G., 93n111
Crawford, R. J., 94n677
Crawford, Richard, 91n1291
Crawford, William "Roy", 94n677
Crawford's dir of city connections 1991, 92n156
Crawley, Tony, 93n1374
Creamer, Thomas, 93n1081
Creative black bk 1989, 90n940
Creative fingerplays & action rhymes, 93n340
Creativity in the later yrs, 93n856
Creedman, Theodore S., 92n111
Creeth, Terry, 93n108
Creighton-Zollar, Ann, 91n894, 94n879
Crellin, John K., 91n1535
Cresswell, Julia, 93n465
Crewe, Ivor, 93n772
Cribb, Joe, 91n983
Cribb, Robert, 94n111
Crimando, William, 91n252
Crime & the elderly, 90n782
Crime in Victorian Britain, 94n590
Crimes & criminals, 93n614
Criminal activity in the deep South, 1700-1930, 90n571
Criminal intelligence & security intelligence, 91n598
Criminal justice ethics, 92n556

Criminal law review: 25 yr index 1954-89, 91n595
Criminology: a reader's gd, 93n606
Criscoe, Betty, 94n1166
Criscoe, Betty L., 91n1110
Crisfield, D. W., 94n823
Critical analyses in English Renaissance drama, 92n1196
Critical dict of sociology, 91n841
Critical dict of the French Revolution, 90n516
Critical gd to Catholic ref bks, 3d ed, 90n1405
Critical gd to horror film series, 93n1354
Critical reception of Charles Dickens 1833-41, 90n1178
Critical survey of ...
    mystery & detective fiction, 90n1106
    poetry: English lang series, rev ed, 93n1236
    short fiction, rev ed, 94n1215
Critical thinking, 94n1483
Crittenden, Mabel, 93n1503, 93n1517
Crofton, Ian, 91n1023
Croissant, Charles R., 93n1273
Cromie, Alice, 91n457
Cromie, Alice Hamilton, 91n456
Cromwellian gazetteer, 91n524
Cronin, Gloria L., 92n1161, 93n1175
Cronquist, Arthur, 93n1500
Crooke, William, 91n100
Crop protection chemicals ref, 1991, 92n1470
Croquet: an annot bibliog from the Rendell Rhoades croquet collection, 93n829
Crosby, Cynthia A., 94n100
Crosby, Gillian, 90n787
Cross index title gd to opera & operetta, 90n1272
Cross, Wilbur, 93n855
Cross-currents of Jungian thought, 93n796
Crossing barriers, 94n17
Cross-ref index, 2d ed, 90n597
Croteau, Maureen, 94n57
Crouch, Archie R., 90n1411
Croucher, Murlin, 94n131
Crowson, Phillip, 94n1978
Crowther, Kelly, 93n68
Cruisers of the US navy 1922-62, 90n671
Crumb, Lawrence N., 94n1522
Crump, Andy, 94n1995
Crutchfield, James A., 90n102
Crystal, David, 94n33
Cuban festivals, 94n1399
Cubberly, W. H., 90n1576, 93n1607
Cucheran, Ruby, 94n1167
Cuddon, J. A., 92n1101
Cuff, Robert H., 91n515
Cullen, J., 90n1491, 94n1652
Cullen, Tony, 91n705
Culligan, Michael, 94n790
Cullum, Carolyn N., 92n625
Cully, Iris V., 91n1413
Cully, Kendig Brubaker, 91n1413
Culotta, Wendy A., 94n1750
Cult baseball players, 91n824
Cult movie stars, 93n1337
Cultivated plants of the tropics & subtropics, 93n1469
Cultural anthropology: a gd to ref & info sources, 92n369
Cultural anthropology of the Middle East, v.1, 93n416
Cultural atlas of France, 93n143
Cultural atlas of Mesopotamia & the ancient Near East, 92n499
Cultural ency of the 1850s in America, 94n507
Culturgrams, 92n1326
Cumming, Jeffrey M., 94n1724
Cummings, David, 90n1229
Cummings, David M., 91n1254, 94n1346
Cummings, Mark, 93n59
Cummings, Pat, 93n1021
Cummings, Steve, 94n1905
Cummins, Blair, 92n330
Cummins, Julie, 92n330, 94n1062
Cumulated abridged index medicus, v.18, 90n1631

Cumulative bibliog of Victorian studies 1985-89, 91n546
Cumulative bk index 1991, 93n23
Cumulative bk index, v.95, no.2, 93n24
Cumulative bk index [CD-ROM], 93n25
Cumulative index to ONLINE, DATABASE & CD-ROM Professional 1986-91, 93n1669
Cuneiform texts in the Metropolitan Museum of Art, 90n989
Cuneo, Michael W., 92n1397
Cunningham, Homer F., 90n478
Cunningham, Lyn Driggs, 90n1286
Cunningham, William A., 92n1597, 94n1759, 94n1760, 94n1761, 94n1762, 94n1763, 94n1764, 94n1765, 94n1766
Curley, Stephen J., 94n1451
Curnow, Judith, 91n1540
Curran, Daniel, 90n1345
Current biog: cum index 1940-90, 92n58
Current biog yrbk 1991, 93n37
Current bks on China 1983-88, 91n98
Current chemical reactions (CCR), v.14, no.2, 93n1718
Current environmental engineering summaries, 1993 ed, 94n1788
Current issues resource builder, 90n88
Current leaders of nations, 92n671
Current research for the info profession 1988/89, 91n632
Current, Richard N., 94n506
Current treaty index, 11th ed, 94n760
Curry, Hayden, 90n556
Curtis, Anthony, 90n1581
Curtis, Melissa C., 93n1432
Cushman, Clare, 94n551
Cushman, Robert F., 91n1605
Custom made, 91n190
CWLA's gd to adoption agencies, 90n800
Cycads of the world, 94n1671
Cyclopedia of literary characters 2, 91n1104
Cyclopedia of world authors 2, 91n1105
Cypess, Sandra Messinger, 91n1242
Cyr, Claude, 90n1801
Cyr, Helen W., 92n102

Dabundo, Laura, 93n531
Daddy Grace: an annot bibliog, 94n1500
Dadmanesh, Ramin, 90n894
Daguerreotypes, 8th ed, 91n820
Dahl, Henry S., 94n552
Dahlo, Ingrid, 94n1769
Dahl's law dict, 94n552
Dakin, Nick, 94n1717
Dakota-English dict, 94n1111
Dale, Alzina Stone, 90n459
Dale, Peter, 94n635
Daley, Basil, 90n1420
Daly, Kathleen N., 92n1322
Daly, M. W., 94n104
Daly, Ronald C., 93n471
Dameron, J. Lasley, 94n61
Damschroder, David, 92n1249
Dance dir 1990, 92n1335
Dance film & video gd, 93n1328
Dance hndbk, 91n1347
Dance in the musical theatre, 90n1317
Dance, S. Peter, 94n1675
Dando, Caroline Z., 92n1486
Dando, William A., 92n1486
Danesh, Abol Hassan, 93n173
Dangerous aquatic animals of the world, 94n1746
Dangerous properties of industrial materials, 7th ed, 90n1758
Daniel, J., 92n130
Daniels, Ger, 91n998
Daniels, Peggy Kneffel, 94n49, 94n50
Daniels, Ted, 93n1399
Danilov, Victor J., 92n129
Danish-English English-Danish dict, 91n1083
Danner, Horace Gerald, 94n1079
Darby, William, 93n1343

Darbyshire, S. J., 91n1531
Dare, Philip N., 91n848
Darnay, Arsen J., 90n242, 92n223, 92n255, 93n204, 93n247, 93n250, 93n1764, 94n193, 94n205
Das, T. K., 92n5
Dashew, Linda, 91n1829
Dashew, Stephen, 91n1829
Data & computer communications, 91n1751
Data bk on the viscosity of liquids, 90n1774
Data map 1989, 90n839
Data: where it is & how to get it, 94n45
Database dict, 91n1743
Datapro dir of ...
    microcomputer hdwr, 91n1734
    microcomputer sftwr, 91n1737
    sftwr, 91n1738
Daugherty, F. Mark, 92n1283, 92n1286, 94n1340, 94n1342
Daughters of the desert, 90n867
Daughtrey, Margery, 93n1499
Daume, Daphne, 92n42
Davey, Gwenda Beed, 94n1390
Daviau, Donald G., 90n1192
David & Charles ency of everyday antiques, 94n1023
David, Jack, 90n1194, 90n1195
David Merrick: a bio-bibliog, 93n1377
Davidian, H. H., 93n1504
Davids, Lewis E., 91n237
Davidson, Linda Kay, 94n1523
Davidson, Robert L., III, 90n549
Davies, Ann, 91n748, 93n743
Davies, Dilys, 94n1653
Davies, J. K., 94n1756
Davies, Julian, 92n833
Davies' medical terminology, 5th ed, 93n1630
Davies, Peter, 94n849
Davies, Stephen, 92n727
Davis, Barbara Kerr, 90n1102
Davis bk of medical abbrevs, 92n1644
Davis, Daniel J., 92n1781, 94n2011
Davis, Donald G., Jr., 90n580
Davis, Evan, 94n159
Davis, Gary A., 92n284
Davis, Gwenn, 90n855, 92n1245, 93n1146
Davis, J. R., 94n1793
Davis, Julie A., 94n2011
Davis, Lansing J., 94n392
Davis, Lee, 94n467, 94n468
Davis, Lenwood G., 90n783, 94n1500
Davis, Linda W., 94n1663
Davis, Lynne, 92n311
Davis, Michael C., 94n277
Davis, Michael D., 93n843
Davis, Mitchell P., 91n943
Davis, Neil M., 94n1817
Davis, P. H., 90n1491
Davis, Robert H., 92n110
Davis's drug gd for nurses, 2d ed, 92n1692
Dawsey, James, 90n1385
Dawson, Joseph G., III, 91n491, 92n663
Dawson, Patricia, 90n473
Day, A. Colin, 94n1542
Day, Alan, 93n98
Day, Alan J., 90n704, 92n82, 93n725
Day, Glenn, 93n748
Day, Heather F., 92n1406
Day, John A., 92n1732
Day, Neil, 93n772
Day, Robert A., 93n958
Day, Ruby, 94n1384
Day, Samuel H., Jr., 90n678
Day, Serenna F., 91n1122
De Angelis, James, 94n163
de Barran, Alicia Casas, 90n147
De Chiara, Joseph, 91n1025, 92n954
de Geest, Gerrit, 93n564

de Lafayette, Jean Maximillien de la Croix, 90n324
De Lorenzo, Barbara, 93n1631
De Parga, Margarita Vazquez, 92n7
De Prisco, Andrew, 92n1573, 92n1574, 94n1706
de Stricker, Ulla, 91n155, 91n161
De Vos, Gail, 92n626
De Vos, Louis, 92n1584
de Vries, Andre, 94n273
De Vries, Mary A., 90n290, 94n300
de Weever, Jacqueline, 90n1176
De Zuane, John, 91n1784
Deacon, Richard, 90n724
Deadly doses: a writer's gd to poisons, 91n1714
Dealers of Polish & Russian bks active abroad 1918 to present, 92n637
Dean, Jan, 94n1627
Dean, Joanna, 92n852
Dean, John A., 91n1777, 93n1716
Dean, Love, 94n90
Dean, Virgil W., 93n513
Deane, Phyllis, 90n166
DeAngelis, Carl, 93n1053
Dear, Ian, 93n842
Death & dying, 92n818
Death row USA reporter 1975-88, 91n596
DeBolt, C. Gerald, 90n933
Debrett's peerage & baronetage, 92n395
Debrett's presidents of the USA, 90n486
Decalo, Samuel, 91n95
Decca hillbilly discography, 1927-45, 91n1310
Deckard, Steve, 91n296
Deconstructionism: a bibliog, 94n1141
Decorative arts & household furnishings in America 1650-1920, 91n978
DeCoste, F. C., 92n853
DeCurtis, Anthony, 94n1367
Deegan, Mary Jo, 93n844
DeFilipps, Robert A., 92n1550
DeFrancis, Beth, 92n894
Defty, Jeff, 93n340
Degen, Bernd, 92n1575
Deger, Joe, 92n938
Degler, Teri, 90n1008, 90n1818
Deglin, Judith Hopfer, 92n1692
DeGregorio, William A., 91n492, 93n514
Del Vecchio, Deborah, 94n1437
DeLancey, Mark W., 90n110, 92n86
Delaplaine, A., 90n1363
Delderfield, Eric R., 91n523
Delgado, James P., 93n1788
Delgado, Jane L., 92n357
Delivering govt servs, 90n735
DellaCava, Frances A., 94n1208
Delli, Bertrun, 92n992
Delnatte, Sabine Y. J., 90n1700
Delong, Marilyn Fuller, 91n1653
Delorme, Robert L., 90n137
Delson, Donn, 91n1367
Delson's dict of motion picture mktg terms, 2d ed, 91n1367
Delvin, Edgard, 93n1600
DeMaggio, Janice A., 92n622
DeMaria, Rusel, 90n1727
Demastes, William W., 92n1377
Demayo, Adrian, 94n1951
DeMiller, Anna L., 92n1007
Demise of the Soviet Union, 94n548
Democracy's dawn, 92n750
Demographic stats 1991, 93n897
Dempsey, Deirdre, 92n1047
Dempsey, Hugh A., 90n368
Dempsey, Michael, 92n43, 93n482
Demsey, David, 94n1324
Denise Levertov: an annot primary & secondary bibliog, 90n1150
Dennis, Marguerite J., 91n1673, 93n371
Dent, David W., 92n722

Dent, N. J. H., 93n1396
Dent, W. Douglas, 90n201, 92n155
Department of Justice Canada, 90n546
Department of the Secretary of State of Canada, 90n546
DePew, John N., 93n663
Derdak, Thomas, 90n177
Derivan, William J., 91n883
Dermine, Pierre, 92n1471
DeRoche, Edward F., 92n277
Derrickson, Margaret Chandler, 90n804, 91n865
Dershem, Larry D., 91n621, 91n622, 92n579, 94n625
DeRuyter, Denise, 92n202
Dervaes, Claudine, 90n431, 92n429
Descartes dict, 94n1493
Descriptionary, 93n1072
Descriptive bibliog of art music by Israeli composers, 90n1218
Descriptive bibliog of Lady Chatterly's Lover, 91n1211
Descriptive cat of the Glenn Gould papers, 93n1254
Descriptive cat of the Jorge Luis Borges collection at the Univ of Va. lib, 94n1300
Descriptive dict & atlas of sexology, 92n832
Desert & mountain plants of the southwest, 94n1645
Deshpande, Bharati, 90n1045
Deshpande, Pandurang Ganesh, 90n1045
Design of bibliogs, 93n690
Desktop bus intelligence sourcebk, 94n171
Desktop dict of info systems tech, 91n1634
Desktop gd to computers in bus, 91n1730
Desktop publisher's legal hndbk, 90n555
Desktop ref to the Intl Reading Assn 1990-91, 92n331
Desktop typographics, 92n644
Desmarais, Barbara, 92n594
Desmarais, Norman, 92n594, 92n1719, 93n659
Despres, Joseph A., 92n301
Destination southwest, 91n910
Destructive & useful insects, 5th ed, 94n1729
Detwiler dir of medical market sources, 94n1834
Detwiler, Susan M., 94n1834
Deuss, Jean, 92n183
Developing lib collections for Calif.'s emerging majority, 92n620
Developing multicultural awareness through children's lit, 94n1178
Development dir 1990, 91n107
Development report card for the states, 1993, 94n170
Developments & research on aging, 94n871
DeVenney, David P., 92n1302, 94n1353
Devine, J. T., 91n1488
Devitt, Phyllis M., 91n145, 91n146
DeVries, Mary A., 90n291
Dewan, John, 94n836
Dewey, Clive, 93n524
Dewey Decimal Classification & relative index, 20th ed, 90n599
Dewey, Donald, 94n831
Dewey, Melvil, 90n599
Dewey, Patrick R., 91n608, 91n638, 91n1728, 91n1705, 94n1400
DeWitt, Donald L., 92n364
Deziron, Mireille, 94n2003
Dhawan, Vibha, 92n1529
di Benedetto, C. Anthony, 91n260
Di Berardino, Angelo, 93n1406
Di Gregorio, Mario A., 92n1525
Di Maso, Peter, 94n1053
Diagram Group, 90n1664, 90n1665, 90n1666, 91n1418, 91n1509, 93n1527, 93n1767, 94n824
Dial 800 for health, 94n1812
Dial in 1992, 93n662
Dial-a-fax dir, 3d ed, 91n1750
Diamant, Lincoln, 90n914
Diamond, David, 93n1023
Diamond, Harold J., 92n1250
Diana, Joan P., 92n834
Diaz, Jacqueline, 94n943
Dibner, Mark D., 90n233
Dibon-Smith, Richard, 94n1924
DiCanio, Margaret, 90n798, 92n1463, 94n586

Dickens glossary, 91n1204
Dickens index, 90n1177
Dickens, Linda, 93n297
Dickerson, Brent C., 94n1628
Dickinson, Dan, 92n781
Dickinson, John R., 91n262
Dickinson, Kieran, 92n781
Dicks, Brian, 91n425
Dickson baseball dict, 90n766
Dickson, Paul, 90n766, 90n1009, 90n1306, 91n451, 91n1061, 92n465, 92n783, 93n1073, 94n730
Dickson's word treasury, 93n1073
Dictionary & hndbk of nuclear medicine & clinical imaging, 92n1657
Dictionary cat, 2d ed, 90n988
Dictionary for ...
    bus & finance, 90n168
    bus & finance, 2d ed, 91n135
    human factors/ergonomics, 94n1791
    the petroleum industry, 93n1743
Dictionary of ...
    abbrevs in medical scis, 91n1644
    acronyms & abbrevs, 94n597
    acronyms & abbrevs in applied linguistics & lang learning, 94n1072
    admirals of the US Navy, 90n664
    Afro-American performers, 91n1259
    Afro-American slavery, 90n493
    AIDS-related terminology, 94n1853
    Alaskan English, 92n1042
    alkaloids, 90n1753
    American biog comprehensive index complete through suppl.8, 91n51
    American children's fiction, 1985-89, 94n1171
    American diplomatic hist, 2d ed, 91n733
    American foreign affairs, 94n731
    American immigration hist, 91n777
    American literary characters, 91n1151
    American pottery marks, 90n933
    American proverbs, 93n1299
    American regional English, v.2, 93n1062
    American religious biog, 2d ed, 94n1509
    ancient Near Eastern architecture, 90n974
    ancient Near Eastern mythology, 92n1323
    animal health terminology, 94n1633
    architecture & construction, 2d ed, 94n1051
    art quotations, 91n1023
    artificial intelligence, 92n1702
    artificial intelligence & neuronal networks, 93n1671
    astronomical names, 90n1746
    Australian artists, 94n1041
    Australian colloquialisms, 92n1052
    automotive engineering, 91n1823
    aviation, 92n1792
    banking, 94n207, 94n210
    banking terms, 91n215
    behavioral sci, 2d ed, 90n90
    bias-free usage, 92n1030
    biblical interpretation, 91n1425
    biblical literacy, 91n1431
    biblical tradition in English lit, 94n1149
    biochemistry & molecular biology, 2d ed, 91n1516
    biomedical acronyms & abbrevs, 2d ed, 92n1645
    blasting tech, 90n1584
    British children's fiction, 90n1094
    British literary characters: 18th- & 19th-century novels, 94n1243
    British studio potters, 91n993
    Buddhist terms & terminologies, 93n1413
    bus quotations, 92n153
    Canadian biog index, 92n59
    Canadian French, 92n1069
    Canadian military hist, 94n517
    Canadian quotations, 93n90
    Canadianisms on histl principles, 92n1049
    card games, 94n841
    Celtic mythology, 93n1304
    chemical engineering, 94n1769
    chemical names & synonyms, 94n1934
    chemistry & chemical tech, 4th ed, 91n1772
    children's fiction from Austral., Canada, India, N.Z., & selected African countries, 94n1172
    Christianity in America, 91n1444
    clinical medicine: English-German, 92n1655
    communication & media studies, 2d ed, 90n888
    composite materials tech, 91n1630
    computer graphics tech & applications, 93n1688
    computer terms, 2d ed, 90n1710
    computer terms, 3d ed, 93n1675
    computing, 3d ed, 91n1722
    concepts in archaeology, 94n487
    concepts in cultural anthropology, 93n418
    concepts in literary criticism & theory, 93n1111
    concepts in physical anthropology, 93n415
    concepts in recreation & leisure studies, 91n807
    conservative & libertarian thought, 92n727
    contemporary pols of Central America & the Caribbean, 92n723
    contemporary pols of S Africa, 90n714
    contemporary pols of S America, 90n730
    contemporary quotations, 2d ed, 92n66
    contrasting pairs, 90n1012
    crime, 93n608
    critical theory, 93n1114
    cults, sects, religions & the occult, 94n1513
    cultural literacy, 90n304
    cultural literacy, 2d ed, 94n305
    dvlpmnt, 91n108
    dicts, 94n1073
    doll marks, 92n935
    drugs, 91n1708
    ecology & environmental sci, 94n1994
    economics, 93n185
    electronic & computer music terminology, 93n1247
    energy, 2d ed, 90n1776
    engineering acronyms & abbrevs, 90n1574
    engineering & tech, 5th ed, 91n1606
    English law, 93n575
    English place names, 93n493
    environment & dvlpmt, 94n1995
    environmental quotations, 93n1777
    environmental sci & tech, rev ed, 94n2000
    epithets & terms of address, 91n1062
    eponyms, 2d ed, 90n1000
    eponyms, 3d ed, 91n1051
    ethology, 90n1478
    evolutionary fish osteology, 93n1558
    eye terminology, 2d ed, 92n1672
    family psychology & family therapy, 2d ed, 94n810
    feminist theory, 91n925
    fictional charaters, rev ed, 93n1148
    finance, 94n204
    finance & investment terms, 3d ed, 92n184
    1st names, 91n419, 92n398
    food & nutrition, 90n1454
    food ingredients, 2d ed, 90n1456
    fracture mechanics, 91n1629
    geographical literacy, 94n466
    global climate change, 94n1949
    historic docs, 92n508
    hypnotism, 92n763
    immunology, 90n1654
    info sci & tech, 93n622
    insurance, 7th ed, 91n237
    insurance terms, 2d ed, 92n210
    intl & comparative law, 93n577
    investing, 94n177
    Irish archaeology, 94n486
    Irish biog, 2d ed, 90n38
    Irish mythology, 90n1304

Dictionary of ... *(continued)*
  Jesus & the Gospels, 93n1428
  Jewish biog, 92n381
  Judaism & Christianity, 93n1405
  Kleinian thought, 90n745
  Lahu, 90n1050
  landscape, 92n1472
  Latin American racial & ethnic terminology, 91n410
  lib & educl tech, 3d ed, 90n353
  literary biog documentary series, v.6, 90n1126
  literary biog documentary series, v.7, 91n1176
  literary biog documentary series, v.10, 94n1154
  literary biog yrbk 88, 91n1101
  literary biog yrbk: 1991, 94n1156
  literary devices: gradus, A-Z, 92n1102
  literary quotations, 91n1107
  literary terms & literary theory, 3d ed, 92n1101
  love, 91n796
  marine tech, 91n1623
  mktg & advertising, 2d ed, 92n241
  materials & manufacturing, 92n1616
  measurement engineering & units, 93n1597
  medical acronyms & abbrevs, 2d ed, 94n1818
  medical & surgical syndromes, 93n1658
  medical terms for the nonmedical person, 2d ed, 90n1655
  mental handicap, 91n854
  Mexican lit, 94n1296
  military, defense contractor, & troop slang acronyms, 91n674
  military quotations, 91n682
  modern medicine, 94n1832
  modern war, 92n647
  musical tech, 93n1246
  mysticism & the esoteric traditions, rev ed, 94n814
  natl biog: missing persons, 94n15
  natl biog 1981-85, 91n13
  Native American mythology, 94n418
  neuropsychology, 91n1658
  Nfld. & Labrador biog, 91n515
  Nfld. English, 2d ed, 92n1051
  N.C. biog, v.4, 92n33
  nursing theory & research, 91n1706
  nutrition & food tech, 92n1481
  obstetrics & gynecology, 90n1641
  occupational titles, 4th ed, 93n301
  optometry, 2d ed, 91n1685
  Oreg. hist, 2d ed, 91n503
  organic compounds, 7th suppl., 5th ed, 91n1766
  organic compounds, 8th suppl., 5th ed, 92n1726
  organometallic compounds, 4th suppl., 90n1754
  organometallic compounds, 5th suppl., 91n1767
  organometallic compounds, 5th suppl., cum structure index, 91n1768
  pastoral care & counseling, 91n1443
  Pentecostal & charismatic movements, 90n1407
  personal finance, 93n243
  petroleum exploration, drilling, & production, 92n1626
  philosophical quotations, 94n1499
  plant pathology, 90n1486
  plant virology, 93n1495
  pol parties & orgs in Russia, 94n779
  pols, 7th ed, 93n722
  polling, 93n103
  Polynesian mythology, 90n1303
  process tech, 91n1609
  protopharmacology, 92n1689
  pseudonyms & their origins, 2d ed, 90n404
  quotations from Shakespeare, 93n1213
  race & ethnic relations, 2d ed, 90n363
  real estate appraisal, 2d ed, 90n293
  real estate lending terms, 90n294
  real numbers, 91n1796
  real people & places in fiction, 94n1159
  religion & philosophy, 91n1414
  religious & spiritual quotations, 91n1420
  Russian personal names, 93n463
  sacred & magical plants, 94n1667
  Scandinavian lit, 92n1240
  sci & creationism, 91n1513
  scientific biog, v.17, suppl.2, 91n1461
  scientific biog, v.18, suppl.2, 91n1462
  scientific literacy, 93n1445
  Scottish bus biog 1860-1960, v.2, 91n129
  selected synonyms in the principal Indo-European langs, 90n1030
  sexual slang, 94n909
  signatures & monograms of American artists, 90n955
  social work: Philippine setting, 90n816
  space tech, 92n1595
  sporting artists 1650-1990, 94n1065
  statistical terms, 5th ed, 92n847
  stats & methodology, 94n79
  steroids, 92n1519
  stylistics, 91n955
  superstitions, 91n798
  surnames, 90n401
  symbolism, 94n979
  symbols, 93n1041
  terms in music, 4th ed, 93n1248
  the African left, 91n764
  the American Indian, 91n399
  the American west, 94n1088
  the Ecumenical movement, 92n1416
  the environment, 3d ed, 90n1791
  the lit of the Iberian Peninsula, 94n1289
  the liturgy, 90n1408
  the martial arts, 93n839
  the Middle Ages, 90n533
  the Napoleonic wars, 94n521
  the Ojibway lang, 94n1124
  the print trade in Ireland, 90n631
  the Russian revolution, 90n524
  the 2d World War, 91n554
  the sport & exercise scis, 92n771
  theatre anthropology, 92n1374
  Third World terms, 93n136
  20th century hist, 91n553
  20th century hist 1914-90, 93n557
  20th century world biog, 93n38
  20th-century Cuban lit, 91n1230
  20th-century design, 92n922
  20th-century world pols, 94n718
  US economic hist, 94n158
  US govt statl terms, 93n903
  visual sci, 4th ed, 90n1691
  war quotations, 91n683
  water & wastewater treatment trademarks & brand names, 93n1772
  W church music, 93n1269
  woodworking tools c.1700-1970, rev ed, 91n1637
  word origins, 92n1022
  world place names derived from British names, 90n429
  world pols, 92n673
Dictionnaire francais, 90n1041
Didik, Frank X., 93n284
Diehm, William J., 93n853
Dienhart, Tom, 92n776, 94n848
Diesel locomotive rosters, 3d ed, 94n2025
Dieter's dict & problem solver, 94n1603
Dietrich, Julia, 93n1211
Dietrich, R. V., 91n1781
Diffor, Elaine N., 90n351, 93n397, 94n375
Diffor, John C., 90n351, 93n397, 94n375
Diffusion of innovations, 91n79
Digest of UK energy stats 1988, 90n1780
Digital systems ref bk, 93n1596
Dihn-Hoa, Ngyuen, 93n1104
Dilbert, Sheila, 94n35
Dillard, Philip H., 93n1274
Diller, Daniel C., 91n536, 92n724
DiMauro, Laurie, 92n1108

Dinan, Desmond, 94n767
Dinosaur & other prehistoric animal factfinder, 94n1959
Dinosaurs: a gd to research, 93n1731
Diodato, Virgil P., 92n140
Diptera types in the Canadian Natl Collection of Insects, pt.1, 92n1579
Diptera types in the Canadian Natl Collection of Insects, pt.2, 94n1724
Dirctory of European environmental orgs, 94n2003
Direct mktg market place [DMMP] 1993, 94n289
Directories in print 1989, 90n57
Directories in print 1993, 94n46
Directories of London, 1677-1977, 91n111
Directors & their films, 94n1453
Directory, 1989-90: Japanese-affiliated cos in USA & Canada, 90n174
Directory, 1990: American society of journalists & authors, 91n936
Directory, 1991-92: Japanese-affiliated cos in USA & Canada, 93n279
Directory, 1992: AAAS consortium of affiliates for intl programs, 94n1572
Directory for exceptional children 1990-91, 91n349
Directory of ...
   AAAS sci & engineering fellows 1973-92, 94n1573
   African American religious bodies, 92n1404
   African film-makers & films, 94n1436
   alcohol & drug treatment resources in Ont. 1989, 91n882
   Alzheimer's disease treatment facilities & home health care programs, 90n1681
   American philosophers 1990-91, 91n1406
   American philosophers 1992-93, 94n1498
   American poets & fiction writers, 1989-90 ed, 91n946
   American youth orgs 1990-91, 91n895
   applications sftwr of the UN system, 92n736
   archives in Manitoba, 90n512
   arctic sci & tech research in Canada, 93n118
   art publishers, bk publishers & record cos, 91n1013
   artist assns & exhibition spaces, art commission, museum curators & art critics, 91n1014
   automated lib systems, 2d ed, 91n637
   biomedical & health care grants 1992, 92n1634
   blacks in the performing arts, 2d ed, 91n1343
   bk printers, 1991 ed, 92n638
   British assns & assns in Ireland, 9th ed, 90n63
   building & equipment grants, 90n807
   building & equipment grants, 2d ed, 93n1035, 94n1772
   business info resources, 1992, 93n192
   business to business cats, 1991, 93n194
   Canadian made products, 91n226
   Canadian manufacturers, 91n227
   Canadian schools 1988, 91n304
   Canadian theatre archives, 94n1476
   catalogers in the SLA, 90n603
   Catholic colleges & univs, 1992, 94n335
   Catholic special educl programs & facilities 1989, 91n299
   Central America classroom resources K-12, 2d ed, 91n118
   chemical engineering consultants, 9th ed, 93n1583
   chemistry sftwr 1992, 94n1939
   college facilities & servs for people with disabilities, 3d ed, 92n321
   community legislation in force, 16th ed, 92n737
   cos offering dividend reinvestment plans, 6th ed, 90n203
   cos offering dividend reinvestment plans, 10th ed, 94n180
   computer & high tech grants, 92n1706
   computer conferencing in libs, 93n656
   computer sftwr & servs, 90n1728
   computerized data files [1989], 91n42
   construction industry consultants, 91n1605
   corporate & fndn givers 1992, 93n872
   corporate affiliations 1989, 90n175
   corporate affiliations 1990, 91n142
   courthouses & abstract & title cos, 1993, 94n559
   credentials in counseling & psychotherapy, 90n750
   current HIV/AIDS research in Canada 1988-91, 93n1651
   dvlpmt research & training insts in Africa, 94n93
   disability support servs in community colleges 1992, 94n371
   E European film-makers & films 1945-91, 93n1348
   editorial resources, 1989-90, 90n894
   educl contests for students K-12, 92n286
   educl sftwr for nursing, 1988, 90n1692
   electronic jls, newsletters & academic discussion lists, 2d ed, 93n72
   employers' assocs, trade unions, joint orgs, 90n253
   ethnic minority professionals in psychology, 90n748
   ethnic professionals in LIS (lib & info sci), 93n625
   European bus, 94n254
   European community trade & professional assns 1992, 94n274
   European industrial & trade assns, 5th ed, 92n242
   European professional & learned societies, 4th ed, 90n58
   European sports orgs, 93n821
   facilities & servs for the learning disabled, 1993-94, 94n373
   faculty contracts & bargaining agents in insts of higher educ, v.15, 90n325
   faculty contracts & bargaining agents in insts of higher educ, v.18, 93n360
   family assns, 92n385
   family assns, 1993-94 ed, 94n431
   fed laboratory & tech resources, 91n1465
   fed libs, 2d ed, 94n651
   fee-based info servs 1989, 90n583
   financial aids for minorities, 1989-90, 90n329
   financial aids for women 1989-90, 90n874
   financial futures exchanges, 90n206
   fine art representatives & corporate art consultants, 90n960
   fine art representatives & corps collecting art, 2d ed, 91n1015
   food & nutrition info for professionals & consumers, 2d ed, 94n1604
   foreign investments in the US: real estate & businesses, 92n138
   foreign law collections in selected law libs, 92n544
   foreign manufacturers in the US, 5th ed, 94n213
   foreign trade orgs in Eastern Europe, 2d ed, 90n176
   fund raising & nonprofit mgmt consultants, 94n901
   galleries for the fine artist, 91n1016
   geosci depts: N America, 29th ed, 92n1736
   govt doc collections & librarians, 6th ed, 93n676
   grants in the humanities 1988, 90n883
   grants in the humanities 1992/93, 93n946
   hospital personnel 1989, 90n1615
   housing attorneys, 1990-91, 92n542
   humor mags & humor orgs in America (& Canada), 2d ed, 90n907
   humor mags & humor orgs in America (& Canada), 3d ed, 93n1188
   Ill. adult literacy programs, 1989 update & suppl, 91n355
   incentives for bus investment & dvlpmt in the US, 3d ed, 93n221
   info mgmt sftwr for libs, info centers, record centers, 1989-90 ed, 91n631
   intentional communities, 1990/91, 92n816
   intl & natl medical & related societies, 2d ed, 92n1666
   intl pers & newsletters on the built environment, 2d ed, 93n1036
   Japanese healthcare industry, 1990 ed, 92n1635
   Japanese technical reports 1992-93, 94n114
   Japanese technical resources in the US 1992, 93n655
   jobs & careers abroad, 8th ed, 94n273
   law school joint degree programs 1989-90, 91n586
   law-related CD-ROMS 1993, 94n560
   leading US export mgmt cos, 3d ed, 92n231
   legislative leaders 1989-90, 90n696
   legislative leaders 1991-92, 93n739
   lib & info orgs in the UK, 94n635
   lib automation sftwr, systems, & servs, 1993 ed, 94n644
   literary mags 1990-91, 91n1106
   literary mags 1993-94, 94n1162
   Lloyd's of London, 91n240
   long-term care centres in Canada, v.9, Sept.90, 91n1646
   low temperature research & dvlpmt in Europe, 7th ed, 94n1964
   mail order catalogs, 4th ed, 91n193
   mailing list cos, 11th ed, 92n252

Directory of ... *(continued)*
  major mailers & what they mail 1990, 91n263
  manufacturing research centers June 1989, 90n234
  medical health care libs in the UK & Republic of Ireland, 7th ed, 92n624
  medical rehabilitation programs, 91n1668
  medical specialists 1989-90, 91n1669
  merger & acquisition firms & professionals 1992, 93n193
  military bases in the US, 92n650
  multinatls, 91n148
  museums in Africa, 91n57
  natl helplines, 91n849
  natl helplines 1993, 94n47
  new & emerging fndns, 2d ed, 92n824
  non-faculty bargaining agents in insts of higher educ, 92n294
  nursing homes 1991-92, 92n1686
  online databases & CD-ROM resources for high schools, 90n344
  online databases, v.13, no.2, 93n1682
  online healthcare databases, 5th ed, 91n1648
  operating grants, 94n889
  overseas summer jobs, 1991, 92n218
  pain treatment centers in the US & Canada, 90n1686
  pan-European orgs 1992, 93n138
  pathology training programs in the US & Canada, 22d ed, 90n1657
  pathology training programs in the US & Canada 1993-94, 93n1643
  pers online: news, law & bus, 5th ed, 91n73
  pers online: sci & tech, 2d ed, 92n1459
  poetry publishers 1990-91, 91n663
  poetry publishers, 8th ed, 94n664
  pol newsletters 1990, 91n739
  popular culture collections, 90n1307
  portable databases, 91n1729
  portable databases, v.3, no.2, 93n1670
  pressure groups in the European Community, 93n768
  publishers in China, 94n672
  publishing 1989, 90n635
  publishing 1993, 94n665
  pubs resources, 1991-92, 92n895
  pubs resources, 1993-94, 94n995
  record & CD retailers, 1990-91 ed, 92n1256
  registered investment advisors with the SEC 1993, 94n179
  religious orgs in the US, 3d ed, 94n1515
  research grants 1989, 90n805
  research grants 1992, 93n873
  residential centers for adults with developmental disabilities, 90n796
  residential centers for adults with mental illnesses, 91n1686
  resources for Australian studies in N America, 94n123
  Russian MPs, 94n523
  school mediation & conflict resolution programs, 90n313
  small pr & mag eds & publs, 22d ed, 92n635
  special collections in W Europe, 94n653
  special collections of research value in Canadian libs, 93n646
  special libs & info centers 1993, 94n650
  special programs for minority group members, 5th ed, 92n221
  state court clerks & county courthouses, 1991 ed, 91n574
  state legislative staff for educ issues, 90n305
  state prison librarians 1990, 92n614
  tech in global financial markets, 91n179
  telefacsimiles sites in N American libs, 6th ed, 92n567
  testing labs, 1991 ed, 92n1614
  Tex. manufacturers, 1991, 92n194
  Tex. wholesalers 1989, 90n275
  the American Psychological Assn, 1989 ed, 90n749
  the canning, freezing, preserving industries 1990-91, 13th ed, 92n1491
  the canning, freezing, preserving industries 1990-91, deluxe ed, 92n1492
  the Ill. lib & info network, 91n609
  the US postsecondary educ, 90n324
  the wood products industry, 1993, 94n1616
  theatre training programs 2, 90n1358
  theatre training programs, 3d ed, 93n1390
  toxicological & related testing labs, 92n1778
  translators & translating agencies in the UK, 2d ed, 92n1014
  travel info sources for the Pacific Islands, 90n461
  UN documentary & archival sources, 93n783
  US govt sftwr for mainframes & microcomputers, 94n1914
  US labor orgs, 1990-91 ed, 92n219
  video, computer & audio-visual products 1993, 94n1887
  W bk publishers & production servs, 92n634
  women's funds 1988, 90n873
  women's health care centers, 90n1616
  women's studies programs & lib resources, 91n927
  world leaders & factbk, 1990 ed, 91n723
  world stock exchanges, 90n204
Directory to ...
  Canadian studies in Canada, 4th ed, 94n126
  fulltext online resources 1992, 93n626
  intl bus educ in Canada, 93n230
Dirksen, P. B., 90n1387
Disability, sexuality & abuse, 93n865
Disarmament & security: 1988-89 yrbk, 92n748
Disciples & American culture, 92n1406
Discover Indian reservations USA, 93n434
Discovering America, 90n922
DISCovering authors [CD-ROM], 94n1146
Discovering wild plants, 91n1523
Discrimination & prejudice, 93n845
Disease & medical care in the US, 94n1802
Disney, Christine, 91n634
Disney's my very 1st dict, 91n1069
Displaced peoples & refugee studies, 92n833
Disputing the dead, 92n549
Distance educ: a selected bibliog, 94n380
Distinguished American lawyers, 91n569
Distinguished classics of ref publishing, 93n18
Distinguished shades, 93n49
Distribution & taxonomy of birds of the world, 92n1570
Dittmar, Joseph J., 91n821
Dividend reinvestment plans, 1992 gd almanac, 94n181
Divinsky, Nathan, 92n789
Division for the Development of Education, UNESCO, for the International Bureau of Education, 94n377
Division of Primary Education, Literacy and Adult Education and Education in Rural Areas, Unesco, 91n353
Divorce & dissolution of marriage laws of the US, 91n862
Dixon, Joan DeVee, 93n1256
Dixon, Penelope, 92n854
Djibouti, 92n87
Dobkin, David S., 93n1541
Dobkowski, Michael N., 94n587
Dobson, David, 90n390
Dobson, Richard, 93n1247
Docherty, James C., 94n124
Dockrill, Michael, 92n497
Doctor, Ronald M., 90n744
Doctoral dissertations on Asia, v.15, nos.1 & 2, 94n108
Doctors bk of home remedies, 91n1675
Doctors' vitamin & mineral ency, 91n1709
Documentation of the European communities, 91n110
Dodge, Meredith D., 91n116
Dodge, Robert K., 92n1318
Doerr, Juergen C., 93n538
Dogs, 94n1705
Dogs, cats, & horses, 91n1116
Doherty, J. E., 92n494
Doing bus in Chicago, 92n161
Doing bus in NYC, 91n141
Doing children's museums, 93n78
Do-it-yourself medical testing, 3d ed, 90n1671
Dolatshahi, Shahpari, 94n264
Doll, Carol A., 91n648
Dolle, Raymond F., 91n1157
Dollinger, Malin, 93n1655
Dominican Republic, 92n112
Donadio, Stephen, 94n71

Donahue, Roy L., 93n1468
Donald Davie: a checklist of his writings, 1946-88, 92n1201
Donald Windham: a bio-bibliog, 92n1184
Donaldson, Sandra, 94n1248
Donavin, Denise Perry, 91n843, 94n1163
Dondale, Charles D., 92n1580, 93n1563
Donna Reed: a bio-bibliog, 92n1342
Donnachie, Ian, 91n533
Donnelly, Danielle J., 90n1483
Donnelly, Dorothy F., 93n1416
Dooley, Patrick K., 93n1172
Doo-wop: the forgotten 3d of rock 'n roll, 93n1290
Dore, Susan Cole, 93n110
Dorf, Michael Ethan, 91n1303
Dorf, Richard C., 91n1748
Dorgan, Charity Anne, 90n216, 91n280, 91n378, 93n310
Dorian, A. F., 90n1643, 94n1800
Dorian, Bob, 92n1360
Dority, G. Kim, 93n8
Dorling Kindersley sci ency, 94n1565
Dorn, Jane L., 92n1562
Dorn, Robert D., 92n1562
Dorney, Lindsay, 92n864
Dorothy Parker: a bio-bibliog, 94n1236
Dorros, Gerald, 93n1646
Dorscheid, Peter, 91n264
Dorton, Claire, 94n1463
Dostal, Cyril A., 90n1600
Doubleday atlas of the USA, 91n431
Doubleday children's dict, 91n1070
Doubleday children's ency, 91n28
Doubleday picture atlas, 91n426
Doughty, Harold R., 92n303
Douglas, Auriel, 91n1052
Douglas, J. D., 90n1395, 92n1417
Douglas, Joel M., 90n325, 92n294, 93n360
Douglass, Jackie Leatherbury, 91n1549
Dove, John C., 94n20, 94n21, 94n771
Dow Jones averages 1885-1990, 92n165
Dow Jones investor's hndbk 1989, 90n205
Dow Jones-Irwin bus & investment almanac, 1990, 91n175
Dow, Susan L., 91n729
Dowell, Richard W., 92n1169
Down Home gd to the blues, 92n1300
Down Home Music, staff of, 92n1300
Downes, John, 92n184
Downey, Pat, 94n1361
Down-home talk, 90n1013
Downing, Douglas, 90n1710, 93n1675
Downs, Buck J., 91n40, 91n741, 93n71, 94n54, 94n744
Downs, Geoff, 94n1939
Downs, Jane B., 92n901
Downs, Robert B., 92n901
Dox, Ida G., 94n1829
Doyle, Paul A., 90n1188
Doyon, Yves, 94n1776
Dr. Axelrod's atlas of freshwater aquarium fishes, 3d ed, 90n1548
Dr. Axelrod's atlas of freshwater aquarium fishes, 6th ed, 93n1553
Dr. Burgess's atlas of marine aquarium fishes, 90n1549
Dr. Burgess's mini-atlas of marine aquarium fishes, 93n1554
Draaijer, Gera E., 93n898
Dragonflies of the Fla. peninsula, Bermuda, & the Bahamas, 90n1553
Drama by women to 1990, 93n1146
Drama criticism, v.1, 94n1201
Drama criticism, v.2, 94n1202
Drama criticism, v.3, 94n1203
Drama dict, 90n1357
Dramatic re-visions, 93n1333
Dramatist's bible 1989, 90n1363
Dramatists sourcebk, 1991-92 ed, 92n1383
Draper, Edythe, 93n1415, 94n1551
Draper, Graham, 92n399
Draper, James P., 91n1186, 92n1107, 93n1115, 93n1119
Draper, Larry W., 91n1435, 94n1501

Draper, Ronald P., 90n1179
Draper's bk of quotations for the Christian world, 94n1551
Drawing instruments 1580-1980, 90n963
Dreisbach, Christopher, 94n1484
Dresser, Peter, 94n1517
Dresser, Peter D., 90n326, 90n694, 94n1801
Dressler, Stephan, 92n1655
Drew, Bernard A., 91n559, 91n1129, 91n1353, 94n1221
Drew, Margaret A., 91n518
Drewes, Athena A., 93n808
Drexel, John, 92n507
Dreyer, M. R., 92n1292
Dreyer, Sharon Spredemann, 93n1123
Dreyfus, Larry, 91n597
Driggers, Stephen G., 90n1151
Driver, Elizabeth, 90n1453
Drost, Harry, 93n953
Drost, Jerome, 90n1103
Drucker, Sally Ann, 93n808
Drug abuse A-Z, 91n881
Drug abuse bibliog for 1988, 93n888
Drug, alcohol, & other addictions, 90n820
Drug, alcohol, & other addictions, 2d ed, 94n914
Drug educ resources dir, 91n887
Drug file, 93n1667
Drug info for the health care professional 1992, 93n1663
Drug interactions gd bk, 93n1664
Drug-alert dict & resource gd, 92n841
Drugs available abroad, 1991, 92n1693
Drugs, vitamins, minerals in pregnancy, 90n1702
Drum: an index to Africa's leading mag 1951-65, 90n107
Drury, George H., 91n1821, 94n2024
Drury, Nevill, 90n1642, 94n814
Drury, Susan, 90n1642
Dubal, David, 91n1287
DuBasky, Mayo, 91n1167
DuBern, Roger, 92n956
Dubin, Michael J., 91n752
DuBlanc, Robin, 90n1072
Dublin stage, 1720-45, 94n1468
Dubois, France, 91n243
Dubreuil, Lorraine, 91n436
Duchac, Joseph, 94n1233
Duchamp, Michel, 93n1725
Duckles, Vincent H., 90n1213
Ducks, 91n1560
Ducks in the wild, 94n1699
Dudenredaktion, 91n1085
Dudley's gear hndbk, 2d ed, 92n1624
Duensing, Edward E., 90n790
Duffy, Susan, 93n1375
Dufour, Pierre, 93n485
Duft, Joseph F., 91n1525
Dugan, Robert E., 91n776
Duggan, Margaret M., 91n1179
Duiker, William J., 90n526
Duke, James A., 91n1536
Duke of Wellington 1769-1852, 91n526
Dulbecco, Renato, 92n1516
Dumouchel, J. Robert, 90n806, 93n874
Dunbar, Gary S., 92n416
Duncan, Helen A., 90n1693
Duncan, Phil, 90n691, 94n749
Duncan's dict for nurses, 2d ed, 90n1693
Dundas, Pamela, 94n46
Dundee, Harold A., 90n1566
Dunford, Penny, 91n1007
Dunkle, Sidney W., 90n1553
Dunkley, David, 91n590
Dunkling, Leslie, 91n1062
Dunlop, Charles E. M., 94n1494
Dunmore, John, 93n487
Dunn, Robert J., 90n1151
Dunn, Thomas P., 94n974
Dunne, Lavon J., 91n1481

Dunne, Pete, 90n1532
Dunning, F. W., 91n1787
Dunning, John S, 90n1533
Dunning, Margaret B., 94n757
Dunn-Wood, Maryjane, 94n1523
Dupayrat, Jacques, 92n1645
Dupre, Jean-Paul, 90n46
Dupre, Louisa, 91n1375
DuPree, Sherry Sherrod, 91n1439
Dupriez, Bernard, 92n1102
Dupuis, Diane L., 93n840
Dupuy, R. Ernest, 94n687
Dupuy, Trevor N., 93n698, 94n687, 94n688
Duryea, Michelle LeBaron, 93n419
Dutch Filipiniana, 93n169
Dutch-English, English-Dutch dict, 92n1065
Dutile, Patty, 94n196
Dutro, J. T., 91n1781
Dutschke, C. W., 90n532
Duursma, E. K., 94n1744
Duxbury, Janet R., 92n1311
Dwight D. Eisenhower: a bibliog of his times & presidency, 92n456
Dwight D. Eisenhower: a centennial bibliog, 1890-1990, 92n464
DWM: a dir of women's media, 16th ed, 94n967
Dworsky, Alan L., 93n590
Dyches, Richard W., 92n1458, 92n1752
Dyer, Alan Frank, 93n1171
Dyer, Donald R., 93n796
Dykhuis, Randy, 91n639
Dynes, Wayne R., 91n870
Dysart, Jane I., 91n155
Dziggel, Oliver C., 94n243, 94n261
Dziki, Sylwester, 91n935

E for environment, 93n1752
Eads, Peter, 92n1198
Eagle, Dorothy, 94n480
Eagle/Walking Turtle, 91n396
Eagles, Brenda M., 90n1287
Eagles, D. Munroe, 93n764
Eagleson, Laurie, 92n1282
Eagleson, Mary, 90n1481
Eaker, Sherry, 90n1364
Earl Blackwell's celebrity register 1990, 91n14
Earle, Michael V., 94n839
Early American music, 91n1253
Early American scientific & technical lit, 91n1454
Early black American playwrights & dramatic writers, 92n1160
Early Christian & Byzantine architecture, 94n1054
Early, John F., 92n1182
Early modern English lexicography, v.1, 91n1044
Early modern English lexicography, v.2, 91n1046
Earnshaw, Jill, 90n254
Earth jl, 1992, 93n1765
Earth's natural forces, 92n1731
Eason, Ron, 94n1563
East & SE Asia material culture in N America, 90n504
East, Roger, 92n83, 92n728, 92n738
Eastern birds, 91n1569
Eastern Europe: a dir & sourcebk 1992, 93n140
Eastern Europe: a market for the 1990s, 92n243
Eastern Europe & the Commonwealth of Independent States 1992, 93n141
Eastern European business dir, 93n284
Eastern islands, 91n432
Eastern wildflowers, 90n1493
Eastman, John, 93n1518
Easton, Patricia, 94n1485
Easton, Robert, 90n968
Easy access to natl parks, 93n499
Easy reading, 2d ed, 91n368
Eating disorders, 90n1684, 92n1684
Eaton, Dian, 90n1010

Eatwell, John, 93n242
Eberhart, George M., 92n570
Eberle, Mark E., 91n1586
Ebert, Roger, 92n1338
Ebert, Samuel H., 90n428
Ebner, David, 91n1379
EBSCO's 1989-90 librarians' hndbk, 90n76
EC agricultural price indices, 91n1480
EC direct, 94n257
EC info hndbk 1993/94, 94n768
Eccardt, Thomas, 94n1122
Eccles, David H., 93n1556
Echols, Anne, 93n933
Echols, John M., 90n1046
Ecker, Ronald L., 91n1513
Eckhardt, Caroline D., 91n1201
Eckhart, Mary Lawrence, 93n517
Eckstein, Richard, 90n807
Eckstein, Richard M., 90n797, 94n1772
Ecologue, 91n189
Economic and Social Policy Department, Statistics Division, 90n1447
Economic indicators hndbk, 93n204
Economic methodology, 90n157
Economic planning 1943-51, 94n263
Economies of Africa, 92n143
Economist atlas, 93n172
Economist atlas of the New Europe, 94n255
Economist desk companion, 93n205
Economist Publications, 90n204
Economist Pubs pocket employer, 90n254
Economist Pubs pocket gd to advertising, 90n276
Ecuador, 91n120
Ecumenism: a bibliographical overview, 94n1524
ECW's biographical gd to Canadian novelists, 94n1273
ECW's biographical gd to Canadian poets, 94n1274
Eddleman, Floyd Eugene, 90n1129, 93n1168
Edelheit, Abraham, 93n550
Edelheit, Abraham J., 91n519, 93n535, 94n532
Edelheit, Hershel, 91n519, 93n535, 93n550, 94n532
Edenbaum, Jesse, 93n1711
Edgar & Dorothy Davidson collection of Canadiana at Mount Allison Univ, 92n6
Edgar, David, 93n1477
Edible garden weeds of Canada, 90n1506
Edible wild fruits & nuts of Canada, 90n1507
Edith Wharton: a descriptive bibliog, 92n1183
Edith Wharton: an annot secondary bibliog, 91n1175
Editing: an annot bibliog, 92n897
Editing docs & texts, 91n951
Editorial Board, 93n1238
Editorial Board, Roth Publishing, Inc., 90n1119
Edmonton, Phil, 93n1781, 93n1782
Education: a gd to ref & info sources, 90n298
Education for older adult learning, 94n389
Education for the Earth, 94n2012
Education in ...
  Canada, 90n300
  England & Wales, 92n316
  Japan, 90n306
  the Arab Gulf states & the Arab world, 93n384
Education index, 93n341
Education Interface gd to corporate support, v.1, no.3, 91n297
Education of women in the US, 93n926
Educational & psychological tests in the Academic Lib, 91n292
Educational film & video locator 1990-91, 91n358
Educational gd to the natl park system, 90n446
Educational media & tech yrbk, v.16, 91n298
Educational media & tech yrbk, v.17, 92n327
Educational media & tech yrbk, v.18, 93n398
Educational opportunity gd, 1993, 94n316
Educational rankings annual 1991, 92n278
Educational Testing Service, Test Collection, 90n302, 91n293
Educator's desk ref, 90n307

Educators gd to ...
    free films, 49th ed, 90n351
    free films, 52d ed, 93n397
    free filmstrips & slides, 45th ed, 94n375
    free guidance materials, 30th ed, 93n400
    free health, physical educ & recreation materials, 26th ed, 94n829
    free home economics & consumer educ materials, 10th ed, 94n886
    free social studies materials, 33d ed, 94n81
    free videotapes, 39th ed, 93n396
Educators grade gd to free teaching aids, 39th ed, 94n317
Educators index of free materials, 101st ed, 93n328
Edward Burlingame Hill: a bio-bibliog, 90n1255
Edward E. Judge & Sons, Inc., 92n1491, 92n1492
Edward Elgar: a gd to research, 94n1327
Edwards, Charles J., 90n822, 91n884, 92n279, 92n825, 94n876
Edwards, Clive, 92n955
Edwards, Elwyn Hartley, 94n1707
Edwards, Ernest P., 90n1534
Edwards, Helen, 92n182
Edwards, John, 94n2021
Edwards, John W., 94n1376
Edwards, Paul M., 94n678, 94n679
Edwin Booth: a bio-bibliog, 93n1379
Eggenberger, David, 93n39
Eggers, Walter, 90n1371
Egypt, 90n148
Egyptian pyramids, 92n505
Ehr, Catherine M., 93n190, 94n167, 94n211
EHR dir of awards: fiscal yr 1990, 93n875
Ehrens, Cheryl, 93n96
Ehresmann, Donald L., 91n1002, 94n1022
Ehrich, Robert W., 94n485
Ehrlich, Eugene, 91n1426, 92n1032
Ehrlich, Paul R., 93n1541
Ei thesaurus, 94n1753
Eichenlaub, Val L., 92n1733
Eichholz, Alice, 90n387, 93n455
Eidenier, Connie Wright, 90n897
Eigen, Lewis D., 90n269, 94n724
1890s: an ency of British lit, art, & culture, 94n981
Eighteenth century: a current bibliog, n.s.11, 92n871
Eighteenth-century British poets, 1st series, 91n1224
Eighteenth-century British poets: 2d series, 92n1222
Eighteenth-century musical chronicle, 91n1258
Eighty silent film stars, 93n1336
Eis, Arlene L., 91n560, 91n561, 91n585, 93n591, 94n560, 94n567, 94n568
Eisenberg, Gerson G., 91n373
Eisenberg, John F., 90n1555, 93n1570
Eisner, Gilbert M., 94n1829
Eiss, Harry, 90n1081
Ekhaml, Leticia T., 92n611
Ekstrom, Brenda L., 90n1514
El Salvador, 90n143
EL&P US electric utility industry dir, 1992, 93n1589
Elazar, Daniel J., 93n726
Elbers, Joan S., 92n1767
Elbert, George A., 90n1469
Elbert, Virginie F., 90n1469
Elder care, 91n845
Elder, Danny, 93n1730
Elder servs 1990-91, 91n844
Elderbroom, Yvette, 92n397
Elderhostels, 90n434
Elderly in America, 92n811
Eldridge, Grant J., 94n52
Eldridge, Wayne Bryant, 91n1575
Eleanor Parker: woman of a 1,000 faces, 91n1357
Election data bk, 94n751
Election Data Services, staff of, 94n751
Election results dir, 1993 ed, 94n738
Elections since 1945, 90n684
Electoral pols dict, 90n695

Electric power in Canada 1989, 92n1761
Electric utility industry sftwr dir, 1992, 93n1590
Electrical engineering materials ref gd, 91n1613
Electronic news financial fact bk & dir 1989-90, 91n176
Electronic packaging & interconnection hndbk, 92n1603
Electronic packaging, microelectronics, & interconnection dict, 94n1781
Electronic post-production terms & concepts, 92n913
Electronic research centres, 2d ed, 90n1580
Electronic style, 94n1002
Electronic univ, 94n376
Elementary school lib collection, 17th ed, 91n649
Elementary school lib collection, 18th ed, 93n667
Elementary teachers gd to free curriculum materials, 50th ed, 94n318
Elements, 2d ed, 93n1712
Elements of English, 2d ed, 90n993
Elements of typographic style, 94n675
Elert, Nicolet V., 91n136
Eleventh mental measurements yrbk, 93n803
Eley, Stephen, 93n828
Elfe, Wolfgang D., 94n1286, 94n1287
El-Hi textbks & serials in print 1989, 90n299
El-Hi textbks & serials in print 1991, 92n285
Eliade gd to world religions, 93n1409
Eliade, Mircea, 93n1409
Elias baseball analyst, 1989, 91n826
Elias, Stephen R., 92n532
Elinor Remick Warren: a bio-bibliog, 94n1321
Elizabeth Barrett Browning: an annot bibliog of the commentary & criticism, 1826-1990, 94n1248
Elkhadem, Saad, 93n1303
Elkin, Judith Laikin, 92n378
Elkington, John, 92n177
Elks, J., 91n1708
Ellen Stewart & La Mama: a bio-bibliog, 94n1410
Ellenbogen, Glenn C., 90n907, 93n1188
Eller, William, 91n356, 93n404
Elliot, Gwen, 92n1528
Elliot, Jeffrey M., 90n675, 91n1174, 92n1185
Elliot, W. Rodger, 92n1504
Elliott, Clark A., 91n1469
Elliott, J. K., 90n1388
Elliott, Pirkko, 91n632
Elliott, Stephen P., 94n42
Elliott, Sydney, 91n759
Ellis, Barbara W., 93n1489, 94n1619
Ellis, Iris, 92n178
Ellis, J. Pamela, 92n1543
Ellis, Martin B., 92n1543
Ellis, Peter Berresford, 90n1304, 93n1304
Ellmore, R. Terry, 92n887
Ellrod, J. G., 90n1323
Elmes, Gregory A., 94n725
Elnicki, Susan E., 91n868
Elrod, J. McRee, 93n598
El-Sanabary, Nagat, 93n384
Elsbree, John J., 90n353
Elsevier's dict of ...
    aquaculture, 93n1467
    civil engineering, 90n1587, 93n1585
    export financing & credit insurance, 91n264
    geoscis, 93n1723
    hydrology & water quality mgmt, 93n1724
    machine tools & elements, 92n1628
    mining & mineralogy, 94n1800
    office automation, 93n323
    physical planning, 91n909
    plant genetic resources, 93n1496
    terrestrial plant ecology, 93n1497
Elsevier's encyclopaedic dict of medicine, pt.B, 90n1643
Elshami, Ahmed M., 91n633
Elster, Robert J., 91n219
Elting, John R., 94n707
Elvis: his life from A to Z, 90n1299

Elwell, Walter A., 90n1394
Elwood, Ann, 90n1
Ely, Charles, 90n1544, 93n1546
Ely, Donald P., 93n398
Embroidery & needlepoint, 90n932
Emergency medical servs for children: innovation bank, 2d ed, 91n1676
Emerging techs & instruction, 93n344
Emerich, Jean, 91n1078
Emerson, John A, 90n1263
Emily Dickinson: a bibliog of secondary sources, 90n1136
Emily Post's etiquette, 15th ed, 93n1307
Emmons, Louise H, 91n1592
Employee assistance progs, 90n259
Employee benefit plans, 8th ed, 94n272
Employee benefits dict, 94n271
Employers' orgs of the world, 92n234
Employment glossary, 91n243
Emsley, John, 93n1712
Encyclopaedia Iranica, v.5, fascicle 1, 92n116
Encyclopaedia Iranica, v.5, fascicle 2, 92n117
Encyclopaedia of Arthurian legends, 93n1190
Encyclopaedia of ...
   Australian plants suitable for cultivation, v.5, 92n1504
   educl media communications & tech, 2d ed, 90n354
   food sci, food tech, & nutrition, 94n1600
   Indian archaeology, 91n479
   Islam, new ed, v.7, 94n151
   Islam, new ed, v.7, fascicules 125-26, 94n150
   lang, 91n1042
   mathematics, 90n1771
   Tamil lit, v.1, 92n1237
   the hist of tech, 91n1464
Encyclopedia Americana, 90n50
Encyclopedia Americana, intl ed, 93n59
Encyclopedia of ...
   adolescence, 92n843
   adoption, 93n866
   African American religions, 94n1514
   African-American civil rights, 93n616
   aging & the elderly, 93n858
   alcoholism, 2d ed, 92n839
   alternative health care, 91n1662
   amazons, 92n862
   American bus hist & biog: banking & finance, 1913-89, 92n185
   American bus hist & biog: banking & finance to 1913, 91n213
   American bus hist & biog: iron & steel in the 19th century, 90n236
   American bus hist & biog: the airline industry, 93n248
   American bus hist & biog: the automobile industry, 1896-1920, 91n228
   American bus hist & biog: the automobile industry, 1920-80, 90n235
   American comics, 92n1327
   American facts & dates, 9th ed, 94n504
   American religions, 3d ed, 91n1415
   American religions, 4th ed, 94n1518
   American scandal, 90n492
   American social hist, 94n505
   American spy films, 91n1379
   American war films, 90n1327
   American wrestling, 91n840
   ancient Egypt, 92n506
   animated cartoons, 93n1347
   antibiotics, 3d ed, 94n1871
   applied physics, v.1, 92n1750
   applied physics, v.2, 93n1733
   applied physics, v.3, 93n1734
   architecture, v.5, 91n1026
   architecture design, engineering & construction, v.2, 90n972
   architecture design, engineering & construction, v.3, 90n973
   arms control & disarmament, 94n797
   assassinations, 92n558
   assns CD-ROM, 94n51
   assns intl orgs 1989, 90n59
   assns intl orgs 1989 suppl, 90n60
   assns intl orgs 1993, 94n48
   assns 1991, v.1, 91n37
   assns 1991, v.2, 91n38
   assns 1994, v.1, 94n49
   assns 1994, v.2, 94n50
   assns: regional, state, & local orgs, 90n61
   assns: regional, state, & local orgs 1992-93, 94n52
   astronomy & astrophysics, 90n1744
   banking & finance, 9th ed, 92n186, 94n208
   biblical & Christian ethics, rev ed, 93n1419
   blindness & vision impairment, 92n1685
   Britain, 94n133
   bus info sources, 7th ed, 90n152
   bus info sources, 9th ed, 93n206
   calligraphy techniques, 92n923
   career change & work issues, 93n409
   career choices for the 1990s, 93n309
   careers & vocational guidance, 8th ed, 91n374
   careers & vocational guidance, 9th ed, 94n386
   censorship, 91n635
   chemical processing & design, v.35, 92n1597
   chemical processing & design, v.36, 94n1759
   chemical processing & design, v.37, 94n1760
   chemical processing & design, v.38, 94n1761
   chemical processing & design, v.39, 94n1762
   chemical processing & design, v.40, 94n1763
   chemical processing & design, v.41, 94n1764
   chemical processing & design, v.42, 94n1765
   chemical processing & design, v.43, 94n1766
   child abuse, 90n576
   childbearing, 94n1831
   colonial & revolutionary America, 91n504
   computer sci & tech, v.19, suppl.4, 90n1711
   computer sci & tech, v.20, suppl.5, 90n1712
   computer sci, 3d ed, 94n1903
   contemporary literary theory, 94n1150
   continental women writers, 92n1232
   cosmology, 94n1926
   deafness & hearing disorders, 93n1656
   death, 90n795
   depression, 92n1683
   drug abuse, 2d ed, 93n890
   early childhood educ, 93n332
   early Christianity, 91n1442
   earth system sci, 93n1721
   educl research, 6th ed, 93n331
   electronic circuits, v.3, 92n1602
   electronic circuits, v.4, 94n1778
   electronics, 2d ed, 91n1616
   environmental control tech, v.4, 92n1774
   environmental studies, 92n1773
   ethics, 93n1395
   evolution, 92n1523
   fermented fresh milk products, 93n1475
   field trips & educl destinations, 93n352
   film, 92n1352
   film festivals, 90n1328
   flora & fauna in English & American lit, 94n1151
   flowers, 94n1654
   fluid mechanics, v.8, 90n1586
   food sci & tech, 93n1473
   franchises & franchising, 90n207
   gambling, 91n806
   genetic disorders & birth defects, 92n1681
   ghosts & spirits, 93n810
   gods, 94n1395
   golf, 93n832
   good health, 90n1644
   governmental advisory orgs 1990-91, 90n694
   governmental advisory orgs 1994-95, 94n747
   handspinning, 90n936
   health info sources, 2d ed, 94n1827
   heresies & heretics, 94n1530
   higher educ, 93n358

Hollywood, 91n1370
homosexuality, 91n870
human biology, 92n1516
human dvlpmt & educ, 91n793
human rights, 92n563
igneous & metamorphic petrology, 91n1782
info systems & servs, 1989, 90n584
Japan, 92n95
Jewish genealogy, v.1, 92n384
Jewish prayer, 94n1556
Jewish symbols, 93n443
Judaism, 91n1449
lasers & optical tech, 92n1604
learning & memory, 94n809
legal info sources, 2d ed, 94n566
lib & info sci, v.44, 94n601
lib & info sci, v.45, 94n602
lib & info sci, v.46, 94n603
lib & info sci, v.47, 94n604
lib & info sci, v.48, 94n605
lib & info sci, v.49, 94n606
lib & info sci, v.50, 94n607
lib & info sci, v.51, 94n608
lit & criticism, 93n1116
living artists, 4th ed, 90n949
living artists in America, 6th ed, 93n1024
major league baseball team hists: American League, 92n778
major league baseball team hists: Natl League, 92n779
major league baseball teams, 94n831
marine scis, 94n1744
marriage, divorce & the family, 90n798
materials characterization, 93n1605
materials sci & engineering, suppl, 90n1599
medical orgs & agencies 1992-93, 93n1632
mental & physical handicaps, 92n322
microbiology, 94n1636
microcomputers, v.6, 92n1707
microcomputers, v.7, 94n1896
microcomputers, v.8, 94n1897
microcomputers, v.9, 94n1898
microcomputers, v.10, 94n1899
minerals, 2d ed, 91n1790
mistresses, 94n961
modern physics, 92n1749
monsters, 90n1310
Mormonism, 93n1420
Mormonism [CD-ROM], 93n1421
music in Canada, 2d ed, 94n1312
nationalism, 91n766
Native American religions, 93n432
natural medicine, 93n1634
Nfld. & Lab., v.3, 93n133
N American sports hist, 93n819
occultism & parapsychology, 3d ed, 92n762
parapsychology & psychical research, 92n761
perennials, 93n1508
pharmaceutical tech, v.2, 91n1710
pharmaceutical tech, v.3, 91n1711
pharmaceutical tech, v.4, 94n1867
pharmaceutical tech, v.5, 94n1868
pharmaceutical tech, v.6, 94n1869
pharmaceutical tech, v.7, 94n1870
phobias, fears, & anxieties, 90n744
physical sci & tech, 1989 yrbk, 90n1425
physical sci & tech 1991 yrbk, 93n1453
physical sci & tech, 2d ed, 94n1566
physical scis & engineering info sources, 90n1424
physics, 2d ed, 92n1747
police sci, 90n567
polymer sci & engineering, index volume, 91n1770
polymer sci & engineering, 2d ed., suppl.v, 91n1771
polymer sci & engineering, 2d ed, v.16, 91n1769
pop, rock & soul, rev ed, 90n1298
pottery techniques, 92n949
recorded sound in the US, 94n1313

religions in the US, 93n1407
rock, rev ed, 90n1294
romanticism, 93n531
Russian hist, 94n524
schizophrenia & the psychotic disorders, 93n799
sci fiction, 94n1211
sculpture techniques, 91n1041
sleep & dreaming, 94n808
social work, 1990 suppl., 18th ed., 91n876
sociology, 93n847
solid earth geophysics, 90n1767
S culture, 90n491
Soviet life, 92n721
sporting firearms, 92n932
statistical scis, suppl, 91n898
strange & unexplained physical phenomena, 94n813
Talmudic sages, 90n1413
telecommunications, 90n1733
telemarketing, 90n273
textiles, 93n1007
the 2d World War, 90n653
the American Constitution, suppl.1, 93n576
the American left, 91n763
the animal world, 90n1516
the blues, 94n1370
the British pr 1422-1992, 94n1008
the central West, 91n502
the Confederacy, 94n506
the early church, 93n1406
the far west, 92n84
the First World, 91n85
the Holocaust, 91n520
the Midwest, 90n100
the N.Y. stage, 1930-40, 90n1367
the N.Y. stage, 1940-50, 94n1474
the reformed faith, 93n1422
the Second World, 92n509
the Third Reich, 92n493
the Third World, 4th ed, 93n137
3d parties in the US, 92n683
tribology, 92n1625
Ukraine, vs. 3-5, 94n138
violence, 94n586
W lawmen & outlaws, 93n609
watercolor techniques, 92n1001
witches & witchcraft, 90n755
women's assns, 94n969
wood, 90n1465
wood joints, 94n1030
world biog, 20th century suppl, v.17, 93n39
world crime, 92n552
world cultures, v.1, 92n334
world cultures, v.2, 92n335
world cultures, v.3, 93n413
world cultures, v.4, 94n395
world cultures, v.5, 94n396
world lit in the 20th century, v.5, 94n1152
world problems & human potential, 3d ed, 92n803
Encyclopedia USA, v.16, 94n509
Encyclopedia USA, v.17, 94n510
Encyclopedia USA index v.1, 94n513
Encyclopedic dict of ...
    accounting & finance, 90n198
    American govt, 93n737
    chemical tech, 94n1936
    economics, 4th ed, 93n180
    electronics, electrical engineering & info processing, 91n1619
    genetics, 92n1521
    psychology, 4th ed, 93n800
    sociology, 4th ed, 93n849
    yoga, 91n1405
Encyclopedic hndbk of cults in America, rev ed, 93n1410
Endangered vertebrates, 91n1553
Endangered wildlife of the world, 94n1676
Ende, Steve, 91n265

Enderlyn, Allyn, 94n243, 94n261
Energy & environmental terms, 90n1775
Energy balances of OECD countries 1980-89, 93n1746
Energy in the dvlpmt of W Africa, 94n1969
Energy info abstracts annual 1988, 90n1781
Energy info abstracts annual 1991, 94n1979
Energy: monthly stats, 91n1802
Energy stats of OECD countries 1980-89, 93n1747
Energy stats sourcebk, 7th ed, 94n1980
Energy stats yrbk 1987, 91n1803
Energy stats yrbk, 1990, 94n1981
Energy supply A-Z, 92n1754
Energy update, 92n1763
Engel, Allison, 92n1493
Engel, Elliot, 91n1203
Engel, Madeline H., 94n1208
Engel, Margaret, 92n1493
Engemann, Thomas S., 90n544
Enggass, Peter M., 90n432
Engineered materials hndbk, v.2, 90n1600
Engineered materials hndbk, v.3, 92n1615
English, Barbara, 94n518
English dict from Cawdrey to Johnson 1604-1755, 92n1013
English lang & orientation programs in the US, 9th ed, 90n994
English lang & orientation programs in the US, 10th ed, 93n1053
English lang criticism on the foreign novel 1965-75, 90n1063
English legal hist, 91n562
English lib, 6th ed, 91n1180
English lit & backgrounds 1660-1700, 91n1179
English novel explication, suppl.4, 91n1194
English origins of American colonists, 92n388
English religion 1500-40, 90n1379
English Renaissance prose fiction, 1500-1660, 93n1203
English Romantic poetry: an annot bibliog, 92n1218
English schoolboy stories, 93n1135
English Slovak dict, 92n1089
English-Chinese glossary of American criminal law & criminal procedure law, 91n571
English-Dakota dict, 94n1112
English-Hausa dict, 91n1086
English-Hindi dict, 92n1074
English-Japanese, Japanese-English dict of computer & data-processing terms, 90n1713
English-Norwegian dict, 90n1052
English-Persian dict, 94n1125
English-Persian dict of legal & commercial terms, 91n570
English-Russian dict with phonetics, 93n1094
English-Serbocroatian dict, 3d ed, 91n1092
English-Serbocroatian, Serbocroatian-English pocket dict, 91n1094
English-Swedish, Swedish-English dict, 92n1092
English-Yiddish, Yiddish-English dict, 93n1105
Enhanced gd for occupational exploration, 92n227
Enns, Paul, 91n1446
Enns, Richard A., 92n99
Enright, Rosemary, 94n1463
Enrique Granados: a bio-bibliog, 93n1259
Enser, A. G. S., 91n547
Enser's filmed bks & plays, 94n1438
Enslen, Richard A., 92n530
Ensminger, M. E., 92n1510
Ensor, Pat, 93n82, 93n660
Entin, Paula B., 90n620
Entomology: a gd to info sources, 2d ed, 91n1589
Entrepreneur & small bus problem solver, 2d ed, 91n152
Environment & behavior, pt.2, 90n1789
Environment abstracts annual 1988, 90n1797
Environment abstracts annual 1991, 93n1766
Environment on file, 93n1767
Environmental accounting, 94n1989
Environmental address bk, 93n1760
Environmental decline & public policy, 94n2019
Environmental dict, 2d ed, 94n1998
Environmental engineering dict, 2d ed, 94n1789
Environmental hazards: air pollution, 90n1790
Environmental hazards: radioactive materials & wastes, 91n1813

Environmental hazards: toxic waste & hazardous material, 93n1770
Environmental industries marketplace, 93n1755
Environmental issues in the Third World, 92n1771
Environmental law index to chemicals, 94n1941
Environmental profiles, 94n2004
Environmental regulatory glossary, 5th ed, 91n1805
Environmental regulatory glossary, 6th ed, 94n2002
Environmental resource dir, Sept 1990, 91n1806
Environmental telephone dir 1992-93, 93n1756
Environmental toxins: psychological, behavioral, & sociocultural aspects 1973-89, 91n789
Environmentalists: a biographical dict, 94n1993
Environmentalist's bkshelf, 94n1992
EPA headquarters telephone dir, 1991 ed, 93n1757
Epic films, 92n1369
Eponyms of behavioral optometry, 94n1866
Epstein, Catherine, 94n411
Epstein, Lee, 90n557, 93n566
Equatorial Guinea, 93n114
Equipment dir of audio-visual, computer & video products 1990-91, 92n915
Era of Napoleon, 92n478
Eraut, Michael, 91n359
Erb, James, 91n1270
Erb, Uwe, 90n1574
Erdos, Dawn Nicole, 91n209, 91n284, 91n285
Eric Gill: a bibliog, 2d ed, 92n965
ERIC identifier authority list (IAL) 1992, 93n636
Erickson, Hal, 90n913, 93n1351, 94n1511
Erickson, Judith B., 91n895
Erickson, Rosemary, 91n187
Ericson, Richard V., 93n606
Erler, Edward J., 90n544
Erlewine, Michael, 94n1314
Erlewine, Stephen Thomas, 94n1314
Erlich, Richard D., 94n974
Ernest Hemingway: a ref gd 1974-89, 92n1172
Ernst & Young, 94n302
Ernst & Young tax gd 1993, 94n302
Ernst Bloch, 92n731
Ernst, Carl H., 90n1567, 91n1601, 93n1576
Ernst Cassirer: an annot bibliog, 90n1371
Ernst Krenek: a bio-bibliog, 90n1240
Ernst, Richard, 91n1606
Erotic art, 90n945
Error analysis, 92n1010
Ertle, Katherine, 93n1462
Ervin, Hazel Arnett, 94n1237
Esanu, Warren H., 93n326
Esenwein, George, 93n790
Espenshade, Edward B., Jr., 91n429
Espig, Gustav, 93n1469
Esposito, Anthony, 92n55
Essay & general lit index 1985-89, 91n52
Essay & general lit index, rev ed, 93n77
Essential gd to ...
  hiking in the US, 93n835
  prescription drugs, 1991 ed, 92n1695
  psychiatric drugs, 91n1712
  the lib IBM PC, v.15, 91n642
  vitamins & minerals, 93n1647
Essential kitchen gardener, 91n1496
Essential Milton, 90n1182
Essential researcher, 94n57
Essential Shakespeare, 2d ed, 94n1256
Estell, Doug, 91n364
Estell, Kenneth, 92n139, 93n190, 93n199, 93n265
Estes, J. Worth, 91n1689
Estes, Sally, 94n1168
Estonian-English, English-Estonian dict, 93n1082
Ethel Merman: a bio-bibliog, 93n1317
Etherton, Michael, 91n1205
Ethical aspects of health care for the elderly, 94n868
Ethical shopper's gd to Canadian supermarket products, 94n248

Ethics: an annot bibliog, 92n1393
Ethiopia, 90n109
Ethnic & native Canadian lit, 92n1226
Ethnic cookbks & food marketplace, 3d ed, 93n1472
Ethnic music on records, v.1, 92n1305
Ethnic pers in contemporary America, 91n383
Ethnographic bibliog of N America, 4th ed. suppl. 1973-1987, 91n380
Ethnologue, 94n1070
Ethnologue index, 12th ed, 94n1069
Ethnomusicology research, 93n1242
Ethridge, James M., 94n662
Ethridge, Karen, 94n662
Etiquette, 90n1309
ETS test collection cat, v.1, 2d ed, 94n304
ETS test collection cat, v.3, 90n302
ETS test collection cat, v.4, 91n293
ETS test collection cat, v.5, 92n273
ETS test collection cat, v.6, 93n329
Ettlinger, John, 94n1384
Ettlinger, John R. T., 90n40
Ettlinger, Steve, 90n1609, 91n1500
Etz, Tony, 90n1334
Euro dict, 94n1108
EUROBrokerS, 94n631
EUROCOM, 94n632
Europa world yr bk 1989, 90n91
Europa world yr bk 1992, 94n82
Europe in figures, 3d ed, 94n935
Europe in transition, 90n514
Europe today, 1990 rev ed, 91n440
European accountancy yrbk 1992/93, 93n271
European advertising mktg & media data 1992, 93n285
European Americana, v.6, 90n488
European artists: signatures & monograms, 1800-1990, 92n985
European business rankings, 93n291, 94n258
European business servs dir, 94n256
European Communities, 94n770
European Communities ency & dir 1992, 92n711
European Community fact bk, 91n109
European cos, 4th ed, 94n260
European compendium of mktg info, 93n286
European consultants dir, 93n287
European consumer lifestyles to 1995, 92n176
European culture, 94n977
European dict, 94n1108
European dir of ...
    business info libs 1990, 92n615
    consumer brands & their owners 1992, 93n288
    consumer goods manufacturers 1989, 90n237
    financial info sources 1990, 92n157
    mktg info sources 1991, 92n244
    trade & bus assns 1990, 92n245
    trade & bus jls 1990, 92n246
European educ thesaurus, 1991 ed, 93n385
European electric utility dir, 1993, 94n1783
European electronics dir 1993, 94n1787
European employment & industrial relations glossary: Belgium, 94n252
European employment & industrial relations glossary: Germany, 94n253
European employment & industrial relations glossary: Spain, 93n295
European employment & industrial relations glossary: UK, 93n297
European faculty dir 1991, 92n313
European garden flora, v.3, 90n1489
European investment in US & Canadian real estate dir 1990, 91n284
European market share reporter, 94n259
European mktg data & stats 1991, 92n247
European markets, 3d ed, 91n266
European markets: a gd to co & industry info sources, 4th ed, 93n289
European petroleum dir, 1993, 94n1972
European pol facts 1918-90, 94n766

European public affair dir 1993, 94n769
European research centres, 7th ed, 90n1431
European research centres, 9th ed, 94n1574
European sources of scientific & technical info, 9th ed, 92n1460
European sources of scientific & technical info, 10th ed, 94n1576
European specialist publishers dir, 94n666
European technical consultancies, 90n1432
European wholesalers & distrs dir, 93n257
European women's almanac, 94n947
European writers, 92n1231
European writers: selected authors, 94n1280
European writers: the 20th century, v.8, 90n1200
European writers: the 20th century, v.10, 90n1201, 91n1231
European writers: the 20th century, v.11, 91n1232
Eurostatistics, 90n185
Eva Hesse sculpture, 90n951
Eva Le Gallienne: a bio-bibliog, 90n1320
Evaluation thesaurus, 4th ed, 93n642
Evan, Frederica, 90n1716, 94n674
Evangelista, Anita, 92n763
Evans, Brenda J., 90n740, 90n741
Evans, Calvin D., 94n1486
Evans, Charles A., Jr., 93n1605
Evans, Eleanor, 90n94
Evans, Eleanor D., 91n749
Evans, Graham, 92n673
Evans, H. Meurig, 94n1136
Evans, Joan, 93n1257
Evans, Marsheela, 91n453
Evans, Philip R., 94n1365
Evenhuis, Neal L., 91n1588
Even-Shoshan, Abraham, 90n1399
Evers, David C., 94n1677
Every bite a delight & other slogans, 94n299
Every little thing, 91n1326
Everyone's gd to cancer therapy, 93n1655
Everything baseball, 91n822
Evetts, Jan, 93n1591
Evinger, William, 94n651
Evinger, William R., 90n686, 92n650, 92n845
Evleth, Donna, 92n491
Evolving constitution, 94n571
Ewart, Neil, 92n1024
Executive branch of the US govt, 90n688
Executive's bus info sourcebk, 91n257
Executives on the move, 91n253
Exegetical dict of ...
    the N.T., v.1, 91n1423
    the N.T., v.2, 93n1426
    the N.T., v.3, 94n1528
Exercise, 90n1645
Expert systems & related topics, 91n1717
Expert systems in geography & environmental studies, 91n445
Explorers & discoverers of the world, 94n463
Explorers & exploration, 94n462
Exploring the world, 92n419
Exploring your world, 91n446
External trade: monthly stats, 91n267
Extinct species of the world, 92n1524
Extinction A-Z, 92n1520
Extraordinary Hispanic Americans, 93n51
Extraterrestrial ency, rev ed, 93n805
Extremely hazardous substances, 90n1798
Eye, ear, nose & throat surgery, 90n1664
Eynon, Derry, 93n491
Eysenck, Michael W., 93n798
Ezell, Edward Clinton, 90n676

F. R. Leavis & Q. D. Leavis, 90n1149
Faber companion to 20th-century popular music, 91n1304
Faber dict of euphemisms, 91n1057
Fabiano, Emily, 90n310, 92n270
Fabre, Michael, 94n1235
Fabulous finds, 92n178

Facciola, Stephen, 92n1549
Faces in the news, 93n40
Facing hist & ourselves: Holocaust & human behavior, 91n518
Facsimile users' dir, 90n1735
Fact bk on aging, 92n815
Fact bk on women in higher educ, 92n311
Factfinder, 94n39
Factory outlet gd to the Mid-Atlantic states, 2d ed, 91n201
Factory outlet gd to the South, 91n200
Facts & figures on govt finance, 1990 ed, 91n214
Facts about ...
    the cities, 93n918
    the presidents, 5th ed, 90n479
    the presidents, 6th ed, 94n499
    the states, 90n706
Facts behind the songs, 94n1366
Facts on File atlas of stars & planets, 94n1925
Facts on File bibliog of American fiction 1866-1918, 94n1229
Facts on File bibliog of American fiction 1919-88, 92n1162
Facts on File children's atlas, 92n400, 94n447
Facts on File dict of ...
    artificial intelligence, 90n1705
    educ, 90n303
    environmental sci, 92n1775
    film & broadcast terms, 93n987
    military sci, 90n652
    new words, 90n1003
    telecommunications, rev ed, 92n1721
    the theatre, 90n1356
    20th-century allusions, 92n878
Facts on File ency of the 20th century, 92n507
Facts on File English/Chinese visual dict, 90n1037
Facts on File English/Spanish visual dict, 93n1101
Facts on File field gd to N Atlantic shorebirds, 90n1531
Facts on File jr visual dict, 90n1018
Facts on File natl profiles: the Benelux countries, 90n132
Facts on File scientific yrbk 1991, 92n1463
Facts on File student's thesaurus, 92n1060
Facts on File world pol almanac, 90n679
Facts on File world pol almanac, 2d ed, 93n719
Faculty white pages 1989, 90n327
Faculty white pages 1991, 93n361
Faherty, Keith F., 90n1589
Fahey, Michael A., 94n1524
Fahim, K., 91n570
Fai, Stephen, 93n1586
Fairchild, Halford H., 93n845
Fairchild's 1990 travel industry personnel dir, 91n453
Fairchild's textile & apparel financial dir 1989-90, 91n229
Fakih, Kimberly Olson, 94n1169
Fales, Susan L., 90n1401
Falk, Kathryn, 91n1135
Falk, Peter Hastings, 90n955, 91n1008, 91n1009, 91n1021, 92n977, 92n978, 92n979, 93n1032, 94n1049
Falklands War: background, conflict, aftermath, 94n684
Falklands/Malvinas campaign, 93n694
Fall wildflowers of N.Mex, 90n1496
Fallen in battle, 90n649
Fallik, Alain, 94n769
Fallon, John P., 90n934
Familiar quotations, 16th ed, 93n89
Families & aging, 93n854
Family ency of child psychology & dvlpmt, 94n807
Family fun & games, 94n824
Family genetic sourcebk, 91n1695
Family health gd to homeopathy, 94n1842
Family law dict, 2d ed, 92n532
Family literacy, 91n357
Family mental health ency, 90n743
Family planning & child survival, 90n801
Family video gd, 93n1329
Family words, 90n1009
Famous animal symbols, v.2, 94n291
Famous Hollywood locations, 94n1421
Famous Indian leaders, 90n371

Famous mineral localities of Canada, 91n1788
Famous movie detectives 2, 92n1365
Famous trials, 93n604
Fan club dir, 94n1400
Fandel, Nancy A., 90n808
Fandom dir no.13, 92n1328
Fanfare for words: bkfairs & bk festivals in N America, 93n682
Fang, Josephine Riss, 92n571
Fang, Nan, 94n672
Fantastic cinema subject gd, 94n1449
Fantasy lit: a reader's gd, 91n1137
Fantasy lit for children & young adults, 3d ed, 90n1083
FAO quarterly bulletin of stats 1990, v.3, 91n1477
FAO species cat, v.13: marine lobsters of the world, 93n1557
FAO species cat, v.15, 94n1719
FAO yrbk: fertilizer, v.39, 91n1478
FAO yrbk: fertilizer, v.41, 94n1590
FAO yrbk: fishery stats, v.66, 91n1581
FAO yrbk: fishery stats, v.72, 94n1715
FAO yrbk: forest products 1976-87, 90n1463
FAO yrbk: forest products 1979-90, 93n1483
FAO yrbk: production, v.45, 94n1591
FAO yrbk: trade, v.41, 90n1447
FAO yrbk: trade, v.45, 94n1592
Far East & Australasia 1991, 92n120
Faragher, John Mack, 91n504
Fargasova, A., 93n1495
Fargues, Philippe, 92n115
Farina, Luciano F., 94n533
Farkas, Emil, 94n855
Farm family financial crisis, 90n1442
Farmer, David Hugh, 94n1527
Farmer, Gene, 92n994
Farr, David F., 90n1501
Farr, J. Michael, 94n387
Farragher, Leslie E., 90n647
Farrand, John, Jr., 90n1536
Farrier, Susan E., 94n1199
Farrow, Nigel, 91n1180
Farson, A. Stuart, 91n598
Fashion in the W world 1500-1990, 93n1011
Fasman, Mark J., 91n1283
Faulkner in the 80s, 93n1173
Faulkner, Kimberly Burton, 94n420
Faulkner's poetry, 90n1141
Fauna of Austral., v.1B, 91n1598
Fax for libs, 91n608
Fay, John J., 90n568, 90n821
FBI most wanted, 90n570
Feczko, Margaret Mary, 90n809, 92n824, 94n890
Federal Computer Products Center, National Technical Information Service, 91n42
Federal data base finder, 3d ed, 92n52
Federal domestic outlays 1983-90, 93n745
Federal educl & scholarship funding gd, 2d ed, 91n329
Federal funding gd 1989, 90n822
Federal Jobs Digest, editors of, 94n284
Federal laboratory tech cat 1989, 91n1463
Federal legal dir, 91n575
Federal regional yellow bk, v.1, no.1, 94n739
Federal regulatory dir, 6th ed, 92n687
Federal staff dir/1, 1990, 91n737
Federal staff dir/1, 1993, 94n735
Federal statistical source, 29th ed, 92n845
Federal systems of the world, 93n726
Federal tax advisor: explanation, 92n263
Federal Writers Project of the Works Progress Administration, 90n442
Federal yellow bk, winter 1990, 91n738
Federalist concordance, 90n544
Federally sponsored training materials, 91n254
Federer, Anne, 91n73, 92n1459
Fedor Dostoevsky: a ref gd, 91n1247
Fedun, Doris, 93n1631
Feed a cold, starve a fever, rev ed, 92n1676

Fegley, Randall, 93n114
Fehrenbach, R. J., 94n598, 94n599
Feigert, Frank, 91n756
Fein, Fiona Morgan, 92n1279
Fein, Richard M., 94n215
Feinberg, Renee, 91n913
Feingold, S. Norman, 90n255
Feinsilber, Mike, 91n1055
Feinstein, Alice, 92n1661
Feldhausen, Jil, 90n1702
Feldman, Lynne B., 91n128
Fell, Derek, 94n1654
Felscher, Harriet, 93n1637
Feltman, John, 93n1636
Female bildungsroman in English, 91n1130
Female detectives in American novels, 94n1208
Female psychology, 93n797
Feminism & psychoanalysis, 93n801
Feminism & women's issues, 92n859
Feminist companion to lit in English, 92n1095
Feminist legal lit, 92n853
Feminist movement: a bibliog, 93n929
Feminist research methods, 92n857
Feminist theory, 94n952
Feminization of poverty in the US, 91n913
Fenlon, Iain, 94n1310
Fentem, P. H., 92n792
Fenton, Ann D., 93n1129
Fenton, Erfert, 91n1034
Fenton, Jill Rubinson, 91n1364
Fenton, Thomas P., 90n572, 91n143, 92n749
Fenwick, Gillian, 94n1261
Fenwick, M. J., 93n1226
Fenza, D. W., 94n993
Feofanov, Dmitry, 91n1275
Ferber, Gene, 90n1713
Ferencz, George J., 92n1262
Ferguson, Chris D., 90n514
Ferguson, Everett, 91n1442
Ferguson, R. Brian, 90n647
Ferguson, Sinclair B., 90n1382
Ferguson, Stephen, 90n517
Ferguson, Tom, 92n1698
Fernald, Anne Conway, 91n161
Fernandez-Armesto, Felipe, 92n408
Fernandez-Shaw, Carlos M., 93n427
Ferns & fern allies of Canada, 90n1490
Ferre, John P., 92n122
Ferreira, Manual, 94n1268
Ferreiro, Alberto, 90n515
Ferris, William, 90n491
Ferruccio Busoni: a bio-bibliog, 92n1275
Fescue grasses of Canada, 91n1531
Festival Europe, 94n479
Fetrow, Alan G., 93n1352
Fetteroll, Eugene, 90n256
Fetters, Linda K., 93n1669
Fetzer, James H., 94n1494, 94n1495
Fetzer, Mary, 93n73
Feuerstein, Georg, 91n1405
Few, Roger, 93n1532
Fhaner, Beth A., 94n1020
FIAF cataloguing rules for film archives, 93n638
Fiber optics standard dict, 2d ed, 91n1754
Fiber optics technical dir 1988, 90n1739
Fiction cat, 12th ed, 92n1137
Fiction for youth, 3d ed, 94n1181
Fiction index for readers 10 to 16, 94n1196
Fiction sequels for readers 10 to 16, 92n1115
Fiction writers gdlines, 2d ed, 93n963
FID dir 1991-92, 93n624
Fidler, Linda M., 91n1263
Field crop diseases hndbk, 2d ed, 90n1449
Field drug ref for emergency care providers, 92n1668
Field equipment of the infantry 1914-45, 90n661

Field gd to ...
    advanced birding, 91n1566
    birds of Britain & Europe, 5th ed, 94n1701
    birds of the W Indies, 5th ed, 94n1693
    coastal wetland plants of the SE US, 94n1661
    E butterflies, 93n1549
    freshwater fishes, 92n1576
    medicinal plants: E & central N America, 91n1536
    Mexican birds, 90n1535
    reptiles & amphibians: E & central N America, 3d ed, 92n1587
    rock art symbols of the greater southwest, 93n508
    shells of the Tex. coast, 93n1522
    Tex. trees, 90n1511
    the acacias of Kenya, 93n1516
    the birds of Mexico, 2d ed, 90n1534
    the ecology of W forests, 94n1681
    the freshwater fishes of Tanzania, 93n1556
    the peat mosses of boreal N America, 91n1539
    the stars & planets, 3d ed, 94n1928
    the waterbirds of Asia, 94n1692
    W birds, 3d ed, 91n1567
    whales, porpoises, & seals from Cape Cod to Nfld., 4th ed, 94n1737
    wildlife habitats of the eastern US, 91n1547
    wildlife habitats of the western US, 91n1548
    wildlife in Tex. & the Southwest, 90n1525
Field, Judith J., 92n514
Fifth dir of pers, 94n986
50 fabulous places to raise your family, 94n944
50 fabulous places to retire in America, 93n921
Fifty finest athletes of the 20th century, 92n768
Fifty yrs among the new words, 93n1064
50 yrs of American autos 1939-89, 90n1807
50 yrs of rock music, 93n1291
Fifty yrs of TV, 93n998
Fighting men of the Indian wars, 93n515
Fighting words, 90n651
Figueroa, Rafael, 94n1381
Filby, Carol, 91n1809
Filby, P. William, 93n460
Fildes, Robert, 90n195
Filichia, Peter, 94n832
Filion, John, 92n1
Filippelli, Ronald L., 92n215
Filisky, Michael, 91n1582
Filler, Louis, 93n49
Filler, Susan M., 90n1241
Film & TV composers, 93n1258
Film & TV hndbk 1990, 91n1388
Film & video finder, 2d ed, 90n352
Film & video finder, 3d ed, 93n1330
Film annual 1992, 93n1369
Film hndbk, 91n1386
Film index, 90n1318
Film news index, 1939-81, 94n1462
Film plots, v.2, 90n1349
Film producers, studios, agents & casting directors gd, 2d ed, 91n1373
Film study, 92n1340
Film superlist: motion pictures in the US public domain 1950-59, 91n1366
Film superlist, updated ed, 94n1439
Film, TV, & video pers, 92n1332
Film writers gd, 2d ed, 91n1374
Film writers gd, 3d ed, 93n1368
Filmmaker's dict, 91n1371
Film-makers's cooperative cat, no.7, 90n1325
Films & videos on photography, 91n999
Films by genre, 94n1444
Films for learning, thinking, & doing, 93n399
Films of the 80s, 92n1361
Films of the Holocaust, 91n1384
Filmstrip & slide set finder, 91n360
Film-video terms & concepts, 93n1345
Final 4 records 1939-91, 94n839

Finance, insurance, & real estate USA, 94n205
Financial aid for ...
　minorities in engineering & sci, 94n1577
　research & creative activities abroad 1992-94, 94n367
　research, study, travel, & other activities abroad 1990-91, 91n346
　study & training abroad 1992-94, 94n368
　vets, military personnel & their dependents 1990-91, 92n651
Financial 1000, 90n230
Financial planners & planning orgs dir, 2d ed, 91n218
Financial resources for intl study, 91n342
Financial Times industrial cos, v.3, 90n1573
Financial Times industrial cos: chemicals, 92n195
Financial Times mining intl yr bk 1989, 90n1800
Financial Times mining intl yr bk 1993, 94n1982
Financial Times oil & gas intl yr bk 1989, 90n1787
Financial Times oil & gas intl yr bk 1993, 93n1748
Financial Times who's who in world oil & gas 1993, 94n1970
Financial Times world insurance yr bk 1990, 91n238
Financial yellow bk, v.5, no.2, 93n239
Finch, Henry, 90n147
Find it fast, updated ed, 91n47
Find that tune, [v.2], 2d ed, 90n1297
Finding Canadian facts fast, rev. ed, 91n647
Findling, John E., 91n733, 91n1336, 94n716
Fine art index, 1992 N American ed, 93n1031
Fine art of copyediting, 92n898
Fine arts, 3d ed, 91n1002
Fine arts pers, 93n1034
Fine, Bernard D., 91n791
Fine flowers by phone, 90n1468
Fink, Donald G., 94n1777
Fink, John M., 90n1658, 94n1859
Fink, Peter E., 92n1415
Finkel, Avraham Yaakov, 91n1450
Finlay, Matthew, 93n1691
Finley, E. G., 90n300
Finn, Bernard S., 93n1593
Finn, Edwin A., Jr., 93n236
Finniston, Monty, 93n1451
Finson, Shelley Davis, 92n1405
Fiore, Silvia Ruffo, 91n715
Fire music, 93n1286
Firefighter's hazardous materials ref bk, 92n1781
Firefighter's hazardous materials ref bk & index, 2d ed, 94n2011
Firnberg, David, 92n1055
First aid for kids, 92n1636
First amendment, 92n684
First American Jewish families, 3d ed, 93n458
First century Palestinian Judaism, 92n1449
First demographic portraits of Russia 1951-90, 94n929
First dict of cultural literacy, 90n312
First editions, 2d ed, 90n643
First ladies, 6th ed, 91n494
First ladies of Ark., 91n922
First math dict, 92n1752
First name reverse dict, 94n442
First sci dict, 92n1458
First stop, 90n75
First suppl. to a comp bibliog of Yugoslav lit in English 1981-85, 90n1212
First whole rehab cat, 91n853
FirstBook of demographics for the republics of the former Soviet Union, 94n930
First-person accounts of genocidal acts in the 20th century, 93n548
FISCAL dir of fee-based info servs in libs, 92n605
FISCAL dir of fee-based research & document supply servs, 4th ed, 94n639
Fisch, Robert W., 90n661
Fischel, Jack, 93n442
Fischer, Andreas, 93n1067
Fischer, Catherine, 93n1158
Fischer, Dennis, 92n1348
Fischer, Gayle V., 93n943
Fischer, Wolfram, 91n563

Fischgrund, Tom, 91n330, 93n366
Fischgrund's insider's gd to the top 25 colleges, 91n330
Fise, Mary Ellen R., 91n191, 94n921
Fish: 5-lang dict of fish, crustaceans & molluscs, 91n1584
Fisher, Charles E., 90n971
Fisher, David, 91n1081
Fisher, Jeffrey D., 92n261
Fisher, Michael, 90n1626
Fisher, William, 92n152
Fishes of ...
　Alta., 2d ed, 94n1720
　Ark., 90n1552
　N.Mex., 91n1585
　the Bahamas & adjacent tropical waters, 2d ed, 94n1713
　the central US, 91n1586
　the Great Barrier Reef & Coral Sea, 92n1577
Fiske, Edward B., 90n338
Fiske gd to colleges 1989, 90n338
Fitch, Donald, 91n1252
Fitch, Thomas P., 91n215
Fitton, Robert A., 91n681
Fitzgerald, Carol Bondhus, 91n480
Fitzgerald, Gerald, 91n1295
Fitzgerald, M. Desmond, 90n206
Fitzgerald, Sheila, 90n1114, 91n1143
Fitzhenry, Robert I., 94n68
Fitzherbert, Andrew, 93n809
Fitzmier, John R., 94n1533
Fitzmyer, Joseph A., 94n1071
Fitzpatrick, Gary L., 91n1757
Fitzpatrick, Sandra, 91n458
Fitzpatrick, Sheila, 91n535
Fitzsimmons, Linda, 90n1355
Fitzsimmons, Richard, 92n834
500 best garden plants, 94n1622
Flackes, W. D., 91n759
Flake, Chad J., 90n1401, 91n1435, 94n1501
Flammability hndbk for plastics, 4th ed, 91n1775
Flammang, James M., 91n1822
Flanagan, Laurence, 94n486
Flanders, Carl N., 92n1677, 94n731
Flanders, Stephen A., 92n1677, 94n731
Flannery, Gerald V., 91n934
Flannery, Tom, 91n1378
Fleeger, Carolyn, 92n1691
Flegg, Jim, 91n1562
Fleischer, Mindy, 90n1596
Fleming, Carrol B., 91n476
Fleming, John, 93n1038
Fleming, Patricia Lockhart, 92n13
Fleming, Steve, 91n838
Flemming, Tom, 91n1650
Fletcher, Katy, 91n1133
Fletcher, Marilyn P., 90n1108
Fletcher, Richard, 92n480
Fletcher, Steve, 90n1100
Fletcher-Janzen, Elaine, 92n320
Fleury, Bruce Edward, 93n1731
Flick, Ernest W., 90n1759, 90n1760, 93n1713
Flieger, Wilhelm, 92n844
Flint, Adam, 93n1761
Flintham, Victor, 91n685
Flodin, Mickey, 93n1098
Flood, James, 92n280
Flora, Joseph M., 94n1222
Flora of Austral., v.3, 91n1519
Flora of North America Editorial Committee, 94n1643
Flora of N America north of Mexico, 94n1643
Flores, Angel, 94n1297
Flores, Arturo A., 91n567, 92n616
Flores-Fowlie, Fay, 91n122
Florida almanac 1992-93, 93n106
Florida statistical abstract 1991, 93n107
Florida's birds, 91n1564
Florida's butterflies & other insects, 90n1547

Flower flies of the subfamily syrphinae of Canada, Alaska, & Greenland, 93n1564
Flowering shrubs & small trees, 92n1541
Flowering trees & shrubs, 90n1508
Flowers, Ann A., 91n1114
Flowers of the Pacific Island seashore, 94n1647
Floyd, Dale E., 93n692
Fluehr-Lobban, Carolyn, 94n105
Fly patterns, 2d ed, 93n837
Flynn, John L., 93n1353
Flynn, Robert A., 93n605
Foard, Elisabeth C., 90n1154
Focal ency of photography, 3d ed, 94n1036
Focus on ...
    addictions, 94n917
    careers, 93n408
    families, 91n859
    fitness, 94n843
    physical impairments, 92n820
    school, 91n308
    teens in trouble, 92n555
Foley, Denise, 94n1805
Foliage plants for decorating indoors, 90n1469
Folk jewelry of the world, 91n998
Folklore & folklife, 93n1300
Folklore of ...
    American holidays, 2d ed, 93n1297
    trees & shrubs, 94n1673
    world holidays, 93n1298
Follet, Robert, 90n1242
Folts, Harold C., 91n1753
Foltz, William, 90n1181
Foner, Eric, 92n468, 94n727
Fonseca, James W., 94n321
Fontaine, George R., 90n1727
Food additives hndbk, 90n1460
Food aid in figures, v.8/2, 93n1480
Food finds, 92n1493
Food hndbk, 91n1490
Food lover's companion, 91n1483
Food pollution, 92n1479
Food sci sourcebk, 2d ed, 92n1489
Foose, R. M., 91n1781
Footage 89: N American film & video sources, 91n966
Football coach quotes, 93n830
Football scholarship gd, 94n844
Foote, Richard H., 94n1725
Foottit, Robert G., 94n1723
Forage resources of China, 93n1510
Fordyce, Rachel, 93n1202
Foreign law, 91n567
Foreign students & intl study, 91n341
Foreign trade stats of Asia & the Pacific 1983-87, 91n268
Foreign visitors to congress, 90n725
Foreman, Dave, 94n1678
Forest inventory terms in Canada, 3d ed, 90n1464
Forest product prices 1971-90, 94n1615
Forestry Department, Statistics and Economic Analysis Staff, 90n1463
Forestry Policy and Planning Division, FAO Forestry Department, 94n1615
Forey, Pamela, 91n1526
Forgay, Beryl, 93n568
Forgotten championships, 90n768
Forman, Robert J., 91n1125
Formulary of cosmetic preparations, v.1, 93n1715
Forrester, Donald J., 93n1569
Forrester, Mary Flanigan, 93n741
Forrester, William, 91n470
Forsberg, Krister, 94n1767
Forschler, Mary, 91n738
Forster, Antonia, 91n1190
Forster, Merlin H., 91n1244
Forsyth, J., 91n216, 92n204
Forty yrs of steel, 94n1382

Foscue, Virginia O., 90n426
Foss, Christopher F., 91n704, 91n705
Fossey, Keith R., 94n844
Foster, Allan, 93n291, 94n258, 94n259
Foster, David William, 91n1243, 93n1227, 94n1298
Foster, Dennis L., 90n207, 92n158
Foster, Donald H., 91n1271
Foster, Janet, 90n507
Foster, Steven, 91n1536
Foudray, Rita Schoch, 93n1120
Found, Peter, 94n1472
Foundation Center, 90n823, 91n144, 93n879, 94n890, 94n892
Foundation dir, 12th ed, 91n866
Foundation dir, 15th ed, 94n890
Foundation dir pt.2, 1993 ed, 94n891
Foundation for Public Affairs, 90n736
Foundation giving, 1993 ed, 94n896
Foundation grants index, 18th ed, 94n823
Foundation grants index quarterly. Mar 1990, 91n867
Foundation grants to individuals, 6th ed, 90n809
Foundation 1000 1992/93, 94n897
Foundation reporter 1993, 94n902
Founders & patriots of America index, 90n396
Fournier, Marion, 93n825
Fowler, Karin J., 93n1318
Fowler Solar Electric, Inc., 92n1627
Fox, Anthony, 93n772
Fox, Daniel M., 91n1655
Fox, James R., 93n577
Fox, Willard, III, 90n1160
Fradkin, Louise G., 94n867
Fragne, R., 90n1454
Fraker, Anne T., 90n1376
France under the German occupation, 1940-44, 92n491
Franchise opportunities, 21st ed, 90n208
Franchising in bus, 90n209
Francillon, Rene J., 90n1802
Francis, June, 93n498
Francis Poulenc: a bio-bibliog, 91n1278
Franck, Irene, 92n23, 92n842, 94n920, 94n1996
Franck, Irene M., 90n238, 90n365, 90n382, 90n1459, 90n1625, 91n553
Francois Villon: a bibliog, 92n1234
Francomano, Clair A., 91n1679, 93n1624
Francouer, Robert T., 92n832
Frank Bridge: a bio-bibliog, 92n1269
Frank, David, 93n526
Frank, Frederick S., 91n1140
Frank, Harry Thomas, 91n1421
Frank Martin: a bio-bibliog, 91n1279
Frank Norris: a descriptive bibliog, 93n1180
Frank, Robyn C., 94n1604
Frank Sinatra: a complete recording hist, 93n1265
Frankel, Benjamin, 94n537
Frankel, Ellen, 93n443
Frankena, Frederick, 92n1768
Frankena, Joann Koelln, 92n1768
Frankfurt Book Fair, 91n658
Franklin, Benjamin, V., 91n1151
Franklin, Constance, 90n960, 91n1013, 91n1014, 91n1015
Franklin-Smith, Constance, 94n1045
Frantz, Donald G., 92n1064
Frantz, J. Paul, 91n248
Frantzve, Kent R., 94n171
Franz, Jeffrey, 90n301, 91n1707
Franz Joseph Haydn: a gd to research, 91n1272
Franz Liszt: a gd to research, 92n1276
Frasca, JoAnn, 91n145, 91n146
Fraser, David, 92n852
Fraser, Janet, 93n1218, 93n1219
Fraser, Robert, 93n266, 93n290, 94n206
Frasier, David K., 91n1354
Frazier, Nancy, 93n444
Frederic, Louis, 93n839
Frederick, Richard G., 93n509

Fredericksen, Burton B., 91n1037
Frederiksen, Elke, 90n856
Fredrickson, Jim, 93n1369
Fredriksen, John C., 91n678
Free & user supported sftwr for the IBM PC, 91n641
Free mags for libs, 3d ed, 90n79
Free money for ...
    athletic scholarships, 94n326
    college, 91n324
    college from the govt, 94n327
    foreign study, 92n292
    graduate school, rev ed, 94n329
    small businesses & entrepreneurs, 91n211
Free money from colleges & univs, 94n328
Free pubs from US govt agencies, 91n44
Free resource builder for librarians & teachers, 2d ed, 93n70
Free speech yrbk, v.29, 92n592
Freed, Melvyn N., 90n307, 92n140
Freedman, Alan, 91n1723, 93n1676
Freedom House Survey Team, 92n561
Freedom in the world, 92n561
Freedom to publish, 91n957
Freedom's lawmakers, 94n727
Freeman, Craig C., 92n1536
Freeman, Harry M., 90n1594
Freeman, Judy, 92n627
Freeman, Michael, 92n141
Freeman, Morton S., 91n1063
Freeman, Paul, 90n1495
Freeman-Grenville, G. S. P., 92n85, 94n460
Freemon, Frank R., 94n493
Frei, Beatrice, 90n68
Freiberg, Marcos, 91n1683
Freidel, Frank, 91n493
Freirman, Richard, 94n1906
Freitag, Werner, 90n227
French & Spanish records of La., 90n464
French, Christopher C., 93n789
French colonial Africa, 94n95
French dict of info tech, 90n610
French feminist theory: Luce Irigaray & Helene Cixous, 92n858
French foreign policy 1918-45, rev ed, 92n720
French lang & lit, 90n1042
French military aviation, 90n660
French nomenclature of N American birds, 92n1566
French novelists since 1960, 90n1203
French, Tom, 94n652
French women writers, 93n1222
French-Canadian authors, 92n1224
French-English agricultural dict, 93n1465
French-English dict of industrial lang, 91n234
Frew, Tim, 90n1736
Frewin, Anthony, 94n494
Frick, G. William, 91n1805
Frick, John P., 92n1620
Fried, Lewis L. B., 94n1491
Friedberg, Joan Brest, 93n1124
Friedes, Harriet, 94n312
Friedlander, Mark P., Jr., 91n177
Friedman, Catherine, 92n159
Friedman, Francine, 94n139
Friedman, Gil, 91n796
Friedman, Norman, 91n696
Friedman, Saul S., 94n538
Friendly advice, 92n71
Friesel, Evyatar, 91n404
Fritz, Linda, 92n365
Fritz, Sara, 93n749
Fritze, Ronald, 94n417
Fritze, Ronald H., 92n500, 93n532
Froelke, Ruth, 90n399
From archetype to zeitgeist, 93n1060
From Belasco to Brook, 92n1381
From day to day, 92n1329
From Erasmus to Tolstoy, 91n774

From page to screen, 93n1359
From real life to reel life, 94n1442
From Stanislavsky to Barrault, 92n1382
From the past to the future, 93n527
From the Titanic to the Challenger, 90n1415
From the top, 90n623
Fromberg, Doris Pronin, 93n332
Frome, Michael, 93n496
Froschl, Merle, 90n311
Fry, C. Hilary, 90n1528
Fry, Gerald M., 92n125
Frye, Fredric L., 92n1588
Fryer, Deborah J., 91n1250
Fuchs, Thomas, 91n530
Fuderer, Laura Sue, 91n1130
Fulford, Margaret, 94n966
Fullerton, B. M., 91n1147
Fullington, Don, 90n460
Fulton, Len, 90n22, 91n663, 92n635, 92n636, 94n664
Fun for kids 2, 93n1006
Fund raiser's gd to ...
    human serv funding, 2d ed, 91n868
    human serv funding 1993, 94n899
    religious philanthropy, 3d ed, 91n1416
    religious philanthropy, 5th ed, 93n1425
Fund your way through college, 93n373
Fundamentals of geriatrics for health professionals, 91n1696
Fundamentals of legal research, 5th ed, 92n548
Funding decision makers 1993, 94n898
Funding for museums, archives & special collections, 90n811
Funding for US study, 91n343
Fungi on plants & plant products in the US, 90n1501
Fungi without gills, 92n1543
Funk & Wagnalls Canadian college dict, rev ed, 90n1025
Funk & Wagnalls standard dict, 2d ed, 94n1077
Funston, Judith E., 92n1174
Furberg, Jon, 93n959
Furet, Francois, 90n516
Furlong, Paul, 93n767
Furness, Raymond, 93n1223
Furtado, Ken, 94n1227
Furtaw, Julia C., 93n421, 93n428, 94n420, 94n1020
Futures markets dict, 91n187
Futurespeak, 92n1145
Fyffe, L. R., 91n1783
FYI, County of Los Angeles Public Library, staff of, 92n605

G. F. Handel: a gd to research, 90n1250
Gabaccia, Donna, 91n914
Gabon, 94n98
Gabosh, Karl, 92n976
Gabriel, Michael R., 90n628
Gaffney, Maureen, 90n828
Gagnon, Louiselle, 94n249
Gaines, Barry, 92n1206
Gainsbrugh, Jeanette, 90n1383
Gainsbrugh, Jonathan, 90n1383
Galante, Steven P., 91n173, 91n174
Galbraith, Leslie R., 92n1406
Gale dir of ....
    databases, 94n1907
    pubs & broadcast media 1990, 91n61
    pubs & broadcast media 1993, 94n988
Gale environmental sourcebk, 93n1768
Gale intl dir of pubs, 1989-90, 90n77
Gale, Robert L., 90n1147, 92n1171, 93n518, 94n507
Galerstein, Carolyn, 90n857
Gale's auto sourcebk, 1991, 92n1795
Gale's literary index [CD-ROM], 94n1161
Gall, Susan, 94n401
Gall, Susan B., 94n201
Gall, Timothy L., 94n201, 94n401
Gallant, Jennifer Jung, 92n617
Gallaudet survival gd to signing, 92n1021

Gallico, Alison, 94n653
Gallivan, Marion F., 93n1006
Gallo, Donald R., 91n1118, 94n1186
Gallup, George, Jr., 92n74
Gallup poll 1990, 92n74
Galvin, Charles O., 92n1669
Gamal Abdel Nasser: a bibliog, 93n543
Gambacinni, Paul, 94n1362
Game fishing bible, 92n798
Gamel, Laurie, 90n277
Gammond, Peter, 92n1297
Gander, Terry, 91n986
Gander, Terry J., 91n708, 92n656
Ganellin, C. R., 91n1708
Gangwere, Blanche M., 92n1252
Ganzl, Kurt, 90n1365
Ganzl's bk of the musical theatre, 90n1365
GAPS, 92n142
Garau, Susan Z., 92n1078
Garber, Eric, 91n1141
Garber, Linda, 94n907
Garcia Ayvens, Francisco, 92n353
Garcia, F. L., 92n186, 94n208
Garcia, Teresa Alvarez, 94n1132
Garden lit, v.1, no.2, 93n1485
Garden trees hndbk, 91n1546
Gardener's companion, 92n1503
Gardener's dict of horticultural terms, 94n1618
Gardener's Latin, 94n1640
Gardener's reading gd, 94n1627
Gardening by mail, 3d ed, 91n1497
Gardiner, C. D., 90n239
Gardinier, David E., 94n98
Gardner, J. Anthony, 90n518
Gardner, James L., 92n1448
Gardner, John C., 90n197
Gareffa, Peter M., 90n33
Gargan, William, 90n1297
Garland, David E., 91n1422
Garland, Ken, 91n1724
Garman, Nancy, 92n138
Garoogian, Andrew, 94n943
Garoogian, Rhoda, 94n943
Garraty, John A., 90n497, 92n468
Garrett, Agnes, 90n1091, 90n1092, 92n1126
Garrett, Martha J., 92n672
Garrett, Wilbur E., 90n468, 91n450
Garrigan, Kristine Ottesen, 92n964
Garrison, Paul, 91n1818
Garrison, Robert H., Jr., 92n1667
Garrison, Stephen, 92n1183
Garrison, Webb, 94n1080
Gartner, Robert, 92n800
Garvey, Geri M., 91n299
Garvey, Mark, 91n1261
Garwood, Alfred N., 92n345, 93n903
Gascoigne, Bamber, 94n133
Gastrow, Shelagh, 92n705, 94n762
Gates, Jean Key, 91n612
Gates, Sheldon, 94n176
Gatten, Jeffrey N., 94n1404
Gattuso, John, 93n431
Gaudier, Maryse, 90n257
Gauthier, Mark A., 94n621
Gavin, Christy, 94n1228
Gay & lesbian American plays, 94n1227
Gay & lesbian characters & themes in mystery novels, 94n1210
Gay Hollywood film & video gd, 94n1460
Gay men & women who enriched the world, 90n814
Gay 90s in America, 93n518
Gays & lesbians in mainstream cinema, 94n1446
Gazukin, Pavel, 94n777
Geahigan, Priscilla C., 90n153
Gealt, Adelheid M., 94n1063
Gean, Constantine J., 90n1701

Gebbie, Amalia, 90n636
Gebbie Pr all-in-one dir 1989, 90n636
Gedridge, Jolen Marya, 94n874
Gee, Bill J., 92n910
Gee, Robin, 93n961, 93n966, 94n994
Geer, Gary, 91n1151
Geist, Christopher D., 90n1307
Gelbert, Doug, 93n820
Geldzahler, Annette, 91n323
Geller, L. D., 90n657
Gellert, Charles Lawrence, 91n405
Gellert, W., 91n1798
GEM, 1991 ed, 92n249
Gemology, 94n1958
Gemstones of E Africa, 94n1955
Gender positive!, 94n1179
Gendron, Celine, 94n817
Genealogical gd to the Burton Histl Collection, 90n394
Genealogical resources in the N.Y. metro area, 90n385
Genealogical resources of the Minn. histl society, 90n391
Genealogies catalogued by the Lib of Congress since 1986, 94n429
Genealogist's address bk, 92n386
Genera & subgenera of the sawflies of Canada & Alaska, 93n1562
Genera of the aphids of Canada, 94n1723
General accounting office, 92n51
General bibliog of C. G. Jung's writings, rev ed, 94n806
General cat of HI observations of galaxies: the ref cat, 91n1758
General Information, Inc., 90n1737, 91n137
General Matthew B. Ridgway: an annot bibliog, 94n678
General sci index, v.14, no.7, 93n1459
General sci index [CD-ROM], 93n1460
Genetic risks: a ref for eye care practitioners, 91n1684
Genetically engineered human therapeutic drugs, 90n1700
Genocide, v.2, 92n560
Genocide in our time, 94n587
Genre in the age of the Baroque, 92n1004
Genre terms, 2d ed, 92n580
Genreflecting, 3d ed, 93n1147
Gentilcore, R. Louis, 94n458
Gentry, Alwyn H., 94n1637
Gentz, William H., 90n898
Genus & species of pathogenic organisms, 92n1660
Geographers: biobibliographical studies, v.13, 92n414
Geography: a resource bk for secondary schools, 90n423
Geography from A to Z, 90n419
Geography on file, 92n401
GeoRef thesaurus & gd to indexing, 5th ed, 90n1765
GeoRef [CD-ROM], 94n1950
Georgakas, Dan, 91n763
George, Bruce, 91n768
George, Daniel P., 92n782
George Eliot: a ref gd 1972-87, 91n1207
George Grenville 1712-70: a bibliog, 94n775
George MacDonald: a bibliographical study, 92n1241
George, Paul S., 91n506
George, Robert Lloyd, 91n178
George Rochberg: a bio-bibliographic gd to his life & works, 93n1256
George, Tracey E., 93n566
George-Warren, Holly, 94n1367
Georgia: the WPA gd to its towns & countryside, 92n441
Georgian-English, English-Georgian dict, 93n1084
Georgopolis, Melissa L., 94n54, 94n744
Geoscience Information Society Guidebooks Committee, 90n1766
Geostatistical glossary & multilingual dict, 92n1738
Gerard, Geoffrey, 90n1551
Gerhan, David R., 90n835
Gerhart, Eugene C., 90n566
Geriatric nursing assistants, 92n1688
German foreign policy 1918-45, rev ed, 92n712
German reunification, 94n522
German sacred polyphonic vocal music between Schutz & Bach, 94n1343
German Section of the Oxford University Press Dictionary Department, 91n1085

German warships 1815-1945, v.1, 91n693
German writers in the age of Goethe, 1789-1832, 91n1235
German-American heritage, 90n365
German-American names, 91n420
German-English genealogical dict, 93n453
Germans after WW II, 91n531
Gerolemou, Chris, 93n215
Geron, Leonard, 94n136
Gerontological social work, 94n872
Gerontology & geriatrics libs & collections in the US & Canada, 94n655
Gerry, Thomas M. F., 94n1138
Gersh, Marjorie, 91n661, 91n662
Gershwin companion, 92n1298
Gertzel, Cherry, 92n90
Gertzman, Jay A., 91n1211
Gervais, Gaeten, 90n511
Gervais, Gilles, 92n1598
Get help, 90n829
Gettysburg: a battlefield atlas, 93n691
Ghana, 92n88
Ghirelli, Michael, 90n392
Ghorayshi, Parvin, 91n244
Ghose, Vijaya, 93n1310
Ghosh, A., 91n479
Ghosh, Shyamali, 90n891
Gianakos, Larry James, 93n993
Giant lizards, 93n1580
Gianturco, Carolyn, 92n1263
Gibb, Mike, 91n1510
Gibberman, Susan R., 93n1331
Gibbon, Laura, 90n230
Gibbons, E. F., Jr., 92n557
Gibbons, Laura, 93n191
Gibilisco, Stan, 90n1591, 91n1616, 92n1607, 93n1594, 94n1567
Gibson, Bob, 93n1701
Gibson, Dyanne, 92n304, 94n310
Gibson, J., 93n1658
Gibson's student gd to W Canadian univs, 94n310
Giese, James R., 90n498, 90n499
Giese, Lester J., 93n919
Giffin, James M., 90n1474
Gifford, Charles S., 93n330
Gifford, Courtney D., 92n219
Gifford, Denis, 91n1035, 91n1365, 93n1344
Gifis, Steven H., 92n531
Gift of life, 94n1823
Gifted & talented info resources, 93n339
Gigging, 91n1303
Gilbar, Annie, 92n1500
Gilbar, Steven, 93n403
Gilbert, Carter R., 94n1716
Gilbert, M. Jean, 94n915
Gilbert, Pamela, 91n1589
Gilbert, Sara D., 90n829, 94n388
Gilbert Sorrentino: a descriptive bibliog, 92n1181
Gilbrant, Thoralf, 92n1422
Gildzen, Alex, 93n1376
Gill, Evan, 92n965
Gill, Kay, 90n77, 90n697, 93n887
Gill, N. W., 92n1525
Gill, Sam D., 94n418
Gillerman, Dorothy, 90n985
Gillespie, Cindy S., 93n1130
Gillespie, John T., 90n1093, 91n1111, 92n1116, 92n1117, 94n1192
Gillette, Gary, 94n833
Gillis, Jack, 90n226, 91n191, 92n1796, 92n1797, 92n1798, 94n921
Gillis, Ruth Jeannette, 91n1112
Gilmore, John, 91n1255
Gimlin, Hoyt, 92n703
Ginell, Cary, 91n1310
Ginsberg, Leon, 94n911
Giordano, Albert G., 91n634
Giovanni Battista Pergolesi: a gd to research, 90n1251

Giovanni Boccaccio: an annot bibliog, 93n1224
Girard, Louise, 90n1372
GIS gd to 4-yr colleges, 91n331
Giscard d'Estaing, Valerie-Ann, 94n1581
Giska, Thomas E., 91n338
Gist of Mencken, 91n1167
Giver's gd, 92n826
Gladstone, Jane, 93n606
Glancy, Ruth F., 94n1251
Glannon, Ann M., 94n378
Glanville, Martyn P., 93n821
Glanze, Walter D., 94n1152
Glasby, John S., 94n1871
Glasnost, 90n136
Glass, Ilana Belle, 92n837
Glassberg, Jeffrey, 94n1703
Glasse, Cyril, 91n1448
Glasser, Michael L., 92n1648
Glasser, Selma, 92n1057
Glazier, Loss Pequeno, 94n659
Glazier, Stephen, 94n1105
Gleason, Henry A., 93n1500
Gledhill, D., 90n1484
Glenn Gould cat, 93n1253
Glenn Miller Army Air Force band, 90n1289
Glenn, Robert W., 94n786
Glick, David M., 92n1517
Glikin, Ronda, 90n858
Glimpses of India, 90n122
Glinert, Lewis, 94n1385
Gloag, John, 92n955
Global atlas, 92n399
Global countertrade, 92n259
Global Tex.: intl trade info sourcebk, 93n267
Global trade white pages 1992, 93n268
Global warming, 94n2014
Global/intl issues & problems, 90n685
Glossarial concordance to the Riverside Chaucer, 94n1250
Glossary: climate change, 92n1734
Glossary construction projects, 92n193
Glossary for the food industries, 92n1487
Glossary geotextiles, 93n1609
Glossary informatics, 91n605
Glossary of ...
    ancient Egyptian nautical titles & terms, 90n1819
    art, architecture, & design since 1945, 3d ed, 94n1043
    automotive terms, 90n1583
    basic archival & lib conservation terms, 90n617
    biochemistry & molecular biology, 92n1517
    Chinese medical terms & acupuncture points, 92n1663
    cognitive sci, 94n1494
    computing terms, 6th ed, 90n1714
    contemporary literary theory, 93n1113
    educl tech terms, 94n377
    epistemology/philosophy of sci, 94n1495
    finance & debt, 93n231
    health care terms, 2d ed, 93n1615
    health servs, 93n1616
    helicopters, 90n1804
    Indian religious terms & concepts, 92n1403
    industrial lang, 91n235
    Islamic economics, 91n133
    Jewish life, 93n449
    medical terminology, 93n1641
    micrographics, 90n1723
    museology, 90n954
    N Indian peasant life, 91n100
    plant tissue culture, 90n1483
    security equipment, 94n1776
    special educ, 90n350
    terms used in pest control, 91n1474
    the Third World, 90n128
    US govt vocabulary, 94n732
    water terms, 94n1951
Glossbrenner, Alfred, 90n1729

Glover, Thomas J., 93n1454, 93n1684
Glutton's glossary, 92n1480
Goble, Alan, 93n1373
Godbolt, Shane, 93n1626
Godden, Irene P., 93n627
Goddesses & wise women, 93n923
Godet, Jean-Denis, 94n1670
Godfrey, Donald G., 93n994
Godfrey-Smith, Anne, 93n131
Godin, Seth, 94n174
Godman, Arthur, 92n1754
Goedan, Juergen Christoph, 93n567
Goehlert, Robert, 90n688
Goehlert, Robert U., 90n705, 91n566, 93n571
Goetsch, Lori, 94n949
Goetz, Philip W., 90n48, 92n41
Goetzfridt, Nicholas J., 90n149, 93n1789
Goetzmann, William H., 94n444
Going places: the gd to travel gds, 90n433
Gold bk: a gd to commonly traded gold bullion coins & bars, 93n226
Goldberg, Lana, 91n332
Goldberg, Lee, 91n332, 91n973
Golden age of top 40 music (1955-1973) on CD, 94n1361
Golden bk ency, 90n51
Golden horizons retirement gd, Calif ed, 90n792
Golden, Richard L., 90n1636
Goldfarb, Sheldon, 90n1187
Goldinger, Carolyn, 91n589
Goldman, Joel, 90n823
Goldman, Jonathan L., 94n1094
Goldman, Martin E., 93n1657
Goldman, Paul, 90n983
Goldner, Susan D., 91n591
Goldstein, Arnold S., 90n1612
Goldstein, Erik, 94n693
Goldstein, Gabriella, 94n856
Goldstein, Martha, 94n42
Goldstein, Sandra E., 90n329
Golemba, Beverly E., 93n934
Golf Digest almanac 1989, 91n834
Golf gadgets, 91n835
GOLF Magazine, editors of, 94n850
GOLF Magazine's ency of golf, 2d ed, 94n850
Golf playoffs, 92n796
Golfers almanac, 93n833
Golob, Richard, 91n1466, 94n1983
Gomez-Gutierrez, J. M., 93n1497
Gone with the Wind on film, 91n1390
Gonzalez, Edgar R., 92n1668
Gonzalez, Raquel Quiroz, 90n1207
Gooch, Bryan N. S., 92n1251
Good bks for the curious traveler: Asia & the S Pacific, 90n453
Good bks for the curious traveler: Europe, 90n456
Good reading, 23d ed, 91n3
Goodenberger, Jennifer, 90n1267
Gooders, John, 91n1560
Goodfellow, William D., 92n1258, 93n1266
Goodheart-Wilcox automotive ency, 90n1808
Goodloe, Alfred M., 91n664
Goodman, Jordan Elliot, 92n184
Goodman, Michael B., 91n1160
Goodman, Robert L., 92n1494
Goodrick, Edward W., 91n1427
Goodsell, Don, 91n1823
Goodwin, Diana M., 91n1658
Goodwin, Maria, 91n458
Gopen, Stuart, 94n1011
Gopen's gd to closed captioned video, 94n1011
Gorbachev's law, 92n525
Gorder, Cheryl, 91n192, 92n179
Gordon, Ann D., 94n964
Gordon, Leonard H. D., 93n521
Gordon MacRae: a bio-bibliog, 92n1309
Gordon, Sarah, 90n1151

Gordon, W. Terrence, 93n1047
Gore, Tom, 90n1474
Goreham, Gary A., 91n1436, 94n1588
Goring, Rosemary, 92n25
Gorlin, Rena A., ed., 91n156
Gorman, G. E., 93n652
Gorman, Jack M., 91n1712
Gorman, Kathleen, 91n951
Gorman, Michael, 90n600
Gorn, Elliot J., 94n505
Goss, Ann, 92n203
Gosselin, Michel, 92n1566
Gotelli, Ilze M., 90n287
Gothic sculpture in America, 90n985
Gotshall, Daniel W., 91n1583
Gottesman, Roberta, 93n1250
Gottlieb, Jean S., 94n1558
Gottlieb, Richard, 91n193
Gotz, Karl-Heinz, 90n1575
Gouke, Mary Noel, 91n860
Goulart, Ron, 91n1036, 92n1327
Gould, Donald P., 90n461
Gould, Katherine, 90n461
Gould, Wilbur A., 92n1487
Goulet, Cyrille, 90n545, 92n550, 94n553
Goulet, Henri, 93n1562
Goulet, Henry, 94n1726
Goulty, George A., 92n1472
Gourman, Jack, 94n357, 94n358
Gourman report: a rating of graduate & professional programs in American & intl univs, 6th ed, 94n357
Gourman report: a rating of undergraduate programs in American & intl univs, 8th ed, 94n358
Goursau, Henri, 94n1108
Goursau, Monique, 94n1108
Gousha new deluxe rd atlas, 93n467
Government assistance almanac 1989-90, 90n806
Government assistance almanac 1992-93, 93n874
Government contracts ref bk, 93n580
Government dir of addresses & telephone nos, 93n740
Government giveaways for entrepreneurs, 3d ed, 93n210
Government Institutes, editorial staff of, 93n1756
Government ref bks 88/89, 91n43
Government ref bks 90/91, 93n74
Government research dir, 5th ed, 90n697
Government research dir 1991-92, 92n688
Government research dir 1993-94, 94n740
Govil, Minnie, 90n194
Goyer, Doreen S., 93n898
Gozdecka-Sanford, Adriana, 94n134
Gozmany, Laszlo, 92n1558
Graber, Kenneth, 90n1243
Graduate curricula in educl communications & tech, 4th ed, 94n379
Graduate scholarship dir, 3d ed, 94n331
Graetzer, Hans G., 94n710
Graf, Rudolf F., 92n1602, 94n1778, 94n1779, 94n1780
Graham, Anne, 93n1387
Graham, Dianne, 91n179
Graham, Glenn A., 90n1577
Graham Greene: a character index & gd, 92n1203
Graham, Joe S., 90n366
Graham, John, 91n179, 92n1721
Graham, John W., 94n802
Graham, Ronnie, 94n1315
Grainge, Michael, 90n1485
Grambs, David, 91n1068
Grambs, Jean Dresden, 92n268
Granatstein, J. L., 94n517
Grand allusions, 91n1055
Grand Natl, Producers Releasing Corp, & Screen Guild/Lippert, 90n1343
Grand trees of America, 94n1672
Grandchamp-Tupula, Mariette, 92n326
Granick, Lois, 91n788

Grant, Carol L., 91n1543
Grant, George C., 93n625
Grant, Janine, 91n234, 91n235
Grant, John A., 91n1543
Grant, Mary A., 93n348
Grant, Michael, 94n1393
Grant seekers gd, 3d ed, 90n810
Grant, Todd W., 93n592
Grant, William E., 90n1133
Grants & awards available to American writers, 17th ed, 93n960
Grant's atlas of anatomy, 9th ed, 92n1646
Grants for libs & info servs, 90n592
Grants register 1991-93, 92n295
GRANTS subject authority gd, 93n637
Grapes of Wrath: a 50 yr bibliographic survey, 92n1182
Graphic art of Roi Partridge, 90n982
Graphic arts ency, 93n1042
Graphic arts vocabulary, 94n1058
Graphics, design & printing terms, 91n1724
Graphics file formats, 93n1687
Grattan, Virginia L., 94n1325
Graubner, Wolfram, 94n1030
Grave, Floyd K., 91n1272
Grave, Margaret G., 91n1272
Graves, Bonnie A., 91n368
Graves, Jane Denker, 90n1247
Graves, Michael F., 91n368
Graves, O. Finley, 91n170
Gray, Anne, 94n1345
Gray, Benita H., 90n1816
Gray, Cecile G., 93n1432
Gray, John, 91n1355, 91n1398, 91n1409, 93n1286, 94n1039
Gray, Mary Taylor, 93n1542
Gray, Michael, 90n1268
Gray, Randal, 92n504, 93n551
Gray, Richard A., 94n1823, 94n2019
Great all-time baseball record bk, rev ed, 94n835
Great American autos of the 50s, 90n1810
Great American baseball stat bk 1993, 94n833
Great American hist fact-finder, 94n512
Great American lighthouses, 91n1830
Great American ships, 93n1788
Great athletes, 93n816
Great battles of the Civil War, 91n507
Great battles of WW I, 90n658
Great bear almanac, 94n1733
Great bk of the sea, 94n1745
Great careers, 2d ed, 91n379
Great cellists, 90n1259
Great combat pictures, 91n1380
Great comic bk artists, v.2, 91n1036
Great cop pictures, 92n1363
Great detective pictures, 91n1381
Great economists before Keynes, 90n161
Great events from ...
    hist 2: arts & culture series, 94n984
    hist 2: human rights series, 93n617
    hist 2: sci & tech series, 92n1465
Great events: the 20th century, 94n539
Great flower bks 1700-1900, 92n1540
Great historians from antiquity to 1800, 91n548
Great historians of the modern age, 92n502
Great Hollywood musical pictures, 93n1360
Great inventions through hist, 93n1447
Great Lakes gd to sunken ships, 94n2029
Great lives: exploration, 90n531
Great lives from hist: Renaissance to 1900 series, 91n549
Great lives from hist: 20th century series, 91n550
Great lives: human rights, 92n562
Great maritime museums of the world, 93n1791
Great modern inventions, 93n1448
Great northerners, 92n24
Great resorts for parents & kids, 92n434
Great sci fiction pictures 2, 91n1382
Great scientific discoveries, 93n1449

Great song thesaurus, 2d ed, 90n1279
Great Spanish films: 1950-90, 93n1365
Great thinkers of the W world, 93n950
Great Torah commentators, 91n1450
Great videos for kids, 94n1426
Great women athletes of the 20th century, 93n815
Great world atlas, 2d ed, 90n406
Great writers of the English lang, 91n1102
Greatest catchers of all time, 92n785
Greaves, Bettina Bien, 94n153
Grechko, A. A., 94n686
Greek & Roman sport, 92n772
Green almanac, 93n1751
Green cathedrals, 94n834
Green co resource gd, 93n1774
Green consumer, 92n177
Green, Diana Huss, 90n1346
Green earth resource gd, 92n179
Green ency, 94n1996
Green index, 91n1809
Green index, 1991-92, 92n1782
Green, Joel B., 93n1428
Green, John, 91n1237
Green, Jonathon, 91n635, 93n1066
Green, Kay Ann, 91n558
Green, Marybeth, 94n1197
Green, Philip, 94n715
Green plants, 93n1498
Green, Scott E., 90n1109
Greenberg, Bruce C., 92n937, 92n939, 92n940, 92n941, 92n943
Greenberg, Martin H., 92n1142
Greenberg, Reva M., 94n389
Greenberg's American Flyer cats 1946-55, 92n937
Greenberg's gd to ...
    American Flyer S gauge, 4th ed, v.1, 92n938
    American Flyer wide gauge, 90n927
    Ives trains 1901-32, v.1, 2d ed, 92n939
    LGB trains, 2d ed, 90n928
    Lionel trains 1945-69, v.1, 8th ed, 92n940
    Lionel trains 1945-69, v.2, 2d ed, 92n941
    Lionel trains 1945-69, v.3, 92n942
    Lionel trains 1970-88, 90n929
    Marklin OO\HO trains, 91n987
    Marx toys, v.2, 91n988
    Marx trains, 90n930
    Marx trains, v.2, 91n989
Greenberg's Lionel catalogs, 92n943
Greene, Cynthia, 94n169
Greene, Edith, 91n568
Greene, Fayal, 92n995
Greene, Jack P., 92n470
Greene, John C., 94n1468
Greene, Robert J., 92n1713
Greene, Stanley A., 94n2016
Greene, Thurston, 93n593
Greenfield, Edward, 91n1292
Greenfield, John R., 92n1219, 93n1193, 94n1243
Greenfield, Stanley R., 93n782
Greenfield, Thomas Allen, 90n911
Greenfieldt, John, 91n52, 92n1137, 94n1481
Greenhouse effect, 91n1804
Greenia, Mark W., 91n1719, 91n1732
Greenland, 93n119
Greenland since 1979, 91n96
Greenline gd to residential architects 1990, 91n1027
Greenspon, Joanna, 92n881
Greenwald, Susan, 90n978
Greenwood annual abstract of legal dissertations & theses, 1985-87, 90n562
Greenwood, Barbara, 92n875, 92n1127
Greenwood, Patti Normandy, 92n764
Greenwood, Val D., 91n417
Greer, Harold E., 94n1631
Greeves, Lydia, 91n468
Gregg, Rodman W., 90n1337

Gregory, Barry, 90n666
Gregory, Hugh, 93n1293
Gregory, K. J., 92n1731
Grehan, Ida, 90n400
Greischar, Lawrence L., 91n1799
Grenham, John, 94n434
Gresh, Alain, 92n118
Gress, Bob, 94n1679
Greulich, Walter, 93n1733, 93n1734
Grey, Mark A., 91n291
Gribben, Arthur, 94n1386
Gribble, Gloria, 92n325
Gribin, Anthony J., 93n1290
Grice, Joel D., 91n1788
Griffel, Margaret Ross, 92n1289
Griffin, Albert Kirby, 92n1420
Griffin, John R., 90n1691
Griffin, Lynne, 93n935
Griffin, William R., 90n1606
Griffith, H. Winter, 90n1667, 94n1839, 94n1877, 94n1884
Griffith, Nancy Snell, 91n1148
Griffiths, Dennis, 94n1008
Griffiths, Peter, 93n828
Griffiths, Stephanie, 92n156
Griffiths, Trevor R., 93n1389, 94n1257
Grimes, Barbara F., 94n1069, 94n1070
Grimes, Janet, 92n1288, 92n1308
Grimes, John, 90n1375
Grimm, Nils R., 91n1634
Grimshaw, Polly Swift, 92n366
Grimsted, Patricia Kennedy, 90n523
Grinstein, Louise S., 93n1738, 94n1923
Grisewood, John, 91n1070
Groe, Harlen, 92n1530
Groener, Erich, 91n693
Grolier world ency of endangered species, 94n1680
Groom, Nigel, 94n1940
Gross, Andrea, 90n453, 90n456
Gross, David C., 93n445, 93n1105
Gross, Dorothy-Ellen, 94n1442
Gross, Ernie, 91n500, 92n1413
Gross, Esther R., 93n445
Gross, Helmut, 91n1772
Gross, Robert F., 94n1232
Grote, David, 93n1068
Groth-Marnat, Gary, 92n759
Ground cover plants, 3d ed, 91n1501
Ground spiders of Canada & Alaska, 93n1563
Groundwater chemicals field gd, 93n1771
Grover-Lizardi, Judith, 93n197
Grow, Michael, 93n149
Grun, Bernard, 93n560
Grundy, Isobel, 92n1095
Grupenhoff, John T., 90n1623
Grzimek's ency of mammals, 91n1593
Gubser, Peter, 93n164
Guelph & Wellington County, 90n510
Guerena, Salvador, 90n1207, 92n618
Guertin, Lucie, 93n1601
Guggenheimer, Eva H., 94n441
Guggenheimer, Heinrich W., 94n441
Guidance Information System, editors of, 91n331
Guide to ...
    academic travel, 91n375
    academic travel, 2d ed, 93n407
    Albert Schweitzer collections, 2d ed, 93n947
    American educl dirs, 6th ed, 92n275
    American graduate schools, 6th ed, 92n303
    American trade cats 1744-1900, 92n258
    Americana: the American collections in the British Lib, 90n43
    amphibians & reptiles, 91n1604
    application programs in BASIC, 92n1713
    archives & mss relating to Kenya & E Africa in the UK, 92n460
    art, 94n1047
    arts & crafts workshops, 91n994
    Asian stock markets, 91n178
    baby products, 90n227
    background investigations, 3d ed, 90n258
    black Washington, 91n458
    British poetry explication, v.1, 92n1221
    British poetry explication, v.2, 94n1265
    British poetry explication, v.3, 94n1266
    campus & non-profit meeting facilities 93, 93n207
    clinical preventive servs, 90n1626
    collections relating to S.D. Norwegian-Americans, 93n451
    cooking schools, 1989, 90n1458
    cooking schools, 1993, 94n1609
    critical reviews, part 2, 3d ed, 92n1333
    Cuban collections in the US, 92n495
    current indexing & abstracting servs in the Third World, 93n652
    dividend reinvestment plans, 94n192
    docs relating to French & British N America in the archives of the sacred congregation "de Propaganda Fide", 93n1424
    drug info & lit, 5th ed, 92n1697
    E Asian collections in N America, 93n120
    European financial centres, 92n187
    fed funding for anti-drug programs 1991, 91n884
    fed funding for child care & early childhood dvlpmt, 93n893
    fed funding for educ, 1991, 92n279
    fed funding for govts & nonprofits, 1991, 92n825
    fed funding for hospitals & health centers, 94n1814
    fed funding for housing & homeless programs, 94n876
    fed funding for volunteer programs, 93n876
    fed gvmt acronyms, 90n686
    475 aircraft museums, 224 city-displayed aircraft, 37 restaurants with aircraft, 6 WWI landmarks, 10th ed, 93n1779
    free computer materials, 90n341
    free computer materials, 10th ed, 93n401
    free computer materials, 11th ed, 94n1911
    French lit: 1789 to the present, 93n1221
    French poetry explication, 94n1284
    funding for intl & foreign programs, 93n880
    genealogical resources in the British Isles, 90n395
    genealogical sftwr, 94n435
    golf schools & camps, 93n834
    govt pubns in Australia, 92n50
    grasses of the lower Rio Grande valley, Tex., 94n1665
    histl resources in the regional municipality of Waterloo, 90n513
    hospitality & tourism educ 1989-90, 91n315
    income tax preparation, 93n326
    info sources for the preparation, editing, & production of docs, 90n896
    info sources in alternative therapy, 90n1661
    intl asset managers, 91n258
    intl educ in the US, 2d ed, 92n314
    intl subscription agencies, 91n664
    Irish churches & graveyards, 92n389
    jls in psychology & educ, 91n795
    Kans. mushrooms, 94n1662
    Latin American & Caribbean census material, 91n119
    law schools in Canada, 94n575
    literary agents & art/photo reps, 1992, 93n961
    mss & docs in the British Isles relating to S & SE Asia, v.1, 90n116
    mss & docs in the British Isles relating to S & SE Asia, v.2, 91n97
    MBA programs in Canada, 93n376
    medieval & renaissance mss in the Huntington Lib, 90n532
    Michigan's endangered wildlife, 94n1677
    microforms in print, 1989 suppl, 90n7
    microforms in print 1991: author-title, 93n1694
    microforms in print 1991: subject, 93n1695
    military installations, 2d ed, 90n656
    military installations, 3d ed, 93n704
    modern Japanese woodblock prints, 1900-75, 93n1043
    multicultural resources 1993/94, 94n400

Guide to ... *(continued)*
  natl monuments & historic sites, 91n460
  N.Y. law firms, 92n541
  official pubns of foreign countries, 92n49
  opera & dance on videocassette, 91n1342
  organ music, 91n1285
  photographic collections at the Smithsonian Inst, v.2, 92n1467
  photographic collections at the Smithsonian Inst, v.3, 94n1038
  pol videos, v.1, no.1, 94n713
  popular US govt pubns, 2d ed, 91n41
  pre-fed records in the Natl Archives, 90n465
  professional orgs for teachers of lang & lit in the US & Canada, 2d ed, 91n1047
  pseudonyms on American records, 1892-1942, 94n1317
  real estate & mortgage banking sftwr, 5th ed, 90n296
  ref bks for school media centers, 4th ed, 93n670
  ref bks, suppl to the 10th ed, 93n12
  ref materials for Canadian libs, 8th ed, 93n16
  research & scholarship in Hungary, 90n309
  research in classical art & mythology, 93n1029
  research in gerontology, 90n793
  research on Martin Luther King, Jr., & the modern black freedom struggle, 91n600
  scholarly resources on the Russian empire & the Soviet Union in the N.Y. metropolitan area, 91n113
  selected natl genetic voluntary orgs, Jan 1989, 91n1694
  selecting & using Bible commentaries, 92n1444
  silent Westerns, 94n1443
  sources in American journalism hist, 90n908
  sources of intl population assistance 1988, 90n836
  southern pols, 1989, 91n754
  special collections in the OCLC database, 90n625
  state environmental programs, 2d ed, 91n1812
  the American occult 1989, 91n799
  the archaeological sites of Israel, Egypt, & N Africa, 91n478
  the archaeological sites of the British Isles, 90n505
  the birds of Alaska, 91n1557
  the birds of Costa Rica, 91n1572
  the birds of Nepal, 93n1543
  the Boris I. Nicolaevsky collection in the Hoover Inst archives, 90n522
  the Canadian financial servs industry 1991, 93n232
  the college lib, 94n658
  the end of the world, 94n1535
  the evaluation of educl experiences in the armed servs, 1992, 94n307
  the fndns of public admin, 91n781
  the gods, 93n1305
  the hist of Calif., 90n500
  the hist of Fla., 91n506
  the hist of Ill., 92n471
  the holdings of the still picture branch of the Natl Archives, 92n450
  the info activities of European dvlpmnt networks, 93n630
  the John D. Crummey peace collection in the Hoover Inst, 93n790
  the laws, regulations & policies of the People's Republic of China on foreign trade & investment, 91n564
  the lit of electronic publishing, 90n628
  the liverworts of N.C., 93n1512
  the mammals of Salta Province, Argentina, 91n1596
  the ms collections at the Univ of Alaska, Anchorage, 92n35
  the ms collections in the rare bk & ms lib of Columbia Univ, 94n28
  the ms collections of the Presbyterian church, US, 92n1412
  the marine isopod crustaceans of the Caribbean, 91n1600
  the marine sport fishes of Atlantic Canada & New England, 93n1555
  the natl wildlife refuges, rev ed, 94n1683
  the Oxford English Dict, 94n1097
  the photographic identification of individual whales based on their natural & acquired markings, 91n1595
  the sources of US military hist, suppl.3, 94n680
  the univs of Europe, 93n382
  the use of libs & info sources, 6th ed, 91n612
  the writings of pioneer Latinamericanists of the US, 91n538
  tourist railroads & railroad museums, 3d ed, 91n1821
  US fndns, their trustees, officers, & donors, 1993 ed, 94n892
  US govt pubns, 1993 ed, 94n55
  US govt stats, 1989 ed, 91n896
  US map resources, 2d ed, 91n447
  videocassettes for children, 90n1346
  worldwide postal-code & address formats, 91n941
  worldwide postal-code & address formats, 1993, 94n989
  Yale Univ Lib Holocaust video testimonies, 91n521
Guides to LC subject headings & classification on peace & intl conflict resolution, 92n581
Guiley, Rosemary, 92n765
Guiley, Rosemary Ellen, 90n755, 93n810
Guilianelli, James, 92n822
Guinness bk of ...
  answers, 7th ed, 90n68
  answers, 8th ed, 93n4
  astronomy, 3d ed, 90n1745
  movie facts & feats, 93n1370
  records 1492, 93n558
  records 1991, 91n1337
  records 1993, 94n1401
  sports records 1993, 94n825
  words, 90n987
  world records, 1990, 90n1308
Guinness ency of popular music, 94n1363
Guinness railway bk, 91n1824
Guinness sports record bk 1990-91, 91n811
Guiougou, Paulette, 90n818
Guitar & lute music in pers, 92n1282
Guitard, Michelle, 93n485
Gulag hndbk, 90n573
Gullong, Jane M., 94n983
Gunderson, Nels L., 91n245
Gunderson, Ted, 90n778
Gunn, Drewey Wayne, 93n1185
Gunn, S. W. A., 92n1656
Gunsmoke: a complete hist & analysis of the legendary broadcast series, 91n970
Gunson, Phil, 90n730, 92n723
Gunston, Bill, 91n686, 91n687
Gunton, Sharon R., 93n1141
Gupta, B. K., 92n1621
Gupta, B. M., 90n608, 93n647, 93n648
Gurney, Gene, 91n177
Gurney, Ireland, Quilter & Warlock, 90n1223
Gustav & Alma Mahler: a gd to research, 90n1241
Gutierrez, Marcos F., 92n1628, 93n1585
Gutman, Israel, 91n520
Gutsche, George J., 90n1210
Guttman, David, 90n784
Guttmann, Hadassah, 94n1326
Gutzman, Philip C., 91n674
Guy, Jeniece, 94n613
Guyana, 90n144
Guzik, Estelle M., 90n385
Gwynn, R. S., 93n1186
Gyorgy Ligeti: a bio-bibliog, 92n1274

H. E. Bates: a bibliographical study, 92n1198
Haag, Enid E., 90n830
Haas, Irvin, 92n435
Haas, Ken, 91n1000
Haas, Lawrence J., 93n731
Haase, Patricia T., 92n1687
Haase, Ynez D., 90n466
Haber, Erika, 92n1088
Haber, Kai, 90n1633
Habibion, J., 91n570
Haboucha, Reginetta, 94n1387
Hackland, Brian, 90n714
Haddon, B. D., 90n1464
Hadjor, Kori Buenor, 93n136

Haertel, Geneva D., 91n300
Hafendorfer, Linda, 90n440
Hager, Philip E., 94n1205
Haggett, Peter, 90n1634, 94n1854
Haggin, B. H., 93n1251
Haglund, Diane, 90n512
Hagood, Margaret B., 91n1416
Hahn, Hannelore, 90n444
Haider, Thomas John, 94n317, 94n318
Haig, Judith, 91n1151
Haile, Suzanne, 91n931, 92n287, 92n573, 92n827, 92n865,
    93n880, 93n881, 93n1411
Haile, Suzanne W., 91n144
Hailes, Julia, 92n177
Haim, S., 94n1125, 94n1126
Haines, Gerald K., 94n752
Haiti: a research hndbk, 91n121
Haiti: gd to the per lit in English, 1800-1990, 92n113
Hajnal, Peter I., 93n783
Hakkert, Adolf M., 94n535
Halachmi, Arie, 90n733
Hale, Kay K., 94n1594
Hale, Linda L., 94n924, 94n925
Hale, Mark, 94n1377
Hale, Terrel D., 94n545
Hale, W. G., 92n1518
Hale, William Storm, 91n1366
Hales, Robert E., 92n1698
Haley, Beverly A., 91n308
Hall, Blaine H., 92n1161, 93n1175
Hall, Bob, 92n1782
Hall, Carl W., 94n1754
Hall, Charles J., 90n1227, 90n1228, 91n1258
Hall, Christine C. Iijima, 90n741
Hall, Clifton D., 91n1234, 94n1200
Hall, Frances Adkins, 92n1078
Hall, George E., 93n908, 94n937
Hall, Hal W., 91n1169, 93n1176, 94n1213
Hall, Joan Houston, 93n1062
Hall, Kermit L., 92n521, 94n554
Hall, R. J., 92n1792
Hall, Rachel, 94n1540
Hall, Robert A., Jr., 92n1078
Hall, Sarah M., 94n666
Hall, Sharon K., 90n1070
Hall, Susan, 91n1113
Hall, Suzanne E., 91n299
Hallam, Elizabeth, 91n525
Halleron, Trish, 90n1678
Hallett, Michael A., 94n588
Halley, Jeanne, 91n1251
Hallgarth, Susan, 93n924
Hallgarth, Susan A., 93n940, 94n967
Halliwell, Brian, 94n1629
Halliwell, Leslie, 90n1332, 90n1347
Halliwell's film gd, 6th ed, 90n1332
Halliwell's filmgoer's & video viewer's companion, 10th ed,
    94n1456
Halliwell's filmgoer's companion, 9th ed, 90n1347
Hallsworth, Gwenda, 90n511
Halpern, Jack, 94n1121
Halpin, Anne, 91n1527
Halstead, Bruce W., 94n1746
Hambly, Maya, 90n963
Hamer, Frank, 92n950
Hamer, Janet, 92n950
Hamilton, A. C., 92n1211
Hamilton, Chris J., 91n1589
Hamilton, David A., 91n1300
Hamilton, Geoff, 93n1488
Hamilton, Lee Templin, 93n1205
Hamilton, Mary, 92n1290
Hamlet in the 1960s, 93n1211
Hammer, Tad Bentley, 92n1372
Hammill, Donald D., 93n333

Hammock, Delia A., 92n1670
Hammond atlas of the world, 94n448
Hammond atlas of the world, concise ed, 94n449
Hammond explorer atlas of the world, 94n450
Hammond gold medallion world atlas, 93n474
Hammond large type world atlas, 90n407
Hammond passport travelmate & US atlas, 91n459
Hammond past worlds, 90n462
Hampton, Barbara, 94n383
Hancock, David A., 91n1563
Hancox, Peter J., 91n1715
Hand, Raymond, Jr., 92n1032
Hand, Richard A, 90n369
Hand, Richard A., 92n799
Handbook for ...
    AACR2 1988 revision, 90n604
    no-load fund investors, 10th ed, 91n180
    no-load fund investors, 1993, 94n189
    scholars, rev ed, 93n973
    the Newbery medal & honor bks, 1980-89, 93n1140
Handbook of ...
    adhesive raw materials, 90n1759
    American diplomacy, 94n757
    American popular culture, 2d ed, 91n1339
    American women's hist, 91n929
    animal sci, 92n1512
    Australian, N.Z. & Antarctic birds, v.1, 92n1563
    behavior therapy & pharmacotherapy for children, 94n1848
    behavioral medicine for women, 90n1663
    campaign spending, 93n749
    contemporary fiction for public libs & school libs, 91n1128
    corrosion data, 91n1624
    denominations in the US, 9th ed, 91n1445
    dvlpmt economics, 91n151
    developmental & physical disabilities, 90n1629
    drinking water quality, 91n1784
    economic cycles, 93n201
    emergency mgmt, 92n78
    English & Celtic studies in the UK and Republic of Ireland,
        2d ed, 90n1169
    environmental fate & exposure data for organic chemicals,
        v.3, 92n1784
    family law, 90n560
    family measurement techniques, 91n863
    financial market indexes, averages, & indicators, 91n171
    fire retardant coatings & fire testing servs, 91n1625
    fish diseases, 91n1587
    gifted educ, 92n284
    good English, rev ed, 93n1061
    heart drugs, 93n1657
    HVAC design, 91n1634
    hydrology, 94n1953
    Indian univs, 92n317
    industrial chemical additives, 93n1709
    industrial org, v.2, 91n232
    industrial stats 1990, 92n196
    Latin American lit, 2d ed, 94n1298
    Latin American studies, no.52, 94n144
    libs, archives & info centers in India, v.6, 90n608
    libs, archives & info centres in India, v.9, 93n647
    libs, archives & info centres in India, v.11, pt.1, 93n648
    marine mammals, v.4, 90n1562
    microwave & optical components, 91n1626
    modern British painting 1900-80, 93n1044
    molecular sieves, 93n1584
    N American Indians, v.4, 90n370
    N American Indians, v.7, 91n397
    natl population censuses: Europe, 93n898
    natural products data, v.1, 92n1723
    old-time radio, 94n1017
    paint raw materials, 2d ed, 90n1760
    pediatric drug therapy, 91n1713
    pesticide toxicology, 92n1783
    plant cell culture, v.5, 91n1517
    plant cell culture, v.6, 91n1518

Handbook of ... *(continued)*
   plants with pest-control properties, 90n1485
   plastic compounds, elastomers, & resins, 93n1710
   plastic materials & tech, 91n1611
   plastics, elastomers, & composites, 2d ed, 93n1714
   pol sci research on Latin America, 92n722
   pol sci research on the USSR & E Europe, 94n781
   polymer sci & tech, 90n1757
   power, utility & boiler terms & phrases, 6th ed, 94n1797
   prescriptive treatments for children & adolescents, 94n1845
   private schools, 70th ed, 90n314
   private schools, 73d ed, 93n349
   protoctista, 91n1515
   psychological assessment, 2d ed, 92n759
   psychotropic drugs, 94n1878
   public admin, 90n737
   real estate terms, rev ed, 93n325
   reconstruction in E Europe & the Soviet Union, 93n536
   research on curriculum, 93n334
   research on music teaching & learning, 93n1252
   research on social studies teaching & learning, 93n336
   research on teaching the English lang arts, 92n280
   research on the educ of young children, 94n314
   research on the illicit drug trade, 93n892
   rocks, minerals, & gemstones, 94n1957
   Rocky Mountain plants, 93n1501
   semiotics, 91n81
   Soviet & E European films & filmmakers, 93n1340
   successful franchising, 3d ed, 91n177
   the American frontier, v.2, 92n367
   the birds of Europe, the Middle East, & N Africa, v.5, 90n1537
   the birds of Europe, the Middle East, & N Africa, v.6, 94n1696
   the birds of Europe, the Middle East, & N Africa, v.7, 94n1697
   the fruit flies (Diptera: Tephritidae) of America north of Mexico, 94n1725
   the nations, 10th ed, 92n676
   toxicologic pathology, 92n1694
   tribology, 92n1621
   United Methodist-related schools, colleges, univs & theological schools, 94n336
   world educ, 92n281
   world stock & commodity exchanges, 1992, 93n222
Handbook on ...
   German military forces, 92n655
   injectable drugs, 7th ed, 94n1885
   intl migration, 92n756
   Japanese military forces, 93n705
Handel, Bernard, 93n1615
Handel's natl dir for the performing arts, 5th ed, 94n1420
Handicapped funding dir 1988-89, 90n797
Handler, Jerome S., 93n541
Handlist of rhetorical terms, 2d ed, 93n1071
Handville, Elizabeth, 91n376
Handweaving: an annot bibliog, 92n948
Hanes, Richard S., 91n1627
Haney, Wayne S., 91n1302, 92n1310
Hanke, Ken, 90n1339, 93n1354
Hankinson, Robert L., 90n1782
Hankinson, Robert L., Jr., 90n1782
Hanks, Patrick, 90n401, 91n419
Hannah Arendt, 90n721
Hannaway, David B., 93n1510
Hannigan, Jane Anne, 91n613, 92n572, 94n616
Hans Rosbaud: a bio-bibliog, 93n1257
Hansard-Winkler, Glenda Ann, 90n255
Hansen, Eric C., 90n1402
Hanson, Charles V., 92n944
Hanson, Gerald T., 90n467
Hanson, Robert P., 93n223, 93n224
HAPI thesaurus & name authority 1970-89, 92n587
Happy birthdays round the world, 94n1402
Haragan, Patricia Dalton, 92n1546
Harborne, Jeffrey B., 94n1639
Harcourt, Caroline S., 93n1484
Harden, Edgar F., 91n1219

Harder, Kelsie B., 93n1299
Hardin, James, 90n1192, 91n1235, 94n1286, 94n1287
Hardin, Steve, 93n82
Harding, Jim, 93n568, 93n569
Hardon, John A., 90n1403
Harduf, David Mendel, 93n1106
Harduf's transliterated Yiddish-English dict, 4th v., 94n1137
Hardy, Gayle J., 94n592
Hardy herbaceous perennials, 3d ed, 92n1538
Hardy, Joan E., 91n1780
Hardy, Phil, 90n1294, 91n1304
Harer, John B., 94n641
Harkanyi, Katalin, 92n1451
Harkavy, Michael David, 90n278
Harkness, Mabel G., 94n1625
Harkness, Richard, 93n1664
Harlem renaissance & beyond, 91n1150
Harman, Jay R., 92n1733
Harmon, Justin, 94n976
Harmon, Robert B., 92n1182
Harmony illus ency of rock, 6th ed, 90n1295
Harmony illus ency of rock, 7th ed, 94n1378
Harmony of the Gospels concerning the greatest life ever lived, 92n1423
Harner, James L., 91n1097, 93n686, 91n1203, 94n1139
Harnsberger, R. Scott, 93n1017
Haroon, Mohammed, 91n101, 93n1239
Harper atlas of world hist, rev ed, 94n528
Harper bk of quotations, 3d ed, 94n68
Harper, Charles A., 92n1603, 93n1714, 94n1781
Harper Collins French dict, college ed, 91n1084
Harper Collins German dict, college ed, 92n1070
Harper Collins Italian dict, college ed, 92n1079
Harper Collins Spanish dict, college ed, 91n1095
Harper concise atlas of the Bible, 92n1439
Harper dict of opera & operetta, 91n1296
Harper ency of military biog, 93n698
Harper ency of military hist, 4th ed, 94n687
Harper religious & inspirational quotation companion, 91n1419
HarperCollins dict of ...
   American govt & pols, 93n736
   art terms & techniques, 2d ed, 93n1025
   astronomy & space sci, 93n1702
   biology, 92n1518
   computer terms, 92n1708
   economics, 92n126
   electronics, 93n1595
   environmental sci, 93n1753
   mathematics, 93n1739
   philosophy, 2d ed, 94n1496
   sociology, 93n848
   stats, 93n904
Harper's Bible pronunciation gd, 91n1428
Harper's ency of mystic & paranormal experience, 92n765
Harper's ency of religious educ, 91n1413
Harpsichord & clavichord music of the 20th century, 94n1335
Harpur, James, 91n1332
Harrigan, Diane E., 91n319
Harrington, Denis J., 92n794
Harrington, Kevin, 91n181
Harrington, Michael, 92n50
Harris, Cyril M., 94n1051
Harris, Eileen, 92n996
Harris, Geraldine, 91n542
Harris, Glen, 90n384
Harris, Godfrey, 90n62
Harris, Ian, 94n1516
Harris Ill. industrial dir, 1991, 92n197
Harris Ind. industrial dir, 1991, 92n198
Harris, Kevin, 91n1200
Harris, Laurie Lanzen, 91n1103, 92n1113, 93n35, 94n11
Harris manufacturers dir, 1993, 94n215
Harris, Maurine, 90n384
Harris, Merle, 93n135
Harris Mich. industrial dir, 1991, 92n199

Harris, Michael, 91n1561
Harris, Nigel G. E., 91n269
Harris Ohio industrial dir, 1991, 92n200
Harris Pa. industrial dir, 1991, 92n201
Harris, Sherry S., 92n290
Harris, Sherwood, 92n609
Harris, Steve, 93n1258
Harris, Wendell V., 93n1111
Harris W.Va. manufacturing dir, 1990, 92n202
Harrison, Charles, 93n350
Harrison, Harriet W., 93n638
Harrison, Hazel, 92n1001
Harrison, James, 94n445
Harrison, Julie, 91n1747
Harrison, R. K., 93n1419
Harrison, Richard, 90n1562
Harrod's librarians' glossary...& ref bk, 7th ed, 92n565
Harrold, Ann, 91n627
Harrower, Gordon III, 90n328
Harry & Wally's favorite TV shows, 91n972
Harry S. Truman ency, 91n505
Harryman, Elizabeth, 90n1683
Hart, C. W., Jr., 90n1550
Hart, Jane Poirier, 91n1308
Hart, John D., 90n1140, 91n1162
Hart, Mary L., 90n1287
Harte, John, 93n1769
Harter, H. Leon, 92n846, 93n902
Hartford, Bill, 93n1784
Hartig, Linda, 92n1264
Hartley, Loyde H., 94n1502
Hartman, Donald K., 90n1103
Hartman, Stephen, 93n243
Hartman, Stephen W., 93n241
Hartmann, Klaus, 91n1609
Hartness, Ann, 93n153
Hartnoll, Phyllis, 94n1472
Hartsock, Ralph, 92n1265
Hartwig, D. Scott, 91n482
Hartzler, Judith, 91n1128
Harvard Bus School core collection 1993, 94n156
Harvey, A. D., 90n508, 91n760
Harvey, Anthony P., 91n1780
Harvey, Joan M., 93n98
Harvey, S. S. K., 92n1625
Haschek, Wanda M., 92n1694
Haseltine, Patricia, 90n504
Hasenfratz, Robert J., 94n1263
Haskins, Jim, 94n475
Hast, Adele, 92n148, 93n260, 94n230
Hasten, Elizabeth, 93n977
Hastenrath, Stefan, 91n1799
Hastings, Baird, 90n1244
Hastings, Elizabeth Hann, 90n734, 94n75
Hastings, Philip K., 90n734, 94n75
Hata, Ikuhiko, 91n511
Hatch, Michael D., 91n1585
Hatch, Stephen L., 94n1664
Hathaway, Gloria J., 92n1786
Hathaway, Thomas, 93n1251
Hattendorf, Lynn C., 92n278
Hauck, Eldon, 92n997
Hauck, Philomena, 90n371
Haule, James M., 92n1216
Havard, C. W. H., 91n1659
Haven't I seen you somewhere before?, 93n1358
Haverland, Bill, 94n861
Havlice, Patricia Pate, 90n1276
Hawai'i, 94n90
Hawaiian insects & their kin, 93n1565
Hawaiian reef animals, rev. ed, 91n1599
Hawcroft, Tim, 91n1511
Hawes, Grace M., 91n732
Hawkins, Joyce M., 90n998, 92n1017
Hawkins, Walter L., 93n423, 94n685

Hawkins-Dady, Mark, 93n1391
Hawks in flight, 90n1532
Hawksworth, David L., 90n1495
Hawley's condensed chemical dict, 12th ed, 94n1933
Hawthorn, Jeremy, 93n1112, 93n1113
Hawthorne, Douglas B., 94n1757
Hay, Fred J., 92n346
Hay, Tony, 92n187
Hayden, Carla D., 94n1170
Hayes, Deborah, 91n1273
Hayes, Greg, 90n433
Hayes, Kevin J., 92n455, 93n1178
Hayes, Nicky, 90n746, 94n811
Hayes, R. M., 90n1340, 94n1440
Hayes, S. V., 91n19
Hayes, Wayland J., Jr., 92n1783
Haymarket affair, 94n786
Haynes, Bruce, 93n1261
Haynes, David, 92n595
Hays, Peter L., 91n1163
Hays, Terence E., 92n335
Hayssen, Virginia, 94n1731
Haythornthwaite, Philip J., 92n492, 94n540
Hayward, Margaret, 91n1502
Hazardous chemicals desk ref, 2d ed, 92n1727
Hazardous substances resource gd, 94n2016
Hazardous waste mgmt facilities dir, 91n1807
Hazel, John, 94n1393
Hazen, Edith P., 91n1250, 93n1235
HBO's gd to movies on videocassette & cable TV 1991, 92n1339
H.D.: a bibliog 1905-90, 94n1234
Head, Honor, 90n68
HeadBangers, 94n1377
Headlam, Catherine, 94n1568
Healers, 90n1625
Healing forest, 91n1538
Health & mental health: dir of key legislators, 90n1617
Health care in Fla., 92n1638
Health care reform terms, advance ed, 94n1804
Health care state rankings 1993, 94n1816
Health care terms, 2d ed, 93n1621
Health, disease, medicine & famine in Ethiopia, 92n1632
Health groups in Washington, 10th ed, 90n1618
Health Media of America, 93n1647
Health of black Americans from post reconstruction to integration, 1871-1960, 91n1642
Health-related cookbks, 93n1471
Healthy aging, 94n869
Healy, Donna Lee, 90n267
Heaney, H. J., 93n2
Heard, J. Norman, 92n367
Hearne, Betsy, 91n1120, 93n1134
Heath, Angela, 94n867
Heaton, Tim B., 93n867
Heavy minerals in colour, 93n1726
Hebel, Udo J., 90n1065
Hecht, Hermann, 94n1427
Heck, Cheva, 93n876
Heckman, Lucy, 90n209
Heckscher, William S., 90n1051
Hector Berlioz: a gd to research, 90n1247
Hede, Agnes Ann, 91n646
Heden, Karel E., 94n2029
Hedgepeth, Chester M., Jr., 92n876
Heeren, Dave, 91n829
Heffron, Mary J., 90n572, 91n143, 92n749
Heidt, Gary A., 91n1597
Heier, Uli, 94n1336
Heim, Kathleen M., 90n596
Heim, Mary Ellen, 90n935
Hein, William S., 94n862
Heineman, James H, 92n1215
Heinrich, Adel, 92n1266
Heinrichs, Wally, 90n717

Hein's cum index to interim precedent decisions of the Board of Immigration Appeals, 93n599
Heintze, James R., 90n1245, 91n1253
Heise, Jon O., 94n473
Heisinger, Barbara B., 94n547
Heister, Rolf, 91n1644
Heitz, Halina, 92n1505
Helbig, Alethea K., 90n1094, 94n1171, 94n1172
Held, Gilbert, 91n1751
Held, John, Jr., 92n966
Helen Hayes: a bio-bibliog, 94n1416
Helfer, Melinda, 91n1135
Heliconia: an identification gd, 92n1535
Helleburst, Lynn, 93n734, 93n750
Hellebust, Lynn, 91n730, 91n739
Hellemans, Alexander, 90n1422
Heller, George N., 93n1240
Hellman, Ronald G., 90n138
Hellner, Nancy, 94n1227
Hellweg, Paul, 92n1060
Helms, Cynthia Newman, 90n947
Help for children from infancy to adulthood, 5th ed, 93n896
Helson, Joan, 94n248
Helt, Marie E., 94n1441
Helt, Richard C., 94n1441
Hemingway: an annot chronology, 93n1174
Hemmerly, Thomas E., 92n1537
Henbest, Nigel, 93n1700
Hench, John B., 94n657
Hendershott, Barbara Sloan, 90n459
Henderson, Alice H., 91n1274
Henderson, C. A. P., 92n45
Henderson, Donald G., 91n1274
Henderson, G. P., 90n63
Henderson, Helene, 92n1113
Henderson, Kathy, 90n899
Henderson, Lesley, 91n1136, 92n1191, 93n1153
Henderson, Robert W., 93n1579
Henderson, S. P. A., 90n63
Henderson's dict of biological terms, 10th ed, 90n1479
Hendler, Sheldon Saul, 91n1709
Hendon, Julia A., 91n381
Hendrickson, Homer, 94n1866
Hendrickson, Robert, 94n1089
Henk Badings, 1907-87: cat of works, 94n1328
Henke, James, 94n1367
Henkes, Robert, 94n1046, 94n1064
Henne, Robert E., 91n319
Hennessey, Gilbert, 91n866
Henning, Charles, 90n713
Henning, Joanne K., 91n1229
Henri Sauguet: a bio-bibliog, 92n1259
Henricus Isaac: a gd to research, 92n1272
Henry, Ann Karen, 90n1702
Henry David Thoreau: an annot bibliog of comment & criticism before 1900, 93n1182
Henry, Dawn, 94n967
Henry Fonda: a bio-bibliog, 93n1323
Henry Holt gd to shells of the world, 90n1513
Henry Holt hndbk of current sci & tech, 93n1455
Henry Holt intl desk ref, 93n269
Henry Holt retirement sourcebk, 93n855
Henry James: a ref gd 1975-87, 92n1174
Henry James ency, 90n1147
Henry, Laurie, 90n902
Henry, Linda, 92n1482
Henry, Marcia Klinger, 93n661
Henry Purcell: a gd to research, 90n1257
Henry, Scott D., 93n1604
Henrysson, Harald, 94n1354
Henslin, James M., 94n877
Hensyl, William R., 91n1664, 93n1623
Hephner, Heather M., 92n1482
Her Majesty's Stationery Office, Central Office of Information, 91n112

Herald, Diana Tixier, 93n1147
Herbal medicine past & present, v.2, 91n1535
Herbert Hoover: a bibliog, 94n496
Herbert Hoover: a bibliog of his times & presidency, 92n454
Herbert, Patricia, 90n1033
Herbert, Patricia M., 93n124
Herbert Spencer: a primary & secondary bibliog, 94n1490
Herbert, Victor, 92n1670
Herbote, Burkhard, 92n439
Herbs, spices, & medicinal plants, v.4, 91n1534
Herbsman, Yael, 93n446
Herbst, Sharon Tyler, 91n1483
Heritage dir 1990, 91n757
Heritage ency of band music, 93n1283
Heritage of music, 90n1231
Heriteau, Jacqueline, 91n1503
Herman, Gerald, 93n552
Herman, Jeff, 91n947
Hermann, Richard, 91n586
Hermann, Richard L., 91n575
Heroines, 91n1129
Herold, Patricia, 92n986
Herren, Ray V., 93n1468
Herrera, Alicia, 92n689
Herring, Susan Davis, 90n1415
Herron, Nancy L., 91n74, 94n820
Hersen, Michel, 90n1629, 94n812, 94n1845, 94n1848
Hersh, George K., Jr., 92n123
Herz, Norman, 91n1786
Herzfeld, Thomas J., 94n190
Herzfeld's gd to closed-end funds, 94n190
Herzhaft, Gerard, 94n1370
Hess, Carol, 94n719
Hess, Carol A., 93n1259
Hess, Robert K., 90n307
Hesse, Carla, 90n517
Hester, M. Thomas, 94n1264
Hetherington, Norriss S., 94n1926
Hewitt, George, 91n533
Hewitt, Joe A., 90n616
Hewitt, John D., 90n845
Hewlett, John, 92n1637
Hexham, Irving, 94n1512
Hiatt, Gerald F. S., 90n1701
Hiatt, Sky, 93n1355
Hicken, Mandy, 94n1438
Hickey, D. J., 92n494
Hickey, Michael, 90n1492
Hickey, Morgen, 92n1147
Hickman, James C., 94n1644
Hickok, Ralph, 93n819
Hicks, Brenda, 92n904
Hicks, Marie L., 93n1512
Hicks, Michael A., 92n483
Hicks, Patrick, 92n1791
Hicks, S. David, 90n172, 94n162, 94n163, 94n898, 94n899
Hidden job market, 93n303
Higbee, Joan Florence, 90n130
Higdon, D. Leon, 90n1146
Higginbotham, R., 90n1603
Higginson, Roy, 92n269
High definition TV, 91n1618
High interest easy reading, 6th ed, 91n366
High/low hndbk, 3d ed, 91n365
Higham, Robin, 94n680
Higher educ in ...
    India, 93n391
    the European community: student hndbk, 6th ed, 91n345
    the UK 1992-93, 93n386
Highfill, John W., 93n1003
Highfill, Philip H., Jr., 92n1378, 92n1379
High-level langs & sftwr applications, 90n1726
Highlights of ...
    fed unemployment compensation laws, Jan 91, 92n224
    state unemployment compensation laws, Jan 90, 91n246

state unemployment compensation laws, Jan 93, 94n219
High-tech hndbk, 92n1700
High-technology editorial gd & stylebk, PC ed, 93n969
Hilado, Carlos J., 91n1775
Hilbert, Robert, 94n1371
Hildebrandt, Darlene Myers, 91n1733, 94n1908
Hildreth, W. Bartley, 90n737
Hilfinger, Ann, 90n1132
Hill, A. David, 90n423
Hill, Anne, 90n888
Hill, C. P., 92n481
Hill, Carolyn N., 90n583, 93n654
Hill, Dennis Auburn, 90n134
Hill, George, 92n855
Hill, George H., 90n1344
Hill, J. E., 92n1581, 94n1734
Hill, Joan, 93n602
Hill, Karen, 90n326, 91n136, 92n1795, 93n412, 93n1768, 94n2017
Hill, Kenneth L., 94n795
Hill, Michelle, 94n1806
Hill, R. A., 92n1519
Hillard, James M., 92n606
Hillstrom, Kevin, 92n591
Hilt, Kathryn, 92n1179
Hilty, Ann, 90n909
Hinckley, Barbara, 90n1130
Hinckley, Karen, 90n1130
Hincks, Joseph, 91n1792
Hinds, Richard deC., 94n2018
Hine, Darlene Clark, 94n965
Hines, Virginia K., 90n831
Hines, W. D., 91n562
Hinkelman, Edward G., 94n290
Hinnells, John R., 93n1404
Hinshelwood, R. D., 90n745
Hinson, Maurice, 91n1288
Hinterauer, Shirley, 91n573
Hipp, James W., 94n1156
Hippocrene companion gd to Romania, 91n473
Hippocrene companion gd to the Soviet Union, rev ed, 91n475
Hippocrene concise dict: English-Hungarian, Hungarian-English, 92n1077
Hippocrene insider's gd to Hungary, 93n505
Hippocrene insiders' gd to Nepal, 9th ed, 93n501
Hippocrene standard dict: Russian-English, English-Russian, 94n1130
Hippocrene USA gd to black America, 93n424
Hippocrene USA gd to historic black south, 94n475
Hirsch, E. D., Jr., 90n304, 90n312, 94n305
Hirsch, N. P., 94n1874
Hirschfelder, Arlene, 93n432
Hirth, Paul, 94n648
His master's voice/la voce del padrone, 90n1226
His master's voice/la voix de son maitre, 91n1257
Hischak, Thomas S., 94n1473
Hispanic Americans: a statistical sourcebk, 1991 ed, 92n354
Hispanic Americans info dir 1990-91, 91n394
Hispanic Americans info dir 1992-93, 93n428
Hispanic heritage, series 4, 93n150
Hispanic image on the silver screen, 93n1363
Hispanic presence in N America from 1492 to today, 93n427
Hispanic rare bks of the golden age (1470-1699) in the Newberry Lib of Chicago, 90n27
Hispanic resource dir 1992-94, 93n429
Hispanic way, 92n355
Hispanic writers, 92n1106
Hispanic writers in Canada, 90n1196
Hispanic-American almanac, 94n412
Hispanic-American material culture, 90n366
Historians of the American frontier, 90n477
Historic docs index, 1972-89, 92n702
Historic docs of 1990, 92n703
Historic docs on presidential elections 1787-1988, 93n753
Historic homes of American authors, 92n435
Historic landmarks of black America, 92n440

Historic ships of Calif., 90n1820
Historic ships of Washington, 90n1821
Historic sites & markers along the Mormon & other great W trails, 90n435
Historic US court cases 1690-1990, 93n578
Historic warships, 94n703
Historical & cultural atlas of African Americans, 92n343
Historical art index A.D. 400-1650, 90n965
Historical atlas of ...
    Ark., 90n467
    Canada, v.2, 94n458
    Canada, v.3, 91n516
    E central Europe, 94n520
    Kans., 2d ed, 90n469
    Mass., 92n451
    pol parties in the US Congress, 1789-1989, 90n687
    S Asia, 2d ed, 94n515
    state power in congress, 1790-1990, 94n725
    Tex., 90n470
    the American West, 90n466
    the Jewish people from the time of the patriarchs to the present, 94n424
    the Middle East, 94n460
    the US, 90n468
Historical dict of ...
    Afghanistan, 93n121
    Angola, 2d ed, 93n112
    Austral., 94n124
    Bangladesh, 90n117
    Botswana, new ed, 91n94
    Buddhism, 94n1519
    Costa Rica, 2d ed, 92n111
    Equatorial Guinea, 2d ed, 90n108
    golfing terms, 94n849
    Hong Kong & Macau, 94n110
    Indonesia, 94n111
    Israel, 94n152
    Laos, 93n128
    Libya, 2d ed, 93n115
    Malawi, 2d ed, 94n100
    Malaysia, 94n118
    Mauritius, 2d ed, 93n147
    modern Spain 1700-1988, 91n116
    Mozambique, 93n116
    Niger, 2d ed, 91n95
    Paraguay, 2d ed, 94n147
    Polynesia, 94n120
    Portugal, 94n135
    reconstruction, 92n469
    revolutionary China, 1839-1976, 93n523
    Singapore, 93n129
    the Central African Republic, 2d ed, 93n113
    the European Community, 94n767
    the French 4th & 5th Republics, 1946-91, 93n537
    the Hashemite kingdom of Jordan, 93n164
    the Korean War, 92n648
    the Progressive Era, 1890-1920, 90n490
    the Republic of Cameroon, 2d ed, 92n86
    the Republic of Korea, 94n117
    the Spanish empire, 1402-1975, 93n540
    the Sudan, 2d ed, 94n105
    the US air force, 94n698
    Tudor England, 1485-1603, 93n532
    Tunisia, 90n113
    Vietnam, 90n526
    world's fairs & expositions 1851-1988, 91n1336
    Zaire, 90n114
    Zimbabwe, 2d ed, 92n91
Historical jls, 2d ed, 94n542
Historical research in music educ, 2d ed, 93n1240
Historical stats of Chile, 90n142
History & folklore of N American wildflowers, 94n1651
History of ...
    agriculture in W Africa, 91n1473
    airlines in Canada, 91n1817

History of ... *(continued)*
American firefighting toys, 92n944
American psychology in notes & news 1883-1945, 90n752
American women's voluntary orgs, 1810-1960, 90n848
biology, 90n1480
Canadian childhood & youth, 94n925
cancer, 90n1682
electrical tech, 93n1593
engineering sci, 90n1572
English in its own words, 92n1023
nursing beginning bibliog, 94n1864
photography, 90n943
sci, 93n1437
sci & tech, 90n1423
sci & tech in the US, v.2, 94n1560
surgery in the US, 1775-1900, 90n1637
surgery in the US 1775-1900, v.2, 94n1822
the Episcopal church in America, 1607-1991, 94n1521
Hitchens, Susan Hayes, 92n1267
Hitler fact bk, 91n530
Hitt, William D., 93n316
Hitzges, Norm, 93n812
Hixson, Richard F., 91n940
Hladczuk, John, 91n356, 93n404
Hladczuk, Sharon, 91n356
HMO/PPO dir, 91n1647
HMO/PPO dir 1993, 94n1815
Ho, Allan, 91n1275
Hoad, Linda, 91n1225
Hobart, Jack, 92n421, 92n1722
Hobbie, Margaret, 93n438
Hobbs, James B., 94n1086
Hobby index 1988, 92n951
Hobbyist sourcebk, 91n977
Hobday, Charles, 92n728
Hobson, Edmund, 91n1599
Hobson, Margaret, 93n1125
Hochmann, Gabriella, 90n1370, 93n1177
Hockey scouting report, 1989-90, 90n775
Hockings, Paul, 93n413, 94n396
Hodd, Michael, 92n143
Hodges, Deborah Robertson, 90n1309
Hodges, Flavia, 90n401, 91n419
Hodgkinson, Virginia Ann, 93n877
Hodgson, Godfrey, 93n520
Hodgson, Michael, 94n476
Hodgson, Terry, 90n1357
Hodson, William K., 93n1603
Hofeller, Thomas B., 90n544
Hoff, Henry B., 92n388
Hoffman, Andrea C., 94n378
Hoffman, Catherine, 91n1680
Hoffman, Eric, 91n466
Hoffman, Herbert H., 93n40
Hoffman, Louise J., 93n96
Hoffman, Verena, 93n725
Hoffmann, Frank, 90n614, 90n1277, 91n1311
Hoffmann, Frank W., 91n1338
Hoffmann, John, 92n471
Hoffmeister, Donald F., 91n1594
Hoffnar, Celeste R., 91n966
Hofstetter, Eleanore O., 91n1236
Hofstetter, Henry W., 90n1691
Hogan, Bill, 91n835
Hogg, Ian, 90n653
Hogg, Ian V., 91n707
Hoggart, Richard, 94n397
Hogue, Charles L., 94n1727
Hoke, John Ray Jr., 90n976
Holder, R. W., 91n1057
Holding, Sue, 94n1044
Holdsworth, Brian, 93n1596
Holdsworth, Deryck W., 91n516
Hole, John W., Jr., 91n1677
Holidays & anniversaries of the world, 2d ed, 91n1341

Holidays & special days project index for young people, 93n1308
Holistic health dir, 1992-93, 94n1808
Holland, David T., 90n50
Holland, F. Ross, Jr, 91n1830
Holland, Lisa, 93n1450
Holland, Patricia G., 94n964
Holland, Ted, 90n1341
Hollander, Zander, 94n852
Hollar, David W., 94n1635
Holley, E. Jens, 94n1507
Holliday, Paul, 90n1486
Hollings, Robert L., 92n51, 94n753
Hollom, P. A. D., 90n1538, 94n1701
Holloway, Joseph E., 94n1081
Holloway, Karen L., 93n268
Hollywood baby boomers, 94n1432
Hollywood greats of the golden yrs, 90n1323
Hollywood Reporter bk of box office hits, 91n1383
Hollywood songsters, 92n1349
Hollywood who's who, 94n1431
Holmen, Marianne, 91n1083
Holmes, Frederic L., 91n1461, 91n1462
Holmes, William M., 90n470
Holocaust, Israel, & the Jews: motion pictures in the Natl Archives, 91n405
Holocaust lit, 94n538
Holography market place, 3d ed, 93n1012
Holography marketplace 1989, 90n941
Hols, Edith, 92n1011
Holston, Kim, 91n1356
Holt, Constance Wall, 94n950
Holt, Dean W., 93n706
Holt foreign film gd, 90n1348
Holt, Linda Hughey, 91n1661, 93n884
Holte, James Craig, 93n1418
Holthuis, L. B., 93n1557
Holtz, Barry W., 94n425
Holtz, W. Bradley, 92n1709
Holtze, Sally Holmes, 90n30
Holy ground: a study of the American camp meeting, 93n1398
Holy spirit, 90n1390
Holy wells & sacred water sources in Britain & Ireland, 94n1386
Holzer, Marc, 90n733, 93n794
Hombs, Mary Ellen, 91n850, 94n1852
Home building & woodworking in colonial America, 93n1612
Home business resource gd, 91n192
Home ency of symptoms, ailments & their natural remedies, 93n1640
Home health care, 93n1620
Home health care equipment, 91n1652
Home improvement cost gd, 2d ed, 91n1029
Home schooling laws in all 50 states, 4th ed, 91n296
Homeless in America, 90n794
Homelessness: abstracts of the psychological & behavioral lit 1967-90, 92n835
Homelessness: an annot bibliog, 94n877
Homoeopathy in the US, 92n1647
Homophones & homographs, 2d ed, 94n1086
Homosexual & society, 91n873
Honduras, 93n155
Honig, Alice Sterling, 93n894
Honig, Donald, 92n785
Honig, Robert, 94n2004
Honour, Hugh, 93n1038
Hony, H. C., 94n1135
Hood, Howard A., 92n1669, 94n1840
Hook, Brian, 93n125
Hook, J. N., 91n1079
Hooper, Brad, 93n1160
Hooper, David, 94n842
Hooper, Judith, 92n180
Hoopes, David S., 92n314
Hoopes, Kathleen R., 92n314
Hoover, Dwight W., 90n845
Hoover, Gary, 92n144, 92n145, 93n208

Hoover's hndbk of ...
    American bus 1992, 93n208
    emerging cos 1993-94, 94n172
    world business 1992, 92n144
Hoover's hndbk: profiles of over 500 major corps, 92n145
Hoover's masterlist of major US cos 1993, 94n164
Hope, Augustine, 91n1011
Hopke, William E., 91n374, 94n386
Hopkins, Mariane S., 92n1328
Hopkins, Nigel J., 93n1740
Hopkins, Richard, 93n959
Hopkinson, Barbara, 90n10, 92n640
Hoppel, Joe, 94n848
Hopple, Gerald W., 91n734
Hopton, Marilyn, 94n980
Horace Greeley: a bio-bibliog, 93n979
Hordeski, Michael F., 91n1735
Horn, Barbara Lee, 93n1377, 93n1378, 94n1410, 94n1411
Horn Bk gd to children's & young adult bks, v.1, no.1, 91n1114
Horn Bk index 1924-89, 91n1122
Horn, Bruce, 94n1662
Horn, Jane, 90n1455
Horn, Judy, 93n676
Horne, Aaron, 91n1276, 93n1260
Horning, Kathleen T., 90n637
Hornor, Edith R., 93n909
Hornor, Louise L., 93n903
Hornsby, Alton, Jr., 92n347
Horowitz, Lois, 91n413
Horror: a connoisseur's gd to lit & film, 90n882
Horror film directors, 1931-90, 92n1348
Horror film stars, 2d ed, 92n1366
Horror lit: a reader's gd, 91n1138
Horse industry dir, 1990-91, 92n1511
Horse owner's vet hndbk, 90n1474
Horses, 94n1707
Horses & tack, rev ed, 92n1510
Horse's name was..., 94n1709
Horst, R. Kenneth, 91n1520
Horton, Carrell Peterson, 92n348
Horton, Stanley M., 92n1424, 92n1425, 92n1426, 92n1427, 92n1428, 92n1429, 92n1430, 92n1431, 92n1432
Hoser, Raymond T., 91n1602
Hoskins, Robert, 92n1203
Hospices, 92n819
Hospital governance, 91n1641
Hospital lit index, v.47, no.1, 92n1643
Hotaling, Edward R., 91n1297
Hotel & restaurant industries, 90n243
Houck, Carter, 92n952
Houdek, Frank G., 91n591, 92n522
Houghton, Patricia, 93n1295
Houk, Rose, 90n1493
Houlden, J. L., 91n1425
Houlette, Forrest, 90n986
House, Jonathan M., 94n681
Houston, James E., 91n302, 93n636
Houze, Herbert, 93n1004
How many calories? how much fat?, 93n1481
How quaint the ways of paradox!, 93n1274
How the new tech works, 92n1699
How to ...
    find bus intelligence in Washington, 10th ed, 91n157
    find info about AIDS, 93n1652
    find info about cos, 8th ed, 92n146
    find info about cos, v.3, 94n173
    locate anyone anywhere without leaving home, 90n778
    locate anyone who is or has been in the military, 90n654
    locate anyone who is or has been in the military, rev ed, 91n679
    read the financial pages & much more, rev ed, 90n218
    research the Supreme Court, 93n571
    talk marketing real good, 91n265
Howard, A. E. Dick, 92n750
Howard, E. Marguerite, 90n270, 90n345

Howard Hanson: a bio-bibliog, 94n1330
Howard, Joyce M., 92n1468
Howard, Philip H., 92n1784, 94n1934
Howard, Vivian, 94n251
Howard-Hill, T. H., 94n1244
Howard-Reguindin, Pamela F., 93n155
Howard-Williams, Jeremy, 94n860
Howarth, Francis G., 93n1565
Howarth, Lynne C., 93n639
Howatson, M. C., 90n1099, 94n1198
Howe-Grant, Mary, 94n1768
Howell, Michael J., 94n311
Howes, Kelly King, 94n1157
Howlett, Charles F., 93n791
Howorth, Lisa N., 90n1287
Hoxie, Frederick E., 92n368
Hoyer, Rudiger, 90n969
Hoyle, Gary D., 93n667
Hoyt, Erich, 92n1520
Hu, Shing Tsung (Peter), 93n1510
Hubbard, Linda S., 90n639, 90n1311, 93n687
Huber, Jeffrey T., 93n1652, 94n1853
Huber, John T., 94n1726
Huber, Kristina Ruth, 93n925
Huchtmeier, W. K., 91n1758
Hudson, Bob, 90n900
Hudson, David, 90n473
Hudson, Grace L., 92n106
Hudson, Howard Penn, 92n891
Hudson, John R., 93n1740
Hudson, Kenneth, 90n458, 92n62
Hudson River school, 92n1002
Hudson, Travis, 91n395
Hudson, Vincent J., 91n1670
Hudson's state capitals news media contacts dir 1991, 92n890
Hudson's subscription newsletter dir 1990, 92n902
Hudson's Washington news media contacts dir 1991, 92n891
Huellmantel, Michael B., 94n256
Huettner, Janet S., 92n828
Huffman, D. M., 90n1502
Huffman, Robert J., 90n64
Hug, Melissa Reiff, 90n1090
Hugh Johnson's modern ency of wine, 3d ed, 92n1488
Hugh Johnson's pocket ency of wine 1992, 93n1474
Hughes, J. M., 94n1096
Hughes, Joan, 91n1075
Hughes, Marija Matich, 92n1710
Hugman, Barry J., 90n759
Hui, Y. H., 93n1473
Hula, Volodymyr, 94n483
Hulbert gd to financial newsletters, 5th ed, 94n191
Hulbert, Mark, 94n191
Hull, Roger, 90n1690
Hulpke, Erika, 91n1165
Huls, Mary Ellen, 94n951
Hultgren, Arland J., 90n1404
Hults, Jan, 90n427
Human anatomy & physiology, 5th ed, 91n1677
Human communication behavior & info processing, 93n956
Human dvlpmt report 1991, 92n75
Human resources glossary, 93n302
Human resources yrbk, 1990 ed, 92n225
Human rights, 90n574
Human rights: a dir of resources, 90n572
Human rights: a ref hndbk, 90n575
Human rights dir: Latin American & the Caribbean, 91n601
Human rights, refugees, migrants & dvlpmt, 94n593
Human rights: 60 major global instruments, 93n615
Human sexuality, 90n1646
Humana, Charles, 94n594
Humanities computing yrbk 1988, 90n884
Humanities computing yrbk 1989-90, 92n880
Humanities index, Apr 89 to Mar 90, 92n881
Humanities index [CD-ROM], 93n948
Humble, Malcolm, 93n1223

Humm, Maggie, 91n925
Humor & cartoon markets 1990, 91n948
Humor in American lit, 93n1189
Humor of the old Southwest, 91n1148
Humor scholarship, 94n1304
Humphrey, Olga, 92n1339
Humphrey, Stephen R., 94n1735
Humphreys, Nancy K., 90n880
Hungary: a complete gd, 4th ed, 92n448
Hunnisett, Basil, 90n979
Hunt, Christopher J., 92n147, 92n336, 92n804
Hunt, Gladys, 94n383
Hunt, Kim, 91n968
Hunt, Thomas C., 90n1377, 93n348
Hunt, Tony, 91n1521
Hunt, V. Daniel, 91n1800
Hunt, William S., 90n422
Hunter, Allan, 93n1346, 93n1356
Hunter, Brian, 92n77
Hunter, Rodney J., 91n1443
Hunting, Anthony L. L., 93n1715
Hunting quotations, 93n836
Hunting the snark: a compendium of new poetic terminology, 91n1178
Hunziker, Ray, 93n1554
Hunziker, Raymond E., III, 90n1549
Hupper, William G., 91n1433, 92n1440, 94n1549
Hurst, Walter E., 91n1366, 94n1439
Hurvitz, David, 91n959
Husband, Janet, 92n1138
Husband, Jonathan F., 92n1138
Husband, Timothy B., 92n989
Hussmann, Jurgen, 91n1703
Hutcheson, Helen, 93n233
Hutchins, Charles R., 90n1496
Hutera, Donald, 91n1347
Huws, Gwilym, 92n105
Hy, Ronald John, 92n78
Hyatt, Edward, 90n1590
Hyman, Mildred, 90n434
Hymenoptera of the world, 94n1726
Hyne, Norman J., 92n1626
Hyper dict, 90n1720
HyperSource on multimedia/hypermedia techs, 91n1745
HyperSource on optical techs, 91n1746
Hysa, Ramazan, 94n1109

Iacono, Domenic J., 90n980
Ian Gorvin, 90n684
Iatridis, Mary D., 94n1559
I.B.I. intl bearing interchange gd, 12th ed, 94n1798
Ibou, Paul, 94n291
Icelandic-English, English-Icelandic dict, 91n1087
Ichthyosis & related disorders, 91n1701
Iconographic index to N.T. subjects represented in photographs & slides of paintings in the visual collections, Fine Arts Lib, Harvard Univ, v.1, 94n1540
Icons, 93n42
Identification gd to the trees of Canada, 91n1544
Identification of flowering plant families, 3d ed, 90n1491
Idi Amin & Uganda, 94n763
IEG dir of sponsorship mktg, 1991, 93n258
Iglitzin, Lynne B., 93n408
Ignashev, Diane M. Nemec, 93n1230
Igoe, Robert S., 90n1456
Igor Stravinsky: an intl bibliog of theses & dissertations, 1925-87, 90n1245
Igor Stravinsky—the composer in the recording studio, 92n1278
Ihrie, Maureen, 94n1289
IIA telephone dir, 90n586
IIE educl assocs 1992-93, 94n366
Illuminated &·decorated medieval mss in the Univ Lib, Utrecht, 91n1039

Illustrated almanac of histl facts, 93n553
Illustrated Ardha-Magadhi dict, 90n1035
Illustrated atlas of Jerusalem, 91n439
Illustrated bio-bibliog of black photographers 1940-88, 90n944
Illustrated chemistry lab terminology, 93n1708
Illustrated computer graphics dict, 94n1912
Illustrated dict of ...
    British steel engravers, 90n979
    electronics, 5th ed, 92n1607
    knitting, 90n931
    microcomputers, 3d ed, 91n1735
    natural health, 90n1642
Illustrated dir of handicapped products 1991-92, 93n863
Illustrated discography of hot rod music 1961-65, 91n1323
Illustrated ency of ...
    active new religions, sects, & cults, 94n1529
    architects & architecture, 93n1040
    fossils, 92n1746
    general aviation, 2d ed, 91n1818
    mankind, 91n75
    N.Z., 91n513
    orchids, 94n1658
    wildlife, 92n1559
    woodworking handtools instruments & devices, rev ed, 93n1610
Illustrated field gd to ferns & allied plants of the British Isles, 92n1531
Illustrated glossary of hand & reconstructive surgery, 91n1703
Illustrated gd to ...
    rocks & minerals, 94n1956
    modern naval warfare, 91n702
    the mountain stream insects of Colo., 93n1568
Illustrated hndbk of desktop publishing & typesetting, 2d ed, 91n667
Illustrated hist of helicopters, 91n689
Illustrated hrdwr bk, 93n1611
Illustrated intl ency of horse breeds & breeding, 91n1577
Illustration index 6, 90n964
Illustration index 7, 94n1050
Image of older adults in the media, 94n870
Images of Poe's works, 91n1171
Images of the other, 92n366
Imaginary people, 90n1105
Imai, Mitsunori, 90n1174
IMF glossary, 93n254
Immell, Myra, 93n1137
Immelmann, Klaus, 90n1478
Immergut, E. H., 91n1773
Immigrant experience, 93n420
Immigrant women in the US, 91n914
Immigrants from the German-speaking countries of Europe, 2d ed, 92n352
Immigration glossary, 91n779
Immigration hist research center, 92n383
Immigration made simple, 91n780
Immigration stats 1987, 91n778
Immigration stats 1991, 94n803
Important peak index of the registry of mass spectral data, 93n1717
Importers manual USA, 1993 ed, 94n290
In Plain English, Inc., 90n292
In search of your Canadian roots, 90n388
In search of your roots: a gd for Canadians, rev ed, 93n456
In the beginning: great 1st lines from your favorite bks, 93n1117
In the field: the lang of the Vietnam War, 92n476
In vitro fertilization clinics, 94n1857
Independent bishops, 91n1447
Independent power 1989 dir, 90n1777
Independent study cat, 4th ed, 90n358
Independent study cat, 5th ed, 94n390
Index & abstract dir, 90n71
Index & dir of industry standards, 90n240
Index by region, usage, & etymology to the Dict of American Regional English, v.1 & 2, 94n1090
Index chemicus, v.125, no.1, 93n1719

Index of ...
    American per verse: 1989, 92n1186
    American per verse: 1990, 93n1187
    college majors, 17th ed, 92n312
    desktop publishing, 1990, 91n673
    economic articles in jls & collective volumes, v.29, 91n165
    English literary mss, v.2, pt.2, 94n1245
    English literary mss, v.3, pt.2, 91n1189
    English literary mss, v.3, pt.3, 94n1246
    English literary mss, v.4, pt.2, 92n1195
    majors & graduate degrees 1994, 94n365
    majors 1991, 91n333
    paintings sold in the British Isles during the 19th century, v.2, 91n1037
Index: the Pacific NW film, video, & audio production index, 7th ed, 90n1338
Index to ...
    America: life & customs - 20th century to 1986, 90n502
    American Ref Bks Annual 1985-89, 90n72
    American short story award collections 1970-90, 94n1230
    AV producers & distrs, 7th ed, 91n975
    black pers 1988, 91n390
    black pers 1991, 94n403
    bk reviews in England 1749-74, 91n1190
    Canadian legal lit 1989, 91n592
    Canadian legal lit 1992, 94n582
    city & regional mags of the US, 91n53
    Commonwealth little mags 1987-89, 93n83
    crime & mystery anthologies, 92n1142
    dance pers: 1991, 94n1424
    dialect maps of Great Britain, 93n1067
    English per lit on the O.T. & ancient Near Eastern studies, v.3, 91n1433
    English per lit on the O.T. & ancient Near Eastern studies, v.4, 92n1440
    English per lit on the O.T. & ancient Near Eastern studies, v.5, 94n1549
    fairy tales 1978-86, 5th suppl, 91n1330
    Fla. Jewish hist in the American Israelite 1854-1900, 93n446
    health info 1988 abstracts, v.1, no.2, 90n1632
    illus of animals & plants, 93n1525
    "Index on Censorship", 91n636
    intl public opinion, 1987-88, 90n734
    intl public opinion, 1991-92, 94n75
    intl stats 1990, 93n915
    Italian architecture, 94n1052
    jls in communication studies through 1990, 93n954
    law school alumni pubns cumulation Jan 1980-June 1989, 90n561
    legal pers [CD-ROM], 93n601
    legal pers: Sept 1990-Aug 1991, 93n600
    legal pers: thesaurus, 91n623
    Negro spirituals, rev ed, 92n1315
    per articles related to law: 30 yr cumulation, 90n564
    per lit on the apostle Paul, 94n1550
    personal names in the NUC of mss collections 1959-84, 90n402
    plays in pers, 1977-87, 91n1126
    poetry for children & young people 1982-87, 90n1096
    proceedings of the Economic & Social Council, 92n739
    proceedings of the General Assembly, 92n740
    proceedings of the Security Council, 43d yr, 91n767
    reviews of bibliographical pubs, v.10, 93n949
    scientific & technical proceedings, no.4, April 1990, 91n1471
    tests used in educl dissertations, 90n310
    the Annenberg TV script archive, v.1, 91n976
    the contents of the per Canadian Lit nos.1-102, 94n1275
    the critical vocabulary of Blackwood's Edinburgh Mag, 1830-40, 94n61
    the decisions rendered by the Immigration Appeal Board, 90n563
    the Hampton Univ newspaper clipping file, 92n349
    the Sporting News, 93n823
    the Wilson authors series, 1991 rev ed, 92n1112
    US invalid pension records 1801-15, 93n459
    who's who bks 1989, 91n54
    who's who bks 1992, 94n14
    women of the world from ancient to modern times, suppl, 90n878
Index Translationum 36, 90n8
Indexing: a basic reading list, 94n638
Indexing from A to Z, 93n653
Indian America, 91n396
Indian music lit, 93n1239
Indian social & economic development, 1987, 90n194
Indian subcontinent in lit for children & young adults, 93n1126
Indiana, 91n102
Indiana bks by Ind. authors, 91n1112
Indiana factbk 1992, 93n108
Indians along the Oregon Trail, expanded ed, 93n436
Indians of ...
    Central & S America, 92n371
    the northeast, 92n360
    the Pacific Northwest, 92n362
    the Southwest, 92n363
Indices to the species of mosses & lichens described by William Mitten, 94n1668
Indigenous navigation & voyaging in the Pacific, 93n1789
Individual investor's gd to investment pubs, 90n210
Individual investor's gd to no-load mutual funds, 8th ed, 90n211
Individuals with disabilities educ act 1980-91, 93n394
Indonesian-English dict, 3d ed, 90n1046
Indonesian-English, English-Indonesian dict, 91n1088
Indoor air quality dir 1992-93, 93n1758
Indoor plants, 92n1505
Industrial chemical thesaurus, 2d ed, 94n1942
Industrial engineering terminology, rev ed, 91n1622, 93n1602
Industrial group index, 93n649
Industrial research in the UK, 14th ed, 93n296
Industrial robot hndbk, 90n1731
Industrial stats yrbk 1990, 94n216
Industrial trends: monthly stats, 91n230
Informal economy, 93n173
Information bks for children, 93n7
Information China, 90n121
Information freedom & censorship: world report 1991, 92n593
Information industry dir, 1991, 92n591
Information marketplace dir, 1993, 93n685
Information Mongolia, 92n96
Information please almanac 1989, 90n2
Information please bus almanac & desk ref, 1994, 94n174
Information please environmental almanac, 1993, 94n1986
Information please kids' almanac, 94n2
Information please sports almanac, 1990, 91n800
Information please sports almanac, 1993, 94n818
Information resources & servs in Austral., 92n588
Information resources dir, fall 1989, 91n1808
Information sci abstracts, v.25, no.2, 91n603
Information security: dict of concepts, standards & terms, 94n1900
Information security hndbk, 93n315
Information sources for virtual reality, 94n1894
Information sources in ...
    cartography, 91n448
    chemistry, 4th ed, 94n1931
    info tech, 92n595
    metallic materials, 91n1632
    patents, 93n587
    pharmaceuticals, 92n1696
    sport & leisure, 94n821
    the earth scis, 2d ed, 91n1780
    the medical scis, 4th ed, 93n1626
Information sources 1989, 90n585
Information studies courses in the UK, 92n589
Informing the nation, 92n619
Ingardia, Richard, 92n1390
Inge, M. Thomas, 91n1339
Ingham, John N., 91n128
Ingle, Lester, 91n1552
Inglis, James, 92n1441
Inherited eye diseases in purebred dogs, 90n1475
INIS: thesaurus, 93n1735

Initial public offering annual 1989, 91n183
Inlander, Charles B., 90n1627, 93n1633
Inman, David, 93n988
Innes, Clive, 91n1541
Insects of Hawaii, v.15, 93n1561
Inside Japanese support 1992, 93n280
Inside the legislative process, 1991 ed, 93n751
Inside US business, 1991 ed, 92n205
Insider's gd to ...
    bk editors & publishers 1990-91, 91n947
    successful US immigration, 93n589
    the colleges 1993, 93n372
Inskipp, Carol, 93n1543
Inskipp, Tim, 93n1543
INSPEC classification 1991, 92n582
INSPEC thesaurus 1991, 92n583
Inspiring African Americans, 92n350
Instant natl locator gd, 93n955
Institute for Brewing Studies, 93n1477
Institute of International Education, 91n342
Institutions of higher educ, 91n312
Institutum Patristicum Augustinianum, 93n1406
Instructions & warnings, 91n248
Instrumental virtuosi, 90n1258
Instrumentation & control consultants, 90n1578
Instrumentation in educ, 94n306
Insurance & alternatives for uninsurables, 91n239
Insurance dict, 90n252
Insurance pers index 1988, 90n251
Intellectual freedom: a ref hndbk, 94n641
Intellectual freedom & censorship, 90n614
Intellectual freedom manual, 4th ed, 94n642
Interavia space dict 1989-90, 91n1819
Intercountry comparisons of agricultural output & productivity, 94n1597
Interdisciplinary approaches to Canadian society, 92n97
Interdisciplinary bibliog of freshwater crayfishes, 90n1550
Interesting athletes, 91n803
Interesting people: black American hist makers, 90n480
Intergenerational readings/resources 1980-93, 94n866
Interior landscape dict, 94n1621
Interlibrary loan policies dir, 4th ed, 93n657
Interlibrary loan servs, 5th ed, 90n615
International affairs dir of orgs, 94n799
International almanac of electoral hist, 3d ed, 92n677
International armed conflict since 1945, 92n661
International art price annual 90, 91n1010
International assn statutes series, 90n69
International auction records 1991, 92n975
International authors & writers who's who, 13th ed, 94n1147
International bibliog 1988, v.16, 90n67
International bibliog of ...
    biog 1970-87, 90n9
    dirs & gds to archival repositories, 92n7
    social & cultural anthropology, v.32, 91n382
    sociology 1985, 90n779
    theatre: 1988-89, 94n1466
International Board for Plant Genetic Resources, 93n1496
International bk trade dir 1989, 90n641
International bks in print 1989, pt.2, 90n10
International brands & their cos 1993-94, 94n228
International bus bibliog, 90n159
International bus dict & ref, 93n255
International bus hndbk: Republic of Korea, 90n285
International bus in S Africa 1988, 90n171
International closeout dir '94, 94n292
International Committee for Social Science Information & Documentation, 91n168
International commodity markets hndbk 1993, 94n188
International cos & their brands 1993-94, 94n229
International corporate 1000 1990, v.3, no.1, 91n255
International corporate yellow bk, v.5, no.1, 93n259
International countermeasures hndbk 1990, 91n703
International current awareness servs: anthropology & related disciplines, v.2, no.1, 92n336

International current awareness servs: economics & related disciplines, v.2, no.1, 92n147
International current awareness servs: sociology & related disciplines, v.2, no.1, 92n804
International debt & the Third World, 90n155
International defense electronic systems hndbk, 93n718
International dvlpmt dict, 92n125
International dict of ...
    adult & continuing educ, 92n333
    anthropologists, 92n337
    architects & architecture, 94n1055
    art & artists, 91n1020
    ballet, 94n1423
    films & filmmakers, v.1, 2d ed, 91n1368
    films & filmmakers, v.2, 2d ed, 92n1353
    films & filmmakers, v.3, 2d ed, 93n1335
    films & filmmakers, v.4, 2d ed, 94n1430
    mgmt, 4th ed, 92n232
    opera, 94n1355
    psychology, 90n747
    the securities industry, 2d ed, 90n217
    theatre, v.1, 93n1391
International dir of ...
    archives, 90n463
    arts, 1991/92 ed, 92n64
    bioethics orgs, 94n1835
    Canadian studies, 93n132
    cinematographers, set- & costume designers in film, v.10, 92n1355
    co hists, 90n177
    co hists, v.2, 91n132
    co hists, v.3, 92n148
    co hists, v.4, 93n260
    co hists, v.5, 94n230
    co hists, v.6, 94n231
    co hists, v.7, 94n232
    contract laboratories, 2d ed, 90n1619
    corporate affiliations, 1989-90, 90n178
    foreign ministers 1589-1989, 91n720
    govt, 91n719
    librarians & lib specialists in the Slavic & E European field, 3d ed, 91n628
    little mags & small prs, 27th ed, 92n636
    non-official statistical sources 1990, 91n899
    occupational safety & health insts, 92n220
    philosophy & philosophers 1990-92, 91n1407
    primatology, 94n1736
    testing labs, 1993 ed, 94n1578
    voluntary work, 5th ed, 94n894
    youth internships with the UN, its related agencies, & non-governmental orgs, 5th ed, 94n790
International dir to Canadian studies, 91n106
International dissertations on fibre reinforced polymers, 90n1750
International ency of ...
    abbrevs & acronyms of orgs, 3d ed, 91n1
    communications, 90n887
    curriculum, 92n274
    educl evaluation, 91n300
    educl tech, 91n359
    fndns, 91n869
    integrated circuits, 90n1591
    integrated circuits, 2d ed, 93n1594
    learned societies & academies, 94n36
    linguistics, 93n1050
International energy stats sourcebk, 2d ed, 94n1984
International exchange locator, 93n387
International film index 1895-1990, 93n1373
International film industry, 90n1329
International film prizes, 92n1372
International financial stats yrbk 1990, 92n188
International gd to children's theatre & educl theatre, 91n1121
International gd to legal deposit, 93n651
International GIS sourcebk, 1993, 93n491
International glossary of hydrology, 2d ed, 94n1952

International hndbk of ...
  addiction behaviour, 92n837
  child care policies & programs, 94n919
  early childhood educ, 94n315
  housing policies & practices, 92n850
  natl parks & nature reserves, 91n452
  reading educ, 93n404
  women's educ, 90n876
International hndbk on ...
  drug control, 94n916
  internal migration, 91n905
  old-age insurance, 92n814
International higher educ, 93n381
International histl stats: Europe 1750-1988, 3d ed, 93n911
International histl stats: the Americas, 1750-1988, 2d ed, 94n936
International illus vocabulary of English-French fingerprint terminology..., 93n607
International imaging source bk 1992, 93n1693
International Labour Review: index 1945-91, 94n285
International legal bibliogs, 93n567
International legal bks in print 1990-91, 92n523
International legal bks in print 1993-94, 94n546
International literary market place 1990, 91n665
International literary market place 1993, 94n667
International lit in English, 92n1193
International mgmt hndbk, 94n238
International mktg data & stats 1991, 92n248
International markets for meat 1990/91, 92n1495
International markets for meat 1992/93, 94n1593
International micrographics source bk, 1989, 91n1736
International Migration Review cum index, 1964-89, 92n339
International military & defense ency, 94n688
International military ency, v.1, 93n702
International monetary fund 1944-92, 94n234
International music jls, 91n1263
International negotiations, 90n726
International opera gd, 92n1292
International orgs: a dict & dir, 3d ed, 94n793
International orgs & world order dict, 93n781
International orgs 1918-45, rev ed, 92n735
International petroleum ency, 90n1783, 93n1744
International proverb scholarship, suppl.1, 91n1331
International proverb scholarship, suppl.2, 94n1388
International research centers dir 1992-93, 93n68
International satellite dir 1989, 4th ed, 90n1738
International satellite dir, 1992, 93n1696
International scholarship dir, 3d ed, 94n332
International schools dir 1990, 25th ed, 91n344
International standard classification of occupations, 92n226
International terrorism in the 1980s, 90n727
International time tables, 91n1757
International trade 89-90, 92n250
International trade 90-91, 93n270
International trade fairs & conferences dir 1991-92, 92n251
International trade stats yrbk, 1987, 91n270
International trade stats yrbk, 1990, 94n233
International translation gd for emergency medicine, 94n1825
International Trotskyism 1929-85, 93n777
International who's who in music, 12th ed, 91n1254
International who's who in music & musicians' dir, 13th ed, 94n1346
International who's who 1989-90, 90n31
International who's who 1990-91, 92n27
International who's who of professional & bus women, 2d ed, 94n958
International writings of Bohdan S. Wynar, 1949-92, 94n80
International yr bk & statesmen's who's who 1992, 94n791
International yrbk of educl & training tech 1991, 92n282
International yrbk of educl & training tech 1992/93, 94n382
International youth hostel hndbk 1991-92, v.1, 92n436
International youth hostel hndbk 1991-92, v.2, 92n437
Internet 1989-90 profiles of intl dvlpmt contractors & grantees, 91n236
Internships, 1991, 92n305
Internships in foreign & defense policy, 91n769

Intertextuality, allusion, & quotation, 90n1065
Interviews & conversations with 20th-century authors writing in English, series 3, 92n1114
International Committee for Social Science Information and Documentation, 90n362, 90n680, 90n779, 90n780
International Council on Archives, Committee on Conservation and Restoration, 90n617
Intner, Sheila S., 91n624, 93n640
Intrep Data Corp., 94n214
Introduction to lib research in anthropology, 92n338
Introduction to US govt info sources, 4th ed, 93n73
Inventing & patenting sourcebk, 92n149
Inventions & discoveries 1993, 94n1581
Inventory of longitudinal studies in the social scis, 93n102
Invertebrates of economic importance in Britain, 4th ed, 91n1556
Investigations of the attack on Pearl Harbor, 91n510
Investment trust dir 1988-89, 90n212
Invisible poets: Afro-Americans of the 19th century, 2d ed, 90n1164
Iowa hist & culture, 90n473
IPA thesaurus & frequency list, 6th ed, 94n1873
IQ debate, 92n266
Iranian short story authors, 91n1237
Iraq-Iran War, 90n518
Ireland, Norma Olin, 90n502, 90n878, 91n1330
Ireland, Sandra L. Jones, 91n383
Ireland's index to inspiration, 94n69
Irene Dunne: a bio-bibliog, 92n1343
Iris, 2d ed., 91n1529
Iris of China, 93n1507
Irish folk music, 90n1285
Irish in America, 93n437
Irish records: sources for family & local hist, 90n383
Irish-American almanac & green pages, rev ed, 91n389
Irish-American heritage, 90n375
Irish/English, English/Irish dict & phrasebk, 93n1088
Irvin, Linda, 93n257, 94n48
Irving, Holly Berry, 94n1604
Is it true what they say about Dixie?, 90n1010
ISA dir of instrumentation 1989, 90n241
Isaac Albeniz: chronological list & thematic cat of his piano works, 94n1320
Isaac Asimov's bk of sci & nature quotations, 90n1440
Isaac Asimov's lib of the universe, 91n1755
Isaacs, Alan, 93n680, 94n204
Isaacs, Jennifer, 91n1038
Isaacs, Katherine M., 94n1084
Isaacs, Ronald H., 93n449
Isbell, P., 92n130
Isbell, Pauline, 91n217
Isbister, Rob, 94n1299
Isely, Duane, 91n1533
Isis cum bibliog 1976-85, 90n1416
Islam & Islamic groups, 94n1553
Islam in N America, 94n1552
Island Pr bibliog of environmental lit, 94n1990
Islands of the S & SE US, 90n451
Isler, Charlotte, 91n1660
Isler's pocket dict, 3d ed, 91n1660
Israel, Guy, 90n1743
ISS dir of overseas schools, 1989/90 ed, 90n346
Italian American material culture, 93n438
Italian Americans & religion, 2d ed, 94n1504
Italian foreign policy 1918-45, rev ed, 92n710
Italian idioms, 92n1078
Italian violin music of the 17th century, 91n1264
Italian-Canadian studies, 90n376
Italian-Canadian writers, 90n1197
Iter Italicum, v.6, 94n978
It's Greek to me!, 92n1026
Iturralde, Mario P., 92n1657
Iversen, Edwin S., 94n1594
Iverson, Cheryl, 90n895
Iverson, Timothy J., 91n602
Iwasaki, George, 92n1700

Ixer, R. A., 92n1740
Iz, Fahir, 94n1135
Izady, Mehrdad R., 93n165
Izawa, Yasuho, 91n511

J. K. Lasser Institute, 93n327
J. K. Lasser's your income tax 1993, 93n327
Jablonski, Stanley, 94n1818
Jacinto, Beatrice, 90n957
Jack, Adrienne, 91n29
Jackson, Alan A., 94n2022
Jackson, Byron M., 92n1762
Jackson, Edward M., 90n1619
Jackson, Frederick H., 93n1080
Jackson, George, 90n524
Jackson, Guida M., 91n921
Jackson, K. David, 91n1244
Jackson, Kathryn A., 94n1053
Jackson, Kathy Merlock, 94n1412
Jackson, Pat, 92n1611, 92n1756, 92n1758, 92n1759
Jackson, Philip W., 93n334
Jackson, Rebecca, 94n863
Jackson, Richard L., 91n1245
Jackson, Susan L., 91n1704
Jacob, Helene, 94n1997
Jacob, Stuart, 91n1367
Jacob, Udo, 90n1569
Jacobs, Arthur, 91n1256
Jacobs, David S., 91n1678
Jacobs, Dick, 90n1278
Jacobs, James E., 90n328
Jacobs, James S., 92n1124
Jacobs, Margaret A., 91n304
Jacobs, William Jay, 92n562
Jacobsen, Roy M., 94n1588
Jacobson, John D., 92n1025
Jacobson, Nancy, 94n83, 94n86
Jacobson, Ronald L., 94n1056
Jacobstein, J. Myron, 90n564, 92n548
Jacques Derrida: an annot primary & secondary bibliog, 94n1491
Jacquet, Constant H., Jr., 90n1384
Jaderstrom, Susan, 93n324
Jain, M. K., 91n102
Jain, S. K., 92n1550
Jakobson, Michael, 90n522
Jakubiak, Joyce, 94n58
Jalas, Jaakko, 90n1494
Jalbert, Gerald, 91n243
James, David E., 90n1767
James Dickey: a descriptive bibliog, 91n1161
James Fenimore Cooper: an annot bibliog of criticism, 93n1171
James, Glenn, 94n1966
James Monroe: a bibliog, 92n452
James, Richard S., 91n1263
James, Robert C., 94n1966
James, Simon, 92n153
James Stewart: a bio-bibliog, 93n1319
Jamison, Martin, 94n763
Jancik, Wayne, 91n1324
Jane's all the world's aircraft 1989-90, 90n1803
Jane's all the world's aircraft 1992-93, 93n1780
Jane's armour & artillery 1989-90, 91n704
Jane's armoured fighting vehicle systems 1989-90, 91n705
Jane's avionics 1991-92, 92n1593
Jane's C3I systems 1989-90, 91n706
Jane's containerisation dir 1991-92, 92n1791
Jane's defence glossary, 94n676
Jane's fighting ships 1990-91, 91n694
Jane's high-speed marine craft 1990, 91n1831
Jane's infantry weapons 1989-90, 91n707
Janes, Michael, 90n1043, 93n1083
Jane's military training systems 1990-91, 92n656
Jane's NATO hndbk 1989-90, 91n768
Jane's NBC protection equipment 1989-90, 91n708

Jane's radar & electronic warfare systems 1989-90, 91n709
Jane's underwater warefare systems 1989-90, 91n710
Jane's urban transport systems 1990, 91n1825
Janet Gaynor: a bio-bibliog, 93n1316
Jankowski, Bernard, 93n1425
Jankowski, Katherine E., 91n864, 93n280, 93n872, 94n1850
Janosik, Robert J., 92n524
Jansma, Pamela E., 94n1991
Japan, 91n103
Japan: an illus ency, 94n115
Japan Chamber of Commerce and Industry, 91n278, 94n245
Japan co hndbks, spring 1990, 91n182
Japan Foundation, 90n1049
Japan trade dir 1990-91, 91n271
Japan trade dir 1993-94, 94n244
Japanese American hist, 94n423
Japanese direct foreign investments, 90n200
Japanese films, 91n1376
Japanese investment in US & Canadian real estate dir 1990, 91n285
Japanese naval aces & fighter units in WW II, 91n511
Japanese plants, 90n1488
Japanese studies from pre-hist to 1990, 93n126
Japanese women writers in English translation, 90n1206
Japanese women writers in English translation, v.2, 94n1295
Japanese/English, English/Japanese glossary of scientific & technical terms, 94n1571
Japan's economy, 90n160
Japan's high tech, 92n1701
Jape, Mijndert, 90n1261
Japonisme, 91n1004
Jarboe, Betty M., 91n414, 92n1421
Jargon: an informal dict of computer terms, 94n1905
Jarock, Beth, 94n993
Jarrell, Howard R., 90n213, 92n160
Jarrett, William S., 90n767, 90n773, 91n812, 91n830, 94n845
Jarvis, Kelvin, 91n1249
Jarvis, M. Todd, 90n1595
Jarvis, Peter, 92n333
Jary, David, 93n848
Jary, Julia, 93n848
Jasion, Jan T., 93n651
Jason, Philip K., 91n1177, 94n514
Jasper, Lisa, 90n1724
Jasper, Lisa R., 93n1686
Jazz & blues lover's gd to the US, 92n1306
Jazz discography, v.1, 93n1287
Jazz discography, v.2, 93n1288
Jazz discography, v.3, 93n1289
Jazz discography, v.5, 94n1373
Jazz discography, v.6, 94n1374
Jazz from A to Z: a graphic dict, 91n1317
Jazz hndbk, 91n1319
Jazz lives, 94n1372
Jazz performers, 91n1316
Jazz portraits, 91n1318
Jean Arthur: a bio-bibliog, 91n1358
Jean Paul Sartre: a bibliog, 94n1489
Jean-Francois Lyotard: a bibliog, 92n873
Jean-Philippe Rameau: a gd to research, 91n1271
Jee, Sharilyn, 91n726
Jefferds, Vincent, 91n1069
Jefferies, Margaret, 94n482
Jeffrey, David Lyle, 94n1149
Jeffri, Joan, 91n877
Jehle, Faustin F., 94n220
Jelitto, Leo, 92n1538
Jenkins, Jon C., 93n784
Jenkins, Russell, 94n726
Jenkins, William A., 90n1022, 90n1023, 92n1061, 92n1062
Jennifer Jones: a bio-bibliog, 91n1351
Jensen, Julie M., 94n1173
Jepson manual, 94n1644
Jepson, Michael H., 90n1703
Jerde, Judith, 93n1007

Jermy, Clive, 92n1531
Jerome, Judson, 90n903
Jerome Rothenberg: a descriptive bibliog, 90n1153
Jerusalem Center for Public Affairs, staff of, 93n726
Jerusalem, the holy city, v.2, 93n544
Jerzy Kosinski: an annot bibliog, 93n1175
Jessica Tandy: a bio-bibliog, 93n1315
Jessie Willcox Smith: a bibliog, 90n984
Jessup, Deborah Hitchcock, 91n1812
Jessup, John E., 90n650
Jessup, Lynne, 90n1282
Jet cutting & cleaning bibliog, 90n1603
Jett-Simpson, Mary, 90n1075
Jewish American fiction writers, 92n1161
Jewish athletes hall of fame, 91n804
Jewish autobiogs & biogs, 90n381
Jewish communities of the world, 4th ed, 90n380
Jewish elderly in the English-speaking countries, 90n784
Jewish family names & their origins, 94n441
Jewish film dir, 93n1357
Jewish genealogy, 92n382
Jewish heritage in America, 90n378
Jewish Holocaust: an annot gd to bks in English, 92n477
Jewish museums of N America, 93n444
Jewish profiles, 93n450
Jewish student's gd to American colleges, 91n332
Jewish time line ency, 91n406
Jewish wisdom, 93n445
Jewish-American hist & culture, 93n442
Jewish-Christian relations, 90n1378
Jezic, Diane Peacock, 90n859
Jim Flegg's field gd to the birds of Britain & Europe, 91n1562
Jimenez, Edgar, 94n356
Joan of Arc in hist, lit, & film, 91n529
Job hunter's gd to 100 great American cities, 93n304
Job hunter's sourcebk, 92n222
Job hunter's sourcebk, 2d ed, 94n279
Job seeker's gd to 1,000 top employers, 94n280
Job seeker's gd to private & public cos, 93n310
Jochum, K. P. S., 92n1217
Joel Whitburn presents daily #1 hits 1940-92, 94n1364
Joel Whitburn's top country singles 1944-88, 91n1313
Johann Michael Haydn (1737-1806): a chronological thematic cat of his works, 94n1332
Johannes Brahms: an annot bibliog, 92n1273
Johannsen, Hano, 92n232
Johansen, Elaine R., 91n716
Johanson, Cynthia J., 94n1032
Johansson, Thomas B., 94n1985
John C. Calhoun: a bibliog, 91n489
John Dewey: the collected works, 1882-1953: index, 93n342
John Donne companion, 91n1206
John Fowles: a ref companion, 93n1208
John Lehmann's 'New Writing': an author-index 1936-50, 92n1205
John McCabe: a bio-bibliog, 92n1261
John Quincy Adams: a bibliog, 94n498
John Ruskin: a ref gd, 90n881
John, Vernon, 92n1616
John Wayne: a bio-bibliog, 93n1320
Johns, Cecily, 92n81
Johnsgard, Paul A., 94n1698, 94n1699
Johnson, Beth Hillman, 94n269
Johnson, Burges, 92n1053
Johnson, Chas Floyd, 92n855
Johnson, Cleveland, 91n1284
Johnson, Craig R., 94n1353
Johnson, Curt, 93n698, 93n974
Johnson, David E., 92n1329
Johnson, Douglas, 91n758
Johnson, Edward D., 93n1061
Johnson, Eric A., 94n1630
Johnson, Eric W., 90n1121
Johnson, Forrest L., 90n1487
Johnson, Helen L., 91n1088

Johnson, Hugh, 92n1488, 93n1474
Johnson, James B., 92n1573, 92n1574, 94n1706
Johnson, Jane G., 92n600
Johnson, Jenny K., 94n379
Johnson, Jerry D., 90n1570
Johnson, John, 94n1449
Johnson, John W., 93n578
Johnson, Joy L., 94n1864
Johnson, Karl E., 93n634
Johnson, Keith, 91n472
Johnson, Ken, 94n455
Johnson, Larry, 90n1808
Johnson, Linda Carlson, 93n1309
Johnson, Lois S., 94n1402
Johnson, Margaret M., 94n479
Johnson, Mary Elizabeth, 94n234
Johnson, Norman L., 91n898
Johnson, Richard S., 90n654, 91n679
Johnson, Rose-Marie, 91n1277
Johnson, Rossall J., 91n1088
Johnson, Stanley H., Jr., 93n1493
Johnson, Tom, 94n1437
Johnson, Victoria L., 92n751
Johnson, Willis L., 92n221
Johnston, Bernard, 92n39, 92n40
Johnston, Robert H., 92n744
Johnston-Des Rochers, Janeen, 91n286, 91n779, 93n252
Joint Chiefs of Staff, 92n649
Jolly, David C., 91n449
Jolma, Dena Jones, 93n836
Jones, Alfred, 91n1429
Jones, Alison, 94n1526
Jones, C. Lee, 92n567, 93n663
Jones, Colin, 93n143
Jones, David L., 92n1504, 94n1671
Jones, Diane Rovena, 90n79
Jones' dict of O.T. proper names, 91n1429
Jones, Dilwyn, 90n1819
Jones, Dolores Blythe, 90n621
Jones, Elizabeth, 92n928
Jones, Errol D., 94n682
Jones, Francine, 94n897, 94n900
Jones, Gareth, 93n1753
Jones, George F., 91n420
Jones, J. Michael, 94n703
Jones, James M., 91n1687
Jones, Jeffrey A., 91n813
Jones, Jimmy, 90n1286
Jones, John Oliver, 91n1565, 93n497
Jones, Kenneth Glyn, 93n1705
Jones, Lawrence K., 93n409
Jones, Lewis P., 93n510
Jones, Linda M., 93n134
Jones, Peter, 91n775
Jones, Sandy, 90n227
Jones, Schuyler, 93n122
Jones, Steve, 94n394
Jones, Susan K., 92n924
Jones, Teresa, 92n1779
Jones, Virginia L., 90n344
Jones, Woodrow, Jr., 91n1642
Jonovic, Donald J., 90n273
Jonsen, Helen, 90n1026
Jopling, Norman, 90n1100
Jordan, Casper LeRoy, 94n1223
Jordan, Michael, 94n1395
Jorgensen, Delores A., 94n547
Jorgensen, Linda, 92n895, 94n995
Jorgenson, Lisa, 94n1672
Joscelyn, Trevor A., 94n1257
Jose, Jim, 93n778
Joseph Chaikin: a bio-bibliog, 93n1376
Joseph Conrad: an annot bibliog, 91n1202
Joseph Conrad's reading, 92n1200
Joseph Jacobs dir of the Jewish pr in America, 3d ed, 92n903

Joseph Jacobs Organization, Inc., 92n903
Joseph, Joel D., 91n197
Joseph Papp: a bio-bibliog, 93n1378
Josephs, Lewis S., 92n1084
Joshi, S. T., 94n1292
Journal of Women's Hist gd to per lit, 93n943
Journalism: a gd to the ref lit, 91n958
Journalists of the US, 92n901
Journals in psychology, 2d ed, 90n753
Journeys of the great explorers, 94n464
Joy, Albert H., 92n1769
Joyce, Beverly A., 90n855, 92n1245, 93n1146
Joyce Cary: a descriptive bibliog, 91n1200
Joyce, Donald Franklin, 93n679
Joyce, P. W., 90n400
Joyce, William L., 91n26
Joys of Hebrew, 94n1385
Joys of Yinglish, 90n1062
Judaica Americana, 92n380
Judaism & Christianity: a gd to the ref lit, 92n1399
Judaism & human rights in contemporary thought, 94n1555
Judd, Karen, 91n949
Judeo-Romance linguistics, 90n1034
Judge, Harry, 90n535
Judicial staff dir, 1990, 91n576
Judicial staff dir, 1993, 94n736
Julia Kristeva, 91n917
Julie Andrews: a bio-bibliog, 90n1322
Juliussen, Egil, 94n1909
Juliussen, Karen Petska, 94n1909
Jull, P., 90n819
Jumonville, Florence M., 90n629
Jung, Heidrun, 94n1072
Jung lexicon, 92n758
Jung, Udo O. H., 94n1072
Junge, Hans-Dieter, 93n1671
Junge, H.-D., 93n1597
Junior ency of Canada, 91n30
Junior high school lib cat, 6th ed, 91n650
Juniorplots 4, 94n1192
Jurgen Habermas (II): a bibliog, 92n1392
Jussi Bjorling phonography, 2d ed, 94n1354
Justice, Keith L., 90n1110

Kabdebo, Thomas, 94n1073
Kadetsky, Jill, 92n58
Kadrey, Richard, 94n76
Kael index, 94n1463
Kagan, Alfred, 91n91
Kahan, Vilem, 92n729
Kahn, Ada P., 90n744, 91n1661, 93n884
Kahn, Ahmed S., 93n1697
Kaiser index to black resources, 1948-86, 93n425
Kaiser, John R., 91n1210, 91n1212
Kajdas, C., 92n1625
Kalck, Pierre, 93n113, 94n97
Kale, Herbert W., II, 91n1564
Kalfatovic, Martin R., 93n163
Kalicki, Anne C., 90n789
Kalk, Suzanne, 92n928
Kalley, Jacqueline A., 90n111, 92n89
Kallmann, Helmut, 94n1312
Kalnay, Alanna, 93n16
Kamp, Jim, 94n962
Kandiuk, Mary, 92n1224
Kane, Joseph Nathan, 90n479, 90n706, 94n499
Kaneko, Anne, 90n1488
Kanellos, Nicolas, 90n1124, 94n412
Kangaroo's comments & wallaby's words, 90n1026
Kanikova, S. I., 94n1281
Kanner, Barbara, 90n860, 91n915
Kansas governors, 91n495
Kansas hist, 93n513
Kantha, Sachi Sri, 92n1649

Kantor, Mattis, 91n406
Kantowicz, Edward R., 90n490
Kapel, David E., 93n330
Kapel, Marilyn B., 93n330
Kaplan, Harold I., 93n1649
Kaplan, Justin, 93n89
Kaplan, Mike, 90n1312, 90n1313
Kapp, Marshall B., 94n868
Karageorgiou, Dimitris, 93n1376
Karamitsanis, Aphrodite, 92n424, 93n492
Karel Husa: a bio-bibliog, 92n1267
Kari, James M., 92n1063
Karkhanis, Sharad, 90n378
Karlowich, Robert A., 91n113, 91n628
Karney, Robyn, 90n1348, 94n1431
Karolides, Melissa, 94n843
Karolides, Nicholas J., 92n820, 94n843
Karp, Rashelle S., 90n158, 92n1129
Karren, Howard, 92n1341
Karst, Kenneth L., 92n684, 93n576
Karsten, Eileen, 94n1442
Kasic, Christopher, 93n68, 94n165
Kasraie, Asadollah, 93n1090
Kasraie, Hassan, 93n1090
Kass, Frederic I., 94n1846
Kastenbaum, Beatrice, 90n795
Kastenbaum, Robert, 90n795
Kaster, Joseph, 92n1324
Katchmer, George A., 93n1336
Kate Chopin companion, 90n1202
Katherine Anne Porter: an annot bibliog, 92n1179
Katlan, Alexander W., 93n1027
Kato, Pamela, 92n751
Katona, Steven, 91n1595
Katona, Steven K., 94n1737
Katz, Bernard S., 90n163, 93n240
Katz, Bill, 90n78, 90n594, 93n84, 93n85
Katz, Linda Sobel, 94n2004
Katz, Linda Sternberg, 90n78, 92n1243, 93n84, 93n85
Katz, William, 92n1243
Kaufman, Kenn, 91n1566
Kaufman, Stephen A., 94n1071
Kaufman, Thomas G., 91n1298
Kaufmann, Walter, 92n1253
Kaur, Amarjit, 94n118
Kavass, Igor I., 92n525, 92n1669, 93n562, 93n759, 94n548, 94n760
Kay, Ann, 91n31
Kay, David C., 93n1687
Kay, Ernest, 90n32, 90n35, 91n16, 94n958, 94n963, 94n1147
Kay, Ian, 94n676
Kay, Lily E., 91n1514
Kay, Richard, 94n1662
Kayar Co., Inc., 92n797
Kaylor, Noel Harold, 94n1487
Kazhdan, Alexander P., 92n510
Kazlauskas, Edward John, 91n631
Kear, Lynn, 94n1413
Kearley, Timothy, 91n563
Keck, George R., 91n1278
Keeble, N. H., 90n1169
Keech, Susan, 90n1737
Keenan, Linda, 93n661
Keeping score: film & TV music, 1980-88, 93n1271
Kehde, Ned, 90n1461, 92n66, 93n823
Kehoe, Timothy, 93n1039
Keienburg, Wolf, 91n1593
Keith, Stuart, 90n1528
Keller, Dean H., 91n1126
Keller, Hans J., 93n1775
Keller, Harald, 90n1574
Keller, Michael A., 90n1213
Keller, Peter C., 94n1955
Kellman, Steven G., 92n1163
Kellner, Bruce, 92n1184

Kelly, Aidan, 94n1517
Kelly, Aidan A., 91n1451
Kelly, Alan, 90n1226, 91n1257
Kelly, Anthony, 91n1628
Kelly, Bernice M., 94n1040
Kelly, Charles, 90n271
Kelly, David H., 90n861
Kelly, Gail P., 90n861, 90n876
Kelly, Joyce, 94n481
Kelly, Melody S., 93n668
Kelly's business dir 1992, 94n265
Kelsey-Wood, Dennis, 91n1576
Kemp, Donna R., 90n259
Kemp, Louis Ward, 91n59
Kemp, Peter, 93n842
Kemp, Thomas Jay, 91n1656
Kempen-van Dommelen, G. J. M., 91n1490
Kendall, Alan, 90n1231, 94n1394
Kennedy, DayAnn M., 91n1455, 91n1456
Kennedy, Frances H., 91n508
Kennedy, Thomas E., 94n1230
Kennedy, William H., 91n79
Kennemer, Phyllis K., 94n694
Kenneth Roberts: the man & his works, 91n1172
Kensley, Brian, 91n1600
Kent, Allen, 90n1711, 90n1712, 92n1707, 94n601, 94n602, 94n603, 94n604, 94n605, 94n606, 94n607, 94n608, 94n1896, 94n1897, 94n1898, 94n1899
Kent, Christopher, 94n1327
Kent, Diana, 91n1650
Kent, James A., 94n1770
Kent, Kathleen L., 94n987
Kentucky ency, 93n109
Kenworthy, James L., 91n564
Kepler, Angela Key, 92n1553
Kepos, Paula, 92n1110, 94n231, 94n232
Kepple, Robert J., 93n1400
Kerber, Jordan E., 92n449
Kerby, Jody L., 91n1687, 93n1650
Kern, Robert W., 91n116
Kernfeld, Barry, 90n1288, 92n1307
Kerr, Donald, 91n516
Kerr, Joan, 94n1041
Kerr, Mary Lee, 90n725, 92n1782
Kerrod, Robin, 90n1519, 90n1520, 92n1456, 93n1530, 93n1703
Kersey, Ethel M., 90n868
Kersten, Dorothy B., 91n625
Kerstitch, Alex, 90n1561
Kesler, C. Peter, 90n690
Kessinger, Roger A., 91n587, 91n588
Kessler, Jack, 93n626
Kessler, Terri, 93n978
Kestenbaum, Ray, 90n890
Kett, Joseph F., 90n304, 94n305
Key ideas in human thought, 94n1497
Key indicators of county growth 1970-2010, 1990 ed, 91n904
Key issues in constitutional hist, 90n501
Key, Jack D., 90n1653
Key works to the fauna & flora of the British Isles & NW Europe, 5th ed, 90n1495
Keyfitz, Natham, 92n844
Keyguide to info sources in ...
   aquaculture, 90n1450
   artificial intelligence/expert systems, 91n1715
   museum studies, 91n60
   online & CD-ROM database searching, 92n590
   paramedical scis, 92n1637
   pharmacy, 90n1703
   public interest law, 92n520
   remote sensing, 90n1590
   vet medicine, 91n1510
Keys Publishing Company Limited, 90n1039
Keys to the insects of the European part of the USSR, v.3, pt.2, 90n1554

Keyser, Daniel J., 93n337, 93n338
Keyworth, C. L., 92n361
Khan, Muhammad Akram, 91n133
Khoee, Debbie, 91n1484
Khorana, Meena, 93n1126
Kiang, Yi-seng, 91n571
Kibbee, Josephine Z., 92n369
Kidd, Charles, 92n395
Kidd, Jane, 91n1577
Kidron, Michael, 93n475
Kid's address bk, 94n53
Kids' catalog collection, 92n181
Kids' favorite bks, 94n1174
Kiehl, Erich H., 90n1397
Kiel, Dyke, 90n1238
Kiell, Norman, 91n786
Kier, Kathleen E., 91n1166
Kies, Cosette, 93n1156
Kiger, Joseph C., 91n869, 94n36
Killens, Camille A., 94n345
Killens, Camille Ann, 92n566
Killingray, David, 92n704
Killpatrick, Frances, 90n760
Killpatrick, James, 90n760
Kilpatrick, Thomas L., 92n596
Kim, David U., 90n645, 92n328
Kim, Douglas M., 92n328
Kim, Hyung-chan, 90n474
Kim, Mi Ja, 90n1694
Kim, Wesley, 94n194
Kimball, Debi, 94n2013
Kimball, Richard L., 90n1038
Kimball, Stanley B, 90n435
Kimbel, Bobby Ellen, 90n1133, 91n1156, 92n1164
Kimber, John, 90n1149
Kimberley, Robert, 92n1714
Kimerling, L. C., 93n1592
Kimes, Beverly Rae, 90n1809
Kimmel, Barbara Brooks, 91n780
Kimmel, Sue, 92n1121
Kimmich, Christoph M., 92n712
Kinch, J. C. B., 90n1156
Kinch, M. B., 90n1149
Kind words: a thesaurus, rev ed, 91n1058
Kindscher, Kelly, 93n1514
Kiner, Larry F., 92n1295, 92n1331, 93n1277, 94n1365
King, Charles W., 91n1279
King, Clive, 90n1492
King, H. G. R., 90n115
King, James J., 94n1998
King, Kamla J., 93n582, 94n748
King, Martha P., 93n594
King, R. C., 92n1521
King, Sally, 90n276
Kingfisher children's ency, 94n37
Kingfisher illus ency of animals, 94n1687
Kingfisher ref atlas, 94n451
Kingfisher sci ency, 94n1568
Kings & queens of England & Great Britain, 91n523
Kingsbury, Stewart A., 93n1299
Kingston, Mike, 93n111
Kinkley, Jeffrey, 94n1279
Kinloch, Adria, 92n156
Kinnaman, William, 93n919
Kinneavy, Gerald Byron, 91n1192
Kinnell, Susan K., 90n537
Kinoshita, Sumie, 90n203, 94n180, 94n181, 94n192
Kinzey, Bert, 94n699
Kipfer, Barbara Ann, 93n1076
Kipps, Harriet Clyde, 92n829
Kirby, Debra M., 92n622, 93n373, 93n377, 94n650
Kirby, Ronald F., 91n814, 91n815, 92n793
Kirby's gd to fitness & motor performance tests, 92n793
Kirk, Mary E., 93n388
Kirk, Tim, 90n723, 93n766

Kirkbride, Joseph H., Jr., 94n1638
Kirkeby, Willy A., 90n1052
Kirkendall, Richard S., 91n505
Kirk-Green, A. H. M., 92n713
Kirkman, L. Katherine, 91n1542
Kirk-Othmer ency of chemical tech, 4th ed, v.7, 94n1768
Kirkpatrick, Betty, 90n995, 92n1016, 94n1098
Kirkpatrick, D. L., 92n1192
Kirkpatrick, Zoe Merriman, 94n1655
Kirsch, George B., 94n826
Kirshon, John W., 91n498
Kirwin, W. J., 92n1051
Kissane, Sharon F. Mrotek, 93n44
Kissling, Mark, 91n945
Kister, Kenneth F., 93n1048
Kister's best dicts for adults & young people, 93n1048
Kits, games & manipulatives for the elementary school classroom, 94n378
Kitty Hawk to NASA, 92n1794
Kivisto, Peter, 90n84
Klapthor, Margaret Brown, 91n494
Klarner, Anne, 91n1714
Kleber, John E., 93n109
Klee as in clay, 94n982
Kleiman, Carol, 93n311
Kleiman, Rhonda H., 90n1462
Klein, Barry, 92n252, 93n1673, 94n293
Klein, Barry T., 91n398, 92n275, 94n419
Klein, Charna, 91n256
Klein, Gerald, 94n207
Klein, Michael L., 94n1539
Kleinbauer, W. Eugene, 94n1054
Kleiner, Diane E. E., 94n1066
Klemanski, John S., 91n718
Klemme, Paul T., 94n1328
Klemp, P. J., 90n1182
Kleper, Michael L., 91n667
Klepper, Robert F., 90n1264, 90n1265
Klett, Dwight A., 94n1288
Klimasauskas, Casimir C., 90n1708
Kline, Ronald R., 91n1614
Kline, Victoria, 92n1246
Kloesel, Christian J. W., 91n1194
Kloos, Helmut, 92n1632
Klossowski, Andrzej, 92n637
Kluepfel, Brian, 93n1012
Knaphus, G., 90n1502
Knapp, Thomas R., 91n1706
Kneifl, Bruce M., 91n1826
Knight, David, 90n1436
Knight, Denise D., 94n1226
Knopf, Kenyon A., 93n181
Knowles, Owen, 93n1207
Knowlton, Jack, 90n419
Knox, Claire E., 92n1167
Knox, Kathleen E., 91n913
Kobylka, Joseph F., 93n566
Kocybala, Arcadia, 91n478
Kodansha's romanized Japanese-English dict, 94n1119
Koehl, Stuart, 92n647
Koek, Karin E., 90n59, 90n60, 93n287
Koen, Willie, 94n1117
Koenigsberg, Ruth, 92n1654
Koeppe, Richard P., 90n303
Kofmel, Kim G., 90n164, 90n231
Kogon, Marilyn, 94n617
Kohl, Herbert, 93n1060
Kohlenberger, John R., III, 91n1427, 92n1442
Kohn, George C., 90n492, 92n508
Kohut, David R., 91n1242
Koike, Hideo, 90n1448
Kokernak, Jane, 93n675
Kolatch, Alfred J., 90n403, 92n398
Kolin, Philip C., 90n1366, 93n1212
Kondratieff, B. C., 93n1568

Kooyman, Mary, 93n128
Koprowicz, Constance L., 90n305
Korch, Rick, 92n795
Korean, 94n1122
Korean war almanac, 92n660
Kornick, Rebecca Hodell, 92n1291
Kornicki, Peter, 94n113
Korros, Alexandra Shecket, 90n379
Korsch, Boris, 91n407, 94n1503
Korsmeyer, Pamela, 91n107
Korzak, Gunter, 91n1629
Koshgarian, Richard, 94n1347
Kosofsky, Rita N., 92n1177
Koszegi, Michael A., 93n1401, 94n1552
Kotz, Samuel, 91n898
Kouri, Mary K., 92n807
Kovacs, Deborah, 94n1193
Kovacs, Diane, 93n72
Kovacs, Ruth, 90n823, 91n317, 91n931, 92n287, 92n573, 92n827, 92n865, 93n880, 93n881, 93n1411, 94n618
Kraeuter, David W., 93n983, 94n1012
Kramer, A. L. N., Sr., 94n1117
Kramer, Jack, 93n1486
Kramer, Jack J., 90n751, 92n760, 93n803
Kramer, Jonathan D., 90n1274
Krane, Willibald, 91n1584
Krantz, Les, 90n942, 90n970
Kraskow, Tina, 93n924
Krause, Chester L., 91n984
Krause, Jerry V., 91n831
Krausse, Gerald H., 90n118
Krausse, Sylvia C. Engelen, 90n118
Krautz, Alfred, 92n1355
Kravitz, Walter, 94n729
Kreamer, Jean Thibodeaux, 92n917
Kreissman, Bern, 92n1789
Kreissman, Bernard, 90n587, 90n588
Kreitner, Kenneth, 91n1246
Kremer, John, 92n638
Kren, Claudia, 91n1763
Kresheck, Janet, 90n1683
Kress, W. John, 92n1535
Kreutzer, W. Brian, 92n672
Krevisky, Joseph, 94n1087
Krewson, Margrit B., 92n352
Kricher, John C., 91n1791, 93n1574, 94n1681
Krieger, Joel, 94n717
Krieger, Tillie, 91n626
Krismann, Carol, 92n233
Kristeller, Paul Oskar, 94n978
Krive, Sarah, 93n1230
Krochalis, Jeanne, 94n29
Kroeger, David, 94n163
Kroeger, Karl, 92n1268
Kroger, Manfred, 93n1475
Krogh, Suzanne Lowell, 93n351
Krogsgaard, Michael, 92n1312
Krohn, Barbara Ehrenwald, 93n1791
Krol, John, 90n1740, 91n61, 93n978, 93n1698, 94n1922
Kronick, David A., 93n1463
Kroschwitz, Jacqueline I., 92n1596
Krstovic, Jelena O., 92n1133, 92n1134
Kruh, David, 94n477
Kruh, Louis, 94n477
Kruk, Leonard, 93n324
Krummel, D. W., 94n1307
Krupa, James J., 90n1565
Kruschke, Earl R., 92n683, 92n1762
Kruse, Janice, 91n303
Kruse, Lenelis, 90n1789
Kruzel, Joseph, 92n652
Ku Klux Klan: an ency, 92n730
Kuhn, Sherman M., 92n1037
Kuipers, B. R., 94n1744
Kuipers, Barbara J., 92n370

Kulich, Jindra, 91n377, 94n391
Kulikowski, Mark, 90n1305
Kuman, Arthur Jr., 93n304
Kuper, Jessica, 90n166
Kuperus, Bart, 93n999
Kurath, Hans, 92n1037
Kurds: a concise hndbk, 93n165
Kurdylo, Kevin Michael, 91n865
Kurian, George, 94n459
Kurian, George Thomas, 90n128, 90n132, 90n569, 91n85, 92n509, 93n137
Kurkowski, David C., 92n671
Kurland, Richard T., 90n563
Kurmann, Joseph A., 93n1475
Kurtz, Edwin B., 93n1598
Kurzweil, Arthur, 92n384
Kushner, Michael G., 94n271
Kutzner, Patricia L., 92n830
KWIC concordance to Samuel Beckett's Murphy, 91n1238
KWIC concordance to Thomas Hardy's Tess of the D'Urbervilles, 90n1180
Kyiv, Ksana, 93n1082

La Cour, Donna Ward, 90n966
La Point, Velma, 90n833
LaBlanc, Michael, 90n1221
LaBlanc, Michael L., 90n33, 93n426, 93n1245
Labor & industrial relations journals & serials, 90n264
Labor conflict in the US, 92n215
Laboratory test hndbk, 2d ed, 91n1678
Labour & population programme, 93n299
Labour force stats 1970-90, 94n235
Labour info, 92n212
Lacasa, Jaime, 92n355
Lachman, Marvin, 94n1231
Lachmann, Richard, 93n849
Lacoff, Cheryl Klein, 94n798, 94n815
Lacy, Charles, 93n1665
Lacy, Norris J., 92n1190
Lacy, Robin Thurlow, 92n1380
LaFrance, David G., 94n682
LaFreniere, Barbara Brumm, 92n442
LaFreniere, Edward N., 92n442
Lagua, Rosalinda T., 92n1485
Lahti, N. E., 90n956
Laine, Claude, 94n1916
Laing, Dave, 90n1294, 91n1304
Lainhart, Ann S., 93n899
Laird, Betty A., 90n720
Laird, Roy D., 90n720
Lake, Sara, 90n711
Lakos, Amos, 90n726, 92n551
Lamar, William W., 90n1564
Lamb, Andrew, 90n1365
Lamb, Annette C., 93n344
Lamb, Connie, 92n1161
Lamba, Navneet, 91n1453
Lambert, David, 93n1531, 94n1960
Lambert, Jean L. F., 93n607
Lambert, Mark, 93n1780
Lambrechts, Eric, 93n1013
Lamme, Linda Leonard, 93n351
Lanasa, Philip J., III, 94n1166
Lancashire, Ian, 90n884, 92n880
Lance, Leonard L., 93n1665
Land use A-Z, 92n1473
Landau, Elaine, 92n1539
Landay, Eugene, 91n1651
Landgraf, Mark J., 94n2028
Landis, Dennis Channing, 90n488
Landman's ency, 3d ed, 90n1782
Landmark yellow pages, 91n1028
Landry, Christine P., 91n1687, 93n1650
Lands & peoples, 90n420

Landsberg, Michele, 92n1118
Lane, Jane-Erik, 93n727
Lane, Leonard G., 92n1021
Lane, Susan, 93n977
Lang, Jovian P., 90n1408, 93n17
Lang, Mabel L, 92n503
Langbart, David A., 94n752
Lange's hndbk of chemistry, 14th ed, 93n1716
Langford, Jeffrey, 90n1247
Langford, Michael, 92n961
Langhans, Edward A., 92n1378, 92n1379
Langley, Winston E., 93n615
Langlois, Denise, 93n252
Langlois, Jennifer, 94n645
Langman, Larry, 90n1327, 91n1379, 92n912, 94n1443
Langston Hughes: a bio-bibliog, 91n1164
Language of ...
 biotech, 90n1597
 computer publishing, 91n659
 real estate, 3d ed, 90n295
 real estate appraisal, 92n261
 sadomasochism, 91n1066
 sex, 93n883
 the Constitution, 93n593
 visual effects, 94n1433
Langworth, Richard M., 90n1810
Lanham, Richard A., 93n1071
Lanier-Graham, Susan D., 93n1759
Lankford, Mary D., 93n399
Lansche, Jerry, 90n768
Lantzy, M. Louise, 93n394
Lanzer, Elizabeth L., 90n145
Laos, 93n127
LaQuey, Tracy L., 92n1715
Large, J. A., 92n1716, 92n1717
Larkin, Colin, 94n1363
Larkin, Gregory V., 91n91
Larkin, Kay, 94n1982
Larkin, Robert P., 94n465
Larkins, William T., 90n667
Larousse ency of precious gems, 93n1725
Larousse gardens & gardening, 91n1504
Larry Eigner: a bibliog of his works, 90n1138
Larson, Kelli A., 92n1172
Larson, Olaf F., 93n846
Larue, C. Steven, 94n1355
LaRue, Jan, 90n1275
LaRue, Robert D., Jr., 90n685
Laser video disc companion, updated ed, 93n997
Laserdisc film gd, 1993-1994 ed, 94n1429
Laskin, David, 91n432
Laskin, Susan L., 91n516
Lass, Abraham H., 92n878
Last, Brian, 91n1180
Last, Cynthia G., 94n1845
Last lines, 92n1246
Last word on making money, 90n219
Late achievers, 93n43
Late 19th century US army, 1865-98, 92n663
Late Victorian & Edwardian writers, 1890-1914, 93n1194
Latest intelligence, 92n646
Latham, Alison, 90n1230
Latham, David, 92n1207
Latham, Robert, 90n1111, 93n1158
Latham, Roy, 93n1688
Latham, Sheila, 92n577, 92n1207
Latin America: a pol dict, 94n784
Latin America & the Caribbean: a critical gd to research sources, 93n148
Latin America, 1983-87, 90n137
Latin America today, rev ed, 91n441
Latin American insects & entomology, 94n1727
Latin American Jewish studies, 92n378
Latin American legal abbrevs, 91n557
Latin American Marxism, 92n734

Latin American military hist, 94n682
Latin American revolutionaries, 91n761
Latin American serial pubs available by exchange, 93n633
Latin American short story, 93n1225
Latin American studies, 2d ed, 91n117
Latin American writers, 90n1208
Latinas of the Americas, 90n863
Latino librarianship, 92n618
Latrobe, Kathy Howard, 93n669
Latvian-English, English-Latvian dict, 94n1123
Lau, Jesus, 94n600
Laube, James, 92n1496
Laudati, Despina, 93n319
Lauer, Joseph J., 91n91
Lauer, Kristin O., 91n1175
Laughlin, Jeannine L., 92n318
Laughlin, Mildred Knight, 93n669
Lauraceae: nectandra, 94n1646
Lauren Bacall: a bio-bibliog, 93n1321
Laurenti, Joseph L., 90n27
Lauriault, Jean, 91n1544
Laurich, Robert Anthony, 92n1680
Lautaret, Ronald, 90n97
Lauther, Howard, 93n1051
Lauther's complete punctuation thesaurus of the English lang, 93n1051
LaVeck, James, 91n379
Lavin, Michael R., 93n209
LaVoie, Roland, 90n929
Law & bus dir of ...
  bankruptcy attorneys 1990, 91n577
  corporate counsel 1990-91, 91n578
  litigation attorneys 1990, 91n579
Law & legal info dir, 5th ed, 90n552
Law & legal info dir, 6th ed, 92n543
Law bk news, 90n539
Law bks in print 1990, 93n570
Law dict, 3d ed, 92n531
Law firms yellow bk, v.2, no.1, 93n584
Law for the layman, 92n522
Law, Jonathan, 94n977
Law lib ref shelf, 90n541
Law lib ref shelf, 2d ed, 93n572
Law lib systems dir, 94n654
Law of war & neutrality, 90n540
Lawless, Robert, 91n121
Lawmen in scarlet, 91n559
Lawrance, Alan, 93n522
Lawrence, Christine C., 92n694
Lawrence, Eleanor, 90n1479
Lawrence, Steven, 94n896
Lawrie, T. D. Veitch, 90n1685
Laws, Edward R., Jr., 92n1783
Lawson, Edward, 92n563
Lawson, Robert W., 91n1574
Lawyers' & creditors' serv dir, 1989 ed, 90n551
Lawyers' & creditors' serv dir, 1993 ed, 94n563
Lax, Roger, 90n1279
Layman, Richard, 90n1126
Layman's gd to new age & spiritual terms, 94n816
Layton, Robert, 91n1292
Lazarus, John, 91n1299
Lazell, Barry, 91n1325
Lazure, Noel, 90n677, 90n1706, 90n1723, 93n1677
LC romanization tables & cataloging policies, 92n586
Le Page, Jean, 90n1426
Lea, Katherine, 94n385
Leach, Marjorie, 93n1305
Leach, Patricia M., 90n72
Lead detection & abatement dir 1993-94, 94n2005
Leadership, 91n71
Leadership: quotations from the military tradition, 91n681
Leafe, David, 91n1388, 94n1455
Leake, Dorothy VanDyke, 94n1645
Leake, John Benjamin, 94n1645

Learning AIDS, 2d ed, 90n1678
Learning vacations, 6th ed, 91n373
Leary, William M., 93n248
Leatherbarrow, W. J., 91n1247
Leatherwood, Stephen, 93n1571
Le-Ba-Khanh, 92n1093
Le-Ba-Kong, 92n1093
Lebanon, rev ed, 93n166
Leccese, Michael, 92n791
Lechner, Jack, 91n1373
Lecker, Robert, 90n1194, 90n1195
LeCompte, Michelle, 92n222, 94n279
Lectionary of music, 90n1232
Lederberg, Joshua, 94n1636
Lederman, Ellen, 91n334
Lee Baxandall's world gd to nude beaches & recreation, 92n773
Lee, C. C., 94n1789, 94n1941
Lee, George L., 90n480, 91n803, 92n350, 94n404
Lee, John, 92n1803
Lee, Lauren K., 93n667
Lee, Mein-ven, 90n1037
Lee, Ming J., 92n1646
Lee, R. Alton, 92n456
Lee, R. R., 92n1599
Lee, Rohama, 94n1462
Lee, Stuart M., 91n1630
Lee, Thomas H., 93n120
Leeds, Mark, 92n443
Lees, Gene, 94n1372
Leeves, Juliet, 91n640
LeFanu, William, 92n1532
Leff, Leonard J., 90n1349
LeFontaine, Joseph Raymond, 92n929
Legacy of the cat, 91n1578
Legal asst's notebk, 93n595
Legal briefs: a lawyer's quotation bk, 91n593
Legal desk bk 1992, 93n597
Legal glossary of fed statutes, 90n546
Legal gd for lesbian & gay couples, 5th ed, 90n556
Legal issues & older adults, 94n572
Legal looseleafs in print 1990, 91n560
Legal looseleafs in print 1993, 94n567
Legal newsletters in print 1990, 91n561
Legal newsletters in print 1993, 94n568
Legal researcher's desk ref 1990, 91n585
Legal researcher's desk ref 1992, 93n591
Legal resource dir, 94n557
Legal thesaurus, 2d ed, 93n574
Legend & lore of the Americas before 1492, 94n417
Leggatt, Alexander, 90n1183
Legislative staff servs 1988, 90n707
Legislative studies in state educ policy 1976-88, 90n308
Legrand, G., 90n1454
Lehto, Mark R., 91n248
Leiby, Bruce R., 92n1309
Leick, Gwendolyn, 90n974, 92n1323
Leif, Irving P., 90n1138
Leininger, Phillip, 92n1155
Leisure lit, 94n820
Leitch, Jay A., 90n1514
Leitch, Thomas M., 94n1239
Leitch, William C., 91n477
Leiter, Richard A., 94n569
Leiter, Samuel L., 90n1367, 92n1381, 92n1382, 94n1474
Lekisch, Barbara, 92n1789
LeMaster, J. R., 94n1240
LeMay, Harold, 90n1003, 90n1004
Lemke, Robert F., 91n984
Lemmon, David, 90n1361
Lemon-aid new car gd 1992, 93n1781
Lemon-aid used car gd 1992, 93n1782
Lems-Dworkin, Carol, 93n1241
Lenburg, Jeff, 93n1347
Lengenfelder, Helga, 90n624
Lenihan, Ayeliffe A., 93n1620

Lenk, John D., 94n1782, 94n1784
Lenk's digital hndbk, 94n1782
Lennon, Mary Beth, 94n1582
Lennon, Thomas M., 94n1485
Lent, John A., 92n886, 94n990, 94n991
Lentz, Harris M., III, 90n1350
Leo, John R., 90n1161
Leo Spitzer on lang & lit, 93n1046
Leonard, Arthur S., 94n570
Leonard, Margaret, 92n902
Leonard, Mark, 94n1061
Leonard, Michelle, 94n1806
Leonard, Robin D., 92n532
Leong, Carol L. H., 90n601
Leppa, Carol J., 90n877
Lepre, J. P., 92n505
Lerman, Anthony, 90n380
Lerner, Loren R., 92n967
Lerner, Richard M., 92n843
Lerner, Rita G., 92n1747
Lerner, Sid, 90n1003, 90n1004, 94n1095
Les Brown's ency of TV, 3d ed, 93n986
Lesbian & gay almanac & events of 1990, 91n871
Lesbian sources, 94n907
Lesbianism: an annot bibliog & gd to the lit 1976-91, 94n908
Lesce, Tony, 91n599
Lesko, Matthew, 90n708, 91n196, 92n52, 93n210, 94n1809
Lesko's info-power, 91n196
Leslie, John, 93n271
Leslie Stephen's life in letters, 94n1261
Lesniak, James G., 92n1096
Lesser, Enid, 94n582
Lesser-known women, 93n934
Lessiter, Mike, 90n761, 90n762
Lester, DeeGee, 93n516
Lester, Meera, 93n962
Lester, Paula E., 94n306
Lester-Massman, Elli, 93n931
Letitia Baldrige's complete gd to the new manners for the 90s, 91n1335
Let's learn French picture dict, 92n1067
Let's learn German picture dict, 92n1071
Let's learn Italian picture dict, 92n1080
Let's learn Spanish picture dict, 92n1090
Leuchtmann, Horst, 93n1248
Leung, Edwin Pak-wah, 93n523
Leventhal, Bennett L., 92n1673
Levey, Judith S., 90n1019, 92n1046
Levi, Anthony, 93n1221
Levie, Howard S., 90n540
Levin, Shirley, 90n318
Levine, Barbara, 93n342
Levine, Caroline, 93n220
Levine, Jeffrey P., 91n141, 92n161
Levine, John R., 93n1687
Levine, Michael, 91n1305, 93n1760, 94n53
Levine, Nancy D., 94n887
Levine, Paula L., 91n1688
Levine, Robert, 91n1342
Levine, Sumner N., 91n175, 93n220
Levinson, David, 92n334
Levinson, Nadine A., 93n797
Levi-Setti, Riccardo, 94n1961
Levit, Fred, 91n1204
Levy, B. Barry, 92n1464
Levy, Leonard W., 92n684, 93n576
Levy, Richard C., 92n149
Lewell, John, 94n1294
Lewin, Paul, 94n1783
Lewinson-Gilboa, Ayelet, 94n489
Lewis, Andy, 91n197
Lewis, Audrey, 93n13
Lewis, Brad Alan, 94n856
Lewis Carroll's Alice: an annot checklist of the Lovett collection, 91n1199

Lewis, Cindy, 92n315
Lewis, D. S., 94n765, 94n783
Lewis, Edward A., 92n1799
Lewis, Ivor, 93n1070
Lewis, Mary S., 90n1214
Lewis, Richard J., 90n1460
Lewis, Richard J., Sr., 90n1758, 91n1776, 92n1682, 92n1727, 94n1933
Lewis, Robert E., 92n1037
Lewis, Samuel, 90n135
Lewis, Shirley, 90n606
Lewis, Thomas P., 90n1215, 93n1261, 94n1316
Lewis, Tom, 92n1165
Lewy, Arieh, 92n274
Lexical semantics, 93n1092
Lexicographical Centre for Canadian English, University of Victoria, 92n1049
Lexicon of ...
    economic thought, 90n165
    economics, 90n166, 93n181
    tax terminology, 90n548
    the Greek & Roman cities & place names in antiquity ca. 1500 B.C. - ca. A.D. 500, fascicule 1, 94n535
Li, Hong-Chan, 90n817
Li, Marjorie H., 91n509
Li, Peter, 91n509
Li, Tze-chung, 91n76
Li, Xia, 94n1002
Liang, Diana F., 93n1741
Liberation theologies, 92n1398
Liberators & patriots of Latin America, 92n108
Librarian's thesaurus, 91n606
Librarianship & info work worldwide 1991, 93n631
Libraries dir 1991-93, 94n634
Libraries in the UK & the Republic of Ireland 1990, 91n627
Libraries, info centers, & databases in sci & tech, 2d ed, 90n624
Library & info sci annual, v.5, 90n593
Library Assn yrbk 1990, 91n614
Library Assn yrbk 1992, 94n636
Library buildings consultant list, 1991, 92n600
Library computer & tech specialists, 92n594
Library hi tech bibliog, v.3, 90n609
Library hi tech bibliog, v.5, 92n597
Library lit. 18, 90n594
Library lit. 19, 91n613
Library lit. 20, 92n572
Library lit. 21, 94n616
Library literature 1992, 94n621
Library literature [CD-ROM], 93n632
Library, media, & archival preservation glossary, 93n663
Library of Congress: a gd to genealogical & histl research, 91n418
Library of Congress classification class KJ-KKZ: law of Europe, 91n621
Library of Congress classification class KK-KKC, 91n622
Library of Congress classification class KL-KWX, 94n625
Library of Congress classification class Z, 92n579
Library of Congress, Subject Cataloging Division, 90n602
Library of Congress subject headings, 12th ed, 90n602
Library pers 1993, 94n622
Library personnel consultants list, 92n601
Library serv to children, 93n665
Library servs for off-campus & distance educ, 92n577
Library systems: a buyer's gd, 2d ed, 91n640
Library use, 2d ed, 93n804
Library-Anthropology Resource Group (LARG), 92n337
LiBretto, Ellen V., 91n365
Lichty, Robert, 92n1804
Lidgren, Karen, 92n260
Lieberman, Jethro K., 94n571
Lieberman-Nissen, Karen, 92n1674
Lien, Jon, 91n1595
Liesner, Thelma, 91n158
Lieutenant-governors of the NW Territories & Alta. 1876-1991, 93n765

Life from death, 90n1677
Lifetime ency of natural remedies, 94n1826
Lifshin, Eric, 94n1795
Light, Nicholas, 91n1485
Lightbody, Andy, 91n689, 91n711
Lighthall, Lynne, 93n643, 94n617
Lighting design on Broadway, 93n1383
Lignor, Amy, 93n194, 93n862
Lilienthal, Nancy, 93n1761
Lima, Carolyn W., 90n1082, 94n1176
Lima, John A., 90n1082, 94n1176
Limb, Peter, 94n103
Limbacher, James L., 93n1271, 93n1358
Limburg, Peter R., 91n1340
Limca bk of records 1991, 93n1310
Linam, Shawn L., 90n1595
Lincoln as a lawyer, 92n526
Lindemann, Erika, 91n1043
Lindfors, Bernth, 90n1190, 93n1110, 94n1148
Lindquist, Richard K., 94n1624
Lindsay, Alexander, 94n1246
Lindsay, Mary P., 91n854
Lineback, Richard H., 91n1406, 91n1407, 93n1397, 94n1498
Lineman's & cableman's hndbk, 8th ed, 93n1598
Lines, Clifford, 91n159
Linfield, Jordan L., 94n1087
Ling, Sum Ngai, 94n110
Linguistic atlas of the gulf states, v.3, 91n1064
Linguistics: a gd to the ref lit, 92n1007
Linguistics ency, 93n1052
Liniger-Goumaz, Max, 90n108
Linscott's dir of immunological & biological reagents, 7th ed, 94n1875
Linton register, 1990-91, 91n247
Linton, Thomas, 94n275
Linton trainer's resource dir, 2d ed, 94n275
Lionel Book Committee, Train Collectors Association, 91n990
Lionel trains: standard of the world, 1900-43, 2d ed, 91n990
Lionel Trilling: an annot bibliog, 94n1239
Lipinski, Kathleen A., 94n1601
Lipinski, Robert A., 94n1601
Lipkin, Midge, 91n350, 92n319
Lippman, Thomas W., 91n950
Lippy, Charles H., 90n1380
Lipsitz, Edmond Y., 92n379
Liptak, Karen, 92n362, 92n363
Lipton, Gladys C., 90n1044, 90n1047, 90n1058
Lisa Birnbach's new & improved college bk, 91n323
Lissauer, Robert, 92n1296
Lissauer's ency of popular music in America, 92n1296
List of authorized customs offices for Community transit/common transit operations, 92n253
List of emigrants from England to America, 1682-92, 90n392
Listen to the music, 90n1274
Listeners' gd to medieval English, 90n991
Listener's musical companion, new ed, 93n1251
Listening to the Beatles, v.1, 92n1314
Liston, Linda L., 92n1735
Liszka, Thomas R., 93n949
Literacy/illiteracy in the world, 91n356
Literary agents of N America, 4th ed, 92n896
Literary exile in the 20th century, 92n1098
Literary lives of Jesus, 90n1064
Literary mss at the Natl Lib of Canada, 2d ed, 91n1225
Literary market place 1990, 90n638
Literary market place 1991, 92n639
Literary market place 1994, 94n668
Literary research gd, 91n1097
Literary research gd, 2d ed, 94n1139
Literary-critical approaches to the Bible, 93n1430
Literature activity bks, 94n1197
Literature & film: an annot bibliog 1978-88, 94n1143
Literature criticism from 1400 to 1800, v.13, 91n1186
Literature criticism from 1400 to 1800, v.15, 92n1107
Literature for young people on war & peace, 90n1081

Literature gd to the hospitality industry, 91n231
Literature of ...
   agricultural engineering, 94n1754
   delight, 94n1169
   music bibliog, 94n1307
   the Great Lakes region, 93n1165
   the nonprofit sector, 90n804
   the nonprofit sector, v.2, 91n865
Literature teacher's bk of lists, 94n1142
Literature-based moral educ, 93n351
Lithuanian Jewish communities, 92n489
Litigation servs resource dir, 92n545
Little black bk of business words, 93n186
Little, Karen R., 92n1269
Littlefield, Carroll D., 92n1564
Littler, Dian Scullion, 90n1505
Litz, A. Walton, 92n1151, 92n1156, 92n1158
Liu, Gongxian, 94n1634
Liungman, Carl G., 93n1041
Livable cities almanac, 93n920
Livesey, Anthony, 90n658
Living with low vision, 94n880
Living with low vision, 2d ed, 91n855
Livingston, Carole Rose, 92n1220
Livo, Norma J., 92n1316
Lizards of the world, 90n1568
Lloyd Alexander: a bio-bibliog, 92n1124
Lobb, Michael L., 90n824
Lobban, Marjorie, 94n906
Lobban, Richard A., Jr., 94n105
Lobenstine, Joy C., 92n808
Local hist & genealogy resources of the Calif. State Lib, rev ed, 92n391
Local hists of Ont. municipalities 1977-87, 91n514
Location photographer's handbk, 91n1000
Location register of 20th-century English literary mss & letters, 90n1168
Lochar, Ruth, 92n623
Locked room murders & other impossible crimes, 93n1150
Locust neurobiology, 93n1566
Loeffelbein, Robert L., 94n827
Loertscher, David V., 92n1130, 93n1144
Loewenstein, C. Jared, 94n1300
Lofland, John, 92n751
Logie, Gordon, 91n909
Lohr, Paul, 91n965
Loiry, William S., 91n272, 92n150, 92n254
Loke, Wing Hong, 91n795
Lomask, Milton, 90n531
Lombardi, Donald P., 91n1764
Lomeli, Francisco A., 90n1123
Lonard, Robert I., 94n1665
London bibliog of the social scis, 24th suppl., 1989, v.47, 91n77
London gd, 91n469
London intl atlas of AIDS, 94n1854
London, Joy, 93n600
London stage 1930-39, 92n1388
London stage 1940-49, 93n1386
London stage 1950-59, 94n1469
Long, Christopher, 94n206
Long, James W., 92n1695
Long, Kim, 90n228, 92n286, 93n352
Long, Mark, 94n1758
Long, Odean, 92n1251
Longley, Dennis, 90n612, 93n315, 94n1900
Longman dict of poetic terms, 90n1118
Longman hndbk of world hist since 1914, 93n559
Longman illus dict of food sci, 91n1485
Longman, Tremper, III, 92n1407
Longstaff, Thomas Richmond Willis, 90n1389
Longstreet, Stephen, 91n1317
Looking at ...
   paintings, 94n1061
   photographs, 92n957
   prints, drawings & watercolours, 90n983

Looney, J. Jefferson, 93n357
Loose cannons & red herrings, 90n1007
Lopez, Daniel, 94n1444
Lopez, Elizabeth I., 91n875
Lopez, Guadalupe, 91n601
Lopez, Manual D., 92n1228
Lopez, Victor D., 91n641
LoPucki, Lynn M., 91n577
LoPucki, Reece J., 91n577
Lord Curzon 1859-1925: a bibliog, 92n486
Lord Dunsany: a bibliog, 94n1292
Lord Grenville 1759-1834: a bibliog, 91n760
Lord Lichfield, 94n472
Lord Nelson 1758-1805: a bibliog, 91n522
Lord, Tom, 93n1287, 93n1288, 93n1289, 94n1373, 94n1374
Lorenzini, Jean A., 90n1651
Lorona, Lionel V., 92n109, 94n145
Los Angeles County histl dir, 90n99
Lossky, Nicholas, 92n1416
Lothrop, Gloria Ricci, 90n500
Lotz, Rainer E., 94n1336
Loughney, Katharine, 92n1332
Loughridge, Brendan, 92n1040
Lougy, Robert E., 91n1205
Louis Sullivan in the Art Institute of Chicago, 91n1030
Louise Bogan: a ref source, 92n1167
Louisiana almanac 1992-93, 93n110
Louisiana governors, 91n491
Lounsbury, Warren C., 90n1368, 94n1470
Loux, Steven B., 92n310
Lovas, Paula M., 90n781
Love, Richard A., 90n1756
Lovece, Frank, 93n995
Loveday, John, 93n1630
Lovejoy's college gd, 19th ed, 91n335
Lover, John G., 91n565
Lovett, Charles C., 91n1199, 92n1202
Lovett, Robert W., 92n1202
Lovett, Stephanie B., 91n1199
Loving Journeys gd to adoption, 94n885
Low, Rosemary, 90n1539
Lowe, Ida B., 94n269
Lowe, Rodney, 94n263
Lowenberg, Carlton, 94n1308
Lowenberg, Susan, 94n1254
Lowens, Irving, 91n1291
Lower, Dorothy M., 93n460
Lowery, Charles D., 93n616
Low-fat supermarket, 94n1612
Lowrey, Joan, 94n435
Lowry, Barbara W., 90n248
Lowry, Philip J., 94n834
Low-water flower gardener, 94n1630
Loyn, H. R., 90n534
Lucas, Amy, 90n584
Lucille Lortel: a bio-bibliog, 94n1414
Luckert, Yelena, 93n447
Ludlow, Daniel H., 93n1420
Ludman, Mark D., 92n1681
Ludwig Tieck: an annot gd to research, 94n1288
Luey, Beth, 91n951
Luginbuhl, Christian B., 91n1759
Luis Leal: a bibliog with interpretative & critical essays, 90n1207
Lukas Foss: a bio-bibliog, 92n1271
Lukas, Viktor, 91n1285
Lulat, Y. G-M., 92n745
Luling, Virginia, 93n1099
Lumpkin, Betty S., 94n1920
Lund, Kimberley, 92n29, 94n19
Lung, Rita Gaston, 93n861
Lusis, Andy, 92n790
Lutheran churches in the world, 90n1410
Luttwak, Edward, 92n647
Lutz, James M., 90n279
Lutz, John, 90n73

Lydersen, Aksel L., 94n1769
Lye, Keith, 92n43
Lyle, William M., 91n1684
Lyme disease, 91n1698
Lynch, Mary Jo, 94n613
Lynch, Richard Chigley, 90n1234, 91n1320
Lynn, M. Stuart, 92n599
Lynn, Martha Drexler, 91n1040
Lynn, Ruth Nadelman, 90n1083
Lyons, Len, 91n1318

M St radio dir, 1990 ed, 92n916
Ma, Lien-sheng, 94n121
Macbeth: an annot bibliog, 2d ed, 91n1216
MacDonald, Barrie, 94n1013
Macdonald, Lynne, 91n1228
MacDonald, Margaret Read, 93n1298
MacDonald, Scott B., 94n916
Macey, Samuel L., 93n14
Macfarlane, Peter W., 90n1685
MacGillivray, Scott, 92n1370
MacGregor, Geddes, 91n1414
Machalski, Andrew, 90n1196
Machlis, Paul, 93n1183
Macintosh bible, 4th ed, 94n1910
Macintosh, Rob, 90n717
Macintyre, J. E., 90n1754, 91n1767, 91n1768
Mack, Roy, 94n1633
MacKay, Charles K., 90n1627
MacKay, Ian, 90n992
Mackenzie, Graham, 93n631
Mackenzie, Harry, 92n1295
Mackenzie, Julia, 92n965
Mackenzie, Leslie, 93n192, 93n862, 94n372, 94n883
Mackerras, Colin, 92n94
Mackey, Douglas A., 91n1220
Mackey, Philip English, 92n826
Mackie, Thomas T., 92n677
Mackin, Bill, 90n923
Mackler, Tasha, 93n1152
Macksey, Kenneth, 93n701
Maclachlan, Graham, 93n1751
MacLennan, Mark, 91n445
Macleod, Iseabail, 90n1054, 91n1091
Macmillan animal ency for children, 93n1532
Macmillan bk of fascinating facts, 90n1
Macmillan bk of the marine aquarium, 94n1717
Macmillan children's gd to dinosaurs & other prehistoric animals, 93n1732
Macmillan dict for children, rev ed, 90n1019
Macmillan dict of pol quotations, 94n724
Macmillan dict of quotations, 91n70
Macmillan dir of leading private cos 1989, 90n179
Macmillan ency of computers, 93n1678
Macmillan ency of sci, 92n1456
Macmillan 1st atlas, 93n476
Macmillan 1st dict, 92n1046
Macmillan gd to correspondence study, 3d ed, 90n359
Macmillan gd to correspondence study, 5th ed, 94n359
Macmillan health ency, 94n1803
Macmillan illus ency of birds, 90n1540
Macmillan illus ency of myths & legends, 91n1333
Macmillan picture wordbk, 92n1047
Macmillan school atlas, 3d ed, 93n471
Macmillan small bus hndbk, 90n186
Macmillan treasury of spices & natural flavorings, 90n1457
Macmillan visual dict, 93n1077
Macnaughton, Elizabeth, 90n513
MacNeice, Jill, 91n460
MacNeil, Anne, 93n1249
Macpherson, Gordon, 93n1629
MacPherson, Lillian, 92n853
Macrae, R., 94n1600
Macrocosm USA, 94n74

Macrone, Michael, 91n1213, 92n1026, 94n1396
Macrothesaurus for info processing in the field of economic & social dvlpmt, 93n641
MacWhinney, Brian, 92n269
Maczuga, Janina, 91n935
Madaus, M. Howard, 93n1004
Madden, Jennifer, 93n1125
Madden, Michael, 91n166
Maddex, Diane, 91n1028
Maddux, Cleborne D., 94n380
Made in ...
    the Ives shops, 92n945
    the USA, 1990 ed, 91n197
    the USA Foundation, staff of, 91n197
Madigan, Carol Orsag, 90n1
Madlem, Peter W., 90n201, 92n155
Maehr, David S., 91n1564
Magarian, Karen, 90n1659
Magay, T., 92n1075, 92n1076
Magazines for ...
    children, 2d ed, 93n87
    libs, 6th ed, 90n78
    libs, 7th ed, 93n85
    young people, 2d ed, 93n84
Mageli, Paul D., 93n420
Mager, N. H., 94n1091
Mager, S. K., 94n1091
Maggio, Rosalie, 92n1030, 94n972
Maggiore, Dolores J., 94n908
Magic, witchcraft, & paganism in America, 2d ed, 93n811
Magill, Frank N., 90n1071, 90n1106, 90n1582, 90n1773, 91n549, 91n550, 91n1104, 91n1105, 91n1127, 91n1765, 91n1778, 92n127, 92n1128, 92n1157, 92n1465, 92n1522, 92n1652, 93, 94n1583
Magill's survey of ...
    American lit, 92n1157
    sci: applied sci series, 94n1583
    sci: earth sci series, 91n1778
    sci: life sci series, 92n1522
    sci: physical sci series, 93n1699
    sci: space exploration series, 90n1582
    world lit, 94n1158
Magliozzi, Ronald S., 90n1326
Magnuson, Norris A., 92n1408
Magnusson, Magnus, 92n25
Magosci, Paul Robert, 94n520
Mahajan, S., 93n1592
Mahar, Mary, 90n315, 93n353
Mahe, Catherine M., 94n2023
Mahler, Gregory, 90n718
Mahn, William J., 92n1728
Mahoney, Dennis J., 92n684
Mahoney, Jim, 91n328, 92n297, 93n359, 94n356
Mahoney, William D., 91n1029
Maidment, David R., 94n1953
Mail art, 92n966
Maintaining good health, 90n1647
Maiorana, Gail, 91n285
Maisel, L. Sandy, 92n685
Maisey, John G., 92n1745
Maizlish, Aaron, 90n422
Major authors & illustrators for children & young adults, 94n1187
Major business orgs of E Europe & the Soviet Union, 92n130
Major chemical & petrochemical cos of Europe 1990/91, 92n204
Major cos of ...
    Europe 1991/92, 92n131
    the Arab world 1991/92, 92n133
    the Far East & Australasia 1991/92, 8th ed, v.1, 93n281
Major decisions, 92n301
Major donors 1993, 94n893
Major energy cos of Europe 1993, 94n1977
Major financial insts of continental Europe 1989/90, 91n216
Major league stadiums, 92n781
Major options, 92n299

Major pol events in ...
    Indo-China 1945-90, 92n708
    Iran, Iraq & the Arabian peninsula 1945-90, 92n725
    S Africa 1948-90, 92n706
Major 20th-century writers, 92n1097
Major weeds of the Near East, 92n1547
Makaryk, Irena R., 94n1150
Make it 2, 90n935
Maker, Ragai N., 90n148
Maki, Kathleen E., 93n213
Makinen, Merja, 91n1200
Making a difference college gd, 1993, 94n348
Making a world of difference, 91n926
Makino, Noboru, 94n116
Makinson, Larry, 91n727, 91n750, 93n752
Makosky, Vivian Parker, 92n311
Makower, Joel, 92n177
Malbin, Michael J., 93n754
Malcom, Shirley M., 94n1561
Maldives, 94n119
Malhotra, Nirmal, 93n391
Malinowsky, H. Robert, 90n1417, 92n1452, 92n1678
Malless, Stan, 90n993
Mallet, Catherine M., 91n1827, 93n1783
Mallett, Daryl F., 93n1157, 94n432
Malloy, Merrit, 92n67
Malmkjaer, Kirsten, 93n1052
Malonis, Jane A., 94n969
Malott, Marcia K., 93n956
Malpas, Pamela G., 94n1616
Mamalakis, Markos J., 90n142
Mammal species of the world, 2d ed, 94n1743
Mammals of ...
    Ill., 91n1594
    Okla., 91n1591
    the central Rockies, 94n1741
    the Indomalayan region, 94n1734
    the neotropics, 90n1555
    the neotropics: the S cone, v.2, 93n1570
Mammals: primates, insect eaters & baleen whales, 90n1520
Mammals: the hunters, 90n1521
Mammals: the large plant-eaters, 90n1522
Mammals: the small plant-eaters, 90n1523
Mamola, Claire Zebroski, 90n1206
Mamola, Claire Zebrowski, 94n1295
Man in Lincoln's nose, 91n1396
Man of magic & mystery, 90n1142
Management of correctional insts, 94n804
Management study abroad 1989-91, 90n270
Manager's bk of quotations, 90n269
Manager's desk ref, 90n266
Managing a nation: the microcomputer sftwr cat, 2d ed, 92n672
Manchel, Frank, 92n1340
Mandell, Judy, 93n963
Mange, Maria A., 93n1726
Mangone, Gerard J., 92n1466
Mangone's concise marine almanac, 92n1466
Mangrum, Charles T., II, 90n349, 94n340
Manley, Deborah, 93n558
Man-made catastrophes, 94n467
Mann, Erick J., 92n87
Mann, Susan Garland, 90n1134
Mann, Thomas E., 93n754
Manning, Beverley, 90n879
Manning, Gail B., 92n691
Manning, Matthew, 91n65
Mansdorf, S. Z., 94n1767
Manser, Martin, 90n987
Manser, Martin H, 90n1031
Manser, Martin H., 91n1060
Mansion: a concordance, 90n1140
Manual of ...
    law French, 2d ed, 91n583
    natural therapy, 90n1669
    old English prose, 91n1188

vascular plants of NE US and adjacent Canada, 2d ed, 93n1500
Manufacturers & miners, 90n238
Manufacturing: a historiographical & bibliographical gd, 92n206
Manufacturing USA, 90n242
Manufacturing USA, 2d ed, 93n247
Manuscripts of Flannery O'Connor at Georgia College, 90n1151
Manwaring, John, 92n559
Many names of country people, 90n1444
Mao Zedong: a bibliog, 93n522
Mapp, Edward, 91n1343
Mapping upper Canada 1780-1867, 92n411
Maps contained in the pubs of the American Bibliog, 1639-1819, 90n425
Maps in British pers, pt.1, 91n449
Maran, Stephen P., 93n1704
Marantz, Kenneth, 93n1022
Marantz, Sylvia, 93n1022
Marcaccio, Kathleen Young, 90n1717, 93n1670, 93n1682, 94n1907
Marcel Proust: a ref gd 1950-70, 92n1235
March, Andrew L., 93n15
March, Ivan, 91n1292
Marcheteau, Michel, 93n182
Marck, Jeffrey C., 93n1080
Marco, Guy A., 94n1313
Marcus, James L., Jr., 93n239
Marcuse, Michael J., 92n872
Marder, Stephen, 93n1096
Mares, Michael A., 91n1596
Margaret Atwood: a ref gd, 92n1225
Margaret Thatcher: a bibliog, 94n776
Margen, Sheldon, 94n1602
Margetts, Juliet, 93n298
Margham, J. P., 92n1518
Margolis, Nadia, 91n529
Margulis, Lynn, 91n1515
Marill, Alvin H., 94n1464
Marine atlas of the Hawaiian Islands, 93n466
Marine invertebrates & plants of the living reef, 90n1560
Marine plants of the Caribbean, 90n1505
Marine tech ref bk, 92n1610
Maritime affairs: a world hndbk, 2d ed, 93n1790
Maritime provinces atlas, new ed, 93n472
Maritime servs dir 1989-90, 91n1832
Mark, H. F., 91n1769
Mark, Herman F., 91n1770, 91n1771
Mark Twain ency, 94n1240
Mark Twain's German critical reception, 1875-1986, 90n1156
Markel, Robert, 94n1349
Markert, Lawrence W., 91n1181
Market gd for young writers, 1988-89 ed, 90n899
Market share reporter 1991, 92n255
Market share reporter 1993, 94n193
Marketing made easier, 94n293
Markevitch, Dimitry, 90n1260
Markey, Kay, 91n832
Markovich, Alex, 93n1786
Markowitz, Harvey, 92n368
Marks, Claude, 92n973
Marks of London goldsmiths & silversmiths (c1697-1837), 90n934
Markwell, F. C., 90n393
Marlin, John Tepper, 91n1491, 93n920
Marlor, Clark S., 92n980
Marr, David G., 94n122
Marra, Jean M., 92n60
Marrandette, David G., 92n796
Marriage licensing laws, 91n587
Marriott, F. H. C., 92n847
Marrs, Suzanne, 90n1158
Marsh, Arthur, 93n305
Marsh, Earle, 90n916
Marsh, James H., 91n30
Marshal Tito: a bibliog, 91n537
Marshall Cavendish ency of ... family health, 93n1617

health, 92n1633
personal relationships: human behavior, 92n757
Marshall Cavendish illus ency of discovery & exploration, 92n417
Marshall Cavendish illus hist of popular music, 91n1306
Marshall Cavendish illus hist of the presidents of the US, 92n462
Marshall Cavendish intl wildlife ency, 90n1515
Marshall Cavendish intl wildlife ency, rev ed, 91n1555
Marshall, Donald G., 94n1140
Marshall, James N., 94n154
Marshall, John, 91n1824
Marshall, Sam A., 91n1001
Marshall, William C., 90n739
Marszalek, John F., 93n616
Marten, James, 94n89
Martens, Hans, 94n257
Marth, Del, 93n106
Marth, Martha J., 93n106
Martin, Christine, 93n966
Martin Chuzzlewit: an annot bibliog, 91n1205
Martin, Daniel R., 90n750
Martin, Daniel W., 91n781
Martin, Dolores Moyano, 94n144
Martin, Elizabeth, 93n680
Martin, Elizabeth A., 91n572
Martin, Fenton S., 90n705, 91n566, 93n571
Martin, G. J., 92n414
Martin, Galen R., 92n125
Martin, Geoffrey Thorndike, 92n501
Martin, Graham R., 93n1596
Martin Heidegger, 91n1402
Martin, Helmut, 94n1279
Martin, Laura C., 91n1528, 94n1673
Martin, Len D., 92n1350, 94n1445
Martin, Linda, 91n1363, 91n1395
Martin, Lucille, 92n1697
Martin Luther King, Jr., Papers Project staff, 91n600
Martin, M. Marlene, 91n380
Martin, Phyllis, 92n1031
Martin, Robert, 94n394
Martin, Robert M., 92n1395
Martin, Robert S., 92n261
Martin, Samuel E., 91n1089
Martin, Susan B., 90n61
Martin, Susan Boyles, 92n170
Martin, William C., 90n1496
Martindale, David, 92n918
Martindale-Hubbell bar register 1990, 91n580
Martindale-Hubbell bar register of preeminent lawyers 1993, 94n561
Martindale-Hubbell law dir 1990, 91n581
Martinez, Arthur D., 92n690
Martinez, Joseph G. R., 92n1221, 94n1265, 94n1266
Martinez, Julio A., 91n1230
Martinez, Nancy C., 92n1221, 94n1265, 94n1266
Marting, Diane E., 91n1246
Martin's pocket dict: English-Japanese, Japanese-English, 91n1089
Martin-Smith's official 1948-89/90 baseball card alphabetical cross-reference gd, 91n980
Martis, Kenneth C., 90n687, 94n725
Marty Robbins: fast cars & country music, 92n1304
Marull, Horacio M., 94n552
Marx, Cheryl E., 93n1467
Mary Martin: a bio-bibliog, 92n1357
Mary McCarthy: an annot bibliog, 93n1177
Mason, Antony, 94n452
Mason, Eileen, 94n70
Mason, Francis, 90n1315
Mason, Francis K., 93n699
Mason, Laura, 90n517
Mason, Robert J., 92n1765
Mason, Sally, 90n619
Mass media & the Constitution, 91n940
Mass media bibliog, 3d ed, 92n885
Mass media: Marconi to MTV, 91n934
Mass media sex & adolescent values, 92n883

Mast, Jennifer Arnold, 94n280
Master dict of food & wine, 91n1486
Master index to poetry, 90n1119
Mastering Greek vocabulary, 92n1073
Masterpieces of African-American lit, 93n1164
Masterpieces of Canadian art from the Natl Gallery of Canada, 91n1006
Masterplots 2: drama series, 91n1127
Masterplots 2: juvenile & young adult fiction series, 92n1128
Masterplots 2: nonfiction, 90n1071
Masterplots 2: poetry series, 93n1237
Masters of lens & light, 93n1343
Masters of mystery & detective fiction, 91n1197
Masthay, Carl, 93n1089
Mastro, Joseph P, 90n525
Matacotta, Barbara, 91n846
Materials & strategies for the educ of trainable mentally retarded learners, 91n351
Materials hndbk, 13th ed, 92n1617
Materials research centres, 3d ed, 90n1601
Materials selection deskbk, 92n1612
Maternal & child health legislation: 1991, 93n594
Mathematical bk review index 1800-1940, 93n1738
Mathematical jls, 93n1741
Mathematical scis professional dir, 1989, 90n1772
Mathematical scis professional dir 1993, 94n1967
Mathematics dict, 5th ed, 94n1966
Mathematics illus dict, rev ed, 91n1793
Mather, George A., 94n1513
Matheson, Ed, 91n671
Mathew, Brian, 91n1529
Mathien, Thomas, 90n1372
Matisoff, James A, 90n1050
Matlon, Ronald J., 93n954
Matray, James I., 92n648
Matsuura, Kumiko, 94n792
Matter of fact, v.14-15, 93n910
Matter of taste, 91n1482
Mattera, Philip, 92n205, 93n272
Matthews, Alison, 93n226
Matthews, Andrew, 91n179
Matthews, Catherine J., 91n598
Matthews, Elizabeth W., 90n541, 92n526, 93n572
Matthews, Geoffrey J., 90n409, 90n417
Matthews, Hugoe, 94n1252
Matthews, John R., 92n1684
Matthews, Joseph, 91n845
Matthews list, v.34, no.1, 91n937
Matthews, Peter, 94n1401
Matthews, Rupert, 90n481
Matthias, Margaret, 94n1968
Mattison, Chris, 90n1568, 92n1589
Mattson, Catherine M., 92n409
Mattson, Mark T., 92n343, 92n409, 92n1765, 94n931
Matuz, Roger, 92n1104
Matz, David, 92n772
Matzke, Eric J., 90n930, 91n989
Maunder, W. John, 94n1949
Maureen O'Sullivan: a bio-bibliog, 91n1349
Maureen Stapleton: a bio-bibliog, 94n1418
Maurer, Heinz F. W., 93n1726
Mauritania, 94n101
Mauritius, 93n146
Mawhinney, Christine, 92n1238
Max Horkheimer, 91n80
Max Weber, 90n86
Max Weber: a bio-bibliog, 90n84
Maxfield, Doris Morris, 93n878
Maxwell, Donald W., 93n1165
Maxwell, F. C., 93n461
Maxwell, Grant L., 94n1337
Maxwell, Margaret F., 90n604
May, Charles E., 91n1142
May, George S., 90n235, 91n228
May, Thomas, 92n1391

Maya civilization, 94n541
Mayall, Donald, 92n227
Mayberry, Debra J., 94n739
Mayer, Janice, 90n162
Mayer, Ralph, 93n1025
Mayer, Sigrid, 90n1371
Mayes, J. T., 92n1704
Mayhew, Susan, 93n489
Mayhew-Smith, Peter, 91n470
Maynard, Thane, 94n1738
Maynard's industrial engineering hndbk, 4th ed, 93n1603
Mayne, Alan J., 94n77
Mayne, John W., 93n1740
Maze, Marilyn, 92n227
Maziarz, Daniel, 93n1775
Mazzeno, Laurence W., 91n1195
McAleese, Ray, 90n354
McAlister, Micheal J., 94n1433
McAlpine, Monica E., 92n1199
McArthur, Feri, 93n1054
McArthur, Tom, 93n1054
McAuliffe, Amy, 94n1814
McBride, Bill, 91n668
McBride, Katharine Winters, 90n1135
McBride, William G., 91n366
McBroom's camera bluebk, 1994 ed, 94n1037
McBroom's price gd to modern cameras, 1991 ed, 92n958
McCabe, Gerard B., 90n587, 90n588
McCabe, James Patrick, 90n1405
McCalla, Robert J., 93n472
McCallum, Heather, 94n1476
McCann, Kelly, 93n935
McCarthy, J. Thomas, 92n533
McCarthy's desk ency of intellectual property, 92n533
McCarty, John, 91n1389
McCarty, Willard, 90n884
McCaskie, A. W., 94n1825
McCaslin, Richard B., 94n495
McCauley, Martin, 94n523
McClain, Gary, 93n269
McClean, Andrew, 94n683
McClelland, Averil Evans, 93n926
McClelland, Doug, 91n1357
McCloskey, Donald N., 92n123
McClure, Arthur F., 90n1319
McCombs, Judith, 92n1225
McConkey, Wilfred J., 94n982
McConnell, Charles N., 91n1636
McConnell, Fraiser, 90n150
McCormick, Curtis W., 90n703, 92n134, 93n744
McCormick, Donald, 91n1133
McCormick, Frank, 94n975
McCormick, Regina, 90n423
McCoy, Judy, 94n1375
McCoy, Sondra Van Meter, 90n427
McCoy, William, 91n1326
McCready, Sam, 94n1414
McCreight, Tim, 93n1008
McCrickard, Eleanor, 92n1263
McCue, Helga, 90n1092
McCue, Helga P., 90n1091, 92n1126
McCullough, Kathleen, 90n1120
McCullough, Prudence, 91n198, 94n203
McCullough, Rita I., 92n856
McCutcheon, Marc, 93n1072, 94n511
McDonald, Arlys L., 90n1248
McDonald, Arthur W., 90n1355
McDonald, Ben, 93n525
McDonald, Charles W., 94n2025
McDonald, Elvin, 94n1617
McDonald, Jiggs, 90n775
McDonald, P. C., 94n1964
McDonnell Douglas aircraft since 1920, 90n1802
McDonough, John E., 93n765
McDougall, D. Blake, 93n765

McDowell, Patricia, 91n401
McElmeel, Sharron L., 91n651, 93n1142, 94n1188
McElrath, Joseph R., Jr., 93n1180
McFarlan, Donald, 90n1308, 91n1337
McFarland, Gertrude K., 90n1694
McGarry, Dorothy, 90n603
McGeary, Mitchell, 91n1326
McGee, Denis C., 94n1595
McGee, Gary B., 90n1407
McGee, Mark Thomas, 90n1351, 91n1369
McGee, Robert W., 94n153
McGillivray, Alice V., 92n696, 94n754, 94n755, 94n756
McGiverin, Rolland H., 91n292
McGovern, Carolyn, 92n702
McGovern, Gail, 91n644
McGovern, Roger, 90n778
McGowen, John, 92n956
McGrath, Daniel F., 91n981, 94n1025
McGraw-Hill circuit ency & troubleshooting gd, v.1, 94n1784
McGraw-Hill concise ency of sci & tech, 2d ed, 90n1427
McGraw-Hill data communications dict, 94n1901
McGraw-Hill dict of ...
    bus acronyms, initials, & abbrevs, 93n170
    info tech & computer acronyms, initials, & abbrevs, 93n1679
    scientific & technical terms, 4th ed, 90n1428
    Wall St acronyms, initials, & abbrevs, 93n171
McGraw-Hill ency of ...
    astronomy, 2d ed, 94n1927
    chemistry, 2d ed, 94n1935
    engineering, 2d ed, 94n1785
    environmental sci & engineering, 3d ed, 94n1999
    physics, 2d ed, 94n1965
    sci & tech, 7th ed, 93n1446
McGraw-Hill Encyclopedia of Science & Technology, staff of, 91n1467
McGraw-Hill personal computer programming ency, 2d ed, 90n1715
McGraw-Hill pocket gd to bus finance, 93n241
McGraw-Hill yrbk of sci & tech 1990, 91n1467
McGraw-Hill's natl electrical code hndbk, 20th ed, 91n1617
McGraw-Hill's natl electrical code hndbk, 21st ed, 94n1786
McGreal, Ian P., 93n950
McGuiness, Colleen, 91n744
McGuire, Paula, 93n41
McGuire, William, 94n78, 94n806
McIlvaine, Eileen, 92n1215
McIlwaine, John, 94n94
McInerny, Derek, 90n1551
McIntire, Dennis K., 91n1254
McKay, David, 93n727
McKeating, Gerald, 92n1565
McKee, Cynthia Ruiz, 94n360
McKee, Patrick, 92n809
McKee, Phillip C., Jr., 94n360
McKeen, William, 91n1327, 94n1379
McKenrick, Robert, 92n556
McKerns, Joseph, 90n905
McKetta, John J., 92n1597, 94n1759, 94n1760, 94n1761, 94n1762, 94n1763, 94n1764, 94n1765, 94n1766
McKim, Donald K., 93n1422
McKnew, Ed, 91n1833, 94n2030
McKnight, Scot, 93n1428
McKusick, Victor A., 91n1679, 93n1624
McLafferty, Fred W., 93n1717
McLanahan, Connie, 91n134
McLanahan, Jack, 91n134
McLane, Audrey M., 90n1694
McLauchlan, Gordon, 91n513
McLean, Barbara E., 91n789
McLean, Bradley H., 93n1429
McLean, Janice, 90n170, 92n128, 93n307
McLean, Janice W., 94n901
McLeish, John A. B., 93n856
McLeish, Kenneth, 90n1104, 94n1258, 94n1497
McLellan, Hilary, 93n1672

McLeod, Donald W., 94n1271, 94n1272
McLerran, Jennifer, 92n809
McMahon, Sean, 92n24
McManus, Gary E., 93n473
McMath, Anne, 91n922
McMillan, James B., 91n1065
McMillon, Bill, 90n436, 93n335, 93n507
McMurray, Emily J., 93n1324
McNamara, Jean, 94n1728
McNamara, Martha J., 92n266
McNamee, Kevin P., 90n1659
McNeil, Barbara, 90n1073, 92n392
McNeil, Ian, 91n1464
McNeil, Robert A., 91n117
McNeill, Allison K., 93n188, 93n189, 94n228, 94n229
McNern, Janet, 93n928
McParland, Stephen J., 91n1323
McPartland, Brian J., 91n1617, 92n1609, 94n1786
McPartland, J. F., 91n1617, 94n1786
McPeek, Gail A., 93n1539
McPhail, Martha E., 93n155
McPheron, William, 90n1131, 92n1181
McPherson, James M., 91n501
McQuain, Jeff, 90n993
McQuain, Jeffrey, 91n1060
McQueen, Barbara, 94n1656
McQueen, Cyrus B., 91n1539
McQueen, Jim, 94n1656
McRae, Barry, 91n1319
McShane, Marilyn D., 94n804
McWilliam, Neil, 93n1018, 93n1019
Meacham, Mary, 93n1122
Mead, Frank S., 91n1445
Meaning of hist, 92n513
Means illus construction dict, new ed, 93n1037
Mearns, Barbara, 90n1541
Mearns, Richard, 90n1541
Measner, Don, 94n458
Measuring global values, 93n729
Mechanisms & mechanical devices sourcebk, 92n1622
Medical abbrevs, 6th ed, 94n1817
Medical acronyms & abbrevs, 2d ed, 91n1653
Medical & health care bks & serials in print 1992, 93n1625
Medical & health info dir, 4th ed, 90n1620
Medical & health info dir 1992-93, 94n1807
Medical dir 1989, 90n1660
Medical English usage & abusage, 92n1671
Medical phrase index, 2d ed, 90n1651
Medical publishing in 19th century America, 91n1640
Medical research centres, 8th ed, 90n1621
Medical terminology with human anatomy, 2d ed, 92n1659
Medical tests & diagnostic procedures, 91n1682
Medical utilization review dir, 1993 ed, 94n1810
Medical word bk A-Z, 93n1631
Medicare made easy, 90n1627
Medicinal plants of India, 92n1550
Medicinal plants of the desert, 91n1537
Medicinal wild plants of the prairie, 93n1514
Medicine in Great Britain from the Restoration to the 19th century, 1660-1800, 94n1821
Medicine, lit, & eponyms, 90n1653
Medieval & renaissance mss in the Walters Art Gallery, v.2, 94n29
Medieval Charlemagne legend, 94n1199
Medieval Consolation of Philosophy: an annot bibliog, 94n1487
Medieval English drama, 91n1191
Medieval rhetoric, 2d ed, 90n529
Medieval Scandinavia, 94n526
Medieval sexuality, 91n874
Medium cos of Europe 1991/92, 92n132
Medvedev, G.S., 90n1554
Meech, Karin Napoleon, 93n1755
Meet the authors & illustrators, 94n1193
Meet the natives: the amateur's field gd to Rocky Mountain wildflowers, trees & shrubs, 9th ed, 93n1505
Meeting the needs of employees with disabilities, 92n228

Meeting the needs of employees with disabilities, 2d ed, 94n881
Mehaffey, Karen Rae, 93n927
Meier, Heinz K., 92n107
Meier, Regula A., 92n107
Meiklejohn, C., 90n372
Mejia, Julia, 92n689
Melaragno, Michele, 92n1748
Meldrum, Marcia, 91n1655
Mellinkoff, David, 93n579
Mellinkoff's dict of American legal usages, 93n579
Melloni, B. John, 94n1829
Melloni's illus medical dict, 3d ed, 94n1829
Melting pot: an annot bibliog & gd to food & nutrition info for ethnic groups in America, 94n1599
Melton, J. Gordon, 91n1415, 91n1451, 92n1402, 93n811, 93n1401, 93n1408, 93n1410, 94n1514, 94n1515, 94n1518, 94n1552
Melville ency: the novels, 91n1166
Melzer, Annabelle Henkin, 92n1368
Men & women of space, 94n1757
Men of achievement, 13th ed, 90n32
Mendelian inheritance in man, 9th ed, 91n1679
Mendelian inheritance in man, 10th ed, 93n1624
Mendelsohn, Henry N., 94n912
Mendenhall, Doris A., 91n1037
Mendenhall, John, 90n981, 92n256
Mendes, Peter, 94n1204
Mene, mene, tekel, 91n1426
Menendez, Albert J., 91n1134
Mental health & psychiatry in Africa, 94n1849
Menville, Douglas, 91n1173
Mercadal, Dennis, 92n1702
Mercer, Anne, 93n1220
Mercer dict of the Bible, 91n1430
Meridith, Robert, 94n1992
Merit student's ency, 92n40
Merkel-Holguin, Lisa A., 94n922
Merkow, Mark S., 91n1725
Merriam-Webster concise hndbk for writers, 93n964
Merriam-Webster concise school & office dict, 93n1058
Merriam-Webster concise school & office thesaurus, 93n1074
Merriam-Webster dict of quotations, 93n91
Merriam-Webster new bk of word hists, 92n1027
Merriam-Webster's collegiate dict, 10th ed, 94n1076
Merriam-Webster's Japanese-English learner's dict, 94n1120
Merritt, Helen, 93n1043
Mersky, Roy M., 90n564, 92n548
Meselson, Sarah, 91n601
Meserole, Mike, 91n800, 94n818
Messadie, Gerald, 93n1447, 93n1448, 93n1449
Messenger, Charles, 90n646
Messier's nebulae & star clusters, 2d ed, 93n1705
Metal cutting tool hndbk, 7th ed, 90n1608
Metals hndbk, 10th ed., v.1, 92n1618
Metals hndbk, 10th ed., v.2, 92n1619
Metaphor 2, 92n1011
Metaphysical Fla., 92n764
Metcalf, Robert A., 94n1729
Metcalf, Robert L., 94n1729
Methodology & method in hist, 91n170
Metzger, Bruce M., 94n1545
Metzger, Linda, 90n1068
Metzler, Susan, 93n1509
Metzler, Van, 93n1509
Mews, Stuart, 91n1417
Mexical legal system, 93n563
Mexican lit, 2d ed, 93n1227
Mexican pol biogs, 1884-1935, 93n775
Meyer, Daniel E., 90n1756
Meyer, Jimmy Elaine Wilkinson, 93n860
Meyer, Linnea, 90n335
Meyer, Manfred, 91n965
Meyer, Michael, 91n910
Meyer, Robert G., 94n1847
Meyer, Ronald, 92n1230

Meyering, Sheryl L., 91n1170
Meyers, Frederick H., 90n1701
Meyers, Robert A., 90n1425, 90n1733, 90n1744, 92n1604, 92n1749, 93n1453, 94n1566
Meza, Fernando A., 91n1286
Michael, Scott W., 94n1718
Michael Singer's film directors, 7th ed, 90n1333
Michael Singer's film directors, 9th ed, 93n1372
Michael Tippett: a bio-bibliog, 91n1280
Michaels, Judith A., 91n880
Michele Landsberg's gd to children's bks, 92n1118
Michelin motoring atlas: France, 3d ed, 90n457
Michelin road atlas of Europe, 90n455
Michigan legal lit, 2d ed, 92n514
Mickolus, Edward F., 90n727, 94n589
Micro computer index, June 89, v.10, no.2, 90n1724
@Micro: educl sftwr evaluations 89/90, 91n361
Microbes & minie balls, 94n493
Microcomputer applications hndbk, 90n1721
Microcomputer index, v.12, 93n1686
Microcomputer market place 1993, 94n1906
Microcomputer sftwr sources, 91n1744
Microcomputers & libs, 92n596
Microelectronics packaging hndbk, 90n1593
Microform market place 1990-91, 92n640
Microform market place 1992-93, 94n669
Micronesia 1975-87, 90n149
Middle ages, 90n534, 91n541
Middle American herpetology, 90n1570
Middle East, 7th ed, 92n724
Middle East: a pol dict, 93n776
Middle East & N Africa 1990, 91n123
Middle East bibliog, 93n162
Middle East today, 91n442
Middle English dict, 92n1037
Middleton, Nick, 90n408, 90n1788
Middletown, 90n845
Mieder, Wolfgang, 91n1331, 93n1299, 94n1388
Miehe, Patrick K., 92n1176
Miethe, Terry L., 90n1396
Mignon, Molly Raymond, 94n487
Mihailovich, Vasa D., 90n1212, 92n1008, 93n1234
Mikdadi, Faysal, 93n543, 94n776
Mikesell, Margaret Lael, 91n1214
Mikhailovskaya, E., 94n782
Miki, Roy, 91n1226
Miko, Chris John, 91n78
Mikolyzk, Thomas A., 91n1164, 94n1262
Mikotowicz, Thomas J., 93n1382
Milby, T. H., 90n1487
Miles, Steven A., 93n69
Miles, Susan G., 93n868
Miles, William, 92n669
Miletich, John J., 90n742, 91n787, 92n1793, 93n889
Miletich, Leo N., 94n1465
Milgate, Murray, 93n242
Milheim, William D., 91n1716, 94n381
Military aircraft: modern bombers & attack planes, 94n700
Military & strategic policy, 91n676
Military fortifications, 93n692
Military hist of the US, 93n700
Military intelligence, 1870-1991, 94n681
Military leaders of the Civil War, 94n701
Military pers, 92n662
Milivojevic, Dragan, 92n1008
Milkias, Paulos, 90n109
Millar, David, 91n1460
Millard, Scott, 94n1630
Millennialism: an intl bibliog, 93n1399
Miller, Connie, 92n857
Miller, E. Willard, 90n1790, 91n1813, 93n1770, 94n1954
Miller, Eugene, 94n168
Miller, Eugene G., 92n1109
Miller, Everitt L., 90n1470
Miller, George, 94n1252

Miller, George Oxford, 90n1525
Miller, Gerald J., 90n737
Miller, Gordon L., 93n1437
Miller, Jacqueline Y., 93n1548
Miller, James M., 91n248
Miller, Joan I., 90n901
Miller, Joanne, 93n324
Miller, Joni, 91n199
Miller, Joseph A., 94n1990
Miller, Kelly S., 91n183
Miller, Kenneth E., 93n119
Miller, Lauri, 91n1017
Miller, Lynn, 90n849
Miller, Martin B., 94n1781
Miller, Oscar J., 92n527, 93n573, 94n549
Miller, Randall M., 90n493
Miller, Richard B., 92n189
Miller, Richard K., 90n1731, 92n1629
Miller, Robert Milton, 92n1359
Miller, Ruby M., 90n1790, 91n1813, 93n1770, 94n1954
Miller, Shelley, 93n633
Miller, Tice L., 94n1479
Miller, Timothy, 91n851
Miller, Warren E., 91n751
Miller, William G., 94n656
Miller-Lachmann, Lyn, 93n1127
Miller-Monzon, John, 94n1457
Millington, Barry, 94n1329
Millman, Linda Josephson, 94n572
Millodet, Michel, 91n1685
Mills, Carlotta, 94n891
Mills, J. J., 92n588, 93n652
Mills, Jane, 93n938
Mills, John, 91n1041
Mills, Watson E., 90n1390, 91n1430, 94n1534, 94n1550
Mills, William J., 91n1715
Millwrights & mechanics gd, 4th ed, 90n1604
Milner, Anita Cheek, 90n386
Milner, Anthony, 90n1033
Milner, J. Edward, 91n1809
Milner, Richard, 92n1523
Milstead, Jessica L., 94n1753
Milward, Peter, 94n1151
Minary, Ruth, 91n1184
Minderovic, Zoran, 92n1133, 92n1134
Miner, Brad, 92n306
Miner, Margaret, 93n1213
Mineral deposits of Europe, v.4/5, 91n1787
Mineral ref manual, 92n1741
Mineral resources A-Z, 92n1739
Minerals hndbk 1992-93, 94n1978
Minerals of the world, 93n1729
Mingei, 90n937
Mini-atlas of cats, 92n1573
Mini-atlas of dog breeds, 92n1574
Miniature gardens, 91n1499
Miniature orchids, 94n1656
Minnesota bus dir 1989-90, 90n180
Minnesota Historical Society, Library & Archives Division, 90n391
Minnick, Wendell L., 94n796
Minor, Barbara B., 93n398
Minor, Mark, 93n1430
Minor oil crops, 93n1464
Minor presidential candidates & parties of 1992, 93n748
Minorities Rights Group, 91n385
Minority consultants & minority-owned consulting firms, 1989 natl dir, 90n271
Minority health resources dir, 93n1618
Minority student enrollments in higher educ, 94n361
Minter, John, 91n338
Mirabile, Lisa, 91n132
Mirando, Louis P., 91n592
Miser, A., 91n200
Mises: an annot bibliog, 94n153

Misey, Johanna L., 92n879
Miska, John, 92n1226, 94n408
Misner, Amy J., 93n71, 94n54, 94n744
Mississippi: the WPA gd, 90n442
Missouri dir of manufacturers, 1991, 92n203
MIT cat of computer scis & artificial intelligence, 90n1709
MIT dict of modern economics, 4th ed, 93n183
Mitchell, Alan, 91n1545
Mitchell, B. R., 93n911, 94n936
Mitchell, Brian, 92n389
Mitchell, Chip, 92n262
Mitchell, G. Clay, 90n1556
Mitchell, James, 91n34
Mitchell, Joanne, 91n1747, 93n1691
Mitchell, Joyce Slayton, 91n372
Mitchell, M. H., 93n1482
Mitchell, P. A., 94n1096
Mitchell, Patricia, 92n410
Mitchell, Robert, 94n337
Mitchell, Robert Cameron, 90n105
Mitchell, Sally, 90n509
Mitchell-Hatton, Sarah Lu, 92n1644
Mitler, Louis, 90n1211
Mizel, Mark S., 94n1820
MLA dir of pers 1993-95, 94n987
MLA dir of scholarly presses in lang & lit, 93n686
MLA intl bibliog, 93n1107
Moavenzadeh, Fred, 91n1631
Mockenhaupt, Robin E., 94n869
Modem USA, 93n1683
Modern American novel, 92n1163
Modern American women writers, 92n1158
Modern & contemporary, 90n1161
Modern arts criticism, v.1, 92n990
Modern British essayists, 1st series, 92n1197
Modern Chinese writers, 94n1279
Modern combat helicopters, 94n711
Modern companion to the European Community, 93n767
Modern dict for the legal profession, 94n555
Modern dict of geography, 2d ed, 90n421
Modern ency of ...
    religions in Russia & the Soviet Union, 90n1381
    Russian & Soviet lit, v.9, 90n1210
    typefaces 1960-90, 92n630
Modern first ladies, 90n484
Modern geography, 92n416
Modern guns, 7th ed, 90n924
Modern Irish lit & culture, 94n1291
Modern Italian hist, 91n532
Modern Japanese novelists, 94n1294
Modern measuring circuit ency, 94n1779
Modern mystery, fantasy & sci fiction writers, 94n1207
Modern power supply & battery charger circuit ency, 94n1780
Modern proverbs & proverbial sayings, 90n1301
Modern writers, 1914-45, 93n1195
Modoc Press, 90n627
Modoc Press, Inc., 90n359, 94n359
Moe, Edward O., 93n846
Moebs, Thomas Truxtun, 90n475
Moen, William E., 90n596
Moersh, Elizabeth Sue, 91n976
Moffat, Riley, 93n900
Mogilner, Alijandra, 94n996
Mohr, Brigitte, 91n345
Moir, Lindsay, 90n368
Mokeba, H. Mbella, 92n86
Mokotoff, Gary, 93n494
Molecules, cells, & life, 91n1514
Molin, Paulette, 93n432
Molinari, Joseph A., 92n912
Molinaro, Lawrence, Jr., 93n249
Moll, Verna Penn, 93n158
Mollman, Sarah C., 91n1030
Mollo, John, 92n657
Molt, Cynthia Marylee, 91n1390, 94n1415

Molyneaux, Gerard, 93n1319
Monaco, 92n106
Monaco, James, 92n1352
Monaghan, Patricia, 91n1334
Monaghan, Robert P., 91n987
Monarchs of Scotland, 91n534
Mondale, Clarence, 90n96
Money for ...
    film & video artists, 92n1356
    intl exchange in the arts, 94n983
    performing artists, 93n1326
    visual artists, 92n991
Money matters, 91n1031
Moneyhon, Carl H., 90n467
Mongeau, Sam, 90n818
Monroe, Burt L., Jr., 92n1570
Montanaro, Ann R., 94n1177
Montgomery, John H., 93n1771
Montgomery, Michael B., 91n1065
Month-by-month atlas of WW II, 91n544
Montney, Charles B., 90n844, 94n46, 94n874
Montserrat, 93n156
Monty, Vivienne, 92n151
Moody, Douglas, 91n305, 91n306, 91n339
Moody hndbk of theology, 91n1446
Moody, Suzanna, 92n383
Moody's hndbk of common stocks, spring 1992, 93n223
Moody's hndbk of dividend achievers 1992, 93n224
Mookini, Esther T., 90n428
Moon, Marjorie, 92n1119
Mooney, Martha T., 92n585
Moons of the solar system, 93n1707
Moore, Bob, 90n723, 93n766, 94n1082
Moore, Burness E., 91n791
Moore, Cory, 91n857
Moore, D. M., 92n1534
Moore, Dianne F., 93n1702
Moore, Jean M., 94n1276
Moore, Mardell, 91n256
Moore, Margaret E., 91n1076
Moore, Maxine, 94n1082
Moore, Michael, 91n1537
Moore, Patrick, 90n1745
Moore, Paula, 94n995
Moore, R. I., 93n545
Moore, Rachelle, 91n1242
Moore, Rhonda D., 91n594
Moore, Robert J., 91n1654
Moore, Stephen, 94n1416
Moorman, Charles, 91n1184
Mora, Juana, 94n915
Moran-Lever, Tery, 91n274, 91n281
Morcos, Selim A., 92n1770
More creative uses of children's lit, v.1, 93n671
More exciting, funny, scary, short, different, & sad bks kids like, 93n1122
More than 100: women sci fiction writers, 90n866
More than words, 92n1418
More theatre, 94n1464
Morehead, Joe, 93n73
Morehead, Philip D., 93n1249
Morehouse, Cynthia T., 94n790
Morgan, Brad, 93n840
Morgan, Bradley J., 92n591, 93n822
Morgan, Hal, 93n312
Morgan, Jean K., 90n271
Morgan, Kathleen O'Leary, 91n901, 93n912, 94n1816
Morgan, Nina, 92n1610
Morgan, Paul W., 94n1580
Morgan, Scott, 91n901, 93n912, 94n1816
Mori, Monica, 93n857, 93n928
Morin, Heather, 91n757
Morinigo, Fernando B., 91n675
Moritz, Charles, 93n37
Morlan, Michael, 92n1794, 94n2026

Morley, Thomas, 92n1533
Morley, William F. E., 91n517
Mormon bibliog 1830-1930: indexes to A Mormon Bibliog and 10 yr suppl, 94n1501
Mormon bibliog 1830-1930: 10 yr suppl, 91n1435
Mormons & Mormonism in US gov docs, 90n1401
Morner, Kathleen, 92n1103
Morningstar closed-end fund sourcebk 1993, 94n194
Morningstar mutual fund 500, 1993, 94n195
Morningstar mutual fund sourcebk 1993, 94n196
Morningstar variable annuity/life sourcebk 1993, 94n197
Moroney, Sean, 90n104
Morreale, Don, 90n1400
Morrill, Dexter, 92n1301
Morris, Christopher, 93n1444
Morris, Derrick, 94n1775
Morris, Dwight, 93n749
Morris, Leslie R., 93n657
Morris, Lori, 90n1372
Morris, Manuel, 92n1284
Morris, Nancy J., 94n90
Morris, Peter, 91n758
Morris, Philip, 92n1014
Morris, Sandra Chass, 93n657
Morrison, Donald George, 90n105
Morrison, Donald R., 90n1373
Morrison, Philip, 91n1457
Morrissett, Christine, 91n1034
Morrow, Blaine Victor, 91n642
Morse, Ronald A., 94n45
Mortenson, Michael E., 91n1797
Morton, Brian, 93n1255
Morton, Fred, 91n94
Morton, L. T., 93n1626
Morton, Leslie T., 91n1654
Morton's medical bibliog, 5th ed, 93n1627
Mosaik's photographic key to the trees & shrubs of Great Britain & N Europe, 94n1670
Mosbaugh, Paige, 92n261
Mosby's emergency dict, 90n1613
Mosby's pocket dict of medicine, nursing, & allied health, 92n1658
Moscow & Leningrad: a topographical gd to Russian cultural hist, v.2, 94n985
Moseley, Charles, 91n669
Moseley, David, 94n1102
Moseley, Robert K., 91n1525
Moser, Diane, 91n1608
Moser, Gerald, 94n1268
Moss, Joyce, 90n139, 92n340, 93n117, 93n160, 93n1359, 94n128, 94n132
Moss, Norman, 93n1069
Moss, Ralph W., 94n1860
Mossman, Jennifer, 91n1341, 93n1
Most complete colored lexicon of cichlids, 94n1711
Moston, Doug, 94n1434
Mostyn, Trevor, 92n725
Mote, James, 91n822
Mother Goose comes 1st, 92n1121
Mothers & daughters in American short fiction, 94n1219
Mothers & daughters of invention, 94n1586
Mothers & mothering, 92n854
Moths of Austral., 92n1578
Motif-index of medieval Catalan folktales, 94n1389
Motion picture annual 1990, 91n1391
Motion picture gd, 1989 annual, 90n1352
Motion picture gd, 1993 annual, 94n1457
Motion picture players' credits, 92n1362
Motion picture serial, 93n1364
Motion picture series & sequels, 91n1353
Motley, Lynne, 93n1683
Motor carrier professional servs dir 1990, 91n1827
Motor carrier professional servs dir 1993, 94n2023
Mottu, Susan, 90n1424
Mount Sinai School of Medicine complete bk of nutrition, 92n1670
Mountfort, Guy, 94n1701

Mouzard, Francois, 90n1804
Movie characters of leading performers of the sound era, 91n1362
Movie classics, 93n1356
Movie list bk, 91n1387
Movie musicals on record, 90n1234
Movie song cat, 94n1309
Movie talk, 91n1397
Moving & relocation sourcebk, 93n917
Moving up, 90n267
Moyles, R. G., 90n1406
Moys classification & thesaurus for legal materials, 3d ed, 94n626
Moys, Elizabeth M., 94n626
Mozart repertory, 92n1279
Mozeson, Isaac E., 90n1002
Mrozek, Donald J., 94n680
MSDS pocket dict, 92n1772
Muccigrosso, Robert, 90n482
Mudge, Bradford K., 93n1196
Mueller, John, 90n85
Muether, John R., 93n1400
Muir, Sarah, 91n910
Mukherjee, Jaydeep, 94n1929
Mula, James J., 90n1345
Muldoon, Maureen, 92n805
Mulherin, Jennifer, 90n1457
Mull, William P., 93n1565
Mullane, Janet, 90n1072
Mullaney, Marie Marmo, 90n483
Mullay, Marilyn, 91n1459, 94n1562
Muller, Georg P., 90n838
Muller, Joachim W., 94n792
Mulligan, Gerald A., 91n1522, 93n1511
Mulliner, K., 93n129
Mullins, June B., 93n1124
Multicultural aspects of lib media programs, 93n669
Multicultural educ, 90n319
Multicultural educ debate, 94n322
Multicultural projects index, 93n1312
Multicultural student's gd to colleges, 94n337
Multilingual dict of ...
    artificial intelligence, 94n1889
    disaster medicine & intl relief, 92n1656
    narcotic drugs & psychotropic substances under intl control, 94n1872
    printing & publishing terms, 92n629
    publishing, printing & bkselling, 93n680
Multimedia ency of mammalian biology [CD-ROM], 94n1739
Mulvaney, Rebekah Michele, 91n1322
Mumford, Laura Stempel, 91n916
Munger, Donna Bingham, 92n390
Municipal yellow bk, v.2, no.1, 93n741
Munn, Glenn G., 92n186, 94n208
Munneke, Gary A., 92n539
Munoz, Olivia, 90n1058
Munro, David, 92n82
Munro, Derek B., 91n1522
Munro, K. M., 92n853
Munroe, Mary Hovas, 92n1131
Munslow, Barry, 91n92
Munson, Danni, 91n871
Munson, Kenneth, 90n1803, 93n1780
Munter, Robert, 90n631
Murder ... by category, 93n1152
Murdock, Jean M., 90n727
Murin, William F., 90n735
Murphey, Cecil B., 91n1431
Murphy, C. Edward, 91n846, 93n879, 93n1653, 94n892
Murphy, Donn B., 94n1416
Murphy, James J., 90n529
Murphy, Larry G., 94n1514
Murphy, Lynn, 92n904
Murphy, Paul C., 90n489
Murray, Andrew, 91n94
Murray, Elaine, 94n816
Murray, Jocelyn, 92n474

Murray, Margaret P., 91n1175
Murray, Michael T., 93n1634
Murray, Paul T., 94n595
Murray resource dir to the nation's historically black colleges & univs, 94n338
Murray, Sterling E., 94n1319
Murray, Thomas E., 91n1066
Murrell, Thomas R., 91n1066
Murry, Velma McBride, 91n892
Murthy, K. Krishna, 93n1413
Museum: a ref gd, 91n59
Museum of American Folk Art ency of 20th-century American folk art & artists, 92n982
Museums of Israel, 91n58
Museums of the world, 4th ed, 94n60
Mushrooms & other fungi of the midcontinental US, 90n1502
Mushrooms & truffles of the Southwest, 92n1545
Mushrooms of N America, 92n1544
Musi*key, 90n1280
Music & dance in Puerto Rico from the age of Columbus to modern times, 93n1243
Music & dance pers, 90n1316
Music & the personal computer, 90n1220
Music & war, 94n1305
Music address bk, 91n1305
Music analyses, 92n1250
Music at auction, 90n1224
Music dir Canada, 5th ed, 91n1260
Music festivals in America, 4th ed, 92n1255
Music for ...
    oboe, 1650-1800, 2d ed, 93n1263
    3 or more pianists, 94n1337
    2 or more players at clavichord, harpsichord, organ, 92n1281
    unaccompanied solo bassoon, 91n1282
Music hist during the Renaissance period, 1425-1520, 92n1252
Music in British libs, 93n650
Music in print master composer index 1988, 90n1249
Music in print master title index 1988, 91n1262
Music lover's gd to Europe, 93n1250
Music of Paul Ben-Haim, 94n1326
Music ref & research materials, 4th ed, 90n1213
Music theory from Zarlino to Schenker, 92n1249
Musical instruments, 91n1281
Musical terms, symbols & theory, 90n1233
Musical woman, v.3, 92n1257
Musicians wrestle everywhere, 94n1308
Muslims of India, 91n101
Musmann, Klaus, 91n79
Musto, Ronald G., 92n1398
Mutual fund ency, 1990 ed, 91n184
Mutual fund ency, 1993-1994 ed, 94n198
My 1st dict, 94n1092
My 1st ency, 94n41
My 1st picture dict, 90n1017, 91n1071
My 1st word bk, 92n1048
My name in bks, 94n1190
My pictionary, 91n1072
My 2d picture dict, 91n1073
My soul looks back, 'less I forget, 94n72
Myers, Eleanor Emlen, 94n529
Myers, J. Wilson, 94n529
Myers, Jack, 90n1118
Myers, Margaret, 94n613
Myers, Robert A., 92n88
Myers, Robin, 91n670
Myers, Sally, 92n838
Myerson, Joel, 94n1241
Mystery reader's walking gd: England, 90n459
Mystery writer's marketplace & sourcebk, 94n994
Mythological & classical world art index, 92n993
Mythologies, 92n1321
Mythology, 93n1302
Myths, gods, & fantasy, 92n1319

Naas, Penelope, 94n787
Nabokov, Peter, 90n968
Nachowitz, Todd, 91n39
Naden, Corinne J., 90n1093, 91n1111, 94n1192
Nader, Jonar C., 94n1902
Nadler, Leonard, 90n256
Nadler, Zeace, 90n256
NAGARA state archives & records mgmt programs, 1989, 90n698
Nagel, Gwen L., 94n1229
Nagel, James, 94n1229
Nahm, Andrew C., 94n117
Naifeh, Steven, 93n1644, 94n562
Naifeh, Steven W., 90n550
Naiman, Arthur, 94n1910
Nakamura, I., 94n1719
Nakamura, Joyce, 90n1098, 91n1119, 92n1125, 94n1187
Nam, Charles B., 91n905
Name is familiar, 94n1459
Names of ...
    countries & their capital cities, 93n104
    plants, 2d ed, 90n1484
    the games, 90n762
Naming of flowers, 91n1527
Naming your child, 92n397
Namovicz, Susan, 94n1810
Nanton, Isabel, 93n503
Napoleonic source bk, 92n492
Napoleonic uniforms, 94n707
Naprawa, Andrew, 94n1809
Nasdaq fact bk & co dir, 1993, 94n182
NASDAQ yellow bk, v.4, no.1, 93n225
Nash, Jay Robert, 92n552, 93n608, 93n609, 93n610, 93n611
Nash, Ralph C., Jr., 93n580
Nasrallah, Wahib, 93n174
Natalis, Constance R., 92n238
Natarajan, G., 90n1774
Nathan, David H., 92n784
Nathanail, Paul, 92n1072
Nathaniel Hawthorne: an annot bibliog of comment & criticism before 1900, 90n1143
Nathaniel Hawthorne ency, 92n1171
National accounts stats 1986, 91n900
National Arboretum bk of outstanding garden plants, 91n1503
National Association of State Development Agencies, 93n221
National black media dir, 90n892
National bk of lists 1992, 93n211
National Conference of Lt. Governors 1990 staff dir, 92n691
National Conference of State Legislatures Education Program, 90n308
National continuing care dir, 2d ed, 90n789
National Council on Aging, 90n788
National data bk of fndns, 16th ed, 93n879
National dir of ...
    addresses & telephone nos, 93n69
    addresses & telephone nos, 1989, 90n181
    AIDS care, 92n1679
    bulletin board systems 1990, 91n1728
    bulletin board systems 1992, 92n1705
    catalogs 1990, 91n194
    catalogs 1992, 94n294
    chiropractic, 3d ed, 93n1645
    corporate giving, 91n144
    corporate public affairs 1991, 92n134
    courts of law 1991, 93n586
    educ libs & collections, 91n655
    educl programs in gerontology & geriatrics 1991, 92n808
    fire chiefs & emergency depts, 1993, 94n878
    grants & aid to individuals in the arts, 7th ed, 90n808
    legal servs, 90n549
    mags 1990, 91n62
    mags 1994, 94n62
    mailing lists 1991, 92n257
    minority-owned business firms, 1990 ed, 91n145
    multi-cultural arts orgs 1990, 92n879
    nonprofit orgs 1992, v.1, 93n195
    retirement facilities 1991, 92n810
    storytelling, 1990 ed, 91n294
    women-owned business firms, 1990 ed, 91n146
National Employment Screening Services, 90n258
National faculty dir 1991, 91n316
National faculty dir 1993, 94n339
National family healthcare hndbk, 94n1813
National fax dir, 90n1736
National fax dir 1990, 90n1737
National gd to ...
    college & univ programmes 1988, 90n339
    educl credit for training programs, 1992-93 ed, 94n392
    fndn funding in health, 90n1622
    fndn funding in higher educ, 91n317
    funding for children, youth & families, 92n827
    funding for elementary & secondary educ, 92n287
    funding for libs & info servs, 92n573
    funding for libs & info servs, 2d ed, 94n618
    funding for the environment & animal welfare, 93n881
    funding for women & girls, 92n865
    funding in aging, 2d ed, 91n846
    funding in arts & culture, 91n931
    funding in religion, 93n1411
National Geographic atlas of the world, 6th ed, 92n402
National Geographic index 1888-1988, 91n450
National health dir 1989, 90n1623
National health dir, 1992, 93n1619
National Hockey League official gd & record bk 1989-90, 91n837
National Hockey League official gd & record bk 1992-93, 94n853
National housing dir for people with disabilities, 1993, 94n883
National index: insurance definitions, 92n207
National index: insurance laws, 92n208
National index: insurance regulations, 92n209
National job bank 1989, 90n260
National park gd 1992, 93n496
National parks, 93n498
National parks fishing gd, 92n800
National Review college gd, 92n306
National Review politically incorrect ref gd, 94n726
National roster of Hispanic elected officials, 1989, 91n740
National Science Resources Center, 90n1418
National Society of Daughters of Founders & Patriots of America, 90n396
National survey of state laws, 94n569
National theatre in N & E Europe, 1746-1900, 92n1384
National trade & professional assns of the US 1990, 91n40
National trade & professional assns of the US 1993, 94n54
National trade policies, 93n320
National Trust for Historic Preservation, 91n1028
National trust gd, rev ed, 91n468
National wildflower research center's wildflower hndbk, 90n1497
Native America, 93n431
Native American architecture, 90n968
Native American women, 94n956
Native American youth & alcohol, 90n824
Native Americans: an annot bibliog, 92n368
Native Americans info dir, 94n420
Native Americans on film & video, v.2, 90n374
Native law bibliog, 2d ed, 92n365
Native peoples of Canada, 90n372
Native peoples of Canada in contemporary society, 91n402
Natural disasters, 94n468
Natural gas industry dir, 1993, 94n1973
Natural hist from A to Z, 93n1523
Natural hist museums, v.1, 93n1524
Natural medicine for children, 91n1681
Natural resources glossary, 92n1790
Natural scis & American scientists in the revolutionary era, 92n1451
Nature dir, 93n1759
Nature in America, 93n1526
Nature of SE Alaska, 93n1528
Nature projects on file, 93n1527
Nature's heartland: native plant communities of the Great Plains, 92n1530

Naughton, Renee, 93n666
Naval Institute gd to ...
    combat fleets of the world 1990/91, 91n695
    combat fleets of the world 1993, 94n704
    maritime museums of N America, 92n1805
    the ships & aircraft of the US fleet, 15th ed, 94n705
    world naval weapons systems, 91n696
Naval officers of the American Revolution, 90n663
Naval terms dict, 5th ed, 90n668
Navarro, Yvonne, 94n442
Navia, Luis E., 91n1401, 94n1488
Navy League of the United States, 91n690
Naylor, Colin, 90n948, 92n921, 93n1028
Naylor, Lynne, 90n919, 93n965
Nazareno, Rodolfo L., 93n1102
Nazi-retro film, 93n1362
NBC hndbk of pronunciation, 4th ed, 92n1032
NBC News Rand McNally world news atlas, 1990 ed, 91n543
NCAA basketball's finest, 93n827
NCAA football's finest, 93n831
NCEA/Ganley's Catholic schools in America 1989, 90n315
NCEA/Ganley's Catholic schools in America 1992, 93n353
NCOA dir of sr centers, 90n788
Neagles, James C., 91n418
Neal, Bill, 94n1640
Neal, Michael, 94n1934
Neal-Schuman index to ...
    card games, 91n832
    performing & creative artists in collective biogs, 92n882
    sports figures in collective biogs, 93n824
Neaman, Judith S., 91n1058
Near-death experiences, 91n785
Neave, Guy R., 93n358
Nebenzahl, Kenneth, 91n427
Nechas, Eileen, 94n1805
Ned Rorem: a bio-bibliog, 90n1248
Neff, Glenda Tennant, 91n945
Neft, David S., 91n823, 92n787, 92n795
Negro almanac, 5th ed, 90n364
Negru, John, 92n644
Nehemiah Grew: a study & bibliog of his writings, 92n1532
Nehmer, Kathleen S., 90n341, 94n317
Nehmer, Kathleen Suttles, 93n401, 94n886, 94n1911
Neibaur, James L., 90n1342
Neill, George W., 90n342, 90n343
Neill, Peter, 93n1791
Neill, Shirley Boes, 90n342, 90n343
Nelson Canadian atlas, 90n417
Nelson, Carl A., 90n1604
Nelson Eddy: a bio-discography, 93n1277
Nelson, Emmanuel S., 94n1224, 94n1290
Nelson, Garrison, 94n741
Nelson intermediate atlas, 90n409
Nelson, Joseph S., 94n1720
Nelson, Marian, 91n664, 91n941, 94n989
Nelson, Michael, 91n745, 93n753, 94n508
Nelson, Ruth Ashton, 93n1501
Nelson, Theodora, 90n453, 90n456
Nelson, Walter R., 92n162, 92n163, 92n164, 92n229
Nelson's concordance of Bible phrases, 93n1431
Nelson's dir of ...
    investment managers 1991, 92n162
    investment research 1991, 92n163
    plan sponsors & tax-exempt funds 1991, 92n164
Nelson's gd to pension fund consultants 1991, 92n229
Nelson's quick ref Bible concordance, 94n1547
Nelson's quick ref Bible dict, 94n1541
Nelson's quick ref Bible hndbk, 94n1544
Nelson's techresources, winter 1993, 94n183
Nemeth, Charles P., 92n538
Nemeth, Gyula, 92n448
Neotropical rainforest mammals, 91n1592
Neo-words, 92n1058
Nestler, Harold, 90n101, 91n88
Netter, Frank H., 90n1635

Netzer, Corinne T., 93n1476
Neu, John, 90n1416
Neufeldt, Victor A., 94n1247
Neugaard, Edward J., 94n1389
NeuralSource, 91n1718
Neuro-computing bibliog, 1989, 90n1708
Neuroscience yr: suppl, 90n1639
Nevada printing hist, 93n678
New age ency, 91n1451
New age music gd, 91n1321
New American dict of music, 93n1249
New American pocket medical dict, 2d ed, 90n1652
New Arthurian ency, 92n1190
New atlas of African hist, 92n85
New A-to-Z of women's health, 90n1675
New bibliog of the Lusophone lits of Africa, 2d ed, 94n1268
New bk of knowledge, 90n52, 93n60
New bk of popular sci, 90n1437, 92n1457, 93n1450
New car buying gd, 1992-93 ed, 93n1784
New, completely rev, greatly expanded, Madam Audrey's
    mostly cheap, all good, useful list of bks for speedy
    ref, 5th ed, 93n13
New concordance of the Bible, 90n1399
New cosmopolitan world atlas, census/environmental ed, 93n477
New dict of sacramental worship, 92n1415
New dict of theology, 90n1382
New ency Britannica, 92n41
New ency of archaeological excavations in the Holy Land, 94n489
New England: a bibliog of its hist, 91n483
New England: additions to the 6 state bibliogs, 91n484
New England planters in the Maritime provinces of Canada
    1759-1800, 94n1589
New Europe: an A to Z compendium on the European
    Community, 92n741
New everyman dict of music, 6th ed, 90n1229
New gardener's hndbk & dict, 93n1486
New Generation gd to the butterflies & day-flying moths of Britain
    & Europe, 90n1546
New Generation gd to the fungi of Britain & Europe, 90n1500
New Good Housekeeping family health & medical gd, 90n1628
New Grolier student ency, 90n53, 93n61
New Grove dict of jazz, 90n1288
New Grove dict of opera, 94n1356
New hacker's dict, 93n1680
New hndbk of health & preventive medicine, 91n1674
New intl atlas, 92n403
New intl dict of acronyms in lib & info sci, 2d ed, 93n621
New Jersey arts, 92n986
New lexicon dict of basic words, new ed, 91n1074
New literary hist intl bibliog of literary theory & criticism,
    90n1066
New lit on fetal alcohol exposure & effects, 91n1692
New Merriam-Webster dict for large print users, 91n1067
New name dict, 90n403
New new words dict, rev ed, 90n1004
New official rules, 90n1306
New Palauan-English dict, 92n1084
New Palgrave dict of money & finance, 93n242
New Penguin dict of geography, 92n418
New Penguin gd to CDs & cassettes, yrbk 1989, 91n1292
New per title abbrevs, 93n86
New pocket Hawaiian dict, 93n1086
New pocket Romanian dict, 90n1053
New pol parties of E Europe & the Soviet Union, 93n770
New prescription drug ref gd, 90n1668
New Princeton ency of poetry & poetics, 94n1302
New quotable woman, rev. ed, 94n973
New read-aloud hndbk, 1989 ed, 91n369
New rhyming dict & poet's hndbk, rev ed, 92n1053
New shorter Oxford English Dict on historical principles, 94n1099
New standard ency, 91n32, 93n62
New standard Jewish ency, 7th ed, 93n448
New state of the world atlas, 4th ed, 93n475
New Testament Christology, 90n1404
New Testament Greek-English dict: Alpha-Gamma, 92n1433

New Testament Greek-English dict: Delta-Epsilon, 92n1434
New Testament Greek-English dict: Lambda-Omicron, 92n1436
New Testament Greek-English dict: Pi-Rho, 92n1437
New Testament Greek-English dict: Sigma-Omega, 92n1438
New Testament Greek-English dict: Zeta-Kappa, 92n1435
New Testament study Bible: Acts, 92n1428
New Testament study Bible: Galatians-Philemon, 92n1430
New Testament study Bible: Hebrews-Jude, 92n1431
New Testament study Bible: John, 92n1427
New Testament study Bible: Luke, 92n1426
New Testament study Bible: Mark, 92n1425
New Testament study Bible: Matthew, 92n1424
New Testament study Bible: Revelation, 92n1432
New Testament study Bible: Romans-Corinthians, 92n1429
New topographical dict of ancient Rome, 94n536
New treasury of scripture knowledge, 93n1434
New Trouser Pr record gd, 3d ed, 90n1235
New 20th-century ency of religious knowledge, 2d ed, 92n1417
New video ency, 92n912
New, W. H., 91n1227
New York Public Library, Black Experience in Children's Book Committee, 90n1079
New York Public Lib bk of ...
  chronologies, 91n27
  how & where to look it up, 92n609
  20th-century American quotations, 94n71
New York Public Lib desk ref, 91n48
New York Times film reviews 1989-90, 94n1458
New York Times theater reviews [1985-86], 91n1399
New Zealand bks in print 1989, 90n26
New Zealand bks in print 1993, 94n5
Newbery & Caldecott awards, 1991 ed, 92n1120
Newbery & Caldecott awards, 1992 ed, 93n1128
Newbery & Caldecott medal & honor bks in other media, 93n1121
Newbery & Caldecott medalists & honor bk winners, 2d ed, 93n1120
Newby, James Edward, 92n1148
Newcomb, Annette, 94n87
Newcomb, Duane, 91n1505
Newcomb, Karen, 91n1505
Newell, James, 92n262
Newman, Eva Jana, 92n969
Newman, Jacqueline M., 94n1599
Newman, John, 90n1132
Newman, Marketa, 92n969
Newman, Oksana, 93n291, 94n258, 94n259
Newman, Peter, 92n484, 93n242
Newman, Peter R., 93n539
Newman, Roxana Ma, 91n1086
Newnham, Jeffrey, 92n673
News media yellow bk of Washington & N.Y., 91n959
Newsletters in print 1993-94, 93n978
Newsmakers, 1988 cum, 90n33
Newson, Cathryn M., 91n749
Newspaper: a ref bk for teachers & librarians, 92n277
Newspaper genealogical column dir, 4th ed, 90n386
Newspapers online, 93n975
Newspapers online, 2d ed, 94n1005
Newstrom, Harvey, 94n1610
Newton, David E., 92n1473, 94n2014
Newton, Derek, 93n1063
Newton, Judy Ann, 90n570, 92n553, 92n730
Newton, Kenneth, 93n727
Newton, Michael, 90n570, 92n553, 92n730
NFB film gd, 93n1342
NGC 2000.0: the complete new general cat & index cats of nebulae & star clusters, 90n1747
NHL Club Public Relations Directors, 94n853
NHL Communications Group, 94n853
Niccolo Machiavelli: an annot bibliog of modern criticism & scholarship, 91n715
Nicholas, Larraine, 94n1423
Nicholas, Vera, 90n803
Nicholls, Ann, 90n458, 92n62
Nicholls, C. S., 91n13, 94n15
Nicholls, Paul T., 94n1917
Nicholls, Peter, 94n1211
Nicholls, Robert P., 90n1472
Nichols, C. Allen, 93n1133
Nichols, Larry A., 94n1513
Nichols, Margaret Irby, 93n670
Nichols, Monte C., 92n1741
Nichols, Tom, 93n1470
Nichols, Victoria, 90n1107
Nicholson, Alison, 92n1501
Nicholson, Carol Avery, 94n654
Nicholson, Frances, 92n714
Nicholson, Peter, 91n1208
Nicholson's access in London, 91n470
Nicholson's children's London, 91n471
Nickel, Ernest H., 92n1741
Nickson, R. Andrew, 94n147
Nicolosi, Lucille, 90n1683
Niebuhr, Gary Warren, 94n1209
Niemeyer, Suzanne, 92n991, 92n1356, 93n1326
Niemi, Richard G., 90n85
Nierenberg, William A., 93n1721
Nigerian artists, 94n1040
Niiya, Brian, 94n423
Nikkei Biotechnology, 91n223
Nikolai Andreevich Rimsky-Korsakov: a gd to research, 90n1252
Nile notes of a howadji, 93n163
Nilsen, Alleen Pace, 92n1123
Nilsen, Don L. F., 93n1189, 94n1304
Nilsen, Kirsti, 93n16
Nilson, Lenore, 90n1084
999 questions about Canada, 90n126
1992-1993 gd to newspaper syndication, 93n977
1990 Health Care Services Committee of the International Foundation of Employee Benefit Plans, 93n1615
1960s: an annot bibliog of social & pol movements in the US, 94n863
1939: the yr in movies, 91n1378
1920 fed population census: cat of microfilm available, 93n901
Nineteenth century American poetry, 91n1177
Nineteenth-century European Catholicism, 90n1402
Nineteenth-century French fiction writers, 94n1283
Nineteenth-century inventors, 93n1439
Nineteenth-century literary criticism, v.22, 90n1072
Nineteenth-century literary criticism, v.29, 92n1108
Nineteenth-century musical chronicle, 90n1227
Nineteenth-century rhetoric, 90n986
Nineteenth-century Russian lit in English, 92n1230
Nineteenth-century writers, 92n1152
99 best residential & recreational communities in America for vacation, retirement & investment planning, 93n919
Nipp, Frank, 93n974
Nisberg, Jay N., 90n167
Nishimura, Mari, 94n1333
Nishiura, Elizabeth, 91n313, 91n680
Nisonger, Thomas E., 93n677
NIV compact dict of the Bible, 90n1395
NIV exhaustive concordance, 91n1427
Niven, David, 94n1371
Nixon, Judith M., 90n243, 93n212
NKJV exhaustive concordance, 94n1548
Nobari, Nuchine, 90n154, 93n187, 94n44
Nobel laureates in ...
  economic scis, 90n163
  lit, 91n1098
  medicine or physiology, 91n1655
Nobel prize winners: chemistry, 91n1765
Nobel prize winners: physics, 90n1773
Nobel prize winners: physiology or medicine, 92n1652
Nobel prize winners: suppl 1987-91, 93n41
Noble, Judith, 92n355
Noel, John V., Jr., 90n668
Noel, Roger, 94n1079
Noether, Dorit, 94n1936
Noether, Herman, 94n1936

Nofsinger, Mary M., 91n861
Nokes, David, 91n1223
Nolan, Kathleen Lopez, 94n1907
Nolan, William F., 92n1166
Nolen, Anita L., 94n1835
Noll, Richard, 93n799
No-Load Fund Investor, editors of, 94n189
Nonbook materials: the org of integrated collections, 3d ed, 90n606
Non-ferrous metal data 1988, 90n1768
Non-ferrous metal data 1990, 93n1727
Nonfiction bks for children, 91n648
Nonprofit almanac 1992-93, 93n877
Nonprofit public policy research orgs, 94n753
Noon, Patrick, 90n244
Noonan, Jon, 93n1439
Noqueira, Carmen Crespo, ed., 90n617
Norback, Craig T., 92n225
Nordquist, Joan, 90n86, 90n136, 90n155, 90n721, 90n794, 90n1684, 91n80, 91n885, 91n886, 91n917, 91n1402, 91n1403, 91n1804, 92n564, 92n731, 92n811, 92n858, 92n873, 92n1392, 94n1855
Norell, Donna M., 94n1285
Norem, Lois, 90n1183
Norena, Carlos G., 91n1404
Norm Hitzges histl sports almanac, 93n812
Norman, Jay, 90n437
Norman, Jeremy M., 93n1627
Norman, Jill, 92n1497
Normandy campaign, 1944, 94n531
Norrbom, Allen L., 94n1725
Norse mythology A to Z, 92n1322
North American brewers resource dir 1992-93, 93n1477
North American dir of programs for runaways, homeless youth, & missing children, 90n831
North American horticulture, 2d ed, 93n1487
North American Indian landmarks, 94n416
North American trees exclusive of Mexico & tropical Fla, 4th ed, 90n1510
Northcutt, Wayne, 93n537
Northern Ireland, 93n145
Northern Ireland: a pol dir 1968-88, 91n759
Northwest weeds, 92n1548
Northwoods wildlife, 90n1512
Norton, Chris, 90n260
Norton, Judith A., 94n1589
Norton, Susan R., 92n1047
Norton/Grove concise ency of music, 90n1230
Norton's 2000.0 star atlas & ref hndbk, 18th ed, 91n1760
Norwegian local hist, 90n134
Norwich, John Julius, 91n932
Nostalgia entertainment sourcebk, 92n1334
Notable black American women, 93n52
Notable Hispanic American women, 94n962
Notable women in the American theatre, 91n924
Notary public hndbk, 91n588
Notes in the cat record based on AACR2 & LC rule interpretations, 90n605
Noth, Winfried, 91n81
Nourie, Alan, 91n63
Nourie, Barbara, 91n63
Nova Scotia newspapers, 92n904
Novallo, Annette, 93n411, 94n58
Novel & short story writer's market, 1989, 90n902
Novel & short story writer's market, 1992, 93n966
Novels of WW II: an annot bibliog, 94n1205
Novels of WW II: an annot bibliog of WW II fiction, 91n1131
Nowak, Ronald M., 93n1572
Nowlan, Gwendolyn Wright, 90n1328, 90n1353, 91n1362, 92n1361, 94n1459
Nowlan, Robert A., 90n1328, 90n1353, 91n1362, 92n1361
Nowlan, Robert Anthony, 94n1459
Noy, Shlomo, 90n1669
Noyes, Gertrude E., 92n1013
NRSV concordance unabridged, 92n1442
NRSV exhaustive concordance, 92n1443

NTC's classical dict, 92n1325
NTC's dict of ...
   direct mail & mailing list terminology & techniques, 91n273
   German false cognates, 93n1085
   grammar terminology, 92n1035
   literary terms, 92n1103
   word origins, 92n1028
NTC's French & English bus dict, 93n182
NTC's mass media dict, 92n887
NTC's new college French & English dict, 92n1068
NTC's new college Greek & English dict, 92n1072
NTC's new Japanese-English character dict, 94n1121
Ntumy, Michael, 94n573
Nuclear energy policy, 92n1762
Nuclear fuel cycle info system, 90n1778
Nuclear heartland, 90n678
Nuclear movies, 93n1349
Nuclear power plants worldwide, 94n1801
Nuclear power reactors in the world, 1991 ed, 93n1749
Nuclear present, 94n709
Nuclear weapons world, 90n674
Nudelman, Edward D, 90n984
Nuessel, Frank, 94n870
Nulman, Macy, 94n1556
Number 1 in the USA, 2d ed, 92n1330
#1 New York Times bestseller, 94n1153
Numbers you need, 93n1740
Nunis, Doyce B., Jr., 90n500
Nunn, Hilary, 93n649
Nurnberger, Fred V., 92n1733
Nurse's quick ref, 91n1704
Nursey-Bray, Paul, 93n778
Nutrients cat, 94n1610
Nutrition, 90n1648
Nutrition almanac, 3d ed, 91n1481
Nutrition & diet therapy dict, 3d ed, 92n1485
Nutrition & disease, 92n1674
Nutrition & health ency, 2d ed, 90n1614
Nutrition desk ref, rev ed, 92n1667
NWO: a dir of natl women's orgs, 93n940
Nyberg, Cheryl Rae, 90n689
Nyvall, Robert F., 90n1449

Oakes, A. J., 91n1532
Oakley, Ruth, 92n462
Ober, Kenneth H., 92n1236
Obituaries: a gd to sources, 2d ed, 91n414
Obituary index 1988, 91n55
O'Brien, Ed, 94n1368
O'Brien, Geoffrey, 91n4
O'Brien, Jacqueline Wasserman, 90n552, 90n841, 91n218, 92n543, 93n913
O'Brien, Nancy Patricia, 92n270
O'Brien, Neal R., 92n1737
O'Brien, Patrick G., 94n496
O'Brien, Robert, 92n839, 93n890
O'Brien, Robert F., 93n1278
O'Brien, Sean K., 90n822
O'Brien, Steven G., 92n681
O'Brien, Tim, 92n774, 94n1688
Observing hndbk & cat of deep-sky objects, 91n1759
Obst, Fritz Jurgen, 90n1569
Occu-facts, 1989-90 ed, 91n376
Occupational entry, 90n596
Occupational outlook hndbk, 1990-91 ed, 91n249
Occupational outlook hndbk, 1992-93 ed, 94n281
Ocean yrbk 8, 92n1744
Oceans Institute of Canada, 93n1790
Ochoa, George, 91n1396
Ockerman, Herbert W., 92n1489, 93n1708
O'Clair, Rita M., 93n1528
Ocokoljich, Natalia, 94n195
O'Connell, Agnes N., 91n918
O'Connor, Diane Vogt, 92n1467, 94n1038

O'Connor, Karen, 90n557
O'Connor, Leo F., 93n1170
O'Connor, W. J., 92n1653
Odell, Rice, 93n1777
O'Donnell, Owen, 90n1311, 93n1324
O'Donnell, Timothy S., 93n95, 93n273
O'Donoghue, Michael, 91n1779, 94n1956
O'Drago, Alicia S., 90n917
O'Driscoll, James E., 90n994
Ody, Penelope, 94n1666
Of a certain age, 92n1141
Off the record, v.1, 93n1292
Off-Hollywood movies, 90n1334
Office for Intellectual Freedom, American Library Association, 94n642
Office International des Epizooties, 94n1633
Office of Communications, American Association for the Advancement of Science, 93n1452
Office of Ethnic Minority Affairs, 90n748
Office of maternal & child health active projects FY 1990, 91n1672
Office sourcebk, 90n290
Official baseball register, 1991 ed, 92n777
Official Catholic dir 1989, 90n1409
Official Catholic dir 1993, 94n1532
Official dir of Canadian museums & related insts, 91n56
Official export gd 1990, 91n274
Official fax dir, 7th Canadian ed, 91n1752
Official gd to ...
    American incomes, 94n283
    household spending, 2d ed, 94n927
    the American marketplace, 93n906
Official museum dir 1989, 90n65
Official museum dir 1992, 93n79
Official museum products & servs dir 1992, 93n80
Official 1991 US golf course dir & gd, 92n797
Official 1992 NFL record & fact bk, 94n846
Official politically correct dict & hndbk, 94n1101
Official professional rodeo media gd, 1990, 91n1838
Official splatter movie gd, 91n1389
Official USGA record bk, 1895-1990, 94n851
Official Whitman coin dealer dir, 2d ed, 91n985
Official Whitman coin dealer dir, 6th ed, 94n1029
Offshore cruising ency, 91n1829
Ogarkov, N. V., 94n686
Ogbondah, Chris W., 91n960
Ogden Nash: a descriptive bibliog, 91n1168
Ogden, Tom, 94n1419
Oggel, L. Terry, 93n1379
O'Grady, Jane, 94n1499
O'Hara, Frederic J., 92n619
O'Herron, Thomas F., 91n275
Oil & gas dict, 90n1784
Oil & Gas Jl exploration index, 93n1750
Ojeda, Ricardo A., 91n1596
Oklahoma botanical lit, 90n1487
Oklahoma herpetology, 90n1565
Oklahoma mammalogy, 90n1557
Okuda, Ted, 90n1343, 92n1370
Old age in myth & symbol, 92n809
Old English proverbs collected by Nathan Bailey, 1736, 94n1384
Old rose advisor, 94n1628
Old Testament commentary survey, 92n1407
Oldenburg, Joseph F., 90n394
Older volunteer, 94n887
Older workers, 92n812
Olderr, Steven, 90n1097, 92n584, 92n1139, 93n1311
Olderr's fiction index 1990, 92n1139
Olderr's fiction subject headings, 92n584
Olderr's young adult fiction index 1988, 90n1097
Oldham, John M., 94n1846
Old-house dict, 90n975
Olea, Ricardo A., 92n1738
O'Leary, Timothy J., 91n380, 92n334
Olendorf, Donna, 90n579

Olevnik, Peter P., 94n323
Olgiatti, Alexandra, 94n268
Olitzky, Kerry M., 93n449, 94n1557
Olive, Steven W., 90n1808
Oliver, A. P. H., 90n1513
Oliver, Pam D., 91n45
Oliver, Paul, 91n1314
Oliviero, Jeffrey, 92n1362
Olsen, Kirsten, 94n959
Olsen, Kristin Gottschalk, 91n1662
Olsen, M. A., 93n226
Olsen, Wallace C., 94n1754
Olshevsky, Moshe, 90n1669
Olson, A. Randall, 94n1659
Olson, James S., 90n1682, 92n371, 93n540, 94n158, 94n497
Olson, Nancy B., 92n578, 94n627, 94n628
Olson, Nancy L., 94n742
Olson, Stan, 90n809, 91n317, 91n866, 91n931, 92n287, 92n573, 92n824, 92n827, 92n865, 93n880, 93n881, 93n1411, 94n618, 94n890, 94n891
Olympic games: complete track & field results 1896-1988, 90n759
Olympic results—Barcelona 1992, 94n856
Olympics factbk, 93n840
Olynyk, Marta D., 94n483
O'Mahony, Kieran, 94n466
O'Malley, William T., 91n1239
O'Meara, Meghan A., 93n261
Omni gazetteer of the USA, 92n425, 93n495
Omnicom index of standards 1989, 91n1753
On account of sex, 91n919, 94n949
On cassette 1991, 92n908
Ondrasik, Allison, 90n839
100 best cos to sell for, 90n278
100 best job$ for the 1990s & beyond, 93n311
100 best small towns in America, 94n942
100 best spare-time bus opportunities today, 91n181
100 best stocks to own in America, 2d ed, 92n169
100 best treatment centers for alcoholism & drug abuse, 90n827
100 families of flowering plants, 2d ed, 90n1492
100 great operas & their stories, 90n1273
100 ways colleges serve adults, 92n332
100 world-class thin bks, 94n1164
One hundred yrs of economic stats, 91n158
One hundred yrs of study on the Passion Narratives, 91n1422
101st congress dir, 90n699
101 business ratios, 94n176
101 microcomputer projects to do in your lib, 91n638
101 stories of the great ballets, 90n1315
1000 brave Canadians, 93n36
1000 cooking substitutions, 91n1484
1000 most obscure words, 91n1054
1000 Russian verbs, 94n1128
1001 Kans. place names, 90n427
1,001 medical facts for every home, 90n1662
1,001 things everyone should know about American hist, 90n497
1001 quips & quotes for bus speeches, 93n219
O'Neal, Bill, 93n515
O'Neill, Patrick B., 90n40, 90n41, 90n42
One-parent children, the growing minority, 91n860
Online Inc.'s top 500 lib microcomputer sftwr application programs, 94n640
Online manual, 93n203
Online programming langs & assemblers, 90n1719
Only the best 1985-89, 90n342
Only the best 1990, 90n343
Ontario central places in 1871, 92n423
OPAC dir 1993, 94n646
O'Pecko, Michael T., 91n1236
Open doors 1990/91, 93n389
Open secrets, 91n750
Open secrets, 2d ed, 93n752
Opening night on Broadway, 92n1387
Opera: an informal gd, 94n1358
Opera annual, US 1984-85, 90n1270
Opera cos of the world, 94n1352

Opera hndbk, 91n1299
Opera mediagraphy, 94n1351
Opera performances in video format, 93n1273
Opera plot index, 91n1300
Operas in German, 92n1289
Opfell, Olga S., 90n869, 94n714
Opie, Iona, 91n798
Opinions '90, 91n78
Opitz, Helmut, 92n623
Opler, Paul A., 93n1549
Optical publishing dir, 1991-92 ed, 92n1720
Opus: America's gd to classical music, summer 1990, 91n1293
Oral hist index, 91n556
Oral hist of contemporary Jewry, 91n408
Orchestral excerpts, 94n1348
Orchid bk, 94n1652
Ordway, Girard, 90n1799
Orenstein, J. A., 93n1685
Orenstein, Ruth M., 90n1725
Organ & harpsichord music by women composers, 92n1266
Organ music in print 1990 suppl, 92n1283
Organization charts, 93n212
Organizational & interorganizational dynamics, 94n864
Organizations of state govt officials dir 1992, 94n742
Orgill, Andrew, 94n684
Origin & evolution of life on Earth, 94n1635
Original martial arts ency, 94n855
Original Scots colonists of early America 1612-1783, 90n390
Orion blue bk: audio 1990, 91n202
Orion blue bk: camera 1990, 91n203
Orion blue bk: car stereo 1990, 91n204
Orion blue bk: computer 1990, 91n205
Orion blue bk: guitars & musical instruments 1990, 91n206
Orion blue bk: professional sound 1989, 91n207
Orion blue bk: video & TV 1990, 91n208
Orlandi, Mario, 90n1644
Orlando di Lasso: a gd to research, 91n1270
Ornamental grasses, 90n1503
Ornamental grasses & grasslike plants, 91n1532
Ornamental shrubs, climbers & bamboos, 94n1632
Ornato, Joseph P., 92n1668
Ornstein, Norman J., 93n754
Orr, Leonard, 90n1067, 93n1114
Orrick, Sarah, 94n2004
Orrmont, Arthur, 92n896
Orson Welles: a bio-bibliog, 91n1361
Orszagh, L., 92n1075, 92n1076
Orthopedic & trauma surgery, 90n1665
Ortiz, Sylvia P., 93n954
Ortolani, Benito, 94n1466
Oryx Press, 90n788
Osborne, C. W., 92n282, 94n382
Osborne, Charles, 90n1271
Oscar Wilde: an annot bibliog, 94n1262
OSI dict of acronyms & related abbrevs, 94n1891
Osier, Donald V., 92n291
Osman, Madina M., 93n1099
Osmond, Jonathan, 94n522
Osterreich, Shelley Anne, 92n372
Ostler, Rosemarie, 93n1049
Ostojic, Branko, 91n1094
Ostraka, 92n503
Ostroff, Harriet, 93n1470
Ostrow, Rona, 90n597
Otchere, Freda E., 94n629
Otfinoski, Steven, 92n1152
Othello: an annot bibliog, 91n1214
Otness, Harold M., 91n1215
O'Toole, Christopher, 90n1521
Ott, Bill, 93n9
Ottesen, Carole, 90n1503
Ottley, John R., 90n928
Otto Luening: a bio-bibliog, 92n1265
Ottoman Turkish writers, 90n1211
Ouellet, Henri, 92n1566

Our family, our friends, our world, 93n1127
Our natl holidays, 93n1313
Our natl symbols, 93n1309
Our Sunday Visitor's Catholic dict, 94n1531
Out of the closet & into the classroom, 94n906
Out of the woodpile, 93n1151
Outhwaite, William, 94n73
Outstanding women athletes, 93n818
Overbury, Stephen, 91n647
Overmier, Judith A., 90n1480
Over-the-counter 1000, 90n214
Owen, Bobbi, 93n1383, 93n1384
Owen, Dolores B., 90n395
Owen, Nancy R., 94n1145
Owen, Robert D., 90n1557
Owls of the N hemisphere, 90n1545
Ownbey, Gerald B., 92n1533
Owners & officers of private cos, 1992, 93n196
Oxbridge dir of newsletters 1990, 91n961
Oxford companion to ...
 American theatre, 2d ed, 94n1480
 Australian folklore, 94n1390
 Australian sport, 94n822
 Canadian theatre, 91n1400
 chess, 2d ed, 94n842
 classical lit, 2d ed, 90n1099
 musical instruments, 94n1338
 pols of the world, 94n717
 popular music, 92n1297
 the Bible, 94n1545
 the English lang, 93n1054
 the Supreme Court of the US, 94n554
Oxford dict for scientific writers & eds, 93n967
Oxford dict of ...
 abbrevs, 93n3
 American legal quotations, 94n584
 Byzantium, 92n510
 modern quotations, 92n68
 new words, 93n1065
 opera, 94n1357
 quotations, 4th ed, 93n92
 saints, 3d ed, 94n1527
Oxford Duden German dict, 91n1085
Oxford ency of European Community law, v.1, 92n534
Oxford encyclopedic English dict, 92n1017
Oxford English dict, 2d ed, 90n1006
Oxford gd to classical mythology in the arts, 1300-1990s, 94n1397
Oxford gd to the French lang, 93n1083
Oxford hist of England: consolidated index, 92n485
Oxford hist of N.Z. lit in English, 92n1239
Oxford illus dict of Australian hist, 94n516
Oxford illus ency, v.3, 90n535
Oxford illus ency, v.4, 90n536
Oxford illus ency of ...
 invention & tech, 93n1451
 peoples & cultures, 94n397
 the arts, 91n932
 the universe, 94n1944
Oxford illus literary gd to Great Britain & Ireland, 2d ed, 94n480
Oxford in fiction, 90n1171
Oxford minidict, 2d ed, 90n998
Oxford minidict of 20th-century world hist, 92n511
Oxford modern English dict, 94n1100
Oxford movement & its leaders, suppl, 94n1522
Oxford paperback French dict, 90n1043
Oxford paperback Italian dict, 90n1048
Oxford thesaurus, American ed, 94n1107
Oxford Turkish dict, 94n1135
Oxford-Duden pictorial Chinese & English dict, 90n1039
Oxford-Duden pictorial Portuguese-English dict, 94n1127
Oxford-Duden pictorial Serbo-Croat & English dict, 90n1055
Oz Clarke's new ency of French wines, 92n1484
Ozer, Jerome S., 90n1270
Ozone layer dict, 94n1945
Ozouf, Mona, 90n516

P. G. Wodehouse: a comprehensive bibliog & checklist, 92n1215
P. T. Forsyth bibliog & index, 94n1520
Pacanowski, John P., 94n1838
Pacific coast inshore fishes, 3d ed, 91n1583
Pacific coast nudibranchs, 93n1573
Pacific research centres, 4th ed, 94n1575
Pacific Rim almanac, 92n137
Paciorek, Michael J., 91n813
Packaging, 90n1426
Packaging engineering resources, 91n1627
Packard, William, 90n1356
Packer, David, 90n1796
Packer, Joan Garrett, 92n1214
Pactor, Howard S., 91n962
Paczulla, Jutta, 92n668
Paden, John Naber, 90n105
Padwick's bibliog of cricket, v.2, 93n828
Paetz, Martin J., 94n1720
Page, G. Terry, 92n232
Page, James A., 92n769
Page, Lawrence M., 92n1576
Page, Penny Booth, 92n840
Paget's disease, 91n1700
Paikeday, Thomas M., 92n1050
Painting of the golden age, 94n1063
Palder, Edward L., 90n791, 91n195
Paleo, Lyn, 91n1141
Palestine question, 92n726
Paletta, Lu Ann, 92n463
Palette of possibilities, 94n1167
Pallay, Steven G., 90n1272
Palliative care of the elderly, 93n857
Palmatier, Robert A., 90n756
Palmegiano, E. M., 94n590
Palmer, Carole L., 92n1225
Palmer, Gregory, 90n43
Palmer, J. J. N., 94n518
Palmer, Jim, 90n321
Palmer, Marlene A., 91n1717
Palmer, Pamela, 94n61
Palmer, Pete, 92n786
Palmer, R. E., 91n614, 94n636
Palmieri, Robert, 90n1262
Palmisano, Joseph M., 92n1795, 93n411, 93n412, 93n878, 94n58
Palmist's companion, 93n809
Palmore, Erdman B., 94n871
Palmquist, Peter E., 92n959, 92n960
Palumbo, Dennis J., 94n588
Pamphlets, pers, & songs of the French revolutionary era in the Princeton Univ Lib, 90n517
Pan-Africanism: an annot bibliog, 94n764
Panero, Julius, 92n954
Pan-European assns, 2d ed, 92n45
Pangallo, Karen L., 91n1207
Pankratz, Tom, 93n1772
Panofsky, Ruth, 94n1277
Panorama of EC industry 93, 94n236
Panovf, Irina, 90n1053
Pantzer, Katharine F., 92n61
Papageorgiou, Markos, 93n1613
Papal encyclicals, 1740-1981, 92n1419
Papal pronouncements, 92n1409
Paperbound bks in print, fall 1990, 91n10
Paperbound bks in print, spring 1989, 90n18
Paperbound bks in print, spring 1992, 93n31
Papers of Elizabeth Cady Stanton and Susan B. Anthony, 94n964
Papp, L., 93n1567
Papua New Guinea, 90n150
Paradis, Line, 92n1471, 94n1058
Paragon House spelling dict, 94n1103
Paraire, Philippe, 93n1291
Parapsychological research with children, 93n808
Parapsychology, new age & the occult, 94n1167
Parapsychology: new sources of info, 1973-89, 92n766
Parasites & diseases of wild mammals in Fla., 93n1569

Parat index of acronyms & abbrevs in electrical & electronic engineering, 90n1592
Paravisini-Gebert, Lizabeth, 94n1301
Parc, Francois, 92n326, 92n1598
Pardes, Herbert, 94n1846
Pare, Michael A., 90n61
Parent, Mary P., 93n328
Parent resource dir, 2d ed, 90n832
Parent, Roger, 90n589
Parent, Roger H., 91n610
Parent's desk ref, 92n842
Parezo, Nancy J., 90n867, 92n373
Parfitt, George, 91n1183
Parham, Iris A., 91n1696, 94n872
Parin, N. V., 94n1719
Paris, Michael, 91n1131
Pariser, E. R., 91n1764
Parish, James Robert, 90n1344, 91n1380, 91n1381, 91n1382, 91n1392, 91n1393, 92n1349, 92n1363, 92n1364, 93n1360, 94n1432, 94n1446, 94n1447
Parisi, Lynn, 90n685
Parisi, Lynn S., 90n344
Park, James, 93n42
Parker, Betty June, 92n316
Parker, Franklin, 92n316
Parker, Geoffrey, 94n530
Parker, Hershel, 93n1178
Parker, Ian, 90n1527
Parker, James G., 92n486
Parker, Lee D., 91n170
Parker, Mark, 91n1833, 94n2030
Parker, Robert, 92n153
Parker, Steve, 90n1518, 90n1523, 94n1819
Parker, Sybil P., 90n1427, 90n1428, 93n1446, 94n1785, 94n1927, 94n1935, 94n1965, 94n1999
Parker-Hale, Mary Ann, 90n1250
Parkes, Geoff, 93n1085
Parkin, Tom, 91n1077
Parkinson, John A., 92n1254
Parks dir of the US, 93n500
Parks, Roger, 91n483, 91n484
Parlett, David, 94n841
Parmley, Robert O., 90n1605
Parness, Jeff, 92n695
Parrinder, Geoffrey, 91n1420
Parrish, Michael, 93n769
Parry, Donald W., 93n1402
Parry, R. B., 91n448
Parsell, Roger, 91n1198
Parsifal on record, 93n1270
Parsons, Charles H., 92n1270
Parsons, Karen Toombs, 91n752
Parsons, Lynn H., 94n498
Parsons, Nicholas T., 93n505
Parsons, Stanley B., 91n752
Partain, Richard B., 90n294
Partington, Angela, 93n92
Partners for Livable Places, 91n847
Partnership almanac, 90n191
Partnow, Elaine, 94n973
Partridge, Michael S., 91n526
Partridge-Brown, Mary, 94n1857
Pasachoff, Jay M., 91n1761, 94n1927, 94n1928
Pascal, Diane, 91n132
Pask, Judith M., 92n598
Paskoff, Paul F., 90n236
Pass, Christopher, 92n126
Passages: a treasure trove of N American exploration, 93n485
Passarelli, Anne B., 90n156
Passenger & immigration lists index, 1992 suppl., 93n460
Passport Books, editors of, 92n1067, 92n1071, 92n1080, 92n1090
Passport's gd to ethnic N.Y., 92n443
Past & promise: lives of N.J. women, 91n923
Past renewed, 94n411
Pastoral responses to older adults & their families, 93n859

Patent, trademark, & copyright laws, 1989 ed, 90n559
Patent, trademark, & copyright laws, 94n576
Pater, Alan F., 90n89
Pater, Jason R., 90n89
Paterson, Ellen R., 93n1666
Patnaik, Pradyot, 94n2015
Paton, John, 91n28, 94n37
Patrias, Karen, 90n1688
Patrick, Gay D., 94n619
Patten, M. N., 91n1632
Patterson, Alex, 93n508
Patterson, Anna Grace, 90n72, 90n593, 93n22, 94n4
Patterson, Austin M., 94n1937
Patterson, Richard, 92n554
Patterson's American educ, v.86, 91n305
Patterson's American educ, v.89, 94n319
Patterson's elementary educ, v.2, 1990 ed, 91n306
Patterson's elementary educ, v.5, 94n320
Patterson's German-English dict for chemists, 4th ed, 94n1937
Patterson's schools classified, v.40, 1990 ed, 91n339
Pauer, Gyula, 90n418
Paul Baker's topical index of contemporary Christian music, 93n1268
Paul, Barbara Dotts, 91n531
Paul, Ellen, 90n799, 93n869
Paul Gauguin: a bio-bibliog, 92n968
Paul, Gregory S., 90n1769
Paul, Shalom M., 93n1435
Paul, T. Otis, 92n1685
Paulin, Mary Ann, 93n671
Paulson, Annie, 90n1497
Paulson, Dennis, 94n1700
Paxton, John, 90n709, 92n427, 93n464, 94n524, 94n766, 94n770
Paying for health care after age 65, 92n1640
Paymer, Marvin E., 90n1251, 94n1366
Payne, Chris, 90n1690
Payne, Peter A., 93n1635
Payne, Wardell J., 92n1404
Payton, Geoffrey, 93n464
PC hdwr & systems implementation, 90n1722
PC-SIG ency of shareware, 4th ed, 93n1689
PDR family gd to prescription drugs, 94n1879
Peace & nuclear war dict, 90n672
Peace & security thesaurus, 91n684
Peace: abstracts of the psychological & behavioral lit 1967-90, 93n789
Peace Corps: an annot bibliog, 90n731
Peace movement orgs & activists in the US, 92n751
Peacekeeping, 91n775
Peacock, John, 92n629, 93n1010
Peake, Hayden B., 94n761
Pearce, David W., 93n183
Pearl Harbor, 1941, 93n696
Pearsall, Derek, 92n1204
Pearsall, Ronald, 94n1023
Pearson, Alison, 94n1682
Pearson, J. D., 90n116, 91n97
Pearson, Steve, 94n1682
Peary, Danny, 91n824, 93n1337
Pecchia, David, 93n1371
Peck, David R., 94n1225
Peck, Terrance W., 92n357
Peckham, Robert D., 92n1234
Pederson, Lee, 91n1064
Pediatric drug hndbk, 2d ed, 90n1698
Pediatrics, 90n1666
Pee Wee speaks, 94n1371
Peggy Glanville-Hicks: a bio-bibliog, 91n1273
Peiris, H. A., 90n715
Pellant, Chris, 91n1789, 93n1728
Pelle, Kimberly D., 91n1336
Peltzman, Barbara R., 91n790
Pemberton, J. Michael, 91n616
Pen is ours, 92n1150
Penguin Canadian dict, 92n1050

Penguin dict for writers & eds, 93n968
Penguin dict of ...
  architecture, 4th ed, 93n1038
  economics, 5th ed, 94n159
  musical performers, 91n1256
  proper names, 93n464
Penguin ency of modern warfare, 93n701
Penguin ency of popular music, 91n1307
Pennell, Allison A., 93n249
Penner, Bob, 90n717
Penney, Barbara, 93n650
Penney, Edmund F., 93n987
Pennsylvania land records, 92n390
Pennsylvania potters 1660-1900, 94n1033
Pennsylvania silversmiths, goldsmiths & pewterers 1684-1900, 94n1034
Pennsylvania workers in brass, copper & tin 1681-1900, 94n1035
Penny, Anne, 93n489
Penny, Nicholas, 94n1067
Penny, Richard, 90n443
Pennypincher, A., 91n200, 91n201
Pension funds, 91n245
Pension funds & their advisors 1992, 94n266
Pension lists of 1792-95, 93n457
Pensions vocabulary, 92n214
People atlas, 93n414
People in the news, 92n23
People in world hist, 1989 ed, 90n537
People speak: American elections in focus, 91n748
People to know, 91n15
People's Almanac presents the bk of lists: the '90s ed, 94n1403
People's chronology, rev ed, 93n554
People's gd to vitamins & minerals from A to zinc, rev ed, 90n1699
People's Medical Society, 94n1812
Peoples of ...
  the American West, 90n1080
  the world: Africans south of the Sahara, 93n117
  the world: Eastern Europe & the post-Soviet republics, 94n132
  the world: Latin Americans, 90n139
  the world: N Americans, 92n340
  the world: the Middle East & N Africa, 93n160
  the world: W Europeans, 94n128
People's Republic of China, State Statistical Bureau, 90n120, 90n184
People's Republic of China yr bk 1991/92, 94n109
Pepermans, Raymond, 91n782
Pepper, Margaret, 91n1419
Percussion discography, 91n1286
Perdue, Lewis, 93n969
Perennial garden plants, 3d ed, 92n1507
Peretz, Annette, 91n1705
Perez, Danny, 90n1300
Perez, Janet, 94n1289
Perez, Louis A., 92n495
Perez-Sabido, Jesus, 90n1670
Perez-Stable, Maria A., 90n1080
Perfume hndbk, 94n1940
Perigee visual dict of signing, rev ed, 93n1098
Perinn, Vincent L., 92n1180
Periodical lit on American music, 1620-1920, 90n1219
PERiodical source index 1847-1985, v.1, 90n397
PERiodical source index 1847-1985, v.3, 90n398
PERiodical source index 1847-1985, v.5-8, 92n393
PERiodical source index 1847-1985, v.9-12, 94n437
PERiodical source index 1989, 92n394
PERiodical source index 1991 annual v., 94n438
Perkins, Agnes, 94n1171
Perkins, Agnes Regan, 90n1094, 94n1172
Perkins, Barbara, 92n1155
Perkins, C. R., 91n448
Perkins, Dorothy, 92n95
Perkins, George, 92n1155
Perkins, Kenneth J., 90n113
Perle, E. Gabriel, 90n558, 94n574

Perlmutter, Barry F., 91n863
Perlo, Don, 91n1318
Perna, Michael L., 92n1242
Pernetta, John, 93n1730
Perone, James E., 94n1330
Perone, Karen L., 92n1271
Perper, Timothy, 92n832
Perren, Richard, 93n126
Perrett, Bryan, 90n653, 94n695
Perretta, Don, 90n1294
Perrin, Robert G., 94n1490
Perritt, Gerald W., 91n184, 94n198
Perry, Gerald J., 92n1678
Perry, Glenn E., 92n726
Perry, Jane Greverus, 91n461
Perry, Jeb H., 93n996
Perry, Jesse P., Jr., 93n1519
Perry, John, 91n461
Perry, Linda, 91n160
Perry, Ruth M., 92n373
Persaud, Tina, 93n4
Persian & English glossary for humanities & social scis, 93n1090
Persian-English dict, 94n1126
Person, James E., Jr., 91n1186, 92n1107, 94n932
Personal info index 1988, 90n565
Personal writings by women to 1900, 90n855
Personnel executives contactbk, 94n286
Persson, Bertil, 91n1447
Persson, Conrad, 92n432
Pesman, M. Walter, 93n1505
Pessin, Allan H., 91n185
Pest control Canada, 6th ed, 91n1479
Pesticide residues in food 1990, 92n1498
Pesticide residues in food 1992, evaluations pt.1, 94n1611
Pesticide users' health & safety hndbk, 90n1451
Pestline, 92n1785
Peter Cushing: the gentle man of horror & his 91 films, 94n1437
Peter Porter: a bibliog 1954-86, 91n1212
Peter Shaffer: an annot bibliog, 92n1208
Peter Taylor: a descriptive bibliog 1934-87, 90n1155
Peterjohn, Bruce G., 91n1559
Peterkin, Karen, 91n1648
Peters atlas of the world, 91n428
Peters, Evelyn J., 92n374
Peters, Gary L., 94n465
Peters, Jacob, 94n864
Peters, Robert, 91n1178
Peters, Susanne, 91n57
Petersen, Neal H., 93n785
Peterson 1st gd to ...
　caterpillars of N America, 94n1730
　clouds & weather, 92n1732
　dinosaurs, 91n1791
　fishes of N America, 91n1582
　reptiles & amphibians, 93n1577
　rocks & minerals, 92n1742
　seashores, 93n1574
　shells of N America, 91n1549
　the solar system, 91n1761
　trees, 94n1674
Peterson, Anne C., 92n843
Peterson, Bernard L., Jr., 92n1160
Peterson, Carolyn Sue, 93n1129
Peterson, Kimberley A., 93n261
Peterson, Linda, 91n277
Peterson, Patricia R., 91n1652
Peterson, Roger Tory, 90n1535, 91n1567, 94n1701
Peterson's bus & mgmt jobs 1989, 90n187
Peterson's college money hndbk 1991, 92n307
Peterson's colleges with programs for students with learning disabilities, 94n340
Peterson's competitive colleges 1990-91, 91n340
Peterson's competitive colleges 1993-94, 94n341
Peterson's dir of college accommodations, 90n437
Peterson's drug & alcohol programs & policies at 4-yr colleges, 90n825
Peterson's engineering, sci, & computer jobs 1989, 90n188
Peterson's gd to ...
　college admissions, 5th ed, 92n308
　colleges with programs for learning-disabled students, 2d ed, 90n349
　4-yr colleges 1991, 91n336
　4-yr colleges 1994, 94n342
　graduate & professional programs 1989, 90n328
　graduate & professional programs, 25th ed, 92n309
　independent secondary schools 1991-92, 92n288
　2-yr colleges 1991, 91n318
　2-yr colleges 1994, 94n343
Peterson's grants for grad study, 3d ed, 93n374
Peterson's grants for postdoctoral study, 93n375
Peterson's register of higher educ 1990, 91n319
Peterson's register of higher educ 1993, 94n344
Peterson's summer opportunities for kids & teenagers 1990, 91n309
Petit, Patrick J., 94n566
Petrides, George A., 94n1674
Petrocelly, K. L., 90n1607
Petroleum fundamentals glossary, 92n1755
Petroleum sftwr dir, 1990, 6th ed, 90n1785
Petroleum sftwr dir, 1994, 94n1974
Petti, Kerstin, 92n1092
Petti, Vincent, 92n1092
Pettijohn, Terry F., 93n800
Petzal, David E., 92n932
Petzet, G. Alan, 93n1750
Pevsner, Nikolaus, 93n1038
Pfaff, Bonnie Shaw, 92n543
Pfaffenberger, Bryan, 91n1726, 92n1711
Pfannl, Beth Kempler, 90n138
Pfautz, Leanne, 92n542
Pfeffer, Glenn B., 94n1820
Pfeffer, Pierre, 90n1526
Pham, Gisele, 93n1600
Pharmaceutical manufacturing ency, 2d ed, 90n1697
Pharmacology from A to Z, 90n1696
Pheby, John, 90n1039
Phelps, Erin, 93n102
Phenix, Katharine, 91n919
Phifer, Paul, 94n362
Philanthropic studies index, 92n828
Philbin, Tom, 90n1609, 93n1611
Philcox, Phil, 91n257
Philip, Alan Butt, 93n768
Philip Lief Group, 90n278, 90n1736
Philip Morrison's long look at the lit, 91n1457
Philipp, Alan, 94n266
Philipp, Hans-Jurgen, 91n124
Philips, Christopher Lee, 94n658
Phillips, Casey R., 94n542
Phillips, Charles, 94n1993
Phillips, Dennis J., 90n776
Phillips, Donald E., 93n956
Phillips, Ellen, 94n1620
Phillips, Gillian, 93n885
Phillips Publishing's telephone industry dir 1989, 90n249
Phillips, Roger, 90n1509, 92n1544
Phillips, Sally, 92n518
Phillips, Steven J., 90n975
Philo of Alexandria: an annot bibliog, 1937-86, 90n1374
Philos, Daphne A., 94n363
Philosopher's dict, 92n1395
Philosopher's index thesaurus, 93n1397
Philosopher's index, v.23, 1989 cum ed, 91n1408
Philosophy bks 1982-86, 92n1391
Philpott, Jane, 91n1535
Phonetics & speech sci, 90n992
Photograde, 92n930
Photographers: a sourcebk for histl research, 93n1014
Photographer's market, 1991, 91n1001

Photography & lit, 93n1013
Phrase that launched 1,000 ships, 92n1059
Phrenology in the British Isles, 90n754
Physical educ index, v.12, 1989, 91n814
Physical educ index, v.13, no.3, 91n815
Physical fitness & sports medicine, 90n1688
Physician-patient relationships, 92n1648
Physicians' desk ref, 1993, 94n1880
Physician's drug hndbk, 5th ed, 94n1881
Physicians' generix 1992, 94n1882
Physicians' gd to rare diseases, 94n1863
Physicians' obituaries, 1989, 91n1656
Phytochemical dict, 94n1639
Pianist's gd to transcriptions, arrangements, & paraphrases, 91n1288
Piano info gd, 90n1262
Piano music by black women, 93n1264
Piano-beds & music by steam, 94n1318
Piantone, Paola, 90n574
Piaseckyj, Oksana, 91n1248
Piccirelli, Annette, 92n688, 93n68, 93n1768, 94n165, 94n345
Pick, James B., 90n145
Pickard, Roy, 90n1324
Picker, Martin, 92n1272
Pickering, David, 90n1356
Pickering, W. R., 92n1696
Pick-up games, 94n823
Pickup, Laurie, 90n842
Pickwell, George V., 94n1750
Pickwick Papers: an annot bibliog, 91n1203
Picquet, D. Cheryn, 94n1892
Picture bks for children, 3d ed, 91n1109
Picture gd to tree leaves, 92n1554
Picture this!, 93n1355
Picturesque scenery of the Lake District 1752-1855, 92n447
Pidgeon, Alice, 93n570
Pierce, Arthur, 91n1358
Pierce, Benjamin A., 91n1695
Pierce, John H., 90n1466
Pierce, Linda C., 91n169
Pierce, Phyllis S., 90n205, 92n165, 94n187
Pierce, Vivienne S., 93n859
Pierce, William L., 93n866
Piers Plowman: a gd to the quotations, 94n1253
Pietraszek, Magdalena, 94n130
Pigs: a hndbk to the breeds of the world, 94n1740
Pike, Linda J., 90n265
Pilbeam, David, 94n394
Pile, John, 92n922
Pilger, Mary Anne, 93n1005, 93n1308, 93n1312, 93n1461
Pilgrimage in the middle ages, 94n1523
Pilipino/English, English/Pilipino concise dict, 90n1061
Pilkington, Michael, 90n1222, 90n1223
Pill bk, 4th ed, 92n1690
Pilla, Marianne Laino, 91n367
Pillsbury, Richard, 94n819
Pimlott, John, 92n658
Pinckney, Cathey, 90n1671
Pinckney, Edward R., 90n1671
Pincoe, Ruth, 94n1476
Pines of Mexico & Central America, 93n1519
Pinfold, John, 93n130
Pinick, Joanna, 92n434
Pinion, F. B., 91n1209
Pinkoski, Karen, 93n135
Pinna, Giovanni, 92n1746
Pinocchio cat, 90n1086
Pinsker, Sanford, 93n442
Pinsky, Maxine A., 91n988
Pirie, Andrew, 91n565
Pisaneschi, Janet, 90n1678
Pisarek, Walery, 91n935
Pistol bk, 2d ed, 90n925
Pit bull dilemma, 91n558
Pitman, Randy, 91n1359

Pitt, Barrie, 91n544
Pitt, Frances, 91n544
Pitt, Robert D. W., 91n515
Pitts, Michael R., 91n1381, 91n1382, 92n1349, 92n1365, 92n1366, 93n1360
Pivato, Joseph, 90n1197
Pivotal conflict: a comprehensive chronology of the 1st World War, 1914-19, 93n552
Pizer, Donald, 92n1169
Pizzorno, Joseph E., 93n1634
Place gd, 1990 ed, 92n422
Place names in Ala., 90n426
Place names of Alta., [v.1], 92n424
Place names of Alta., v.2, 93n492
Place-names in classical mythology: Greece, 90n1302
Places, 90n444
Places rated almanac, 91n908
Places, towns & townships, 94n937
Plain talk about art, 2d ed, 90n956
Planets, potions & parchments, 92n1464
Planning lib facilities, 91n643
Plano, Jack C., 94n784
Plant, animal & anatomical illus in art & sci, 92n1513
Plant closings, 93n300
Plant engineer's ref bk, 93n1608
Plant life, 92n1534
Plant life of W Austral., 92n1527
Plant names of medieval England, 91n1521
Plant resources of SE Asia, no.2, 92n1475
Plant tissue culture, 92n1529
Plantagenet ency, 91n525
Plants & flowers of Great Britain & N Europe, 94n1657
Plants for ground-cover, 91n1507
Plastics additives & modifiers hndbk, 93n1711
Plastics technical dict, 94n1938
Platnick, Norman I., 93n1563
Platt, Suzy, 90n82
Play index 1988-92, 94n1481
Play, learn, & grow, 94n1184
Plays for children & young adults, 92n1129
Plevin, Arlene, 92n791
Pleyel as music publisher, 91n1251
Ploski, Harry A., 90n364
Plot locator, 92n1140
Pluhar, Jennifer, 94n1664
Plumbers & pipe fitters lib, 4th ed, 91n1636
Plumbers hndbk, 8th ed, 92n1599
Plunkett, Michael, 91n391
Pocket drug gd, 90n1701
Pocket ency, 91n29
Pocket factfinder, 91n31
Pocket gd to ...
    electrical equipment & instrumentation, 2d ed, 93n1599
    nursing diagnoses, 3d ed, 90n1694
    the identification of 1st eds, 4th ed, 91n668
Pocket Oxford dict of current English, 8th ed, 94n1078
Pocket PCref, 93n1684
Pocket place names of Hawai'i, 90n428
Pocket ref, 93n1454
Pockney, B. P., 93n142
Podell, Janet, 90n706
Podrazik, Walter J., 91n972
Poems of Emily Dickinson: an annot gd to commentary published in English, 94n1233
Poetry by American women, 1975-89, 92n1187
Poetry by women to 1900, 92n1245
Poetry criticism, v.1, 92n1247
Poetry criticism, v.5, 94n1303
Poetry index annual 1990, 93n1238
Poets & Writers, Inc., staff of, 91n946
Poet's market 1990, 90n903
Poggi, Isotta, 93n811
Pogonowski, Iwo Cyprian, 90n521, 91n1090
Pohanish, Richard P., 94n2016
Poirot, Jean-Paul, 93n1725

Poisonous plants of Canada, 91n1522
Poisonous snakes of the world, 93n1578
Pok, Attila, 93n546
Polach, Dilette, 90n1762
Poland, rev ed, 94n134
Poland: a histl atlas, rev ed, 90n521
Polangin, Richard F., 92n1638
Pole, J. R., 92n470
Polic, Edward F., 90n1289
Police dict & ency, 90n568
Police, firefighter, & paramedic stress, 91n787
Police products hndbk, 91n599
Policies of ...
    AV producers & distrs, 2d ed, 91n616
    educl sftwr pubIs, 92n328
    publishers, 1989 ed, 90n645
Polisar, Donna, 90n785
Polish biographical dict, 93n44
Polish music, 90n1216
Polish roots, 94n433
Polish-English, English-Polish dict with complete phonetics, rev ed, 91n1090
Political & economic ency of ...
    S America & the Caribbean, 93n774
    the Pacific, 91n126
    the Soviet Union & Eastern Europe, 92n104
    W Europe, 92n714
Political corruption: scope & resource, 91n716
Political data hndbk: OECD countries, 93n727
Political dict of the state of Israel, suppl. 1987-93, 2d ed, 94n785
Political hndbk of the world 1989, 91n722
Political leaders in black Africa, 93n761
Political leaders in Weimar Germany, 94n774
Political leaders of the contemporary Middle East & N Africa, 91n762
Political left in the American theatre of the 30's, 93n1375
Political parties & elections in the US, 92n685
Political parties in Sri Lanka since independence, 90n715
Political parties of ...
    Asia & the Pacific, 94n765
    the Americas and the Caribbean, 94n783
    the Americas, 1980s to 1990s, 94n720
Political quotations, 91n724
Political resource dir 1989, 90n682
Political resource dir 1993, 94n719
Political scandals & causes celebres since 1945, 92n678
Political sci, 91n717
Polk, Noel, 90n1140, 91n1162
Polking, Kirk, 91n952
Polkinhorn, Harry, 90n1153
Pollack, Martin, 90n892, 91n938
Pollack, Sandra, 94n1226
Pollin, Burton R., 91n1171
Pollock, Bruce, 90n1281, 93n1279
Pollock, Sean R., 94n932
Pollock, Steve, 94n1686, 94n1987
Pollock, Zailig, 94n1278
Polmar, Norman, 93n556, 94n705
Polner, Murray, 93n450
Polymer hndbk, 3d ed, 91n1773
Polymer sci dict, 90n1751
Ponko, Vincent, Jr., 91n125
Pool player's natl pocket billiard dir, 1992 ed, 94n858
Pool player's road atlas 1994, 94n859
Poole, Chris, 90n1810
Poorman, Susan, 92n882
Pope, Rex, 90n151
Pope, Stephen, 91n554
Popp, Judy, 91n218
Popular dict of Sikhism, 91n1452
Popular entertainment research, 93n1327
Popular gd to classical music, 94n1345
Popular music, v.13, 90n1281
Popular music, v.15, 93n1279
Popular reading for children 3, 94n1168

Popular song index, 3d suppl, 90n1276
Population hist of E US cities & towns, 1790-1870, 93n900
Pop-up & movable bks, 94n1177
Porkess, Roger, 93n904
Porteous, Andrew, 94n2000
Porter, A. N., 92n487
Porter, Allison I., 92n230
Porter, David L., 90n757, 90n769, 93n817
Porter, George S., 92n1468
Porter, James, 90n1283
Porter, Valerie, 93n1491, 94n1740
Porterfield, Kay Marie, 94n917
Porter-Shirley, Bunny, 90n825
Portmanteau dict, 94n1083
Portraits of American women, 93n932
Portraying persons with disabilities: an annot bibliog of fiction, 3d ed, 93n1132
Portraying persons with disabilities: an annot bibliog of nonfiction, 2d ed, 93n1124
Position descriptions in special libs, 2d ed, 94n624
Positively Bob Dylan, 92n1312
Posner, Julia L., 90n800, 90n822
Post, Elizabeth L., 93n1307
Post, Joyce A., 94n655
Post-feminist Hollywood actress, 91n1363
Post-harvest & processing techs of African staple foods, 93n1478
Post-release assistance programs for prisoners, 94n910
Potato terms, 91n1487
Potparic, O., 93n1658
Potter, Robert B., 94n148
Potter, Vilma Raskin, 94n1009
Potter's dict of materials & techniques, 3d ed, 92n950
Pottker, Jan, 94n155
Potts, George, 94n1679
Potts, William F., 94n1901
Pough, Frederick H., 92n1742
Poultney, David, 93n1269
Pouyez, Christian, 93n132
Poverty in developing countries, 94n905
Poverty row horrors, 94n1461
Povsic, Frances, 92n1229
Powell, Anton, 91n540
Powell, Charles C., 94n1624
Powell, Mark Allan, 93n1432
Powell, William S., 92n33
Power brokers, 90n481
Power media selects, 5th ed, 92n889
Power quotes, 93n730
PowerBoat gd, 2d ed, 91n1833
PowerBoat gd, 3d ed, 94n2030
Powers, Bethel Ann, 91n1706
Powers, John, 93n1414
Poyer, Joe, 91n689, 91n711
Pozin, Mikhail A., 94n160
Practical approach series cum methods index, 92n1526
Practical English-Chinese pronouncing dir, 94n1110
Practical English-Japanese dict, 92n1082
Prance, Ghillean T., 90n1498
Pranin, Stanley A., 93n838, 94n854
Prather, Ronald, 94n1324
Pratt, Douglas, 93n997
Pratt, Frantz, 92n113
Pratt, Vernon, 91n1180
Pratt's gd to venture capital sources, 1992 ed, 93n197
Pravda, Alex, 93n788, 94n136
PRC Year Book, Beijing, Editorial Department, 94n109
Prebish, Charles S., 94n1519
Pre-cinema hist, 94n1427
Predators & predation, 90n1526
Predatory dinosaurs of the world, 90n1769
Prelinger, Richard, 91n966
Preller, James, 94n1193
Premiere gd to movies on video, 92n1341
Premiere Magazine, 92n1341
Preminger, Alex, 94n1302

Prentice, Ann E., 90n593
Prentice Hall banking yrbk, 92n189
Prentice Hall Editorial Staff, 90n291
Prentice Hall encyclopedic dict of English usage, 2d ed, 94n1091
Prentice Hall good reading gd, 90n1104
Prentice Hall gd to English lit, 91n1187
Prentice Hall real estate investor's ency, 91n287
Prentice Hall's illus dict of computing, 94n1902
Prentice-Hall pocket ency: house plants, 90n1471
Prentice-Hall pocket ency of ...
    creative photography, 92n961
    home decorating, 92n956
    organic gardening, 93n1488
Prepas, Ellie, 92n410
Presbyterians, 94n1533
Preschool resource gd, 94n312
Prescription drugs & their side effects, 94n1884
Presenting children's authors, illustrators & performers, 92n1127
Preservation & access tech, 92n599
Presidency A to Z, 94n508
President, Patricia A., 93n1618
Presidential landmarks, 94n477
Presidential primaries & caucuses 1992, 94n755
Presidents' last years, 90n478
Presidents of the USA, 12th ed, 91n493
Presidents' wives, 90n485
Presner, Lewis A., 93n255
Presocratic philosophers, 94n1488
Press in Nigeria, 91n960
Preston, Cathy Lynn, 90n1180
Preston, John, 93n886
Preston, Richard J., Jr., 90n1510
Preston, Virginia, 93n144
Preston-Mafham, Ken, 92n1551
Preston-Mafham, Rod, 92n1551
Prevention educ, 91n883
Prevention how-to dict of healing remedies & techniques, 93n1636
Prevention magazine, editors of, 94n1805
Prevention Magazine Health Books, editors of, 91n1675, 92n1639, 92n1661, 93n1636
Prevention's giant bk of health facts, 92n1639
Prezelin, Bernard, 91n695, 94n704
Pribic, Rado, 91n1098
Pribylovski, Vladimir, 94n262
Pribylovskii, Vladimir, 94n779
Price, Anne, 92n610
Price, David H., 90n361
Price, H. Marcus, III, 92n549
Price of admission, 91n727
Price, Robert L., 90n445
Price, Taff, 93n837
Prickett, Robert L., 93n343
Pridgeon, Alec, 94n1658
Primaryplots, 90n1095
Prime sources of Calif. & Nev. local hist, 93n511
Primm, E. Russell, 91n371
Prince, Mary Miles, 90n538, 90n543, 93n562, 94n543, 94n544
Princeton Alciati companion, 90n1051
Princetonians 1784-90, 93n356
Princetonians 1791-94, 93n357
Pringle, David, 90n1105, 92n1144
Pringle, Peter K., 90n912
Print price index '93, 93n1032
Print Project, 94n203
Prints of Robert Motherwell, 92n1003
Prisma's Swedish-English & English-Swedish dict, 4th ed, 90n1060
Prison pictures from Hollywood, 92n1364
Prison slang, 93n603
Pritchard, James B., 92n1439
Private independent schools 1988, 90n316
Private law dict & bilingual lexicons, 90n547
Private libs in renaissance England, v.1, 94n598
Private libs in renaissance England, v.2, 94n599
Private schools of the US, 90n317

Prizewinning lit: UK literary award winners, 91n1185
Pro basketball stats, 94n840
Pro football bio-bibliog, 90n774
Pro football hall of fame, 92n794
Pro/Am bk of music & mythology, 94n1316
Pro/Am gd to US bks about music, 1987 suppl, 90n1215
Probe dir of foreign direct investment in the US, 6th ed, 90n215
Process plant machinery, 90n1585
Prochner, Lawrence, 94n315
Pro-choice/pro-life, 92n834
Proctor & Hughes' chemical hazards of the workplace, 3d ed, 92n1786
Proctor, William, 94n1104
Produced & abandoned, 92n1345
Product design mgmt, 90n244
Product dvlpmt dir 1993, 94n1836
Product SOS 1993, 94n1837
Professional & occupational licensing dir, 94n800
Professional baseball franchises, 94n832
Professional careers sourcebk, 91n378
Professional careers sourcebk, 2d ed, 93n411
Professional codes of conduct in the UK, 91n269
Professional football, 94n847
Professional goldsmithing, 92n953
Professional gd to diseases, 3d ed, 90n1676
Professional gd to diseases, 4th ed, 94n1841
Professional Secretaries Intl complete office hndbk, 93n324
Professional secretary's encyclopedic dict, 4th ed, 90n291
Professional secretary's hndbk, rev ed, 94n301
Proffer, Carl R., 92n1230
ProFile 1991-92, 92n998
Profiles 1989-90, 93n390
Profiles in childhood educ 1931-60, 94n313
Program for Art on Film, 93n1016
Project BREED dir, 94n1708
Projected pulp & paper mills in the world 1990-2000, 92n1502
Prominent families of the USA, 92n387
Pronouncing dict of proper names, 94n1084
Propagation of alpine plant & dwarf bulbs, 94n1629
Propas, Sharon W., 93n533
Proper noun speller, 91n1078
Prosocial dvlpmt in children, 93n894
Prospect researcher's gd to biographical research collections, 93n675
Prostitutes in medical lit, 92n1649
Prostitution: a gd to sources, 1960-90, 93n882
Prostitution in Hollywood films, 94n1447
Prosyniuk, Joann, 92n990
Protectionism, 90n279
Protestant sensibility in the American novel, 93n1170
Proulx, Daniel, 92n559
Provose, Carl, 93n918
Provost, Foster, 92n457, 92n512
Prucha, Francis Paul, 92n375
Prue, Donald, 90n1644
Pruett, Barbara J., 92n1304, 93n1327
Prunckun, Henry W., Jr., 92n528
Prune bk: the 60 toughest sci & tech jobs in Washington, 93n757
Pryce, David, 91n114
Prydain companion, 90n1089
Pryor, Judith, 90n735
Prytherch, Ray, 90n360, 90n763, 92n565, 93n21, 93n631, 93n1125
Przecha, Donna, 94n435
Pschyrembel's Klinisches Worterbuch, editorial staff, 90n1641
P.S.I. gd, 94n1799
Psoriasis: professional educl materials, 91n1702
PsycBOOKS 1989, 91n788
Psychiatric dict, 6th ed, 90n1672
Psychoanalysis, psychology, & lit: a bibliog, suppl. to the 2d ed, 91n786
Psychoanalytic terms & concepts, 91n791
Psychology: a gd to ref & info sources, 94n805
Psycholsocial aspects of AIDS, 91n1688
Psychopathology in adulthood, 94n812
Public admin & mgmt vocabulary, 91n782

Public admin desk bk, 91n776
Public admin in the Third World, 91n783
Public admin research gd, 93n794
Public budgeting & financial mgmt, 92n754
Public gardens & parks of Niagara, 90n1466
Public info contact dir 1988-89, 90n1433
Public interest law, 93n566
Public interest law groups, 90n557
Public interest profiles 1988-89, 90n736
Public interest profiles 1992-93, 93n795
Public intl law, 92n516
Public lib cat, 9th ed, 90n620
Public opinion polls & survey research, 91n82
Public relations & ethics, 92n122
Public relations bibliog 1986-87, 92n235
Public relations in bus, govt, & society, 90n156
Public schooling in America, 93n354
Public schools USA, 2d ed, 93n350
Public sector productivity, 90n733
Public utilities, 92n1605
Public welfare dir, 1990/91, 91n879
Public welfare dir, 1993/94, 94n913
Publication peer review, 94n997
Publication sources in educl leadership, 93n343
Public-domain sftwr & shareware, 2d ed, 90n1727
Publicity & media resources for bk pubs, 1992-1993 ed, 94n670
Publishers dir, 1989, 90n639
Publishers dir, 1992, 93n687
Publishers, distrs & wholesalers of ...
 the US 1989-90, 90n640
 the US 1990-91, 92n641
 the US 1991-92, 93n688
 the US 1993-94, 94n671
Publishers' intl ISBN dir, 16th ed, 91n666
Publishers trade list annual 1989, 90n19
Publishers trade list annual, 1992, 94n660
Publishing law hndbk, 1989 suppl, 90n558
Publishing law hndbk, 2d ed, 94n574
Puccio, Joseph, 90n1718
Puccio, Joseph A., 90n618
Puckett, Katharyn E., 93n1131
Pukui, Mary Kawena, 90n428, 93n1086
Pulp & paper industry in the OECD member countries 1990, 94n237
Pulsiano, Phillip, 90n1165, 94n526
Pun my word, 92n1034
Punctuation handbk, 90n901
Purcell, Catherine, 93n376, 94n575
Purcell, L. Edward, 94n500
Purchasing an ency, 3d ed, 91n33
Purchasing an ency, 4th ed, 94n38
Purkis, R. H. A., 91n148
Pursell, Frances Josephson, 90n356
Purver, Ron, 92n667, 92n668
Purvis, James D., 93n544
Pusan perimeter, Korea, 1950, 94n679
Putnam, Paul A., 92n1512
Putnam's concise mythological dict, 92n1324
Putz, Manfred, 90n712
Pyatt, Sherman E., 91n842
Pycroft, Christopher, 91n92
Pyle, Gerald F., 94n1802
Pynsent, Robert B., 94n1281
Pyott, Patty, 92n310
Pyper, T. R., 90n610
Pythagoras: an annot bibliog, 91n1401

Quaglieri, Philip L., 90n261
Quah, Jon S. T., 90n123
Quah, Stella R., 90n123
Quality control, 92n233
Quality declared seed, 94n1596
Quantification in sci, 92n1748
Quarks, critters, & chaos, 94n1585

Quarles, Sandra L., 93n595
Quebedeaux, Richard, 93n511
Queens, empresses, grand duchesses & regents, 90n869
Quentin Crisp's bk of quotations, 91n872
Quertermous, Russell C., 90n924
Quertermous, Steven C., 90n924
Que's computer user's dict, 91n1726
Que's computer user's dict, 2d ed, 92n1711
Quick gd to food additives, 2d ed, 92n1494
Quick look drug bk with indications index, 93n1665
Quick ref gd to Astronomy mag 1973-90, 92n1722
Quick ref gd to Natl Geographic 1955-mid 1990, 92n421
Quick reference Chinese, 90n1038
Quick selection gd to chemical protective clothing, 2d ed, 94n1767
Quigley, Ellen, 90n1194, 90n1195
Quigley, Thomas, 92n1273
Quilt ency illus, 92n952
Quilt groups today, 94n1031
Quinlan, David, 93n1338
Quinlan's illus dir of film comedy actors, 93n1338
Quinn, Karen J., 91n1188
Quinn, Kenneth P., 91n1188
Quitno, Neal, 91n901, 93n912, 94n1816
Quotable business, 93n218
Quotable quote bk, 92n67
Quotable woman, 92n870
Quotation location, 91n67
Quote it 2, 90n566
"Quote me", 91n68

R. G. Collingwood: a bibliographical checklist, 94n1484
R. R. Bowker Database Publishing Group, 90n1420
R&D ratios & budgets, 94n295
Rabin, Carol Price, 92n1255
Rabin, Jack, 90n737, 92n754
Rabinovitz, Rubin, 91n1238
Rabson, Carolyn, 94n1348
Rachel Carson Council, staff of, 94n2009
Racial & religious violence in America, 92n553
Racism in the US, 91n384
Rackham, Peter, 91n706
Radford, F. L., 91n546
Radice, Roberto, 90n1374
Radie Britain: a bio-bibliog, 91n1265
Radio: a ref gd, 90n911
Radio & TV pioneers: a patent bibliog, 93n983
Radio & TV, suppl.2, 90n912
Radio broadcasting from 1920 to 1990, 92n907
Radio dial radio station gd, 90n917
Radioactive waste as a social & pol issue, 92n1768
Radiocarbon dating lit, 90n1762
Radon dir 1990-91, 91n1810
Radon industry dir 1989, 90n1795
Radu, Michael, 91n761
Raeburn, Michael, 90n1231
Rafailovich, Miriam H., 94n1923
Raffauf, Robert F., 91n1538
Ragan, David, 93n1339
Ragazzini, Giuseppe, 92n1081
Rageau, Jean-Pierre, 91n714, 94n712
Raglin, Lorraine, 92n855
Rahman, H. U., 90n519
Rahman, Syedur, 90n117
Rahr, Alexander, 92n715
Rai, Priya Muhar, 90n1414
RAIC dir of scholarships & awards for architecture, 93n1039
Railway dict, 94n2022
Rainey, Buck, 91n1394, 92n1367, 93n1361
Rainforest plants of E Austral., 94n1682
Raintree illus sci ency, 94n1569
Raj, Prakash A., 93n501
Rake, Alan, 93n760
Ralph Pickard Bell Library, staff of, 92n6
Ralph Vaughan Williams: a gd to research, 91n1267

Ralson, Anthony, 94n1903
Rama, Eller D., 92n1760
Ramsay, Jeff, 91n94
Ramsey, Patricia G., 90n319
Ramsey/Sleeper architectural graphic standards, 8th ed, 90n976
Ramson, W. S., 90n1027, 94n1096
Rand McNally atlas of American frontiers, 94n490
Rand McNally atlas of world hist, 1992 ed, 93n545
Rand McNally children's atlas of ...
    native Americans, 94n421
    the environment, 92n1766
    the US, 90n412
Rand McNally children's world atlas, 90n410
Rand McNally Goode's world atlas, 18th ed, 91n429
Rand McNally handy railroad atlas of the US, 90n1811
Rand McNally 1990 commercial atlas & mktg gd, 91n276
Rand McNally photographic world atlas, 90n411
Rand McNally picture atlas of prehistoric life, 94n1962
Rand McNally picture atlas of the world, 92n404
Rand McNally pocket city atlas, 90n413
Rand McNally pocket road atlas, 90n414
Rand McNally road atlas, 67th ed, 93n468
Rand McNally road atlas: US, Canada, Mexico, 65th ed, 90n415
Rand McNally the explorer world atlas, 92n405
Rand McNally traveler's world atlas & gd, 90n438
Rand McNally world atlas, 93n478
Rand McNally world facts & maps, 90n424
Rand McNally zip code atlas & market planner, 2d ed, 91n147
Randall, Bernice, 92n1033
Randall, John E., 92n1577
Randall, Lilian M. C., 94n29
Randall Thompson: a bio-bibliog, 92n1260
Randolph, Ruth Elizabeth, 91n1150
Random House atlas of the oceans, 93n1730
Random House college dict, rev ed, 90n999
Random House compact world atlas, rev ed, 93n479
Random House crossword puzzle dict, 90n1011
Random House dict for writers & readers, 91n1068
Random House ency, 3d ed, 91n34
Random House gd to grammar, usage, & punctuation, 92n1036
Random House hndbk of bus terms, 90n167
Random House health & medicine dict, 94n1830
Random House Portuguese dict, 93n1091
Random House Webster's college dict, 93n1059
Random House word menu, 94n1105
Rangel-Ribeiro, Victor, 94n1349
Ransley, John, 93n721
Ranson, K. Anne, 90n45
Rao, D. S. Prasada, 94n1597
Rap music in the 1980s, 94n1375
Rape: a bibliog, 92n564
Rape: a bibliog 1976-88, 93n620
Raper, Ann Trueblood, 90n789
Raper, Richard, 92n485
Rapid gd to hazardous chemicals in the workplace, 2d ed, 91n1776
Rapp, George R., Jr., 91n1790
Rare & endangered biota of Fla., v.1, 94n1735
Rare & endangered biota of Fla., v.2, 94n1716
Rasic, Jeremija Lj., 93n1475
Rasinski, Timothy V., 93n1130
Rasmussen, Carl G., 90n1386
Rasmussen, Jorg, 90n952
Rasmussen, R. Kent, 92n91
Rasor, Eugene L., 91n527, 93n693, 93n694, 94n527
Rastafari & reggae, 91n1322
Rather, L. J., 92n1650
Rating gd to franchises, rev ed, 92n158
Rating gd to life in America's small cities, 91n911
Ratliff, A. H. C., 91n1699
Ratnachandra, 90n1035
Ratsch, Christian, 94n1667
Raub, Deborah Fineblum, 90n229
Rausch, Ralph, 92n1103
Rawson, Hugh, 93n1213
Ray, Donald I., 91n764

Ray, Harold L., 90n756
Ray, Martin S., 90n1179
Ray, Martyn S., 91n1610
Ray, Mary Helen, 90n1472
Ray, Robert H., 91n1206
Raymond, Eric S., 93n1680
Raymond, Walter John, 93n722
Rayner, Lynn, 91n1674
Raza, Moonis, 93n391
Reaching out, 91n1649
Read all your life, 90n1102
Read for your life, 94n383
Read more about it, v.3, 91n555
Read, Phyllis J., 94n970
Reader dvlpmt bibliog, 4th ed, 92n324
Reader's cat, 91n4
Reader's companion to American hist, 92n468
Reader's companion to the novels & short stories of Evelyn Waugh, 90n1188
Reader's Digest children's world atlas, 93n480
Reader's ency of E European lit, 94n1281
Readers' gd abstracts, v.1, no.4, 90n74
Reader's gd for parents of children with mental, physical, or emotional disabilities, 3d ed, 91n857
Reader's gd to ...
    Australian fiction, 94n1269
    intelligence pers, 94n761
    rational expectations, 93n175
    the American novel of detection, 94n1231
    the private eye novel, 94n1209
    20th century sci fiction, 90n1108
Readers' gd to per lit 1990, 92n60
Reader's quotation bk, 93n403
Reading about the environment, 94n1991
Reading lists for college-bound students, 91n364
Reading the numbers, 91n1794
Ready, Barbara C., 90n358
Reagan, Michael, 93n661
Realms of gold, 92n406
Realty, 2d ed, 91n286
Reardon, Joan, 92n1187
Rebach, Howard M., 93n891
Rebecca West: an annot bibliog, 92n1214
Recent American opera, 92n1291
Recent studies in myths & lit, 1970-90, 93n1301
Recipes into type, 94n1613
Recipex, 92n1500
Recommended family resorts in the US, Canada, & the Caribbean, 91n463
Recommended pubs for legal research 1970/71, 94n549
Recommended pubs for legal research 1989, 92n527
Recommended pubs for legal research 1990, 93n573
Recommended ref bks in paperback, 2d ed, 93n15
Recommended ref bks 1989, 90n6
Recommended ref bks 1990, 91n6
Recommended ref bks 1991, 92n10
Recommended ref bks 1992, 93n22
Recommended ref bks 1993, 94n4
Recommended videos for schools, 92n325
Record of writing: an annot & illus bibliog of George Bowering, 91n1226
Record repositories in Great Britain, 9th ed, 92n488
Record Shelf gd to the classical repertoire, 90n1269
Recorded performances of Gerard Souzay, 92n1284
Records of the presidency, 90n487
Recovery resource bk, 91n891
Recreation & entertainment industries, 91n802
Recreation hndbk, 94n827
Recursos: a dir of Mexican-American insts, orgs, & univ programs, 92n689
Recycling in America, 94n2013
Recycling sourcebk, 94n2017
Red bk, 1993, 94n1883
Red data birds in Britain, 92n1561

Red Sea, Gulf of Aden & Suez Canal, 92n1770
Redden, Kenneth R., 94n555
Redding, Thomas A., 91n577
Reddy, Marlita A., 94n193, 94n282, 94n422
Redfern, Bernice, 90n862
Redford, Kent H., 93n1570
Rediscovery of creation, 93n1417
Redman, Deborah A., 90n157, 93n175
Redner, James H., 92n1580
Reed, Jeffrey G., 93n804
Reed, John H., 90n777
Reeder, DeeAnn M., 94n1743
Reeder, Ray, 94n1331
Reef sharks & rays of the world, 94n1718
Rees, Alan M., 91n1680, 93n1614, 94n1827
Rees, Dafydd, 91n1325, 92n1313
Rees, Mary Noel, 93n738
Rees, Nigel, 90n83, 92n1059
Rees, Philip, 92n732
Rees, Robin, 94n1684
Reeves, Diane Lindsey, 94n923
Reeves, Randall R., 93n1571
Reference and Adult Services Division, American Library Association, 93n17
Reference & info servs, 92n604
Reference bks bulletin 1987-88, 90n5
Reference bks bulletin 1988-89, 91n5
Reference bks bulletin 1989-90, 92n8
Reference bks bulletin 1991-92, 94n3
Reference bks for children, 4th ed, 93n1129
Reference Books Committee, 1989, 90n1078
Reference Department, John Davis Williams Library, University of Mississippi, 92n1140
Reference ency of the American Indian, 5th ed, 91n398
Reference ency of the American Indian, 6th ed, 94n419
Reference gd for English studies, 92n872
Reference gd to ...
    addiction counseling, 92n836
    Afro-American publications & eds 1827-1946, 94n1009
    clean air, 92n1776
    English lit, 2d ed, 92n1192
    sci fiction, fantasy, & horror, 93n1155
    US military hist 1607-1815, 92n466
    US military hist 1815-65, 94n501
    US military hist 1865-1919, 94n502
    world hunger, 92n1486
Reference readiness, 4th ed, 91n646
Reference sources for small & medium-sized libs, 5th ed, 93n17
Reference sources in hist, 92n500
Reference works for theological research, 3d ed, 93n1400
Reference works in British & American lit, v.1, 91n1096
Reference works in British & American lit, v.2, 92n1094
Reflections on childhood, 93n895
Reform Judaism in America, 94n1557
Refugee & immigrant resource dir 1990-91, 91n878
Rega, Regina, 94n175, 94n646, 94n1919
Regan, Geoffrey, 92n659
Reginald, Robert, 90n675, 92n1185, 93n1157, 94n1214
Reginald's sci fiction & fantasy awards, 2d ed, 93n1157
Region & regionalism in the US, 90n96
Regional economic growth in the US, 91n163
Regional interest mags of the US, 92n905
Regional theatre dir 1989-90, 90n1359
Regional theatre dir 1992-93, 93n1388
Register of ...
    Canadian honours, 92n396
    N American hospitals, 1993, 94n1806
    N American insurance cos, 1993, 94n221
Rehabilitation resource manual: vision, 91n856, 94n884
Reher, Ernst-Otto, 91n1609
Rehm, Sigmund, 93n1469
Rehrig, William H., 93n1283
Reich, Bernard, 91n762, 91n770, 94n152
Reichel, Brian J., 90n1443
Reichler, Joseph L., 90n764, 94n835

Reid, Alison, 91n1375
Reid, Bruce J., 90n1703, 91n1715
Reid, Daniel G., 91n1444
Reid, Francis, 94n1475
Reid, Jane Davidson, 94n1397
Reilly, Bernard F., Jr., 93n735
Reilly, Edwin D., 94n1903
Reilly, John W., 90n295
Reimer, Carol J., 93n1362
Reimer, Robert C., 93n1362
Reinberg, Linda, 92n476
Reinehr, Robert C., 94n1017
Reithmaier, Larry, 91n1607
Rela, Walter, 91n1243
RELEX for Russian, 93n1093
Religion & American life, 90n1376
Religion & the American experience, 1620-1900, 94n1507
Religion in pols, 91n1417
Religion in the Soviet Union, 94n1503
Religions on file, 91n1418
Religious bodies in the US, 93n1408
Religious holidays & calendars, 94n1517
Religious info sources, 93n1401
Religious leaders, 93n1403
Religious leaders of America, 92n1402
Religious proverbs, 92n1420
Religious radio & TV in the US, 1921-91, 94n1511
Religious seminaries in America, 90n1377
Religious writer's marketplace, 3d ed, 90n898
Remark, John F., 91n980
Remember the ladies, 94n959
Remini, Robert V., 92n458
Remley, Mary L., 92n767
Remnant, Mary, 91n1281
Renaud, Alix, 92n1490
Renewable energy, 94n1985
Renkiewicz, Frank, 91n961
Renouf, John P., 94n581
Renshaw, Jeffrey H., 93n1284
Renstrom, Peter G., 90n695, 92n530, 92n535
Rentschler, Cathy, 94n621
Renyi picture dict: Hebrew & English, 94n1116
Renyi picture dict: Russian & English, 94n1131
Renz, Loren, 94n896
Report on bus: Canada co hndbk, fall 1989, 91n186
Report on bus: Canada co hndbk 1993, 94n250
Reproduction: a gd to materials in the Women's Educl Resource Centre, 93n885
Reptile care, 92n1588
Reptiles & amphibians, 90n1524, 94n1748
Reptiles & amphibians of Austral., 5th ed, 93n1575
Republic chapterplays, 94n1440
Republic of China yrbk 1991-92, 94n121
Reruns on file, 93n994
Research & dvlpmt growth trends, 1992 ed, 94n209
Research centers dir 1990, 90n326
Research centers dir 1993, 94n345
Research gd for studies in infancy & childhood, 90n830
Research gd to American hist biog, 90n482
Research gd to libs & archives in the Low Countries, 92n607
Research in critical theory since 1965, 90n1067
Research servs dir, 4th ed, 90n64
Research servs dir, 5th ed, 94n165
Researcher's gd to ...
    American genealogy, 2d ed, 91n417
    B.C. 19th century dirs, 90n73
    sources on Soviet social hist in the 1930s, 91n535
Researching copyright renewal, 91n630
Researching modern evangelicalism, 91n1441
Resinger, H., 93n1497
Resource dir for the disabled, 93n864
Resource gd of pubns supported by multiculturalism programs, 94n398
Resource reading list 1990, 91n401

Resources for ...
    educl equity, 90n311
    elders with disabilities, 91n858
    elders with disabilities, 2d ed, 94n873
    people with disabilities & chronic conditions, 92n821
    people with disabilities & chronic conditions, 2d ed, 94n882
    research in legal ethics, 93n592
    teaching thinking, 91n303
    the future, 94n77
    writers, 93n971
Resources in ...
    ancient philosophy, 93n1393
    human-computer interaction, 92n1712
    sacred dance, rev ed, 92n1336
Respectfully quoted, 90n82
Response recordings, 91n1302
Ress, Lisa, 94n806
Restaurateurs & innkeepers, 90n1459
Restoration & 18th-century dramatists, 90n1170
Restoration drama, 91n1193
Restum, Eric J., 94n988
Retfalvi, Andrea, 90n909
Retirement sourcebk, 90n791
Retrospective bibliog of American demographic hist from colonial times to 1983, 90n835
Rettig, James, 93n18
Reuther, David, 91n828, 92n786
Revell Bible dict, 91n1432
Revell concise Bible dict, 93n1433
Revenge of the creature features movie gd, 3d ed, 90n1330
Revere, Alan, 92n953
Reverse symbolism dict, 93n1311
Revolutionary & dissident movements, 3d ed, 93n728
Revolutionary orgs & revolutionaries in interbellum Poland, 93n779
Rew, John, 91n240
Rewards offered by the US, 91n597
Reynolds, C. H. B., 94n119
Reynolds, Cecil R., 92n320
Reynolds, Hugh, 90n688
Reynolds, Jacqueline, 93n1456
Reynolds, Jean E., 90n52, 90n420
Reynolds, Michael, 93n1174
Reynolds, Thomas H., 91n567
Rezak, Ira, 91n1655
Rhoades, Nancy L., 93n829
Rhododendron hybrids, 2d ed, 94n1631
Rhododendron portraits, 93n1506
Rhododendron species, v.3, 93n1504
Ribar, Carlotta, 91n789
Ricci, Patricia L., 91n160
Rice, C. David, 90n1319
Rice, Jane, 92n1659
Rice, Jonathan, 94n1362
Rice, M. Katherine, 91n1663
Rice, Mitchell F., 91n1642
Rice, Tim, 94n1362
Richard, Alfred Charles, Jr., 93n1363, 94n1448
Richard Brautigan: an annot bibliog, 92n1168
Richard Burton: a bio-bibliog, 93n1322
Richard Eberhart: a descriptive bibliog 1921-87, 90n1137
Richard, Francois, 91n1635, 92n1601, 93n1609
Richard Jefferies: a bibliographical study, 94n1252
Richard Rodney Bennett: a bio-bibliog, 91n1268
Richard Widmark: a bio-bibliog, 91n1356
Richard Wilbur: a ref gd, 93n1184
Richards, Betty W., 90n1488
Richards, Gillian, 92n1383
Richards, Laurence O., 93n1433
Richards, Nanci B., 90n792
Richards, William R., 94n1723
Richardson, B. J., 91n1598
Richardson, David T., 94n1737
Richardson, Doug, 91n688
Richardson, Elizabeth P., 91n1019
Richardson, J., 92n588
Richardson, L., Jr., 94n536
Richardson, Michael D., 93n343
Richardson, Selma K., 93n87
Richart, Robert W., 92n1274
Richey, Virginia H., 93n1131
Richmond, W. Edson, 90n1284
Richter, Alan, 94n909
Richter, Klaus, 90n1569
Richter, O.-G., 91n1758
Ricigliano, Lorraine, 94n1293
Ricks, David A., 94n213
Ricks, Stephen D., 93n167, 93n1402
Rickson, R., 94n260
Riddick, John F., 90n122
Ridge, John Drew, 92n1743
Ridge, Martin, 94n490
Ridgway, Sam H., 90n1562
Ridinger, Robert B. Marks, 90n731, 91n873, 94n488
Ridpath, Ian, 91n1760, 94n1925
Riegel, Martin P., 90n1820, 90n1821
Riegel's hndbk of industrial chemistry, 9th ed, 94n1770
Rietz, Sandra A., 92n1316
Riggar, T. F., 91n252
Riggin, Judith M., 93n1320
Riggle, Judith, 90n1077
Riggs, Stephen Return, 94n1111
Right college 1991, 91n337
Right gd, 94n787
Righter, Robert, 94n1689
Riley, Dorothy Winbush, 94n72
Riley, Eileen, 92n706
Riley, Laura, 94n1683
Riley, Sam G., 90n906, 91n53, 91n963, 92n905, 93n217, 94n267
Riley, William, 94n1683
Riley-Smith, Jonathan, 92n498
Rimler, Walter, 92n1298
Rimmer, Robert H., 93n1332
Rinderknecht, Carol, 90n20, 90n21, 92n18, 92n19, 93n32, 94n10
Rinehart, Julia R., 94n473
Ringelheim, Joan, 93n528
Ringgren, Helmer, 91n1424
Ringler, William A., Jr., 90n1166, 94n1267
Rintoul, M. C., 94n1159
Rinzler, Carol Ann, 91n1492, 92n1675, 92n1676
Riotte, J. C. E., 93n1550
Ripley, Gordon, 93n1220
Rip-roaring reads for reluctant teen readers, 94n1182
Rise & fall of the Soviet Union, 93n535
Ritchie, Donald A., 94n758
Ritchie, L. A., 94n2031
Ritchie, Maureen, 91n912
Ritt, Eva L., 92n479
Ritter, Charles F., 90n692
Rivadue, Barry, 91n1360, 92n1357
Rivard, Denis, 94n1945, 94n2001
Riviello, Barbara Jo, 92n54
Rix, Martyn, 90n1509
Rix, Sara E., 92n812
RMA annual statement studies 1993, 94n217
Roadside wildflowers of the S Great Plains, 92n1536
Roaf, Michael, 92n499
Robb, David S., 93n1206
Robbins, Ira A., 90n1235, 93n1281
Robbins, Samuel D., Jr., 92n1567
Roberge, Marc-Andre, 92n1275
Roberson, William H., 93n1179
Robert Bridges: an annot bibliog, 1873-1988, 93n1205
Robert Burton & The Anatomy of Melancholy, 90n1673
Robert Creeley, Edward Dorn, & Robert Duncan, 90n1160
Robert D. Murphy: a register of his papers in the Hoover Inst Archives, 91n732
Robert Frost: a ref gd 1974-90, 92n1170
Robert, Henry M., 92n679
Robert Lehman collection, 90n952

Robert Lowell papers at the Houghton Lib, Harvard Univ, 92n1176
Robert Mitchum: a bio-bibliog, 94n1417
Robert Russell Bennett: a bio-bibliog, 92n1262
Robert Ward: a bio-bibliog, 90n1246
Roberts, Carol, 91n1228
Roberts, D. Hywel E., 92n105
Roberts, Elfed Vaughan, 94n110
Roberts, Gary Boyd, 94n439
Roberts, Helene E., 94n1540
Roberts, Jerry, 94n1417
Roberts, Margaret, 90n690
Roberts, Nancy L., 92n752
Roberts, Patricia L., 91n1115, 94n1178, 94n1179
Roberts, Vera Mowry, 91n924
Roberts, Willard Lincoln, 91n1790
Roberts, William, 91n532
Robertson, Allen, 91n1347
Robertson, Dave, 93n498
Robertson, David B., 90n652
Robertson, Debra E. J., 93n1132
Robertson, H. Rocke, 91n1045
Robertson, J. Wesley, 91n1045
Robertson, Patrick, 93n1370
Robin, Kathe, 91n1135
Robinson, Alice M., 91n924
Robinson Crusoe: a bibliographical checklist of English lang editions (1719-1979), 92n1202
Robinson, Doris, 90n1316, 92n934, 93n1034
Robinson, Francis, 91n99
Robinson, Gerard A., 92n945
Robinson, Jane, 91n454
Robinson, John C., 91n1568
Robinson, Judith Schiek, 94n56
Robinson, Lesley, 93n203
Robinson, R. K., 94n1600
Robinson, Richard, 91n130
Robinson, Sinclair, 92n1069
Robinson, Thomas A., 92n1073
Robison, Henry W., 90n1552
Robomatix reporter annual 1988, v.6, 90n1732
Robotics abstracts annual 1989, v.7, 91n1749
Robson, T. O., 92n1547
Rochelle, Mercedes, 90n965, 92n993
Rock & roll movie ency of the 1950s, 91n1369
Rock movers & shakers, 91n1325
Rock movers & shakers, [rev ed], 92n1313
Rock 'n' roll through 1969, 94n1376
Rockabilly, 92n1310
Rockett, Melanie E., 92n962
Rockin' the classics & classicizin' the rock, 1st suppl., 92n1311
Rocks & minerals, 91n1779, 93n1728
Rocks, David T., 94n1428
Rocks, minerals & fossils of the world, 91n1789
Rodale Press, editors of, 91n49
Rodale's all-new ency of organic gardening, 93n1489, 94n1619
Rodale's good-times almanac, 91n49
Rodale's illus ency of perennials, 94n1620
Rodes, Barbara K., 93n1777
Rodger, Richard, 90n846
Rodger, Robin W. A., 91n224
Rodgers, Raymond S., 92n592
Rodin, Alvin E., 90n1653
Rodriguez, Paul Anthony, 94n1016, 94n1435
Roebuck, Wendy, 91n426
Roeder, Marcelotte Leake, 94n1645
Roehlkepartain, Eugene C., 90n1412
Roes, Nicholas A., 92n296
Roesch, Roberta, 92n1683
Roess, Anne C., 92n1605
Rogal, Samuel J., 92n1100, 94n1821
Roger Corman: the best of the cheap acts, 90n1351
Roger Ebert's movie home companion 1991 ed, 92n1338
Rogers, Alisdair, 92n76
Rogers, Chester B., 90n695
Rogers, D. M., 91n1440

Rogers, Earl M., 90n1441
Rogers, Susan H., 90n1441
Rogerson, John, 94n1546
Roget's children's thesaurus, 92n1061
Roget's intl thesaurus, 5th ed, 93n1075
Roget's student thesaurus, 92n1062
Roget's thesaurus of the Bible, 94n1542
Roget's 21st century thesaurus, 93n1076
Roget's II, expanded ed, 90n1032
Roginski, Jim, 90n1087, 93n1120, 93n1121
Rogondino, Michael, 92n645
Rogow, Roberta, 92n1145
Rohmann, Chris, 94n1397
Rohsenow, John S., 92n1317
Rohwer, Jens G., 94n1646
Rojo, Alfonso L., 93n1558
Rokala, D. A., 90n372
Roland, Albert E., 94n1659
Roland, Charles G., 90n1636
Roland, Tom, 92n1303
Rolef, Susan Hattis, 94n785
Roller coasters, 94n828
Rollin, Jack, 92n801
Rolling Stone album gd, 94n1367
Rolling Stone index, 94n1404
Rollings, Neil, 94n263
Rollins, Alden, 93n547
Rollins, Arline McClarty, 91n860
Rollock, Barbara, 93n1139
Rollyson, Carl, 94n16
Romaine, Lawrence B., 92n258
Romaine-Davis, Ada, 93n1620
Roman Catholics, 91n1525
Roman de la rose: an annot bibliog, 94n1282
Roman Jakobson 1896-1982: a complete bibliog of his writings, 92n1009
Roman sculpture, 94n1066
Romance reader's hndbk, 91n1135
Romanian-English, English-Romanian dict, 92n1085
Romaniuk, Bohdan R., 93n870, 94n898, 94n902
Rome in the 4th century AD, 93n547
Romiszowski, Alexander J., 93n345
Ronald Reagan: his 1st career, 90n1319
Roney, Alex, 91n109
Rood, Karen L., 91n1176
Rookledge, Sarah, 94n1563
Rookledge's intl hndbk of type designers, 94n1563
Room, Adrian, 90n404, 90n429, 90n1012, 90n1746, 92n1028, 92n1325, 93n184, 94n440
Rooney, John F., Jr., 94n819
Roosa, Dean M., 90n1499
Roosens, Laurent, 90n943
Roosevelt research, 93n516
Root, Betty, 94n1092, 94n1093
Root, Terry, 90n1542
Roots of English, 91n1053
Roper, Nancy, 90n1652
Rosaler, Robert C., 91n1634
Rosato, Dominick V., 94n1771
Rosato's plastics ency & dict, 94n1771
Rose, Barry, 94n1842
Rose, Chris, 91n1573
Rose, Clive, 90n728
Rose, Jonathan, 93n689
Rose, Richard, 92n677
Rose, Rose K., 94n1923
Rosen, Fred S., 90n1654
Rosen, Nathan Aaron, 90n577
Rosen, Stephen, 93n600
Rosenak, Chuck, 92n982
Rosenak, Jan, 92n982
Rosenbaum, Barbara, 92n1195
Rosenbaum, Ernest H., 93n1655
Rosenberg, Betty, 93n1147
Rosenberg, Jerry, 92n741

Rosenberg, Jerry M., 93n170, 93n171, 93n1679, 94n177, 94n210
Rosenberg, Judith K., 93n1133
Rosenberg, Kenneth V., 92n1569
Rosenberg, Kenyon C., 90n353, 91n1294
Rosenberg, Lee, 93n921, 94n944
Rosenberg, Saralee, 93n921, 94n944
Rosenblatt, Arthur, 94n1309
Rosenblum, Joseph, 93n1214
Rosenstiel, Leonie, 92n896
Roser, Nancy L., 94n1173
Roses, Lorraine Elena, 91n1150
Rosovsky, Nitza, 91n58
Rospond, Mary Chris, 90n947
Ross, Deane, 92n1506
Ross, Franz, 90n941, 93n1012
Ross gd to rose growing, 92n1506
Ross, John A., 90n801
Ross, Joseph A., 91n185
Ross, Linda M., 94n1201, 94n1517
Ross, Lynn C., 94n270
Ross, Mabel, 90n936
Ross, Robert L., 90n1191
Ross, Robert L., ed, 92n1193
Ross, Stewart, 91n534
Rossi, Ernest E., 94n784
Rossi, Jacques, 90n573
Rossi, John, 94n1751
Rossman, Douglas A., 90n1566
Rosten, Leo, 90n1062
Rotenburg, Gerald N., 93n1661
Roth, John K., 92n1393
Roth, Martin, 91n953
Roth Publishing, Inc., Editorial Board, 90n1074, 90n1101, 90n1113, 90n1159, 90n1163
Roth, Wendy, 93n499
Rothbart, Linda S., 90n1812, 91n1827, 93n1783, 94n2023
Rothenberg, Marc, 94n1560
Rothenberg, Mikel A., 90n1655
Rothman, Barbara Katz, 94n1831
Roth's American poetry annual 1988, 90n1163
Roth's essay index, 90n1101
Roth's index to literary criticism, 90n1074
Roth's index to short stories, 90n1113
Rothwell, Kenneth S., 92n1368
Roudane, Matthew C., 90n1128
Rough, Valerie, 94n1737
Rouleau, Claudia, 91n810
Rourke dinosaur dict, 91n1792
Rousseau dict, 93n1396
Rousseaux, Colin G., 92n1694
Routh, C. R. N., 92n482
Routledge dict of 20th-century pol thinkers, 94n715
Rovin, Jeff, 90n1310, 94n1429
Rowe, Fred A., 93n410
Rowe, William M., 90n1739
Rowell, C. H. F., 93n1566
Rowland, Ian, 94n112
Rowland, J. F. B., 94n1931
Rowland-Entwhistle, Theodore, 91n36, 94n39
Rowlinson, William, 93n1083
Roy, Archie, 94n1944
Roy, F. Hampton, 93n858
Roy Harris: a bio-bibliog, 92n1277
Royal descents of 500 immigrants to the American colonies or the US, 94n439
Royal Histl Society annual bibliog of British & Irish hist: pubs of 1992, 94n518
Royal Institute of International Affairs, 91n552
Royce, Brenda Scott, 92n1342, 93n1321
Royle, Trevor, 91n682
Rozakis, Laurie, 92n1036
Rozmovits, Linda, 94n1278
Rubash, Joyce, 91n1486
Rubens, Philip, 93n970
Rubert, Steven C., 92n91

Rubin, Harvey W., 92n210
Rubin, Irvin I., 91n1611
Rubin, Leona G., 92n230
Rubin, Lionel F., 90n1475
Rubin, Rhea Joyce, 91n644, 92n1141
Rubin, Steven Jay, 92n1354
Rubinger, Richard, 90n306
Rubinstein, Chaim T., 91n439
Rubinstein, Charlotte Streifer, 92n1005
Rubinstein, W. D., 93n462
Rudd, Amanda S., 91n357
Ruddick, Nicholas, 93n1204
Ruddy, James F., 92n930
Rudi, Marilynn J., 92n1227
Rudin, Claire, 91n652
Rudisill, Richard, 93n1014
Rudman, Masha Kabakow, 90n738
Rudoff, Carol, 91n1690
Rudy, Stephen, 92n1009
Rugg, Frederick E., 94n364
Rugg's recommendations on the colleges, 10th ed, 94n364
Rugh, Archie, 90n10
Rulau, Russell, 90n922, 92n931
Rumbold, Valerie, 94n1310
Rumney, Thomas A., 94n461
Runkel, Sylvan T., 90n1499
Running Pr cyclopedia, 94n40
Ruoff, A. LaVonne Brown, 92n1149
Rupp, Richard V., 92n211
Rupp, Robert O., 92n458
Ruppert, James, 90n1162
Ruppli, Michel, 92n1299
Rupp's insurance & risk mgmt glossary, 92n211
Rural church in America, 91n1436
Rural dvlpmt, 92n213, 93n922
Rusch, Frederic E., 92n1169
Ruse, Christina, 94n980
Rushing, Brian C., 92n305
Russ Meyer: the life & films, 91n1354
Russell, Charles, 93n858
Russell, Cheryl, 93n906, 94n283
Russell, Jeff, 90n1296
Russell, John J., 91n40
Russell, Nancy R., 92n225
Russell, Norma Jean, 92n1064
Russell, Percy, 90n1614
Russia & the Commonwealth A to Z, 94n525
Russia 1993: pol & economic analysis & bus dir, 94n137
Russian & Soviet educ 1731-1989, 93n383
Russian dicts: selected bibliog 1960-90, 92n1086
Russian emigre serials, 91n411
Russian govt today, spring 1993, 94n780
Russian phrasebk & dict, 92n1088
Russian-English dict of verbal collocations (REDVC), 94n1129
Russian-English dict with phonetics, 92n1087
Russian-English sci & engineering dict, 90n1429
Russian-English/English-Russian dict of free market era economics, 94n160
Russin, Mildred M., 92n1692
Russo, Nancy Felipe, 91n918
Rutherford, Donald, 93n185
Rutkow, Ira M., 90n1637, 94n1822
Rutsohn, Rita G., 92n216
Rutter, Joseph W., 92n1806
Ryan, Beverly A., 90n598
Ryan, Bryan, 92n1097, 92n1106
Ryan, Elizabeth A., 91n1080
Ryan, James G., 90n383
Ryan, Joe, 90n75
Ryan, Joseph M., 90n307
Ryan, Mary C., 90n484
Rycroft, Michael, 92n1592
Ryder, Randall J., 91n368
Rymaszewski, Eugene J., 90n1593

S. N. Behrman: a research & production sourcebk, 94n1232
Sable, Martin H., 91n538
Sabljic, John, 91n149
Sabosik, Patricia E., 92n57
Sabrosky, Curtis W., 91n1590
Sacarto, Douglas, 90n710
Sachs, Michael, 90n641, 92n1461
Sack, Sallyann Amdur, 93n494
Sackett, Susan, 91n1383
Sacred choral music in print: master index 1992, 94n1341
Sacred choral music in print: 1992 suppl, 94n1340
Sacred Dance Guild, 92n1336
Sader, Marion, 92n9
Sadie, Stanley, 90n1230, 94n1356
Sadler, Geoff, 92n1153
Sadler, M. J., 94n1600
Sadock, Benjamin J., 93n1649
Saenger, Paul, 91n551
Safety & health at work, ILO-CIS bulletin: 5-yearly index 1984-88, 91n250
Saffady, William, 90n611, 91n1618
Saffle, Michael, 92n1276
Safir, Leonard, 91n71, 91n72
Safire, William, 91n71, 91n72
Sagar, D. J., 92n708, 94n765
Sage, Andrew P., 91n1727
Sagebrush country, 94n1660
Saha, Santosh C., 91n1473
Sahibs, nabobs & boxwallahs, 93n1070
Sailing dir, 94n860
Saint: a complete hist in print, radio, film & TV, 94n1249
Saint-Gilles, Amaury, 90n937
Saint-Louis, Jean-Marc, 91n779
Saints, 94n1526
Saito, Toshio, 90n1174
Sajdak, Bruce T., 93n1215
Sakelliou-Schultz, Liana, 90n1150
Saks, Norman, 94n1369
Salaman, R. A., 91n1637
Salem, Dorothy C., 94n960
Salem, James M., 92n1333
Sales prospecting & territory planning dir, 91n279
Saliba, John A., 91n1410
Salisbury, Joyce E., 91n874
Salley, Columbus, 94n406
Salley, Homer E., 94n1631
Sallis, Lela, 92n297, 93n359
Salmon, Richard D., 93n304
Salmonson, Jessica Amanda, 92n862
Salomon, Brownell, 92n1196
Salons of America 1922-36, 92n980
Salsa & related genres, 94n1381
Salu, Luc, 90n943, 93n1013
Salvatore, Dominick, 93n320
Salwak, Dale, 93n1209
Salzman, Jack, 91n485
Sambhi, Piara Singh, 91n1452
Sammons, Vivian Ovelton, 92n351
Samson, Jim, 91n968
Samuel Beckett: a ref gd, 90n1204
Samuel Butler: an annot bibliog of writings about him, 91n1198
Samuels, Jeffrey M., 90n559, 94n576
San Miguel, Rachel, 93n1103
Sanborn, Lavonne Hayes, 93n402
Sandak, Cass R., 92n1776
Sander, Daryl, 92n555
Sander, Reinhard, 93n1110, 94n1148
Sandinista Nicaragua, 90n146
Sandler, Todd, 90n727
Sandorfy, Michael, 93n360
Sands, Kathleen M., 92n358
Sandys, Julian, 91n240
Sanford, George, 94n134
Saniga, Richard D., 92n318
Santana fossils, 92n1745

Santi, Albert, 92n262
Sarah Vaughan: a discography, 93n1285
Sardegna, Jill, 92n1685
Sarfoh, Joseph A., 94n1969
Sarg, Michael J., 94n1858
Sarna, Jonathan D., 90n379
Sartori, Eva Martin, 93n1222
Satchwell, Michele L., 91n364
Sater, Ana Lya, 92n378
Saterstrom, Mary H., 93n400
Sattler, Martha J., 90n1139
Sattler, S. C., 94n392
Sauber, S. Richard, 94n810
Saudi Arabia: bibliog on society, pols, economics, v.2, 91n124
Saul, Pauline, 90n393, 93n461
Saunders, Tom, 94n861
Sauvant, Karl P., 94n792
Savage, Kathleen M., 91n378, 93n411, 93n412
Savageau, David, 91n908
Savaiano, Eugene, 92n1091
Savarese, Nicola, 92n1374
Savidge, Charlotte, 90n1356
Saving endangered mammals, 94n1738
Savola, Kristen L., 93n102
Sawin, Philip, 91n231
Sawoniak, Henryk, 93n621
Sawusch, Mark R., 91n1739
Sawyer, Malcolm, 93n177
Sax, N. Irving, 90n1758
Saxophone recital music, 94n1339
Saye, Jerry D., 90n605
Sayer, Jeffrey A., 92n1764, 93n1484
Sayers, Scott P., Jr., 94n1368
Sbrega, John J., 91n486
SCAD bulletin 20—1991, 92n716
Scale modeling buyer's gd, 2d ed, 92n946
Scammon, Richard M., 92n696, 94n756
Scandinavian-American heritage, 90n382
Scanlan, Jean M., 91n161
Scarborough, Katharine T. A., 92n620
Scarre, Chris, 94n534
Scarrett, Douglas, 90n297
Scenic design on Broadway, 93n1384
Schaad, Evelyn, 92n213, 93n922
Schaafsma, Gertjan, 92n1631
Schacht, Wilhelm, 92n1538
Schadel, Erwin, 90n1391, 90n1392
Schaefer, Glenn, 90n1704, 90n1707, 90n1732
Schaefer, Vincent J., 92n1732
Schaeffer, Deborah L., 90n1285
Schafer, Jurgen, 91n1044, 91n1046
Schaffer, Ellen G., 92n544
Schanke, Robert A., 90n1320
Scharnhorst, Gary, 90n1143, 93n1182
Schayes, Terry Lee, 94n294
Scheiber, Jodie, 91n736
Scheina, Robert L., 91n697
Schellinger, Paul E., 92n34, 93n1159
Schellmann, Jorg, 90n953
Schenk, Trudy, 90n399
Scherzer, Norman A., 92n832
Schetgen, Robert, 94n1015
Scheven, Yvette, 90n106
Schiavone, Giuseppe, 94n793
Schick, Frank L., 90n487, 92n356
Schick, Renee, 90n487, 92n356
Schieber, Philip, 90n625
Schiff, Matthew M., 93n1290
Schiller, Andrew, 90n1022, 90n1023, 92n1061, 92n1062
Schimmelman, Janice G., 91n1003
Schinabeck, Michael J., 94n271
Schlachter, Gail Ann, 90n329, 90n874, 91n346, 92n651, 94n1367, 94n368
Schlebecker, John T., 90n1444
Schlesser, Jerry L., 92n1693

Schlessinger, Bernard S., 90n158, 92n28
Schlessinger, June H., 92n28, 92n1129
Schleuter, Stanley L., 94n1339
Schlicke, Priscilla, 91n1459, 94n1562
Schlundt, Christena L., 90n1317
Schmalensee, Richard, 91n232
Schmalleger, Frank, 92n556
Schmick's Mahican dict, 93n1089
Schmidly, David J., 92n1583
Schmidt, Arno, 92n1499
Schmidt, Jonathan K., 94n137
Schmittroth, Linda, 92n866
Schmitz, Cecilia M., 94n1823
Schneider, Arthur, 92n913
Schneider, Craig W., 93n1513
Schneider, Gerhard, 91n1423, 93n1426, 94n1528
Schneider, Janet Carney, 90n825
Schneider, Terry, 91n309
Schneider, Walter, 91n67
Schneier, Betsy R., 90n792
Schnell, Gary D., 90n1557
Schniewind, Arno P., 91n1495
Schocken gd to Jewish bks, 94n425
Schoenburg, Nancy, 92n489
Schoenburg, Stuart, 92n489
Schoenhals, Kai, 92n112
Schofield, Eileen K., 92n1536
Schofield, Janice J., 91n1523
Scholar's gd to ...
   academic journals in religion, 90n1385
   geographical writing on the American & Canadian past, 94n461
   Washington, D.C. for Latin American & Caribbean studies, 2d ed, 93n149
   Washington, D.C. for SW European studies, 90n130
Scholarship bk, 3d ed, 91n314
Scholarship bk, 4th ed, 94n333
Scholarships, fellowships & grants for programs abroad, 91n347
Scholarships, fellowships & loans 1992-93, 93n377
Scholtz, James, 90n619
Scholtz, James C., 92n621
Schomp, Virginia, 92n172
Schon, Isabel, 90n1085, 93n150, 94n1180
Schonberg, Bent, 94n1425
Schonkron, Marcel, 92n1085
School lib media annual 1989, 90n622
School lib media annual 1990, 91n653
School lib media annual 1991, 92n612
School lib media annual 1992, 93n672
School librarian's sourcebk, 91n652
School Search gd to private schools for students with learning disabilities, 91n350
School songs of America's colleges & univs, 93n1278
Schools abroad of interest to Americans 1988-89, 90n347
Schoolsearch gd to colleges with programs or servs for students with disabilities, 92n319
Schooner, Steven L., 93n580
Schorr, Alan Edward, 91n878, 92n426, 93n429
Schotte, Marilyn, 91n1600
Schraeder, Peter J., 92n87
Schuker, Eleanor, 93n797
Schulman, Martin, 93n223
Schult, Joachim, 94n860
Schultes, Ricard Evans, 91n1538
Schultz, Margie, 91n1352, 92n1343
Schultz, William R., 94n1491
Schulze, Suzanne, 93n979
Schumacher, Rose, 90n189, 90n659, 91n86, 91n942
Schumann, Walter, 93n1729, 94n1957
Schur, Norman W., 91n1054
Schuster, Danny, 92n1552
Schuster, James Vincent, 91n884, 92n279, 92n825
Schutt, David, 93n197
Schutz, Wayne, 93n1364
Schuursma, Ann Briegleb, 93n1242

Schuweiler, Alan R., 90n927
Schuyler, Michael, 93n662
Schwab, Arnold T., 90n1198
Schwager, Edith, 92n1671
Schwann artist issue, 14th ed, 90n1236
Schwartz, Albert, 93n1579
Schwartz, Carol A., 93n213, 94n49
Schwartz, David, 92n1314
Schwartz, Mel M., 93n1606
Schwartz, Mortimer D., 92n527, 93n573, 94n549
Schwartz, Philip J., 90n581
Schwartz, Ronald, 93n1365
Schwartzberg, Joseph E., 94n515
Schwarz, Catherine, 90n996, 93n1057
Schwarz, Lawrence J., 90n560
Schwarz, Volker, 90n1789
Schwarzkopf, LeRoy C., 91n43, 93n74
Schwegel, Janet, 91n421
Schweikart, Larry, 91n213, 92n185
Schweitzer, Christoph E., 91n1235
Schweitzer, Darrell, 94n1292
Schweitzer, David, 93n773
Schweitzer, Marjorie M., 92n813
Schweitzer, Philip A., 90n1602
Schwing, Ned, 93n1004
Science & technical writing: a manual of style, 93n970
Science & tech annual ref review 89, 90n1417
Science & tech desk ref, 94n1584
Science & tech in fact & fiction: a gd to children's bks, 91n1455
Science & tech in fact & fiction: a gd to young adult bks, 91n1456
Science & tech 1989: a purchase gd, 91n1458
Science Bks & Films best bks for children 1988-91, 94n1561
Science experiments index for young people update 91, 93n1461
Science experiments on file, 90n1438
Science fair project index 1985-89, 93n1462
Science.fiction & fantasy bk review annual 1988, 90n1111
Science fiction & fantasy bk review annual 1990, 93n1158
Science fiction & fantasy lit 1975-91, 94n1214
Science fiction & fantasy ref index 1985-91, 94n1213
Science fiction, fantasy & horror, 1987, 90n1112
Science fiction, fantasy & horror ref, 90n1110
Science fiction, horror & fantasy film & TV credits suppl-1987, 90n1350
Science fiction stars & horror heroes, 92n1371
Science for children, 90n1418
Science sources 1991, 93n1452
Science teacher's bk of lists, 94n1580
Science yr, 1990, 90n1439
Science-fiction: the early yrs, 92n1143
Scientific & technical bks & serials in print 1989, 90n1419
Scientific & technical bks & serials in print 1991, 92n1453
Scientific & technical pers of the 17th & 18th centuries, 93n1463
Scientific American cum index 1978-88, 91n1472
Scientific English, 93n958
Scientific traveler, 93n1456
Scivally, Bruce, 90n1331
Sclater, Neil, 91n1616
SCOLMA dir of libs & special collections on Africa in the UK & in Europe, 5th ed, 94n652
Scoor-oot, 90n1054
Scotchmer, Sarah Parker, 94n399
Scotland: a literary gd, 91n474
Scots thesaurus, 91n1091
Scott, David H., 91n1426
Scott dramatized, 93n1210
Scott, Foresman advanced dict, 90n1020
Scott, Foresman beginning dict, 90n1021
Scott, Foresman beginning thesaurus, 90n1022
Scott, Foresman intermediate dict, 90n1024
Scott, Foresman jr thesaurus, 90n1023
Scott, Foresman Robert's rules of order, 1990 ed, 92n679
Scott, Frank, 92n1300
Scott, Gregory E. J., 92n557
Scott, Henry W., 91n569
Scott, Julian, 91n1681

Scott, Mark W., 90n1184, 94n893
Scott, Mona L., 94n630
Scott, Randall W., 94n1405
Scott, Thomas, 90n1481
Scott, William, 94n1350
Scott-Roberts, Fiona, 91n258
Scott's dirs: Ont. manufacturers, 17th ed, 90n245
Scouting report: 1993, 94n836
Screen gems: a hist of Columbia Pictures TV from Cohn to coke, 1948-83, 93n996
Screen sleuths, 93n1350
Screen world 1988, 90n1354
Screwball comedy films, 92n1359
Scribner writers series on CD-ROM, 94n1160
Scriven, Michael, 93n642
Scrivener, David, 91n712
Scuttlebutt, 90n1818
Sea of Cortez marine invertebrates, 90n1561
Seabourne, Joan, 93n879, 94n892
Seal, Graham, 94n1390
Sealander, John A., 91n1597
Seale, Doris, 90n373, 93n433
Seaman, Gerald R., 90n1252
Search for security: the ACCESS gd to fndns, 91n772
Search sheets for OPACs on the Internet, 93n661
Searing, Susan, 93n931
Searles, Richard B., 93n1513
Sears list of subject headings, 14th ed, 92n585
Sears list of subject headings: Canadian companion, 4th ed, 93n643
Seashores, rev ed, 91n1552
Seaton, Anne, 90n997
Seaweeds of the SE US, 93n1513
Sebba, Gregor, 94n1485
Second 50 yrs: a ref manual for sr citizens, 93n853
Second suppl. to a comp bibliog of Yugoslav lit in English 1986-90, 93n1234
Secretary's key, 92n260
Sectional maps of W Canada, 1871-1955, 91n436
Secular choral music in print: 1991 suppl., 92n1286
Secular choral music in print: 1993 suppl., 94n1342
Security, arms control, & conflict reduction in E Asia & the Pacific, 94n683
Security in computing, 1990 ed, 91n1732
Seeds of woody plants in N America, rev ed, 93n1521
Seeley, Charlotte Palmer, 93n707
Seeley, Darrell, 93n1646
Seeley, Frank E., 93n853
Sefami, Jacobo, 93n1228
Segal, Aaron, 94n428
Segal, Audrey, 94n385
Segal, David, 94n1216, 94n1217
Segal, Gerald, 91n126
Segal, Marilyn, 91n602
Segal, Ronald, 93n475
Segen, J. C., 94n1832
Segrave, Kerry, 91n1363, 91n1395, 93n612
Segsworth, R. V., 92n755
Segulin, Fran, 92n201
Selden, Holly M., 93n245
Select index to Svoboda, v.1, 93n980
Select index to Svoboda, v.2, 93n981
Selected & annot bibliog of American naval hist, rev ed, 90n665
Selected bibliog of modern historiography, 93n546
Selected bibliog of the foot & ankle with commentary, 94n1820
Selected musical terms of non-Western cultures, 92n1253
Selected refs in orthopaedic trauma, 91n1699
Selected state enactments 1990, 92n697
Selection of lib materials for area studies, pt.1, 92n81
Selective bibliog of American lit, 1775-1900, 91n1147
Selective gd to the collections, 90n44
Selective inventory of social sci info & doc servs, 3d ed, 90n87
Self, Huber, 90n469
Selice, Stephanie, 90n741
Sellen, Betty-Carol, 94n1032

Sellen, Mary K., 94n623
Seller's gd to govt purchasing, 92n139
Selnow, Gary W., 91n53, 92n905
Selvon, Sydney, 93n147
Semantics: a bibliog, 1986-91, 93n1047
Seminar Clearinghouse International, Inc., 92n46
Seminars dir, 2d ed, 92n46
Semsel, Craig, 91n1614
Senecal, A. J., 93n19
Senecal, Michael D., 93n519
Senelick, Laurence, 92n1384
Senick, Gerard J., 90n1090, 93n1141
Senior citizen servs, 94n874
Senior high school lib cat, 14th ed, 93n673
Senior movement, 93n861
Seniorplots, 90n1093
Senn, Bryan, 94n1449
Sennitt, Andrew G., 93n1000
Sennitt, Andy, 93n999
Sensibar, Judith L., 90n1141
Sensitive issues: an annot gd to children's lit K-6, 93n1130
Senter, Janet P., 92n859
Sentman, Catherine, 93n1250
Sentz, Lilli, 93n1659
Sequels: an annot gd to novels in series, 2d ed, 92n1138
Serafica-de Guzman, Leonora, 90n816
Serafin, Steven, 92n1154, 93n50
Serafin, Steven R., 94n1152
Serbocroatian-English dict, 3d ed, 91n1093
Seredich, John, 92n1787
Serials cataloging hndbk, 90n601
Serials dir, 4th ed, 91n64
Serials dir, 7th ed, 94n63
Serials dir: EBSCO CD-ROM, summer 1993, 94n64
Serials gd to ethnoart, 91n1022
Serials ref work, 90n618
Serio, Joseph, 93n613
Serow, William J., 91n905, 92n756
Service industries USA, 93n250
Setting up a co in the European Community, 91n162
Settlement lit of the Greater Punjab, 93n524
Seubert, Emelia, 90n374
Seven-lang thesaurus of European animals, 92n1558
Seventeenth-century British nondramatic poets, 94n1264
Sewer, June, 93n1583
Sex & gender issues: a hndbk of tests & measures, 92n831
Sex differences & learning, 92n268
Sexual assault & child sexual abuse, 90n578
Sexuality & the law, 94n570
Sexuality educ, 90n813
Seychelles, 94n140
Seymore, Bruce II, 94n799
Seymour, Paul R., 91n1556
Seymour-Smith, Martin, 93n1148
Shaberman, Raphael B., 92n1241
Shackman, Joshua, 94n787
Shade & color with water-conserving plants, 93n1520
Shadily, Hassan, 90n1046
Shadowcatchers: a dir of women in Calif. photography before 1901, 92n960
Shaeffer, Claire, 91n995
Shafritz, Jay M., 90n303, 90n652, 92n557, 93n736, 94n718
Shafritz, Todd J. A., 90n652
Shaikh, Farzana, 94n1553
Shailor, Barbara A., 94n30
Shain, Michael, 90n612, 93n315, 94n1900
Shake, rattle & roll, 90n1293
Shakespeare: a bibliographical gd, new ed, 92n1210
Shakespeare A to Z, 92n1209
Shakespeare: an annot bibliog, 93n1214
Shakespeare & feminist criticism, 93n1212
Shakespeare & the musical stage, 91n1297
Shakespeare folio hndbk & census, 91n1215
Shakespeare index, 93n1215
Shakespeare music cat, 92n1251

Shakespeare on screen, 92n1368
Shakespearean criticism, v.9, 90n1184
Shakespearean criticism, v.11, 91n1217
Shakespearean criticism, v.18, 94n1260
Shakespearean criticism, v.19, yrbk 1991, 94n1259
Shakespeare's characters, 94n1258
Shakespeare's Othello, 90n1185
Shakespeare's quotations, 94n1257
Shaland, Irene, 92n1385
Shamley, Sarah L., 92n911
Shank, Robert, 92n1423
Shannon, Gary W., 94n1802
Shannon, Michael Owen, 93n145
Shannon, Moira D., 93n1620
Shape under the sheet, 92n1175
Shapiro, Fay, 91n961
Shapiro, Fred R., 94n584
Shapiro, Lillian L., 94n1181
Shapiro, Michael Steven, 91n59
Shapiro, Mitchell E., 90n920
Sharkey, Paulette Bochnig, 93n824, 93n1121
Sharks & other creatures of the deep, 92n1585
Sharma, Sue, 90n1297
Sharp, Avery T., 91n1290
Sharp, Daryl, 92n758
Sharp, Dennis, 93n1040
Sharpe, Anne S., 93n342
Sharpe, Richard, 91n694
Sharylen, Maria, 94n1042
Shatzkin, Mike, 91n825
Shaughnessy, Roseann, 93n957
Shaver, James P., 93n336
Shavit, David, 90n729, 92n746, 93n786
Shaw, Frank, 91n1569, 91n1570
Shaw, Gareth, 90n133
Shaw, Jean M., 92n1458, 92n1752
Shaw, John, 90n124
Shaw, Marion, 90n1186
Shaw, Warren, 91n114
She said, he said, 93n914
Shearing, Clifford D., 93n606
Shedding the veil: mapping the European discovery of America & the world, 93n470
Sheehan, Michael, 91n712
Sheets, William, 94n1778
Sheldon, Joseph K., 93n1417
Shellow, Jill R., 90n810
Shells, 94n1675
Shelly, Mack C. II, 90n1443
Shelnutt, Eve, 93n936
Sheng, Jin, 94n672
Shenhom, Daisy E., 93n1046
Shepard, Leslie, 92n762
Shepard, Thomas H., 90n1638, 93n1628
Shepherd, Simon, 91n1183
Sheppard, Howard R., 92n545
Sheppard, Jocelyn, 90n1131
Sheppard, Julia, 90n507
Sherby, Louise S., 92n1215
Sherman, Andrew J., 94n199
Sherman, Charles H., 94n1332
Sherman, Gale W., 93n1140, 94n1182
Sherman, Joan R., 90n1164
Sherman, Mark A., 93n1416
Shermis, Michael, 90n1378
Shermyen, Anne H., 93n107
Shiel, Suzanne, 91n906
Shield of republic/sword of empire, 91n678
Shields-West, Eileen, 93n732
Shiflett, Lee, 92n459
Shih, Catherine, 91n255, 93n225, 93n259
Shih, Tian-Chu, 93n1471
Shim, Jae K., 90n198, 93n241, 93n243
Shimomura, Ruth H., 90n1765
Shimoni, Yaacov, 93n161

Shimpock-Vieweg, Kathy, 93n596
Shinn, Marybeth, 92n835
Shipbuilding industry, 94n2031
Shipman, David, 91n1397
Shipman, Robert Oliver, 92n1034
Shipping lit of the Great Lakes, 93n1778
Ships of the royal navy, v.2, 91n692
Shiri, Keith, 94n1436
Shirley, Carl R., 90n1123
Shoebridge, Michele, 94n821
Shoemaker, Thomas M., 93n1598
Shook, R. J., 92n166
Shook, Robert L., 92n166
Shoot-em-ups ride again, 92n1367
Shore, Irma, 90n957
Shorebirds of the Pacific Northwest, 94n1700
Short, David, 90n1750
Short story criticism, v.2, 90n1114
Short story criticism, v.3, 91n1143
Short story criticism, v.11, 94n1216
Short story criticism, v.12, 94n1217
Short story cycle, 90n1134
Short story index 1984-88, 90n1115
Short story writers & their work, 2d ed, 93n1160
Short title cat of the emblem bks...in the Stirling Maxwell collection, rev ed, 90n632
Shorter English-Nepali dict, 92n1083
Short-term economic stats: Central & E Europe, 93n292
Short-title cat of bks printed in England, Scotland & Ireland...1475-1640, v.3, 92n61
Short-title cat of music printed before 1825 in the Fitzwilliam Museum, Cambride, 94n1310
Showers, Victor, 90n92
Shrader, Charles R., 93n710
Shrader, Charles Reginald, 92n466, 94n501, 94n502
Shreir, Sally, 90n875
Shrout, Richard Neil, 93n864
Shroyer, Jo Ann, 94n1585
Shrubs, 90n1509
Shtasel, Philip, 91n1682
Shuffelton, Frank, 93n512
Shugar, Gershon J., 91n1777
Shulman, Frank Joseph, 91n103, 94n108
Shulman, Jason A., 90n1440
Shulman, Jeffrey, 92n841
Shult, Linda, 93n931
Shumaker, David, 94n611
Shuman, R. Baird, 93n971, 93n1380
Shurts, Mary M., 91n1406
Shuster, Robert D., 91n1441
SIBD 92-93, 93n293
Siberia & the Soviet Far East, 93n139
Sibley, Barbara, 91n234, 91n235
Sibley, Charles G., 92n1570
Sibley, David, 90n1532
Sickness & wellness pubs, 90n1610
Siddiqui, Dilnawaz A., 90n357
Siddons, James, 90n1253
Sieber, Mary, 92n1800, 92n1801
Siebert, Donald T., 92n1194
Siegel, Alice, 94n2
Siegel, Barbara, 91n1370
Siegel, Barry, 92n777
Siegel, David S., 94n1027, 94n1028
Siegel, Joel G., 90n198, 93n241, 93n243
Siegel, Jonathan P., 90n269, 94n724
Siegel, Martha S., 93n589
Siegel, Scott, 91n1370
Siegel, Susan, 94n1027, 94n1028
Siegman, Gita, 90n56, 90n66, 93n66, 93n1314
Sienkewicz, Thomas J., 92n1135
Sierra Club gd to the natural areas of New England, 91n461
Sierra Club hndbk of seals & sirenians, 93n1571
Sierra Club naturalist's gd to the S Rockies, 92n444
Sierra Leone, 94n102

Sifakis, Carl, 91n806, 92n558
Sifakis, Stewart, 93n711, 93n712, 93n713, 93n714, 93n715
Sigler, David Burns, 93n716
Sikhism & the Sikhs, 90n1414
Sikhs in N America, 93n1436
Sikhs: their lit on culture, hist, philosophy, pols, religion & traditions, 91n1453
Silent witnesses: Russian films 1908-19, 91n1385
Silk stalkings: when women write of murder, 90n1107
Silkworm diseases, 92n1477
Silver, Carole G., 91n1058
Silverburg, Sanford R., 91n770, 93n162
Silverman, Buddy Robert S., 91n804
Silverman, Pamela B., 93n893
Silverstein, Natalie Anne, 91n883
Silverstone, Paul H., 90n669, 91n698
Similes dict, 90n1014
Simko, Jan, 92n1089
Simley, John, 90n177
Simmons, Ann, 90n268
Simmons, Henry C., 93n859
Simmons, James C., 91n455
Simms, Ena G., 94n1110
Simms, Michael, 90n1118
Simms, Norman, 93n1229
Simon & Schuster pocket gd to fortified & dessert wines, 91n1493
Simon & Schuster pocket gd to shells of the world, 91n1550
Simon & Schuster's gd to reptiles & amphibians of the world, 91n1603
Simon, Dolores, 94n1613
Simon, Harriet Furst, 93n342
Simon, Henry W., 90n1273
Simon, James E., 91n1534
Simon, Seymour, 93n1706
Simon, Susan H., 92n1286, 94n1340, 94n1342
Simoncini, Gabriele, 93n779
Simone de Beauvoir: a bibliog, 93n930
Simone de Beauvoir: an annot biblig, 90n1370
Simoneau, Karin, 91n907
Simony, Maggie, 94n474
Simora, Filomena, 90n590, 91n611
Simplified dict of modern Tongan, 94n1134
Simpson, Allan, 91n817, 91n818
Simpson, Benny J., 90n1511
Simpson, Colin MacLeod, 94n1891
Simpson, J. A., 90n1006
Simpson, James B., 93n94
Simpson, John, 93n1296
Simpson, Kieran, 92n26
Simpson, Marcus B., Jr., 93n1545
Simpson, Martha Seif, 94n1194
Simpson, Mary, 93n503
Sims, Reginald W., 90n1495
Sims, William J., 90n93
Sinatra: the man & his music, 94n1368
Since 1776, 90n489
Sinclair, Brett Jason, 94n1843
Sinclair, Ian R., 92n1708, 93n1595
Sinclair, Louis, 91n765
Sinclair, Patti K., 93n1752
Sineath, Timothy W., 92n576
Singapore, 90n123
Singer, David, 93n439
Singer, Michael, 90n1333, 93n1372
Singerman, Robert, 92n380, 94n426
Singh, Madan G., 94n1570
Singh, Maheep, 92n317
Singh, Rajwant, 91n1453
Singh, Sunita, 94n953
Singleton, Laurel R., 90n498, 90n499
Singleton, Ralph S., 91n1371
Singson, Karen P., 91n313, 93n871
Sinkankas, John, 94n1958
Sinnott, Roger W., 90n1747
Sinnott, Susan, 93n51

SIPRI yrbk 1990: world armaments & disarmament, 91n713
Sir Gawain & the Green Knight: an annot bibliog, 1978-89, 93n1217
Sir Harry Lauder discography, 92n1331
Sir John Vanbrugh: a ref gd, 94n975
Sir Richard F. Burton: a biobibliographical study, 91n444
Sir Thomas Malory: an anecdotal bibliog of editions, 1485-1985, 92n1206
Sir William Osler: an annot bibliog with illustrations, 90n1636
Sirotof, Gene, 90n1359, 93n1387, 93n1388
Sitarz, Daniel, 90n555, 91n862
Sitsky, Larry, 91n1289
Sitter, John, 91n1224, 92n1222
Sittig, Marshall, 90n1697
Sitwell, Sacheverell, 92n1540
Siwoff, Seymour, 91n826
Sixteen modern American authors, v.2, 91n1153
Sixth bk of jr authors & illustrators, 90n30
Skapura, Robert, 91n964, 93n916, 94n1006, 94n1007
Skeen, Molly, 94n622
Skeete, Charles, 94n249
Skidmore, Thomas E., 94n142
Skiff, Brian A., 91n1759
Skinner, Robert E., 94n1235
Skinner's dir of security dealer name & address changes 1992, 94n184
Skipper, James K., Jr., 93n826
Skirball, Sheba F., 91n1384
Skorman, Richard, 90n1334
Skoss, Diane, 94n854
Skretvedt, Randy, 92n1334
Skutch, Alexander F., 91n1572
Slade, Alexander L., 92n577
Slang!, 91n1061
Slapin, Beverly, 90n373, 93n433
Slater, Courtenay M., 93n908, 94n937
Slater, Michael, 90n1177
Slater, Thomas J., 93n1340
Slater-Putt, Dawne, 92n393
Slatt, Roger M., 92n1737
Slattery, William J., 94n1463
Slaven, Anthony, 91n129
Slavens, Thomas P., 92n1330
Slavic studies, 94n131
Slee, Debora A., 93n1621, 94n1804
Slee, Vergil N., 93n1621, 94n1804
Slesser, Malcolm, 90n1776
Slide, Anthony, 90n1329, 92n914, 94n1210
Slide buyers' gd, 6th ed, 91n1012
Sloan, Dave, 92n776, 94n848
Sloan, Jane E., 94n1450
Sloan, Wm. David, 90n904
Sloane, Sally Jo, 92n1281
Slomanson, William R., 90n159
Slonimsky, Nicolas, 90n1232, 93n1244
Slovak, Irene, 91n348
Sly, David F., 91n905
Small arms today, 2d ed, 90n676
Small business info hndbk, 92n136
Small business sourcebk, 3d ed, 90n216
Small business sourcebk, 5th ed, 93n213
Small business start-up index, 91n166
Small, John, 90n421
Small pr: an annot gd, 94n659
Small pr center dir, 94n673
Small pr record of bks in print 1989-90, 90n22
Small ruminant production & the small ruminant genetic resource in tropical Africa, 92n1476
Smallman-Raynor, Matthew, 94n1854
Smallwood, Carol, 90n88, 90n446, 93n70
Smart consumer's dir, 1993 ed, 94n202
Smart, Giles, 94n894
Smeeton, Donald Dean, 90n1379
Smialek, William, 90n1216
Smith, Adeline Mercer, 90n79

Smith, Brenda, 93n673
Smith, Candace P., 90n1097
Smith, Carolyn J., 90n1254
Smith, Carter, 90n260, 90n496, 90n501
Smith, Colin, 90n1056, 93n1100, 94n1133
Smith, Cyd, 91n811
Smith, Darren L., 90n77, 91n392, 91n394, 93n500
Smith, David, 93n1063
Smith, Devon Cottrell, 91n379
Smith, Diann Sutherlin, 90n1013
Smith, Donald, 92n1069
Smith, Doreen L., 94n864
Smith, Dorman H., 92n1282
Smith, Frederick, 90n1279
Smith, G. B., 94n1874
Smith, Gary A., 92n1369
Smith, Gregory White, 90n550, 93n1644, 94n562
Smith, Hilda L., 91n1182
Smith, Hobart M., 94n1752
Smith, Jane Bandy, 90n622, 91n653, 92n612, 93n672
Smith, Jerome H., 93n1434
Smith, Jessie Carney, 92n348, 93n52
Smith, John David, 90n493
Smith, John Hazel, 90n1185
Smith, John W., 91n718
Smith, Judith Scharman, 94n1612
Smith, Kathie Billingslea, 93n469
Smith, Laura, 94n1195
Smith, Leon, 94n1421
Smith, Linda C., 92n604
Smith, Margaret, 91n1189
Smith, Margaret M., 94n1246
Smith, Martin A., 90n1424
Smith, Mary M., 92n1660
Smith, Murphy D., 92n406
Smith, Myron J., Jr., 90n774, 91n699, 93n695, 93n696, 94n837, 94n847
Smith, Nancy Kegan, 90n484
Smith, Paul, 94n1383
Smith, Philip H., Jr., 92n1216
Smith, Raoul, 90n1705
Smith, Richard M., 90n98
Smith, Robert Ellis, 94n577
Smith, Robert H., 92n1805
Smith, Robert Selles, 93n581
Smith, Roger, 94n469
Smith, Ronald L., 93n1325
Smith, Rozella B., 94n1752
Smith, Scott D., 94n1612
Smith, Stanley H., 91n510
Smith, Stephen L. J., 91n807
Smith, Tom W., 90n85
Smith, William, 94n1541
Smith-Morris, Miles, 92n738
Smithsonian gd to historic America: the Plains states, 91n464
Smithsonian timelines of the ancient world, 94n534
Smolik, Jane, 92n181
Smucker, Donovan E., 92n1410
Smyers, Jennifer, 90n249
Snaith, Clifton U., 90n1186
Snakes of ...
   E N America, 91n1601
   the US & Canada, v.1, 94n1751
   the world, 90n1571
Snarr, Neil, 90n146
Snodgrass, Mary Ellen, 92n289, 93n43, 93n1143, 94n17
Snoke, Elizabeth R., 92n464
Snow, Dennis A., 93n1608
Snow, Kathleen M., 90n371
Snyder, Louis L., 91n766
Snyder, Paula, 94n947
Sobel, Audrey J., 94n922
Sobel, Robert, 91n731
Sobel, Stuart, 94n855
Sobsey, Dick, 93n865

Social & religious hist of the Jews, 2d ed: index to vs.9-18, 94n427
Social correlates of infant & reproductive mortality in the US, 94n879
Social dimensions of intl bus, 94n222
Social sci & the cults, 91n1410
Social sci ref sources, 2d ed, 91n76
Social scis: a cross-disciplinary gd to selected sources, 91n74
Social scis: an intl bibliog of serial lit, 1830-1985, 93n100
Social scis index, 93n97
Social scis index: April 1990-March 1991, 93n96
Social support networks, 1983-87, 90n815
Social work almanac, 94n911
Social work educ 2, 90n817
Socioeconomics of sustainable agriculture, 94n1588
Sociology in govt, 93n846
Sociology of ...
   Mennonites, Hutterites & Amish, v.2, 92n1410
   mental illness, 90n1674
   religion, 92n1397
   work, 91n244
Socolofsky, Homer E., 90n469, 91n495, 93n513
Sodowsky, Kay, 92n1139
Software ency 1989, 90n1730
Software ency 1993, 94n1915
Software info! for ...
   Apple II computers, 91n1740
   LANs, 91n1741
   Novell NetWare compatible products, 91n1742
Soil mechanics & fndns, 92n1601
Sokol, Stanley S., 93n44
Solar electric independent home bk, 92n1627
Sole, Carlos A., 90n1208
Solid waste educ recycling dir, 92n1779
Solis, Beatriz, 94n915
Solo cello, 90n1260
Solomon, David H., 94n875
Solomon, Sheila A. B., 92n1672
Solorzano, Lucia, 91n321, 93n364
Somalia, 90n110
Somali-English dict, 2d ed, 93n1099
Some of the common & uncommon birds of B.C. & where to find them, 91n1563
Somer, Elizabeth, 92n1667, 93n1647
Somerset, J. Alan B., 92n1386
Somerville, James, 92n38
Something about the author, v.8, 91n1119
Something about the author autobiog series, v.12, 92n1125
Sommer, Elyse, 90n1014
Sommer, Mike, 90n1014
Song & dance, 92n1351
Song on record, 90n1266
Songe, Alice H., 92n571
Songs, odes, glees, & ballads, 92n669
Songwriter's market, 1991, 91n1261
Sontz, Ann H. L., 92n271
Soos, A., 93n1567
Soothill, Eric, 90n1543, 91n1571
Soothill, Richard, 91n1571
Soper, Elizabeth W., 90n303
Soper, Mary Ellen, 91n606
Soper, Nan, 90n584
Soren Kierkegaard bibliogs, 94n1486
Sorensen, Shauna, 92n67
Sorrow, Barbara Head, 94n1920
Sosa, Maria, 94n1561
Sosare, M., 94n1123
Sotheby's concise ency of porcelain, 92n933
Soukup, Paul A., 90n886
Soul music A-Z, 93n1293
Soul of America, 90n495
Sound films, 1927-39, 93n1352
Soundies distributing corp of America, 92n1370
Source bk 1989-90: social & health servs in the greater NY area, 90n818
Source bk of franchise opportunities, 1990-91 ed., 92n154

Source gd to the music of Percy Grainger, 93n1261
Sourcebook for sci, mathematics, & tech educ 1990-91, 92n1462
Sourcebook for sci, mathematics, & tech educ 1992, 94n1582
Sourcebook of ...
    American literary journalism, 93n976
    automatic identification & data collection, 91n1612
    Canadian health stats, 91n1650
    contemporary N American architecture, 90n977
    county demographics, census ed, 94n933
Sourcebook on standards info, 92n574
Sources: an annot bibliog of women's issues, 92n856
Sources in ...
    electrical hist, 91n1614
    European pol hist, v.2, 90n723
    European pol hist, v.3, 93n766
Sources of property market info, 90n297
Sources on the hist of women's mags, 1792-1960, 92n861
Sources: the dir of contacts for editors, reporters & researchers, summer 1990, 26th ed, 91n939
South Africa, 90n112
South Africa under apartheid, 90n111
South Africa's road to change, 1987-1990, 92n89
South America, Central America, & the Caribbean 1993, 94n146
South American birds, 90n1533
South American population censuses since independence, 91n907
South America's natl parks, 91n477
South Asian hndbk, 1992, 93n502
South Carolina: the WPA gd, 90n447
South Pacific islands legal systems, 94n573
Southard, Samuel, 92n818
South-east Asia langs & lits, 90n1033
Southern Africa: a concise gd for independent travellers, 92n446
Southern Africa: annual review 1987/88, 91n92
Southern Calif.'s best ghost towns, 91n462
Southern, Eileen, 92n874
Southern wildflowers, 91n1528
Southon, I. W., 90n1753
Southwest Native American arts & material culture, 92n373
Southwest publishing marketplace, 1991 ed, 91n662
Sova, Dawn B., 94n961
Sova, Gordon, 90n127
Sova, Harry W., 93n982
Sova, Patricia L., 93n982
Soviet foreign policy 1918-45, 92n744
Soviet Jewish hist, 1917-91, 93n447
Soviet lexicon, 90n720
Soviet military ency, abridged English-lang ed, 94n686
Soviet nomenklatura, 3d ed, 92n718
Soviet perception of Canada, 1917-87, 91n105
Soviet propaganda network, 90n728
Soviet pubs on Judaism, Zionism, & the state of Israel 1984-88, 91n407
Soviet security & intelligence orgs 1917-90, 93n769
Soviet stats since 1950, 93n142
Soviet Union, 3d ed, 91n536
Soviet Union: a biographical dict, 92n22
Soviet Union in lit, 92n1229
Soybean diseases, 94n1595
Space almanac, 90n1581
Space atlas, 93n1700
Space exploration, 92n1590, 94n1756
Space people from A-Z, 91n1608
Space station glossary, 93n1581
Space war glossary, 90n677
Space words, 93n1706
Spaghetti westerns, 93n1367
Spain: 1001 sights, 93n506
Spain, Patrick J., 92n145, 93n208, 94n172
Spalding, Frances, 92n970
Spangenburg, Ray, 91n1608
Spangler, Stella S., 91n1455, 91n1456
Spanish American authors, 94n1297
Spanish American women writers, 91n1246
Spanish & Portuguese Jewry, 94n426
Spanish Armada of 1588, 94n527

Spanish, Catalan, & Galician literary authors of the 20th century, 93n1233
Spanish idioms, 92n1091
Spanish-American war, 91n488
Spanish-English, English-Spanish dict of computer terms, 94n1895
Spanish-English hndbk for medical professionals, 3d ed, 90n1670
Spanish-lang ref bks, 90n367
Spar, Ira, 90n989
Sparhawk, Ruth M., 90n758
Sparkes, A. W., 92n1396
Sparkman, Lisa, 90n190
Sparks, Andrew N., 94n1094
Sparks, Linda, 91n312, 94n324
Spatial Terminology Standardization Committee, 93n1581
Speake, Jennifer, 93n1296
Speaker's treasury of sports anecdotes, stories, & humor, 91n816
Speaking for ourselves, 91n1118
Speaking for ourselves, too, 94n1186
Spear, Hilda D., 93n1206
Spears, Richard A., 92n1035, 92n1041
Special access required, 92n528
Special collections in college & univ libs, 90n627
Special educ hndbk, 92n323
Special effects & stunts gd, 90n1331
Special effects & stunts gd, 2d ed, 94n1454
Specialty cookbks, v.1, 93n1470
Specialty cut flowers, 94n1623
Specifications & standards for plastics & composites, 91n1633
Speck, Bruce W., 92n897, 94n997
Spector, Robert D., 90n1167
Spectrum guides: African wildlife safaris, 90n1527
Spectrum: your gd to today's music, summer 1990, 91n1308
Spence, Annette, 90n1645, 90n1646, 90n1648, 90n1649, 90n1650
Spence, Bruce, 93n569
Spencer, Donald D., 93n1681, 94n1904, 94n1912
Spencer, James R., 92n1344
Spencer, Michael D. G., 91n44
Spencer, Peter, 93n1280
Spenser ency, 92n1211
Spicer, Dorothy Gladys, 94n1406
Spies & provocateurs, 94n796
Spies & sleuths, 90n1345
Spies, Karen, 93n1313
Spiewak, Scott A., 92n1606
Spignesi, Stephen J., 92n1175
Spilhaus, Athelstan, 92n407
Spille, Henry A., 94n392
Spillner, Bernd, 92n1010
Spillner, Paul, 91n1
Spindle, Les, 90n1322
Spinelli, Donald C., 90n1042
Spinoza in English, 93n1394
Spivack, Carol, 91n1344
Spivak, Steven M., 92n574
Splittstoesser, Walter E., 91n1506
Spodek, Bernard, 94n314
Spokes, Penny, 90n5, 91n5, 92n8
Spomer, Cynthia Russell, 91n977, 93n306, 94n286
Sponsored research in the hist of art, 7, 90n946
Sport in Britain, 93n814
Sporting News complete baseball record bk, 1993 ed, 94n838
Sporting News complete Super Bowl bk, 1993 ed, 94n848
Sports & fitness, 90n763
Sports & recreation for the disabled, 91n813
Sports ency: baseball, 9th ed, 91n823
Sports ency: pro basketball, 3d ed, 92n787
Sports ency: pro football, 8th ed, 92n795
Sports fan's connection, 93n822
Sports federation of Canada sports dir 1990, 91n810
Sports halls of fame, 93n820
Sports Illustrated, editors of, 93n813
Sports Illustrated 1992 sports almanac, 93n813
Sports in N America, v.3, 94n826
Sports rules ency, 2d ed, 91n808
Sports talk, 90n756

Spottswood, Richard K., 92n1305
Sprackland, Robert George, 93n1580
Spring wildflowers, 94n1659
Springberg, Judith, 93n582, 94n748
Sproccati, Sandro, 94n1047
Sprug, Joseph W., 91n1330, 94n69
Sprung, Barbara, 90n311
Spurgeon, Charles H., 90n1393, 90n1398
Spy fiction, 91n1133
Spycatcher's ency of espionage, 93n787
Spyclopedia, 90n724
Squire, Larry R., 94n809
Squitier, Karl A., 91n1123
Sragow, Michael, 92n1345
Srinivasan, T. N., 91n151
St. Claire, Allison, 92n438
St. James ency of mortgage & real estate finance, 92n262
St. James gd to biog, 92n34
St. James mutual fund dir, 92n167
St. James world futures & options dir 1991-92, 92n168
St John, Ronald Bruce, 93n115
St. Vincent & the Grenadines, 94n148
Staake, Bob, 91n948
Staar, Richard F., 93n780
Stable vet hndbk, 91n1512
Stachura, Peter D., 94n774
Stade, George, 90n1200, 90n1201, 91n1231, 91n1232, 92n1231, 93n1191, 94n1280
Staff dirs on CD-ROM, 1993/1, 94n737
Staff training, 91n252
Stafford, Beth, 91n927
Stafford, D. C., 91n148
Stage deaths, 92n1376
Stage it with music, 94n1473
Stained glass before 1700 in American collections: midwestern & W states, 91n996
Stained glass before 1700 in American collections: silver-stained roundels & unipartite panels, 92n989
Stainsby, Meg, 93n1217
Stainton, Elsie Myers, 92n898
Stake, Donald Wilson, 93n1423
Staley, Thomas F., 90n1173, 91n1196, 91n1240
Stambaugh, James, 91n1441
Stambler, Irwin, 90n1298
Stamp, Robert M., 90n37, 94n18
Stamps, coins, postcards & related materials, 92n934
Standard & Poor's register of corporations, directors & executives 1991, 92n135
Standard & Poor's stock & bond gd, 1993 3d, 94n200
Standard cat of ...
    American cars 1805-1942, 2d ed, 90n1809
    American cars 1976-86, 2d ed, 91n1822
    Buick 1912-90, 92n1800
    Cadillac 1912-90, 92n1801
    Chevrolet 1912-90, 92n1802
    Chrysler 1924-90, 92n1803
    firearms, 2d ed, 93n1004
    Ford 1903-90, 92n1804
    US military vehicles 1940-65, 94n691
    US paper money, 9th ed, 91n984
Standard cataloging for school & public libs, 91n624
Standard dir of ...
    advertisers 1989, 90n280
    advertisers 1993, 94n296
    advertisers tradename index 1989, 90n281
    advertising agencies, Feb-May 1989, 90n282
    advertising agencies, Jan 1993, 94n297
    intl advertisers & agencies 1993, 94n226
    worldwide mktg 1990, 91n277
Standard hndbk for electrical engineers, 13th ed, 94n1777
Standard hndbk of ...
    environmental engineering, 91n1620
    fastening & joining, 2d ed, 90n1605
    hazardous waste treatment & disposal, 90n1594

Standard industrial classification applied to histl data: the 1871 industrial census, 91n150
Standard per dir 1990, 91n65
Standard per dir 1993, 94n67
Standard trade index of Japan 1990-91, 91n278
Standard trade index of Japan 1992-93, 94n245
Standards: a resource & gd for identification, selection, & acquisition, 91n160
Standish, Peter, 94n1299
Stanford companion to Victorian fiction, 90n1172
Stanford, Quentin H., 94n456
Stange, Scott, 94n988
Stanke, Don, 94n1432
Stankus, Tony, 93n1440
Stanley, Autumn, 94n1586
Stanley, Colin, 91n1221
Stanley, Janet L., 94n1040
Stanley, John, 90n1330
Stansfield, Geoffrey, 91n60
Stansfield, W. D., 92n1521
Stansifer, Charles L., 93n154
Stanton, Shelby, 94n708
Stape, J. H., 90n1189
Star & planet spotting, 91n1756
Star gd, 1990-91, 90n36
Star Trek: an annot gd to resources, 93n1331
Starck, Marcia, 93n1648
Starer, Daniel, 94n166
Stark, Richard W., 93n1667
Starkey, Edward D., 92n1399
StarList 2000, 94n1924
Starnes, De Witt T., 92n1013
State & local stats sources 1990-91, 91n897
State & local stats sources, 2d ed, 94n934
State & province vital records gd, 94n432
State & regional assns of the US 1989, 90n95
State & regional assns of the US, 1992 ed, 93n71
State blue bks, legislative manuals & ref pubns, 91n730
State census records, 93n899
State data & database finder, 90n708
State doc checklists, 91n729
State educ docs, 91n295
State elective officials & the legislatures 1991-92, 92n692
State issues 1989, 90n710
State issues 1992, 93n755
State lead poisoning prevention dir 1992, 94n2006
State legislative leadership, committees & staff 1991-92, 92n698
State legislative sourcebk 1992, 93n750
State legislative staff dir 1991, 93n738
State parks of Utah, 90n452
State rankings, 1990, 91n901
State rankings, 1991, 93n912
State ref pubns 1991-92, 93n734
State yellow bk, 90n700
State yellow bk, v.5, no.1, 94n743
State-by-state gd to children's & young adult authors & illustrators, 92n1130
States, Jack S., 92n1545
States of awareness, 90n742
Statesman's yr-bk histl companion, 90n709
Statesman's yr-bk 1991-92, 92n77
Statesman's yr-bk world gazetteer, 4th ed, 92n427
Statesmen who changed the world, 94n716
Stationary engineering hndbk, 90n1607
Stationers' co archive, 91n670
Statistical abstract of N.D. 1988, 90n840
Statistical abstract of the US 1992, 94n938
Statistical forecasts of the US, 94n932
Statistical hndbk on ...
    the American family, 93n867
    US Hispanics, 92n356
    women in America, 92n867
Statistical record of ...
    Asian Americans, 94n401
    black America, 92n348

Statistical record of ... *(continued)*
   native N Americans, 94n422
   the environment, 93n1764
   women worldwide, 92n866
Statistical ref index 1990 annual, 92n848
Statistical report on road accidents in 1990, 94n2027
Statistical Study Center, 92n642
Statistical yrbk, 1987, 92n849
Statistical yrbk for ...
   Asia & the Pacific 1988, 91n902
   Asia & the Pacific 1991, 94n939
   Latin America & the Caribbean, 1991 ed, 93n151
Statistics and Economic Analysis Staff of the Forestry Department, FAO, 93n1483
Statistics & surveys vocabulary, 93n905
Statistics of road traffic accidents in Europe, v.34, 90n1813
Statistics of road traffic accidents in Europe 1991, 93n1785
Statistics on alcohol & drug abuse in Canada & other countries, 90n819
Statistics sources, 13th ed, 90n841
Statistics sources 1993, 93n913
STATS, Inc., 94n836
Statt, David A., 91n792, 93n317
Stauffer, Douglas B., 93n1717
Steadman, Susan M., 93n1333
Steam locomotive dir of N America, 90n1806
Steam locomotives of the Reading & P & R railroads, 90n1817
Steam passenger serv dir 1989, 90n1814
Stearn, William T., 94n1641, 94n1642
Stearn's dict of plant names for gardeners, 94n1642
Stebbins, Robert C., 93n1577
Stedman, Preston, 91n1329
Stedman's abbrev., 93n1623
Stedman's medical dict, 25th ed, 91n1664
Stedman's medical speller, 93n1637
Stedman's pathology lab medicine words, 93n1638
Steele, Apollonia, 91n1229, 94n1276
Steele, J. Valerie, 91n40, 91n741, 93n744
Steele, Joelle, 94n1621
Steele, Philip, 92n1585, 93n414
Steen, Sara J., 90n1311
Steen, Sarah J., 93n392, 93n393
Steene, Roger C., 92n1577
Steep, Barbara J., 91n887
Steeves, Paul D., 90n1381
Stegall, Nancy L., 90n1141
Stegemeyer, Anne, 90n938
Stehman, Dan, 92n1277
Stein, Alice P., 93n1659
Stein, Barbara L., 94n1181
Stein, Barry Jason, 94n696
Stein, J. Stewart, 94n1773
Stein, Jess, 90n999
Stein, Robert M., 93n745
Steinbeck, George, 91n187
Steiner, Dale R., 94n542
Steiner, Lisa A., 90n1654
Steiner, Michael, 90n96
Steinfirst, Susan, 93n1300
Steinhart, Peter, 91n1551
Steinmetz, Sol, 91n1059
Steinzor, Curt Efram, 90n1217
Steis, Drew, 90n961
Stelbecker-Pountney, Barbro E., 93n597
Stella, Nancy C., 90n810
Stelter, Gilbert A., 90n510
Stelter, Jeffrey S., 94n563
Stelter, Thomas, 90n551, 94n563
Stendahl, Karen L., 91n247
Stenesh, J., 91n1516
Stepchuk, Roman, 93n981
Stephan, Aurelia, 91n1705
Stephen Crane: an annot bibliog of secondary scholarship, 93n1172
Stephen King companion, 90n1148
Stephen, Marg, 93n135

Stephens, A. Ray, 90n470
Stephens, Gloria, 91n1578
Stephens, Meic, 91n1107, 94n480
Stephens, Thomas M., 91n410
Stephenson, Mary Sue, 91n643
Stephenson, Richard W., 90n648
Stepnich, Ivan C., 92n1700
Stern, Edward L., 94n1884
Stern, Ephraim, 94n489
Stern, Geoffrey, 92n733
Stern, Malcolm H., 93n458, 94n1557
Stetler, Susan L., 90n28, 90n918, 93n188, 93n189, 94n228, 94n229
Stevens, Gregory I., 94n399
Stevens, Joseph E., 92n445
Stevens, Mark, 90n186
Stevens, Paul, 90n1784
Stevens, Serita Deborah, 91n1714
Stevenson, George A., 93n1042
Stevenson, James A. C., 90n1054
Stevenson, Joan C., 93n415
Stevenson, John, 90n506, 93n529, 93n559
Stevenson, L. Harold, 92n1775
Steverson, Tyrone, 93n1322
Stewart, Brent S., 93n1571
Stewart, Donna, 91n1689
Stewart, John, 90n503, 92n92, 93n1707
Stewart, Julia, 94n443
Stewart, Robert, 93n553
Stewart, Steve, 93n1369, 94n1460
Stewart, William T., 90n1319
Stibili, Edward C., 94n1504
Stidworthy, John, 90n1521, 90n1522, 90n1524
Stievater, Susan M., 92n877
Stiles, F. Gary, 91n1572
Stiling, Peter D., 90n1547
Still more words of Wall Street, 91n185
Stinson, Shirley M., 94n1864
Stirling, David, 91n1563
Stitt, Fred A., 91n1032
Stitt, J. Michael, 92n1318
Stock, Janet C., 92n1235
Stock market & investment vocabulary, 90n202
Stockdale, F. M., 92n1292
Stoddart colour visual dict: French-English, 94n1114
Stokes, Donald, 93n1551
Stokes, Lillian, 93n1551
Stokes, Roy, 90n630
Stone, Jon R., 94n1535
Stone, Norman, 91n545
Stonehouse, Bernard, 94n464
Stoner, K. Lynn, 90n863
Storey, Dee, 94n1183
Storied N.Mex., 92n1165
Story, G. M., 92n1051
Storytelling folklore sourcebk, 92n1316
Storytelling for young adults, 92n626
Storytime sourcebk, 92n625
Stoumen, Tatiana, 90n444
Stoutenburgh, John, Jr., 91n399
Strachan, Anne, 91n1185
Straight from the horse's mouth, 90n1008
Strain, Philip S., 90n1629
Stramler, James H., Jr., 94n1791
Strammiello, Rosemary, 92n60
Strangelove, Michael, 93n72
Strategic atlas, rev. ed, 91n714
Strategic atlas, 3d ed, 94n712
Stratford festival story, 92n1386
Stratton, Peter, 90n746, 94n811
Straub, Deborah Gillan, 93n45
Straughn, Barbarasue Lovejoy, 91n335
Straughn, Charles T., II, 91n335
Straus, Murray A., 91n863
Strauss, Herbert A., 91n409

Straussman, David, 94n1457
Stravinskas, Peter M. J., 94n1531
Stravinsky, John, 91n836
Strawbridge, Donna, 91n1458
Strayer, Joseph R., 90n533
Streimann, Heinar, 91n1540
Stress and mental health, 90n1649
Stress, strain, & Vietnam, 90n739
Stretch, Robert H., 90n739
Strichart, Stephen S., 90n349, 94n340
Strickland, Charlene, 91n1116
Strickland, Jennifer, 94n197
Strickland-Hodge, Barry, 90n1703
Strickler, Carol, 93n1009
Strier, Franklin D., 91n568
Strijp, Ruud, 93n416
String music of black composers, 93n1260
Stroebel, Leslie, 94n1036
Stroff, Stephen M., 94n1358
Strong, Cynthia B., 93n1614
Strong, Gary E., 92n391
Strong, Lisa L., 94n409
Strong, William S., 94n637
Stroud's judicial dict of words & phrases, 5th cum suppl. to the 5th ed, 92n536
Strouf, Judie L. H., 94n1142
Stroynowski, Juliusz, 91n18
Struk, Danylo Husar, 94n138
Stuart, Chris, 90n1558
Stuart, Douglas, 92n1444
Stuart, Philip, 92n1278
Stuart, Tilde, 90n1558
Stuart-Fox, David J., 93n123
Stuart-Fox, Martin, 93n128
Stubbendieck, James, 90n1504
Stubblebine, Donald J., 93n1272
Student atlas of the world, 94n453
Student contact bk, 94n58
Student pol activism, 90n683
Student thesaurus, 91n1080
Student-Bilharz, Barbara, 90n1584
Student's complete vocabulary gd to the Greek N.T., 94n1543
Student's dict of psychology, 90n746
Student's dict of psychology, 2d ed, 94n811
Student's gd to Ont. univs, 92n304
Studies in begoniaceae 4, 94n1649
Studwell, William E., 91n1300, 93n640
Study abroad 1989-91, 90n348
Study holidays, 17th ed, 94n369
Stultz, Newell M., 90n112
Sturge, Charles, 91n240
Sturgis' illus dict of architecture & building, 91n1033
Sturgis, Russell, 91n1033
Sturino, Franc, 90n376
Sturm, Gary L., 94n2028
Sturm, Terry, 92n1239
Suarez, Thomas, 93n470
Subak-Sharpe, Genell J., 92n1670
Subject access to films & videos, 93n640
Subject bibliog of the 2d World War, & aftermath, 91n547
Subject bibliogs of govt pubns, 91n45
Subject collections, 7th ed, 94n656
Subject comps of state laws 1985-88, 90n689
Subject dir of special libs & info centers 1991, 92n622
Subject gd to ...
    bks in print 1990-91, 91n11
    bks in print 1991-92, 92n15
    children's bks in print 1989-90, 90n17
    children's bks in print 1991-92, 92n17
    classical instrumental music, 90n1267
Subject headings for church or synagogue libs, 2d ed, 91n625
Subject headings for the lit of law & intl law, & index to LC K schedules, 4th ed, 91n626
Subject index to feature articles & special reports in ency yrbks 1975-91, 94n35

Subject is murder, v.2, 91n1134
Sublette, James E., 91n1585
Sublette, Mary, 91n1585
Subramaniam, V., 91n783
Sub-Saharan African films & filmmakers, 90n1321
Substance abuse, 90n1650
Substance abuse: a resource gd for secondary schools, 92n838
Substance abuse among ethnic minorities in America, 93n891
Substance abuse & kids, 90n826
Substance abuse 1: drug abuse, 91n885
Substance abuse residential treatment centers for teens, 91n888
Substance abuse 2: alcohol abuse, 91n886
Successful industrial product innovation, 91n260
Succulents, 91n1541
Sudan, rev ed, 94n104
Sugar, Bert Randolph, 91n827
Sugar-cane diseases, 90n1448
Suichmezian, Louis, 92n259
Sukiennik, Adelaide Weir, 93n1124
Sulanowski, James S., 94n577
Sullivan, Eugene, 94n393
Sullivan, George, 94n700, 94n711
Sullivan, Howard A., 90n1042
Sullivan, Irene F., 94n418
Sullivan, Lester, 94n1235
Sullivan, Mark W., 92n1002
Sullivan, Michael J., III, 93n729
Sullivan, Shirley G., 90n285
Sullivan, Thomas F. P., 91n1805, 94n2002
Summer employment dir of the US, 1991, 92n217
Summer on campus, 90n318
Summer reading clubs, 94n1194
Summer theatre dir 1989, 90n1360
Summer theatre dir 1992, 93n1387
Summers, Harry G., Jr., 92n660
Summers, Wilford I., 93n1587
Summerscales, John, 90n1750
Sumrall, Amber Coverdale, 93n944
Sunshine, Linda, 90n827
Suominen, Juha, 90n1494
Superconductivity sourcebk, 91n1800
Supernatural fiction for teens, 2d ed, 93n1156
$upertrader's almanac, 2d ed, 93n321
Supplement to ...
    a gd to source materials for the study of Barbados hist, 1627-1834, 93n541
    the dict of American lib biog, 91n604
    the 10th mental measurements yrbk, 92n760
    Who's Who in America 1991-92, 93n53
Supplementary Russian-English dict, 93n1096
Supreme Court A to Z, 94n556
Supreme Court at work, 91n589
Supreme Court justices, 94n551
Supreme Court yrbk 1990-91, 93n588
Surfin'ary, 92n802
Suriname & the Netherlands Antilles, 94n149
Surrency, Erwin C., 93n756
Survey of social sci: economics series, 92n127
Survey Research Consultants International, 94n75
Survey Research Consultants International, Inc., 90n734
Surviving the nuclear age...1945-1983 table of contents, 92n667
Surviving the nuclear age, 1987 update, 92n668
Suskin, Steven, 91n1309, 92n1387
Suspect chemicals sourcebk, 1989 ed, 90n1761
Sussman, Allen E., 93n1656
Sussman, Lance J., 94n1557
Sutherland, John, 90n1172
Sutherland, Linda, 91n586
Sutherland, Linda P., 91n575
Sutherland, Neil, 94n924, 94n925
Sutherland, Stuart, 90n747
Sutherland, Zena, 93n1134
Suttles, Sharon F., 94n81
Suttles, Steven A., 94n81
Suttles, Wayne, 91n397

Sutton, Alan, 94n1317
Sutton, Clay, 90n1532
Sutton, Elizabeth, 93n389
Sutton, Roger, 93n1134
Svejda, Jim, 90n1269
Swain, Tony, 92n1411
Swallows & martins, 91n1573
Swanborough, Gordon, 91n700
Swanick, Eric L., 93n526
Swannell, Julia, 94n1100
Swanson, Elliott, 91n1359
Swarbrick, James, 91n1710, 91n1711, 94n1867, 94n1868, 94n1869, 94n1870
Swarthout, Douglas, 91n1358
Swartz, Jon D., 94n1017
Swatos, William H., Jr., 90n84
Swedberg, Harriett, 91n979
Swedberg, Robert W., 91n979
Sweeney, Del, 94n624
Sweeney, Jerry K., 94n757
Sweeney, Kevin, 93n1323
Sweeney, Patricia E., 91n920
Sweet, hot & blue: St. Louis' musical heritage, 90n1286
Sweethearts of the sage, 93n1361
Sweetland, Richard C., 93n337, 93n338
Swenson, Mary, 91n118
Swift, Gay, 92n947
Switzerland, 92n107
Swortzell, Lowell, 91n1121
Sydnor, William, 92n1418
Sygall, Susan, 92n315
Sykes, Charles, 92n306
Sykes, Egerton, 94n1394
Sylvia Plath: a ref gd 1973-88, 91n1170
Symonds, Craig L., 93n691
Symphony: a research & info gd, v.1, 91n1329
Syndicated TV, 90n913
SYNERJY, summer-fall 1989, v.16, 91n1801
Synopsis of the herpetofauna of Mexico, v.7, 94n1752
Synoptic problem, 90n1389
Systems & control ency, suppl. v.2, 94n1570
Szajkowski, Bogdan, 93n770
Szczawinski, Adam F., 90n1506, 90n1507
Szladits, Charles, 90n542
Szostak, R., 93n1584
Szycher, Michael, 93n1639
Szycher's dict of biomaterials & medical devices, 93n1639

Tabbert, Russell, 92n1042
Taber's cyclopedic medical dict, 17th ed, 94n1833
Taber's medical word bk with pronunciations, 91n1663
Tabler, Judith, 91n741, 93n71
Tackling toxics in everyday products, 93n1761
Taeuber, Cynthia, 92n867
Taft gd to corporate giving contacts, 6th ed, 91n864
Tagalog slang dict, 93n1103
Tager, Jack, 92n451
Takacs, G., 92n1077
Talbot, Dawn E., 92n1701
Tale of two cities: an annot bibliog, 94n1251
Tale type & motif index of early US almanacs, 92n1318
Talk shows & hosts on radio, 93n990
Talking philosophy, 92n1396
Talking with artists, 93n1021
Tallulah Bankhead: a bio-bibliog, 92n1337
Tamblyn, Eldon W., 92n628
Tambo, David C., 90n845
Tamerius, Steve D., 90n1299
Tamm, Boris, 94n1775
Tanford, Charles, 93n1456
T.A.P.P. sources: a natl dir of teenage pregnancy prevention programs, 91n875
Tapper, Lawrence F., 94n410
Tapping the govt grapevine, 2d ed, 94n56

Taragano, Martin, 92n788, 94n840
Taras, Raymond C., 94n781
Tarboton, Warwick, 92n1571
Tardiff, Joseph C., 94n1260
Targumic mss in the Cambridge Genizah collections, 94n1539
Tarr, Rodger L., 90n1209
Tarutz, Judith A., 93n972
Tate, Michael L., 92n376
Tatem, Moira, 91n798
Tatla, Darshan Singh, 93n1436
Tatro, David S., 90n1698
Taucher, Frank A., 93n321
Tax companion 1991, 92n264
Tax havens, 94n186
Tax lexicon 1989, 90n548
Taxation glossary, 3d ed, 91n288
Taylor, Arnold R., 91n1087
Taylor, Barbara, 94n1702
Taylor, Bruce, 90n901
Taylor, Charles A., 94n400
Taylor, D. A., 91n1623
Taylor, David, 91n1579
Taylor, Desmond, 94n1205
Taylor, James, 91n554
Taylor, Jane, 93n674
Taylor, John W. R., 90n1803
Taylor, Marian, 90n1003, 90n1004
Taylor, Michael J. H., 90n1803, 93n1780
Taylor, Patrick, 94n1622
Taylor, Peter J., 92n674
Taylor, Robert H., 92n93
Taylor, Ronald J., 92n1548, 94n1660
Taylor, Thomas J., 91n1193, 93n1381
Taylor, Vic, 91n1630
Taylor, Wendell Hertig, 91n1132
Taylor, William R., 90n1815
Tayyeb, Rashid, 94n597
TCG theatre dir 1993-94, 94n1477
Teacher educ program evaluation, 91n289
Teaching, coaching, & learning tennis, 90n776
Teaching sci to children, 2d ed, 94n1559
Teague, Edward H., 92n999, 94n1052
Teasdale, Karen H., 94n583
Technical dict of lib & info sci, 94n600
Technical editing, 93n972
Technology Assessment Advisory Committee to the Commission on Preservation and Access, 92n599
Teed, Peter, 93n557
Teens' favorite bks, 94n1175
Teets, Bruce, 91n1202
Teitelman, Jodi L., 91n1696
Telecommunications abstract annual 1988, v.4, 90n1742
Telecommunications dir, 5th ed, 93n1698
Telecommunications dir 1994-95, 94n1922
Telecommunications fact bk & illus dict, 93n1697
Telecommunications systems & servs dir, 4th ed, 90n1740
Telegen reporter annual 1988, 90n1596
Television & audio hndbk for technicians & engineers, 91n1615
Television & ethics, 90n910
Television & young people, 91n965
Television detective shows of the 70s, 92n918
Television drama series programming, 93n993
Television engineering hndbk, rev ed, 93n1588
Television horror movie hosts, 93n985
Television industry, 92n914
Television interviews 1951-55, 92n911
Television network prime-time programming, 1948-88, 90n920
Television writers gd, 90n919
Television writers gd, 2d ed, 93n965
Television yrbk, 93n995
Television-related cartoons in the New Yorker, 94n1056
Telfer, Dorothy, 93n1503
Telgen, Diane, 94n962
Template dir for libs 1989-90, 91n639
Ten precisionist artists, 93n1017

Ten yrs of Ethnic Forum, 1980-89 & cum index, 92n341
Tener, Jean F., 94n1276
Tennessee almanac & bk of facts 1989-90, 90n102
Tennessee attorneys dir, 1992, 93n585
Tennessee govt officials dir, 1991, 93n742
Tennessee Williams: a bibliog, 2d ed, 93n1185
Tenney, Merrill C., 90n1395
Tenth mental measurements yrbk, 90n751
Terborg-Penn, Rosalyn, 94n965
Terenzio, Maurice, 92n1370
Terenzio, Stephanie, 92n1003
Teresi, Dick, 92n180
Terleckyj, Nestor E., 91n163
Terminology of communication disorders, 3d ed, 90n1683
Terms of trade, 91n275
Terrace, Vincent, 91n1392, 91n1393, 93n998
Terrell, Dirk, 94n1929
Terrell, Peter, 94n1115
Terres, John K., 92n1556, 93n1537
Terrible speller, 94n1104
Terrorism: a ref hndbk, 94n585
Terrorism, assassination, espionage & propaganda, 91n771
Terrorism, 1980-90, 92n551
Terrorism, 1988-91, 94n589
Terry, Edwin, 91n1705
Terry, John V., 90n168, 91n135, 94n238
Terry, Max, 94n903
Terry, Michael, 93n297
Terzibaschitsch, Stefan, 90n670, 90n671
Test Collection, Educational Testing Service, 92n273, 93n329, 94n304
Test critiques, v.9, 93n337
Tests: a comprehensive ref for assessments in psychology, educ, & bus, 3d ed, 93n338
Teutsch, Betsy Platin, 93n443
Texas, 94n89
Texas almanac & state industrial gd, 1992-93, 93n111
Texas fact bk 1989, 90n190
Texas mushrooms, 93n1509
Texas range plants, 94n1664
Texas state dir 1989, 90n701
Texas trade & prof assns 1989, 90n277
Text retrieval: a dir of sftwr, 3d ed, 92n1714
Text storage & retrieval systems, 90n611
Textile industry, 90n248
Thackeray, Frank W., 94n716
That old time rock & roll, 90n1291
Thatcher, David, 92n1251
Theatre backstage from A to Z, 3d ed, 90n1368
Theatre lighting from A to Z, 94n1470
Theatrical designers, 93n1382
Theil, Gordon, 91n1280
Thematic list of ...
    descriptors: anthropology, 90n362
    descriptors: economics, 91n168
    descriptors: pol sci, 90n680
    descriptors: sociology, 90n780
Themes & settings in fiction, 90n1103
Themes in American painting, 94n1064
The-Mulliner, Lian, 93n129
Theodicy: an annot bibliog, 94n1506
Theodore Dreiser: a primary bibliog & ref gd, 2d ed, 92n1169
Theodore M. Hesburgh: a bio-bibliog, 91n311
Theological dict of the OT, v.6, 91n1424
Theoretical syntax 1980-90, 93n1049
Theriault, Yves, 93n905
Thermal treatment of hazardous wastes, 90n1793
Thermodynamic properties of inorganic materials, 91n1762
Thesaurus gd, 1992, 94n631
Thesaurus linguae Graecae, 3d ed, 91n1123
Thesaurus of ...
    ERIC descriptors, 12th ed, 91n302
    psychological index terms, 6th ed, 93n645
    subject headings for TV, 91n619
    word roots of the English lang, 94n1079

Theses on English-Canadian lit, 91n1229
Theuns, Leo, 93n504
They wrote for children too, 90n1076
Thibault, Danielle, 91n954
Thiessen, Diane, 94n1968
Things precious & wild, 92n1556
Third Barnhart dict of new English, 91n1059
Third opinion, 90n1658
Third opinion, 2d ed, 94n1859
Third World gd 89/90, 90n129
Third World hndbk, 92n101
Third World in film & video, 1984-90, 92n102
Third World struggle for peace with justice, 92n749
Third World tourism research 1950-84, 93n504
This day in American hist, 91n500
This day in religion, 92n1413
Thode, Ernest, 93n453, 93n454
Thoene, Jess G., 94n1863
Thomas, Anne N., 90n1189
Thomas Carlyle: a descriptive bibliog, 90n1209
Thomas, Carol H., 92n321
Thomas, Clayton L., 94n1833
Thomas, Eberle, 92n1208
Thomas, Edmund J., 92n1109
Thomas, Fannette H., 91n645
Thomas, G. Scott, 91n911, 94n945
Thomas, Graham Stuart, 91n1507, 92n1507, 94n1632
Thomas Hardy dict, 91n1209
Thomas, James L., 92n321, 94n1184
Thomas Jefferson, 1981-90: an annot bibliog, 93n512
Thomas, Jeffrey, 94n1382
Thomas, John C., 91n279
Thomas, Nicholas, 91n1368, 92n1353, 93n1335
Thomas, Page A., 90n1389
Thomas, R. Murray, 91n793
Thomas, Rebecca L., 90n1095
Thomas, Richard K., 90n1674
Thomas, T. Donley, 94n1332
Thomas, Wendy, 92n396
Thomison, Dennis, 93n1033
Thompson, Alice K., 93n584
Thompson, Andrew, 90n730
Thompson, Andrews, 92n723
Thompson, Annie F., 93n1243
Thompson, Bard, 91n1437
Thompson, Della, 94n1078
Thompson, Don, 94n1407
Thompson, Donald, 93n1243
Thompson, Harry F., 93n451
Thompson, Henry O., 94n1536
Thompson, M. M., 94n1825
Thompson, Maggie, 94n1407
Thompson, Max C., 90n1544, 93n1546
Thompson, Susan, 90n1107
Thompson, Trisha, 90n1647
Thomsett, Michael C., 90n252, 90n1233, 91n167, 93n186
Thomson, Ashley, 90n511
Thomson, Ellen Mazur, 94n1059
Thomson, Ian, 91n110
Thorn, John, 91n828, 92n786
Thorndike, E. L., 90n1020, 90n1021, 90n1024
Thorne, Eunice, 91n671
Thornton, L. Anne, 93n919
Thornton Wilder: a ref gd 1926-90, 94n1242
Thorson, Marcie Kisner, 90n340, 93n378
Those fabulous serial heroines, 91n1394
Thoughts on leadership, 93n316
Threatened birds of the Americas, pt.2, 3d ed, 94n1695
Three decadent poets, 91n1222
3 decades of TV, 91n967
300 1st words, 94n1093
300 most selective colleges, 91n320
3-D movies, 90n1340
Thro, Ellen, 91n1743, 92n1703
Throgmorton, Todd H., 94n828

Through Indian eyes, 93n433
Through the pale door, 91n1140
Thum, Marcella, 93n424
Thurner, Dick, 94n1083
Thurston, Anne, 92n460
Tibet, 93n130
Tice, Janet, 91n463
Tiemstra, Suzanne Spicer, 93n1267
Tierney, Helen, 90n872, 92n863, 93n939
Tiffany, L. H., 90n1502
Tightwad, A., 91n201
Tillema, Herbert K., 92n661
Tiller, Veronica E., 93n434
Timber design & construction sourcebk, 90n1575
Time: a bibliographic gd, 93n14
Time dimension, 92n5
Timelines, 92n465
Times atlas of ...
    world exploration, 92n408
    world hist, 3d ed, 91n545
    world hist, 4th ed, 94n530
Time's flotsam: overseas collections of Calif. Indian material culture, 91n395
Times London hist atlas, 93n534
Time-saver standards for building types, 3d ed, 91n1025
Time-saver standards for interior design & space planning, 92n954
Timetables of ...
    hist, 3d ed, 93n560
    sci, 90n1422
    sports hist: baseball, 90n767
    sports hist: basketball, 91n830
    sports hist: football, 90n773, 94n845
    sports hist: the Olympic games, 91n812
Timme, S. Lee, 91n1530
Timor, 94n112
Timothy Findley: an annot bibliog, 91n1228
Timpe, A. Dale, 90n196, 91n253
Tiner, Ralph W., 94n1661
Tingley, Kenneth W., 93n765
Tinker gd to Latin American & Caribbean policy & scholarly resources in metro NY, 90n138
Tinling, Marion, 90n870
Tipper, Allison, 90n133
Tischler, Alice, 90n1218
Tismaneanu, Vladimir, 91n761
Tiwari, Udayanarayan, 92n1074
Tobias, Norman, 93n702
Tobias, Richard C., 92n1188
Tobias, Russell R., 92n1594
Tobiasen, Linda, 94n891
Tobolt, William K., 90n1808
Today's world: a new world atlas, 93n481
Todd, David Keith, 91n1785
Todd, Janet, 90n864
Toenjes, Leonard P., 90n1588
Tolf, Robert W., 94n533
Tolkien thesaurus, 92n1213
Tolnai, Marton, 90n309
Tolz, Vera, 92n490
Tolzmann, Don Heinrich, 91n393
Tomasi, Silvano M., 94n1504
Tomassi, Noreen, 94n983
Tomassini, Christine, 92n591, 94n1020
Tomelleri, Joseph, 91n1586
Tomlinson, Gerald, 91n816, 93n1412
Tompane, Michael, 93n499
Tony Harrison: a bibilog 1957-87, 91n1210
Toogood, Alan, 91n1546
Tools of the profession, 2d ed, 93n674
Top professions, 91n1242
Topical ref bks, 92n9
Topographical dict of Scotland, 2d ed, 90n135
Toposaurus, 92n1025
Torikashvili, John J., 93n1084
Torres, Arturo L., 91n557

Torres-Seda, Olga, 94n1301
Torrington, Derek, 90n254
Tosh, Dennis S., Jr., 93n325
Total baseball, 2d ed, 92n786
Total forecast: Japan 1990s, 94n116
Total TV bk, 94n1016
Toth, A. G., 92n534
Toth, Georgetta, 94n897, 94n900
Totten, Samuel, 92n272, 93n548
Toucan Valley Publications, research staff of, 94n928, 94n941
Touchton, Judith G., 92n311
Tough guy: the American movie macho, 90n1342
Touliatos, John, 91n863
Tour gd to the Civil War, 3d ed, 91n456
Tour gd to the old West, 2d ed, 91n457
Tourism & the travel industry, 90n432
Tourneau, Isabelle, 91n1489
Tousignaut, Dwight R., 94n1873
Towell, Julie E., 90n57, 90n844
Towers, Deirdre, 93n1328
Townley, John M., 90n448
Townsend, Dennis P., 92n1624
Townsend, Kiliaen V. R., 90n320
Townsend, Shelley, 90n900
Toxic substances controls gd, 90n1799
Toxicological evaluations, 1, 92n1729
Toxics A to Z, 93n1769
Toy buying gd, 90n229
Toy, Ernest W., Jr., 90n1822
Traceski, Frank T., 91n1633
Tracey, Patrick Austin, 94n701
Tracey, William R., 93n302
Tracing your Irish ancestors, 94n434
Tracy, Martin B., 92n814
Trade & professional assns in Calif., 4th ed, 90n287
Trade & professional assns in Calif., 5th ed, 93n67
Trade names dict 1989, 90n283
Trade names dict: co index 1989, 90n284
Trade shows worldwide 1990, 91n280
Trade shows worldwide 1993, 94n298
Trade union hndbk, 5th ed, 93n305
Trade unions of the world 1989-90, 90n262
Trade unions of the world 1992-93, 93n313
Tradeshow week data bk, 1992, 93n322
Traditional music of Britain & Ireland, 90n1283
Trafzer, Clifford E., 93n435
Trager, James, 93n554
Trail west, 90n448
Train robbery era, 92n554
Train times in Mexico, 2d ed, 91n1828
Trainer's resource 1989, 90n256
Training & dvlpmt orgs dir, 5th ed, 93n307
Training dir for bus & industry 1989-90, 90n263
Train-watcher's gd to N American railroads, 2d ed, 94n2024
Transcript/video index, 1991, 93n1001
Transcript/video index, 1992, 94n1021
Transliterated English-Yiddish, Yiddish-English dict, 93n1106
Transnational corps & labor, 91n143
Transnational corps in ...
    biotech, 90n247
    S Africa, 93n276
    S Africa & Namibia, 91n127
Transnational corps 1983-87, 90n246
Transportation glossary, 90n1801
Transportation mgmt assn dir, 1989 ed, 91n1815
Transportation-logistics dict, 3d ed, 91n1814
Transylvanian lib, 94n1212
Trapani, Margi, 90n1678
Trash cash, fizzbos, & flatliners, 94n1095
Trattner, John H., 93n757
Traugott, Santa, 91n751
Travel & older adults, 92n438
Travel & tourism data, 90n430
Travel bk, 2d ed, 94n473
Travel dict, 90n431, 92n429

Traveler's country music radio atlas 1993, 94n1018
Traveler's gd to ...
    American crafts east of the Miss., 91n992
    American gardens, rev ed, 90n1472
    major US airports, 90n440
    native America: the Great Lakes region, 94n413
    world radio, 1992 ed, 93n999
Traveler's reading gd, rev & updated ed, 94n474
Traveling Jewish in America, 3d ed, 93n441
Travellers: Canada to 1900, 91n467
Travis, Carole, 91n119
Travis, Cheryl Brown, 91n789
Travis, William G., 92n1408
Treasure, Geoffrey, 94n519
Treasure hunting bibliog & index to per articles, 90n777
Treasures from the film archives, 90n1326
Treasury of ...
    business quotations, 91n167
    humor, 90n1121
    religious quotations, 93n1412
    cocaine abuse, 93n889
Treboux, Dominique, 91n875
Trees, 91n1545, 94n1669
Trees & shrubs for Pacific Northwest gardens, 2d ed, 91n1543
Trees & shrubs of Great Britain & N Europe, 94n1670
Trees for American gardens, 92n1508
Trees of ...
    Ga. & adjacent states, 91n1542
    Hawai'i, 92n1553
    the West, 93n1517
Trefil, James, 90n304, 94n305
Trefousse, Hans L., 92n469
Trehub, Aaron, 94n130
Treitel, Corinna, 92n857
Trelease, Jim, 91n369
Tremblay, Florent A., 90n990
Trenchard, Warren C., 94n1543
Trends in public opinion, 90n85
Triffin, Nicholas, 93n570
Trigg, George L., 92n1747, 92n1750, 93n1733, 93n1734
Trillo, Robert L., 91n1831
Trilobites, 2d ed, 94n1961
Trinder, Barrie, 94n484
Trinick, Michael, 91n468
Tripp, F. R., 94n702
Trissel, Lawrence A., 94n1885
Troike, Rudolph C., 92n1006
Troise, Fred L., 91n1785
Troll student atlas, 93n482
Troll student ency, 92n43
Troll young people's dict, 93n1063
Tropicals, 90n1482
Trotsky: a bibliog, 91n765
Trotsky, Susan M., 93n1108, 93n1109
Trouble is their bus: private eyes in fiction, film & TV, 1927-88, 91n930
Trouser Press record gd, 4th ed, 93n1281
Trout & salmon hndbk, 90n772
Troxell, Kay, 92n1336
Troy, Leo, 90n191, 91n233
Truck, van & 4X4 bk, 92n1797
Trucksource 1989, 90n1812
Trucksource 1992, 93n1783
Trudeau, Lawrence J., 94n1201, 94n1202, 94n1203
True grits, 91n199
Truett, Carol, 91n1744
Truhart, Peter, 91n720
Trzyna, Thaddeus C., 91n1811, 93n1773, 94n2007
Tseng, Sally C., 92n586
Tsivian, Yuri, 91n1385
Tsouras, Peter, 92n664
Tsouras, Peter G., 94n697
Tucker, John Mark, 90n580
Tucker, Kerry, 93n312
Tucker, Martin, 92n1098

Tudor, Dean, 90n4, 93n10
Tufts, Eleanor, 90n865
Tufts, Susan E., 90n697
Tu'inukuafe, Edgar, 94n1134
Tuleja, Tad, 90n1015
Tuller, Lawrence W., 94n239
Tullis, LaMond, 93n892
Tulloch, Paulette P., 93n940
Tulloch, Sara, 93n1065
Tummala, Rao R., 90n1593
Tung Hua Book Company Limited, 90n1039
Tung, Louise Watanbe, 94n1571
Tunnell, James E., 92n646
Tunnell, Michael O., 90n1089, 92n1124
Turecki, Gwen E., 93n1682, 93n1698, 94n1907, 94n1922
Turkington, Carol, 93n1656
Turks & Caicos Islands, 93n157
Turnbull, Deborah A., 90n1450
Turnbull, N. B., 92n792
Turner, Angela, 91n1573
Turner, Arnella K., 92n1159
Turner, Carlton E., 90n1695
Turner, Deborah Ann, 93n1183
Turner, Harold W., 91n1411, 92n1400, 92n1401, 94n1505
Turner, Jane, 91n234, 91n235
Turner, Mary Jane, 90n711
Turner Moss Company, Composite Group, 91n154
Turner, Nancy J., 90n1506, 90n1507
Turner, Norma H., 91n1688
Turner, Patricia, 91n1259
Turner, Rufus P., 92n1607
Turtles of the world, 90n1567
Tutein, David W., 92n1200
Tuten-Puckett, Katharyn E., 94n1190
Tuttle dict of ...
    antiques & collectibles terms, 94n1024
    1st names, 93n465
    new words: since 1960, 93n1066
    quotations for speeches, 93n93
Tuttle, Marcia, 91n615
Tuttle's concise Indonesian dict, 94n1117
TV & studio cast musicals on record, 91n1320
TV ency, 93n988
Tver, Betty M., 92n322
Tver, David F., 90n1614, 92n322
Twenties, 1917-29, 90n1127
20th century American folk, self taught, & outsider art, 94n1032
Twentieth century European short story, 91n1142
20th century painters & sculptors, 92n970
Twentieth century short story explication, suppl.4 to 3d ed, 90n1116
Twentieth-century African-American writers & artists, 92n876
Twentieth-century Caribbean & black African writers, 1st series, 93n1110
Twentieth-century Caribbean & black African writers, 2d series, 94n1148
Twentieth-century children's writers, 3d ed, 90n1088
Twentieth-century choral music, 2d ed, 92n1287
Twentieth-century composer speaks, 94n1333
Twentieth-century crime & mystery writers, 3d ed, 93n1153
Twentieth-century evangelicalism, 91n1434
Twentieth-century German dramatists, 1889-1918, 94n1286
Twentieth-century German dramatists, 1919-92, 94n1287
Twentieth-century German novel, 91n1236
Twentieth-century inventors, 92n1454
Twentieth-century literary criticism, v.39, 92n1110
Twentieth-century literary movements index, 92n1113
Twentieth-century musical chronicle, 90n1228
Twentieth-century romance & histl fiction writers, 2d ed, 91n1136
Twentieth-century sci-fiction writers, 3d ed, 93n1159
Twentieth-century shapers of American popular religion, 90n1380
Twentieth-century short story explication: an index, 93n1161
Twentieth-century short story explication: new series, v.1, 94n1218
Twentieth-century short story explication: suppl.5 to the 3d ed, 92n1146

Twentieth-century Spanish poets, 1st series, 92n1242
Twentieth-century W writers, 2d ed, 92n1153
Twins in children's & adolescent lit, 94n1183
Twitchett, Denis, 93n125
Two hundred yrs of the American circus, 94n1419
Tyckoson, David A., 90n1679
Tyler, Linda L., 90n1255
Tynan, Daniel J., 90n1125
Tyning, Thomas F., 91n1604
Types & motifs of the Judeo-Spanish folktales, 94n1387

UFO ency, v.2, 93n807
UFOs in the 1980s, 91n797
Uganda: an annot bibliog of source materials, 92n90
Ujifusa, Grant, 91n725, 94n746
UK bus finance dir 1990/91, 91n217
UK hotel groups dir 1989/90, 91n472
Ukman, Lesa, 93n258
Ukraine, 91n115
Ukraine: a tourist gd, 94n483
Ukraine: pol parties & orgs, 94n782
Ukraine top 100 exporters, 93n294
Ulack, Richard, 90n418
Ulrich's intl pers dir 1989-90, 90n80
Ulrich's intl pers dir 1990-91, 91n66
Ulrich's intl pers dir 1991-92, 92n65
Ulrich's intl pers dir 1992-93, 93n88
Ulrich's intl pers dir 1993-94, 94n65
Ulrich's plus [CD-ROM], 94n66
Ultimate black bk, 90n62
Ultimate cat bk, 91n1579
Ultimate dinosaur bk, 94n1960
Ultimate gd to sci fiction, 92n1144
Ultimate teddy bear bk, 92n936
Unanue, Emil R., 90n1654
UNCTAD commodity yrbk 1988, 91n282
Under its generous dome, 2d ed, 94n657
Understanding abilities, disabilities, & capabilities, 92n318
Understanding Asian Americans, 91n509
Understanding British English, 91n1076
Understanding lasers, 93n1646
Underwood, Lorraine A., 90n285
Unemployment insurance glossary, 93n252
Unesco list of docs & pubs 1984-86, 90n722
Unesco Social & Human Sciences Documentation Centre, 90n87
Unesco yrbk on peace & conflict studies 1988, 92n753
Ungerleider-Mayerson, Joy, 91n58
Uniforms & insignia of the navies of WW II, 92n665
Uniforms of the American Revolution in color, 92n657
Union army 1861-65: org & operations, 90n662
Union cat of letters to Clemens, 93n1183
Union list of geologic field trip gdbks of N America, 5th ed, 90n1766
Union of International Associations, 90n69, 92n803, 93n75
United Nations Development Programme, 93n1776
United Nations disarmament yrbk, 1987, 90n732
United Nations Environment Programme, 93n1776
United Nations juridical yrbk 1985, 94n578
United States, 93n520
United States air force, 93n709
United States army: a dict, 92n664
United States atlas for young people, 93n469
United States business hist, 1602-1988, 91n130
United States, Canada, & Mexico road atlas, 91n433
United States congressional districts 1883-1913, 91n752
United States corporation hists, 2d ed, 93n174
United States Department of Labor, 91n249
United States foreign policy & the Middle East/N Africa, 91n770
United States govt docs on women, 1800-1990, 94n951
United States importers & exporters dir, 90n286
United States in ...
    Africa, 90n729
    Asia, 92n746
    Latin America, 93n786

United States intelligence, 91n734
United States military road atlas, 94n677
United States navy: a dict, 92n666
United States navy aircraft since 1911, 91n700
United States sanctions & S Africa, 94n545
United States today, 91n434
United States treaty index: 1776-1990 consolidation, 93n759
Universal almanac 1991, 92n2
Universal English-Gujarati dict, 90n1045
Universal horrors, 92n1358
University of California at Berkeley Wellness Letter, editors of, 92n1642, 94n1602
University of North Dakota, Bureau of Business & Economic Research, 90n840
University pr bks for public & secondary school libs 1991, 93n664
University pr bks for public libs, 12th ed, 92n603
Unlocking the files of the FBI, 94n752
Unmacht, Robert, 92n916
Unreal! Hennepin County lib subject headings for fictional characters & places, 2d ed, 93n644
Unsold TV pilots 1955-88, 91n973
Unsworth, Michael E., 92n662
Unterburger, Amy L., 90n1434, 92n357
Untergasser, Dieter, 91n1587
Unwin, Derick, 90n354
Unwin, Linda, 91n472
Up from the roots: growing a vocabulary, 94n1082
Upham, Martin, 92n234, 93n313
Upshall, Michael, 94n42
Upstream people, 92n376
Uranian worlds, 2d ed, 91n1141
Urban, Emil K., 90n1528
Urban hist yrbk 1988, 90n846
Urban informal sector in Africa in retrospect & prospect, 93n277
Urban pols dict, 91n718
Urban public transportation glossary, 90n1816
Urban South, 90n843
Urban transport & planning, 90n842
Urbanic, Allan, 91n411
Urdang, Laurence, 94n299, 94n1107
Urrows, David Francis, 92n1260
Uruguay, 90n147
U.S. aging policy interest groups, 93n860
U.S. agricultural groups, 91n1476
U.S. aircraft & armament of Operation Desert Storm in detail & scale, 94n699
U.S. & Canadian businesses, 1955-87, 90n153
U.S. & foreign diplomatic contacts, 92n747
U.S. army heraldic crests, 94n696
U.S. army uniforms of the Korean war, 94n708
U.S. Central Intelligence Agency, 92n676
U.S. Coast Guard cutters & craft, 1946-90, 91n697
U.S. combat: America's land-based weaponry, 91n711
U.S. criminal justice interest groups, 94n588
U.S. custom house gd 1990, 91n281
U.S. defence & military fact bk, 92n654
U.S. Department of Commerce, National Technical Information Service, Office of Business Development, 94n114
U.S. Department of Commerce, National Technical Information Service, Office of International Affairs, 93n655
U.S. Department of Commerce, Technology Administration, 94n1914
U.S. Department of Labor Employment and Training Administration, 93n301
U.S. Department of the Navy (Bureau of Medicine and Surgery), 93n1578
U.S. Dept of Defense dict of military terms, rev ed, 92n649
U.S. energy & environmental interest groups, 92n1753
U.S. Environmental Protection Agency, 90n1798, 91n1807
U.S. govt: a resource bk for secondary schools, 90n711
U.S. govt pubns for the school lib media center, 2d ed, 92n611
U.S. hist: a resource bk for secondary schools, v.1, 90n498
U.S. hist: a resource bk for secondary schools, v.2, 90n499
U.S. import stats for animal related commodities 1981-86, 91n283
U.S. industrial outlook '93, 94n218

U.S. Jl's 1991 natl treatment dir, 91n889
U.S. Latino lit, 93n1166
U.S. master tax gd, 1991, 92n265
U.S. merchant tokens 1845-60, 3d ed, 92n931
U.S. military logistics, 1607-1991, 93n710
U.S. National Arboretum, staff and consultants of, 91n1503
U.S. natl security policy groups, 91n784
US Naval Intelligence, 92n665
U.S. Navy aircraft 1921-41 & U.S. Marine Corps aircraft 1914-59, 90n667
U.S. Navy ships & Coast Guard cutters, 91n701
U.S. outdoor atlas & recreation gd, 93n497
U.S. reference-iana, 90n475
U.S. relations with S Africa, 92n745
U.S. Securities & Exchange Commission, 94n802
U.S. sourcebk of R&D spenders, 1992 ed, 94n240
U.S. student Fulbright grants & other grants for graduate study & research abroad, 94n346
U.S. Supreme Court, 91n566
U.S. War Department, 92n655, 93n705
US warships of WW II, 90n669
USA & Canada 1990, 91n87
U.S.A. Gulf Coast oil & gas industry dir, 1992, 93n1745
U.S.A. oil industry dir, 1993, 94n1975
U.S.A. oil industry's environmental dir, 1993, 93n1762
U.S.A. oilfield serv, supply & manufacturers dir, 1989, 90n1786
U.S.A. oilfield serv, supply & manufacturers dir, 1993, 94n1976
USA travel phone bk, 92n432
USAN & the USP dict of drug names, 92n1691
USAtlas, 91n435
U.S.-E European trade sourcebk, 92n150
Use of criminal penalties for pollution of the environment, 91n594
Used bk lover's gd to New England, 94n1027
Used bk lover's gd to the mid-Atlantic states, 94n1028
Used car bk, 1989 ed, 90n226
Used car bk, 1991 ed, 92n1798
Used car buying gd, 1992-93 ed, 93n1786
User educ for online systems in libs, 92n598
User's dir of computer networks, 92n1715
User's gd to the Bluebk, 93n590
Ushkevich, Alexander, 93n1079
Using children's bks in reading/lang arts programs, 93n402
Using govt docs, 93n668
Using lit to teach middle grades about war, 94n694
Using media to make kids feel good, 90n828
Using picture storybks to teach literary devices, 91n1113
U.S.-Soviet trade dir, 1990, 91n272
U.S.-Soviet trade sourcebk, 92n254
USSR calendar of events 1987, 90n525
USSR crime stats & summaries, 93n613
USSR in 1989, 92n490
Utah place names, 92n428
Utilization of tropical foods: fruits & leaves, 92n1474
Utsey, Keith, 90n271
Utts, Janet R., 90n1610

V. S. Naipaul: a selective bibliog with annots, 1957-87, 91n1249
Vacation study abroad, 42d ed, 93n393
Vagts, Detlev, 91n490
Vaillancourt, Veronica, 91n757
Valentine, Stuart, 90n217
Valk, Barbara G., 90n476, 91n117, 92n587
Vallerand, April Hazard, 92n1692
Valverde, Antonio Martin, 93n295
Vampire in lit, 91n1139
Vamplew, Wray, 94n822
Van Cott, John W., 92n428
Van Daele, Lori A., 91n285
Van de Sande, Wendy S., 93n687, 94n407
van den Dungen, Peter, 91n774
van den Muijzenberg, Otto, 93n169
van der Heij, D. G., 91n1487
Van der Heij, Dirk G., 92n1631
van der Horst, Koert, 91n1039
van der Leeden, Frits, 91n1785
van der Muelen, Jan, 90n969
van der Tuin, J. D., 93n1724
Van Egmond, Peter, 92n1170
van Gelderen, D. M., 93n1506
Van Gorder, Barbara E., 90n585
Van Hasselt, Vincent B., 90n1629, 94n1848
van Hoey Smith, J. R. P., 93n1506
Van Keuren, Frances, 93n1029
van Leunen, Mary-Claire, 93n973
van Loon, C. D., 91n1487
Van Noppen, Jean-Pierre, 92n1011
Van Nostrand, Brian, 92n423
Van Nostrand Reinhold dict of info tech, 3d ed, 90n612
Van Nostrand's scientific ency, 7th ed, 90n1430
Van Orden, M. D., 91n701
Van Orden, Phyllis, 93n665
Van Scotter, Richard D., 93n354
Van Son, Victoria, 94n750
Van Tassel, David D., 93n860
van Tienhoven, Ans, 94n1731
van Tienhoven, Ari, 94n1731
Van Tighem, Kevin, 93n1533
Van Vliet, Willem, 92n850
Van Vynckt, Randall J., 94n1055
Van Willigen, John, 93n417
Van Zandt, Eleanor, 94n445
VanArsdel, Rosemary T., 91n528
Vance, Timothy J., 94n1119
Vancil, David E., 94n1074
Vanden Bloock, Cecile, 93n784
Vanden, Harry E., 92n734
Vandenberg, Martina E., 90n287
Vandervort-Jones, Pamela A., 90n301, 91n1707
Vanderwerf, Mary Ann, 91n1455, 91n1456
Vandome, Nick, 93n614
Vane, Sylvia Brakke, 91n400
VanGrasstek, Craig, 93n149
Vanguardism in Latin American lit, 91n1244
Vanicky, Donna, 93n194
VanMeter, Vandelia, 91n487, 93n561
Vann, J. Don, 91n528
Vardara, Dena R., 91n1663
Variety & Daily Variety TV reviews, v.16, 94n1019
Variety intl film gd 1991, 92n1373
Variety obituaries, v.12, 91n1345
Variety's complete home video dir 1989, 2d ed, 90n1335
Variety's complete home video dir 1989: adult titles suppl, 90n1336
Variety's dir of major US show bus awards, 90n1312
Variety's film reviews, v.20, 92n1346
Variety's film reviews, v.21, 92n1347
Variety's who's who in show bus, rev ed, 90n1313
Varney, Philip, 91n462
Vasarhelyi, Miklos A., 90n197
Vascular flora of the southeastern US, v.3, pt.2, 91n1533
Vascular plants of Ky., 93n1494
Vascular plants of Minn., 92n1533
Vash, Peter, 94n1603
Vasilevsky, Andrei, 94n777
Vass, Winifred K., 94n1081
Vassilian, Hamo, 92n342, 92n496
Vassilian, Hamo B., 91n386, 93n530, 93n1472, 94n129
Vassiliou, M. S., 93n1685
Vas-Zoltan, Peter, 90n309
Vaubel, Ekkehard, 91n1703
Vaughan, Andrew, 91n1312
Vaughn, Virginia Mason, 91n1214
Vegetable growing hndbk, 3d ed, 91n1506
Veglahn, Nancy J., 93n1441
Vehicle identification 1988-89, 90n1805
Veilleux, Gaston, 90n574
Vellucci, Sherry L., 90n605
Vendor Study Group of the Association for Higher Education of North Texas, 90n595

Venezuela, 92n114
Venomous animals, 90n1563
Venomous reptiles of Latin America, 90n1564
Venomous reptiles of N America, 93n1576
Venomous sea snakes, 94n1750
Venture into cultures, 94n1170
Venzon, Anne Cipriano, 91n488
Vera, Eduardo S., 93n1733, 93n1734
Verdi & his major contemporaries, 91n1298
Verheij, E. W. M., 92n1475
Verkler, Linda A., 90n643
Vermont almanac 1991, 91n89
Vernau, Judi, 91n636
Veron, J. E. N., 94n1747
Verrall, Catherine, 91n401
Versar, Inc., 91n1807
Verseform: a comparative bibliog, 90n1117
Vertical file index, 92n575
Veterans benefits manual, 93n708
Vibbert, Spencer, 94n1810
Vickery, William Edward, 91n236
Victorian American women 1840-80, 93n927
Victorian art reproductions in modern sources, 92n964
Victorian Britain, 90n509
Victorian criticism of American writers, 92n1159
Victorian music publishers, 92n1254
Victorian novel, 91n1195
Victorian pers, v.2, 91n528
Victorian studies, 93n533
Victorian writers, 1832-1890, 93n1197
Vidal, Dominique, 92n118
Vidali, Carole F., 94n1334
Vidaver, William E., 90n1483
Video annual 1991, 92n917
Video for libs, 90n619
Video game quest, 91n839
Video movies, 91n1359
Video policies & procedures for libs, 92n621
Video source bk, 12th ed, 92n909
Video source bk 1993, 94n1020
Videodisc compendium for educ & training, 90n355
Videos for bus & training 1989, 90n192
Videos for understanding diversity, 94n399
Vienna Institute for Comparative Economic Studies, 91n153, 93n907
Vierck, Elizabeth, 92n815, 92n1640
Vietnam, 94n122
Vietnam battle chronology, 93n716
Vietnam bk list, 93n525
Vietnam coastal & riverine forces hndbk, 90n666
Vietnam: the decisive battles, 92n658
Vietnam vet films, 93n1366
Vietnam war: hndbk of the lit & research, 94n497
Vietnam war in lit, 94n514
Vietnam war lit, 2d ed, 90n1132
Vietnamese-English dict, 93n1104
Vietnamese-English, English-Vietnamese dict, 92n1093
Viewers' choice gd to movies on video, 93n1334
Vilcinskas, Mara M., 90n212
Villa, Jaime, 90n1570
Villeneuve, Joseph J., 90n218
Vince, Ronald W., 90n1369
Vinson, James, 91n1020
Vinyard, Denis W., 92n1433, 92n1434, 92n1435, 92n1436, 92n1437, 92n1438
Viola, Lynne, 91n535
Violence against women, 94n596
Violet Archer: a bio-bibliog, 92n1264
Violin music by women composers, 91n1277
Virgin Islands, 93n158
Virology: dir & dict of animal, bacterial & plant viruses, 90n1690
Virtes, John J., 94n726
Virtual reality: a selected bibliog, 93n1672
Viruses & reproduction, 90n1689
Visigoths in Gaul & Spain AD 418-711, 90n515

Visual dict of ...
   animals, 93n1534
   cars, 93n1787
   dinosaurs, 94n1963
   everyday things, 93n1078
   flight, 94n2020
   military uniforms, 93n703
   plants, 93n1502
   ships & sailing, 93n1792
   special military forces, 94n689
   the Earth, 94n1946
   the human body, 93n1492
   the universe, 94n1930
Visual ency of natural healing, 92n1661
Visual literacy, 91n354
Viswanath, D.S., 90n1774
Vital & health stats series, 92n1641
Vital stats on congress, 1991-92, 93n754
Vittor, F., 91n570
Vives bibliog, 91n1404
Viviano, Benedict T., 93n1435
Vivien Leigh: a bio-bibliog, 94n1415
VNR concise ency of mathematics, 2d ed, 91n1798
Vocabulary of ...
   advanced ceramics, 92n1598
   agriculture, 92n1471
   cell engineering, v.1, 93n1600
   educl tech & training, 92n326
   food additives, 92n1490
   free trade, 93n233
   genetic engineering, 91n1621
   global warming, v.1, 94n2001
   hazardous materials in the workplace, 94n1997
   medical signs & symptoms, 91n1665
   public sector auditing, 94n249
   safety & security equipment, 93n1601
   signs & symptoms of the musculoskeletal system, v.1, 91n1666
   Soviet society & culture, 93n1095
Vocal compositions in German organ tablatures 1550-1650, 91n1284
Vocational careers sourcebk, 93n412
Vocelli, Virginia S., 90n158
Vocino, Michael C., Jr., 90n264
Vockeroth, J. R., 93n1564
Voedisch, Virginia G., 90n625
Voegelin-Carleton, Ardis, 90n921, 92n906
Vogel, Charles O., 92n976
Vogel, Colin J., 91n1512
Vogel, J. Thomas, 90n248
Vogt, W. Paul, 94n79
Vohra, Anjali, 92n904
Voices from the underground, 94n1010
Vold, Edwina Battle, 90n319
Voll, John Obert, 94n105
Vollnhals, Otto, 94n1889
Volunteer! 1992-1993 ed, 94n903
Volunteer vacations, rev ed, 90n436
Volunteer work, 94n904
Volunteerism, 3d ed, 92n829
Volunteerism & older adults, 92n807
Voous, Karel H., 90n1545
Voss, Roger, 91n1493
Votteler, Thomas, 91n1143
Vox everyday Spanish & English dict, 90n1059
Vrana, Stan A., 92n1114
Vronskaya, Jeanne, 90n39
Vyas, Anju, 94n953
Vyhnanek, Louis A., 92n500

W. B. Yeats: a census of the mss, 92n1238
W. B. Yeats: a classified bibliog of criticism, 2d ed, 92n1217
W. C. Fields—an annot gd, 94n1428
Wachsberger, Ken, 94n1010
Waddell, D. A. G., 92n114

Waddick, James W., 93n1507
Wade, Carlson, 93n1640
Wade, William A., 90n1735, 94n347
Wading birds of the world, 91n1571
Wagner compendium, 94n1329
Wagner, Pat, 90n513
Wai, Lokky, 91n402
Waithe, Deborah, 94n67
Wakeley, H., 90n234
Wakelyn, Jon L., 90n692
Walberg, Herbert J., 91n300
Walch, Margaret, 91n1011
Walde, Rolf, 91n1609
Walden, Gene, 92n169
Walden, Graham R., 91n82
Walder, Ronald H., 94n458
Waldhorn, Arthur, 91n3
Waldman, Carl, 91n1403, 93n488
Waldo, Andrew B., 94n2018
Waldon, Freda Farrell, 91n517
Waldrup, Carole Chandler, 90n485
Wales, 92n105
Wales, Katie, 91n955
Walford, A. J., 91n1459
Walford's concise gd to ref material, 2d ed, 93n20
Walford's gd to ...
    ref material, v.1, 5th ed: sci & tech, 91n1459
    ref material, v.1, 6th ed: sci & tech, 6th ed, 94n1562
    ref material, v.2, 5th ed: social & histl scis, 93n98
    ref material, v.3, 5th ed: generalia, 93n21
Walker, Aidan, 90n1465
Walker, Albert, 92n235
Walker, Alvin, Jr., 93n645
Walker, Barbara K., 93n1161
Walker, Betty K., 92n1412
Walker, Diane Parr, 94n1343
Walker, Elaine L., 94n885
Walker, John, 94n1456
Walker, John A., 94n1043
Walker, John M., 90n1597
Walker, Leo, 90n1290
Walker, Mark, 93n1366
Walker, Mary, 94n676
Walker, Michael, 90n165
Walker, Neil E., 93n1145, 94n59
Walker, P. M. B., 92n1591, 93n1720, 93n1742
Walker, Paul, 94n1343
Walker, Peter M. B., 90n1477
Walker, Samuel, 94n550
Walker, Warren S., 90n1116, 92n1146, 93n1161, 94n1218
Walker, William O., Jr., 91n1428
Walker-Hill, Helen, 93n1264
Walker's mammals of the world, 5th ed, 93n1572
Walker's manual of W corps 1992, 93n214
Walkiewicz, Lynn, 93n1397
Walkowicz, Chris, 91n1580, 94n1710
Wall, C. Edward, 90n609, 92n597, 93n910
Wall, Elizabeth J., 93n223
Wall St dict, 92n166
Wallace, Amy, 94n1403
Wallace, Steven P., 93n861
Wallach, Van, 90n1571
Walle, Dennis F., 92n35
Wallechinsky, David, 93n841, 94n1403
Wallen, Denise, 90n811
Wallenfeldt, Jeffrey H., 90n1345
Waller, Adrian, 91n956
Waller, Robert, 92n717
Walliman, Isidor, 94n587
Wallis, Lawrence W., 92n630
Wallman, Lester, 90n560
Walls, David, 94n865
Walmer, Max, 91n702
Walsh, Claudette, 94n1242
Walsh, James E., 92n36, 94n31

Walsh, Jim, 90n425, 92n1641
Walsh, John Michael, 91n1159
Walt Disney: a bio-bibliog, 94n1412
Walt Whitman: a descriptive bibliog, 94n1241
Walter Benjamin, 91n1403
Walter, John, 90n925
Walter M. Miller, Jr.: a bio-bibliog, 93n1179
Walter, Virginia A., 94n1185
Walters, David, 91n1328
Walters, James E., 93n1520
Walters, LeRoy, 90n1611
Walters, S. M., 90n1489
Walthall, Barbara, 92n1462, 94n1582
Walton, D. W., 90n1559, 91n1598
Walton, Richard K., 91n1574
Wanda Gag: a cat raisonne of the prints, 94n1060
Wang, Jing, 91n341
Want, Robert S., 91n574, 91n723, 94n564, 94n579, 94n1478
Want's fed-state court dir, 1990 ed, 91n582
Want's fed-state court dir, 1993 ed, 94n564
Want's theater dir, 1993 ed, 94n1478
War against Japan, 1941-45, 91n486
War & peace lit for children & young adults, 94n1185
War & peace through women's eyes, 93n1169
Ward, Adrienne Marie, 91n1047
Ward, Charles A., 94n985
Ward, Gary L., 91n1447, 94n1514
Ward, Geoffrey C., 93n54
Ward, Gerald W. R., 91n978
Ward, James V., 93n1568
Ward, John L., 93n178
Ward, Martha E., 91n1117
Ward's bus dir of US private & public cos 1989, 90n182
Ward's bus dir of US private & public cos 1992, 93n198
Ward's sales prospector, 93n199
Warfare & armed conflicts, 94n692
Warner, Jay, 94n1359
Warner, Thomas E., 90n1219
Warner, Timothy, 90n244
Warr, Wendy, 94n1939
Warr, Wendy A., 90n1756
Warrack, John, 94n1357
Warren G. Harding: a bibliog, 93n509
Warren, Gretchen Ward, 91n1348
Warren, Major T., 92n1083
Warrior's words, 94n697
Wars & peace treaties 1816-1991, 94n693
Wars in the Third World since 1945, 92n653
Warships of the Civil War navies, 91n698
Washburn, Wilcomb E., 90n370
Washington almanac, 93n731
Washington area lib dir, 94n611
Washington art, 90n961
Washington info dir 1989-90, 90n702
Washington info dir 1992-93, 93n743
Washington Irving bibliog, 90n1144
Washington '90, 91n741
Washington '93, 94n744
Washington Post deskbk on style, 2d ed, 91n950
Washington Post gd to Washington, 2d ed, 90n445
Washington representatives 1989, 90n703
Washington representatives 1992, 93n744
Washington Researchers Publishing, 91n157, 91n266, 91n753, 92n240, 93n251, 93n274, 93n289, 94n173
Washington, Valora, 90n833
Wasik, John F., 93n1774
Wasserman, Ellen S., 91n55
Wasserman, Philip D., 91n1718
Wasserman, Steven, 90n552, 90n1424, 91n218, 92n543, 93n917
Wasserman, Steven R., 90n841, 93n913
Wassink, Jan, 92n1572
Wassink, Jan L., 94n1741
Wastewater treatment tech, 90n1794
Watchable birds of the Rocky Mountains, 93n1542
Watching Kans. wildlife, 94n1679

Water ency, 2d ed, 91n1785
Water quality & availability, 94n1954
Waterjet cutting, 92n1629
Waters of the Nile, 92n473
Waters, William J., 90n1220
Water-soluble resins, 2d ed, 93n1713
Waterston, Elizabeth, 91n467
Watkins, Mel, 94n127
Watson, Benjamin, 93n1135
Watson, Bruce W., 91n734, 92n664, 92n666, 93n709
Watson, Carol, 94n41
Watson, Cynthia, 91n784
Watson, Elena M., 93n985
Watson, G. Llewellyn, 92n859
Watson, James, 90n888
Watson, Noelle, 91n132, 91n313, 92n1191, 93n1159
Watson, Susan M., 91n734, 92n664, 92n666, 93n709
Watstein, Sarah B., 94n949
Watstein, Sarah Barbara, 92n1680
Watt, David L., 94n1588
Watt, Evan, 94n1951
Watters, Carolyn, 93n622
Watterson, Andrew, 90n1451
Watterson, Ronald M., 91n558
Watts, Thomas D., 90n824
Waugh, William L., Jr., 92n78
WAVE: women's audio-visuals in English, 94n954
Way, Frederick, Jr., 92n1806
Way nature works, 94n1684
Way's steam towboat dir, 92n1806
Wayward women: a gd to women travellers, 91n454
We shall be heard, 90n879
Wear, Terri A., 94n1709
Wearing, J. P., 92n1388, 93n1386, 94n1469
Weather almanac, 6th ed, 93n1722
Weather hndbk, 92n1735
Weather of US cities, 4th ed, 94n1947
Weatherford, Elizabeth, 90n374
Weaver, David D., 93n1654
Weaver, Norma Wright, 94n1311
Weaver, Robert Lamar, 94n1311
Weaver, Tom, 92n1358, 92n1371, 94n1461
Weaver's bk of 8-shaft patterns, 93n1009
Webb, C. Anne, 94n648
Webb, James L. A., Jr., 94n101
Webb, Walter, 93n215
Webber, Bert, 93n436
Webber, Elizabeth, 91n1055
Webber, F. R., 94n1048
Weber, George H., 92n1688
Weber, Lynn, 94n955
Weber, Mary K., 93n585, 93n742
Weber, Olga S., 91n3
Weber, R. David, 91n346, 92n651, 92n1763, 94n367, 94n368
Weber, William A., 91n1524
Weberg, Brian, 90n707
Webster, Linda, 90n578
Webster, Valerie J., 91n280, 94n298
Webster, Virginia, 94n559
Webster's dict of English usage, 90n1005
Webster's illus dict ency, 91n35
Webster's new biog dict, 90n34
Webster's new ideal dict, 2d ed, 91n1049
Webster's new world dict, 92n1018
Webster's new world dict for young adults, 94n1094
Webster's new world dict of eponyms, 91n1052
Webster's new world dict of media & communications, 92n888
Webster's new world ency, 93n63
Webster's new world ency, college ed, 94n42
Webster's new world ency, pocket ed, 94n43
Webster's new world Hebrew dict, 93n1087
Webster's new world secretarial hndbk, 4th ed, 90n292
Webster's 9th new collegiate dict, 91n1050
Webster's II New Riverside desk quotations, 93n94
Webster's II New Riverside desk ref, home & office ed, 93n5

Webster's II New Riverside pocket dict, rev ed, 92n1019
Webster's word hists, 91n1056
Wedborn, Helena, 90n871
Wedding music, 93n1266
Wedgeworth, Robert, 94n609
Wedgwood, C. G., 94n1787
Weed seeds of the Great Plains, 94n1663
Weeds & words, 90n1445
Weeds of Ky. and adjacent states, 92n1546
Weeds of the woods, 93n1515
Weeg, Carol, 91n343
Weeks, Albert L., 92n718
Weeks, John M., 92n338, 94n541
Weevils of Canada & Alaska, v.1, 94n1722
Wegener, Larry Edward, 92n1178
Wehmann, Howard H., 90n465
Weihs, Jean, 90n606, 91n624
Weik, Martin H., 90n889, 91n1754
Weilant, Edward, 91n78
Weimer, Ferne, 91n1441
Weinberg, Meyer, 91n384, 93n99, 93n618
Weiner, David, 90n192
Weiner, David J., 92n909
Weiner, E. S. C., 90n1006
Weiner, Ed, 94n1838
Weiner, Miriam, 92n384
Weiner, Richard, 92n888
Weinstein, Amy, 91n879
Weinstein, Amy J., 94n913
Weinstein, Miriam, 94n348
Weinstock, Richard A., 91n1344
Weintraub, Stanley, 93n1216
Weird! the complete bk of Halloween words, 91n1340
Weisberg, Gabriel P., 91n1004
Weisberg, Yvonne M. L., 91n1004
Weiskel, Timothy C., 94n2019
Weiss, Allan, 90n1199
Weiss, Anne D., 93n895
Weiss, Carla M., 93n300
Weiss, David M., 91n846
Weiss, Irving, 93n895
Weiss, Manfred, 94n253
Weissberg, Nancy C., 90n1680
Weisser, Thomas, 93n1367
Welch, Jeffrey Egan, 94n1143
Welch, John W., 92n1445, 93n1402
Welcher, Frank J., 90n662
Well-appointed bath, 90n971
Wellek, Alex, 93n737
Weller, Carolyn R., 93n636
Wellisch, Hans H., 93n653, 94n638
Wellness ency, 92n1642
Wellness ency of food & nutrition, 94n1602
Wells, John, 91n309, 91n319
Wells, John H., 90n358
Wells, Robert V., 90n835
Wells, Shirley E., 91n310
Wells, Stanley, 92n1210
Wellsprings of imagination, 94n478
Welsh, Brian W. W., 91n108
Welsh, Doris Varner, 91n7
Welsh women, 94n950
Welsh-English, English-Welsh dict, 94n1136
Welton, Ann, 94n462
Welty collection, 90n1158
Wenner, Lettie McSpadden, 92n1753
Wennrich, Peter, 91n1, 91n1619
Wepsiec, Jan, 93n100
Werner, Craig, 91n1149
Werner's manual for prison law libs, 2d ed, 92n616
Wertsmas, Vladimir F., 92n1015
Wesley quotations, 92n1421
West, Ewan, 94n1357
West, Geoffrey P., 90n1476, 93n1490
West German cinema 1985-90, 94n1441

West, Jim, 93n1744
West, John G., Jr., 93n576
West, Mark I., 94n478
Westcott's plant disease hndbk, 5th ed, 91n1520
Westerman-Alkire, Cheryl, 93n86
Western birds, 90n1536, 91n1570
Western Europe 1989: a pol & economic survey, 90n131
Western European economic orgs, 93n290
Western fiction in the LC classification scheme, 90n598
Western lang lit on pre-Islamic central Arabia, 93n167
Western reader's gd, 94n88
Western series & sequels, 2d ed, 94n1221
Westfall, Gloria D., 94n95
Westin, Richard A., 90n548
Westley, David, 94n1849
Weston, David, 90n632
Weston, Geoff, 92n1014
West's tax law dict, 1992 ed, 93n581
Westwood, Jennifer, 91n1332
WetCoast words, 91n1077
Wetland economics & assessment, 90n1514
Wetta, Frank J., 94n1451
Wetterau, Bruce, 91n27
Wexler, Alan, 93n488
Wexler, Paul, 90n1034
Weyd, Donna L., 91n394
Weyers warships of the world 1992/93, 94n706
Whalen, Lucille, 90n575
Whaley, Gould, Jr., 91n657
What a piece of work is man!, 91n69
What about murder? 1981-91, 94n1206
What do I read next?, 92n1136
What do you call a person from...?, 91n451
What they said in 1988, 90n89
What to do when you can't afford health care, 94n1809
What you need to know about psychiatric drugs, 92n1698
What's new for parents, 94n920
What's what, rev ed, 91n1081
Wheal, Elizabeth-Anne, 91n554
Wheeler, Douglas L., 94n135
Wheeler, James O., 91n443
Wheeler, Leslie, 94n78
Wheeler, Thomas, 91n1216
Whelan, Keith, 92n1256
When is a pig a hog?, 92n1033
Where do we come from? What are we? Where are we going?, 90n785
Where once we walked, 93n494
Where the animals are, 94n1688
Where the birds are, 91n1565
Where the jobs are, 90n255
Where the whales are, 92n1582
Where to find what, 3d ed, 92n606
Where to make money, 94n945
Where walls once stood, 93n388
Where's that tune?, 92n1258
Wheye, Darryl, 93n1541
Which dict?, 92n1040
Whisenhunt, Donald W., 94n509, 94n510, 94n513
Whisker, James Biser, 94n732, 94n1033, 94n1034, 94n1035
Whissen, Thomas Reed, 93n1149
Whistler, W. Arthur, 94n1647
Whistlin' Dixie: a dict of S expressions, 94n1089
Whitaker, Cathy Seitz, 91n672
Whitaker, Jerry C., 91n1615, 93n1588
Whitaker, Joseph, 93n6
Whitaker, Marian, 90n613
Whitaker's almanack 1992, 93n6
Whitaker's bks in print 1993, 94n6
Whitburn, Joel, 92n1293, 92n1294, 93n1282
White, Adam, 91n1301
White, Anthony R., 90n982
White, Barbara A., 91n1155
White, Glenn D., 92n1608
White, J. Perry, 92n1287
White, James J., 92n1513
White, James P., 91n351
White, Jess R., 91n808
White, Joseph L., 93n585, 93n742
White, R. E. O., 92n69
White, R. Steven, 90n233
White, Rhea A., 92n766
White, Rolf B., 90n219
White, Stephen, 92n104, 93n536
Whitehead, Ella, 92n1205
Whitehead ency of deer, 94n1742
Whitehead, G. Kenneth, 94n1742
Whitehead, Peter, 90n1543
Whiteley, Sandy, 90n5, 91n5, 92n8, 94n3
Whiteside, Alicja, 92n190
Whitewater sourcebk, 90n443
Whitfield, James R., 90n740, 91n1689
Whitfield, Philip, 90n1540, 93n1732
Whiting, Bartlett Jere, 90n1301
Whitman, Joan, 94n1613
Whitmore, Timothy C., 92n1764
Whitney, Barry L., 94n1506
Whitney, David C., 91n496
Whittaker, William, 93n502
Whitten, Bessie E., 92n206
Whitten, David O., 92n206
Whitworth, Terry L., 91n1590
Who is who at the Earth Summit, Rio de Janeiro, 1992, 93n1763
Who is who in ...
    serv to the earth, 93n1775
    the Russian govt, 94n777
    the Russian govt, suppl.1, 94n778
Who is who [in] govt, pol, banking & industry: in Latin America, 2d ed, 90n140
Who knows: a gd to Washington experts, 10th ed, 91n753
Who knows about foreign industries & markets, 13th ed, 93n274
Who knows about industries & markets, 13th ed, 93n251
Who knows what, 94n166
Who owns corporate America 1993, 94n167
Who played who on the screen, 90n1324
Who said what when, 92n70
Who was who: a cum index 1897-1990, 93n47
Who was who in ...
    America with world notables, index 1993, 94n23
    native American hist, 91n403
    the American Revolution, 94n500
    world exploration, 93n488
Who was who 1981-90, 93n46
Who wrote that song?, 90n1278
Whole baseball cat, 91n828
Whole lib hndbk, 92n570
Wholesale-by-mail cat 1991, 91n198
Wholesale-by-mail cat 1993, 94n203
Who's inventing what?, 91n164
Who's succeeding, 91n149
Who's wealthy in America 1990, 91n219
Who's wealthy in America 1993, 94n211
Who's who among black Americans 1990/91, 91n388
Who's who among Hispanic Americans 1991-92, 92n357
Who's who at the Frankfurt Bk Fair 1989, 91n658
Who's who: Chicano officeholders, 1990-91, 92n690
Who's Who in China, editorial board, 92n30
Who's who in ...
    Africa, 93n760
    Alaskan arts & crafts, 3d ed, 91n997
    America 1989-91: jr & sr high school version, 91n21
    America 1990-91, 91n22
    America 1992-93, 94n24
    America: jr & sr high school version, v.5-v.8, 93n55
    American art 1989-90, 90n950
    American art 1991-92, 92n971
    American educ, 1988-89, 90n301
    American nursing 1988-89, 91n1707
    American nursing 1993-94, 94n1865
    American pols 1989-90, 90n693

Who's who in ... *(continued)*
    American pols 1991-92, 92n682
    art, 24th ed, 92n972
    Asian & Australasian pols, 93n762
    athletics in American colleges & univs, 91n805
    athletics in American high schools, 92n770
    Australasia & the Far East, 91n16
    bus & industry in the UK 1991, 93n298
    Canada, 92n29
    Canada, 1992, 94n19
    Canadian bus 1989-90, 90n164
    Canadian film & TV 1989, 91n1375
    Canadian film & TV 1991-92, 93n1341
    Canadian finance 1988-89, 90n231
    Canadian lit 1992-93, 93n1220
    China, 92n30
    classical mythology, 94n1393
    comedy, 93n1325
    community, technical, & jr colleges 1991, 92n297
    congress 1991-92, 92n693
    early Hanoverian Britain (1714-1789), 94n519
    European bus, 94n223
    European insts & enterprises 1993, 94n771
    European pols, 92n719
    European pols, 2d ed, 94n772
    fashion, 2d ed, 90n938
    finance & industry 1992-93, 93n179
    Hollywood, 93n1339
    interior design, 90n939
    intl affairs, 92n742
    intl banking 1990/91, 92n190
    intl banking, 6th ed, 94n224
    intl orgs, 93n784
    Italy 1992, 94n20
    Japan 1991-92, 93n48
    late medieval England (1272-1485), 92n483
    Lebanon 1990-91, 91n17
    mass communication, 2d ed, 91n935
    Mexico today, 2d ed, 94n12
    new country music, 91n1312
    non-classical mythology, 94n1394
    Pacific navigation, 93n487
    religion 1992-93, 94n1510
    Roman Britain & Anglo-Saxon England, 92n480
    Russia & the new states, 94n136
    sci & engineering 1992-93, 94n1564
    sci in Europe, 7th ed, 93n1442
    S African pols, 3d ed, 92n705
    S African pols, 4th ed, 94n762
    space: the intl space yr ed, 94n1755
    Spain 1992, 94n21
    Stuart Britain, 92n481
    tech, 6th ed, 90n1434
    the Arab world 1990-91, 92n119
    the east 1991-92, 91n23
    the east 1993-94, 94n25
    the fed executive branch 1993, 94n745
    the midwest 1990-91, 91n24
    the motion picture industry, 6th ed, 90n1337
    the N.T., 94n1537
    the O.T., together with the Apocrypha, 94n1538
    the Peace Corps, 1993 ed, 94n798
    the People's Republic of China, 3d ed, 92n21
    the socialist countries of Europe, 91n18
    the south & southwest, 23d ed, 94n26
    the UN & related agencies, 2d ed, 93n782
    the West 1989-90, 91n25
    the world 1993-94, 94n22
    the Writers' Union of Canada, 4th ed, 94n998
    Tudor England, 92n482
    world insurance, 93n253
    writers, eds & poets, 1992-93, 93n974
Who's who 1989: deans & directors in mgmt & admin studies at Canadian univs, 90n272
Who's who 1991, 92n31

Who's who of ...
    American women 1991-92, 93n56
    emerging leaders in America 1993-94, 94n27
    jazz in Montreal, 91n1255
    Nobel prize winners 1901-90, 2d ed, 92n28
    S Africa, 91n19
    the Asian Pacific Rim, 1992 ed, 93n168
    women in world pols, 93n937
    world religions, 93n1404
Why do we quote...?, 90n83
Why you say it, 94n1080
Whyld, Kenneth, 94n842
Wicker, Gerald L., 93n339
Wickremasinghe, Walter, 92n281
Widdowson, J. D. A., 92n1051
Wiedensohler, Pat, 94n639
Wiegand, Wayne A., 91n604
Wiener, Allen J., 94n1380
Wiersma, John H., 94n829
Wiersma, Tina M., 94n829
Wiesner, Hillary S., 93n1409
Wiggers, Raymond, 92n1554
Wigoder, Geoffrey, 91n1449, 92n381, 93n448, 93n1435
Wilbur, C. Keith, 93n1612
Wilcock, Helen, 90n1573, 90n1787
Wilcox, Bonnie, 91n1580, 94n1710
Wilcox, Derk Arend, 94n787
Wilcox, Laird, 91n771, 91n799
Wild animals of W Canada, 93n1533
Wild Austral., 90n454
Wild flowers, 91n1526
Wilderness U: opportunities for outdoor educ in the US & abroad, 93n335
Wildflowers around the world, 92n1539
Wildflowers for all seasons, 90n1498
Wildflowers of ...
    Miss., 91n1530
    Prince Edward Island, 94n1650
    the central south, 92n1537
    the tallgrass prairie: the upper Midwest, 90n1499
    the W plains, 94n1655
    the west, 93n1503
Wildfowl of the world, 90n1543
Wildhaber, Michael E., 93n708
Wildman, Iris J., 91n630
Wiley, Elizabeth, 90n1152
Wilford, Jane, 91n463
Wilhoit, Frances Goins, 92n885
Wilkes, Angela, 92n1048
Wilkes, G. A., 92n1052
Wilkes, Joseph A., 90n972, 90n973, 91n1026
Wilkie, Richard W., 92n451
Wilkinson, Carroll Wetzel, 92n860
Wilkinson, Charles F., 90n103
Wilks, Daniel S., 94n1948
Willett, Peter, 94n1939
Willey, Joy, 93n1641
William D. Wittliff & the Encino Pr, 91n657
William J. Fellner: a bio-bibliog, 94n154
William Makepeace Thackeray: an annot bibliog 1976-87, 90n1187
William Mason (1829-1908): an annot bibliog & cat of works, 90n1243
William Pitt the Younger 1759-1806: a bibliog, 90n508
William S. Burroughs: a ref gd, 91n1160
William Saroyan: a ref gd, 90n1154
William Walton: a bio-bibliog, 90n1254
William Walton: a cat, rev ed, 91n1269
William Walton: a source bk, 94n1323
William Wilberforce 1759-1833: a bibliog, 93n771
Williams, Beverly, 94n1197
Williams, Brian, 93n656, 94n451
Williams, Christine, 91n586
Williams, David, 92n1662
Williams, David Russell, 92n1249
Williams, Donald, 92n1436

Williams, Donald F., 92n1433, 92n1434, 92n1435, 92n1437, 92n1438
Williams, Ernest, 93n1551
Williams, Frank P., III, 94n804
Williams, Glyndwr, 94n444
Williams, Gwyneth, 90n714
Williams, Helen E., 92n1122
Williams, Hermine W., 90n1251
Williams, James, 90n364
Williams, James G., 90n1711, 90n1712, 92n1707, 94n1896, 94n1897, 94n1898, 94n1899
Williams, Jane, 90n1596, 90n1742
Williams, Jeanne M., 94n876
Williams, John Taylor, 90n558, 94n574
Williams, Kenneth L., 90n1571
Williams, Kim, 92n915
Williams, Leslie R., 90n319, 93n332
Williams, Lisa, 92n295
Williams, Martha E., 92n569, 93n628, 94n614
Williams, Marty, 93n933
Williams, Michael W., 94n402, 94n764
Williams, Peter W., 94n505
Williams, Phil, 94n718
Williams, Phillip, 90n350, 92n323
Williams, Phillip G., 90n1677
Williams, R., 90n819
Williams, Robin, 94n1905
Williams, Robyn, 93n778
Williams, Roger L., 93n1501
Williams, Sally, 93n1485
Williams, Tim Guyse, 92n80
Williamson, David, 90n486, 92n395
Williamson, John B., 93n861
Williamson, John P., 94n1112
Williamson, Mark, 92n1595
Williamson, Mary F., 92n967
Williamson, Sandra L., 90n1184, 91n1217
Williamson, Thomas G., 90n1589
Williamson, William B., 93n1407
Willig, Robert D., 91n232
Willihnganz, Shirley C., 92n122
Willis, Alan, 94n946
Willis, John, 90n1354
Willis, Roy, 94n1398
Willis, Stephen, 93n21
Willis-Thomas, Deborah, 90n944
Willmington, Harold L., 92n1446
Willmington's complete gd to Bible knowledge: N.T. people, 92n1446
Wilmeth, Don B., 94n1479
Wilson, A., 91n216, 92n131, 92n132, 92n204, 94n1977
Wilson, Andrew, 91n1819, 94n525
Wilson bus abstracts, 93n176
Wilson, Carol R., 92n191
Wilson, Charles Reagan, 90n491
Wilson, Clyde N., 91n489
Wilson, Craig A., 90n645
Wilson, Cynthia, 94n1861
Wilson, Diana Hardy, 92n923
Wilson dir of emerging market funds, 1992-1993 ed, 94n185
Wilson, Don E., 94n1743
Wilson, George, 90n139, 92n340, 93n117, 93n160, 93n1359, 94n128, 94n132
Wilson, Ian M., 94n185
Wilson, James D., 94n1240
Wilson, Janet O., 94n866
Wilson, Joyce M., 93n10
Wilson, Katharina M., 92n1232
Wilson, Kenneth G., 94n1085
Wilson, Larry David, 90n1570
Wilson, Miriam J. Williams, 93n896
Wilson, Pamela M., 90n813
Wilson, R. E., 94n1929
Wilson, R. Trevor, 92n1476
Wilson, Robert, 91n742

Wilson, Robert Thomas, 90n1072
Wilson, Shaun, 93n1605
Wilusz, E., 92n1625
Winaker, Lesley Richman, 94n632
Winckler, Suzanne, 91n464
Wind, Barry, 92n1004
Windrow, Martin, 93n699
Windsor, Alan, 93n1044
Winearls, Joan, 92n411
Wingard, Helene F., 92n890, 92n891
Winget, Lynn W., 92n1091
Wingfield, Mary Ann, 94n1065
Winkel, Lois, 91n649, 92n1121
Winklepleck, Julie, 90n1740, 94n988
Winnan, Audur H., 94n1060
Winning edge, 90n760
Winning scholarships, 94n311
Winokur, Jon, 92n71
Winsell, Keith A., 92n574
Winship, Michael, 91n1144
Winstanley, Dean, 90n441
Winter, Arthur, 94n1844
Winter, Georgie, 91n892
Winter, Ruth, 93n1754, 94n1844
Winters, Christopher, 92n337
Winthrop, Robert H., 93n418
Wintle, Justin, 91n683
WIP: a dir of work-in-progress & recent pubs, 93n924
Wischnath, Lothar, 94n1721
Wischnitzer, Saul, 90n1656
Wisconsin birdlife, 92n1567
Wise garden ency, 91n1508
Wise, Tess, 92n479
Wiseberg, Laurie S., 91n601
Wiseman, John A., 93n761, 94n99
Wiseman, Nigel, 92n1663
Wissolik, Richard David, 91n1005
Wiswesser, Edward H., 90n1817
Wit & wisdom of pols, 90n713
Witcher, Curt B., 94n438
Witherick, Michael, 90n421
Witkam, J. J., 90n520
Witlieb, Bernard L., 94n970
Witt, Elder, 91n746, 94n556
Witt, Maria, 93n621
Witten, Matthew, 94n1634
Wittfoht, A. M., 94n1938
Wittig, Alice J., 92n611
Wittman, Sandra M., 91n512
Wittmer, Donna Sasse, 93n894
Witty words, 94n70
Wladaver-Morgan, Susan, 94n158
WLN interlib loan policies dir, 93n658
WLN interlib loan policies dir, 2d ed, 94n643
Woddis, Carole, 93n1389
Woelfel, Charles J., 92n186, 94n208
Wolcott, Roger T., 91n1412
Woldman's engineering alloys, 7th ed, 92n1620
Wolf, Carolyn, 94n620
Wolf, Kirsten, 94n526
Wolf, Laura M., 90n1461
Wolf, Leonard, 90n882
Wolf, Richard, 94n620
Wolf spiders, nurseryweb spiders, & lynx spiders of Canada & Alaska, 92n1580
Wolfe, J. S., 90n1442
Wolfe, Josephine Brace, 91n1074
Wolfgang Amadeus Mozart: a gd to research, 90n1244
Wolke, Howie, 94n1678
Wolman, Benjamin B., 90n90
Woltjer, Richard K., 90n1338
Womanwords, 93n938
Women & aging: a selected, annot bibliog, 90n854
Women & aging: an annot bibliog, 93n928
Women & AIDS, 94n1855

Women & mass communications, 92n886
Women & religion, 92n1405
Women & tech, 94n948
Women & the lit of the 17th century, 91n1182
Women & writing in Russia & the USSR, 93n1230
Women artists in the US, 91n928
Women authors of modern Hispanic S America, 91n1242
Women composers, 90n859
Women In International Security, 91n769
Women in ...
   chemistry & physics, 94n1923
   English social hist 1800-1914, v.1, 91n915
   English social hist 1800-1914, v.2, 90n860
   Japanese society, 93n925
   psychology, 91n918
   sociology, 93n844
   sport, 92n767
   the 1st & 2d world wars, 90n871
   the West, 93n941
Women into the unknown, 90n870
Women of ...
   classical mythology, 92n1320
   color & S women annual suppl, 1991/92, 94n955
   color in the US, 90n862
   E and S Africa, 90n851
   N, W, and central Africa, 90n852
Women outdoors, 92n851
Women patriots of the American Revolution, 92n461
Women philosophers: a bibliog of bks through 1990, 93n1392
Women philosophers: a bio-critical source bk, 90n868
Women prime ministers & presidents, 94n714
Women public speakers in the US, 1800-1925, 94n957
Women, race, & ethnicity, 93n931
Women scientists, 93n1441
Women serial & mass murderers, 93n612
Women who ruled, 91n921
Women working in nontraditional fields, 92n860
Women writers: from page to screen, 91n1364
Women writers of Germany, Austria, & Switzerland, 90n856
Women's archives gd, 92n852
Women's diaries, journals, & letters, 90n853
Women's educ in the Third World, 91n861
Women's ency of health & emotional healing, 94n1805
Women's health perspectives, v.2, 90n877
Women's info dir, 94n968
Women's issues, 91n916
Women's movements of the world, 90n875
Women's Project of New Jersey Inc., 91n923
Women's recovery programs, 91n890
Women's studies: a gd to info sources, 91n912
Women's studies ency, 90n872
Women's studies ency, v.2, 92n863
Women's studies ency, v.3, 93n939
Women's studies in India, 94n953
Women's studies index 1989, 92n869
Women's studies research hndbk, 3d ed, 92n864
Wonchul, Oh, 94n1122
Wonderful world of mathematics, 94n1968
Wonders of the world, 92n1000
Wong, Nancy C., 93n23
Wood, Bret, 91n1361
Wood, Clement, 92n1054
Wood, Clifford H., 93n473
Wood, David N., 91n1780
Wood, Donna, 90n283, 90n284, 91n164, 91n259
Wood, Elizabeth H., 92n1697
Wood, Elizabeth J., 93n914
Wood engineering & construction hndbk, 90n1589
Wood, Floris W., 92n79, 93n914
Wood, Jenny, 94n454
Wood, Marion, 92n472
Wood, R. Kent, 91n298, 92n327
Wood, Robert Muir, 92n1557, 94n1962
Woodhead, Peter, 91n60
Woodhouse, William, 93n701

Woodill, Gary A., 94n315
Woodman, William F., 90n1443
Woodrow Wilson: a bibliog of his times & presidency, 91n728
Woods, Christopher, 93n1508
Woods, Jeannie M., 94n1418
Woodson, Dorothy C., 90n107
Woodward, Ralph Lee Jr., 90n143
Woodward, Ruth L., 93n356, 93n357
Woodwind music of black composers, 91n1276
Woodworker's dict, 92n1630
Woodworth, David, 92n218, 94n894
Woody Herman: a gd to the big band recordings, 1936-87, 92n1301
Woolery, George W., 91n974
Woolls, Blanche, 92n838
Woolum, Janet, 93n818
Worcester, Wayne, 94n57
Word for word: a dict of synonyms, 92n1056
Word perfect: a dict of current English usage, 92n1029
Word: the dict that reveals the Hebrew source of English, 90n1002
Word traps, 94n1087
Word watcher's hndbk, 3d ed, 92n1031
Word wise: a dict of English idioms, 92n1038
Wordless/almost wordless picture bks, 93n1131
Words of the Vietnam War, 92n475
Words of wisdom, 91n72
Words on cassette 1992, 93n984
Words on tape 1989, 90n921
Words to the wise: a writer's gd to feminist & lesbian pers & pubs, 92n900
Wordwatcher's gd to good writing & grammar, 91n1063
Work of ...
   Brian W. Aldiss, 93n1154
   Chad Oliver, 91n1169
   Charles Beaumont, 2d ed, 92n1166
   Colin Wilson, 91n1221
   Dean Ing, 92n1173
   George Zebrowski, 2d ed, 92n1185
   Ian Watson, 91n1220
   Louis L'Amour, 93n1176
   Pamela Sargent, 91n1174
   Reginald Bretnor, 91n1158
   Robert Reginald, 2d ed, 94n1238
   Ross Rocklynne, 91n1173
Work-at-home sourcebk, 4th ed, 93n308
Workers of the Writers' Program of the Works Progress Administration, 90n1318
Workers of the Writers' Program of the Works Progress Administration in New Mexico, 90n450
Workers of the Writer's Program of the Works Progress Administration in the State of Georgia, 92n441
Workers of the Writers' Program of the Works Progress Administration of Arizona, 90n449
Workers' participation in mgmt, 90n257
Working for your uncle, 94n284
Working holidays 1993, 94n370
Working with older adults, 3d ed, 91n644
Working women on the Hollywood screen, 90n857
World agricultural stats 1987, 90n1452
World almanac & bk of facts 1989, 90n3
World Almanac gd to good word usage, 91n1060
World Almanac infopedia, 91n36
World almanac of ...
   1st ladies, 92n463
   presidential campaigns, 93n732
   the Soviet Union, 91n114
   US pols, 91n726
World apparel fibre consumption survey, 90n250
World architecture index, 92n999
World artists 1980-90, 92n973
World authors 1980-85, 92n1099
World ballet & dance 1992-93, 94n1425
World Bank depository lib program dir of libs, 90n626
World Bank group, 92n191
World Bank group dir, Sept 1990, 91n220

World beat: a listener's gd to contemporary world music on CD, 93n1280
World Book atlas, 93n483
World Book dict, 92n1020
World Book ency, 90n54, 93n64
World Book ency of people & places, 93n490
World Book health & medical annual 1989, 90n1630
World bk of America's presidents, 91n497
World Book yr bk 1989, 90n55
World Book-Rush-Presbyterian-St. Luke's Medical Center medical ency, 92n1664
World business dir, 93n261
World chamber of commerce dir 1989, 90n288
World class business, 93n272
World communication & transportation data, 91n942
World Cup 1930-90, 92n801
World currency monitor annual 1976-89: pound sterling, 91n221
World currency monitor annual 1976-89: US dollar, 91n222
World debt tables, 90n232
World debt tables 1991-92, 93n244
World defense forces, 2d ed, 90n659
World dvlpmt dir, 92n738
World dict of legal abbrevs, 93n562
World dir of ...
 diplomatic representation, 93n723
 environmental orgs, 3d ed, 91n1811
 environmental orgs, 4th ed, 93n1773
 human rights research & training insts, 2d ed, 93n619
 minorities, 91n385
 peace research & training insts, 7th ed, 93n792
 social sci insts 1990, 91n83
 teaching & research insts in intl law 1990, 92n546
World economic data, 2d ed, 90n189
World economic data, 3d ed, 93n273
World economy, 94n157
World ency of ...
 lib & info servs, 3d ed, 94n609
 organized crime, 93n610
 police forces & penal systems, 90n569
 20th century murder, 93n611
World energy & nuclear dir, 2d ed, 94n2008
World energy dir, 3d ed, 90n1779
World explorers & discoverers, 93n486
World fact file, 92n83
World factbk 1991-92, 93n105
World facts & figures, 3d ed, 90n92
World financial system, 2d ed, 94n206
World fishes important to N Americans, 93n1559
World gd to ...
 abbrevs of orgs, 9th ed, 93n2
 lib, archive, & info sci assns, 92n571
 libs, 10th ed, 92n568
 libs, 11th ed, 94n612
 scientific assns & learned societies, 5th ed, 92n1461
 special libs, 2d ed, 92n623
World govt, 92n674
World hist for children & young adults, 93n561
World human rights gd, 3d ed, 94n594
World hunger, 92n830
World in turmoil, 93n550
World index of economic forecasts, 3d ed, 90n195
World investment dir 1992, v.1, 94n227
World Jewish dir, 92n379
World law school dir, 1993 ed, 94n565
World list of mammalian species, 3d ed, 92n1581
World list of social sci pers 1991, 93n101
World lit criticism 1500 to the present, 93n1119
World map dir 1989, 90n422
World markets desk bk, 94n239
World media hndbk, 1990 ed, 92n892
World media hndbk 1992-94, 94n992
World music: a source bk for teaching, 90n1282
World mythology, 94n1398
World news digest, v.1, no.2, 90n93

World of ...
 African music, 94n1315
 cacti, 92n1552
 games, 90n771
 learning 1990, 91n301
 learning 1993, 94n308
 options for the 90's, 92n315
 W. E. B. Du Bois, 93n99
 winners, 90n66
 winners, 2d ed, 93n1314
World philosophy, 94n1482
World population growth & aging, 92n844
World quality of life indicators, 91n86
World quality of life indicators, 2d ed, 93n95
World racism & related inhumanities, 93n618
World radio TV hndbk, 1992 ed, 93n1000
World record of major conflict areas, 92n82
World resources 1992-93, 93n1776
World Resources Institute, 93n1776, 94n1986
World retail dir & sourcebk 1991, 93n262
World satellite annual, 1993/94, 94n1758
World satellite dir, 1989, 11th ed, 90n1741
World statistical compendium for raw hides & skins, leather, & leather footwear 1972-90, 5th ed, 94n1598
World stats in brief, 14th ed, 94n940
World tables, 1988-89 ed, 90n193
World tech policies, 94n1587
World trade resources gd, 93n265
World trade system, 93n266
World War I source bk, 94n540
World War II: America at war 1941-45, 93n556
World War II at sea, 91n699
World who's who of women, 9th ed, 90n35
World who's who of women, 11th ed, 94n963
World wildlife habitats, 93n1535
World's greatest brands, 93n275
World's master paintings from the early Renaissance to the present day, 93n1045
World's news media, 93n953
Worldscope financial & serv co profiles, 90n220
Worldscope industrial co profiles, 90n221
Worldwide bibliog of art exhibition cats 1963-87, 93n1020
Worldwide franchise dir, 92n170
Worldwide govt dir 1990, 91n721
Worldwide govt dir 1992, 93n724
Worldwide gd to equivalent irons & steels, 3d ed, 94n1796
Worldwide interesting people, 94n404
Worldwide natural gas industry dir, 1991, 92n1758
Worldwide offshore contractors & equipment dir, 1991, 92n1611
Worldwide petrochemical dir, 1990, 92n1759
Worldwide petroleum phone/fax/telex dir, 1991, 92n1760
Worldwide travel info contact bk 1991-92, 92n439
Worobec, Mary Devine, 90n1799
Woroby, Maria, 93n980
Worth, Fred L., 90n1299
Worthen, William B., 92n919, 92n920
Would the Buddha wear a walkman?, 92n180
Woy, James, 90n152, 93n206
WPA gd to 1930s Ariz., 90n449
WPA gd to 1930s N.Mex., 90n450
Wray, James D., 90n1748
Wray, William D., 90n160
Wren, Brenda, 90n1579
Wrestling college & univ dir, 2d ed, 94n862
Wright, A. J., 90n571
Wright, Amy Bartlett, 94n1730
Wright, Becky A., 90n625
Wright, Christopher, 93n1045
Wright, David, 92n400, 94n447
Wright, David F., 90n1382
Wright, Derek J., 92n624
Wright, Elizabeth, 93n801
Wright, H. Stephen, 93n1271
Wright Investors' Serv, 90n220, 90n221
Wright, Jill, 92n400, 94n447

Wright, Joan, 90n433
Wright, John W., 90n827, 92n2
Wright, Josephine, 92n874
Wright, Martin, 92n738
Wright, Nicola, 93n476
Wright, Patricia S., 91n364
Wright, Peter, 93n787
Wright, Rita J., 90n190, 90n277
Wright, Sarah Bird, 90n451
Wright, Stuart, 90n1137, 90n1155, 92n1201
Wright, Sylvia Hart, 90n977
Write to the heart, 93n944
Writers after WW II, 1945-60, 93n1198
Writers & philosophers, 92n1109
Writers & publs gd to Tex. markets, 92n893
Writer's complete crime ref bk, 91n953
Writers dir 1990-92, 91n1100
Writers dir 1992-94, 93n1118
Writers for young adults, 3d ed, 90n1098
Writers from the S Pacific, 93n1229
Writer's gd to everyday life in the 1800s, 94n511
Writer's gd to metropolitan Washington, 92n894
Writers' gd to Tex. markets, 90n893
Writer's hndbk, 91n944
Writer's hndbk, 1993 ed, 94n999
Writer's market, 1991, 91n945
Writers of ...
    the Caribbean & Central America, 93n1226
    the Indian diaspora, 94n1290
    the middle ages & renaissance before 1660, 93n1199
    the restoration & 18th century, 1660-1789, 93n1200
    the romantic period, 1789-1832, 93n1201
Writers' Program of the Works Projects Administration, South Carolina, 90n447
Writing A to Z, 91n952
Writing about music, 90n1237
Writing about Vietnam, 91n512
Writing for the ethnic markets, 93n962
Wu, Emily, 94n251
Wuerch, William L., 90n149
Wuerttemberg emigration index, v.5, 90n399
Wunder, John R., 90n477
Wunderlich, Richard, 90n1086
Wurl, Joel, 92n383
Wurman, Richard Saul, 91n435
Wurth, Shirley, 94n1165
Wye, Kenneth R., 91n1550
Wyman, Bruce, 92n1775
Wyman, Donald, 92n1508
Wyman, Hastings, Jr., 91n754
Wynar, Bohdan S., 90n6, 90n593, 91n6, 91n115, 92n10, 93n8, 93n22, 94n4, 94n80
Wynar, Lubomyr, 92n341
Wynbrandt, James, 92n1681
Wynn, Graeme, 94n461
Wynne-Davies, Marion, 91n1187
Wyoming birds, 92n1562

X-rated videotape gd 2, 93n1332

Yaakov, Juliette, 90n620, 90n1115, 91n650, 92n610, 92n1137, 93n673, 94n1481
Yachmetz, Kathy A., 93n351
Yakima, Palouse, Cayuse, Umatilla, Walla Walla, & Wanapum Indians, 93n435
Yale Daily News, staff of, 93n372
Yamada, Nanako, 93n1043
Yamada, Osamu, 93n1206
Yanak, Ted, 94n512
Yang, Hiyol, 93n215
Yannone, Mark J. A., 93n586
Yarshater, Ehsan, 92n116, 92n117
Yarwood, Doreen, 93n1011
Yawching, Donna, 91n104
Year bk of labour stats 1991, 93n314
Year bk of labour stats: retrospective ed on population censuses 1945-89, 91n251
Yearbook of ...
    American & Canadian churches 1989, 90n1384
    English festivals, 94n1406
    experts, authorities & spokespersons, 8th ed, 91n943
    intl orgs 1991/92, 93n75
    sci & the future 1991, 91n1468
    Soviet foreign relations, 1991 ed, 93n788
    the European Communities & of the other European orgs, 12th ed, 94n773
Yearbook on intl communist affairs 1991, 93n780
Yearbook suppl. to McGraw-Hill's Natl Electrical Code Hndbk, 1991, 92n1609
Yellin, Jean Fagan, 92n1150
Yellow pages industry source bk, 1992-93 ed, 94n674
Yenal, Edith, 91n1233
Yentis, S. M., 94n1874
Yerkes, Elizabeth, 90n941
Yntema, Sharon K., 90n866
Yoder, Barbara, 91n891
Yoell, John H., 93n1262
Yogacara school of Buddhism, 93n1414
Yogi, Stan, 90n1122
Yogis, John A., 92n537
Yokoyama, Kevin M., 91n283
Yolton, John W., 93n555
York, Henry E., 91n717
Yorke, Amanda, 92n94
Yorkshire stage 1766-1803, 90n1355
You can say that again, 92n69
You got to be original, man!, 91n1315
Young adult 1991 annual bklist, 93n1136
Young adult reader's adviser, 93n1137
Young, Arthur P., 90n847, 94n1507
Young Canada dict, 2d ed, 90n1028
Young Canada thesaurus, 90n1029
Young, Cheryl G., 93n1521
Young, Copeland H., 93n102
Young, George, 90n73
Young, Ian, 94n1856
Young, James A., 93n1521
Young, John V, 90n452
Young, Jordan R., 92n1334
Young, Josiah U., III, 94n1508
Young, Mark, 94n825, 94n1581
Young, Michael L., 93n103
Young, Millie M., 93n1684
Young Oxford companion to the congress of the US, 94n758
Young people's atlas of the US, 94n445
Young people's bks in series, 93n1133
Young reader's companion, 94n1189
Young, Robert J., 92n720
Young, Robyn V., 92n1247, 94n1303
Young, W. Murray, 90n1256
Youngberg, Harold W., 93n1510
Youngblood, Ronald F., 94n1547
Yount, Lisa, 93n1443
Your 1991/92 gd to Social Security benefits, rev ed, 92n230
Your reading, 8th ed, 92n1123
Your reading, 9th ed, 94n648
Your resource gd to environmental orgs, 92n1787
Youth ministry resource bk, 90n1412
Yudofsky, Stuart, 92n1698
Yugoslav linguistics in English 1900-80, 92n1008
Yugoslavia: a comprehensive English-lang bibliog, 94n139
Yup-lian, Lu, 92n1477
Yvorra, James G., 90n1613

Zagaris, Bruce, 94n916
Zaimont, Judith Lang, 92n1257
Zak, Victoria, 94n1603
Zakalik, Joanna M., 94n650
Zakia, Richard, 94n1036
Zalewski, Wojciech, 92n637
Zalucky, Henry K., 93n1097
Zanichelli new college Italian & English dict, 92n1081
Zaslaw, Neal, 92n1279, 92n1280
Zauner, Georg, 92n1555
Zeiger, Arthur, 91n3
Zein, Zein Ahmed, 92n1632
Zeitak, G., 92n1666
Zeleny, Robert O., 90n47, 90n54, 90n55, 90n1439, 90n1630, 93n58, 93n64
Zeleznik, Karen, 93n1462
Zell, Hans, 90n642
Zell, Hans M., 91n93
Zelnik, Martin, 92n954
Zempel, Edward N., 90n643
Zemtsov, Ilya, 92n721
Zen Buddhism: a classified bibliog, 92n1448
Zentner, Christian, 92n493
Zepper, John T., 93n383
Zera, Richard S., 93n219
Zerden, Sheldon, 91n1643
Zezulin, Alexandra, 93n1079
Zhao, Yu-tang, 93n1507
Ziegler, Ronald, 91n20
Zikopoulos, Marianthi, 93n389, 93n390
Zilla, Karin, 94n624
Zilm, Glennis, 94n1864

Zim, Herbert S., 91n1552
Zimdahl, Robert L., 90n1445
Zimmerman, David R., 94n1886
Zimmerman, Dorothy Wynne, 93n1222
Zimmerman, Franklin B., 90n1257
Zimmerman, Julie N., 93n846
Zimmerman, Marc, 93n1166
Zimmerman's complete gd to nonprescription drugs, 2d ed, 94n1886
Zinkewych, Osyp, 94n483
Ziring, Lawrence, 93n776
Zito, Dorothea R., 90n793
Zito, George V., 90n793
Zminda, Don, 94n836
Zondervan NIV atlas of the Bible, 90n1386
Zoo animals, 91n1554
Zoological cat of Austral., v.5, 90n1559
Zophy, Angela Howard, 91n929
Zorc, R. David, 93n1099, 93n1103
Zubatsky, David S., 90n381, 92n382, 93n1233
Zuck, Virpi, 92n1240
Zucker, Isabel, 92n1541
Zuckerman, Edward L., 91n794
Zuckerman, Mary Ellen, 92n861
Zuker, R. Fred, 92n308
Zurawicki, Leon, 92n259
Zurick, Tim, 93n717
Zvirin, Stephanie, 94n926
Zwang, Moses, 90n1669
Zweifel, Richard G., 94n1748
Zwicker, Barrie, 91n939
Zwirn, Jerrold, 91n4

Subject Index

Reference is to year and entry number.

ABBREVIATIONS. *See also* **ACRONYMS**
Acronyms, initialisms & abbrevs dict 1992, v.1, 93n1
Common abbrevs in clinical medicine, 90n1633
Dictionary of acronyms & abbrevs, 94n597
Dictionary of acronyms & abbrevs in applied linguistics & lang learning, 94n1072
Dictionary of medical acronyms & abbrevs, 2d ed, 94n1818
International ency of abbrevs & acronyms of orgs, 3d ed, 91n1
OSI dict of acronyms & related abbrevs, 94n1891
Oxford dict of abbrevs, 93n3
Stedman's abbrev., 93n1623
World gd to abbrevs of orgs, 9th ed, 93n2

ABBREVIATIONS, RUSSIAN—DICTIONARIES—ENGLISH
Compressed Russian, 93n1097

ABILITY—TESTING
ETS test collection cat, v.4, 91n293

ABNORMALITIES, HUMAN
Encyclopedia of genetic disorders & birth defects, 92n1681

ABORTION
Abortion: a ref hndbk, 93n851
Abortion & family planning bibliog for 1989-90, 93n850
Abortion debate in the US and Canada, 92n805
Abortion in the US, 92n1669
Abortion in the US, 1992 suppl, 94n1840
Pro-choice/pro-life, 92n834

ABSALOM! ABSALOM!
Absalom! Absalom! a concordance to the novel, 91n1162

ABSTRACTING & INDEXING SERVICES
Guide to current indexing & abstracting servs in the Third World, 93n652
Index & abstract dir, 90n71

ABSTRACTS
Matter of fact, v.14-15, 93n910

ABUSED WIVES
Battered wives, 90n577

ACACIA
Field gd to the acacias of Kenya, 93n1516

ACADEMIC LIBRARIES. *See* **LIBRARIES, UNIVERSITY & COLLEGE**

ACADIENSIS (FREDERICTON, N.B.)
Acadiensis index, 1971-91, 93n526

ACCADIAN LANGUAGE. *See* **AKKADIAN LANGUAGE**

ACCIDENTS
Field drug ref for emergency care providers, 92n1668
Maintaining good health, 90n1647
Vocabulary of safety & security equipment, 93n1601

ACCOUNTING
Accountants' index, 37th suppl, 91n169
Accounting research dir, 2d ed, 90n197
Encyclopedic dict of accounting & finance, 90n198
Environmental accounting, 94n1989
European accountancy yrbk 1992/93, 93n271

Methodology & method in hist, 91n170
National accounts stats 1986, 91n900

ACHIEVEMENT TESTS
ETS test collection cat, v.3, 90n302
ETS test collection cat, v.4, 91n293
ETS test collection cat, v.5, 92n273
ETS test collection cat, v.6, 93n329

ACID RAIN
Acid rain: a bibliog of Canadian fed & provincial govt docs, 92n1769
Acid rain abstracts annual 1988, 90n1796

ACQUIRED IMMUNE DEFICIENCY SYNDROME. *See* **AIDS (DISEASE)**

ACQUISITION OF AUDIO-VISUAL MATERIALS
Policies of AV producers & distrs, 2d ed, 91n616

ACQUISITION OF GOVERNMENT PUBLICATIONS
Free pubs from US govt agencies, 91n44
U.S. govt pubns for the school lib media center, 2d ed, 92n611

ACQUISITIONS (LIBRARIES)
AHE vendor dir for acquisitions librarians, 90n595
EBSCO's 1989-90 librarians' hndbk, 90n76
Magazines for libs, 6th ed, 90n78
Policies of publishers, 1989 ed, 90n645

ACRONYMS. *See also* **ABBREVIATIONS**
Acronyms, initialisms & abbrevs dict 1992, v.1, 93n1
Dictionary of acronyms & abbrevs, 94n597
Dictionary of acronyms & abbrevs in applied linguistics & lang learning, 94n1072
Guide to fed gvmt acronyms, 90n686
International ency of abbrevs & acronyms of orgs, 3d ed, 91n1
New intl dict of acronyms in lib & info sci, 2d ed, 93n621
OSI dict of acronyms & related abbrevs, 94n1891
Stedman's abbrev., 93n1623
World gd to abbrevs of orgs, 9th ed, 93n2

ACTING
Back Stage hndbk for performing artists, 90n1364
Coming to terms with acting, 94n1434
Regional theatre dir 1989-90, 90n1359

ACTIVITY PROGRAMS IN EDUCATION
Literature activity bks, 94n1197
Literature-based moral educ, 93n351
More creative uses of children's lit, v.1, 93n671

ACTORS. *See also* **MOTION PICTURE ACTORS & ACTRESSES**
Agnes Moorehead: a bio-bibliog, 94n1413
Biographical dict of actors, actresses, musicians, dancers, managers & other stage personnel in London, 1660-1800, v.13, 92n1378
Biographical dict of actors, actresses, musicians, dancers, managers & other stage personnel in London, 1660-1800, v.14, 92n1379
Boris Karloff: a bio-bibliog, 94n1409
Cary Grant: a bio-bibliog, 91n1350
Colleen Dewhurst: a bio-bibliog, 94n1411
Edwin Booth: a bio-bibliog, 93n1379

Eva Le Gallienne: a bio-bibliog, 90n1320
Helen Hayes: a bio-bibliog, 94n1416
Jessica Tandy: a bio-bibliog, 93n1315
Joseph Chaikin: a bio-bibliog, 93n1376
Julie Andrews: a bio-bibliog, 90n1322
Maureen Stapleton: a bio-bibliog, 94n1418
Orson Welles: a bio-bibliog, 91n1361
Regional theatre dir 1989-90, 90n1359
Richard Burton: a bio-bibliog, 93n1322
Tallulah Bankhead: a bio-bibliog, 92n1337
Vivien Leigh: a bio-bibliog, 94n1415

ACUPUNCTURE
Glossary of Chinese medical terms & acupuncture points, 92n1663

ADA (COMPUTER PROGRAM LANGUAGE)
Ada lang vocablary, 93n1677

ADAMS, JOHN QUINCY
John Quincy Adams: a bibliog, 94n498

ADEN, GULF OF
Red Sea, Gulf of Aden & Suez Canal, 92n1770

ADHESIVES
Handbook of adhesive raw materials, 90n1759

ADMINISTRATION. *See* **MANAGEMENT**

ADMINISTRATIVE AGENCIES. *See also* **EXECUTIVE ADVISORY BODIES**
Access to US govt info, 91n46
Encyclopedia of govtl advisory orgs 1990-91, 90n694
Federal regional yellow bk, v.1, no.1, 94n739
Federal regulatory dir, 6th ed, 92n687
Federal staff dir/1, 1993, 94n735
Federal yellow bk, winter 1990, 91n738
Guide to fed gvmt acronyms, 90n686
Heritage dir 1990, 91n757
Latest intelligence, 92n646
Prune bk: the 60 toughest sci & tech jobs in Washington, 93n757
Public info contact dir 1988-89, 90n1433
Staff dirs on CD-ROM, 1993/1, 94n737
State yellow bk, v.5, no.1, 94n743
Who knows: a gd to Washington experts, 10th ed, 91n753
Who's who in the fed executive branch 1993, 94n745

ADMINISTRATIVE SCIENCE QUARTERLY
Administrative sci quarterly cum index 1956-85, 90n265

ADMIRALS
Admirals of the new steel navy, 91n691
Dictionary of admirals of the US Navy, 90n664

ADOLESCENCE
Black adolescence, 91n892
Encyclopedia of adolescence, 92n843

ADOLESCENT PSYCHIATRY
Bibliography for training in child & adolescent mental health, 92n1673
Handbook of prescriptive treatments for children & adolescents, 94n1845

ADOLESCENT PSYCHOLOGY
Best yrs of their lives, 94n926

ADOLESCENTS. *See* **YOUTH**

ADOPTION
Adoption dir, 90n799
Adoption lit for children & young adults, 93n868
Adoption resource gd, 2d ed, 92n822
CWLA's gd to adoption agencies, 90n800
Encyclopedia of adoption, 93n866
Loving Journeys gd to adoption, 94n885

ADOPTION AGENCIES
Adoption choices, 93n869

ADS. *See* **ADVERTISING**

ADULT CHILD ABUSE VICTIMS
Sexual assault & child sexual abuse, 90n578

ADULT CHILDREN OF ALCOHOLICS
Children of alcoholics, 92n840

ADULT CHILDREN—SERVICES FOR
Caregiving of older adults, 94n867

ADULT EDUCATION
Adult basic educ collection, 91n352
Adult educ in continental Europe 1986-88, 91n377
Adult educ in continental Europe 1989-91, 94n391
Adult learner's gd to alternative & external degree programs, 94n393
Annotated bibliog of natl sources of adult educ stats, 91n353
Comparative adult educ, 90n357
Education for older adult learning, 94n389
Elderhostels, 90n434
Guide to academic travel, 91n375
Guide to academic travel, 2d ed, 93n407
International dict of adult & continuing educ, 92n333
100 ways colleges serve adults, 92n332

ADULTS ABUSED AS CHILDREN. *See* **ADULT CHILD ABUSE VICTIMS**

ADVENTURE AND ADVENTURERS
Power brokers, 90n481

ADVENTURE DI PINOCCHIO
Pinocchio cat, 90n1086

ADVENTURE FILMS
Black action films, 90n1344

ADVENTURE STORIES. *See* **DETECTIVE & MYSTERY STORIES**

ADVERSARY SYSTEMS (LAW)
Adversary system, 91n568

ADVERTISING
Advertising ratios & budgets, 94n287
Adweek agency dir 1992, 92n238
Co-op source dir: spring 1993, 94n288
Dictionary of mktg & advertising, 2d ed, 92n241
Economist Pubs pocket gd to advertising, 90n276
NTC's dict of direct mail & mailing list terminology & techniques, 91n273
Power media selects, 5th ed, 92n889
Shipping lit of the Great Lakes, 93n1778
Standard dir of advertisers 1989, 90n280
Standard dir of advertisers 1993, 94n296
Standard dir of advertising tradename index 1989, 90n281
Standard dir of advertising agencies: Feb-May 1989, 90n282
Standard dir of advertising agencies: Jan 1993, 94n297
Standard dir of intl advertisers & agencies 1993, 94n226

AERONAUTICS
Acronym bk: acronyms in aerospace & defense, 91n675
Aviation/space dict, 7th ed, 91n1607
Cambridge air & space dict, 92n1591
Dictionary of aviation, 92n1792
Illustrated ency of general aviation, 2d ed, 91n1818
Kitty Hawk to NASA, 92n1794
Visual dict of flight, 94n2020

AERONAUTICS, COMMERCIAL
Airline safety, 92n1793
Encyclopedia of American bus hist & biog: the airline industry, 93n248

AERONAUTICS, MILITARY
French military aviation, 90n660
United States air force, 93n709

AEROPHYTES
Shade & color with water-conserving plants, 93n1520

AESTHETICS
Companion to aesthetics, 94n1492
Walter Benjamin, 91n1403

AFGHANISTAN
Afghanistan, 93n122

Historical dict of Afghanistan, 93n121

AFRICA
Africa, 92n474
Africa, rev ed, 90n104
Africa: a gd to ref material, 94n94
Africa today, 1990 rev. ed, 91n437
African archaeology, 94n488
African bk world & pr, 4th ed, 90n642
African music, 93n1241
African names, 94n443
African socio-economic indicators 1989, 94n92
African states & rulers, 90n503
African studies companion, 91n93
African women: a general bibliog, 1976-85, 90n850
American & Canadian doctoral dissertations & master's theses on Africa, 1974-87, 91n91
Bibliographies for African studies 1970-86, 90n106
Black theatre & performance, 91n1398
Blacks in film & TV, 91n1355
Conservation atlas of tropical forests: Africa, 93n1484
Dictionary of the African left, 91n764
Directory of African film-makers & films, 94n1436
Directory of dvlpmt research & training insts in Africa, 94n93
Directory of museums in Africa, 91n57
Drum: an index to "Africa's leading mag 1951-65", 90n107
Economies of Africa, 92n143
Ethiopia, 90n109
Mental health & psychiatry in Africa, 94n1849
New atlas of African hist, 92n85
Post-harvest & processing techs of African staple foods, 93n1478
SCOLMA dir of libs & special collections on Africa in the UK & in Europe, 5th ed, 94n652
Small ruminant production & the small ruminant genetic resource in tropical Africa, 92n1476
Somalia, 90n110
South Africa, 90n112
Spectrum guides: African wildlife safaris, 90n1527
Sub-Saharan African films & filmmakers, 90n1321
Urban informal sector in Africa in retrospect & prospect, 93n277
Waters of the Nile, 92n473
Women of N, W, and central Africa, 90n852
World of African music, 94n1315

AFRICA, EAST
Adventuring in E Africa, 91n465
Guide to archives & mss relating to Kenya & E Africa in the UK, 92n460
Women of E and S Africa, 90n851

AFRICA, EASTERN
Gemstones of E Africa, 94n1955

AFRICA—FOREIGN RELATIONS—UNITED STATES
United States in Africa, 90n729

AFRICA, FRENCH-SPEAKING EQUATORIAL
French colonial Africa, 94n95

AFRICA, FRENCH-SPEAKING WEST
French colonial Africa, 94n95

AFRICA, NORTH
Biographical dict of the Middle East, 93n161
Guide to the archaeological sites of Israel, Egypt, & N Africa, 91n478
Handbook of the birds of Europe, the Middle East, & N Africa, v.6, 94n1696
Handbook of the birds of Europe, the Middle East, & N Africa, v.7, 94n1697
Middle East & N Africa 1990, 91n123
Peoples of the world: the Middle East & N Africa, 93n160
Political leaders of the contemporary Middle East & N Africa, 91n762
Women of N, W, and central Africa, 90n852

AFRICA, NORTH—FOREIGN RELATIONS—UNITED STATES
United States foreign policy & the Middle East/N Africa, 91n770

AFRICA—POLITICS & GOVERNMENT
African pol facts since 1945, 2d ed, 92n704
Pan-Africanism: an annot bibliog, 94n764

AFRICA, SOUTHERN
African birds of prey, 92n1571
Chris & Tilde Stuart's field gd to the mammals of S Africa, 90n1558
Dictionary of contemporary pols of S Africa, 90n714
Southern Africa: a concise gd for independent travellers, 92n446
Southern Africa: annual review 1987/88, 91n92
Who's who of S Africa, 91n19
Women of E and S Africa, 90n851

AFRICA, SUB-SAHARAN
Africa south of the Sahara 1990, 91n90
Africa south of the Sahara 1993, 94n91
African studies thesaurus, 94n629
African theology, 94n1508
Ashe, traditional religion & healing in sub-Saharan Africa & the Diaspora, 91n1409
Bibliography on educ in dvlpmt & social change in sub-Saharan Africa, 91n291
Black Africa: a comparative hndbk, 2d ed, 90n105
Peoples of the world: Africans south of the Sahara, 93n117
Political leaders in Black Africa, 93n761
Who's who in Africa, 93n760

AFRICA, WEST
Energy in the dvlpmt of W Africa, 94n1969
History of agriculture in W Africa, 91n1473
Women of N, W, and central Africa, 90n852

AFRICAN AMERICANS. *See* **AFRO-AMERICANS**

AFRICAN LANGUAGES—INFLUENCE ON ENGLISH
African heritage of American English, 94n1081

AFRICAN LITERATURE (ENGLISH)
Black African lit in English, 1982-86, 90n1190

AFRICAN LITERATURE (PORTUGUESE)
New bibliog of the Lusophone lits of Africa, 2d ed, 94n1268

AFRICAN NATIONAL CONGRESS
ANC & black workers in S Africa, 1912-92, 94n103

AFRICANS
Worldwide interesting people, 94n404

AFRO-AMERICAN ADMIRALS
African American generals, 94n685

AFRO-AMERICAN AGED
Black aged in the US, 2d ed, 90n783

AFRO-AMERICAN ART
Art of black American women, 94n1046
Black artist in America, 93n1033

AFRO-AMERICAN ARTISTS
Black authors & illustrators of children's bks, 2d ed, 93n1139
Twentieth-century African-American writers & artists, 92n876

AFRO-AMERICAN ARTS
African-American traditions in song, sermon, tale, & dance, 1600s-1920, 92n874

AFRO-AMERICAN ATHLETES
Interesting athletes, 91n803

AFRO-AMERICAN AUTHORS
African American writers, 92n1156
Ann Petry: a bio-bibliog, 94n1237
Black authors, 92n1148
Black authors & illustrators of children's bks, 2d ed, 93n1139
Black writers, 90n1068
Invisible poets: Afro-Americans of the 19th century, 2d ed, 90n1164
Twentieth-century African-American writers & artists, 92n876

AFRO-AMERICAN CHILDREN
Black children & American institutions, 90n833

AFRO-AMERICAN CHURCHES
Encyclopedia of African American religions, 94n1514

AFRO-AMERICAN COMPOSERS
Woodwind music of black composers, 91n1276

AFRO-AMERICAN DRAMATISTS
Early black American playwrights & dramatic writers, 92n1160

AFRO-AMERICAN ENGLISH. See BLACK ENGLISH

AFRO-AMERICAN GENERALS
African American generals, 94n685

AFRO-AMERICAN LIBRARIANS
Directory of ethnic professionals in LIS (lib & info sci), 93n625

AFRO-AMERICAN LITERATURE (ENGLISH). See AMERICAN LITERATURE—AFRO-AMERICAN AUTHORS

AFRO-AMERICAN MOTION PICTURE ACTORS & ACTRESSES
Blacks in film & TV, 91n1355

AFRO-AMERICAN MUSICIANS
Dictionary of Afro-American performers, 91n1259

AFRO-AMERICAN PENTECOSTALS
Biographical dict of African-American, Holiness-Pentecostals 1880-1990, 91n1439

AFRO-AMERICAN PERIODICALS
Index to black pers 1988, 91n390
Index to black pers 1991, 94n403
Reference gd to Afro-American pubs & eds 1827-1946, 94n1009

AFRO-AMERICAN PHOTOGRAPHERS
Illustrated bio-bibliog of black photographers 1940-88, 90n944

AFRO-AMERICAN SCIENTISTS
Black scientists, 93n1443

AFRO-AMERICAN TEENAGERS
Black adolescence, 91n892

AFRO-AMERICAN UNIVERSITIES & COLLEGES
America's black colleges, 94n330

AFRO-AMERICAN WOMEN
African American women, 94n960
Art of black American women, 94n1046
Bibliographical gd to African-American women writers, 94n1223
Black American women in lit, 90n858
Black American women in Olympic track & field, 93n843
Black American women novelists, 91n1149
Black females in the US, 90n741
Black women in America, 94n965
Black women in TV, 92n855
Harlem renaissance & beyond, 91n1150
Notable black American women, 93n52
Pen is ours, 92n1150
Piano music by black women, 93n1264
Women of color & S women annual suppl, 1991/92, 94n955

AFRO-AMERICANS
African American biogs, 93n423
African American ency, 94n402
African American: social & economic conditions, 94n405
African-American community studies from N America, 92n346
Afro-American sources in Va., 91n391
Black Americans: a statl sourcebk, 92n345
Black Americans info dir, 91n392
Black Americans info dir 1994-95, 94n407
Black arts annual 1987/88, 90n962
Black authors, 92n1148
Black bk publishers in the US, 93n679
Black elected officials, 20th ed, 94n733
Black males in the US, 90n740
Black Olympian medalists, 92n769
Black 100, 94n406
Black resource gd, 10th ed, 93n422
Black resource gd, 1990-91 ed, 91n387

Blacks in sci & medicine, 92n351
Books by African-American authors & illustrators for children & young adults, 92n1122
Chronology of African-American hist, 92n347
Civil rights movement, 94n595
Directory of African American religious bodies, 92n1404
Encyclopedia of African-American civil rights, 93n616
Freedom's lawmakers, 94n727
Guide to black Washington, 91n458
Health of black Americans from post reconstruction to integration, 1871-1960, 91n1642
Hippocrene USA gd to black America, 93n424
Hippocrene USA gd to historic black south, 94n475
Historic landmarks of black America, 92n440
Historical & cultural atlas of African Americans, 92n343
Index to the Hampton Univ newspaper clipping file, 92n349
Inspiring African Americans, 92n350
Interesting people: black American hist makers, 90n480
Invisible poets: Afro-Americans of the 19th century, 2d ed, 90n1164
Kaiser index to black resources, 1948-86, 93n425
Langston Hughes: a bio-bibliog, 91n1164
My soul looks back, 'less I forget, 94n72
National black media dir, 90n892
Negro almanac, 5th ed, 90n364
Statistical record of black America, 92n348
Who's who among black Americans 1990/91, 91n388
Women of color in the US, 90n862
World of W. E. B. Du Bois, 93n99
Worldwide interesting people, 94n404

AFRO-AMERICANS IN LITERATURE
American ethnic lits, 94n1225
Black experience in children's bks 1989, 90n1079
Chester Himes: an annot primary & secondary bibliog, 94n1235
Harlem renaissance & beyond, 91n1150
Invisible poets: Afro-Americans of the 19th century, 2d ed, 90n1164
Masterpieces of African-American lit, 93n1164
Out of the woodpile, 93n1151

AFRO-AMERICANS IN MOTION PICTURES
Black action films, 90n1344

AFRO-AMERICANS—LANGUAGE—DICTIONARIES
African heritage of American English, 94n1081

AFRO-AMERICANS—MUSIC
African-American traditions in song, sermon, tale, & dance, 1600s-1920, 92n874
Cash Box black contemporary album charts, 1975-87, 90n1277

AFRO-AMERICANS—RELIGION
Ashe, traditional religion & healing in sub-Saharan Africa & the Diaspora, 91n1409
Encyclopedia of African American religions, 94n1514

AGE & EMPLOYMENT
Older workers, 92n812

AGED. See also AGING; GERONTOLOGY; RETIREMENT
Aging with style & savvy, 91n843
America's elderly, 90n790
Anthropology of aging, 92n813
Bibliography of seniors & the family research 1980-91, 93n852
Black aged in the US, 2d ed, 90n783
Caregiving of older adults, 94n867
Congregate care by county, 90n786
Consumer's gd to aging, 94n875
CPA world dir of old age, 90n787
Creativity in the later yrs, 93n856
Crime & the elderly, 90n782
Education for older adult learning, 94n389
Elder care, 91n845
Elder servs 1990-91, 91n844
Elderhostels, 90n434
Elderly in America, 92n811
Encyclopedia of aging & the elderly, 93n858
Families & aging, 93n854

Golden horizons retirement gd, Calif. ed, 90n792
Guide to research in gerontology, 90n793
Jewish elderly in the English-speaking countries, 90n784
Image of older adults in the media, 94n870
Late achievers, 93n43
Legal issues & older adults, 94n572
National gd to funding in aging, 2d ed, 91n846
NCOA dir of sr centers, 90n788
Resources for elders with disabilities, 91n858
Resources for elders with disabilities, 2d ed, 94n873
Retirement sourcebk, 90n791
Second 50 yrs: a ref manual for sr citizens, 93n853
Senior movement, 93n861
Senior citizen servs, 94n874
Travel & older adults, 92n438
U.S. aging policy interest groups, 93n860
Working with older adults, 3d ed, 91n644

AGED—CRIMES AGAINST
Crime & the elderly, 90n782

AGED—HEALTH & HYGIENE
Complete gd to symptoms, illness & surgery for people over 50, 94n1839
Ethical aspects of health care for the elderly, 94n868
Healthy aging, 94n869
Palliative care of the elderly, 93n857

AGED—RELIGIOUS LIFE
Pastoral responses to older adults & their families, 93n859

AGED VOLUNTEERS. *See also* **VOLUNTARISM**
Older volunteer, 94n887
Volunteerism & older adults, 92n807

AGED WOMEN
Women & aging, 90n854

AGED WORKERS. *See* **AGE & EMPLOYMENT**

AGENTS PROVOCATEURS
Spies & provocateurs, 94n796

AGING
Aging & sensory change, 90n781
Anthropology of aging, 92n813
Building lib collections on aging, 92n806
Consumer's gd to aging, 94n875
Encyclopedia of aging & the elderly, 93n858
Fact bk on aging, 92n815
Fundamentals of geriatrics for health professionals, 91n1696
Gerontology & geriatrics libs & collections in the US & Canada, 94n655
Healthy aging, 94n869
Old age in myth & symbol, 92n809
Where do we come from? What are we? Where are we going?, 90n785
Women & aging: a selected annot bibliog, 90n854
Women & aging: an annot bibliog, 93n928
World population growth & aging, 92n844

AGORA
Ostraka, 92n503

AGRICULTURAL CHEMICALS
Crop protection chemicals ref, 1991, 92n1470
Pestline, 92n1785

AGRICULTURAL ENGINEERING
Literature of agricultural engineering, 94n1754

AGRICULTURAL PRODUCTIVITY
FAO yrbk: production, v.45, 94n1591
Intercountry comparisons of agricultural output & productivity, 94n1597

AGRICULTURE
Agricultural research centres, 9th ed, 90n1446
Agricultural sftwr dir 1990, 91n1475
Agriculture dict, 93n1468
American farm crisis, 90n1441
Biological & agricultural index [CD-ROM], 93n1458

Biological & agricultural index, v.75, no.6, 91n1470
EC agricultural price indices, 91n1480
FAO quarterly bulletin of stats 1990, v.3, 91n1477
FAO yrbk: trade 1987, v.41, 90n1447
Farm family financial crisis, 90n1442
French-English agricultural dict, 93n1465
History of agriculture in W Africa, 91n1473
Many names of country people, 90n1444
U.S. agricultural groups, 91n1476
Vocabulary of agriculture, 92n1471
Who's who in sci in Europe, 7th ed, 93n1442
World agricultural stats 1987, 90n1452

AGRICULTURAL PRODUCTIVITY
Commodity review & outlook 1990-91, 93n1466

AHTENA LANGUAGE
Ahtna Athabaskan dict, 92n1063

AID TO DEPENDENT CHILDREN. *See* **CHILD WELFARE**

AIDS (DISEASE)
AIDS, 92n1677
AIDS: abstracts of the psychological & behavioral lit 1983-89, 2d ed, 91n1687
AIDS: abstracts of the psychological & behavioral lit 1983-91, 3d ed, 93n1650
AIDS & women, 92n1680
AIDS bibliog for 1981-86, 90n1680
AIDS crisis in America, 94n1852
AIDS dir, 94n1850
AIDS dissidents, 94n1856
AIDS funding, 93n1653
AIDS info sourcebk 1991-92, 92n1678
AIDS 1988 pt.2, 90n1679
AIDS: 1,000 full-text statistical abstracts from the A Matter of Fact database, 1984-92, 94n1851
Dictionary of AIDS-related terminology, 94n1853
Directory of current HIV/AIDS research in Canada 1988-91, 93n1651
How to find info about AIDS, 93n1652
Learning AIDS, 2d ed, 90n1678
National dir of AIDS care, 92n1679
Psycholsocial aspects of AIDS, 91n1688
Women & AIDS, 94n1855

AIKIDO
Aiki News ency of aikido, 93n838
Aiki News 1994 dojo finder, 94n854

AIR CONDITIONING
Air-conditioning glossary, 91n1635
Handbook of HVAC design, 91n1634

AIR—POLLUTION
Air pollution control, 90n1792
Environmental hazards: air pollution, 90n1790
Reference gd to clean air, 92n1776

AIR POWER
Jane's all the world's aircraft 1992-93, 93n1780

AIR QUALITY MANAGEMENT
Reference gd to clean air, 92n1776

AIR TRANSPORT. *See* **AERONAUTICS, COMMERCIAL**

AIR TRAVEL
United States military road atlas, 94n677

AIR WARFARE
Air wars & aircraft, 91n685

AIRCRAFT CARRIERS
Aircraft carriers of the US navy, 2d ed, 90n670
Naval Institute gd to combat fleets of the world 1993, 94n704

AIRCRAFT INDUSTRY
Encyclopedia of American bus hist & biog: the airline industry, 93n248
McDonnell Douglas aircraft since 1920, 90n1802

AIRLINES
Encyclopedia of American bus hist & biog: the airline industry, 93n248

AIRPLANES
Guide to 475 aircraft museums, 224 city-displayed aircraft, 37 restaurants with aircraft, 6 WWI landmarks, 10th ed, 93n1779
History of airlines in Canada, 91n1817
Jane's all the world's aircraft 1989-90, 90n1803
McDonnell Douglas aircraft since 1920, 90n1802
Visual dict of flight, 94n2020

AIRPLANES, MILITARY
U.S. aircraft & armament of Operation Desert Storm in detail & scale, 94n699
U.S. Navy aircraft 1921-41 & U.S. Marine Corps aircraft 1914-59, 90n667

AIRPORTS
Traveler's gd to major US airports, 90n440

AKKADIAN LANGUAGE
Cuneiform texts in the Metropolitan Museum of Art, 90n989

ALABAMA
Place names in Ala., 90n426

ALADDIN (RECORD COMPANY)
Aladdin/Imperial labels, 92n1299

ALASKA
Alaska place names, 4th ed, 92n426
Alaska wilderness milepost 1989, 90n439
Alaskan histl docs since 1867, 90n97
Checklist of beetles of Canada & Alaska, 93n1560
Dictionary of Alaskan English, 92n1042
Discovering wild plants, 91n1523
Encyclopedia of the far west, 92n84
Guide to the ms collections at the Univ of Alaska, Anchorage, 92n35
Nature of SE Alaska, 93n1528
Weevils of Canada & Alaska, v.1, 94n1722

ALBANIAN LANGUAGE—DICTIONARIES—ENGLISH
Albanian-English dict, 94n1109

ALBENIZ, ISAAC
Isaac Albeniz: chronological list & thematic cat of his piano works, 94n1320

ALBERTA
Alberta bibliog, 93n135
Fishes of Alta., 2d ed, 94n1720
From the past to the future, 93n527
Place names of Alta., [v.1], 92n424
Place names of Alta., v.2, 93n492

ALCHEMY
Alchemy in Europe, 91n1763

ALCIATI, ANDREA
Princeton Alciati companion, 90n1051

ALCOHOL ABUSE. *See* SUBSTANCE ABUSE

ALCOHOLIC BEVERAGES
Biomedical & social aspects of alcohol use, 92n1631
Complete beverage dict, 94n1601

ALCOHOLISM
Children of alcoholics, 4th ed, 91n880
Directory of alcohol & drug treatment resources in Ont. 1989, 91n882
Drug, alcohol & other addictions, 90n820
Encyclopedia of alcoholism, 2d ed, 92n839
Focus on addictions, 94n917
Native American youth & alcohol, 90n824
New lit on fetal alcohol exposure & effects, 91n1692
100 best treatment centers for alcoholism & drug abuse, 90n827
Prevention educ, 91n883
Substance abuse: a resource gd for secondary schools, 92n838
Substance abuse residential treatment centers for teens, 91n888
Substance abuse 2: alcohol abuse, 91n886
Women's recovery programs, 91n890

ALDISS, BRIAN W.
Work of Brian W. Aldiss, 93n1154

ALEXANDER, LLOYD
Lloyd Alexander: a bio-bibliog, 92n1124
Prydain companion, 90n1089

ALGAE
Handbook of protoctista, 91n1515

ALICE'S ADVENTURES IN WONDERLAND
Lewis Carroll's Alice: an annot checklist of the Lovett collection, 91n1199

ALIENS
Hein's cum index to interim precedent decisions of the Board of Immigration Appeals, 93n599

ALKALOIDS
Dictionary of alkaloids, 90n1753
Handbook of natural products data, v.1, 92n1723

ALLIED ARTISTS PICTURE CORPORATION
Allied Artists checklist, 94n1445

ALLIUMS
Alliums, 94n1653

ALLOYS
Woldman's engineering alloys, 7th ed, 92n1620

ALLUSIONS
Facts on File dict of 20th-century allusions, 92n878
Grand allusions, 91n1055
Intertextuality, allusion, & quotation, 90n1065

ALMANACS
Canadian global almanac 1993, 94n1
Chase's annual events 1990, 91n2
Information please almanac 1989, 90n2
Information please kids' almanac, 94n2
Information please sports almanac, 1993, 94n818
Macmillan bk of fascinating facts, 90n1
Rodale's good-times almanac, 91n49
Tale type & motif index of early US almanacs, 92n1318
Texas almanac & state industrial gd, 1992-93, 93n111
Universal almanac 1991, 92n2
Webster's II New Riverside desk ref, home & office ed, 93n5
Whitaker's almanac 1992, 93n6
World almanac & bk of facts 1989, 90n3

ALPINE FAUNA
Illustrated gd to the mountain stream insects of Colo., 93n1568

ALPINE FLORA
Alpine wildflowers of the Rocky Mountains, 91n1525
Desert & mountain plants of the southwest, 94n1645
Propagation of alpine plant & dwarf bulbs, 94n1629

ALTERNATIVE MEDICINE
Alternative health care resources, 94n1843
Complete hndbk of natural healing, 93n1648
Encyclopedia of alternative health care, 91n1662
Guide to info sources in alternative therapy, 90n1661
Manual of natural therapy, 90n1669
Third opinion, 2d ed, 94n1859

ALTERNATIVE PRESS
Voices from the underground, 94n1010

ALZHEIMER'S DISEASE
Alzheimer's disease: abstracts of the psychological & behavioral lit, 91n1689
Directory of Alzheimer's disease treatment facilities & home health care programs, 90n1681

AMAZON RIVER VALLEY
Healing forest, 91n1538

AMBASSADORS
Dictionary of American diplomatic hist, 2d ed, 91n733

AMERICA
Christopher Columbus ency, 92n415
Columbus dict, 92n512
Columbus' dict, 93n517
Shedding the veil: mapping the European discovery of America & the world, 93n470

AMERICAN ANTIQUARIAN SOCIETY
Under its generous dome, 2d ed, 94n657

AMERICAN ASSOCIATION OF LAW LIBRARIES
AALL annual meetings: an annot index of the recordings, 91n591

AMERICAN BAND OF THE ALLIED EXPEDITIONARY FORCES
Glenn Miller Army Air Force band, 90n1289

AMERICAN CIVIL LIBERTIES UNION
American Civil Liberties Union: an annot bibliog, 94n550

AMERICAN CRISIS, THE
Concordance to Thomas Paine's Common Sense & The American Crisis, 90n712

AMERICAN DRAMA
American drama criticism: suppl.2 to the 2d ed, 90n1129
American drama criticism, suppl.3 to the 2d ed, 93n1168
American drama 1918-60, 93n1380
American playwrights since 1945, 90n1366
American theater & drama research, 92n1385
American women playwrights, 1900-30, 93n1167
American women playwrights 1964-89, 94n1228
Clifford Odets: a research & production sourcebk, 92n1377
Clifford Odets: an annot bibliog 1935-89, 91n1154
Contemporary authors bibliographical series, v.3, 90n1128
Drama by women to 1990, 93n1146
Gay & lesbian American plays, 94n1227
Political left in the American theatre of the 30's, 93n1375

AMERICAN FICTION
American best sellers, 90n1130
American short-story writers, 1910-45, 1st series, 91n1156
American women's fiction 1790-1870, 91n1155
Bibliography of contemporary American fiction, 1945-88, 90n1131
Black American women novelists, 91n1149
Contemporary fiction writers of the South, 94n1222
Dictionary of American literary characters, 91n1151
Facts on File bibliog of American fiction 1866-1918, 94n1229
Facts on File bibliog of American fiction 1919-88, 92n1162
Female bildungsroman in English, 91n1130
Genreflecting, 3d ed, 93n1147
Heroines, 91n1129
Jewish American fiction writers, 92n1161
Modern American novel, 92n1163
Of a certain age, 92n1141
Protestant sensibility in the American novel, 93n1170
Short story cycle, 90n1134
Storied N.Mex., 92n1165
War & peace through women's eyes, 93n1169

AMERICAN FIELD SERVICE
American field serv archives of WW I, 1914-17, 90n657

AMERICAN ISRAELITE
Index to Fla. Jewish hist in the American Israelite 1854-1900, 93n446

AMERICAN LEAGUE OF PROFESSIONAL CLUBS
Encyclopedia of major league baseball team hists: American League, 92n778

AMERICAN LITERATURE. *See also names of individual authors*
American ethnic lits, 94n1225
American literary biographers: 1st series, 92n1154
American writers, suppl.3, 92n1151
Appalachian authors, 91n1146
Asian American lit, 90n1122
Bibliography of American lit, v.9, 93n1162
Bibliography of women & lit, 90n849

Biographical dict of contemporary Catholic American writing, 90n1125
Biographical dict of Hispanic lit in the US, 90n1124
Collector's bkshelf, 92n929
Contemporary gay American novelists, 94n1224
Encyclopedia of flora & fauna in English & American lit, 94n1151
Great writers of the English lang, 91n1102
Humor in American lit, 93n1189
Masterpieces of African-American lit, 93n1164
Recent studies in myths & lit, 1970-90, 93n1301
Reference gd for English studies, 92n872
Reference works in British & American lit, v.1, 91n1096
Reference works in British & American lit, v.2, 92n1094
Vietnam war in lit, 94n514

AMERICAN LITERATURE—AFRO-AMERICAN AUTHORS
Bibliographical gd to African-American women writers, 94n1223

AMERICAN LITERATURE—GREAT LAKES REGION
Literature of the Great Lakes region, 93n1165

AMERICAN LITERATURE—INDIAN AUTHORS
American Indian lits, 92n1149

AMERICAN LITERATURE—MEXICAN-AMERICAN AUTHORS
Chicano writers, 90n1123
U.S. Latino lit, 93n1166

AMERICAN LITERATURE—19TH CENTURY
Characters in 19th century lit, 94n1157
Selective bibliog of American lit, 1775-1900, 91n1147
Nineteenth-century writers, 92n1152
Victorian criticism of American writers, 92n1159
Washington Irving bibliog, 90n1144

AMERICAN LITERATURE—REVOLUTIONARY PERIOD, 1775-1785
Selective bibliog of American lit, 1775-1900, 91n1147

AMERICAN LITERATURE—20TH CENTURY
Age of maturity, 1929-41, 90n1069
American literary mags, 93n1163
American women writers on Vietnam, 91n1145
Black American women in lit, 90n858
Bohemian register, 92n1147
Broadening views, 1968-88, 91n1152
Harlem renaissance & beyond: literary biogs of 100 black women writers 1900-45, 91n1150
Sixteen modern American authors, v.2, 91n1153
Twenties, 1917-29, 90n1127

AMERICAN LITERATURE—WOMEN AUTHORS
Contemporary Canadian & US women of letters, 94n1138
Contemporary lesbian writers of the US, 94n1226

AMERICAN NEWSPAPERS
Ethnic pers in contemporary America, 91n383

AMERICAN PERIODICALS
American literary mags, 93n1163
American mass-market mags, 91n63
Directory of literary mags 1990-91, 91n1106
Directory of literary mags 1993-94, 94n1162
Ethnic pers in contemporary America, 91n383
Index to city & regional mags of the US, 91n53
Regional interest mags of the US, 92n905

AMERICAN POETRY
Colonial & 19th century, 90n1162
Concordance to the minor poetry of Edward Taylor (1642?-1729), 93n1181
Critical survey of poetry: English lang series, rev ed, 93n1236
Hunting the snark, 91n1178
Index of American per verse: 1990, 93n1187
Invisible poets: Afro-Americans of the 19th century, 2d ed, 90n1164
Modern & contemporary, 90n1161
Nineteenth century American poetry, 91n1177
Poetry by American women, 1975-89, 92n1187
Poetry by women to 1900, 92n1245

AMERICAN PROSE LITERATURE
Sourcebook of American literary journalism, 93n976

AMERICAN PSYCHOLOGICAL ASSOCIATION
APA membership register, 1991, 93n802

AMERICAN REFERENCE BOOKS ANNUAL
Index to American Ref Bks Annual 1985-89, 90n72

AMERICAN WIT & HUMOR
American pol prints 1766-1876, 93n735
Humor in American lit, 93n1189
Humor of the old Southwest, 91n1148
New official rules, 90n1306
Official politically correct dict & hndbk, 94n1101
Television-related cartoons in the New Yorker, 94n1056

AMERICANA
Bookman's gd to Americana, 10th ed, 92n459
European Americana, v.6, 90n488
Guide to Americana: the American collections in the British Lib, 90n43

AMERICANISMS
American Heritage college dict, 3d ed, 94n1075
Columbia gd to standard American English, 94n1085
Dictionary of American regional English, v.2, 93n1062
Dictionary of the American west, 94n1088
Family words, 90n1009
Homophones & homographs, 2d ed, 94n1086
Index by region, usage, & etymology to the Dict of American Regional English, v.1 & 2, 94n1090
Is it true what they say about Dixie?, 90n1010
NBC hndbk of pronunciation, 4th ed, 92n1032
Oxford thesaurus, American ed, 94n1107
Trash cash, fizzbos, & flatliners, 94n1095
Whistlin' Dixie: a dict of S expressions, 94n1089

AMERICANS—FRANCE—PARIS
Americans in Paris, 1900-30, 90n472

AMIN, IDI
Idi Amin & Uganda, 94n763

AMINO ACIDS IN NUTRITION
Nutrients cat, 94n1610

AMISH
Sociology of Mennonites, Hutterites & Amish, v.2, 92n1410

AMPHIBIANS
Amphibians & reptiles in Kans., 3d ed, 94n1749
Amphibians & reptiles of La., 90n1566
Amphibians & reptiles of the W Indies, 93n1579
Completely illus atlas of reptiles & amphibians for the terrarium, 90n1569
Field gd to reptiles & amphibians: E & central N America, 3d ed, 92n1587
Guide to amphibians & reptiles, 91n1604
Oklahoma herpetology, 90n1565
Peterson 1st gd to reptiles & amphibians, 93n1577
Reptiles & amphibians, 90n1524
Reptiles & amphibians, 94n1748
Reptiles & amphibians of Austral., 5th ed, 93n1575
Simon & Schuster's gd to reptiles & amphibians of the world, 91n1603

AMPHIBIOUS WARFARE
Jane's underwater warefare systems 1989-90, 91n710

AMUSEMENT PARKS
Amusement park gd, 92n774
Roller coasters, 94n828

ANARCHISTS
Anarchist thinkers & thought, 93n778

ANATOMY, COMPARATIVE
Animal anatomy on file, 91n1509

ANATOMY, HUMAN
Atlas of human anatomy, 90n1635
Body atlas, 94n1819
Elsevier's encyclopaedic dict of medicine, pt.B, 90n1643
Grant's atlas of anatomy, 9th ed, 92n1646
Human anatomy & physiology, 5th ed, 91n1677
Medical terminology with human anatomy, 2d ed, 92n1659

ANATOMY OF MELANCHOLY
Robert Burton & The Anatomy of Melancholy, 90n1673

ANDREWS, JULIE
Julie Andrews: a bio-bibliog, 90n1322

ANESTHESIA
Anaesthesia A-Z, 94n1874

ANGIOSPERMS
Colorado flora: E slope, 91n1524
Flora of Austral., v.3, 91n1519
Flora of N America north of Mexico, 94n1643
Great flower bks 1700-1900, 92n1540
Identification of flowering plant families, 3d ed, 90n1491
100 families of flowering plants, 2d ed, 90n1492
Vascular flora of the southeastern US, v.3, pt.2, 91n1533

ANGLICAN COMMUNION
History of the Episcopal church in America, 1607-1991, 94n1521
Oxford movement & its leaders, suppl, 94n1522

ANGLO-AMERICAN CATALOGING RULES
AACR2 decisions & rule interpretations, 5th ed, 93n639
Cataloging computer files, 94n628
Handbook for AACR2 1988 revision, 90n604
Notes in the cat record based on AACR2 & LC rule interpretations, 90n605
Serials cataloging hndbk, 90n601

ANGLO-INDIAN DIALECT. See HOBSON-JOBSON

ANGLO-NORMAN DIALECT
Manual of law French, 2d ed, 91n583

ANGLO-SAXONS
Kings & queens of England & Great Britain, 91n523

ANGOLA
Angola, 94n96
Historical dict of Angola, 2d ed, 93n112

ANHINGIDAE
Cormorants, darters, & pelicans of the world, 94n1698

ANIMAL BEHAVIOR
Dictionary of ethology, 90n1478

ANIMAL HEALTH
Animal health yrbk 1990, 92n1509
Dictionary of animal health terminology, 94n1633

ANIMAL INDUSTRY
Handbook of animal sci, 92n1512
U.S. import stats for animal related commodities 1981-86, 91n283

ANIMAL PRODUCTS
Animal production: quarterly stats 1—1991, 92n1469
Handbook of animal sci, 92n1512

ANIMALS
Animal anatomy on file, 91n1509
Animals around the world, 93n1530
Encyclopedia of the animal world, 90n1516
Key works to the fauna & flora of the British Isles & NW Europe, 5th ed, 90n1495
Kingfisher illus ency of animals, 94n1687
Macmillian animal ency for children, 93n1532
Marshall Cavendish intl wildlife ency, 90n1515
National gd to funding for the environment & animal welfare, 93n881
Natural hist from A to Z, 93n1523
Spectrum guides: African wildlife safaris, 90n1527
Straight from the horse's mouth, 90n1008
Visual dict of animals, 93n1534
Wild animals of W Canada, 93n1533

ANIMALS, FOSSIL. *See* **PALEONTOLOGY**

ANIMALS IN LITERATURE
Encyclopedia of flora & fauna in English & American lit, 94n1151

ANIMATED FILMS
American animated films: the silent era, 1897-1929, 91n1365
Animated TV specials, 91n974
Encyclopedia of animated cartoons, 93n1347

ANIMATORS
Walt Disney: a bio-bibliog, 94n1412

ANKLE
Selected bibliog of the foot & ankle with commentary, 94n1820

ANNALS. *See* **CHRONOLOGY, HISTORICAL**

ANNENBERG, SCHOOL OF COMMUNICATIONS (UNIVERSITY OF PENNSYLVANIA)
Index to the Annenberg TV script archive, v.1, 91n976

ANNIVERSARIES
From day to day, 92n1329
Holidays & anniversaries of the world, 2d ed, 91n1341

ANNOTATIONS & CITATIONS (LAW)
Bieber's dict of legal citations, 3d ed, 90n543

ANONYMS & PSEUDONYMS
Dictionary of pseudonyms & their origins, 2d ed, 90n404
Guide to pseudonyms on American records, 1892-1942, 94n1317

ANOREXIA NERVOSA
Eating disorders, 90n1684

ANTARCTIC REGIONS
Antarctica: an ency, 92n92
Handbook of Australian, New Zealand & Antarctic birds, v.1, 92n1563

ANTHOLOGIES
Ireland's index to inspiration, 94n69

ANTHONY, SUSAN B.
Papers of Elizabeth Cady Stanton and Susan B. Anthony, 94n964

ANTHROPO-GEOGRAPHY
Atlas of world cultures, 90n361
AUSMAP atlas of Austral., 94n455
Cultural atlas of France, 93n143
Economist atlas of the New Europe, 94n255
Region & regionalism in the US, 90n96
World Bk ency of people & places, 93n490

ANTHROPOLOGISTS
Daughters of the desert, 90n867
International dict of anthropologists, 92n337

ANTHROPOLOGY. *See also* **ARCHAEOLOGY**
Anthropological lit: an index to per articles & essays, v.2, nos.1-2, 91n381
Anthropology in use, 93n417
Anthropology of war, 90n647
Cultural anthropology: a gd to ref & info sources, 92n369
Dictionary of theatre anthropology, 92n1374
International current awareness servs: anthropology & related disciplines, v.2, no.1, 92n336
Introduction to lib research in anthropology, 92n338

ANTIBIOTICS
Encyclopedia of antibiotics, 3d ed, 94n1871

ANTIQUARIAN BOOKSELLERS
Antiquarian cats of musical interest, 90n1225
Antiquarian, specialty, & used bk sellers 1993, 94n662

ANTIQUE DEALERS
Antiquing in England, 91n979

ANTIQUES
David & Charles ency of everyday antiques, 94n1023

ANTIQUITIES
Chronologies in old world archaeology, 3d ed, 94n485
Glossary of ancient Egyptian nautical titles & terms, 90n1819

ANTISEMITISM
Antisemitism: an annot bibliog, v.2, 92n377
Bibliography on antisemitism, 91n409

ANXIETY
Encyclopedia of phobias, fears, & anxieties, 90n744

APARTHEID
Apartheid: a selective annotated bibliog, 1979-87, 91n842
South Africa under apartheid, 90n111
South Africa's road to change, 1987-1990, 92n89

APHIDIDAE
Genera of the aphids of Canada, 94n1723

APOCRYPHAL BOOKS
Catalogue of English Bible translations, 93n1427

APPALACHIAN REGION IN LITERATURE
Appalachian authors, 91n1146

APPLICATION SOFTWARE
Guide to application programs in BASIC, 92n1713

APPLIED ARTS. *See* **DECORATIVE ARTS**

APPLIED LINGUISTICS
Dictionary of acronyms & abbrevs in applied linguistics & lang learning, 94n1072
Error analysis, 92n1010

APPORTIONMENT (ELECTION LAW)
Historical atlas of state power in congress, 1790-1990, 94n725

APPRENTICES
Child apprentices in America from Christ's Hospital, London 1617-1778, 91n415

APTITUDE TESTS. *See* **ABILITY-TESTING**

AQUACULTURE
Aquaculture sourcebk, 94n1594
Elsevier's dict of aquaculture, 93n1467
Keyguide to info sources in aquaculture, 90n1450

AQUARIUM FISHES
Atlas of livebearers of the world, 94n1721
Dr. Axelrod's atlas of freshwater aquarium fishes, 3d ed, 90n1548
Dr. Axelrod's atlas of freshwater aquarium fishes, 6th ed, 93n1553
Dr. Burgess's atlas of marine aquarium fishes, 90n1549
Dr. Burgess's mini-atlas of marine aquarium fishes, 93n1554

AQUARIUMS
Completely illus atlas of reptiles & amphibians for the terrarium, 90n1569

AQUARIUMS, PUBLIC
Where the animals are, 94n1688

AQUATIC ANIMALS
Dangerous aquatic animals of the world, 94n1746

AQUATIC SPORTS
Adventurers afloat: a nautical bibliog, 90n1822

ARAB COUNTRIES
Atlas of the Arab world, 92n115
Education in the Arab Gulf states & the Arab world, 93n384
Who's who in the Arab world 1990-91, 92n119

ARABIC LANGUAGE—DICTIONARIES—ENGLISH
Glossary of Islamic economics, 91n133

ARAMAIC LANGUAGE
New concordance of the Bible, 90n1399
NIV exhaustive concordance, 91n1427

ARAMAIC PHILOLOGY
Aramaic bibliog, pt.1, 94n1071

ARCHAEOLOGY
African archaeology, 94n488
Archaeology hndbk, 93n507
Atlas of world cultures, 90n361
Dictionary of concepts in archaeology, 94n487
Encyclopaedia of Indian archaeology, 91n479

Guide to the archaeological sites of the British Isles, 90n505
Hammond past worlds, 90n462
Radiocarbon dating lit, 90n1762

ARCHER, VIOLET
Violet Archer: a bio-bibliog, 92n1264

ARCHITECTS
American architects, 90n970
Illustrated ency of architects & architecture, 93n1040
International dict of architects & architecture, 94n1055
ProFile 1991-92, 92n998

ARCHITECTURAL DESIGN
Encyclopedia of architecture design, engineering & construction, v.2, 90n972
Encyclopedia of architecture design, engineering & construction, v.3, 90n973

ARCHITECTURAL DRAWING
Architectural detailing for commercial construction, 92n994
Ramsey/Sleeper architectural graphic standards, 8th ed, 90n976

ARCHITECTURE
Anatomy of a house, 92n995
Architect's detail lib, 91n1032
Art & architecture in Canada, 92n967
Art & architecture thesaurus, 91n618
Art & architecture thesaurus, suppl.1, 93n635
Bibliographic gd to art & architecture 1990, 92n963
British architectural bks & writers 1556-1785, 92n996
Canadian architecture collection, 94n1053
Chartres: sources & literary interpretation, 90n969
Dictionary of ancient Near Eastern architecture, 90n974
Dictionary of architecture & construction, 2d ed, 94n1051
Directory of intl pers & newsletters on the built environment, 2d ed, 93n1036
Early Christian & Byzantine architecture, 94n1054
Encyclopedia of architecture, v.5, 91n1026
Greenline gd to residential architects 1990, 91n1027
Home building & woodworking in colonial America, 93n1612
Illustrated ency of architects & architecture, 93n1040
Index to Italian architecture, 94n1052
International dict of architects & architecture, 94n1055
Native American architecture, 90n968
Old-house dict, 90n975
Penguin dict of architecture, 4th ed, 93n1038
RAIC dir of scholarships & awards for architecture, 93n1039
Sourcebook of contemporary N American architecture, 90n977
Sturgis' illus dict of architecture & building, 91n1033
Wonders of the world, 92n1000
World architecture index, 92n999

ARCHIVAL RESOURCES
Guide to Cuban collections in the US, 92n495
Preservation & access tech, 92n599

ARCHIVES
Archives accessions annual 1988, 91n26
Archives & mss repositories in the USSR: Ukraine & Moldavia, 90n523
Archives of data-processing hist, 91n1731
British archives, 2d ed, 90n507
Directory of archives in Manitoba, 90n512
Glossary of basic archival & lib conservation terms, 90n617
Guelph & Wellington County, 90n510
Guide to archives & mss relating to Kenya & E Africa in the UK, 92n460
Guide to mss & docs in the British Isles relating to S & SE Asia, v.2, 91n97
Guide to the Boris I. Nicolaevsky collection in the Hoover Institution archives, 90n522
Guide to the hist of Calif., 90n500
Guide to the holdings of the still picture branch of the Natl Archives, 92n450
Handbook of libs, archives & info centers in India, v.6, 90n608
International bibliog of dirs & gds to archival repositories, 92n7
International dir of archives, 90n463
Record repositories in Great Britain, 9th ed, 92n488
Selective gd to the collections, 90n44
Sources in European pol hist, v.3, 93n766
World gd to lib, archive, & info sci assns, 92n571

ARCTIC REGIONS
Arctic, 90n115
Directory of arctic sci & tech research in Canada, 93n118
Greenland since 1979, 91n96
Passages: a treasure trove of N American exploration, 93n485

ARDHAMAGADHI LANGUAGE—DICTIONARIES—ENGLISH
Illustrated Ardha-Magadhi dict, 90n1035

ARDHAMAGADHI LANGUAGE—DICTIONARIES—GUJARATI
Illustrated Ardha-Magadhi dict, 90n1035

ARDHAMAGADHI LANGUAGE—DICTIONARIES—HINDI
Illustrated Ardha-Magadhi dict, 90n1035

ARDHAMAGADHI LANGUAGE—DICTIONARIES—SANSKRIT
Illustrated Ardha-Magadhi dict, 90n1035

AREA STUDIES
BBC World Service glossary of current affairs, 92n80
Selection of lib materials for area studies, pt.1, 92n81
World record of major conflict areas, 92n82

ARENDT, HANNAH
Hannah Arendt, 90n721

ARGENTINA
Argentina, 93n152
Guide to the mammals of Salta Province, Argentina, 91n1596

ARIZONA
Arizona game birds, 90n1529
Arizona legal research gd, 93n596
WPA gd to 1930s Ariz, 90n449

ARKANSAS
Arkansas made, v.1, 92n919
Arkansas made, v.2, 92n920
Arkansas mammals, rev ed, 91n1597
Atlas of Ark., 90n98
First ladies of Ark., 91n922
Historical atlas of Ark., 90n467

ARMADA, 1588
Spanish Armada of 1588, 94n527

ARMAMENTS. See ARMED FORCES; ARMS CONTROL; DISARMAMENT

ARMED FORCES
Directory of military bases in the US, 92n650
Guide to the evaluation of educl experiences in the armed servs, 1992, 94n307
International countermeasures hndbk 1990, 91n703
World defense forces, 2d ed, 90n659

ARMENIA
Armenians: a colossal bibliographic gd to bks published in the English lang, 94n129

ARMENIAN MASSACRES, 1915-1923
Armenian genocide, 93n530

ARMENIAN-AMERICANS
Armenian American almanac, 2d ed, 91n386
Armenian yellow pages 1991, 92n342

ARMENIANS
Armenians & Iran, 92n496

ARMORED VEHICLES, MILITARY
Jane's armoured fighting vehicle systems 1989-90, 91n705

ARMS & ARMOR
Jane's armour & artillery 1989-90, 91n704
Jane's infantry weapons 1989-90, 91n707

ARMS CONTROL
Arms control & disarmament, defense & military, intl security, & peace, 90n673
Arms control, disarmament, & military security dict, 90n675
Bibliography of arms control verification, 91n712
Canada & intl peace & security, 91n773
Encyclopedia of arms control & disarmament, 94n797
Peace & security thesaurus, 91n684
Security, arms control, & conflict reduction in E Asia & the Pacific, 94n683
SIPRI yrbk 1990: world armaments & disarmament, 91n713
Surviving the nuclear age...1945-1983 table of contents, 92n667
Surviving the nuclear age, 1987 update, 92n668

ART. *See also* ARTS
Aboriginality, 91n1038
Annual & biennial exhibition record of the Whitney Museum of American Art 1918-89, 92n977
Annual exhibition record of the Art Inst of Chicago 1888-1950, 92n978
Annual exhibition record of the Natl Academy of Design 1901-50, 91n1021
Annual exhibition record of the Pa. Academy of the Fine Arts, v.2, 91n1008
Annual exhibition record of the Pa. Academy of the Fine Arts, v.3, 91n1009
Arkansas made, v.2, 92n920
Art & architecture in Canada, 92n967
Art & architecture thesaurus, 91n618
Art & architecture thesaurus, suppl.1, 93n635
Art diary intl 1990, 92n987
Art on screen, 93n1016
Artists in quotation, 90n966
Benet's reader's ency of American lit, 92n1155
Bibliographic gd to art & architecture 1990, 92n963
Biennial exhibition record of the Corcoran Gallery of Art 1907-67, 92n979
Boston Art Club: exhibition record 1873-1909, 92n976
Bulfinch pocket dict of art terms, 3d ed, 93n1023
Concise Oxford dict of art & artists, 92n981
Contemporary masterworks, 93n1028
Dictionary of art quotations, 91n1023
Directory of fine art representatives & corps collecting art, 2d ed, 91n1015
Fine arts, 3d ed, 91n1002
Fine arts pers, 93n1034
Glossary of art, architecture, & design since 1945, 3d ed, 94n1043
Guide to art, 94n1047
HarperCollins dict of art terms & techniques, 2d ed, 93n1025
International art price annual 90, 91n1010
International auction records 1991, 92n975
Looking at prints, drawings & watercolours, 90n983
Modern arts criticism, v.1, 92n990
Money for visual artists, 92n991
Plain talk about art, 2d ed, 90n956
Robert Lehman collection, 90n952
Slide buyers' gd, 6th ed, 91n1012
Sponsored research in the hist of art, 7, 90n946
Victorian art reproductions in modern sources, 92n964
Worldwide bibliog of art exhibition cats 1963-87, 93n1020

ART, AMERICAN
American art dir 1989-90, 90n958
American art dir 1991-92, 92n983
American imprints on art through 1865, 91n1003
Artists in Mich., 1900-76, 90n947
Gothic sculpture in America, 90n985
Salons of America 1922-36, 92n980
Who's who in American art 1989-90, 90n950
Who's who in American art 1991-92, 92n971

ART, BRITISH
1890s: an ency of British lit, art, & culture, 94n981
Victorian art reproductions in modern sources, 92n964

ART, CLASSICAL
Guide to research in classical art & mythology, 93n1029
Mythological & classical world art index, 92n993

ART CONSULTANTS
Directory of fine art representatives & corporate art consultants, 90n960

ART CRITICISM
Bibliography of salon criticism in Paris from the ancien regime to the Restoration, 1699-1827, 93n1018
Bibliography of salon criticism in Paris from the July Monarchy to the Second Republic, 1831-51, 93n1019

ART CRITICS
Directory of artist assns & exhibition spaces, art commission, museum curators & art critics, 91n1014

ART—INDEXES
Art index, 93n1030
Art index, Nov 89-Oct 90, 92n992
Art price index intl '94, 94n1049
Fine art index, 1992 North American ed, 93n1031
Historical art index A.D. 400-1650, 90n965
Illustration index 6, 90n964

ART INSTITUTE OF CHICAGO
Annual exhibition record of the Art Inst of Chicago 1888-1950, 92n978
Louis Sullivan in the Art Institute of Chicago, 91n1030

ART—MARKETING
Art mktg sourcebk, 94n1045
Artist's market, 1991, 91n1017
Directory of artist assns & exhibition spaces, art commission, museum curators & art critics, 91n1014

ART, MODERN
Annual bibliog of modern art, 1990, 93n1015
Art of black American women, 94n1046
ArtSpeak, 92n988
Biographical dict of women artists in Europe & America since 1850, 91n1007
Christo prints & objects 1963-87, 90n953
Contemporary artists, 3d ed, 90n948
Encyclopedia of living artists, 4th ed, 90n949
Japonisme, 91n1004
Mail art, 92n966
Twentieth-century African-American writers & artists, 92n876
Victorian art reproductions in modern sources, 92n964
World artists 1980-90, 92n973

ART MUSEUM CURATORS
Directory of artist assns & exhibition spaces, art commission, museum curators & art critics, 91n1014

ART MUSEUMS
Directory of galleries for the fine artist, 91n1016
International dir of arts, 1991/92 ed, 92n64
Washington art, 90n961

ART, NIGERIAN
Nigerian artists, 94n1040

ART PATRONAGE
Money for intl exchange in the arts, 94n983

ART, PRIMITIVE
Serials gd to ethnoart, 91n1022

ARTHUR, JEAN
Jean Arthur: a bio-bibliog, 91n1358

ARTHUR, KING
New Arthurian ency, 92n1190

ARTHURIAN ROMANCES
Arthurian dict, 91n1184
Encyclopaedia of Arthurian legends, 93n1190
New Arthurian ency, 92n1190
Sir Thomas Malory: an anecdotal bibliog of eds, 1485-1985, 92n1206

ARTICLE 19 (ORGANIZATION)
Information freedom & censorship: world report 1991, 92n593

ARTIFICIAL INTELLIGENCE
Artificial intelligence abstracts annual 1988, 90n1704
Artificial intelligence abstracts annual 1991, 94n1888
Artificial intelligence & instruction, 91n1716
Artificial intelligence dict, 92n1703
Artificial intelligence vocabulary, 90n1706
Dictionary of artificial intelligence, 92n1702
Dictionary of artificial intelligence & neuronal networks, 93n1671
Facts on File dict of artificial intelligence, 90n1705
Keyguide to info sources in artificial intelligence/expert systems, 91n1715
MIT cat of computer scis & artificial intelligence, 90n1709
Multilingual dict of artificial intelligence, 94n1889
NeuralSource, 91n1718

ARTIFICIAL SATELLITES
International satellite dir, 1992, 93n1696
Space almanac, 90n1581
World satellite annual, 1993/94, 94n1758

ARTISANS
Traveler's gd to American crafts east of the Miss., 91n992

ARTISTS
American artists: signatures & monograms, 1800-1989, 91n1018
American cultural leaders from colonial times to the present, 94n976
American women artists past & present, v.2, 90n865
Artisthelp, 91n877
Artists in Mich., 1900-76, 90n947
Artists of the Pacific Northwest, 94n1042
Biographical dict of Sask. artists: women artists, 92n969
Biographies of creative artists, 92n877
Concise Oxford dict of art & artists, 92n981
Contemporary artists, 3d ed, 90n948
Dictionary of Australian artists, 94n1041
Dictionary of signatures & monograms of American artists, 90n955
Encyclopedia of living artists, 4th ed, 90n949
Encyclopedia of living artists in America, 6th ed, 93n1024
European artists: signatures & monograms, 1800-1990, 92n985
International dict of art & artists, 91n1020
Klee as in clay, 94n982
Moscow & Leningrad: a topographical gd to Russian cultural hist, v.2, 94n985
Neal-Schuman index to performing & creative artists in collective biogs, 92n882
Nigerian artists, 94n1040
Who's who in American art 1989-90, 90n950
World artists 1980-90, 92n973

ARTISTS' MARKS
Artists as illustrators, 90n959
Artists' monograms & indiscernible signatures, 92n984

ARTISTS' MATERIALS
American artists' materials, v.2, 93n1027

ARTS
Art world dir: arts review yrbk 1993, 94n1044
Biographies of creative artists, 92n877
Black arts annual 1987/88, 90n962
Black arts annual 1989/90, 93n1026
Fine art index, 1992 North American ed, 93n1031
International dict of art & artists, 91n1020
Money for intl exchange in the arts, 94n983
National gd to funding in arts & culture, 91n931
New Jersey arts, 92n986
Oxford illus ency of the arts, 91n932

ARTS & CRAFTS MOVEMENT
Guide to arts & crafts workshops, 91n994
Who's who in Alaskan arts & crafts, 3d ed, 91n997

ARTS & SOCIETY
Great events from hist 2: arts & culture series, 94n984

ARTS, AMERICAN
American cultural leaders from colonial times to the present, 94n976

ARTS, MODERN
Action art, 94n1039
American cultural leaders from colonial times to the present, 94n976
Clockworks, 94n974
Great events from hist 2: arts & culture series, 94n984
Neal-Schuman index to performing & creative artists in collective biogs, 92n882
Oxford gd to classical mythology in the arts, 1300-1990s, 94n1397

ASHMOLEAN MUSEUM
Catalogue of European sculpture in the Ashmolean Museum 1540 to the present day, 94n1067

ASIA. See also ASIA, SOUTHEASTERN; names of countries
Asia & the Pacific, 92n93
Asia 1992 yrbk, 94n106
Asia today, rev ed, 92n412
Asian markets, 2d ed, 92n240
Bibliographic gd to E Asian studies 1991, 94n107
Doctoral dissertations on Asia, v.15, nos.1 & 2, 94n108
Foreign trade stats of Asia & the Pacific 1983-87, 91n268
Guide to Asian stock markets, 91n178
Political parties of Asia & the Pacific, 94n765
Statistical yrbk for Asia & the Pacific 1988, 91n902
Statistical yrbk for Asia & the Pacific 1991, 94n939
Who's who in Asian & Australasian pols, 93n762
Who's who in Australasia & the Far East, 91n16
World investment dir 1992, v.1, 94n227

ASIA—FOREIGN RELATIONS—UNITED STATES
United States in Asia, 92n746

ASIA, SOUTHEASTERN
Atlas of SE Asia, 90n418
Brunei, 90n118
Good bks for the curious traveler: Asia & the S Pacific, 90n453
Guide to mss & docs in the British Isles relating to S & SE Asia, v.1, 90n116
Guide to mss & docs in the British Isles relating to S & SE Asia, v.2, 91n97
Historical dict of Vietnam, 90n526
Mammals of the Indomalayan region, 94n1734
Plant resources of SE Asia, no.2, 92n1475
Singapore, 90n123
South-east Asia langs & lits, 90n1033

ASIAN WOMEN
Women of color & S women annual suppl, 1991/92, 94n955

ASIAN-AMERICAN LIBRARIANS
Directory of ethnic professionals in LIS (lib & info sci), 93n625

ASIAN-AMERICAN WOMEN
Women of color & S women annual suppl, 1991/92, 94n955

ASIAN-AMERICANS
Asian American lit, 90n1122
Asian American media ref gd, 2d ed, 92n910
Asian American studies, 90n474
Asian Americans info dir, 93n421
East & SE Asia material culture in N America, 90n504
Statistical record of Asian Americans, 94n401
Understanding Asian Americans, 91n509

ASIAN-AMERICANS IN LITERATURE
American ethnic lits, 94n1225

ASSASSINATION
Encyclopedia of assassinations, 92n558
Terrorism, assassination, espionage & propaganda, 91n771

ASSEMBLER LANGUAGE (COMPUTER PROGRAM LANGUAGE)
Online programming langs & assemblers, 90n1719
PC hdwr & systems implementation, 90n1722

ASSEMBLY, RIGHT OF
Intellectual freedom: a ref hndbk, 94n641

ASSOCIATIONS, INSTITUTIONS, ETC. *See also* TRADE & PROFESSIONAL ASSOCIATIONS
Alternative dir of nongovtl orgs in S Asia, rev. ed, 91n39
Associations Canada 1991, 92n44
Associations Canada 1992, 93n65
Capital source, fall 1989, 90n94
Consultants & consulting orgs dir 1989, 90n170
Detwiler dir of medical market sources, 94n1834
Dictionary of pol parties & orgs in Russia, 94n779
Directory of British assns & assns in Ireland, 9th ed, 90n63
Directory of European professional & learned societies, 4th ed, 90n58
Directory of religious orgs in the US, 3d ed, 94n1515
Encyclopedia of assns CD-ROM, 94n51
Encyclopedia of assns intl orgs 1989, 90n59
Encyclopedia of assns intl orgs 1989 suppl, 90n60
Encyclopedia of assns intl orgs 1993, 94n48
Encyclopedia of assns 1991, v.1, 91n37
Encyclopedia of assns 1991, v.2, 91n38
Encyclopedia of assns 1994, v.1, 94n49
Encyclopedia of assns 1994, v.2, 94n50
Encyclopedia of assns: regional, state, & local orgs, 90n61
Encyclopedia of assns: regional, state, & local orgs 1992-93, 94n52
Encyclopedia of medical orgs & agencies 1992-93, 93n1632
Encyclopedia of women's assns, 94n969
IMF glossary, 93n254
International assn statutes series, 90n69
International ency of learned societies & academies, 94n36
State & regional assns of the US 1989, 90n95
World gd to scientific assns & learned societies, 5th ed, 92n1461

ASTHMA
Asthma resources dir, 91n1690

ASTROLOGY IN LITERATURE
Chaucer name dict, 90n1176

ASTRONAUTICS
Acronym bk: acronyms in aerospace & defense, 91n675
Aerospace tech centres, 90n1579
America in space, 92n1594
Aviation/space dict, 7th ed, 91n1607
Cambridge air & space dict, 92n1591
Cambridge ency of space, 92n1592
Dictionary of space tech, 92n1595
Magill's survey of sci, 90n1582
Space exploration, 92n1590

ASTRONAUTS
Men & women of space, 94n1757
Space people from A-Z, 91n1608

ASTRONOMY
Astronomer's sourcebk, 93n1701
Astronomy & astrophysics ency, 93n1704
Cambridge atlas of astronomy, 2d ed, 90n1743
Children's space atlas, 93n1703
Color atlas of galaxies, 90n1748
Dictionary of astronomical names, 90n1746
Encyclopedia of astronomy & astrophysics, 90n1744
Facts on File atlas of stars & planets, 94n1925
Field gd to the stars & planets, 3d ed, 94n1928
Guinness bk of astronomy, 3d ed, 90n1745
HarperCollins dict of astronomy & space sci, 93n1702
McGraw-Hill ency of astronomy, 2d ed, 94n1927
NGC 2000.0: the complete new general cat & index cats of nebulae & star clusters, 90n1747
Norton's 2000.0 star atlas & ref hndbk, 18th ed, 91n1760
Observing hndbk & cat of deep-sky objects, 91n1759
Peterson 1st gd to the solar system, 91n1761
Quick ref gd to Astronomy Mag 1973-90, 92n1722
Space atlas, 93n1700
Space words, 93n1706
Visual dict of the universe, 94n1930

ASTROPHYSICS
Astronomy & astrophysics ency, 93n1704
Encyclopedia of astronomy & astrophysics, 90n1744

ATHEISM
Religion in the Soviet Union, 94n1503

ATHLETES
Biographical dict of American sports: basketball & other indoor sports, 90n769
Biographical dict of American sports, 1989-92 suppl, 93n817
Biographical dict of American sports: outdoor sports, 90n757
Black Olympian medalists, 92n769
Fifty finest athletes of the 20th century, 92n768
Great athletes, 93n816
Greek & Roman sport, 92n772
Interesting athletes, 91n803
Neal-Schuman index to sports figures in collective biogs, 93n824
Oxford companion to Australian sport, 94n822
Who's who in athletics in American high schools, 92n770

ATHLETIC CLUBS
Can you name that team?, 92n775
College names of the games, 90n761
Names of the games, 90n762

ATHLETICS
Who's who in athletics in American colleges & univs, 91n805
Winning edge, 90n760

ATLANTIC COAST (CANADA)
Guide to the marine sport fishes of Atlantic Canada & New England, 93n1555

ATLANTIC COAST (U.S.)
Eastern islands, 91n432

ATLANTIC OCEAN
Fishes of the Bahamas & adjacent tropical waters, 2d ed, 94n1713

ATLANTIC PROVINCES
Acadiensis index, 1971-91, 93n526
Atlantic Canadian imprints, 1801-20, 92n13

ATLASES
Associated Pr world atlas, 90n405
Atlas of Columbus & the great discoveries, 91n427
Atlas of the world, 2d ed, 94n446
Atlas of the world with geophysical boundaries, 92n407
Bantam illus world atlas, 91n422
Bibliographic gd to maps & atlases 1990, 92n413
Children's atlas of people & places, 94n454
Children's atlas of world hist, 90n527
Concise Earth bk world atlas, 91n423
Courage children's illus world atlas, 91n425
Doubleday picture atlas, 91n426
Facts on File children's atlas, 92n400
Facts on File children's atlas, 94n447
Geography on file, 92n401
Global atlas, 92n399
Great world atlas, 2d ed, 90n406
Hammond atlas of the world, 94n448
Hammond atlas of the world, concise ed, 94n449
Hammond explorer atlas of the world, 94n450
Hammond gold medallion world atlas, 93n474
Hammond large type world atlas, 90n407
Macmillan 1st atlas, 93n476
National Geographic atlas of the world, 6th ed, 92n402
New cosmopolitan world atlas, census/environmental ed, 93n477
New intl atlas, 92n403
New state of the world atlas, 4th ed, 93n475
Peters atlas of the world, 91n428
Rand McNally children's world atlas, 90n410
Rand McNally Goode's world atlas, 18th ed, 91n429
Rand McNally photographic world atlas, 90n411
Rand McNally picture atlas of the world, 92n404
Rand McNally road atlas: US, Canada, Mexico, 65th ed, 90n415
Rand McNally the explorer world atlas, 92n405
Rand McNally traveler's world atlas & gd, 90n438
Rand McNally world atlas, 93n478
Random House compact world atlas, rev ed, 93n479
Reader's Digest children's world atlas, 93n480
Realms of gold, 92n406

Student atlas of the world, 94n453
Today's world: a new world atlas, 93n481
Troll student atlas, 93n482
World Bk atlas, 93n483
Young people's atlas of the US, 94n445

ATLASES, CANADA
Canadian Oxford intermediate atlas, 94n457
Canadian Oxford school atlas, 6th ed, 94n456
Macmillan school atlas, 3d ed, 93n471
Rand McNally road atlas: US, Canada, Mexico, 65th ed, 90n415

ATLASES, MEXICO
Rand McNally road atlas: US, Canada, Mexico, 65th ed, 90n415

ATOMIC BOMB
Atomic bomb, 94n710

ATOMIC WARFARE. *See* **NUCLEAR WARFARE**

ATTACK & DEFENSE (MILITARY SCIENCE)
Congress & defense 1990, 91n749
Jane's defence glossary, 94n676

ATTACK PLANES
Combat arms: modern attack aircraft, 91n686
Military aircraft: modern bombers & attack planes, 94n700

ATWOOD, MARGARET
Margaret Atwood: a ref gd, 92n1225

AUCTIONS
Music at auction, 90n1224

AUDIOCASSETTES
British words on tape 1991, 92n906
On cassette 1991, 92n908
Words on cassette 1992, 93n984

AUDIOCASSETTES IN EDUCATION
Audiocassette & CD finder, 3d ed, 94n374

AUDIO-VISUAL AIDS. *See* **AUDIO-VISUAL MATERIALS**

AUDIO-VISUAL EDUCATION
Encyclopaedia of educl media communications & tech, 2d ed, 90n354

AUDIO-VISUAL EQUIPMENT
Dictionary of lib & educl tech, 3d ed, 90n353
Directory of video, computer & audio-visual products 1993, 94n1887
Equipment dir of audio-visual, computer & video products 1990-91, 92n915

AUDIO-VISUAL LIBRARY SERVICE
School lib media annual, v.10, 93n672

AUDIO-VISUAL MATERIALS
American Lib Assn best of the best for children, 94n1163
AMI, v.9, issue 1, 91n968
Asian American media ref gd, 2d ed, 92n910
Audio video review digest, 90n918
AV market place 1990, 91n969
AV market place 1992, 93n991
Educators gd to free guidance materials, 30th ed, 93n400
Elementary school lib collection, 17th ed, 91n649
Elementary school lib collection, 18th ed, 93n667
Encyclopaedia of educl media communications & tech, 2d ed, 90n354
Index to AV producers & distrs, 7th ed, 91n975
Play, learn, & grow, 94n1184
Policies of AV producers & distrs, 2d ed, 91n616
WAVE: women's audio-visuals in English, 94n954

AUDIO-VISUAL MATERIALS CENTER. *See* **INSTRUCTIONAL MATERIALS CENTER**

AUGUSTINE, SAINT, BISHOP OF HIPPO
Augustine's De Civitate Dei: an annot bibliog of modern criticism, 1960-90, 93n1416

AUSTRALASIA
Asia & the Pacific, 92n93

Catalog of the diptera of the Australasian & oceanian regions, 91n1588
Far East & Australasia 1991, 92n120
Major cos of the Far East & Australasia 1991/92, 8th ed, v.1, 93n281
Who's who in Asian & Australasian pols, 93n762
Who's who in Australasia & the Far East, 91n16

AUSTRALIA
Aboriginal religions in Austral., 92n1411
Aboriginality, 91n1038
Adventuring in Austral., 91n466
AUSMAP atlas of Austral., 94n455
Australian bks in print 1989, 90n23
Australian bks in print by subject 1989, 90n24
Australian natl dict, 90n1027
Australian pers in print 1989, 90n25
Australian pers in print 1991, 93n81
Australian plant name index, 94n1648
Australian plants identified, 92n1528
Australian ref dict, 93n131
Australian reptiles & frogs, 91n1602
Business who's who of Austral., 22d ed, 90n162
Cambridge dict of Australian places, 94n471
Catalogue of mosses of Austral. & its external territories, 91n1540
Concise ency of Austral., 2d ed, 90n124
Corals of Austral. & the Indo-Pacific, 94n1747
Dictionary of Australian artists, 94n1041
Dictionary of Australian colloquialisms, 92n1052
Directory of resources for Australian studies in N America, 94n123
Encyclopaedia of Australian plants suitable for cultivation, v.5, 92n1504
Fauna of Austral., v.1B, 91n1598
Fishes of the Great Barrier Reef & Coral Sea, 92n1577
Flora of Austral., v.3, 91n1519
Guide to govt pubns in Austral., 92n50
Handbook of Australian, N.Z. & Antarctic birds, v.1, 92n1563
Historical dict of Austral., 94n124
Information resources & servs in Austral., 92n588
Kangaroo's comments & wallaby's words, 90n1026
Oxford companion to Australian folklore, 94n1390
Oxford companion to Australian sport, 94n822
Oxford illus dict of Australian hist, 94n516
Plant life of W Austral., 92n1527
Rainforest plants of E Austral., 94n1682
Reptiles & amphibians of Austral., 5th ed, 93n1575
Who's who in Australasia & the Far East, 91n16
Wild Austral., 90n454
Zoological cat of Austral., v.5, 90n1559

AUSTRALIAN ABORIGINES
Aboriginal religions in Austral., 92n1411
Aboriginality, 91n1038

AUSTRALIAN LITERATURE
Australian literary criticism, 1945-88, 90n1191
Reader's gd to Australian fiction, 94n1269

AUSTRIA
Where once we walked, 93n494

AUSTRIAN LITERATURE
Companion to 20th-century German lit, 93n1223

AUTHORITY FILES (CATALOGING)
ERIC identifier authority list (IAL) 1992, 93n636

AUTHORS
Author biogs master index, 3d ed, 90n1073
Author profile collection, 93n1138
Authors: critical & biographical refs, 2d ed, 94n1145
Bestsellers 89, 90n579
Biographical index to children's & young adult authors & illustrators, 93n1144
Bookpeople: a multicultural album, 93n1142
Contemporary authors, v.133, 93n1108
Contemporary authors, v.134, 93n1109
Contemporary authors cumulative index, 92n1111
Contemporary authors: new revision series, v.32, 92n1096

Contemporary world writers, 2d ed, 94n1144
Critical survey of mystery & detective fiction, 90n1106
Cyclopedia of world authors 2, 91n1105
Directory, 1990: American society of journalists & authors, 91n936
DISCovering authors [CD-ROM], 94n1146
Gale's literary index [CD-ROM], 94n1161
Index to the Wilson authors series, 1991 rev ed, 92n1112
International authors & writers who's who, 13th ed, 94n1147
Interviews & conversations with 20th-century authors writing in English, series 3, 92n1114
Magill's survey of world lit, 94n1158
Major 20th-century writers, 92n1097
Nobel laureates in lit, 91n1098
Scribner writers series on CD-ROM, 94n1160
Sixth bk of jr authors & illustrators, 90n30
Something about the author, v.8, 91n1119
Twentieth-century children's writers, 3d ed, 90n1088
Twentieth-century romance & histl fiction writers, 2d ed, 91n1136
Who's who in writers, eds & poets, 1992-93, 93n974
World authors 1980-85, 92n1099
Writers dir 1990-92, 91n1100
Writers dir 1992-94, 93n1118

AUTHORS & PUBLISHERS
Publishing law hndbk, 2d ed, 94n574

AUTHORS, AFRICAN
New bibliog of the Lusophone lits of Africa, 2d ed, 94n1268
Twentieth-century Caribbean & black African writers, 1st series, 93n1110
Twentieth-century Caribbean & black African writers, 2d series, 94n1148

AUTHORS, AFRO-AMERICAN. See AFRO-AMERICAN AUTHORS

AUTHORS, AMERICAN
Age of maturity, 1929-41, 90n1069
American mag journalists, 1900-60: 1st series, 91n963
American peace writers, editors, & pers, 92n752
American short-story writers, 1880-1910, 90n1133
American writers, suppl.3, 92n1151
Bibliography of American lit, v.8, 91n1144
Biographical dict of contemporary Catholic American writing, 90n1125
Birthday bk, 92n1131
Broadening views, 1968-88, 91n1152
Contemporary fiction writers of the South, 94n1222
Dictionary of literary biog documentary series, v.7, 91n1176
Directory of American poets & fiction writers, 1989-90 ed, 91n946
Dorothy Parker: a bio-bibliog, 94n1236
Grants & awards available to American writers, 17th ed, 93n960
Great writers of the English lang, 91n1102
Hemingway: an annot chronology, 93n1174
Historic homes of American authors, 92n435
Lloyd Alexander: a bio-bibliog, 94n1124
Mark Twain ency, 94n1240
Nineteenth-century writers, 92n1152
Speaking for ourselves, 91n1118
Speaking for ourselves, too, 94n1186
State-by-state gd to children's & young adult authors & illustrators, 92n1130
Twenties, 1917-29, 90n1127
Twentieth-century W writers, 2d ed, 92n1153
Wellsprings of imagination, 94n478

AUTHORS & PUBLISHER
Publishing law hndbk, 1989 suppl, 90n558

AUTHORS, AUSTRIAN
Austrian fiction writers, 1875-1913, 90n1192

AUTHORS, BLACK
Black authors & illustrators of children's bks, 2d ed, 93n1139
Black lit criticism, 93n1115

AUTHORS, BRITISH
Children's fiction sourcebk, 93n1125

AUTHORS, CANADIAN
Canadian writers & their works: cum index, fiction series, 94n1271
Canadian writers & their works: fiction series, 90n1194
Canadian writers & their works: poetry series, 90n1195
CANSCAIP companion, 92n875
Comprehensive bibliog of English-Canadian short stories 1950-83, 90n1199
Hispanic writers in Canada, 90n1196
Who's who in Canadian lit 1992-93, 93n1220
Who's who in the Writers' Union of Canada, 4th ed, 94n998

AUTHORS, CARIBBEAN
Twentieth-century Caribbean & black African writers, 1st series, 93n1110
Twentieth-century Caribbean & black African writers, 2d series, 94n1148

AUTHORS, CHILEAN
Hispanic writers in Canada, 90n1196

AUTHORS, CHINESE
Modern Chinese writers, 94n1279

AUTHORS, DUTCH
Dutch Filipiniana, 93n169

AUTHORS, ENGLISH
British writers, suppl.2, 93n1191
Dictionary of British children's fiction, 90n1094
Great writers of the English lang, 91n1102
Joseph Conrad: an annot bibliog, 91n1202
Location register of 20th-century English literary mss & letters, 90n1168
Modern British essayists, 1st series, 92n1197
Oxford illus literary gd to Great Britain & Ireland, 2d ed, 94n480
Speaking for ourselves, 91n1118
Speaking for ourselves, too, 94n1186
Wellsprings of imagination, 94n478
Writers of the middle ages & Renaissance before 1660, 93n1199

AUTHORS, ENGLISH—EARLY MODERN, 1500-1700
British prose writers, 1660-1800, 2d series, 92n1194

AUTHORS, ENGLISH—18TH CENTURY
British prose writers, 1660-1800, 2d series, 92n1194
British Romantic novelists, 1789-1832, 93n1196

AUTHORS, ENGLISH—19TH CENTURY
Late Victorian & Edwardian writers, 1890-1914, 93n1194

AUTHORS, ENGLISH—20TH CENTURY
British mystery writers, 1920-39, 90n1173
Contemporary novelists, 5th ed, 92n1191
Contemporary writers, 1960 to the present, 93n1192
Modern writers, 1914-45, 93n1195

AUTHORS, EXILED
Literary exile in the 20th century, 92n1098

AUTHORS, GERMAN
German writers in the age of Goethe, 1789-1832, 91n1235
Ludwig Tieck: an annot gd to research, 94n1288

AUTHORS, INDIC
Writers of the Indian diaspora, 94n1290

AUTHORS, IRISH
Anglo-Irish lit, 91n1239
Annotated critical bibliog of James Joyce, 91n1240
Location register of 20th-century English literary mss & letters, 90n1168
Lord Dunsany: a bibliog, 94n1292
Oxford illus literary gd to Great Britain & Ireland, 2d ed, 94n480

AUTHORS, LATIN AMERICAN
Latin American writers, 90n1208

AUTHORS, RUSSIAN
Fedor Dostoevsky, 91n1247
Moscow & Leningrad: a topographical gd to Russian cultural hist, v.2, 94n985

AUTHORS, SCOTTISH
Location register of 20th-century English literary mss & letters, 90n1168
Thomas Carlyle, 90n1209

AUTHORS, SPANISH AMERICAN
Hispanic writers, 92n1106
Spanish American authors, 94n1297

AUTHORS, TURKISH
Ottoman Turkish writers, 90n1211

AUTHORSHIP. See also PUBLISHERS & PUBLISHING
American short-story writers, 1910-45: 2d series, 92n1164
California and Hawaii publishing market place, 91n661
Canadian writer's market, 9th ed, 91n956
Children's writer's & illustrator's market, 1989, 90n897
Children's writer's & illustrator's market, 1992, 93n957
Directory of poetry pubs 1990-91, 91n663
Directory of publication resources, 1993-94, 94n995
Dramatist's bible 1989, 90n1363
Fiction writers gdlines, 2d ed, 93n963
Handbook for scholars, rev ed, 93n973
Ireland's index to inspiration, 94n69
Mystery writer's marketplace & sourcebk, 94n994
Novel & short story writer's market, 1989, 90n902
Novel & short story writer's market, 1992, 93n966
Poet's market 1990, 90n903
Religious writer's marketplace, 3d ed, 90n898
Writers & pubs gd to Tex. markets, 92n893
Writer's complete crime ref bk, 91n953
Writer's gd to metropolitan Washington, 92n894
Writers' gd to Tex. markets, 90n893
Writer's hndbk, 91n944
Writer's hndbk, 1993 ed, 94n999
Writer's market, 1991, 91n945
Writing A to Z, 91n952
Writing for the ethnic markets, 93n962

AUTHORSHIP—STYLE MANUALS
Chicago manual of style, 14th ed, 94n1001
Christian writer's manual of style, 90n900
High-technology editorial gd & stylebk, PC ed, 93n969

AUTOBIOGRAPHY—WOMEN AUTHORS
Personal writings by women to 1900, 90n855

AUTOGRAPHS
Artists' monograms & indiscernible signatures, 92n984
Dictionary of signatures & monograms of American artists, 90n955

AUTOMATIC SPEECH RECOGNITION
Sourcebook of automatic identification & data collection, 91n1612

AUTOMATION
Automation ency, 4th ed, 90n1577
Breaking through technical jargon, 91n1725

AUTOMATION IN DOCUMENTATION. See INFORMATION STORAGE & RETRIEVAL SYSTEMS

AUTOMOBILE INDUSTRY & TRADE
Encyclopedia of American bus hist & biog: the automobile industry, 1896-1920, 91n228
Encyclopedia of American bus hist & biog: the automobile industry, 1920-80, 90n235

AUTOMOBILES
American automobile collections & museums, 94n2026
Auto dict, 94n2021
Auto museum dir USA suppl with Canadian museums, 90n1815
Car bk, 1991 ed, 92n1796
Chevrolet restoration dir, 91n1826
Dictionary of automotive engineering, 91n1823
50 yrs of American autos 1939-89, 90n1807
Gale's auto sourcebk, 1991, 92n1795
Glossary of automotive terms, 90n1583
Goodheart-Wilcox automotive ency, 90n1808
Great American autos of the 50s, 90n1810
Lemon-aid new car gd 1992, 93n1781
New car buying gd, 1992-93 ed, 93n1784
Orion blue bk: car stereo 1990, 91n204
Standard cat of American cars, 1805-1942, 2d ed, 90n1809
Standard cat of American cars 1976-86, 2d ed, 91n1822
Standard cat of Buick 1912-90, 92n1800
Standard cat of Cadillac 1912-90, 92n1801
Standard cat of Chevrolet 1912-90, 92n1802
Standard cat of Chrysler 1924-90, 92n1803
Standard cat of Ford 1903-90, 92n1804
Used car bk, 1989 ed, 90n226
Vehicle identification 1988-89, 90n1805
Visual dict of cars, 93n1787

AVANT-GARDE (AESTHETICS)
Vanguardism in Latin American lit, 91n1244

AVIATION. See AERONAUTICS

AVIATION INDUSTRY. See AIRLINES

AVIONICS
Jane's avionics 1991-92, 92n1593

AWARDS. See REWARDS (PRIZES, ETC.)

AWARENESS
States of awareness, 90n742

AWKWARD AGE, THE
Concordance to Henry James's The Awkward Age, 90n1145

BABLYONIAN LANGUAGE. See AKKADIAN LANGUAGE

BACALL, LAUREN
Lauren Bacall: a bio-bibliog, 93n1321

BACH, JOHANN SEBASTIAN
Bach English-title index, 94n1331
Cantatas of J. S. Bach, 90n1256

BACTERIAL DISEASES
Viruses & reproduction, 90n1689

BACTERIOLOGY, MEDICAL
Genus & species of pathogenic organisms, 92n1660

BADINGS, HENK
Henk Badings, 1907-87: cat of works, 94n1328

BAHAI FAITH
Bibliography of English-lang works on the Babi & Baha'i faiths 1844-1985, 92n1447

BAHAMAS
Dragonflies of the Fla peninsula, Bermuda, & the Bahamas, 90n1553
Fishes of the Bahamas & adjacent tropical waters, 2d ed, 94n1713

BALANCE OF NATURE. See ECOLOGY

BALDNESS
Alopecia, 91n1691

BALI ISLAND (INDONESIA)
Bibliography of Bali, 93n123

BALLADS
Ballad scholarship, 90n1284
British broadside ballads of the 16th century, 92n1220

BALLET
Classical ballet technique, 91n1348
Dance hndbk, 91n1347
International dict of ballet, 94n1423
World ballet & dance 1992-93, 94n1425

BALLETS
Guide to opera & dance on videocassette, 91n1342
101 stories of the great ballets, 90n1315

BAMBOO
Ornamental shrubs, climbers & bamboos, 94n1632

BAND MUSIC
American Wind Symphony commissioning project, 93n1284

Heritage ency of band music, 93n1283
BANGLADESH
Cambridge ency of India, Pakistan, Bangladesh, Sri Lanka, Nepal, Bhutan & the Maldives, 91n99
Historical dict of Bangladesh, 90n117
South Asian hndbk, 1992, 93n502
BANJO MUSIC
Banjo on record, 94n1336
BANK BUILDINGS
Money matters: a critical look at bank architecture, 91n1031
BANK EMPLOYEES
Who's who in intl banking, 6th ed, 94n224
BANKERS
Encyclopedia of American business hist & bio: banking & finance to 1913, 91n213
BANKHEAD, TALLULAH
Tallulah Bankhead: a bio-bibliog, 92n1337
BANKING. See **BANKS & BANKING**
BANKRUPTCY
Law & bus dir of bankruptcy attorneys 1990, 91n577
BANKS & BANKING
American Banker's banking factbk 1991, 93n236
Banking in the US, 92n183
Banking terminology, 3d ed, 91n210
Canadian Payments Assn dir 1990, 91n212
Corporate finance sourcebk 1991, 93n238
Dictionary of banking, 94n210
Encyclopedia of American bus hist & bio: banking & finance to 1913, 91n213
Encyclopedia of American bus hist & bio: banking & finance, 1913-89, 92n185
Encyclopedia of banking & finance, 9th ed, 92n186, 94n208
Law & bus dir of bankruptcy attorneys 1990, 91n577
Prentice Hall banking yrbk, 92n189
Who's who in intl banking 1990/91, 92n190
World Bank group, 92n191
BANKS & BANKING—ENGLAND
Dictionary of banking, 94n207
BANKS & BANKING, INTERNATIONAL
International business dict & ref, 93n255
Who's who in intl banking, 6th ed, 94n224
BARBADOS
Supplement to a gd to source materials for the study of Barbados hist, 1627-1834, 93n541
BARBARY STATES. See **AFRICA, NORTH**
BASEBALL
Ballplayers, 91n825
Baseball: a comp bibliog, suppl.1, 94n837
Baseball America's 1990 almanac, 91n817
Baseball America's 1990 dir, 91n818
Baseball autograph hndbk, 92n925
Baseball chronology, 92n780
Baseball ency, 7th ed, 90n764
Baseball ency, 9th ed, 94n830
Baseball ency update, 1989, 91n819
Baseball file, 93n825
Baseball gd, 1991 ed, 92n776
Baseball quotations, 92n784
Baseball vacations, 92n782
Baseballistics, 91n827
Baseball's benchmark boxscores, 91n821
Baseball's greatest quotations, 92n783
Daguerreotypes, 8th ed, 91n820
Dickson baseball dict, 90n766
Elias baseball analyst, 1989, 91n826
Encyclopedia of major league baseball team hists: American League, 92n778
Encyclopedia of major league baseball teams, 94n831

Everything baseball, 91n822
Forgotten championships, 90n768
Great all-time baseball record bk, rev ed, 94n835
Great American baseball stat bk 1993, 94n833
Greatest catchers of all time, 92n785
Names of the games, 90n762
Official baseball register, 1991 ed, 92n777
Professional baseball franchises, 94n832
Scouting report: 1993, 94n836
Sporting News complete baseball record bk, 1993 ed, 94n838
Sports ency: baseball, 9th ed, 91n823
Timetables of sports hist: baseball, 90n767
Total baseball, 2d ed, 92n786
Whole baseball cat, 91n828
BASEBALL CARDS
Baseball card dealer dir, 1990, 92n926
Martin-Smith's official 1948-89/90 baseball card alphabetical cross-reference gd, 91n980
BASEBALL FIELDS
Ballparks of N America, 90n765
Green cathedrals, 94n834
Major league stadiums, 92n781
BASEBALL FILMS
Baseball in the movies, 93n1351
BASEBALL PLAYERS
Baseball nicknames, 93n826
Baseball vacations, 92n782
Cult baseball players, 91n824
BASIC (COMPUTER PROGRAM LANGUAGE)
Guide to application programs in BASIC, 92n1713
BASKETBALL
Basketball abstract 1989-90, 91n829
Basketball resource gd, 2d ed, 91n831
Biographical dict of American sports: basketball & other indoor sports, 90n769
Final 4 records 1939-91, 94n839
Names of the games, 90n762
NCAA basketball's finest, 93n827
Pro basketball stats, 94n840
Sports ency: pro basketball, 3d ed, 92n787
Timetables of sports hist: basketball, 91n830
BASKETBALL—COACHES
Basketball biogs, 92n788
BASKETBALL PLAYERS
Basketball biogs, 92n788
Pro basketball stats, 94n840
BASQUE LANGUAGE—DICTIONARIES—ENGLISH
Basque-English dict, 90n1036
BASSOON MUSIC
Music for unaccompanied solo bassoon, 91n1282
BATES, H. E. (HERBERT ERNEST)
H. E. Bates: a bibliographical study, 92n1198
BATS
Bats of Tex., 92n1583
BATTERED WIVES. See **ABUSED WIVES**
BATTERY CHARGERS
Modern power supply & battery charger circuit ency, 94n1780
BATTLEFIELDS
America's natl battlefield parks, 92n445
BATTLES
Battle bk, 94n695
Battles & battlescenes of WW II, 90n655
Great battles of the Civil War, 91n507
Great battles of WW I, 90n658
Vietnam: the decisive battles, 92n658
BAXTER, ANNE
Anne Baxter: a bio-bibliog, 93n1318

BAYEUX TAPESTRY
Bayeux tapestry, 2d ed, 91n1005

BEACON COLLEGE PROJECT
Beacon college project dir, 94n325

BEARINGS (MACHINERY)
I.B.I. intl bearing interchange gd, 12th ed, 94n1798
P.S.I. gd, 94n1799

BEARS
Great bear almanac, 94n1733

BEAT GENERATION. *See* **BOHEMIANS**

BEATLES
Beatles: a bio-bibliog, 91n1327
Beatles album file & complete discography, rev ed, 90n1296
Beatles: the ultimate recording gd, 94n1380
Every little thing: the definitive gd to Beatles recording variations, 91n1326
Listening to the Beatles, v.1, 92n1314

BEAUMONT, CHARLES
Work of Charles Beaumont, 2d ed, 92n1166

BEAUTY. *See* **AESTHETICS**

BEAUVOIR, SIMONE DE
Simône de Beauvoir: a bibliog, 93n930
Simone de Beauvoir: an annot bibliog, 90n1370

BECKETT, SAMUEL
KWIC concordance to Samuel Beckett's Murphy, 91n1238
Samuel Beckett, 90n1204

BEETLES
Catalog of types of Coleoptera in the Canadian Natl Collection of Insects, suppl.3, 94n1728
Checklist of beetles of Canada & Alaska, 93n1560
Weevils of Canada & Alaska, v.1, 94n1722

BEGONIACEAE
Studies in begoniaceae 4, 94n1649

BEHAVIOR THERAPY
Handbook of behavior therapy & pharmacotherapy for children, 94n1848
Handbook of prescriptive treatments for children & adolescents, 94n1845

BEHAVIORAL OPTOMETRY
Eponyms of behavioral optometry, 94n1866

BEHAVIORAL TOXICOLOGY
Environmental toxins: psychological, behavioral, & sociocultural aspects 1973-89, 91n789

BEHRMAN, S. N.
S. N. Behrman: a research & production sourcebk, 94n1232

BEINECKE RARE BOOK & MANUSCRIPT LIBRARY
Catalogue of medieval & renaissance mss in the Beinecke Rare Bk & Mss Lib, Yale Univ, v.3, 94n30

BELGIUM
European employment & industrial relations glossary: Belgium, 94n252
Facts on File national profiles: the Benelux countries, 90n132

BENEFICIAL INSECTS
Destructive & useful insects, 5th ed, 94n1729

BENELUX COUNTRIES
Facts on File national profiles: the Benelux countries, 90n132
Research gd to libs & archives in the Low Countries, 92n607

BEN-HAIM, PAUL
Music of Paul Ben-Haim, 94n1326

BENJAMIN, WALTER
Walter Benjamin, 91n1403

BENNETT, RICHARD RODNEY
Richard Rodney Bennett: a bio-bibliog, 91n1268

BENNETT, ROBERT RUSSELL
Robert Russell Bennett: a bio-bibliog, 92n1262

BEOWULF
Beowulf scholarship, 94n1263
Listeners' gd to medieval English, 90n991

BEREAVEMENT
Books to help children cope with separation & loss, v.3, 90n738

BERLIOZ, HECTOR
Hector Berlioz: a gd to research, 90n1247

BERMUDA ISLANDS
Dragonflies of the Fla. peninsula, Bermuda, & the Bahamas, 90n1553

BEST SELLERS
American best sellers, 90n1130
#1 New York Times bestseller, 94n1153

BEVERAGES
Complete beverage dict, 94n1601

BHUTAN
Cambridge ency of India, Pakistan, Bangladesh, Sri Lanka, Nepal, Bhutan & the Maldives, 91n99
South Asian hndbk, 1992, 93n502

BIBLE
Almanac of the Bible, 93n1435
Atlas of the Bible lands, rev ed, 91n1421
Baker ency of the Bible, 90n1394
Bible & modern literary criticism, 93n1432
Bible: cultural atlas for young people, 94n1546
Building your biblical studies lib, 90n1397
Classic Bible study lib for today, 90n1398
Commenting & commentaries, rev ed, 90n1393
Compact topical Bible, 92n1441
Dictionary of biblical interpretation, 91n1425
Dictionary of biblical literacy, 91n1431
Harper concise atlas of the Bible, 92n1439
Harper's Bible pronunciation gd, 91n1428
Judaism & Christianity: a gd to the ref lit, 92n1399
Literary-critical approaches to the Bible, 93n1430
Mercer dict of the Bible, 91n1430
Nelson's quick ref Bible dict, 94n1541
Nelson's quick ref Bible hndbk, 94n1544
New ency of archaeological excavations in the Holy Land, 94n489
NIV compact dict of the Bible, 90n1395
Oxford companion to the Bible, 94n1545
Revell Bible dict, 91n1432
Revell concise Bible dict, 93n1433
Roget's thesaurus of the Bible, 94n1542
Zondervan NIV atlas of the Bible, 90n1386

BIBLE AS LITERATURE
Bible & modern literary criticism, 93n1432

BIBLE—COMMENTARIES
Guide to selecting & using Bible commentaries, 92n1444

BIBLE—CONCORDANCES
Nelson's concordance of Bible phrases, 93n1431
Nelson's quick ref Bible concordance, 94n1547
NIV exhaustive concordance, 91n1427
NKJV exhaustive concordance, 94n1548
NRSV concordance unabridged, 92n1442

BIBLE—CROSS REFERENCES
New treasury of Scripture knowledge, 93n1434

BIBLE, ENGLISH—VERSIONS
Catalogue of English Bible translations, 93n1427
Mene, mene, tekel, 91n1426

BIBLE IN LITERATURE
Chaucer & the Bible, 90n1175
Dictionary of biblical tradition in English lit, 94n1149

BIBLE. N.T.
Bibliography of Greek N.T. mss, 90n1388
Complete biblical lib, 92n1422

Exegetical dict of the N.T., v.1, 91n1423
Exegetical dict of the N.T., v.2, 93n1426
Exegetical dict of the N.T., v.3, 94n1528
Harmony of the Gospels concerning the greatest life ever lived, 92n1423
New Testament Christology, 90n1404
New Testament Greek-English dict: Alpha-Gamma, 92n1433
New Testament Greek-English dict: Delta-Epsilon, 92n1434
New Testament Greek-English dict: Lambda-Omicron, 92n1436
New Testament Greek-English dict: Pi-Rho, 92n1437
New Testament Greek-English dict: Sigma-Omega, 92n1438
New Testament Greek-English dict: Zeta-Kappa, 92n1435
New Testament study Bible: Acts, 92n1428
New Testament study Bible: Galatians-Philemon, 92n1430
New Testament study Bible: Hebrews-Jude, 92n1431
New Testament study Bible: John, 92n1427
New Testament study Bible: Luke, 92n1426
New Testament study Bible: Mark, 92n1425
New Testament study Bible: Matthew, 92n1424
New Testament study Bible: Revelation, 92n1432
New Testament study Bible: Romans-Corinthians, 92n1429
Synoptic problem, 90n1389
The student's complete vocabulary gd to the Greek N.T., 94n1543
Who's who in the N.T., 94n1537
Willmington's complete gd to Bible knowledge: N.T. people, 92n1446

BIBLE. N.T. EPISTLES OF PAUL
Index to per lit on the apostle Paul, 94n1550

BIBLE. N.T. GOSPELS
Dictionary of Jesus & the Gospels, 93n1428

BIBLE. N.T.—ILLUSTRATIONS
Iconographic index to N.T. subjects represented in photographs & slides of paintings in the visual collections, Fine Arts Lib, Harvard Univ, v.1, 94n1540

BIBLE. O.T.
Annotated bibliog of the Peshitta of the O.T., 90n1387
Citations & allusions to Jewish scripture in early Christian & Jewish writings through 180 CE, 93n1429
Great Torah commentators, 91n1450
Index to English per lit on the O.T. & ancient Near Eastern studies, v.3, 91n1433
Index to English per lit on the O.T. & ancient Near Eastern studies, v.4, 92n1440
Index to English per lit on the O.T. & ancient Near Eastern studies, v.5, 94n1549
New concordance of the Bible, 90n1399
Old Testament commentary survey, 92n1407
Targumic mss in the Cambridge Genizah collections, 94n1539
Theological dict of the O.T., v.6, 91n1424
Who's who in the O.T., together with the Apocrypha, 94n1538

BIBLE. O.T. DANIEL
Book of Daniel: an annot bibliog, 94n1536

BIBLIOGRAPHIC SEARCHING ONLINE. See **ON-LINE BIBLIOGRAPHIC SEARCHING**

BIBLIOGRAPHICAL CITATIONS
Bibliographic style manual, 91n954

BIBLIOGRAPHY
ABC for bk collectors, 94n1026
American bk publishing record cum 1991, 93n26
Australian bks in print 1989, 90n23
Australian bks in print by subject 1989, 90n24
B&T link module 2, world ed, 93n27
Basic bus lib, 2d ed, 90n158
Bibliographic index 1990, 92n4
Bibliographical companion, 90n630
Bibliography of contemporary American fiction, 1945-88, 90n1131
Books & pers online, v.2, no.1, 90n154
Books in print 1989-90, 90n12
Books in print 1989-90: subject gd, 90n13
Books in print 1990-91, 91n9
Books in print 1991-92, 92n14, 93n29
Books in print 1993-94, 94n7
Books in print plus, 94n8
Books in print plus with bk reviews plus, 93n28
Books out-of-print 1984-88, 90n15
Canadian bk review annual 1988, 90n4
Canadian bks in print 1991: author & title index, 92n11
Canadian bks in print 1991: subject index, 92n12
Checklist of American imprints for 1840, 92n18
Checklist of American imprints for 1841, 92n19
Checklist of American imprints for 1842, 93n32
Children's bks in print 1989-90, 90n16
Children's bks in print 1991-92, 92n16
Cumulative bk index 1991, 93n23
Cumulative bk index, v.95, no.2, 93n24
Cumulative bk index [CD-ROM], 93n25
Design of bibliogs, 93n690
Dictionary of British children's fiction, 90n1094
Guide to ref materials for Canadian libs, 8th ed, 93n16
Guide to selecting & using Bible commentaries, 92n1444
Index to reviews of bibliographical pubs, v.10, 93n949
International bks in print 1989, pt.2, 90n10
International legal bibliogs, 93n567
Junior high school lib cat, 6th ed, 91n650
Literary research gd, 91n1097
Music ref & research materials, 4th ed, 90n1213
New Zealand bks in print 1989, 90n26
Paperbound bks in print, fall 1990, 91n10
Paperbound bks in print, spring 1989, 90n18
Paperbound bks in print, spring 1992, 93n31
Small pr record of bks in print 1989-90, 90n22
Subject gd to bks in print 1990-91, 91n11
Subject gd to bks in print 1991-92, 92n15
Subject gd to children's bks in print 1989-90, 90n17
Subject gd to children's bks in print 1991-92, 92n17
Whitaker's bks in print 1993, 94n6

BIBLIOGRAPHY—BEST BOOKS
Adventuring with bks, 9th ed, 90n1075
Adventuring with bks, 10th ed, 94n1173
American Lib Assn best of the best for children, 94n1163
Award-winning bks for children & young adults, 91n1110
Best bks for children, 4th ed, 91n1111
Best bks for jr high readers, 92n1116
Best bks for public libs, 94n647
Best bks for sr high readers, 92n1117
Best in children's bks, 93n1134
Best of Children's Choices, 90n1084
Best ref bks 1986-90, 93n8
Bibliography [of] bks for children, 90n1078
Books for new adult readers, 4th ed, 90n356
Books for you, 11th ed, 94n1165
Books kids will sit still for, 2d ed, 92n627
Catholic lifetime reading plan, 90n1403
Dictionary of American children's fiction, 1985-89, 94n1171
Dictionary of children's fiction from Austral., Canada, India, N.Z., & selected African countries, 94n1172
Distinguished classics of ref publishing, 93n18
Dogs, cats, & horses, 91n1116
Fiction cat, 12th ed, 92n1137
Good reading, 23d ed, 91n3
Guide to ref bks for school media centers, 4th ed, 93n670
Handbook of contemporary fiction for public libs & school libs, 91n1128
Kister's best dicts for adults & young people, 93n1048
Literature teacher's bk of lists, 94n1142
New, completely rev, greatly expanded, Madam Audrey's mostly cheap, all good, useful list of bks for speedy ref, 5th ed, 93n13
Newbery & Caldecott awards, 1992 ed, 93n1128
100 world-class thin bks, 94n1164
Play, learn, & grow, 94n1184
Prentice Hall good reading gd, 90n1104
Reader's cat, 91n4
Reading lists for college-bound students, 91n364
Recommended ref bks in paperback, 2d ed, 93n15
Science & tech in fact & fiction: a gd to young adult bks, 91n1456

Science Bks & Films best bks for children 1988-91, 94n1561
Supernatural fiction for teens, 2d ed, 93n1156
Walford's gd to ref material, 5th ed, v.3: generalia, 93n21
Young adult reader's adviser, 93n1137
Your reading, 9th ed, 94n648

BIBLIOGRAPHY—BIBLIOGRAPHY
British literary bibliog, 1970-79, 94n1244

BIBLIOGRAPHY CITATION
Electronic style, 94n1002

BIBLIOGRAPHY—EARLY PRINTED BOOKS
Contemporary printed lit of the English counter-reformation between 1558 & 1640, v.1, 91n1440
Short-title cat of bks printed in England, Scotland & Ireland...1475-1640, v.3, 92n61

BIBLIOGRAPHY—FIRST EDITIONS
Catalog of 1st eds, 92n928
Edgar & Dorothy Davidson collection of Canadiana at Mount Allison Univ, 92n6
Pocket gd to the identification of 1st eds, 4th ed, 91n668

BIBLIOGRAPHY, INTERNATIONAL
Index Translationum 36, 90n8
International bibliog 1988, v.16, 90n67

BIBLIOMETRICS
Bibliometrics: an annot bibliog, 1970-90, 94n623

BIBLIOTHERAPY FOR CHILDREN
Books to help children cope with separation & loss, v.3, 90n738

BICYCLES
Bicyclist's sourcebk, 92n791

BIELORUSSIA
Active figures of the trade union & working class movement of Russia, Ukraine, Bielorussia, & Kazakhstan, 94n262

BIG BAND MUSIC
Woody Herman: a gd to the big band recordings, 1936-87, 92n1301

BIG BANDS
Big band almanac, rev ed, 90n1290

BILLINGS, WILLIAM
Catalog of the musical works of William Billings, 92n1268

BILLY GRAHAM CENTER
Researching modern evangelicalism, 91n1441

BIOCHEMISTRY
Concise ency biochemistry, 2d ed, 90n1481
Dictionary of biochemistry & molecular biology, 2d ed, 91n1516
Glossary of biochemistry & molecular biology, 92n1517
Molecules, cells, & life, 91n1514

BIOENGINEERING
Biotechnology sourcebk, 90n1595

BIOETHICS
Bibliography of bioethics, v.15, 90n1611

BIOGRAPHERS
American literary biographers: 1st series, 92n1154

BIOGRAPHICAL FILMS
From real life to reel life, 94n1442

BIOGRAPHY
Almanac of famous people, 4th ed, 90n28
American literary biographers, 2d series, 93n50
American originals, 93n54
Annual obituary 1986, 90n29
Annual obituary 1990, 92n20
Biography: an annot bibliog, 94n16
Biography & genealogy master index 1991, 92n392
Biography & genealogy master index [CD-ROM], 94n436
Biography index Sept 1990-Aug 1991, 93n33
Biography index [CD-ROM], 93n34
Biography today, 1992 annual cum, 94n11
Biography today, v.1, issue 1, 93n35

British biographical index, 92n55
Cambridge biographical dict, 92n25
Canadian obituary record, 90n37
Concise dict of American biog, 4th ed, 92n32
Concise dict of natl bibliog, 94n13
Contemporary heroes & heroines, 91n12
Current biog: cum index 1940-90, 92n58
Current biog yrbk 1991, 93n37
Dictionary of Canadian biog index, 92n59
Dictionary of natl biog 1981-85, 91n13
Dictionary of N.C. biog, v.4, 92n33
Dictionary of 20th century world biog, 93n38
Distinguished shades, 93n49
Encyclopedia of world biog, 20th century suppl, v.17, 93n39
Great lives from hist: Renaissance to 1900 series, 91n549
Great lives from hist: 20th century series, 91n550
Index to who's who bks 1989, 91n54
Index to who's who bks 1992, 94n14
International authors & writers who's who, 13th ed, 94n1147
International bibliog of biog 1970-87, 90n9
International who's who 1989-90, 90n31
International who's who 1990-91, 92n27
Men of achievement, 13th ed, 90n32
Newsmakers, 1988 cum, 90n33
People in the news, 92n23
People to know, 91n15
Prospect researcher's gd to biographical research collections, 93n675
St. James gd to biog, 92n34
Supplement to Who's Who in America 1991-92, 93n53
Webster's new biog dict, 90n34
Who was who: a cum index 1897-1990, 93n47
Who was who in America with world notables, index 1993, 94n23
Who was who 1981-90, 93n46
Who's who in America 1989-91: jr & sr high school version, 91n21
Who's who in America 1990-91, 91n22
Who's who in America 1992-93, 94n24
Who's who in America: jr & sr high school version, v.5-v.8, 93n55
Who's who in American nursing 1993-94, 94n1865
Who's who in Canada, 92n29
Who's who in European insts & enterprises 1993, 94n771
Who's who in Italy 1992, 94n20
Who's who in Mexico today, 2d ed, 94n12
Who's Who in the east 1991-92, 91n23
Who's who in the east 1993-94, 94n25
Who's who in the south & southwest, 23d ed, 94n26
Who's who in the world 1993-94, 94n22
Who's who of American women 1991-92, 93n56
Who's who of emerging leaders in America 1993-94, 94n27
Who's who 1991, 92n31
World who's who of women, 9th ed, 90n35
World who's who of women, 11th ed, 94n963

BIOGRAPHY—20TH CENTURY
Celebrity sources, 91n20
Contemporary heroes & heroines, bk 2, 93n45
Crossing barriers, 94n17
Faces in the news, 93n40
Icons, 93n42
Nobel prize winners: suppl 1987-91, 93n41

BIOGRAPHY AS A LITERARY FORM
Biography: an annot bibliog, 94n16

BIOLOGICAL REAGENTS
Linscott's dir of immunological & biological reagents, 7th ed, 94n1875

BIOLOGY
Biolexicon, 92n1514
Biological & agricultural index, 93n1458
Biological & agricultural index, v.75, no.6, 91n1470
Chambers biology dict, 90n1477
Concise dict of biology, new ed, 92n1515
Concise ency of biological & biomedical measurement systems, 93n1635

Dictionary of biomedical acronyms & abbreviations, 2d ed, 92n1645
HarperCollins dict of biology, 92n1518
Henderson's dict of biological terms, 10th ed, 90n1479
History of biology, 90n1480
Multimedia ency of mammalian biology [CD-ROM], 94n1739
Plant, animal & anatomical illus in art & sci, 92n1513
Practical approach series cum methods index, 92n1526

BIOMEDICAL MATERIALS
Concise ency of medical & dental materials, 92n1662
Szycher's dict of biomaterials & medical devices, 93n1639

BIOPHYSICS
Molecules, cells, & life, 91n1514

BIOTECHNOLOGY
Biotechnology & the research enterprise, 90n1443
Biotechnology from A to Z, 94n1790
Biotechnology sourcebk, 90n1595
Language of biotech, 91n1597
Telegen reporter annual 1988, 90n1596
Vocabulary of cell engineering, v.1, 93n1600

BIOTECHNOLOGY INDUSTRIES
Biotechnology gd Japan 1990-91, 91n223
Biotechnology Japan, 90n233
Transnational corps in biotech, 90n247

BIRD POPULATIONS
Atlas of wintering N American birds, 90n1542

BIRD WATCHERS
Biographies for birdwatchers, 90n1541

BIRDS
Bird atlas, 94n1702
Birding by ear, 91n1574
Birds alternative names, 93n1544
Birds in jeopardy, 93n1541
Birds: the aerial hunters, 90n1517
Birds: the plant- & seed-eaters, 90n1518
Cambridge ency of ornithology, 93n1540
Distribution & taxonomy of birds of the world, 92n1570
Facts on File field gd to N Atlantic shorebirds, 90n1531
Field gd to advanced birding, 91n1566
Hawks in flight, 90n1532
Macmillan illus ency of birds, 90n1540
Swallows & martins, 91n1573
Threatened birds of the Americas, pt.2, 3d ed, 94n1695
Wading birds of the world, 91n1571

BIRDS—AFRICA
Birds of Africa, v.3, 90n1528
Birds of the Middle East & N Africa, 90n1538
Handbook of the birds of Europe, the Middle East, & N Africa, v.6, 94n1696
Handbook of the birds of Europe, the Middle East, & N Africa, v.7, 94n1697

BIRDS—ALASKA
Guide to the birds of Alaska, 91n1557

BIRDS—ANTARCTICA
Handbook of Australian, N.Z. & Antarctic birds, v.1, 92n1563

BIRDS—AUSTRALIA
Handbook of Australian, N.Z. & Antarctic birds, v.1, 92n1563

BIRDS—BLUE RIDGE MOUNTAIN REGION
Birds of the Blue Ridge Mountains, 93n1545

BIRDS—BRITISH COLUMBIA
Some of the common & uncommon birds of B.C. & where to find them, 91n1563

BIRDS—CANADA
Birds of Toronto & vicinity, 92n1565
Field gd to W birds, 3d ed, 91n1567
Where the birds are, 91n1565

BIRDS—COLORADO
Colorado birds, 94n1689

BIRDS—COLORADO RIVER VALLEY
Birds of the lower Colorado River Valley, 92n1569

BIRDS—COSTA RICA
Guide to the birds of Costa Rica, 91n1572

BIRDS—EUROPE
Field gd to birds of Britain & Europe, 5th ed, 94n1701
Handbook of the birds of Europe, the Middle East & N Africa, v.5, 90n1537
Jim Flegg's field gd to the birds of Britain & Europe, 91n1562

BIRDS, EXTINCT
Birds in jeopardy, 93n1541

BIRDS—FLORIDA
Florida's birds, 91n1564

BIRDS—GALAPAGOS ISLANDS
Collins field gd to the birds of Galapagos, 91n1561

BIRDS—GREAT BRITAIN
Field gd to birds of Britain & Europe, 5th ed, 94n1701
Jim Flegg's field gd to the birds of Britain & Europe, 91n1562
Red data birds in Britain, 92n1561

BIRDS—GUATEMALA
Birds of Tikal, 94n1691

BIRDS—ILLINOIS
Birds of Ill., 91n1558

BIRDS—JAPAN
Birds of Japan, 93n1538

BIRDS—KANSAS
Birds in Kans., 90n1544
Birds in Kans., v.2, 93n1546

BIRDS—MEXICO
Field gd to Mexican birds, 90n1535
Field gd to the birds of Mexico, 2d ed, 90n1534

BIRDS—MICHIGAN
Atlas of breeding birds of Mich., 93n1539

BIRDS—MIDDLE EAST
Birds of the Middle East & N Africa, 90n1538

BIRDS—NEPAL
Guide to the birds of Nepal, 93n1543

BIRDS—NEW ZEALAND
Handbook of Australian, New Zealand & Antarctic birds, v.1, 92n1563

BIRDS—NORTH AMERICA
Atlas of wintering N American birds, 90n1542
Audubon Society ency of N American birds, 93n1537
Birds of N America: W region, 90n1530
Eastern birds, 91n1569
Facts on File field gd to N Atlantic shorebirds, 90n1531
French nomenclature of North American birds, 92n1566
Western birds, 90n1536
Western birds, 91n1570

BIRDS—NORTHWEST, PACIFIC
Shorebirds of the Pacific Northwest, 94n1700

BIRDS OF PREY
African birds of prey, 92n1571

BIRDS—OHIO
Birds of Ohio, 91n1559

BIRDS—OREGON
Birds of Malheur Natl Wildlife Refuge, Oreg., 92n1564

BIRDS—PAKISTAN
Birds of Pakistan, v.1, 92n1568

BIRDS—PENNSYLVANIA
Atlas of breeding birds in Pa., 94n1694

BIRDS—ROCKY MOUNTAINS
Birds of the central Rockies, 92n1572
Watchable birds of the Rocky Mountains, 93n1542

BIRDS—SOUTH AMERICA
South American birds, 90n1533

BIRDS—TENNESSEE
Annotated checklist of the birds of Tenn., 91n1568

BIRDS—UNITED STATES
Where the birds are, 91n1565

BIRDS—WEST
Field gd to W birds, 3d ed, 91n1567

BIRDS—WEST INDIES
Field gd to birds of the W Indies, 5th ed, 94n1693

BIRDS—WISCONSIN
Wisconsin birdlife, 92n1567

BIRDS—WYOMING
Wyoming birds, 92n1562

BIRTH CONTROL
Abortion & family planning bibliog for 1989-90, 93n850
Family planning & child survival, 90n801
T.A.P.P. sources: a natl dir of teenage pregnancy prevention programs, 91n875

BIRTH DEFECTS. *See* **ABNORMALITIES, HUMAN**

BIRTHDAYS
Birthday bk, 92n1131
From day to day, 92n1329
Happy birthdays round the world, 94n1402
State-by-state gd to children's & young adult authors & illustrators, 92n1130

BIRTHPLACES
Birthday bk, 92n1131
State-by-state gd to children's & young adult authors & illustrators, 92n1130

BJORLING, JUSSI
Jussi Bjorling phonography, 2d ed, 94n1354

BLACK AMERICANS. *See* **AFRO-AMERICANS**

BLACK ENGLISH
African heritage of American English, 94n1081

BLACK LITERATURE. *See* **AMERICAN LITERATURE—AFRO-AMERICAN AUTHORS**

BLACK THEATER
Black theatre & performance, 91n1398

BLACKFOOT LANGUAGE. *See* **SIKSIKA LANGUAGE**

BLACKS
Ashe, traditional religion & healing in sub-Saharan Africa & the Diaspora, 91n1409
Bibliographic gd to black studies 1990, 92n344
Contemporary black biog, v.1, 93n426
Kaiser index to black resources, 1948-86, 93n425
My soul looks back, 'less I forget, 94n72
Worldwide interesting people, 94n404

BLACKS—DANCING
Black dance, 90n1314

BLACKS IN TELEVISION BROADCASTING
Black women in TV, 92n855

BLACKS IN THE PERFORMING ARTS
Directory of blacks in the performing arts, 2d ed, 91n1343

BLACKWOOD'S EDINBURGH MAGAZINE
Index to the critical vocabulary of Blackwood's Edinburgh Mag, 1830-40, 94n61

BLAISE, CLARK
Clark Blaise papers, 92n1223

BLAKE, WILLIAM
Blake set to music, 91n1252

BLASTING
Dictionary of blasting tech, 90n1584

BLINDNESS
Encyclopedia of blindness & vision impairment, 92n1685

BLOCH, ERNST
Ernst Bloch, 92n731

BLOOMSBURY GROUP
Bloomsbury group, 91n1181
Bloomsbury iconography, 91n1019

BLOWFLIES
Bird blow flies in N America, 91n1590

BLUES (MUSIC)
Blackwell gd to blues records, 91n1314
Blues: a bibliographic gd, 90n1287
Down Home gd to the blues, 92n1300
Encyclopedia of the blues, 94n1370

BOARD OF GOVERNORS OF THE FEDERAL RESERVE SYSTEM (U.S.)
Biographical dict of the board of governors of the Fed Reserve, 93n240

BOARDING SCHOOLS
Boarding school gd, 90n320
Boarding schools dir 1991, 92n283

BOARDS OF TRADE
American Chamber of Commerce in Italy dir 1992, 94n268
Anglo-American trade dir 1993, 94n264
Directory of foreign trade orgs in E Europe, 2d ed. 90n176
World chamber of commerce dir 1989, 90n288

BOATS & BOATING
Adventurers afloat: a nautical bibliog, 90n1822
Marine atlas of the Hawaiian Islands, 93n466
PowerBoat gd, 3d ed, 94n2030

BOCCACCIO, GIOVANNI
Giovanni Boccaccio: an annot bibliog, 93n1224

BODY, HUMAN
Visual dict of the human body, 93n1492

BOETHIUS
Medieval Consolation of Philosophy: an annot bibliog, 94n1487

BOGAN, LOUISE
Louise Bogan: a ref source, 92n1167

BOHEMIANS
Bohemian register, 92n1147

BOILERS
Handbook of power, utility & boiler terms & phrases, 6th ed, 94n1797

BOMBERS
Military aircraft: modern bombers & attack planes, 94n700

BONDS
Bond buyer 1990 yrbk, 91n172
Standard & Poor's stock & bond gd, 1993 3d, 94n200

BONES
Dictionary of evolutionary fish osteology, 93n1558
Paget's disease, 91n1700

BOOK COLLECTING
ABC for bk collectors, 94n1026
Bibliographical companion, 90n630
Collector's bkshelf, 92n929

BOOK DESIGN
Design of bibliogs, 93n690

BOOK INDUSTRIES & TRADE
ABC for bk collectors, 94n1026
Award-winning bks for children & young adults 1990-91, 94n1166
Bodian's publishing desk ref, 90n644
Book industry trends 1991, 92n642
Books & mags: a gd to publishing & bkselling courses in the US, 93n681
Bowker annual lib & bk trade almanac 1990-91, 91n611

Children's bk awards intl, 94n1195
Fanfare for words: bkfairs & bk festivals in N America, 93n682

BOOK REVIEWING
Historical jls, 2d ed, 94n542

BOOK SELECTION
Selection of lib materials for area studies, pt.1, 92n81

BOOK TALKS
Juniorplots 4, 94n1192

BOOKLIST
Popular reading for children 3, 94n1168

BOOKS
Bodian's publishing desk ref, 90n644
Books & pers online, 94n44

BOOKS & READING
Good reading, 23d ed, 91n3
#1 New York Times bestseller, 94n1153
Reader's quotation bk, 93n403

BOOKS—CENSORSHIP. *See* **CENSORSHIP**

BOOKS—CONSERVATION & RESTORATION
Glossary of basic archival & lib conservation terms, 90n617
Library, media, & archival preservation glossary, 93n663

BOOKS—REVIEWS
B&T link module 2, world ed, 93n27
Bestsellers 89, 90n579
Book review digest, 86th annual cum, 92n54
Book review digest [CD-ROM], 93n76
Book review index 1988, 90n70
Book review index, 1991 cum, 94n59
Booklist's gd to the yr's best bks, 1992 ed, 93n9
Books in print plus with bk reviews plus, 93n28
Canadian bk review annual 1990, 93n10
Children's bk review index, v.16, 93n1145
Index to bk reviews in England 1749-74, 91n1190
New, completely rev, greatly expanded, Madam Audrey's mostly cheap, all good, useful list of bks for speedy ref, 5th ed, 93n13
Recommended ref bks 1991, 92n10

BOOKSELLERS & BOOKSELLING
African bk world & pr, 4th ed, 90n642
American bk trade dir 1990-91, 91n660
American bk trade dir 1991-92, 92n631
American bk trade dir 1993-94, 94n661
Antiquarian, specialty, & used bk sellers 1993, 94n662
Bodian's publishing desk ref, 90n644
BookGuide 1991, 92n927
Books & mags: a gd to publishing & bkselling courses in the US, 93n681
Bowker annual lib & bk trade almanac, 37th ed, 93n629
Bowker annual lib & bk trade almanac, 38th ed, 94n615
Colorado bk gd, 93n683
Dealers of Polish & Russian bks active abroads 1918 to present, 92n637
Dictionary of the print trade in Ireland, 90n631
Directory of publishing 1989, 90n635
Guide to intl subscription agencies, 91n664
International literary market place 1990, 91n665
International literary market place 1993, 94n667
Literary market place 1994, 94n668
Multilingual dict of publishing, printing & bkselling, 93n680
Publishers trade list annual, 1992, 94n660

BOOKSTORES
Used bk lover's gd to New England, 94n1027
Used bk lover's gd to the mid-Atlantic states, 94n1028

BOOTH, EDWIN
Edwin Booth: a bio-bibliog, 93n1379

BORDEN, LIZZIE
Borden murders, 93n605

BORGES, JORGE LUIS
Concordance to the works of Jorge Luis Borges (1899-1986), Argentine author, 94n1299
Descriptive cat of the Jorge Luis Borges collection at the Univ of Va. lib, 94n1300

BOSTON ART CLUB
Boston Art Club: exhibition record 1873-1909, 92n976

BOSWELL, JAMES
Boswellian studies, 3d ed, 93n1231
Boswell's literary art, 93n1232

BOTANICAL CHEMISTRY
Phytochemical dict, 94n1639

BOTANY. *See also* divisions; classification of the vegetable kingdom; words beginning with Plant; and names of plants
Australian plant name index, 94n1648
Australian plants identified, 92n1528
Bignoniaceae—pt.2 (tribe tecomeae), 94n1637
Botanical Latin, 4th ed, 94n1641
Cleveland herbal, botanical, & horticultural collections, 93n1493
Desert & mountain plants of the southwest, 94n1645
Elsevier's dict of terrestrial plant ecology, 93n1497
Gardener's Latin, 94n1640
Green plants, 93n1498
Jepson manual, 94n1644
Key works to the fauna & flora of the British Isles & NW Europe, 5th ed, 90n1495
Lauraceae: nectandra, 94n1646
Manual of vascular plants of NE US and adjacent Canada, 2d ed, 93n1500
Names of plants, 2d ed, 90n1484
Nature's heartland: native plant communities of the Great Plains, 92n1530
Nehemiah Grew: a study & bibliog of his writings, 92n1532
Oklahoma botanical lit, 90n1487
100 families of flowering plants, 2d ed, 90n1492
Plant life of W Austral., 92n1527
Vascular plants of Ky., 93n1494
Vascular plants of Minn., 92n1533

BOTSWANA
Botswana, 94n99
Historical dict of Botswana, new ed, 91n94

BOUNDARY DISPUTES
Atlas of world pol flashpoints, 94n794
Border & territorial disputes, 3d ed, 94n722

BOWERING, GEORGE
Record of writing: an annot & illus bibliog of George Bowering, 91n1226

BOYS IN LITERATURE
English schoolboy stories, 93n1135

BRADLEY, FRANCIS HERBERT
Bradley: a research bibliog, 92n1390

BRADSTREET, ANNE
Anne Bradstreet: a ref gd, 91n1157

BRAHMS, JOHANNES
Johannes Brahms: an annot bibliog, 92n1273

BRAND NAME PRODUCTS
Brands & their cos, 8th ed, 91n259

BRASS INSTRUMENTS
Brass bibliog, 91n1283

BRAUTIGAN, RICHARD
Richard Brautigan: an annot bibliog, 92n1168

BRAZIL
Brazil in ref bks, 1965-89, 93n153
Santana fossils, 92n1745

BRAZILIAN LITERATURE
Brazilian lit, 91n1243

BRETNOR, REGINALD
Work of Reginald Bretnor, 91n1158

BREWERS
North American brewers resource dir 1992-93, 93n1477

BRIDGE, FRANK
Frank Bridge: a bio-bibliog, 92n1269

BRIDGES, ROBERT SEYMOUR
Robert Bridges: an annot bibliog, 1873-1988, 93n1205

BRITAIN, RADIE
Radie Britain: a bio-bibliog, 91n1265

BRITISH COLUMBIA
Adventuring in B.C., 93n503
Bibliography on old-growth forests in B.C., 92n1501
WetCoast words, 91n1077
Researcher's gd to B.C. 19th century dirs, 90n73

BRITISH ISLES
Great northerners, 92n24

BRITISH LIBRARY
Guide to Americana: the American collections in the British Lib, 90n43

BRITISH POETRY. *See* **ENGLISH POETRY**

BRITTEN, BENJAMIN
Benjamin Britten discography, 92n1270

BROADCASTING
American-Jewish media dir, 1989, 90n890
AMI, v.9, issue 1, 91n968
Broadcast communications dict, 3d ed, 90n914
Broadcasting & cable market place 1992, 93n992
Broadcasting in the UK, 2d ed, 94n1013
Gale dir of pubs & broadcast media 1993, 94n988
Matthews list, v.34, no.1, 91n937
Radio & TV, suppl.2, 90n912

BROADSIDES
British broadside ballads of the 16th century, 92n1220

BROADWAY (NEW YORK, N.Y.)
Broadway: an encyclopedic gd to the hist, people & places of Times Square, 92n467

BRONTE, PATRICK BRAMWELL
Bibliography of the mss of Patrick Branwell Bronte, 94n1247

BROOKS, CLEANTH
Cleanth Brooks: an annot bibliog, 91n1159

BROWN, GEORGE MACKAY
Contribution to lit of Orcadian writer George Mackay Brown, 93n1206

BROWNING, ELIZABETH BARRETT
Elizabeth Barrett Browning: an annot bibliog of the commentary & criticism, 1826-1990, 94n1248

BRUNEI
Brunei, 90n118

BUDDHISM
Buddhist America, 90n1400
Dictionary of Buddhist terms & terminologies, 93n1413
Historical dict of Buddhism, 94n1519
Yogacara school of Buddhism, 93n1414
Zen Buddhism: a classified bibliog, 92n1448

BUDGET
Public budgeting & financial mgmt, 92n754

BUDGET IN BUSINESS
R&D ratios & budgets, 94n295

BUILDING
Building construction illus, 2d ed, 92n1600
Building trades dict, 90n1588
Construction glossary, 2d ed, 94n1773
Construction tech info sources, 93n1586
Dictionary of architecture & construction, 2d ed, 94n1051
Directory of intl pers & newsletters on the built environment, 2d ed, 93n1036
Means illus construction dict, new ed, 93n1037
Ramsey/Sleeper architectural graphic standards, 8th ed, 90n976

BUILDING MATERIALS
Concise ency of building & construction materials, 91n1631
Time-saver standards for building types, 3d ed, 91n1025
Wood engineering & construction hndbk, 90n1589

BUILDING SITES
Glossary construction projects, 92n193

BUILDING STONES
Architect's hndbk of marble, granite, & stone, 91n1024

BUILDING, WOODEN
Timber design & construction sourcebk, 90n1575
Wood engineering & construction hndbk, 90n1589

BUILDINGS
Directory of building & equipment grants, 2d ed, 93n1035
Directory of building & equipment grants, 2d ed, 94n1772
Complete custodial hndbk, 90n1606
Sturgis' illus dict of architecture & building, 91n1033

BULBS
Bulbs, 91n1498
Propagation of alpine plant & dwarf bulbs, 94n1629

BULIMIA
Eating disorders, 90n1684

BURMA
Burma, 93n124
Burma: a study gd, 90n119

BURROUGHS, WILLIAM S.
William S. Burroughs: a ref gd, 91n1160

BURTON HISTORICAL COLLECTION
Genealogical gd to the Burton Histl Collection, 90n394

BURTON, RICHARD
Richard Burton: a bio-bibliog, 93n1322

BURTON, RICHARD FRANCIS
Sir Richard F. Burton: a biobibliographical study, 91n444

BURTON, ROBERT
Robert Burton & The Anatomy of Melancholy, 90n1673

BUSINESS. *See also* **ACCOUNTING; CORPORATIONS**
Basic bus lib, 2d ed, 90n158
Bibliographic gd to bus & economics 1990, 92n121
Books & pers online, v.2, no.1, 90n154
Business info desk ref, 92n140
Business info sourcebk, 93n200
Business jls of the US, 92n152
Business pers index, 93n216
Business rankings annual 1989, 90n183
Business rankings annual, 1992, 93n202
Canadian bus in the Pacific Rim, 94n251
Data: where it is & how to get it, 94n45
Dow Jones-Irwin bus & investment almanac, 1990, 91n175
Executive's bus info sourcebk, 91n257
Harvard Bus School core collection 1993, 94n156
International bus bibliog, 90n159
International bus hndbk: Republic of Korea, 90n285
Peterson's bus & mgmt jobs 1989, 90n187
Quotable business, 93n218
Random House hndbk of bus terms, 90n167
Treasury of business quotations, 91n167
Who's who in bus & industry in the UK 1991, 93n298
Wilson bus abstracts, 93n176

BUSINESS ADMINISTRATION. *See* **INDUSTRIAL MANAGEMENT**

BUSINESS COMMUNICATION
Better said & clearly written, 91n933
1001 quips & quotes for bus speeches, 93n219

BUSINESS CONSULTANTS
European consultants dir, 93n287

BUSINESS CYCLES
Handbook of economic cycles, 93n201

BUSINESS—DATA BASES
Books & pers online, 1992 ed, 93n187
Business online: a Canadian gd, 91n155
Business online: the professional's gd, 91n161
Online manual, 93n203

BUSINESS—DICTIONARIES
Biz words, 91n131
Concise dict of business, 92n124
Dictionary for bus & finance, 90n168
Dictionary for bus & finance, 2d ed, 91n135
Dictionary of bus quotations, 92n153
Encyclopedia of bus info sources, 7th ed, 90n152
International dict of mgmt, 4th ed, 92n232
Little black bk of bus words, 93n186
McGraw-Hill dict of bus acronyms, initials, & abbrevs, 93n170
NTC's French & English bus dict, 93n182
Professional secretary's encyclopedic dict, 4th ed, 90n291
Terms of trade, 91n275

BUSINESS—DIRECTORIES
Business sftwr dir 1990/91, 91n138
China business dir 1992, 93n278
Columbine fax dir, 91n140
Directory of business info resources, 1992, 93n192
Directory of business to business cats, 1991, 93n194
Directory of pers online: news, law & bus, 5th ed, 91n73
Encyclopedia of bus info sources, 9th ed, 93n206

BUSINESS EDUCATION
Bricker's intl dir 1989, 90n268
Directory to intl bus educ in Canada, 93n230
Management study abroad 1989-91, 90n270

BUSINESS ENTERPRISES
Business & legal CD-ROMS in print 1993, 94n175
Business connexions 1992, 93n228
Contemporary entrepreneurs, 93n178
Directory, 1991-92: Japanese-affiliated cos in USA & Canada, 93n279
Doing bus in Chicago, 92n161
Doing bus in N.Y. City, 91n141
Eastern European bus dir, 93n284
Hoover's hdnbk of American bus 1992, 93n208
Hoover's hndbk of emerging cos 1993-94, 94n172
Hoover's hndbk of world bus 1992, 92n144
Hoover's hndbk: profiles of over 500 major corps, 92n145
Hoover's masterlist of major US cos 1993, 94n164
How to find bus intelligence in Washington, 10th ed, 91n157
How to find info about cos, 8th ed, 92n146
Kelly's business dir 1992, 94n265
McGraw-Hill pocket gd to bus finance, 93n241
Minnesota bus dir 1989-90, 90n180
National bk of lists 1992, 93n211
National dir of addresses & telephone numbers 1989, 90n181
100 best cos to sell for, 90n278
UK bus finance dir 1990/91, 91n217
United States bus hist, 1602-1988, 91n130
U.S. & Canadian businesses, 1955-87, 90n153
Ward's bus dir of US private & public cos 1992, 93n198
Western European economic orgs, 93n290
Work-at-home sourcebk, 4th ed, 93n308

BUSINESS FORECASTING
Book of European forecasts, 93n282

BUSINESS—INFORMATION SERVICES
Desktop bus intelligence sourcebk, 94n171
Information please bus almanac & desk ref, 1994, 94n174
Who knows what, 94n166

BUSINESS LIBRARIES
Basic bus lib, 2d ed, 90n158
European dir of bus info libs 1990, 92n615

BUSINESS MERGERS. See CONSOLIDATION & MERGER OF CORPORATIONS

BUSINESS NAMES
Brands & their cos 1992, 93n188
Companies & their brands 1992, 93n189
Corporate eponymy, 93n184
International brands & their cos 1993-94, 94n228
International cos & their brands 1993-94, 94n229
Trade names dict 1989, 90n283
Trade names dict: co index 1989, 90n284
World's greatest brands, 93n275

BUSINESS—PERIODICALS
Books & pers online, 1992 ed, 93n187
Business pers index: Aug 1990-July 1991, 93n215

BUSINESS RELOCATION
Craighead's intl bus, travel, & relocation gd to 71 countries 1992-93, 93n264

BUSINESS—RESEARCH
Business info: how to find it, how to use it, 2d ed, 93n209

BUSINESS SCHOOLS
Barron's gd to graduate bus schools, 8th ed, 94n168
Business Week's gd to the best bus schools, 91n139
Business Week's gd to the best executive educ programs, 94n169

BUSINESSMEN
Business who's who of Austral., 22d ed, 90n162
Contemporary American bus leaders, 91n128
Contemporary entrepreneurs, 93n178
Corporate eponymy, 93n184
United States bus hist, 1602-1988, 91n130
Who's who in Canadian bus 1989-90, 90n164
Who's who in European bus, 94n223

BUSONI, FERRUCCIO
Ferruccio Busoni: a bio-bibliog, 92n1275

BUTLER, SAMUEL
Samuel Butler: an annot bibliog of writings about him, 91n1198

BUTTERFLIES
Annotated list of Ont. lepidoptera, 93n1550
Butterflies & moths, 93n1547
Butterflies through binoculars, 94n1703
Butterfly bk, 93n1551
Common names of N American butterflies, 93n1548
Field gd to E butterflies, 93n1549
Florida's butterflies & other insects, 90n1547
New Generation gd to the butterflies & day-flying moths of Britain & Europe, 90n1546

BUYERS' GUIDES. See CONSUMER EDUCATION

BYELORUSSIAN LANGUAGE—DICTIONARIES—ENGLISH
Byelorussian-English, English-Byelorussian dict with complete phonetics, 93n1079

BYZANTINE EMPIRE
Oxford dict of Byzantium, 92n510

CABINET OFFICERS
Biographical dir of the US executive branch, 1774-1989, 91n731

CABLE TELEVISION
Broadcasting & cable market place 1992, 93n992

CACTUS
Cacti: the illus dict, 92n1551
World of cacti, 92n1552

CAD/CAM SYSTEMS
CAD/CAM abstracts annual 1988, 90n1707
CAD/CAM abstracts annual 1991, 93n1690
Combinatory vocabulary of CAD/CAM in mechanical engineering, 94n1916

CAHUILLA INDIANS
Cahuilla landscape, 92n359

CALDECOTT MEDAL BOOKS
Newbery & Caldecott awards, 1991 ed, 92n1120
Newbery & Caldecott awards, 1992 ed, 93n1128
Newbery & Caldecott medal & honor bks in other media, 93n1121
Newbery & Caldecott medalists & honor bk winners, 2d ed, 93n1120

CALENDARS
Chase's annual events 1990, 91n2
Religious holidays & calendars, 94n1517
Yorkshire stage 1766-1803, 90n1355

CALHOUN, JOHN C.
John C. Calhoun: a bibliog, 91n489

CALIFORNIA
Cahuilla landscape, 92n359
California: an environmental atlas & gd, 92n1789
California & Hawaii publishing market place, 91n661
California environmental dir, 5th ed, 94n2007
California Indians: primary resources, rev ed, 91n400
California initiatives & referendums 1912-90, 93n793
California legal hist mss in the Huntington Lib, 90n554
California museum dir, 2d ed, 92n63
California water resources dir, 2d ed, 92n1757
Catalog of Calif. state grants assistance 1989, 90n803
Developing lib collections for Calif.'s emerging majority, 92n620
Famous Hollywood locations, 94n1421
Guide to the hist of Calif., 90n500
Historic ships of Calif., 90n1820
Jepson manual, 94n1644
Legal asst's notebk, 93n595
Local hist & genealogy resources of the Calif. State Lib, rev ed, 92n391
Los Angeles County histl dir, 90n99
Prime sources of Calif. & Nev. local hist, 93n511
Shadowcatchers: a dir of women in Calif. photography before 1901, 92n960
Southern Calif.'s best ghost towns, 91n462
Trade & professional assns in Calif., 4th ed, 90n287
Trade & professional assns in Calif., 5th ed, 93n67

CALL GIRLS. *See* **PROSTITUTES**

CALLIGRAPHY
Encyclopedia of calligraphy techniques, 92n923

CAMBODIAN LANGUAGE—DICTIONARIES—ENGLISH
Cambodian-English English-Cambodian dict, 91n1082

CAMERAS
McBroom's camera bluebk, 1994 ed, 94n1037
McBroom's price gd to modern cameras, 1991 ed, 92n958
Orion blue bk: camera 1990, 91n203

CAMEROON
Historical dict of the Republic of Cameroon, 2d ed, 92n86

CAMP MEETINGS
Holy ground: a study of the American camp meeting, 93n1398

CAMP SITES, FACILITIES, ETC.
Allstate Motor Club RV park & campground dir 1990, 91n809

CAMPAIGN FUNDS
Handbook of campaign spending, 93n749
Open secrets, 91n750
Open secrets, 2d ed, 93n752

CAMPAIGN SONGS
Songs, odes, glees, & ballads, 92n669

CAMPS
Peterson's summer opportunities for kids & teenagers 1990, 91n309

CANADA
Aboriginal self-govt in Canada, 92n374
Abortion debate in the US and Canada, 92n805
Acadiensis index, 1971-91, 93n526

ACCC dir of Canadian colleges & insts, 93n362
Access Canada 1990, 91n104
Access register 1988, 90n553
Acid rain: a bibliog of Canadian fed & provincial govt docs, 92n1769
African-American community studies from N America, 92n346
Agricultural sftwr dir 1990, 91n1475
Almanac of Canadian pols, 93n764
Alphabetical list of titles of fed statues, 92n550
American garden gdbk west, 90n1470
American lib dir 1993-94, 94n610
Annotated bibliog of Canadian demography 1983-89, 91n906
Annotated bibliog of the official langs of Canada, 94n1068
Annotated list of Ont. lepidoptera, 93n1550
Aquaculture sourcebk, 94n1594
Art & architecture in Canada, 92n967
Associations Canada 1991, 92n44
Associations Canada 1992, 93n65
Atlantic Canadian imprints, 1801-20, 92n13
Atlas of Alta. lakes, 92n410
Baseball: a comp bibliog, suppl.1, 94n837
Best doctors in America 1992-93, 93n1644
Best of Children's Choices, 90n1084
Bibliographies in hist, 90n528
Bibliography of N.B. geology (1839-1988), 91n1783
Bibliography of Ont. hist 1976-1986, 90n511
Bibliography of philosophy in Canada, 90n1372
Biographical dict of Canadian Jewry 1909-14, 94n410
Birds in jeopardy, 93n1541
Book trade in Canada with who's where, 1989/90, 91n671
BookGuide 1991, 92n927
Business connexions 1992, 93n228
Business online: a Canadian gd, 91n155
Canada, 94n127
Canada: a reader's gd, 93n19
Canada legal dir 1990, 91n573
Canada legal dir 1992, 93n583
Canada media dir, 91n938
Canada tax cases: index & citator, 94n581
Canada votes 1935-88, 91n756
Canadia oil industry dir, 1991, 92n1756
Canadian almanac & dir 1991, 92n98
Canadian architecture collection, 94n1053
Canadian Assn of Law Libs dir, 94n649
Canadian bk review annual 1990, 93n10
Canadian bks in print 1991: author & title index, 92n11
Canadian bks in print 1991: subject index, 92n12
Canadian bus & economics, 3d ed, 94n246
Canadian bus in the Pacific Rim, 94n251
Canadian children's dict, 92n1043
Canadian dict of bus & economics, 94n247
Canadian dirs 1790-1987, 90n125
Canadian Educ Assn hdnbk 1991, 92n276
Canadian feminist thesaurus, 91n620
Canadian global almanac 1993, 94n1
Canadian Health Libs Assn dir 1990-91, 92n613
Canadian hospital dir, v.38, Sept 90, 91n1645
Canadian human rights yrbk 1989-90, 92n559
Canadian illus news, Montreal 1869-83, 90n909
Canadian ISBN publs' dir 1990, 92n633
Canadian law dict, 2d ed, 92n537
Canadian law symposia index, 93n598
Canadian legal sftwr dir 1991, 92n540
Canadian lib hndbk, 94n617
Canadian lit index: cum index to 1986 pubs, 93n1218
Canadian markets 1990, 91n903
Canadian media list 1992/93, 93n952
Canadian medical device dir, 93n1642
Canadian obituary record, 90n37
Canadian Oxford intermediate atlas, 94n457
Canadian Oxford school atlas, 6th ed, 94n456
Canadian parliamentary hndbk, 1988 ed, 90n716
Canadian peace dir, 90n717
Canadian per index, v.43, 92n56
Canadian picture dict, 92n1044

Canadian primary dict, 92n1045
Canadian quaternary vocabulary, 94n1943
Canadian who's who 1990, 92n26
Canadian women's movement, 1960-90, 94n966
Canadian world almanac & bk of facts 1991, 92n1
Canadian writers, 1920-59, 2d series, 91n1227
Canadian writer's market, 9th ed, 91n956
Canadian yrbk of intl law, v.27, 92n547
CANSCAIP companion, 92n875
Catalog of types of Coleoptera in the Canadian Natl Collection of Insects, suppl.3, 94n1728
Catalogue of the mss in the Irving Layton collection, 90n1193
Checklist of beetles of Canada & Alaska, 93n1560
CLE research gd, v.2, 94n583
Climatological atlas of snowfall & snow depth for the NE US and SE Canada, 94n1948
COGEL blue bk, 9th ed, 94n801
Collection of definitions in fed statutes, 90n545
Common & botanical names of weeds in Canada, 1992 ed, 93n1511
Common names of N American butterflies, 93n1548
Comparative adult educ, 90n357
Consolidated index to the Canadian yrbk of intl law v.1-25, 91n590
Construction tech info sources, 93n1586
Contemporary bks reflecting Canada's cultural diversity, 94n409
Contemporary Canadian childhood & youth, 94n924
Corpus almanac & Canadian sourcebk, 1989, 90n127
Corpus almanac & Canadian sourcebk, 1993, 94n125
Descriptive cat of the Glenn Gould papers, 93n1254
Dictionary of Canadian biog index, 92n59
Dictionary of Canadian quotations, 93n90
Dictionary of Nfld. English, 2d ed, 92n1051
Diesel locomotive rosters, 3d ed, 94n2025
Diptera types in the Canadian Natl Collection of Insects, pt.1, 92n1579
Diptera types in the Canadian Natl Collection of Insects, pt.2, 94n1724
Directory, 1991-92: Japanese-affiliated cos in USA & Canada, 93n279
Directory of alcohol & drug treatment resources in Ont. 1989, 91n882
Directory of archives in Manitoba, 90n512
Directory of Canadian made products, 91n226
Directory of Canadian manufacturers, 91n227
Directory of Canadian schools 1988, 91n304
Directory of Canadian theatre archives, 94n1476
Directory of computer sftwr & servs, 90n1728
Directory of long-term care centres in Canada, v.9, Sept.90, 91n1646
Directory of pain treatment centers in the US & Canada, 90n1686
Directory of special collections of research value in Canadian libs, 93n646
Directory to Canadian studies in Canada, 4th ed, 94n126
Directory to intl bus educ in Canada, 93n230
Discovering wild plants, 91n1523
Drug file, 93n1667
Edgar & Dorothy Davidson collection of Canadiana at Mount Allison Univ, 92n6
Education in Canada, 90n300
Electric power in Canada 1989, 92n1761
Electronic univ, 94n376
Employment glossary, 91n243
Encyclopedia of music in Canada, 2d ed, 94n1312
Environmental resource dir, Sept 1990, 91n1806
Ethical shopper's gd to Canadian supermarket products, 94n248
Ethnic cookbks & food marketplace, 3d ed, 93n1472
Famous mineral localities of Canada, 91n1788
Ferns & fern allies of Canada, 90n1490
Field gd to medicinal plants: E & central N America, 91n1536
Field gd to the peat mosses of boreal N America, 91n1539
Finding Canadian facts fast, rev. ed, 91n647
Flora of N America north of Mexico, 94n1643
French-Canadian authors, 92n1224
French-English dict of industrial lang, 91n234
From the past to the future, 93n527

GAPS, 92n142
Gardening by mail, 3d ed, 91n1497
Genera of the aphids of Canada, 94n1723
Gerontology & geriatrics libs & collections in the US & Canada, 94n655
Gibson's student gd to W Canadian univs, 94n310
Global atlas, 92n399
Glossary construction projects, 92n193
Glossary of industrial lang, 91n235
Glossary of security equipment, 94n1776
Guelph & Wellington County, 90n510
Guide to docs relating to French & British N America in the archives of the sacred congregation "de Propaganda Fide", 93n1424
Guide to histl resources in the regional municipality of Waterloo, 90n513
Guide to law schools in Canada, 94n575
Guide to MBA programs in Canada, 93n376
Guide to ref materials for Canadian libs, 8th ed, 93n16
Guide to the Canadian financial servs industry 1991, 93n232
Guide to the college lib, 94n658
Guide to the marine sport fishes of Atlantic Canada & New England, 93n1555
Heritage dir 1990, 91n757
Hispanic writers in Canada, 90n1196
Hispanic-American material culture, 90n366
Historical atlas of Canada, v.2, 94n458
History of airlines in Canada, 91n1817
History of Canadian childhood & youth, 94n925
History of nursing beginning bibliog, 94n1864
Hospital governance, 91n1641
Hymenoptera of the world, 94n1726
Identification gd to the trees of Canada, 91n1544
Immigration glossary, 91n779
Immigration stats 1987, 91n778
Immigration stats 1991, 94n803
In search of your roots: a gd for Canadians, rev ed. 93n456
Index to Canadian legal lit 1989, 91n592
Index to Canadian legal lit 1992, 94n582
Index to the decisions rendered by the Immigration Appeal Board, 90n563
Interdisciplinary approaches to Canadian society, 92n97
Interlibrary loan servs, 5th ed, 90n615
International dir of Canadian studies, 93n132
International dir to Canadian studies, 91n106
Italian-Canadian studies, 90n376
Italian-Canadian writers, 90n1197
Jewish museums of N America, 93n444
Junior ency of Canada, 91n30
Legal desk bk 1992, 93n597
Legal glossary of fed statutes, 90n546
Lemon-aid new car gd 1992, 93n1781
Lemon-aid used car gd 1992, 93n1782
Lieutenant-governors of the NW territories & Alta. 1876-1991, 93n765
Major league stadiums, 92n781
Mapping upper Canada 1780-1867, 92n411
Margaret Atwood: a ref gd, 92n1225
Maritime provinces atlas, new ed, 93n472
Masterpieces of Canadian art from the Natl Gallery of Canada, 91n1006
Matthews list, v.34, no.1, 91n937
Meet the authors & illustrators, 94n1193
Money for performing artists, 93n1326
Music dir Canada, 5th ed, 91n1260
Native law bibliog, 2d ed, 92n365
Native peoples of Canada, 90n372
NFB film gd, 93n1342
999 questions about Canada, 90n126
North American horticulture, 2d ed, 93n1487
North American trees exclusive of Mexico & tropical Fla., 4th ed, 90n1510
Nova Scotia newspapers, 92n904
Official dir of Canadian museums & related insts, 91n56
100 best spare-time bus opportunities today, 91n181

Oxford companion to Canadian theatre, 91n1400
Penguin Canadian dict, 92n1050
Personal info index 1988, 90n565
Poisonous plants of Canada, 91n1522
Political parties of the Americas, 1980s to 1990s, 94n720
Presenting children's authors, illustrators & performers, 92n1127
Private law dict & bilingual lexicons, 90n547
Public gardens & parks of Niagara, 90n1466
RAIC dir of scholarships & awards for architecture, 93n1039
Realty, 2d ed, 91n286
Recommended family resorts in the US, Canada, & the Caribbean, 91n463
Recreation & entertainment industries, 91n802
Register of Canadian honours, 92n396
Report on bus: Canada co hndbk 1993, 94n250
Reruns on file, 93n994
Researcher's gd to British Columbia 19th century dirs, 90n73
Resource gd of pubns supported by multiculturalism programs, 94n398
Resource reading list 1990, 91n401
Roller coasters, 94n828
Scott's dirs: Ont. manufacturers, 17th ed, 90n245
Sears list of subject headings: Canadian companion, 4th ed, 93n643
Secretary's key, 92n260
Sociology of Mennonites, Hutterites & Amish, v.2, 92n1410
Some of the common & uncommon birds of B.C. & where to find them, 91n1563
Sourcebook of Canadian health stats, 91n1650
Sources: the dir of contacts for editors, reporters & researchers, summer 1990, 26th ed, 91n939
Soviet perception of Canada, 1917-87, 91n105
Sports federation of Canada sports dir 1990, 91n810
Standard industrial classification applied to histl data: the 1871 industrial census, 91n150
State & province vital records gd, 94n432
Statistics & surveys vocabulary, 93n905
Statistics on alcohol & drug abuse in Canada & other countries, 90n819
Steam locomotive dir of N America, 90n1806
Stroud's judicial dict of words & phrases, 5th cum suppl. to the 5th ed, 92n536
Student's gd to Ont. univs, 92n304
Taxation glossary, 3d ed, 91n288
Train-watcher's gd to N American railroads, 2d ed, 94n2024
Travellers: Canada to 1900, 91n467
Unemployment insurance glossary, 93n252
U.S. & Canadian buses, 1955-87, 90n153
Vocabulary of advanced ceramics, 92n1598
Vocabulary of agriculture, 92n1471
Vocabulary of cell engineering, v.1, 93n1600
Vocabulary of educl tech & training, 92n326
Vocabulary of food additives, 92n1490
Vocabulary of free trade, 93n233
Vocabulary of global warming, v.1, 94n2001
Vocabulary of safety & security equipment, 93n1601
Weeds of the woods, 93n1515
Weevils of Canada & Alaska, v.1, 94n1722
Who's succeeding, 91n149
Who's who 1989: deans & directors in mgmt & admin studies at Canadian univs, 90n272
Who's who in Canada, 92n29
Who's who in Canada, 1992, 94n19
Who's who in Canadian bus 1989-90, 90n164
Who's who in Canadian film & TV 1989, 91n1375
Who's who in Canadian film & TV 1991-92, 93n1341
Who's who of jazz in Montreal, 91n1255
Wild animals of W Canada, 93n1533
Winning scholarships, 94n311
Women's archives gd, 92n852
Women's studies research hndbk, 3d ed, 92n864
Yearbook of American & Canadian churches 1989, 90n1384

CANADA—ARMED FORCES
Courage in the air, 93n697

CANADA. ARMY
Canada's army in WW II, 94n702

CANADA—ATLASES
United States, Canada, & Mexico road atlas, 91n433

CANADA—BIOGRAPHY
Canadian obituary record 1991, 94n18
1000 brave Canadians, 93n36

CANADA—BUSINESS HANDBOOKS
Report on bus: Canada company hndbk, fall 1989, 91n186

CANADA—CONSTITUTIONAL LAW
Constitutional glossary, 94n553

CANADA—ECONOMIC CONDITIONS
Canadian bus & economics, 3d ed, 94n246
Who's who in Canadian finance 1988-89, 90n231

CANADA—EMIGRATION & IMMIGRATION
New England planters in the Maritime provinces of Canada 1759-1800, 94n1589

CANADA—FOREIGN RELATIONS—JAPAN
Directory, 1989-90: Japanese-affiliated cos in USA & Canada, 90n174

CANADA—GENEALOGY
In search of your Canadian roots, 90n388

CANADA—HISTORICAL GEOGRAPHY
Historical atlas of Canada, v.3, 91n516
Scholar's gd to geographical writing on the American & Canadian past, 94n461

CANADA—HISTORY—TO 1763 (NEW FRANCE)
Bibliography of Canadiana published in Great Britain, 1519-1763, 91n517

CANADA—HISTORY, MILITARY
Courage in the air, 93n697
Dictionary of Canadian military hist, 94n517

CANADA—IMPRINTS
Checklist of Canadian copyright deposits in the British Museum 1895-1923, v.3, pt.2, 90n40
Checklist of Canadian copyright deposits in the British Museum 1895-1923, v.4, 90n41
Checklist of Canadian copyright deposits in the British Museum 1895-1923, v.5, 90n42

CANADA—MAPS
Nelson Canadian atlas, 90n417
Nelson intermediate atlas, 90n409
Rand McNally road atlas: US, Canada, Mexico, 65th ed, 90n415
Sectional maps of W Canada, 1871-1955, 91n436

CANADA—NATIVE RACES
Annotated bibliog of aboriginal-controlled justice programs in Canada, 93n569
Breaking down the walls, 93n568

CANADA. PARLIAMENT
Almanac of Canadian pols, 93n764
Canadian parliamentary hndbk, 93n763

CANADA—PERIODICALS
Canadian studies: foreign pubs & theses, 4th ed, 93n134

CANADA—POLITICS & GOVERNMENT
Almanac of transatlantic pols 1991-92, 92n675
Canadian parliamentary gd, spring 1990, 91n755
Canadian public admin: bibliog, suppl. 5, 92n755
Contemporary Canadian pol, 90n718

CANADA—POPULAR CULTURE
Directory of popular culture collections, 90n1307

CANADIAN FICTION
Canadian writers & their works: cum index, fiction series, 94n1271
Canadian writers & their works: fiction series, 90n1194
Comprehensive bibliog of English-Canadian short stories 1950-83, 90n1199
ECW's biographical gd to Canadian novelists, 94n1273

CANADIAN ILLUSTRATED NEWS
Canadian illus news, Montreal 1869-83, 90n909

CANADIAN LITERATURE
Atlantic Canadian lit in English, 92n1227
Canadian lit index: cum index to 1986 pubs, 93n1218
Canadian lit index: cum index to 1987 pubs, 93n1219
Canadian writers, 1920-59, 2d series, 91n1227
Contemporary Canadian & US women of letters, 94n1138
Ethnic & native Canadian lit, 92n1226
Index to the contents of the per Canadian Lit nos.1-102, 94n1275
Italian-Canadian writers, 90n1197
Lawmen in scarlet, 91n559
Literary mss at the Natl Lib of Canada, 2d ed, 91n1225
Theses on English-Canadian lit, 91n1229
Who's who in Canadian lit 1992-93, 93n1220

CANADIAN NATIONAL COLLECTION OF INSECTS
Catalog of types of Coleoptera in the Canadian Natl Collection of Insects, suppl.3, 94n1728
Diptera types in the Canadian Natl Collection of Insects, pt.2, 94n1724

CANADIAN POETRY
Canadian writers & their works: cum index, poetry series, 94n1272
Canadian writers & their works: poetry series, 90n1195
ECW's biographical gd to Canadian poets, 94n1274

CANADIAN YEARBOOK OF INTERNATIONAL LAW
Consolidated index to the Canadian yrbk of intl law v.1-25, 91n590

CANADIANISMS
Dictionary of Canadianisms on histl principles, 92n1049

CANCER
Cancer dict, 94n1858
Cancer sourcebk, v.1, 91n1693
Cancer therapy, 94n1860
Everyone's gd to cancer therapy, 93n1655
History of cancer, 90n1682
Third opinion, 90n1658
Third opinion, 2d ed, 94n1859

CANCER CAUSING AGENTS. *See* CARCINOGENS

CANTATAS
Cantatas of J. S. Bach, 90n1256

CANTERBURY TALES
Chaucer's general prologue to the Canterbury Tales, 91n1201

CARCINOGENS
Carcinogenically active chemicals, 92n1682

CARD GAMES. *See* CARDS

CARDIOVASCULAR AGENTS
Handbook of heart drugs, 93n1657

CARDS
Book of card games, 90n770
Dictionary of card games, 94n841
Neal-Schuman index to card games, 91n832

CARE OF CHILDREN. *See* CHILD CARE

CAREER CHANGES
Encyclopedia of career change & work issues, 93n409

CAREER DEVELOPMENT
Career advancement for women in the fed serv, 94n270
Focus on careers, 93n408
Professional careers sourcebk, 2d ed, 93n411

CAREER EDUCATION
Career index, 91n370
Career training sourcebk, 94n388
Chronicle career index, 93n405
Major options, 92n299

CAREER PLANNING. *See* CAREER DEVELOPMENT; VOCATIONAL GUIDANCE

CAREGIVING—SERVICES FOR
Caregiving of older adults, 94n867

CARIBBEAN AREA
Adventuring in the Caribbean, 91n476
Ballparks of N America, 90n765
Bibliographic gd to Caribbean mass comm, 94n990
Bibliography of Latin American & Caribbean bibliogs: annual report, 1989-90, 92n109
Bibliography of Latin American & Caribbean bibliogs, 1985-89: social scis & humanities, 94n145
Black theatre & performance, 91n1398
Cambridge ency of Latin America & the Caribbean, 94n142
Caribbean 1975-80, 94n143
Colonial British Caribbean newspapers, 91n962
Dictionary of contemporary pols of Central America & the Caribbean, 92n723
Guide to Latin American & Caribbean census material, 91n119
Latin America & the Caribbean: a critical gd to research sources, 93n148
Marine plants of the Caribbean, 90n1505
Political & economic ency of S America & the Caribbean, 93n774
Political parties of the Americas and the Caribbean, 94n783
Recommended family resorts in the US, Canada, & the Caribbean, 91n463
St. Vincent & the Grenadines, 94n148
Scholars' gd to Washington, DC for Latin American & Caribbean studies, 2d ed, 93n149
South American, Central American, & the Caribbean 1993, 94n146
Statistical yrbk for Latin America & the Caribbean, 1991 ed, 93n151

CARIBBEAN LITERATURE
Caribbean women novelists, 94n1301
Writers of the Caribbean & Central America, 93n1226

CARICATURES & CARTOONS
Encyclopedia of American comics, 92n1327
Great comic bk artists, v.2, 91n1036
Humor & cartoon markets 1990, 91n948

CARING
Prosocial dvlpmt in children, 93n894

CARLYLE, THOMAS
Thomas Carlyle: a descriptive bibliog, 90n1209

CAROLINIAN LANGUAGE—DICTIONARIES—ENGLISH
Carolinian-English dict, 93n1080

CARROLL, LEWIS
Lewis Carroll's Alice: an annot checklist of the Lovett collection, 91n1199

CARS (AUTOMOBILES). *See* AUTOMOBILES

CARTOGRAPHY
Atlas of disease distributions, 90n1634
Civil War newspaper maps: a cartobibliography of the N daily pr, 94n492
Civil War newspaper maps: a histl atlas, 94n491
Information sources in cartography, 91n448
Shedding the veil: mapping the European discovery of America & the world, 93n470

CARTOONS, ANIMATED. *See* ANIMATED FILMS

CARY, JOYCE
Joyce Cary: a descriptive bibliog, 91n1200

CASSIRER, ERNST
Ernst Cassirer: an annot bibliog, 90n1371

CATALAN LITERATURE
Spanish, Catalan, & Galician literary authors of the 20th century, 93n1233

CATALOGERS
Directory of catalogers in the SLA, 90n603

CATALOGING
Cataloger's gd to MARC coding & tagging for AV material, 94n627
Cataloging computer files, 94n628
Cataloging serv bulletin, no.1-52, 92n578

Children's cat, 16th ed, 92n610
EUROCOM, 94n632
Genre terms, 2d ed, 92n580
LC romanization tables & cataloging policies, 92n586
Library of Congress classification class KK-KKC, 91n622
Nonbook materials: the org of integrated collections, 3d ed, 90n606
Serials cataloging hndbk, 90n601
Sourcebook on standards info, 92n574
Subject access to films & videos, 93n640

CATALOGS, CLASSIFIED (DEWEY DECIMAL)
Junior high school lib cat, 6th ed, 91n650

CATALOGS, COMMERCIAL
Catalogue of Canadian catalogues, 2d ed, 91n188
Catalogue of Canadian catalogues, 3d ed, 93n227
Guide to American trade cats 1744-1900, 92n258
Kids's catalog collection, 92n181
National dir of catalogs 1992, 94n294

CATALOGS, ON-LINE
Dial in 1992, 93n662
OPAC dir 1993, 94n646
Search sheets for OPACs on the Internet, 93n661
User educ for online systems in libs, 92n598

CATALOGS, SUBJECT
A to zoo, 3d ed, 90n1082
Subject collections, 7th ed, 94n656

CATALOGS, UNION
New England: a bibliog of its hist, 91n483
New England: additions to the 6 state bibliogs, 91n484
Shipping lit of the Great Lakes, 93n1778

CATHEDRALE DE CHARTRES
Chartres: sources & literary interpretation, 90n969

CATHOLIC AUTHORS
Biographical dict of contemporary Catholic American writing, 90n1125
Catholic lifetime reading plan, 90n1403

CATHOLIC CHURCH
Catholic lifetime reading plan, 90n1403
Critical gd to Catholic ref bks, 3d ed, 90n1405
Dictionary of the liturgy, 90n1408
Guide to docs relating to French & British N America in the archives of the sacred congregation "de Propaganda Fide", 93n1424
New dict of sacramental worship, 92n1415
Nineteenth-century European Catholicism, 90n1402
Official Catholic dir 1989, 90n1409
Official Catholic dir 1993, 94n1532
Our Sunday Visitor's Catholic dict, 94n1531
Roman Catholics, 94n1525

CATS
Atlas of cats of the world, 91n1576
Dogs, cats, & horses, 91n1116
Legacy of the cat, 91n1578
Mini-atlas of cats, 92n1573
Ultimate cat bk, 91n1579

CATTLE
Cattle: a hndbk to the breeds of the world, 93n1491
Cowboy & gunfighter collectibles, 90n923

CAVES
Atlas of the great caves of the world, 91n833

CD-I TECHNOLOGY
CD-ROMs in print 1993, 94n1919

CD-ROM
Books & pers online, 1992 ed, 93n187
CD-ROM 1992, 94n645
CD-ROM buyer's gd & hndbk, 3d ed, 94n1917
CD-ROM dir 1990, 91n1747
CD-ROM dir 1992, 93n1691
CD-ROM finder, 1993 ed, 94n1918
CD-ROM for librarians & educators, 94n1920

CD-ROM info products: an evaluative gd & dir, 92n1716
CD-ROM info products: the evaluative gd, 92n1717
CD-ROM market place 1991, 92n1718
CD-ROMS in print 1991, 92n1719
CD-ROMS in print 1993, 94n1919
Directory of law-related CD-ROMS 1993, 94n560
Directory of online databases & CD-ROM resources for high schools, 90n344
Optical publishing dir, 1991-92 ed, 92n1720

CD-ROM INDUSTRY
CD-ROM per index, 93n82

CD-ROM PROFESSIONAL
Cumulative index to ONLINE, DATABASE & CD-ROM Professional 1986-91, 93n1669

CD-ROMs
Applied sci & tech index [CD-ROM], 93n1457
Art index [CD-ROM], 93n1030
B&T link module 2 [CD-ROM], 93n27
Beacon: college & career planning on CD-ROM, 94n349
Biography & genealogy master index [CD-ROM], 94n436
Biography index [CD-ROM], 93n34
Biological & agricultural index [CD-ROM], 93n1458
Book review digest [CD-ROM], 93n76
Books in print plus, 94n8
Books in print plus with book reviews plus, 93n28
Business pers index [CD-ROM], 93n216
CD-ROMS in print [CD-ROM], 93n1692
Children's ref plus [CD-ROM], 93n11
Cumulative bk index [CD-ROM], 93n25
DISCovering authors [CD-ROM], 94n1146
Essay & general lit index [CD-ROM], 93n77
Encyclopedia of assns CD-ROM, 94n51
Encyclopedia of Mormonism [CD-ROM], 93n1421
Gale's literary index [CD-ROM], 94n1161
General sci index [CD-ROM], 93n1460
GeoRef [CD-ROM], 94n1950
Index to legal pers [CD-ROM], 93n601
Library lit [CD-ROM], 93n632
MLA intl bibliog [CD-ROM], 93n1107
Multimedia ency of mammalian biology [CD-ROM], 94n1739
Omni gazetteer of the USA [CD-ROM], 93n495
Scribner writers series on CD-ROM, 94n1160
Serials dir: EBSCO CD-ROM, summer 1993, 94n64
Social scis index [CD-ROM], 93n97
Ulrich's plus [CD-ROM], 94n66
Wilson bus abstracts [CD-ROM], 93n176

CELEBRITIES
American originals, 93n54
Authors & artists for young adults, v.1, 90n1091
Authors & artists for young adults, v.2, 90n1092
Celebrity sources, 91n20
Earl Blackwell's celebrity register 1990, 91n14
Icons, 93n42
Kid's address bk, 94n53
Late achievers, 93n43
Newsmakers, 1988 cum, 90n33
People in the news, 92n23
Star gd, 1990-91, 90n36

CELLS
Vocabulary of cell engineering, v.1, 93n1600

CELTIC LANGUAGES
Handbook of English & Celtic studies in the UK and Republic of Ireland, 2d ed, 90n1169

CELTIC LITERATURE
Handbook of English & Celtic studies in the UK and Republic of Ireland, 2d ed, 90n1169

CEMETERIES
American military cemeteries, 93n706
Disputing the dead: US law on aboriginal remains & grave goods, 92n549
Guide to Irish churches & graveyards, 92n389

CENSORSHIP
Encyclopedia of censorship, 91n635
Index to "Index on Censorship", 91n636
Information freedom & censorship: world report 1991, 92n593
Intellectual freedom: a ref hndbk, 94n641
Intellectual freedom & censorship, 90n614

CENSUS
Census snapshot for all US places, 1990, 94n928
1920 fed population census: cat of microfilm available, 93n901
State census records, 93n899

CENTRAL AFRICAN REPUBLIC
Central African Republic, 94n97
Historical dict of the Central African Republic, 2d ed, 93n113

CENTRAL AMERICA. See also LATIN AMERICA
Ballparks of N America, 90n765
Dictionary of contemporary pols of Central America & the Caribbean, 92n723
Directory of Central America classroom resources K-12, 2d ed, 91n118
Pines of Mexico & Central America, 93n1519
South American, Central America, & the Caribbean 1993, 94n146

CENTRAL AMERICAN LITERATURE
Writers of the Caribbean & Central America, 93n1226

CENTRAL EUROPE
Democracy's dawn, 92n750

CERAMIC MATERIALS
Potter's dict of materials & techniques, 3d ed, 92n950

CERAMICS
Ceramics & glass: intl auctions from Jan 1st to Dec 31st, 92n974
Clay today, 91n1040
Vocabulary of advanced ceramics, 92n1598

CHAIKIN, JOSEPH
Joseph Chaikin: a bio-bibliog, 93n1376

CHAMBER MUSIC
Chamber music: an intl gd to works & their instrumentation, 94n1349
Conductor's repertory of chamber music, 94n1350
Piano music by black women, 93n1264
Saxophone recital music, 94n1339

CHANDLER, RAYMOND
Dictionary of literary biog documentary series, v.6, 90n1126

CHANNELING (SPIRITUALISM)
Channeling: a bibliographic exploration, 93n806

CHARACTERS & CHARACTERISTICS IN LITERATURE
Characters from young adult lit, 93n1143
Characters in 19th century lit, 94n1157
Characters in 20th-century lit, 91n1103
Companion to literary myths, heroes & archetypes, 94n1155
Cyclopedia of literary characters 2, 91n1104
Dictionary of American literary characters, 91n1151
Dictionary of British literary characters: 18th- & 19th-century novels, 94n1243
Dictionary of fictional charaters, rev ed, 93n1148
My name in bks, 94n1190
Shakespeare's characters, 94n1258

CHARACTERS & CHARACTERISTICS IN MOTION PICTURES
Movie characters of leading performers of the sound era, 91n1362
Name is familiar, 94n1459
Who played who on the screen, 90n1324

CHARACTERS & CHARACTERISTICS IN LITERATURE
Imaginary people, 90n1105

CHARISMATIC MOVEMENT. See PENTECOSTALISM

CHARITABLE USES, TRUSTS, & FOUNDATIONS
AIDS funding, 93n1653
Corporate fndn profiles, 7th ed, 94n900
Foundation reporter 1993, 94n902

CHARITIES
Charitable orgs of the US 1992-92, 93n878
Giver's gd, 92n826

CHARLEMAGNE, EMPEROR, 742-814—ROMANCES
Medieval Charlemagne legend, 94n1199

CHARTERIS, LESLIE
Saint: a complete hist in print, radio, film & TV, 94n1249

CHARTS, DIAGRAMS, ETC.
Charts, graphics & stats index 1988-91, 93n916

CHAUCER, GEOFFREY
Chaucer & the Bible, 90n1175
Chaucer name dict, 90n1176
Chaucer's general prologue to the Canterbury Tales, 91n1201
Chaucer's Knight's Tale: an annot bibliog 1900-85, 92n1199
Glossarial concordance to the Riverside Chaucer, 94n1250
Listeners' gd to medieval English, 90n991

CHECKLIST OF NEGRO NEWSPAPERS IN THE UNITED STATES
Reference gd to Afro-American publications & eds 1827-1946, 94n1009

CHEMICAL ELEMENTS
Elements, 2d ed, 93n1712

CHEMICAL ENGINEERING
Chemical engineering bibliog (1967-88), 91n1610
Dictionary of chemical engineering, 94n1769
Dictionary of process tech, 91n1609
Directory of chemical engineering consultants, 9th ed, 93n1583
Encyclopedia of chemical processing & design, v.35, 92n1597
Encyclopedia of chemical processing & design, v.36, 94n1759
Encyclopedia of chemical processing & design, v.37, 94n1760
Encyclopedia of chemical processing & design, v.38, 94n1761
Encyclopedia of chemical processing & design, v.39, 94n1762
Encyclopedia of chemical processing & design, v.40, 94n1763
Encyclopedia of chemical processing & design, v.41, 94n1764
Encyclopedia of chemical processing & design, v.42, 94n1765
Encyclopedia of chemical processing & design, v.43, 94n1766
Handbook of molecular sieves, 93n1584
Industrial chemical thesaurus, 2d ed, 94n1942
Quick selection gd to chemical protective clothing, 2d ed, 94n1767

CHEMICAL INDUSTRY
Financial Times industrial cos: chemicals, 92n195
Major chemical & petrochemical cos of Europe 1990/91, 92n204
Process plant machinery, 90n1585

CHEMICAL LABORATORIES
Academic laboratory chemical hazards gdbk, 92n1728
Illustrated chemistry lab terminology, 93n1708

CHEMICAL LITERATURE
Information sources in chemistry, 4th ed, 94n1931

CHEMICALS
Academic laboratory chemical hazards gdbk, 92n1728
Bretherick's hndbk of reactive chemical hazards, 4th ed, 92n1724
Chemical exposure & human health, 94n1861
Chemical structure sftwr for personal computers, 90n1756
Chemical tradenamed dict, 94n1932
Comprehensive gd to the hazardous properties of chemical substances, 94n2015
Dictionary of chemical names & synonyms, 94n1934
Handbook of industrial chemical additives, 93n1709
Suspect chemicals sourcebk, 1989 ed, 90n1761
Toxic substances controls gd, 90n1799

CHEMISTRY
Chemical lit 1700-1860, 90n1749
Chemical research faculties 1988, 90n1755
Chemist's ready ref hndbk, 91n1777
Comprehensive polymer sci, 91n1774
Concise dict of chemistry, new ed, 92n1725
Current chemical reactions (CCR), v.14, no.2, 93n1718
Dictionary of chemistry & chemical tech, 4th ed, 91n1772
Directory of chemistry sftwr 1992, 94n1939

Hawley's condensed chemical dict, 12th ed, 94n1933
Index chemicus, v.125, no.1, 93n1719
Industrial chemical thesaurus, 2d ed, 94n1942
Lange's hndbk of chemistry, 14th ed, 93n1716
McGraw-Hill ency of chemistry, 2d ed, 94n1935

CHEMISTRY—DICTIONARIES—GERMAN LANGUAGE
Patterson's German-English dict for chemists, 4th ed, 94n1937

CHEMISTRY, ORGANIC
Condensed ency of surfactants, 90n1752
Dictionary of organic compounds, 7th suppl., 5th ed, 91n1766
Dictionary of organic compounds, 8th suppl., 5th ed., 92n1726
Dictionary of organometallic compounds, 4th suppl, 90n1754

CHEMISTRY, PHARMACEUTICAL
Pharmaceutical manufacturing ency, 2d ed, 90n1697

CHEMISTRY, TECHNICAL
Encyclopedia of chemical processing & design, v.35, 92n1597
Encyclopedia of chemical processing & design, v.36, 94n1759
Encyclopedia of chemical processing & design, v.37, 94n1760
Encyclopedia of chemical processing & design, v.38, 94n1761
Encyclopedia of chemical processing & design, v.39, 94n1762
Encyclopedia of chemical processing & design, v.40, 94n1763
Encyclopedia of chemical processing & design, v.41, 94n1764
Encyclopedia of chemical processing & design, v.42, 94n1765
Encyclopedia of chemical processing & design, v.43, 94n1766
Encyclopedic dict of chemical tech, 94n1936
Kirk-Othmer ency of chemical tech, 4th ed, v.7, 94n1768
Riegel's hndbk of industrial chemistry, 9th ed, 94n1770
Suspect chemicals sourcebk, 1989 ed, 90n1761

CHEMISTS
Nobel prize winners: chemistry, 91n1765

CHEMOTHERAPY
AARP Pharmacy Serv prescription drug hndbk, 2d ed, 93n1660

CHESS
Chess: an annot bibliog 1969-88, 92n790
Chess ency, 92n789
Oxford companion to chess, 2d ed, 94n842

CHICAGO METROPOLITAN AREA (ILL.)
Doing bus in Chicago, 92n161

CHICANO LITERATURE (ENGLISH). *See* **AMERICAN LITERATURE—MEXICAN AMERICAN AUTHORS**

CHILD ABUSE
Child abuse & neglect, 91n602
Encyclopedia of child abuse, 90n576
Maintaining good health, 90n1647
Sexual assault & child sexual abuse, 90n578

CHILD ANALYSIS
Anna Freud: a gd to research, 91n790

CHILD CARE
Child care, 91n893
Child care crisis, 94n923
Childwise cat, 3d ed, 94n921
Guide to fed funding for child care & early childhood dvlpmt, 93n893
International hndbk of child care policies & programs, 94n919

CHILD DEVELOPMENT
Best of Bkfinder, 93n1123
Black children & American insts, 90n833
Childwise cat, rev ed, 91n191
Family ency of child psychology & dvlpmt, 94n807
Guide to fed funding for child care & early childhood dvlpmt, 93n893
Handbook of research on the educ of young children, 94n314
Help for children from infancy to adulthood, 5th ed, 93n896
Prosocial dvlpmt in children, 93n894
What's new for parents, 94n920

CHILD HEALTH SERVICES
Abstracts of active projects FY 1990, 91n1671
Bibliography for training in child & adolescent mental health, 92n1673
Caring for kids with special needs, 94n918
Childhood symptoms, 94n1838
Emergency medical servs for children: innovation bank, 2d ed, 91n1676
Maternal & child health legislation: 1991, 93n594
Natural medicine for children, 91n1681
Office of maternal & child health active projects FY 1990, 91n1672
Reaching out, 91n1649
Substance abuse & kids, 90n826
Using media to make kids feel good, 90n828

CHILD PSYCHIATRY
Bibliography for training in child & adolescent mental health, 92n1673
Handbook of behavior therapy & pharmacotherapy for children, 94n1848
Handbook of prescriptive treatments for children & adolescents, 94n1845

CHILD PSYCHOLOGY
Family ency of child psychology & dvlpmt, 94n807

CHILD REARING
Parent's desk ref, 92n842
Preschool resource gd, 94n312
What's new for parents, 94n920

CHILD STUDY. *See* **CHILD DEVELOPMENT; CHILD PSYCHOLOGY**

CHILD WELFARE
Child welfare stat bk 1993, 94n922
Feminization of poverty in the US, 91n913

CHILDBIRTH
Encyclopedia of childbearing, 94n1831

CHILDHOOD
Handbook of research on the educ of young children, 94n314
Reflections on childhood, 93n895

CHILDREN
CHILDES/BIB: an annot bibliog of child lang & lang disorders, 92n269
Childwise cat, rev ed, 91n191
Contemporary Canadian childhood & youth, 94n924
History of Canadian childhood & youth, 94n925
Literature-based moral educ, 93n351
Research gd for studies in infancy & childhood, 90n830

CHILDREN—BOOKS & READING
Author a month (for dimes), 94n1188
Behind the covers, v.2, 90n1087
Bookpeople: a 1st album, 91n651
Books to read aloud with children through age 8, 91n363
Choosing bks for children, rev. ed, 91n1120
Information bks for children, 93n7
Library serv to children, 93n665
Literature of delight, 94n1169
Michele Landsberg's gd to children's bks, 92n1118
More exciting, funny, scary, short, different, & sad bks kids like, 93n1122
Sensitive issues: an annot gd to children's lit K-6, 93n1130
Using children's bks in reading/lang arts programs, 93n402
Primaryplots, 90n1095

CHILDREN—CARE. *See* **CHILD CARE**

CHILDREN—MEDICAL CARE. *See* **CHILD HEALTH SERVICES**

CHILDREN—MORTALITY
Family planning & child survival, 90n801

CHILDREN OF ALCOHOLICS
Children of alcoholics, 92n840

CHILDREN OF DIVORCED PARENTS
Children & adjustment to divorce, 91n861

CHILDREN OF SINGLE PARENTS
One-parent children, the growing minority, 91n860

CHILDREN—PSYCHIC ABILITY
Parapsychological research with children, 93n808

CHILDREN—SERVICES FOR
Children's servs in the American public lib, 91n645

CHILDREN—SURGERY
Pediatrics, 90n1666

CHILDREN'S ATLASES
Kingfisher ref atlas, 94n451

CHILDREN'S BOOKS. See CHILDREN'S LITERATURE

CHILDREN'S ENCYCLOPEDIAS & DICTIONARIES
Barron's jr fact finder, 90n46
Childcraft, 90n47
Childcraft: the how & why lib, 93n58
Children's Britannica, 92n38
Compton's ency, 90n48
Compton's ency & fact-index, 94n34
Doubleday children's ency, 91n28
Factfinder, 94n39
First math dict, 92n1752
First sci dict, 92n1458
Golden bk ency, 90n51
Junior ency of Canada, 91n30
Kingfisher children's ency, 94n37
Kingfisher sci ency, 94n1568
My 1st dict, 94n1092
My 1st ency, 94n41
My 1st picture dict, 91n1071
My 2d picture dict, 91n1073
My first picture dict, 90n1017
My pictionary, 91n1072
My 1st word bk, 92n1048
New bk of knowledge, 90n52
New bk of knowledge, 93n60
New Grolier student ency, 90n53
New Grolier student ency, 93n61
Pocket ency, 91n29
Pocket factfinder, 91n31
Scott, Foresman beginning thesaurus, 90n1022
Scott, Foresman jr thesaurus, 90n1023
Troll student ency, 92n43
World Almanac infopedia, 91n36

CHILDREN'S FILMS
Best videos for children & young adults, 92n617
Best yrs of their lives, 94n926

CHILDREN'S LIBRARIES. See LIBRARIES, CHILDREN'S

CHILDREN'S LITERATURE. See also CHILDREN'S STORIES
Adventuring with bks, 9th ed, 90n1075
Adventuring with bks, 10th ed, 94n1173
Author profile collection, 93n1138
Authors & artists for young adults, v.1, 90n1091
Authors & artists for young adults, v.2, 90n1092
Authors & artists for young adults, v.6, 92n1126
Authors of bks for young people, 3d ed, 91n1117
Behind the covers, v.2, 90n1087
Biographical index to children's & young adult authors & illustrators, 93n1144
Birthday bk, 92n1131
Black authors & illustrators of children's bks, 2d ed, 93n1139
Black experience in children's bks 1989, 90n1079
Bookpeople: a multicultural album, 93n1142
Books by African-American authors & illustrators for children & young adults, 92n1122
Children's bk review index, v.14, 91n50
Children's bk review index, v.16, 93n1145
Children's bks: awards & prizes, 1992 ed, 94n1191
Children's lit review, v.16, 90n1090
Children's lit review, v.25, 93n1141
Children's media market place, 3d ed, 90n621
Children's writer's & illustrator's market, 1992, 93n957
Children's writer's word bk, 94n996
Choosing bks for children, rev. ed, 91n1120
Counting bks are more than numbers, 91n1115
Hispanic heritage, series 4, 93n150
Horn Bk index 1924-89, 91n1122
Library lit. 20, 92n572
Lloyd Alexander: a bio-bibliog, 92n1124
Major authors & illustrators for children & young adults, 94n1187
Masterplots 2: juvenile & young adult fiction series, 92n1128
Meet the authors & illustrators, 94n1193
More creative uses of children's lit, v.1, 93n671
My name in bks, 94n1190
New read-aloud hndbk, 1989 ed, 91n369
Our family, our friends, our world, 93n1127
Palette of possibilities, 94n1167
Peoples of the American West, 90n1080
Pinocchio cat, 90n1086
Play, learn, & grow, 94n1184
Presenting children's authors, illustrators & performers, 92n1127
Sixth bk of jr authors & illustrators, 90n30
Something about the author autobiog series, v.12, 92n1125
Something about the author, v.8, 91n1119
State-by-state gd to children's & young adult authors & illustrators, 92n1130
Summer reading clubs, 94n1194
They wrote for children too, 90n1076
Twentieth-century children's writers, 3d ed, 90n1088
Understanding abilities, disabilities, & capabilities, 92n318
Using children's bks in reading/lang arts programs, 93n402
Venture into cultures, 94n1170
Wellsprings of imagination, 94n478
Wordless/almost wordless picture bks, 93n1131
Writers for young adults, 3d ed, 90n1098
Young reader's companion, 94n1189

CHILDREN'S LITERATURE—BIBLIOGRAPHY
A to zoo, 3d ed, 90n1082
A to zoo, 4th ed, 94n1176
Adoption lit for children & young adults, 93n868
Alternative pr publs of children's bks, 3d ed, 90n637
American Lib Assn best of the best for children, 94n1163
Award-winning bks for children & young adults, 91n1110
Award-winning bks for children & young adults 1990-91, 94n1166
Best bks for children: preschool through grade 6, 4th ed, 91n1111
Best in children's bks, 93n1134
Best of Bkfinder, 93n1123
Best of Children's Choices, 90n1084
Best sci & tech ref bks for young people, 92n1452
Beyond picture bks, 90n1077
Bibliography [of] bks for children, 90n1078
Books kids will sit still for, 2d ed, 92n627
Books to read aloud with children through age 8, 91n363
Books without bias: through indian eyes, 90n373
Children's bk awards intl, 94n1195
Children's bks in print 1989-90, 90n16
Children's bks in print 1991-92, 92n16
Children's bks in print 1992, 94n9
Children's bks of the yr, 1990 ed, 91n1108
Children's cat, 16th ed, 92n610
Children's fiction sourcebk, 93n1125
Children's ref plus, 93n11
E for environment, 93n1752
Elementary school lib collection, 17th ed, 91n649
Elementary school lib collection, 18th ed, 93n667
Fantasy lit for children & young adults, 3d ed, 90n1083
Fiction for youth, 3d ed, 94n1181
From page to screen, 93n1359
Gender positive!, 94n1179
High interest easy reading, 6th ed, 91n366
Horn Bk gd to children's & young adult bks, v.1, no.1, 91n1114
Indian subcontinent in lit for children & young adults, 93n1126
Indiana bks by Ind. authors, 91n1112
Junior high school lib cat, 6th ed, 91n650
Kids' favorite bks, 94n1174
Literature activity bks, 94n1197

Michele Landsberg's gd to children's bks, 92n1118
More exciting, funny, scary, short, different, & sad bks kids like, 93n1122
Mother Goose comes 1st, 92n1121
Newbery & Caldecott awards, 1991 ed, 92n1120
Newbery & Caldecott awards, 1992 ed, 93n1128
Newbery & Caldecott medal & honor bks in other media, 93n1121
Newbery & Caldecott medalists & honor bk winners, 2d ed, 93n1120
Nonfiction bks for children, 91n648
Picture bks for children, 3d ed, 91n1109
Popular reading for children 3, 94n1168
Pop-up & movable bks, 94n1177
Primaryplots, 90n1095
Science & tech in fact & fiction: a gd to children's bks, 91n1455
Sensitive issues: an annot gd to children's lit K-6, 93n1130
Soviet Union in lit, 92n1229
Subject gd to children's bks in print 1989-90, 90n17
Subject gd to children's bks in print 1991-92, 92n17
Through Indian eyes, 93n433
University pr bks for public & secondary school libs 1991, 93n664
Using lit to teach middle grades about war, 94n694
War & peace lit for children & young adults, 94n1185
Your reading, 8th ed, 92n1123
Your reading, 9th ed, 94n648

CHILDREN'S LITERATURE IN SERIES
Young people's bks in series, 93n1133

CHILDREN'S LITERATURE, SPANISH
Books in Spanish for children & young adults, 90n1085
Books in Spanish for children & young adults, 94n1180

CHILDREN'S MUSEUMS
Doing children's museums, 93n78

CHILDREN'S PARAPHERNALIA
Childwise cat, 3d ed, 94n921

CHILDREN'S PERIODICALS
Magazines for children, 2d ed, 93n87
Magazines for young people, 2d ed, 93n84

CHILDREN'S PLAYS
International gd to children's theatre & educl theatre, 91n1121
Plays for children & young adults, 92n1129

CHILDREN'S POETRY
Index to poetry for children & young people 1982-87, 90n1096

CHILDREN'S REFERENCE BOOKS
Children's ref plus, 93n11
Guide to ref bks for school media centers, 4th ed, 93n670
Reference bks for children, 4th ed, 93n1129

CHILDREN'S STORIES
Benjamin Tabart's juvenile lib, 92n1119
Best yrs of their lives, 94n926
Children's writer's & illustrator's market, 1989, 90n897
Dictionary of British children's fiction, 90n1094
Dictionary of children's fiction from Austral., Canada, India, N.Z., & selected African countries, 94n1172
Fiction index for readers 10 to 16, 94n1196
Fiction sequels for readers 10 to 16, 92n1115
Portraying persons with disabilities: an annot bibliog of fiction, 3d ed, 93n1132
Portraying persons with disabilities: an annot bibliog of nonfiction, 2d ed, 93n1124
Prydain companion, 90n1089
Twins in children's & adolescent lit, 94n1183
Using picture storybks to teach literary devices, 91n1113

CHILDREN'S STORIES, AMERICAN
Dictionary of American children's fiction, 1985-89, 94n1171

CHILDREN'S STORIES, COMMONWEALTH OF NATIONS (ENGLISH)
Dictionary of children's fiction from Austral., Canada, India, N.Z., & selected African countries, 94n1172

CHILDREN'S STORIES, ENGLISH
English schoolboy stories, 93n1135

CHILDREN'S WRITINGS
Market gd for young writers, 1988-89 ed, 90n899

CHILE
Chile, 90n141
Historical stats of Chile, 90n142

CHINA
Atlas of China, 91n438
Bibliography of Sun Yat-sen in China's Republican Revolution, 1885-1925, 93n521
Biographical dict & analysis of China's party leadership 1922-88, 92n707
Cambridge ency of China, 2d ed, 93n125
Cambridge hndbk of contemporary China, 92n94
China business dir 1992, 93n278
China leading cos, 94n242
China statistical abstract 1989, 90n120
China trade & price stats 1988, 90n184
Christianity in China, 90n1411
Current bks on China 1983-88, 91n98
Directory of publishers in China, 94n672
Forage resources of China, 93n1510
Glossary of Chinese medical terms & acupuncture points, 92n1663
Historical dict of revolutionary China, 1839-1976, 93n523
Information China, 90n121
Iris of China, 93n1507
People's Republic of China yr bk 1991/92, 94n109
Silkworm diseases, 92n1477
Who's who in China, 92n30
Who's who in the People's Republic of China, 3d ed, 92n21

CHINESE DRAMA
Chinese drama, 92n1228

CHINESE ESSAYS
Modern Chinese writers, 94n1279

CHINESE LANGUAGE—DICTIONARIES—ENGLISH
Chinese-English dict of enigmatic folk similes, 92n1317
Chinese-English dict of the Wu dialect, 93n1081
English-Chinese glossary of American criminal law & criminal procedure law, 91n571
Facts on File English/Chinese visual dict, 90n1037
Oxford-Duden pictorial Chinese & English dict, 90n1039
Quick reference Chinese, 90n1038

CHIROPRACTIC
Chiropractic college admissions & curriculum dir, 1988-89, 90n1659
National dir of chiropractic, 3d ed, 93n1645

CHITIN
Chitin sourcebk, 91n1764

CHOICE
Choice annual cum index, v.28, 92n57

CHOPIN, KATE
Kate Chopin companion, 90n1202

CHORAL MUSIC
Choral music in print master index 1991, 92n1285
Choral music of Latin America, 93n1267
Choral music reviews index 2, 1986-88, 91n1290
Chorus in opera, 94n1353
Sacred choral music in print: 1992 suppl, 94n1340
Schwann artist issue, 14th ed, 90n1236
Secular choral music in print, 1991 suppl., 92n1286

CHORUSES
Twentieth-century choral music, 2d ed, 92n1287

CHRISTIAN ART & SYMBOLISM
Church symbolism, 2d ed, 94n1048

CHRISTIAN CHURCH (DISCIPLES OF CHRIST)
Disciples & American culture, 92n1406

CHRISTIAN EDUCATION
Harper's ency of religious educ, 91n1413

CHRISTIAN ETHICS
Encyclopedia of biblical & Christian ethics, rev ed, 93n1419

CHRISTIAN LITERATURE
Christian writer's manual of style, 90n900
Encyclopedia of the early church, 93n1406
Protestant sensibility in the American novel, 93n1170

CHRISTIAN PILGRIMS & PILGRIMAGES
Pilgrimage in the middle ages, 94n1523

CHRISTIAN SECTS
Encyclopedia of religions in the US, 93n1407

CHRISTIANITY
Almanac of the Christian world, 93n1415
Christianity in China, 90n1411
Dictionary of Christianity in America, 91n1444
Dictionary of Judaism & Christianity, 93n1405
Judaism & Christianity: a gd to the ref lit, 92n1399
Resources in ancient philosophy, 93n1393

CHRISTIANITY IN LITERATURE
Chaucer & the Bible, 90n1175

CHRISTIANITY—MIDDLE AGES, 600-1500
Pilgrimage in the middle ages, 94n1523

CHRISTINE DE PISAN
Christine de Pizan, 2d ed, 91n1233

CHRISTO
Christo prints & objects 1963-87, 90n953

CHRONIC DISEASES
Directory of pain treatment centers in the US & Canada, 90n1686
Nutrition & disease, 92n1674

CHRONICALLY ILL
Resources for people with disabilities & chronic conditions, 92n821
Resources for people with disabilities & chronic conditions, 2d ed, 94n882

CHRONOLOGY, HISTORICAL
Asimov's chronology of the world, 93n549
Chronology of conflict & resolution, 1945-85, 90n650
New York Public Lib bk of chronologies, 91n27
People's chronology, rev ed, 93n554

CHURCH COLLEGES
Choose a Christian college, 3d ed, 94n334
Directory of Catholic colleges & univs, 1992, 94n335

CHURCH DECORATION & ORNAMENT
Chartres: sources & literary interpretation, 90n969

CHURCH HISTORY
Christianity in China, 90n1411
Dictionary of Christianity in America, 91n1444
Encyclopedia of early Christianity, 91n1442
Encyclopedia of the early church, 93n1406
Researching modern evangelicalism, 91n1441
Rural church in America, 91n1436
Twentieth-century evangelicalism, 91n1434

CHURCH LIBRARIES
Subject headings for church or synagogue libs, 2d ed, 91n625

CHURCH MUSIC
Dictionary of W church music, 93n1269
Henry Purcell: a gd to research, 90n1257
Sacred choral music in print: 1992 suppl, 94n1340

CHURCH OF ENGLAND
Oxford movement & its leaders, suppl, 94n1522

CHURCH OF JESUS CHRIST OF LATTER-DAY SAINTS
Encyclopedia of Mormonism, 93n1420
Encyclopedia of Mormonism [CD-ROM], 93n1421
Mormons & Mormonism in US gov docs, 90n1401

CHURCH SCHOOLS
Catholic school educ in the US, 93n348
Directory of Catholic special educl programs & facilities 1989, 91n299
NCEA/Ganley's Catholic schools in America 1989, 90n315
NCEA/Ganley's Catholic schools in America 1992, 93n353

CHURCH WORK
Christian resource dir, 90n1383
Youth ministry resource bk, 90n1412

CHURCHES
Guide to Irish churches & graveyards, 92n389
Yearbook of American & Canadian churches 1989, 90n1384

CHURCHES OF CHRIST
Disciples & American culture, 92n1406

CINEMATOGRAPHERS
Cinematographers, production designers, costume designers & film editors gd, 2d ed, 91n1372
Cinematographers, production designers, costume designers & film editors gd, 3d ed, 93n1371
International dir of cinematographers, set- & costume designers in film, v.10, 92n1355
Masters of lens & light, 93n1343

CINEMATOGRAPHY
Delson's dict of motion picture mktg terms, 2d ed, 91n1367
Filmmaker's dict, 91n1371
Film-video terms & concepts, 93n1345
Language of visual effects, 94n1433
Special effects & stunts gd, 90n1331
Special effects & stunts gd, 2d ed, 94n1454

CIPHERS
Latest intelligence, 92n646

CIRCUS
Two hundred yrs of the American circus, 94n1419

CITATION OF LEGAL AUTHORITIES
Bieber's dict of legal abbrevs, 4th ed, 94n543
Bieber's dict of legal citations, 4th ed, 94n544
User's gd to the Bluebk, 93n590

CITIES & TOWNS
American small city profiles, 94n941
America's top rated cities, 1992 ed, 94n943
Cities & churches, 94n1502
Cities & towns in American hist, 90n847
City & state dirs in print 1990-91, 90n844
Facts about the cities, 93n918
Instant natl locator gd, 93n955
100 best small towns in America, 94n942
Places rated almanac, 91n908
Rand McNally pocket city atlas, 90n413
Rating gd to life in America's small cities, 91n911
Southern Calif.'s best ghost towns, 91n462
Urban hist yrbk 1988, 90n846
Urban south, 90n843
Where to make money, 94n945
World facts & figures, 3d ed, 90n92

CITY CHURCHES
Cities & churches, 94n1502

CITY LIGHTS BOOKS
City Lights bks, 94n1220

CITY PLANNING. See also URBAN POLICY
Elsevier's dict of physical planning, 91n909
Urban transport & planning, 90n842

CIVIC IMPROVEMENT
Better community cat, 91n847

CIVIL AVIATION. See AERONAUTICS, COMMERCIAL

CIVIL ENGINEERING
Elsevier's dict of civil engineering, 90n1587
Elsevier's dict of civil engineering, 93n1585

CIVIL RIGHTS. See also HUMAN RIGHTS
Civil rights movement, 94n595
Encyclopedia of African-American civil rights, 93n616
Encyclopedia of human rights, 92n563
Freedom in the world, 92n561
Public interest law groups, 90n557
World human rights gd, 3d ed, 94n594

CIVIL SERVICE POSITIONS
America's fed jobs, 92n216

CIVILIZATION
Blackwell dict of 20th-century social thought, 94n73
Catalogue of the pre-1500 W manuscript bks at the Newberry Lib, 91n551
Classical scholarship, 91n1124
Covert culture sourcebk, 94n76
Dictionary of cultural literacy, 90n304
Dictionary of cultural literacy, 2d ed, 94n305
Harper atlas of world hist, rev ed, 94n528
Middle ages, 91n541

CLARKE, AUSTIN
Austin Clarke: a ref gd, 94n1293

CLASSICAL DICTIONARIES
Concise Oxford companion to classical lit, 94n1198
Oxford companion to classical lit, 2d ed, 90n1099

CLASSICAL LITERATURE
Classical & medieval lit criticism, v.6, 92n1133
Classical & medieval lit criticism, v.7, 92n1134
Classical Greek & Roman drama, 91n1125
Concise Oxford companion to classical lit, 94n1198
Oxford companion to classical lit, 2d ed, 90n1099
Recent studies in myths & lit, 1970-90, 93n1301

CLASSICAL PHILOLOGY
Cambridge ritualists, 92n1132
Classical scholarship, 91n1124

CLASSICISTS
Classical scholarship, 91n1124

CLASSIFICATION
EUROCOM, 94n632
FIAF cataloguing rules for film archives, 93n638
INSPEC classification 1991, 92n582
INSPEC thesaurus 1991, 92n583

CLASSIFICATION, DEWEY DECIMAL
Abridged DDC & relative index, 12th ed, 91n617
Conversion tables: LC-Dewey, Dewey-LC, 94n630
Dewey Decimal Classification & relative index, 20th ed, 90n599

CLASSIFICATION, LIBRARY OF CONGRESS
Conversion tables: LC-Dewey, Dewey-LC, 94n630
Library of Congress classification class KJ-KKZ: law of Europe, 91n621
Library of Congress classification class KK-KKC, 91n622
Library of Congress classification class KL-KWX, 94n625
Library of Congress classification class Z, 92n579
Western fiction in the LC classification scheme, 90n598

CLAVICHORD MUSIC
Harpsichord & clavichord music of the 20th century, 94n1335

CLEANING
Jet cutting & cleaning bibliog, 90n1603

CLERGY—MALPRACTICE
Clergy malpractice, 92n515

CLERKS OF COURT
BNA's dir of state & fed courts, judges, & clerks, 4th ed, 93n582

CLEVELAND PUBLIC LIBRARY
Index to Negro spirituals, rev ed, 92n1315

CLIMATIC CHANGES
Dictionary of global climate change, 94n1949
Weather hndbk, 92n1735

CLIMATOLOGY
Climatic atlas of Mich., 92n1733
Climatic atlas of the Indian Ocean, pt.3, 91n1799
Climatological atlas of snowfall & snow depth for the NE US and SE Canada, 94n1948
Glossary: climate change, 92n1734

CLIMBING PLANTS
Ornamental shrubs, climbers & bamboos, 94n1632

CLOSED CAPTIONED TELEVISION
Gopen's gd to closed captioned video, 94n1011

CLOTHING, PROTECTIVE
Jane's NBC protection equipment 1989-90, 91n708
Quick selection gd to chemical protective clothing, 2d ed, 94n1767

CLOUDS
Peterson 1st gd to clouds & weather, 92n1732

COASTAL ARCHAEOLOGY
Coastal & maritime archaeology, 92n449

COASTAL FLORA
Field gd to coastal wetland plants of the SE US, 94n1661

COCAINE
Cocaine, 90n1695
Treatment of cocaine abuse, 93n889

CO-DEPENDENCE (PSYCHOLOGY)
Recovery resource bk, 91n891

CODES. See CIPHERS

COGENERATION OF ELECTRIC POWER & HEAT
Cogeneration & small power production manual, 3d ed, 92n1606

COGNITION IN CHILDREN
Resources for teaching thinking, 91n303

COGNITIVE PSYCHOLOGY
Blackwell dict of cognitive psychology, 93n798

COIN DEALERS
Official Whitman coin dealer dir, 2d ed, 91n985
Official Whitman coin dealer dir, 6th ed, 94n1029

COINS
Coin atlas, 91n983
Coin World almanac, 6th ed, 91n982
Commemorative coins of the US, 93n1002
Comprehensive US silver dollar ency, 93n1003
Photograde, 92n930
U.S. merchant tokens 1845-60, 3d ed, 92n931

COLD WAR
Cold war chronology, 94n795
Cold war 1945-91, 94n537

COLETTE
Colette: an annot primary & secondary bibliog, 94n1285

COLLECTIBLES
Collectibles market gd & price index, 8th ed, 92n924
Stamps, coins, postcards & related materials, 92n934
Tuttle dict of antiques & collectibles terms, 94n1024

COLLECTION AGENCIES
Collection agency dir, 2d ed, 93n237

COLLECTION DEVELOPMENT (LIBRARIES)
Collection evaluation in academic libs, 93n677
Subject collections, 7th ed, 94n656

COLLECTIVE BARGAINING
BNA's 1993 source bk on collective bargaining & employee relations, 94n277
Collective bargaining in higher educ & the professions, bibliog no.20, 94n269
Directory of faculty contracts & bargaining agents in insts of higher ed, v.15, 90n325
Directory of non-faculty bargaining agents in insts of higher educ, 92n294

COLLECTIVE SETTLEMENTS
American communes 1860-1960, 91n851
American communes to 1860, 91n848

COLLECTORS & COLLECTING
Antiquing in England, 91n979

COLLEGE & RESEARCH LIBRARIES
College & Research Libs & College & Research Libs News: index for vs.41-50 (1980-89), 92n628

COLLEGE & RESEARCH LIBRARIES NEWS
College & Research Libs & College & Research Libs News: index for vs.41-50 (1980-89), 92n628

COLLEGE, CHOICE OF
Barron's top 50, 93n366
Lovejoy's college gd, 19th ed, 91n335
Peterson's gd to 4-yr colleges 1991, 91n336

COLLEGE COSTS
America's lowest cost colleges, 92n296
Barron's 300 best buys in college educ, 91n321
Best dollar values in American colleges, 91n322
College costs & financial aid hndbk 1994, 94n353
College price bk 1990, 91n338

COLLEGE FACILITIES
Elderhostels, 90n434
Peterson's dir of college accommodations, 90n437

COLLEGE MAJORS
College majors & careers, rev ed, 94n362

COLLEGE PRESIDENTS
American college president, 1636-1989, 92n271

COLLEGE SPORTS
College admissions index of majors & sports 1989-90, 90n336
College names of the games, 90n761
Wrestling college & univ dir, 2d ed, 94n862

COLLEGE STUDENTS
Peterson's drug & alcohol programs & policies at 4-yr colleges, 90n825
Reading lists for college-bound students, 91n364
Student pol activism, 90n683

COLLEGE TEACHERS
Faculty white pages 1989, 90n327

COLLINGWOOD, R. G.
R. G. Collingwood: a bibliographical checklist, 94n1484

COLLODI, CARLO
Pinocchio cat, 90n1086

COLOMBIA
Colombia, 92n110

COLONIAL ADMINISTRATORS
Biographical dict of the British Colonial Serv 1939-66, 92n713

COLONIZATION
English origins of American colonists, 92n388

COLOR
Color compendium, 91n1011

COLOR PRINTS
Guide to modern Japanese woodblock prints, 1900-75, 93n1043

COLORADO
Colorado flora: E slope, 91n1524
Colorado gd, 90n441
Colorado place names, 94n470
Illustrated gd to the mountain stream insects of Colo., 93n1568

COLUMBIA PICTURES CORPORATION
Columbia checklist, 92n1350

COLUMBIA PICTURES TELEVISION
Screen gems: a hist of Columbia Pictures TV from Cohn to coke, 1948-83, 93n996

COLUMBUS, CHRISTOPHER
Atlas of Columbus & the great discoveries, 91n427
Christopher Columbus ency, 92n415
Columbus: an annot gd to the scholarship on his life & writings, 1750-1988, 92n457
Columbus dict, 92n512
Columbus' dict, 93n517
Columbus docs, 94n533

COMBAT
Stress, strain, & Vietnam, 90n739

COMBAT VEHICLES. See ARMORED VEHICLES, MILITARY

COMEDIANS
Quinlan's illus dir of film comedy actors, 93n1338
Who's who in comedy, 93n1325

COMEDY FILMS
Screwball comedy films, 92n1359

COMIC BOOKS, STRIPS, ETC.
American comic strip collections, 1884-1939, 91n1035
Comic art collection cat, 94n1405
Comic-bk superstars, 94n1407
Encyclopedia of American comics, 92n1327
Great comic bk artists, v.2, 91n1036

COMMAND OF TROOPS
Leadership: quotations from the military tradition, 91n681

COMMERCE
External trade: monthly stats, 91n267

COMMERCIAL ART
American graphic design, 94n1059

COMMERCIAL BUILDINGS
Architectural detailing for commercial construction, 92n994

COMMERCIAL FISHING. See FISHERIES

COMMERCIAL LAW
English-Persian dict of legal & commercial terms, 91n570

COMMERCIAL LOANS
Free money for small businesses & entrepreneurs, 91n211

COMMERCIAL POLICY
National trade policies, 93n320

COMMERCIAL PRODUCTS
Consumer product & manufacturer ratings 1961-90, 94n214
Eastern European business dir, 93n284
Factory outlet gd to the mid-atlantic states, 2d ed, 91n201
Factory outlet gd to the south, 91n200

COMMERCIAL STATISTICS
Business rankings annual, 1989, 90n183
Business rankings annual, 1992, 93n202

COMMODITY CONTROL
UNCTAD commodity yrbk 1988, 91n282

COMMODITY EXCHANGES
Commodity prices, 2d ed, 92n159
Directory of financial futures exchanges, 90n206
Futures markets dict, 91n187
Handbook of world stock & commodity exchanges, 1992, 93n222

COMMODITY FUTURES
Commodities price locator, 90n274
Commodity review & outlook 1990-91, 93n1466
International commodity markets hndbk 1993, 94n188

COMMON SENSE
Concordance to Thomas Paine's Common Sense & The American Crisis, 90n712

COMMONWEALTH OF INDEPENDENT STATES
Eastern Europe & the Commonwealth of Independent States 1992, 93n141
Russia & the Commonwealth A to Z, 94n525

COMMONWEALTH OF NATIONS
Bibliography of Commonwealth law reports, 92n518
Commonwealth yrbk 1991, 92n100
International lit in English, 92n1193

COMMONWEALTH OF NATIONS PERIODICALS
Index to Commonwealth little mags 1987-89, 93n83

COMMUNAL LIVING
American communes 1860-1960, 91n851
American communes to 1860, 91n848
Directory of intentional communities, 1990/91, 92n816

COMMUNICATION
Christian communication, 90n886
Communication & the mass media, 92n884
Communication serials, 1992/1993 ed, 93n982
Control of the media in the US, 93n951
Dictionary of communication & media studies, 2d ed, 90n888
Directory of computer conferencing in libs, 93n656
Family words, 90n1009
Graduate curricula in educl communications & tech, 4th ed, 94n379
Handbook of semiotics, 91n81
Human communication behavior & info processing, 93n956
Index to jls in communication studies through 1990, 93n954
International ency of communications, 90n887
Social dimensions of intl bus, 94n222
Webster's new world dict of media & communications, 92n888
Who's who in mass communication, 2d ed, 91n935
World communication & transportation data, 91n942
World's news media, 93n953

COMMUNICATIVE DISORDERS
Terminology of communication disorders, 3d ed, 90n1683

COMMUNISM
Atlas of communism, 92n733
Communist & Marxist parties of the world, 2d ed, 92n728
Encyclopedia of the American left, 91n763
Ernst Bloch, 92n731
Handbook of pol sci research on the USSR & E Europe, 94n781
International Trotskyism 1929-85, 93n777
Latin American Marxism, 92n734
Revolutionary orgs & revolutionaries in interbellum Poland, 93n779
Soviet perception of Canada, 1917-87, 91n105
Yearbook on intl communist affairs 1991, 93n780

COMMUNISM
Encyclopedia of the 2d World, 92n509
Handbook of pol sci research on the USSR & E Europe, 94n781
Revolutionary orgs & revolutionaries in interbellum Poland, 93n779
Soviet perception of Canada, 1917-87, 91n105
Who's who in the socialist countries of Europe, 91n18

COMMUNIST INTERNATIONAL
Bibliography of the communist intl (1919-79), v.1, 92n729

COMMUNITY COLLEGES
AACJC membership dir 1989, 90n321
AACJC membership dir 1992, 93n359
Beacon college project dir, 94n325
Community, technical, & jr colleges statistical yrbk, 1990 ed, 91n328
Community, technical, & jr colleges statistical yrbk, 1992 ed, 94n356
Peterson's gd to 2-yr colleges 1994, 94n343
Who's who in community, technical, & jr colleges 1991, 92n297

COMMUNITY DEVELOPMENT
Better community cat, 91n847

COMMUNITY LIFE
Middletown, 90n845

COMPACT DISC READ-ONLY MEMORY. *See* **CD-ROM**

COMPACT DISCS
Audiocassette & CD finder, 3d ed, 94n374

Basic classical & operatic recordings collection on CD for libs, 91n1294
Directory of record & CD retailers, 1990-91 ed, 92n1256
New Penguin gd to CDs & cassettes, yrbk 1989, 91n1292

COMPARATIVE EDUCATION
Comparative adult educ, 90n357
International hndbk of women's educ, 90n876

COMPARATIVE LAW
Bibliography on foreign & comparative law, 90n542
Dictionary of intl & comparative law, 93n577
Foreign law, 91n567

COMPASSION (ETHICS). *See* **CARING**

COMPOSERS
Contemporary composers, 93n1255
Italian violin music of the 17th century, 91n1264
Listener's musical companion, new ed, 93n1251
Songwriter's market, 1991, 91n1261
String music of black composers, 93n1260

COMPOSERS, AFRO-AMERICAN. *See* **AFRO-AMERICAN COMPOSERS**

COMPOSERS—AUSTRIA
Compleat Mozart, 92n1265
Ernst Krenek: a bio-bibliog, 90n1240
Franz Joseph Haydn: a gd to research, 91n1272
Franz Liszt: a gd to research, 92n1276
Gustav & Alma Mahler: a gd to research, 90n1241
Hans Rosbaud: a bio-bibliog, 93n1257
Johann Michael Haydn (1737-1806): a chronological thematic cat of his works, 94n1332
Twentieth-century composer speaks, 94n1333
Wolfgang Amadeus Mozart: a gd to research, 90n1244

COMPOSERS—CANADA
Violet Archer: a bio-bibliog, 92n1264

COMPOSERS—CZECHOSLOVAKIA
Antonin Dvorak on records, 93n1262

COMPOSERS—ENGLAND
Edward Elgar: a gd to research, 94n1327

COMPOSERS—FLANDERS
Orlando di Lasso: a gd to research, 91n1270

COMPOSERS—FRANCE
Albert Roussel: a bio-bibliog, 90n1242
Claude Debussy: a gd to research, 91n1266
Francis Poulenc: a bio-bibliog, 91n1278
Hector Berlioz: a gd to research, 90n1247
Henri Sauguet: a bio-bibliog, 92n1259
Jean-Philippe Rameau: a gd to research, 91n1271

COMPOSERS—GERMANY
Carl Maria von Weber: a gd to research, 91n1274
G. F. Handel: a gd to research, 90n1250
Johannes Brahms: an annot bibliog, 92n1273
Wagner compendium, 94n1329

COMPOSERS—GREAT BRITAIN
Anthony Milner: a bio-bibliog, 90n1253
Benjamin Britten discography, 92n1270
Frank Bridge: a bio-bibliog, 92n1269
Henry Purcell: a gd to research, 90n1257
John McCabe: a bio-bibliog, 92n1261
Michael Tippett: a bio-bibliog, 91n1280
Ralph Vaughan Williams: a gd to research, 91n1267
Richard Rodney Bennett: a bio-bibliog, 91n1268
William Walton: a bio-bibliog, 90n1254
William Walton: a cat, rev ed, 91n1269
William Walton: a source bk, 94n1323

COMPOSERS—HUNGARY
Gyorgy Ligeti: a bio-bibliog, 92n1274

COMPOSERS—ISRAEL
Descriptive bibliog of art music by Israeli composers, 90n1218
Music of Paul Ben-Haim, 94n1326

COMPOSERS—ITALY
Alessandro & Domenico Scarlatti: a gd to research, 94n1334
Claudio Monteverdi: a gd to research, 90n1238
Ferruccio Busoni: a bio-bibliog, 92n1275
Giovanni Battista Pergolesi: a gd to research, 90n1251

COMPOSERS—NETHERLANDS
Henk Badings, 1907-87: cat of works, 94n1328

COMPOSERS—RUSSIA
Alexander Tcherepnin: a bio-bibliog, 90n1239
Igor Stravinsky—the composer in the recording studio, 92n1278
Nikolai Andreevich Rimsky-Korsakov: a gd to research, 90n1252

COMPOSERS—SPAIN
Enrique Granados: a bio-bibliog, 93n1259

COMPOSERS—SWITZERLAND
Frank Martin: a bio-bibliog, 91n1279

COMPOSERS—UNITED STATES
Alec Wilder: a bio-bibliog, 94n1324
Catalog of the musical works of William Billings, 92n1268
Edward Burlingame Hill: a bio-bibliog, 90n1255
Elinor Remick Warren: a bio-bibliog, 94n1321
George Rochberg: a bio-bibliographic gd to his life & works, 93n1256
Howard Hanson: a bio-bibliog, 94n1330
Karel Husa: a bio-bibliog, 92n1267
Lukas Foss: a bio-bibliog, 92n1271
Ned Rorem: a bio-bibliog, 90n1248
Otto Luening: a bio-bibliog, 92n1265
Peggy Glanville-Hicks: a bio-bibliog, 91n1273
Radie Britain: a bio-bibliog, 91n1265
Randall Thompson: a bio-bibliog, 92n1260
Robert Russell Bennett: a bio-bibliog, 92n1262
Robert Ward: a bio-bibliog, 90n1246
Roy Harris: a bio-bibliog, 92n1277
William Mason (1829-1908): an annot bibliog & cat of works, 90n1243

COMPOSERS—WALES
Alun Hoddinott: a bio-bibliog, 94n1322

COMPOSITE MATERIALS
Composite materials hndbk, 2d ed, 93n1606
Composites: an insider's gd to corporate America's activities, 91n154
Concise ency of composite materials, 91n1628
Dictionary of composite materials tech, 91n1630
Specifications & standards for plastics & composites, 91n1633

COMPOSITION (LANGUAGE ARTS)
CCCC bibliog of composition & rhetoric 1987, 91n1043

COMPOSITION (LAW)
Law & bus dir of bankruptcy attorneys 1990, 91n577

COMPULSIVE BEHAVIOR
Focus on addictions, 94n917
International hndbk of addiction behaviour, 92n837

COMPUTER BULLETIN BOARDS
National dir of bulletin board systems 1990, 91n1728
National dir of bulletin board systems 1992, 91n1705

COMPUTER CONFERENCING
Computer mediated communication, 93n345
Directory of computer conferencing in libs, 93n656

COMPUTER CRIMES
Computer law & sftwr protection, 94n1892

COMPUTER EDUCATION
Only the best 1990, 90n343

COMPUTER ENGINEERING
Computer engineering hndbk, 94n1774

COMPUTER GRAPHICS
Dictionary of computer graphics tech & applications, 93n1688
Footage 89: N American film & video sources, 91n966
Graphics, design & printing terms, 91n1724
Graphics file formats, 93n1687
Illustrated computer graphics dict, 94n1912

COMPUTER INDUSTRY
Canadian legal sftwr dir 1991, 92n540
Computer industry 1993 almanac, 94n1909
Directory of computer sftwr & servs, 90n1728

COMPUTER INTERFACES
Computer professional's quick ref, 93n1685
Virtual reality: a selected bibliog, 93n1672

COMPUTER MUSIC
Dictionary of electronic & computer music terminology, 93n1247
Dictionary of musical tech, 93n1246

COMPUTER NETWORKS
Computer professional's quick ref, 93n1685
McGraw-Hill data communications dict, 94n1901
OSI dict of acronyms & related abbrevs, 94n1891
User's dir of computer networks, 92n1715

COMPUTER OPERATING SYSTEMS. See OPERATING SYSTEMS (COMPUTERS)

COMPUTER PROGRAMS
Humanities computing yrbk 1988, 90n884

COMPUTER SCIENCE
Dictionary of acronyms & abbrevs, 94n597
Encyclopedia of computer sci, 3d ed, 94n1903
Magill's survey of sci: physical sci series, 93n1699

COMPUTER SCIENCE LITERATURE
ACM gd to computing lit 1988, 91n1720
Bibliographic gd to computer sci 1991, 94n1893
Breaking through technical jargon, 91n1725
Computer glossary, 4th ed, 91n1723
Computer sci abbreviations & acronyms, 1990 ed, 91n1719
Computing info dir, 7th ed, 91n1733
Dictionary of computing, 3d ed, 91n1722
Jargon: an informal dict of computer terms, 94n1905
Que's computer user's dict, 91n1726
Que's computer user's dict, 2d ed, 92n1711

COMPUTER SIMULATION
Computer-based simulations in educ & training, 94n381
Concise ency of modelling & simulation, 93n1674

COMPUTER SOFTWARE
Agricultural sftwr dir 1990, 91n1475
Alfred Glossbrenner's master gd to free sftwr for IBMs & compatible computers, 90n1729
Business sftwr dir 1990/91, 91n138
Computer catalogs, 93n1673
Datapro dir of microcomputer sftwr, 91n1737
Datapro dir of sftwr, 91n1738
Desktop gd to computers in bus, 91n1730
Directory of applications sftwr of the UN system, 92n736
Directory of chemistry sftwr 1992, 94n1939
Directory of computer sftwr & servs, 90n1728
Directory of educl sftwr for nursing, 1988, 90n1692
Directory of info mgmt sftwr for libs, info centers, record centers, 1989-90 ed, 91n631
Directory of US govt sftwr for mainframes & microcomputers, 94n1914
Electric utility industry sftwr dir, 1992, 93n1590
Free & user supported sftwr for the IBM PC, 91n641
Guide to free computer materials, 11th ed, 94n1911
Guide to genealogical sftwr, 94n435
Guide to real estate & mortgage banking sftwr, 5th ed, 90n296
High-level langs & sftwr applications, 90n1726
Humanities computing yrbk 1989-90, 92n880
Managing a nation: the microcomputer sftwr cat, 2d ed, 92n672
McGraw-Hill personal computer programming ency, 2d ed, 90n1715
@Micro: educl sftwr evaluations 89/90, 91n361
Microcomputer applications hndbk, 90n1721
Microcomputer sftwr sources, 91n1744

Online Inc.'s top 500 lib microcomputer sftwr application programs, 94n640
Only the best 1985-89, 90n342
Petroleum sftwr dir, 1990, 6th ed, 90n1785
Petroleum sftwr dir, 1994, 94n1974
Public-domain sftwr & shareware, 2d ed, 90n1727
Software ency 1989, 90n1730
Software ency 1993, 94n1915
Software info! for Apple II computers, 91n1740
Software info! for LANs, 91n1741
Software info! for Novell NetWare compatible products, 91n1742

COMPUTER SYSTEMS
Basic gd to online info systems for health care professionals, 90n1624

COMPUTER TERMINALS
Directory of video, computer & audio-visual products 1993, 94n1887

COMPUTER-AIDED DESIGN
CAD rating gd, 2d ed, 92n1709

COMPUTER-AIDED TRANSCRIPTION
Court reporting computer compatible machine shorthand dict, 90n289

COMPUTER-ASSISTED INSTRUCTION
CD-ROM for librarians & educators, 94n1920
Computer mediated communication, 93n345
Computer-based simulations in educ & training, 94n381

COMPUTERS. See also **INFORMATION STORAGE & RETRIEVAL SYSTEMS; MICROCOMPUTERS**
AMI, v.9, issue 1, 91n968
AV market place 1990, 91n969
Bibliographic gd to the hist of computing, computers, & the info processing industry, 91n1721
Computer acronyms & abbrevs, 94n1890
Computer catalogs, 93n1673
Computer dict, 3d ed, 93n1681
Computer dict, 4th ed, 94n1904
Computer glossary, 5th ed, 93n1676
Computer health hazards, 92n1710
Computer law & sftwr protection, 94n1892
Computer pers currently received in the LC, 2d ed, 90n1718
Computer publishers & pubs, 1988-89 ed, 90n1716
Computer publishers & pubs, 1992-93 ed, 93n684
Consumer gd computer buying gd, new ed, 90n225
Desktop gd to computers in bus, 91n1730
Dictionary of computer terms, 2d ed, 90n1710
Dictionary of computer terms, 3d ed, 93n1675
Directory of computer & high tech grants, 92n1706
Encyclopedia of computer sci & tech, v.19, suppl.4, 90n1711
Encyclopedia of computer sci & tech, v.20, suppl.5, 90n1712
English-Japanese, Japanese-English dict of computer & data-processing terms, 90n1713
Equipment dir of audio-visual, computer & video products 1990-91, 92n915
Glossary of computing terms, 6th ed, 90n1714
Guide to free computer materials, 10th ed, 93n401
HarperCollins dict of computer terms, 92n1708
Macmillan ency of computers, 93n1678
McGraw-Hill dict of info tech & computer acronyms, initials, & abbrevs, 93n1679
MIT cat of computer scis & artificial intelligence, 90n1709
New hacker's dict, 93n1680
Orion blue bk: computer 1990, 91n205
Peterson's engineering, sci, & computer jobs 1989, 90n188
Prentice Hall's illus dict of computing, 94n1902
Security in computing, 1990 ed, 91n1732
Spanish-English, English-Spanish dict of computer terms, 94n1895

COMPUTING LITERATURE
Computing info dir, 10th ed, 94n1908

CONCENTRATION CAMPS—SOVIET UNION
Gulag hndbk, 90n573

CONCERTS
Music lover's gd to Europe, 93n1250

CONCORDIA UNIVERSITY. LIBRARIES. SPECIAL COLLECTIONS
Catalogue of the letters, tapes & photographs in the Irving Layton collection, 94n1270

CONCRETE POETRY
Concrete poetry, 90n1120

CONDIMENTS
Complete bk of herbs, spices & condiments, 91n1492

CONDUCT OF LIFE
Words of wisdom, 91n72

CONFEDERATE STATES OF AMERICA. See also **UNITED STATES—HISTORY—CIVIL WAR, 1861-1865**
Compendium of the Confederate armies: Ala., 93n711
Compendium of the Confederate armies: Fla. & Ark., 93n712
Compendium of the Confederate armies: N.C., 93n713
Compendium of the Confederate armies: Tenn., 93n714
Encyclopedia of the Confederacy, 94n506
Military leaders of the Civil War, 94n701
Warships of the Civil War navies, 91n698

CONFERENCE FACILITIES. See **CONVENTION FACILITIES**

CONFERENCE PROCEEDINGS
Bibliographic gd to conference pubns 1990, 92n3

CONFESSIO AMANTIS
Annotated index to the commentary on John Gower's Confessio Amantis, 91n1208

CONFLICT MANAGEMENT
Annotated bibliog for teaching conflict resolution in schools, 2d ed, 91n290
Conflict & culture, rev ed, 93n419

CONGREGATIONAL CHURCHES
Concordance of The Pilgrim Hymnal, 90n1265

CONIFERS
Coniferous trees, 92n1555

CONRAD, JOSEPH
Annotated critical bibliog of Joseph Conrad, 93n1207
Joseph Conrad: an annot bibliog, 91n1202
Joseph Conrad's reading, 92n1200

CONSERVATION OF NATURAL RESOURCES
Conservation atlas of tropical forests: Africa, 93n1484
Conservation atlas of tropical forests: Asia & the Pacific, 92n1764
Environmentalists: a biographical dict, 94n1993
North American horticulture, 2d ed, 93n1487

CONSERVATISM
Biographical dict of the extreme right since 1890, 92n732
Dictionary of conservative & libertarian thought, 92n727
Right gd, 94n787

CONSERVATIVE LITERATURE
National Review politically incorrect ref gd, 94n726

CONSOLATION OF PHILOSOPHY
Medieval Consolation of Philosophy: an annot bibliog, 94n1487

CONSOLIDATION & MERGER OF CORPORATIONS
Buyouts: dir of M & A intermediaries, 1990 ed, 91n174
Corporate trendtrac 1988, 90n196
Directory of merger & acquisition firms & professionals 1992, 93n193

CONSTRUCTION INDUSTRY
Building construction cost data 1991, 92n192
Construction glossary, 2d ed, 94n1773
Construction index, v.2, no.3, 90n978
Construction tech info sources, 93n1586
Glossary construction projects, 92n193

CONSULTANTS
American Consultants League dir 1989, 90n199
Consultants & consulting orgs dir 1989, 90n170
Consultants & consulting orgs dir 1991, 92n128
Consultants ref gd, 91n256
Directory of construction industry consultants, 91n1605
Directory of fund raising & nonprofit mgmt consultants, 94n901
European technical consultancies, 90n1432
Instrumentation & control consultants, 90n1578
Minority consultants & minority-owned consulting firms, 1989 natl dir, 90n271
Who knows: a gd to Washington experts, 10th ed, 91n753

CONSUMER EDUCATION
Almanac of consumer markets 1990-91, 90n222
American forecaster almanac 1990, 90n228
Better Bus Bureau A-Z buying gd, 92n172
Buying gd issue, 1989, 90n224
Childwise cat, rev ed, 91n191
Childwise cat, 3d ed, 94n921
Complete gd to medical tests, 90n1667
Consumer Europe 1991, 92n173
Consumer gd computer buying gd, new ed, 90n225
Consumer power, 92n171
Consumer Reports 1992 buying gd issue, 93n234
Consumer sourcebk 1992-93, 93n235
Consumer Spain 1991, 92n175
Consumer's gd to free medical info by phone & by mail, 94n1844
Consumers gd to Social Security benefits including Medicare, 12th ed, 90n223
Consumers index to product evaluations & info sources, 1990 annual, 92n174
Custom made, 91n190
Ecologue, 91n189
Educators gd to free home economics & consumer educ materials, 10th ed, 94n886
Elder care, 91n845
Ethical shopper's gd to Canadian supermarket products, 94n248
European consumer lifestyles to 1995, 92n176
Green consumer, 92n177
Green Earth resource gd, 92n179
Lemon-aid new car gd 1992, 93n1781
Lemon-aid used car gd 1992, 93n1782
Lesko's info-power, 91n196
New car buying gd, 1992-93 ed, 93n1784
Orion blue bk: audio 1990, 91n202
Orion blue bk: camera 1990, 91n203
Orion blue bk: car stereo 1990, 91n204
Orion blue bk: computer 1990, 91n205
Orion blue bk: guitars & musical instruments 1990, 91n206
Orion blue bk: professional sound 1989, 91n207
Orion blue bk: video & TV 1990, 91n208
Retirement sourcebk, 90n791
Smart consumer's dir, 1993 ed, 94n202
Toxics A to Z, 93n1769
Toy buying gd, 90n229
What you need to know about psychiatric drugs, 92n1698
Wholesale-by-mail cat 1991, 91n198
Wholesale-by-mail cat 1993, 94n203

CONSUMER PROTECTION
Consumers's gd to product grades & terms, 94n201
Smart consumer's dir, 1993 ed, 94n202

CONSUMPTION (ECONOMICS)
European dir of consumer goods manufacturers 1989, 90n237
World apparel fibre consumption survey, 90n250

CONTAINERIZATION
Jane's containerisation dir 1991-92, 92n1791

CONTEMPORARY CHRISTIAN MUSIC
Paul Baker's topical index of contemporary Christian music, 93n1268

CONTINUING EDUCATION
Adult learner's gd to alternative & external degree programs, 94n393
Guide to academic travel, 2d ed, 93n407
Independent study cat, 5th ed, 94n390
International dict of adult & continuing educ, 92n333
Macmillan gd to correspondence study, 5th ed, 94n359
National gd to educl credit for training programs, 1992-93 ed, 94n392

CONTRACTORS
Internet 1989-90 profiles of intl dvlpmt contractors & grantees, 91n236

CONVENTION FACILITIES
Guide to campus & non-profit meeting facilities 93, 93n207
Places, 90n444

CONVERTS
Conversion experience in America, 93n1418

COOK, ARTHUR BERNARD
Cambridge ritualists, 92n1132

COOKERY
American regional cookery index, 90n1462
Bibliography of cookery bks published in Britain 1875-1914, 90n1453
Chef's bk of formulas, yields, & sizes, 92n1499
Cooking A to Z, 90n1455
Cook's index, 90n1461
Cooksource, 91n1489
Edible garden weeds of Canada, 90n1506
Ethnic cookbks & food marketplace, 3d ed, 93n1472
Food lover's companion, 91n1483
Glutton's glossary, 92n1480
Guide to cooking schools, 1989, 90n1458
Health-related cookbks, 93n1471
Master dict of food & wine, 91n1486
Matter of taste, 91n1482
Recipes into type, 94n1613
Recipex, 92n1500
Specialty cookbks, v.1, 93n1470
True grits, 91n199

COOKING SCHOOLS
Guide to cooking schools, 1989, 90n1458
Guide to cooking schools, 1993, 94n1609

COOPER, JAMES FENIMORE
James Fenimore Cooper: an annot bibliog of criticism, 93n1171

COOPERATION
Prosocial dvlpmt in children, 93n894

COOPERATIVE LIVING. *See* COMMUNAL LIVING

COPTIC CHURCH
Coptic ency, 92n1414

COPY ART
Canned art: clip art for the Macintosh, 91n1034

COPY-READING
Copy-editing, 3d ed, 94n1000
Copyediting: a practical gd, 2d ed, 91n949
Editing docs & texts, 91n951
Fine art of copyediting, 92n898

COPYRIGHT
Copyright bk, 4th ed, 94n637
Copyright dir 1990-91, 91n629
Patent, trademark, & copyright laws, 1989 ed, 90n559
Patent, trademark, & copyright laws, 94n576
Publishing law hndbk, 2d ed, 94n574
Researching copyright renewal, 91n630

COPYRIGHT DEPOSIT. *See* LEGAL DEPOSIT (OF BOOKS, ETC.)

CORAL REEF FAUNA
Reef sharks & rays of the world, 94n1718

CORAL SEA
Fishes of the Great Barrier Reef & Coral Sea, 92n1577

CORAL SEA, BATTLES OF THE, 1942
Battles of Coral Sea & Midway, 1942, 93n695

CORALS
Corals of Austral. & the Indo-Pacific, 94n1747

CORCORAN GALLERY OF ART
Biennial exhibition record of the Corcoran Gallery of Art 1907-67, 92n979

CORIOLANUS
Coriolanus: an annotated bibliog, 90n1183

CORMAN, ROGER
Roger Corman: the best of the cheap acts, 90n1351

CORMORANTS
Cormorants, darters, & pelicans of the world, 94n1698

CORNFORD, FRANCIS MACDONALD
Cambridge ritualists, 92n1132

CORPORATE BUYOUTS. *See* CONSOLIDATION & MERGER OF CORPORATIONS

CORPORATE SPONSORSHIP
IEG dir of sponsorship mktg, 1991, 93n258

CORPORATION LAW
Law & bus dir of corporate counsel 1990-91, 91n578
Setting up a co in the European community, 91n162

CORPORATIONS
All-in-one business contactbk 1990, 91n136
American big businesses dir, 1993 ed, 94n161
America's phone bk 1989-90, 91n137
Brands & their cos 1992, 93n188
Companies & their brands 1992, 93n189
Corporate 500, 9th ed, 92n823
Corporate 1000, winter 1988-89, 90n173
Corporate dir 1989, 90n172
Corporate dir of US public cos 1993, 94n178
Corporate tech dir 1992, 93n246
Corporate trendtrac 1988, 90n196
Corporate yellow bk, v.8, no.3, 93n191
Directory of corporate affiliations 1989, 90n175
Directory of corporate affiliations 1990, 91n142
Dow Jones-Irwin bus & investment almanac, 1990, 91n175
Electronic news financial fact bk & dir 1989-90, 91n176
Ethical shopper's gd to Canadian supermarket products, 94n248
Fairchild's textile & apparel financial dir 1989-90, 91n229
Hoover's hndbk of American bus 1992, 93n208
Hoover's hndbk of emerging cos 1993-94, 94n172
Hoover's hndbk of world business 1992, 92n144
Hoover's hndbk: profiles of over 500 major corps, 92n145
Hoover's masterlist of major US cos 1993, 94n164
How to find info about cos, v.3, 94n173
International corporate 1000 1990, v.3, no.1, 91n255
International dir of co hists, 90n177
International dir of co hists, v.2, 91n132
International dir of co hists, v.3, 92n148
International dir of co hists, v.4, 93n260
International dir of corporate affiliations, 1989-90, 90n178
Japan co hndbks, spring 1990, 91n182
Macmillan dir of leading private cos 1989, 90n179
Major business orgs of E Europe & the Soviet Union, 92n130
Major cos of Europe 1991/92, 92n131
Major cos of the Arab world 1991/92, 92n133
Major cos of the Far East & Australasia 1991/92, 8th ed, v.1, 93n281
Medium cos of Europe 1991/92, 92n132
National dir of corporate public affairs 1991, 92n134
Nelson's techresources, winter 1993, 94n183
100 best cos to sell for, 90n278
Standard & Poor's register of corporations, directors & executives 1991, 92n135
Transnational corporations in S Africa & Namibia, 91n127
United States corporation hists, 2d ed, 93n174
Vocabulary of public sector auditing, 94n249
Walker's manual of W corps 1992, 93n214

Ward's bus dir of US private & public cos, 90n182
Who owns corporate America 1993, 94n167
Who's succeeding, 91n149

CORPORATIONS—CHARITABLE CONTRIBUTIONS
Corporate giving dir 1993, 94n163
Corporate giving yellow pages 1993, 94n162
Foundation dir, 15th ed, 94n890
Foundation dir pt.2, 1993 ed, 94n891
Foundation giving, 1993 ed, 94n896
Guide to US fndns, their trustees, officers, & donors, 1993 ed, 94n892

CORPORATIONS—FINANCE
McGraw-Hill pocket gd to bus finance, 93n241

CORPORATIONS, FOREIGN—UNITED STATES
Directory of foreign manufacturers in the US, 5th ed, 94n213

CORPORATIONS, NONPROFIT
National dir of nonprofit orgs 1992, v.1, 93n195

CORRECTIONAL INSTITUTIONS
Management of correctional insts, 94n804

CORRECTIONS
Management of correctional insts, 94n804
World ency of police forces & penal systems, 90n569

CORRESPONDENCE SCHOOLS & COURSES
Bear's gd to earning college degrees non-traditionally, 94n350
College degrees by mail, 94n351
Electronic univ, 94n376
Independent study cat, 5th ed, 94n390
Macmillan gd to correspondence study, 3d ed, 90n359
Macmillan gd to correspondence study, 5th ed, 94n359

CORROSION & ANTI-CORROSIVES
Corrosion & corrosion protection hndbk, 2d ed, 90n1602
Handbook of corrosion data, 91n1624

CORRUPTION (IN POLITICS)
Political corruption: scope & resource, 91n716
Political scandals & causes celebres since 1945, 92n678

COSMETICS
Formulary of cosmetic preparations, v.1, 93n1715

COSMOLOGY
Encyclopedia of cosmology, 94n1926
Isaac Asimov's lib of the universe, 91n1755

COSTA RICA
Costa Rica, 93n154
Historical dict of Costa Rica, 2d ed, 92n111

COSTUME
Chronicle of W fashion, 93n1010

COSTUME DESIGN
Cinematographers, production designers, costume designers & film editors gd, 2d ed, 91n1372
Cinematographers, production designers, costume designers & film editors gd, 3d ed, 93n1371
International dir of cinematographers, set- & costume designers in film, v.10, 92n1355

COTTAGE INDUSTRIES
Home business resource gd, 91n192

COUNCIL FOR MUTUAL ECONOMIC ASSISTANCE
Comecon data 1988, 91n153

COUNSELORS
Directory of credentials in counseling & psychotherapy, 90n750

COUNTER CULTURE. *See* SUBCULTURE; UNDERGROUND PRESS

COUNTER-REFORMATION
Contemporary printed lit of the English counter-reformation between 1558 & 1640, v.1, 91n1440

COUNTERTRADE
Global countertrade, 92n259

COUNTING
Counting bks are more than numbers, 91n1115

COUNTRY LIFE
Down-home talk, 90n1013
Many names of country people, 90n1444

COUNTRY MUSIC
Billboard bk of no.1 country hits, 92n1303
Cash Box country album charts, 1964-88, 91n1311
Decca hillbilly discography, 1927-45, 91n1310
Joel Whitburn's top country singles 1944-88, 91n1313
Traveler's country music radio atlas 1993, 94n1018
Who's who in new country music, 91n1312

COUNTY COURTS
County courthouse bk, 91n584
Directory of state court clerks & county courthouses, 1991 ed, 91n574

COUNTY GOVERNMENT
Municipal yellow bk, v.2, no.1, 93n741

COURT REPORTING. *See* **LAW REPORTING**

COURTESANS
Encyclopedia of mistresses, 94n961

COURTS
BNA's dir of state & fed courts, judges, & clerks, 4th ed, 93n582
Directory of state court clerks & county courthouses, 1991 ed, 91n574
Judicial staff dir, 1990, 91n576
National dir of courts of law 1991, 93n586
Want's fed-state court dir, 1990 ed, 91n582
Want's fed-state court dir, 1993 ed, 94n564

COURTS OF LAST RESORT
Congressional Quarterly's gd to the US Supreme Court, 2d ed, 91n746
Supreme Court at work, 91n589
U.S. Supreme Court, 91n566

COWBOYS
Cowboy & gunfighter collectibles, 90n923

CRAFTS (HANDICRAFTS). *See* **HANDICRAFTS**

CRAFTSMEN. *See* **ARTISANS**

CRANE, STEPHEN
Stephen Crane: an annot bibliog of secondary scholarship, 93n1172

CRAYFISH
Interdisciplinary bibliog of freshwater crayfishes, 90n1550

CREATION
Rediscovery of creation, 93n1417

CREATIONISM
Dictionary of sci & creationism, 91n1513

CREATIVE ABILITY
Creativity in the later yrs, 93n856

CREATIVE WRITING
AWP official gd to writing programs, 6th ed, 94n993

CREDIT BUREAUS
Lawyers' & creditors' serv dir, 1989 ed, 90n551

CREDIT UNIONS
Cooperative/credit union dict & ref, 91n134

CREELEY, ROBERT
Robert Creeley, Edward Dorn, & Robert Duncan, 90n1160

CRETE (GREECE)
Aerial atlas of ancient Crete, 94n529

CRICKET
Padwick's bibliog of cricket, v.2, 93n828

CRIME & CRIMINALS
Burs under the saddle, 90n471
Comparative criminology, 93n602
Crime in Victorian Britain, 94n590
Crimes & criminals, 93n614
Criminal activity in the deep South, 1700-1930, 90n571
Criminal intelligence & security intelligence, 91n598
Criminology: a reader's gd, 93n606
Encyclopedia of world crime, 92n552
FBI most wanted, 90n570
World ency of organized crime, 93n610
Writer's complete crime ref bk, 91n953

CRIME IN LITERATURE. *See* **DETECTIVE & MYSTERY STORIES**

CRIMINAL INVESTIGATION
Lawyers' & creditors' serv dir, 1989 ed, 90n551

CRIMINAL JUSTICE, ADMINISTRATION OF
Anderson's dir of criminal justice educ 1991, 92n538
Annotated bibliog of aboriginal-controlled justice programs in Canada, 93n569
Breaking down the walls, 93n568
Criminal justice ethics, 92n556
Dictionary of crime, 93n608
U.S. criminal justice interest groups, 94n588

CRIMINAL LAW
Criminal law review: 25 yr index 1954-89, 91n595
Dictionary of crime, 93n608
World ency of police forces & penal systems, 90n569

CRIMINAL STATISTICS
USSR crime stats & summaries, 93n613

CRIMINOLOGY. *See* **CRIME & CRIMINALS**

CRITICAL THINKING
Critical thinking, 94n1483

CRITICISM
Australian literary criticism, 1945-88, 90n1191
Children's lit review, v.16, 90n1090
Classical & medieval lit criticism, v.6, 92n1133
Classical & medieval lit criticism, v.7, 92n1134
Concise glossary of contemporary literary theory, 93n1112
Contemporary Canadian & US women of letters, 94n1138
Contemporary critical theory, 94n1140
Contemporary literary criticism, v.63, 92n1104
Contemporary literary criticism annual cum title index for 1991, 92n1105
Contemporary literary criticism: yrbk 1987, 90n1070
Deconstructionism: a bibliog, 94n1141
Dictionary of concepts in literary criticism & theory, 93n1111
Encyclopedia of contemporary literary theory, 94n1150
Encyclopedia of lit & criticism, 93n1116
English lang criticism on the foreign novel 1965-75, 90n1063
F. R. Leavis & Q. D. Leavis, 90n1149
Glossary of contemporary literary theory, 93n1113
Literature criticism from 1400 to 1800, v.13, 91n1186
Literature criticism from 1400 to 1800, v.15, 92n1107
Mark Twain's German critical reception, 1875-1986, 90n1156
New literary hist intl bibliog of literary theory & criticism, 90n1066
Nineteenth-century literary criticism, v.22, 90n1072
Nineteenth-century literary criticism, v.29, 92n1108
Research in critical theory since 1965, 90n1067
Roth's index to literary criticism, 90n1074
Shakespearean criticism, v.9, 90n1184
Short story criticism, v.2, 90n1114
Short story criticism, v.3, 91n1143
Short story criticism, v.11, 94n1216
Short story criticism, v.12, 94n1217
Twentieth-century literary criticism, v.39, 92n1110
Victorian criticism of American writers, 92n1159
World lit criticism 1500 to the present, 93n1119

CROPS
Weeds & words, 90n1445

CROQUET
Croquet: an annot bibliog from the Rendell Rhoades croquet collection, 93n829

CROSS REFERENCES (CATALOGING)
Cross-ref index, 2d ed, 90n597

CROSSWORD PUZZLES
Random House crossword puzzle dict, 90n1011

CRUELTY TO CHILDREN. *See* **CHILD ABUSE**

CRUISERS (WARSHIPS)
Cruisers of the US navy 1922-62, 90n671

CRUSADES
Atlas of the Crusades, 92n498

CRUSTACEA
Fish: 5-lang dict of fish, crustaceans & molluscs, 91n1584
Guide to the marine isopod crustaceans of the Caribbean, 91n1600

CUBA
Bibliography of Cuban mass communications, 94n991
Cuban festivals, 94n1399
Guide to Cuban collections in the US, 92n495

CUBAN AMERICAN LITERATURE
Biographical dict of Hispanic lit in the US, 90n1124

CUBAN LITERATURE
Dictionary of 20th-century Cuban lit, 91n1230
U.S. Latino lit, 93n1166

CUCUMIS
Biosystematic monograph of the genus Cucumis (Cucurbitaceae), 94n1638

CULTS
Bibliography of new religious movements in primal societies, v.4, 92n1400
Dictionary of cults, sects, religions & the occult, 94n1513
Encyclopedic hndbk of cults in America, rev ed, 93n1410
Illustrated ency of active new religions, sects, & cults, 94n1529
Social sci & the cults, 91n1410
Sociology of religion, 92n1397

CULTURAL ANTHROPOLOGY. *See* **ETHNOLOGY**

CULTURAL GEOGRAPHY. *See* **ANTHROPO-GEOGRAPHY**

CULTURAL POLICY
Oxford illus ency of peoples & cultures, 94n397

CULTURAL PROPERTY, PROTECTION OF
Landmark yellow pages, 91n1028

CULTURE
European culture, 94n977
Oxford illus ency of peoples & cultures, 94n397

CULTURED MILKS
Encyclopedia of fermented fresh milk products, 93n1475

CUMMINGS, E. E.
Concordance to the complete poems of E. E. Cummings, 90n1135

CUNEIFORM TABLETS
Cuneiform texts in the Metropolitan Museum of Art, 90n989

CURIOSITIES & WONDERS
Guinness bk of answers, 7th ed, 90n68

CURZON, GEORGE NATHANIEL CURZON, MARQUIS OF, 1859-1925
Lord Curzon 1859-1925: a bibliog, 92n486

CUSHING, PETER
Peter Cushing: the gentle man of horror & his 91 films, 94n1437

CUSTOM HOUSES
U.S. custom house gd 1990, 91n281

CUSTOMS ADMINISTRATION
List of authorized customs offices for Community transit/common transit operations, 92n253

CUT FLOWER INDUSTRY
Fine flowers by phone, 90n1468

CUT FLOWERS
Specialty cut flowers, 94n1623

CYCADACEAE
Cycads of the world, 94n1671

CYCLING
Bicyclist's sourcebk, 92n791

DAKOTA LANGUAGE—DICTIONARIES—ENGLISH
Dakota-English dict, 94n1111
English-Dakota dict, 94n1112

DANCE. *See* **DANCING**

DANCE ORCHESTRAS
Glenn Miller Army Air Force band, 90n1289

DANCING
Bibliographic gd to dance 1989, 91n1346
Bibliographic gd to dance 1991, 94n1422
Black dance, 90n1314
Dance dir 1990, 92n1335
Dance film & video gd, 93n1328
Dance hndbk, 91n1347
Dance in the musical theatre, 90n1317
Dictionary of theatre anthropology, 92n1374
Index to dance pers: 1991, 94n1424
Music & dance in Puerto Rico from the age of Columbus to modern times, 93n1243
Music & dance pers, 90n1316
World ballet & dance 1992-93, 94n1425

DANGEROUS MATERIALS. *See* **HAZARDOUS SUBSTANCES**

DANISH LANGUAGE—DICTIONARIES—ENGLISH
Danish-English English-Danish dict, 91n1083

DARWIN, CHARLES
Charles Darwin's marginalia, v.1, 92n1525

DATA BASES
Business online: the professional's gd, 91n161
CD-ROM for librarians & educators, 94n1920
CD-ROM per index, 93n82
CD-ROM research collections, 93n660
Directory of online databases, v.13, no.2, 93n1682
Directory of online healthcare databases, 5th ed, 91n1648
Directory of portable databases, 91n1729
Directory of portable databases, v.3, no.2, 93n1670
Directory to fulltext online resources 1992, 93n626
Electronic style, 94n1002
Federal data base finder, 3d ed, 92n52
Gale dir of databases, 94n1907
Keyguide to info sources in online & CD-ROM database searching, 92n590
OPAC dir 1993, 94n646

DATA LIBRARIES
CD-ROM research collections, 93n660

DATA PROCESSING. *See* **ELECTRONIC DATA PROCESSING; INFORMATION STORAGE & RETRIEVAL SYSTEMS**

DATA PROTECTION
Computer law & sftwr protection, 94n1892

DATA TRANSMISSION SYSTEMS
Computer-readable databases, 5th ed, 90n1717
Data & computer communications, 91n1751
Database dict, 91n1743
McGraw-Hill data communications dict, 94n1901
OSI dict of acronyms & related abbrevs, 94n1891

DATABASES
Cumulative index to ONLINE, DATABASE & CD-ROM Professional 1986-91, 93n1669
Sourcebook on standards info, 92n574
User educ for online systems in libs, 92n598

DATES. *See* **CHRONOLOGY, HISTORICAL**

DAVIE, DONALD
Donald Davie: a checklist of his writings, 1946-88, 92n1201

DAVIS, BERTRAM R.
Catalogue of the Bertam R. Davis "Robert Southey" collection, 91n1218

DAY CARE CENTERS FOR THE AGED
Golden horizons retirement gd, Calif ed, 90n792

DE CIVITATE DEI
Augustine's De Civitate Dei: an annot bibliog of modern criticism, 1960-90, 93n1416

DEAFNESS
Encyclopedia of deafness & hearing disorders, 93n1656

DEATH
Affairs in order, 92n817
Challenge of euthanasia, 91n852
Death & dying, 92n818
Encyclopedia of death, 90n795

DEATH ROW
Death row USA reporter 1975-88, 91n596

DEBTOR & CREDITOR
Lawyers' & creditors' serv dir, 1993 ed, 94n563

DEBTS, EXTERNAL
International debt & the Third World, 90n155

DEBUSSY, CLAUDE
Claude Debussy: a gd to research, 91n1266

DECCA RECORDS (FIRM)
Decca hillbilly discography, 1927-45, 91n1310

DECONSTRUCTION
Deconstructionism: a bibliog, 94n1141

DECORATIONS OF HONOR
Register of Canadian honours, 92n396

DECORATIVE ARTS
Applied & decorative arts, 2d ed, 94n1022
Arkansas made, v.1, 92n919
Arkansas made, v.2, 92n920
Art & architecture in Canada, 92n967
Decorative arts & household furnishings in America 1650-1920, 91n978
Tuttle dict of antiques & collectibles terms, 94n1024

DEER
Whitehead ency of deer, 94n1742

DEFENSE INDUSTRIES
Dictionary of military, defense contractor, & troop slang acronyms, 91n674

DEFENSE POLICY. *See* **MILITARY POLICY**

DEFENSIVE (MILITARY STRATEGY)
International countermeasures hndbk 1990, 91n703

DEFOE, DANIEL
Robinson Crusoe: a bibliographical checklist of English lang editions (1719-1979), 92n1202

DEFORMITIES. *See* **ABNORMALITIES, HUMAN**

DEGREES, ACADEMIC
Bear's gd to earning college degrees non-traditionally, 94n350
Campus-free college degrees, 5th ed, 93n378
College degrees by mail, 94n351
College majors, 91n334

DELAWARE
Used bk lover's gd to the mid-Atlantic states, 94n1028

DELEGATED LEGISLATION
BNA's dir of state administrative codes & registers, 94n748

DEMOCRACY
Democracy's dawn, 92n750

DEMOGRAPHY
Annotated bibliog of Canadian demography 1983-89, 91n906
Canadian markets 1990, 91n903
Demographic stats 1991, 93n897
First demographic portraits of Russia 1951-90, 94n929
Retrospective bibliog of American demographic hist from colonial times to 1983, 90n835
Social work almanac, 94n911
Sourcebook of county demographics, census ed, 94n933
Statistical forecasts of the US, 94n932

DENOMINATIONS, CHRISTIAN. *See* **CHRISTIAN SECTS**

DENTAL MATERIALS
Concise ency of medical & dental materials, 92n1662

DENTISTRY
Barron's gd to medical & dental schools, 4th ed, 90n1656

DENTISTRY—DICTIONARIES—SPANISH
Bilingual dict of dental terms: Spanish-English, 91n1683

DEPENDENCY
Public admin in the Third World, 91n783

DEPRESSION
Encyclopedia of depression, 92n1683

DERRIDA, JACQUES
Jacques Derrida: an annot primary & secondary bibliog, 94n1491

DESCARTES, RENE
Descartes dict, 94n1493

DESCRIPTION (RHETORIC)
Descriptionary, 93n1072

DESCRIPTIVE CATALOGING
Bibliographic style manual, 91n954
Cataloging computer files, 94n628
Dewey Decimal Classification & relative index, 20th ed, 90n599
Handbook for AACR2 1988 revision, 90n604
Notes in the cat record based on AACR2 & LC rule interpretations, 90n605
Serials cataloging hndbk, 90n601

DESERT PLANTS
Desert & mountain plants of the southwest, 94n1645
Low-water flower gardener, 94n1630

DESIGN
American graphic design, 94n1059
Construction index, v.2, no.3, 90n978
Contemporary designers, 2d ed, 92n921
Dictionary of 20th-century design, 92n922
Product design mgmt, 90n244

DESKTOP PUBLISHING
Canned art: clip art for the Macintosh, 91n1034
Collier's rules for desktop design & typography, 92n643
Computer type, 92n645
Design of bibliogs, 93n690
Desktop publisher's legal hndbk, 90n555
Desktop typographics, 92n644
Guide to the lit of electronic publishing, 90n628
Illustrated hndbk of desktop publishing & typesetting, 2d ed, 91n667
Index of desktop publishing, 1990, 91n673

DETECTIVE & MYSTERY FILMS
Famous movie detectives 2, 92n1365
Great detective pictures, 91n1381
Saint: a complete hist in print, radio, film & TV, 94n1249
Screen sleuths, 93n1350
Spies & sleuths, 90n1345

DETECTIVE & MYSTERY STORIES. *See also* **HORROR TALES**
British mystery & thriller writers since 1940, 1st series, 91n1196
British mystery writers, 1920-39, 90n1173
Catalogue of crime, rev ed, 91n1132
Critical survey of mystery & detective fiction, 90n1106
Dictionary of literary biog documentary series, v.6, 90n1126

Female detectives in American novels, 94n1208
Gay & lesbian characters & themes in mystery novels, 94n1210
Index to crime & mystery anthologies, 92n1142
Locked room murders & other impossible crimes, 93n1150
Man of magic & mystery, 90n1142
Masters of mystery & detective fiction, 91n1197
Modern mystery, fantasy & sci fiction writers, 94n1207
Murder ... by category, 93n1152
Mystery writer's marketplace & sourcebk, 94n994
Out of the woodpile, 93n1151
Reader's gd to the American novel of detection, 94n1231
Reader's gd to the private eye novel, 94n1209
Saint: a complete hist in print, radio, film & TV, 94n1249
Silk stalkings: when women write of murder, 90n1107
Subject is murder, v.2, 91n1134
Twentieth-century crime & mystery writers, 3d ed, 93n1153
What about murder? 1981-91, 94n1206
Writer's complete crime ref bk, 91n953

DETECTIVE & MYSTERY TELEVISION PROGRAMS
Television detective shows of the 70s, 92n918

DETECTIVES IN MASS MEDIA
Trouble is their bus: private eyes in fiction, film & TV, 1927-88, 91n930

DETROIT PUBLIC LIBRARY
Genealogical gd to the Burton Histl Collection, 90n394

DEVELOPING COUNTRIES
Atlas of the Third World, 2d ed, 94n459
Bibliography of new religious movements in primal societies, v.4, 92n1400
Development dir 1990, 91n107
Dictionary of dvlpmt, 91n108
Dictionary of Third World terms, 93n136
Directory of dvlpmt research & training insts in Africa, 94n93
Encyclopedia of the Third World, 4th ed, 93n137
Glossary of the Third World, 90n128
Guide to current indexing & abstracting servs in the Third World, 93n652
Guide to sources of intl population assistance 1988, 90n836
Guide to the info activities of European dvlpmt networks, 93n630
International debt & the Third World, 90n155
International dvlpmt dict, 92n125
Poverty in developing countries, 94n905
Public admin in the Third World, 91n783
Third World gd 89/90, 90n129
Third World hndbk, 92n101
Third World in film & video, 1984-90, 92n102
Third World struggle for peace with justice, 92n749
Third World tourism research 1950-84, 93n504
Urban informal sector in Africa in retrospect & prospect, 93n277
Wars in the Third World since 1945, 92n653
Women's educ in the Third World, 90n861
World debt tables, 90n232
World debt tables 1991-92, 93n244
World dvlpmt dir, 92n738

DEVELOPMENTAL PSYCHOLOGY
Encyclopedia of human dvlpmt & educ, 91n793

DEWEY, JOHN
John Dewey: the collected works, 1882-1953: index, 93n342

DEWHURST, COLLEEN
Colleen Dewhurst: a bio-bibliog, 94n1411

DIAGNOSIS
Complete gd to medical tests, 90n1667
Concise ency of biological & biomedical measurement systems, 93n1635
Do-it-yourself medical testing, 3d ed, 90n1671
Isler's pocket dict, 3d ed, 91n1660
Medical tests & diagnostic procedures, 91n1682
Pocket gd to nursing diagnoses, 3d ed, 90n1694

DIAGNOSTIC IMAGING
Dictionary & hndbk of nuclear medicine & clinical imaging, 92n1657

DICKENS, CHARLES
Critical reception of Charles Dickens 1833-41, 90n1178
Dickens glossary, 91n1204
Dickens index, 90n1177
Martin Chuzzlewit: an annot bibliog, 91n1205
Pickwick Papers: an annot bibliog, 91n1203
Tale of two cities: an annot bibliog, 94n1251

DICKEY, JAMES
James Dickey: a descriptive bibliog, 91n1161

DICKINSON, EMILY
Emily Dickinson: a bibliog of secondary sources, 90n1136
Musicians wrestle everywhere, 94n1308
Poems of Emily Dickinson: an annot gd to commentary published in English, 94n1233

DICTIONARIES, POLYGLOT
Dictionary cat, 2d ed, 90n988
Dictionary of animal health terminology, 94n1633
Dictionary of evolutionary fish osteology, 93n1558
Dictionary of process tech, 91n1609
Elsevier's dict of aquaculture, 93n1467
Elsevier's dict of civil engineering, 93n1585
Elsevier's dict of export financing & credit insurance, 91n264
Elsevier's dict of hydrology & water quality mgmt, 93n1724
Elsevier's dict of machine tools & elements, 92n1628
Elsevier's dict of mining & mineralogy, 94n1800
Elsevier's dict of office automation, 93n323
Euro dict, 94n1108
European dict, 94n1108
International illus vocabulary of English-French fingerprint terminology..., 93n607
IMF glossary, 93n254
Multilingual dict of disaster medicine & intl relief, 92n1656
Potato terms, 91n1487

DICTIONARY OF AMERICAN BIOGRAPHY
Dictionary of American biog comprehensive index complete through suppl.8, 91n51

DICTIONARY OF AMERICAN REGIONAL ENGLISH
Index by region, usage, & etymology to the Dict of American Regional English, v.1 & 2, 94n1090

DIESEL LOCOMOTIVES
Diesel locomotive rosters, 3d ed, 94n2025

DIET
Melting pot: an annot bibliog & gd to food & nutrition info for ethnic groups in America, 94n1599

DIET THERAPY
Health-related cookbks, 93n1471
Mount Sinai School of Medicine complete bk of nutrition, 92n1670
Nutrition & diet therapy dict, 3d ed, 92n1485

DIETARY SUPPLEMENTS
Doctors' vitamin & mineral ency, 91n1709
Nutrients cat, 94n1610

DIFFUSION OF INNOVATIONS
Diffusion of innovations, 91n79

DIGITAL COMMUNICATIONS
Preservation & access tech, 92n599

DIGITAL ELECTRONICS
Digital systems ref bk, 93n1596
Lenk's digital hndbk, 94n1782

DINOSAURS
Dinosaur & other prehistoric animal factfinder, 94n1959
Dinosaurs: a gd to research, 93n1731
Macmillan children's gd to dinosaurs & other prehistoric animals, 93n1732
Peterson 1st gd to dinosaurs, 91n1791
Predatory dinosaurs of the world, 90n1769
Rand McNally picture atlas of prehistoric life, 94n1962
Rourke dinosaur dict, 91n1792
Ultimate dinosaur bk, 94n1960
Visual dict of dinosaurs, 94n1963

DIPLOMATS
Dictionary of American diplomatic hist, 2d ed, 91n733
International dir of foreign ministers 1589-1989, 91n720
Statesmen who changed the world, 94n716
U.S. & foreign diplomatic contacts, 92n747
Who's who in intl affairs, 92n742
World dir of diplomatic representation, 93n723

DIPTERA
Catalog of the diptera of the Australasian & oceanian regions, 91n1588
Catalogue of palaearctic diptera, v.7, 93n1567
Diptera types in the Canadian Natl Collection of Insects, pt.2, 94n1724

DIRECT MARKETING
Direct mktg market place [DMMP] 1993, 94n289
Directory of major mailers & what they mail 1990, 91n263

DIRECTORIES
British dirs, 90n133
Directories in print 1989, 90n57
Directories in print 1993, 94n46

DISABLED. *See* HANDICAPPED

DISARMAMENT
Arms control & disarmament, defense & military, intl security, & peace, 90n673
Arms control, disarmament, & military security dict, 90n675
Canada & intl peace & security, 91n773
Disarmament & security: 1988-89 yrbk, 92n748
Encyclopedia of arms control & disarmament, 94n797
Peace & security thesaurus, 91n684
SIPRI yrbk 1990: world armaments & disarmament, 91n713
Surviving the nuclear age, 1987 update, 92n668
Surviving the nuclear age...1945-1983 table of contents, 92n667
Unesco yrbk on peace & conflict studies 1988, 92n753
United Nations disarmament yrbk, 1987, 90n732

DISASTER FILMS
Nuclear movies, 93n1349

DISASTER MEDICINE
Multilingual dict of disaster medicine & intl relief, 92n1656

DISASTER RELIEF
Handbook of emergency mgmt, 92n78
Multilingual dict of disaster medicine & intl relief, 92n1656

DISASTERS
Catastrophes & disasters, 94n469
From the Titanic to the Challenger, 90n1415
Man-made catastrophes, 94n467
Natural disasters, 94n468

DISCOVERIES (IN GEOGRAPHY)
Children's atlas of exploration, 94n452
Explorers & exploration, 94n462
Marshall Cavendish illus ency of discovery & exploration, 92n417
Times atlas of world exploration, 92n408

DISCRIMINATION
Discrimination & prejudice, 93n845
World racism & related inhumanities, 93n618

DISCUS (FISH)
Atlas of discus of the world, 92n1575

DISEASES
Are you at risk?, 92n1675
Health, disease, medicine & famine in Ethiopia, 92n1632
Health of black Americans from post reconstruction to integration, 1871-1960, 91n1642
Physicians' gd to rare diseases, 94n1863
Professional gd to diseases, 3d ed, 90n1676
Professional gd to diseases, 4th ed, 94n1841

DISNEY, WALT
Walt Disney: a bio-bibliog, 94n1412

DISPUTE RESOLUTION (LAW)
Alternative dispute resolution for the community, 91n565
Alternative dispute resolution sourcebk, 1993-94 ed, 94n579

DISSENTERS
Revolutionary & dissident movements, 3d ed, 93n728

DISSERTATIONS—ABSTRACTS
Greenwood annual abstract of legal dissertations & theses, 1985-87, 90n562

DISSERTATIONS, ACADEMIC
American & Canadian doctoral dissertations & master's theses on Africa, 1974-87, 91n91
Anglo-Irish lit, 91n1239
Canadian studies: foreign pubs & theses, 4th ed, 93n134
Cities & towns in American hist, 90n847
Igor Stravinsky: an intl bibliog of theses & dissertations, 90n1245
Religion & the American experience, 1620-1900, 94n1507
Theses on English-Canadian lit, 91n1229

DISTANCE EDUCATION
Distance educ: a selected bibliog, 94n380
Electronic univ, 94n376
Library servs for off-campus & distance educ, 92n577

DISTANT EARLY WARNING SYSTEM
Jane's C3I systems 1989-90, 91n706

DISTRICT COURTS
Want's fed-state court dir, 1990 ed, 91n582

DIVIDENDS
Guide to dividend reinvestment plans, 94n192
Moody's hndbk of dividend achievers 1992, 93n224

DIVORCE
Children & adjustment to divorce, 91n861
Divorce & dissolution of marriage laws of the US, 91n862
Encyclopedia of marriage, divorce & the family, 90n798
Handbook of family law, 90n560

DJIBOUTI (REPUBLIC)
Djibouti, 92n87

DOCUMENTARY FILMS
NFB film gd, 93n1342

DOCUMENTS IN MACHINE-READABLE FORM
Directory of computerized data files [1989], 91n42

DOCUMENTS LIBRARIANS
Directory of govt doc collections & librarians, 6th ed, 93n676

DOGS
Atlas of dog breeds of the world, 91n1580
Atlas of dog breeds of the world, 94n1710
Canine lexicon, 94n1706
Complete dog bk, 18th ed, 93n1552
Dogs, 94n1705
Dogs, cats, & horses, 91n1116
Inherited eye diseases in purebred dogs, 90n1475
Mini-atlas of dog breeds, 92n1574
Pit bull dilemma, 91n558
Project BREED dir, 94n1708

DOLLS
Dictionary of doll marks, 92n935

DOMESTIC RELATIONS
Family law dict, 2d ed, 92n532
Handbook of family law, 90n560

DOMINICAN REPUBLIC
Dominican Republic, 92n112

DONATION OF ORGANS, TISSUES, ETC.
Life from death, 90n1677

DONNE, JOHN
John Donne companion, 91n1206

DOPING IN SPORTS
Drug file, 93n1667

DORN, EDWARD
Robert Creeley, Edward Dorn, & Robert Duncan, 90n1160

DOSTOEVSKY, FEDOR
Fedor Dostoevsky: a ref gd, 91n1247

DOWSON, ERNEST CHRISTOPHER
Three decadent poets, 91n1222

DRAGONFLIES
Dragonflies of the Fla. peninsula, Bermuda, & the Bahamas, 90n1553

DRAMA
Back Stage theater gd, 93n1389
Book of 1000 plays, 90n1100
Companion to the medieval theatre, 90n1369
Drama dict, 90n1357
Dramatic re-visions, 93n1333
Dramatist's bible 1989, 90n1363
Index to plays in pers, 1977-87, 91n1126
International dict of theatre, v.1, 93n1391
International gd to children's theatre & educl theatre, 91n1121
Masterplots 2: drama series, 91n1127
More theatre, 94n1464
Play index 1988-92, 94n1481

DRAMATIC CRITICISM
American drama criticism, suppl.2 to the 2d ed, 90n1129
American drama criticism, suppl.3 to the 2d ed, 93n1168
Drama criticism, v.1, 94n1201
Drama criticism, v.2, 94n1202
Drama criticism, v.3, 94n1203

DRAMATIC MUSIC
Chronology of music in the Florentine theater 1751-1800, 94n1311

DRAMATISTS
American playwrights since 1945, 90n1366
Contemporary authors bibliographical series, v.3, 90n1128
Contemporary dramatists, 5th ed, 94n1467
Samuel Beckett: a ref gd, 90n1204
Twentieth-century German dramatists, 1889-1918, 94n1286
Twentieth-century German dramatists, 1919-92, 94n1287
William Saroyan: a ref gd, 90n1154

DRAWING INSTRUMENTS
Drawing instruments 1580-1980, 90n963

DREAMS
Encyclopedia of sleep & dreaming, 94n808

DREISER, THEODORE
Theodore Dreiser: a primary bibliog & ref gd, 2d ed, 92n1169

DROPOUTS
At-risk youth, 91n310

DROUGHT-ENDURNG PLANTS. *See* AEROPHYTES

DRUG ABUSE. *See* SUBSTANCE ABUSE

DRUG THERAPY. *See* CHEMOTHERAPY

DRUG TRAFFIC
Handbook of research on the illicit drug trade, 93n892
International hndbk on drug control, 94n916

DRUGS. *See also* PHARMACOLOGY
AARP Pharmacy Serv prescription drug hndbk, 2d ed, 93n1660
British pharmacopoeia 1993, 94n1876
Canadian Medical Assn gd to prescription & over-the-counter drugs, 93n1661
Complete drug ref, 1992 ed, 93n1662
Complete gd to prescription & non-prescription drugs, 94n1877
Davis's drug gd for nurses, 2d ed, 92n1692
Dictionary of drugs, 91n1708
Drug educ resources dir, 91n887
Drug info for the health care professional 1992, 93n1663
Drug interactions gd bk, 93n1664
Drugs available abroad, 1991, 92n1693
Drugs, vitamins, minerals in pregnancy, 90n1702
Encyclopedia of drug abuse, 2d ed, 93n890
Essential gd to prescription drugs, 1991 ed, 92n1695
Field drug ref for emergency care providers, 92n1668
Genetically engineered human therapeutic drugs, 90n1700
Guide to fed funding for anti-drug programs 1991, 91n884
Handbook of pediatric drug therapy, 91n1713
Handbook on injectable drugs, 7th ed, 94n1885
Multilingual dict of narcotic drugs & psychotropic substances under intl control, 94n1872
New prescription drug ref gd, 90n1668
PDR family gd to prescription drugs, 94n1879
Pediatric drug hndbk, 2d ed, 90n1698
Pharmaceutical manufacturing ency, 2d ed, 90n1697
Pharmacology from A to Z, 90n1696
Physicians' desk ref, 1993, 94n1880
Physician's drug hndbk, 5th ed, 94n1881
Physicians' generix 1992, 94n1882
Pill bk, 4th ed, 92n1690
Pocket drug gd, 90n1701
Prescription drugs & their side effects, 94n1884
Quick look drug bk with indications index, 93n1665
Red bk, 1993, 94n1883
USAN & the USP dict of drug names, 92n1691
Zimmerman's complete gd to nonprescription drugs, 2d ed, 94n1886

DRUGS IN SPORTS. *See* DOPING IN SPORTS

DRUM (SOUTH AFRICA EDITION)
Drum: an index to "Africa's leading mag 1951-65", 90n107

DU BOIS, W. E. B. (WILLIAM EDWARD BURGHARDT)
World of W. E. B. Du Bois, 93n99

DUCKS
Ducks, 91n1560
Ducks in the wild, 94n1699

DUNCAN, ROBERT EDWARD
Robert Creeley, Edward Dorn, & Robert Duncan, 90n1160

DUNNE, IRENE
Irene Dunne: a bio-bibliog, 92n1343

DUNSANY, EDWARD JOHN MORETON DRAX PLUNKETT, BARON
Lord Dunsany: a bibliog, 94n1292

DUTCH LANGUAGE—DICTIONARIES—ENGLISH
Dutch-English, English-Dutch dict, 92n1065

DVORAK, ANTONIN
Antonin Dvorak on records, 93n1262

DWELLINGS
Affordable housing, 90n967
Complete bk of home environmental hazards, 92n1780
Home improvement cost gd, 2d ed, 91n1029

DYLAN, BOB
Bob Dylan: a bio-bibliog, 94n1379
Positively Bob Dylan, 92n1312

EAR—DISEASES
Encyclopedia of deafness & hearing disorders, 93n1656

EARLY CHILDHOOD EDUCATION
Encyclopedia of early childhood educ, 93n332
Handbook of research on the educ of young children, 94n314
International hndbk of early childhood educ, 94n315
Profiles in childhood educ 1931-60, 94n313

EARTH SATELLITES. *See* ARTIFICIAL SATELLITES

EARTH SCIENCES. *See also* GEOGRAPHY; GEOLOGY
Chambers earth scis dict, 93n1720
Concise Oxford dict of earth scis, 92n1730
Earth's natural forces, 92n1731
Encyclopedia of earth system sci, 93n1721
Information sources in the earth scis, 2d ed, 91n1780
Magill's survey of sci: earth sci series, 91n1778
Nature in America, 93n1526
Oxford illus ency of the universe, 94n1944
Visual dict of the Earth, 94n1946

EAST (U.S.)—POPULATION
Population hist of E US cities & towns, 1790-1870, 93n900

EAST ASIA
Far East & Australasia 1991, 92n120
Guide to E Asian collections in N America, 93n120
Major cos of the Far East & Australasia 1991/92, 8th ed, v.1, 93n281
Security, arms control, & conflict reduction in E Asia & the Pacific, 94n683

EAST EUROPEAN LITERATURE
Reader's ency of E European lit, 94n1281

EAST EUROPEANS
International dir of librarians & lib specialists in the Slavic & E European field, 3d ed, 91n628
Peoples of the world: Eastern Europe & the post-Soviet republics, 94n132

EATING. *See* FOOD HABITS

EATING DISORDERS
Eating disorders, 92n1684
Focus on addictions, 94n917

EBERHART, RICHARD
Richard Eberhart: a descriptive bibliog, 90n1137

ECOLOGY
Atlas of the natural world, 92n1557
Conservation dir 1991, 92n1788
Dictionary of ecology & environmental sci, 94n1994
Dictionary of environmental quotations, 93n1777
Dictionary of the environment, 3d ed, 90n1791
Encyclopedia of environmental studies, 92n1773
Energy & environmental terms, 90n1775
Expert systems in geography & environmental studies, 91n445
Island Pr bibliog of environmental lit, 94n1990

ECOLOGY IN LITERATURE
E for environment, 93n1752

ECONOMETRICS
World tables, 1988-89 ed, 90n193

ECONOMIC ASSISTANCE, CANADIAN
GAPS, 92n142

ECONOMIC ASSISTANCE, DOMESTIC
Assistance & benefits info dir, 93n887
Federal domestic outlays 1983-90, 93n745
Federal funding gd 1989, 90n822
Government assistance almanac 1989-90, 90n806
Government assistance almanac 1992-93, 93n874

ECONOMIC ASSISTANCE, JAPANESE
Inside Japanese support 1992, 93n280

ECONOMIC CONDITIONS. *See* ECONOMIC HISTORY

ECONOMIC CYCLES. *See* BUSINESS CYCLES

ECONOMIC DEVELOPMENT
Development report card for the states, 1993, 94n170
Dictionary of environment & dvlpmt, 94n1995
Handbook of dvlpmt economics, 91n151
Indian social & economic dvlpmt, 1987, 90n194
International dvlpmt dict, 92n125
Lexicon of economic thought, 90n165

ECONOMIC FORECASTING
Handbook of economic cycles, 93n201
World index of economic forecasts, 3d ed, 90n195

ECONOMIC GEOGRAPHY
New state of the world atlas, 4th ed, 93n475

ECONOMIC HISTORY
Atlas of the world economy, 92n141
World economy, 94n157
World fact file, 92n83
World tables, 1988-89 ed, 90n193

ECONOMIC INDICATORS
Atlas of the world economy, 92n141
Economic indicators hndbk, 93n204
Measuring global values, 93n729

ECONOMIC POLICY
Economic planning 1943-51, 94n263
Economist atlas, 93n172
Lexicon of economic thought, 90n165
Short-term economic stats: Central & E Europe, 93n292

ECONOMIC SANCTIONS, AMERICAN
United States sanctions & S Africa, 94n545

ECONOMIC SURVEYS
World economic data, 2d ed, 90n189

ECONOMICS. *See also* BUSINESS; COMMERCE; ECONOMISTS; FINANCE; INDUSTRY; STATISTICS; TAXATION; WEALTH
Bibliographic gd to bus & economics 1990, 92n121
Bibliography of histl economics to 1980, 92n123
Bibliography of law & economics, 93n564
Business & legal CD-ROMS in print 1993, 94n175
Canadian dict of bus & economics, 94n247
Dictionary of economics, 93n185
Economic methodology, 90n157
Encyclopedic dict of economics, 4th ed, 93n180
Glossary of Islamic economics, 91n133
HarperCollins dict of economics, 92n126
Index of economic articles in jls & collective volumes, v.29, 91n165
International current awareness servs: economics & related disciplines, v.2, no.1, 92n147
International writings of Bohdan S. Wynar, 1949-92, 94n80
Last word on making money, 90n219
Lexicon of economics, 90n166
Lexicon of economics, 93n181
Macrothesaurus for info processing in the field of economic & social dvlpmt, 93n641
MIT dict of modern economics, 4th ed, 93n183
One hundred yrs of economic stats, 91n158
Penguin dict of economics, 5th ed, 94n159
Rand McNally 1990 commercial atlas & mktg gd, 91n276
Survey of social sci: economics series, 92n127
Thematic list of descriptors: economics, 91n168
William J. Fellner: a bio-bibliog, 94n154

ECONOMICS—DICTIONARIES—RUSSIAN
Russian-English/English-Russian dict of free market era economics, 94n160

ECONOMISTS
Biographical dict of dissenting economists, 93n177
Great economists before Keynes, 90n161
Nobel laureates in economic scis, 90n163
William J. Fellner: a bio-bibliog, 94n154

ECUADOR
Ecuador, 91n120

ECUMENICAL MOVEMENT
Dictionary of the Ecumenical movement, 92n1416
Ecumenism: a bibliographical overview, 94n1524

EDDY, NELSON
Nelson Eddy: a bio-discography, 93n1277

EDITING
American Medical Assn manual of style, 8th ed, 90n895
Chicago manual of style, 14th ed, 94n1001
Copy-editing, 3d ed, 94n1000
Copyediting: a practical gd, 2d ed, 91n949
Directory of editorial resources, 1989-90, 90n894
Directory of pubn resources, 1991-92, 92n895
Directory of pubn resources, 1993-94, 94n995
Editing: an annot bibliog, 92n897
Editing docs & texts, 91n951
Fine art of copyediting, 92n898

Guide to info sources for the preparation, editing, & production of docs, 90n896
Insider's gd to bk editors & pubs 1990-91, 91n947
Publication peer review, 94n997

EDITORS
Insider's gd to bk editors & pubs 1990-91, 91n947
Who's who in writers, eds & poets, 1992-93, 93n974

EDUCATION
Advanced research methodology, 92n73
American educators' ency, 93n330
Bibliographic gd to educ 1991, 94n303
Bibliographic gd to educl research, 3d ed, 92n267
Bibliography on educ in dvlpmt & social change in sub-Saharan Africa, 91n291
Canadian Educ Assn hdnbk 1991, 92n276
Core list of bks & jls in educ, 92n270
Directory of state legislative staff for educ issues, 90n305
Education: a gd to ref & info sources, 90n298
Education in Canada, 90n300
Education in England & Wales, 92n316
Education in Japan, 90n306
Education in the Arab Gulf states & the Arab world, 93n384
Education index, 93n341
Educational rankings annual 1991, 92n278
Educator's desk ref, 90n307
Encyclopedia of educl research, 6th ed, 93n331
Facts on File dict of educ, 90n303
Guide to American educl dirs, 6th ed, 92n275
Guide to free computer materials, 90n341
Guide to journals in psychology & educ, 91n795
Higher educ in India, 93n391
Higher educ in the UK 1992-93, 93n386
International yrbk of educl & training tech 1991, 92n282
Legislative studies in state educ policy 1976-88, 90n308
@Micro: educl sftwr evaluations 89/90, 91n361
Only the best 1985-89, 90n342
Only the best 1990, 90n343
Public schooling in America, 93n354
Publication sources in educl leadership, 93n343
Resources for educl equity, 90n311
Russian & Soviet educ 1731-1989, 93n383
State educ docs, 91n295
Thesaurus of ERIC descriptors, 12th ed, 91n302
Who's who in American educ, 1988-89, 90n301
Women's educ in the Third World, 90n861
World of learning 1993, 94n308

EDUCATION—CURRICULA
Guide to the evaluation of educl experiences in the armed servs, 1992, 94n307
Handbook of research on curriculum, 93n334
International ency of curriculum, 92n274

EDUCATION, ELEMENTARY
Directory of Canadian schools 1988, 91n304
Elementary teachers gd to free curriculum materials, 50th ed, 94n318
El-Hi textbks & serials in print 1989, 90n299
El-Hi textbks & serials in print 1991, 92n285
Kits, games & manipulatives for the elementary school classroom, 94n378
Multicultural educ, 90n319
National gd to funding for elementary & secondary educ, 92n287
Patterson's elementary educ, v.2, 1990 ed, 91n306
Patterson's elementary educ, v.5, 94n320
Private independent schools 1988, 90n316
Private schools of the US, 90n317

EDUCATION—EUROPE
European educ thesaurus, 1991 ed, 93n385

EDUCATION—GRADUATE WORK
Graduate curricula in educl communications & tech, 4th ed, 94n379
Peterson's gd to graduate & professional programs 1989, 90n328
Peterson's gd to graduate & professional programs, 25th ed, 92n309

EDUCATION, HIGHER
Academic yr abroad 1989/90, 90n345
Accredited insts of postsecondary educ, 1990-91, 92n290
Accredited insts of postsecondary educ, programs, candidates, 1992-93, 94n347
Almanac of higher educ 1989-90, 90n332
Almanac of higher educ 1992, 93n355
American higher educ, 94n323
Atlas of American higher educ, 94n321
Bear's gd to earning non-traditional college degrees, 10th ed, 90n323
Chronicle 4-yr college databk, 1988-89, 90n333
Chronicle 4-yr college databk for 1991-92 school yr, 93n368
Chronicle 2-yr college databk, 1988-89, 90n334
Chronicle 2-yr college databk for 1991-92 school yr, 93n369
Collective bargaining in higher educ & the professions, bibliog no.20, 94n269
College admissions data hndbk 1989-90, 90n335
Directory of faculty contracts & bargaining agents in insts of higher ed, v.15, 90n325
Directory of non-faculty bargaining agents in insts of higher educ, 92n294
Directory of the US postsecondary educ, 90n324
Encyclopedia of higher educ, 93n358
Fact bk on women in higher educ, 92n311
Faculty white pages 1989, 90n327
Faculty white pages 1991, 93n361
National gd to fndn funding in higher educ, 91n317
Peterson's gd to colleges with programs for learning-disabled students, 2d ed, 90n349
Peterson's register of higher educ 1990, 91n319
Peterson's register of higher educ 1993, 94n344

EDUCATION LIBRARIES
National dir of educ libs & collections, 91n655

EDUCATION OF ADULTS. *See* **ADULT EDUCATION**

EDUCATION, SECONDARY. *See also* **PRIVATE SCHOOLS**
College Board gd to high schools, 91n307
Directory of Canadian schools 1988, 91n304
Directory of online databases & CD-ROM resources for high schools, 90n344
El-Hi textbks & serials in print 1989, 90n299
National gd to funding for elementary & secondary educ, 92n287
Patterson's American educ, v.86, 91n305
Patterson's American educ, v.89, 94n319
Peterson's gd to independent secondary schools 1991-92, 92n288

EDUCATION—SOFTWARE
Policies of educl sftwr publs, 92n328

EDUCATION, SPECIAL. *See* **SPECIAL EDUCATION**

EDUCATIONAL EQUALIZATION
Resources for educl equity, 90n311

EDUCATIONAL EVALUATION
International ency of educl evaluation, 91n300

EDUCATIONAL EXCHANGES
Foreign students & intl study, 91n341

EDUCATIONAL GAMES
Kits, games & manipulatives for the elementary school classroom, 94n378

EDUCATIONAL LITERATURE
Educators gd to free videotapes, 39th ed, 93n396
Educators index of free materials, 101st ed, 93n328
Guide to journals in psychology & educ, 91n795

EDUCATIONAL MEDIA. *See* **TEACHING—AIDS & DEVICES**

EDUCATIONAL MEDIA CENTERS. *See* **INSTRUCTIONAL MATERIALS CENTERS**

EDUCATIONAL PUBLISHING
Cabell's dir of publ opportunities in educ, 3d ed, 94n663

EDUCATIONAL TECHNOLOGY
Educational media & tech yrbk, v.16, 91n298
Educational media & tech yrbk, v.17, 92n327
Educational media & tech yrbk, v.18, 93n398
Emerging techs & instruction, 93n344
Glossary of educl tech terms, 94n377
Graduate curricula in educl communications & tech, 4th ed, 94n379
International ency of educl tech, 91n359
International yrbk of educl & training tech 1992/93, 94n382
Vocabulary of educl tech & training, 92n326

EDUCATIONAL TESTING SERVICE
ETS test collection cat, v.1, 2d ed, 94n304
ETS test collection cat, v.3, 90n302
ETS test collection cat, v.4, 91n293
ETS test collection cat, v.5, 92n273
ETS test collection cat, v.6, 93n329

EDUCATIONAL TESTS & MEASUREMENTS
Educational & psychological tests in the Academic Lib, 91n292
ETS test collection cat, v.1, 2d ed, 94n304
ETS test collection cat, v.3, 90n302
ETS test collection cat, v.4, 91n293
ETS test collection cat, v.5, 92n273
ETS test collection cat, v.6, 93n329
Index to tests used in educl dissertations, 90n310
Instrumentation in educ, 94n306
Supplement to the 10th mental measurements yrbk, 92n760
Test critiques, v.9, 93n337
Tests: a comprehensive ref for assessments in psychology, educ, & bus, 3d ed, 93n338

EGYPT
Ancient Egypt, 91n542
Bibliography of the Amarna period & its aftermath, 92n501
Egypt, 90n148
Egyptian pyramids, 92n505
Encyclopedia of ancient Egypt, 92n506
Gamal Abdel Nasser: a bibliog, 93n543
Guide to the archaeological sites of Israel, Egypt, & N Africa, 91n478
Nile notes of a howadji, 93n163

EIGHTEENTH CENTURY
Eighteenth century: a current bibliog, n.s.11, 92n871

EIGNER, LARRY
Larry Eigner: a bibliog of his works, 90n1138

EISENHOWER, DWIGHT D.
Dwight D. Eisenhower: a bibliog of his times & presidency, 92n456
Dwight D. Eisenhower: a centennial bibliog, 1890-1990, 92n464

EKG. *See* ELECTROCARDIOGRAPHY

EL SALVADOR
El Salvador, 90n143

ELASTOMERS
Handbook of plastics, elastomers, & composites, 2d ed, 93n1714

ELECTIONS
Almanac of Canadian pols, 93n764
America votes 19, 92n696
America votes 20, 94n756
American natl election studies data sourcebk, 1952-86, 91n751
British electorate, 1963-87, 93n772
Canada votes 1935-88, 91n756
Congressional Quarterly's pols in America 1990, 90n691
Congressional Quarterly's pols in America 1994, 94n749
Election data bk, 94n751
Elections since 1945, 90n684
Electoral pols dict, 90n695
Historic docs on presidential elections 1787-1988, 93n753
Historical atlas of state power in congress, 1790-1990, 94n725
International almanac of electoral hist, 3d ed, 92n677
People speak: American elections in focus, 91n748
Political parties & elections in the US, 92n685
Price of admission, 91n727

ELECTIONEERING
World almanac of presidential campaigns, 93n732

ELECTRIC APPARATUS & APPLIANCES
Pocket gd to electrical equipment & instrumentation, 2d ed, 93n1599

ELECTRIC CABLES
Lineman's & cableman's hndbk, 8th ed, 93n1598

ELECTRIC ENGINEERING
American electricians' hndbk, 12th ed, 93n1587
Dictionary of measurement engineering & units, 93n1597
Electrical engineering materials ref gd, 91n1613
Encyclopedic dict of electronics, electrical engineering & info processing, 91n1619
History of electrical tech, 93n1593
McGraw-Hill's natl electrical code hndbk, 20th ed, 91n1617
McGraw-Hill's natl electrical code hndbk, 21st ed, 94n1786
Parat index of acronyms & abbrevs in electrical & electronic engineering, 90n1592
Pocket gd to electrical equipment & instrumentation, 2d ed, 93n1599
Sources in electrical hist, 91n1614
Standard hndbk for electrical engineers, 13th ed, 94n1777
Yearbook suppl. to McGraw-Hill's natl electrical code hndbk, 1991, 92n1609

ELECTRIC INDUSTRIES
Electric utility industry sftwr dir, 1992, 93n1590

ELECTRIC LINES
Lineman's & cableman's hndbk, 8th ed, 93n1598

ELECTRIC POWER
Electric power in Canada 1989, 92n1761

ELECTRIC UTILITIES
EL&P US electric utility industry dir, 1992, 93n1589
European electric utility dir, 1993, 94n1783

ELECTROCARDIOGRAPHY
Comprehensive electrocardiology, 90n1685

ELECTRONIC APPARATUS & APPLIANCES
Electronic packaging, microelectronics, & interconnection dict, 94n1781

ELECTRONIC CIRCUITS
Encyclopedia of electronic circuits, v.3, 92n1602
Encyclopedia of electronic circuits, v.4, 94n1778
McGraw-Hill circuit ency & troubleshooting gd, v.1, 94n1784
Modern measuring circuit ency, 94n1779

ELECTRONIC DATA PROCESSING
Archives of data-processing hist, 91n1731
Bibliographic gd to the hist of computing, computers, & the info processing industry, 91n1721
Computer dict, 3d ed, 93n1681
Computer dict, 4th ed, 94n1904
Computer glossary, 4th ed, 91n1723
Concise ency of info processing in systems & orgs, 91n1727
Desktop dict of info systems tech, 91n634
English-Japanese, Japanese-English dict of computer & data-processing terms, 90n1713
Glossary informatics, 91n605
Glossary of computing terms, 6th ed, 90n1714
HarperCollins dict of computer terms, 92n1708
High-technology editorial gd & stylebk, PC ed, 93n969
Libraries, info centers, & databases in sci & tech, 2d ed, 90n624
New hacker's dict, 93n1680

ELECTRONIC MEASUREMENTS
Modern measuring circuit ency, 94n1779

ELECTRONIC MUSIC
Dictionary of musical tech, 93n1246

ELECTRONIC PUBLISHING
Directory of electronic jls, newsletters & academic discussion lists, 2d ed, 93n72
Guide to the lit of electronic publishing, 90n628
Language of computer publishing, 91n659

ELECTRONICS
Computer engineering hndbk, 94n1774
Electronic news financial fact bk & dir 1989-90, 91n176
Electronic packaging & interconnection hndbk, 92n1603
Electronic packaging, microelectronics, & interconnection dict, 94n1781
Electronic packaging, microelectronics, & interconnection dict, 94n1781
Electronic research centres, 2d ed, 90n1580
Encyclopedia of electronics, 2d ed, 91n1616
Encyclopedic dict of electronics, electrical engineering & info processing, 91n1619
European electronics dir 1993, 94n1787
Guide to the lit of electronic publishing, 90n628
HarperCollins dict of electronics, 93n1595
Illustrated dict of electronics, 5th ed, 92n1607
International defense electronic systems hndbk, 93n718
Parat index of acronyms & abbrevs in electrical & electronic engineering, 90n1592

ELECTRONICS IN MILITARY ENGINEERING
Jane's radar & electronic warfare systems 1989-90, 91n709

ELEMENTARY SCHOOL LIBRARIES
Adventuring with bks, 9th ed, 90n1075
Elementary school lib collection, 18th ed, 93n667

ELEMENTARY SCHOOLS
Directory of school mediation & conflict resolution programs, 90n313

ELGAR, EDWARD
Edward Elgar: a gd to research, 94n1327

ELIOT, GEORGE
George Eliot: a ref gd 1972-87, 91n1207

EMBASSIES. *See* **AMBASSADORS**

EMBLEM BOOKS
Century of emblems, 91n669
Princeton Alciati companion, 90n1051
Short title cat of the emblem bks...in the Stirling Maxwell collection, rev ed, 90n632

EMBLEMS
Our natl symbols, 93n1309
Reverse symbolism dict, 93n1311

EMBROIDERY
Batsford ency of embroidery techniques, 92n947
Embroidery & needlepoint, 90n932

EMERGENCIES. *See* **ACCIDENTS**

EMERGENCY MEDICINE
International translation gd for emergency medicine, 94n1825
Mosby's emergency dict, 90n1613
National dir of fire chiefs & emergency depts, 1993, 94n878
Police, firefighter, & paramedic stress, 91n787

EMERGING NATIONS. *See* **DEVELOPING COUNTRIES**

EMIGRATION. *See* **IMMIGRATION**

EMIGRATION & IMMIGRATION
Atlas of intl migration, 94n428
Complete bk of emigrants 1661-99, 91n416
Complete bk of emigrants 1751-76, 94n430
Handbook on intl migration, 92n756
Immigration glossary, 91n779
Immigration made simple, 91n780
Immigration stats 1987, 91n778
Immigration stats 1991, 94n803
Index to the decisions rendered by the Immigration Appeal Board, 90n563
International Migration Review cum index, 1964-89, 92n339
Passenger & immigration lists index, 1992 suppl., 93n460
Refugee & immigrant resource dir 1990-91, 91n878
Wuerttemberg emigration index, v.5, 90n399

EMIGRATION & IMMIGRATION LAW
Hein's cum index to interim precedent decisions of the Board of Immigration Appeals, 93n599
Insider's gd to successful US immigration, 93n589

EMPLOYEE ASSISTANCE PROGRAMS
Employee assistance progs, 90n259

EMPLOYEE FRINGE BENEFITS
Companies that care, 93n312
Employee benefit plans, 8th ed, 94n272
Employee benefits dict, 94n271

EMPLOYEES' MAGAZINES, HANDBOOKS, ETC.
Corporate mags of the US, 93n217

EMPLOYEES, RATING OF
Guide to background investigations, 3d ed, 90n258

EMPLOYEES, TRAINING OF
Linton register, 1990-91, 91n247
Linton trainer's resource dir, 2d ed, 94n275
National gd to educl credit for training programs, 1992-93 ed, 94n392
Staff training, 91n252
Trainer's resource 1989, 90n256
Training & dvlpmt orgs dir, 5th ed, 93n307
Training dir for bus & industry 1989-90, 90n263
Videos for bus & training 1989, 90n192

EMPLOYERS' ASSOCIATIONS
Employers' orgs of the world, 92n234

EMPLOYER-SUPPORTED DAY CARE
Companies that care, 93n312

EMPLOYMENT (ECONOMIC THEORY)
Employment glossary, 91n243
European employment & industrial relations glossary: Spain, 93n295
European employment & industrial relations glossary: UK, 93n297
Urban informal sector in Africa in retrospect & prospect, 93n277

EMPLOYMENT IN FOREIGN COUNTRIES
Directory of jobs & careers abroad, 8th ed, 94n273
Directory of overseas summer jobs, 1991, 92n218

ENCINO PRESS
William D. Wittliff & the Encino Pr, 91n657

ENCYCLICALS, PAPAL
Papal encyclicals, 1740-1981, 92n1419
Papal pronouncements: a gd, 1740-1981, 92n1409

ENCYCLOPEDIAS & DICTIONARIES. *See also* **CHILDREN'S ENCYCLOPEDIAS & DICTIONARIES**
Academic American ency, 90n45
Academic American ency, 93n57
Australian ref dict, 93n131
Barron's new student's concise ency, 2d ed, 94n32
Britannica bk of the yr, 1991, 92n42
Cambridge ency, 94n33
Cassell ency dict, 92n37
Collier's ency, 92n39
Compton's ency, 90n48
Compton's ency & fact-index, 94n34
Concise Columbia ency, 2d ed, 90n49
Dictionary for bus & finance, 90n168
Dictionary of dicts, 94n1073
Encyclopedia Americana, 90n50
Encyclopedia Americana, intl ed, 93n59
First stop, 90n75
From archetype to zeitgeist, 93n1060
Information China, 90n121
Merit student's ency, 92n40
New bk of knowledge, 93n60
New ency Britannica, 92n41
New standard ency, 91n32

New standard ency, 93n62
Oxford illus ency, v.3, 90n535
Oxford illus ency, v.4, 90n536
People's Almanac presents the bk of lists: the '90s ed, 94n1403
Professional secretary's encyclopedic dict, 4th ed, 90n291
Purchasing an ency, 3d ed, 91n33
Purchasing an ency, 4th ed, 94n38
Random House ency, 3d ed, 91n34
Running Pr cyclopedia, 94n40
Webster's II New Riverside desk ref, home & office ed, 93n5
Webster's illus dict ency, 91n35
Webster's new world ency, 93n63
Webster's new world ency, college ed, 94n42
Webster's new world ency, pocket ed, 94n43
World Bk dict, 92n1020
World bk ency, 90n54
World Bk ency, 93n64

ENCYCLOPEDIAS & DICTIONARIES—YEARBOOKS—INDEXES
Subject index to feature articles & special reports in ency yrbks 1975-91, 94n35

END OF THE WORLD
Millennialism: an intl bibliog, 93n1399

ENDANGERED SPECIES. *See also* WILDLIFE CONSERVATION
Atlas of endangered animals, 94n1686
California's wild heritage, 91n1551
Endangered vertebrates, 91n1553
Endangered wildlife of the world, 94n1676
Extinction A-Z, 92n1520
Grolier world ency of endangered species, 94n1680
Guide to Michigan's endangered wildlife, 94n1677
Threatened birds of the Americas, pt.2, 3d ed, 94n1695

ENDOWMENTS
America's new fndns 1992, 93n870
Annual register of grant support, 26th ed, 94n888
Corporate 500, 9th ed, 92n823
Corporate fndn profiles, 7th ed, 94n900
Directory of new & emerging fndns, 2d ed, 92n824
Education Interface gd to corporate support, v.1, no.3, 91n297
EHR dir of awards: fiscal yr 1990, 93n875
Foundation dir, 12th ed, 91n866
Foundation dir, 15th ed, 94n890
Foundation dir pt.2, 1993 ed, 94n891
Foundation giving, 1993 ed, 94n896
Foundation grants index, 18th ed, 90n823
Foundation grants index quarterly. Mar 1990, 91n867
Foundation 1000 1992/93, 94n897
Foundation reporter 1993, 94n902
Free money for small businesses & entrepreneurs, 91n211
Fund raiser's gd to human serv funding, 2d ed, 91n868
Fund raiser's gd to religious philanthropy, 3d ed, 91n1416
Funding for museums, archives & special collections, 90n811
Grant seekers gd, 3d ed, 90n810
Guide to funding for intl & foreign programs, 93n880
Guide to US fndns, their trustees, officers, & donors, 1993 ed, 94n892
Inside Japanese support 1992, 93n280
International ency of fndns, 91n869
Literature of the nonprofit sector, 90n804
Literature of the nonprofit sector, v.2, 91n865
Major donors 1993, 94n893
National data bk of fndns, 16th ed, 93n879
National dir of corporate giving, 91n144
National gd to fndn funding in higher educ, 91n317
National gd to funding for children, youth & families, 92n827
National gd to funding for elementary & secondary educ, 92n287
National gd to funding for libs & info servs, 92n573
National gd to funding for libs & info servs, 2d ed, 94n618
National gd to funding for the environment & animal welfare, 93n881
National gd to funding for women & girls, 92n865
National gd to funding in arts & culture, 91n931
National gd to funding in religion, 93n1411
Philanthropic studies index, 92n828
Taft gd to corporate giving contacts, 6th ed, 91n864

ENERGY. *See* FORCE & ENERGY; POWER RESOURCES

ENERGY DEVELOPMENT
SYNERJY, summer-fall 1989, v.16, 91n1801

ENERGY POLICY
Energy balances of OECD countries 1980-89, 93n1746
Energy info abstracts annual 1988, 90n1781
Energy stats of OECD countries 1980-89, 93n1747
Independent power 1989 dir, 90n1777
U.S. energy & environmental interest groups, 92n1753
World energy dir, 3d ed, 90n1779

ENGINEERING. *See also specific types of engineering*
Aerospace tech centres, 90n1579
Dictionary of engineering & tech, 5th ed, 91n1606
Dictionary of engineering acronyms & abbrevs, 90n1574
Directory of AAAS sci & engineering fellows 1973-92, 94n1573
Directory, 1992: AAAS consortium of affiliates for intl programs, 94n1572
Ei thesaurus, 94n1753
Encyclopedia of applied physics, v.2, 93n1733
Encyclopedia of applied physics, v.3, 93n1734
Encyclopedia of architecture design, engineering & construction, v.2, 90n972
Encyclopedia of architecture design, engineering & construction, v.3, 90n973
Encyclopedia of physical scis & engineering info sources, 90n1424
Financial Times industrial cos, v.3, 90n1573
History of engineering sci, 90n1572
Japanese/English, English/Japanese glossary of scientific & technical terms, 94n1571
Macmillan ency of sci, 92n1456
Magill's survey of sci: applied sci series, 94n1583
McGraw-Hill ency of engineering, 2d ed, 94n1785
Peterson's engineering, sci, & computer jobs 1989, 90n188
Russian-English sci & engineering dict, 90n1429
Scientific & technical pers of the 17th & 18th centuries, 93n1463
Wood engineering & construction hndbk, 90n1589

ENGINEERING INSTRUMENTS
Comprehensive dict of instrumentation & control, 90n1576

ENGINEERING MEASUREMENTS
Comprehensive dict of measurement & control, 2d ed, 93n1607

ENGINEERS
Biographies of scientists for sci-tech libs, 93n1440

ENGLAND
Antiquing in England, 91n979
Biographical dict of actors, actresses, musicians, dancers, managers & other stage personnel in London, 1660-1800, v.13, 92n1378
Biographical dict of actors, actresses, musicians, dancers, managers & other stage personnel in London, 1660-1800, v.14, 92n1379
British dirs, 90n133
Butterworths law dir 1993, 94n558
Concise dict of law, 2d ed, 91n572
Contemporary printed lit of the English counter-reformation between 1558 & 1640, v.1, 91n1440
Dictionary of banking, 94n207
Dictionary of English law, 93n575
Dictionary of English place names, 93n493
Education in England & Wales, 92n316
Index to bk reviews in England 1749-74, 91n1190
List of emigrants from England to America, 1682-92, 90n392
London stage 1930-39, 92n1388
London stage 1940-49, 93n1386
London stage 1950-59, 94n1469
Mystery reader's walking gd: England, 90n459
Oxford hist of England: consolidated index, 92n485
Private libs in renaissance England, v.1, 94n598
Private libs in renaissance England, v.2, 94n599

Women in English social hist 1800-1914, v.1, 91n915
Yearbook of English festivals, 94n1406

ENGLAND—CHURCH HISTORY
English religion 1500-40, 90n1379

ENGLAND—CIVILIZATION
Historical dict of Tudor England, 1485-1603, 93n532

ENGLAND—HISTORY
Plant names of medieval England, 91n1521
Who's who in late medieval England (1272-1485), 92n483

ENGLISH DRAMA
Caroline drama, 2d ed, 93n1202
Critical analyses in English Renaissance drama, 92n1196
Drama by women to 1990, 93n1146
Medieval English drama, 91n1191
Restoration & 18th-century dramatists, 90n1170
Restoration drama, 91n1193
Scott dramatized, 93n1210
Sir John Vanbrugh: a ref gd, 94n975

ENGLISH DRAMA—IRISH AUTHORS
Contemporary Irish dramatists, 90n1205

ENGLISH FICTION
Dictionary of British literary characters: 18th- & 19th-century novels, 94n1243
English novel explication, suppl.4, 91n1194
English Renaissance prose fiction, 1500-1660, 93n1203
Female bildungsroman in English, 91n1130
Genreflecting, 3d ed, 93n1147
Heroines, 91n1129
Novels of WW II, 91n1131
Of a certain age, 92n1141
Out of the closet & into the classroom, 94n906
Oxford in fiction, 90n1171
Victorian novel, 91n1195

ENGLISH IMPRINTS
Twentieth-century German novel, 91n1236

ENGLISH LANGUAGE
American Heritage college dict, 3d ed, 94n1075
Collection of definitions in fed statutes, 90n545
Collection of dicts & related works illustrating the dvlpmt of the English dict, 91n1045
Dictionary of chemistry & chemical tech, 4th ed, 91n1772
Dictionary of cultural literacy, 2d ed, 94n305
Dictionary of engineering & tech, 5th ed, 91n1606
Dictionary of process tech, 91n1609
Elsevier's dict of civil engineering, 90n1587
Elsevier's dict of export financing & credit insurance, 91n264
English-Japanese, Japanese-English dict of computer & data-processing terms, 90n1713
Fifth dir of pers, 94n986
Forest inventory terms in Canada, 3d ed, 90n1464
French dict of info tech, 90n610
French-English dict of industrial lang, 91n234
Glossary informatics, 91n605
Glossary of helicopters, 90n1804
Glossary of museology, 90n954
Handbook of English & Celtic studies in the UK and Republic of Ireland, 2d ed, 90n1169
Human rights, 90n574
Medical English usage & abusage, 92n1671
Merriam-Webster concise hndbk for writers, 93n964
Oxford companion to the English lang, 90n1054
Packaging, 90n1426
Penguin dict for writers & eds, 93n968
Scientific English, 93n958
Space war glossary, 90n677
Spanish-English hndbk for medical professionals, 3d ed, 90n1670

ENGLISH LANGUAGE—ACRONYMS. See ACRONYMS

ENGLISH LANGUAGE—AUSTRALIA—DICTIONARIES
Australian concise Oxford dict, 94n1096
Australian natl dict, 90n1027
Australian words & their origins, 91n1075
Dictionary of Australian colloquialisms, 92n1052
Kangaroo's comments & wallaby's words, 90n1026

ENGLISH LANGUAGE—CANADA—DICTIONARIES
Dictionary of Canadianisms on histl principles, 92n1049
Funk & Wagnalls Canadian college dict, rev ed, 90n1025
Penguin Canadian dict, 92n1050
Straight from the horse's mouth, 90n1008
Young Canada dict, 2d ed, 90n1028
Young Canada thesaurus, 90n1029

ENGLISH LANGUAGE—COLLECTIVE NOUNS
Crash of rhinoceroses, 94n1106

ENGLISH LANGUAGE—COMPOUND WORDS
Portmanteau dict, 94n1083

ENGLISH LANGUAGE—DIALECTS. See also AMERICANISMS; ENGLISH LANGUAGE—PROVINCIALISMS
Dictionary of American regional English, v.2, 93n1062
Dictionary of the American west, 94n1088
Index by region, usage, & etymology to the Dict of American Regional English, v.1 & 2, 94n1090
Index to dialect maps of Great Britain, 93n1067
Linguistic atlas of the gulf states, v.3, 91n1064

ENGLISH LANGUAGE—DICTIONARIES. See also PICTURE DICTIONARIES
American Heritage dict, 2d college ed, 93n1055
American Heritage dict of the English lang, 3d ed, 93n1056
British English for American readers, 93n1068
Canadian primary dict, 92n1045
Cassell pocket English dict, 92n1016
Chambers concise dict, 93n1057
Concise Oxford dict of current English, 8th ed, 91n1048
Dictionary of Alaskan English, 92n1042
Dictionary of epithets & terms of address, 91n1062
Early modern English lexicography, v.1, 91n1044
Funk & Wagnalls standard dict, 2d ed, 94n1077
In the field: the lang of the Vietnam War, 92n476
Kister's best dicts for adults & young people, 93n1048
Merriam-Webster concise school & office dict, 93n1058
Merriam-Webster's collegiate dict, 10th ed, 94n1076
New lexicon dict of basic words, new ed, 91n1074
New Merriam-Webster dict for large print users, 91n1067
New shorter Oxford English Dict on historical principles, 94n1099
1000 most obscure words, 91n1054
Oxford encyclopedic English dict, 92n1017
Oxford modern English dict, 94n1100
Pocket Oxford dict of current English, 8th ed, 94n1078
Random House college dict, rev ed, 90n999
Random House Webster's college dict, 93n1059
Scott, Foresman advanced dict, 90n1020
Third Barnhart dict of new English, 91n1059
Webster's II new Riverside pocket dict, rev ed, 92n1019
Webster's new ideal dict, 2d ed, 91n1049
Webster's new world dict, 92n1018
Webster's 9th new collegiate dict, 91n1050
Words of the Vietnam War, 92n475

ENGLISH LANGUAGE—DICTIONARIES—ALBANIAN
Albanian-English dict, 94n1109

ENGLISH LANGUAGE—DICTIONARIES—BASQUE
Basque-English dict, 90n1036

ENGLISH LANGUAGE—DICTIONARIES—BIBLIOGRAPHY
Catalog of dicts, word bks, & philological texts, 1440-1900, 94n1074

ENGLISH LANGUAGE—DICTIONARIES—BYELORUSSIAN
Byelorussian-English, English-Byelorussian dict with complete phonetics, 93n1079

ENGLISH LANGUAGE—DICTIONARIES—CAMBODIAN
Cambodian-English English-Cambodian dict, 91n1082

ENGLISH LANGUAGE—DICTIONARIES—CHINESE
English-Chinese glossary of American criminal law & criminal procedure law, 91n571
Facts on File English/Chinese visual dict, 90n1037
Oxford-Duden pictorial Chinese & English dict, 90n1039
Practical English-Chinese pronouncing dir, 94n1110
Quick reference Chinese, 90n1038

ENGLISH LANGUAGE—DICTIONARIES—DAKOTA
Dakota-English dict, 94n1111
English-Dakota dict, 94n1112

ENGLISH LANGUAGE—DICTIONARIES—DANISH
Danish-English, English-Danish dict, 91n1083

ENGLISH LANGUAGE—DICTIONARIES—DUTCH
Dutch-English, English-Dutch dict, 92n1065

ENGLISH LANGUAGE—DICTIONARIES—ESTONIAN
Estonian-English, English-Estonian dict, 93n1082

ENGLISH LANGUAGE—DICTIONARIES—FRENCH
Ada lang vocablary, 93n1677
Adrienne's dict: English/French, 92n1066
Air-conditioning glossary, 91n1635
Ashley dict, 90n1040
Beginning French bilingual dict, 2d ed, 90n1044
Canadian quaternary vocabulary, 94n1943
Collins-Robert French-English, English-French dict, 2d ed, 94n1113
Combinatory vocab of CAD/CAM in mechanical engineering, 94n1916
Constitutional glossary, 94n553
Dictionary of Canadian French, 92n1069
Dictionnaire francais, 90n1041
Employment glossary, 91n243
French-English agricultural dict, 93n1465
Glossary geotextiles, 93n1609
Glossary of security equipment, 94n1776
Glossary of water terms, 94n1951
Graphic arts vocabulary, 94n1058
Harper Collins French dict, college ed, 91n1084
Immigration glossary, 91n779
International illus vocabulary of English-French fingerprint terminology..., 93n607
Let's learn French picture dict, 92n1067
NTC's French & English bus dict, 93n182
NTC's new college French & English dict, 92n1068
Oxford paperback French dict, 90n1043
Ozone layer dict, 94n1945
Phonetics & speech sci, 90n992
Public admin & mgmt vocabulary, 91n782
Space station glossary, 93n1581
Statistics & surveys vocabulary, 93n905
Stoddart colour visual dict: French-English, 94n1114
Taxation glossary, 3d ed, 91n288
Unemployment insurance glossary, 93n252
Vocabulary of cell engineering, v.1, 93n1600
Vocabulary of genetic engineering, 91n1621
Vocabulary of free trade, 93n233
Vocabulary of hazardous materials in the workplace, 94n1997
Vocabulary of medical signs & symptoms, 91n1665
Vocabulary of public sector auditing, 94n249
Vocabulary of safety & security equipment, 93n1601
Vocabulary of signs & symptoms of the musculoskeletal system, v.1, 91n1666

ENGLISH LANGUAGE—DICTIONARIES—GEORGIAN
Georgian-English, English-Georgian dict, 93n1084

ENGLISH LANGUAGE—DICTIONARIES—GERMAN
Collins German-English, English-German dict unabridged, 2d ed, 94n1115
Dictionary of clinical medicine: English-German, 92n1655
Dictionary of terms in music, 4th ed, 93n1248
Harper Collins German dict, college ed, 92n1070
Let's learn German picture dict, 92n1071
Oxford Duden German dict, 91n1085

ENGLISH LANGUAGE—DICTIONARIES—GREEK
NTC's new college Greek & English dict, 92n1072

ENGLISH LANGUAGE—DICTIONARIES—HAUSA
English-Hausa dict, 91n1086

ENGLISH LANGUAGE—DICTIONARIES—HAWAIIAN
New pocket Hawaiian dict, 93n1086

ENGLISH LANGUAGE—DICTIONARIES—HEBREW
Renyi picture dict: Hebrew & English, 94n1116
Webster's new world Hebrew dict, 93n1087

ENGLISH LANGUAGE—DICTIONARIES—HINDI
English-Hindi dict, 92n1074

ENGLISH LANGUAGE—DICTIONARIES—HUNGARIAN
Concise English-Hungarian dict, 14th ed, 92n1075
Hippocrene concise dict: English-Hungarian, Hungarian-English, 92n1077

ENGLISH LANGUAGE—DICTIONARIES—ICELANDIC
Icelandic-English, English-Icelandic dict, 91n1087

ENGLISH LANGUAGE—DICTIONARIES—INDONESIAN
Indonesian-English, English-Indonesian dict, 91n1088
Tuttle's concise Indonesian dict, 94n1117

ENGLISH LANGUAGE—DICTIONARIES—IRISH
Irish/English, English/Irish dict & phrasebk, 93n1088

ENGLISH LANGUAGE—DICTIONARIES—ITALIAN
Beginning Italian bilingual dict, 2d ed, 90n1047
Harper Collins Italian dict, college ed, 92n1079
Italian idioms, 92n1078
Let's learn Italian picture dict, 92n1080
Oxford paperback Italian dict, 90n1048
Zanichelli new college Italian & English dict, 92n1081

ENGLISH LANGUAGE—DICTIONARIES—JAPANESE
Collins Shubun English-Japanese dict, 94n1118
Japanese/English, English/Japanese glossary of scientific & technical terms, 94n1571
Martin's pocket dict: English-Japanese, Japanese-English, 91n1089
Practical English-Japanese dict, 92n1082

ENGLISH LANGUAGE—DICTIONARIES, JUVENILE
Canadian children's dict, 92n1043
Childcraft dict, 90n1016
Disney's my very 1st dict, 91n1069
Doubleday children's dict, 91n1070
Facts on File jr visual dict, 90n1018
First dict of cultural literacy, 90n312
Macmillan 1st dict, 92n1046
Macmillan dict for children, rev ed, 90n1019
Macmillan picture wordbk, 92n1047
Scott, Foresman beginning dict, 90n1021
Scott, Foresman intermediate dict, 90n1024
Troll young people's dict, 93n1063
Webster's new world dict for young adults, 94n1094

ENGLISH LANGUAGE—DICTIONARIES—KOREAN
Korean, 94n1122

ENGLISH LANGUAGE—DICTIONARIES—LATVIAN
Latvian-English, English-Latvian dict, 94n1123

ENGLISH LANGUAGE—DICTIONARIES—NEPALI
Shorter English-Nepali dict, 92n1083

ENGLISH LANGUAGE—DICTIONARIES—NORWEGIAN
English-Norwegian dict, 90n1052

ENGLISH LANGUAGE—DICTIONARIES—OJIBWA
Dictionary of the Ojibway lang, 94n1124

ENGLISH LANGUAGE—DICTIONARIES—PERSIAN
English-Persian dict, 94n1125
English-Persian dict of legal & commercial terms, 91n570

ENGLISH LANGUAGE—DICTIONARIES—POLISH
Polish-English, English-Polish dict with complete phonetics, rev ed, 91n1090

ENGLISH LANGUAGE—DICTIONARIES—PORTUGUESE
Oxford-Duden pictorial Portuguese-English dict, 94n1127
Random House Portuguese dict, 93n1091

ENGLISH LANGUAGE—DICTIONARIES—ROMANIAN
New pocket Romanian dict, 90n1053
Romanian-English, English-Romanian dict, 92n1085

ENGLISH LANGUAGE—DICTIONARIES—RUSSIAN
English-Russian dict with phonetics, 93n1094
Hippocrene standard dict: Russian-English, English-Russian, 94n1130
Lexical semantics, 93n1092
Renyi picture dict: Russian & English, 94n1131
Russian phrasebk & dict, 92n1088
Russian-English/English-Russian dict of free market era economics, 94n160

ENGLISH LANGUAGE—DICTIONARIES—SERBO-CROATIAN
English-Serbocroatian dict, 3d ed, 91n1092
English-Serbocroatian, Serbocroatian-English pocket dict, 91n1094
Oxford-Duden pictorial Serbo-Croat & English dict, 90n1055
Serbocroatian-English dict, 3d ed, 91n1093

ENGLISH LANGUAGE—DICTIONARIES—SLOVAK
English Slovak dict, 92n1089

ENGLISH LANGUAGE—DICTIONARIES—SPANISH
Beginning Spanish bilingual dict, 2d ed, 90n1058
Bilingual dict of dental terms: Spanish-English, 91n1683
Collins Spanish-English, English-Spanish dict, 94n1132
Collins Spanish-English, English-Spanish dict, 2d ed, 90n1056
Collins Spanish-English, English-Spanish dict unabridged, 3d ed, 94n1133
Collins Spanish-English/English-Spanish dict, 3d ed, 93n1100
Concise American Heritage Larousse Spanish dict, 90n1057
Dahl's law dict, 94n552
Elsevier's dict of terrestrial plant ecology, 93n1497
Harper Collins Spanish dict, college ed, 91n1095
Let's learn Spanish picture dict, 92n1090
Spanish idioms, 92n1091
Spanish-English, English-Spanish dict of computer terms, 94n1895
Vox everyday Spanish & English dict, 90n1059

ENGLISH LANGUAGE—DICTIONARIES—SWEDISH
English-Swedish, Swedish-English dict, 92n1092
Prisma's Swedish-English & English-Swedish dict, 4th ed, 90n1060

ENGLISH LANGUAGE—DICTIONARIES—TAGALOG
Pilipino/English, English/Pilipino concise dict, 90n1061

ENGLISH LANGUAGE—DICTIONARIES—TONGAN
Simplified dict of modern Tongan, 94n1134

ENGLISH LANGUAGE—DICTIONARIES—TURKISH
Oxford Turkish dict, 94n1135

ENGLISH LANGUAGE—DICTIONARIES—VIETNAMESE
Vietnamese-English, English-Vietnamese dict, 92n1093

ENGLISH LANGUAGE—DICTIONARIES—WELSH
Welsh-English, English-Welsh dict, 94n1136

ENGLISH LANGUAGE—DICTIONARIES—YIDDISH
English-Yiddish, Yiddish-English dict, 93n1105
Harduf's transliterated Yiddish-English dict, 4th v., 94n1137
Transliterated English-Yiddish, Yiddish-English dict, 93n1106

ENGLISH LANGUAGE—EARLY MODERN, 1500-1700
Early modern English lexicography, v.1, 91n1044
Early modern English lexicography, v.2, 91n1046
English dict from Cawdrey to Johnson 1604-1755, 92n1013

ENGLISH LANGUAGE—ENGLAND—DICTIONARIES
British English for American readers, 93n1068
British/American lang dict, 93n1069
Cassell concise English dict, new ed, 94n1098
Chambers English dict, 7th ed, 90n996
Oxford English dict, 2d ed, 90n1006
Oxford minidict, 2d ed, 90n998

ENGLISH LANGUAGE—EPONYMS
Dictionary of eponyms, 2d ed, 90n1000
Dictionary of eponyms, 3d ed, 91n1051
Webster's new world dict of eponyms, 91n1052

ENGLISH LANGUAGE—ETYMOLOGY
Book of roots, 90n1001
Cassell everyday phrases, new ed, 92n1024
Dictionary of word origins, 92n1022
Dictionary of world place names derived from British names, 90n429
Grand allusions, 91n1055
Guide to the Oxford English Dict, 94n1097
Guinness bk of words, 90n987
History of English in its own words, 92n1023
It's Greek to me!, 92n1026
Loose cannons & red herrings, 90n1007
Many names of country people, 90n1444
Merriam-Webster new bk of word hists, 92n1027
NTC's dict of word origins, 92n1028
1000 most obscure words, 91n1054
Portmanteau dict, 94n1083
Roots of English, 91n1053
Scuttlebutt, 90n1818
Straight from the horse's mouth, 90n1008
Thesaurus of word roots of the English lang, 94n1079
Toposaurus, 92n1025
Up from the roots: growing a vocabulary, 94n1082
Webster's word hists, 91n1056
What do you call a person from...?, 91n451
Why you say it, 94n1080
Word: the dict that reveals the Hebrew source of English, 90n1002

ENGLISH LANGUAGE—EUPHEMISM
Faber dict of euphemisms, 91n1057

ENGLISH LANGUAGE—FOREIGN ELEMENTS—HEBREW
Word: the dict that reveals the Hebrew source of English, 90n1002

ENGLISH LANGUAGE—FOREIGN WORDS & PHRASES
Joys of Yinglish, 90n1062
Toposaurus, 92n1025

ENGLISH LANGUAGE—GLOSSARIES, VOCABULARIES, ETC.
Children's writer's word bk, 94n996
Dickson's word treasury, 93n1073

ENGLISH LANGUAGE—GRAMMAR
Handbook of good English, rev ed, 93n1061
Nineteenth-century rhetoric, 90n986
NTC's dict of grammar terminology, 92n1035

ENGLISH LANGUAGE—HOMONYMS
Homophones & homographs, 2d ed, 94n1086
Word traps, 94n1087

ENGLISH LANGUAGE—IDIOMS
Catch phrases, cliches & idioms, 92n1039
Cat's pajamas: a fabulous fictionary of familiar phrases, 90n1015
Word wise: a dict of English idioms, 92n1038

ENGLISH LANGUAGE—MIDDLE ENGLISH, 1100-1500
Annotated bibliog of N American doctoral dissertations on old English lang & lit, 90n1165
Early modern English lexicography, v.1, 91n1044
Early modern English lexicography, v.2, 91n1046
Glossarial concordance to the Riverside Chaucer, 94n1250
Listeners' gd to medieval English, 90n991
Middle English dict, 92n1037

ENGLISH LANGUAGE—NEW WORDS. *See* WORDS, NEW—ENGLISH

ENGLISH LANGUAGE—OLD ENGLISH, CA. 450-1100
Annotated bibliog of N American doctoral dissertations on old English lang & lit, 90n1165

ENGLISH LANGUAGE—ORTHOGRAPHY & SPELLING
Canadian spelling dict, 7th ed, 94n1102

Cassell spelling dict, 92n1055
Paragon House spelling dict, 94n1103
Terrible speller, 94n1104

ENGLISH LANGUAGE—PRONUNCIATION
NBC hndbk of pronunciation, 4th ed, 92n1032
Pronouncing dict of proper names, 94n1084

ENGLISH LANGUAGE—PROVINCIALISMS
Annotated bibliog of S American English, 91n1065
Dictionary of Nfld. English, 2d ed, 92n1051
Down-home talk, 90n1013
Is it true what they say about Dixie?, 90n1010
Understanding British English, 91n1076
WetCoast words, 91n1077

ENGLISH LANGUAGE—PUNCTUATION
Lauther's complete punctuation thesaurus of the English lang, 93n1051
Punctuation handbk, 90n901

ENGLISH LANGUAGE—RHETORIC
Elements of English, 2d ed, 90n993
Handlist of rhetorical terms, 2d ed, 93n1071
Nineteenth-century rhetoric, 90n986
Random House dict for writers & readers, 91n1068

ENGLISH LANGUAGE—RHYME
Complete rhyming dict revised, 92n1054
New rhyming dict & poet's hndbk, rev ed, 92n1053

ENGLISH LANGUAGE—SLANG
Cat's pajamas: a fabulous fictionary of familiar phrases, 90n1015
Contemporary American slang, 92n1041
Family words, 90n1009
Slang!, 91n1061
Trash cash, fizzbos, & flatliners, 94n1095

ENGLISH LANGUAGE—SOUTHERN STATES
Whistlin' Dixie: a dict of S expressions, 94n1089

ENGLISH LANGUAGE—STUDY & TEACHING—FOREIGN SPEAKERS
Adult basic educ English as a 2d lang collection, 92n329
English lang & orientation programs in the US, 9th ed, 90n994
English lang & orientation programs in the US, 10th ed, 93n1053

ENGLISH LANGUAGE—SYNONYMS & ANTONYMS
Analogy bk of related words, 92n1057
Appropriate word, 91n1079
Chambers dict of synonyms & antonyms, 90n1031
Chambers thesaurus, 90n997
Descriptionary, 93n1072
Dictionary of contrasting pairs, 90n1012
Facts on File student's thesaurus, 92n1060
Merriam-Webster concise school & office thesaurus, 93n1074
Oxford thesaurus, American ed, 94n1107
Random House word menu, 94n1105
Roget's children's thesaurus, 92n1061
Roget's international thesaurus, 5th ed, 93n1075
Roget's student thesaurus, 92n1062
Roget's 21st century thesaurus, 93n1076
Roget's II, expanded ed, 90n1032
Scott, Foresman beginning thesaurus, 90n1022
Scott, Foresman jr thesaurus, 90n1023
Thesaurus of word roots of the English lang, 94n1079
Word for word: a dict of synonyms, 92n1056
Young Canada thesaurus, 90n1029

ENGLISH LANGUAGE—TERMS & PHRASES
Cassell dict of literary & lang terms, 94n980
Catch phrases, cliches & idioms, 92n1039
Concise glossary of contemporary literary theory, 93n1112
Crash of rhinoceroses, 94n1106
Dictionary of concepts in literary criticism & theory, 93n1111
Fighting words, 90n651
Glossary of contemporary literary theory, 93n1113
Grand allusions, 91n1055
Guinness bk of words, 90n987
Mene, mene, tekel, 91n1426

Neo-words, 92n1058
Phrase that launched 1,000 ships, 92n1059
Random House word menu, 94n1105
Scuttlebutt, 90n1818
Sports talk, 90n756
Straight from the horse's mouth, 90n1008
Whistlin' Dixie: a dict of S expressions, 94n1089

ENGLISH LANGUAGE—USAGE
Columbia gd to standard American English, 94n1085
Dictionary of bias-free usage, 92n1030
Facts on File dict of new words, 90n1003
Prentice Hall encyclopedic dict of English usage, 2d ed, 94n1091
Pun my word, 92n1034
Random House dict for writers & readers, 91n1068
Random House gd to grammar, usage, & punctuation, 92n1036
Webster's dict of English usage, 90n1005
When is a pig a hog?, 92n1033
Which dict?, 92n1040
Word perfect: a dict of current English usage, 92n1029
Word watcher's hndbk, 3d ed, 92n1031
Wordwatcher's gd to good writing & grammar, 91n1063
World Almanac gd to good word usage, 91n1060

ENGLISH LANGUAGE—VERSIFICATION
Complete rhyming dict revised, 92n1054
Hunting the snark: a compendium of new poetic terminology, 91n1178

ENGLISH LITERATURE
Bibliography of women & lit, 90n849
British literary bibliog, 1970-79, 94n1244
British women writers, 90n864
Collector's bkshelf, 92n929
Dictionary of biblical tradition in English lit, 94n1149
Encyclopedia of flora & fauna in English & American lit, 94n1151
English lib, 6th ed, 91n1180
Fifth dir of pers, 94n986
Great writers of the English lang, 91n1102
Handbook of English & Celtic studies in the UK and Republic of Ireland, 2d ed, 90n1169
Index of English literary mss, v.2, pt.2, 94n1245
Index of English literary mss, v.3, pt.2, 91n1189
Index of English literary mss, v.4, pt.2, 92n1195
International lit in English, 92n1193
Prentice Hall gd to English lit, 91n1187
Recent studies in myths & lit, 1970-90, 93n1301
Reference gd for English studies, 92n872
Reference gd to English lit, 2d ed, 92n1192
Reference works in British & American lit, v.1, 91n1096
Reference works in British & American lit, v.2, 92n1094
Women & the lit of the 17th century, 91n1182

ENGLISH LITERATURE—AFRICAN AUTHORS. See AFRICAN LITERATURE (ENGLISH)

ENGLISH LITERATURE—AUSTRALIA. See AUSTRALIAN LITERATURE

ENGLISH LITERATURE—EARLY MODERN, 1500-1700
Backgrounds to Restoration & 18th-century English lit, 90n1167
English lit & backgrounds 1660-1700, 91n1179
Literature criticism from 1400 to 1800, v.13, 91n1186
Writers of the Restoration & 18th century, 1660-1789, 93n1200

ENGLISH LITERATURE—18TH CENTURY
Backgrounds to Restoration & 18th-century English lit, 90n1167
Biographical dict of English women writers 1580-1720, 91n1183
Eighteenth-century British poets, 1st series, 91n1224
Index of English literary mss, v.3, pt.3, 94n1246
Index to bk reviews in England 1749-74, 91n1190
Writers of the Restoration & 18th century, 1660-1789, 93n1200

ENGLISH LITERATURE—IRISH AUTHORS
Modern Irish lit & culture, 94n1291

ENGLISH LITERATURE—MANUSCRIPTS
Index of English literary mss, v.3, pt.3, 94n1246

ENGLISH LITERATURE—MIDDLE ENGLISH, 1100-1500
Annotated bibliog of N American doctoral dissertations on old English lang & lit, 90n1165
Annotated index to the commentary on John Gower's Confessio Amantis, 91n1208
Writers of the middle ages & Renaissance before 1660, 93n1199

ENGLISH LITERATURE—19TH CENTURY
Annotated critical bibliog of Thomas Hardy, 90n1179
Bibliographies of studies in Victorian lit for the 10 yrs 1975-84, 92n1188
Characters in 19th century lit, 94n1157
Critical reception of Charles Dickens 1833-41, 90n1178
1890s: an ency of British lit, art, & culture, 94n981
KWIC concordance to Thomas Hardy's Tess of the D'Urbervilles, 90n1180
Victorian writers, 1832-1890, 93n1197
William Makepeace Thackeray: an annot bibliog 1976-87, 90n1187
Writers of the Romantic period, 1789-1832, 93n1201

ENGLISH LITERATURE—OLD ENGLISH, CA. 450-1100
Annotated bibliog of N American doctoral dissertations on old English lang & lit, 90n1165

ENGLISH LITERATURE—RESEARCH
Literary research gd, 2d ed, 94n1139

ENGLISH LITERATURE—20TH CENTURY
Bloomsbury group, 91n1181
British writers, suppl.2, 93n1191
Contemporary writers, 1960 to the present, 93n1192
Location register of 20th-century English literary mss & letters, 90n1168
Writers after WW II, 1945-60, 93n1198

ENGLISH NEWSPAPERS
Colonial British Caribbean newspapers, 91n962

ENGLISH PERIODICALS
Victorian criticism of American writers, 92n1159
Victorian pers, v.2, 91n528

ENGLISH PHILOLOGY
Catalog of dicts, word bks, & philological texts, 1440-1900, 94n1074
Elements of English, 2d ed, 90n993

ENGLISH POETRY. *See also names of individual poets*
Bibliography & index of English verse, 1476-1558, 90n1166
British broadside ballads of the 16th century, 92n1220
Columbia Granger's index to poetry, 9th ed, 91n1250
Critical survey of poetry: English lang series, rev ed, 93n1236
English Romantic poetry: an annot bibliog, 92n1218
Guide to British poetry explication, v.1, 92n1221
Guide to British poetry explication, v.2, 94n1265
Last lines, 92n1246
Poetry by women to 1900, 92n1245
Three decadent poets, 91n1222

ENGLISH POETRY—EARLY MODERN, 1500-1700
Annotated critical bibliog of Augustan poetry, 91n1223
Bibliography & index of English verse in ms 1501-58, 94n1267

ENGLISH POETRY—18TH CENTURY
Annotated critical bibliog of Augustan poetry, 91n1223
Eighteenth-century British poets: 2d series, 92n1222

ENGLISH POETRY—EXPLICATION
Guide to British poetry explication, v.3, 94n1266

ENGLISH POETRY—19TH CENTURY
British Romantic poets, 1789-1832, 1st series, 92n1219

ENGLISH PROSE LITERATURE
British prose writers, 1660-1800, 2d series, 92n1194
British Romantic prose writers, 1789-1832, 2d series, 93n1193
Manual of old English prose, 91n1188

ENGRAVERS
Eric Gill: a bibliog, 2d ed, 92n965
Illustrated dict of British steel engravers, 90n979

ENLIGHTENMENT
Blackwell companion to the enlightenment, 93n555

ENSEMBLES (MUSIC). *See* INSTRUMENTAL MUSIC

ENTERTAINERS
Alice Faye: a bio-bibliog, 91n1360
Celebrity sources, 91n20
Variety obituaries, v.12, 91n1345

ENTOMOLOGY
Entomology: a gd to info sources, 2d ed, 91n1589

ENTREPRENEURSHIP
Entrepreneur & small bus problem solver, 2d ed, 91n152
Government giveaways for entrepreneurs, 3d ed, 93n210
100 best spare-time bus opportunities today, 91n181
Pratt's gd to venture capital sources, 1992 ed, 93n197

ENVIRONMENT. *See* ANTHROPO-GEOGRAPHY; HUMAN ECOLOGY; ZOOLOGY

ENVIRONMENTAL CHEMISTRY
Environmental law index to chemicals, 94n1941

ENVIRONMENTAL CONTROL. *See* ENVIRONMENTAL ENGINEERING; ENVIRONMENTAL LAW; ENVIRONMENTAL POLICY

ENVIRONMENTAL EDUCATION
Business & the environment, 93n249
Wilderness U: opportunities for outdoor educ in the US & abroad, 93n335

ENVIRONMENTAL ENGINEERING
Current environmental engineering summaries, 1993 ed, 94n1788
Dictionary of environmental sci & tech, rev ed, 94n2000
Environmental engineering dict, 2d ed, 94n1789
Facts on File dict of environmental sci, 92n1775
McGraw-Hill ency of environmental sci & engineering, 3d ed, 94n1999
Standard hndbk of environmental engineering, 91n1620

ENVIRONMENTAL HEALTH
Atlas of world issues, 90n408
Chemical exposure & human health, 94n1861
Complete bk of home environmental hazards, 92n1780
Livable cities almanac, 93n920
Toxics A to Z, 93n1769

ENVIRONMENTAL LAW
Environmental hazards: toxic waste & hazardous material, 93n1770
Green ency, 94n1996
Guide to state environmental programs, 2d ed, 91n1812
Use of criminal penalties for pollution of the environment, 91n594

ENVIRONMENTAL LITERATURE
E for environment, 93n1752
Island Pr bibliog of environmental lit, 94n1990

ENVIRONMENTAL MONITORING
Environment on file, 93n1767

ENVIRONMENTAL POLICY
Atlas of environmental issues, 90n1788
Bibliographic gd to the environment 1991, 94n1988
California: an environmental atlas & gd, 92n1789
California environmental dir, 5th ed, 94n2007
Dictionary of ecology & environmental sci, 94n1994
Dictionary of environment & dvlpmt, 94n1995
Earth jl, 1992, 93n1765
Environment & behavior, pt.2, 90n1789
Environment abstracts annual 1988, 90n1797
Environment abstracts annual 1991, 93n1766
Environment on file, 93n1767
Environmental accounting, 94n1989
Environmental decline & public policy, 94n2019
Environmental dict, 2d ed, 94n1998
Environmental hazards: air pollution, 90n1790
Environmental issues in the Third World, 92n1771
Environmental law index to chemicals, 94n1941

Environmental profiles, 94n2004
Environmental regulatory glossary, 5th ed, 91n1805
Environmental regulatory glossary, 6th ed, 94n2002
Environmental resource dir, Sept 1990, 91n1806
Environmental telephone dir 1992-93, 93n1756
Environmentalist's bkshelf, 94n1992
Gale environmental sourcebk, 93n1768
Green almanac, 93n1751
Green co resource gd, 93n1774
Green index, 91n1809
Green index, 1991-92, 92n1782
Guide to state environmental programs, 2d ed, 91n1812
HarperCollins dict of environmental sci, 93n1753
Information please environmental almanac, 1993, 94n1986
National gd to funding for the environment & animal welfare, 93n881
Reading about the environment, 94n1991
Red Sea, Gulf of Aden & Suez Canal, 92n1770
Statistical record of the environment, 93n1764
Toxic substances controls gd, 90n1799
U.S. energy & environmental interest groups, 92n1753
U.S.A. oil industry's environmental dir, 1993, 93n1762
Who is who at the Earth Summit, Rio de Janeiro, 1992, 93n1763
Who is who in serv to the earth, 93n1775
World dir of environmental orgs, 3d ed, 91n1811
World dir of environmental orgs, 4th ed, 93n1773

ENVIRONMENTAL PROTECTION
Canadian environmental dir 1991, 92n1777
Data: where it is & how to get it, 94n45
Dictionary of environmental sci & tech, rev ed, 94n2000
Dirctory of European environmental orgs, 94n2003
E for environment, 93n1752
Ecologue, 91n189
Education for the Earth, 94n2012
Encyclopedia of environmental studies, 92n1773
Environmental address bk, 93n1760
Environmental industries marketplace, 93n1755
Environmentalists: a biographical dict, 94n1993
Environmentalist's bkshelf, 94n1992
Extremely hazardous substances, 90n1798
Facts on File dict of environmental sci, 92n1775
Green consumer, 92n177
Green Earth resource gd, 92n179
Green ency, 94n1996
McGraw-Hill ency of environmental sci & engineering, 3d ed, 94n1999
Nature dir, 93n1759
Nature projects on file, 93n1527
Reading about the environment, 94n1991
World resources 1992-93, 93n1776
Your resource gd to environmental orgs, 92n1787

ENVIRONMENTAL PROTECTION AGENCY
EPA headquarters telephone dir, 1991 ed, 93n1757
Information resources dir, fall 1989, 91n1808

ENVIRONMENTAL PSYCHOLOGY
Environment & behavior, pt.2, 90n1789

ENVIRONMENTALISTS
Environmental address bk, 93n1760
Environmental profiles, 94n2004
Environmentalists: a biographical dict, 94n1993

ENVIRONMENTALLY INDUCED DISEASES
Chemical exposure & human health, 94n1861

EPIC POETRY
Beowulf scholarship, 94n1263
Classical epic: an annot bibliog, 92n1135

EPIDEMIOLOGY
Disease & medical care in the US, 94n1802

EPISCOPAL CHURCH
Concordance of The Hymnal 1982, 90n1264
History of the Episcopal church in America, 1607-1991, 94n1521

EPITHETS
Dictionary of epithets & terms of address, 91n1062

EPONYMS
Corporate eponymy, 93n184
Eponyms of behavioral optometry, 94n1866
Medicine, lit, & eponyms, 90n1653

EQUATORIAL GUINEA
Equatorial Guinea, 93n114
Historical dict of Equatorial Guinea, 2d ed, 90n108

ERASMUS, DESIDERIUS
Catalogue of the Erasmus collection in the City Lib of Rotterdam, 92n1394

EROTIC ART
Erotic art, 90n945

EROTIC FILMS
Russ Meyer: the life & films, 91n1354
X-rated videotape gd 2, 93n1332

EROTIC LITERATURE
Clandestine erotic fiction in English 1800-1930, 94n1204

ESCHLEMAN, CLAYTON
Clayton Eshleman: a descriptive bibliog, 90n1139

ESKIMOS
Aboriginal self-govt in Canada, 92n374
Native peoples of Canada in contemporary society, 91n402
Resource reading list 1990, 91n401

ESPIONAGE
Spycatcher's ency of espionage, 93n787
Spyclopedia, 90n724
Terrorism, assassination, espionage & propaganda, 91n771

ESSAYS
Essay & general lit index 1985-89, 91n52
Essay & general lit index, rev ed, 93n77
Modern British essayists, 1st series, 92n1197
Roth's essay index, 90n1101

ESTONIAN LANGUAGE—DICTIONARIES—ENGLISH
Estonian-English, English-Estonian dict, 93n1082

ETHICS
Bibliographic gd to the comparative study of ethics, 92n1389
Encyclopedia of ethics, 93n1395
Ethics: an annot bibliog, 92n1393
Judaism & human rights in contemporary thought, 94n1555
Television & ethics, 90n910

ETHICS IN THE BIBLE
Encyclopedia of biblical & Christian ethics, rev ed, 93n1419

ETHIOPIA
Ethiopia, 90n109
Health, disease, medicine & famine in Ethiopia, 92n1632

ETHNIC ART
Serials gd to ethnoart, 91n1022
Southwest Native American arts & material culture, 92n373

ETHNIC ARTS
National dir of multi-cultural arts orgs 1990, 92n879

ETHNIC GROUPS. See also MINORITIES
Atlas of world cultures, 90n361
Developing lib collections for Calif.'s emerging majority, 92n620
Dictionary of American immigration hist, 91n777
Directory of ethnic professionals in LIS (lib & info sci), 93n625
Ethnographic bibliog of N America, 4th ed. suppl. 1973-1987, 91n380
Melting pot: an annot bibliog & gd to food & nutrition info for ethnic groups in America, 94n1599
Passport's gd to ethnic N.Y., 92n443
Peoples of the world: Africans south of the Sahara, 93n117
Peoples of the world: N Americans, 92n340
Peoples of the world: the Middle East & N Africa, 93n160
Writing for the ethnic markets, 93n962

ETHNIC GROUPS IN LITERATURE
American ethnic lits, 94n1225
Our family, our friends, our world, 93n1127
Venture into cultures, 94n1170

ETHNIC JEWELRY
Folk jewelry of the world, 91n998

ETHNIC PRESS
Ethnic pers in contemporary America, 91n383
Joseph Jacobs dir of the Jewish pr in America, 3d ed, 92n903

ETHNIC RELATIONS
Conflict & culture, rev ed, 93n419
International writings of Bohdan S. Wynar, 1949-92, 94n80

ETHNOBOTANY
Medicinal wild plants of the prairie, 93n1514

ETHNOLOGICAL MUSEUMS & COLLECTIONS
Time's flotsam: overseas collections of Calif. Indian material culture, 91n395

ETHNOLOGY
Cultural anthropology of the Middle East, v.1, 93n416
Dictionary of concepts in cultural anthropology, 93n418
Encyclopedia of world cultures, v.1, 92n334
Encyclopedia of world cultures, v.2, 92n335
Encyclopedia of world cultures, v.3, 93n413
Encyclopedia of world cultures, v.4, 94n395
Encyclopedia of world cultures, v.5, 94n396
Glossary of the Third World, 90n128
Illustrated ency of mankind, 91n75
International bibliog of social & cultural anthropology, v.32, 91n382
Micronesia 1975-87, 90n149
Multicultural aspects of lib media programs, 93n669
People atlas, 93n414

ETHNOLOGY—LATIN AMERICA—DICTIONARIES—PORTUGUESE
Dictionary of Latin American racial & ethnic terminology, 91n410

ETHNOLOGY—LATIN AMERICA—DICTIONARIES—SPANISH
Dictionary of Latin American racial & ethnic terminology, 91n410

ETHNOMUSICOLOGY
Ethnomusicology research, 93n1242
Selected musical terms of non-Western cultures, 92n1253

ETIQUETTE
Emily Post's etiquette, 15th ed, 93n1307
Etiquette, 90n1309
Letitia Baldrige's complete gd to the new manners for the 90s, 91n1335

EUPHEMISM
Kind words: a thesaurus, rev ed, 91n1058
Official politically correct dict & hndbk, 94n1101

EUROPE
Trees & shrubs of Great Britain & N Europe, 94n1670
Adult educ in continental Europe 1986-88, 91n377
Adult educ in continental Europe 1989-91, 94n391
Alchemy in Europe, 91n1763
Annotated bibliogs of mineral deposits in Europe, pt.2, 92n1743
Annotated index of medieval women, 93n933
Ballad scholarship, 90n1284
Bibliography of law & economics, 93n564
Book of European forecasts, 93n282
Cambridge gd to the museums of Europe, 92n62
Catalogue of European sculpture in the Ashmolean Museum 1540 to the present day, 94n1067
Coniferous trees, 92n1555
Consumer Europe 1991, 92n173
Continental actress, 91n1395
Dirctory of European environmental orgs, 94n2003
Directory of European bus, 94n254
Directory of European community trade & professional assns 1992, 94n274
Directory of European industrial & trade assns, 5th ed, 92n242
Directory of European sports orgs, 93n821
Directory of special collections in W Europe, 94n653
Era of Napoleon, 92n478
Ethnic music on records, v.1, 92n1305
Europe in figures, 3d ed, 94n935
Europe today, 1990 rev ed, 91n440
European accountancy yrbk 1992/93, 93n271
European advertising mktg & media data 1992, 93n285
European artists: signatures & monograms, 1800-1990, 92n985
European business rankings, 94n258
European cos, 4th ed, 94n260
European compendium of mktg info, 93n286
European consumer lifestyles to 1995, 92n176
European culture, 94n977
European dir of consumer brands & their owners 1992, 93n288
European dir of consumer goods manufacturers 1989, 90n237
European dir of financial info sources 1990, 92n157
European dir of mktg info sources 1991, 92n244
European dir of trade & bus jls 1990, 92n246
European electric utility dir, 1993, 94n1783
European electronics dir 1993, 94n1787
European faculty dir 1991, 92n313
European garden flora, v.3, 90n1489
European market share reporter, 94n259
European markets, 3d ed, 91n266
European research centres, 9th ed, 94n1574
European sources of scientific & technical info, 10th ed, 94n1576
European specialist publishers dir, 94n666
European wholesalers & distrs dir, 93n257
European women's almanac, 94n947
Festival Europe, 94n479
From Stanislavsky to Barrault, 92n1382
Good bks for the curious traveler: Europe, 90n456
Guide to European financial centres, 92n187
Handbook of natl population censuses: Europe, 93n898
Handbook of the birds of Europe, the Middle East, & N Africa, v.6, 94n1696
Handbook of the birds of Europe, the Middle East, & N Africa, v.7, 94n1697
International histl stats: Europe 1750-1988, 3d ed, 93n911
Key works to the fauna & flora of the British Isles & NW Europe, 5th ed, 90n1495
Major cos of Europe 1991/92, 92n131
Major financial insts of continental Europe 1989/90, 91n216
Matter of taste, 91n1482
Medium cos of Europe 1991/92, 92n132
Mineral deposits of Europe, v.4/5, 91n1787
Mosaik's photographic key to the trees & shrubs of Great Britain & N Europe, 94n1670
Music lover's gd to Europe, 93n1250
National theatre in N & E Europe, 1746-1900, 92n1384
New Generation gd to the butterflies & day-flying moths of Britain & Europe, 90n1546
New Generation gd to the fungi of Britain & Europe, 90n1500
Painting of the golden age, 94n1063
Panorama of EC industry 93, 94n236
Peoples of the world: W Europeans, 94n128
Plants & flowers of Great Britain & N Europe, 94n1657
Political & economic ency of W Europe, 92n714
Scholar's gd to Washington, D.C. for SW European studies, 90n130
Scientific traveler, 93n1456
Seven-lang thesaurus of European animals, 92n1558
Slavic studies, 94n131
Spaghetti westerns, 93n1367
Who's who in European bus, 94n223
Who's who in European insts & enterprises 1993, 94n771
Who's who in European pols, 92n719

EUROPE, EASTERN
American bibliog of Slavic & E European studies for 1990, 94n130
Bibliographic gd to Soviet & E European studies 1990, 92n103
Comecon data 1990, 93n907
Consumer E Europe 1992, 93n283
Cracking Eastern Europe, 94n261

Democracy's dawn, 92n750
Directory of E European film-makers & films 1945-91, 93n1348
Directory of foreign trade orgs in E Europe, 2d ed, 90n176
Eastern Europe & the Commonwealth of Independent States 1992, 93n141
Eastern Europe: a dir & sourcebk 1992, 93n140
Eastern Europe: a market for the 1990s, 92n243
Eastern European business dir, 93n284
Handbook of pol sci research on the USSR & E Europe, 94n781
Handbook of reconstruction in E Europe & the Soviet Union, 93n536
Handbook of Soviet & E European films & filmmakers, 93n1340
Historical atlas of E central Europe, 94n520
Major business orgs of E Europe & the Soviet Union, 92n130
Mineral deposits of Europe, v.4/5, 91n1787
New pol parties of E Europe & the Soviet Union, 93n770
Political & economic ency of the Soviet Union & E Europe, 92n104
Short-term economic stats: Central & E Europe, 93n292
Slavic studies, 94n131
Where once we walked: a gd to the Jewish communities destroyed in the Holocaust, 93n494
Who's who in Russia & the new states, 94n136
Who's who in the socialist countries of Europe, 91n18

EUROPE—ECONOMIC CONDITIONS
Economist atlas of the New Europe, 94n255
Western Europe 1989: a pol & economic survey, 90n131

EUROPE—HISTORY
Columbia dict of European pol hist since 1914, 93n529
Dictionary of the Napoleonic wars, 94n521
Europe in transition, 90n514

EUROPE—MAPS
Economist atlas of the New Europe, 94n255
Michelin road atlas of Europe, 90n455

EUROPE—POLITICS & GOVERNMENT
Almanac of transatlantic pols 1991-92, 92n675
Sources in European pol hist, v.3, 93n766
European pol facts 1918-90, 94n766
Sources in European pol hist, v.2, 90n723
Western Europe 1989: a pol & economic survey, 90n131
Who's who in European pols, 2d ed, 94n772

EUROPEAN COMMUNITIES
Countdown 2000, v.2, 94n789
Directory of community legislation in force, 16th ed, 92n737
Documentation of the European Communities, 91n110
EC info hndbk 1993/94, 94n768
EUROCOM, 94n632
European Communities ency & dir 1992, 92n711
European Community fact bk, 91n109
European public affair dir 1993, 94n769
Historical dict of the European Community, 94n767
Modern companion to the European Community, 93n767
Panorama of EC industry 93, 94n236
SCAD bulletin 20—1991, 92n716

EUROPEAN COOPERATION
European public affair dir 1993, 94n769

EUROPEAN ECONOMIC COMMUNITY
EC direct, 94n257
European Xommunities, 94n770
New Europe: an A to Z compendium on the European Community, 92n741
Oxford ency of European Community law, v.1, 92n534
Yearbook of the European Communities & of the other European orgs, 12th ed, 94n773

EUROPEAN FEDERATION
Directory of pan-European orgs 1992, 93n138

EUROPEAN LITERATURE
European writers, 92n1231
European writers: selected authors, 94n1280
European writers: the 20th century, v.8, 90n1200
European writers: the 20th century, v.9, 90n1201
European writers: the 20th century, v.10, 91n1231
European writers: the 20th century, v.11, 91n1232
Twentieth century European short story, 91n1142
Women writers of Germany, Austria, & Switzerland, 90n856

EUTHANASIA
Challenge of euthanasia, 91n852

EVALUATIONS
Evaluation thesaurus, 4th ed, 93n642

EVANGELICALISM
American evangelicalism, 92n1408
Researching modern evangelicalism, 91n1441
Twentieth-century evangelicalism, 91n1434

EVIDENCE, EXPERT
Litigation servs resource dir, 92n545

EVOLUTION (BIOLOGY)
Origin & evolution of life on Earth, 94n1635

EXAMINATIONS
Supplement to the 10th mental measurements yrbk, 92n760

EXCAVATIONS (ARCHAEOLOGY)
Dictionary of Irish archaeology, 94n486
New ency of archaeological excavations in the Holy Land, 94n489
Spain: 1001 sights, 93n506

EXCHANGE OF BIBLIOGRAPHIC INFORMATION—STANDARDS
Sourcebook on standards info, 92n574

EXCHANGE OF PERSONS PROGRAMS
Money for intl exchange in the arts, 94n983

EXCHANGE RATE. *See* **FOREIGN EXCHANGE**

EX-CONVICTS—SERVICES FOR
Post-release assistance programs for prisoners, 94n910

EXECUTIVE ADVISORY BODIES
Encyclopedia of governmental advisory orgs 1994-95, 94n747
Encyclopedia of govtl advisory orgs 1990-91, 90n694

EXECUTIVE AGENCIES. *See* **ADMINISTRATIVE AGENCIES**

EXECUTIVE DEPARTMENTS. *See* **ADMINISTRATIVE AGENCIES**

EXECUTIVES
Executives on the move, 91n253
Who's who in European bus, 94n223

EXECUTIVES, TRAINING OF
Bricker's short-term executive programs, 90n169
Moving up, 90n267

EXERCISE
Benefits of exercise, 92n792
Dictionary of the sport & exercise scis, 92n771
Exercise, 90n1645
Focus on fitness, 94n843

EXHIBITIONS
Agenda world: Jan 1991, worldwide ed, 92n239
Books of the fairs, 93n1306
Historical dict of world's fairs & expositions 1851-1988, 91n1336
International trade fairs & conferences dir 1991-92, 92n251
Trade shows worldwide 1990, 91n280
Trade shows worldwide 1993, 94n298
Tradeshow week data bk, 1992, 93n322

EXHUMATION
Disputing the dead, 92n549

EXILES' WRITING, RUSSIAN
Russian emigre serials, 91n411

EXISTENTIALISM
Work of Colin Wilson, 91n1221

EXPERT SYSTEMS (COMPUTER SCIENCE)
Expert systems & related topics, 91n1717

Expert systems in geography & environmental studies, 91n445

EXPLORERS
Atlas of N American exploration, 94n444
Children's atlas of exploration, 94n452
Explorers & discoverers of the world, 94n463
Great lives: exploration, 90n531
Journeys of the great explorers, 94n464
Sir Richard F. Burton: a biobibliographical study, 91n444
Times atlas of world exploration, 92n408
Who was who in world exploration, 93n488
Who's who in Pacific navigation, 93n487
World explorers & discoverers, 93n486

EXPLORERS, WOMEN
Women into the unknown, 90n870

EXPORT MARKETING
Elsevier's dict of export financing & credit insurance, 91n264
Global Tex.: intl trade info sourcebk, 93n267
Global trade white pages 1992, 93n268
International business dict & ref, 93n255
International trade stats yrbk, 1990, 94n233
World markets desk bk, 94n239
World trade resources gd, 93n265

EXPORT TRADING COMPANIES
Directory of leading US export mgmt cos, 3d ed, 92n231
Official export gd 1990, 91n274
United States importers & exporters dir, 90n286

EXPORTS
American export register 1992, 93n318
Official export gd 1990, 91n274
Ukraine top 100 exporters, 93n294
U.S. custom house gd 1990, 91n281

EXTINCT ANIMALS
Extinct species of the world, 92n1524

EXTINCT BIRDS. *See* **BIRDS, EXTINCT**

EXTINCTION (BIOLOGY)
Extinction A-Z, 92n1520

EXTRATERRESTRIAL LIFE. *See* **LIFE ON OTHER PLANETS**

EYE
Eye, ear, nose & throat surgery, 90n1664
Genetic risks: a ref for eye care practitioners, 91n1684

FABLES
Brewer's dict of 20th-century phrase & fable, 93n1294

FACSIMILE TRANSMISSION
Bowker's bk trade fax & phone dir 1989, 90n634
Columbine fax dir, 91n140
Dial-a-fax dir, 3d ed, 91n1750
Directory of telefacsimiles sites in N American libs, 6th ed, 92n567
Facsimile users' dir, 90n1735
Fax for libs, 91n608
National fax dir, 90n1736
National fax dir 1990, 90n1737
Official fax dir, 7th Canadian ed, 91n1752

FADS
Arts & entertainment fads, 91n1338

FAIRS
Festival Europe, 94n479

FAIRY TALES
Index to fairy tales 1978-86, 5th suppl, 91n1330

FAKEBOOKS (MUSIC)
Where's that tune?, 92n1258

FALKLAND ISLANDS WAR, 1982
Falklands War: background, conflict, aftermath, 94n684
Falklands/Malvinas campaign, 93n694

FAMILY
Dictionary of family psychology & family therapy, 2d ed, 94n810
Encyclopedia of marriage, divorce & the family, 90n798
Families & aging, 93n854
Family mental health ency, 90n743
Focus on families, 91n859
Handbook of family measurement techniques, 91n863
Statistical hndbk on the American family, 93n867

FAMILY LAW. *See* **DOMESTIC RELATIONS**

FAMILY LIFE SURVEYS
50 fabulous places to raise your family, 94n944

FAMILY PLANNING. *See* **BIRTH CONTROL**

FAMILY POLICY
Feminization of poverty in the US, 91n913

FAMILY PSYCHOTHERAPY
Dictionary of family psychology & family therapy, 2d ed, 94n810

FAMILY RECREATION
Great resorts for parents & kids, 92n434
National parks, 93n498
Recommended family resorts in the US, Canada, & the Caribbean, 91n463

FAMILY-OWNED BUSINESS ENTERPRISES
Born to power, 94n155

FAMINES
Health, disease, medicine & famine in Ethiopia, 92n1632
World hunger, 92n830

FAMOUS PEOPLE. *See* **CELEBRITIES**

FANS—SOCIETIES & CLUBS
Fan club dir, 94n1400

FANTASTIC FICTION
British sci fiction, 93n1204
Modern mystery, fantasy & sci fiction writers, 94n1207
Prydain companion, 90n1089
Reference gd to sci fiction, fantasy, & horror, 93n1155
Science fiction & fantasy lit 1975-91, 94n1214
Science fiction & fantasy ref index 1985-91, 94n1213
Science fiction, fantasy & horror, 1987, 90n1112
Science fiction, fantasy & horror ref, 90n1110
Supernatural fiction for teens, 2d ed, 93n1156
Tolkien thesaurus, 92n1213

FANTASTIC FILMS
Fantastic cinema subject gd, 94n1449
Science fiction, horror & fantasy film & TV credits suppl-1987, 90n1350

FANTASTIC LITERATURE
Fantasy lit: a reader's gd, 91n1137
Fantasy lit for children & young adults, 3d ed, 90n1083
Reginald's sci fiction & fantasy awards, 2d ed, 93n1157
Science fiction & fantasy bk review annual 1988, 90n1111
Uranian worlds, 2d ed, 91n1141

FANTASTIC POETRY
Contemporary sci fiction, fantasy, & horror poetry, 90n1109

FANTASY—FILM CATALOGS
Fantastic cinema subject gd, 94n1449

FARM ANIMALS. *See* **LIVESTOCK**

FARMERS
New England planters in the Maritime provinces of Canada 1759-1800, 94n1589

FARMS
American farm crisis, 90n1441

FASHION
Chronicle of W fashion, 93n1010
Fashion in the W world 1500-1990, 93n1011
Who's who in fashion, 2d ed, 90n938

FASHION DESIGN. *See* **COSTUME DESIGN**

FASTENERS
Standard handbk of fastening & joining, 2d ed, 90n1605

FASTS & FEASTS
Religious holidays & calendars, 94n1517

FAULKNER, WILLIAM
Absalom! Absalom! a concordance to the novel, 91n1162
Faulkner in the 80s, 93n1173
Faulkner's poetry, 90n1141
Mansion: a concordance, 90n1140

FAUNA. *See* **ANIMALS**

FAX. *See* **FACSIMILE TRANSMISSION**

FAYE, ALICE
Alice Faye: a bio-bibliog, 91n1360

FEAR
Encyclopedia of phobias, fears, & anxieties, 90n744

FEDERAL AID. *See* **ECONOMIC ASSISTANCE, DOMESTIC**

FEDERAL AID TO COMMUNITY DEVELOPMENT
Free money for small businesses & entrepreneurs, 91n211

FEDERAL AID TO EDUCATION
Free money for college from the govt, 94n327
Guide to fed funding for educ, 1991, 92n279
U.S. student Fulbright grants & other grants for graduate study & research abroad, 94n346

FEDERAL AID TO THE ARTS
Artisthelp, 91n877

FEDERAL GOVERNMENT
Election results dir, 1993 ed, 94n738
Federal data base finder, 3d ed, 92n52
Federal legal dir, 91n575
Government dir of addresses & telephone nos, 93n740

FEDERAL GRANTS. *See* **GRANTS-IN-AID**

FEDERALIST
Federalist concordance, 90n544

FELLNER, WILLIAM JOHN
William J. Fellner: a bio-bibliog, 94n154

FEMINISM
American women's mags, 90n880
Canadian feminist per index, 1972-85, 92n868
Canadian women's movement, 1960-90, 94n966
Dictionary of feminist theory, 91n925
Feminism & women's issues, 92n859
Feminist legal lit, 92n853
Feminist movement: a bibliog, 93n929
Feminist research methods, 92n857
Feminist theory, 94n952
French feminist theory: Luce Irigaray & Helene Cixous, 92n858
Goddesses & wise women, 93n923
Mothers & mothering, 92n854
Papers of Elizabeth Cady Stanton and Susan B. Anthony, 94n964
Simone de Beauvoir: a bibliog, 93n930
Women & religion: a bibliographic gd to Christian feminist liberation theology, 92n1405
Women public speakers in the US, 1800-1925, 94n957
Women's issues: an annot bibliog, 91n916
Women's movements of the world, 90n875
Women's studies ency, v.3, 93n939
Women's studies research hndbk, 3d ed, 92n864
Words to the wise: a writer's gd to feminist & lesbian pers & publs, 3d ed, 92n900

FEMINISM & LITERATURE
Feminist companion to lit in English, 92n1095
Shakespeare & feminist criticism, 93n1212

FEMINISM & THEATER
Dramatic re-visions, 93n1333

FEMINIST CRITICISM
Dramatic re-visions, 93n1333

FEMINIST THEOLOGY
Liberation theologies, 92n1398
Women & religion: a bibliographic gd to Christian feminist liberation theology, 92n1405

FERMENTED MILK
Encyclopedia of fermented fresh milk products, 93n1475

FERNS
Ferns & fern allies of Canada, 90n1490
Illustrated field gd to ferns & allied plants of the British Isles, 92n1531

FERTILITY CLINICS
In vitro fertilization clinics, 94n1857

FERTILIZERS
FAO yrbk: fertilizer, v.39, 91n1478
FAO yrbk: fertilizer, v.41, 94n1590

FESCUE
Fescue grasses of Canada, 91n1531

FESTIVALS
Best festivals of N America, 3d ed, 91n1344
Chase's annual events 1990, 91n2
Cuban festivals, 94n1399
East & SE Asia material culture in N America, 90n504
Fanfare for words: bkfairs & bk festivals in N America, 93n682
Festival Europe, 94n479
Folklore of American holidays, 2d ed, 93n1297
Folklore of world holidays, 93n1298
Multicultural projects index, 93n1312
Yearbook of English festivals, 94n1406

FETAL ALCOHOL SYNDROME
New lit on fetal alcohol exposure & effects, 91n1692

FETUS
Catalog of prenatally diagnosed conditions, 2d ed, 93n1654
Drugs, vitamins, minerals in pregnancy, 90n1702

FIBER OPTICS
Fiber optics standard dict, 2d ed, 91n1754
Fiber optics technical dir 1988, 90n1739

FIBERS
World apparel fibre consumption survey, 90n250

FICTION. *See also* **DETECTIVE & MYSTERY STORIES; HORROR TALES; SCIENCE FICTION**
Angus Wilson: a bibliog 1947-87, 90n1189
Classic cult fiction, 93n1149
English lang criticism on the foreign novel 1965-75, 90n1063
Fiction cat, 12th ed, 92n1137
Fiction for youth, 3d ed, 94n1181
Fiction writers gdlines, 2d ed, 93n963
Genreflecting, 3d ed, 93n1147
Handbook of contemporary fiction for public libs & school libs, 91n1128
Olderr's fiction index 1990, 92n1139
Prentice Hall good reading gd, 90n1104
Read all your life, 90n1102
Sequels: an annot gd to novels in series, 2d ed, 92n1138
Stanford companion to Victorian fiction, 90n1172
Themes & settings in fiction, 90n1103
Unreal! Hennepin County lib subject headings for fictional characters & places, 2d ed, 93n644
What do I read next?, 92n1136
Novels of WW II, 94n1205

FIELD CROPS
Field crop diseases hndbk, 2d ed, 90n1449
Quality declared seed, 94n1596

FIELD SPORTS. *See* **HUNTING**

FIELDS, W. C.
W. C. Fields—an annot gd, 94n1428

FIGHTER PILOTS
Japanese naval aces & fighter units in WW II, 91n511

FIGHTING. *See* **COMBAT**

FIGURES OF SPEECH
Descriptionary, 93n1072
Handlist of rhetorical terms, 2d ed, 93n1071

FILIPINO LANGUAGE. *See* **TAGALOG LANGUAGE**

FILIPINOS
Ang mahalaga sa buhay, 93n1102

FILM ADAPTATIONS
Books & plays in films 1896-1915, 93n1344
Enser's filmed bks & plays, 94n1438
From page to screen, 93n1359
More theatre, 94n1464
Movie characters of leading performers of the sound era, 91n1362
Women writers: from page to screen, 91n1364

FILM FESTIVALS
Encyclopedia of film festivals, 90n1328

FILM GENRES
Films by genre, 94n1444

FILM NEWS
Film news index, 1939-81, 94n1462

FILMSTRIPS
Educators gd to free filmstrips & slides, 45th ed, 94n375
Filmstrip & slide set finder, 91n360

FINANCE. *See also* **INVESTMENTS**
Bibliography of finance, 92n182
Business & legal CD-ROMS in print 1993, 94n175
Corporate finance sourcebk 1991, 93n238
Dictionary for bus & finance, 90n168
Dictionary for bus & finance, 2d ed, 91n135
Dictionary of banking terms, 91n215
Dictionary of finance, 94n204
Dictionary of finance & investment terms, 3d ed, 92n184
Dictionary of personal finance, 93n243
Encyclopedia of American business hist & biog: banking & finance to 1913, 91n213
Encyclopedia of American business hist & biog: banking & finance, 1913-89, 92n185
Encyclopedia of banking & finance, 9th ed, 92n186
Encyclopedic dict of accounting & finance, 90n198
Facts & figures on govt finance, 1990 ed, 91n214
Finance, insurance, & real estate USA, 94n205
Financial 1000, 90n230
Financial yellow bk, v.5, no.2, 93n239
Glossary of finance & debt, 93n231
Guide to European financial centres, 92n187
Guide to the Canadian financial servs industry 1991, 93n232
International financial stats yrbk 1990, 92n188
Major financial insts of continental Europe 1989/90, 91n216
New Palgrave dict of money & finance, 93n242
Pacific Rim almanac, 92n137
Partnership almanac, 90n191
Still more words of Wall St, 91n185
Wall St dict, 92n166
Who's who in Canadian finance 1988-89, 90n231
Who's who in finance & industry 1992-93, 93n179
World debt tables 1991-92, 93n244
World financial system, 2d ed, 94n206
Worldscope financial & serv co profiles, 90n220
Worldscope industrial co profiles, 90n221

FINANCE, PUBLIC
Public budgeting & financial mgmt, 92n754
Vocabulary of public sector auditing, 94n249

FINANCIAL AID, STUDENT. *See* **STUDENT AID**

FINANCIAL FUTURES
Directory of financial futures exchanges, 90n206
Futures markets dict, 91n187

FINANCIAL PLANNERS
Financial planners & planning orgs dir, 2d ed, 91n218

FINDLEY, TIMOTHY
Timothy Findley: an annot bibliog, 91n1228

FINE ARTS. *See* **ART**

FINGER PLAY
Creative fingerplays & action rhymes, 93n340

FIRE EXTINCTION
History of American firefighting toys, 92n944

FIRE FIGHTERS
National dir of fire chiefs & emergency depts, 1993, 94n878
Police, firefighter, & paramedic stress, 91n787

FIRE PREVENTION
Firefighter's hazardous materials ref bk, 92n1781
Firefighter's hazardous materials ref bk & index, 2d ed, 94n2011

FIRE RESISTANT MATERIALS
Handbook of fire retardant coatings & fire testing servs, 91n1625

FIREARMS
Cowboy & gunfighter collectibles, 90n923
Encyclopedia of sporting firearms, 92n932
Modern guns: identification & values, 7th ed, 90n924
Small arms today, 2d ed, 90n676
Standard cat of firearms, 2d ed, 93n1004

FIRST AID IN ILLNESS & INJURY
First aid for kids, 92n1636

FISHERIES
Canadian fisheries & ocean industries dir, 3d ed, 91n224
FAO yrbk: fishery stats, v.66, 91n1581
FAO yrbk: fishery stats, v.72, 94n1715
Keyguide to info sources in aquaculture, 90n1450
Mangone's concise marine almanac, 92n1466

FISHES
Catalogue of freshwater & marine fishes of Ala., 94n1714
Cichlids of N & Central America, 94n1712
Dictionary of evolutionary fish osteology, 93n1558
Field gd to freshwater fishes, 92n1576
Field gd to the freshwater fishes of Tanzania, 93n1556
Fish: 5-lang dict of fish, crustaceans & molluscs, 91n1584
Fishes of Alta., 2d ed, 94n1720
Fishes of Ark., 90n1552
Fishes of N.Mex., 91n1585
Fishes of the central US, 91n1586
Fishes of the Great Barrier Reef & Coral Sea, 92n1577
Guide to the marine sport fishes of Atlantic Canada & New England, 93n1555
Handbook of fish diseases, 91n1587
Hawaiian reef animals, rev ed, 91n1599
Most complete colored lexicon of cichlids, 94n1711
Pacific Coast inshore fishes, 3d ed, 91n1583
Sharks & other creatures of the deep, 92n1585
World fishes important to N Americans, 93n1559

FISHING
Bookman's gd to hunting, shooting, angling, & related subjects, 92n799
Game fishing bible, 92n798
National parks fishing gd, 92n800
Trout & salmon hndbk, 90n772

FITNESS, PHYSICAL. *See* **PHYSICAL FITNESS**

FITZWILLIAM MUSEUM
Short-title cat of music printed before 1825 in the Fitzwilliam Museum, Cambridge, 94n1310

FLIES. *See* **DIPTERA**

FLORA. *See* **BOTANY**

FLORENCE (ITALY)
Chronology of music in the Florentine theater 1751-1800, 94n1311

FLORIDA
Complete gd to life in Fla., 92n442
Dragonflies of the Fla. peninsula, Bermuda, & the Bahamas, 90n1553
Florida almanac 1992-93, 93n106
Florida statistical abstract 1991, 93n107
Florida's butterflies & other insects, 90n1547
Guide to the hist of Fla., 91n506
Health care in Fla., 92n1638
Index to Fla. Jewish hist in the American Israelite 1854-1900, 93n446
Metaphysical Fla., 92n764
Parasites & diseases of wild mammals in Fla., 93n1569
Rare & endangered biota of Fla., v.1, 94n1735
Rare & endangered biota of Fla., v.2, 94n1716

FLORISTS
Fine flowers by phone, 90n1468

FLORSHEIM, RICHARD A.
Catalogue raisonne of the graphic work of Richard Florsheim, 90n980

FLOWER PAINTING & ILLUSTRATION
Great flower bks 1700-1900, 92n1540
Wildflowers for all seasons, 90n1498

FLOWERING PLANTS. *See* ANGIOSPERMS; FLOWERS

FLOWERS. *See also* WILDFLOWERS; *names of plants*
Encyclopedia of flowers, 94n1654
Flowering shrubs & small trees, 92n1541
Heliconia: an identification gd, 92n1535
Identification of flowering plant families, 3d ed, 90n1491
Japanese plants, 90n1488
Naming of flowers, 91n1527
100 families of flowering plants, 2d ed, 90n1492
Plants & flowers of Great Britain & N Europe, 94n1657

FLUID MECHANICS
Encyclopedia of fluid mechanics, v.8, 90n1586

FLY FISHING
Fly patterns, 2d ed, 93n837

FLYING SAUCERS. *See* UNIDENTIFIED FLYING OBJECTS

FOLIAGE PLANTS
Foliage plants for decorating indoors, 90n1469

FOLK ART
Arkansas made, v.1, 92n919
Arkansas made, v.2, 92n920
Mingei, 90n937
Museum of American Folk Art ency of 20th-century American folk art & artists, 92n982
20th century American folk, self taught, & outsider art, 94n1032

FOLK ARTISTS
Motif-index of medieval Catalan folktales, 94n1389
Museum of American Folk Art ency of 20th-century American folk art & artists, 92n982
20th century American folk, self taught, & outsider art, 94n1032
Types & motifs of the Judeo-Spanish folktales, 94n1387

FOLK MEDICINE
Ashe, traditional religion & healing in sub-Saharan Africa & the Diaspora, 91n1409
Feed a cold, starve a fever, rev ed, 92n1676
Medicinal plants of India, 92n1550

FOLK MUSIC
Aladdin/Imperial labels, 92n1299
Ethnic music on records, v.1, 92n1305
Irish folk music, 90n1285
Traditional music of Britain & Ireland, 90n1283
World music: a source bk for teaching, 90n1282
World of African music, 94n1315

FOLKLORE
Folklore & folklife, 93n1300
Folklore of American holidays, 2d ed, 93n1297
Folklore of world holidays, 93n1298
Index to fairy tales 1978-86, 5th suppl, 91n1330
Oxford companion to Australian folklore, 94n1390
Storytelling folklore sourcebk, 92n1316

FOLK-SONGS
Irish folk music, 90n1285

FONDA, HENRY
Henry Fonda: a bio-bibliog, 93n1323

FOOD. *See also* NUTRITION
Better Homes & Gardens complete gd to food & cooking, 92n1482
Cassell food dict, 92n1483
Codex alimentarius, v.1, 93n1479
Cooksource, 91n1489
Corinne T. Netzer ency of food values, 93n1476
Dictionary of food & nutrition, 90n1454
Dictionary of food ingredients, 2d ed, 90n1456
Dictionary of nutrition & food tech, 92n1481
Directory of food & nutrition info for professionals & consumers, 2d ed, 94n1604
Encyclopaedia of food sci, food tech, & nutrition, 94n1600
Food finds, 92n1493
Food pollution, 92n1479
Food sci sourcebk, 2d ed, 92n1489
Glutton's glossary, 92n1480
How many calories? how much fat?, 93n1481
Master dict of food & wine, 91n1486
Melting pot: an annot bibliog & gd to food & nutrition info for ethnic groups in America, 94n1599
Nutrition, 90n1648
Nutrition almanac, 3d ed, 91n1481
1000 cooking substitutions, 91n1484
Pesticide residues in food 1990, 92n1498
Post-harvest & processing techs of African staple foods, 93n1478
True grits, 91n199
Wellness ency of food & nutrition, 94n1602

FOOD ADDITIVES
Compendium of food additive specifications, addendum 1, 94n1608
Food additives hndbk, 90n1460
Quick gd to food additives, 2d ed, 92n1494
Vocabulary of food additives, 92n1490

FOOD HABITS
Melting pot: an annot bibliog & gd to food & nutrition info for ethnic groups in America, 94n1599

FOOD INDUSTRY & TRADE
Encyclopaedia of food sci, food tech, & nutrition, 94n1600
Encyclopedia of food sci & tech, 93n1473
Food finds, 92n1493
Food hndbk, 91n1490
Glossary for the food industries, 92n1487
U.S. agricultural groups, 91n1476

FOOD, NATURAL
Catalogue of healthy food, 91n1491

FOOD—PRESERVATION
Almanac of the canning, freezing, preserving industries 1990-91, 92n1478
Directory of the canning, freezing, preserving industries 1990-91, 13th ed, 92n1491
Directory of the canning, freezing, preserving industries 1990-91, deluxe ed, 92n1492

FOOD RELIEF
Food aid in figures, v.8/2, 93n1480

FOOD SUPPLY
Reference gd to world hunger, 92n1486
World hunger, 92n830

FOOT
Selected bibliog of the foot & ankle with commentary, 94n1820

FOOTBALL
Football coach quotes, 93n830
Football scholarship gd, 94n844
Names of the games, 90n762
NCAA football's finest, 93n831
Official 1992 NFL record & fact bk, 94n846
Pro football bio-bibliog, 90n774
Pro football hall of fame, 92n794
Professional football, 94n847
Sporting News complete Super Bowl bk, 1993 ed, 94n848
Sports ency: pro football, 8th ed, 92n795
Timetables of sports hist: football, 90n773
Timetables of sports hist: football, 94n845

FORAGE PLANTS
Forage resources of China, 93n1510

FORCE & ENERGY
Data: where it is & how to get it, 94n45
Digest of UK energy stats 1988, 90n1780
Energy & environmental terms, 90n1775
Energy info abstracts annual 1991, 94n1979
Energy: monthly stats, 91n1802
Energy stats sourcebk, 7th ed, 94n1980
Energy stats yrbk 1987, 91n1803
Energy stats yrbk, 1990, 94n1981
Energy update, 92n1763
International energy stats sourcebk, 2d ed, 94n1984

FORCED MIGRATION
Atlas of intl migration, 94n428

FORECASTING
American forecaster almanac 1990, 90n228
Resources for the future, 94n77

FOREIGN AGENTS
Washington representatives 1992, 93n744

FOREIGN EXCHANGE
World currency monitor annual 1976-89: pound sterling, 91n221
World currency monitor annual 1976-89: US dollar, 91n222

FOREIGN STUDY
Academic yr abroad, 93n392
Academic yr abroad 1989/90, 90n345
Financial aid for research & creative activities abroad 1992-94, 94n367
Financial aid for research, study, travel, & other activities abroad 1990-91, 91n346
Financial aid for study & training abroad 1992-94, 94n368
Foreign students & intl study, 91n341
Free money for foreign study, 92n292
International scholarship dir, 3d ed, 94n332
Scholarships, fellowships & grants for programs abroad, 91n347
Schools abroad of interest to Americans 1988-89, 90n347
Study abroad 26 1989-91, 90n348
Study holidays, 17th ed, 94n369
Vacation study abroad, 42d ed, 93n393
Working holidays 1993, 94n370

FOREIGN TRADE. *See* INTERNATIONAL TRADE

FOREIGN TRADE PROMOTION
United States importers & exporters dir, 90n286

FOREIGNERS. *See* ALIENS; IMMIGRANTS

FORENSIC ACCOUNTING
Litigation servs resource dir, 92n545

FOREST ECOLOGY
Book of forest & thicket, 93n1518
Field gd to the ecology of W forests, 94n1681

FOREST FLORA
Book of forest & thicket, 93n1518

FOREST PRODUCTS
Directory of the wood products industry, 1993, 94n1616
FAO yrbk: forest products 1976-87, 90n1463
FAO yrbk: forest products 1979-90, 93n1483

Forest product prices 1971-90, 94n1615

FORESTRY
Bibliography, 1988-90, 93n1482

FORESTS & FORESTRY
Australia's native forests, 91n1494
Forest inventory terms in Canada, 3d ed, 90n1464
Parks dir of the US, 93n500

FORSYTH, PETER TAYLOR
P. T. Forsyth bibliog & index, 94n1520

FORTIFICATION
Military fortifications, 93n692

FORTUNOFF VIDEO ARCHIVE FOR HOLOCAUST TESTIMONIES
Guide to Yale Univ Lib Holocaust video testimonies, 91n521

FOSS, LUKAS
Lukas Foss: a bio-bibliog, 92n1271

FOSSILS. *See* PALEONTOLOGY

FOUNDATION FOR PUBLIC AFFAIRS (WASHINGTON, D.C.)
Public interest profiles 1992-93, 93n795

FOUNDATIONS
Soil mechanics & fndns, 92n1601

FOUNDATIONS (ENDOWMENTS). *See* CHARITABLE USES, TRUSTS, & FOUNDATIONS; ENDOWMENTS

FOUNDATIONS (PHILANTHROPY). *See* PHILANTHROPY

FOWLES, JOHN
John Fowles: a ref companion, 93n1208

FOX, CHARLES JAMES
Charles James Fox 1749-1806: a bibliog, 93n773

FRACTURE MECHANICS
Dictionary of fracture mechanics, 91n1629

FRACTURES
Selected refs in orthopaedic trauma, 91n1699

FRANCE
Biographical dict of French pol leaders since 1870, 91n758
Cultural atlas of France, 93n143
France under the German occupation, 1940-44, 92n491
French military aviation, 90n660
French women writers, 93n1222
His master's voice/la voix de son maitre, 91n1257
Historical dict of the French 4th & 5th Republics, 1946-91, 93n537
Medieval & renaissance mss in the Walters Art Gallery, v.2, 94n29
Napoleonic source bk, 92n492
Napoleonic uniforms, 94n707
Oz Clarke's new ency of French wines, 92n1484
Visigoths in Gaul & Spain AD 418-711, 90n515

FRANCE—COLONIES—AFRICA
French colonial Africa, 94n95

FRANCE—FOREIGN RELATIONS
French foreign policy 1918-45, rev ed, 92n720

FRANCE—HISTORY
Critical dict of the French Revolution, 90n516
Dictionary of the Napoleonic wars, 94n521
Pamphlets, pers, & songs of the French revolutionary era in the Princeton Univ Lib, 90n517
Tale of two cities: an annot bibliog, 94n1251

FRANCE—MAPS
Michelin motoring atlas: France, 3d ed, 90n457

FRANCHISES (RETAIL TRADE)
Encyclopedia of franchises & franchising, 90n207
Franchise opportunities, 21st ed, 90n208
Franchising in bus, 90n209
Handbook of successful franchising, 3d ed, 91n177
Rating gd to franchises, rev ed, 92n158

Source bk of franchise opportunities, 1990-91 ed., 92n154
Worldwide franchise dir, 92n170

FRANKFORT BOOK FAIR
Who's who at the Frankfurt Bk Fair 1989, 91n658

FREE MATERIAL
Alfred Glossbrenner's master gd to free sftwr for IBMs & compatible computers, 90n1729
Current issues resource builder, 90n88
Educators gd to free films, 49th ed, 90n351
Educators gd to free filmstrips & slides, 45th ed, 94n375
Educators gd to free health, physical educ & recreation materials, 26th ed, 94n829
Educators gd to free home economics & consumer educ materials, 10th ed, 94n886
Educators gd to free social studies materials, 33d ed, 94n81
Educators gd to free videotapes, 39th ed, 93n396
Educators grade gd to free teaching aids, 39th ed, 94n317
Educators index of free materials, 101st ed, 93n328
Elementary teachers gd to free curriculum materials, 50th ed, 94n318
Free mags for libs, 3d ed, 90n79
Free resource builder for librarians & teachers, 2d ed, 93n70
Guide to free computer materials, 90n341
Guide to free computer materials, 11th ed, 94n1911

FREE TRADE & PROTECTION
Protectionism, 90n279
Vocabulary of free trade, 93n233

FREEDOM OF INFORMATION
Access register 1988, 90n553
Information freedom & censorship: world report 1991, 92n593
Intellectual freedom & censorship, 90n614
Intellectual freedom manual, 4th ed, 94n642

FREEDOM OF RELIGION
Intellectual freedom: a ref hndbk, 94n641

FREEDOM OF SPEECH
First amendment, 92n684
Free speech yrbk, v.29, 92n592
Intellectual freedom: a ref hndbk, 94n641

FREEDOM OF THE PRESS
Freedom to publish, 91n957
Intellectual freedom: a ref hndbk, 94n641

FRENCH CANADIAN LITERATURE
Canadian writers, 1920-59, 2d series, 91n1227

FRENCH LANGUAGE—DICTIONARIES—ENGLISH
Ada lang vocablary, 93n1677
Air-conditioning glossary, 91n1635
Alphabetical list of titles of fed statues, 92n550
Artificial intelligence vocabulary, 90n1706
Ashley dict, 90n1040
Beginning French bilingual dict, 2d ed, 90n1044
Canadian quaternary vocabulary, 94n1943
Central heating: glossary, 92n1623
Collection of definitions in fed statutes, 90n545
Collins-Robert French-English, English-French dict, 2d ed, 94n1113
Combinatory vocabulary of CAD/CAM in mechanical engineering, 94n1916
Constitutional glossary, 94n553
Dictionary of Canadian French, 92n1069
Dictionnaire francais, 90n1041
Elsevier's dict of export financing & credit insurance, 91n264
Employment glossary, 91n243
Forest inventory terms in Canada, 3d ed, 90n1464
French dict of info tech, 90n610
French nomenclature of N American birds, 92n1566
French-English agricultural dict, 93n1465
French-English dict of industrial lang, 91n234
Glossary geotextiles, 93n1609
Glossary informatics, 91n605
Glossary of helicopters, 90n1804
Glossary of micrographics, 90n1723

Glossary of museology, 90n954
Glossary of security equipment, 94n1776
Glossary of water terms, 94n1951
Graphic arts vocabulary, 94n1058
Harper Collins French dict, college ed, 91n1084
Human rights, 90n574
Immigration glossary, 91n779
International illus vocabulary of English-French fingerprint terminology..., 93n607
Legal glossary of fed statutes, 90n546
NTC's French & English bus dict, 93n182
NTC's new college French & English dict, 92n1068
Oxford gd to the French lang, 93n1083
Oxford paperback French dict, 90n1043
Ozone layer dict, 94n1945
Packaging, 90n1426
Pensions vocabulary, 92n214
Phonetics & speech sci, 90n992
Potato terms, 91n1487
Public admin & mgmt vocabulary, 91n782
Soil mechanics & fndns, 92n1601
Space station glossary, 93n1581
Space war glossary, 90n677
Statistics & surveys vocabulary, 93n905
Stock market & investment vocabulary, 90n202
Stoddart colour visual dict: French-English, 94n1114
Taxation glossary, 3d ed, 91n288
Unemployment insurance glossary, 93n252
Vocabulary of advanced ceramics, 92n1598
Vocabulary of cell engineering, v.1, 93n1600
Vocabulary of free trade, 93n233
Vocabulary of genetic engineering, 91n1621
Vocabulary of hazardous materials in the workplace, 94n1997
Vocabulary of medical signs & symptoms, 91n1665
Vocabulary of public sector auditing, 94n249
Vocabulary of safety & security equipment, 93n1601
Vocabulary of signs & symptoms of the musculoskeletal system, v.1, 91n1666

FRENCH LANGUAGE—GRAMMAR
Oxford gd to the French lang, 93n1083

FRENCH LANGUAGE—PROVINCIALISMS
Dictionary of Canadian French, 92n1069

FRENCH LITERATURE
Christine de Pizan: a bibliog, 2d ed, 91n1233
French lang & lit, 90n1042
French novelists since 1960, 90n1203
French women writers, 93n1222
Guide to French lit: 1789 to the present, 93n1221
Medieval Charlemagne legend, 94n1199
Nineteenth-century French fiction writers, 94n1283

FRENCH PHILOLOGY
French lang & lit, 90n1042

FRENCH POETRY
Guide to French poetry explication, 94n1284

FRENCH-CANADIAN LITERATURE
Contemporary Canadian & US women of letters, 94n1138
French-Canadian authors, 92n1224

FRESHWATER INVERTEBRATES
Interdisciplinary bibliog of freshwater crayfishes, 90n1550

FREUD, ANNA
Anna Freud: a gd to research, 91n790

FROGS
Australian reptiles & frogs, 91n1602

FRONTIER & PIONEER LIFE
Cowboy & gunfighter collectibles, 90n923
Handbook of the American frontier, v.2, 92n367
Rand McNally atlas of American frontiers, 94n490

FROST, ROBERT
Robert Frost: a ref gd 1974-90, 92n1170

FRUIT
Edible wild fruits & nuts of Canada, 90n1507
European garden flora, v.3, 90n1489
Plant resources of SE Asia, no.2, 92n1475
Utilization of tropical foods: fruits & leaves, 92n1474

FRUIT JUICES
Codex alimentarius, 2d ed, v.6, 94n1606

FRUIT-FLIES
Handbook of the fruit flies (Diptera: Tephritidae) of America North of Mexico, 94n1725

FUNCTION TESTS (MEDICINE)
Concise ency of biological & biomedical measurement systems, 93n1635
Medical tests & diagnostic procedures, 91n1682

FUND RAISING
Annual register of grant support 1989, 90n802
Annual register of grant support, 26th ed, 94n888
Directory of building & equipment grants, 90n807
Directory of fund raising & nonprofit mgmt consultants, 94n901
Fund raiser's gd to human serv funding, 2d ed, 91n868
Fund raiser's gd to human serv funding 1993, 94n899
Fund raiser's gd to religious philanthropy, 3d ed, 91n1416
Fund raiser's gd to religious philanthropy, 5th ed, 93n1425
Funding decision makers 1993, 94n898
Grant seekers gd, 3d ed, 90n810
Handicapped funding dir 1988-89, 90n797
Literature of the nonprofit sector, 90n804
National gd to fndn funding in health, 90n1622
National gd to fndn funding in higher educ, 91n317
Philanthropic studies index, 92n828
Taft gd to corporate giving contacts, 6th ed, 91n864

FUNDAMENTALISM
American Evangelicalism, 92n1408

FUNGI. *See also* MUSHROOMS
Fungi on plants & plant products in the US, 90n1501
Fungi without gills, 92n1543
Mushrooms & truffles of the southwest, 92n1545
New Generation gd to the fungi of Britain & Europe, 90n1500

FUR TRADE
Bibliography of N Manitoba, 92n99

FURNITURE
Complete dict of furniture, rev ed, 92n955

FUTURES MARKET
U.S. industrial outlook '93, 94n218

GABON
Gabon, 94n98

GAG, WANDA
Wanda Gag: a cat raisonne of the prints, 94n1060

GALAPAGOS ISLANDS
Collins field gd to the birds of Galapagos, 91n1561

GALAXIES
Color atlas of galaxies, 90n1748
General cat of HI observations of galaxies: the ref cat, 91n1758

GALLEGAN LITERATURE
Spanish, Catalan, & Galician literary authors of the 20th century, 93n1233

GAMBLING
Encyclopedia of gambling, 91n806

GAME & GAME-BIRDS
Arizona game birds, 90n1529

GAMES
Biographical dict of American sports: basketball & other indoor sports, 90n769
Creative fingerplays & action rhymes, 93n340
Family fun & games, 94n824
Multicultural projects index, 93n1312
Pick-up games, 94n823
Recreation hndbk, 94n827
World of games, 90n771

GARDANO, ANTONIO
Antonio Gardano: Venetian music printer 1538-69, 90n1214

GARDEN TOOLS
Complete illus gd to everything sold in garden centers (except the plants), 91n1500

GARDENING
American Horticultural Society ency of gardening, 94n1617
Complete illus gd to everything sold in garden centers (except the plants), 91n1500
Garden lit, v.1, no.2, 93n1485
Gardener's companion, 92n1503
Gardener's reading gd, 94n1627
Gardening by mail, 3d ed, 91n1497
Larousse gardens & gardening, 91n1504
New gardener's hndbk & dict, 93n1486
North American horticulture, 2d ed, 93n1487
Wise garden ency, 91n1508

GARDENS
American garden gdbk west, 90n1470
Miniature gardens, 91n1499
Public gardens & parks of Niagara, 90n1466
Traveler's gd to American gardens, rev ed, 90n1472

GAS INDUSTRY
Financial Times oil & gas intl yr bk 1993, 93n1748
Financial Times oil & gas intl yrbk 1989, 90n1787
Worldwide natural gas industry dir, 1991, 92n1758

GASES
Radon industry dir 1989, 90n1795

GAUGUIN, PAUL
Paul Gauguin: a bio-bibliog, 92n968

GAWAIN (LEGENDARY CHARACTER)
Sir Gawain & the Green Knight: an annot bibliog, 1978-89, 93n1217

GAYNOR, JANET
Janet Gaynor: a bio-bibliog, 93n1316

GAYS
Big gay bk, 93n886
Gay men & women who enriched the world, 90n814
Lesbian & gay almanac & events of 1990, 91n871
Out of the closet & into the classroom, 94n906
Quentin Crisp's bk of quotations, 91n872
Sexuality & the law, 94n570

GAYS IN LITERATURE
Contemporary gay American novelists, 94n1224
Gay & lesbian American plays, 94n1227
Gay & lesbian characters & themes in mystery novels, 94n1210

GAYS IN MOTION PICTURES
Gay Hollywood film & video gd, 94n1460

GAZETTEERS
Dictionary of world place names derived from British names, 90n429
Omni gazetteer of the USA, 93n495
Statesman's yr-bk world gazetteer, 4th ed, 92n427

GEARING
Dudley's gear hndbk, 2d ed, 92n1624

GEMPYLIDAE
FAO species cat, v.15, 94n1719

GEMS
Gemology, 94n1958

GENEALOGY
Address bk for Germanic genealogy, 4th ed, 93n454

American wills & admins in the Prerogative Court of Canterbury, 1610-1857, 90n389
Ancestry's concise genealogical dict, 90n384
Ancestry's red bk, rev ed, 93n455
A-Z gd to tracing ancestors in Britain, 3d ed, 90n393
A-Z gd to tracing ancestors in Britain, 4th ed, 93n461
Bibliography of genealogy & local hist pers with union list of major US collections, 91n412
Biography & genealogy master index 1991, 92n392
Biography & genealogy master index [CD-ROM], 94n436
Child apprentices in America from Christ's Hospital, London 1617-1778, 91n415
Directory of family assns, 92n385
Directory of family assns, 1993-94 ed, 94n431
Encyclopedia of Jewish genealogy, v.1, 92n384
English origins of American colonists, 92n388
First American Jewish families, 3d ed, 93n458
Genealogical gd to the Burton Histl Collection, 90n394
Genealogies catalogued by the Lib of Congress since 1986, 94n429
Genealogist's address bk, 92n386
German-English genealogical dict, 93n453
Guide to genealogical sftwr, 94n435
Guide to Irish churches & graveyards, 92n389
In search of your roots: a gd for Canadians, rev ed, 93n456
Irish-American heritage, 90n375
Library of Congress: a gd to genealogical & histl research, 91n418
Local hist & genealogy resources of the Calif. State Lib, rev ed, 92n391
PERiodical source index 1847-1985, v.1, 90n397
PERiodical source index 1847-1985, v.3, 90n398
PERiodical source index 1847-1985, v.5-8, 92n393
PERiodical source index 1847-1985, v.9-12, 94n437
PERiodical source index 1989, 92n394
PERiodical source index 1991 annual v., 94n438
Polish roots, 94n433
Prominent families of the USA, 92n387
Researcher's gd to American genealogy, 2d ed, 91n417
Royal descents of 500 immigrants to the American colonies or the US, 94n439
State & province vital records gd, 94n432
State census records, 93n899
Tracing your Irish ancestors, 94n434

GENERALS
Concise dict of military biog, 93n699
Military leaders of the Civil War, 94n701

GENETIC DISORDERS
Encyclopedia of genetic disorders & birth defects, 92n1681
Genetic risks: a ref for eye care practitioners, 91n1684
Guide to selected natl genetic voluntary orgs, Jan 1989, 91n1694

GENETIC ENGINEERING
Genetically engineered human therapeutic drugs, 90n1700
Telegen reporter annual 1988, 90n1596
Vocabulary of genetic engineering, 91n1621

GENETICS
Encyclopedic dict of genetics, 92n1521

GENIZAH
Targumic mss in the Cambridge Genizah collections, 94n1539

GENOCIDE
Facing hist & ourselves: Holocaust & human behavior, 91n518
First-person accounts of genocidal acts in the 20th century, 93n548
Genocide, v.2, 92n560
Genocide in our time, 94n587

GENRE PAINTING
Genre in the age of the Baroque, 92n1004

GEOGRAPHERS
Biographical dict of geography, 94n465
Geographers: biobibliographical studies, v.13, 92n414

GEOGRAPHICAL MYTHS
Atlas of legendary places, 91n1332

GEOGRAPHICAL NAMES. See NAMES, GEOGRAPHICAL

GEOGRAPHY. *See also* Maps *under names of places*
Bibliography of geographic thought, 91n443
Concise Earth facts, 91n424
Concise Earth hist, 92n420
Concise Oxford dict of geography, 93n489
Dictionary of geographical literacy, 94n466
Encyclopedia of the 1st world, 91n85
Europa world yr bk 1989, 90n91
Expert systems in geography & environmental studies, 91n445
Exploring the world, 92n419
Exploring your world, 91n446
Geography: a resource bk for secondary schools, 90n423
Geography from A to Z, 90n419
Geography on file, 92n401
International GIS sourcebk, 1993, 93n491
Lands & peoples, 90n420
Modern dict of geography, 2d ed, 90n421
Modern geography, 92n416
National Geographic index 1888-1988, 91n450
NBC News Rand McNally world news atlas, 1990 ed, 91n543
New Penguin dict of geography, 92n418
Rand McNally children's world atlas, 90n410
Rand McNally world facts & maps, 90n424
Strategic atlas, rev. ed, 91n714
World economic data, 3d ed, 93n273
World facts & figures, 3d ed, 90n92

GEOGRAPHY, HISTORICAL
Atlas of world affairs, 9th ed, 93n720
Harper atlas of world hist, rev ed, 94n528
Rand McNally atlas of world hist, 1992 ed, 93n545
Shedding the veil: mapping the European discovery of America & the world, 93n470
Times atlas of world hist, 3d ed, 91n545
Times atlas of world hist, 4th ed, 94n530

GEOLOGY
AGI data sheets, 3d ed, 91n1781
Bibliography & index of geology, 1988, 90n1763
Bibliography & index of geology, v.53, no.9, 90n1764
Bibliography of N.B. geology (1839-1988), 91n1783
Canadian quaternary vocabulary, 94n1943
Directory of geosci depts: N America, 29th ed, 92n1736
Elsevier's dict of geoscis, 93n1723
GeoRef thesaurus & gd to indexing, 5th ed, 90n1765
GeoRef [CD-ROM], 94n1950
Geostatistical glossary & multilingual dict, 92n1738
Union list of geologic field trip gdbks of N America, 5th ed, 90n1766

GEOMETRY
Computer graphics hndbk: geometry & mathematics, 91n1797

GEOPHYSICS
Encyclopedia of solid earth geophysics, 90n1767

GEOPOLITICS
Atlas of world pol flashpoints, 94n794
Strategic atlas, 3d ed, 94n712

GEORGIA
Georgia: the WPA gd to its towns & countryside, 92n441
Trees of Ga. & adjacent states, 91n1542

GEORGIAN LANGUAGE—DICTIONARIES—ENGLISH
Georgian-English, English-Georgian dict, 93n1084

GEOTEXTILES
Glossary geotextiles, 93n1609

GERIATRIC NURSING
Geriatric nursing assistants, 92n1688

GERIATRICS
Fundamentals of geriatrics for health professionals, 91n1696
Gerontology & geriatrics libs & collections in the US & Canada, 94n655

GERMAN LANGUAGE—DICTIONARIES—ENGLISH
Collins German-English, English-German dict unabridged, 2d ed, 94n1115

Dictionary of chemistry & chemical tech, 4th ed, 91n1772
Dictionary of engineering & tech, 5th ed, 91n1606
Dictionary of terms in music, 4th ed, 93n1248
Glossary of educl tech terms, 94n377
Harper Collins German dict, college ed, 92n1070
NTC's dict of German false cognates, 93n1085
Oxford Duden German dict, 91n1085
Patterson's German-English dict for chemists, 4th ed, 94n1937

GERMAN LITERATURE
Austrian fiction writers, 1875-1913, 90n1192
Companion to 20th-century German lit, 93n1223
German writers in the age of Goethe, 1789-1832, 91n1235
Twentieth-century German novel, 91n1236

GERMAN REUNIFICATION QUESTION (1949-1990)
Big Powers & the German question, 1941-90, 93n538

GERMAN-AMERICANS
Catalog of the German-Americana collection, Univ of Cincinnati, 91n393
German-American heritage, 90n365
Immigrants from the German-speaking countries of Europe, 2d ed, 92n352
Past renewed, 94n411

GERMANY
Charles Szladits' gd to foreign legal materials: German, 2d ed, 91n563
European employment & industrial relations glossary: Germany, 94n253
German reunification, 94n522
German warships 1815-1945, v.1, 91n693
Max Weber, 90n86
Max Weber: a bio-bibliog, 90n84
Nazi-retro film, 93n1362
Operas in German, 92n1289
Twentieth-century German dramatists, 1889-1918, 94n1286
Twentieth-century German dramatists, 1919-92, 94n1287
Where once we walked: a gd to the Jewish communities destroyed in the Holocaust, 93n494

GERMANY—ARMED FORCES
Handbook on German military forces, 92n655

GERMANY—FOREIGN RELATIONS
German foreign policy 1918-45, rev ed, 92n712

GERMANY—GENEALOGY
Address bk for Germanic genealogy, 4th ed, 93n454

GERMANY—HISTORY
Encyclopedia of the Third Reich, 92n493
Germans after WW II, 91n531

GERMANY—POLITICS & GOVERNMENT
Political leaders in Weimar Germany, 94n774

GERMPLASM RESOURCES, PLANT
Elsevier's dict of plant genetic resources, 93n1496

GERNON, JOHN TALBOT—LIBRARY
Matter of taste, 91n1482

GERONTOLOGY. *See also* AGED; AGING
Anthropology of aging, 92n813
Building lib collections on aging, 92n806
Developments & research on aging, 94n871
Encyclopedia of aging & the elderly, 93n858
Gerontology & geriatrics libs & collections in the US & Canada, 94n655
Guide to research in gerontology, 90n793
National dir of educl programs in gerontology & geriatrics 1991, 92n808
Where do we come from? What are we? Where are we going?, 90n785

GERSHWIN, GEORGE
Gershwin companion, 92n1298

GETTYSBURG (PA.), BATTLE OF, 1863
Gettysburg: a battlefield atlas, 93n691

GHANA
Ghana, 92n88

GHOST DANCE
American Indian ghost dance, 1870 & 1890, 92n372

GHOSTS
Encyclopedia of ghosts & spirits, 93n810

GIBSON, WALTER BROWN
Man of magic & mystery, 90n1142

GIDE, ANDRE
Annotated bibliog of criticism on Andre Gide 1973-88, 92n1233

GIFTED CHILDREN
Educational opportunity gd, 1993, 94n316
Gifted & talented info resources, 93n339
Handbook of gifted educ, 92n284

GILA MONSTER
Venomous reptiles of N America, 93n1576

GILBERT, W. S. (WILLIAM SCHWENCK)
How quaint the ways of paradox!, 93n1274

GILL, ERIC
Eric Gill: a bibliog, 2d ed, 92n965

GIRLS
National gd to funding for women & girls, 92n865

GLANVILLE-HICKS, PEGGY
Peggy Glanville-Hicks: a bio-bibliog, 91n1273

GLASS PAINTING & STAINING
Stained glass before 1700 in American collections: midwestern & W states, 91n996
Stained glass before 1700 in American collections: silver-stained roundels & unipartite panels, 92n989

GLOBAL WARMING
Global warming, 94n2014
Vocabulary of global warming, v.1, 94n2001

GOD
Bibliotheca Trinitariorum, v.1, 90n1391
Bibliotheca Trinitariorum, v.2, 90n1392

GODDESSES
Ancient & shining ones, 94n1392
Book of goddesses & heroines, rev ed, 91n1334
Guide to the gods, 93n1305
Women of classical mythology, 92n1320

GODS
Ancient & shining ones, 94n1392
Encyclopedia of gods, 94n1395
Guide to the gods, 93n1305

GOLD COINS
Gold bk: a gd to commonly traded gold bullion coins & bars, 93n226

GOLDSMITHS
Pennsylvania silversmiths, goldsmiths & pewterers 1684-1900, 94n1034

GOLDWORK
Marks of London goldsmiths & silversmiths (c1697-1837), 90n934
Professional goldsmithing, 92n953

GOLF
Complete golfer's cat, 91n836
Encyclopedia of golf, 93n832
Golf Digest almanac 1989, 91n834
Golf gadgets, 91n835
GOLF Magazine's ency of golf, 2d ed, 94n850
Golf playoffs, 92n796
Golfers almanac, 93n833
Guide to golf schools & camps, 93n834
Historical dict of golfing terms, 94n849
Official 1991 US golf course dir & gd, 92n797
Official USGA record bk, 1895-1990, 94n851

GONE WITH THE WIND (MOTION PICTURE)
Complete Gone with the Wind sourcebk, 94n1452
Gone with the Wind on film, 91n1390

GOSPEL MUSIC
Down Home gd to the blues, 92n1300

GOTHIC LITERATURE
Through the pale door, 91n1140

GOTTFRIED VON STRASSBURG
Complete concordance to Gottfried Von Strassburg's Tristan, 94n1200

GOULD, GLENN
Descriptive cat of the Glenn Gould papers, 93n1254
Glenn Gould cat, 93n1253

GOVERNMENT AGENCIES. *See* ADMINISTRATIVE AGENCIES

GOVERNMENT BUILDINGS. *See* PUBLIC BUILDINGS

GOVERNMENT CONSULTANTS
Nonprofit public policy research orgs, 94n753

GOVERNMENT CONTRACTS. *See* PUBLIC CONTRACTS

GOVERNMENT DEPARTMENTS. *See* ADMINISTRATIVE AGENCIES

GOVERNMENT EXECUTIVES
Prune bk: the 60 toughest sci & tech jobs in Washington, 93n757

GOVERNMENT OFFICIALS. *See* PUBLIC OFFICERS

GOVERNMENT PRODUCTIVITY
Public sector productivity, 90n733

GOVERNMENT PUBLICATIONS. *See also under names of countries*
Access to US govt info, 91n46
Bibliographic gd to govt pubs—foreign: 1990, 92n47
Bibliographic gd to govt pubs—US: 1990, 92n48
Directory of computerized data files [1989], 91n42
Free pubs from US govt agencies, 91n44
Guide to official pubs of foreign countries, 92n49
Guide to popular US govt pubs, 2d ed, 91n41
Guide to US govt pubs, 1993 ed, 94n55
Guide to US govt stats, 1989 ed, 91n896
Informing the nation: a hndbk of govt info for librarians, 92n619
International bibliog 1988, v.16, 90n67
Introduction to US govt info sources, 4th ed, 93n73
State doc checklists, 91n729
Subject bibliogs of govt pubs, 91n45
Tapping the govt grapevine, 2d ed, 94n56
Unesco list of docs & pubs 1984-86, 90n722
U.S. govt pubs for the school lib media center, 2d ed, 92n611
Using govt docs, 93n668

GOVERNMENT PUBLICATIONS—AFRICA
French colonial Africa, 94n95

GOVERNMENT PUBLICATIONS—AUSTRALIA
Guide to govt pubs in Austral., 92n50

GOVERNMENT PUBLICATIONS—CANADA
Acid rain: a bibliog of Canadian fed & provincial govt docs, 92n1769
Canadian bus & economics, 3d ed, 94n246

GOVERNMENT PURCHASING
Government contracts ref bk, 93n580
Seller's gd to govt purchasing, 92n139

GOVERNORS
American leaders 1789-1991, 92n680
Biographical dir of the governors of the US 1983-88, 90n483
Kansas governors, 91n495
Louisiana governors, 91n491

GOVERNORS—WIVES
First ladies of Ark., 91n922

GOWER, JOHN
Annotated index to the commentary on John Gower's Confessio Amantis, 91n1208

GRABLE, BETTY
Betty Grable: a bio-bibliog, 94n1408

GRACE, DADDY
Daddy Grace: an annot bibliog, 94n1500

GRADUATE STUDENTS
Free money for graduate school, rev ed, 94n329
Graduate scholarship dir, 3d ed, 94n331

GRADUATE WORK. *See* UNIVERSITIES & COLLEGES—GRADUATE WORK

GRAINGER, PERCY
Source gd to the music of Percy Grainger, 93n1261

GRAMMAR, COMPARATIVE & GENERAL
Theoretical syntax 1980-90, 93n1049

GRAMOPHONE COMPANY
His master's voice/la voce del padrone, 90n1226
His master's voice/la voix de son maitre, 91n1257

GRANADOS, ENRIQUE
Enrique Granados: a bio-bibliog, 93n1259

GRANIVORES
Birds: the plant- & seed-eaters, 90n1518

GRANT, CARY
Cary Grant: a bio-bibliog, 91n1350

GRANTS-IN-AID
Action gd to govt grants, loans, & giveaways, 94n895
America's new fndns 1992, 93n870
Annual register of grant support 1989, 90n802
Awards almanac 1991, 91n313
Awards almanac 1992, 93n871
Catalog of Calif. state grants assistance 1989, 90n803
Directory of building & equipment grants, 90n807
Directory of building & equipment grants, 2d ed, 93n1035
Directory of computer & high tech grants, 92n1706
Directory of corporate & fndn givers 1992, 93n872
Directory of grants in the humanities 1992/93, 93n946
Directory of operating grants, 94n889
Directory of research grants 1989, 90n805
Directory of research grants 1992, 93n873
Directory of women's funds 1988, 90n873
Federal domestic outlays 1983-90, 93n745
Federal educl & scholarship funding gd, 2d ed, 91n329
Federal funding gd 1989, 90n822
Financial aid for research, study, travel, & other activities abroad 1990-91, 91n346
Foundation grants to individuals, 6th ed, 90n809
Government assistance almanac 1989-90, 90n806
Government giveaways for entrepreneurs, 3d ed, 93n210
Grants & awards available to American writers, 17th ed, 93n960
Grants for libs & info servs, 90n592
Grants register 1991-93, 92n295
Guide to fed funding for anti-drug programs 1991, 91n884
Guide to fed funding for govts & nonprofits, 1991, 92n825
Guide to fed funding for hospitals & health centers, 94n1814
Money for visual artists, 92n991
National dir of grants & aid to individuals in the arts, 7th ed, 90n808
National gd to fndn funding in health, 90n1622
Sources: the dir of contacts for editors, reporters & researchers, summer 1990, 26th ed, 91n939

GRAPES OF WRATH
Grapes of Wrath: a 50 yr bibliographic survey, 92n1182

GRAPHIC ARTS
American graphic design, 94n1059
Graphic art of Roi Partridge, 90n982
Graphic arts ency, 93n1042

GRASSES
Fescue grasses of Canada, 91n1531
Guide to grasses of the lower Rio Grande valley, Tex., 94n1665

GRASSLAND FAUNA
Mammals: the large plant-eaters, 90n1522

GRAVEYARDS. See CEMETERIES

GRAY, JOHN
Three decadent poets, 91n1222

GRAY POWER. See SENIOR POWER

GRAZING
Mammals: the large plant-eaters, 90n1522

GREAT BASIN
Sagebrush country, 94n1660

GREAT BRITAIN
Art world dir: arts review yrbk 1993, 94n1044
A-Z gd to tracing ancestors in Britain, 4th ed, 93n461
A-Z of UK brands, 2d ed, 92n236
A-Z of UK mktg data, 4th ed, 92n237
Benjamin Tabart's juvenile lib, 92n1119
BFI film & TV hndbk 1993, 94n1455
Bibliography of cookery bks published in Britain 1875-1914, 90n1453
Biographical dict of life peers, 93n462
Black theatre & performance, 91n1398
Britain 1990, 91n112
British archives, 2d ed, 90n507
British biographical index, 92n55
British broadside ballads of the 16th century, 92n1220
British electorate, 1963-87, 93n772
British English for American readers, 93n1068
British hit albums, 5th ed, 94n1362
British librarianship & info work 1986-90, v.2, 94n633
British lib dir, 90n607
British literary publishing houses, 1881-1965, 93n689
British pharmacopoeia 1993, 94n1876
British printmakers 1855-1955, 94n1057
British radio & TV pioneers, 94n1012
British theatre yrbk 1989, 90n1361
British trademarks of the 1920s & 30s, 90n981
Broadcasting in the UK, 2d ed, 94n1013
Cambridge gd to the historic places of Britain & Ireland, 90n458
Campion, Dowland & the lutenist songwriters, 90n1222
Careers & educl opportunities, 90n360
Cassell concise English dict, new ed, 94n1098
Commonwealth yrbk 1991, 92n100
Concise dict of natl bibliog, 94n13
Consumer mags of the British Isles, 94n267
Contemporary Britain: an annual review 1992, 93n144
Crawford's dir of city connections 1991, 92n156
Crime in Victorian Britain, 94n590
Debrett's peerage & baronetage, 92n395
Dictionary of British studio potters, 91n993
Dictionary of natl biog 1981-85, 91n13
Dictionary of world place names derived from British names, 90n429
Digest of UK energy stats 1988, 90n1780
Directory of employers' assocs, trade unions, joint orgs, 90n253
Directory of lib & info orgs in the UK, 94n635
Directory of medical health care libs in the UK & Republic of Ireland, 7th ed, 92n624
Economic planning 1943-51, 94n263
Economist Pubs pocket gd to advertising, 90n276
Encyclopedia of Britain, 94n133
Encyclopedia of romanticism, 93n531
Encyclopedia of the British pr 1422-1992, 94n1008
English legal hist, 91n562
English religion 1500-40, 90n1379
Famous trials, 93n604
Film & TV hndbk 1990, 91n1388
From Belasco to Brook, 92n1381
Guide to mss & docs in the British Isles relating to S & SE Asia, v.2, 91n97
Guide to the archaeological sites of the British Isles, 90n505
Handbook of English & Celtic studies in the UK and Republic of Ireland, 2d ed, 90n1169
Illustrated dict of British steel engravers, 90n979
Index of paintings sold in the British Isles during the 19th century, v.2, 91n1037
Index to dialect maps of Great Britain, 93n1067
Invertebrates of economic importance in Britain, 4th ed, 91n1556
Investment trust dir 1988-89, 90n212
Julie Andrews: a bio-bibliog, 90n1322
Kelly's business dir 1992, 94n265
Key works to the fauna & flora of the British Isles & NW Europe, 5th ed, 90n1495
Kings & queens of England & Great Britain, 91n523
Libraries dir 1991-93, 94n634
Libraries in the UK & the Republic of Ireland 1990, 91n627
Manual of law French, 2d ed, 91n583
Maps in British pers, pt.1, 91n449
Medical dir 1989, 90n1660
Medicine in Great Britain from the Restoration to the 19th century, 1660-1800, 94n1821
Mosaik's photographic key to the trees & shrubs of Great Britain & N Europe, 94n1670
Music in British libs, 93n650
National trust gd, rev ed, 91n468
New Generation gd to the butterflies & day-flying moths of Britain & Europe, 90n1546
New Generation gd to the fungi of Britain & Europe, 90n1500
Oxford dict of saints, 3d ed, 94n1527
Oxford hist of England: consolidated index, 92n485
Oxford illus literary gd to Great Britain & Ireland, 2d ed, 94n480
Pension funds & their advisors 1992, 94n266
Phrenology in the British Isles, 90n754
Plants & flowers of Great Britain & N Europe, 94n1657
Professional codes of conduct in the UK, 91n269
Record repositories in Great Britain, 9th ed, 92n488
Recreation & entertainment industries, 91n802
Red data birds in Britain, 92n1561
Reruns on file, 93n994
Richard Burton: a bio-bibliog, 93n1322
Shipbuilding industry, 94n2031
Sport in Britain, 93n814
Stationers' co archive, 91n670
Trade union hndbk, 5th ed, 93n305
Traditional music of Britain & Ireland, 90n1283
Trees & shrubs of Great Britain & N Europe, 94n1670
UK bus finance dir 1990/91, 91n217
UK hotel groups dir 1989/90, 91n472
Understanding British English, 91n1076
Urban hist yrbk 1988, 90n846
Victorian criticism of American writers, 92n1159
Victorian music publishers, 92n1254
Victorian pers, v.2, 91n528
Victorian studies, 93n533
Vivien Leigh: a bio-bibliog, 94n1415
Whitaker's bks in print 1993, 94n6
Who's who in art, 24th ed, 92n972
William Pitt the Younger 1759-1806: a bibliog, 90n508
Yorkshire stage 1766-1803, 90n1355

GREAT BRITAIN—BIOGRAPHY
Dictionary of natl biog: missing persons, 94n15
Who's who in early Hanoverian Britain (1714-1789), 94n519

GREAT BRITAIN—CIVILIZATION
Backgrounds to Restoration & 18th-century English lit, 90n1167
1890s: an ency of British lit, art, & culture, 94n981

GREAT BRITAIN—COLONIES
Atlas of British overseas expansion, 92n487
Biographical dict of the British Colonial Serv 1939-66, 92n713
Encyclopedia of colonial & revolutionary America, 91n504

GREAT BRITAIN—ECONOMIC CONDITIONS
Atlas of British social & economic hist since c. 1700, 90n151
Companion to the Industrial Revolution, 91n159

GREAT BRITAIN—FOREIGN RELATIONS—LIBRARY RESOURCES
British foreign policy 1918-45, rev ed, 92n709

GREAT BRITAIN—FOREIGN RELATIONS—MIDDLE EAST
Britain in the Middle East 1921-56, 91n125

GREAT BRITAIN—GENEALOGY
A-Z gd to tracing ancestors in Britain, 3d ed, 90n393
Guide to genealogical resources in the British Isles, 90n395

GREAT BRITAIN—HISTORY
Bayeux tapestry, 2d ed, 91n1005
British histl facts, 1688-1760, 90n506
British naval hist since 1815, 91n527
Companion to the English civil wars, 92n484
Cromwellian gazetteer, 91n524
1890s: an ency of British lit, art, & culture, 94n981
Historical dict of Tudor England, 1485-1603, 93n532
Plantagenet ency, 91n525
Royal Histl Society annual bibliog of British & Irish hist: pubs of 1992, 94n518
Spanish Armada of 1588, 94n527
Victorian Britain, 90n509
Who's who in early Hanoverian Britain (1714-1789), 94n519
Who's who in Roman Britain & Anglo-Saxon England, 92n480
Who's who in Stuart Britain, 92n481
Who's who in Tudor England, 92n482

GREAT BRITAIN. PARLIAMENT
Britain votes 4, 90n719

GREAT BRITAIN—POLITICS & GOVERNMENT
Almanac of British pols, 4th ed, 92n717
Charles James Fox 1749-1806: a bibliog, 93n773
George Grenville 1712-70: a bibliog, 94n775
Lord Grenville 1759-1834: a bibliog, 91n760
Margaret Thatcher: a bibliog, 94n776
William Wilberforce 1759-1833: a bibliog, 93n771

GREAT BRITAIN. ROYAL NAVY
Ships of the royal navy, v.2, 91n692

GREAT LAKES
Great Lakes gd to sunken ships, 94n2029
Literature of the Great Lakes region, 93n1165
Shipping lit of the Great Lakes, 93n1778
Traveler's gd to native America: the Great Lakes region, 94n413

GREAT PLAINS
Common legumes of the Great Plains, 90n1504
Nature's heartland: native plant communities of the Great Plains, 92n1530
Smithsonian gd to historic America: the Plains states, 91n464
Weed seeds of the Great Plains, 94n1663
Wildflowers of the W plains, 94n1655

GREAT POWERS
Strategic atlas, 3d ed, 94n712

GREECE
Ancient Greece, 91n540
Greek & Roman sport, 92n772
Ostraka, 92n503
Place-names in classical mythology: Greece, 90n1302

GREEK LANGUAGE, BIBLICAL
Exegetical dict of the N.T., v.1, 91n1423
Exegetical dict of the N.T., v.2, 93n1426
Exegetical dict of the N.T., v.3, 94n1528
Mastering Greek vocabulary, 92n1073
NIV exhaustive concordance, 91n1427
The student's complete vocabulary gd to the Greek N.T., 94n1543

GREEK LANGUAGE—DICTIONARIES—ENGLISH
NTC's new college Greek & English dict, 92n1072

GREEK LITERATURE
Thesaurus linguae Graecae, 3d ed, 91n1123

GREELEY, HORACE
Horace Greeley: a bio-bibliog, 93n979

GREENE, GRAHAM
Graham Greene: a character index & gd, 92n1203

GREENHOUSE EFFECT, ATMOSPHERIC
Greenhouse effect, 91n1804
Vocabulary of global warming, v.1, 94n2001

GREENHOUSE PLANTS
Ball field gd to diseases of greenhouse ornamentals, 93n1499

GREENLAND
Greenland, 93n119
Greenland since 1979, 91n96

GRENVILLE, GEORGE
George Grenville 1712-1770: a bibliog, 94n775

GRENVILLE, WILLIAM WYNTHAM GRENVILLE, BARON
Lord Grenville 1759-1834: a bibliog, 91n760

GREW, NEHEMIAH
Nehemiah Grew: a study & bibliog of his writings, 92n1532

GRIEF
Death & dying, 92n818

GROCERY TRADE
Cooksource, 91n1489
Ethnic cookbks & food marketplace, 3d ed, 93n1472

GROUND COVER PLANTS
Ground cover plants, 3d ed, 91n1501
Plants for ground-cover, 91n1507

GROUP HOMES
Caring for kids with special needs, 94n918

GROUP WORK IN EDUCATION
Cooperative learning, 92n272

GUERRILLAS
Latin American revolutionaries, 91n761

GUIANA
Caribbean 1975-80, 94n143

GUILLAUME DE LORRIS
Roman de la rose: an annot bibliog, 94n1282

GUITAR
Orion blue bk: guitars & musical instruments 1990, 91n206

GUITAR MUSIC
Classical guitar music in print, 90n1261
Guitar & lute music in pers, 92n1282

GUJARATI LANGUAGE—DICTIONARIES—ENGLISH
Universal English-Gujarati dict, 90n1045

GUMS & RESINS
Water-soluble resins, 2d ed, 93n1713

GUNS. *See* FIREARMS

GUNSMOKE (RADIO PROGRAM)
Gunsmoke: a complete hist & analysis of the legendary broadcast series, 91n970

GUNSMOKE (TELEVISION PROGRAM)
Gunsmoke: a complete hist & analysis of the legendary broadcast series, 91n970

GURNEY, IVOR
Gurney, Ireland, Quilter & Warlock, 90n1223

GUYANA
Guyana, 90n144

GYNECOLOGY
A-Z of women's sexuality, 91n1661
Dictionary of obstetrics & gynecology, 90n1641

HABERMAS, JURGEN
Jurgen Habermas (II): a bibliog, 92n1392

HABITAT (ECOLOGY)
Field gd to wildlife habitats of the eastern US, 91n1547
Field gd to wildlife habitats of the western US, 91n1548
World wildlife habitats, 93n1535

HAITI
Haiti: a research hndbk, 91n121
Haiti: gd to the per lit in English, 1800-1990, 92n113

HALLOWEEN
Weird! the complete bk of Halloween words, 91n1340

HALLS OF FAME
Sports halls of fame, 93n820

HAMLET
Hamlet in the 1960s, 93n1211

HAMMETT, DASHIELL
Dictionary of literary biog documentary series, v.6, 90n1126

HAND WEAVING
Handweaving: an annot bibliog, 92n948
Weaver's bk of 8-shaft patterns, 93n1009

HANDBOOKS, VADE-MECUMS, ETC.
Courvoisier's bk of the best, 94n472
Essential researcher, 94n57
Guinness bk of answers, 8th ed, 93n4
Macmillan visual dict, 93n1077
Matter of fact, v.14-15, 93n910
Pocket ref, 93n1454

HANDEL, GEORGE FRIDERIC
G. F. Handel: a gd to research, 90n1250

HANDICAPPED. See also PHYSICALLY HANDICAPPED
Complete dir for people with disabilities, 1992, 93n862
Directory of college facilities & servs for people with disabilities, 3d ed, 92n321
Directory of residential centers for adults with developmental disabilities, 90n796
Disability, sexuality & abuse, 93n865
Handicapped funding dir 1988-89, 90n797
Meeting the needs of employees with disabilities, 92n228
Meeting the needs of employees with disabilities, 2d ed, 94n881
National housing dir for people with disabilities, 1993, 94n883
Portraying persons with disabilities: an annot bibliog of fiction, 3d ed, 93n1132
Portraying persons with disabilities: an annot bibliog of nonfiction, 2d ed, 93n1124
Resources for people with disabilities & chronic conditions, 92n821
Resources for people with disabilities & chronic conditions, 2d ed, 94n882
Sports & recreation for the disabled, 91n813
Understanding abilities, disabilities, & capabilities, 92n318

HANDICAPPED CHILDREN
Concise ency of special educ, 92n320
Individuals with disabilities educ act 1980-91, 93n394
Parent resource dir, 2d ed, 90n832
Reader's gd for parents of children with mental, physical, or emotional disabilities, 3d ed, 91n857
School Search gd to private schools for students with learning disabilities, 91n350
Special educ hndbk, 92n323
Teaching sci to children, 2d ed, 94n1559

HANDICRAFT
Crafts index for young people, 93n1005
Crafts supply sourcebk, 91n991
Custom made, 91n190
Fun for kids 2, 93n1006
Guide to arts & crafts workshops, 91n994
Make it 2, 90n935
Multicultural projects index, 93n1312
Traveler's gd to American crafts east of the Miss., 91n992

Who's who in Alaskan arts & crafts, 3d ed, 91n997

HANSON, HOWARD
Howard Hanson: a bio-bibliog, 94n1330

HAPPINESS
Medieval Consolation of Philosophy: an annot bibliog, 94n1487

HARDING, WARREN G.
Warren G. Harding: a bibliog, 93n509

HARDWARE
Complete illus gd to everything sold in hdwr stores, 90n1609
Illustrated hrdwr bk, 93n1611

HARDY, THOMAS
Annotated critical bibliog of Thomas Hardy, 90n1179
KWIC concordance to Thomas Hardy's Tess of the D'Urbervilles, 90n1180
Thomas Hardy dict, 91n1209

HARPSICHORD MUSIC
Harpsichord & clavichord music of the 20th century, 94n1335
Organ & harpsichord music by women composers, 92n1266

HARRIS, ROY
Roy Harris: a bio-bibliog, 92n1277

HARRISON, JANE ELLEN
Cambridge ritualists, 92n1132

HARRISON, TONY
Tony Harrison: a bibliog 1957-87, 91n1210

HARVARD BUSINESS SCHOOL. BAKER LIBRARY
Harvard Bus School core collection 1993, 94n156

HARVARD UNIVERSITY. FINE ARTS LIBRARY
Iconographic index to N.T. subjects represented in photographs & slides of paintings in the visual collections, Fine Arts Lib, Harvard Univ, v.1, 94n1540

HARVARD UNIVERSITY—LIBRARY
Catalogue of the 15th-century printed bks in the Harvard Univ Lib, v.1, 92n36
Catalogue of the 15th-century printed bks in the Harvard Univ Lib, v.2, 94n31

HAWAII
Encyclopedia of the far west, 92n84
Hawai'i, 94n90
Hawaiian insects & their kin, 93n1565
Hawaiian reef animals, rev ed, 91n1599
Insects of Hawaii, v.15, 93n1561
Marine atlas of the Hawaiian Islands, 93n466
Pocket place names of Hawai'i, 90n428
Trees of Hawai'i, 92n1553

HAWAIIAN LANGUAGE—DICTIONARIES—ENGLISH
New pocket Hawaiian dict, 93n1086

HAWTHORNE, NATHANIEL
Nathaniel Hawthorne: an annot bibliog of comment & criticism before 1900, 90n1143
Nathaniel Hawthorne ency, 92n1171

HAYDN, JOSEPH
Franz Joseph Haydn: a gd to research, 91n1272

HAYDN, MICHAEL
Johann Michael Haydn (1737-1806): a chronological thematic cat of his works, 94n1332

HAYES, HELEN
Helen Hayes: a bio-bibliog, 94n1416

HAYMARKET SQUARE RIOT, CHICAGO, ILL, 1886
Haymarket affair, 94n786

HAZARDOUS SUBSTANCES
Book of lists for regulated hazardous substances 1993, 94n2010
Bretherick's hndbk of reactive chemical hazards, 4th ed, 92n1724
Dangerous properties of industrial materials, 7th ed, 90n1758
Extremely hazardous substances, 90n1798
Firefighter's hazardous materials ref bk, 92n1781

Firefighter's hazardous materials ref bk & index, 2d ed, 94n2011
Hazardous chemicals desk ref, 2d ed, 92n1727
Hazardous substances resource gd, 94n2016
MSDS pocket dict, 92n1772
Rapid gd to hazardous chemicals in the workplace, 2d ed, 91n1776
Toxic substances controls gd, 90n1799
Toxicological evaluations, 1, 92n1729
Vocabulary of hazardous materials in the workplace, 94n1997

HAZARDOUS WASTES
Encyclopedia of environmental control tech, v.4, 92n1774
Environmental hazards: toxic waste & hazardous material, 93n1770
Hazardous waste mgmt facilities dir, 91n1807
Radioactive waste as a social & pol issue, 92n1768
Standard hndbk of hazardous waste treatment & disposal, 90n1594
Thermal treatment of hazardous wastes, 90n1793
Toxic substances controls gd, 90n1799

H.D. (HILDA DOOLITTLE)
H.D.: a bibliog 1905-90, 94n1234

HEADS OF STATE
Columbia dict of pol biog, 92n670
Liberators & patriots of Latin America, 92n108
Who's who in European pols, 92n719

HEALTH
Best of health, 91n1643
CHID search ref gd, June 1990, 91n1638
CHID word list, June 1990, 91n1639
Consumer health info source bk, 3d ed, 91n1680
Dieter's dict & problem solver, 94n1603
Encyclopedia of good health, 90n1644
Exercise, 90n1645
Focus on fitness, 94n843
Health & mental health: dir of key legislators, 90n1617
Human sexuality, 90n1646
Illustrated dict of natural health, 90n1642
Index to health info 1988 abstracts, v.1, no.2, 90n1632
Macmillan health ency, 94n1803
Maintaining good health, 90n1647
Marshall Cavendish ency of family health, 93n1617
Marshall Cavendish ency of health, 92n1633
Medical & health info dir, 4th ed, 90n1620
National gd to fndn funding in health, 90n1622
Nutrition, 90n1648
Nutrition & health ency, 2d ed, 90n1614
Random House health & medicine dict, 94n1830
Stress and mental health, 90n1649
Substance abuse, 90n1650
Wellness ency, 92n1642
World Book health & medical annual 1989, 90n1630

HEALTH CARE. *See* **MEDICAL CARE**

HEALTH ECOLOGY. *See* **ENVIRONMENTAL HEALTH**

HEALTH EDUCATION
Educators gd to free health, physical educ & recreation materials, 26th ed, 94n829
Guide to clinical preventive servs, 90n1626
Sickness & wellness pubs, 90n1610

HEALTH FACILITIES
Health care in Fla., 92n1638

HEALTH FOOD. *See* **FOOD, NATURAL**

HEALTH MAINTENANCE ORGANIZATIONS
HMO/PPO dir, 91n1647
HMO/PPO dir 1993, 94n1815

HEALTH OCCUPATIONS
Keyguide to info sources in paramedical scis, 92n1637

HEALTH RISK ASSESSMENT
Chemical hazard communication gdbk, 2d ed, 94n2018
Computer health hazards, 92n1710

HEALTH SERVICES ADMINISTRATION
Aspen dict of health care admin, 90n1612

HEATING
Central heating: glossary, 92n1623
Handbook of HVAC design, 91n1634

HEAVY MINERALS
Heavy minerals in colour, 93n1726

HEBREW IMPRINTS
Planets, potions & parchments, 92n1464

HEBREW LANGUAGE
New concordance of the Bible, 90n1399

HEBREW LANGUAGE—DICTIONARIES—ENGLISH
Renyi picture dict: Hebrew & English, 94n1116
Theological dict of the O.T., v.6, 91n1424
Webster's new world Hebrew dict, 93n1087

HEIDEGGER, MARTIN
Martin Heidegger, 91n1402

HELICONIA
Heliconia: an identification gd, 92n1535

HELICOPTERS
Combat arms: modern helicopters, 91n687
Glossary of helicopters, 90n1804
Illustrated hist of helicopters, 91n689

HELPING BEHAVIOR IN CHILDREN
Prosocial dvlpmt in children, 93n894

HEMINGWAY, ERNEST
Concordance to Hemingway's In Our Time, 91n1163
Ernest Hemingway: a ref gd 1974-89, 92n1172
Hemingway: an annot chronology, 93n1174

HERALDRY
Debrett's peerage & baronetage, 92n395

HERBIVORES
Birds: the plant- & seed-eaters, 90n1518
Mammals: the small plant-eaters, 90n1523

HERBS
Cleveland herbal, botanical, & horticultural collections, 93n1493
Complete bk of herbs, spices & condiments, 91n1492
Complete medicinal herbal, 94n1666
Herbal medicine past & present, v.2, 91n1535
Herbs, spices, & medicinal plants, v.4, 91n1534
Lifetime ency of natural remedies, 94n1826
Macmillan treasury of spices & natural flavorings, 90n1457

HERESIES, CHRISTIAN
Encyclopedia of heresies & heretics, 94n1530

HERMAN, WOODY
Woody Herman: a gd to the big band recordings, 1936-87, 92n1301

HEROES
Contemporary heroes & heroines, bk 2, 93n45
Courage in the air, 93n697

HEROINES
Contemporary heroes & heroines, bk 2, 93n45

HERPETOLOGY
Synopsis of the herpetofauna of Mexico, v.7, 94n1752

HESBURGH, THEODORE MARTIN
Theodore M. Hesburgh: a bio-bibliog, 91n311

HESSE, EVA
Eva Hesse sculpture, 90n951

HIGH ALTITUDE GARDENING
Low-water flower gardener, 94n1630

HIGH DEFINITION TELEVISION
High definition TV, 91n1618

HIGH INTEREST-LOW VOCABULARY BOOKS
Best: high/low bks for reluctant readers, 91n367
Choices, v.2, 92n330
Easy reading, 2d ed, 91n368

High interest easy reading, 6th ed, 91n366
High/low hndbk, 3d ed, 91n365

HIGH SCHOOL LIBRARIES—BOOK LISTS
Books for you, 11th ed, 94n1165
Seniorplots, 90n1093

HIGH SCHOOL STUDENTS
Best bks for sr high readers, 92n1117
Focus on school, 91n308

HIGH SCHOOLS
Who's who in athletics in American high schools, 92n770

HIGH TECHNOLOGY
Directory of computer & high tech grants, 92n1706
High-tech hndbk, 92n1700
How the new tech works, 92n1699
Japan's high tech, 92n1701
Library hi tech bibliog, v.5, 92n597

HIGH TECHNOLOGY INDUSTRIES
Hidden job market, 93n303

HIGHER EDUCATION. *See* **EDUCATION, HIGHER**

HIKING
Essential gd to hiking in the US, 93n835

HILL, EDWARD BURLINGAME
Edward Burlingame Hill: a bio-bibliog, 90n1255

HIMES, CHESTER B.
Chester Himes: an annot primary & secondary bibliog, 94n1235

HISPANIC AMERICAN PERIODICALS INDEX
HAPI thesaurus & name authority 1970-89, 92n587

HISPANIC-AMERICAN WOMEN
Notable Hispanic American women, 94n962
Women of color & S women annual suppl, 1991/92, 94n955

HISPANIC-AMERICANS
Alcohol-related issues in the Latino population 1980-90, 94n915
American ethnic lits, 94n1225
At-risk youth, 91n310
Directory of ethnic professionals in LIS (lib & info sci), 93n625
Extraordinary Hispanic Americans, 93n51
Hispanic Americans: a statistical sourcebk, 1991 ed, 92n354
Hispanic Americans info dir 1990-91, 91n394
Hispanic Americans info dir 1992-93, 93n428
Hispanic heritage, series 4, 93n150
Hispanic image on the silver screen, 93n1363
Hispanic presence in N America from 1492 to today, 93n427
Hispanic resource dir 1992-94, 93n429
Hispanic-American almanac, 94n412
Hispanic-American material culture, 90n366
Latino librarianship, 92n618
National roster of Hispanic elected officials, 1989, 91n740
Statistical hndbk on US Hispanics, 92n356
Who's who among Hispanic Americans 1991-92, 92n357
Who's who: Chicano officeholders, 1990-91, 92n690

HISPANISTS
Hispanic way, 92n355

HISPANOLA
Caribbean 1975-80, 94n143

HISTORIANS
Blackwell dict of historians, 90n530
Great historians from antiquity to 1800, 91n548
Great historians of the modern age, 92n502
Past renewed, 94n411

HISTORIC BUILDINGS
Guide to black Washington, 91n458
Landmark yellow pages, 91n1028
National trust gd, rev ed, 91n468

HISTORIC SHIPS
Great American ships, 93n1788
Historic warships, 94n703

HISTORIC SITES
Cambridge gd to the historic places of Britain & Ireland, 90n458
East & SE Asia material culture in N America, 90n504
Hippocrene USA gd to black America, 93n424
Hippocrene USA gd to historic black south, 94n475
Historic landmarks of black America, 92n440
Historic sites & markers along the Mormon & other great W trails, 90n435
Parks dir of the US, 93n500
Smithsonian gd to historic America: the Plains states, 91n464
Tour gd to the Civil War, 3d ed, 91n456
Tour gd to the old west, 2d ed, 91n457

HISTORICAL FICTION
Twentieth-century romance & histl fiction writers, 2d ed, 91n1136

HISTORICAL FILMS
Epic films, 92n1369

HISTORICAL GEOGRAPHY. *See* **GEOGRAPHY, HISTORICAL**

HISTORICAL LIBRARIES
Guide to the hist of Calif., 90n500

HISTORICAL MARKERS
Historic sites & markers along the Mormon & other great W trails, 90n435

HISTORICAL MUSEUMS
East & SE Asia material culture in N America, 90n504

HISTORIOGRAPHY
Methodology & method in hist, 91n170
Selected bibliog of modern historiography, 93n546

HISTORY. *See also* History *under specific subjects and names of countries, states, etc.*
Annual register 1988, 90n704
Dictionary of historic docs, 92n508
Meaning of hist, 92n513
Reference sources in hist, 92n500
Timetables of hist, 3d ed, 93n560
Walford's gd to ref material, 5th ed, v.2: social & histl scis, 93n98

HISTORY, ANCIENT
Chronologies in old world archaeology, 3d ed, 94n485
Historical jls, 2d ed, 94n542
Lexicon of the Greek & Roman cities & place names in antiquity ca. 1500 B.C.—ca. A.D. 500, fascicule 1, 94n535
Smithsonian timelines of the ancient world, 94n534

HISTORY IN ART
Historical art index A.D. 400-1650, 90n965

HISTORY, MODERN
Dictionary of 20th century hist, 91n553
Facts on File ency of the 20th century, 92n507
First-person accounts of genocidal acts in the 20th century, 93n548
Great events: the 20th century, 94n539
Longman hndbk of world hist since 1914, 93n559
Oxford minidict of 20th-century world hist, 92n511

HITCHCOCK, ALFRED
Alfred Hitchcock: a gd to refs & resources, 94n1450

HITLER, ADOLF
Hitler fact bk, 91n530

HMOs. *See* **HEALTH MAINTENANCE ORGANIZATIONS**

HOBBIES
Hobbyist sourcebk, 91n977

HOBSON-JOBSON
Sahibs, nabobs & boxwallahs, 93n1070

HOCKEY
Complete ency of hockey, 4th ed, 94n852
Hockey scouting report, 1989-90, 90n775
Names of the games, 90n762
National Hockey League official gd & record bk 1989-90, 91n837
National Hockey League official gd & record bk 1992-93, 94n853

HODDINOTT, ALUN
Alun Hoddinott: a bio-bibliog, 94n1322

HOLIDAYS
Chase's annual events 1990, 91n2
Folklore of American holidays, 2d ed, 93n1297
Folklore of world holidays, 93n1298
Holidays & anniversaries of the world, 2d ed, 91n1341
Holidays & special days project index for young people, 93n1308
Our natl holidays, 93n1313

HOLISTIC MEDICINE
Holistic health dir, 1992-93, 94n1808

HOLOCAUST, JEWISH (1939-1945)
Bibliography of the Holocaust Memorial Resource & Educ Center of central Fla., 92n479
Bibliography on Holocaust lit: suppl., 91n519
Bibliography on Holocaust lit, suppl. v.2, 94n532
Catalogue of audio & video collections of Holocaust testimony, 2d ed, 93n528
Encyclopedia of the Holocaust, 91n520
Facing hist & ourselves: Holocaust & human behavior, 91n518
Films of the Holocaust, 91n1384
Guide to Yale Univ Lib Holocaust video testimonies, 91n521
Holocaust, Israel, & the Jews: motion pictures in the Natl Archives, 91n405
Holocaust lit, 94n538
Jewish Holocaust: an annot gd to bks in English, 92n477
Lithuanian Jewish communities, 92n489
World in turmoil, 93n550

HOLOGRAPHY
Holography market place, 3d ed, 93n1012
Holography marketplace 1989, 90n941

HOLY SPIRIT
Bibliography of the nature & role of the holy spirit in 20th-century writings, 94n1534
Holy spirit, 90n1390

HOLY WELLS
Holy wells & sacred water sources in Britain & Ireland, 94n1386

HOME CARE SERVICES
Home health care, 93n1620

HOME CONSTRUCTION. *See* HOUSE CONSTRUCTION

HOME ECONOMICS
Educators gd to free home economics & consumer educ materials, 10th ed, 94n886

HOME FURNISHINGS. *See* HOUSE FURNISHINGS

HOME LABOR
Work-at-home sourcebk, 4th ed, 93n308

HOME SCHOOLING
Home schooling laws in all 50 states, 4th ed, 91n296

HOME VIDEO SYSTEMS
New video ency, 92n912

HOME-BASED BUSINESSES
Work-at-home sourcebk, 4th ed, 93n308

HOMELESS YOUTH
North American dir of programs for runaways, homeless youth, & missing children, 90n831

HOMELESSNESS
American homelessness, 91n850
Guide to fed funding for housing & homeless programs, 94n876
Homeless in America, 90n794
Homelessness: abstracts of the psychological & behavioral lit 1967-90, 92n835
Homelessness: an annot bibliog, 94n877

HOMEOPATHY
Family health gd to homeopathy, 94n1842
Homoeopathy in the US, 92n1647

HOMER
Classical epic: an annot bibliog, 92n1135

HOMOSEXUALITY
Alyson almanac: a treasury of info for the gay & lesbian community, 90n812
Encyclopedia of homosexuality, 91n870
Gay men & women who enriched the world, 90n814
Homosexual & society, 91n873
Legal gd for lesbian & gay couples, 5th ed, 90n556
Lesbian & gay almanac & events of 1990, 91n871
Quentin Crisp's bk of quotations, 91n872
Uranian worlds, 2d ed, 91n1141

HOMOSEXUALITY & LITERATURE
Contemporary gay American novelists, 94n1224
Gay & lesbian American plays, 94n1227
Gay & lesbian characters & themes in mystery novels, 94n1210

HOMOSEXUALITY IN LITERATURE
Out of the closet & into the classroom, 94n906

HOMOSEXUALITY IN MOTION PICTURES
Gays & lesbians in mainstream cinema, 94n1446

HOMOSEXUALS. *See* GAYS; LESBIANS

HONDURAS
Honduras, 93n155

HONG KONG
Historical dict of Hong Kong & Macau, 94n110

HOOVER, HERBERT
Herbert Hoover: a bibliog, 94n496
Herbert Hoover: a bibliog of his times & presidency, 92n454

HOPKINS, GERARD MANLEY
Concordance to the sermons of Gerard Manley Hopkins, 90n1181

HORKHEIMER, MAX
Max Horkheimer, 91n80

HORN BOOK MAGAZINE
Horn Bk index 1924-89, 91n1122

HORROR FILMS
Critical gd to horror film series, 93n1354
Fantastic cinema subject gd, 94n1449
Horror: a connoisseur's gd to lit & film, 90n882
Horror film directors, 1931-90, 92n1348
Horror film stars, 2d ed, 92n1366
Official splatter movie gd, 91n1389
Peter Cushing: the gentle man of horror & his 91 films, 94n1437
Poverty row horrors, 94n1461
Revenge of the creature features movie gd, 3d ed, 90n1330
Science fiction, horror & fantasy film & TV credits suppl-1987, 90n1350
Science fiction stars & horror heroes, 92n1371
Television horror movie hosts, 93n985
Universal horrors, 92n1358

HORROR TALES
Horror: a connoisseur's gd to lit & film, 90n882
Horror lit: a reader's gd, 91n1138
Science fiction & fantasy lit 1975-91, 94n1214
Science fiction, fantasy & horror, 1987, 90n1112
Science fiction, fantasy & horror ref, 90n1110
Shape under the sheet, 92n1175
Stephen King companion, 90n1148
Through the pale door, 91n1140
Transylvanian lib, 94n1212

HORROR TELEVISION PROGRAMS
Television horror movie hosts, 93n985

HORSES
A-Z of horse diseases & health problems, 91n1511
Dogs, cats, & horses, 91n1116
Horse industry dir, 1990-91, 92n1511
Horse owner's vet hndbk, 90n1474
Horses, 94n1707
Horses & tack, rev ed, 92n1510

Horse's name was..., 94n1709
Illustrated intl ency of horse breeds & breeding, 91n1577
Stable vet hndbk, 91n1512

HORTICULTURE
Gardener's dict of horticultural terms, 94n1618
Gardening by mail, 3d ed, 91n1497
North American horticulture, 2d ed, 93n1487

HOSPICE (TERMINAL CARE)
Hospices, 92n819
Palliative care of the elderly, 93n857

HOSPITALITY INDUSTRY
Guide to hospitality & tourism educ 1989-90, 91n315
Literature gd to the hospitality industry, 91n231

HOSPITALS
Canadian hospital dir, v.38, Sept 90, 91n1645
Directory of hospital personnel 1989, 90n1615
Directory of medical rehabilitation programs, 91n1668
Directory of women's health care centers, 90n1616
Hospital governance, 91n1641
Hospital lit index, v.47, no.1, 92n1643
Register of N American hospitals, 1993, 94n1806

HOTELS, TAVERNS, ETC.
Hotel & restaurant industries, 90n243
Peterson's dir of college accommodations, 90n437
UK hotel groups dir 1989/90, 91n472

HOTLINES (COUNSELING)
Directory of natl helplines, 91n849
Directory of natl helplines 1993, 94n47

HOUSE CONSTRUCTION
Building construction illus, 2d ed, 92n1600
Home building & woodworking in colonial America, 93n1612

HOUSE FURNISHINGS
Decorative arts & household furnishings in America 1650-1920, 91n978
Well-appointed bath, 90n971

HOUSE ORGANS
Corporate mags of the US, 93n217

HOUSE PLANTS
Foliage plants for decorating indoors, 90n1469
Indoor plants, 92n1505
Prentice-Hall pocket ency: house plants, 90n1471

HOUSEHOLD SUPPLIES
Consumer's dict of household, yard & office chemicals, 93n1754

HOUSEHOLD SURVEYS
Official gd to household spending, 2d ed, 94n927

HOUSING
Congregate care by county, 90n786
Directory of housing attorneys, 1990-91, 92n542
Guide to fed funding for housing & homeless programs, 94n876
International hndbk of housing policies & practices, 92n850

HOUSING & HEALTH
Consumer's dict of household, yard & office chemicals, 93n1754
Tackling toxics in everyday products, 93n1761

HUDSON RIVER SCHOOL
Hudson River school, 92n1002

HUGHES, LANGSTON
Langston Hughes: a bio-bibliog, 91n1164

HUMAN ANATOMY. *See* **ANATOMY, HUMAN**

HUMAN BODY. *See* **BODY, HUMAN**

HUMAN BIOLOGY
Encyclopedia of human biology, 92n1516

HUMAN CAPITAL
Human dvlpmt report 1991, 92n75
Human resources yrbk, 1990 ed, 92n225

HUMAN CHROMOSOMES
Mendelian inheritance in man, 9th ed, 91n1679
Mendelian inheritance in man, 10th ed, 93n1624

HUMAN ECOLOGY
Changing wilderness values,1930-90, 92n1767
Environmentalist's bkshelf, 94n1992
Island Pr bibliog of environmental lit, 94n1990
Rand McNally children's atlas of the environment, 92n1766
Reading about the environment, 94n1991
Rediscovery of creation, 93n1417

HUMAN ENGINEERING
Dictionary for human factors/ergonomics, 94n1791

HUMAN EVOLUTION
Cambridge ency of human evolution, 94n394
Encyclopedia of evolution, 92n1523

HUMAN GEOGRAPHY. *See* **ANTHROPO-GEOGRAPHY**

HUMAN REPRODUCTION
Encyclopedia of childbearing, 94n1831
In vitro fertilization clinics, 94n1857
Language of sex, 93n883
Reproduction: a gd to materials in the Women's Educl Resource Centre, 93n885

HUMAN RESOURCES. *See* **HUMAN CAPITAL**

HUMAN RIGHTS. *See also* **CIVIL RIGHTS**
Amnesty Intl: the 1993 report on human rights around the world, 94n591
Canadian human rights yrbk 1989-90, 92n559
Encyclopedia of human rights, 92n563
Freedom in the world, 92n561
Great events from hist 2: human rights series, 93n617
Great lives: human rights, 92n562
Guide to research on Martin Luther King, Jr., & the modern black freedom struggle, 91n600
Human rights, 90n574
Human rights: a dir of resources, 90n572
Human rights: a ref hndbk, 90n575
Human rights dir: Latin American & the Caribbean, 91n601
Human rights, refugees, migrants & dvlpmt, 94n593
Human rights: 60 major global instruments, 93n615
Judaism & human rights in contemporary thought, 94n1555
World dir of human rights research & training insts, 2d ed, 93n619
World dir of peace research & training insts, 7th ed, 93n792
World human rights gd, 3d ed, 94n594
World racism & related inhumanities, 93n618

HUMAN SERVICES
Artisthelp, 91n877
Fund raiser's gd to human serv funding, 2d ed, 91n868
Fund raiser's gd to human serv funding 1993, 94n899
Source bk 1989-90: social & health servs in the greater NY area, 90n818

HUMAN SETTLEMENTS
Urban south, 90n843

HUMAN-COMPUTER INTERACTION
Abstracts in human-computer interaction, v.1: issue 2, June 1990, 92n1704
Information sources for virtual reality, 94n1894
Resources in human-computer interaction, 92n1712
Virtual reality: a selected bibliog, 93n1672

HUMANISM
Iter Italicum, v.6, 94n978

HUMANITIES
American humanities index for 1987, v.13, 90n885
American humanities index for 1991, v.17, 93n945
Directory of grants in the humanities 1988, 90n883
Directory of grants in the humanities 1992/93, 93n946
Guide to research & scholarship in Hungary, 90n309
Humanities computing yrbk 1988, 90n884
Humanities computing yrbk 1989-90, 92n880
Humanities index, 93n948

Humanities index, Apr 89 to Mar 90, 92n881
Key ideas in human thought, 94n1497
Persian & English glossary for humanities & social scis, 93n1090

HUNGARIAN LANGUAGE—DICTIONARIES—ENGLISH
Concise Hungarian-English dict, 92n1076
Hippocrene concise dict: English-Hungarian, Hungarian-English, 92n1077

HUNGARIAN-CANADIANS
Canadian studies on Hungarians: a bibliog. Suppl., 94n408

HUNGARY
Canadian studies on Hungarians: a bibliog. Suppl., 94n408
Guide to research & scholarship in Hungary, 90n309
Hippocrene insider's gd to Hungary, 93n505
Hungary: a complete gd, 4th ed, 92n448

HUNGER
Reference gd to world hunger, 92n1486
World hunger, 92n830

HUNTING
Bookman's gd to hunting, shooting, angling, & related subjects, 92n799
Hunting quotations, 93n836

HUSA, KAREL
Karel Husa: a bio-bibliog, 92n1267

HUTTERITE BRETHREN
Sociology of Mennonites, Hutterites & Amish, v.2, 92n1410

HYDROGEN
General cat of HI observations of galaxies: the ref cat, 91n1758

HYDROLOGY
Elsevier's dict of hydrology & water quality mgmt, 93n1724
Handbook of hydrology, 94n1953
International glossary of hydrology, 2d ed, 94n1952
Water ency, 2d ed, 91n1785

HYGIENE, SEXUAL
A-to-Z of women's sexuality, rev ed, 93n884
Language of sex, 93n883

HYMENOPTERA
Hymenoptera of the world, 94n1726

HYMNAL 1982
Concordance of The Hymnal 1982, 90n1264

HYMNS
American sacred music imprints 1698-1810, 91n1291
Concordance of The Pilgrim Hymnal, 90n1265

HYPERTEXT SYSTEMS
Emerging techs & instruction, 93n344

HYPNOTISM
Dictionary of hypnotism, 92n763

IBERIAN LITERATURE
Dictionary of the lit of the Iberian Peninsula, 94n1289

IBM PERSONAL COMPUTER
Best of shareware: IBM PC utilities, 91n1739

ICE HOCKEY. *See* **HOCKEY**

ICELAND
Mineral deposits of Europe, v.4/5, 91n1787

ICELANDIC LANGUAGE—DICTIONARIES—ENGLISH
Icelandic-English, English-Icelandic dict, 91n1087

ICELANDIC LITERATURE
Bibliography of modern Icelandic lit in translation, suppl., 1971-80, 92n1236

ILLINOIS
Awesome almanac—Ill., 94n84
Carnegie lib in Ill., 92n602
Guide to the hist of Ill., 92n471

ILLINOIS LIBRARY AND INFORMATION NETWORK
Directory of the Ill. lib & info network, 91n609

ILLITERACY. *See* **LITERACY**

ILLUMINATION OF BOOKS AND MANUSCRIPTS, MEDIEVAL
Illuminated & decorated medieval mss in the Univ Lib, Utrecht, 91n1039

ILLUSTRATED BOOKS
Photography & lit, 93n1013

ILLUSTRATED BOOKS, CHILDREN'S
Artists of the page, 93n1022
Children's bk illus & design, 94n1062
Children's writer's & illustrator's market, 1989, 90n897
Newbery & Caldecott awards, 1992 ed, 93n1128
Newbery & Caldecott medal & honor bks in other media, 93n1121
Newbery & Caldecott medalists & honor bk winners, 2d ed, 93n1120

ILLUSTRATORS
Artists as illustrators, 90n959
Artists of the page, 93n1022
Author profile collection, 93n1138
Biographical index to children's & young adult authors & illustrators, 93n1144
CANSCAIP companion, 92n875
Children's bk illus & design, 94n1062
Jessie Willcox Smith: a bibliog, 90n984
Major authors & illustrators for children & young adults, 94n1187
Meet the authors & illustrators, 94n1193
Presenting children's authors, illustrators & performers, 92n1127
Sixth bk of jr authors & illustrators, 90n30
Talking with artists, 93n1021

IMAGE TRANSMISSION
AIIM speakers dir 1992-93, 93n1668

IMAGING SYSTEMS
International imaging source bk 1992, 93n1693

IMMIGRANTS
Complete bk of emigrants 1700-50, 93n452
Immigrant experience, 93n420
Immigrant women in the US, 91n914
Immigration hist research center, 92n383
Resource gd of pubns supported by multiculturalism programs, 94n398

IMMUNOLOGY
Dictionary of immunology, 90n1654
Linscott's dir of immunological & biological reagents, 7th ed, 94n1875

IMPERIAL (RECORD COMPANY)
Aladdin/Imperial labels, 92n1299

IMPERIALISM
Atlas of British overseas expansion, 92n487

IMPORTS
Bergano's register of intl importers 1992/93, 93n256
Global Tex.: intl trade info sourcebk, 93n267
Global trade white pages 1992, 93n268
Importers manual USA, 1993 ed, 94n290
U.S. import stats for animal related commodities 1981-86, 91n283
World trade resources gd, 93n265

IN OUR TIME
Concordance to Hemingway's In Our Time, 91n1163

INCOME
Official gd to American incomes, 94n283

INCOME TAX
Guide to income tax preparation, 93n326

INCUNABULA
Catalogue of the 15th-century printed bks in the Harvard Univ Lib, v.1, 92n36

Catalogue of the 15th-century printed bks in the Harvard Univ Lib, v.2, 94n31

INDEPENDENT CATHOLIC CHURCHES
Independent bishops, 91n1447

INDEPENDENT SCHOOLS. *See* PRIVATE SCHOOLS

INDEPENDENT STUDY
Independent study cat, 4th ed, 90n358

INDEX ON CENSORSHIP
Index to "Index on Censorship", 91n636

INDEX TO LEGAL PERIODICALS
Index to legal pers: thesaurus, 91n623

INDEXES
Roth's essay index, 90n1101

INDEXING
Indexing: a basic reading list, 94n638
Indexing from A to Z, 93n653

INDEXING & ABSTRACTING SERVICES. *See* ABSTRACTING & INDEXING SERVICES

INDIA
Cambridge ency of India, Pakistan, Bangladesh, Sri Lanka, Nepal, Bhutan & the Maldives, 91n99
Concise dict of Indian philosophy, 90n1375
Encyclopaedia of Indian archaeology, 91n479
Glimpses of India, 90n122
Glossary of N Indian peasant life, 91n100
Handbook of Indian univs, 92n317
Handbook of libs, archives & info centers in India, v.6, 90n608
Handbook of libs, archives & info centres in India, v.9, 93n647
Handbook of libs, archives & info centres in India, v.11, pt.1, 93n648
Higher educ in India, 93n391
Indian music lit, 93n1239
Indian social & economic dvlpmt, 1987, 90n194
Indiana, 91n102
Limca bk of records 1991, 93n1310
Medicinal plants of India, 92n1550
Muslims of India, 91n101
Popular dict of Sikhism, 91n1452
Sikhs: their lit on culture, hist, philosophy, pols, religion & traditions, 91n1453
South Asian hndbk, 1992, 93n502
Women's studies in India, 94n953

INDIA—LITERATURE. *See* INDIC LITERATURE

INDIA—RELIGION
Glossary of Indian religious terms & concepts, 92n1403

INDIAN LITERATURE
American Indian lits, 92n1149

INDIAN OCEAN
Climatic atlas of the Indian Ocean, pt.3, 91n1799

INDIANA
Awesome almanac—Ind., 94n86
Indiana bks by Ind. authors, 91n1112
Indiana factbk 1992, 93n108

INDIANA STATE UNIVERSITY. CORDELL COLLECTION
Catalog of dicts, word bks, & philological texts, 1440-1900, 94n1074

INDIANS IN LITERATURE
American ethnic lits, 94n1225
Peoples of the American West, 90n1080

INDIANS OF NORTH AMERICA
Aboriginal self-govt in Canada, 92n374
Alaskan histl docs since 1867, 90n97
American Indian ghost dance, 1870 & 1890, 92n372
American Indian ref bks for children & young adults, 92n370
American Indian resource materials in the W hist collections, Univ of Okla., 92n364
American Indian women, 92n358
Ancient America, 92n472
Atlas of American Indian affairs, 92n375
Bibliography of Indian law per articles published 1980-90, 2d ed, 94n547
Bibliography of native N Americans on disc, 94n415
Bibliography of the Blackfoot, 90n368
Biographical dict of Indians of the Americas, 93n430
Blackfoot dict of stems, roots, & affixes, 92n1064
Bookman's gd to the Indians of the Americas, 90n369
Books without bias: through Indian eyes, 90n373
California Indians, 92n361
California Indians: primary resources, rev ed, 91n400
Daughters of the desert, 90n867
Dictionary of Native American mythology, 94n418
Dictionary of the American Indian, 91n399
Discover Indian reservations USA, 93n434
Disputing the dead, 92n549
Encyclopedia of Native American religions, 93n432
Famous Indian leaders, 90n371
Field gd to rock art symbols of the greater southwest, 93n508
Fighting men of the Indian wars, 93n515
Handbook of N American Indians, v.4, 90n370
Handbook of N American Indians, v.7, 91n397
Handbook of the American frontier, v.2, 92n367
Images of the other: a gd to microform mss on Indian-White relations, 92n366
Indian America, 91n396
Indians along the Oregon Trail, expanded ed, 93n436
Indians of the northeast, 92n360
Indians of the Pacific Northwest, 92n362
Indians of the southwest, 92n363
Legend & lore of the Americas before 1492, 94n417
Medicinal wild plants of the prairie, 93n1514
Native America, 93n431
Native American architecture, 90n968
Native American women, 94n956
Native American youth & alcohol, 90n824
Native Americans: an annot bibliog, 92n368
Native Americans info dir, 94n420
Native Americans on film & video, v.2, 90n374
Native law bibliog, 2d ed, 92n365
North American Indian landmarks, 94n416
Rand McNally children's atlas of Native Americans, 94n421
Reference ency of the American Indian, 5th ed, 91n398
Reference ency of the American Indian, 6th ed, 94n419
Resource reading list 1990, 91n401
Southwest Native American arts & material culture, 92n373
Statistical record of native N Americans, 94n422
Through Indian eyes, 93n433
Time's flotsam: overseas collections of Calif. Indian material culture, 91n395
Traveler's gd to native America: the Great Lakes region, 94n413
Upstream people, 92n376
Who was who in native American hist, 91n403
Women of color & S women annual suppl, 1991/92, 94n955
Yakima, Palouse, Cayuse, Umatilla, Walla Walla, & Wanapum Indians, 93n435

INDIANS OF NORTH AMERICA—CANADA
Aboriginal self-govt in Canada, 92n374
Bibliography of N Manitoba, 92n99
Native peoples of Canada, 90n372
Native peoples of Canada in contemporary society, 91n402

INDIANS OF SOUTH AMERICA
Healing forest, 91n1538

INDIC LANGUAGES
Universal English-Gujarati dict, 90n1045

INDIC LITERATURE
Encyclopaedia of Tamil lit, v.1, 92n1237
Writers of the Indian diaspora, 94n1290

INDOCHINA
America & the Indochina wars, 1945-90, 93n733
Major pol events in Indo-China 1945-90, 92n708

INDOCHINA—RELATIONS—UNITED STATES
America & the Indochina wars, 1945-90, 93n733

INDOCHINESE WAR, 1946-1954
Vietnam coastal & riverine forces hndbk, 90n666

INDO-EUROPEAN LANGUAGES
Bibliography of bibliogs of the langs of the world, v.1, 92n1006
Dictionary of selected synonyms in the principal Indo-European langs, 90n1030

INDONESIA
Historical dict of Indonesia, 94n111

INDONESIAN LANGUAGE—DICTIONARIES—ENGLISH
Indonesian-English dict, 3d ed, 90n1046
Indonesian-English, English-Indonesian dict, 91n1088
Tuttle's concise Indonesian dict, 94n1117

INDOOR AIR POLLUTION
Indoor air quality dir 1992-93, 93n1758
Tackling toxics in everyday products, 93n1761

INDOOR GARDENING
Indoor plants, 92n1505

INDO-PACIFIC REGION
Corals of Austral. & the Indo-Pacific, 94n1747

INDUSTRIAL ARCHAEOLOGY
Blackwell ency of industrial archaeology, 94n484

INDUSTRIAL CHEMISTRY. *See* **CHEMICAL ENGINEERING; CHEMISTRY, TECHNICAL**

INDUSTRIAL ENGINEERING
Industrial engineering terminology, rev ed, 91n1622
Industrial engineering terminology, rev ed, 93n1602
Maynard's industrial engineering hndbk, 4th ed, 93n1603

INDUSTRIAL EQUIPMENT
Directory of building & equipment grants, 2d ed, 94n1772

INDUSTRIAL HYGIENE
Proctor & Hughes' chemical hazards of the workplace, 3d ed, 92n1786

INDUSTRIAL MANAGEMENT
Business & the environment, 93n249

INDUSTRIAL MOBILIZATION
International defense electronic systems hndbk, 93n718

INDUSTRIAL ORGANIZATION (ECONOMIC THEORY)
Handbook of industrial org, v.2, 91n232

INDUSTRIAL PRODUCTIVITY
Industrial stats yrbk 1990, 94n216

INDUSTRIAL PROMOTIONS
Directory of incentives for bus investment & dvlpmt in the US, 3d ed, 93n221

INDUSTRIAL RELATIONS
BNA's 1993 source bk on collective bargaining & employee relations, 94n277
European employment & industrial relations glossary: Belgium, 94n252
European employment & industrial relations glossary: Germany, 94n253
Labor & industrial relations journals & serials, 90n264

INDUSTRIAL SAFETY
International dir of occupational safety & health insts, 92n220
Safety & health at work, ILO-CIS bulletin: 5-yearly index 1984-88, 91n250

INDUSTRIAL SOCIOLOGY
Sociology of work, 91n244

INDUSTRIAL STATISTICS
RMA annual statement studies 1993, 94n217

INDUSTRIAL TOXICOLOGY
Proctor & Hughes' chemical hazards of the workplace, 3d ed, 92n1786

INDUSTRIALISTS
Corporate eponymy, 93n184
Scott's dirs: Ont. manufacturers, 17th ed, 90n245

INDUSTRY
Almanac of bus & industrial financial ratios, 1990 ed, 91n233
Directory of Canadian manufacturers, 91n227
Directory of Tex. wholesalers 1989, 90n275
Financial Times industrial cos, v.3, 90n1573
French-English dict of industrial lang, 91n234
Glossary of industrial lang, 91n235
Handbook of industrial stats 1990, 92n196
Harris Ill. industrial dir, 1991, 92n197
Harris Ind. industrial dir, 1991, 92n198
Harris Mich. industrial dir, 1991, 92n199
Harris Ohio industrial dir, 1991, 92n200
Harris Pa. industrial dir, 1991, 92n201
Harris W.Va. manufacturing dir, 1990, 92n202
Industrial research in the UK, 14th ed, 93n296
Industrial trends: monthly stats, 91n230
Inside US business, 1991 ed, 92n205
Manufacturing: a historiographical & bibliographical gd, 92n206
Manufacturing USA, 2d ed, 93n247
Missouri dir of manufacturers, 1991, 92n203
Service industries USA, 93n250
Standard industrial classification applied to histl data: the 1871 industrial census, 91n150
U.S. industrial outlook '93, 94n218
Who knows about industries & markets, 13th ed, 93n251
Who's who in bus & industry in the UK 1991, 93n298
Who's who in finance & industry 1992-93, 93n179

INFANTRY
Field equipment of the infantry 1914-45, 90n661
Jane's infantry weapons 1989-90, 91n707

INFANTS
Childwise cat, 3d ed, 94n921
Guide to baby products, 90n227
Social correlates of infant & reproductive mortality in the US, 94n879

INFORMAL SECTOR (ECONOMICS)
Informal economy, 93n173

INFORMATION INDUSTRY ASSOCIATION
IIA telephone dir, 90n586
Information sources 1989, 90n585

INFORMATION NETWORKS
Guide to the info activities of European dvlpmt networks, 93n630

INFORMATION RESOURCES MANAGEMENT
AIIM speakers dir 1992-93, 93n1668
Lesko's info-power, 91n196

INFORMATION RETRIEVAL
Keyguide to info sources in online & CD-ROM database searching, 92n590

INFORMATION SCIENCE
ALISE library & info sci educ statl report 1991, 92n576
Annotated bibliog of faculty status in lib & info sci, 93n634
Annual review of info sci & tech, v.25, 92n569
Annual review of info sci & tech, v.26, 93n628
Annual review of info sci & tech, v.27, 94n614
British librarianship & info work 1986-90, v.2, 94n633
Current research for the info profession 1988/89, 91n632
Dictionary of acronyms & abbrevs, 94n597
Dictionary of info sci & tech, 93n622
Encyclopedia of computer sci, 3d ed, 94n1903
Encyclopedia of lib & info sci, v.44, 94n601
Encyclopedia of lib & info sci, v.45, 94n602
Encyclopedia of lib & info sci, v.46, 94n603
Encyclopedia of lib & info sci, v.47, 94n604
Encyclopedia of lib & info sci, v.48, 94n605
Encyclopedia of lib & info sci, v.49, 94n606
Encyclopedia of lib & info sci, v.50, 94n607
Encyclopedia of lib & info sci, v.51, 94n608
Information sci abstracts, v.25, no.2, 91n603

Information studies courses in the UK, 92n589
Librarian's thesaurus, 91n606
Librarianship & info work worldwide 1991, 93n631
Library & info sci annual, v.5, 90n593
Library lit. 21, 94n616
Library lit 1992, 94n621
Library lit [CD-ROM], 93n632
National gd to funding for libs & info servs, 2d ed, 94n618
New intl dict of acronyms in lib & info sci, 2d ed, 93n621
Sourcebook on standards info, 92n574
Thesaurus gd, 1992, 94n631
World ency of lib & info servs, 3d ed, 94n609
World gd to lib, archive, & info sci assns, 92n571

INFORMATION SCIENCE LIBRARIES
National gd to funding for libs & info servs, 92n573

INFORMATION SCIENCE LITERATURE
Library pers 1993, 94n622

INFORMATION SERVICES
Access Canada 1990, 91n104
ALA yearbk of lib & info servs, v.14, 90n589
ALA yrbk of lib & info servs 1990, v.15, 91n610
Data: where it is & how to get it, 94n45
Directory of fee-based info servs 1989, 90n583
Directory of Japanese technical resources in the US 1992, 93n655
Directory of natl helplines 1993, 94n47
Directory to fulltext online resources 1992, 93n626
Encyclopedia of info systems & servs, 1989, 90n584
Find it fast, updated ed, 91n47
Finding Canadian facts fast, rev. ed, 91n647
FISCAL dir of fee-based research & document supply servs, 4th ed, 94n639
Grants for libs & info servs, 90n592
IIA telephone dir, 90n586
Information industry dir, 1991, 92n591
Information marketplace dir, 1993, 93n685
Information resources & servs in Austral., 92n588
Information security: dict of concepts, standards & terms, 94n1900
Information sources 1989, 90n585
Keyguide to info sources in paramedical scis, 92n1637
Libraries, info centers, & databases in sci & tech, 2d ed, 90n624
Reference & info servs, 92n604
Selective inventory of social sci info & doc servs, 3d ed, 90n87
Third World struggle for peace with justice, 92n749
Ultimate black bk, 90n62

INFORMATION SERVICES INDUSTRY
Burwell dir of info brokers 1992, 93n654
Clearinghouse dir 1991-92, 92n566
European dir of financial info sources 1990, 92n157
Position descriptions in special libs, 2d ed, 94n624

INFORMATION RETRIEVAL
Encyclopedia of bus info sources, 9th ed, 93n206

INFORMATION STORAGE & RETRIEVAL SYSTEMS
Books & pers online, v.2, no.1, 90n154
Business info desk ref, 92n140
Business online: a Canadian gd, 91n155
Business online: the professional's gd, 91n161
Directory of automated lib systems, 2d ed, 91n637
Directory of info mgmt sftwr for libs, info centers, record centers, 1989-90 ed, 91n631
Encyclopedia of info systems & servs, 1989, 90n584
Entomolgy: a gd to info sources, 2d ed, 91n1589
Handbook of libs, archives & info centres in India, v.9, 93n647
Information industry dir, 1991, 92n591
Information resources dir, fall 1989, 91n1808
Library systems: a buyer's gd, 2d ed, 91n640
Macrothesaurus for info processing in the field of economic & social dvlpmt, 93n641
Online manual, 93n203
Van Nostrand Reinhold dict of info tech, 3d ed, 90n612

INFORMATION TECHNOLOGY
Bibliography of info tech, 90n613
CD-ROM tech for info managers, 91n633
Desktop dict of info systems tech, 91n634
Dictionary of info sci & tech, 93n622
Directory of tech in global financial markets, 91n179
French dict of info tech, 90n610
Handbook of libs, archives & info centers in India, v.6, 90n608
Handbook of libs, archives & info centres in India, v.11, pt.1, 93n648
Information sources in info tech, 92n595
Library hi tech bibliog, v.3, 90n609
McGraw-Hill dict of info tech & computer acronyms, initials, & abbrevs, 93n1679
Van Nostrand Reinhold dict of info tech, 3d ed, 90n612

INFORMERS
Rewards offered by the US, 91n597

ING, DEAN
Work of Dean Ing, 92n1173

INITIALISMS. See ACRONYMS

INJURIES. See ACCIDENTS

INORGANIC COMPOUNDS
Thermodynamic properties of inorganic materials, 91n1762

INSECT PESTS
Destructive & useful insects, 5th ed, 94n1729

INSECTIVORA
Mammals: primates, insect eaters & baleen whales, 90n1520

INSECTS
Catalogue of palaearctic diptera, v.7, 93n1567
Diptera types in the Canadian Natl Collection of Insects, pt.1, 92n1579
Dragonflies of the Fla peninsula, Bermuda, & the Bahamas, 90n1553
Florida's butterflies & other insects, 90n1547
Genera of the aphids of Canada, 94n1723
Hawaiian insects & their kin, 93n1565
Illustrated gd to the mountain stream insects of Colo., 93n1568
Insects of Hawaii, v.15, 93n1561
Keys to the insects of the European part of the USSR, v.3, pt.2, 90n1554
Latin American insects & entomology, 94n1727
Wolf spiders, nurseryweb spiders, & lynx spiders of Canada & Alaska, 92n1580

IN-SERVICE TRAINING. See EMPLOYEES, TRAINING OF

INSTITUTIONS, ASSOCIATIONS, ETC. See ASSOCIATIONS, INSTITUTIONS, ETC.

INSTRUCTIONAL MATERIALS. See TEACHING—AIDS & DEVICES

INSTRUCTIONAL MATERIALS CENTERS
ACRL dir of curriculum materials centers 1990, 92n291
Educational media & tech yrbk, v.18, 93n398
Recommended ref bks 1993, 94n4
School lib media annual 1989, v.7, 90n622
School lib media annual, v.10, 93n672

INSTRUCTIONAL MATERIALS INDUSTRY
Children's media market place, 3d ed, 90n621
Policies of AV producers & distrs, 2d ed, 91n616

INSTRUMENT MANUFACTURE
ISA dir of instrumentation 1989, 90n241

INSTRUMENTAL ENSEMBLES
Conductor's repertory of chamber music, 94n1350

INSTRUMENTAL MUSIC
Instrumental virtuosi, 90n1258
Subject gd to classical instrumental music, 90n1267

INSURANCE
Dictionary of insurance, 7th ed, 91n237
Dictionary of insurance terms, 2d ed, 92n210
Directory of Lloyd's of London, 91n240
Finance, insurance, & real estate USA, 94n205
Financial Times world insurance yr bk 1990, 91n238

Insurance & alternatives for uninsurables, 91n239
Insurance dict, 90n252
Insurance pers index 1988, 90n251
Medical utilization review dir, 1993 ed, 94n1810
Morningstar variable annuity/life sourcebk 1993, 94n197
National index: insurance definitions, 92n207
National index: insurance laws, 92n208
National index: insurance regulations, 92n209
Register of N American insurance cos, 1993, 94n221
Rupp's insurance & risk mgmt glossary, 92n211
Tax companion 1991, 92n264
Who's who in world insurance, 93n253

INSURANCE, UNEMPLOYMENT
Highlights of fed unemployment compensation laws, Jan 91, 92n224
Highlights of state unemployment compensation laws, Jan 90, 91n246
Highlights of state unemployment compensation laws, Jan 93, 94n219
Unemployment insurance glossary, 93n252

INTEGRATED CIRCUITS
International ency of integrated circuits, 90n1591
International ency of integrated circuits, 2d ed, 93n1594

INTELLECTUAL FREEDOM. *See* CENSORSHIP; FREEDOM OF INFORMATION; FREEDOM OF SPEECH

INTELLECTUAL PROPERTY
McCarthy's desk ency of intellectual property, 92n533

INTELLECTUALS
Biographical dict of the extreme right since 1890, 92n732

INTELLIGENCE LEVELS
IQ debate, 92n266

INTELLIGENCE OFFICERS
Soviet security & intelligence orgs 1917-90, 93n769
Spies & provocateurs, 94n796

INTELLIGENCE SERVICE
American intelligence, 1775-1990, 93n785
Latest intelligence, 92n646
Reader's gd to intelligence pers, 94n761
Soviet security & intelligence orgs 1917-90, 93n769
Special access required, 92n528
United States intelligence, 91n734

INTERCOUNTRY ADOPTION
Loving Journeys gd to adoption, 94n885

INTERCULTURAL COMMUNICATIONS
Culturgrams, 92n1326
Social dimensions of intl bus, 94n222

INTERCULTURAL EDUCATION
Developing multicultural awareness through children's lit, 94n1178
Multicultural educ, 90n319
Multicultural projects index, 93n1312
Videos for understanding diversity, 94n399

INTERDISCIPLINARY APPROACH IN EDUCATION
Using lit to teach middle grades about war, 94n694

INTERGENERATIONAL RELATIONS
Intergenerational readings/resources 1980-93, 94n866

INTERIOR ARCHITECTURE
Time-saver standards for interior design & space planning, 92n954

INTERIOR DECORATION
Prentice-Hall pocket ency [of] home decorating, 92n956
Time-saver standards for interior design & space planning, 92n954
Who's who in interior design, 90n939

INTERIOR LANDSCAPING
Interior landscape dict, 94n1621

INTER-LIBRARY LOANS
Fax for libs, 91n608
Interlibrary loan policies dir, 4th ed, 93n657
Interlibrary loan servs, 5th ed, 90n615
WLN interlib loan policies dir, 93n658
WLN interlib loan policies dir, 2d ed, 94n643

INTERNAL SECURITY
Information security hndbk, 93n315
Soviet security & intelligence orgs 1917-90, 93n769
Special access required, 92n528

INTERNATIONAL AGENCIES
Books in print of the UN system, 94n788
European pol facts 1918-90, 94n766
International orgs: a dict & dir, 3d ed, 94n793
International orgs & world order dict, 93n781
International orgs 1918-45, rev ed, 94n735
International yr bk & statesmen's who's who 1992, 94n791
Soviet propaganda network, 90n728
Who's who in intl affairs, 92n742
Who's who in intl orgs, 93n784
Who's who in the UN & related agencies, 2d ed, 93n782
Yearbook of intl orgs 1991/92, 93n75

INTERNATIONAL BUSINESS ENTERPRISES
Access Nippon '92 business hndbk, 94n241
Bricker's intl dir, 24th ed, 94n225
China leading cos, 94n242
CIFAR's global co hndbk, 1992 ed, 93n263
Cracking E Europe, 94n261
Cracking the Pacific Rim, 94n243
Directory of European bus, 94n254
Directory of multinatls, 91n148
Economic planning 1943-51, 94n263
European advertising mktg & media data 1992, 93n285
European business rankings, 93n291, 94n258
European business servs dir, 94n256
European cos, 4th ed, 94n260
European consultants dir, 93n287
European dir of consumer brands & their owners 1992, 93n288
European market share reporter, 94n259
European markets: a gd to co & industry info sources, 4th ed, 93n289
International bus in S Africa 1988, 90n171
International corporate yellow bk, v.5, no.1, 93n259
International dir of co hists, v.5, 94n230
International dir of co hists, v.6, 94n231
International dir of co hists, v.7, 94n232
International dir of corporate affiliations, 1989-90, 90n178
International mgmt hndbk, 94n238
International trade stats yrbk, 1987, 91n270
International trade stats yrbk, 1990, 94n233
Japan trade dir 1993-94, 94n244
Major cos of the Far East & Australasia 1991/92, 8th ed, v.1, 93n281
Major energy cos of Europe 1993, 94n1977
Panorama of EC industry 93, 94n236
Report on bus: Canada co hndbk 1993, 94n250
SIBD 92-93, 93n293
Standard dir of intl advertisers & agencies 1993, 94n226
Transnational corps & labor, 91n143
Transnational corps in biotech, 90n247
Transnational corps in S Africa, 93n276
Transnational corps 1983-87, 90n246
World business dir, 93n261
World class business, 93n272

INTERNATIONAL COOPERATION
Guide to funding for intl & foreign programs, 93n880

INTERNATIONAL ECONOMIC RELATIONS
Directory, 1989-90: Japanese-affiliated cos in USA & Canada, 90n174
International business dict & ref, 93n255
International dvlpmt dict, 92n125

INTERNATIONAL EDUCATION
Access to UK higher educ, 93n380
Financial resources for intl study, 91n342
Guide to intl educ in the US, 2d ed, 92n314

Handbook of world educ, 92n281
Higher educ in the European Community: student hndbk, 6th ed, 91n345
IIE educl assocs 1992-93, 94n366
International exchange locator, 93n387
International higher educ, 93n381
International schools dir 1990, 25th ed, 91n344
ISS dir of overseas schools, 1989/90 ed, 90n346
Open doors 1990/91, 93n389
Profiles 1989-90, 93n390
Where walls once stood, 93n388
World of options for the 90's, 92n315

INTERNATIONAL FINANCE
IMF glossary, 93n254
International business dict & ref, 93n255
International monetary fund 1944-92, 94n234

INTERNATIONAL LABOUR REVIEW
International Labour Review: index 1945-91, 94n285

INTERNATIONAL LAW
Bibliography on foreign & comparative law, 90n542
Canadian yrbk of intl law, v.27, 92n547
Consolidated index to the Canadian yrbk of intl law v.1-25, 91n590
Dictionary of intl & comparative law, 93n577
International business dict & ref, 93n255
International legal bks in print 1990-91, 92n523
Public intl law, 92n516
Subject headings for the lit of law & intl law, & index to LC K schedules, 4th ed, 91n626
World dir of teaching & research insts in intl law 1990, 92n546

INTERNATIONAL LIBRARIANSHIP
Biographical dir of natl librarians, 90n581

INTERNATIONAL MONETARY FUND
IMF glossary, 93n254
International monetary fund 1944-92, 94n234

INTERNATIONAL NUCLEAR INFORMATION SYSTEM
INIS: thesaurus, 93n1735

INTERNATIONAL ORGANIZATIONS. See also INTERNATIONAL AGENCIES
Europa world yr bk 1992, 94n82
Index to proceedings of the Economic & Social Council, 92n739
Managing a nation: the microcomputer sftwr cat, 2d ed, 92n672
Unesco list of docs & pubs 1984-86, 90n722
World dvlpmt dir, 92n738
World govt, 92n674
Worldwide govt dir 1990, 91n721

INTERNATIONAL POLITICS. See WORLD POLITICS

INTERNATIONAL RELATIONS
Guides to LC subject headings & classification on peace & intl conflict resolution, 92n581
International business dict & ref, 93n255
International negotiations, 90n726
International orgs & world order dict, 93n781
International orgs 1918-45, rev ed, 92n735
Internships in foreign & defense policy, 91n769
Protectionism, 90n279
Sources in European pol hist, v.2, 90n723

INTERNATIONAL STANDARD BOOK NUMBERS
Canadian ISBN publs' dir 1990, 92n633
Publishers' intl ISBN dir, 16th ed. 91n666

INTERNATIONAL TRADE
Directory to intl bus educ in Canada, 93n230
Henry Holt intl desk ref, 93n269
International trade 89-90, v.2, 92n250
International trade 90-91, 93n270
U.S.-E European trade sourcebk, 92n150
Who knows about foreign industries & markets, 13th ed, 93n274
World markets desk bk, 94n239

INTERNSHIP PROGRAMS
Complete gd to Washington internships, 2d ed, 92n695
Great careers, 2d ed, 91n379
International dir of youth internships with the UN, its related agencies, & non-governmental orgs, 5th ed, 94n790
Internships, 1991, 92n305

INTERSTELLAR COMMUNICATIONS
Extraterrestrial ency, rev ed, 93n805

INTERTEXTUALITY
Intertextuality, allusion, & quotation, 90n1065

INUIT. See ESKIMOS

INVENTIONS
Catalog of govt inventions available for licensing 1989, 91n225
Great inventions through hist, 93n1447
Great modern inventions, 93n1448
Inventing & patenting sourcebk, 92n149
Inventions & discoveries 1993, 94n1581
Nineteenth-century inventors, 93n1439
Oxford illus ency of invention & tech, 93n1451
Who's inventing what?, 91n164

INVENTORS
British radio & TV pioneers, 94n1012
Nineteenth-century inventors, 93n1439
Radio & TV pioneers: a patent bibliog, 93n983
Twentieth-century inventors, 92n1454

INVERTEBRATES
Invertebrates of economic importance in Britain, 4th ed, 91n1556

INVESTIGATIONS
Guide to background investigations, 3d ed, 90n258
How to locate anyone anywhere without leaving home, 90n778

INVESTMENT ADVISERS
Directory of registered investment advisors with the SEC 1993, 94n179
Pension funds & their advisors 1992, 94n266

INVESTMENT ANALYSIS
Hulbert gd to financial newsletters, 5th ed, 94n191

INVESTMENT TRUSTS. See MUTUAL FUNDS

INVESTMENTS
Business One Irwin bus & investment almanac, 1992, 93n220
Business One Irwin investor's hndbk 1993, 94n187
Complete gd to closed-end funds, 90n201
Complete gd to closed-end funds, 2d ed, 92n155
Corporate finance sourcebk 1991, 93n238
Dictionary of finance & investment terms, 3d ed, 92n184
Dictionary of investing, 94n177
Directory of cos offering dividend reinvestment plans, 6th ed, 90n203
Directory of cos offering dividend reinvestment plans, 10th ed, 94n180
Dividend reinvestment plans, 1992 gd almanac, 94n181
Dow Jones-Irwin bus & investment almanac, 1990, 91n175
Guide to intl asset managers, 91n258
Guide to the Canadian financial servs industry 1991, 93n232
Handbook for no-load fund investors, 10th ed, 91n180
Handbook for no-load fund investors, 1993, 94n189
How to read the financial pages & much more, rev ed, 90n218
Hulbert gd to financial newsletters, 5th ed, 94n191
Individual investor's gd to investment pubs, 90n210
Individual investor's gd to no-load mutual funds, 8th ed, 90n211
Market share reporter 1993, 94n193
McGraw-Hill dict of Wall St acronyms, initials, & abbrevs, 93n171
Morningstar closed-end fund sourcebk 1993, 94n194
Morningstar mutual fund sourcebk 1993, 94n196
Morningstar variable annuity/life sourcebk 1993, 94n197
NASDAQ yellow bk, v.4, no.1, 93n225
Nelson's dir of investment managers 1991, 92n162
Nelson's dir of investment research 1991, 92n163
Over-the-counter 1000, 90n214
Pacific Rim almanac, 92n137
Still more words of Wall Street, 91n185

Stock market & investment vocabulary, 90n202
Wall St dict, 92n166
World investment dir 1992, v.1, 94n227
Worldscope financial & serv co profiles, 90n220
Worldscope industrial co profiles, 90n221

INVESTMENTS, FOREIGN
Asian finance dir, 1990 ed, 91n209
Guide to Asian stock markets, 91n178
Wilson dir of emerging market funds, 1992-1993 ed, 94n185

INVESTMENTS, FOREIGN—CANADA
European investment in US & Canadian real estate dir 1990, 91n284

INVESTMENTS, FOREIGN—UNITED STATES
Directory of foreign investments in the US: real estate & businesses, 92n138
European investment in US & Canadian real estate dir 1990, 91n284
Probe dir of foreign direct investment in the US, 6th ed, 90n215

INVESTMENTS, JAPANESE
Japanese direct foreign investments, 90n200
Japanese investment in US & Canadian real estate dir 1990, 91n285

IOWA
Iowa hist & culture, 90n473

IQ. *See* **INTELLIGENCE LEVELS**

IRAN
Armenians & Iran, 92n496
Encyclopaedia Iranica, v.5, fascicle 1, 92n116
Encyclopaedia Iranica, v.5, fascicle 2, 92n117
Iranian short story authors, 91n1237
Persian & English glossary for humanities & social scis, 93n1090

IRAQ
BBC World Service Gulf Crisis chronology, 93n542
Cultural atlas of Mesopotamia & the ancient Near East, 92n499

IRAQI-IRANIAN CONFLICT
Iraq-Iran War, 90n518

IRELAND
Anglo-Irish lit, 91n1239
Book of Irish names, 90n400
British lib dir, 90n607
Cambridge gd to the historic places of Britain & Ireland, 90n458
Chronology of Irish hist since 1500, 92n494
Companion to Irish hist 1603-1921, 93n539
Connoisseur's gd to Ireland, 90n460
Dictionary of Irish archaeology, 94n486
Dictionary of Irish biog, 2d ed, 90n38
Dictionary of Irish mythology, 90n1304
Dublin stage, 1720-45, 94n1468
Guide to Irish churches & graveyards, 92n389
Guide to the archaeological sites of the British Isles, 90n505
Handbook of English & Celtic studies in the UK and Republic of Ireland, 2d ed, 90n1169
Irish folk music, 90n1285
Irish records: sources for family & local hist, 90n383
Modern Irish lit & culture, 94n1291
Oxford dict of saints, 3d ed, 94n1527
Traditional music of Britain & Ireland, 90n1283

IRELAND—HISTORY
Royal Histl Society annual bibliog of British & Irish hist: publications of 1992, 94n518

IRELAND IN LITERATURE
Contemporary Irish dramatists, 90n1205

IRELAND, JOHN
Gurney, Ireland, Quilter & Warlock, 90n1223

IRIS (PLANT)
Iris, 2d ed., 91n1529
Iris of China, 93n1507

IRISH
Tracing your Irish ancestors, 94n434

IRISH LANGUAGE—DICTIONARIES—ENGLISH
Irish/English, English/Irish dict & phrasebk, 93n1088

IRISH LITERATURE
Modern Irish lit & culture, 94n1291

IRISH-AMERICANS
Irish in America, 93n437
Irish-American almanac & green pages, rev ed, 91n389
Irish-American heritage, 90n375

IRON
Worldwide gd to equivalent irons & steels, 3d ed, 94n1796

IRON & STEEL WORKERS
Encyclopedia of American bus hist & biog: iron & steel in the 19th century, 90n236

IRVING, WASHINGTON
Washington Irving bibliog, 90n1144

ISLAM
Concise ency of Islam, 91n1448
Encyclopaedia of Islam, new ed, v.7, 94n151
Encyclopaedia of Islam, new ed, v.7, fascicules 125-26, 94n150
Islam & Islamic groups, 94n1553
Islam in N America, 94n1552

ISLAMIC COUNTRIES
Chronology of Islamic hist 570-1000 CE, 90n519
Encyclopaedia of Islam, new ed, v.7, 94n151
Encyclopaedia of Islam, new ed, v.7, fascicules 125-26, 94n150

ISLANDS
Asia & the Pacific, 92n93
Eastern islands, 91n432
Islands of the S & SE US, 90n451

ISRAEL
Glossary of Jewish life, 93n449
Historical dict of Israel, 94n152
Holocaust, Israel, & the Jews: motion pictures in the Natl Archives, 91n405
Museums of Israel, 91n58
Oral hist of contemporary Jewry, 91n408
Political dict of the state of Israel, suppl. 1987-93, 2d ed, 94n785

ISRAEL-ARAB CONFLICTS
Palestine question, 92n726

ITALIAN LANGUAGE—DICTIONARIES—ENGLISH
Beginning Italian bilingual dict, 2d ed, 90n1047
Harper Collins Italian dict, college ed, 92n1079
Italian idioms, 92n1078
Oxford paperback Italian dict, 90n1048
Zanichelli new college Italian & English dict, 92n1081

ITALIAN-AMERICANS
Italian American material culture, 93n438
Italian Americans & religion, 2d ed, 94n1504

ITALIAN-CANADIAN AUTHORS
Italian-Canadian writers, 90n1197

ITALIAN-CANADIANS
Italian American material culture, 93n438
Italian-Canadian studies, 90n376

ITALY
American Chamber of Commerce in Italy dir 1992, 94n268
Architect's hndbk of marble, granite, & stone, 91n1024
Index to Italian architecture, 94n1052
Modern Italian hist, 91n532
Who's who in Italy 1992, 94n20

ITALY—FOREIGN RELATIONS
Italian foreign policy 1918-45, rev ed, 92n710

JACKSON, ANDREW
Andrew Jackson: a bibliog, 92n458

JAKOBSON, ROMAN
Roman Jakobson 1896-1982: a complete bibliog of his writings, 92n1009

JAMES BOND FILMS
Complete James Bond movie ency, 92n1354

JAMES, HENRY
Concordance to Henry James's The Awkward Age, 90n1145
Concordance to Henry James's The Spoils of Poynton, 90n1146
Concordance to Henry James's What Maisie Knew, 91n1165
Henry James: a ref gd 1975-87, 92n1174
Henry James ency, 90n1147

JAMESTOWN (VA.)
Captain John Smith: a ref gd, 92n455

JAPAN
Access Nippon '92 business hndbk, 94n241
Asian finance dir, 1990 ed, 91n209
Biotechnology gd Japan 1990-91, 91n223
Biotechnology Japan, 90n233
Birds of Japan, 93n1538
Cambridge ency of Japan, 94n113
Directory, 1991-92: Japanese-affiliated cos in USA & Canada, 93n279
Directory of Japanese healthcare industry, 1990 ed, 92n1635
Directory of Japanese technical reports 1992-93, 94n114
Directory of Japanese technical resources in the US 1992, 93n655
Education in Japan, 90n306
Encyclopedia of Japan, 92n95
Guide to modern Japanese woodblock prints, 1900-75, 93n1043
Japan, 91n103
Japan: an illus ency, 94n115
Japan co hndbks, spring 1990, 91n182
Japan trade dir 1990-91, 91n271
Japanese films, 91n1376
Japanese naval aces & fighter units in WW II, 91n511
Japanese studies from pre-hist to 1990, 93n126
Japan's high tech, 92n1701
Mingei, 90n937
Standard trade index of Japan 1990-91, 91n278
Standard trade index of Japan 1992-93, 94n245
Total forecast: Japan 1990s, 94n116
Who's who in Japan 1991-92, 93n48
Women in Japanese society, 93n925

JAPAN—ARMED FORCES
Handbook on Japanese military forces, 93n705

JAPAN—ECONOMIC CONDITIONS
Consumer Japan 1990, 91n261
Japan's economy, 90n160

JAPAN—FOREIGN RELATIONS—CANADA
Directory, 1989-90: Japanese-affiliated cos in USA & Canada, 90n174

JAPAN—FOREIGN RELATIONS—UNITED STATES
Directory, 1989-90: Japanese-affiliated cos in USA & Canada, 90n174

JAPANESE LANGUAGE—DICTIONARIES—ENGLISH
Basic Japanese-English dict, 90n1049
English-Japanese, Japanese-English dict of computer & data-processing terms, 90n1713
Japanese/English, English/Japanese glossary of scientific & technical terms, 94n1571
Kodansha's romanized Japanese-English dict, 94n1119
Martin's pocket dict: English-Japanese, Japanese-English, 91n1089
Merriam-Webster's Japanese-English learner's dict, 94n1120
NTC's new Japanese-English character dict, 94n1121
Practical English-Japanese dict, 92n1082

JAPANESE LITERATURE
Japanese women writers in English translation, 90n1206
Japanese women writers in English translation, v.2, 94n1295
Modern Japanese novelists, 94n1294

JAPANESE-AMERICANS
Japanese American hist, 94n423

JAZZ MUSIC
Aladdin/Imperial labels, 92n1299
Best rated CDs 1992: jazz, popular, etc., 93n1275
Blackwell gd to recorded jazz, 92n1307
CD review digest annual 1990: jazz, popular, etc., 92n1308
Charlie Parker discography, 94n1369
Fire music, 93n1286
Jazz & blues lover's gd to the US, 92n1306
Jazz discography, v.1, 93n1287
Jazz discography, v.2, 93n1288
Jazz discography, v.3, 93n1289
Jazz discography, v.5, 94n1373
Jazz discography, v.6, 94n1374
Jazz from A to Z: a graphic dict, 91n1317
Jazz hndbk, 91n1319
New Grove dict of jazz, 90n1288
You got to be original, man!, 91n1315

JAZZ MUSICIANS
Big band almanac, rev ed, 90n1290
Jazz lives, 94n1372
Jazz performers, 91n1316
Jazz portraits, 91n1318
Pee Wee speaks, 94n1371
Sarah Vaughan: a discography, 93n1285
Who's who of jazz in Montreal, 91n1255

JEAN DE MEUN
Roman de la rose: an annot bibliog, 94n1282

JEFFERIES, RICHARD
Richard Jefferies: a bibliographical study, 94n1252

JEFFERSON, THOMAS
Thomas Jefferson, 1981-90: an annot bibliog, 93n512

JERUSALEM
Illustrated atlas of Jerusalem, 91n439
Jerusalem, the holy city, v.2, 93n544

JESUS CHRIST
Literary lives of Jesus, 90n1064
New Testament Christology, 90n1404

JET CUTTING
Jet cutting & cleaning bibliog, 90n1603

JEWELRY MAKING
Professional goldsmithing, 92n953

JEWISH ART & SYMBOLISM
Encyclopedia of Jewish symbols, 93n443

JEWISH ATHLETES
Jewish athletes hall of fame, 91n804

JEWISH LAW
Biblical law bibliog, 92n1445

JEWISH LITERATURE
Jewish American fiction writers, 92n1161
Schocken gd to Jewish bks, 94n425

JEWISH MUSEUMS
Jewish museums of N America, 93n444

JEWISH NEWSPAPERS
American-Jewish media dir, 1989, 90n890

JEWISH PERIODICALS
American-Jewish media dir, 1989, 90n890

JEWISH TRAVELERS
Traveling Jewish in America, 3d ed, 93n441

JEWISH-ARAB RELATIONS
A to Z of the Middle East, 92n118

JEWS
American Jewish yr bk 1989, 90n377
American Jewish yr bk 1992, 93n439
Atlas of medieval Jewish hist, 93n440

Atlas of modern Jewish hist, 91n404
Bibliography on antisemitism, 91n409
Biographical dict of Canadian Jewry 1909-14, 94n410
Dictionary of Jewish biog, 92n381
Encyclopedia of Jewish genealogy, v.1, 92n384
Encyclopedia of Jewish symbols, 93n443
First American Jewish families, 3d ed, 93n458
Genealogical resources in the N.Y. metro area, 90n385
Glossary of Jewish life, 93n449
Historical atlas of the Jewish people from the time of the patriarchs to the present, 94n424
Holocaust, Israel, & the Jews: motion pictures in the Natl Archives, 91n405
Index to Fla. Jewish hist in the American Israelite 1854-1900, 93n446
Jewish autobiogs & biogs, 90n381
Jewish communities of the world, 4th ed, 90n380
Jewish elderly in the English-speaking countries, 90n784
Jewish genealogy, 92n382
Jewish heritage in America, 90n378
Jewish museums of N America, 93n444
Jewish profiles, 93n450
Jewish time line ency, 91n406
Jewish wisdom, 93n445
Jewish-American hist & culture, 93n442
Jewish film dir, 93n1357
Joseph Jacobs dir of the Jewish pr in America, 3d ed, 92n903
Judaica Americana, 92n380
Judeo-Romance linguistics, 90n1034
Latin American Jewish studies, 92n378
Lithuanian Jewish communities, 92n489
New standard Jewish ency, 7th ed, 93n448
Oral hist of contemporary Jewry, 91n408
Reform Judaism in America, 94n1557
Schocken gd to Jewish bks, 94n425
Social & religious hist of the Jews, 2d ed: index to vs.9-18, 94n427
Soviet Jewish hist, 1917-91, 93n447
Soviet pubns on Judaism, Zionism, & the state of Israel 1984-88, 91n407
Spanish & Portuguese Jewry, 94n426
Traveling Jewish in America, 3d ed, 93n441
Where once we walked: a gd to the Jewish communities destroyed in the Holocaust, 93n494
World Jewish dir, 92n379

JEWS—GERMANY
World in turmoil, 93n550

JEWS—PORTUGAL
Spanish & Portuguese Jewry, 94n426

JEWS—SPAIN
Spanish & Portuguese Jewry, 94n426

JOAN OF ARC, SAINT
Joan of Arc in hist, lit, & film, 91n529

JOB DESCRIPTIONS
America's top 300 jobs, 94n276
Healers, 90n1625
Manufacturers & miners, 90n238
Occupational outlook hndbk, 1992-93 ed, 94n281
100 best job$ for the 1990s & beyond, 93n311
Restaurateurs & innkeepers, 90n1459

JOB HUNTING
Complete gd for occupational exploration, 1993 ed, 94n387
Enhanced gd for occupational exploration, 92n227
Hidden job market, 93n303
Job hunter's gd to 100 great American cities, 93n304
Job hunter's sourcebk, 92n222
Job hunter's sourcebk, 2d ed, 94n279
Job seeker's gd to 1,000 top employers, 94n280
Job seeker's gd to private & public cos, 93n310

JOB STRESS
Police, firefighter, & paramedic stress, 91n787

JOB TRAINING. *See* **OCCUPATIONAL TRAINING**

JOB VACANCIES
Career gd to America's top industries, 94n278
National job bank 1989, 90n260
Where the jobs are, 90n255

JOHN D. CRUMMEY PEACE COLLECTION (HOOVER INSTITUTION ON WAR, REVOLUTION & PEACE)
Guide to the John D. Crummey peace collection in the Hoover Inst, 93n790

JOHNSON, ANDREW
Andrew Johnson: a bibliog, 94n495

JOHNSON, LIONEL PIGOT
Three decadent poets, 91n1222

JOINTS (ENGINEERING)
Standard handbk of fastening & joining, 2d ed, 90n1605

JOLSON, AL
Al Jolson: a bio-discography, 94n1365

JONES, JENNIFER
Jennifer Jones: a bio-bibliog, 91n1351

JORDAN
Historical dict of the Hashemite kingdom of Jordan, 93n164

JOURNALISM
American journalism hist, 90n904
Biographical dict of American journalism, 90n905
Directory of pers online: news, law & bus, 5th ed, 91n73
Encyclopedia of the British pr 1422-1992, 94n1008
Guide to sources in American journalism hist, 90n908
Index to city & regional mags of the US, 91n53
Journalism: a gd to the ref lit, 91n958
Press in Nigeria, 91n960
Publication peer review, 94n997
Regional interest mags of the US, 92n905
Sourcebook of American literary journalism, 93n976
Washington Post deskbk on style, 2d ed, 91n950

JOURNALISTS
American mag journalists, 1850-1900, 90n906
American mag journalists, 1900-60: 1st series, 91n963
Biographical dict of American journalism, 90n905
Directory, 1990: American society of journalists & authors, 91n936
Encyclopedia of the British pr 1422-1992, 94n1008
Horace Greeley: a bio-bibliog, 93n979
Journalists of the US, 92n901
Sources: the dir of contacts for editors, reporters & researchers, summer 1990, 26th ed, 91n939

JOYCE, JAMES
Annotated critical bibliog of James Joyce, 91n1240

JUDAISM
American synagogue hist, 90n379
Blackwell dict of Judaica, 94n1554
Dictionary of Judaism & Christianity, 93n1405
Encyclopedia of Jewish prayer, 94n1556
Encyclopedia of Jewish symbols, 93n443
Encyclopedia of Judaism, 91n1449
First century Palestinian Judaism, 92n1449
Glossary of Jewish life, 93n449
Jewish profiles, 93n450
Jewish wisdom, 93n445
Judaism & Christianity: a gd to the ref lit, 92n1399
Judaism & human rights in contemporary thought, 94n1555
Schocken gd to Jewish bks, 94n425
Social & religious hist of the Jews, 2d ed: index to vs.9-18, 94n427
Soviet pubns on Judaism, Zionism, & the state of Israel 1984-88, 91n407

JUDAISM—RELATIONS—CHRISTIANITY
Jewish-Christian relations, 90n1378

JUDGES
BNA's dir of state & fed courts, judges, & clerks, 4th ed, 93n582
Supreme Court justices, 94n551

JUDICIAL DISTRICTS
Judicial staff dir, 1993, 94n736
Staff dirs on CD-ROM, 1993/1, 94n737

JUNG, CARL GUSTAV
Cross-currents of Jungian thought, 93n796
General bibliog of C. G. Jung's writings, rev ed, 94n806
Jung lexicon, 92n758

JUNIOR COLLEGES
AACJC membership dir 1989, 90n321
AACJC membership dir 1992, 93n359
Chronicle 2-yr college databk for 1991-92, 93n369
Community, technical, & jr colleges statistical yrbk, 1990 ed, 91n328
Community, technical, & jr colleges statistical yrbk, 1992 ed, 94n356
Peterson's gd to 2-yr colleges 1991, 91n318
Peterson's gd to 2-yr colleges 1994, 94n343
Who's who in community, technical, & jr colleges 1991, 92n297

JUNIOR HIGH SCHOOL LIBRARIES
Best bks for jr high readers, 92n1116
Junior high school lib cat, 6th ed, 91n650
Your reading, 8th ed, 92n1123
Your reading, 9th ed, 94n648

JUSTICES
American leaders 1789-1991, 92n680

JUTLAND, BATTLE OF, 1916
Battle of Jutland, 93n693

JUVENILE DELINQUENCY
Focus on teens in trouble, 92n555

KAEL, PAULINE
Kael index, 94n1463

KANSAS
Amphibians & reptiles in Kans., 3d ed, 94n1749
Birds in Kans., 90n1544
Guide to Kans. mushrooms, 94n1662
Historical atlas of Kans., 2d ed, 90n469
Kansas governors, 91n495
Kansas hist, 93n513
1001 Kans. place names, 90n427
Watching Kans. wildlife, 94n1679

KARLOFF, BORIS
Boris Karloff: a bio-bibliog, 94n1409

KAVIA INDIANS (SHOSHONEANS). See CAHUILLA INDIANS

KAZAKHSTAN
Active figures of the trade union & working class movement of Russia, Ukraine, Bielorussia, & Kazakhstan, 94n262

KENNEDY, JOHN F. (JOHN FITZGERALD)
Assassination of John F. Kennedy, 94n494

KENTUCKY
Appalachian authors, 91n1146
Kentucky ency, 93n109
Vascular plants of Ky., 93n1494
Weeds of Ky. and adjacent states, 92n1546

KENYA
Field gd to the acacias of Kenya, 93n1516
Guide to archives & mss relating to Kenya & E Africa in the UK, 92n460

KEYBOARD INSTRUMENT MUSIC
Music for 2 or more players at clavichord, harpsichord, organ, 92n1281

KIERKEGAARD, SOREN
Soren Kierkegaard bibliogs, 94n1486

KING, MARTIN LUTHER, JR.
Guide to research on Martin Luther King, Jr., & the modern black freedom struggle, 91n600

KING, STEPHEN
Shape under the sheet, 92n1175
Stephen King companion, 90n1148

KINGS & RULERS
Encyclopedia of mistresses, 94n961
Kings & queens of England & Great Britain, 91n523
Monarchs of Scotland, 91n534
Power brokers, 90n481
Statesmen who changed the world, 94n716

KLEIN, ABRAHAM MOSES
A. M. Klein: an annot bibliog, 94n1278

KLEINIAN GROUPS
Dictionary of Kleinian thought, 90n745

KNIGHT'S TALE
Chaucer's Knight's Tale: an annot bibliog 1900-85, 92n1199

KNITTING
Illustrated dict of knitting, 90n931

KNOWLEDGE, THEORY OF
Glossary of cognitive sci, 94n1494
Glossary of epistemology/philosophy of sci, 94n1495

KOREA
Asian finance dir, 1990 ed, 91n209
Historical dict of the Korean War, 92n648
Historical dict of the Republic of Korea, 94n117
International bus hndbk: Republic of Korea, 90n285

KOREAN WAR, 1950-1953
Historical dict of the Korean War, 92n648
Korean war almanac, 92n660
Pusan perimeter, Korea, 1950, 94n679
U.S. army uniforms of the Korean war, 94n708

KOSINSKI, JERZY
Jerzy Kosinski: an annot bibliog, 93n1175

KRENEK, ERNST
Ernst Krenek, 90n1240

KRISTEVA, JULIA
Julia Kristeva, 91n917

KU KLUX KLAN
Ku Klux Klan: an ency, 92n730

KURDS
Kurds: a concise hndbk, 93n165

KUWAIT
BBC World Service Gulf Crisis chronology, 93n542

LA MAMA EXPERIMENTAL THEATRE CLUB
Ellen Stewart & La Mama: a bio-bibliog, 94n1410

LABOR & LABORING CLASSES
Encyclopedia of career change & work issues, 93n409
International Labour Review: index 1945-91, 94n285
Labour force stats 1970-90, 94n235
Labour info, 92n212
Transnational corporations & labor, 91n143
Year bk of labour stats 1991, 93n314
Year bk of labour stats: retrospective ed on population censuses 1945-89, 91n251
Workers' participation in mgmt, 90n257

LABOR MARKET. See LABOR SUPPLY

LABOR POLICY
Labour & population programme, 93n299

LABOR SUPPLY
America's top 300 jobs, 91n241
100 best job$ for the 1990s & beyond, 93n311

LABRADOR (NFLD.)
Atlas of Nfld. & Lab., 93n473
Encyclopedia of Nfld. & Lab., v.3, 93n133

LADINO . *See* **SPANISH JEWS**

LADY CHATTERLY'S LOVER
Descriptive bibliog of Lady Chatterly's Lover, 91n1211

LAHU LANGUAGE—DICTIONARIES—ENGLISH
Dictionary of Lahu, 90n1050

LAKE DISTRICT (ENGLAND)
Picturesque scenery of the Lake District 1752-1855, 92n447

LAKES—ALBERTA
Atlas of Alta. lakes, 92n410

L'AMOUR, LOUIS
Work of Louis L'Amour, 93n1176

LAND SETTLEMENT
Cahuilla landscape, 92n359
Pennsylvania land records, 92n390

LAND USE
Land use A-Z, 92n1473

LANDSCAPE
Dictionary of landscape, 92n1472

LANDSCAPE GARDENING
National Arboretum bk of outstanding garden plants, 91n1503
Shade & color with water-conserving plants, 93n1520

LANDSCAPE PAINTING
Hudson River school, 92n1002

LANGLAND, WILLIAM
Annotated critical bibliog of Langland, 92n1204
Piers Plowman: a gd to the quotations, 94n1253

LANGUAGE & CULTURE
Official politically correct dict & hndbk, 94n1101

LANGUAGE & LANGUAGES
Annotated bibliog of the official langs of Canada, 94n1068
Bibliography of bibliogs of the langs of the world, v.1, 92n1006
Compendium of the world's langs, 92n1012
Dictionary of dicts, 94n1073
Dictionary of stylistics, 91n955
Encyclopaedia of lang, 91n1042
Error analysis, 92n1010
Study holidays, 17th ed, 94n369

LANGUAGE ARTS
Handbook of research on teaching the English lang arts, 92n280
Using children's bks in reading/lang arts programs, 93n402

LANGUAGE DISORDERS
CHILDES/BIB: an annot bibliog of child lang & lang disorders, 92n269

LANGUAGE, UNIVERSAL
Ethnologue, 94n1070
Ethnologue index, 12th ed, 94n1069

LAOS
Historical dict of Laos, 93n128
Laos, 93n127

LARGE TYPE BOOKS
Complete dir of large print bks & serials 1992, 93n30
New Merriam-Webster dict for large print users, 91n1067

LASERS
Encyclopedia of lasers & optical tech, 92n1604
Laser video disc companion, updated ed, 93n997

LASERS IN MEDICINE
Understanding lasers, 93n1646

LASSO, ORLANDO DI
Orlando di Lasso: a gd to research, 91n1270

LATIN AMERICA
Annotated bibliog of Latin American sport, 91n801
Annotated bibliog on rodent research in Latin America, 1960-85, 90n1556
Bibliographic gd to Latin American studies 1991, 94n141
Bibliography of Latin American & Caribbean bibliogs: annual report, 1989-90, 92n109
Bibliography of Latin American & Caribbean bibliogs, 1985-89: social scis & humanities, 94n145
Bignoniaceae—pt.2 (tribe tecomeae), 94n1637
Cambridge ency of Latin America & the Caribbean, 94n142
Choral music of Latin America, 93n1267
El Salvador, 90n143
Guide to Latin American & Caribbean census material, 91n119
Guide to the writings of pioneer Latinamericanists of the US, 91n538
Handbook of Latin American studies, no.52, 94n144
Handbook of pol sci research on Latin America, 92n722
Hispanic heritage, series 4, 93n150
Latin America & the Caribbean: a critical gd to research sources, 93n148
Latin America, 1983-87, 90n137
Latin America today, rev ed, 91n441
Latin American insects & entomology, 94n1727
Latin American Jewish studies, 92n378
Latin American legal abbrevs, 91n557
Latin American revolutionaries, 91n761
Latin American studies, 2d ed, 91n117
Latinas of the Americas, 90n863
Lauraceae: nectandra, 94n1646
Neotropical rainforest mammals, 91n1592
Oral hist of contemporary Jewry, 91n408
People of the world: Latin Americans, 90n139
Sandinista Nicaragua, 90n146
Statistical yrbk for Latin America & the Caribbean, 1991 ed, 93n151
Tinker gd to Latin American & Caribbean policy & scholarly resources in metro N.Y., 90n138
Vanguardism in Latin American lit, 91n1244

LATIN AMERICA—HISTORY
Latin American military hist, 94n682
Liberators & patriots of Latin America, 92n108

LATIN AMERICA—LIBRARY RESOURCES
Scholars' gd to Washington, DC for Latin American & Caribbean studies, 2d ed, 93n149

LATIN AMERICA—POLITICS & GOVERNMENT
Latin America: a pol dict, 94n784
Political parties of the Americas and the Caribbean, 94n783
Political parties of the Americas, 1980s to 1990s, 94n720
Who is who [in] govt, pol, banking & industry: in Latin America, 2d ed, 90n140

LATIN AMERICA—RELATIONS—UNITED STATES
United States in Latin America, 93n786

LATIN AMERICAN LITERATURE
Contemporary Latin American fiction, 91n1241
Handbook of Latin American lit, 2d ed, 94n1298
Latin American writers, 90n1208
Luis Leal: a bibliog with interpretative & critical essays, 90n1207
Vanguardism in Latin American lit, 91n1244

LATIN AMERICANS
Hispanic-American material culture, 90n366

LATIN AMERICANS IN MOTION PICTURES
Censorship & Hollywood's Hispanic image, 94n1448

LATIN LANGUAGE
Weeds & words, 90n1445

LATIN LANGUAGE—DICTIONARIES—ENGLISH
Names of plants, 2d ed, 90n1484

LATIN LANGUAGE, MEDIEVAL & MODERN
Bibliotheca lexicologiae medii aevi, 90n990
Iter Italicum, v.6, 94n978
Princeton Alciati companion, 90n1051

LATVIAN LANGUAGE—DICTIONARIES—ENGLISH
Latvian-English, English-Latvian dict, 94n1123

LAUDER, HARRY
Sir Harry Lauder discography, 92n1331

LAW
Abortion in the US, 92n1669
American law dict, 92n535
Bibliographic gd to law 1990, 92n517
Bibliography of Commonwealth law reports, 92n518
Bibliography of Indian law per articles published 1980-90, 2d ed, 94n547
Bibliography of law & economics, 93n564
Bieber's dict of legal abbrevs, 3d ed, 90n538
Bieber's dict of legal abbrevs, 4th ed, 94n543
Bieber's dict of legal citations, 3d ed, 90n543
Bieber's dict of legal citations, 4th ed, 94n544
Black's law dict, 6th ed, 92n529
Books & pers online, v.2, no.1, 90n154
Bowker's law bks & serials in print 1991, 93n565
Business & legal CD-ROMS in print 1993, 94n175
California legal hist mss in the Huntington Lib, 90n554
Canada legal dir 1990, 91n573
Canada tax cases: index & citator, 94n581
Canadian law dict, 2d ed, 92n537
Canadian law symposia index, 93n598
Charlemagne Tower collection of American colonial laws, 92n519
Charles Szladits' gd to foreign legal materials: German, 2d ed, 91n563
CLE research gd, v.2, 94n583
Collection of definitions in fed statutes, 90n545
Comprehensive bibliog of American constitutional & legal hist, suppl., 1980-87, 92n521
Concise dict of law, 2d ed, 91n572
Dahl's law dict, 94n552
Demise of the Soviet Union, 94n548
Dictionary of English law, 93n575
Directory of foreign law collections in selected law libs, 92n544
Directory of law-related CD-ROMS 1993, 94n560
Directory of pers online: news, law & bus, 5th ed, 91n73
Encyclopedia of legal info sources, 2d ed, 94n566
English legal hist, 91n562
English-Chinese glossary of American criminal law & criminal procedure law, 91n571
English-Persian dict of legal & commercial terms, 91n570
Family law dict, 2d ed, 92n532
Foreign law, 91n567
Gorbachev's law, 92n525
Greenwood annual abstract of legal dissertations & theses, 1985-87, 90n562
Historic US court cases 1690-1990, 93n578
Index to law school alumni pubns cumulation Jan 1980-June 1989, 90n561
Index to legal pers: Sept 1990-Aug 1991, 93n600
Index to legal pers [CD-ROM], 93n601
Index to per articles related to law: 30 yr cumulation, 90n564
Index to the decisions rendered by the Immigration Appeal Board, 90n563
International legal bibliogs, 93n567
International legal bks in print 1993-94, 94n546
Latin American legal abbrevs, 91n557
Law & legal info dir, 5th ed, 90n552
Law & legal info dir, 6th ed, 92n543
Law bk news, 90n539
Law bks in print 1990, 93n570
Law dict, 3d ed, 92n531
Law for the layman, 92n522
Law lib ref shelf, 90n541
Law lib ref shelf, 2d ed, 93n572
Legal asst's notebk, 93n595
Legal briefs: a lawyer's quotation bk, 91n593
Legal desk bk 1992, 93n597
Legal glossary of fed statutes, 90n546
Legal looseleafs in print 1993, 94n567
Legal newsletters in print 1990, 91n561

Legal newsletters in print 1993, 94n568
Legal thesaurus, 2d ed, 93n574
Lexicon of tax terminology, 90n548
Martindale-Hubbell law dir 1990, 91n581
Mellinkoff's dict of American legal usages, 93n579
Mexical legal system, 93n563
Michigan legal lit, 2d ed, 92n514
Modern dict for the legal profession, 94n555
National dir of legal servs, 90n549
National survey of state laws, 94n569
Oxford dict of American legal quotations, 94n584
Oxford ency of European Community law, v.1, 92n534
Quote it 2, 90n566
Recommended pubs for legal research 1970/71, 94n549
Recommended pubs for legal research 1990, 93n573
South Pacific islands legal systems, 94n573
Stroud's judicial dict of words & phrases, 5th cum suppl. to the 5th ed, 92n536
Subject headings for the lit of law & intl law, & index to LC K schedules, 4th ed, 91n626
West's tax law dict, 1992 ed, 93n581
World dict of legal abbrevs, 93n562

LAW—CANADA
Private law dict & bilingual lexicons, 90n547

LAW—CHINA
Guide to the laws, regulations & policies of the People's Republic of China on foreign trade & investment, 91n564

LAW—CLASSIFICATION
Library of Congress classification class KJ-KKZ: law of Europe, 91n621
Moys classification & thesaurus for legal materials, 3d ed, 94n626

LAW ENFORCEMENT
Dictionary of crime, 93n608
Latest intelligence, 92n646
Police dict & ency, 90n568
Rewards offered by the US, 91n597
Special access required, 92n528
Unlocking the files of the FBI, 94n752

LAW FIRMS
Guide to N.Y. law firms, 92n541
Law firms yellow bk, v.2, no.1, 93n584

LAW LIBRARIES
AALL annual meetings: an annot index of the recordings, 91n591
Canadian Assn of Law Libs dir, 94n649
Law lib systems dir, 94n654
Werner's manual for prison law libs, 2d ed, 92n616

LAW OFFICES
Canadian legal sftwr dir 1991, 92n540
Federal legal dir, 91n575

LAW REPORTING
Court reporting computer compatible machine shorthand dict, 90n289

LAW SCHOOLS
Barron's gd to law schools, 9th ed, 92n539
Directory of law school join degree programs 1989-90, 91n586
Guide to law schools in Canada, 94n575
Index to law school alumni pubns cumulation Jan 1980-June 1989, 90n561
World law school dir, 1993 ed, 94n565

LAW (THEOLOGY)
Biblical law bibliog, 92n1445

LAWRENCE, D. H.
Descriptive bibliog of Lady Chatterly's Lover, 91n1211

LAWYERS
Best lawyers in America 1989-90, 90n550
Best lawyers in America 1993-94, 94n562
Butterworths law dir 1993, 94n558
Canada legal dir 1992, 93n583
Directory of housing attorneys, 1990-91, 92n542

Distinguished American lawyers, 91n569
Law & bus dir of corporate counsel 1990-91, 91n578
Law & bus dir of litigation attorneys 1990, 91n579
Lawyers' & creditors' serv dir, 1993 ed, 94n563
Lincoln as a lawyer, 92n526
Martindale-Hubbell bar register 1990, 91n580
Martindale-Hubbell bar register of preeminent lawyers 1993, 94n561
Tennessee attorneys dir, 1992, 93n585

LAYTON, IRVING
Catalogue of the letters, tapes & photographs in the Irving Layton collection, 94n1270
Catalogue of the mss in the Irving Layton collection, 90n1193

LE GALLIENNE, EVA
Eva Le Gallienne: a bio-bibliog, 90n1320

LEAD
Childhood lead poisoning prevention, 91n1697
Lead detection & abatement dir 1993-94, 94n2005
State lead poisoning prevention dir 1992, 94n2006

LEADERSHIP
Leadership, 91n71
Leadership: quotations from the military tradition, 91n681
Thoughts on leadership, 93n316

LEAL, LUIS
Luis Leal: a bibliog with interpretative & critical essays, 90n1207

LEARNED INSTITUTIONS & SOCIETIES
Directory of European professional & learned societies, 4th ed, 90n58
International ency of learned societies & academies, 94n36
World gd to scientific assns & learned societies, 5th ed, 92n1461
World of learning 1990, 91n301

LEARNING
Sex differences & learning, 92n268
World of learning 1993, 94n308

LEARNING DISABILITIES
BOSC dir, 1990 ed, 91n348
Complete dir for people with learning disabilities, 1993/94, 94n372
Directory of facilities & servs for the learning disabled, 1993-94, 94n373
Peterson's colleges with programs for students with learning disabilities, 94n340

LEARNING DISABLED YOUTH
Peterson's colleges with programs for students with learning disabilities, 94n340
Peterson's gd to colleges with programs for learning-disabled students, 2d ed, 90n349
Schoolsearch gd to colleges with programs or servs for students with disabilities, 92n319

LEARNING, PSYCHOLOGY OF
Encyclopedia of learning & memory, 94n809

LEARNING RESOURCE CENTERS. *See* INSTRUCTIONAL MATERIALS CENTERS

LEATHER GOODS
World statistical compendium for raw hides & skins, leather, & leather footwear 1972-90, 5th ed, 94n1598

LEAVES
Picture gd to tree leaves, 92n1554

LEAVIS, F. R.
F. R. Leavis & Q. D. Leavis, 90n1149

LEAVIS, Q. D.
F. R. Leavis & Q. D. Leavis, 90n1149

LEBANON
Lebanon, rev ed, 93n166
Who's who in Lebanon 1990-91, 91n17

LECTURERS
Yearbook of experts, authorities & spokespersons, 8th ed, 91n943

LEGAL AID
Legal resource dir, 94n557

LEGAL ASSISTANCE TO PRISONERS
Legal resource dir, 94n557
Werner's manual for prison law libs, 2d ed, 92n616

LEGAL DEPOSIT (OF BOOKS, ETC.)
International gd to legal deposit, 93n651

LEGAL ETHICS
Resources for research in legal ethics, 93n592

LEGAL LAWS
Selected state enactments 1990, 92n697

LEGAL LITERATURE
Index to Canadian legal lit 1989, 91n592
Index to Canadian legal lit 1992, 94n582

LEGAL RESEARCH
Arizona legal research gd, 93n596
Congress & law-making, 2d ed, 90n705
Fundamentals of legal research, 5th ed, 92n548
Legal researcher's desk ref 1990, 91n585
Legal researcher's desk ref 1992, 93n591
Mexical legal system, 93n563
Recommended pubs for legal research 1989, 92n527

LEGAL SERVICES
Public interest law groups, 90n557

LEGENDS
Brewer's bk of myth & legend, 94n1391
Contemporary legend, 94n1383
Macmillan illus ency of myths & legends, 91n1333
Medieval Charlemagne legend, 94n1199

LEGISLATION
Alphabetical list of titles of fed statues, 92n550
Congress & law-making, 2d ed, 90n705
Congressional Quarterly's American congressional dict, 94n729

LEGISLATIVE BODIES
Directory of legislative leaders 1989-90, 90n696
Directory of legislative leaders 1991-92, 93n739
Legislative staff servs 1988, 90n707
State legislative leadership, committees & staff 1991-92, 92n698
State yellow bk, v.5, no.1, 94n743

LEGISLATORS
American leaders 1789-1991, 92n680
American legislative leaders, 1850-1910, 90n692
Congressional roll call 1989, 91n747
Who's who in European pols, 92n719

LEGUMES
Common legumes of the Great Plains, 90n1504
Vascular flora of the southeastern US, v.3, pt.2, 91n1533

LEHMANN, JOHN
John Lehmann's 'New Writing': an author-index 1936-50, 92n1205

LEIGH, VIVIEN
Vivien Leigh: a bio-bibliog, 94n1415

LEISURE
Dictionary of concepts in recreation & leisure studies, 91n807
Information sources in sport & leisure, 94n821
Leisure lit, 94n820

LEISURE INDUSTRY
Recreation & entertainment industries, 91n802

LESBIANISM
Contemporary lesbian writers of the US, 94n1226
Lesbian sources, 94n907
Lesbianism: an annot bibliog & gd to the lit 1976-91, 94n908
Words to the wise: a writer's gd to feminist & lesbian pers & pubs, 3d ed, 92n900

LESBIANS
Contemporary lesbian writers of the US, 94n1226

Gay & lesbian American plays, 94n1227
Gay & lesbian characters & themes in mystery novels, 94n1210
Lesbian & gay almanac & events of 1990, 91n871
Lesbian sources, 94n907

LEVERAGED BUYOUTS
Buyouts: dir of LBO financing sources, 1990 ed, 91n173

LEVERTOV, DENISE
Denise Levertov: an annot primary & secondary bibliog, 90n1150

LEWIS, C. S.
C. S. Lewis: a ref gd 1972-88, 94n1254

LEXICOGRAPHY
Catalog of dicts, word bks, & philological texts, 1440-1900, 94n1074

LIBERALISM
Dictionary of conservative & libertarian thought, 92n727

LIBERATION THEOLOGY
Liberation theologies, 92n1398
Women & religion: a bibliographic gd to Christian feminist liberation theology, 92n1405

LIBRARIANS
Supplement to the dict of American lib biog, 91n604

LIBRARIES. *See also specific types, e.g.* PUBLIC LIBRARIES
Advances in lib automation & networking, v.3, 90n616
ALA yearbk of lib & info servs, v.14, 90n589
American lib dir 1989-90, 90n582
American lib dir 1990-91, 91n607
American lib dir 1992-93, 93n623
American lib dir 1993-94, 94n610
American lib hist, 90n580
Basic lib skills, 3d ed, 94n620
Bowker annual lib & bk trade almanac 1989-90, 90n590
Bowker annual lib & bk trade almanac 1990-91, 91n611
British lib dir, 90n607
Building the ref collection, 94n619
Grants for libs & info servs, 90n592
Guide to scholarly resources on the Russian empire & the Soviet Union in the N.Y. metropolitan area, 91n113
Guide to the use of libs & info sources, 6th ed, 91n612
Interlibrary loan policies dir, 4th ed, 93n657
Libraries dir 1991-93, 94n634
Libraries, info centers, & databases in sci & tech, 2d ed, 90n624
Library lit. 18, 90n594
Library lit. 19, 91n613
Library lit [CD-ROM], 93n632
New York Public Lib bk of how & where to look it up, 92n609
Washington area lib dir, 94n611
Whole lib hndbk, 92n570
WLN interlib loan policies dir, 93n658
World gd to lib, archive, & info sci assns, 92n571
World gd to libs, 10th ed, 92n568
World gd to libs, 11th ed, 94n612

LIBRARIES & PUBLISHING
Library lit. 18, 90n594
Library lit. 19, 91n613
Policies of publishers, 1989 ed, 90n645

LIBRARIES & THE AGED
Working with older adults, 3d ed, 91n644

LIBRARIES—AUTOMATION
CD-ROM 1992, 94n645
Directory of automated lib systems, 2d ed, 91n637
Directory of lib automation sftwr, systems, & servs, 1993 ed, 94n644
Essential gd to the lib IBM PC, v.15, 91n642
Information sources in info tech, 92n595
Library computer & tech specialists, 92n594
Microcomputers & libs, 92n596
101 microcomputer projects to do in your lib, 91n638
Template dir for libs 1989-90, 91n639
User educ for online systems in libs, 92n598

LIBRARIES—CANADA
Canadian lib yrbk, 4th ed, 90n591

LIBRARIES—CENSORSHIP
Intellectual freedom & censorship, 90n614
Intellectual freedom manual, 4th ed, 94n642

LIBRARIES, CHILDREN'S
Author a month (for dimes), 94n1188
Beyond picture bks, 90n1077
Bookpeople: a 1st album, 91n651
Building the ref collection, 94n619
Children's cat, 16th ed, 92n610
Children's media market place, 3d ed, 90n621
Children's servs in the American public lib, 91n645
Library serv to children, 93n665
Primaryplots, 90n1095
Storytime sourcebk, 92n625
Summer reading clubs, 94n1194
Using children's bks in reading/lang arts programs, 93n402

LIBRARIES, DEPOSITORY
International gd to legal deposit, 93n651
World Bank depository lib program dir of libs, 90n626

LIBRARIES—GIFTS, LEGACIES
National gd to funding for libs & info servs, 92n573

LIBRARIES, GOVERNMENTAL, ADMINISTRATIVE, ETC.
Directory of fed libs, 2d ed, 94n651

LIBRARIES, INTERNATIONAL
World Bank depository lib program dir of libs, 90n626

LIBRARIES, NATIONAL
Biographical dir of natl librarians, 90n581

LIBRARIES—PERIODICALS
Free mags for libs, 3d ed, 90n79
Magazines for libs, 7th ed, 93n85

LIBRARIES, PRIVATE
Private libs in renaissance England, v.1, 94n598
Private libs in renaissance England, v.2, 94n599

LIBRARIES, SCHOOL. *See* SCHOOL LIBRARIES

LIBRARIES, SPECIAL
Directory of special libs & info centers 1993, 94n650
From the top, 90n623
Position descriptions in special libs, 2d ed, 94n624
Subject dir of special libs & info centers 1991, 92n622
Tools of the profession, 2d ed, 93n674
World gd to special libs, 2d ed, 92n623

LIBRARIES—SPECIAL COLLECTIONS
Best videos for children & young adults, 92n617
CD-ROM research collections, 93n660
Directory of special collections in W Europe, 94n653
Directory of special collections of research value in Canadian libs, 93n646
Educational & psychological tests in the Academic Lib, 91n292
Free & user supported sftwr for the IBM PC, 91n641
Free resource builder for librarians & teachers, 2d ed, 93n70
Gerontology & geriatrics libs & collections in the US & Canada, 94n655
Guide to special collections in the OCLC database, 90n625
Informing the nation: a hndbk of govt info for librarians, 92n619
Latino librarianship, 92n618
Nonbook materials: the org of integrated collections, 3d ed, 90n606
Selection of lib materials for area studies, pt.1, 92n81
Special collections in college & univ libs, 90n627
State doc checklists, 91n729
Video for libs, 90n619
Video movies, 91n1359
Video policies & procedures for libs, 92n621
Voices from the underground, 94n1010

LIBRARIES, UNIVERSITY & COLLEGE
ACRL univ lib stats 1988-89, 91n656
Collection evaluation in academic libs, 93n677
Educational & psychological tests in the Academic Lib, 91n292

Guide to the college lib, 94n658
Search sheets for OPACs on the Internet, 93n661
Special collections in college & univ libs, 90n627

LIBRARY ADMINISTRATION
Advances in lib admin & org, v.7, 90n587
Advances in lib admin & org, v.8, 90n588
Library lit. 20, 92n572

LIBRARY ASSOCIATION
Library Assn yrbk 1992, 94n636

LIBRARY ASSOCIATION INDUSTRIAL GROUP
Industrial group index, 93n649

LIBRARY AUTHORITY FILES. *See* **AUTHORITY FILES (CATALOGING)**

LIBRARY BUILDINGS
Carnegie lib in Ill., 92n602
Library buildings consultant list, 1991, 92n600
Planning lib facilities, 91n643

LIBRARY CATALOGS & READERS
Search sheets for OPACs on the Internet, 93n661

LIBRARY COLLECTION
Building lib collections on aging, 92n806

LIBRARY CONSULTANTS
Library buildings consultant list, 1991, 92n600
Library computer & tech specialists, 92n594
Library personnel consultants list, 92n601

LIBRARY COOPERATION
Latin American serial pubs available by exchange, 93n633

LIBRARY EDUCATION
Occupational entry, 90n596

LIBRARY EMPLOYEES
Library computer & tech specialists, 92n594
Library personnel consultants list, 92n601

LIBRARY INFORMATION NETWORKS
Directory of computer conferencing in libs, 93n656
Sourcebook on standards info, 92n574

LIBRARY MATERIALS
Current issues resource builder, 90n88

LIBRARY OF CONGRESS. COPYRIGHT OFFICE
Researching copyright renewal, 91n630

LIBRARY PERSONNEL MANAGEMENT
Position descriptions in special libs, 2d ed, 94n624

LIBRARY PLANNING
Planning lib facilities, 91n643

LIBRARY RESOURCES
Directory of govt doc collections & librarians, 6th ed, 93n676
Directory of special collections of research value in Canadian libs, 93n646
Find it fast, updated ed, 91n47
Guide to Cuban collections in the US, 92n495
Guide to the use of libs & info sources, 6th ed, 91n612
How to find info about cos, 8th ed, 92n146
Information resources & servs in Austral., 92n588
Scholars' gd to Washington, DC for Latin American & Caribbean studies, 2d ed, 93n149
SCOLMA dir of libs & special collections on Africa in the UK & in Europe, 5th ed, 94n652
Special collections in college & univ libs, 90n627

LIBRARY SCIENCE
Advances in librarianship, v.15, 93n627
Advances in lib admin & org, v.8, 90n588
ALA yrbk of lib & info servs 1990, v.15, 91n610
ALISE Library & info sci educ statl report 1991, 92n576
American lib hist, 90n580
Annotated bibliog of faculty status in lib & info sci, 93n634
Annual review of info sci & tech, v.25, 92n569
Bowker annual lib & bk trade almanac, 37th ed, 93n629

Bowker annual lib & bk trade almanac, 38th ed, 94n615
British librarianship & info work 1986-90, v.2, 94n633
Dictionary of acronyms & abbrevs, 94n597
Dictionary of info sci & tech, 93n622
Encyclopedia of lib & info sci, v.44, 94n601
Encyclopedia of lib & info sci, v.45, 94n602
Encyclopedia of lib & info sci, v.46, 94n603
Encyclopedia of lib & info sci, v.47, 94n604
Encyclopedia of lib & info sci, v.48, 94n605
Encyclopedia of lib & info sci, v.49, 94n606
Encyclopedia of lib & info sci, v.50, 94n607
Encyclopedia of lib & info sci, v.51, 94n608
Guide to the use of libs & info sources, 6th ed, 91n612
Harrod's librarians' glossary...& ref bk, 7th ed, 92n565
International writings of Bohdan S. Wynar, 1949-92, 94n80
Librarian's thesaurus, 91n606
Librarianship & info work worldwide 1991, 93n631
Library & info sci annual, v.5, 90n593
Library Assn yrbk 1990, 91n614
Library lit [CD-ROM], 93n632
Library lit 1992, 94n621
Library lit. 20, 92n572
Library lit. 21, 94n616
Library pers 1993, 94n622
Library serv to children, 93n665
National gd to funding for libs & info servs, 2d ed, 94n618
New intl dict of acronyms in lib & info sci, 2d ed, 93n621
Research gd to libs & archives in the Low Countries, 92n607
Whole lib hndbk, 92n570
World ency of lib & info servs, 3d ed, 94n609

LIBRARY SCIENCE—DICTIONARIES—SPANISH
Technical dict of lib & info sci, 94n600

LIBRARY SCIENCE—SOCIETIES, ETC.
Directory of lib & info orgs in the UK, 94n635
FID dir 1991-92, 93n624

LIBRARY STATISTICS
ACRL univ lib stats 1988-89, 91n656

LIBYA
Historical dict of Libya, 2d ed, 93n115

LICENSES
Professional & occupational licensing dir, 94n800

LICHENS
Indices to the species of mosses & lichens described by William Mitten, 94n1668

LIEUTENANT-GOVERNORS
Lieutenant-governors of the NW territories & Alta. 1876-1991, 93n765
National Conference of Lt. Governors 1990 staff dir, 92n691

LIFE
Origin & evolution of life on Earth, 94n1635

LIFE CARE COMMUNITIES
Golden horizons retirement gd, Calif ed, 90n792
National continuing care dir, 2d ed, 90n789
99 best residential & recreational communities in America for vacation, retirement & investment planning, 93n919

LIFE ON OTHER PLANETS
Extraterrestrial ency, rev ed, 93n805

LIFE SCIENCES
Magill's survey of sci: life sci series, 92n1522

LIFE SKILLS
Friendly advice, 92n71

LIGHTHOUSES
Great American lighthouses, 91n1830

LINCOLN, ABRAHAM
Lincoln as a lawyer, 92n526

LINGUISTICS
Career opportunities for bilinguals & multilinguals, 92n1015
Encyclopaedia of lang, 91n1042

International ency of linguistics, 93n1050
Linguistics: a gd to the ref lit, 92n1007
Linguistics ency, 93n1052
Yugoslav lingustics in English 1900-80, 92n1008

LIONEL CORPORATION
Greenberg's Lionel catalogs, 92n943

LIQUIDS
Data bk on the viscosity of liquids, 90n1774

LISZT, FRANZ
Franz Liszt: a gd to research, 92n1276

LITERACY
Dictionary of cultural literacy, 90n304
Directory of Ill. adult literacy programs, 1989 update & suppl, 91n355
Family literacy, 91n357
International hndbk of reading educ, 93n404
Library lit. 20, 92n572
Literacy/illiteracy in the world, 91n356
Reader dvlpmt bibliog, 4th ed, 92n324

LITERARY AGENTS
Guide to literary agents & art/photo reps, 1992, 93n961
Literary agents of N America, 4th ed, 92n896

LITERARY CALENDARS
Calendar of literary facts, 92n1100

LITERARY CHARACTERS. *See* **CHARACTERS & CHARACTERISTICS IN LITERATURE**

LITERARY CRITICISM. *See* **CRITICISM**

LITERARY LANDMARKS
Historic homes of American authors, 92n435
Mystery reader's walking gd: England, 90n459
Oxford illus literary gd to Great Britain & Ireland, 2d ed, 94n480
Scotland: a literary gd, 91n474
Wellsprings of imagination, 94n478

LITERARY MOVEMENTS
Twentieth-century literary movements index, 92n1113

LITERARY PRIZES
Index to American short story award collections 1970-90, 94n1230
Prizewinning lit: UK literary award winners, 91n1185

LITERARY STYLE. *See* **STYLE, LITERARY**

LITERATURE
Author a month (for dimes), 94n1188
Authors: critical & biographical refs, 2d ed, 94n1145
Benet's reader's ency of American lit, 92n1155
Bookpeople: a 1st album, 91n651
Cassell dict of literary & lang terms, 94n980
Concise Oxford dict of literary terms, 91n1099
Cyclopedia of literary characters 2, 91n1104
Cyclopedia of world authors 2, 91n1105
Dictionary of concepts in literary criticism & theory, 93n1111
Dictionary of literary biog documentary series, v.10, 94n1154
Dictionary of literary biog yrbk 88, 91n1101
Dictionary of literary biog yrbk: 1991, 94n1156
Dictionary of literary terms & literary theory, 3d ed, 92n1101
Directory of literary mags 1990-91, 91n1106
Elements of English, 2d ed, 90n993
Encyclopedia of lit & criticism, 93n1116
Essay & general lit index 1985-89, 91n52
Essay & general lit index, rev ed, 93n77
Gale's literary index [CD-ROM], 94n1161
Literature teacher's bk of lists, 94n1142
Magill's survey of world lit, 94n1158
Masterplots 2: nonfiction, 90n1071
New literary hist intl bibliog of literary theory & criticism, 90n1066
NTC's dict of literary terms, 92n1103
Photography & lit, 93n1013
Plot locator, 92n1140
Women writers: from page to screen, 91n1364
Writers dir 1992-94, 93n1118

LITERATURE & MEDICINE
Medicine, lit, & eponyms, 90n1653

LITERATURE—BLACK AUTHORS
Black lit criticism, 93n1115

LITERATURE, MEDIEVAL
Concordance to middle English metrical romances, 90n1174
Medieval Charlemagne legend, 94n1199

LITERATURE, MODERN
City Lights bks, 94n1220
Concise glossary of contemporary literary theory, 93n1112
Contemporary world writers, 2d ed, 94n1144
Encyclopedia of contemporary literary theory, 94n1150
Encyclopedia of continental women writers, 92n1232
Encyclopedia of world lit in the 20th century, v.5, 94n1152
Glossary of contemporary literary theory, 93n1113
Literary exile in the 20th century, 92n1098
MLA intl bibliog, 93n1107
Twentieth-century literary movements index, 92n1113
World authors 1980-85, 92n1099

LITERATURE—19TH CENTURY
Nineteenth-century lit criticism, v.22, 90n1072

LITERATURE PUBLISHING
British literary publishing houses, 1881-1965, 93n689
Small pr: an annot gd, 94n659

LITHOGRAPHY
Catalogue raisonne of the graphic work of Richard Florsheim, 90n980

LITHUANIA
Lithuanian Jewish communities, 92n489

LITTLE MAGAZINES
Directory of literary mags 1993-94, 94n1162

LITTLE PRESS BOOKS
Small pr center dir, 94n673

LITTLE PRESSES
Directory of small pr & mag eds & publs, 22d ed, 92n635
International dir of little mags & small prs, 27th ed, 92n636
Small pr: an annot gd, 94n659

LITURGICS
Bibliography of Christian worship, 91n1437
Dictionary of the liturgy, 90n1408
New dict of sacramental worship, 92n1415

LIVERWORTS
Guide to the liverworts of N.C., 93n1512

LIVESTOCK
Handbook of animal sci, 92n1512

LIZARDS
Giant lizards, 93n1580
Lizards of the world, 90n1568

LLOYD'S (FIRM)
Directory of Lloyd's of London, 91n240

LOANS, INTERLIBRARY. *See* **INTER-LIBRARY LOANS**

LOBBYING
COGEL blue bk, 9th ed, 94n801

LOBBYISTS
Activist's almanac, 94n865
American lobbyists dir 1990, 91n742
Beacham's gd to key lobbyists, 90n690
Directory of pressure groups in the European Community, 93n768
Political resource dir 1989, 90n682
Public interest profiles 1988-89, 90n736
Washington representatives 1989, 90n703
Washington representatives 1992, 93n744

LOBSTERS
FAO species cat, v.13: marine lobsters of the world, 93n1557

LOCAL GOVERNMENT
Government dir of addresses & telephone nos, 93n740

LOCAL LAWS
Subject comps of state laws 1985-88, 90n689

LOCAL TRANSIT
Urban public transportation glossary, 90n1816

LOCOMOTIVES
Steam locomotive dir of N America, 90n1806
Steam locomotives of the Reading & P & R railroads, 90n1817

LOCUSTS
Locust neurobiology, 93n1566

LONDON (ENGLAND)
Directories of London, 1677-1977, 91n111
London gd, 91n469
Nicholson's access in London, 91n470
Nicholson's children's London, 91n471
Times London hist atlas, 93n534

LONG-TERM CARE OF THE SICK
Directory of long-term care centres in Canada, v.9, Sept 90, 91n1646
Elder care, 91n845

LOOSE-LEAF PUBLICATIONS, LEGAL
Legal looseleafs in print 1990, 91n560

LORTEL, LUCILLE
Lucille Lortel: a bio-bibliog, 94n1414

LOS ANGELES COUNTY MUSEUM OF ART
Clay today, 91n1040

LOSS (PSYCHOLOGY)
Books to help children cope with separation & loss, v.3, 90n738

LOST CONTINENTS
Atlas of legendary places, 91n1332

LOUISIANA
Amphibians & reptiles of La., 90n1566
Bibliography of New Orleans imprints 1764-1864, 90n629
French & Spanish records of La., 90n464
Louisiana almanac 1992-93, 93n110
Louisiana governors, 91n491

LOVE
Dictionary of love, 91n796

LOVE POETRY
Roman de la rose: an annot bibliog, 94n1282

LOW TEMPERATURE RESEARCH
Directory of low temperature research & dvlpmt in Europe, 7th ed, 94n1964

LOWELL, ROBERT
Robert Lowell papers at the Houghton Lib, Harvard Univ, 92n1176

LOWER RIO GRANDE VALLEY (TEX.)
Guide to grasses of the lower Rio Grande valley, Tex., 94n1665

LOW-FAT DIET
Low-fat supermarket, 94n1612

LUENING, OTTO
Otto Luening: a bio-bibliog, 92n1265

LUTE MUSIC
Guitar & lute music in pers, 92n1282

LUTHERAN CHURCH
Lutheran churches in the world, 90n1410

LUXEMBOURG
Facts on File national profiles: the Benelux countries, 90n132

LYME DISEASE
Lyme disease, 91n1698

LYOTARD, JEAN-FRANCOIS
Jean-Francois Lyotard: a bibliog, 92n873

MACAO
Historical dict of Hong Kong & Macau, 94n110

MACBETH
Macbeth: an annot bibliog, 2d ed, 91n1216

MACDONALD, GEORGE
George MacDonald: a bibliographical study, 92n1241

MACDONALD, ROSS
Dictionary of literary biog documentary series, v.6, 90n1126

MACHIAVELLI, NICCOLO
Niccolo Machiavelli: an annot bibliog of modern criticism & scholarship, 91n715

MACHINE-TOOLS
Elsevier's dict of machine tools & elements, 92n1628

MACHINE-READABLE BIBLIOGRAPHIC DATA
Sourcebook on standards info, 92n574

MACHISMO IN MOTION PICTURES
Tough guy: the American movie macho, 90n1342

MACINTOSH (COMPUTER)
Bob Brant's best of Macintosh shareware, 94n1913
Hyper dict, 90n1720
Macintosh bible, 4th ed, 94n1910

MACRAE, GORDON
Gordon MacRae: a bio-bibliog, 92n1309

MAGIC
Ancient & shining ones, 94n1392
Magic, witchcraft, & paganism in America, 2d ed, 93n811

MAGNETIC MATERIALS
Concise ency of magnetic & superconducting materials, 93n1591

MAHICAN LANGUAGE
Schmick's Mahican dict, 93n1089

MAHLER, ALMA
Gustav & Alma Mahler, 90n1241

MAHLER, GUSTAV
Gustav & Alma Mahler, 90n1241

MAIL ART
Mail art, 92n966

MAIL-ORDER BUSINESS
Wholesale-by-mail cat 1993, 94n203

MAILING LISTS
Directory of mailing list cos, 11th ed, 92n252
National dir of mailing lists 1991, 92n257

MAIL-ORDER BUSINESS
Catalogue of Canadian catalogues, 2d ed, 91n188
Catalogue of Canadian catalogues, 3d ed, 93n227
Directory of mail order catalogs, 4th ed, 91n193
Gardening by mail, 3d ed, 91n1497
Kids's catalog collection, 92n181
National dir of catalogs 1990, 91n194
Wholesale-by-mail catalog 1991, 91n198

MAJOLICA, ITALIAN
Robert Lehman collection, 90n952

MALAMUD, BERNARD
Bernard Malamud: a descriptive bibliog, 92n1177

MALAWI
Historical dict of Malawi, 2d ed, 94n100

MALAYSIA
Historical dict of Malaysia, 94n118

MALDIVES
Cambridge ency of India, Pakistan, Bangladesh, Sri Lanka, Nepal, Bhutan & the Maldives, 91n99
Maldives, 94n119
South Asian hndbk, 1992, 93n502

MALEBRANCHE, NICOLAS
Bibliographia Malebranchiana, 94n1485

MALHEUR NATIONAL WILDLIFE REFUGE
Birds of Malheur Natl Wildlife Refuge, Oreg., 92n1564

MALNUTRITION
Reference gd to world hunger, 92n1486
World hunger, 92n830

MALORY, THOMAS, SIR
Sir Thomas Malory: an anecdotal bibliog of editions, 1485-1985, 92n1206

MAMMALS. See also names of families, genera, species, etc.
Arkansas mammals, rev ed, 91n1597
Asdell's patterns of mammalian reproduction, 94n1731
Chris & Tilde Stuart's field gd to the mammals of S Africa, 90n1558
Fauna of Austral., v.1B, 91n1598
Grzimek's ency of mammals, 91n1593
Guide to the mammals of Salta Province, Argentina, 91n1596
Mammal species of the world, 2d ed, 94n1743
Mammals of Ill., 91n1594
Mammals of Okla., 91n1591
Mammals of the central Rockies, 94n1741
Mammals of the Indomalayan region, 94n1734
Mammals of the neotropics, 90n1555
Mammals of the neotropics: the S cone, v.2, 93n1570
Mammals: primates, insect eaters & baleen whales, 90n1520
Mammals: the hunters, 90n1521
Mammals: the large plant-eaters, 90n1522
Mammals: the small plant-eaters, 90n1523
Multimedia ency of mammalian biology [CD-ROM], 94n1739
Neotropical rainforest mammals, 91n1592
Oklahoma mammalogy, 90n1557
Parasites & diseases of wild mammals in Fla., 93n1569
Saving endangered mammals, 94n1738
Seven-lang thesaurus of European animals, 92n1558
Walker's mammals of the world, 5th ed, 93n1572
World list of mammalian species, 3d ed, 92n1581
Zoological cat of Austral., v.5, 90n1559

MAN
Illustrated ency of mankind, 91n75

MAN—INFLUENCE ON NATURE
Atlas of endangered places, 94n1987
Conservation atlas of tropical forests: Africa, 93n1484
Rand McNally children's atlas of the environment, 92n1766
Random House atlas of the oceans, 93n1730

MAN, PREHISTORIC
African archaeology, 94n488
Chronologies in old world archaeology, 3d ed, 94n485

MANAGEMENT
Administrative sci quarterly cum index 1956-85, 90n265
Business Week's gd to the best executive educ programs, 94n169
Concise dict of mgmt, 93n317
Executive's bus info sourcebk, 91n257
International dict of mgmt, 4th ed, 92n232
Management study abroad 1989-91, 90n270
Manager's bk of quotations, 90n269
Manager's desk ref, 90n266
Moving up, 90n267
Peterson's bus & mgmt jobs 1989, 90n187
Public admin & mgmt vocabulary, 91n782
Quality control, 92n233
Quotable business, 93n218
Treasury of business quotations, 91n167
Who's who 1989: deans & directors in mgmt & admin studies at Canadian univs, 90n272

MANAGERIAL ACCOUNTING
101 business ratios, 94n176

MANITOBA
Bibliography of N Manitoba, 92n99
Directory of archives in Manitoba, 90n512

MANNED SPACE FLIGHT
Who's who in space: the intl space yr ed, 94n1755

MANNERS & CUSTOMS
Culturgrams, 92n1326
Hispanic way, 92n355
People atlas, 93n414

MANPOWER POLICY
Plant closings, 93n300

MANSION, THE
Mansion: a concordance, 90n1140

MANUFACTURES
American manufacturers dir, 1993 ed, 94n212
Brands & their cos 1992, 93n188
Companies & their brands 1992, 93n189
Consumer product & manufacturer ratings 1961-90, 94n214
Directory of Canadian made products, 91n226
Directory of Tex. manufacturers, 1991, 92n194
European dir of consumer goods manufacturers 1989, 90n237
Harris manufacturers dir, 1993, 94n215
Made in the USA, 1990 ed, 91n197
Manufacturing USA, 90n242
Manufacturing USA, 2d ed, 93n247
Official museum products & servs dir 1992, 93n80
RMA annual statement studies 1993, 94n217

MANUFACTURING
Harris Ill. industrial dir, 1991, 92n197
Harris Ind. industrial dir, 1991, 92n198
Harris Mich. industrial dir, 1991, 92n199
Harris Ohio industrial dir, 1991, 92n200
Harris Pa. industrial dir, 1991, 92n201
Harris W.Va. manufacturing dir, 1990, 92n202
Missouri dir of manufacturers, 1991, 92n203

MANUFACTURING PROCESSES
Automation ency, 4th ed, 90n1577
Dictionary of materials & manufacturing, 92n1616
Dictionary of process tech, 91n1609
Directory of manufacturing research centers June 1989, 90n234

MANUSCRIPT PREPARATION (AUTHORSHIP)
Chicago manual of style, 14th ed, 94n1001
Directory of pub resources, 1993-94, 94n995
Editing: an annot bibliog, 92n897
Guide to info sources for the preparation, editing, & production of docs, 90n896
Publication peer review, 94n997

MANUSCRIPTS
California legal hist mss in the Huntington Lib, 90n554
Catalog of pre-1900 vocal mss in the music lib, univ of Calif. at Berkeley, 90n1263
Catalogue of Arabic mss, fascicule 5, 90n520
Catalogue of medieval & renaissance mss in the Beinecke Rare Bk & Mss Lib, Yale Univ, v.3, 94n30
Catalogue of the mss in the Irving Layton collection, 90n1193
Guide to medieval & renaissance mss in the Huntington Lib, 90n532
Guide to mss & docs in the British Isles relating to S & SE Asia, v.1, 90n116
Guide to mss & docs in the British Isles relating to S & SE Asia, v.2, 91n97
Guide to the ms collections at the Univ of Alaska, Anchorage, 92n35
Guide to the ms collections in the rare bk & ms lib of Columbia Univ, 94n28
Index to personal names in the NUC of mss collections 1959-84, 90n402
Literary mss at the Natl Lib of Canada, 2d ed, 91n1225
Location register of 20th-century English literary mss & letters, 90n1168
Manuscripts of Flannery O'Connor at Georgia College, 90n1151
Papers of Elizabeth Cady Stanton and Susan B. Anthony, 94n964
Robert Lowell papers at the Houghton Lib, Harvard Univ, 92n1176

Union cat of letters to Clemens, 93n1183
Welty collection, 90n1158

MANUSCRIPTS, CANADIAN
From the past to the future, 93n527

MANUSCRIPTS, ENGLISH
Bibliography & index of English verse in ms 1501-58, 94n1267
Bibliography of the mss of Patrick Branwell Bronte, 94n1247
George Grenville 1712-1770: a bibliog, 94n775
Index of English literary mss, v.2, pt.2, 94n1245
Index of English literary mss, v.3, pt.2, 91n1189
Index of English literary mss, v.3, pt.3, 94n1246
Manual of old English prose, 91n1188
W. B. Yeats: a census of the mss, 92n1238

MANUSCRIPTS—ITALIAN
Columbus docs, 94n533

MANUSCRIPTS, MEDIEVAL
Catalogue of the pre-1500 W manuscript bks at the Newberry Lib, 91n551
Illuminated & decorated medieval mss in the Univ Lib, Utrecht, 91n1039
Medieval & renaissance mss in the Walters Art Gallery, v.2, 94n29

MANUSCRIPTS, RENAISSANCE
Bibliography & index of English verse in ms 1501-58, 94n1267
Catalogue of the pre-1500 W manuscript bks at the Newberry Lib, 91n551
Iter Italicum, v.6, 94n978
Medieval & renaissance mss in the Walters Art Gallery, v.2, 94n29

MAO, TSE-TUNG
Mao Zedong: a bibliog, 93n522

MAP COLLECTIONS
Guide to US map resources, 2d ed, 91n447
World map dir 1989, 90n422

MAPPING (CARTOGRAPHY). *See* CARTOGRAPHY

MAPS
Bibliographic gd to maps & atlases 1990, 92n413
Maps in British pers, pt.1, 91n449

MAPS, TOURIST
Rand McNally pocket city atlas, 90n413

MARC SYSTEM
Cataloger's gd to MARC coding & tagging for AV material, 94n627

MARDI: AND A VOYAGE THITHER
Concordance to Herman Melville's Mardi, 92n1178

MARINE ALGAE
Marine plants of the Caribbean, 90n1505
Seaweeds of the SE US, 93n1513

MARINE AQUARIUM FISHES
Macmillan bk of the marine aquarium, 94n1717

MARINE AQUARIUMS
Macmillan bk of the marine aquarium, 94n1717

MARINE BIOLOGY
Great bk of the sea, 94n1745
Random House atlas of the oceans, 93n1730

MARINE ENGINEERING
Dictionary of marine tech, 91n1623

MARINE FAUNA
Seashores, rev ed, 91n1552
Sharks & other creatures of the deep, 92n1585

MARINE FISHES
Fishes of the Bahamas & adjacent tropical waters, 2d ed, 94n1713
Guide to the marine sport fishes of Atlantic Canada & New England, 93n1555

MARINE FLORA
Marine plants of the Caribbean, 90n1505
Seashores, rev ed, 91n1552

MARINE INVERTEBRATES
Hawaiian reef animals, rev. ed, 91n1599
Marine invertebrates & plants of the living reef, 90n1560
Sea of Cortez marine invertebrates, 90n1561

MARINE MAMMALS
Handbook of marine mammals, v.4, 90n1562
Sierra Club hndbk of seals & sirenians, 93n1571

MARINE RESOURCES
Mangone's concise marine almanac, 92n1466
Random House atlas of the oceans, 93n1730

MARINE SCIENCES
Encyclopedia of marine scis, 94n1744

MARITIME ARCHAEOLOGY
Coastal & maritime archaeology, 92n449

MARITIME PROVINCES
Atlantic Canadian imprints, 1801-20, 92n13
Maritime provinces atlas, new ed, 93n472

MARKET SURVEYS
Almanac of consumer markets 1990-91, 90n222
Market share reporter 1991, 92n255

MARKETING
Art mktg sourcebk, 94n1045
A-Z of UK brands, 2d ed, 92n236
A-Z of UK mktg data, 4th ed, 92n237
Book of European forecasts, 93n282
Consumer E Europe 1992, 93n283
Dictionary of mktg & advertising, 2d ed, 92n241
European advertising mktg & media data 1992, 93n285
European compendium of mktg info, 93n286
European dir of consumer brands & their owners 1992, 93n288
European dir of mktg info sources 1991, 92n244
European dir of trade & bus jls 1990, 92n246
European mktg data & stats 1991, 92n247
European markets, 3d ed, 91n266
European wholesalers & distrs dir, 93n257
FAO yrbk: trade, v.41, 90n1447
FAO yrbk: trade, v.45, 94n1592
Foreign trade stats of Asia & the Pacific 1983-87, 91n268
GEM, 1991 ed, 92n249
How to talk marketing real good, 91n265
IEG dir of sponsorship mktg, 1991, 93n258
International closeout dir '94, 94n292
International mktg data & stats 1991, 92n248
Japan trade dir 1990-91, 91n271
Marketing made easier, 94n293
National dir of mailing lists 1991, 92n257
Pacific Rim almanac, 92n137
Standard dir of worldwide mktg 1990, 91n277
Standard trade index of Japan 1990-91, 91n278
$upertrader's almanac, 2d ed, 93n321
Terms of trade, 91n275
Trade names dict: co index 1989, 90n284
Trade names dict 1989, 90n283
Tradeshow week data bk, 1992, 93n322
World retail dir & sourcebk 1991, 93n262
World trade system, 93n266

MARKETING RESEARCH
Asian markets, 2d ed, 92n240
Bibliography of mktg research methods, 3d ed, 91n262

MARLOWE, CHRISTOPHER
Christopher Marlowe in the 80s, 94n1255

MARRIAGE
Encyclopedia of marriage, divorce & the family, 90n798
Marriage licensing laws, 91n587
Medieval sexuality, 91n874

MARTIAL ARTS
Aiki News ency of aikido, 93n838
Dictionary of the martial arts, 93n839
Original martial arts ency, 94n855

MARTIN CHUZZLEWIT
Martin Chuzzlewit: an annot bibliog, 91n1205

MARTIN, FRANK
Frank Martin: a bio-bibliog, 91n1279

MARTIN, MARY
Mary Martin: a bio-bibliog, 92n1357

MARXISM. See COMMUNISM

MARYLAND
Battle of Antietam & the Md. campaign of 1862, 91n482

MASOCHISM
Language of sadomasochism, 91n1066

MASON, WILLIAM
William Mason: (1828-1908): an annot bibliog & cat of works, 90n1243

MASS MEDIA
Bibliographic gd to Caribbean mass communications, 94n990
Bibliography of Cuban mass communications, 94n991
Canada media dir, 91n938
Communication & the mass media, 92n884
Control of the media in the US, 93n951
Facts on File dict of film & broadcast terms, 93n987
Gale dir of pubs & broadcast media 1993, 94n988
Hudson's state capitals news media contacts dir 1991, 92n890
Hudson's Washington news media contacts dir 1991, 92n891
Mass media & the Constitution, 91n940
Mass media bibliog, 3d ed, 92n885
Mass media: Marconi to MTV, 91n934
National black media dir, 90n892
NTC's mass media dict, 92n887
Reruns on file, 93n994
Webster's new world dict of media & communications, 92n888
World media hndbk, 1990 ed, 92n892
World media hndbk 1992-94, 94n992
Writing A to Z, 91n952

MASS MEDIA & CHILDREN
Using media to make kids feel good, 90n828

MASS MEDIA & TEENAGERS
Mass media sex & adolescent values, 92n883

MASS MEDIA & WOMEN
DWM: a dir of women's media, 16th ed, 94n967
Women & mass communications, 92n886

MASS MEDIA IN RELIGION
Christian communication, 90n886

MASS SPECTROMETRY
Important peak index of the registry of mass spectral data, 93n1717

MASSACHUSETTS
Historial atlas of Mass., 92n451

MASSACHUSETTS INSTITUTE OF TECHNOLOGY. INSTITUTE ARCHIVES
Selective gd to the collections, 90n44

MASSES
American masses & requiems, 92n1302

MASTER OF BUSINESS ADMINISTRATION DEGREE
Guide to MBA programs in Canada, 93n376

MATERIALS
ASM engineered materials ref bk, 90n1598
ASM materials engineering dict, 94n1793
Compilation of ASTM standard definitions, 7th ed, 92n1613
Concise ency of materials characterizations, 94n1795
Concise ency of materials economics, policy & mgmt, 94n1794
Concise ency of mineral resources, 91n1786
Dictionary of materials & manufacturing, 92n1616
Encyclopedia of materials sci & engineering, suppl, 90n1599
Engineered materials hndbk, v.3, 92n1615
Information sources in metallic materials, 91n1632
Materials hndbk, 13th ed, 92n1617
Materials research centres, 3d ed, 90n1601
Materials selection deskbk, 92n1612

MATHEMATICAL MODELS
Concise ency of modelling & simulation, 93n1674

MATHEMATICAL STATISTICS
Encyclopedia of statistical scis, suppl, 91n898

MATHEMATICIANS
Combined membership list 1989-90, 90n1770
Mathematical scis professional dir, 1989, 90n1772
Pythagoras: an annot bibliog, 91n1401

MATHEMATICS
A. J. Lohwater's Russian-English dict of the mathematical scis, 2d ed, 91n1795
Biographical dict of mathematicians, 93n1736
Combined membership list 1992-93, 93n1737
Computer graphics hndbk: geometry & mathematics, 91n1797
Concise dict of math, 92n1751
Encyclopaedia of mathematics, 90n1771
First math dict, 92n1752
HarperCollins dict of mathematics, 93n1739
Mathematical bk review index 1800-1940, 93n1738
Mathematical jls, 93n1741
Mathematical scis professional dir 1993, 94n1967
Mathematics dict, 5th ed, 94n1966
Mathematics illus dict, rev ed, 91n1793
Numbers you need, 93n1740
Sourcebook for sci, mathematics, & tech educ 1990-91, 92n1462
Sourcebook for sci, mathematics, & tech educ 1992, 94n1582
VNR concise ency of mathematics, 2d ed, 91n1798
Wonderful world of mathematics, 94n1968

MAURITANIA
Mauritania, 94n101

MAURITIUS
Historical dict of Mauritius, 2d ed, 93n147
Mauritius, 93n146

MAYAS
Archaeological gd to Mexico's Yucatan peninsula, 94n481
Maya civilization, 94n541

MCCABE, JOHN
John McCabe: a bio-bibliog, 92n1261

MCCARTHY, MARY
Mary McCarthy: an annot bibliog, 93n1177

MEASURING INSTRUMENTS
Economist desk companion, 93n205

MEAT
International markets for meat 1990/91, 92n1495
International markets for meat 1992/93, 94n1593

MECHANICAL ENGINEERING
Combinatory vocabulary of CAD/CAM in mechanical engineering, 94n1916
Handbook of tribology, 92n1621
Millwrights & mechanics gd, 4th ed, 90n1604

MECHANICAL MOVEMENTS
Mechanisms & mechanical devices sourcebk, 92n1622

MEDIA PROGRAMS (EDUCATION)
Brown's dir of instructional programs, 1992: 7-12, 93n347
Brown's dir of instructional programs, 1992: K-8, 93n346
Guide to ref bks for school media centers, 4th ed, 93n670
School lib media annual, v.7, 90n622
School lib media annual, v.8, 91n653
School lib media annual, v.9, 92n612
School lib media annual, v.10, 93n672
School librarian's sourcebk, 91n652

MEDIATION
Directory of school mediation & conflict resolution programs, 90n313

MEDICAL BACTERIOLOGY. See BACTERIOLOGY, MEDICAL

MEDICAL CARE
Basic gd to online info systems for health care professionals, 90n1624
Consumer health & nutrition index, v.8, no.1, 93n1614
Dial 800 for health, 94n1812
Directory of biomedical & health care grants 1992, 92n1634
Directory of Japanese healthcare industry, 1990 ed, 92n1635
Directory of online healthcare databases, 5th ed, 91n1648
Encyclopedia of health info sources, 2d ed, 94n1827
Glossary of health care terms, 2d ed, 93n1615
Glossary of health servs, 93n1616
Guide to fed funding for hospitals & health centers, 94n1814
Health care in Fla., 92n1638
Health care reform terms, advance ed, 94n1804
Health care state rankings 1993, 94n1816
Health care terms, 2d ed, 93n1621
Health groups in Washington, 10th ed, 90n1618
Health of black Americans from post reconstruction to integration, 1871-1960, 91n1642
Medical & health care bks & serials in print 1992, 93n1625
Medical utilization review dir, 1993 ed, 94n1810
Minority health resources dir, 93n1618
National family healthcare hndbk, 94n1813
New Good Housekeeping family health & medical gd, 90n1628
What to do when you can't afford health care, 94n1809

MEDICAL DIAGNOSIS. *See* DIAGNOSIS

MEDICAL EDUCATION
Barron's gd to financing a medical school educ, 91n1673

MEDICAL ETHICS
International dir of bioethics orgs, 94n1835

MEDICAL GENETICS
Family genetic sourcebk, 91n1695
Mendelian inheritance in man, 9th ed, 91n1679
Mendelian inheritance in man, 10th ed, 93n1624

MEDICAL GEOGRAPHY
Atlas of disease distributions, 90n1634
Disease & medical care in the US, 94n1802

MEDICAL INSTRUMENTS & APPARATUS
Canadian medical device dir, 93n1642
Szycher's dict of biomaterials & medical devices, 93n1639

MEDICAL LIBRARIES
Annual stats of medical school libs in the US & Canada 1987-88, 91n654
Canadian Health Libs Assn dir 1990-91, 92n613
Core collection in nursing & the allied health scis, 91n1705
Directory of medical health care libs in the UK & Republic of Ireland, 7th ed, 92n624

MEDICAL LITERATURE
Information sources in the medical scis, 4th ed, 93n1626

MEDICAL MATERIALS. *See* BIOMEDICAL MATERIALS

MEDICAL OFFICES
Computer News for Physicians dir of medical office computer system vendors, 91n1670

MEDICAL PUBLISHING
Medical publishing in 19th century America, 91n1640

MEDICAL SCIENTISTS
Nobel prize winners: physiology or medicine, 92n1652

MEDICAL STATISTICS
Sourcebook of Canadian health stats, 91n1650
Vital & health stats series, 92n1641

MEDICAL SUPPLIES
Product dvlpmt dir 1993, 94n1836
Product SOS 1993, 94n1837

MEDICAL WRITING
American Medical Assn manual of style, 8th ed, 90n895
Medical English usage & abusage, 92n1671

MEDICARE
Complete & easy gd to social security & medicare, 10th ed, 94n220
Complete Medicare hndbk, 91n1651
Medicare made easy, 90n1627
Paying for health care after age 65, 92n1640

MEDICINAL PLANTS
Cleveland herbal, botanical, & horticultural collections, 93n1493
Cornucopia, 92n1549
Field gd to medicinal plants: E & central N America, 91n1536
Healing forest, 91n1538
Herbs, spices, & medicinal plants, v.4, 91n1534
History & folklore of N American wildflowers, 94n1651
Medicinal plants of India, 92n1550
Medicinal plants of the desert, 91n1537

MEDICINE
ABMS compendium suppl., 1991, 92n1665
Advanced research methodology, 92n73
Barron's gd to medical & dental schools, 4th ed, 90n1656
Bibliography of medical & biomedical biog, 91n1654
Black's medical dict, 36th ed, 91n1659
Black's medical dict, 37th ed, 93n1629
Charles Press hndbk of current medical abbrevs, 3d ed, 93n1622
Checklist of the Newberry Lib's printed bks in sci, medicine, tech, & the pseudosciences ca. 1460-1750, 94n1558
Churchill Livingstone's medical word gd, 92n1654
Churchill's illus medical dict, 90n1640
Common abbrevs in clinical medicine, 90n1633
Comprehensive electrocardiology, 90n1685
Consumer's gd to free medical info by phone & by mail, 94n1844
Consumer's gd to medical lingo, 93n1633
Core collection in nursing & the allied health scis, 91n1705
Cumulated abridged index medicus, v.18, 90n1631
Davies' medical terminology, 5th ed, 93n1630
Davis bk of medical abbrevs, 92n1644
Detwiler dir of medical market sources, 94n1834
Dictionary of abbrevs in medical scis, 91n1644
Dictionary of biomedical acronyms & abbrevs, 2d ed, 92n1645
Dictionary of clinical medicine: English-German, 92n1655
Dictionary of medical acronyms & abbrevs, 2d ed, 94n1818
Dictionary of medical terms for the nonmedical person, 2d ed, 90n1655
Dictionary of modern medicine, 94n1832
Directory of intl & natl medical & related societies, 2d ed, 92n1666
Elsevier's encyclopaedic dict of medicine, pt.B, 90n1643
Encyclopedia of health info sources, 2d ed, 94n1827
Encyclopedia of medical orgs & agencies 1992-93, 93n1632
Glossary of Chinese medical terms & acupuncture points, 92n1663
History of surgery in the US, 1775-1900, 90n1637
Information sources in the medical scis, 4th ed, 93n1626
Lifetime ency of natural remedies, 94n1826
Macmillan health ency, 94n1803
Medical abbrevs, 6th ed, 94n1817
Medical acronyms & abbrevs, 2d ed, 91n1653
Medical & health care bks & serials in print 1992, 93n1625
Medical & health info dir, 4th ed, 90n1620
Medical phrase index, 2d ed, 90n1651
Medical publishing in 19th century America, 91n1640
Medical research centres, 8th ed, 90n1621
Medical terminology with human anatomy, 2d ed, 92n1659
Medical word bk A-Z, 93n1631
Medicine in Great Britain from the Restoration to the 19th century, 1660-1800, 94n1821
Medicine, lit, & eponyms, 90n1653
Melloni's illus medical dict, 3d ed, 94n1829
Morton's medical bibliog, 5th ed, 93n1627
Mosby's pocket dict of medicine, nursing, & allied health, 92n1658
New American pocket medical dict, 2d ed, 90n1652
Nobel laureates in medicine or physiology, 91n1655
Planets, potions & parchments, 92n1464
Practical approach series cum methods index, 92n1526
Professional gd to diseases, 3d ed, 90n1676
Professional gd to diseases, 4th ed, 94n1841
Random House health & medicine dict, 94n1830

Sir William Osler: an annot bibliog with illustrations, 90n1636
Stedman's abbrev., 93n1623
Stedman's medical dict, 25th ed, 91n1664
Stedman's medical speller, 93n1637
Stedman's pathology lab medicine words, 93n1638
Taber's cyclopedic medical dict, 17th ed, 94n1833
Taber's medical word bk with pronunciations, 91n1663
Who's who in sci in Europe, 7th ed, 93n1442
World Book-Rush-Presbyterian-St. Luke's Medical Center medical ency, 92n1664

MEDICINE & PSYCHOLOGY
Handbook of behavioral medicine for women, 90n1663

MEDICINE—DICTIONARIES—SPANISH
Spanish-English hndbk for medical professionals, 3d ed, 90n1670

MEDICINE, MAGIC, MYSTIC, & SPAGIRIC
Dictionary of sacred & magical plants, 94n1667

MEDICINE, MILITARY
Microbes & minie balls, 94n493

MEDICINE, POPULAR
American Medical Assn ency of medicine, 91n1657
Are you at risk?, 92n1675
Complete gd to medical tests, 90n1667
Consumer health info source bk, 3d ed, 91n1680
Doctors bk of home remedies, 91n1675
Feed a cold, starve a fever, rev ed, 92n1676
Home ency of symptoms, ailments & their natural remedies, 93n1640
New Good Housekeeping family health & medical gd, 90n1628
New hndbk of health & preventive medicine, 91n1674
1,001 medical facts for every home, 90n1662
Prevention's giant bk of health facts, 92n1639
Visual ency of natural healing, 92n1661

MEDICINE, PREVENTIVE
Guide to clinical preventive servs, 90n1626
Maintaining good health, 90n1647
New hndbk of health & preventive medicine, 91n1674
Wellness ency, 92n1642

MEDICINE—SPECIALTIES & SPECIALISTS
ABMS compendium of certified medical specialists 1990-91, 91n1667
Directory of medical specialists 1989-90, 91n1669

MELANCHOLY IN LITERATURE
Robert Burton & The Anatomy of Melancholy, 90n1673

MELANESIA
Indigenous navigation & voyaging in the Pacific, 93n1789

MELVILLE, HERMAN
Checklist of Melville reviews, 93n1178
Concordance to Herman Melville's Mardi, 92n1178
Melville ency: the novels, 91n1166

MEMORY
Encyclopedia of learning & memory, 94n809

MEN IN MOTION PICTURES
Tough guy: the American movie macho, 90n1342

MENCKEN, H. L.
Gist of Mencken, 91n1167

MENNONITES
Sociology of Mennonites, Hutterites & Amish, v.2, 92n1410

MENTAL DISORDERS. *See* MENTAL ILLNESS

MENTAL HEALTH
Family mental health ency, 90n743
Get help, 90n829
Health & mental health: dir of key legislators, 90n1617
Stress and mental health, 90n1649

MENTAL ILLNESS
Clinician's hndbk, 3d ed, 94n1847

Columbia Univ College of Physicians & Surgeons complete home gd to mental health, 94n1846
Encyclopedia of mental & physical handicaps, 92n322
Female psychology, 93n797
Mental health & psychiatry in Africa, 94n1849
Sociology of mental illness, 90n1674

MENTALLY HANDICAPPED
Dictionary of mental handicap, 91n854
Directory of residential centers for adults with mental illnesses, 91n1686
Encyclopedia of mental & physical handicaps, 92n322
Handbook of developmental & physical disabilities, 90n1629
Materials & strategies for the educ of trainable mentally retarded learners, 91n351

MENTALLY ILL
Directory of residential centers for adults with mental illnesses, 91n1686
Reader's gd for parents of children with mental, physical, or emotional disabilities, 3d ed, 91n857

MERMAN, ETHEL
Ethel Merman: a bio-bibliog, 93n1317

MERRICK, DAVID
David Merrick: a bio-bibliog, 93n1377

METAL TRADE
Pennsylvania workers in brass, copper & tin 1681-1900, 94n1035

METAL-CUTTING TOOLS
Metal cutting tool hndbk, 7th ed, 90n1608

METALS
ASM hndbk, v.3, 94n1792
ASM hndbk, v.18, 93n1604
Information sources in metallic materials, 91n1632
Metals hndbk, 10th ed., v.1, 92n1618
Metals hndbk, 10th ed., v.2, 92n1619

METAL-WORK
Complete metalsmith, rev ed, 93n1008

METAL-WORKERS
Pennsylvania workers in brass, copper & tin 1681-1900, 94n1035

METAPHOR
Loose cannons & red herrings, 90n1007
Metaphor 2, 92n1011
Sports talk, 90n756

METIS. *See* INDIANS OF NORTH AMERICA—CANADA

METROPOLITAN AREAS
50 fabulous places to raise your family, 94n944
Livable cities almanac, 93n920
Moving & relocation sourcebk, 93n917
Where to make money, 94n945

METROPOLITAN OPERA (NEW YORK, N.Y.)
Annals of the Metropolitan opera, 91n1295

MEULEN, JACOB TER
From Erasmus to Tolstoy, 91n774

MEXICAN LITERATURE
Dictionary of Mexican lit, 94n1296
Luis Leal: a bibliog with interpretative & critical essays, 90n1207
Mexican lit, 2d ed, 93n1227

MEXICAN-AMERICAN AUTHORS
Chicano writers, 90n1123

MEXICAN-AMERICAN BORDER REGION
BorderLine, 90n476

MEXICAN-AMERICAN LITERATURE
Luis Leal, 90n1207

MEXICAN-AMERICAN WOMEN
Chicana studies index, 94n971

MEXICAN-AMERICANS
Chicano anthology index, 92n353

MEXICO
Aquaculture sourcebk, 94n1594
Archaeological gd to Mexico's Yucatan peninsula, 94n481
Atlas of Mexico, 90n145
Diesel locomotive rosters, 3d ed, 94n2025
Latin American serial pubs available by exchange, 93n633
Mexical legal system, 93n563
Mexican pol biogs, 1884-1935, 93n775
Mushrooms & truffles of the Southwest, 92n1545
Pines of Mexico & Central America, 93n1519
Steam locomotive dir of N America, 90n1806
Synopsis of the herpetofauna of Mexico, v.7, 94n1752
Train times in Mexico, 2d ed, 91n1828
Train-watcher's gd to N American railroads, 2d ed, 94n2024
United States, Canada, & Mexico road atlas, 91n433
Who's who in Mexico today, 2d ed, 94n12

MENTAL TESTS. *See* EDUCATIONAL TESTS & MEASUREMENTS; PSYCHOLOGICAL TESTS

MEXICO—FOREIGN RELATIONS—UNITED STATES
BorderLine, 90n476

MEXICO—MAPS
Atlas of Mexico, 90n145
Rand McNally road atlas: US, Canada, Mexico, 65th ed, 90n415

MEXICO—RELATIONS—UNITED STATES
Recursos: a dir of Mexican-American insts, orgs, & univ programs, 92n689

MEYER, RUSS
Russ Meyer: the life & films, 91n1354

MICHIGAN
Artists in Mich., 1900-76, 90n947
Atlas of breeding birds of Mich., 93n1539
Awesome almanac—Mich., 94n87
Climatic atlas of Mich., 92n1733
Guide to Michigan's endangered wildlife, 94n1677
Michigan legal lit, 2d ed, 92n514

MICHIGAN STATE UNIVERSITY
Comic art collection cat, 94n1405

MICROBIOLOGY
Encyclopedia of microbiology, 94n1636
Handbook of protoctista, 91n1515

MICROCOMPUTERS
Chemical structure sftwr for personal computers, 90n1756
Datapro dir of microcomputer hdwr, 91n1734
Datapro dir of microcomputer sftwr, 91n1737
Directory of automated lib systems, 2d ed, 91n637
Encyclopedia of microcomputers, v.6, 92n1707
Encyclopedia of microcomputers, v.7, 94n1896
Encyclopedia of microcomputers, v.8, 94n1897
Encyclopedia of microcomputers, v.9, 94n1898
Encyclopedia of microcomputers, v.10, 94n1899
Essential gd to the lib IBM PC, v.15, 91n642
High-technology editorial gd & stylebk, PC ed, 93n969
Illustrated dict of microcomputers, 3d ed, 91n1735
McGraw-Hill personal computer programming ency, 2d ed, 90n1715
Micro computer index, June 89, v.10, no.2, 90n1724
Microcomputer applications hndbk, 90n1721
Microcomputer index, v.12, 93n1686
Microcomputer market place 1993, 94n1906
Microcomputer sftwr sources, 91n1744
Microcomputers & libs, 92n596
Music & the personal computer, 90n1220
101 microcomputer projects to do in your lib, 91n638
PC hdwr & systems implementation, 90n1722
Pocket PCref, 93n1684

MICROELECTRONICS
Electronic packaging, microelectronics, & interconnection dict, 94n1781

Microelectronics packaging hndbk, 90n1593

MICROFICHES
Roth's index to literary criticism, 90n1074

MICROFORMS
Bibliographic gd to microform pubns 1991, 94n1921
Guide to microforms in print, 1989 suppl, 90n7
Guide to microforms in print 1991: author-title, 93n1694
Guide to microforms in print 1991: subject, 93n1695
Images of the other: a gd to microform mss on Indian-White relations, 92n366
Microform market place 1992-93, 94n669

MICROGRAPHICS
Glossary of micrographics, 90n1723
International micrographics source bk, 1989, 91n1736

MICRONESIA
Indigenous navigation & voyaging in the Pacific, 93n1789
Micronesia 1975-87, 90n149

MICRONESIA (FEDERATED STATES)
Flowers of the Pacific Island seashore, 94n1647

MICROORGANISMS
Westcott's plant disease hndbk, 5th ed, 91n1520

MICROPUBLISHING
Microform market place 1990-91, 92n640

MICROWAVE DEVICES
Handbook of microwave & optical components, 91n1626

MIDDLE AGED
Late achievers, 93n43
Women & aging, 90n854

MIDDLE AGES
Dictionary of the Middle Ages, 90n533
Guide to medieval & renaissance mss in the Huntington Lib, 90n532
Middle ages, 90n534
Smithsonian timelines of the ancient world, 94n534

MIDDLE EARTH (IMAGINARY PLACE)
Tolkien thesaurus, 92n1213

MIDDLE EAST
A to Z of the Middle East, 92n118
Atlas of the Middle East, 90n416
Bibliographic gd to Middle Eastern studies 1990, 93n159
Bibliography on temples of the ancient Near East & Mediterranean world, 93n1402
Biographical dict of the Middle East, 93n161
Cultural anthropology of the Middle East, v.1, 93n416
Cultural atlas of Mesopotamia & the ancient Near East, 92n499
Dictionary of ancient Near Eastern architecture, 90n974
Handbook of the birds of Europe, the Middle East, & N Africa, v.6, 94n1696
Handbook of the birds of Europe, the Middle East, & N Africa, v.7, 94n1697
Historical atlas of the Middle East, 94n460
Index to English per lit on the O.T. & ancient Near Eastern studies, v.3, 91n1433
Index to English per lit on the O.T. & ancient Near Eastern studies, v.4, 91n1440
Index to English per lit on the O.T. & ancient Near Eastern studies, v.5, 94n1549
Iraq-Iran War, 90n518
Kurds: a concise hndbk, 93n165
Major cos of the Arab world 1991/92, 92n133
Major pol events in Iran, Iraq & the Arabian peninsula 1945-90, 92n725
Major weeds of the Near East, 92n1547
Middle East & N Africa 1990, 91n123
Middle East, 7th ed, 92n724
Middle East: a pol dict, 93n776
Middle East bibliog, 93n162
Middle East today, 91n442
Peoples of the world: the Middle East & N Africa, 93n160

Political leaders of the contemporary Middle East & N Africa, 91n762

MIDDLE EAST—FOREIGN RELATIONS—GREAT BRITAIN
Britain in the Middle East 1921-56, 91n125

MIDDLE EAST—FOREIGN RELATIONS—UNITED STATES
United States foreign policy & the Middle East/N Africa, 91n770

MIDDLE EAST—POLITICS & GOVERNMENT
Middle East: a pol dict, 93n776

MIDDLE WEST
Encyclopedia of the central West, 91n502
Encyclopedia of the Midwest, 90n100
Field gd to medicinal plants: E & central N America, 91n1536
Who's who in the Midwest 1990-91, 91n24

MIDWAY, BATTLE OF, 1942
Battles of Coral Sea & Midway, 1942, 93n695

MIGRANT LABOR
Human rights, refugees, migrants & dvlpmt, 94n593

MIGRATION, INTERNAL
International hndbk on internal migration, 91n905

MILITARY AIRPLANES. *See* **AIRPLANES, MILITARY**

MILITARY ART & SCIENCE
Acronym bk: acronyms in aerospace & defense, 91n675
Army dict & desk ref, 93n717
Book of military blunders, 92n659
Dictionary of military, defense contractor, & troop slang acronyms, 91n674
Dictionary of military quotations, 91n682
Dictionary of modern war, 92n647
Facts on File dict of military sci, 90n652
Fighting words, 90n651
Harper ency of military hist, 4th ed, 94n687
International military & defense ency, 94n688
International military ency, v.1, 93n702
Military pers, 92n662
Soviet military ency, abridged English-lang ed, 94n686
U.S. Dept of Defense dict of military terms, rev ed, 92n649

MILITARY BASES
Directory of military bases in the US, 92n650
Guide to military installations, 2d ed, 90n656
United States military road atlas, 94n677

MILITARY BIOGRAPHY
Concise dict of military biog, 93n699
Harper ency of military biog, 93n698

MILITARY DEPENDENTS
Financial aid for vets, military personnel & their dependents 1990-91, 92n651

MILITARY EDUCATION
Jane's military training systems 1990-91, 92n656

MILITARY HELICOPTERS
Modern combat helicopters, 94n711

MILITARY HISTORY
Air wars & aircraft, 91n685
Chronology of conflict & resolution, 1945-85, 90n650
Harper ency of military hist, 4th ed, 94n687
International armed conflict since 1945, 92n661
Using lit to teach middle grades about war, 94n694
Warfare & armed conflicts, 94n692
Wars & peace treaties 1816-1991, 94n693

MILITARY INTELLIGENCE
Military intelligence, 1870-1991, 94n681
United States intelligence, 91n734

MILITARY LEADERSHIP. *See* **COMMAND OF TROOPS**

MILITARY POLICY
Military & strategic policy, 91n676

Nuclear weapons world, 90n674

MILITARY POWER. *See* **DISARMAMENT**

MILITARY SURVEILLANCE
Latest intelligence, 92n646

MILITARY SCHOOLS. *See* **MILITARY EDUCATION**

MILITARY UNIFORMS. *See* **UNIFORMS, MILITARY**

MILLENNIALISM
Guide to the end of the world, 94n1535
Millennialism: an intl bibliog, 93n1399

MILLER, GLENN
Glenn Miller Army Air Force band, 90n1289

MILLER, WALTER M.
Walter M. Miller, Jr.: a bio-bibliog, 93n1179

MILLIONAIRES
Who's wealthy in America 1990, 91n219

MILLWRIGHTS
Millwrights & mechanics gd, 4th ed, 90n1604

MILNER, ANTHONY
Anthony Milner: a bio-bibliog, 90n1253

MILTON, JOHN
Essential Milton, 90n1182

MINERAL INDUSTRIES
Canadian mines hndbk 1989-90, 90n239
Financial Times mining intl yrbk 1989, 90n1800

MINERALOGY
Atlas of opaque & ore minerals in their assns, 92n1740
Elsevier's dict of mining & mineralogy, 94n1800
Encyclopedia of minerals, 2d ed, 91n1790
Famous mineral localities of Canada, 91n1788
Gemstones of E Africa, 94n1955
Handbook of rocks, minerals, & gemstones, 94n1957
Heavy minerals in colour, 93n1726
Illustrated gd to rocks & minerals, 94n1956
Mineral deposits of Europe, v.4/5, 91n1787
Mineral ref manual, 92n1741
Minerals of the world, 93n1729
Peterson 1st gd to rocks & minerals, 92n1742
Rocks & minerals, 93n1728
Rocks, minerals & fossils of the world, 91n1789

MINERALS. *See* **MINERALOGY**

MINERALS IN HUMAN NUTRITION
Doctors' vitamin & mineral ency, 91n1709
Essential gd to vitamins & minerals, 93n1647

MINERALS IN THE BODY
Nutrients cat, 94n1610
People's gd to vitamins & minerals from A to zinc, rev ed, 90n1699

MINES & MINERAL RESOURCES
Famous mineral localities of Canada, 91n1788
Financial Times mining intl yr bk 1989, 90n1800
Financial Times mining intl yr bk 1993, 94n1982
Mineral resources A-Z, 92n1739
Minerals hndbk 1992-93, 94n1978

MINIATURE BOOKS
Bibliography of miniature bks (1470-1965), 91n7

MINIATURE ROSES
Australian gd to miniature roses, 91n1502

MINING ENGINEERING
Elsevier's dict of mining & mineralogy, 94n1800

MINISTRY. *See* **CHURCH WORK**

MINNESOTA
Awesome almanac—Minn., 94n85
Genealogical resources of the Minn. Histl Society, 90n391
Vascular plants of Minn., 92n1533

MINNESOTA HISTORICAL SOCIETY
Genealogical resources of the Minn. Histl Society, 90n391

MINORITIES
Cities & churches, 94n1502
Contemporary bks reflecting Canada's cultural diversity, 94n409
Developing multicultural awareness through children's lit, 94n1178
Directory of ethnic professionals in LIS (lib & info sci), 93n625
Directory of financial aids for minorities, 1989-90, 90n329
Directory of special programs for minority group members, 5th ed, 92n221
Financial aid for minorities in engineering & sci, 94n1577
Immigrant experience, 93n420
Immigration hist research center, 92n383
Minority student enrollments in higher educ, 94n361
Our family, our friends, our world, 93n1127
Racial & religious violence in America, 92n553
Racism in the US, 91n384
Resource gd of pubns supported by multiculturalism programs, 94n398
Substance abuse among ethnic minorities in America, 93n891
Third World in film & video, 1984-90, 92n102
Venture into cultures, 94n1170
Women, race, & ethnicity, 93n931
World dir of minorities, 91n385

MINORITY BUSINESS ENTERPRISES
Minority consultants & minority-owned consulting firms, 1989 natl dir, 90n271
National dir of minority-owned bus firms, 1990 ed, 91n145

MINORITY STUDENTS
Multicultural aspects of lib media programs, 93n669
Multicultural educ debate, 94n322
Multicultural student's gd to colleges, 94n337

MISCELLANEOUS FACTS. See ALMANACS

MISES, LUDWIG VON
Mises: an annot bibliog, 94n153

MISSING PERSONS
How to locate anyone anywhere without leaving home, 90n778

MISSISSIPPI
Mississippi: the WPA gd, 90n442
Wildflowers of Miss., 91n1530

MISSISSIPPI DEPARTMENT OF ARCHIVES AND HISTORY
Welty collection, 90n1158

MISSISSIPPI RIVER REGION
Way's steam towboat dir, 92n1806

MISTRESSES
Encyclopedia of mistresses, 94n961

MITCHUM, ROBERT
Robert Mitchum: a bio-bibliog, 94n1417

MOBILE HOMES
Affordable housing, 90n967

MODELS & MODELMAKING
Hobby index 1988, 92n951
Scale modeling buyer's gd, 2d ed, 92n946

MODEMS
Modem USA, 93n1683

MODULAR COORDINATION (ARCHITECTURE)
Time-saver standards for building types, 3d ed, 91n1025

MOLDAVIA
Archives & mss repositories in the USSR: Ukraine & Moldavia, 90n523

MOLECULAR BIOLOGY
Bibliography on computational molecular biology, 94n1634
Dictionary of biochemistry & molecular biology, 2d ed, 91n1516
Glossary of biochemistry & molecular biology, 92n1517

MOLLUSKS
Fish: 5-lang dict of fish, crustaceans & molluscs, 91n1584

MONACO
Monaco, 92n106

MONETARY POLICY
Comecon data 1988, 91n153

MONEY
Last word on making money, 90n219
New Palgrave dict of money & finance, 93n242

MONEY MAKING. See FUND RAISING

MONGOLIA (PEOPLE'S REPUBLIC)
Information Mongolia, 92n96

MONOGRAMS
Artists' monograms & indiscernible signatures, 92n984
European artists: signatures & monograms, 1800-1990, 92n985

MONROE, JAMES
James Monroe: a bibliog, 92n452

MONSTERS
Encyclopedia of monsters, 90n1310
Encyclopedia of strange & unexplained physical phenomena, 94n813

MONTEVERDI, CLAUDIO
Claudio Monteverdi: a gd to research, 90n1238

MONTSERRAT
Monserrat, 93n156

MOON
Moons of the solar system, 93n1707

MOOREHEAD, AGNES
Agnes Moorehead: a bio-bibliog, 94n1413

MORAL EDUCATION
Literature-based moral educ, 93n351

MORMON BIBLIOGRAPHY, 1830-1930
Mormon bibliog 1830-1930: indexes to A Mormon Bibliog and 10 yr suppl, 94n1501

MORMON CHURCH
Encyclopedia of Mormonism, 93n1420
Encyclopedia of Mormonism [CD-ROM], 93n1421
Mormon bibliog 1830-1930: 10 yr suppl, 91n1435

MORMONS
Mormons & Mormonism in US gov docs, 90n1401

MORRIS, WILLIAM
Annotated critical bibliog of William Morris, 92n1207

MORTGAGES
Guide to real estate & mortgage banking sftwr, 5th ed, 90n296

MOSSES
Catalogue of mosses of Austral. & its external territories, 91n1540
Indices to the species of mosses & lichens described by William Mitten, 94n1668

MOTHERHOOD
Mothers & mothering, 92n854

MOTHERS
Mothers & mothering, 92n854
Social correlates of infant & reproductive mortality in the US, 94n879

MOTHERS & DAUGHTERS IN LITERATURE
Mothers & daughters in American short fiction, 94n1219

MOTHERWELL, ROBERT
Prints of Robert Motherwell, 92n1003

MOTHS
Butterflies & moths, 93n1547
Moths of Australia, 92n1578
New Generation gd to the butterflies & day-flying moths of Britain & Europe, 90n1546

MOTION PICTURE ACTORS & ACTRESSES
Ann Sothern: a bio-bibliog, 91n1352
Anne Baxter: a bio-bibliog, 93n1318
B western actors ency, 90n1341
Betty Grable: a bio-bibliog, 94n1408
Continental actress, 91n1395
Cult movie stars, 93n1337
Henry Fonda: a bio-bibliog, 93n1323
Hollywood baby boomers, 94n1432
Hollywood greats of the golden yrs, 90n1323
Hollywood songsters, 92n1349
Hollywood who's who, 94n1431
Horror film stars, 2d ed, 92n1366
International dict of films & filmmakers, v.3, 2d ed, 93n1335
Irene Dunne: a bio-bibliog, 92n1343
Jean Arthur: a bio-bibliog, 91n1358
Jennifer Jones: a bio-bibliog, 91n1351
John Wayne: a bio-bibliog, 93n1320
Lauren Bacall: a bio-bibliog, 93n1321
Man in Lincoln's nose, 91n1396
Mary Martin: a bio-bibliog, 92n1357
Motion picture players' credits, 92n1362
Movie characters of leading performers of the sound era, 91n1362
Movie talk, 91n1397
Name is familiar, 94n1459
Post-feminist Hollywood actress, 91n1363
Resources for writers, 93n971
Richard Widmark: a bio-bibliog, 91n1356
Robert Mitchum: a bio-bibliog, 94n1417
Ronald Reagan: his 1st career, 90n1319
Science fiction stars & horror heroes, 92n1371
Sweethearts of the sage, 91n1361
Those fabulous serial heroines, 91n1394
Tough guy: the American movie macho, 90n1342
Who's who in Hollywood, 93n1339

MOTION PICTURE AUTHORSHIP
Film writers gd, 3d ed, 93n1368

MOTION PICTURE EDITORS
Cinematographers, production designers, costume designers & film editors gd, 2d ed, 91n1372
Cinematographers, production designers, costume designers & film editors gd, 3d ed, 93n1371

MOTION PICTURE FESTIVALS. *See* FILM FESTIVALS

MOTION PICTURE FILM
Footage 89: N American film & video sources, 91n966

MOTION PICTURE INDUSTRY
Delson's dict of motion picture mktg terms, 2d ed, 91n1367
Encyclopedia of Hollywood, 91n1370
Film & TV hndbk 1990, 91n1388
International film industry, 90n1329
Movie talk, 91n1397

MOTION PICTURE LOCATIONS
Famous Hollywood locations, 94n1421

MOTION PICTURE MUSIC
Cinema sheet music, 93n1272
Film & TV composers, 93n1258
Keeping score: film & TV music, 1980-88, 93n1271
Movie musicals on record, 90n1234
Movie song cat, 94n1309

MOTION PICTURE PRODUCERS & DIRECTORS
Big screen bk, 94n1435
Directors & their films, 94n1453
Directory of African film-makers & films, 94n1436
Directory of E European film-makers & films 1945-91, 93n1348
Film hndbk, 91n1386
Film producers, studios, agents & casting directors gd, 2d ed, 91n1373
Handbook of Soviet & E European films & filmmakers, 93n1340
Hollywood who's who, 94n1431
International dict of films & filmmakers, v.1, 2d ed, 91n1368
International dict of films & filmmakers, v.2, 2d ed, 92n1353
International dict of films & filmmakers, v.3, 2d ed, 93n1335
International dict of films & filmmakers, v.4, 2d ed, 94n1430
Michael Singer's film directors, 7th ed, 90n1333
Michael Singer's film directors, 9th ed, 93n1372
Orson Welles: a bio-bibliog, 91n1361
Roger Corman: the best of the cheap acts, 90n1351
Science fiction stars & horror heroes, 92n1371
Sub-Saharan African films & filmmakers, 90n1321
Who's who in Canadian film & TV 1989, 91n1375
Who's who in Canadian film & TV 1991-92, 93n1341
Who's who in the motion picture industry, 6th ed, 90n1337

MOTION PICTURE REMAKES
Haven't I seen you somewhere before?, 93n1358

MOTION PICTURE SEQUELS
Haven't I seen you somewhere before?, 93n1358

MOTION PICTURE SERIALS
Motion picture serial, 93n1364
Republic chapterplays, 94n1440
Those fabulous serial heroines, 91n1394

MOTION PICTURE STUDIOS
Grand Natl, Producers Releasing Corp, & Screen Guild/Lippert, 90n1343

MOTION PICTURES
Allied Artists checklist, 94n1445
AMI, v.9, issue 1, 91n968
AV market place 1990, 91n969
BFI film & TV hndbk 1993, 94n1455
Blacks in film & TV, 91n1355
Chambers concise ency of film & TV, 93n1346
Chambers film quotes, 93n1374
Charlie Chan at the movies, 90n1339
Cinema sequels & remakes, 1903-87, 90n1353
Columbia checklist, 92n1350
Complete Gone with the Wind sourcebk, 94n1452
Complete James Bond movie ency, 92n1354
Contemporary theatre, film, & TV, v.7, 90n1311
Contemporary theatre, film, & TV, v.9, 93n1324
Continental actress, 91n1395
Directors & their films, 94n1453
Directory of E European film-makers & films 1945-91, 93n1348
Encyclopedia of film, 92n1352
Encyclopedia of film festivals, 90n1328
FIAF cataloguing rules for film archives, 93n638
Film & video finder, 3d ed, 93n1330
Film index, 90n1318
Film plots, v.2, 90n1349
Film producers, studios, agents & casting directors gd, 2d ed, 91n1373
Film study, 92n1340
Film superlist: motion pictures in the US public domain 1950-59, 91n1366
Film superlist, updated ed, 94n1439
Film, TV, & video pers, 92n1332
Filmmaker's dict, 91n1371
Film-makers's cooperative cat, no.7, 90n1325
Films by genre, 94n1444
Gays & lesbians in mainstream cinema, 94n1446
Grand Natl, Producers Releasing Corp, & Screen Guild/Lippert, 90n1343
Guinness bk of movie facts & feats, 93n1370
Handbook of Soviet & E European films & filmmakers, 93n1340
Hispanic image on the silver screen, 93n1363
Index: the Pacific NW film, video, & audio production index, 7th ed, 90n1338
International dict of films & filmmakers, v.1, 2d ed, 91n1368
International film index 1895-1990, 93n1373
International film prizes, 92n1372
Man in Lincoln's nose, 91n1396
Masters of lens & light, 93n1343
Money for film & video artists, 92n1356
Motion picture series & sequels, 91n1353

Movie list bk, 91n1387
Native Americans on film & video, v.2, 90n374
1939: the yr in movies, 91n1378
Nostalgia entertainment sourcebk, 92n1334
Prostitution in Hollywood films, 94n1447
Revenge of the creature features movie gd, 3d ed, 90n1330
Screen world 1988, 90n1354
Silent witnesses: Russian films 1908-19, 91n1385
Sub-Saharan African films & filmmakers, 90n1321
Third World in film & video, 1984-90, 92n102
Variety's who's who in show bus, rev ed, 90n1313
Women writers: from page to screen, 91n1364

MOTION PICTURES & CHILDREN
Family video gd, 93n1329

MOTION PICTURES & LITERATURE
Literature & film: an annot bibliog 1978-88, 94n1143

MOTION PICTURES IN EDUCATION
AFVA evaluations 1991, 93n395
Educational film & video locator 1990-91, 91n358
Educators gd to free films, 49th ed, 90n351
Educators gd to free films, 52d ed, 93n397
Film & video finder, 2d ed, 90n352
Films for learning, thinking, & doing, 93n399
Understanding abilities, disabilities, & capabilities, 92n318

MOTION PICTURES—GERMANY
Nazi-retro film, 93n1362
West German cinema 1985-90, 94n1441

MOTION PICTURES IN MEDICINE
Catalogue of films & videos in the British Medical Assn lib, 94n1824

MOTION PICTURES—REVIEWS
Bob Dorian's classic movies, 92n1360
Encyclopedia of American war films, 90n1327
Family video gd, 93n1329
Film annual 1992, 93n1369
Film news index, 1939-81, 94n1462
Films of the 80s, 92n1361
Great cop pictures, 92n1363
Great Spanish films: 1950-90, 93n1365
Guide to critical reviews, part 2, 3d ed, 92n1333
Guide to videocassettes for children, 90n1346
Halliwell's film gd, 6th ed, 90n1332
Halliwell's filmgoer's & video viewer's companion, 10th ed, 94n1456
Halliwell's filmgoer's companion, 9th ed, 90n1347
HBO's gd to movies on videocassette & cable TV 1991, 92n1339
Hollywood Reporter bk of box office hits, 91n1383
Holt foreign film gd, 90n1348
Japanese films, 91n1376
Kael index, 94n1463
Laser video disc companion, updated ed, 93n997
Laserdisc film gd, 1993-1994 ed, 94n1429
Motion picture annual 1990, 91n1391
Motion picture gd, 1989 annual, 90n1352
Motion picture gd, 1993 annual, 94n1457
Movie classics, 93n1356
New York Times film reviews 1989-90, 94n1458
NFB film gd, 93n1342
Off-Hollywood movies, 90n1334
Picture this! a gd to over 300 environmentally, socially, & politically relevant films & videos, 93n1355
Premiere gd to movies on video, 92n1341
Produced & abandoned, 92n1345
Roger Ebert's movie home companion 1991 ed, 92n1338
Shoot-em-ups ride again, 92n1367
Sound films, 1927-39, 93n1352
3-D movies, 90n1340
Variety intl film gd 1991, 92n1373
Variety's complete home video dir 1989, 2d ed, 90n1335
Variety's complete home video dir 1989: adult titles suppl, 90n1336
Variety's film reviews, v.20, 92n1346
Variety's film reviews, v.21, 92n1347
Video movies, 91n1359
Viewers' choice gd to movies on video, 93n1334
Working women on the Hollywood screen, 90n857

MOTOR ABILITY
Kirby's gd to fitness & motor performance tests, 92n793

MOTORBOATS
Powerboat gd, 2d ed, 91n1833

MOVING, HOUSEHOLD
Moving & relocation sourcebk, 93n917

MOZAMBIQUE
Historical dict of Mozambique, 93n116

MOZART, WOLFGANG AMADEUS
Compleat Mozart, 92n1280
Mozart repertory, 92n1279
Wolfgang Amadeus Mozart: a gd to research, 90n1244

MUHAMMAD, PROPHET
Chronology of Islamic hist 570-1000 CE, 90n519

MULTICULTURALISM. *See* **PLURALISM (SOCIAL SCIENCES)**

MUNCIE (INDIANA)
Middletown, 90n845

MUNICIPAL GOVERNMENT
Municipal yellow bk, v.2, no.1, 93n741
Urban pols dict, 91n718

MUNICIPAL SERVICES
Delivering govt servs, 90n735

MURDER
Borden murders, 93n605
World ency of 20th century murder, 93n611

MURPHY
KWIC concordance to Samuel Beckett's Murphy, 91n1238

MURPHY, ROBERT D.
Robert D. Murphy: a register of his papers in the Hoover Inst Archives, 91n732

MURRAY, GILBERT
Cambridge ritualists, 92n1132

MUSCULOSKELETAL SYSTEM
Vocabulary of signs & symptoms of the musculoskeletal system, v.1, 91n1666

MUSEUMS
Auto museum dir USA suppl with Canadian museums, 90n1815
California museum dir, 2d ed, 92n63
Cambridge gd to the museums of Europe, 92n62
Corporate museums, galleries, & visitor centers, 92n129
Directory of museums in Africa, 91n57
Funding for museums, archives & special collections, 90n811
Glossary of museology, 90n954
Guide to 475 aircraft museums, 224 city-displayed aircraft, 37 restaurants with aircraft, 6 WWI landmarks, 10th ed, 93n1779
International dir of arts, 1991/92 ed, 92n64
Keyguide to info sources in museum studies, 91n60
Museum: a ref gd, 91n59
Museums of Israel, 91n58
Museums of the world, 4th ed, 94n60
Official dir of Canadian museums & related insts, 91n56
Official museum dir 1989, 90n65
Official museum dir 1992, 93n79
Official museum products & servs dir 1992, 93n80
Public info contact dir 1988-89, 90n1433

MUSEUMS & THE VISUALLY HANDICAPPED
Access to art: a museum dir for blind & visually impaired people, 90n957

MUSEUMS FOR CHILDREN. *See* **CHILDREN'S MUSEUMS**

MUSHROOMS
All that the rain promises & more, 92n1542
Guide to Kans. mushrooms, 94n1662
Mushrooms & other fungi of the midcontinental US, 90n1502
Mushrooms of N America, 92n1544
Texas mushrooms, 93n1509

MUSIC
African music, 93n1241
All music gd, 94n1314
American masses & requiems, 92n1302
American orchestral music, 94n1347
American Wind Symphony commissioning project, 93n1284
AMI, v.9, issue 1, 91n968
Antiquarian cats of musical interest, 90n1225
Antonio Gardano: Venetian music printer 1538-69, 90n1214
Art of the piano, 91n1287
Baker's biographical dict of musicians, 8th ed, 93n1244
Baroque music: a research & info gd, 94n1306
Basic classical & operatic recordings collection on compact disc for libs, 91n1294
Benet's reader's ency of American lit, 92n1155
Best rated CDs: classical 1992, 94n1344
Bibliographic gd to music 1990, 92n1248
Billboard bk of gold & platinum records, 91n1301
Biographical dict of Russian/Soviet composers, 91n1275
CD review digest annual 1990: classical, v.4, 92n1288
Checklist of Canadian copyright deposits in the British Museum 1895-1923, v.4, 90n41
Classical music discographies, 1976-88, 90n1268
Dictionary of terms in music, 4th ed, 93n1248
Early American music, 91n1253
Eighteenth-century musical chronicle, 91n1258
Encyclopedia of music in Canada, 2d ed, 94n1312
Handbook of research on music teaching & learning, 93n1252
Harpsichord & clavichord music of the 20th century, 94n1335
Heritage of music, 90n1231
His master's voice/la voix de son maitre, 91n1257
Historical research in music educ, 2d ed, 93n1240
Indian music lit, 93n1239
International music jls, 91n1263
International who's who in music, 12th ed, 91n1254
Lectionary of music, 90n1232
Literature of music bibliog, 94n1307
Music & dance in Puerto Rico from the age of Columbus to modern times, 93n1243
Music & dance pers, 90n1316
Music & the personal computer, 90n1220
Music dir Canada, 5th ed, 91n1260
Music for oboe, 1650-1800, 2d ed, 93n1263
Music hist during the Renaissance period, 1425-1520, 92n1252
Music in print master composer index 1988, 90n1249
Music in print master title index 1988, 91n1262
Music ref & research materials, 4th ed, 90n1213
Music theory from Zarlino to Schenker, 92n1249
Musical terms, symbols & theory, 90n1233
New American dict of music, 93n1249
New everyman dict of music, 6th ed, 90n1229
Nineteenth-century musical chronicle, 90n1227
Norton/Grove concise ency of music, 90n1230
Nostalgia entertainment sourcebk, 92n1334
Opera performances in video format, 93n1273
Opus: America's gd to classical music, summer 1990, 91n1293
Periodical lit on American music, 1620-1920, 90n1219
Pleyel as music publisher, 91n1251
Polish music, 90n1216
Pro/Am gd to US bks about music, 1987 suppl, 90n1215
Record Shelf gd to the classical repertoire, 90n1269
Short-title cat of music printed before 1825 in the Fitzwilliam Museum, Cambride, 94n1310
Twentieth-century composer speaks, 94n1333
Twentieth-century musical chronicle, 90n1228
Vocal compositions in German organ tablatures 1550-1650, 91n1284
Writing about music, 90n1237

MUSIC & MYTHOLOGY
Pro/Am bk of music & mythology, 94n1316

MUSIC & WAR
Music & war, 94n1305

MUSIC APPRECIATION
Anthologies of music, 2d ed, 94n1319
Listener's musical companion, new ed, 93n1251
Popular gd to classical music, 94n1345

MUSIC FESTIVALS
Music festivals in America, 4th ed, 92n1255
Music lover's gd to Europe, 93n1250

MUSIC, HINDUSTANI
Indian music lit, 93n1239

MUSIC, INDIC
Indian music lit, 93n1239

MUSIC, ITALIAN
His master's voice/la voce del padrone, 90n1226

MUSIC LIBRARIES
Music in British libs, 93n650

MUSIC PUBLISHING
Literature of music bibliog, 94n1307
Victorian music publishers, 92n1254

MUSIC TRADE
Music at auction, 90n1224

MUSICAL ANALYSIS
Anthologies of music, 2d ed, 94n1319
Music analyses, 92n1250

MUSICAL CRITICISM
Writing about music, 90n1237

MUSICAL FILMS
Great Hollywood musical pictures, 93n1360
Movie musicals on record, 90n1234
Song & dance, 92n1351
Soundies distributing corp of America, 92n1370

MUSICAL INSTRUMENTS
Indian music lit, 93n1239
Musical instruments, 91n1281
Orion blue bk: guitars & musical instruments 1990, 91n206
Oxford companion to musical instruments, 94n1338

MUSICAL INVENTIONS & PATENTS
Piano-beds & music by steam, 94n1318

MUSICAL LANDMARKS
Jazz & blues lover's gd to the US, 92n1306
Music lover's gd to Europe, 93n1250

MUSICAL REVUE, COMEDY, ETC.
American musical theatre: a chronicle, 2d ed, 93n1385
Berlin, Kern, Rodgers, Hart, & Hammerstein, 91n1309
Broadway's prize-winning musicals, 94n1465
Dance in the musical theatre, 90n1317
Ganzl's bk of the musical theatre, 90n1365
Guide to critical reviews, part 2, 3d ed, 92n1333
Opening night on Broadway, 92n1387
Opera plot index, 91n1300
Stage it with music, 94n1473
TV & studio cast musicals on record, 91n1320

MUSIC-HALLS
Gigging, 91n1303

MUSICIANS
Baker's biographical dict of musicians, 8th ed, 93n1244
Billboard bk of no.1 hits, rev ed, 90n1292
Billboard bk of no.1 hits, 3d ed, 94n1360
Billboard bk of 1-hit wonders, 91n1324
Contemporary musicians, 90n1221
Contemporary musicians, v.6, 93n1245
Instrumental virtuosi, 90n1258

International who's who in music & musicians' dir, 13th ed, 94n1346
Moscow & Leningrad: a topographical gd to Russian cultural hist, v.2, 94n985
Penguin dict of musical performers, 91n1256
Sweet, hot & blue: St. Louis' musical heritage, 90n1286
World of African music, 94n1315

MUSICOLOGY
American musicologists 1890-1945, 90n1217

MUSLIMS
Muslims of India, 91n101

MUTUAL FUNDS
Herzfeld's gd to closed-end funds, 94n190
Investment trust dir 1988-89, 90n212
Morningstar mutual fund 500, 1993, 94n195
Mutual fund ency, 1990 ed, 91n184
Mutual fund ency, 1993-1994 ed, 94n198
St. James mutual fund dir, 92n167

MYSTERIES & MIRACLE-PLAYS
Concordance to The Towneley Plays, 91n1192
Medieval English drama, 91n1191

MYSTERY & DETECTIVE STORIES. *See* DETECTIVE & MYSTERY STORIES

MYSTICISM
Dictionary of mysticism & the esoteric traditions, rev ed, 94n814

MYTHOLOGY
Ancient & shining ones, 94n1392
Bibliography of Slavic mythology, 90n1305
Book of goddesses & heroines, rev ed, 91n1334
Brewer's bk of myth & legend, 94n1391
Dictionary of Irish mythology, 90n1304
Dictionary of Polynesian mythology, 90n1303
Index to fairy tales 1978-86, 5th suppl, 91n1330
Macmillan illus ency of myths & legends, 91n1333
Mythologies, 92n1321
Mythology, 93n1302
Myths, gods, & fantasy, 92n1319
Norse mythology A to Z, 92n1322
NTC's classical dict, 92n1325
Place-names in classical mythology: Greece, 90n1302
Pro/Am bk of music & mythology, 94n1316
Putnam's concise mythological dict, 92n1324
Who's who in classical mythology, 94n1393
Who's who in non-classical mythology, 94n1394

MYTHOLOGY, ASSYRO
Dictionary of ancient Near Eastern mythology, 92n1323

MYTHOLOGY, CELTIC
Dictionary of Celtic mythology, 93n1304

MYTHOLOGY, CLASSICAL
By Jove!, 94n1396
Guide to research in classical art & mythology, 93n1029
Mythological & classical world art index, 92n993
Oxford gd to classical mythology in the arts, 1300-1990s, 94n1397
Women of classical mythology, 92n1320

MYTHOLOGY, EGYPTIAN
Concise dict of Greek, Roman, Norse, & Egyptian mythology, 93n1303

MYTHOLOGY, GREEK
Concise dict of Greek, Roman, Norse, & Egyptian mythology, 93n1303

MYTHOLOGY IN LITERATURE
Recent studies in myths & lit, 1970-90, 93n1301

MYTHOLOGY, NORSE
Concise dict of Greek, Roman, Norse, & Egyptian mythology, 93n1303

MYTHOLOGY, ORIENTAL
Dictionary of ancient Near Eastern mythology, 92n1323

MYTHOLOGY, ROMAN
Concise dict of Greek, Roman, Norse, & Egyptian mythology, 93n1303

MYXOMYCETES
Handbook of protoctista, 91n1515

NAIPAUL, V. S.
V. S. Naipaul: a selective bibliog with annotations, 1957-87, 91n1249

NAMES
Klee as in clay, 94n982
Penguin dict of proper names, 93n464
Pronouncing dict of proper names, 94n1084

NAMES, GEOGRAPHICAL
Book of Irish names, 90n400
Brewer's dict of names, 94n440
Cahuilla landscape, 92n359
Colorado place names, 94n470
Dictionary of English place names, 93n493
Dictionary of real people & places in fiction, 94n1159
Dictionary of world place names derived from British names, 90n429
Lexicon of the Greek & Roman cities & place names in antiquity ca. 1500 B.C.—ca. A.D. 500, fascicule 1, 94n535
Omni gazetteer of the USA, 92n425
Omni gazetteer of the USA [CD-ROM], 93n495
1001 Kans. place names, 90n427
Place gd, 1990 ed, 92n422
Place names in Ala., 90n426
Place names of Alta., [v.1], 92n424
Place-names in classical mythology: Greece, 90n1302
Pocket place names of Hawai'i, 90n428
Toposaurus, 92n1025
Utah place names, 92n428
What do you call a person from...?, 91n451

NAMES IN LITERATURE
Chaucer name dict, 90n1176
Dictionary of real people & places in fiction, 94n1159
My name in bks, 94n1190

NAMES IN THE BIBLE
Harper's Bible pronunciation gd, 91n1428
Jones' dict of O.T. proper names, 91n1429

NAMES, IRISH
Book of Irish names, 90n400

NAMES, PERSONAL
African names, 94n443
Baby name countdown, 91n421
Book of Irish names, 90n400
Brewer's dict of names, 94n440
Dictionary of 1st names, 91n419
Dictionary of 1st names, 92n398
Dictionary of real people & places in fiction, 94n1159
Dictionary of Russian personal names, 93n463
Dictionary of surnames, 90n401
First name reverse dict, 94n442
German-American names, 91n420
Jewish family names & their origins, 94n441
Naming your child, 92n397
New name dict, 90n403
Proper noun speller, 91n1078
Tuttle dict of 1st names, 93n465
Webster's new world dict of eponyms, 91n1052

NAMIBIA
Transnational corporations in S Africa & Namibia, 91n127

NAPOLEONIC WARS, 1800-1814
Era of Napoleon, 92n478
Napoleonic source bk, 92n492

NARCOTICS
Drug, alcohol & other addictions, 90n820
Handbook of research on the illicit drug trade, 93n892
International hndbk on drug control, 94n916

NASH, OGDEN
Ogden Nash: a descriptive bibliog, 91n1168

NASSER, GAMAL ABDEL
Gamal Abdel Nasser: a bibliog, 93n543

NATIONAL CEMETERIES
American military cemeteries, 93n706

NATIONAL GEOGRAPHIC
National Geographic index 1888-1988, 91n450
Quick ref gd to Natl Geographic 1955-mid 1990, 92n421

NATIONAL HOCKEY LEAGUE
Complete ency of hockey, 4th ed, 94n852

NATIONAL LEAGUE OF PROFESSIONAL BASEBALL CLUBS
Elias baseball analyst, 1989, 91n826
Encyclopedia of major league baseball team hists: Natl League, 92n779

NATIONAL LIBERATION MOVEMENTS
Latin American revolutionaries, 91n761

NATIONAL LIBRARIANS
Biographical dir of natl librarians, 90n581

NATIONAL LIBRARY OF CANADA
Passages: a treasure trove of N American exploration, 93n485

NATIONAL MONUMENTS
Guide to natl monuments & historic sites, 91n460

NATIONAL MUSEUM OF AMERICAN HISTORY (U.S.)— PHOTOGRAPHY COLLECTION
Guide to photographic collections at the Smithsonian Inst, v.2, 92n1467
Guide to photographic collections at the Smithsonian Inst, v.3, 94n1038

NATIONAL PARKS & RESERVES
Adventuring in Austral., 91n466
America's natl battlefield parks, 92n445
Easy access to natl parks, 93n499
Educational gd to the natl park system, 90n446
Guide to natl monuments & historic sites, 91n460
Guide to the natl wildlife refuges, rev ed, 94n1683
International hndbk of natl parks & nature reserves, 91n452
National park gd 1992, 93n496
National parks, 93n498
National parks fishing gd, 92n800
South America's natl parks, 91n477
U.S. outdoor atlas & recreation gd, 93n497
Wild Australia, 90n454

NATIONAL SCIENCE FOUNDATIONS
EHR dir of awards: fiscal yr 1990, 93n875

NATIONAL SECURITY
Military & strategic policy, 91n676
Security, arms control, & conflict reduction in E Asia & the Pacific, 94n683

NATIONAL SOCIALISM IN MOTION PICTURES
Nazi-retro film, 93n1362

NATIONAL UNION CATALOG OF MANUSCRIPT COLLECTIONS
Index to personal names in the NUC of mss collections 1959-84, 90n402

NATIONALISM
Encyclopedia of nationalism, 91n766

NATIVE PLANTS. See BOTANY

NATURAL AREAS
Adventuring in Austral., 91n466
Sierra Club gd to the natural areas of New England, 91n461

NATURAL FOOD. See FOOD, NATURAL

NATURAL HISTORY
Atlas of the natural world, 92n1557
Birds of the Blue Ridge Mountains, 93n1545
California's wild heritage, 91n1551
Dictionary of the environment, 3d ed, 90n1791
Index to illus of animals & plants, 93n1525
Natural hist museums, v.1, 93n1524
Nature in America, 93n1526
Nature of SE Alaska, 93n1528
Nature projects on file, 93n1527
New bk of popular sci, 90n1437
New bk of popular sci, 92n1457
New bk of popular sci, 93n1450
Sierra Club naturalist's gd to the S Rockies, 92n444
Things precious & wild, 92n1556
Way nature works, 94n1684

NATURAL PESTICIDES
Handbook of plants with pest-control properties, 90n1485

NATURAL RESOURCES
Atlas of the Third World, 2d ed, 94n459
Atlas of US environmental issues, 92n1765
Dictionary of environmental sci & tech, rev ed, 94n2000
Natural resources glossary, 92n1790

NATURAL SCIENCE. See PHYSICS

NATURALISTS
Environmentalists: a biographical dict, 94n1993

NATURE
Dictionary of environmental quotations, 93n1777
Rediscovery of creation, 93n1417
Things precious & wild, 92n1556

NATURE CONSERVATION
Atlas of environmental issues, 90n1788
Atlas of US environmental issues, 92n1765
Changing wilderness values,1930-90, 92n1767
Extinct species of the world, 92n1524
Green ency, 94n1996
Nature dir, 93n1759

NATURE IN LITERATURE
E for environment, 93n1752

NATURE STUDY
Wilderness U: opportunities for outdoor educ in the US & abroad, 93n335

NATUROPATHY
Encyclopedia of natural medicine, 93n1634

NAUTICAL CHARTS
Marine atlas of the Hawaiian Islands, 93n466

NAVAL ART & SCIENCE
Glossary of ancient Egyptian nautical titles & terms, 90n1819
Illustrated gd to modern naval warfare, 91n702
Naval terms dict, 5th ed, 90n668
Scuttlebutt, 90n1818
United States navy: a dict, 92n666

NAVAL MUSEUMS
Great maritime museums of the world, 93n1791
Historic warships, 94n703
Naval Institute gd to maritime museums of N America, 92n1805

NAVIES
Mangone's concise marine almanac, 92n1466
Naval Institute gd to combat fleets of the world 1990/91, 91n695
Uniforms & insignia of the navies of WW II, 92n665

NAVIGATION
Indigenous navigation & voyaging in the Pacific, 93n1789
Maritime affairs: a world hndbk, 2d ed, 93n1790
Maritime servs dir 1989-90, 91n1832

NAVIGATION (AERONAUTICS)
Air almanac 1990, 91n1816

NEAR-DEATH EXPERIENCES
Near-death experiences, 91n785

NEBULAE
Messier's nebulae & star clusters, 2d ed, 93n1705
NGC 2000.0: the complete new general cat & index cats of nebulae & star clusters, 90n1747

NELSON, HORATIO NELSON, VISCOUNT
Lord Nelson 1758-1805: a bibliog, 91n522

NEPAL
Cambridge ency of India, Pakistan, Bangladesh, Sri Lanka, Nepal, Bhutan & the Maldives, 91n99
Guide to the birds of Nepal, 93n1543
Hippocrene insiders' gd to Nepal, 9th ed, 93n501
South Asian hndbk, 1992, 93n502

NEPALI LANGUAGE—DICTIONARIES—ENGLISH
Shorter English-Nepali dict, 92n1083

NETHERLANDS
Facts on File national profiles: the Benelux countries, 90n132

NETHERLANDS ANTILLES
Suriname & the Netherlands Antilles, 94n149

NEURAL CIRCUITRY
Neuro-computing bibliog, 1989, 90n1708

NEURAL COMPUTERS
NeuralSource, 91n1718
Neuro-computing bibliog, 1989, 90n1708

NEUROLOGIC MANIFESTATIONS OF GENERAL DISEASES
Alzheimer's, stroke, & 29 other neurological disorders sourcebk, 94n1862

NEUROLOGY
Neuroscience yr: suppl, 90n1639

NEUROPSYCHOLOGY
Dictionary of neuropsychology, 91n1658
Neuroscience yr: suppl, 90n1639

NEVADA
Nevada printing hist, 93n678
Prime sources of Calif. & Nev. local hist, 93n511

NEW AGE MOVEMENT
Layman's gd to new age & spiritual terms, 94n816
Metaphysical Fla., 92n764
New age ency, 91n1451
Parapsychology, new age & the occult, 94n815
Would the Buddha wear a walkman?, 92n180

NEW AGE MUSIC
New age music gd, 91n1321

NEW BUSINESS ENTERPRISES
100 best spare-time bus opportunities today, 91n181
Where to make money, 94n945

NEW ENGLAND
Guide to the marine sport fishes of Atlantic Canada & New England, 93n1555
New England: a bibliog of its hist, 91n483
New England: additions to the 6 state bibliogs, 91n484
Sierra Club gd to the natural areas of New England, 91n461
Used bk lover's gd to New England, 94n1027

NEW JERSEY
New Jersey arts, 92n986
Past & promise: lives of N.J. women, 91n923
Used bk lover's gd to the mid-Atlantic states, 94n1028

NEW LEFT. *See* RIGHT & LEFT (POLITICAL SCIENCE)

NEW MEXICO
Fall wildflowers of N.Mex., 90n1496
Fishes of N.Mex., 91n1585
WPA gd to 1930s N.Mex., 90n450

NEW ORLEANS (LA.)—IMPRINTS
Bibliography of New Orleans imprints 1764-1864, 90n629

NEW PRODUCTS
Successful industrial product innovation, 91n260

NEW WORDS. *See* WORDS, NEW

NEW WRITING
John Lehmann's 'New Writing': an author-index 1936-50, 92n1205

NEW YORK (CITY)
Encyclopedia of the N.Y. stage, 1930-1940, 90n1367
Guide to N.Y. law firms, 92n541
Passport's gd to ethnic N.Y., 92n443

NEW YORK (STATE)
Bibliography of N.Y. state communities, rev ed, 90n101
Bibliography of N.Y. state communities, 3d ed, 91n88
Used bk lover's gd to the mid-Atlantic states, 94n1028

NEW YORK METROPOLITAN AREA
Doing bus in N.Y. City, 91n141
Genealogical resources in the N.Y. metro area, 90n385
Guide to scholarly resources on the Russian empire & the Soviet Union in the N.Y. metropolitan area, 91n113

NEW YORKER
Television-related cartoons in the New Yorker, 94n1056

NEW ZEALAND
Adventuring in N.Z., 94n482
Handbook of Australian, N.Z. & Antarctic birds, v.1, 92n1563
Illustrated ency of N.Z., 91n513
New Zealand bks in print 1989, 90n26
New Zealand bks in print 1993, 94n5

NEW ZEALAND LITERATURE
Oxford hist of N.Z. lit in English, 92n1239

NEWBERRY LIBRARY
Checklist of the Newberry Lib's printed bks in sci, medicine, tech, & the pseudosciences ca. 1460-1750, 94n1558
Hispanic rare bks of the golden age (1470-1699) in the Newberry Lib of Chicago, 90n27

NEWBERY MEDAL BOOKS
Handbook for the Newbery medal & honor bks, 1980-89, 93n1140
Newbery & Caldecott awards, 1991 ed, 92n1120
Newbery & Caldecott awards, 1992 ed, 93n1128
Newbery & Caldecott medal & honor bks in other media, 93n1121
Newbery & Caldecott medalists & honor bk winners, 2d ed, 93n1120

NEWFOUNDLAND
Atlantic Canadian imprints, 1801-20, 92n13
Atlas of Nfld. & Lab., 93n473
Dictionary of Nfld. & Labrador biog, 91n515
Encyclopedia of Nfld. & Lab., v.3, 93n133

NEWSLETTERS
Hudson's subscription newsletter dir 1990, 92n902
Legal newsletters in print 1990, 91n561
Newsletters in print 1993-94, 93n978
Oxbridge dir of newsletters 1990, 91n961

NEWSPAPER EDITORS
Horace Greeley: a bio-bibliog, 93n979

NEWSPAPER PUBLISHING
Gebbie Pr all-in-one dir 1989, 90n636

NEWSPAPER SYNDICATES. *See* SYNDICATES (JOURNALISM)

NEWSPAPERS
Bacon's media calendar dir 1993, 94n1003
Bacon's newspaper/mag dir 1993, 94n1004
Bacon's publicity checker 1991, 92n899
Canadian illus news, Montreal 1869-83, 90n909
Gale dir of pubs & broadcast media 1990, 91n61
Gale dir of pubs & broadcast media 1993, 94n988
Matthews list, v.34, no.1, 91n937

News media yellow bk of Washington & N.Y., v.1, no.1, 91n959
Newspapers online, 93n975
Newspapers online, 2d ed, 94n1005
1992-1993 gd to newspaper syndication, 93n977
Nova Scotia newspapers, 92n904

NEWSPAPERS IN EDUCATION
Newspaper: a ref bk for teachers & librarians, 92n277

NEWSWEEK
Cover story index 1960-89, 91n964

NIAGARA FALLS (N.Y. & ONT.)
Public gardens & parks of Niagara, 90n1466

NICARAGUA
Sandinista Nicaragua, 90n146

NICOLAEVSKY, BORIS I.
Guide to the Boris I. Nicolaevsky collection in the Hoover Inst archives, 90n522

NIGER
Historical dict of Niger, 2d ed, 91n95

NIGERIA
Nigerian artists, 94n1040
Press in Nigeria, 91n960

NILE RIVER VALLEY
Waters of the Nile, 92n473

NINETEENTH CENTURY
Cumulative bibliog of Victorian studies 1985-89, 91n546

NOBEL PRIZES
Nobel laureates in economic scis, 90n163
Nobel laureates in lit, 91n1098
Nobel laureates in medicine or physiology, 91n1655
Nobel prize winners: chemistry, 91n1765
Nobel prize winners: physics, 90n1773
Nobel prize winners: physiology or medicine, 92n1652
Nobel prize winners: suppl 1987-91, 93n41
Who's who of Nobel prize winners 1901-90, 2d ed, 92n28

NOBILITY
Biographical dict of life peers, 93n462

NONFERROUS METALS
Non-ferrous metal data 1988, 90n1768
Non-ferrous metal data 1990, 93n1727

NON-FORMAL EDUCATION
Bear's gd to earning college degrees non-traditionally, 11th ed, 94n350
Bear's gd to earning non-traditional college degrees, 10th ed, 90n323
Campus-free college degrees, 4th ed, 90n340
Campus-free college degrees, 5th ed, 93n378
College degrees by mail, 92n300, 94n351

NON-GOVERNMENTAL ORGANIZATIONS
Alternative dir of nongovtl orgs in S Asia, rev. ed, 91n39

NONMETALLIC MINERALS
Concise ency of mineral resources, 91n1786

NONSEXIST LANGUAGE. See SEXISM IN LANGUAGE

NORMANDY (FRANCE)
Normandy campaign, 1944, 94n531

NORM-REFERENCED TESTS
Consumer's gd to tests in print, 2d ed, 93n333

NORRIS, FRANK
Frank Norris: a descriptive bibliog, 93n1180

NORSEMEN. See NORTHMEN

NORTH AMERICA
Bibliographic gd to N American hist 1990, 92n453
History & folklore of N American wildflowers, 94n1651
USA & Canada 1990, 91n87

NORTH AMERICA—DISCOVERY & EXPLORATION
Atlas of N American exploration, 94n444
Passages: a treasure trove of N American exploration, 93n485

NORTH ATLANTIC TREATY ORGANIZATION
Jane's NATO hndbk 1989-90, 91n768

NORTH CAROLINA
Dictionary of N.C. biog, v.4, 92n33
Guide to the liverworts of N.C., 93n1512

NORTH DAKOTA
Statistical abstract of N.D. 1988, 90n840

NORTHEASTERN STATES
Butterflies through binoculars, 94n1703
Climatological atlas of snowfall & snow depth for the NE US and SE Canada, 94n1948

NORTHERN IRELAND
Contemporary Irish dramatists, 90n1205
Dictionary of Irish archaeology, 94n486
Dictionary of Irish mythology, 90n1304
Modern Irish lit & culture, 94n1291
Northern Ireland, 93n145
Northern Ireland: a pol dir 1968-88, 91n759

NORTHMEN
Medieval Scandinavia, 94n526

NORTHWEST, PACIFIC
Artists of the Pacific Northwest, 94n1042
Trees & shrubs for Pacific Northwest gardens, 2d ed, 91n1543

NORWAY
Norwegian local hist, 90n134

NORWEGIAN LANGUAGE—DICTIONARIES—ENGLISH
English-Norwegian dict, 90n1052

NORWEGIAN-AMERICANS
Guide to collections relating to S.D. Norwegian-Americans, 93n451

NOTARIES
Notary public hndbk, 91n588

NOTES (CATALOGING)
Notes in the cat record based on AACR2 & LC rule interpretations, 90n605

NOVA SCOTIA
Spring wildflowers, 94n1659

NOVELISTS
Concordance to Henry James's The Awkward Age, 90n1145
Contemporary gay American novelists, 94n1224
Critical survey of short fiction, rev ed, 94n1215
Henry James ency, 90n1147

NOVELISTS, AUSTRALIAN
Reader's gd to Australian fiction, 94n1269

NOVELISTS, CANADIAN
ECW's biographical gd to Canadian novelists, 94n1273

NOVELISTS, ENGLISH
British Romantic novelists, 1789-1832, 93n1196
John Fowles: a ref companion, 93n1208

NOVELISTS, FRENCH
French novelists since 1960, 90n1203

NOVELS. See FICTION

NOWLAN, ALDEN
Alden Nowlan papers, 94n1276

NUCLEAR ARMS CONTROL
Nuclear present, 94n709
Peace & nuclear war dict, 90n672

NUCLEAR ENERGY
Chambers nuclear energy & radiation dict, 93n1742
Nuclear energy policy, 92n1762
World energy & nuclear dir, 2d ed, 94n2008

NUCLEAR FUELS
Nuclear fuel cycle info system, 90n1778

NUCLEAR INDUSTRY
Nuclear energy policy, 92n1762
Nuclear present, 94n709

NUCLEAR MEDICINE
Dictionary & hndbk of nuclear medicine & clinical imaging, 92n1657

NUCLEAR POWER. *See* **NUCLEAR ENERGY**

NUCLEAR POWER PLANTS
Nuclear power plants worldwide, 94n1801

NUCLEAR REACTORS
Nuclear power reactors in the world, 1991 ed, 93n1749

NUCLEAR WARFARE
Nuclear present, 94n709
Peace & nuclear war dict, 90n672

NUCLEAR WARFARE IN MOTION PICTURES
Nuclear movies, 93n1349

NUCLEAR WEAPONS
Disarmament & security: 1988-89 yrbk, 92n748
Jane's NBC protection equipment 1989-90, 91n708
Nuclear heartland, 90n678
Nuclear weapons world, 90n674
Surviving the nuclear age...1945-1983 table of contents, 92n667
Surviving the nuclear age, 1987 update, 92n668

NUDIBRANCHIATA
Pacific coast nudibranchs, 93n1573

NUDIST CAMPS
Lee Baxandall's world gd to nude beaches & recreation, 92n773

NUMBERS, REAL
Dictionary of real numbers, 91n1796

NUMISMATICS
Discovering America, 90n922

NURSES
American nursing, v.2, 93n1659

NURSING
Associate degree nursing educ, 92n1687
Core collection in nursing & the allied health scis, 91n1705
Davis's drug gd for nurses, 2d ed, 92n1692
Dictionary of nursing theory & research, 91n1706
Directory of educl sftwr for nursing, 1988, 90n1692
Duncan's dict for nurses, 2d ed, 90n1693
Geriatric nursing assistants, 92n1688
History of nursing beginning bibliog, 94n1864
Mosby's pocket dict of medicine, nursing, & allied health, 92n1658
Nurse's quick ref, 91n1704
Pocket gd to nursing diagnoses, 3d ed, 90n1694
Professional gd to diseases, 4th ed, 94n1841
Who's who in American nursing 1988-89, 91n1707

NURSING HOMES
Directory of nursing homes 1991-92, 92n1686
Golden horizons retirement gd, Calif ed, 90n792

NUTRITION
Best of health, 91n1643
Consumer health & nutrition index, v.8, no.1, 93n1614
Dictionary of food & nutrition, 90n1454
Dictionary of nutrition & food tech, 92n1481
Dieter's dict & problem solver, 94n1603
Directory of food & nutrition info for professionals & consumers, 2d ed, 94n1604
Encyclopaedia of food sci, food tech, & nutrition, 94n1600
Longman illus dict of food sci, 91n1485
Melting pot: an annot bibliog & gd to food & nutrition info for ethnic groups in America, 94n1599
Mount Sinai School of Medicine complete bk of nutrition, 92n1670
Nutrients cat, 94n1610
Nutrition, 90n1648

Nutrition almanac, 3d ed, 91n1481
Nutrition & diet therapy dict, 3d ed, 92n1485
Nutrition & disease, 92n1674
Nutrition & health ency, 2d ed, 90n1614
Nutrition desk ref, rev ed, 92n1667
Wellness ency of food & nutrition, 94n1602

NUTS
Edible wild fruits & nuts of Canada, 90n1507
European garden flora, v.3, 90n1489
Plant resources of SE Asia, no.2, 92n1475

OBESITY
Eating disorders, 90n1684

OBITUARIES
Obituaries: a gd to sources, 2d ed, 91n414
Obituary index 1988, 91n55
Stage deaths, 92n1376
Variety obituaries, v.12, 91n1345

OBOE MUSIC
Music for oboe, 1650-1800, 2d ed, 93n1263

OBSTETRICS
A-Z of women's sexuality, 91n1661
Dictionary of obstetrics & gynecology, 90n1641

OCCULTISM
Checklist of the Newberry Lib's printed bks in sci, medicine, tech, & the pseudosciences ca. 1460-1750, 94n1558
Dictionary of cults, sects, religions & the occult, 94n1513
Dictionary of mysticism & the esoteric traditions, rev ed, 94n814
Encyclopedia of occultism & parapsychology, 3d ed, 92n762
Guide to the American occult 1989, 91n799
Harper's ency of mystic & paranormal experience, 92n765
Parapsychology, new age & the occult, 94n815

OCCUPATIONAL APTITUDE TESTS
ETS test collection cat, v.5, 92n273
ETS test collection cat, v.6, 93n329
Tests: a comprehensive ref for assessments in psychology, educ, & bus, 3d ed, 93n338

OCCUPATIONAL HEALTH & SAFETY. *See* **INDUSTRIAL HYGIENE**

OCCUPATIONAL TRAINING
Career training sourcebk, 94n388
Chronicle vocational school manual for 1991-92 school yr, 93n406

OCCUPATIONS
Complete gd for occupational exploration, 1993 ed, 94n387
Dictionary of occupational titles, 4th ed, 93n301
Encyclopedia of careers & vocational guidance, 8th ed, 91n374
Encyclopedia of careers & vocational guidance, 9th ed, 94n386
International standard classification of occupations, 92n226
Occupational outlook hndbk, 1990-91 ed, 91n249
Occupational outlook hndbk, 1992-93 ed, 94n281
Top professions, 91n242
Vocational careers sourcebk, 93n412

OCEAN
Ocean yrbk 8, 92n1744
Random House atlas of the oceans, 93n1730

OCEAN ENGINEERING
Marine tech ref bk, 92n1610

OCEAN TRAVEL
Offshore cruising ency, 91n1829

OCEANIA
Bibliography of new religious movements in primal societies, v.3, 91n1411
Catalog of the diptera of the Australasian & oceanian regions, 91n1588
Directory of travel info sources for the Pacific Islands, 90n461
Far East & Australasia 1991, 92n120
Good bks for the curious traveler: Asia & the S Pacific, 90n453

South Pacific islands legal systems, 94n573

OCEANIAN LITERATURE
Writers from the S Pacific, 93n1229

OCEANOGRAPHY
Mangone's concise marine almanac, 92n1466

OCEAN LIFE. *See* **MARINE BIOLOGY**

OCLC
Guide to special collections in the OCLC database, 90n625

O'CONNOR, FLANNERY
Manuscripts of Flannery O'Connor at Georgia College, 90n1151

ODETS, CLIFFORD
Clifford Odets: a research & production sourcebk, 92n1377
Clifford Odets: an annot bibliog 1935-89, 91n1154

OFFICE PRACTICE
Complete secretary's hndbk, 7th ed, 94n300
Elsevier's dict of office automation, 93n323
Office sourcebk, 90n290
Professional Secretaries Intl complete office hndbk, 93n324
Professional secretary's encyclopedic dict, 4th ed, 90n291
Professional secretary's hndbk, rev ed, 94n301
Secretary's key, 92n260
Webster's new world secretarial hndbk, 4th ed, 90n292

OFFSHORE OIL INDUSTRY
Worldwide offshore contractors & equipment dir, 1991, 92n1611

OIL & GAS JOURNAL
Oil & Gas Jl exploration index, 93n1750

OIL FIELD EQUIPMENT & SUPPLIES INDUSTRY
U.S.A. oilfield serv, supply & manufacturers dir, 1989, 90n1786

OILS & FATS
Codex alimentarius, v.8, 94n1607
Minor oil crops, 93n1464

OJIBWA LANGAUGE—DICTIONARIES—ENGLISH
Dictionary of the Ojibway lang, 94n1124

OKLAHOMA
American Indian resource materials in the W hist collections, Univ of Okla., 92n364
Mammals of Okla., 91n1591
Oklahoma botanical lit, 90n1487
Oklahoma herpetology, 90n1565
Oklahoma mammalogy, 90n1557

OLD AGE
Aging with style & savvy, 91n843
Of a certain age, 92n1141
Old age in myth & symbol, 92n809

OLD AGE ASSISTANCE
National gd to funding in aging, 2d ed, 91n846

OLD AGE PENSIONS
International hndbk on old-age insurance, 92n814

OLD GROWTH FORESTS
Bibliography on old-growth forests in B.C., 92n1501

OLIVER, CHAD
Work of Chad Oliver, 91n1169

OLYMPICS
Black American women in Olympic track & field, 93n843
Black Olympian medalists, 92n769
Complete bk of the Olympics, 1992 ed, 93n841
Olympic games: complete track & field results 1896-1988, 90n759
Olympics factbk, 93n840
Olympic results—Barcelona 1992, 94n856
Timetables of sports hist: the Olympic games, 91n812

OMAHA INDIANS
Upstream people, 92n376

ONLINE
Cumulative index to ONLINE, DATABASE & CD-ROM Professional 1986-91, 93n1669

ON-LINE BIBLIOGRAPHIC SEARCHING
BiblioData fulltext sources online, 90n1725
Books & pers online, 94n44
Keyguide to info sources in online & CD-ROM database searching, 92n590
Newspapers online, 93n975
Newspapers online, 2d ed, 94n1005
Search sheets for OPACs on the Internet, 93n661
User educ for online systems in libs, 92n598

ON-LINE DATA PROCESSING
Directory of online databases, v.13, no.2, 93n1682
Modem USA, 93n1683

ONTARIO
Bibliography of Ont. hist 1976-1986, 90n511
Farm family financial crisis, 90n1442
Local hists of Ont. municipalities 1977-87, 91n514
Mapping upper Canada 1780-1867, 92n411
Ontario central places in 1871, 92n423
Public gardens & parks of Niagara, 90n1466
Scott's dirs: Ont. manufacturers, 17th ed, 90n245

OPENING SENTENCES. *See* **OPENINGS (RHETORIC)**

OPENINGS (RHETORIC)
In the beginning: great 1st lines from your favorite bks, 93n1117

OPERA
Annals of the Metropolitan opera, 91n1295
Chorus in opera, 94n1353
Cross index title gd to opera & operetta, 90n1272
Harper dict of opera & operetta, 91n1296
International dict of opera, 94n1355
International opera gd, 92n1292
Music lover's gd to Europe, 93n1250
New Grove dict of opera, 94n1356
Opera: an informal gd, 94n1358
Operas in German, 92n1289
Oxford dict of opera, 94n1357
Recent American opera, 92n1291
Schwann artist issue, 14th ed, 90n1236
Verdi & his major contemporaries, 91n1298
Wagner compendium, 94n1329

OPERA COMPANIES
Opera cos of the world, 94n1352

OPERAS
Basic classical & operatic recordings collection on compact disc for libs, 91n1294
Complete operas of Richard Strauss, 90n1271
Ganzl's bk of the musical theatre, 90n1365
Guide to opera & dance on videocassette, 91n1342
Nikolai Andreevich Rimsky-Korsakov: a gd to research, 90n1252
100 great operas & their stories, 90n1273
Opera annual, US 1984-85, 90n1270
Opera hndbk, 91n1299
Opera performances in video format, 93n1273
Opera plot index, 91n1300
Shakespeare & the musical stage, 91n1297

OPERAS—FILM & VIDEO ADAPTATIONS
Opera mediagraphy, 94n1351

OPERATING SYSTEMS (COMPUTERS)
Computer professional's quick ref, 93n1685
PC hdwr & systems implementation, 90n1722

OPERETTA
Cross index title gd to opera & operetta, 90n1272
Harper dict of opera & operetta, 91n1296

OPTHALMOLOGY
Dictionary of eye terminology, 2d ed, 92n1672
Dictionary of visual sci, 4th ed, 90n1691

OPTICAL CHARACTER RECOGNITION DEVICES
Sourcebook of automatic identification & data collection, 91n1612

OPTICAL COMMUNICATIONS
Fiber optics standard dict, 2d ed, 91n1754

OPTICAL DISKS
CD-ROM reviews 1987-90, 93n659
CD-ROM tech for info managers, 91n633

OPTICAL STORAGE DEVICES
CD-ROM reviews 1987-90, 93n659
CD-ROM tech for info managers, 91n633
HyperSource on multimedia/hypermedia techs, 91n1745
HyperSource on optical techs, 91n1746

OPTICS
Encyclopedia of lasers & optical tech, 92n1604

OPTOMETRY
Dictionary of optometry, 2d ed, 91n1685

ORAL HISTORY
Catalogue of audio & video collections of Holocaust testimony, 2d ed, 93n528
Oral hist index, 91n556

ORAL READING
New read-aloud hndbk, 1989 ed, 91n369

ORCHESTRAL MUSIC
American orchestral music, 94n1347
Listen to the music, 90n1274
Orchestral excerpts, 94n1348
Schwann artist issue, 14th ed, 90n1236

ORCHIDS
Illustrated ency of orchids, 94n1658
Miniature orchids, 94n1656
Orchid bk, 94n1652

ORDER STATISTICS
Chronological annot bibliog of order stats, v.3, 92n846
Chronological annot bibliog of order stats, v.4, 93n902

ORDNANCE, NAVAL
Naval Institute gd to world naval weapons systems, 91n696

ORE DEPOSITS
Annotated bibliogs of mineral deposits in Europe, pt.2, 92n1743

OREGON
Birds of Malheur Natl Wildlife Refuge, Oreg., 92n1564
Dictionary of Oreg. hist, 2d ed, 91n503

OREGON TRAIL
Indians along the Oregon Trail, expanded ed, 93n436

ORES
Atlas of opaque & ore minerals in their assns, 92n1740

ORGAN MUSIC
Guide to organ music, 91n1285
Organ & harpsichord music by women composers, 92n1266
Organ music in print 1990 suppl, 91n1283
Vocal compositions in German organ tablatures 1550-1650, 91n1284

ORGANIC CHEMISTRY. *See* CHEMISTRY, ORGANIC

ORGANIC GARDENING
Essential kitchen gardener, 91n1496
Prentice-Hall pocket ency [of] organic gardening, 93n1488
Rodale's all-new ency of organic gardening, 93n1489, 94n1619

ORGANIZATION
Administrative sci quarterly cum index 1956-85, 90n265
Organizational & interorganizational dynamics, 94n864

ORGANIZATIONAL EFFECTIVENESS
Organization charts, 93n212

ORGANIZATIONS. *See* ASSOCIATIONS, INSTITUTIONS, ETC.

ORGANOMETALLIC COMPOUNDS
Dictionary of organometallic compounds, 4th suppl, 90n1754
Dictionary of organometallic compounds, 5th suppl, 91n1767
Dictionary of organometallic compounds, 5th suppl., cum structure index, 91n1768

ORIENTAL LANGUAGES
LC romanization tables & cataloging policies, 92n586

ORKNEY (SCOTLAND) IN LITERATURE
Contribution to lit of Orcadian writer George Mackay Brown, 93n1206

ORNAMENTAL GRASSES
Ornamental grasses, 90n1503
Ornamental grasses & grasslike plants, 91n1532

ORNAMENTAL SHRUBS
Ornamental shrubs, climbers & bamboos, 94n1632
Trees & shrubs for Pacific Northwest gardens, 2d ed, 91n1543

ORNAMENTAL TREES
Trees & shrubs for Pacific Northwest gardens, 2d ed, 91n1543
Trees for American gardens, 92n1508

ORNITHOLOGY. *See* BIRDS

ORTHODONTICS
Bilingual dict of dental terms: Spanish-English, 91n1683

ORTHOPEDIA
Orthopedic & trauma surgery, 90n1665
Selected refs in orthopaedic trauma, 91n1699

OSLER, WILLIAM
Sir William Osler: an annot bibliog with illustrations, 90n1636

OSTEITIS DEFORMANS
Paget's disease, 91n1700

OSTEOPATHY
Barron's gd to medical & dental schools, 4th ed, 90n1656

OSTRAKA
Ostraka, 92n503

O'SULLIVAN, MAUREEN
Maureen O'Sullivan: a bio-bibliog, 91n1349

OTHELLO
Othello: an annot bibliog, 91n1214
Shakespeare's Othello, 90n1185

OTOLARYNGOLOGY
Eye, ear, nose & throat surgery, 90n1664

OUTDOOR EDUCATION
Wilderness U: opportunities for outdoor educ in the US & abroad, 93n335

OUTDOOR RECREATION
Adventure vacations, 92n433
Adventuring in B.C., 93n503
Alaska wilderness milepost 1989, 90n439
Big bk of adventure travel, 91n455
Colorado gd, 90n441

OUTER SPACE
Children's space atlas, 93n1703
Magill's survey of sci, 90n1582
Space almanac, 90n1581
Space atlas, 93n1700
Space exploration, 94n1756
Space words, 93n1706

OUTLAWS
Encyclopedia of W lawmen & outlaws, 93n609

OUTLET STORES
Fabulous finds, 92n178
Factory outlet gd to the Mid-Atlantic states, 2d ed, 91n201
Factory outlet gd to the South, 91n200

OUT-OF-PRINT BOOKS
Bookman's gd to Americana, 10th ed, 92n459
Bookman's price index, v.38, 91n981
Books in print 1989-90, 90n12
Books in print 1990-91, 91n9
Books out-of-print 1984-88, 90n15

OWLS
Owls of the N hemisphere, 90n1545

OXFORD ENGLISH DICTIONARY
Early modern English lexicography, v.2, 91n1046
Guide to the Oxford English Dict, 94n1097

OXFORD HISTORY OF ENGLAND
Oxford hist of England: consolidated index, 92n485

OXFORD MOVEMENT
Oxford movement & its leaders, suppl, 94n1522

OZONE LAYER
Ozone layer dict, 94n1945

PACIFIC AREA
Canadian bus in the Pacific Rim, 94n251
Central Pacific campaign, 1943-44, 91n677
Cracking the Pacific Rim, 94n243
Flowers of the Pacific Island seashore, 94n1647
Foreign trade stats of Asia & the Pacific 1983-87, 91n268
Pacific Rim almanac, 92n137
Political & economic ency of the Pacific, 91n126
Political parties of Asia & the Pacific, 94n765
Security, arms control, & conflict reduction in E Asia & the Pacific, 94n683
Statistical yrbk for Asia & the Pacific 1991, 94n939
War against Japan, 1941-45, 91n486
Who's who in Pacific navigation, 93n487
Who's who of the Asian Pacific Rim, 1992 ed, 93n168
World investment dir 1992, v.1, 94n227

PACIFIC COAST (NORTH AMERICA)
Pacific coast nudibranchs, 93n1573

PACIFIC NORTHWEST. *See* **NORTHWEST, PACIFIC**

PACIFIC REGION. *See* **PACIFIC AREA**

PACIFISTS
American peace writers, editors, & pers, 92n752

PACKAGING
Packaging, 90n1426
Packaging engineering resources, 91n1627

PACS. *See* **POLITICAL ACTION COMMITTEES**

PAGANISM
Magic, witchcraft, & paganism in America, 2d ed, 93n811

PAIN
Directory of pain treatment centers in the US & Canada, 90n1686

PAINE, THOMAS
Concordance to Thomas Paine's Common Sense & The American Crisis, 90n712

PAINT MATERIALS
Handbook of paint raw materials, 2d ed, 90n1760

PAINTERS
Painting of the golden age, 94n1063
20th century painters & sculptors, 92n970

PAINTERS' MATERIAL. *See* **ARTISTS' MATERIAL**

PAINTING
Handbook of modern British painting 1900-80, 93n1044
Iconographic index to N.T. subjects represented in photographs & slides of paintings in the visual collections, Fine Arts Lib, Harvard Univ, v.1, 94n1540
Index of paintings sold in the British Isles during the 19th century, v.2, 91n1037
Looking at paintings, 94n1061
Painting of the golden age, 94n1063
Themes in American painting, 94n1064
World's master paintings from the early Renaissance to the present day, 93n1045

PAKISTAN
Birds of Pakistan, v.1, 92n1568
Cambridge ency of India, Pakistan, Bangladesh, Sri Lanka, Nepal, Bhutan & the Maldives, 91n99
South Asian hndbk, 1992, 93n502

PALAUAN LANGUAGE—DICTIONARIES—ENGLISH
New Palauan-English dict, 92n1084

PALEONTOLOGY
Dinosaur & other prehistoric animal factfinder, 94n1959
Illustrated ency of fossils, 92n1746
Macmillan children's gd to dinosaurs & other prehistoric animals, 93n1732
Rand McNally picture atlas of prehistoric life, 94n1962
Rocks, minerals & fossils of the world, 91n1789
Santana fossils, 92n1745

PALESTINE
Guide to the archaeological sites of Israel, Egypt, & N Africa, 91n478
New ency of archaeological excavations in the Holy Land, 94n489
Palestine question, 92n726

PALMISTRY
Palmist's companion, 93n809

PAN-AFRICANISM
Pan-Africanism: an annot bibliog, 94n764

PANAMA
Latin American serial pubs available by exchange, 93n633
Mammals of the neotropics, 90n1555
Mammals of the neotropics: the S cone, v.2, 93n1570

PAPAL DOCUMENTS
Papal encyclicals, 1740-1981, 92n1419
Papal pronouncements, 92n1409

PAPER INDUSTRY
Projected pulp & paper mills in the world 1990-2000, 92n1502
Pulp & paper industry in the OECD member countries 1990, 94n237

PAPER MONEY
Standard cat of US paper money, 9th ed, 91n984

PAPERBACKS
Recommended ref bks in paperback, 2d ed, 93n15
Supernatural fiction for teens, 2d ed, 93n1156

PAPP, JOSEPH
Joseph Papp: a bio-bibliog, 93n1378

PAPUA NEW GUINEA
Papua New Guinea, 90n150

PARAGUAY
Historical dict of Paraguay, 2d ed, 94n147

PARAPSYCHOLOGY. *See* **PSYCHICAL RESEARCH**

PARENT & CHILD
Sexuality educ, 90n813

PARENTING
Parent's desk ref, 92n842
What's new for parents, 94n920

PARENTS OF HANDICAPPED CHILDREN
Parent resource dir, 2d ed, 90n832

PARIS (FRANCE)
Americans in Paris, 1900-30, 90n472

PARKER, DOROTHY
Dorothy Parker: a bio-bibliog, 94n1236

PARKER, ELEANOR
Eleanor Parker: woman of a 1,000 faces, 91n1357

PARKS
Easy access to natl parks, 93n499
Parks dir of the US, 93n500
State parks of Utah, 90n452

PARLIAMENTARY PRACTICE
Scott, Foresman Robert's rules of order, 1990 ed, 92n679

PARROTS
Atlas of conures, 94n1690

Atlas of parrots of the world, 92n1560
Complete bk of parrots, 90n1539

PARSIFAL (LEGENDARY CHARACTER). *See* **PERCEVAL (LEGENDARY CHARACTER)**
Parsifal on record, 93n1270

PARTNERSHIP
Partnership almanac, 90n191

PARTRIDGE, ROI
Graphic art of Roi Partridge, 90n982

PARZIVAL (LEGENDARY CHARACTER). *See* **PERCEVAL (LEGENDARY CHARACTER)**

PASSION NARRATIVES (GOSPELS)
One hundred yrs of study on the Passion Narratives, 91n1422

PASTORAL COUNSELING
Dictionary of pastoral care & counseling, 91n1443

PASTORAL THEOLOGY
Dictionary of pastoral care & counseling, 91n1443

PATENT LAWS & LEGISLATION
Patent, trademark, & copyright laws, 94n576

PATENTS
Information sources in patents, 93n587
Inventing & patenting sourcebk, 92n149
Patent trademark & copyright laws, 1989 ed, 90n559
Piano-beds & music by steam, 94n1318
Radio & TV pioneers: a patent bibliog, 93n983

PATHOLOGICAL LABORATORIES
Laboratory test hndbk, 2d ed, 91n1678

PATHOLOGISTS
Commentary on the medical writings of Rudolf Virchow, 92n1650

PATHOLOGY
Directory of pathology training programs in the US & Canada, 22d ed, 90n1657
Directory of pathology training programs in the US & Canada 1993-94, 93n1643

PATIENT EDUCATION
Medical tests & diagnostic procedures, 91n1682

PAUL THE APOSTLE, SAINT
Index to per lit on the apostle Paul, 94n1550

PEACE
American peace movement, 93n791
Canadian peace dir, 90n717
Democracy's dawn, 92n750
From Erasmus to Tolstoy, 91n774
Guide to the John D. Crummey peace collection in the Hoover Inst, 93n790
Guides to LC subject headings & classification on peace & intl conflict resolution, 92n581
International affairs dir of orgs, 94n799
Literature for young people on war & peace, 90n1081
Peace: abstracts of the psychological & behavioral lit 1967-90, 93n789
Peacekeeping, 91n775
Search for security: the ACCESS gd to fndns, 91n772
Soviet propaganda network, 90n728
Third World struggle for peace with justice, 92n749
Unesco yrbk on peace & conflict studies 1988, 92n753
War & peace lit for children & young adults, 94n1185
War & peace through women's eyes, 93n1169
World dir of peace research & training insts, 7th ed, 93n792

PEACE CORPS (UNITED STATES)
Peace Corps, 90n731
Who's who in the Peace Corps, 94n798

PEACE MOVEMENTS
American peace writers, editors, & pers, 92n752
Amnesty Intl: the 1993 report on human rights around the world, 94n591
Peace movement orgs & activists in the US, 92n751

Who's who in the Peace Corps, 1993 ed, 94n798

PEACE OFFICERS
Encyclopedia of W lawmen & outlaws, 93n609

PEACE PALACE (HAGUE, NETHERLANDS)
From Erasmus to Tolstoy, 91n774

PEARL HARBOR (HAWAII), ATTACK ON, 1941
Investigations of the attack on Pearl Harbor, 91n510
Pearl Harbor, 1941, 93n696

PEAT MOSSES
Field gd to the peat mosses of boreal N America, 91n1539

PEDIATRIC PHARMACOLOGY
Handbook of pediatric drug therapy, 91n1713
Pediatric drug hndbk, 2d ed, 90n1698

PEER REVIEW
Publication peer review, 94n997

PELICANS
Cormorants, darters, & pelicans of the world, 94n1698

PENNSYLVANIA
Atlas of Pa., 91n430
Pennsylvania land records, 92n390
Pennsylvania potters 1660-1900, 94n1033
Pennsylvania silversmiths, goldsmiths & pewterers 1684-1900, 94n1034
Pennsylvania workers in brass, copper & tin 1681-1900, 94n1035
Used bk lover's gd to the mid-Atlantic states, 94n1028

PENNSYLVANIA ACADEMY OF THE FINE ARTS
Annual exhibition record of the Pa. Academy of the Fine Arts, v.2, 91n1008
Annual exhibition record of the Pa. Academy of the Fine Arts, v.3, 91n1009

PENSION TRUSTS
Nelson's dir of plan sponsors & tax-exempt funds 1991, 92n164
Nelson's gd to pension fund consultants 1991, 92n229
Pension funds, 91n245

PENSIONS
Index to US invalid pension records 1801-15, 93n459
Pensions vocabulary, 92n214

PENSIONS, MILITARY
Pension lists of 1792-95, 93n457
Veterans benefits manual, 93n708

PENTECOSTALISM
American evangelicalism, 92n1408
Dictionary of Pentecostal & charismatic movements, 90n1407
Holy spirit, 90n1390

PERCEVAL (LEGENDARY CHARACTER)
Complete concordance to Wolfram Von Eschenbach's Parzival, 91n1234
Parsifal on record, 93n1270

PERCUSSION MUSIC
Percussion discography, 91n1286

PERENNIALS
Encyclopedia of perennials, 93n1508
Handbook of plant cell culture, v.6, 91n1518
Hardy herbaceous perennials, 3d ed, 92n1538
Perennial garden plants, 3d ed, 92n1507
Rodale's illus ency of perennials, 94n1620

PERFORMANCE ART
Action art, 94n1039

PERFORMING ARTS. *See also* **BALLET; DANCING; MOTION PICTURES; THEATER**
Back Stage hndbk for performing artists, 90n1364
Best festivals of N America, 3d ed, 91n1344
Biographical dict of actors, actresses, musicians, dancers, managers & other stage personnel in London, 1660-1800, v.13, 92n1378

Biographical dict of actors, actresses, musicians, dancers, managers & other stage personnel in London, 1660-1800, v.14, 92n1379
Communication serials, 1992/1993 ed, 93n982
Drama dict, 90n1357
Handel's natl dir for the performing arts, 5th ed, 94n1420
Money for performing artists, 93n1326
Nostalgia entertainment sourcebk, 92n1334
Popular entertainment research, 93n1327
Reference gd for English studies, 92n872
Stage deaths, 92n1376
Variety's dir of major US show bus awards, 90n1312
Variety's who's who in show bus, rev ed, 90n1313

PERFUMES
Perfume hndbk, 94n1940

PERGOLESI, GIOVANNI BATTISTA
Giovanni Battista Pergolesi: a gd to research, 90n1251

PERIODICALS
Australian pers in print 1989, 90n25
Australian pers in print 1991, 93n81
Bacon's media calendar dir 1993, 94n1003
Bacon's newspaper/mag dir 1993, 94n1004
Bacon's publicity checker 1991, 92n899
BiblioData fulltext sources online, 90n1725
Bodian's publishing desk ref, 90n644
Books & pers online, 94n44
Canadian media list 1992/93, 93n952
Canadian per index, v.43, 92n56
CD-ROM per index, 93n82
Consumer mags of the British Isles, 94n267
Cover story index 1960-89, 91n964
Cover story index 1960-91, 94n1006
Cover story index: 1992 suppl, 94n1007
Directory of electronic jls, newsletters & academic discussion lists, 2d ed, 93n72
Directory of humor mags & humor orgs in America (& Canada), 2d ed, 90n907
Directory of humor mags & humor orgs in America (& Canada), 3d ed, 93n1188
Directory of pers online: news, law & bus, 5th ed, 91n73
Directory of pers online: sci & tech, 2d ed, 92n1459
Directory of small pr & mag eds & publs, 22d ed, 92n635
EBSCO's 1989-90 librarians' hndbk, 90n76
Gale intl dir of pubs, 1989-90, 90n77
Gebbie Pr all-in-one dir 1989, 90n636
Index & abstract dir, 90n71
Index of American per verse: 1990, 93n1187
Index to Commonwealth little mags 1987-89, 93n83
Index to legal pers: Sept 1990-Aug 1991, 93n600
Index to plays in pers, 1977-87, 91n1126
International dir of little mags & small prs, 27th ed, 92n636
Journal of Women's Hist gd to per lit, 93n943
Labor & industrial relations journals & serials, 90n264
Magazines for libs, 6th ed, 90n78
Magazines for libs, 7th ed, 93n85
Maps in British pers, pt.1, 91n449
Mathematical jls, 93n1741
MLA dir of pers 1993-95, 94n987
National dir of mags 1990, 91n62
National dir of mags 1994, 94n62
New per title abbrevs, 93n86
Readers' gd abstracts, v.1, no.4, 90n74
Readers' gd to per lit 1990, 92n60
Serials dir, 4th ed, 91n64
Serials dir, 7th ed, 94n63
Serials dir: EBSCO CD-ROM, summer 1993, 94n64
Standard per dir 1990, 91n65
Standard per dir 1993, 94n67
Ulrich's intl pers dir 1989-90, 90n80
Ulrich's intl pers dir 1990-91, 91n66
Ulrich's intl pers dir 1991-92, 92n65
Ulrich's intl pers dir 1992-93, 93n88
Ulrich's intl pers dir 1993-94, 94n65
Ulrich's plus [CD-ROM], 94n66

World list of social sci pers 1991, 93n101

PERSIAN GULF REGION
Major pol events in Iran, Iraq & the Arabian peninsula 1945-90, 92n725

PERSIAN GULF WAR, 1991
BBC World Service Gulf Crisis chronology, 93n542
U.S. aircraft & armament of Operation Desert Storm in detail & scale, 94n699

PERSIAN LANGUAGE—DICTIONARIES—ENGLISH
Persian & English glossary for humanities & social scis, 93n1090
Persian-English dict, 94n1126

PERSONAL COMPUTERS. *See* MICROCOMPUTERS

PERSONAL NAMES. *See* NAMES, PERSONAL

PERSONALITY ASSESSMENT
Handbook of psychological assessment, 2d ed, 92n759

PERSONNEL MANAGEMENT
Economist Pubs pocket employer, 90n254
Human resources glossary, 93n302
Manager's desk ref, 90n266
Personnel executives contactbk, 94n286

PESTICIDAL PLANTS
Handbook of plants with pest-control properties, 90n1485

PESTICIDES
Ball pest & disease manual, 94n1624
Basic gd to pesticides, 94n2009
Handbook of environmental fate & exposure data for organic chemicals, v.3, 92n1784
Handbook of pesticide toxicology, 92n1783
Pesticide residues in food 1990, 92n1498
Pesticide residues in food 1992, evaluations pt.1, 94n1611
Pesticide users' health & safety hndbk, 90n1451
Pestline, 92n1785

PESTS
Glossary of terms used in pest control, 91n1474
Pest control Canada, 6th ed, 91n1479

PETAWAWA NATIONAL FORESTRY INSTITUTE
Bibliography, 1988-90, 93n1482

PETROLEUM
Petroleum fundamentals glossary, 92n1755
Petroleum sftwr dir, 1990, 6th ed, 90n1785

PETROLEUM CHEMICALS INDUSTRY
Major chemical & petrochemical cos of Europe 1990/91, 92n204

PETROLEUM ENGINEERING
Dictionary of petroleum exploration, drilling, & production, 92n1626

PETROLEUM INDUSTRY & TRADE
Asia-Pacific/Africa-Middle East petroleum dir, 1993, 94n1971
Canadia oil industry dir, 1991, 92n1756
Dictionary for the petroleum industry, 93n1743
Dictionary of petroleum exploration, drilling, & production, 92n1626
European petroleum dir, 1993, 94n1972
Financial Times oil & gas intl yrbk 1989, 90n1787
Financial Times who's who in world oil & gas 1993, 94n1970
International petroleum ency, 90n1783, 93n1744
Landman's ency, 3d ed, 90n1782
Natural gas industry dir, 1993, 94n1973
Oil & gas dict, 90n1784
Oil & Gas Jl exploration index, 93n1750
Petroleum sftwr dir, 1994, 94n1974
U.S.A Gulf Coast oil & gas industry dir, 1992, 93n1745
U.S.A. oil industry dir, 1993, 94n1975
U.S.A. oil industry's environmental dir, 1993, 93n1762
U.S.A. oilfield serv, supply & manufacturers dir, 1993, 94n1976
Worldwide petrochemical dir, 1990, 92n1759
Worldwide petroleum phone/fax/telex dir, 1991, 92n1760

PETRY, ANN
Ann Petry: a bio-bibliog, 94n1237

PETS
Best pet name bk ever, 91n1575

PHARMACEUTICAL TECHNOLOGY
Encyclopedia of pharmaceutical tech, v.2, 91n1710
Encyclopedia of pharmaceutical tech, v.3, 91n1711
Encyclopedia of pharmaceutical tech, v.4, 94n1867
Encyclopedia of pharmaceutical tech, v.5, 94n1868
Encyclopedia of pharmaceutical tech, v.6, 94n1869
Encyclopedia of pharmaceutical tech, v.7, 94n1870
IPA thesaurus & frequency list, 6th ed, 94n1873

PHARMACOLOGY. *See also* **DRUGS**
Dictionary of protopharmacology, 92n1689
Information sources in pharmaceuticals, 92n1696
Pharmaceutical manufacturing ency, 2d ed, 90n1697
Pharmacology from A to Z, 90n1696

PHARMACY
Information sources in pharmaceuticals, 92n1696
Keyguide to info sources in pharmacy, 90n1703

PHILANTHROPISTS
Major donors 1993, 94n893

PHILANTHROPY. *See* **CHARITIES; ENDOWMENTS**

PHILIPPINE LITERATURE
Dutch Filipiniana, 93n169

PHILIPPINES
Dictionary of social work: Philippine setting, 90n816
Dutch Filipiniana, 93n169

PHILO OF ALEXANDRIA
Philo of Alexandria: an annot bibliog 1937-86, 90n1374

PHILOLOGY
Guide to professional orgs for teachers of lang & lit in the US & Canada, 2d ed, 91n1047

PHILOSOPHERS
Bradley: a research bibliog, 92n1390
Descartes dict, 94n1493
Directory of American philosophers 1990-91, 91n1406
Directory of American philosophers 1992-93, 94n1498
Ernst Cassirer, 90n1371
International dir of philosophy & philosophers 1990-92, 91n1407
Jean Paul Sartre: a bibliog, 94n1489
Jurgen Habermas (II): a bibliog, 92n1392
Leo Spitzer on lang & lit, 93n1046
Presocratic philosophers, 94n1488
Pythagoras: an annot bibliog, 91n1401
Simone de Beauvoir, 90n1370
Simone de Beauvoir: a bibliog, 93n930
Soren Kierkegaard bibliogs, 94n1486
Spinoza in English, 93n1394
Vives bibliog, 91n1404

PHILOSOPHY
Bibliography of eds, translations, & commentary on Xenophon's Socratic writings, 90n1373
Bibliography of philosophy in Canada, 90n1372
Blackwell dict of 20th-century social thought, 94n73
Concise dict of Indian philosophy, 90n1375
Dictionary of philosophical quotations, 94n1499
Dictionary of religion & philosophy, 91n1414
Glossary of cognitive sci, 94n1494
Great thinkers of the W world, 93n950
HarperCollins dict of philosophy, 2d ed, 94n1496
International dir of philosophy & philosophers 1990-92, 91n1407
Key ideas in human thought, 94n1497
Philosopher's dict, 92n1395
Philosopher's index thesaurus, 93n1397
Philosopher's index, v.23, 1989 cum ed, 91n1408
Philosophy bks 1982-86, 92n1391
Resources in ancient philosophy, 93n1393
Talking philosophy, 92n1396

Walford's gd to ref material, 5th ed, v.2: social & histl scis, 93n98
Women philosophers, 90n868
Women philosophers, 93n1392
World philosophy, 94n1482

PHILOSOPHY & RELIGION
Medieval Consolation of Philosophy: an annot bibliog, 94n1487

PHILOSOPHY IN LITERATURE
Writers & philosophers, 92n1109

PHOBIAS
Encyclopedia of phobias, fears, & anxieties, 90n744

PHONETICS
Phonetics & speech sci, 90n992

PHONOTAPES
Words on tape 1989, 90n921

PHOTOGRAPHERS
American photographers, 90n942
Bibliography of writings by & about women in photography 1850-1950, 92n959
Dictionary of Australian artists, 94n1041
Guide to literary agents & art/photo reps, 1992, 93n961
Photographers: a sourcebk for histl research, 93n1014
Shadowcatchers: a dir of women in Calif. photography before 1901, 92n960

PHOTOGRAPHY
Arkansas made, v.2, 92n920
Canadian photo market, 92n962
Checklist of Canadian copyright deposits in the British Museum 1895-1923, v.5, 90n42
Creative black bk 1989, 90n940
Films & videos on photography, 91n999
Focal ency of photography, 3d ed, 94n1036
Guide to the photographic identification of individual whales based on their natural & acquired markings, 91n1595
History of photography, 90n943
Illustrated bio-bibliog of black photographers 1940-88, 90n944
Location photographer's handbk, 91n1000
Looking at photographs, 92n957
McBroom's camera bluebk, 1994 ed, 94n1037
Photographer's market, 1991, 91n1001
Photography & lit, 93n1013
Prentice-Hall pocket ency [of] creative photography, 92n961

PHRENOLOGY
Phrenology in the British Isles, 90n754

PHYLLOXERIDAE
Genera of the aphids of Canada, 94n1723

PHYSICAL ANTHROPOLOGY
Dictionary of concepts in physical anthropology, 93n415

PHYSICAL EDUCATION & TRAINING
Acrosport, 94n817
Educators gd to free health, physical educ & recreation materials, 26th ed, 94n829
Physical educ index, v.12, 1989, 91n814
Physical educ index, v.13, no.3, 91n815

PHYSICAL FITNESS
Dieter's dict & problem solver, 94n1603
Focus on fitness, 94n843
Kirby's gd to fitness & motor performance tests, 92n793
Leisure lit, 94n820
Marshall Cavendish ency of health, 92n1633
Physical fitness & sports medicine, 90n1688

PHYSICAL GEOGRAPHY
Atlas of the natural world, 92n1557

PHYSICAL SCIENCES
Encyclopedia of physical sci & tech, 2d ed, 94n1566
Magill's survey of sci: physical sci series, 93n1699

PHYSICALLY HANDICAPPED
Directory of disability support servs in community colleges 1992, 94n371

Encyclopedia of mental & physical handicaps, 92n322
First whole rehab cat, 91n853
Focus on physical impairments, 92n820
Handbook of developmental & physical disabilities, 90n1629
Illustrated dir of handicapped products 1991-92, 93n863
Resources for elders with disabilities, 91n858

PHYSICIAN & PATIENT
Physician-patient relationships, 92n1648

PHYSICIANS
Best doctors in America 1992-93, 93n1644
Biographical dict of medicine, 92n1651
Medical dir 1989, 90n1660
Nobel laureates in medicine or physiology, 91n1655
Physicians' obituaries, 1989, 91n1656

PHYSICISTS
Nobel prize winners: physics, 90n1773

PHYSICS
Encyclopedia of applied physics, v.1, 92n1750
Encyclopedia of applied physics, v.2, 93n1733
Encyclopedia of applied physics, v.3, 93n1734
Encyclopedia of modern physics, 92n1749
Encyclopedia of physics, 2d ed, 92n1747
McGraw-Hill ency of physics, 2d ed, 94n1965
Quantification in sci, 92n1748
Superconductivity sourcebk, 91n1800

PHYSICS, ASTRONOMICAL. *See* **ASTROPHYSICS**

PHYSIOLOGISTS
British physiologists 1885-1914, 92n1653
Nobel laureates in medicine or physiology, 91n1655

PHYSIOLOGY
Human anatomy & physiology, 5th ed, 91n1677
Molecules, cells, & life, 91n1514

PHYTOGEOGRAPHY
Atlas florae Europaeae, 90n1494
Plant life, 92n1534
Vascular plants of Minn., 92n1533

PIANISTS
Art of the piano, 91n1287
Glenn Gould cat, 93n1253
William Mason (1829-1908): an annot bibliog & cat of works, 90n1243

PIANO
Piano info gd, 90n1262

PIANO MUSIC
Descriptive cat of the Glenn Gould papers, 93n1254
Isaac Albeniz: chronological list & thematic cat of his piano works, 94n1320
Music for 3 or more pianists, 94n1337
Pianist's gd to transcriptions, arrangements, & paraphrases, 91n1288
Piano music by black women, 93n1264
Source gd to the music of Percy Grainger, 93n1261

PICKWICK PAPERS
Pickwick Papers: an annot bibliog, 91n1203

PICTURE DICTIONARIES
Canadian picture dict, 92n1044
Facts on File jr visual dict, 90n1018
Macmillan visual dict, 93n1077
My 1st dict, 94n1092
Oxford-Duden pictorial Chinese & English dict, 90n1039
Oxford-Duden pictorial Portuguese-English dict, 94n1127
Renyi picture dict: Hebrew & English, 94n1116
Renyi picture dict: Russian & English, 94n1131
Running Pr cyclopedia, 94n40
Stoddart colour visual dict: French-English, 94n1114
Visual dict of animals, 93n1534
Visual dict of cars, 93n1787
Visual dict of dinosaurs, 94n1963
Visual dict of everyday things, 93n1078

Visual dict of flight, 94n2020
Visual dict of military uniforms, 93n703
Visual dict of plants, 93n1502
Visual dict of ships & sailing, 93n1792
Visual dict of the human body, 93n1492

PICTURE DICTIONARIES, CHINESE
Facts on File English/Chinese visual dict, 90n1037
Oxford-Duden pictorial Chinese & English dict, 90n1039
What's what, rev ed, 91n1081

PICTURE DICTIONARIES, FRENCH
Stoddart colour visual dict: French-English, 94n1114

PICTURE DICTIONARIES, SPANISH
Facts on File English/Spanish visual dict, 93n1101

PICTURE TRANSMISSION. *See* **IMAGE TRANSMISSION**

PICTURE-BOOKS FOR CHILDREN
A to zoo, 3d ed, 90n1082
A to zoo, 4th ed, 94n1176
Palette of possibilities, 94n1167
Picture bks for children, 3d ed, 91n1109
Using picture storybks to teach literary devices, 91n1113
Wordless/almost wordless picture bks, 93n1131

PICTURES
Illustration index 7, 94n1050

PICTURE-WRITING
Dictionary of symbols, 93n1041

PIERS THE PLOWMAN
Piers Plowman: a gd to the quotations, 94n1253

PILGRIM HYMNAL
Concordance of The Pilgrim Hymnal, 90n1265

PINES
Pines of Mexico & Central America, 93n1519

PIPE-FITTING
Plumbers & pipe fitters lib, 4th ed, 91n1636

PISTOLS
Combat pistols, 91n986
Pistol bk, 2d ed, 90n925

PIT BULL TERRIERS
Pit bull dilemma, 91n558

PITT, WILLIAM
William Pitt the Younger 1759-1806: a bibliog, 90n508

PLACE-NAMES. *See* **NAMES, GEOGRAPHICAL**

PLANETS
Field gd to the stars & planets, 3d ed, 94n1928
Oxford illus ency of the universe, 94n1944
Star & planet spotting, 91n1756

PLANNED COMMUNITIES
99 best residential & recreational communities in America for vacation, retirement & investment planning, 93n919

PLANNED PARENTHOOD. *See* **BIRTH CONTROL**

PLANT CELL CULTURE
Handbook of plant cell culture, v.5, 91n1517
Handbook of plant cell culture, v.6, 91n1518

PLANT CLOSINGS. *See* **PLANT SHUTDOWNS**

PLANT COMMUNITIES
Nature's heartland: native plant communities of the Great Plains, 92n1530

PLANT DISEASES
Ball field gd to diseases of greenhouse ornamentals, 93n1499
Dictionary of plant pathology, 90n1486
Field crop diseases hndbk, 2d ed, 90n1449
Sugar-cane diseases, 90n1448
Westcott's plant disease hndbk, 5th ed, 91n1520

PLANT DISTRIBUTION. *See* **PHOTOGEOGRAPHY**

PLANT ECOLOGY. *See* **BOTANY—ECOLOGY**

PLANT ENGINEERING
Plant engineer's ref bk, 93n1608

PLANT NAMES, POPULAR
Plant names of medieval England, 91n1521

PLANT SHUTDOWNS
Plant closings, 93n300

PLANT TISSUE CULTURE
Glossary of plant tissue culture, 90n1483
Plant tissue culture, 92n1529

PLANT VIRUSES
Dictionary of plant virology, 93n1495

PLANTAGENET, HOUSE OF
Plantagenet ency, 91n525

PLANTS. *See also names of individual plants*
Atlas florae Europaeae, 90n1494
Australian plants identified, 92n1528
Colorado flora: E slope, 91n1524
Cornucopia, 92n1549
Crop protection chemicals ref, 1991, 92n1470
Cultivated plants of the tropics & subtropics, 93n1469
Discovering wild plants, 91n1523
Encyclopedia of flora & fauna in English & American lit, 94n1151
Flora of Austral., v.3, 91n1519
Gardener's Latin, 94n1640
Green plants, 93n1498
Handbook of Rocky Mountain plants, 93n1501
Jepson manual, 94n1644
Manual of vascular plants of NE US and adjacent Canada, 2d ed, 93n1500
Plant life, 92n1534
Stearn's dict of plant names for gardeners, 94n1642
Succulents, 91n1541
Visual dict of plants, 93n1502

PLANTS, ORNAMENTAL
American Horticultural Society ency of garden plants, 90n1467
Atlas florae Europaeae, 90n1494
Ball field gd to diseases of greenhouse ornamentals, 93n1499
Ball pest & disease manual, 94n1624
Bernard E. Harkness seedlist hndbk, 2d ed, 94n1625
Blooms of Bressingham garden plants, 94n1626
Colorado flora: E slope, 91n1524
Cycads of the world, 94n1671
European garden flora, v.3, 90n1489
500 best garden plants, 94n1622
Flora of Austral., v.3, 91n1519
Handbook of plant cell culture, v.5, 91n1517
National Arboretum bk of outstanding garden plants, 91n1503
New gardener's hndbk & dict, 93n1486
Ornamental grasses & grasslike plants, 91n1532
Tropicals, 90n1482

PLASTICS
Engineered materials hndbk, v.2, 90n1600
Flammability hndbk for plastics, 4th ed, 91n1775
Handbook of plastic compounds, elastomers, & resins, 93n1710
Handbook of plastic materials & tech, 91n1611
Handbook of plastics, elastomers, & composites, 2d ed, 93n1714
Plastics additives & modifiers hndbk, 93n1711
Plastics technical dict, 94n1938
Rosato's plastics ency & dict, 94n1771
Specifications & standards for plastics & composites, 91n1633

PLATH, SYLVIA
Sylvia Plath: a ref gd 1973-88, 91n1170

PLAYER-PIANO ROLLS
Classical reproducing piano roll, 91n1289

PLEYEL, IGNAZ
Pleyel as music publisher, 91n1251

PLUMBING
Plumbers & pipe fitters lib, 4th ed, 91n1636
Plumbers hndbk, 8th ed, 92n1599
Well-appointed bath, 90n971

PLURALISM (SOCIAL SCIENCES)
Bookpeople: a multicultural album, 93n1142
Guide to multicultural resources 1993/94, 94n400
Venture into cultures, 94n1170
Videos for understanding diversity, 94n399

POE, EDGAR ALLAN
Concordance to the poetry of Edgar Allan Poe, 90n1152
Images of Poe's works, 91n1171

POETICS
Dictionary of literary devices: gradus, A-Z, 92n1102
Longman dict of poetic terms, 90n1118
New Princeton ency of poetry & poetics, 94n1302

POETRY
American poetry index, v.4, 90n1159
Clayton Eshleman, 90n1139
Columbia Granger's gd to poetry anthologies, 92n1243
Columbia Granger's index to poetry, 9th ed, 91n1250
Concrete poetry, 90n1120
Directory of poetry publishers 1990-91, 91n663
Directory of poetry publishers, 8th ed, 94n664
Index of American per verse, 1989, 92n1186
Jerome Rothenberg: a descriptive bibliog, 90n1153
Last lines, 92n1246
Master index to poetry, 90n1119
Masterplots 2: poetry series, 93n1237
New Princeton ency of poetry & poetics, 94n1302
Poetry criticism, v.1, 92n1247
Poetry criticism, v.5, 94n1303
Poetry index annual 1990, 93n1238
Poet's market 1990, 90n903
Roth's American poetry annual 1988, 90n1163
Verseform: a comparative bibliog, 90n1117

POETS
Concordance to the complete poems of E. E. Cummings, 90n1135
Contemporary poets, 5th ed, 92n1244
Faulkner's poetry, 90n1141
Who's who in writers, eds & poets, 1992-93, 93n974

POETS, AMERICAN
American poets since WW II, 3d series, 93n1186
Contemporary sci fiction, fantasy, & horror poetry. 90n1109
Critical survey of poetry: English lang series, rev ed, 93n1236
Dictionary of literary biog documentary series, v.7, 91n1176
Directory of American poets & fiction writers, 1989-90 ed, 91n946
James Dickey: a descriptive bibliog, 91n1161
Richard Eberhart: a descriptive bibliog 1927-87, 90n1137
Robert Creeley, Edward Dorn, & Robert Duncan, 90n1160

POETS, CANADIAN
A. M. Klein: an annot bibliog, 94n1278
Canadian poets: vital facts, 90n1198
Canadian writers & their works: cum index, poetry series, 94n1272
ECW's biographical gd to Canadian poets, 94n1274
Record of writing: an annot & illus bibliog of George Bowering, 91n1226

POETS, ENGLISH
Annotated critical bibliog of Alfred, Lord Tennyson, 90n1186
British Romantic poets, 1789-1832, 1st series, 92n1219
Concordance to the sermons of Gerard Manley Hopkins, 90n1181
Critical survey of poetry: English lang series, rev ed, 93n1236
Eighteenth-century British poets, 1st series, 91n1224
Essential Milton, 90n1182
John Donne companion, 91n1206
Seventeenth-century British nondramatic poets, 94n1264

POETS, IRISH
Austin Clarke: a ref gd, 94n1293

POETS, SPANISH
Twentieth-century Spanish poets, 1st series, 92n1242

POISONOUS ANIMALS
Venomous animals, 90n1563

POISONOUS PLANTS
Healing forest, 91n1538
Poisonous plants of Canada, 91n1522

POISONOUS SNAKES
Poisonous snakes of the world, 93n1578
Venomous reptiles of Latin America, 90n1564
Venomous reptiles of N America, 93n1576

POISONS
Deadly doses: a writer's gd to poisons, 91n1714

POLAND
Poland, rev ed, 94n134
Poland: a histl atlas, rev ed, 90n521
Polish biographical dict, 93n44
Polish music, 90n1216
Polish roots, 94n433
Revolutionary orgs & revolutionaries in interbellum Poland, 93n779

POLICE
Encyclopedia of police sci, 90n567
Great cop pictures, 92n1363
Police dict & ency, 90n568
Police, firefighter, & paramedic stress, 91n787
Police products hndbk, 91n599

POLICY SCIENTISTS
Nonprofit public policy research orgs, 94n753

POLISH LANGUAGE—DICTIONARIES—ENGLISH
Polish-English, English-Polish dict with complete phonetics, rev ed, 91n1090

POLITICAL ACTION COMMITTEES
Open secrets, 91n750
Open secrets, 2d ed, 93n752

POLITICAL CONSULTANTS
Political resource dir 1993, 94n719

POLITICAL ETHICS
COGEL blue bk, 9th ed, 94n801

POLITICAL LEADERSHIP
Who's who: Chicano officeholders, 1990-91, 92n690

POLITICAL PARTICIPATION
Electoral pols dict, 90n695

POLITICAL PARTIES
Dictionary of pol parties & orgs in Russia, 94n779
Historical atlas of pol parties in the US Congress, 1789-1989, 90n687
Minor presidential candidates & parties of 1992, 93n748
New pol parties of E Europe & the Soviet Union, 93n770
People speak: American elections in focus, 91n748
Political parties & elections in the US, 92n685
Political parties of Asia & the Pacific, 94n765
Political parties of the Americas and the Caribbean, 94n783
Political parties of the Americas, 1980s to 1990s, 94n720

POLITICAL PLANNING
Washington almanac, 93n731

POLITICAL PLAYS
Political left in the American theatre of the 30's, 93n1375

POLITICAL SCIENCE
Chambers dict of pol biog, 93n721
Dictionary of pols, 7th ed, 93n722
Dictionary of 20th-century world pols, 94n718
Directory of pol newsletters 1990, 91n739
Encyclopedia of Soviet life, 92n721
Guide to pol videos, v.1, no.1, 94n713
Handbook of pol sci research on Latin America, 92n722
Macmillan dict of pol quotations, 94n724
Oxford companion to pols of the world, 94n717
Political sci, 91n717
Routledge dict of 20th-century pol thinkers, 94n715
Thematic list of descriptors: pol sci, 90n680

POLITICAL SCIENTISTS
Hannah Arendt, 90n721

POLITICAL STATISTICS
Political data hndbk: OECD countries, 93n727
Statesman's yr-bk 1991-92, 92n77

POLITICAL VIOLENCE. See TERRORISM

POLITICIANS
American natl election studies data sourcebk, 1952-86, 91n751
Biographical dict of French pol leaders since 1870, 91n758
Horace Greeley: a bio-bibliog, 93n979
Political leaders in Black Africa, 93n761
Political leaders in Weimar Germany, 94n774
Who's who in Asian & Australasian pols, 93n762
Who's who in European pols, 92n719
Who's who in S African pols, 3d ed, 92n705

POLITICS & LITERATURE
Political left in the American theatre of the 30's, 93n1375

POLITICS IN MOTION PICTURES
American pol movies, 91n1377

POLITICS, PRACTICAL
Political quotations, 91n724
Wit & wisdom of pol, 90n713

POLLUTANTS
Handbook of environmental fate & exposure data for organic chemicals, v.3, 92n1784

POLLUTION
Atlas of endangered places, 94n1987
Atlas of environmental issues, 90n1788
Atlas of US environmental issues, 92n1765
Complete bk of home environmental hazards, 92n1780
Environmental hazards: toxic waste & hazardous material, 93n1770
Environmental toxins: psychological, behavioral, & sociocultural aspects 1973-89, 91n789
Statistical record of the environment, 93n1764
Use of criminal penalties for pollution of the environment, 91n594

POLYGLOT PERIODICALS
Gale intl dir of pubs, 1989-90, 90n77

POLYMERS & POLYMERIZATION
Chitin sourcebk, 91n1764
Comprehensive polymer sci, 91n1774
Concise ency of polymer processing & applications, 93n1582
Concise ency of polymer sci & engineering, 92n1596
Encyclopedia of polymer sci & engineering, 2d ed, v.16, 91n1769
Encyclopedia of polymer sci & engineering, index volume, 91n1770
Encyclopedia of polymer sci & engineering, 2d ed., suppl.v, 91n1771
Handbook of polymer sci & tech, 90n1757
International dissertations on fibre reinforced polymers, 90n1750
Polymer hndbk, 3d ed, 91n1773
Polymer sci dict, 90n1751

POLYNESIA
Dictionary of Polynesian mythology, 90n1303
Flowers of the Pacific Island seashore, 94n1647
Historical dict of Polynesia, 94n120
Indigenous navigation & voyaging in the Pacific, 93n1789

POOL (GAME)
Billiard industry source bk, 1992/1993 ed, 94n857
Pool player's natl pocket billiard dir, 1992 ed, 94n858
Pool player's road atlas 1994, 94n859

POOR
Feminization of poverty in the US, 91n913
World hunger, 92n830

POPULAR CULTURE
Arts & entertainment fads, 91n1338
Communication serials, 1992/1993 ed, 93n982

Encyclopedia of monsters, 90n1310
Fan club dir, 94n1400
Fandom dir no.13, 92n1328
Handbook of American popular culture, 2d ed, 91n1339

POPULAR LITERATURE
American best sellers, 90n1130
Classic cult fiction, 93n1149
#1 New York Times bestseller, 94n1153

POPULAR MUSIC
Aladdin/Imperial labels, 92n1299
Banjo on record, 94n1336
Basic musical lib, "P" series, 1-1000, 92n1295
Berlin, Kern, Rodgers, Hart, & Hammerstein, 91n1309
Best rated CDs 1992: jazz, popular, etc., 93n1275
Billboard bk of American singing groups, 94n1359
Billboard bk of no.1 hits, rev ed, 90n1292
Billboard bk of no.1 hits, 3d ed, 94n1360
Billboard bk of 1-hit wonders, 91n1324
Billboard bk of top 40 albums, 92n1293
Billboard 1990 music & video yrbk, 92n1294
Billboard top 1000 singles 1955-90, 93n1282
Billboard's hottest hot 100 hits, 93n1276
Blues: a bibliographic gd, 90n1287
British hit albums, 5th ed, 94n1362
Cash Box black contemporary album charts, 1975-87, 90n1277
CD review digest annual 1990: jazz, popular, etc., 92n1308
Contemporary musicians, 90n1221
Encyclopedia of pop, rock & soul, rev ed, 90n1298
Ethnic music on records, v.1, 92n1305
Faber companion to 20th-century popular music, 91n1304
Facts behind the songs, 94n1366
Find that tune, [v.2], 2d ed, 90n1297
Gigging, 91n1303
Golden age of top 40 music (1955-1973) on CD, 94n1361
Great song thesaurus, 2d ed, 90n1279
Guinness ency of popular music, 94n1363
Joel Whitburn presents daily #1 hits 1940-92, 94n1364
Lissauer's ency of popular music in America, 92n1296
Marshall Cavendish illus hist of popular music, 91n1306
Movie song cat, 94n1309
Musi*key, 90n1280
Music address bk, 91n1305
New Trouser Pr record gd, 3d ed, 90n1235
Oxford companion to popular music, 92n1297
Penguin ency of popular music, 91n1307
Popular music, v.13, 90n1281
Popular music, v.15, 93n1279
Popular song index, 3d suppl, 90n1276
Response recordings, 91n1302
Rolling Stone album gd, 94n1367
Songwriter's market, 1991, 91n1261
Spectrum: your gd to today's music, summer 1990, 91n1308
Trouser Pr record gd, 4th ed, 93n1281
Who wrote that song?, 90n1278
World beat: a listener's gd to contemporary world music on CD, 93n1280
World of African music, 94n1315

POPULATION
Century of population growth, 90n834
Guide to sources of intl population assistance 1988, 90n836
Key indicators of county growth 1970-2010, 1990 ed, 91n904
Labour & population programme, 93n299
South American population censuses since independence, 91n907
World population growth & aging, 92n844

POPULATION CONTROL. *See* **BIRTH CONTROL**

PORCELAIN
Sotheby's concise ency of porcelain, 92n933

PORPOISES
Field gd to whales, porpoises, & seals from Cape Cod to Nfld., 4th ed, 94n1737

PORTER, KATHERINE ANNE
Katherine Anne Porter: an annot bibliog, 92n1179

PORTER, PETER
Peter Porter: a bibliog 1954-86, 91n1212

PORTUGAL
Dictionary of the lit of the Iberian Peninsula, 94n1289
Historical dict of Portugal, 94n135

PORTUGUESE LANGUAGE—BRAZIL
Random House Portuguese dict, 93n1091

PORTUGUESE LANGUAGE—DICTIONARIES—ENGLISH
Latin American legal abbrevs, 91n557
Oxford-Duden pictorial Portuguese-English dict, 94n1127
Random House Portuguese dict, 93n1091

PORTUGUESE LITERATURE—AFRICAN AUTHORS.
See **AFRICAN LITERATURE (PORTUGUESE)**

POSTAL ADDRESSES. *See* **STREET ADDRESSES**

POSTAL SERVICE
Guide to worldwide postal-code & address formats, 91n941
Guide to worldwide postal-code & address formats, 1993, 94n989

POTATOES
Potato terms, 91n1487

POTTERS
Pennsylvania potters 1660-1900, 94n1033

POTTERY
Ceramics & glass: intl auctions from Jan 1st to Dec 31st, 92n974
Dictionary of American pottery marks, 90n933
Dictionary of British studio potters, 91n993
Encyclopedia of pottery techniques, 92n949
Potter's dict of materials & techniques, 3d ed, 92n950
Robert Lehman collection, 90n952

POULENC, FRANCIS
Francis Poulenc: a bio-bibliog, 91n1278

POVERTY
Poverty in developing countries, 94n905

POWER (MECHANICS)
Dictionary of energy, 2d ed, 90n1776

POWER RESOURCES
Digest of UK energy stats 1988, 90n1780
Energy in the dvlpmt of W Africa, 94n1969
Energy supply A-Z, 92n1754

POWER-PLANTS
Handbook of power, utility & boiler terms & phrases, 6th ed, 94n1797

PRACTICAL APPROACH SERIES
Practical approach series cum methods index, 92n1526

PRACTICE OF LAW
Lincoln as a lawyer, 92n526

PRAYER
Encyclopedia of Jewish prayer, 94n1556

PRECIOUS STONES
Gemology, 94n1958
Gemstones of E Africa, 94n1955
Handbook of rocks, minerals, & gemstones, 94n1957
Larousse ency of precious gems, 93n1725

PREDATION (BIOLOGY)
Predators & predation, 90n1526

PREDATORY ANIMALS
Mammals: the hunters, 90n1521
Predators & predation, 90n1526
Predatory dinosaurs of the world, 90n1769

PREFABRICATED HOUSES
Affordable housing, 90n967

PREFERRED PROVIDER ORGANIZATIONS (MEDICAL CARE)
HMO/PPO dir 1993, 94n1815

PREGNANCY
Drugs, vitamins, minerals in pregnancy, 90n1702
Encyclopedia of childbearing, 94n1831

PREHISTORIC ANIMALS. *See* PALEONTOLOGY

PREJUDICES
Discrimination & prejudice, 93n845

PRENATAL CONDITIONS
Catalog of prenatally diagnosed conditions, 2d ed, 93n1654

PRESBYTERIAN CHURCH
Encyclopedia of the reformed faith, 93n1422
Guide to the ms collections of the Presbyterian church, US, 92n1412
Presbyterians, 94n1533

PRESCHOOL CHILDREN
Mother Goose comes 1st, 92n1121
Play, learn, & grow, 94n1184
Preschool resource gd, 94n312

PRESIDENTIAL CANDIDATES
Minor presidential candidates & parties of 1992, 93n748

PRESIDENTS
Almanac of American presidents from 1789 to the present, 93n519
American leaders 1789-1991, 92n680
American presidents, 7th ed, 91n496
American presidents: an annotated bibliog, 91n481
Biographical dir of the US executive branch, 1774-1989, 91n731
Charles A. Beard's the presidents in American hist, rev. ed, 91n490
Complete bk of US presidents, 2d ed, 91n492
Complete bk of US presidents, 3d ed, 93n514
Congressional Quarterly's gd to the presidency, 91n745
Debrett's presidents of the USA, 90n486
Encyclopedia of mistresses, 94n961
Facts about the presidents, 5th ed, 90n479
Facts about the presidents, 6th ed, 94n499
Marshall Cavendish illus hist of the presidents of the US, 92n462
Presidency A to Z, 94n508
Presidential landmarks, 94n477
Presidential primaries & caucuses 1992, 94n755
Presidents' last years, 90n478
Presidents of the USA, 12th ed, 91n493
Records of the presidency, 90n487
Songs, odes, glees, & ballads, 92n669
Warren G. Harding: a bibliog, 93n509
World almanac of presidential campaigns, 93n732
World bk of America's presidents: portraits of the presidents, 91n497

PRESIDENTS—WIVES
First ladies, 6th ed, 91n494
Modern first ladies, 90n484
Presidents' wives, 90n485
World almanac of 1st ladies, 92n463

PRESLEY, ELVIS
Elvis: his life from A to Z, 90n1299

PRESS
Encyclopedia of the British pr 1422-1992, 94n1008

PRESS LAW
Desktop publisher's legal hndbk, 90n555
Publishing law hndbk, 1989 suppl, 90n558
Publishing law hndbk, 2d ed, 94n574

PRESSURE GROUPS
Political resource dir 1989, 90n682
Public interest profiles 1988-89, 90n736
Public interest profiles 1992-93, 93n795
U.S. aging policy interest groups, 93n860
U.S. criminal justice interest groups, 94n588
U.S. energy & environmental interest groups, 92n1753
Washington representatives 1989, 90n703

PRIMARIES
Congressional & gubernatorial primaries 1991-92, 94n754
Presidential primaries & caucuses 1992, 94n755

PRIMATES
Audiovisual resources in primatology, Wis Regional Primate Research Center, 94n1732
International dir of primatology, 94n1736
Mammals: primates, insect eaters & baleen whales, 90n1520

PRINCE EDWARD ISLAND
Wildflowers of Prince Edward Island, 94n1650

PRINCETON UNIVERSITY—ALUMNI
Princetonians 1784-90, 93n356
Princetonians 1791-94, 93n357

PRINCETON UNIVERSITY LIBRARY
Pamphlets, pers, & songs of the French revolutionary era in the Princeton Univ Lib, 90n517

PRINTERS
Dictionary of the print trade in Ireland, 90n631
Directory of bk printers, 1991 ed, 92n638
Stationers' co archive, 91n670
Yellow pages industry source bk, 1992-93 ed, 94n674

PRINTING
Bibliography of New Orleans imprints 1764-1864, 90n629
Graphic arts ency, 93n1042
Graphic arts vocabulary, 94n1058
Modern ency of typefaces 1960-90, 92n630
Multilingual dict of printing & publishing terms, 92n629
Multilingual dict of publishing, printing & bkselling, 93n680
Nevada printing hist, 93n678

PRINTING, PRACTICAL
Elements of typographic style, 94n675
Graphics, design & printing terms, 91n1724

PRINTMAKERS
British printmakers 1855-1955, 94n1057

PRINTS
Catalogue raisonne of the graphic work of Richard Florsheim, 90n980
Print price index '93, 93n1032

PRISON FILMS
Prison pictures from Hollywood, 92n1364

PRISON LIBRARIES
Directory of state prison librarians 1990, 92n614
Gulag hndbk, 90n573
Prison slang, 93n603
Werner's manual for prison law libs, 2d ed, 92n616

PRIVACY, RIGHT OF
Compilation of state & fed privacy laws, 1992 ed, 94n577
Personal info index 1988, 90n565

PRIVATE COMPANIES
Owners & officers of private cos, 1992, 93n196

PRIVATE SCHOOLS
Boarding school gd, 90n320
Catholic school educ in the US, 93n348
Handbook of private schools, 70th ed, 90n314
Handbook of private schools, 73d ed, 93n349
ISS dir of overseas schools, 1989/90 ed, 90n346
NCEA/Ganley's Catholic schools in America 1989, 90n315
NCEA/Ganley's Catholic schools in America 1992, 93n353
Private independent schools 1988, 90n316
Private schools of the US, 90n317
School Search gd to private schools for students with learning disabilities, 91n350

PRO FOOTBALL HALL OF FAME (U.S.)
Pro football hall of fame, 92n794

PROCESS CONTROL
Comprehensive dict of instrumentation & control, 90n1576
Comprehensive dict of measurement & control, 2d ed, 93n1607

PRO-CHOICE MOVEMENT
Abortion debate in the US and Canada, 92n805

Pro-choice/pro-life, 92n834

PRODUCE TRADE
FAO yrbk: trade, v.45, 94n1592
U.S. agricultural groups, 91n1476

PRODUCT CODING
Sourcebook of automatic identification & data collection, 91n1612

PRODUCT SAFETY
Product SOS 1993, 94n1837

PROFESSIONAL EMPLOYEES
International who's who of professional & bus women, 2d ed, 94n958
Who knows: a gd to Washington experts, 10th ed, 91n753

PROFESSIONAL ETHICS
Codes of professional responsibility, 2d ed, 91n156
Professional codes of conduct in the UK, 91n269
Public relations & ethics, 92n122

PROGRAM MUSIC
Subject gd to classical instrumental music, 90n1267

PROGRAMMING LANGUAGES (ELECTRONIC COMPUTERS)
High-level langs & sftwr applications, 90n1726
Online programming langs & assemblers, 90n1719

PROJECTORS
Pre-cinema hist, 94n1427

PRO-LIFE MOVEMENT
Abortion debate in the US and Canada, 92n805
Pro-choice/pro-life, 92n834

PROOFREADING
Copy-editing, 3d ed, 94n1000

PROPAGANDA
Encyclopedia of Soviet life, 92n721
Soviet propaganda network, 90n728
Terrorism, assassination, espionage & propaganda, 91n771

PROPOSAL WRITING FOR GRANTS
Action gd to govt grants, loans, & giveaways, 94n895

PROSTITUTION
Prostitutes in medical lit, 92n1649
Prostitution: a gd to sources, 1960-90, 93n882
Prostitution in Hollywood films, 94n1447

PROTECTION OF CHILDREN. *See* **CHILD WELFARE**

PROTECTIVE CLOTHING. *See* **CLOTHING, PROTECTIVE**

PROTESTANTISM & LITERATURE
Protestant sensibility in the American novel, 93n1170

PROTISTA
Handbook of protoctista, 91n1515

PROTOZOA
Handbook of protoctista, 91n1515

PROUST, MARCEL
Marcel Proust: a ref gd 1950-70, 92n1235

PROVERBS
Cassell bk of proverbs, 93n1295
Chinese-English dict of enigmatic folk similes, 92n1317
Concise Oxford dict of proverbs, 2d ed, 93n1296
Dictionary of American proverbs, 93n1299
International proverb scholarship, suppl.1, 91n1331
International proverb scholarship, suppl.2, 94n1388
Jewish wisdom, 93n445
Joys of Hebrew, 94n1385
Modern proverbs & proverbial sayings, 90n1301
Old English proverbs collected by Nathan Bailey, 1736, 94n1384
Religious proverbs, 92n1420
Witty words, 94n70

PRYDAIN (IMAGINARY PLACE)
Prydain companion, 90n1089

PSEUDONYMS. *See* **ANONYMS & PSEUDONYMS**

PSORIASIS
Psoriasis: professional educl materials, 91n1702

PSYCHIATRY
Columbia Univ College of Physicians & Surgeons complete home gd to mental health, 94n1846
Comprehensive glossary of psychiatry & psychology, 93n1649
Mental health & psychiatry in Africa, 94n1849
Psychiatric dict, 6th ed, 90n1672

PSYCHICAL RESEARCH
Encyclopedia of ghosts & spirits, 93n810
Encyclopedia of occultism & parapsychology, 3d ed, 92n762
Encyclopedia of parapsychology & psychical research, 92n761
Harper's ency of mystic & paranormal experience, 92n765
Parapsychological research with children, 93n808
Parapsychology, new age & the occult, 94n815
Parapsychology: new sources of info, 1973-89, 92n766

PSYCHOANALYSIS
Anna Freud: a gd to research, 91n790
Cross-currents of Jungian thought, 93n796
Feminism & psychoanalysis, 93n801
Jung lexicon, 92n758
Psychoanalytic terms & concepts, 91n791

PSYCHOANALYTIC THEORY
Female psychology, 93n797

PSYCHOLOGICAL LITERATURE
Guide to journals in psychology & educ, 91n795
Library use, 2d ed, 93n804

PSYCHOLOGICAL TESTS
Handbook of family measurement techniques, 91n863
Handbook of psychological assessment, 2d ed, 92n759
Instrumentation in educ, 94n306
Tests: a comprehensive ref for assessments in psychology, educ, & bus, 3d ed, 93n338

PSYCHOLOGY
Advanced research methodology, 92n73
AIDS: abstracts of the psychological & behavioral lit 1983-89, 2d ed, 91n1687
Black females in the US, 90n741
Black males in the US, 90n740
Clinician's thesaurus, rev ed, 91n794
Comprehensive glossary of psychiatry & psychology, 93n1649
Concise dict of psychology, 2d ed, 91n792
Dictionary of behavioral sci, 2d ed, 90n90
Dictionary of Kleinian thought, 90n745
Directory of ethnic minority professionals in psychology, 90n748
Directory of the American Psychological Assn, 1989 ed, 90n749
Encyclopedic dict of psychology, 4th ed, 93n800
General bibliog of C. G. Jung's writings, rev ed, 94n806
Guide to journals in psychology & educ, 91n795
History of American psychology in notes & news 1883-1945, 90n752
International dict of psychology, 90n747
Journals in psychology, 2d ed, 90n753
Marshall Cavendish ency of personal relationships: human behavior, 92n757
PsycBOOKS 1989, 91n788
Psychoanalysis, psychology, & lit: a bibliog, suppl. to the 2d ed, 91n786
Psychology: a gd to ref & info sources, 94n805
Psychopathology in adulthood, 94n812
States of awareness, 90n742
Student's dict of psychology, 90n746
Student's dict of psychology, 2d ed, 94n811
Thesaurus of psychological index terms, 6th ed, 93n645
Women in psychology, 91n918

PSYCHOLOGY—LIBRARY RESOURCES
Library use, 2d ed, 93n804

PSYCHOMETRICS
Eleventh mental measurements yrbk, 93n803

Instrumentation in educ, 94n306
Supplement to the 10th mental measurements yrbk, 92n760
Tenth mental measurements yrbk, 90n751

PSYCHOTHERAPISTS
Directory of credentials in counseling & psychotherapy, 90n750

PSYCHOTHERAPY
Clinician's hndbk, 3d ed, 94n1847

PSYCHOTROPIC DRUGS
Essential gd to psychiatric drugs, 91n1712
Handbook of psychotropic drugs, 94n1878
Multilingual dict of narcotic drugs & psychotropic substances under intl control, 94n1872
What you need to know about psychiatric drugs, 92n1698

PUBLIC ADMINISTRATION
Administrative sci quarterly cum index 1956-85, 90n265
Canadian public admin: bibliog, suppl.5, 92n755
Guide to the fndns of public admin, 91n781
Handbook of public admin, 90n737
National dir of corporate public affairs 1991, 92n134
Public admin & mgmt vocabulary, 91n782
Public admin desk bk, 91n776
Public admin in the Third World, 91n783
Public admin research gd, 93n794
Public sector productivity, 90n733

PUBLIC BUILDINGS
American capitols, 92n997

PUBLIC CONTRACTS
Government contracts ref bk, 93n580

PUBLIC DOMAIN
Film superlist: motion pictures in the US public domain 1950-59, 91n1366

PUBLIC HEALTH
Health care terms, 2d ed, 93n1621
Health, disease, medicine & famine in Ethiopia, 92n1632
Index to health info 1988 abstracts, v.1, no.2, 90n1632
Source bk 1989-90: social & health servs in the greater NY area, 90n818

PUBLIC HEALTH ADMINISTRATION
National health dir, 1989, 90n1623
National health dir, 1992, 93n1619

PUBLIC INTEREST LAW
Keyguide to info sources in public interest law, 92n520
Public interest law, 93n566
Public interest law groups, 90n557

PUBLIC LIBRARIES
Carnegie lib in Ill., 92n602
Children's servs in the American public lib, 91n645

PUBLIC LIBRARIES—BOOK LISTS
Best bks for public libs, 94n647
Books for the teen age 1990, 91n362
Handbook of contemporary fiction for public libs & school libs, 91n1128
Public lib cat, 9th ed, 90n620
Science & tech 1989: a purchase gd, 91n1458
University pr bks for public & secondary school libs 1991, 93n664
University pr bks for public libs, 12th ed, 92n603

PUBLIC LIBRARIES—COLLECTION DEVELOPMENT
Video for libs, 90n619

PUBLIC OFFICERS
Nuclear weapons world, 90n674

PUBLIC OPINION
American profile—opinions & behavior, 1972-89, 92n79
American public opinion index 1989, 92n72
Index to intl public opinion 1987-88, 90n734
Index to intl public opinion, 1991-92, 94n75
Opinions '90, 91n78
Soviet pubs on Judaism, Zionism, & the state of Israel 1984-88, 91n407

Trends in public opinion, 90n85

PUBLIC OPINION POLLS
Dictionary of polling, 93n103
Gallup poll 1990, 92n74
Public opinion polls & survey research, 91n82

PUBLIC RELATIONS
Gebbie Pr all-in-one dir 1989, 90n636
National dir of corporate public affairs 1991, 92n134
Public relations & ethics, 92n122
Public relations bibliog 1986-87, 92n235
Public relations in bus, govt, & society, 90n156
Publicity & media resources for bk pubs, 1992-1993 ed, 94n670

PUBLIC SCHOOLS
Public schooling in America, 93n354
Public schools USA, 2d ed, 93n350

PUBLIC SPEAKING
1001 quips & quotes for bus speeches, 93n219
Speaker's treasury of sports anecdotes, stories, & humor, 91n816

PUBLIC UTILITIES
Public utilities, 92n1605

PUBLIC WELFARE
Public welfare dir, 1993/94, 94n913

PUBLIC WORSHIP
ABCs of worship, 93n1423
Bibliography of Christian worship, 91n1437

PUBLICITY
Marketing made easier, 94n293

PUBLISHERS & PUBLISHING
African bk world & pr, 4th ed, 90n642
Alternative pr publishers of children's bks, 3d ed, 90n637
Alternative pubs, 91n672
Association of American univ prs dir 1988-89, 90n633
Association of American univ prs dir 1990-91, 92n632
Black bk publishers in the US, 93n679
Bodian's publishing desk ref, 90n644
Book trade in Canada with who's where, 1989/90, 91n671
Books & mags: a gd to publishing & bkselling courses in the US, 93n681
Books in print 1990-91, 91n9
Books in print of the UN system, 94n788
British literary publishing houses, 1881-1965, 93n689
Canadian writer's market, 9th ed, 91n956
Colonial British Caribbean newspapers, 91n962
Colorado bk gd, 93n683
Computer publishers & pubs, 1988-89, 90n1716
Computer publishers & pubs, 1992-93 ed, 93n684
Directory of art publishers, bk publishers & record cos, 91n1013
Directory of poetry publishers 1990-91, 91n663
Directory of poetry publishers, 8th ed, 94n664
Directory of publishers in China, 94n672
Directory of publishing 1989, 90n635
Directory of publishing 1993, 94n665
Directory of small pr & mag eds & publishers, 22d ed, 92n635
Directory of W bk publs & production servs, 92n634
European specialist publishers dir, 94n666
First editions, 2d ed, 90n643
Gebbie Pr all-in-one dir 1989, 90n636
IIA telephone dir, 90n586
Information marketplace dir, 1993, 93n685
Information sources 1989, 90n585
Insider's gd to bk editors & publs 1990-91, 91n947
International bk trade dir 1989, 90n641
International dir of little mags & small prs, 27th ed, 92n636
International literary market place 1990, 91n665
Literary market place 1990, 90n638
Literary market place 1991, 92n639
Literary market place 1994, 94n668
Multilingual dict of printing & publishing terms, 92n629
Multilingual dict of publishing, printing & bkselling, 93n680
New Zealand bks in print 1993, 94n5

Policies of publishers, 1989 ed, 90n645
Publicity & media resources for bk pubs, 1992-1993 ed, 94n670
Publishers dir, 1989, 90n639
Publishers dir, 1992, 93n687
Publishers, distrs & wholesalers of the US 1989-90, 90n640
Publishers, distrs & wholesalers of the US 1990-91, 92n641
Publishers, distrs & wholesalers of the US 1991-92, 93n688
Publishers, distrs & wholesalers of the US 1993-94, 94n671
Publishers trade list annual, 1989, 90n19
Publishers trade list annual, 1992, 94n660
Small pr: an annot gd, 94n659
Southwest publishing marketplace, 1991 ed, 91n662
Stationers' co archive, 91n670
Who's who at the Frankfurt Bk Fair 1989, 91n658
William D. Wittliff & the Encino Pr, 91n657
Writers' gd to Tex. markets, 90n893
Writers & publs gd to Tex. markets, 92n893
Writer's gd to metropolitan Washington, 92n894
Yellow pages industry source bk, 1992-93 ed, 94n674

PUERTO RICAN LITERATURE
Biographical dict of Hispanic lit in the US, 90n1124
U.S. Latino lit, 93n1166

PUERTO RICO
Annotated bibliog of Puerto Rican bibliogs, 91n122
Birds in jeopardy, 93n1541
Music & dance in Puerto Rico from the age of Columbus to modern times, 93n1243

PULPWOOD INDUSTRY
Compendium of pulp & paper training & research insts, 94n1614
Projected pulp & paper mills in the world 1990-2000, 92n1502

PUNJAB
Settlement lit of the Greater Punjab, 93n524

PURCELL, HENRY
Henry Purcell: a gd of research, 90n1257

PUTTICK AND SIMPSON
Music at auction, 90n1224

PYM, BARBARA
Barbara Pym: a ref gd, 93n1209

PYRAMIDS
Egyptian pyramids, 92n505

PYTHAGORAS
Pythagoras: an annot bibliog, 91n1401

QUAILS
Atlas of quails, 93n1536

QUALITY CONTROL
Quality control, 92n233

QUALITY OF LIFE
Better community cat, 91n847
50 fabulous places to raise your family, 94n944
Livable cities almanac, 93n920
100 best small towns in America, 94n942
World quality of life indicators, 91n86
World quality of life indicators, 2d ed, 93n95

QUEENS
Women who ruled, 91n921

QUESTIONS & ANSWERS
Guinness bk of answers, 8th ed, 93n4

QUILTER, ROGER
Gurney, Ireland, Quilter & Warlock, 90n1223

QUILTING
Quilt ency illus, 92n952
Quilt groups today, 94n1031

QUOTATIONS
Artists in quotation, 90n966
Baseball quotations, 92n784
Baseball's greatest quotations, 92n783
Beacon bk of quotations by women, 94n972
Brush up your Shakespeare!, 91n1213
Columbia Granger's dict of poetry quotations, 93n1235
Concise Columbia dict of quotations, 90n81
Dictionary of bus quotations, 92n153
Dictionary of Canadian quotations, 93n90
Dictionary of contemporary quotations, 2d ed, 92n66
Dictionary of environmental quotations, 93n1777
Dictionary of literary quotations, 91n1107
Dictionary of military quotations, 91n682
Dictionary of philosophical quotations, 94n1499
Dictionary of quotations from Shakespeare, 93n1213
Dictionary of religious & spiritual quotations, 91n1420
Dictionary of war quotations, 91n683
Draper's bk of quotations for the Christian world, 94n1551
Familiar quotations, 16th ed, 93n89
Friendly advice, 92n71
Gist of Mencken, 91n1167
Harper bk of quotations, 3d ed, 94n68
Intertextuality, allusion, & quotation, 90n1065
Isaac Asimov's bk of sci & nature quotations, 90n1440
Jewish wisdom, 93n445
Joys of Hebrew, 94n1385
Leadership, 91n71
Leadership: quotations from the military tradition, 91n681
Legal briefs: a lawyer's quotation bk, 91n593
Macmillan dict of pol quotations, 94n724
Macmillan dict of quotations, 91n70
Manager's bk of quotations, 90n269
Meaning of hist, 92n513
Merriam-Webster dict of quotations, 93n91
Movie talk, 91n1397
My soul looks back, 'less I forget, 94n72
New quotable woman, rev ed, 94n973
New York Public Lib bk of 20th-century American quotations, 94n71
Oxford dict of American legal quotations, 94n584
Oxford dict of modern quotations, 92n68
Oxford dict of quotations, 4th ed, 93n92
Political quotations, 91n724
Power quotes, 93n730
Quentin Crisp's bk of quotations, 91n872
Quotable quote bk, 92n67
Quotable woman, 92n870
Quotation location, 91n67
"Quote me", 91n68
Reader's quotation bk, 93n403
Reflections on childhood, 93n895
Religious proverbs, 92n1420
Respectfully quoted, 90n82
Shakespeare's quotations, 94n1257
Things precious & wild, 92n1556
Thoughts on leadership, 93n316
Treasury of business quotations, 91n167
Treasury of religious quotations, 93n1412
Tuttle dict of quotations for speeches, 93n93
Webster's II New Riverside desk quotations, 93n94
What a piece of work is man!, 91n69
What they said in 1988, 90n89
Who said what when, 92n70
Why do we quote..?, 90n83
Wit & wisdom of pol, 90n713
Witty words, 94n70
Words of wisdom, 91n72
World of W. E. B. Du Bois, 93n99
You can say that again, 92n69

RABBINICAL SEMINARIES
Religious seminaries in America, 90n1377

RABBIS
Encyclopedia of Talmudic sages, 90n1413

Great Torah commentators, 91n1450

RACE RELATIONS
Dictionary of race & ethnic relations, 2d ed, 90n363

RACISM
Racism in the US, 91n384
World racism & related inhumanities, 93n618

RADAR DEFENSE NETWORKS
Jane's radar & electronic warfare systems 1989-90, 91n709

RADIATION
Environmental hazards: radioactive materials & wastes, 91n1813

RADICALS
Biographical dict of the extreme right since 1890, 92n732

RADIO
ARRL hndbk for radio amateurs 1993, 94n1015
Bacon's radio/TV dir 1993, 94n1014
British radio & TV pioneers, 94n1012
Broadcasting & cable market place 1992, 93n992
Canadian media list 1992/93, 93n952
Gale dir of pubs & broadcast media 1990, 91n61
Gale dir of pubs & broadcast media 1993, 94n988
Radio & TV pioneers: a patent bibliog, 93n983
Radio & TV, suppl.2, 90n912
World radio TV hndbk, 1992 ed, 93n1000

RADIO BROADCASTING
Nostalgia entertainment sourcebk, 92n1334
Radio: a ref gd, 90n911
Radio broadcasting from 1920 to 1990, 92n907

RADIO IN RELIGION
Religious radio & TV in the US, 1921-91, 94n1511

RADIO PROGRAMS
Children's hour: radio progs for children 1929-56, 91n971
Handbook of old-time radio, 94n1017

RADIO STATIONS
Gigging, 91n1303
M St radio dir, 1990 ed, 92n916
Radio dial radio station gd, 90n917
Traveler's country music radio atlas 1993, 94n1018
Traveler's gd to world radio, 1992 ed, 93n999

RADIOACTIVE POLLUTION
Environmental hazards: radioactive materials & wastes, 91n1813

RADIOCARBON DATING
Radiocarbon dating lit, 90n1762

RADON
Radon dir 1990-91, 91n1810
Radon industry dir 1989, 90n1795

RAFTING (SPORTS)
Whitewater sourcebk, 90n443

RAILROAD MOTOR-CARS
Steam passenger serv dir 1989, 90n1814

RAILROAD MUSEUMS
Guide to tourist railroads & railroad museums, 3d ed, 91n1821
Steam passenger serv dir 1989, 90n1814

RAILROADS
American shortline railway gd, 4th ed, 92n1799
Century of Pullman cars, v.2, 91n1820
Compendium of American railroad radio frequencies, 12th ed, 94n2028
Guide to tourist railroads & railroad museums, 3d ed, 91n1821
Guinness railway bk, 91n1824
Railway dict, 94n2022
Rand McNally handy railroad atlas of the US, 90n1811
Train times in Mexico, 2d ed, 91n1828
Train-watcher's gd to N American railroads, 2d ed, 94n2024

RAILROADS—MODELS
Greenberg's American Flyer cats 1946-55, 92n937
Greenberg's gd to American Flyer S gauge, 4th ed, v.1, 92n938

Greenberg's gd to American Flyer wide gauge, 90n927
Greenberg's gd to Ives trains 1901-32, v.1, 2d ed, 92n939
Greenberg's gd to LGB trains, 2d ed, 90n928
Greenberg's gd to Lionel trains 1945-69, v.1, 8th ed, 92n940
Greenberg's gd to Lionel trains 1945-69, v.2, 2d ed, 92n941
Greenberg's gd to Lionel trains 1945-69, v.3, 92n942
Greenberg's gd to Lionel trains 1970-88, 90n929
Greenberg's gd to Marklin OO\HO trains, 91n987
Greenberg's gd to Marx trains, 90n930
Greenberg's gd to Marx trains, v.2, 91n989
Greenberg's Lionel catalogs, 92n943
Lionel trains: standard of the world, 1900-43, 2d ed, 91n990
Made in the Ives shops, 92n945

RAIN FOREST PLANTS
Rainforest plants of E Austral., 94n1682

RAIN FORESTS
Conservation atlas of tropical forests: Africa, 93n1484
Conservation atlas of tropical forests: Asia & the Pacific, 92n1764
Neotropical rainforest mammals, 91n1592

RAMEAU, JEAN-PHILIPPE
Jean-Philippe Rameau: a gd to research, 91n1271

RAND, AYN
Ayn Rand: 1st descriptive bibliog, 92n1180

RANGE PLANTS—TEXAS
Texas range plants, 94n1664

RAPE
Rape: a bibliog, 92n564
Rape: a bibliog 1976-88, 93n620

RAPE VICTIMS
Sexual assault & child sexual abuse, 90n578

RAPPING (MUSIC)
Rap music in the 1980s, 94n1375

RARE ANIMALS
California's wild heritage, 91n1551

RARE BIRDS
Birds in jeopardy, 93n1541

RARE BOOKS
BookGuide 1991, 92n927
Bookman's price index, v.38, 91n981
Bookman's price index, v.46, 94n1025
Catalog of 1st eds, 92n928
Edgar & Dorothy Davidson collection of Canadiana at Mount Allison Univ, 92n6
Hispanic rare bks of the golden age (1470-1699) in the Newberry Lib of Chicago, 90n27

RARE FISHES
Rare & endangered biota of Fla., v.2, 94n1716

RARE MAMMALS
Rare & endangered biota of Fla., v.1, 94n1735

RAS TAFARI MOVEMENT
Rastafari & reggae, 91n1322

RATIO ANALYSIS
101 business ratios, 94n176

RATIONAL EXPECTATIONS (ECONOMIC THEORY)
Reader's gd to rational expectations, 93n175

RAW MATERIALS
World statistical compendium for raw hides & skins, leather, & leather footwear 1972-90, 5th ed, 94n1598

RAYS (FISHES)
Reef sharks & rays of the world, 94n1718

READERS
Beyond picture bks, 90n1077
Easy reading, 2d ed, 91n368
Reader dvlpmt bibliog, 4th ed, 92n324

READING
Books for new adult readers, 4th ed, 90n356
Desktop ref to the Intl Reading Assn 1990-91, 92n331
International hndbk of reading educ, 93n404
Library lit. 20, 92n572
Literature activity bks, 94n1197
Read for your life, 94n383

REAGAN, RONALD
Ronald Reagan: his 1st career, 90n1319

REAGENTS, BIOLOGICAL. *See* BIOLOGICAL REAGENTS

REAL ESTATE. *See* REAL PROPERTY

REAL ESTATE BUSINESS
Dictionary of real estate lending terms, 90n294
Handbook of real estate terms, rev ed, 93n325
Japanese investment in US & Canadian real estate dir 1990, 91n285
Language of real estate, 3d ed, 90n295
Prentice Hall real estate investor's ency, 91n287
Realty, 2d ed, 91n286
St. James ency of mortgage & real estate finance, 92n262

REAL ESTATE INVESTMENT
Sources of property market info, 90n297

REAL PROPERTY
Dictionary of real estate appraisal, 2d ed, 90n293
Dictionary of real estate lending terms, 90n294
Finance, insurance, & real estate USA, 94n205
Guide to real estate & mortgage banking sftwr, 5th ed, 90n296
Handbook of real estate terms, rev ed, 93n325
Language of real estate, 3d ed, 90n295
Language of real estate appraisal, 92n261
Realty, 2d ed, 91n286
Sources of property market info, 90n297

RECONNAISSANCE AIRCRAFT
Combat arms: modern spyplanes, 91n688

RECONSTRUCTION
Freedom's lawmakers, 94n727
Historical dict of reconstruction, 92n469

RECORDS
NAGARA state archives & records mgmt programs, 1989, 90n698

RECREATION
Acrosport, 94n817
Dictionary of concepts in recreation & leisure studies, 91n807
Educators gd to free health, physical educ & recreation materials, 26th ed, 94n829
Information sources in sport & leisure, 94n821
Sports & recreation for the disabled, 91n813
Women outdoors, 92n851

RECREATION AREAS
Allstate Motor Club RV park & campground dir 1990, 91n809
America's secret recreation areas, 94n476
Parks dir of the US, 93n500
United States military road atlas, 94n677
U.S. outdoor atlas & recreation gd, 93n497

RECYCLING (WASTE, ETC.)
Recycling in America, 94n2013
Recycling sourcebk, 94n2017
Solid waste educ recycling dir, 92n1779

REDUCING DIETS
Dieter's dict & problem solver, 94n1603

REED, DONNA
Donna Reed: a bio-bibliog, 92n1342

REFERENCE BOOKS
Best.ref bks 1986-90, 93n8
Business info: how to find it, how to use it, 2d ed, 93n209
Canada: a reader's gd, 93n19
Canadian bk review annual 1988, 90n4
Canadian bus & economics, 3d ed, 94n246
Communication & the mass media, 92n884
Cultural anthropology: a gd to ref & info sources, 92n369
Distinguished classics of ref publishing, 93n18
Government ref bks 88/89, 91n43
Government ref bks 90/91, 93n74
Guide to ref bks, suppl to the 10th ed, 93n12
Guide to ref materials for Canadian libs, 8th ed, 93n16
Guide to the college lib, 94n658
Index to American Ref Bks Annual 1985-89, 90n72
Introduction to lib research in anthropology, 92n338
Law lib ref shelf, 90n541
Literary research gd, 91n1097
Literary research gd, 2d ed, 94n1139
New, completely rev, greatly expanded, Madam Audrey's mostly cheap, all good, useful list of bks for speedy ref, 5th ed, 93n13
New York Public Lib desk ref, 91n48
Recommended ref bks 1989, 90n6
Recommended ref bks 1990, 91n6
Recommended ref bks 1991, 92n10
Recommended ref bks 1992, 93n22
Recommended ref bks 1993, 94n4
Reference bks bulletin 1987-88, 90n5
Reference bks bulletin 1988-89, 91n5
Reference bks bulletin 1989-90, 92n8
Reference bks bulletin 1991-92, 94n3
Reference readiness, 4th ed, 91n646
Reference sources for small & medium-sized libs, 5th ed, 93n17
Reference works in British & American lit, v.1, 91n1096
Reference works in British & American lit, v.2, 92n1094
Serials ref work, 90n618
Slavic studies, 94n131
Spanish-lang ref bks, 90n367
Student contact bk, 94n58
Topical ref bks, 92n9
Walford's concise gd to ref material, 2d ed, 93n20
Walford's gd to ref material, 5th ed, v.1: sci & tech, 91n1459
Walford's gd to ref material, 6th ed, v.1: sci & tech, 94n1562
Walford's gd to ref material, 5th ed, v.2: social & histl scis, 93n98
Walford's gd to ref material, 5th ed, v.3: generalia, 93n21
Where to find what, 3d ed, 92n606

REFERENCE BOOKS FOR CHILDREN. *See* CHILDREN'S REFERENCE BOOKS

REFERENCE SERVICES (LIBRARIES)
FISCAL dir of fee-based info servs in libs, 92n605
Reference & info servs, 92n604
Reference readiness, 4th ed, 91n646
Serials ref work, 90n618
Topical ref bks, 92n9
Where to find what, 3d ed, 92n606

REFERENDUM
California initiatives & referendums 1912-90, 93n793

REFORM JUDAISM
Reform Judaism in America, 94n1557

REFORMATION
English religion 1500-40, 90n1379

REFORMED CHURCH
Encyclopedia of the reformed faith, 93n1422

REFORMERS
Great lives: human rights, 92n562

REFUGEES
Displaced peoples & refugee studies, 92n833
Human rights, refugees, migrants & dvlpmt, 94n593
Refugee & immigrant resource dir 1990-91, 91n878

REFUSE & REFUSE DISPOSAL
Solid waste educ recycling dir, 92n1779

REGENTS
Queens, empresses, grand duchesses & regents, 90n869

REGGAE MUSIC
Rastafari & reggae, 91n1322

REGINALD, R.
Work of Robert Reginald, 2d ed, 94n1238

REGIONAL PLANNING
Elsevier's dict of physical planning, 91n909

REGIONALISM
Region & regionalism in the US, 90n96

REGISTER OF BIRTHS, ETC.
State & province vital records gd, 94n432

REGULATORY AGENCIES. *See* ADMINISTRATIVE AGENCIES

REHABILITATION
Directory of medical rehabilitation programs, 91n1668
Handbook of developmental & physical disabilities, 90n1629

REINFORCED SOLIDS. *See* COMPOSITE MATERIALS

RELIGION
Bibliographic gd to the comparative study of ethics, 92n1389
Bibliography of new religious movements in primal societies, v.3, 91n1411
Bibliography of new religious movements in primal societies, v.4, 92n1400
Bibliography of new religious movements in primal societies, v.5, 92n1401
Bibliography of new religious movements in primal societies, v.6, 94n1505
Concise dict of religion, 94n1512
Dictionary of Pentecostal & charismatic movements, 90n1407
Dictionary of religion & philosophy, 91n1414
Dictionary of religious & spiritual quotations, 91n1420
Directory of African American religious bodies, 92n1404
Directory of religious orgs in the US, 3d ed, 94n1515
Encyclopedia of American religions, 3d ed, 91n1415
Encyclopedia of American religions, 4th ed, 94n1518
Fund raiser's gd to religious philanthropy, 3d ed, 91n1416
Fund raiser's gd to religious philanthropy, 5th ed, 93n1425
Handbook of denominations in the US, 9th ed, 91n1445
Harper religious & inspirational quotation companion, 91n1419
Illustrated ency of active new religions, sects, & cults, 94n1529
Italian Americans & religion, 2d ed, 94n1504
Modern ency of religions in Russia & the Soviet Union, 90n1381
National gd to funding in religion, 93n1411
Reference works for theological research, 3d ed, 93n1400
Religion & American life, 90n1376
Religion in the Soviet Union, 94n1503
Religious bodies in the US, 93n1408
Religious info sources, 93n1401
Religious leaders, 93n1403
Religious leaders of America, 92n1402
Scholar's gd to academic journals in religion, 90n1385
Subject headings for church or synagogue libs, 2d ed, 91n625
This day in religion, 92n1413
Treasury of religious quotations, 93n1412
Walford's gd to ref material, 5th ed, v.2: social & histl scis, 93n98
Who's who in religion 1992-93, 94n1510

RELIGION & LITERATURE
Dictionary of biblical tradition in English lit, 94n1149

RELIGION & MYTHOLOGY
Dictionary of Native American mythology, 94n418

RELIGION & POLITICS
Religion in pols, 91n1417

RELIGION & SOCIOLOGY
Church & social action, 91n1412
Social sci & the cults, 91n1410
Sociology of religion, 92n1397

RELIGION, PRIMITIVE
Ashe, traditional religion & healing in sub-Saharan Africa & the Diaspora, 91n1409
Bibliography of new religious movements in primal societies, v.3, 91n1411

Bibliography of new religious movements in primal societies, v.4, 92n1400
Bibliography of new religious movements in primal societies, v.5, 92n1401
Bibliography of new religious movements in primal societies, v.6, 94n1505
Encyclopedia of Native American religions, 93n432
Mythologies, 92n1321

RELIGIONS
Ancient & shining ones, 94n1392
Contemporary religions: a world gd, 94n1516
Dictionary of cults, sects, religions & the occult, 94n1513
Eliade gd to world religions, 93n1409
Religions on file, 91n1418
Sociology of religion, 92n1397

RELIGIOUS BIOGRAPHY
Dictionary of American religious biog, 2d ed, 94n1509
Twentieth-century shapers of American popular religion, 90n1380
Who's who of world religions, 93n1404

RELIGIOUS DANCE, MODERN
Resources in sacred dance, rev ed, 92n1336

RELIGIOUS LIFE
Religious proverbs, 92n1420

RELIGIOUS FREEDOM. *See* FREEDOM OF RELIGION

RELIGIOUS LITERATURE
Religious writer's marketplace, 3d ed, 90n898

REMOTE SENSING
Keyguide to info sources in remote sensing, 90n1590

RENAISSANCE. *See also* MIDDLE AGES
Guide to medieval & renaissance mss in the Huntington Lib, 90n532

RENEWABLE ENERGY SOURCES
Almanac of renewable energy, 94n1983
Renewable energy, 94n1985

REPORT WRITING
College style sheet, 3d ed, 93n959
Guide to info sources for the preparation, editing, & production of docs, 90n896
100 world-class thin bks, 94n1164

REPRODUCTION
Asdell's patterns of mammalian reproduction, 94n1731
Viruses & reproduction, 90n1689

REPTILES
Amphibians & reptiles in Kans., 3d ed, 94n1749
Amphibians & reptiles of La., 90n1566
Amphibians & reptiles of the W Indies, 93n1579
Australian reptiles & frogs, 91n1602
Completely illus atlas of reptiles & amphibians for the terrarium, 90n1569
Field gd to reptiles & amphibians: E & central N America, 3d ed, 92n1587
Guide to amphibians & reptiles, 91n1604
Middle American herpetology, 90n1570
Oklahoma herpetology, 90n1565
Peterson 1st gd to reptiles & amphibians, 93n1577
Reptile care, 92n1588
Reptiles & amphibians, 90n1524
Reptiles & amphibians, 94n1748
Reptiles & amphibians of Austral., 5th ed, 93n1575
Simon & Schuster's gd to reptiles & amphibians of the world, 91n1603
Snakes of E North America, 91n1601
Turtles of the world, 90n1567
Venomous reptiles of Latin America, 90n1564

REPUBLIC PICTURE CORPORATION
Republic chapterplays, 94n1440

REQUIEMS
American masses & requiems, 92n1302

RESEARCH
Finding Canadian facts fast, rev ed, 91n647
Guide to research & scholarship in Hungary, 90n309
Handbook of research on teaching the English lang arts, 92n280
International research centers dir 1992-93, 93n68
New York Public Lib bk of how & where to look it up, 92n609
Prospect researcher's gd to biographical research collections, 93n675
Research servs dir, 5th ed, 94n165
Scientific traveler, 93n1456
Sponsored research in the hist of art, 7, 90n946
Student contact bk, 94n58
Where to find what, 3d ed, 92n606

RESEARCH & DEVELOPMENT CONTRACTS
R&D ratios & budgets, 94n295
Research & dvlpmt growth trends, 1992 ed, 94n209
U.S. sourcebk of R&D spenders, 1992 ed, 94n240

RESEARCH GRANTS
Action gd to govt grants, loans, & giveaways, 94n895
Directory of grants in the humanities 1988, 90n883
Directory of research grants 1989, 90n805
GRANTS subject authority gd, 93n637
Peterson's grants for grad study, 3d ed, 93n374
Peterson's grants for postdoctoral study, 93n375
Scholarships, fellowships & loans 1992-93, 93n377

RESEARCH INSTITUTES
Chemical research faculties 1988, 90n1755
Directory of dvlpmt research & training insts in Africa, 94n93
Directory of manufacturing research centers June 1989, 90n234
Electronic research centres, 2d ed, 90n1580
European research centres, 7th ed, 90n1431
European research centres, 9th ed, 94n1574
Government research dir, 5th ed, 90n697
Government research dir 1991-92, 92n688
Government research dir 1993-94, 94n740
Guide to research & scholarship in Hungary, 90n309
Guide to scholarly resources on the Russian empire & the Soviet Union in the N.Y. metropolitan area, 91n113
International ency of learned societies & academies, 94n36
Materials research centres, 3d ed, 90n1601
Medical research centres, 8th ed, 90n1621
Nonprofit public policy research orgs, 94n753
Public info contact dir 1988-89, 90n1433
Research centers dir 1990, 90n326
Research centers dir 1993, 94n345
Research servs dir, 4th ed, 90n64

RESEARCH LIBRARIES
CD-ROM research collections, 93n660
Center for Research Libs hndbk, 92n608

RESORTS
Great resorts for parents & kids, 92n434
99 best residential & recreational communities in America for vacation, retirement & investment planning, 93n919

RESTAURANTS, LUNCH ROOMS, ETC.
Hotel & restaurant industries, 90n243

RETIREMENT
Consumer's gd to aging, 94n875
Destination southwest, 91n910
Henry Holt retirement sourcebk, 93n855
Older workers, 92n812
Retirement sourcebk, 90n791

RETIREMENT COMMUNITIES
50 fabulous places to retire in America, 93n921
Golden horizons retirement gd, Calif ed, 90n792
National continuing care dir, 2d ed, 90n789
National dir of retirement facilities 1991, 92n810
99 best residential & recreational communities in America for vacation, retirement & investment planning, 93n919

RETIREMENT INCOMES
Pensions vocabulary, 92n214

REVIEWING (BOOKS). *See* BOOK REVIEWING

REVOLUTIONISTS
Liberators & patriots of Latin America, 92n108
Revolutionary orgs & revolutionaries in interbellum Poland, 93n779

REVOLUTIONS
Historical dict of revolutionary China, 1839-1976, 93n523

REWARDS (PRIZES, ETC.)
Awards, honors, & prizes, 8th ed, 90n56
Awards, honors, & prizes, 9th ed, 93n66
Award-winning bks for children & young adults, 91n1110
Children's bks: awards & prizes, 1992 ed, 94n1191
Variety's dir of major US show bus awards, 90n1312
World of winners, 90n66
World of winners, 2d ed, 93n1314

RHETORIC
Dictionary of literary devices: gradus, A-Z, 92n1102
Medieval rhetoric, 2d ed, 90n529

RHODODENDRON
Rhododendron hybrids, 2d ed, 94n1631
Rhododendron portraits, 93n1506
Rhododendron species, v.3, 93n1504

RIDGWAY, MATTHEW B.
General Matthew B. Ridgway: an annot bibliog, 94n678

RIGHT & LEFT (POLITICAL SCIENCE)
Encyclopedia of the American left, 91n763
Political left in the American theatre of the 30's, 93n1375

RIMSKY-KORSAKOV, NICOLAI ANDREYEVICH
Nikolai Andreevich Rimsky-Korsakov: a gd to research, 90n1252

RIPARIAN ECOLOGY
Birds of the lower Colorado River Valley, 92n1569

RISK COMMUNICATION
Instructions & warnings, 91n248

RISK MANAGEMENT
Rupp's insurance & risk mgmt glossary, 92n211

RIVERS
Whitewater sourcebk, 90n443

ROAD MAPS
Gousha new deluxe rd atlas, 93n467
Rand McNally pocket road atlas, 90n414
Rand McNally road atlas, 67th ed, 93n468

ROBBINS, MARTY
Marty Robbins: fast cars & country music, 92n1304

ROBERT LEHMAN COLLECTION
Robert Lehman collection, 90n952

ROBERTS, KENNETH
Kenneth Roberts: the man & his works, 91n1172

ROBINSON CRUSOE
Robinson Crusoe: a bibliographical checklist of English lang editions (1719-1979), 92n1202

ROBOT INDUSTRY
Industrial robot hndbk, 90n1731

ROBOTICS
Concise intl ency of robotics, 91n1748
Industrial robot hndbk, 90n1731
Robomatix reporter annual 1988, v.6, 90n1732
Robotics abstracts annual 1989, v.7, 91n1749

ROCHBERG, GEORGE
George Rochberg: a bio-bibliographic gd to his life & works, 93n1256

ROCK FILMS
Rock & roll movie ency of the 1950s, 91n1369

ROCK MUSIC
Billboard bk of no.1 hits, rev ed, 90n1292

Billboard bk of no.1 hits, 3d ed, 94n1360
Children of Nuggets, 91n1328
Doo-wop: the forgotten 3d of rock 'n roll, 93n1290
Encyclopedia of pop, rock & soul, rev ed, 90n1298
Encyclopedia of rock, rev ed, 90n1294
50 yrs of rock music, 93n1291
Find that tune, [v.2], 2d ed, 90n1297
Harmony illus ency of rock, 6th ed, 90n1295
Harmony illus ency of rock, 7th ed, 94n1378
Illustrated discography of hot rod music 1961-65, 91n1323
Marshall Cavendish illus hist of popular music, 91n1306
Off the record, v.1, 93n1292
Rock 'n' roll through 1969, 94n1376
Rockin' the classics & classicizin' the rock, 1st suppl, 92n1311
Shake, rattle & roll, 90n1293
That old time rock & roll, 90n1291

ROCK MUSICIANS
Beatles: a bio-bibliog, 91n1327
Beatles album file & complete discography, rev ed, 90n1296
Bob Dylan: a bio-bibliog, 94n1379
Elvis: his life from A to Z, 90n1299
HeadBangers, 94n1377
Listening to the Beatles, v.1, 92n1314
Rock movers & shakers, 91n1325
Rock movers & shakers, [rev ed], 92n1313

ROCK PAINTINGS
Field gd to rock art symbols of the greater southwest, 93n508

ROCKABILLY MUSIC
Rockabilly, 92n1310

ROCKETRY
Cambridge ency of space, 92n1592
Dictionary of space tech, 92n1595

ROCKETS (AERONAUTICS)
Space almanac, 90n1581

ROCKLYNNE, ROSS
Work of Ross Rocklynne, 91n1173

ROCKS
Encyclopedia of igneous & metamorphic petrology, 91n1782
Handbook of rocks, minerals, & gemstones, 94n1957
Illustrated gd to rocks & minerals, 94n1956
Peterson 1st gd to rocks & minerals, 92n1742
Rocks & minerals, 93n1728
Rocks, minerals & fossils of the world, 91n1789

ROCKY MOUNTAINS
Handbook of Rocky Mountain plants, 93n1501
Mammals of the central Rockies, 94n1741
Meet the natives: the amateur's field gd to Rocky Mountain wildflowers, trees & shrubs, 9th ed, 93n1505
Sierra Club naturalist's gd to the S Rockies, 92n444

RODENTS
Annotated bibliog on rodent research in Latin America, 1960-85, 90n1556

RODEOS
Official professional rodeo media gd, 1990, 91n838

ROLAND (LEGENDARY CHARACTER)
Medieval Charlemagne legend, 94n1199

ROLLER COASTERS
Roller coasters, 94n828

ROLLING STONE
Rolling Stone index, 94n1404

ROMAN DE LA ROSE
Roman de la rose: an annot bibliog, 94n1282

ROMANCE LANGUAGES
Judeo-Romance linguistics, 90n1034

ROMANCE LITERATURE
Romance reader's hndbk, 91n1135
Twentieth-century romance & histl fiction writers, 2d ed, 91n1136

ROMANCES
Concordance to middle English metrical romances, 90n1174

ROMANIA
Hippocrene companion gd to Romania, 91n473

ROMANIAN LANGUAGE—DICTIONARIES—ENGLISH
New pocket Romanian dict, 90n1053
Romanian-English, English-Romanian dict, 92n1085

ROMANTICISM
British Romantic poets, 1789-1832, 1st series, 92n1219
Classic cult fiction, 93n1149
Encyclopedia of romanticism, 93n531
English Romantic poetry: an annot bibliog, 92n1218

ROME
Ancient Rome, 91n539
Greek & Roman sport, 92n772
Rome in the 4th century AD, 93n547

ROME (ITALY)—BUILDINGS, STRUCTURES, ETC.
New topographical dict of ancient Rome, 94n536

ROOSEVELT, ELEANOR
Roosevelt research, 93n516

ROOSEVELT FAMILY
Roosevelt research, 93n516

ROOSEVELT, FRANKLIN D.
Roosevelt research, 93n516

ROOSEVELT, THEODORE
Roosevelt research, 93n516

ROREM, NED
Ned Rorem: a bio-bibliog, 90n1248

ROSBAUD, HANS
Hans Rosbaud: a bio-bibliog, 93n1257

ROSES
Old rose advisor, 94n1628
Ross gd to rose growing, 92n1506

ROTHENBERG, JEROME
Jerome Rothenberg: a descriptive bibliog, 90n1153

ROTI (INDONESIA)
Timor, 94n112

ROUSSEAU, JEAN-JACQUES
Rousseau dict, 93n1396

ROUSSEL, ALBERT
Albert Roussel: a bio-bibliog, 90n1242

ROYAL CANADIAN MOUNTED POLICE
Lawmen in scarlet, 91n559

ROYAL DESCENT, FAMILIES OF
Royal descents of 500 immigrants to the American colonies or the US, 94n439

RUMINANTS
Small ruminant production & the small ruminant genetic resource in tropical Africa, 92n1476

RUNAWAY TEENAGERS
North American dir of programs for runaways, homeless youth, & missing children, 90n831

RURAL CHURCHES
Rural church in America, 91n1436

RURAL DEVELOPMENT
Rural dvlpmt, 92n213, 93n922

RURAL FAMILIES
Farm family financial crisis, 90n1442

RURAL POPULATION
Many names of country people, 90n1444

RUSKIN, JOHN
John Ruskin: a ref gd, 90n881

RUSSELL, PEE WEE
Pee Wee speaks, 94n1371

RUSSIA. *See also* **SOVIET UNION; FORMER SOVIET UNION**
Active figures of the trade union & working class movement of Russia, Ukraine, Bielorussia, & Kazakhstan, 94n262
Directory of Russian MPs, 94n523
Encyclopedia of Russian hist, 94n524
First demographic portraits of Russia 1951-90, 94n929
Moscow & Leningrad: a topographical gd to Russian cultural hist, v.2, 94n985
Russia & the Commonwealth A to Z, 94n525
Russia 1993: pol & economic analysis & bus dir, 94n137
Who's who in Russian & the new states, 94n136

RUSSIA—POLITICS & GOVERNMENT
Dictionary of pol parties & orgs in Russia, 94n779
Russian govt today, spring 1993, 94n780
Who is who in the Russian govt, 94n777
Who is who in the Russian govt, suppl.1, 94n778

RUSSIAN LANGUAGE
Dictionary of Russian personal names, 93n463

RUSSIAN LANGUAGE—ACRONYMS
Compressed Russian, 93n1097

RUSSIAN LANGUAGE—DICTIONARIES
Russian dicts: selected bibliog 1960-90, 92n1086
Vocabulary of Soviet society & culture, 93n1095

RUSSIAN LANGUAGE—DICTIONARIES—ENGLISH
A. J. Lohwater's Russian-English dict of the mathematical scis, 2d ed, 91n1795
Compressed Russian, 93n1097
Elsevier's dict of civil engineering, 90n1587
Elsevier's dict of geoscis, 93n1723
Hippocrene standard dict: Russian-English, English-Russian, 94n1130
Lexical semantics, 93n1092
1000 Russian verbs, 94n1128
Renyi picture dict: Russian & English, 94n1131
Russian phrasebk & dict, 92n1088
Russian-English dict of verbal collocations (REDVC), 94n1129
Russian-English dict with phonetics, 92n1087
Russian-English sci & engineering dict, 90n1429
Russian-English/English-Russian dict of free market era economics, 94n160
Supplementary Russian-English dict, 93n1096
Vocabulary of Soviet society & culture, 93n1095

RUSSIAN LITERATURE
Modern ency of Russian & Soviet lit, v.9, 90n1210
Nineteenth-century Russian lit in English, 92n1230
Women & writing in Russian & the USSR, 93n1230

SACRED BOOKS
Religious proverbs, 92n1420

SACRED VOCAL MUSIC
German sacred polyphonic vocal music between Schutz & Bach, 94n1343
Sacred choral music in print: master index 1992, 94n1341
Sacred choral music in print: 1992 suppl, 94n1340

SADISM
Language of sadomasochism, 91n1066

SAFARIS
Adventuring in E Africa, 91n465
Big bk of adventure travel, 91n455

SAFETY APPLIANCES
Vocabulary of safety & security equipment, 93n1601

SAFETY EDUCATION
Maintaining good health, 90n1647

SAILING
A-Z of sailing terms, 93n842
Sailing dir, 94n860
Visual dict of ships & sailing, 93n1792

SAILING SHIPS
Offshore cruising ency, 91n1829

SAINT (FICTICIOUS CHARACTER)
Saint: a complete hist in print, radio, film & TV, 94n1249

SAINTS
Book of saints, 6th ed, 91n1438
Oxford dict of saints, 3d ed, 94n1527
Saints, 94n1526

SALES
100 best cos to sell for, 90n278
Sales prospecting & territory planning dir, 91n279
Ward's sales prospector, 93n199

SALMON
Trout & salmon hndbk, 90n772

SALON (EXHIBITION: PARIS, FRANCE)
Bibliography of salon criticism in Paris from the ancien regime to the Restoration, 1699-1827, 93n1018
Bibliography of salon criticism in Paris from the July Monarchy to the Second Republic, 1831-51, 93n1019
Salons of America 1922-36, 92n980

SALSA
Salsa & related genres, 94n1381

SALVATION ARMY
Bibliography of Salvation Army lit in English, 90n1406

SANITATION
Statistical record of the environment, 93n1764

SANSKRIT LANGUAGE
Concise dict of Indian philosophy, 90n1375

SARGENT, PAMELA
Work of Pamela Sargent, 91n1174

SAROYAN, WILLIAM
William Saroyan: a ref gd, 90n1154

SASQUATCH
Big footnotes, 90n1300

SATELLITES
International satellite dir 1989, 4th ed, 90n1738
Moons of the solar system, 93n1707
World satellite dir, 1989, 11th ed, 90n1741

SATELLITES, ARTIFICIAL. *See* **ARTIFICIAL SATELLITES**

SATIRISTS
Samuel Butler: an annot bibliog of writings about him, 91n1198

SAUDI ARABIA
Saudi Arabia: bibliog on society, pols, economics, v.2, 91n124
Western lang lit on pre-Islamic central Arabia, 93n167

SAUGUET, HENRI
Henri Sauguet: a bio-bibliog, 92n1259

SAXOPHONE MUSIC
Saxophone recital music, 94n1339

SAXOPHONISTS
Charlie Parker discography, 94n1369

SCALING (SOCIAL SCIENCES)
Instrumentation in educ, 94n306

SCANDALS
Encyclopedia of American scandal, 90n492

SCANDINAVIA
Medieval Scandinavia, 94n526
Norse mythology A to Z, 92n1322

SCANDINAVIAN LITERATURE
Dictionary of Scandinavian lit, 92n1240

SCANDINAVIAN-AMERICANS
Scandinavian-American heritage, 90n382

SCARLATTI, ALESSANDRO
Alessandro & Domenico Scarlatti: a gd to research, 94n1334

SCARLATTI, DOMENICO
Alessandro & Domenico Scarlatti: a gd to research, 94n1334

SCENE PAINTERS
Biographical dict of scenographers, 92n1380

SCHIZOPHRENIA
Encyclopedia of schizophrenia & the psychotic disorders, 93n799

SCHOLARS, JEWISH
Great Torah commentators, 91n1450

SCHOLARSHIPS. See also GRANTS-IN-AID; STUDENT AID
America's new fndns 1992, 93n870
A's & B's of academic scholarships, 12th ed, 90n330
A's & B's of academic scholarships, 16th ed, 94n363
Awards almanac 1991, 91n313
Awards almanac 1992, 93n871
Cash for college, 94n360
College check mate, 3d ed, 90n331
Directory of financial aids for minorities, 1989-90, 90n329
Directory of grants in the humanities 1992/93, 93n946
Directory of research grants 1992, 93n873
EHR dir of awards: fiscal yr 1990, 93n875
Federal educl & scholarship funding gd, 2d ed, 91n329
Financial aid for research & creative activities abroad 1992-94, 94n367
Financial aid for research, study, travel, & other activities abroad 1990-91, 91n346
Financial aid for study & training abroad 1992-94, 94n368
Football scholarship gd, 94n844
Free money for athletic scholarships, 94n326
Free money for college, 91n324
Free money for foreign study, 92n292
Free money for graduate school, rev ed, 94n329
Free money from colleges & univs, 94n328
Funding for US study, 91n343
Inside Japanese support 1992, 93n280
International scholarship dir, 3d ed, 94n332
Money for film & video artists, 92n1356
Money for intl exchange in the arts, 94n983
Money for performing artists, 93n1326
Money for visual artists, 92n991
Peterson's grants for grad study, 3d ed, 93n374
Peterson's grants for postdoctoral study, 93n375
RAIC dir of scholarships & awards for architecture, 93n1039
Scholarship bk, 3d ed, 91n314
Scholarship bk, 4th ed, 94n333
Scholarships, fellowships & loans 1992-93, 93n377
Sources: the dir of contacts for editors, reporters & researchers, summer 1990, 26th ed, 91n939
U.S. student Fulbright grants & other grants for graduate study & research abroad, 94n346
Winning edge, 90n760
Winning scholarships, 94n311

SCHOOL CHILDREN IN LITERATURE
English schoolboy stories, 93n1135

SCHOOL CONTESTS
Contests for students, 92n289
Directory of educl contests for students K-12, 92n286

SCHOOL DISTRICTS
Public schools USA, 2d ed, 93n350

SCHOOL EXCURSIONS
Encyclopedia of field trips & educl destinations, 93n352

SCHOOL LIBRARIES
Author a month (for dimes), 94n1188
Book Reports & Library Talk dir of sources, 93n666
Building the ref collection, 94n619
Canadian lib hndbk, 94n617
More creative uses of children's lit, v.1, 93n671
Multicultural aspects of lib media programs, 93n669
Nonfiction bks for children, 91n648
School lib media annual 1989, v.7, 90n622
School lib media annual 1990, v.8, 91n653
School lib media annual 1991, v.9, 92n612
School lib media annual 1992, v.10, 93n672
School librarian's sourcebk, 91n652
Using children's bks in reading/lang arts programs, 93n402
Using govt docs, 93n668

SCHOOL LIBRARIES—BOOK LISTS
Best bks for children, 4th ed, 91n1111
Books kids will sit still for, 2d ed, 92n627
Children's cat, 16th ed, 92n610
Guide to ref bks for school media centers, 4th ed, 93n670
Reference bks for children, 4th ed, 93n1129
Science Bks & Films best bks for children 1988-91, 94n1561
Senior high school lib cat, 14th ed, 93n673
University pr bks for public & secondary school libs 1991, 93n664
U.S. govt pubns for the school lib media center, 2d ed, 92n611

SCHOOL LIBRARIES (ELEMENTARY). See ELEMENTARY SCHOOL LIBRARIES

SCHOOL MEDIA CENTERS. See INSTRUCTIONAL MATERIALS CENTERS

SCHWEITZER, ALBERT
Guide to Albert Schweitzer collections, 2d ed, 93n947

SCIENCE
AAAS hndbk 1993/94, 94n1579
Academic Pr dict of sci & tech, 93n1444
Album of sci, 90n1421
Almanac of sci & tech, 91n1466
American men & women of sci 1992-93, 93n1438
Applied sci & tech index, 93n1457
Applied sci & tech index 1990, 92n1468
Best sci & tech ref bks for young people, 92n1452
Black scientists, 93n1443
Checklist of the Newberry Lib's printed bks in sci, medicine, tech, & the pseudosciences ca. 1460-1750, 94n1558
Companion to the physical scis, 90n1436
Concise illus dict of sci & tech, 94n1567
Concise sci dict, 2d ed, 92n1455
Dictionary of scientific literacy, 93n1445
Directory of AAAS sci & engineering fellows 1973-92, 94n1573
Directory of pers online: sci & tech, 2d ed, 92n1459
Dorling Kindersley sci ency, 94n1565
Early American scientific & technical lit, 91n1454
Economic methodology, 90n157
Encyclopedia of physical sci & tech 1989 yrbk, 90n1425
Encyclopedia of physical sci & tech 1991 yrbk, 93n1453
Encyclopedia of physical scis & engineering info sources, 90n1424
European research centres, 9th ed, 94n1574
European sources of scientific & technical info, 9th ed, 92n1460
European sources of scientific & technical info, 10th ed, 94n1576
Facts on File scientific yrbk 1991, 92n1463
First sci dict, 92n1458
General sci index, v.14, no.7, 93n1459
General sci index [CD-ROM], 93n1460
Glossary of epistemology/philosophy of sci, 94n1495
Great events from hist 2: sci & tech series, 92n1465
Great scientific discoveries, 93n1449
Great thinkers of the W world, 93n950
Henry Holt hndbk of current sci & tech, 93n1455
History of engineering sci, 90n1572
History of sci, 93n1437
History of sci & tech, 90n1423
History of sci & tech in the US, v.2, 94n1560
Index to scientific & technical proceedings, no.4, April 1990, 91n1471
Isaac Asimov's bk of sci & nature quotations, 90n1440
Isis cum bibliog 1976-85, 90n1416

Japanese/English, English/Japanese glossary of scientific & technical terms, 94n1571
Key ideas in human thought, 94n1497
Kingfisher sci ency, 94n1568
Macmillan ency of sci, 92n1456
Magill's survey of sci: applied sci series, 94n1583
McGraw-Hill concise ency of sci & tech, 2d ed, 90n1427
McGraw-Hill dict of scientific & technical terms, 4th ed, 90n1428
McGraw-Hill ency of sci & tech, 7th ed, 93n1446
McGraw-Hill yrbk of sci & tech 1990, 91n1467
Natural scis & American scientists in the revolutionary era, 92n1451
New bk of popular sci, 90n1437
New bk of popular sci, 92n1457
New bk of popular sci, 93n1450
Peterson's engineering, sci, & computer jobs 1989, 90n188
Philip Morrison's long look at the lit, 91n1457
Planets, potions & parchments, 92n1464
Quarks, critters, & chaos, 94n1585
Raintree illus sci ency, 94n1569
Russian-English sci & engineering dict, 90n1429
Science & tech annual ref review 89, 90n1417
Science & tech desk ref, 94n1584
Science & tech in fact & fiction: a gd to children's bks, 91n1455
Science & tech in fact & fiction: a gd to young adult bks, 91n1456
Science & tech 1989: a purchase gd, 91n1458
Science Bks & Films best bks for children 1988-91, 94n1561
Science experiments index for young people update 91, 93n1461
Science experiments on file, 90n1438
Science for children, 90n1418
Science sources 1991, 93n1452
Science teacher's bk of lists, 94n1580
Science yr, 1990, 90n1439
Scientific & technical bks & serials in print 1989, 90n1419
Scientific & technical bks & serials in print 1991, 92n1453
Scientific & technical pers of the 17th & 18th centuries, 93n1463
Scientific American cum index 1978-88, 91n1472
Scientific traveler, 93n1456
Sourcebook for sci, math, & tech educ 1990-91, 92n1462
Sourcebook for sci, math, & tech educ 1992, 94n1582
Systems & control ency, suppl. v.2, 94n1570
Teaching sci to children, 2d ed, 94n1559
Timetables of sci, 90n1422
Van Nostrand's scientific ency, 7th ed, 90n1430
Walford's gd to ref material, 5th ed, v.1: sci & tech, 91n1459
Walford's gd to ref material, 6th ed, v.1: sci & tech, 94n1562
Way nature works, 94n1684
Who's who in sci & engineering 1992-93, 94n1564
Who's who in sci in Europe, 7th ed, 93n1442
Women scientists, 93n1441
Yearbook of sci & the future 1991, 91n1468

SCIENCE & STATE
Prune bk: the 60 toughest sci & tech jobs in Washington, 93n757

SCIENCE FICTION
British sci fiction, 93n1204
Clockworks, 94n974
Encyclopedia of sci fiction, 94n1211
Futurespeak, 92n1145
Modern mystery, fantasy & sci fiction writers, 94n1207
More than 100: women sci fiction writers, 90n866
Reader's gd to 20th century sci fiction, 90n1108
Reference gd to sci fiction, fantasy, & horror, 93n1155
Reginald's sci fiction & fantasy awards, 2d ed, 93n1157
Science fiction & fantasy bk review annual 1988, 91n1111
Science fiction & fantasy bk review annual 1990, 93n1158
Science fiction & fantasy lit 1975-91, 94n1214
Science fiction & fantasy ref index 1985-91, 94n1213
Science fiction, fantasy & horror, 1987, 90n1112
Science fiction, fantasy & horror ref, 90n1110
Science-fiction: the early yrs, 92n1143
Twentieth-century sci-fiction writers, 3d ed, 93n1159
Ultimate gd to sci fiction, 92n1144
Uranian worlds, 2d ed, 91n1141
Walter M. Miller, Jr.: a bio-bibliog, 93n1179

Work of Brian W. Aldiss, 93n1154
Work of Chad Oliver, 91n1169
Work of Charles Beaumont, 2d ed, 92n1166
Work of Dean Ing, 92n1173
Work of George Zebrowski, 2d ed, 92n1185
Work of Ian Watson, 91n1220
Work of Pamela Sargent, 91n1174
Work of Reginald Bretnor, 91n1158
Work of Ross Rocklynne, 91n1173

SCIENCE FICTION FILMS
Fantastic cinema subject gd, 94n1449
Great sci fiction pictures 2, 91n1382
Science fiction, horror & fantasy film & TV credits suppl-1987, 90n1350
Science fiction stars & horror heroes, 92n1371

SCIENCE PROJECTS
Nature projects on file, 93n1527
Science fair project index 1985-89, 93n1462

SCIENCE—SOCIETIES, ETC.
AAAS hndbk 1989-90, 90n1435
Directory, 1992: AAAS consortium of affiliates for intl programs, 94n1572
Public info contact dir 1988-89, 90n1433
World gd to scientific assns & learned societies, 5th ed, 92n1461

SCIENTIFIC AMERICAN
Philip Morrison's long look at the lit, 91n1457
Scientific American cum index 1978-88, 91n1472

SCIENTISTS
American men & women of sci 1989-90, 90n1420
Biographical index to American sci, 91n1469
Biographies of scientists for sci-tech libs, 93n1440
Blacks in sci & medicine, 92n351
Chambers concise dict of scientists, 91n1460
Dictionary of scientific biog, v.17, suppl.2, 91n1461
Dictionary of scientific biog, v.18, suppl.2, 91n1462

SCOTLAND
British dirs, 90n133
Butterworths law dir 1993, 94n558
Companion to Scottish hist from the Reformation to the present, 91n533
Contribution to lit of Orcadian writer George Mackay Brown, 93n1206
Monarchs of Scotland, 91n534
Scotland: a literary gd, 91n474
Topographical dict of Scotland, 2d ed, 90n135

SCOTS LANGUAGE—DICTIONARIES—ENGLISH
Scoor-oot, 90n1054
Scots thesaurus, 91n1091

SCOTT, SIR WALTER
Scott dramatized, 93n1210

SCOTTISH LANGUAGE. See SCOTS LANGUAGE—DICTIONARIES—ENGLISH

SCOTTISH LITERATURE
Boswellian studies, 3d ed, 93n1231

SCOTTISH-AMERICANS
Original Scots colonists of early America 1612-1783, 90n390

SCREENWRITERS
Film writers gd, 2d ed, 91n1374
International dict of films & filmmakers, 2d ed, v.4, 94n1430
Man in Lincoln's nose, 91n1396

SCULPTORS
American women sculptors, 92n1005
Eva Hesse sculpture, 90n951
20th century painters & sculptors, 92n970

SCULPTURE
Annual exhibition record of the Natl Academy of Design 1901-50, 91n1021

Catalogue of European sculpture in the Ashmolean Museum 1540 to the present day, 94n1067
Encyclopedia of sculpture techniques, 91n1041
Gothic sculpture in America, 90n985
Roman sculpture, 94n1066

SEA COWS. *See* **SIRENIA**

SEA LIFE. *See* **MARINE BIOLOGY**

SEA SNAKES
Venomous sea snakes, 94n1750

SEALS (ANIMALS)
Field gd to whales, porpoises, & seals from Cape Cod to Nfld., 4th ed, 94n1737
Sierra Club hndbk of seals & sirenians, 93n1571

SEAMANSHIP
A-Z of sailing terms, 93n842

SEARCHING, BIBLIOGRAPHICAL
Basic lib skills, 3d ed, 94n620
Guide to info sources in alternative therapy, 90n1661

SEASHORE
Flowers of the Pacific Island seashore, 94n1647
Peterson 1st gd to seashores, 93n1574

SEAWEED. *See* **MARINE ALGAE**

SECOND CAREERS. *See* **CAREER CHANGES**

SECONDHAND BOOKSELLERS. *See* **ANTIQUARIAN BOOKSELLERS**

SECRET SERVICE
Soviet security & intelligence orgs 1917-90, 93n769

SECRETARIAL PRACTICE. *See* **OFFICE PRACTICE**

SECRETARIES
Complete secretary's hndbk, 7th ed, 94n300
Office sourcebk, 90n290
Professional secretary's hndbk, rev ed, 94n301
Secretary's key, 92n260
Webster's new world secretarial hndbk, 4th ed, 90n292

SECTS
Bibliography of new religious movements in primal societies, v.4, 92n1400
Dictionary of cults, sects, religions & the occult, 94n1513
Encyclopedic hndbk of cults in America, rev ed, 93n1410
Handbook of denominations in the US, 9th ed, 91n1445
Illustrated ency of active new religions, sects, & cults, 94n1529
Social sci & the cults, 91n1410

SECURITIES
How to read the financial pages & much more, rev ed, 90n218
International dict of the securities industry, 2d ed, 90n217
McGraw-Hill dict of Wall St acronyms, initials, & abbrevs, 93n171
Still more words of Wall Street, 91n185

SECURITY, INTERNATIONAL
Arms control & disarmament, defense & military, intl security, & peace, 90n673
Arms control, disarmament, & military security dict, 90n675
Canada & intl peace & security, 91n773
International affairs dir of orgs, 94n799
Internships in foreign & defense policy, 91n769
Peace & security thesaurus, 91n684

SECURITY SYSTEMS
Glossary of security equipment, 94n1776

SELECTION OF NONBOOK MATERIALS
Selection of lib materials for area studies, pt.1, 92n81

SELF-ACTUALIZATION (PSYCHOLOGY)
Would the Buddha wear a walkman?, 92n180

SELF-CARE, HEALTH
Complete hndbk of natural healing, 93n1648
Illustrated dict of natural health, 90n1642

SELF-EXAMINATION, MEDICAL
Do-it-yourself medical testing, 3d ed, 90n1671

SELF-HELP DEVICES FOR THE DISABLED
Home health care equipment, 91n1652
Meeting the needs of employees with disabilities, 92n228
Meeting the needs of employees with disabilities, 2d ed, 94n881
Resource dir for the disabled, 93n864

SELF-HELP GROUPS
Sickness & wellness pubs, 90n1610

SEMANTICS
Semantics: a bibliog, 1986-91, 93n1047

SEMICONDUCTORS
Concise ency of semiconducting materials & related techs, 93n1592

SEMINARS
Seminars dir, 2d ed, 92n46

SEMIOTICS
Handbook of semiotics, 91n81
Julia Kristeva, 91n917

SENIOR CITIZENS. *See* **AGED**

SENIOR POWER
Senior movement, 93n861

SENSE ORGANS
Aging & sensory change, 90n781

SEPARATION (PSYCHOLOGY)
Books to help children cope with separation & loss, v.3, 90n738

SEQUELS (LITERATURE)
Sequels: an annot gd to novels in series, 2d ed, 92n1138
Western series & sequels, 2d ed, 94n1221

SERBO-CROATIAN LANGUAGE—DICTIONARIES—ENGLISH
English-Serbocroatian dict, 3d ed, 91n1092
English-Serbocroatian, Serbocroatian-English pocket dict, 91n1094
Oxford-Duden pictorial Serbo-Croat & English dict, 90n1055
Serbocroatian-English dict, 3d ed, 91n1093

SERIAL MURDERS
Women serial & mass murderers, 93n612

SERIAL PUBLICATIONS
Advances in serials mgmt, v.3, 91n615
Communication serials, 1992/1993 ed, 93n982
Directory of electronic jls, newsletters & academic discussion lists, 2d ed, 93n72
El-Hi textbks & serials in print 1989, 90n299
El-Hi textbks & serials in print 1991, 92n285
Gale dir of pubs & broadcast media 1990, 91n61
Gale dir of pubs & broadcast media 1993, 94n988
Latin American serial pubs available by exchange, 93n633
National dir of mags 1994, 94n62
Readers' gd to per lit 1990, 92n60
Russian emigre serials, 91n411
Serials dir, 4th ed, 91n64
Serials dir, 7th ed, 94n63
Serials dir: EBSCO CD-ROM, summer 1993, 94n64
Serials ref work, 90n618
Standard per dir 1993, 94n67
Ulrich's intl pers dir 1989-90, 90n80
Ulrich's intl pers dir 1990-91, 91n66
Ulrich's intl pers dir 1991-92, 92n65
Ulrich's intl pers dir 1992-93, 93n88
Ulrich's intl pers dir 1993-94, 94n65
Ulrich's plus [CD-ROM], 94n66

SERIES
Books in series 1985-89: cum 1985-88, 90n14
Western series & sequels, 2d ed, 94n1221
Young people's bks in series, 93n1133

SERMONS
Concordance to the sermons of Gerard Manley Hopkins, 90n1181

SERVICES INDUSTRIES
Best nonfranchise bus opportunities, 94n199

SET DESIGNERS
Biographical dict of scenographers, 92n1380
Scenic design on Broadway, 93n1384
Theatrical designers, 93n1382

SEWAGE
Wastewater treatment tech, 90n1794

SEWING
Claire Shaeffer's fabric sewing gd, 91n995

SEX
A-to-Z of women's sexuality, rev ed, 93n884
Descriptive dict & atlas of sexology, 92n832
Dictionary of sexual slang, 94n909
Language of sex, 93n883
Mass media sex & adolescent values, 92n883
Sex & gender issues: a hndbk of tests & measures, 92n831
Variety's complete home video dir 1989: adult titles suppl, 90n1336

SEX & LAW
Feminist legal lit, 92n853
Sexuality & the law, 94n570

SEX CRIMES
Disability, sexuality & abuse, 93n865

SEX CUSTOMS
Medieval sexuality, 91n874

SEX DIFFERENCES IN EDUCATION
Sex differences & learning, 92n268

SEX DISCRIMINATION
On account of sex, 94n949

SEX INSTRUCTION
Human sexuality, 90n1646
Sexuality educ, 90n813
T.A.P.P. sources: a natl dir of teenage pregnancy prevention programs, 91n875

SEX ROLE
Shakespeare & feminist criticism, 93n1212
Womanwords, 93n938

SEXISM
Dictionary of bias-free usage, 92n1030
Gender positive!, 94n1179
She said, he said, 93n914
Womanwords, 93n938

SEXISM IN LANGUAGE
Dictionary of bias-free usage, 92n1030
Womanwords, 93n938

SEXUALLY TRANSMITTED DISEASES
Prostitutes in medical lit, 92n1649

SEYCHELLES
Seychelles, 94n140

SHADE TREES
Shade & color with water-conserving plants, 93n1520

SHAFFER, PETER
Peter Shaffer: an annot bibliog, 92n1208

SHAKESPEARE, WILLIAM
Brush up your Shakespeare!, 91n1213
Coriolanus: an annotated bibliog, 90n1183
Dictionary of quotations from Shakespeare, 93n1213
Essential Shakespeare, 2d ed, 94n1256
Hamlet in the 1960s, 93n1211
Macbeth: an annot bibliog, 2d ed, 91n1216
Othello: an annot bibliog, 91n1214
Shakespeare: a bibliographical gd, new ed, 92n1210
Shakespeare A to Z, 92n1209
Shakespeare: an annot bibliog, 93n1214
Shakespeare & feminist criticism, 93n1212
Shakespeare & the musical stage, 91n1297
Shakespeare folio hndbk & census, 91n1215
Shakespeare index, 93n1215
Shakespeare music cat, 92n1251
Shakespeare on screen, 92n1368
Shakespearean criticism, v.9, 90n1184
Shakespearean criticism, v.11, 91n1217
Shakespearean criticism, v.18, 94n1260
Shakespearean criticism, v.19, yrbk 1991, 94n1259
Shakespeare's characters, 94n1258
Shakespeare's Othello, 90n1185
Shakespeare's quotations, 94n1257
Stratford festival story, 92n1386

SHALE
Argillaceous rock atlas, 92n1737

SHAREWARE (COMPUTER SOFTWARE)
Bob Brant's best of Macintosh shareware, 94n1913
PC-SIG ency of shareware, 4th ed, 93n1689

SHARKS
Reef sharks & rays of the world, 94n1718

SHAW, BERNARD
Bernard Shaw: a gd to research, 93n1216

SHELLS
Field gd to shells of the Tex. coast, 93n1522
Henry Holt gd to shells of the world, 90n1513
Peterson 1st gd to shells of N America, 91n1549
Shells, 94n1675
Simon & Schuster pocket gd to shells of the world, 91n1550

SHIPBUILDING INDUSTRY
Shipbuilding industry, 94n2031

SHIPPING
Shipping lit of the Great Lakes, 93n1778

SHIPS
Historic ships of Calif., 90n1820
Historic ships of Washington, 90n1821
Jane's high-speed marine craft 1990, 91n1831
Naval Institute gd to combat fleets of the world 1993, 94n704
Naval Institute gd to the ships & aircraft of the US fleet, 15th ed, 94n705
Visual dict of ships & sailing, 93n1792

SHIPS—PASSENGER LISTS
Passenger & immigration lists index, 1992 suppl., 93n460

SHIPWRECKS
Great Lakes gd to sunken ships, 94n2029

SHOOTING
Bookman's gd to hunting, shooting, angling, & related subjects, 92n799

SHOPPING
Ethical shopper's gd to Canadian supermarket products, 94n248

SHORE BIRDS
Facts on File field gd to N Atlantic shorebirds, 90n1531
Shorebirds of the Pacific Northwest, 94n1700

SHORT FILMS
Soundies distributing corp of America, 92n1370

SHORT STORIES
American short-story writers, 1880-1910, 90n1133
American short-story writers, 1910-45, 1st series, 91n1156
American short-story writers, 1910-45: 2d series, 92n1164
Comprehensive bibliog of English-Canadian short stories 1950-83, 90n1199
Critical survey of short fiction, rev ed, 94n1215
H. E. Bates: a bibliographical study, 92n1198
Index to American short story award collections 1970-90, 94n1230
Iranian short story authors, 91n1237
Kate Chopin companion, 90n1202
Latin American short story, 93n1225
Mothers & daughters in American short fiction, 94n1219
Novel & short story writer's market, 1989, 90n902

Novel & short story writer's market, 1992, 93n966
Reader's companion to the novels & short stories of Evelyn Waugh, 90n1188
Roth's index to short stories, 90n1113
Short story index 1984-88, 90n1115
Short story writers & their work, 2d ed, 93n1160
Twentieth century European short story, 91n1142
Twentieth-century short story explication: new series, v.1, 94n1218
Twentieth-century short story explication: suppl.5 to the 3d ed, 92n1146

SHORT STORY
Critical survey of short fiction, rev ed, 94n1215
Short story criticism, v.2, 90n1114
Short story criticism, v.3, 91n1143
Short story criticism, v.11, 94n1216
Short story criticism, v.12, 94n1217
Short story cycle, 90n1134
Twentieth century short story explication, suppl.4 to 3d ed, 90n1116
Twentieth-century short story explication: an index, 93n1161

SHRUBS
Flowering trees & shrubs, 90n1508
Folklore of trees & shrubs, 94n1673
Meet the natives: the amateur's field gd to Rocky Mountain wildflowers, trees & shrubs, 9th ed, 93n1505
Mosaik's photographic key to the trees & shrubs of Great Britain & N Europe, 94n1670
Shrubs, 90n1509
Trees & shrubs of Great Britain & N Europe, 94n1670
Trees of Hawai'i, 92n1553
Weeds of the woods, 93n1515

SIBERIA
Siberia & the Soviet Far East, 93n139

SICK CHILDREN
Using media to make kids feel good, 90n828

SIERRA LEONE
Sierra Leone, 94n102

SIGN LANGUAGE
Gallaudet survival gd to signing, 92n1021
Perigee visual dict of signing, rev ed, 93n1098

SIGNS & SYMBOLS
Dictionary of symbolism, 94n979
Dictionary of symbols, 93n1041
Famous animal symbols, v.2, 94n291
Instructions & warnings, 91n248

SIKH-AMERICANS
Sikhs in N America, 93n1436

SIKHISM
Popular dict of Sikhism, 91n1452
Sikhism & the Sikhs, 90n1414
Sikhs: their lit on culture, hist, philosophy, pols, religion & traditions, 91n1453

SIKHS
Sikhs in N America, 93n1436

SIKSIKA INDIANS
Bibliography of the Blackfoot, 90n368
Blackfoot dict of stems, roots, & affixes, 92n1064

SILENT FILMS
American animated films: the silent era, 1897-1929, 91n1365
Guide to silent Westerns, 94n1443
Resources for writers, 93n971
Treasures from the film archives, 90n1326

SILKWORMS
Silkworm diseases, 92n1477

SILVERSMITHS
Pennsylvania silversmiths, goldsmiths & pewterers 1684-1900, 94n1034

SILVERWORK
Marks of London goldsmiths & silversmiths (c1697-1837), 90n934

SIMILE
Similes dict, 90n1014

SINATRA, FRANK
Frank Sinatra: a complete recording hist, 93n1265
Sinatra: the man & his music, 94n1368

SINGAPORE
Historical dict of Singapore, 93n129
Singapore, 90n123

SINGERS
Billboard bk of American singing groups, 94n1359
Hollywood songsters, 92n1349
Julie Andrews: a bio-bibliog, 90n1322

SINGLE-PARENT FAMILY
One-parent children, the growing minority, 91n860

SIR GAWAIN & THE GREEN KNIGHT
Sir Gawain & the Green Knight: an annot bibliog, 1978-89, 93n1217

SIRENIA
Sierra Club hndbk of seals & sirenians, 93n1571

SIOUX LANGUAGE. *See* **DAKOTA LANGUAGE**

SKIN
Ichthyosis & related disorders, 91n1701
Psoriasis: professional educl materials, 91n1702

SLANG
Brewer's dict of 20th-century phrase & fable, 93n1294

SLAVERY
Dictionary of Afro-American slavery, 90n493

SLAVIC COUNTRIES
American bibliog of Slavic & E European studies for 1990, 94n130
Slavic studies, 94n131

SLAVIC LANGUAGES
LC romanization tables & cataloging policies, 92n586

SLAVS
International dir of librarians & lib specialists in the Slavic & E European field, 3d ed, 91n628

SLEEP
Encyclopedia of sleep & dreaming, 94n808

SLIDES (PHOTOGRAPHY)
Educators gd to free filmstrips & slides, 45th ed, 94n375

SLOGANS
Brewer's dict of 20th-century phrase & fable, 93n1294
Every bite a delight & other slogans, 94n299

SLOW LEARNING CHILDREN
Best: high/low bks for reluctant readers, 91n367
High/low hndbk, 3d ed, 91n365

SMALL BUSINESS
Action gd to govt grants, loans, & giveaways, 94n895
Best nonfranchise bus opportunities, 94n199
Canadian small business hndbk, 2d ed, 92n151
Entrepreneur & small bus problem solver, 2d ed, 91n152
Free money for small businesses & entrepreneurs, 91n211
Macmillan small bus hndbk, 90n186
Pratt's gd to venture capital sources, 1992 ed, 93n197
Small business info hndbk, 92n136
Small business sourcebk, 3d ed, 90n216
Small business sourcebk, 5th ed, 93n213
Small business start-up index, 91n166

SMALL LIBRARIES—BOOK LISTS
Reference sources for small & medium-sized libs, 5th ed, 93n17

SMITH, JESSIE WILLCOX
Jessie Willcox Smith: a bibliog, 90n984

SMITH, JOHN
Captain John Smith: a ref gd, 92n455

SMITHSONIAN INSTITUTION. LIBRARIES
Books of the fairs, 93n1306

SNAKE MACKERALS. *See* GEMPYLIDAE

SNAKES
Atlas of snakes of the world, 92n1586
A-Z of snake keeping, 92n1589
Snakes of E North America, 91n1601
Snakes of the US & Canada, v.1, 94n1751
Snakes of the world, 90n1571

SNOW
Climatological atlas of snowfall & snow depth for the NE US and SE Canada, 94n1948

SOCCER
World Cup 1930-90, 92n801

SOCIAL ACTION
Activist's almanac, 94n865

SOCIAL CHANGE
Atlas of social issues, 92n76

SOCIAL HISTORY
Atlas of social issues, 92n76
Atlas of world issues, 90n408
Covert culture sourcebk, 94n76
Encyclopedia of American social hist, 94n505
Macrothesaurus for info processing in the field of economic & social dvlpmt, 93n641
World fact file, 92n83

SOCIAL INDICATORS
50 fabulous places to raise your family, 94n944
Livable cities almanac, 93n920
Measuring global values, 93n729
100 best small towns in America, 94n942

SOCIAL INTERACTION IN CHILDREN
Prosocial dvlpmt in children, 93n894

SOCIAL MOVEMENTS
1960s: an annot bibliog of social & pol movements in the US, 94n863

SOCIAL NETWORKS
Social support networks, 1983-87, 90n815

SOCIAL PROBLEMS
Atlas of world issues, 90n408
Encyclopedia of world problems & human potential, 3d ed, 92n803
New state of the world atlas, 4th ed, 93n475
Picture this! a gd to over 300 environmentally, socially, & politically relevant films & videos, 93n1355
Sensitive issues: an annot gd to children's lit K-6, 93n1130

SOCIAL REFORMERS
Activist's almanac, 94n865
American social leaders, 94n78

SOCIAL SCIENCES
Advanced research methodology, 92n73
Blackwell dict of 20th-century social thought, 94n73
Dictionary of stats & methodology, 94n79
Educators gd to free social studies materials, 33d ed, 94n81
Guide to research & scholarship in Hungary, 90n309
Handbook of research on social studies teaching & learning, 93n336
Inventory of longitudinal studies in the social scis, 93n102
Key ideas in human thought, 94n1497
London bibliog of the social scis, 24th suppl., 1989, v.47, 91n77
Macrocosm USA, 94n74
Persian & English glossary for humanities & social scis, 93n1090
Selective inventory of social sci info & doc servs, 3d ed, 90n87
Social sci ref sources, 2d ed, 91n76
Social scis: a cross-disciplinary gd to selected sources, 91n74
Social scis: an intl bibliog of serial lit, 1830-1985, 93n100
Social scis index, 93n97
Social scis index: April 1990-March 1991, 93n96
Thematic list of descriptors: anthropology, 90n362
Thematic list of descriptors: economics, 91n168
Walford's gd to ref material, 5th ed, v.2: social & histl scis, 93n98
World dir of social sci insts 1990, 91n83
World list of social sci pers 1991, 93n101

SOCIAL SCIENTISTS
Max Weber, 90n86
Max Weber: a bio-bibliog, 90n84

SOCIAL SECURITY
Complete & easy gd to social security & medicare, 10th ed, 94n220
Consumers gd to Social Security benefits including Medicare, 12th ed, 90n223
International hndbk on old-age insurance, 92n814
Your 1991/92 gd to Social Security benefits, rev ed, 92n230

SOCIAL SERVICE
Author's gd to social work jls, 3d ed, 94n912
Delivering govt servs, 90n735
Dictionary of social work: Philippine setting, 90n816
Encyclopedia of social work, 1990 suppl., 18th ed., 91n876
Public welfare dir, 1990/91, 91n879
Social support networks, 1983-87, 90n815
Social work almanac, 94n911
Source bk 1989-90: social & health servs in the greater NY area, 90n818

SOCIAL SURVEYS
Public opinion polls & survey research, 91n82
Trends in public opinion, 90n85

SOCIAL WELFARE. *See* SOCIAL PROBLEMS

SOCIAL WORK ADMINISTRATION
Dictionary of social work: Philippine setting, 90n816

SOCIAL WORK EDUCATION
Social work educ 2, 90n817

SOCIAL WORK WITH CHILDREN
Child abuse & neglect, 91n602

SOCIAL WORK WITH THE AGED
Gerontological social work, 94n872

SOCIAL WORKERS
Directory of credentials in counseling & psychotherapy, 90n750

SOCIALISM
Encyclopedia of the American left, 91n763
Guide to the Boris I. Nicolaevsky collection in the Hoover Inst archives, 90n522
Latin American Marxism, 92n734

SOCIALLY HANDICAPPED YOUTH
At-risk youth, 91n310

SOCIOLOGISTS
Max Weber, 90n86
Max Weber: a bio-bibliog, 90n84

SOCIOLOGY
Church & social action, 91n1412
Critical dict of sociology, 91n841
Encyclopedia of sociology, 93n847
Encyclopedia of world problems & human potential, 3d ed, 92n803
Encyclopedic dict of sociology, 4th ed, 93n849
HarperCollins dict of sociology, 93n848
International bibliog of sociology 1985, 90n779
International current awareness servs: sociology & related disciplines, v.2, no.1, 92n804
Sociology in govt, 93n846
Thematic list of descriptors: sociology, 90n780

SOCRATES
Bibliography of eds, translations, & commentary on Xenophon's Socratic writings, 90n1373

SOFTWARE ENGINEERING
Concise ency of sftwr engineering, 94n1775

SOFTWARE PROTECTION
Computer law & sftwr protection, 94n1892

SOIL MECHANICS
Soil mechanics & fndns, 92n1601

SOLAR ENERGY
Solar electric independent home bk, 92n1627

SOLAR SYSTEM
Children's space atlas, 93n1703
Space almanac, 90n1581
Space atlas, 93n1700

SOLDIERS
Fallen in battle, 90n649
Fighting men of the Indian wars, 93n515
Financial aid for vets, military personnel & their dependents 1990-91, 92n651
Warrior's words, 94n697
Words of the Vietnam War, 92n475

SOMALI LANGUAGE—DICTIONARIES—ENGLISH
Somali-English dict, 2d ed, 93n1099

SOMALIA
Somalia, 90n110

SONGS
American women songwriters, 94n1325
Campion, Dowland & the lutenist songwriters, 90n1222
Great song thesaurus, 2d ed, 90n1279
Gurney, Ireland, Quilter & Warlock, 90n1223
Popular song index, 3d suppl, 90n1276
Song on record, 90n1266

SONGWRITERS. *See* **COMPOSERS**

SORRENTINO, GILBERT
Gilbert Sorrentino: a descriptive bibliog, 92n1181

SOTHERN, ANN
Ann Sothern: a bio-bibliog, 91n1352

SOUL MUSIC
Encyclopedia of pop, rock & soul, rev ed, 90n1298
Soul music A-Z, 93n1293

SOUND
Audio dict, 2d ed, 92n1608
Orion blue bk: audio 1990, 91n202
Orion blue bk: professional sound 1989, 91n207
Television & audio hndbk for technicians & engineers, 91n1615

SOUND MOTION PICTURES
Sound films, 1927-39, 93n1352

SOUND RECORDING INDUSTRY
Directory of art publishers, bk publishers & record cos, 91n1013

SOUND RECORDINGS
Billboard bk of no.1 hits, rev ed, 90n1292
Billboard bk of no.1 hits, 3d ed, 94n1360
Dictionary of musical tech, 93n1246
Directory of record & CD retailers, 1990-91 ed, 92n1256
Encyclopedia of recorded sound in the US, 94n1313
Guide to pseudonyms on American records, 1892-1942, 94n1317
His master's voice/la voce del padrone, 90n1226
His master's voice/la voix de son maitre, 91n1257
Jussi Bjorling phonography, 2d ed, 94n1354
New Trouser Pr record gd, 3d ed, 90n1235
Rolling Stone album gd, 94n1367
Song on record, 90n1266
Trouser Pr record gd, 4th ed, 93n1281

SOUNDIES DISTRIBUTING CORPORATION OF AMERICA
Soundies distributing corp of America, 92n1370

SOUTH AFRICA
ANC & black workers in S Africa, 1912-92, 94n103
Apartheid: a selective annotated bibliog, 1979-87, 91n842
International bus in S Africa 1988, 90n171
Major pol events in S Africa 1948-90, 92n706
South Africa, 90n112
South Africa under apartheid, 90n111
South Africa's road to change, 1987-1990, 92n89
Transnational corps in S Africa, 93n276
Transnational corps in S Africa & Namibia, 91n127
Who's who in S African pols, 3d ed, 92n705
Who's who in S African pols, 4th ed, 94n762

SOUTH AFRICA—FOREIGN RELATIONS—UNITED STATES
United States sanctions & S Africa, 94n545
U.S. relations with S Africa, 92n745

SOUTH AMERICA
Atlas of S America, 93n484
Dictionary of contemporary pols of S Amer, 90n730
Guyana, 90n144
Mammals of the neotropics, 90n1555
Political & economic ency of S America & the Caribbean, 93n774
South American, Central America, & the Caribbean 1993, 94n146
South American population censuses since independence, 91n907
South America's natl parks, 91n477
Uruguay, 90n147

SOUTH ASIA
Alternative dir of nongovtl orgs in S Asia, rev. ed, 91n39
Guide to mss & docs in the British Isles relating to S & SE Asia, v.1, 90n116
Guide to mss & docs in the British Isles relating to S & SE Asia, v.2, 91n97
Historical atlas of S Asia, 2d ed, 94n515
Indian subcontinent in lit for children & young adults, 93n1126
Mammals of the Indomalayan region, 94n1734

SOUTH CAROLINA
Books & articles on S.C. hist, 2d ed, 93n510
John C. Calhoun, 91n489
South Carolina: the WPA gd, 90n447

SOUTH DAKOTA
Guide to collections relating to S.D. Norwegian-Americans, 93n451

SOUTHEAST ASIAN LITERATURE
South-east Asia langs & lits, 90n1033

SOUTHERN STATES
Annotated bibliog of S American English, 91n1065
Contemporary fiction writers of the South, 94n1222
Criminal activity in the deep south, 1700-1930, 90n571
Encyclopedia of S culture, 90n491
Guide to S pols, 1989, 91n754
Hippocrene USA gd to historic black south, 94n475
Humor of the old Southwest, 91n1148
Is it true what they say about Dixie?, 90n1010
Islands of the S & SE US, 90n451
Urban south, 90n843
Vascular flora of the southeastern US, v.3, pt.2, 91n1533
Whistlin' Dixie: a dict of S expressions, 94n1089

SOUTHEY, ROBERT
Catalogue of the Bertam R. Davis "Robert Southey" collection, 91n1218

SOUTHWEST, NEW
Destination southwest, 91n910
Mushrooms & truffles of the southwest, 92n1545
Shade & color with water-conserving plants, 93n1520
Southwest publishing marketplace, 1991 ed, 91n662

SOUTHWEST, OLD
Humor of the old southwest, 91n1148

SOUTHWESTERN STATES
Desert & mountain plants of the southwest, 94n1645

SOUZAY, GERARD
Recorded performances of Gerard Souzay, 92n1284

SOVIET UNION. *See also* **FORMER SOVIET UNION;** *former republics, e.g.,* **RUSSIA; UKRAINE**
Bibliographic gd to Soviet & E European studies 1990, 92n103

Biographical dict of Russian/Soviet composers, 91n1275
Biographical dict of the Soviet Union 1917-88, 90n39
Biographical dir of 100 leading Soviet officials, 92n715
Dictionary of the Russian revolution, 90n524
Encyclopedia of Russian hist, 94n524
Encyclopedia of Soviet life, 92n721
Glasnost, 90n136
Gorbachev's law, 92n525
Guide to scholarly resources on the Russian empire & the Soviet Union in the N.Y. metropolitan area, 91n113
Guide to the Boris I. Nicolaevsky collection in the Hoover Inst archives, 90n522
Hippocrene companion gd to the Soviet Union, rev ed, 91n475
International writings of Bohdan S. Wynar, 1949-92, 94n80
Keys to the insects of the European part of the USSR, v.3, pt.2, 90n1554
Modern ency of religions in Russia & the Soviet Union, 90n1381
Religion in the Soviet Union, 94n1503
Researcher's gd to sources on Soviet social hist in the 1930s, 91n535
Rise & fall of the Soviet Union, 93n535
Russia & the Commonwealth A to Z, 94n525
Russian & Soviet educ 1731-1989, 93n383
SIBD 92-93, 93n293
Soviet Jewish hist, 1917-91, 93n447
Soviet lexicon, 90n720
Soviet military ency, abridged English-lang ed, 94n686
Soviet nomenklatura, 3d ed, 92n718
Soviet propaganda network, 90n728
Soviet pubs on Judaism, Zionism, & the state of Israel 1984-88, 91n407
Soviet security & intelligence orgs 1917-90, 93n769
Soviet stats since 1950, 93n142
Soviet Union, 3d ed, 91n536
Soviet Union: a biographical dict, 92n22
Soviet Union in lit, 92n1229
USSR calendar of events 1987, 90n525
USSR crime stats & summaries, 93n613
USSR in 1989, 92n490
Women & writing in Russian & the USSR, 93n1230
World almanac of the Soviet Union, 91n114

SOVIET UNION—COMMERCE—UNITED STATES
U.S.-Soviet trade dir, 1990, 91n272
U.S.-Soviet trade sourcebk, 92n254

SOVIET UNION—FOREIGN RELATIONS
Soviet foreign policy 1918-45, 92n744
Yearbook of Soviet foreign relations, 1991 ed, 93n788

SOVIET UNION—FOREIGN RELATIONS—UNITED STATES
Cold war chronology, 94n795

SOVIET UNION—POLITICS & GOVERNMENT
Demise of the Soviet Union, 94n548
Dictionary of pol parties & orgs in Russia, 94n779
Handbook of pol sci research on the USSR & E Europe, 94n781
Political & economic ency of the Soviet Union & Eastern Europe, 92n104

SOYBEAN—DISEASES & PESTS
Soybean diseases, 94n1595

SPACE FLIGHT
Interavia space dict 1989-90, 91n1819
Kitty Hawk to NASA, 92n1794
Men & women of space, 94n1757

SPACE SCIENCES
Cambridge air & space dict, 92n1591
HarperCollins dict of astronomy & space sci, 93n1702

SPACE STATIONS
Space almanac, 90n1581
Space station glossary, 93n1581

SPACE WARFARE
Space war glossary, 90n677

SPAIN
Consumer Spain 1991, 92n175
Dictionary of the lit of the Iberian Peninsula, 94n1289
European employment & industrial relations glossary: Spain, 93n295
Great Spanish films: 1950-90, 93n1365
Hispanic heritage, series 4, 93n150
Historical dict of modern Spain 1700-1988, 91n116
Historical dict of the Spanish empire, 1402-1975, 93n540
Motif-index of medieval Catalan folktales, 94n1389
Spain: 1001 sights, 93n506
Spanish Armada of 1588, 94n527
Visigoths in Gaul & Spain AD 418-711, 90n515
Who's who in Spain 1992, 94n21

SPANISH AMERICAN LITERATURE
Afro-Spanish American author 2: the 1980s, 91n1245
Spanish American women writers, 91n1246
Women authors of modern Hispanic S America, 91n1242

SPANISH AMERICAN POETRY
Contemporary Spanish American poets, 93n1228

SPANISH ARMADA. *See* **ARMADA, 1588**

SPANISH IMPRINTS
Hispanic rare bks of the golden age (1470-1699) in the Newberry Lib of Chicago, 90n27

SPANISH JEWS
Types & motifs of the Judeo-Spanish folktales, 94n1387

SPANISH LANGUAGE
Spanish-lang ref bks, 90n367

SPANISH LANGUAGE—DICTIONARIES—ENGLISH
Beginning Spanish bilingual dict, 2d ed, 90n1058
Bilingual dict of dental terms: Spanish-English, 91n1683
Collins Spanish-English, English-Spanish dict, 94n1132
Collins Spanish-English, English-Spanish dict, 2d ed, 90n1056
Collins Spanish-English, English-Spanish dict unabridged, 3d ed, 94n1133
Collins Spanish-English/English-Spanish dict, 3d ed, 93n1100
Concise American Heritage Larousse Spanish dict, 90n1057
Dahl's law dict, 94n552
Elsevier's dict of terrestrial plant ecology, 93n1497
Facts on File English/Spanish visual dict, 93n1101
Harper Collins Spanish dict, college ed, 91n1095
Latin American legal abbrevs, 91n557
Spanish idioms, 92n1091
Spanish-English, English-Spanish dict of computer terms, 94n1895
Spanish-English hndbk for medical professionals, 3d ed, 90n1670

SPANISH LITERATURE
Biographical dict of Hispanic lit in the US, 90n1124
Spanish, Catalan, & Galician literary authors of the 20th century, 93n1233

SPECIAL EDUCATION
Concise ency of special educ, 92n320
Directory for exceptional children 1990-91, 91n349
Directory of Catholic special educl programs & facilities 1989, 91n299
Encyclopedia of mental & physical handicaps, 92n322
Glossary of special educ, 90n350
Special educ hndbk, 92n323

SPECIAL FORCES (MILITARY SCIENCE)
Visual dict of special military forces, 94n689

SPECIAL LIBRARIANS
Directory of catalogers in the SLA, 90n603
International dir of librarians & lib specialists in the Slavic & E European field, 3d ed, 91n628

SPECIAL LIBRARIES. *See* **LIBRARIES, SPECIAL**

SPEEDWRITING. *See* **STENOTYPY**

SPEECH ERRORS
Error analysis, 92n1010

SPELLERS
Canadian spelling dict, 7th ed, 94n1102
Paragon House spelling dict, 94n1103
Proper noun speller, 91n1078

SPENCER, HERBERT
Herbert Spencer: a primary & secondary bibliog, 94n1490

SPENSER, EDWARD
Spenser ency, 92n1211

SPICES
Complete bk of herbs, spices & condiments, 91n1492
Complete bk of spices, 92n1497
Herbs, spices, & medicinal plants, v.4, 91n1534
Macmillan treasury of spices & natural flavorings, 90n1457

SPIES
Spies & provocateurs, 94n796

SPINNING
Encyclopedia of handspinning, 90n936

SPINOZA, BENEDICTUS DE,
Spinoza in English, 93n1394

SPIRITS
Encyclopedia of ghosts & spirits, 93n810

SPIRITUAL LIFE
Dictionary of religious & spiritual quotations, 91n1420

SPIRITUALS (SONGS)
Index to Negro spirituals, rev ed, 92n1315

SPITZER, LEO
Leo Spitzer on lang & lit, 93n1046

SPOILS OF POYNTON, THE
Concordance to Henry James's The Spoils of Poynton, 90n1146

SPONGES
Atlas of sponge morphology, 92n1584

SPORTING NEWS, THE
Index to the Sporting News, 93n823

SPORTS
Acrosport, 94n817
Annotated bibliog of Latin American sport, 91n801
Atlas of American sport, 94n819
Biographical dict of American sports: outdoor sports, 90n757
College admissions index of majors & sports 1992-93, 93n379
Directory of European sports orgs, 93n821
Drug file, 93n1667
Encyclopedia of N American sports hist, 93n819
Free money for athletic scholarships, 94n326
Guinness bk of sports records 1993, 94n825
Guinness sports record bk 1990-91, 91n811
Information please sports almanac, 1990, 91n800
Information please sports almanac, 1993, 94n818
Information sources in sport & leisure, 94n821
Leisure lit, 94n820
Norm Hitzges histl sports almanac, 93n812
Oxford companion to Australian sport, 94n822
Pick-up games, 94n823
Speaker's treasury of sports anecdotes, stories, & humor, 91n816
Sport in Britain, 93n814
Sports & fitness, 90n763
Sports fan's connection, 93n822
Sports federation of Canada sports dir 1990, 91n810
Sports Illustrated 1992 sports almanac, 93n813
Sports in N America, v.3, 94n826
Sports rules ency, 2d ed, 91n808

SPORTS ART
Dictionary of sporting artists 1650-1990, 94n1065

SPORTS FOR CHILDREN
Recreation hndbk, 94n827

SPORTS FOR WOMEN
American women in sport, 1887-1987, 90n758
Outstanding women athletes, 93n818
Women in sport, 92n767

SPORTS MEDICINE
Collected papers on sports medicine research, 1982-87, 90n1687
Physical fitness & sports medicine, 90n1688

SPORTS MUSEUMS
Sports halls of fame, 93n820

SPORTS PROMOTERS
Biographical dict of American sports: outdoor sports, 90n757

SPORTS SCIENCES
Dictionary of the sport & exercise scis, 92n771

SPORTS STORIES
Index to the Sporting News, 93n823

SPRINGS
Holy wells & sacred water sources in Britain & Ireland, 94n1386

SPY FILMS
Encyclopedia of American spy films, 91n1379
Spies & sleuths, 90n1345

SPY STORIES
Catalogue of crime, rev ed, 91n1132
Spy fiction, 91n1133

SPYING. See ESPIONAGE

SRI LANKA
Cambridge ency of India, Pakistan, Bangladesh, Sri Lanka, Nepal, Bhutan & the Maldives, 91n99
Political parties in Sri Lanka since independence, 90n715
South Asian hndbk, 1992, 93n502

STADIA
Major league stadiums, 92n781

STAGE LIGHTING
ABC of stage lighting, 94n1475
Lighting design on Broadway, 93n1383
Theatre lighting from A to Z, 94n1470

STAGE MACHINERY
Theatre backstage from A to Z, 3d ed, 90n1368

STAINED GLASS. See GLASS PAINTING & STAINING

STANDARD INDUSTRIAL CLASSIFICATION MANUAL
Standard industrial classification applied to histl data: the 1871 industrial census, 91n150

STANDARDIZATION
Index & dir of industry standards, 90n240
Standards: a resource & gd for identification, selection, & acquisition, 91n160

STANDARDS, ENGINEERING
Standards: a resource & gd for identification, selection, & acquisition, 91n160

STANTON, ELIZABETH CADY
Papers of Elizabeth Cady Stanton and Susan B. Anthony, 94n964

STAPLETON, MAUREEN
Maureen Stapleton: a bio-bibliog, 94n1418

STAR TREK (TELEVISION PROGRAM)
Star Trek: an annot gd to resources, 93n1331

STAR TREK FILMS
Star Trek: an annot gd to resources, 93n1331

STARS
Binary stars, 94n1929
Facts on File atlas of stars & planets, 94n1925
Field gd to the stars & planets, 3d ed, 94n1928
Messier's nebulae & star clusters, 2d ed, 93n1705
NGC 2000.0: the complete new general cat & index cats of nebulae & star clusters, 90n1747
Star & planet spotting, 91n1756
StarList 2000, 94n1924

STATE AID TO EDUCATION
Free money for college from the govt, 94n327

STATE GOVERNMENTS
Almanac of American pols 1994, 94n746
Book of the states, v.28, 1990-91 ed, 91n743
Book of the states, v.29, 94n721
CQ's state fact finder, 94n750
Directory of legislative leaders 1989-90, 90n696
Directory of legislative leaders 1991-92, 93n739
Election results dir, 1993 ed, 94n738
Facts about the states, 90n706
Government dir of addresses & telephone nos, 93n740
Inside the legislative process, 1991 ed, 93n751
Legislative staff servs 1988, 90n707
NAGARA state archives & records mgmt programs, 1989, 90n698
Organizations of state govt officials dir 1992, 94n742
Selected state enactments 1990, 92n697
State blue bks, legislative manuals & ref pubns, 91n730
State data & database finder, 90n708
State elective officials & the legislatures 1991-92, 92n692
State issues 1989, 90n710
State issues 1992, 93n755
State legislative leadership, committees & staff 1991-92, 92n698
State legislative sourcebk 1992, 93n750
State legislative staff dir 1991, 93n738
State ref pubs 1991-92, 93n734
State yellow bk, 90n700
State yellow bk, v.5, no.1, 94n743
Subject comps of state laws 1985-88, 90n689
Texas state dir 1989, 90n701

STATE TREES
Grand trees of America, 94n1672

STATESMEN
Biographical dir of the US executive branch, 1774-1989, 91n731
Columbia dict of pol biog, 92n670
Mexican pol biogs, 1884-1935, 93n775
Political leaders of the contemporary Middle East & N Africa, 91n762
Statesmen who changed the world, 94n716
Who's who in Africa, 93n760
Who's who in European pols, 92n719
Who's who in S African pols, 3d ed, 92n705

STATISTICIANS
Federal statistical source, 29th ed, 92n845

STATISTICS
Almanac of the 50 states, 1992 ed, 93n909
America votes 19, 92n696
Charts, graphics & stats index 1988-91, 93n916
Comparative world data, 90n838
County & city extra, 1992, 93n908
Data map 1989, 90n839
Demographic stats 1991, 93n897
Dictionary of statistical terms, 5th ed, 92n847
Dictionary of US govt statistical terms, 93n903
Encyclopedia of statistical scis, suppl, 91n898
Energy stats yrbk 1987, 91n1803
Europe in figures, 3d ed, 94n935
Eurostatistics, 90n185
FAO quarterly bulletin of stats 1990, v.3, 91n1477
Guide to US govt stats, 1989 ed, 91n896
Handbook of industrial stats 1990, 92n196
HarperCollins dict of stats, 93n904
Index to intl stats 1990, 93n915
International dir of non-official statistical sources 1990, 91n899
International histl stats: Europe 1750-1988, 3d ed, 93n911
International histl stats: the Americas, 1750-1988, 2d ed, 94n936
Official gd to the American marketplace, 93n906
Places, towns & townships, 94n937
Political data hndbk: OECD countries, 93n727
She said, he said, 93n914
Short-term economic stats: Central & E Europe, 93n292
State & local stats sources, 2d ed, 94n934
Statistical abstract of N.D. 1988, 90n840
Statistical abstract of the US 1992, 94n938
Statistical hndbk on women in America, 92n867
Statistical record of black America, 92n348
Statistical ref index 1990 annual, 92n848
Statistical yrbk, 1987, 92n849
Statistical yrbk for Asia & the Pacific 1988, 91n902
Statistical yrbk for Asia & the Pacific 1991, 94n939
Statistics & surveys vocabulary, 93n905
Statistics sources, 13th ed, 90n841
Statistics sources 1993, 93n913
Supplement to the 10th mental measurements yrbk, 92n760
World facts & figures, 3d ed, 90n92
World stats in brief, 14th ed, 94n940
World tables, 1988-89 ed, 90n193
Year bk of labour stats: retrospective ed on population censuses 1945-89, 91n251

STEAM ENGINEERING
Stationary engineering hndbk, 90n1607

STEAM MOTOR-CARS
Steam passenger serv dir 1989, 90n1814

STEAMBOATS
Way's steam towboat dir, 92n1806

STEEL
Worldwide gd to equivalent irons & steels, 3d ed, 94n1796

STEEL BAND MUSIC
Forty yrs of steel, 94n1382

STEEL INDUSTRY & TRADE
Encyclopedia of American bus hist & biog: iron & steel in the 19th century, 90n236

STENOTYPY
Court reporting computer compatible machine shorthand dict, 90n289

STEPHENS, LESLIE
Leslie Stephen's life in letters, 94n1261

STERLING MAXWELL COLLECTION
Short title cat of the emblem bks...in the Stirling Maxwell collection, rev ed, 90n632

STEROIDS
Anabolic steroids & sports, 93n1666
Dictionary of steroids, 92n1519

STEWART, ELLEN
Ellen Stewart & La Mama: a bio-bibliog, 94n1410

STEWART, JAMES
James Stewart: a bio-bibliog, 93n1319

STOCK COMPANIES
Nasdaq fact bk & co dir, 1993, 94n182

STOCK INDEX FUTURES
St. James world futures & options dir 1991-92, 92n168

STOCK OPTIONS
St. James world futures & options dir 1991-92, 92n168

STOCK PRICE INDEXES
Dow Jones averages 1885-1990, 92n165
Handbook of financial market indexes, averages, & indicators, 91n171

STOCK QUOTATIONS
Common stock newspaper abbrevs & trading symbols, suppl.1, 92n160

STOCKBROKERS
Skinner's dir of security dealer name & address changes 1992, 94n184

STOCK-EXCHANGE
Common stock newspaper abbrevs & trading symbols, 90n213
Common stock newspaper abbrevs & trading symbols, suppl.1, 92n160
Crawford's dir of city connections 1991, 92n156
Directory of tech in global financial markets, 91n179

Directory of world stock exchanges, 90n204
Handbook of financial market indexes, averages, & indicators, 91n171
Handbook of world stock & commodity exchanges, 1992, 93n222
McGraw-Hill dict of Wall St acronyms, initials, & abbrevs, 93n171
Stock market & investment vocabulary, 90n202

STOCKS. *See also* **INVESTMENTS**
Business One Irwin investor's hndbk 1993, 94n187
Complete gd to closed-end funds, 90n201
Directory of cos offering dividend reinvestment plans, 6th ed, 90n203
Dow Jones averages 1885-1990, 92n165
Dow Jones investor's handbk 1989, 90n205
Individual investor's gd to no-load mutual funds, 8th ed, 90n211
Initial public offering annual 1989, 91n183
International dict of the securities industry, 2d ed, 90n217
Moody's hndbk of common stocks, spring 1992, 93n223
100 best stocks to own in America, 2d ed, 92n169
Standard & Poor's stock & bond gd, 1993 3d, 94n200

STONE INDUSTRY & TRADE
Architect's hndbk of marble, granite, & stone, 91n1024

STORYTELLING
National dir of storytelling, 1990 ed, 91n294
Storytelling folklore sourcebk, 92n1316
Storytelling for young adults, 92n626
Storytime sourcebk, 92n625

STRADELLA, ALESSANDRO
Alessandro Stradella (1639-1682): a thematic cat of his compositions, 92n1263

STRATEGIC DEFENSE INITIATIVE
Space war glossary, 90n677

STRATFORD FESTIVAL (ONT.)
Stratford festival story, 92n1386

STRAUSS, RICHARD
Complete operas of Richard Strauss, 90n1271

STRAVINSKY, IGOR
Igor Stravinsky: an intl bibliog of theses & dissertations, 1925-87, 90n1245
Igor Stravinsky—the composer in the recording studio, 92n1278

STREET ADDRESSES
Guide to worldwide postal-code & address formats, 91n941
Guide to worldwide postal-code & address formats, 1993, 94n989
National dir of addresses & telephone nos, 93n69

STRESS (PHYSIOLOGY)
Stress, strain, & Vietnam, 90n739

STRESS (PSYCHOLOGY)
Stress and mental health, 90n1649

STRIKES & LOCKOUTS
Labor conflict in the US, 92n215

STRUCTURAL DESIGN
Timber design & construction sourcebk, 90n1575

STUDENT AID. *See also* **GRANTS-IN-AID; SCHOLARSHIPS**
A's & B's of academic scholarships, 12th ed, 90n330
A's & B's of academic scholarships, 16th ed, 94n363
Barron's gd to financing a medical school educ, 91n1673
Cash for college, 94n360
Chronicle financial aid gd for 1991-92 school yr, 93n367
College check mate, 3d ed, 90n331
College costs & financial aid hndbk 1994, 94n353
College price bk 1990, 91n338
Complete college financing gd, 2d ed, 93n371
Directory of financial aids for minorities, 1989-90, 90n329
Directory of financial aids for women 1989-90, 90n874
Financial aid for minorities in engineering & sci, 94n1577
Financial aid for research & creative activities abroad 1992-94, 94n367
Financial aid for study & training abroad 1992-94, 94n368
Financial aid for vets, military personnel & their dependents 1990-91, 92n651
Financial resources for intl study, 91n342
Foundation grants to individuals, 6th ed, 90n809
Free money for college, 91n324
Free money for college from the govt, 94n327
Free money from colleges & univs, 94n328
Fund your way through college, 93n373
Graduate scholarship dir, 3d ed, 94n331
International scholarship dir, 3d ed, 94n332
National dir of grants & aid to individuals in the arts, 7th ed, 90n808
Scholarship bk, 3d ed, 91n314
Scholarship bk, 4th ed, 94n333
Scholarships, fellowships & loans 1992-93, 93n377
Winning edge, 90n760

STUDENT LOAN FUNDS
Complete college financing gd, 2d ed, 93n371
Graduate scholarship dir, 3d ed, 94n331

STUDENT MOVEMENTS
Student pol activism, 90n683

STUDENT NEWSPAPERS & PERIODICALS
College media dir 1989, 90n891
Freedom to publish, 91n957

STUDENTS, FOREIGN
College hndbk foreign student suppl. 1992, 92n302
Funding for US study, 91n343
Open doors 1990/91, 93n389
Profiles 1989-90, 93n390

STUDENTS, JEWISH
Jewish student's gd to American colleges, 91n332

STUDENTS' SONGS
School songs of America's colleges & univs, 93n1278

STUNT MEN & WOMEN
Special effects & stunts gd, 90n1331
Special effects & stunts gd, 2d ed, 94n1454

STYLE, LITERARY
Dictionary of stylistics, 91n955
Random House dict for writers & readers, 91n1068
Using picture storybks to teach literary devices, 91n1113

SUBCULTURE
Covert culture sourcebk, 94n76
Voices from the underground, 94n1010

SUBJECT HEADINGS
African studies thesaurus, 94n629
Art & architecture thesaurus, 91n618
Art & architecture thesaurus, suppl.1, 93n635
Canadian feminist thesaurus, 91n620
Cross-ref index, 2d ed, 90n597
Ei thesaurus, 94n1753
GRANTS subject authority gd, 93n637
HAPI thesaurus & name authority 1970-89, 92n587
Index to legal pers: thesaurus, 91n623
Industrial chemical thesaurus, 2d ed, 94n1942
Olderr's fiction subject headings, 92n584
Sears list of subject headings, 14th ed, 92n585
Sears list of subject headings: Canadian companion, 4th ed, 93n643
Subject access to films & videos, 93n640
Subject headings for church or synagogue libs, 2d ed, 91n625
Thesaurus of psychological index terms, 6th ed, 93n645
Thesaurus of subject headings for TV, 91n619
Unreal! Hennepin County lib subject headings for fictional characters & places, 2d ed, 93n644

SUBJECT HEADINGS, LIBRARY OF CONGRESS
Guides to LC subject headings & classification on peace & intl conflict resolution, 92n581
Library of Congress subject headings, 12th ed, 90n602
Subject headings for the lit of law & intl law, & index to LC K schedules, 4th ed, 91n626

SUB-SAHARAN AFRICA. *See* **AFRICA, SUB-SAHARAN**

SUBSTANCE ABUSE
Alcohol/drug abuse dict & ency, 90n821
Children of alcoholics, 4th ed, 91n880
Cocaine, 90n1695
Drug abuse A-Z, 91n881
Drug abuse bibliog for 1988, 93n888
Drug, alcohol, & other addictions, 90n820
Drug, alcohol, & other addictions, 2d ed, 94n914
Drug educ resources dir, 91n887
Drug-alert dict & resource gd, 92n841
Encyclopedia of drug abuse, 2d ed, 93n890
Guide to drug info & lit, 5th ed, 92n1697
Guide to fed funding for anti-drug programs 1991, 91n884
International hndbk of addiction behaviour, 92n837
100 best treatment centers for alcoholism & drug abuse, 90n827
Peterson's drug & alcohol programs & policies at 4-yr colleges, 90n825
Recovery resource bk, 91n891
Reference gd to addiction counseling, 92n836
Statistics on alcohol & drug abuse in Canada & other countries, 90n819
Substance abuse, 90n1650
Substance abuse: a resource gd for secondary schools, 92n838
Substance abuse among ethnic minorities in America, 93n891
Substance abuse & kids, 90n826
Substance abuse 1: drug abuse, 91n885
Substance abuse residential treatment centers for teens, 91n888
Substance abuse 2: alcohol abuse, 91n886
U.S. Jl's 1991 natl treatment dir, 91n889
Women's recovery progams, 91n890

SUCCESS
Book of women's firsts, 94n970

SUDAN
Historical dict of the Sudan, 2d ed, 94n105
Sudan, rev ed, 94n104

SUDDEN INFANT DEATH SYNDROME
Social correlates of infant & reproductive mortality in the US, 94n879

SUEZ CANAL (EGYPT)
Red Sea, Gulf of Aden & Suez Canal, 92n1770

SUGARCANE
Sugar-cane diseases, 90n1448

SULLIVAN, ARTHUR, SIR
How quaint the ways of paradox!, 93n1274

SULLIVAN, LOUIS H.
Louis Sullivan in the Art Institute of Chicago, 91n1030

SUMERIAN LANGUAGE
Cuneiform texts in the Metropolitan Museum of Art, 90n989

SUMMER EMPLOYMENT
Directory of overseas summer jobs, 1991, 92n218
Summer employment dir of the US, 1991, 92n217

SUMMER SCHOOLS
Peterson's summer opportunities for kids & teenagers 1990, 91n309

SUMMER THEATER
Summer theatre dir 1992, 93n1387

SUN YAT-SEN
Bibliography of Sun Yat-sen in China's Republican Revolution, 1885-1925, 93n521

SUPER BOWL GAME (FOOTBALL)
Sporting News complete Super Bowl bk, 1993 ed, 94n848

SUPERCONDUCTIVITY
Superconductivity sourcebk, 91n1800

SUPERCONDUCTORS
Concise ency of magnetic & superconducting materials, 93n1591

SUPERNATURAL
Harper's ency of mystic & paranormal experience, 92n765
Supernatural fiction for teens, 2d ed, 93n1156

SUPERSTITION
Dictionary of superstitions, 91n798

SURFACE ACTIVE AGENTS
Condensed ency of surfactants, 90n1752

SURFACES (TECHNOLOGY)
Encyclopedia of materials characterization, 93n1605

SURFING
Surfin'ary, 92n802

SURGERY
History of surgery in the US 1775-1900, 90n1637
History of surgery in the US 1775-1900, v.2, 94n1822

SURGERY, PLASTIC
Illustrated glossary of hand & reconstructive surgery, 91n1703

SURINAM
Suriname & the Netherlands Antilles, 94n149

SUSTAINABLE AGRICULTURE
Socioeconomics of sustainable agriculture, 94n1588

SVOBODA
Select index to Svoboda, v.1, 93n980
Select index to Svoboda, v.2, 93n981

SWEDISH LANGUAGE—DICTIONARIES—ENGLISH
English-Swedish, Swedish-English dict, 92n1092
Prisma's Swedish-English & English-Swedish dict, 4th ed, 90n1060

SWIMMING POOLS
ALSA swimmer's gd, 1993 ed, 94n861

SWINE
Pigs: a hndbk to the breeds of the world, 94n1740

SWISS LITERATURE (GERMAN)
Companion to 20th-century German lit, 93n1223

SWITZERLAND
Switzerland, 92n107

SYMBOLISM
Reverse symbolism dict, 93n1311

SYMONS, ARTHUR
Arthur Symons: a bibliog, 92n1212

SYMPHONIES
Catalogue of 18th-century symphonies, 90n1275

SYMPHONY
Symphony: a research & info gd, v.1, 91n1329

SYMPTOMATOLOGY
Vocabulary of medical signs & symptoms, 91n1665

SYNAGOGUE LIBRARIES
Subject headings for church or synagogue libs, 2d ed, 91n625

SYNAGOGUES
American synagogue hist, 90n379

SYNDICATES (JOURNALISM)
1992-1993 gd to newspaper syndication, 93n977

SYNDROMES
Dictionary of medical & surgical syndromes, 93n1658

SYNOPTIC PROBLEM
Synoptic problem, 90n1389

SYSTEM FAILURES (ENGINEERING)
From the Titanic to the Challenger, 90n1415

TAGALOG LANGUAGE
Tagalog slang dict, 93n1103

TAGALOG LANGUAGE—DICTIONARIES—ENGLISH
Ang mahalaga sa buhay, 93n1102
Pilipino/English, English/Pilipino concise dict, 90n1061

TAIWAN
Republic of China yrbk 1991-92, 94n121

TAKEOVERS, CORPORATE. *See* CONSOLIDATION & MERGER OF CORPORATIONS

TALE OF TWO CITIES
Tale of two cities: an annot bibliog, 94n1251

TALENTED STUDENTS
Handbook of gifted educ, 92n284

TALES
Tale type & motif index of early US almanacs, 92n1318

TALK SHOWS
Talk shows & hosts on radio, 93n990

TALMUD
Encyclopedia of Talmudic sages, 90n1413
Great Torah commentators, 91n1450

TAMIL LITERATURE
Encyclopaedia of Tamil lit, v.1, 92n1237

TANDY, JESSICA
Jessica Tandy: a bio-bibliog, 93n1315

TANZANIA
Field gd to the freshwater fishes of Tanzania, 93n1556

TARIFF
Protectionism, 90n279

TAX HAVENS
Tax havens, 94n186

TAX INCENTIVES
Directory of incentives for bus investment & dvlpmt in the US, 3d ed, 93n221

TAX PLANNING
Tax companion 1991, 92n264

TAX RETURNS
Ernst & Young tax gd 1993, 94n302
Guide to income tax preparation, 93n326

TAXATION
Canadian master tax gd, 1992, 93n229
Facts & figures on govt finance, 1990 ed, 91n214
Federal tax advisor: explanation, 92n263
J. K. Lasser's your income tax 1993, 93n327
Lexicon of tax terminology, 90n548
Taxation glossary, 3d ed, 91n288
U.S. master tax gd, 1991, 92n265
West's tax law dict, 1992 ed, 93n581

TAYLOR, EDWARD
Concordance to the minor poetry of Edward Taylor (1642?-1729), 93n1181

TAYLOR, PETER HILLSMAN
Peter Taylor: a descriptive bibliog 1934-87, 90n1155

TCHEREPNIN, ALEXANDER
Alexander Tcherepnin: a bio-bibliog, 90n1239

TEACHERS
Teacher educ program evaluation, 91n289

TEACHERS' UNIONS
Directory of faculty contracts & bargaining agents in insts of higher educ, v.18, 93n360

TEACHING—AIDS & DEVICES
Brown's dir of instructional programs, 1992: K-8, 93n346
Brown's dir of instructional programs, 1992: 7-12, 93n347
Current issues resource builder, 90n88
Educators gd to free filmstrips & slides, 45th ed, 94n375
Educators gd to free health, physical educ & recreation materials, 26th ed, 94n829
Educators gd to free home economics & consumer educ materials, 10th ed, 94n886
Educators gd to free social studies materials, 33d ed, 94n81
Educators grade gd to free teaching aids, 39th ed, 94n317
Elementary teachers gd to free curriculum materials, 50th ed, 94n318
Guide to free computer materials, 11th ed, 94n1911
Geography: a resource bk for secondary schools, 90n423

TEAM LEARNING APPROACH TO EDUCATION
Cooperative learning, 92n272

TECHNICAL EDITING
Oxford dict for scientific writers & eds, 93n967
Technical editing, 93n972

TECHNICAL WRITING
Oxford dict for scientific writers & eds, 93n967
Science & technical writing: a manual of style, 93n970
Technical editing, 93n972

TECHNOLOGY
Academic Pr dict of sci & tech, 93n1444
Almanac of sci & tech, 91n1466
Applied sci & tech index 1990, 92n1468
Applied sci & tech index [CD-ROM], 93n1457
Best sci & tech ref bks for young people, 92n1452
Bibliographic gd to tech 1990, 92n1450
Checklist of the Newberry Lib's printed bks in sci, medicine, tech, & the pseudosciences ca. 1460-1750, 94n1558
Concise illus dict of sci & tech, 94n1567
Corporate tech dir 1992, 93n246
Dictionary of engineering & tech, 5th ed, 91n1606
Directory of fed laboratory & tech resources, 91n1465
Directory of pers online: sci & tech, 2d ed, 92n1459
Early American scientific & technical lit, 91n1454
Encyclopaedia of the hist of tech, 91n1464
Encyclopedia of physical sci & tech, 1989 yrbk, 90n1425
Encyclopedia of physical sci & tech, 1991 yrbk, 93n1453
Encyclopedia of physical sci & tech, 2d ed, 94n1566
European research centres, 9th ed, 94n1574
European sources of scientific & technical info, 9th ed, 92n1460
European sources of scientific & technical info, 10th ed, 94n1576
Facts on File scientific yrbk 1991, 92n1463
Federal laboratory tech cat 1989, 91n1463
General sci index, v.14, no.7, 93n1459
Great events from hist 2: sci & tech series, 92n1465
Henry Holt hndbk of current sci & tech, 93n1455
History of sci & tech, 90n1423
History of sci & tech in the US, v.2, 94n1560
Index to scientific & technical proceedings, no.4, April 1990, 91n1471
Macmillan ency of sci, 92n1456
McGraw-Hill concise ency of sci & tech, 2d ed, 90n1427
McGraw-Hill dict of scientific & technical terms, 4th ed, 90n1428
McGraw-Hill ency of sci & tech, 7th ed, 93n1446
McGraw-Hill yrbk of sci & tech 1990, 91n1467
New bk of popular sci, 90n1437
New bk of popular sci, 92n1457
New bk of popular sci, 93n1450
Oxford illus ency of invention & tech, 93n1451
Science & tech desk ref, 94n1584
Science & tech in fact & fiction: a gd to children's bks, 91n1455
Science & tech in fact & fiction: a gd to young adult bks, 91n1456
Science & tech 1989: a purchase gd, 91n1458
Science and tech annual ref review 89, 90n1417
Science yr, 1990, 90n1439
Scientific & technical bks & serials in print 1989, 90n1419
Scientific & technical bks & serials in print 1991, 92n1453
Sourcebook for sci, mathematics, & tech educ 1990-91, 92n1462
Sourcebook for sci, mathematics, & tech educ 1992, 94n1582
Systems & control ency, suppl. v.2, 94n1570
Walford's gd to ref material, 5th ed, v.1: sci & tech, 91n1459
Walford's gd to ref material, 6th ed, v.1: sci & tech, 94n1562
Who's who in sci & engineering 1992-93, 94n1564

Who's who in sci in Europe, 7th ed, 93n1442
Who's who in tech, 6th ed, 90n1434
World tech policies, 94n1587
Yearbook of sci & the future 1991, 91n1468

TECHNOLOGY & STATE
Prune bk: the 60 toughest sci & tech jobs in Washington, 93n757

TECHNOLOGY TRANSFER
Diffusion of innovations, 91n79

TEDDY BEARS
Button in ear, 90n926
Ultimate teddy bear bk, 92n936

TEEN-AGE. *See* ADOLESCENCE

TEENAGE PARENTS
Adolescent pregnancy & parenthood, 91n894

TEENAGE PREGNANCY
Adolescent pregnancy & parenthood, 91n894
T.A.P.P. sources: a natl dir of teenage pregnancy prevention programs, 91n875

TEENAGERS
Best yrs of their lives, 94n926
Bibliography for training in child & adolescent mental health, 92n1673
Caring for kids with special needs, 94n918
Get help, 90n829
Juniorplots 4, 94n1192
Mass media sex & adolescent values, 92n883
Rip-roaring reads for reluctant teen readers, 94n1182
Substance abuse residential treatment centers for teens, 91n888

TELECOMMUNICATION
Communications standard dict, 2d ed, 90n889
Data & computer communications, 91n1751
Directory of computer conferencing in libs, 93n656
Distance educ: a selected bibliog, 94n380
Encyclopedia of telecommunications, 90n1733
Facts on File dict of telecommunications, rev ed, 92n1721
Fax for libs, 91n608
Telecommunications abstract annual 1988, v.4, 90n1742
Telecommunications dir 1994-95, 94n1922
Telecommunications dir, 5th ed, 93n1698
Telecommunications fact bk & illus dict, 93n1697
World satellite dir, 1989, 11th ed, 90n1741

TELECOMMUNICATION SYSTEMS
International satellite dir 1989, 4th ed, 90n1738
Omnicom index of standards 1989, 91n1753
Telecommunications systems & servs dir, 4th ed, 90n1740

TELEMARKETING
Encyclopedia of telemarketing, 90n273

TELEPHONE—DIRECTORIES
Bowker's bk trade fax & phone dir 1989, 90n634
Business connexions 1992, 93n228
Checklist of Canadian copyright deposits in the British Museum 1895-1923, v.3, pt.2, 90n40
(Code) bk area code dir, rev ed, 90n1734
Instant natl locator gd, 93n955
National dir of addresses & telephone nos, 93n69
Phillips Publishing's telephone industry dir 1989, 90n249
USA travel phone bk, 92n432

TELEVISION
American-Jewish media dir, 1989, 90n890
Bacon's radio/TV dir 1993, 94n1014
BFI film & TV hndbk 1993, 94n1455
British radio & TV pioneers, 94n1012
Canadian media list 1992/93, 93n952
Chambers concise ency of film & TV, 93n1346
Contemporary theatre, film, & TV, v.7, 90n1311
Contemporary theatre, film, & TV, v.9, 93n1324
FIAF cataloguing rules for film archives, 93n638
Film, TV, & video pers, 92n1332
Filmmaker's dict, 91n1371

Gale dir of pubs & broadcast media 1990, 91n61
Gale dir of pubs & broadcast media 1993, 93n988
New video ency, 92n912
Orion blue bk: video & TV 1990, 91n208
Radio & TV pioneers: a patent bibliog, 93n983
Radio & TV, suppl.2, 90n912
Television & audio hndbk for technicians & engineers, 91n1615
Television drama series programming, 93n993
Television horror movie hosts, 93n985
Television writers gd, 2d ed, 93n965
Television engineering hndbk, rev ed, 93n1588
Television-related cartoons in the New Yorker, 94n1056
Thesaurus of subject headings for TV, 91n619
World radio TV hndbk, 1992 ed, 93n1000

TELEVISION ACTORS & ACTRESSES
Complete actors' TV credits, 1948-88, v.1, 2d ed, 91n1392
Complete actors' TV credits, 1948-88, v.2, 2d ed, 91n1393

TELEVISION ADAPTATIONS
More theatre, 94n1464

TELEVISION & CHILDREN
Television & young people, 91n965

TELEVISION BROADCASTING
Film & TV hndbk 1990, 91n1388
Les Brown's ency of TV, 3d ed, 93n986
Matthews list, v.34, no.1, 91n937
NBC hndbk of pronunciation, 4th ed, 92n1032
Religious radio & TV in the US, 1921-91, 94n1511
Television & ethics, 90n910
Television interviews 1951-55, 92n911
TV ency, 93n988
Variety & Daily Variety TV reviews, v.16, 94n1019

TELEVISION MUSIC
Film & TV composers, 93n1258
TV & studio cast musicals on record, 91n1320

TELEVISION PRODUCERS & DIRECTORS
Who's who in Canadian film & TV 1989, 91n1375
Who's who in Canadian filn & TV 1991-92, 93n1341

TELEVISION—PRODUCTION & DIRECTION
Back Stage: TV, film & tape production dir, 1989 ed, 90n915
Total TV bk, 94n1016

TELEVISION PROGRAMS
Children's media market place, 3d ed, 90n621
Complete actors' TV credits, 1948-88, v.1, 2d ed, 91n1392
Complete actors' TV credits, 1948-88, v.2, 2d ed, 91n1393
Complete dir to prime time network TV shows 1946-present, 4th ed, 90n916
Famous Hollywood locations, 94n1421
Fifty yrs of TV, 93n998
Syndicated TV, 90n913
Television drama series programming, 93n993
Television interviews 1951-55, 92n911
Television network prime-time programming, 1948-88, 90n920
Television yrbk, 93n995
3 decades of TV, 91n967
Transcript/video index, 1991, 93n1001
Unsold TV pilots 1955-88, 91n973
Variety & Daily Variety TV reviews, v.16, 94n1019

TELEVISION SCRIPTS
Index to the Annenberg TV script archive, v.1, 91n976
Transcript/video index, 1991, 93n1001

TELEVISION SERIALS
Harry & Wally's favorite TV shows, 91n972
Television detective shows of the 70s, 92n918

TELEVISION SPECIALS
Animated TV specials, 91n974

TELEVISION WRITERS
Television writers gd, 90n919

TELL EL-AMARNA
Bibliography of the Amarna period & its aftermath, 92n501

TEMPLES
Bibliography on temples of the ancient Near East & Mediterranean world, 93n1402

TENNESSEE
Tennessee almanac & bk of facts 1989-90, 90n102
Tennessee attorneys dir, 1992, 93n585
Tennessee govt officials dir, 1991, 93n742

TENNIS
Teaching, coaching, & learning tennis, 90n776

TENNYSON, ALFRED TENNYSON, BARON
Annotated critical bibliog of Alfred, Lord Tennyson, 90n1186

TERATOGENIC AGENTS
Catalog of teratogenic agents, 6th ed, 90n1638
Catalog of teratogenic agents, 7th ed, 93n1628

TERMINAL CARE
Death & dying, 92n818

TERRORISM
Almanac of modern terrorism, 92n557
International terrorism in the 1980s, 90n727
Latin American revolutionaries, 91n761
Terrorism: a ref hndbk, 94n585
Terrorism, assassination, espionage & propaganda, 91n771
Terrorism, 1980-90, 92n551
Terrorism, 1988-91, 94n589

TESS OF THE D'URBERVILLES
KWIC concordance to Thomas Hardy's Tess of the D'Urbervilles, 90n1180

TESTING LABORATORIES
Directory of testing labs, 1991 ed, 92n1614
International dir of testing labs, 1993 ed, 94n1578

TEXAS
Bats of Tex., 92n1583
Directory of Tex. manufacturers, 1991, 92n194
Field gd to shells of the Tex. coast, 93n1522
Field gd to Tex. trees, 90n1511
Field gd to wildlife in Tex. & the Southwest, 90n1525
Historical atlas of Tex., 90n470
Texas, 94n89
Texas almanac & state industrial gd, 1992-93, 93n111
Texas fact bk 1989, 90n190
Texas mushrooms, 93n1509
Texas state dir 1989, 90n701
Texas trade & prof assns 1989, 90n277
William D. Wittliff & the Encino Pr, 91n657
Writers & publishers gd to Tex. markets, 92n893
Writers' gd to Tex. markets, 90n893

TEXT PROCESSING (COMPUTER SCIENCE)
Text retrieval: a dir of sftwr, 3d ed, 92n1714
Text storage & retrieval systems, 90n611

TEXTBOOKS
El-Hi textbks & serials in print 1989, 90n299
El-Hi textbks & serials in print 1991, 92n285

TEXTILE FABRICS
Claire Shaeffer's fabric sewing gd, 91n995
Encyclopedia of textiles, 93n1007

TEXTILE INDUSTRY
Fairchild's textile & apparel financial dir 1989-90, 91n229
Textile industry, 90n248

THACKERAY, WILLIAM MAKEPEACE
Annotations for the selected works of William Makepeace Thackeray, 91n1219
William Makepeace Thackeray, 90n1187

THATCHER, MARGARET
Margaret Thatcher: a bibliog, 94n776

THEATER. *See also* DRAMA
American drama criticism: suppl.2 to the 2d ed, 90n1129
American drama criticism, suppl.3 to the 2d ed, 93n1168
American drama 1918-60, 93n1380
American theater & drama research, 92n1385
American theatre hist, 93n1381
Back Stage theater gd, 93n1389
Bibliographic gd to theatre arts 1990, 92n1375
British theatre yrbk 1989, 90n1361
Cambridge gd to American theatre, 94n1479
Cambridge gd to theatre, updated ed, 94n1471
Cambridge gd to world theatre, 90n1362
Companion to the medieval theatre, 90n1369
Concise Oxford companion to the theatre, 94n1472
Contemporary theatre, film, & TV, v.7, 90n1311
Contemporary theatre, film, & TV, v.9, 93n1324
Dictionary of theatre anthropology, 92n1374
Directory of Canadian theatre archives, 94n1476
Directory of theatre training programs 2, 90n1358
Directory of theatre training programs, 3d ed, 93n1390
Dramatist's bible 1989, 90n1363
Dramatists sourcebk, 1991-92 ed, 92n1383
Dublin stage, 1720-45, 94n1468
Ellen Stewart & La Mama: a bio-bibliog, 94n1410
Encyclopedia of the N.Y. stage, 1930-40, 90n1367
Encyclopedia of the N.Y. stage, 1940-50, 94n1474
Eva Le Gallienne: a bio-bibliog, 90n1320
Facts on File dict of the theatre, 90n1356
Guide to critical reviews, part 2, 3d ed, 92n1333
International bibliog of theater: 1988-89, 94n1466
International dict of theatre, v.1, 93n1391
Joseph Papp: a bio-bibliog, 93n1378
London stage 1930-39, 92n1388
London stage 1940-49, 93n1386
London stage 1950-59, 94n1469
Lucille Lortel: a bio-bibliog, 94n1414
More theatre, 94n1464
National theatre in N & E Europe, 1746-1900, 92n1384
New York Times theater reviews [1985-86], 91n1399
Oxford companion to American theatre, 2d ed, 94n1480
Oxford companion to Canadian theatre, 91n1400
Regional theatre dir 1992-93, 93n1388
Stage deaths, 92n1376
Summer theatre dir 1989, 90n1360
TCG theatre dir 1993-94, 94n1477
Theatre backstage from A to Z, 3d ed, 90n1368
Want's theater dir, 1993 ed, 94n1478
Yorkshire stage 1766-1803, 90n1355

THEATER CRITICISM. *See* DRAMATIC CRITICISM

THEATRICAL MANAGERS
Biographical dict of actors, actresses, musicians, dancers, managers & other stage personnel in London, 1660-1800, v.13, 92n1378
Biographical dict of actors, actresses, musicians, dancers, managers & other stage personnel in London, 1660-1800, v.14, 92n1379

THEATRICAL PRODUCERS & DIRECTORS
David Merrick: a bio-bibliog, 93n1377
Ellen Stewart & La Mama: a bio-bibliog, 94n1410
From Belasco to Brook, 92n1381
From Stanislavsky to Barrault, 92n1382
Joseph Chaikin: a bio-bibliog, 93n1376
Lucille Lortel: a bio-bibliog, 94n1414

THEME PARKS. *See* AMUSEMENT PARKS

THEODICY
Theodicy: an annot bibliog, 94n1506

THEOLOGICAL SEMINARIES
Religious seminaries in America, 90n1377

THEOLOGY
African theology, 94n1508
Compact dict of doctrinal words, 90n1396
Dictionary of Judaism & Christianity, 93n1405
Draper's bk of quotations for the Christian world, 94n1551
Great thinkers of the W world, 93n950
Moody hndbk of theology, 91n1446

More than words, 92n1418
New 20th-century ency of religious knowledge, 2d ed, 92n1417
New dict of theology, 90n1382
Reference works for theological research, 3d ed, 93n1400
Scholar's gd to academic journals in religion, 90n1385
Wesley quotations, 92n1421

THERAPEUTICS
Lifetime ency of natural remedies, 94n1826
Manual of natural therapy, 90n1669
Prevention how-to dict of healing remedies & techniques, 93n1636

THERMODYNAMICS
Thermodynamic properties of inorganic materials, 91n1762

THESAURI
Scott, Foresman beginning thesaurus, 90n1022
Scott, Foresman jr thesaurus, 90n1023
Student thesaurus, 91n1080

THIRD PARTIES (UNITED STATES POLITICS)
Encyclopedia of 3d parties in the US, 92n683

THOMPSON, RANDALL
Randall Thompson: a bio-bibliog, 92n1260

THOREAU, HENRY DAVID
Henry David Thoreau: an annot bibliog of comment & criticism before 1900, 93n1182

TIBET
Tibet, 93n130

TIECK, LUDWIG
Ludwig Tieck: an annot gd to research, 94n1288

TIMBER JOINTS
Encyclopedia of wood joints, 94n1030

TIME
Cover story index 1960-89, 91n964
International time tables, 91n1757
Time: a bibliographic gd, 93n14
Time dimension, 92n5

TIMES SQUARE (NEW YORK, N.Y.)
Broadway: an encyclopedic gd to the hist, people & places of Times Square, 92n467

TIMOR
Timor, 94n112

TIPPETT, MICHAEL
Michael Tippett: a bio-bibliog, 91n1280

TITLE COMPANIES
Directory of courthouses & abstract & title cos, 1993, 94n559

TITO, JOSIP BROZ
Marshal Tito: a bibliog, 91n537

TOBACCO HABIT
Focus on addictions, 94n917

TOLKIEN, J. R. R.
Tolkien thesaurus, 92n1213

TONGAN LANGUAGE—DICTIONARIES—ENGLISH
Simplified dict of modern Tongan, 94n1134

TOURISM. See TOURIST TRADE

TOURIST TRADE
Beam's dir of intl tourist events 1991, 92n431
Fairchild's 1990 travel industry personnel dir, 91n453
Guide to hospitality & tourism educ 1989-90, 91n315
Leisure lit, 94n820
Third World tourism research 1950-84, 93n504
Tourism & the travel industry, 90n432
Travel & tourism data, 90n430
Worldwide travel info contact bk 1991-92, 92n439

TOWBOATS
Way's steam towboat dir, 92n1806

TOWNELEY PLAYS
Concordance to The Towneley Plays, 91n1192

TOXIC SUBSTANCES. See POISONS

TOXICOLOGY
Chemical exposure & human health, 94n1861
Comprehensive gd to the hazardous properties of chemical substances, 94n2015
Handbook of toxicologic pathology, 92n1694
International dir of contract laboratories, 2d ed, 90n1619
Toxicological evaluations, 1, 92n1729
Toxics A to Z, 93n1769

TOXICOLOGY LABORATORIES
Directory of toxicological & related testing labs, 92n1778
International dir of contract laboratories, 2d ed, 90n1619

TOY & MOVABLE BOOKS
Pop-up & movable bks, 94n1177

TOYS
Greenberg's gd to Marx toys, v.2, 91n988
History of American firefighting toys, 92n944
Toy buying gd, 90n229

TRADE. See COMMERCE

TRADE & PROFESSIONAL ASSOCIATIONS
Associations yellow bk, v.2, no.1, 93n319
Business orgs, agencies, & pubs dir, 6th ed, 93n190
Directory of European community trade & professional assns 1992, 94n274
Directory of European industrial & trade assns, 5th ed, 92n242
European dir of trade & bus assns 1990, 92n245
National trade & professional assns of the US 1990, 91n40
National trade & professional assns of the US 1993, 94n54
Pan-European assns, 2d ed, 92n45
Professional codes of conduct in the UK, 91n269
State & regional assns of the US, 1992 ed, 93n71
Texas trade & prof assns 1989, 90n277
Trade & professional assns in Calif., 4th ed, 90n287
Trade & professional assns in Calif., 5th ed, 93n67

TRADE CATALOGS. See CATALOGS, COMMERCIAL

TRADE NAMES. See BUSINESS NAMES

TRADE SCHOOLS
Who's who in community, technical, & jr colleges 1991, 92n297

TRADEMARKS
British trademarks of the 1920s & 30s, 90n981
Character trademarks, 92n256
Patent, trademark, & copyright laws, 94n576
Trade names dict: co index 1989, 90n284
Trade names dict 1989, 90n283

TRADE-UNIONS
Active figures of the trade union & working class movement of Russia, Ukraine, Bielorussia, & Kazakhstan, 94n262
American dir of organized labor, 93n306
America's labor leaders, 90n261
Directory of employers' assocs, trade unions, joint orgs, 90n253
Directory of US labor orgs, 1990-91 ed, 92n219
Trade union hndbk, 5th ed, 93n305
Trade unions of the world 1989-90, 90n262
Trade unions of the world 1992-93, 93n313
Transnational corporations & labor, 91n143

TRADING COMPANIES
Directory of foreign trade orgs in Eastern Europe, 2d ed, 90n176

TRADITIONAL ANGLICAN CHURCHES
Independent bishops, 91n1447

TRAFFIC ACCIDENTS
Statistical report on road accidents in 1990, 94n2027
Statistics of road traffic accidents in Europe, v.34, 90n1813
Statistics of road traffic accidents in Europe 1991, 93n1785

TRAFFIC ENGINEERING
Concise ency of traffic & transportation systems, 93n1613

TRAILS
Historic sites & markers along the Mormon & other great W trails, 90n435
Trail West: A bibliog-index to W American trails, 90n448

TRAIN ROBBERIES
Train robbery era, 92n554

TRAINING OF EMPLOYEES. *See* EMPLOYEES, TRAINING OF

TRANSCENDENTALISM (NEW ENGLAND)
Nathaniel Hawthorne: an annot bibliog of comment & criticism before 1900, 90n1143

TRANSFER STUDENTS
College hndbk for transfer students 1991, 91n326
College hndbk for transfer students 1994, 94n354

TRANSLATORS
Directory of translators & translating agencies in the UK, 2d ed, 92n1014

TRANSPLANTATION OF ORGANS, TISSUES, ETC.
Gift of life, 94n1823
Life from death, 90n1677

TRANSPORTATION
Concise ency of traffic & transportation systems, 93n1613
Motor carrier professional servs dir 1990, 91n1827
Transportation glossary, 90n1801
Transportation mgmt assn dir, 1989 ed, 91n1815
Transportation-logistics dict, 3d ed, 91n1814
Urban public transportation glossary, 90n1816
World communication & transportation data, 91n942

TRANSPORTATION ENGINEERING
Concise ency of traffic & transportation systems, 93n1613

TRAUMATOLOGY
Selected refs in orthopaedic trauma, 91n1699

TRAVEL
Aware traveler's dir, 1991 ed, 92n430
Baseball vacations, 92n782
Fairchild's 1990 travel industry personnel dir, 91n453
Going places: the gd to travel gds, 90n433
Kitty Hawk to NASA, 92n1794
Leisure lit, 94n820
Rand McNally traveler's world atlas & gd, 90n438
Travel & older adults, 92n438
Travel dict, 90n431
Travel dict, 92n429
Traveler's reading gd, rev & updated ed, 94n474
USA travel phone bk, 92n432
Washington Post gd to Washington, 2d ed, 90n445

TREASURE-TROVE
Treasure hunting bibliog & index to per articles, 90n777

TREATIES
Current treaty index, 11th ed, 94n760
United States treaty index: 1776-1990 consolidation, 93n759

TREE CROPS
Seeds of woody plants in N America, rev ed, 93n1521

TREES
Field gd to Tex. trees, 90n1511
Flowering trees & shrubs, 90n1508
Folklore of trees & shrubs, 94n1673
Garden trees hndbk, 91n1546
Identification gd to the trees of Canada, 91n1544
Meet the natives: the amateur's field gd to Rocky Mountain wildflowers, trees & shrubs, 9th ed, 93n1505
Mosaik's photographic key to the trees & shrubs of Great Britain & N Europe, 94n1670
North American trees exclusive of Mexico & tropical Fla., 4th ed, 90n1510
Picture gd to tree leaves, 92n1554
Trees, 91n1545
Trees, 94n1669

Trees & shrubs of Great Britain & N Europe, 94n1670
Trees of Ga. & adjacent states, 91n1542
Trees of Hawai'i, 92n1553
Trees of the west, 93n1517

TRIALS
Famous trials, 93n604

TRIALS (ANARCHY)
Haymarket affair, 94n786

TRIBOLOGY
Encyclopedia of tribology, 92n1625
Handbook of tribology, 92n1621

TRICHIURIDAE
FAO species cat, v.15, 94n1719

TRILLING, LIONEL
Lionel Trilling: an annot bibliog, 94n1239

TRILOBITES
Trilobites, 2d ed, 94n1961

TRINITY
Bibliotheca Trinitariorum, v.1, 90n1391
Bibliotheca Trinitariorum, v.2, 90n1392

TRISTAN
Complete concordance to Gottfried Von Strassburg's Tristan, 94n1200

TRIVIA. *See* CURIOSITIES & WONDERS

TROPICAL FISHES
All about tropical fish, 4th ed, 90n1551

TROPICAL PLANTS
Cultivated plants of the tropics & subtropics, 93n1469
Tropicals, 90n1482

TROPICS
Bignoniaceae—pt.2 (tribe tecomeae), 94n1637
Cultivated plants of the tropics & subtropics, 93n1469
Utilization of tropical foods: fruits & leaves, 92n1474

TROTSKY, LEON
International Trotskyism 1929-85, 93n777
Trotsky: a bibliog, 91n765

TROUT
Trout & salmon hndbk, 90n772

TRUCKING
Motor carrier professional serv dir 1993, 94n2023
Trucksource 1989, 90n1812
Trucksource 1992, 93n1783

TRUCKS
Truck, van & 4X4 bk, 92n1797

TRUFFLES
Mushrooms & truffles of the Southwest, 92n1545

TRUMAN, HARRY S.
Harry S. Truman ency, 91n505

TUDOR, HOUSE OF
Historical dict of Tudor England, 1485-1603, 93n532

TUMORS
Third opinion, 90n1658

TUNISIA
Historical dict of Tunisia, 90n113

TURKISH LANGUAGE—DICTIONARIES—ENGLISH
Oxford Turkish dict, 94n1135

TURKS & CAICOS ISLANDS
Turks & Caicos Islands, 93n157

TURTLES
Turtles of the world, 90n1567

TWAIN, MARK
Mark Twain ency, 94n1240
Mark Twain's German critical reception, 1875-1986, 90n1156

Union cat of letters to Clemens, 93n1183

TWELFTH CENTURY
Europe in transition, 90n514

TWENTIETH CENTURY
Chronicle of the 1st World War, v.2, 93n551
Dictionary of 20th century hist 1914-90, 93n557

TWINS
Twins in children's & adolescent lit, 94n1183

TYPE & TYPE-FOUNDING
Computer type, 92n645
Elements of typographic style, 94n675
Modern ency of typefaces 1960-90, 92n630

TYPE DESIGNERS
Rookledge's intl hndbk of type designers, 94n1563

UGANDA
Idi Amin & Uganda, 94n763
Uganda: an annot bibliog of source materials, 92n90

UKRAINE
Active figures of the trade union & working class movement of Russia, Ukraine, Bielorussia, & Kazakhstan, 94n262
Archives & mss repositories in the USSR: Ukraine & Moldavia, 90n523
Encyclopedia of Ukraine, vs. 3-5, 94n138
International writings of Bohdan S. Wynar, 1949-92, 94n80
Ukraine, 91n115
Ukraine: a tourist gd, 94n483
Ukraine: pol parties & orgs, 94n782
Ukraine top 100 exporters, 93n294

UKRAINIAN LITERATURE
Bibliography of Ukrainian lit in English & French, 91n1248

UKRAINIAN NEWSPAPERS
Select index to Svoboda, v.1, 93n980
Select index to Svoboda, v.2, 93n981

UNDERCOVER OPERATIONS
Rewards offered by the US, 91n597

UNDERDEVELOPED AREAS. *See* **DEVELOPING COUNTRIES**

UNDERGROUND PRESS
Alternative pr index, Jan-Mar 1991, v.23, no.1, 92n53
Alternative pubs, 91n672
Voices from the underground, 94n1010

UNDERWATER ARCHAEOLOGY
Coastal & maritime archaeology, 92n449

UNEMPLOYMENT BENEFITS. *See* **INSURANCE, UNEMPLOYMENT**

UNIDENTIFIED FLYING OBJECTS
Encyclopedia of strange & unexplained physical phenomena, 94n813
UFO ency, v.2, 93n807
UFOs in the 1980s, 91n797

UNIFORM SYSTEM OF CITATION
User's gd to the Bluebk, 93n590

UNIFORMS, MILITARY
Napoleonic uniforms, 94n707
Uniforms of the American Revolution in color, 92n657
Visual dict of military uniforms, 93n703

UNITED KINGDOM
Access to UK higher educ, 93n380
European employment & industrial relations glossary: UK, 93n297
Higher educ in the UK 1992-93, 93n386
Who's who in bus & industry in the UK 1991, 93n298

UNITED METHODIST CHURCH
Handbook of United Methodist-related schools, colleges, univs & theological schools, 94n336

UNITED NATIONS
Chronology & fact bk of the UN 1941-91, 94n792
Directory of applications sftwr of the UN system, 92n736
Directory of UN documentary & archival sources, 93n783
Index to proceedings of the Economic & Social Council, 92n739
Index to proceedings of the General Assembly, 92n740
Index to proceedings of the Security Council, 43d yr, 91n767
International yr bk & statesmen's who's who 1992, 94n791
United Nations juridical yrbk 1985, 94n578
Who's who in the UN & related agencies, 2d ed, 93n782

UNITED NATIONS EDUCATION, SCIENCE & CULTURAL ORGANZATION
Unesco list of docs & pubs 1984-86, 90n722

UNITED STATES
Archaeology hndbk, 93n507
Peoples of the world: N Americans, 92n340
United States, 93n520
United States, Canada, & Mexico road atlas, 91n433
United States today, 91n434

UNITED STATES. AIR FORCE
Historical dict of the US air force, 94n698
United States air force, 93n709

UNITED STATES—ARMED FORCES
African American generals, 94n685
American women & the US armed forces, 93n707
America's top military careers, 94n690
Bibliography of military name lists from pre-1675 to 1900, 91n413
Central Pacific campaign, 1943-44, 91n677
Dictionary of military, defense contractor, & troop slang acronyms, 91n674
Fallen in battle, 90n649
Guide to military installations, 2d ed, 90n656
Guide to military installations, 3d ed, 93n704
How to locate anyone who is or has been in the military, 90n654
How to locate anyone who is or has been in the military, rev ed, 91n679
Shield of republic/sword of empire, 91n678
U.S. defence & military fact bk, 92n654

UNITED STATES. ARMED FORCES RADIO SERVICE
Basic musical lib, "P" series, 1-1000, 92n1295

UNITED STATES. ARMY
Army dict & desk ref, 93n717
Late 19th century US army, 1865-98, 92n663
Military leaders of the Civil War, 94n701
Union army 1861-65: org & operations, 90n662
United States army: a dict, 92n664
U.S. army heraldic crests, 94n696
U.S. army uniforms of the Korean war, 94n708
U.S. military logistics, 1607-1991, 93n710
Vietnam battle chronology, 93n716

UNITED STATES—BIOGRAPHY
American leaders 1789-1991, 92n680
Research gd to American hist biog, 90n482

UNITED STATES—CAPITAL & CAPITOL
American capitols, 92n997

UNITED STATES—CENSUS
Atlas of the 1990 census, 94n931
Historical atlas of state power in congress, 1790-1990, 94n725

UNITED STATES—CHURCH HISTORY
Guide to the end of the world, 94n1535
Roman Catholics, 94n1525

UNITED STATES—CIVILIZATION
American studies, 91n485
Extraordinary Hispanic Americans, 93n51
First dict of cultural literacy, 90n312
Gay 90s in America, 93n518

Jewish-American hist & culture, 93n442

UNITED STATES. COAST GUARD
U.S. Coast Guard cutters & craft, 1946-90, 91n697
U.S. Navy aircraft 1921-41 & U.S. Marine Corps aircraft 1914-59, 90n667
U.S. Navy ships & Coast Guard cutters, 91n701

UNITED STATES—COMMERCE—SOVIET UNION
U.S.-Soviet trade dir, 1990, 91n272
U.S.-Soviet trade sourcebk, 92n254

UNITED STATES. CONGRESS
Access to US govt info, 91n46
CIS 4-yr cum index, 1987-90, 93n758
CIS index to unpublished US house of representatives committee hearings 1833-1936, 92n700
CIS index to unpublished US house of representatives committee hearings 1937-46, 92n701
Commitees in the US Congress 1947-92, v.1, 94n741
Condensed [congressional] dir, 92n686
Congress A to Z, 2d ed, 94n728
Congress & defense 1990, 91n749
Congress & the nation, v.7, 91n744
Congress dict, 94n730
Congressional Quarterly almanac, v.45, 92n694
Congressional Quarterly's American congressional dict, 94n729
Congressional Quarterly's gd to Congress, 4th ed, 93n747
Congressional Quarterly's pols in America 1990, 90n691
Congressional Quarterly's pols in America 1994, 94n749
Congressional roll call 1989, 91n747
Congressional staff dir/1, 1990, 91n735
Congressional staff dir/1, 1993, 94n734
Congressional voting gd: a 10 yr compilation, 4th ed, 93n746
Congressional yellow bk, spring 1990, v.16, no.1, 91n736
Handbook of campaign spending, 93n749
101st congress dir, 90n699
Open secrets, 91n750
Staff dirs on CD-ROM, 1993/1, 94n737
United States congressional districts 1883-1913, 91n752
Vital stats on congress, 1991-92, 93n754
Who's who in congress 1991-92, 92n693
Young Oxford companion to the congress of the US, 94n758

UNITED STATES—CONSTITUTION
American constitution, 92n524
Bicentennial concordance, 94n580
First amendment, 92n684

UNITED STATES—CONSTITUTIONAL HISTORY
Comprehensive bibliog of American constitutional & legal hist, suppl., 1980-87, 92n521
Key issues in constitutional hist, 90n501

UNITED STATES—CONSTITUTIONAL LAW
Constitutional law dict, v.1, 92n530
Encyclopedia of the American constitution, suppl.1, 93n576
Evolving constitution, 94n571
Federalist concordance, 90n544
Language of the constitution, 93n593

UNITED STATES—DEFENSES
American defense annual, 1990-91, 92n652
U.S. defense & military fact bk, 92n654

UNITED STATES—DESCRIPTION & TRAVEL
Rand McNally 1990 commercial atlas & mktg gd, 91n276

UNITED STATES—ECONOMIC CONDITIONS
Contemporary atlas of the US, 92n409
Dictionary of US economic hist, 94n158
Regional economic growth in the US, 91n163

UNITED STATES—ECONOMIC POLICY
Development report card for the states, 1993, 94n170
Washington almanac, 93n731

UNITED STATES—EMIGRATION & IMMIGRATION
Dictionary of American immigration hist, 91n777
Immigrant experience, 93n420
Immigrants from the German-speaking countries of Europe, 2d ed, 92n352
Immigration hist research center, 92n383

UNITED STATES—ETHINC RELATIONS
Asian American studies, 90n474

UNITED STATES—EXECUTIVE DEPARTMENTS
CIS index to US executive branch docs, 1789-1909, pt.1, 92n699
Executive branch of the US govt, 90n688
Federal yellow bk, winter 1990, 91n738
Washington info dir 1989-90, 90n702
Washington info dir 1992-93, 93n743

UNITED STATES. FEDERAL BUREAU OF INVESTIGATION
Unlocking the files of the FBI, 94n752

UNITED STATES—FOREIGN RELATIONS
American foreign policy index, v.1, no.1, 94n759
Chronological hist of US foreign relations, v.3, 92n743
Consolidated treaties & intl agreements, 93n756
Dictionary of American diplomatic hist, 2d ed, 91n733
Dictionary of American foreign affairs, 94n731
Foreign visitors to congress, 90n725
Handbook of American diplomacy, 94n757
Peace Corps: an annot bibliog, 90n731
Robert D. Murphy: a register of his papers in the Hoover Inst Archives, 91n732
United States treaty index: 1776-1990 consolidation, 93n759

UNITED STATES—FOREIGN RELATIONS—AFRICA
United States in Africa, 90n729

UNITED STATES—FOREIGN RELATIONS—ASIA
United States in Asia, 92n746

UNITED STATES—FOREIGN RELATIONS—EUROPE, EASTERN
U.S.-E European trade sourcebk, 92n150

UNITED STATES—FOREIGN RELATIONS—INDOCHINA
America & the Indochina wars, 1945-90, 93n733

UNITED STATES—FOREIGN RELATIONS—JAPAN
Directory, 1989-90: Japanese-affiliated cos in USA & Canada, 90n174

UNITED STATES—FOREIGN RELATIONS—LATIN AMERICA
United States in Latin America, 93n786

UNITED STATES—FOREIGN RELATIONS—MEXICO
BorderLine, 90n476
Recursos: a dir of Mexican-American insts, orgs, & univ programs, 92n689

UNITED STATES—FOREIGN RELATIONS—MIDDLE EAST
United States foreign policy & the Middle East/N Africa, 91n770

UNITED STATES—FOREIGN RELATIONS—NORTH AFRICA
United States foreign policy & the Middle East/N Africa, 91n770

UNITED STATES—FOREIGN RELATIONS—SOUTH AFRICA
United States sanctions & S Africa, 94n545
U.S. relations with S Africa, 92n745

UNITED STATES—FOREIGN RELATIONS—SOVIET UNION
Cold war chronology, 94n795

UNITED STATES—GAZETTEERS
Omni gazetteer of the USA, 92n425
Omni gazetteer of the USA [CD-ROM], 93n495

UNITED STATES—GENEALOGY
Ancestry's red bk, 90n387
Bibliography of military name lists from pre-1675 to 1900, 91n413
Founders & patriots of America index, 90n396

List of emigrants from England to America, 1682-92, 90n392
Newspaper genealogical column dir, 4th ed, 90n386
Prominent families of the USA, 92n387

UNITED STATES. GOVERNMENT ACCOUNTING OFFICE
General accounting office, 92n51

UNITED STATES—GOVERNMENT PUBLICATIONS
Bibliographic gd to govt pubs—US: 1990, 92n48
Government ref bks 88/89, 91n43
Government ref bks 90/91, 93n74
Mormons & Mormonism in US gov docs, 90n1401

UNITED STATES—HISTORICAL GEOGRAPHY
Historical atlas of Kans., 2d ed, 90n469
Historical atlas of the US, 90n468
Rand McNally atlas of American frontiers, 94n490
Region & regionalism in the US, 90n96
Scholar's gd to geographical writing on the American & Canadian past, 94n461

UNITED STATES—HISTORY
American Heritage illus hist of the US, 90n494
American hist: a bibliographic review, v.4, 91n480
American hist for children & young adults, 91n487
Bibliographies in hist, 90n528
Chronicle of America, 91n498
Cultural ency of the 1850s in America, 94n507
Dictionary of Afro-American slavery, 90n493
Encyclopedia of American facts & dates, 9th ed, 94n504
Encyclopedia of American scandal, 90n492
Encyclopedia USA, v.16, 94n509
Encyclopedia USA, v.17, 94n510
Encyclopedia USA index v.1, 94n513
European Americana, v.6, 90n488
Facts about the states, 90n706
Great American hist fact-finder, 94n512
Guide to pre-fed records in the Natl Archives, 90n465
Handbook of the American frontier, v.2, 92n367
Herbert Hoover: a bibliog of his times & presidency, 92n454
Historians of the American frontier, 90n477
Index to America: life & customs—20th century to 1986, 90n502
Interesting people: black American hist makers, 90n480
Iowa hist & culture, 90n473
Naval officers of the American Revolution, 90n663
1,001 things everyone should know about American hist, 90n497
Reader's companion to American hist, 92n468
Since 1776, 90n489
Soul of America, 90n495
This day in American hist, 91n500
Timelines, 92n465
U.S. hist: a resource bk for secondary schools, v.1, 90n498
U.S. hist: a resource bk for secondary schools, v.2, 90n499
U.S. reference-iana, 90n475

UNITED STATES—HISTORY—CIVIL WAR, 1861-1865
Battle chronicles of the Civil War, 91n501
Battle of Antietam & the Md. campaign of 1862, 91n482
Civil War, 90n496
Civil War battlefield gd, 91n508
Civil War maps, 2d ed, 90n648
Civil War newspaper maps: a cartobibliography of the N daily pr, 94n492
Civil War newspaper maps: a histl atlas, 94n491
Compendium of the Confederate armies: Ala., 93n711
Compendium of the Confederate armies: Fla. & Ark., 93n712
Compendium of the Confederate armies: N.C., 93n713
Compendium of the Confederate armies: Tenn., 93n714
Great battles of the Civil War, 91n507
Microbes & minie balls, 94n493
Military leaders of the Civil War, 94n701
Tour gd to the Civil War, 3d ed, 91n456
Union army 1861-65: org & operations, 90n662

UNITED STATES—HISTORY—COLONIAL PERIOD
Charlemagne Tower collection of American colonial laws, 92n519

Encyclopedia of colonial & revolutionary America, 91n504

UNITED STATES—HISTORY, MILITARY
Celluloid wars, 94n1451
Guide to the sources of US military hist, suppl.3, 94n680
Military hist of the US, 93n700
Reference gd to US military hist 1607-1815, 92n466
Reference gd to US military hist 1815-65, 94n501
Reference gd to US military hist 1865-1919, 94n502
Shield of republic/sword of empire, 91n678

UNITED STATES—HISTORY—REVOLUTION, 1775-1783
American Revolution 1775-1783: an ency, 94n503
Blackwell ency of the American Revolution, 92n470
Encyclopedia of colonial & revolutionary America, 91n504
Uniforms of the American Revolution in color, 92n657
Who was who in the American Revolution, 94n500
Women patriots of the American Revolution, 92n461

UNITED STATES—HISTORY—WAR OF 1898
Spanish-American war, 91n488

UNITED STATES—IMPRINTS
American bk publishing record cum 1988, 90n11
American bk publishing record cum 1989, 91n8
American bk publishing record cum 1991, 93n26
Checklist of American imprints 1830-39: author index, 90n20
Checklist of American imprints 1830-39: title index, 90n21
Checklist of American imprints for 1842, 93n32
Checklist of American imprints for 1843, 94n10

UNITED STATES—MAPS
Contemporary atlas of the US, 92n409
Doubleday atlas of the USA, 91n431
Hammond passport travelmate & US atlas, 91n459
Maps contained in the pubs of the American Bibliog, 1639-1819, 90n425
Rand McNally children's atlas of the US, 90n412
Rand McNally pocket road atlas, 90n414
United States atlas for young people, 93n469
USAtlas, 91n435

UNITED STATES. MARINE CORPS
Almanac of US seapower 1989, 91n690
U.S. Navy aircraft 1921-41 & U.S. Marine Corps aircraft 1914-59, 90n667
Vietnam battle chronology, 93n716

UNITED STATES. NATIONAL ARCHIVES & ADMINISTRATION
Guide to pre-fed records in the Natl Archives, 90n465
Guide to the holdings of the still picture branch of the Natl Archives, 92n450

UNITED STATES—NATIONAL SECURITY
U.S. natl security policy groups, 91n784

UNITED STATES. NAVY
Admirals of the new steel navy, 91n691
Aircraft carriers of the US navy, 2d ed, 90n670
Almanac of US seapower 1989, 91n690
Cruisers of the US navy 1922-62, 90n671
Dictionary of admirals of the US Navy, 90n664
Naval Institute gd to the ships & aircraft of the US fleet, 15th ed, 94n705
Naval officers of the American Revolution, 90n663
Selected & annotated bibliog of American naval hist, rev ed, 90n665
United States navy: a dict, 92n666
U.S. Navy aircraft 1921-41 & U.S. Marine Corps aircraft 1914-59, 90n667
United States navy aircraft since 1911, 91n700
U.S. Navy ships & Coast Guard cutters, 91n701
US warships of WW II, 90n669
Warships of the Civil War navies, 91n698

UNITED STATES—OCCUPATIONS
Career connection, rev ed, 93n410

UNITED STATES—OFFICIALS & EMPLOYEES
Biographical dir of the US executive branch, 1774-1989, 91n731

Federal staff dir/1, 1990, 91n737
Freedom's lawmakers, 94n727
Working for your uncle, 94n284

UNITED STATES—POLITICS & GOVERNMENT
Almanac of American pols 1990, 91n725
Almanac of American pols 1994, 94n746
Almanac of American presidents from 1789 to the present, 93n519
Almanac of transatlantic pols 1991-92, 92n675
American legislative leaders, 1850-1910, 90n692
American natl election studies data sourcebk, 1952-86, 91n751
American pol leaders from colonial times to the present, 92n681
American pol prints 1766-1876, 93n735
American presidents: an annotated bibliog, 91n481
Congressional Quarterly's American congressional dict, 94n729
Congressional voting gd: a 10 yr compilation, 4th ed, 93n746
Dwight D. Eisenhower: a bibliog of his times & presidency, 92n456
Encyclopedic dict of American govt, 93n737
Glossary of US govt vocabulary, 94n732
Guide to S pols, 1989, 91n754
HarperCollins dict of American govt & pols, 93n736
Harry S. Truman ency, 91n505
Historic docs index, 1972-89, 92n702
Historic docs of 1990, 92n703
Historical atlas of pol parties in the US Congress, 1789-1989, 90n687
Historical dict of reconstruction, 92n469
Historical dict of the Progressive Era, 1890-1920, 90n490
John C. Calhoun: a bibliog, 91n489
Minor presidential candidates & parties of 1992, 93n748
National Review politically incorrect ref gd, 94n726
1960s: an annot bibliog of social & pol movements in the US, 94n863
Public admin desk bk, 91n776
U.S. govt: a resource bk for secondary schools, 90n711
Washington '90, 91n741
Washington '93, 94n744
Washington almanac, 93n731
Washington representatives 1992, 93n744
Who's who in American pols 1989-90, 90n693
Who's who in American pols 1991-92, 92n682
Woodrow Wilson: a bibliog of his times & presidency, 91n728
World almanac of US pols, 91n726

UNITED STATES—POPULAR CULTURE
Directory of popular culture collections, 90n1307
Handbook of American popular culture, 2d ed, 91n1339
Timelines, 92n465

UNITED STATES—POPULATION
Atlas of the 1990 census, 94n931
Retrospective bibliog of American demographic hist from colonial times to 1983, 90n835

UNITED STATES—RACE RELATIONS
Civil rights movement, 94n595
Racism in the US, 91n384

UNITED STATES—RELIGION
Encyclopedia of religions in the US, 93n1407
Religion & American life, 90n1376
Religion & the American experience, 1620-1900, 94n1507
Religious bodies in the US, 93n1408
Twentieth-century shapers of American popular religion, 90n1380

UNITED STATES—RURAL CONDITIONS
Sociology in govt, 93n846

UNITED STATES. SECURITIES & EXCHANGE COMMISSION
U.S. Securities & Exchange Commission, 94n802

UNITED STATES—SOCIAL CONDITIONS
Contemporary atlas of the US, 92n409
Encyclopedia of American social hist, 94n505
1960s: an annot bibliog of social & pol movements in the US, 94n863
Trends in public opinion, 90n85

UNITED STATES—SOCIAL LIFE & CUSTOMS
Encyclopedia of American social hist, 94n505
Writer's gd to everyday life in the 1800s, 94n511

UNITED STATES—STATISTICS
Almanac of the 50 states, 1992 ed, 93n909
American stats index 1988, 90n837
CQ's state fact finder, 94n750
Federal statistical source, 29th ed, 92n845
State & local stats sources 1990-91, 91n897
State rankings, 1990, 91n901
State rankings, 1991, 93n912

UNITED STATES. SUPREME COURT
Congressional Quarterly's gd to the US Supreme Court, 2d ed, 91n746
Evolving constitution, 94n571
How to research the Supreme Court, 93n571
Oxford companion to the Supreme Court of the US, 94n554
Supreme Court A to Z, 94n556
Supreme Court at work, 91n589
Supreme Court justices, 94n551
Supreme Court yrbk 1990-91, 93n588
U.S. Supreme Court, 91n566

UNITS
Quantification in sci, 92n1748

UNIVERSITIES & COLLEGES
Adult learner's gd to alternative & external degree programs, 94n393
American univs & colleges, 14th ed, 93n363
America's lowest cost colleges, 92n296
Barron's best buys in college educ, 2d ed, 93n364
Barron's compact gd to colleges, 7th ed, 92n298
Barron's profiles of American colleges, 19th ed, 93n365
Barron's 300 best buys in college educ, 91n321
Barron's top 50, 93n366
Beacon: college & career planning on CD-ROM, 94n349
Best dollar values in American colleges, 91n322
Cash for college, 94n360
Chronicle financial aid gd for 1991-92 school yr, 93n367
Chronicle 2-yr college databk, 1988-89, 90n334
Chronicle 4-yr college databk for 1991-92 school yr, 93n368
Chronicle 4-yr college databk, 1988-89, 90n333
College admissions data hndbk 1992-93, 93n370
College hndbk for transfer students 1991, 91n326
College hndbk for transfer students 1994, 94n354
College hndbk foreign student suppl. 1992, 92n302
College hndbk 1991, 91n327
College hndbk 1994, 94n355
College majors, 91n334
Common-sense gd to American colleges 1991-92, 92n310
Compact gd to colleges, 6th ed, 90n337
Comparative gd to American colleges, 15th ed, 92n293
Directory of Catholic colleges & univs, 1992, 94n335
Directory of college facilities & servs for people with disabilities, 3d ed, 92n321
Directory of the US postsecondary educ, 90n324
Electronic univ, 94n376
Fischgrund's insider's gd to the top 25 colleges, 91n330
Fiske gd to colleges 1989, 90n338
GIS gd to 4-yr colleges, 91n331
Gourman report: a rating of undergraduate programs in American & intl univs, 8th ed, 94n358
Guide to hospitality & tourism educ 1989-90, 91n315
Guide to the univs of Europe, 93n382
Handbook of Indian univs, 92n317
Handbook of United Methodist-related schools, colleges, univs & theological schools, 94n336
Insider's gd to the colleges 1993, 93n372
Institutions of higher educ, 91n312
Jewish student's gd to American colleges, 91n332
Lisa Birnbach's new & improved college bk, 91n323
Lovejoy's college gd, 19th ed, 91n335
Making a difference college gd, 1993, 94n348
Multicultural student's gd to colleges, 94n337

National Review college gd, 92n306
Peterson's competitive colleges 1990-91, 91n340
Peterson's drug & alcohol programs & policies at 4-yr colleges, 90n825
Peterson's gd to colleges with programs for learning-disabled students, 2d ed, 90n349
Peterson's gd to 4-yr colleges 1991, 91n336
Peterson's gd to 4-yr colleges 1994, 94n342
Peterson's register of higher educ 1993, 94n344
Right college 1991, 91n337
School songs of America's colleges & univs, 93n1278
Schoolsearch gd to colleges with programs or servs for students with disabilities, 92n319
300 most selective colleges, 91n320
Who's who in athletics in American colleges & univs, 91n805
World of learning 1990, 91n301

UNIVERSITIES & COLLEGES—ADMISSION
College admissions, 94n324
College admissions data hndbk 1989-90, 90n335
Peterson's competitive colleges 1993-94, 94n341
Peterson's gd to college admissions, 5th ed, 92n308

UNIVERSITIES & COLLEGES, BLACK
America's black colleges, 94n330
Murray resource dir to the nation's historically black colleges & univs, 94n338

UNIVERSITIES & COLLEGES—CANADA
ACCC dir of Canadian colleges & institutes, 93n362
Gibson's student gd to W Canadian univs, 94n310
National gd to college & univ programmes 1988, 90n339
Student's gd to Ont. univs, 92n304
Who's who 1989: deans & directors in mgmt & admin studies at Canadian univs, 90n272

UNIVERSITIES & COLLEGES—CURRICULA
Barron's profiles of American colleges, 16th ed, 90n322
College admissions index of majors & sports 1989-90, 90n336
College admissions index of majors & sports 1992-93, 93n379
College Board gd to 150 popular college majors, 94n352
Directory of theatre training programs 2, 90n1358
Index of college majors, 17th ed, 92n312
Index of majors & graduate degrees 1994, 94n365
Index of majors 1991, 91n333
Major decisions, 92n301
Patterson's schools classified, v.40, 1990 ed, 91n339
Peterson's colleges with programs for students with learning disabilities, 94n340
Rugg's recommendations on the colleges, 10th ed, 94n364
Summer on campus, 90n318

UNIVERSITIES & COLLEGES—FACULTY
Directory of faculty contracts & bargaining agents in institutions of higher educ, v.18, 93n360
European faculty dir 1991, 92n313
Faculty white pages 1989, 90n327
Faculty white pages 1991, 93n361
National faculty dir 1991, 91n316
National faculty dir 1993, 94n339

UNIVERSITIES & COLLEGES—FINANCE
College cost bk 1991, 91n325
Peterson's college money hndbk 1991, 92n307

UNIVERSITIES & COLLEGES—GRADUATE WORK
Barron's gd to graduate bus schools, 8th ed, 94n168
Gourman report: a rating of graduate & professional programs in American & intl univs, 6th ed, 94n357
Guide to American graduate schools, 6th ed, 92n303
Peterson's gd to graduate & professional programs 1989, 90n328

UNIVERSITIES & COLLEGES—GREAT BRITAIN
Careers & educl opportunities, 90n360

UNIVERSITIES & COLLEGES—HONORS COURSES
Summer on campus, 90n318

UNIVERSITIES & COLLEGES IN LITERATURE
Oxford in fiction, 90n1171

UNIVERSITY EXTENSION
Campus-free college degrees, 5th ed, 93n378

UNIVERSITY OF ALASKA, ANCHORAGE. LIBRARY.
Guide to the ms collections at the Univ of Alaska, Anchorage, 92n35

UNIVERSITY OF ALBERTA
From the past to the future, 93n527

UNIVERSITY OF CALGARY. LIBRARIES. SPECIAL COLLECTIONS DIVISION
Alden Nowlan papers, 94n1276
Clark Blaise papers, 92n1223

UNIVERSITY OF NOTRE DAME
Theodore M. Hesburgh: a bio-bibliog, 91n311

UNIVERSITY OF VIRGINIA LIBRARY
Descriptive cat of the Jorge Luis Borges collection at the Univ of Va. lib, 94n1300

UNIVERSITY OF WATERLOO LIBRARY
Catalogue of the Bertram R. Davis "Robert Southey" collection, 91n1218

UNIVERSITY PRESSES
MLA dir of scholarly presses in lang & lit, 93n686

URBAN FOLKLORE
Contemporary legend, 94n1383

URBAN HEALTH
Livable cities almanac, 93n920

URBAN POLICY
American suburbs, 94n946
Middletown, 90n845
Urban hist yrbk 1988, 90n846

URBAN RENEWAL
Better community cat, 91n847

URBAN STUDIES. *See* URBAN POLICY

URBAN TRANSPORTATION
Jane's urban transport systems 1990, 91n1825
Urban public transportation glossary, 90n1816
Urban transport & planning, 90n842

URBAN-RURAL MIGRATION
Rating gd to life in America's small cities, 91n911

URUGUAY
Uruguay, 90n147

US NEWS & WORLD REPORT
Cover story index 1960-89, 91n964

USED CARS
Lemon-aid used car gd 1992, 93n1782
Used car bk, 1991 ed, 92n1798
Used car buying gd, 1992-93 ed, 93n1786

UTAH
State parks of Utah, 90n452
Utah place names, 92n428

UTILITIES (COMPUTER PROGRAMS)
Best of shareware: IBM PC utilities, 91n1739

VACATION SCHOOLS
Learning vacations, 6th ed, 91n373

VACATIONS
Adventure vacations, 92n433
Volunteer vacations, rev ed, 90n436

VALUES
What a piece of work is man!, 91n69

VAMPIRE FILMS
Cinematic vampires, 93n1353

VAMPIRES
Transylvanian lib, 94n1212
Vampire in lit, 91n1139

VANBRUGH, JOHN, SIR
Sir John Vanbrugh: a ref gd, 94n975

VANS
Truck, van & 4X4 bk, 92n1797

VAUGHAN WILLIAMS, RALPH
Ralph Vaughan Williams: a gd to research, 91n1267

VAUGHN, SARAH
Sarah Vaughan: a discography, 93n1285

VEGETABLE GARDENING
Complete vegetable gardener's sourcebk, rev ed, 91n1505
Essential kitchen gardener, 91n1496
Vegetable growing hndbk, 3d ed, 91n1506

VEHICLES, MILITARY
Standard cat of US military vehicles 1940-1965, 94n691

VENDORS & PURCHASERS
AHE vendor dir for acquisitions librarians, 90n595
BiblioData fulltext sources online, 90n1725

VENEZUELA
Venezuela, 92n114

VENTILATION
Handbook of HVAC design, 91n1634

VENTURE CAPITAL
Pratt's gd to venture capital sources, 1992 ed, 93n197

VERDI, GIUSEPPE
Verdi & his major contemporaries, 91n1298

VERMONT
Vermont almanac 1991, 91n89

VERTEBRATES
Endangered vertebrates, 91n1553

VERTICAL FILES (LIBRARIES)
Vertical file index, 92n575

VETERANS
Financial aid for vets, military personnel & their dependents 1990-91, 92n651
How to locate anyone who is or has been in the military, 90n654
How to locate anyone who is or has been in the military, rev ed, 91n679
Vietnam vet films, 93n1366

VETERINARY MEDICINE
Black's vet dict, 16th ed, 90n1476
Black's vet dict, 17th ed, 93n1490
Concise vet dict, 90n1473
Dictionary of animal health terminology, 94n1633
Directory of intl & natl medical & related societies, 2d ed, 92n1666
Horse owner's vet hndbk, 90n1474
Inherited eye diseases in purebred dogs, 90n1475
Keyguide to info sources in vet medicine, 91n1510
Stable vet hndbk, 91n1512

VICE-PRESIDENTS
American leaders 1789-1991, 92n680
Biographical dir of the US executive branch, 1774-1989, 91n731

VIDEO ART
Money for film & video artists, 92n1356

VIDEO DISCS
Bowker's complete video dir 1992, 93n989
Laserdisc film gd, 1993-1994 ed, 94n1429
Laser video disc companion, updated ed, 93n997
Videodisc compendium for educ & training, 90n355

VIDEO GAMES
Video game quest, 91n839

VIDEO RECORDINGS
Back Stage: TV, film & tape production dir, 1989 ed, 90n915
Best videos for children & young adults, 92n617
Billboard 1990 music & video yrbk, 92n1294
Bowker's complete video dir 1992, 93n989
Equipment dir of audio-visual, computer & video products 1990-91, 92n915
Family video gd, 93n1329
Film & video finder, 2d ed, 90n352
Film, TV, & video pers, 92n1332
Great videos for kids, 94n1426
Guide to pol videos, v.1, no.1, 94n713
Off-Hollywood movies, 90n1334
Orion blue bk: video & TV 1990, 91n208
Premiere gd to movies on video, 92n1341
Roger Ebert's movie home companion 1991 ed, 92n1338
Third World in film & video, 1984-90, 92n102
Variety's complete home video dir 1989, 2d ed, 90n1335
Variety's complete home video dir 1989: adult titles suppl, 90n1336
Video annual 1991, 92n917
Video for libs, 90n619
Video movies, 91n1359
Video policies & procedures for libs, 92n621
Video source bk, 12th ed, 92n909
Viewers' choice gd to movies on video, 93n1334
X-rated videotape gd 2, 93n1332
Film-video terms & concepts, 93n1345

VIDEO TAPES
AMI, v.9, issue 1, 91n968
Bowker's complete video dir 1992, 93n989
Complete gd to special interest videos, 1991 ed, 92n1344
Educational film & video locator 1990-91, 91n358
Educators gd to free videotapes, 39th ed, 93n396
Electronic post-production terms & concepts, 92n913
Film & video finder, 3d ed, 93n1330
Footage 89: N American film & video sources, 91n966
Halliwell's filmgoer's & video viewer's companion, 10th ed, 94n1456
Native Americans on film & video, v.2, 90n374
Recommended videos for schools, 92n325
Transcript/video index, 1992, 94n1021
Video source bk 1993, 94n1020
Videos for bus & training 1989, 90n192
Videos for understanding diversity, 94n399

VIDEO TAPES IN EDUCATION
AFVA evaluations 1991, 93n395
Films for learning, thinking, & doing, 93n399

VIDEO TAPES IN MEDICINE
Catalogue of films & videos in the British Medical Assn lib, 94n1824

VIDEOCASSETTES
Guide to opera & dance on videocassette, 91n1342
Guide to videocassettes for children, 90n1346
HBO's gd to movies on videocassette & cable TV 1991, 92n1339
Transcript/video index, 1991, 93n1001

VIETNAM
Historical dict of Vietnam, 90n526
Vietnam, 94n122

VIETNAMESE CONFLICT, 1961-1975
America & the Indochina wars, 1945-90, 93n733
American women writers on Vietnam, 91n1145
In the field: the lang of the Vietnam War, 92n476
Stress, strain, & Vietnam, 90n739
Vietnam battle chronology, 93n716
Vietnam bk list, 93n525
Vietnam coastal & riverine forces hndbk, 90n666
Vietnam: the decisive battles, 92n658
Vietnam vet films, 93n1366
Vietnam war: hndbk of the lit & research, 94n497
Vietnam war in lit, 94n514
Vietnam war lit, 2d ed, 90n1132
Voices from the underground, 94n1010

Words of the Vietnam War, 92n475
Writing about Vietnam, 91n512

VIETNAMESE LANGUAGE—DICTIONARIES—ENGLISH
Vietnamese-English dict, 93n1104
Vietnamese-English, English-Vietnamese dict, 92n1093

VILLON, FRANCOIS
Francois Villon: a bibliog, 92n1234

VINES. See CLIMBING PLANTS

VIOLENCE
Encyclopedia of violence, 94n586
Racial & religious violence in America, 92n553

VIOLIN MUSIC
Italian violin music of the 17th century, 91n1264
Violin music by women composers, 91n1277

VIOLONCELLISTS
Great cellists, 90n1259

VIOLONCELLO MUSIC
Solo cello, 90n1260

VIRCHOW, RUDOLF LUDWIG KARL
Commentary on the medical writings of Rudolf Virchow, 92n1650

VIRGIL
Classical epic: an annot bibliog, 92n1135

VIRGIN FORESTS. See OLD GROWTH FORESTS

VIRGIN ISLANDS
Virgin Islands, 93n158

VIRGINIA
Afro-American sources in Va., 91n391
Captain John Smith: a ref gd, 92n455

VIRTUAL REALITY
Information sources for virtual reality, 94n1894
Virtual reality: a selected bibliog, 93n1672

VIRUSES
Virology: dir & dict of animal, bacterial & plant viruses, 90n1690

VISCOSITY
Data bk on the viscosity of liquids, 90n1774

VISIGOTHS
Visigoths in Gaul & Spain AD 418-711, 90n515

VISION
Dictionary of visual sci, 4th ed, 90n1691

VISITORS' CENTERS
Corporate museums, galleries, & visitor centers, 92n129

VISITORS, FOREIGN
Foreign visitors to congress, 90n725

VISUAL LITERACY
Visual literacy, 91n354

VISUALLY HANDICAPPED
Encyclopedia of blindness & vision impairment, 92n1685
Living with low vision, 94n880
Living with low vision, 2d ed, 91n855
Rehabilitation resource manual: vision, 91n856
Rehabilitation resource manual: vision, 94n884

VITAL STATISTICS
Indiana factbk 1992, 93n108
Vital & health stats series, 92n1641

VITAMINS
Doctors' vitamin & mineral ency, 91n1709
Drugs, vitamins, minerals in pregnancy, 90n1702
People's gd to vitamins & minerals from A to zinc, rev ed, 90n1699

VITAMINS IN HUMAN NUTRITION
Essential gd to vitamins & minerals, 93n1647
Nutrients cat, 94n1610

VIVES, JUAN LUIS
Vives bibliog, 91n1404

VOCABULARY
Analogy bk of related words, 92n1057
Children's writer's word bk, 94n996
Dickson's word treasury, 93n1073
300 1st words, 94n1093

VOCAL MUSIC
Catalog of pre-1900 vocal mss in the music lib, univ of Calif at Berkeley, 90n1263
Recorded performances of Gerard Souzay, 92n1284

VOCATIONAL EDUCATION
Chronicle vocational school manual for 1991-92 school yr, 93n406

VOCATIONAL GUIDANCE
America's top military careers, 94n690
America's top 300 jobs, 91n241
Beacon: college & career planning on CD-ROM, 94n349
Career discovery ency, 91n371
Career discovery ency, 94n384
Career index, 91n370
Careers & educl opportunities, 90n360
Cassell careers ency, 13th ed, 94n385
College Board gd to jobs & career planning, 91n372
College majors & careers, rev ed, 94n362
Complete gd for occupational exploration, 1993 ed, 94n387
Educators gd to free guidance materials, 30th ed, 93n400
Encyclopedia of career change & work issues, 93n409
Encyclopedia of career choices for the 1990s, 93n309
Encyclopedia of careers & vocational guidance, 8th ed, 91n374
Encyclopedia of careers & vocational guidance, 9th ed, 94n386
Enhanced gd for occupational exploration, 92n227
Focus on careers, 93n408
Great careers, 2d ed, 91n379
Occu-facts, 1989-90 ed, 91n376
Professional careers sourcebk, 91n378
Professional careers sourcebk, 2d ed, 93n411
Top professions, 91n242
Vocational careers sourcebk, 93n412
Where the jobs are, 90n255

VOCATIONAL QUALIFICATIONS
Career connection, rev ed, 93n410
Encyclopedia of career choices for the 1990s, 93n309

VOCATIONAL REHABILITATION
Meeting the needs of employees with disabilities, 92n228
Meeting the needs of employees with disabilities, 2d ed, 94n881

VOCATIONAL TRAINING. See OCCUPATIONAL TRAINING

VOLUNTARISM
Great careers, 2d ed, 91n379
Guide to fed funding for volunteer programs, 93n876
International dir of voluntary work, 5th ed, 94n894
Nonprofit almanac 1992-93, 93n877
Philanthropic studies index, 92n828
Volunteer! 1992-1993 ed, 94n903
Volunteer work, 94n904
Volunteerism & older adults, 92n807
Volunteerism, 3d ed, 92n829

VOLUNTEERS
Volunteer vacations, rev ed, 90n436

VOTING
American natl election studies data sourcebk, 1952-86, 91n751
British electorate, 1963-87, 93n772

VOYAGES & TRAVELS
Children's atlas of exploration, 94n452
Going places: the gd to travel gds, 90n433
Travel bk, 2d ed, 94n473

WAGES
American salaries & wages survey, 92n223
American salaries & wages survey, 2d ed, 94n282

WAGNER, RICHARD
Parsifal on record, 93n1270
Wagner compendium, 94n1329

WALES
British dirs, 90n133
Butterworths law dir 1993, 94n558
Education in England & Wales, 92n316
Wales, 92n105
Welsh women, 94n950

WALKER, ALICE MALSENIOR
Alice Walker: an annot bibliog 1968-86, 90n1157

WALTERS ART GALLERY (BALTIMORE, MD.)
Medieval & renaissance mss in the Walters Art Gallery, v.2, 94n29

WALTON, WILLIAM
William Walton: a bio-bibliog, 90n1254
William Walton: a cat, rev ed, 91n1269
William Walton: a source bk, 94n1323

WAR
American women writers on Vietnam, 91n1145
Anthropology of war, 90n647
Dictionary of war quotations, 91n683
International affairs dir of orgs, 94n799
Law of war & neutrality, 90n540
Using lit to teach middle grades about war, 94n694
War & peace lit for children & young adults, 94n1185
Wars in the Third World since 1945, 92n653
World record of major conflict areas, 92n82

WAR FILMS
Celluloid wars, 94n1451
Encyclopedia of American war films, 90n1327
Great combat pictures, 91n1380

WAR IN LITERATURE
Literature for young people on war & peace, 90n1081
Vietnam bk list, 93n525

WAR MEMORIALS
American battle monuments, 91n680

WAR POETRY
Vietnam war in lit, 94n514

WAR STORIES
Novels of WW II, 94n1205
Vietnam war in lit, 94n514
War & peace through women's eyes, 93n1169

WARD, ROBERT
Robert Ward: a bio-bibliog, 90n1246

WARFARE, CONVENTIONAL
Penguin ency of modern warfare, 93n701

WARLOCK, PETER
Gurney, Ireland, Quilter & Warlock, 90n1223

WARREN, ELINOR REMICK
Elinor Remick Warren: a bio-bibliog, 94n1321

WARSHIPS
German warships 1815-1945, v.1, 91n693
Illustrated gd to modern naval warfare, 91n702
Jane's fighting ships 1990-91, 91n694
U.S. Navy ships & Coast Guard cutters, 91n701
US warships of WW II, 90n669
Warships of the Civil War navies, 91n698
Weyers warships of the world 1992/93, 94n706

WASHINGTON (D.C.)
Capital source, fall 1989, 90n94
Guide to black Washington, 91n458
Health groups in Washington, 10th ed, 90n1618
Hudson's Washington news media contacts dir 1991, 92n891
Washington area lib dir, 94n611
Washington art, 90n961
Washington info dir 1989-90, 90n702
Washington info dir 1992-93, 93n743
Washington '90, 91n741
Washington '93, 94n744
Washington Post gd to Washington, 2d ed, 90n445

WASHINGTON (STATE)
Historic ships of Washington, 90n1821

WASHINGTON METROPOLITAN AREA
Writer's gd to metropolitan Washington, 92n894

WASHINGTON POST
Washington Post deskbk on style, 2d ed, 91n950

WATER
California water resources dir, 2d ed, 92n1757
Dictionary of water & wastewater treatment trademarks & brand names, 93n1772
Glossary of water terms, 94n1951
Handbook of drinking water quality, 91n1784
Water ency, 2d ed, 91n1785

WATER BIRDS
Birds: the waterbirds, 90n1519
Field gd to the waterbirds of Asia, 94n1692
Wildfowl of the world, 90n1543

WATER SPORTS. See AQUATIC SPORTS

WATER QUALITY
Elsevier's dict of hydrology & water quality mgmt, 93n1724
Water quality & availability, 94n1954

WATER REUSE
Dictionary of water & wastewater treatment trademarks & brand names, 93n1772

WATER SOLUBLE POLYMERS
Water-soluble resins, 2d ed, 93n1713

WATER, UNDERGROUND
Groundwater chemicals field gd, 93n1771
Wastewater treatment tech, 90n1794

WATERCOLOR PAINTING
Encyclopedia of watercolor techniques, 92n1001

WATER-JET
Waterjet cutting, 92n1629

WATERLOO (ONT.)
Guide to histl resources in the regional municipality of Waterloo, 90n513

WATER-SUPPLY
Water quality & availability, 94n1954

WATSON, IAN
Work of Ian Watson, 91n1220

WAUGH, EVELYN
Reader's companion to the novels & short stories of Evelyn Waugh, 90n1188

WAYNE, JOHN
John Wayne: a bio-bibliog, 93n1320

WEALTH
Who's wealthy in America 1993, 94n211

WEAPONS SYSTEMS
Jane's underwater warefare systems 1989-90, 91n710
Naval Institute gd to world naval weapons systems, 91n696
U.S. combat: America's land-based weaponry, 91n711

WEATHER
Peterson 1st gd to clouds & weather, 92n1732
Weather almanac, 6th ed, 93n1722
Weather hndbk, 92n1735
Weather of US cities, 4th ed, 94n1947

WEBER, CARL MARIA VON
Carl Maria von Weber: a gd to research, 91n1274

WEBER, MAX
Max Weber, 90n86
Max Weber: a bio-bibliog, 90n84

WEDDING MUSIC
Wedding music, 93n1266

WEEDS
Common & botanical names of weeds in Canada, 1992 ed, 93n1511
Edible garden weeds of Canada, 90n1506
Major weeds of the Near East, 92n1547
Northwest weeds, 92n1548
Weed seeds of the Great Plains, 94n1663
Weeds & words, 90n1445
Weeds of Ky. and adjacent states, 92n1546

WEIGHTS & MEASURES
Quantification in sci, 92n1748
Reading the numbers, 91n1794

WELLES, ORSON
Orson Welles: a bio-bibliog, 91n1361

WELLINGTON, ARTHUR WELLESLEY, DUKE OF
Duke of Wellington 1769-1852, 91n526

WELSH-AMERICANS
Welsh women, 94n950

WELSH LANGUAGE—DICTIONARIES—ENGLISH
Welsh-English, English-Welsh dict, 94n1136

WELTY, EUDORA
Welty collection, 90n1158

WESLEY, JOHN
Wesley quotations, 92n1421

WEST AFRICA. *See* **AFRICA, WEST**

WEST INDIES
Amphibians & reptiles of the W Indies, 93n1579
Caribbean 1975-80, 94n143
Political parties of the Americas, 1980s to 1990s, 94n720
Tinker gd to Latin American & Caribbean policy & scholarly resources in metro NY, 90n138

WEST, REBECCA
Rebecca West: an annot bibliog, 92n1214

WEST (U.S.)
All that the rain promises & more, 92n1542
American garden gdbk west, 90n1470
American west, 90n103
Birds of N America: W region, 90n1530
Burs under the saddle, 90n471
Dictionary of the American West, 94n1088
Encyclopedia of the far west, 92n84
Encyclopedia of W lawmen & outlaws, 93n609
Field gd to the ecology of W forests, 94n1681
Fighting men of the Indian wars, 93n515
Graphic art of Roi Partridge, 90n982
Historic sites & markers along the Mormon & other great W trails, 90n435
Historical atlas of the American west, 90n466
Northwest weeds, 92n1548
Peoples of the American west, 90n1080
Smithsonian gd to historic America: the Plains states, 91n464
Tour gd to the old west, 2d ed, 91n457
Trail west: a bibliog-index to w American trails, 90n448
Trees of the west, 93n1517
Twentieth-century W writers, 2d ed, 92n1153
Western reader's gd, 94n88
Western series & sequels, 2d ed, 94n1221
Who's who in the west 1989-90, 91n25
Wildflowers of the west, 93n1503
Women in the west, 93n941

WESTERN FILMS
B western actors ency, 90n1341
Guide to silent westerns, 94n1443
Shoot-em-ups ride again, 92n1367
Spaghetti westerns, 93n1367
Sweethearts of the sage, 93n1361

WESTERN STORIES
Western fiction in the LC classification scheme, 90n598
Western series & sequels, 2d ed, 94n1221
Work of Louis L'Amour, 93n1176

WETLAND FLORA
Field gd to coastal wetland plants of the SE US, 94n1661

WETLANDS
Wetland economics & assessment, 90n1514

WHALES
Field gd to whales, porpoises, & seals from Cape Cod to Nfld., 4th ed, 94n1737
Guide to the photographic identification of individual whales based on their natural & acquired markings, 91n1595
Mammals: primates, insect eaters & baleen whales, 90n1520
Where the whales are, 92n1582

WHARTON, EDITH
Edith Wharton: a descriptive bibliog, 92n1183
Edith Wharton: an annot secondary bibliog, 91n1175

WHAT MAISIE KNEW
Concordance to Henry James's What Maisie Knew, 91n1165

WHITE-WATER CANOEING
Whitewater sourcebk, 90n443

WHITMAN, WALT
Walt Whitman: a descriptive bibliog, 94n1241

WHITNEY MUSEUM OF AMERICAN ART
Annual & biennial exhibition record of the Whitney Museum of American Art 1918-89, 92n977

WHOLESALE TRADE
American wholesalers & distrs dir, 93n245

WIDMARK, RICHARD
Richard Widmark: a bio-bibliog, 91n1356

WIFE ABUSE
Battered wives, 90n577

WILBERFORCE, WILLIAM
William Wilberforce 1759-1833: a bibliog, 93n771

WILBUR, RICHARD
Richard Wilbur: a ref gd, 93n1184

WILD FLOWER GARDENING
Encyclopaedia of Australian plants suitable for cultivation, v.5, 92n1504

WILD FLOWERS
Alpine wildflowers of the Rocky Mountains, 91n1525
Eastern wildflowers, 90n1493
Fall wildflowers of N.Mex., 90n1496
History & folklore of N American wildflowers, 94n1651
Meet the natives: the amateur's field gd to Rocky Mountain wildflowers, trees & shrubs, 9th ed, 93n1505
National wildflower research center's wildflower hndbk, 90n1497
Roadside wildflowers of the S Great Plains, 92n1536
Sagebrush country, 94n1660
Southern wildflowers, 91n1528
Spring wildflowers, 94n1659
Wild flowers, 91n1526
Wildflowers around the world, 92n1539
Wildflowers for all seasons, 90n1498
Wildflowers of Miss., 91n1530
Wildflowers of Prince Edward Island, 94n1650
Wildflowers of the central south, 92n1537
Wildflowers of the tallgrass prairie: the upper midwest, 90n1499
Wildflowers of the W plains, 94n1655
Wildflowers of the west, 93n1503

WILD PLANTS, EDIBLE
Edible garden weeds of Canada, 90n1506
Edible wild fruits & nuts of Canada, 90n1507

WILDE, OSCAR
Oscar Wilde: an annot bibliog, 94n1262

WILDER, ALEC
Alec Wilder: a bio-bibliog, 94n1324

WILDER, THORNTON
Thornton Wilder: a ref gd 1926-90, 94n1242

WILDERNESS AREAS
America's secret recreation areas, 94n476
Big outside, rev ed, 94n1678
Changing wilderness values, 1930-90, 92n1767
U.S. outdoor atlas & recreation gd, 93n497

WILDERNESS SURVIVAL
Wilderness U: opportunities for outdoor educ in the US & abroad, 93n335

WILDLIFE. *See* **ANIMALS; ZOOLOGY**

WILDLIFE CONSERVATION
Atlas of endangered animals, 94n1686
Endangered wildlife of the world, 94n1676
Grolier world ency of endangered species, 94n1680
Guide to Michigan's endangered wildlife, 94n1677
Saving endangered mammals, 94n1738

WILDLIFE DISEASES
Parasites & diseases of wild mammals in Fla., 93n1569

WILDLIFE REFUGES
Guide to the natl wildlife refuges, rev ed, 94n1683
Where the animals are, 94n1688

WILDLIFE WATCHING
Mammals of the central Rockies, 94n1741
Northwoods wildlife, 90n1512
Watching Kans. wildlife, 94n1679

WILKINSON, TATE
Yorkshire stage 1766-1803, 90n1355

WILLIAMS, TENNESSEE
Tennessee Williams: a bibliog, 2d ed, 93n1185

WILLS
Affairs in order, 92n817
American wills & admins in the Prerogative Court of Canterbury, 1610-1857, 90n389

WILSON, ANGUS
Angus Wilson: a bibliog 1947-87, 90n1189

WILSON, COLIN
Work of Colin Wilson, 91n1221

WILSON, WOODROW
Woodrow Wilson: a bibliog of his times & presidency, 91n728

WIND ENSEMBLES
American Wind Symphony commissioning project, 93n1284

WINE & WINE MAKING
Buyer's gd to American wines, 2d ed, 94n1605
California's great chardonnays, 92n1496
Hugh Johnson's modern ency of wine, 3d ed, 92n1488
Hugh Johnson's pocket ency of wine 1992, 93n1474
Master dict of food & wine, 91n1486
Oz Clarke's new ency of French wines, 92n1484
Simon & Schuster pocket gd to fortified & dessert wines, 91n1493

WINERIES
California wine winners 1989, 91n1488

WISCONSIN
Awesome almanac—Wis., 94n83
Wisconsin birdlife, 92n1567

WISEMAN, ADELE
Adele Wiseman: an annot bibliog, 94n1277

WIT & HUMOR
Directory of humor mags & humor orgs in America (& Canada), 2d ed, 90n907

Directory of humor mags & humor orgs in America (& Canada), 3d ed, 93n1188
Humor & cartoon markets 1990, 91n948
Humor scholarship, 94n1304
Literature of delight, 94n1169
1001 quips & quotes for bus speeches, 93n219
Treasury of humor, 90n1121
Witty words, 94n70

WITCHCRAFT
Encyclopedia of witches & witchcraft, 90n755
Magic, witchcraft, & paganism in America, 2d ed, 93n811

WITTLIFF, WILLIAM D.
William D. Wittliff & the Encino Pr, 91n657

WODEHOUSE, P. G.
P. G. Wodehouse: a comprehensive bibliog & checklist, 92n1215

WOLFRAM VON ESCHENBACH
Complete concordance to Wolfram Von Eschenbach's Parzival, 91n1234

WOMEN
African women: a general bibliog, 1976-85, 90n850
AIDS & women, 92n1680
Annotated index of medieval women, 93n933
A-to-Z of women's sexuality, rev ed, 93n884
Bibliography of writings by & about women in photography 1850-1950, 92n959
Biographies of American women, 91n920
Book of women, 93n935
Book of women's firsts, 94n970
Canadian feminist thesaurus, 91n620
Directory of financial aids for women 1989-90, 90n874
Directory of women's funds 1988, 90n873
Education of women in the US, 93n926
European women's almanac, 94n947
Fact bk on women in higher educ, 92n311
Female psychology, 93n797
Feminist legal lit, 92n853
Feminist research methods, 92n857
Handbook of American women's hist, 91n929
Handbook of behavioral medicine for women, 90n1663
Index to women of the world from ancient to modern times, suppl, 90n878
International hndbk of women's educ, 90n876
Journal of Women's Hist gd to per lit, 93n943
Latinas of the Americas, 90n863
Lesser-known women, 93n934
Modern first ladies, 90n484
National gd to funding for women & girls, 92n865
Native American women, 94n956
New A-to-Z of women's health, 90n1675
Past & promise: lives of N.J. women, 91n923
Portraits of American women, 93n932
Presidents' wives, 90n485
Quotable woman, 92n870
Remember the ladies, 94n959
Shadowcatchers: a dir of women in Calif. photography before 1901, 92n960
Statistical hndbk on women in America, 92n867
Statistical record of women worldwide, 92n866
United States govt docs on women, 1800-1990, 94n951
Victorian American women 1840-80, 93n927
We shall be heard, 90n879
Welsh women, 94n950
Who's who of American women 1991-92, 93n56
Womanwords, 93n938
Women & aging, 93n928
Women & AIDS, 94n1855
Women in English social hist 1800-1914, v.1, 91n915
Women in English social hist 1800-1914, v.2, 90n860
Women in Japanese society, 93n925
Women in the west, 93n941
Women into the unknown, 90n870
Women of classical mythology, 92n1320
Women of color in the US, 90n862

Women of E and S Africa, 90n851
Women of N, W, and central Africa, 90n852
Women outdoors, 92n851
Women patriots of the American Revolution, 92n461
Women working in nontraditional fields, 92n860
Women's archives gd, 92n852
Women's diaries, journals, & letters, 90n853
Women's educ in the Third World, 90n861
Women's ency of health & emotional healing, 94n1805
Women's health perspectives, v.2, 90n877
Women's info dir, 94n968
Women's issues: an annot bibliog, 91n916
Women's movements of the world, 90n875
Women's recovery progams, 91n890
Women's studies: a gd to info sources, 91n912
Women's studies ency, v.3, 93n939
World who's who of women, 9th ed, 90n35
World who's who of women, 11th ed, 94n963

WOMEN, AFRO-AMERICAN. *See* AFRO-AMERICAN WOMEN

WOMEN & LITERATURE
American women playwrights, 1900-30, 93n1167
American women playwrights 1964-89, 94n1228
American women's fiction 1790-1870, 91n1155
Bibliographical gd to African-American women writers, 94n1223
Black American women novelists, 91n1149
British women writers, 90n864
Female bildungsroman in English, 91n1130
Mothers & daughters in American short fiction, 94n1219
Shakespeare & feminist criticism, 93n1212
Silk stalkings: when women write of murder, 90n1107
War & peace through women's eyes, 93n1169
Women & the lit of the 17th century, 91n1182

WOMEN & RELIGION
Goddesses & wise women, 93n923

WOMEN & THE MILITARY
American women & the US armed forces, 93n707

WOMEN ARTISTS
American women artists past & present, v.2, 90n865
Biographical dict of Sask. artists: women artists, 92n969
Biographical dict of women artists in Europe & America since 1850, 91n1007
Women artists in the US, 91n928

WOMEN ATHLETES
American women in sport, 1887-1987, 90n758
Great women athletes of the 20th century, 93n815
Outstanding women athletes, 93n818

WOMEN AUTHORS
Bibliography of women & lit, 90n849
Bloomsbury gd to women's lit, 93n942
Confidence woman, 93n936
Drama by women to 1990, 93n1146
Encyclopedia of continental women writers, 92n1232
Feminist companion to lit in English, 92n1095
More than 100: women sci fiction writers, 90n866
Personal writings by women to 1900, 90n855
Silk stalkings: when women write of murder, 90n1107
Spanish American women writers, 91n1246
Women in English social hist 1800-1914, v.2, 90n860
Women writers of Germany, Austria, & Switzerland, 90n856

WOMEN AUTHORS, AMERICAN
Alice Walker: an annot bibliog 1968-86, 90n1157
American women writers on Vietnam, 91n1145
American women's fiction 1790-1870, 91n1155
Black American women in lit, 90n858
Modern American women writers, 92n1158

WOMEN AUTHORS, ENGLISH
Biographical dict of English women writers 1580-1720, 91n1183
British women writers, 90n864
Checklist of women writers 1801-1900, 92n1189
George Eliot: a ref gd 1972-87, 91n1207

WOMEN AUTHORS, FRENCH
French women writers, 93n1222
Simone de Beauvoir: a bibliog, 93n930

WOMEN AUTHORS, JAPANESE
Japanese women writers in English translation, 90n1206
Women in Japanese society, 93n925

WOMEN AUTHORS, SPANISH AMERICAN
Women authors of modern Hispanic S America, 91n1242

WOMEN CHEMISTS
Women in chemistry & physics, 94n1923

WOMEN CIVIL RIGHTS WORKERS
American women civil rights activists, 94n592

WOMEN COMPOSERS
American women songwriters, 94n1325
Musical woman, v.3, 92n1257
Organ & harpsichord music by women composers, 92n1266
Piano music by black women, 93n1264
Violin music by women composers, 91n1277
Women composers, 90n859

WOMEN—CRIMES AGAINST
Violence against women, 94n596

WOMEN DETECTIVES IN LITERATURE
Female detectives in American novels, 94n1208

WOMEN DRAMATISTS
American women playwrights, 1900-30, 93n1167

WOMEN ENTERTAINERS
Notable women in the American theatre, 91n924

WOMEN ENVIRONMENTALISTS
Making a world of difference, 91n926

WOMEN HEADS OF HOUSEHOLDS
Feminization of poverty in the US, 91n913

WOMEN HEADS OF STATE
Women prime ministers & presidents, 94n714
Women who ruled, 91n921

WOMEN IMMIGRANTS
Immigrant women in the US, 91n914

WOMEN IN BUSINESS
International who's who of professional & bus women, 2d ed, 94n958
National dir of women-owned bus firms, 1990 ed, 91n146
United States business hist, 1602-1988, 91n130

WOMEN IN CHRISTIANITY
Women & religion: a bibliographic gd to Christian feminist liberation theology, 92n1405

WOMEN IN CIVIL SERVICE
Career advancement for women in the fed serv, 94n270

WOMEN IN INFORMATION SCIENCE
On account of sex 1982-86, 91n919
On account of sex 1987-92, 94n949

WOMEN IN LIBRARY SCIENCE
On account of sex 1982-86, 91n919
On account of sex 1987-92, 94n949

WOMEN IN LITERATURE
Bibliography of women & lit, 90n849
Bloomsbury gd to women's lit, 93n942
Female bildungsroman in English, 91n1130
Heroines, 91n1129

WOMEN IN MOTION PICTURES
Working women on the Hollywood screen, 90n857

WOMEN IN POLITICS
Who's who of women in world pols, 93n937
Women prime ministers & presidents, 94n714

WOMEN IN SCIENCE
Women in chemistry & physics, 94n1923

Women scientists, 93n1441

WOMEN IN TECHNOLOGY
Mothers & daughters of invention, 94n1586
Women & tech, 94n948

WOMEN IN TELEVISION BROADCASTING
Black women in TV, 92n855

WOMEN IN THE THEATER
Dramatic re-visions, 93n1333
Notable women in the American theatre, 91n924

WOMEN INTERNATIONAL SPECIALISTS
Making a world of difference, 91n926

WOMEN MURDERERS
Women serial & mass murderers, 93n612

WOMEN ORATORS
We shall be heard, 90n879
Women public speakers in the US, 1800-1925, 94n957

WOMEN PHILOSOPHERS
Simone de Beauvoir, 90n1370
Women philosophers: a bibliog of bks through 1990, 93n1392
Women philosophers: a bio-critical source bk, 90n868

WOMEN POETS
Anne Bradstreet: a ref gd, 91n1157
Denise Levertov: an annot primary & secondary bibliog, 90n1150
Emily Dickinson: a bibliog of secondary sources, 90n1136
Poetry by American women, 1975-89, 92n1187
Poetry by women to 1900, 92n1245
Sylvia Plath: a ref gd 1973-88, 91n1170

WOMEN PSYCHOLOGISTS
Women in psychology, 91n918

WOMEN—QUOTATIONS
Beacon bk of quotations by women, 94n972
New quotable woman, rev. ed, 94n973
Write to the heart, 93n944

WOMEN SCULPTORS
American women sculptors, 92n1005

WOMEN SOCIAL REFORMERS
Women public speakers in the US, 1800-1925, 94n957

WOMEN SOCIAL SCIENTISTS
Making a world of difference, 91n926

WOMEN—SOCIETIES & CLUBS
NWO: a dir of natl women's orgs, 93n940

WOMEN SOCIOLOGISTS
Women in sociology, 93n844

WOMEN SOLDIERS
Encyclopedia of amazons, 92n862

WOMEN—SOVIET UNION
Women & writing in Russian & the USSR, 93n1230

WOMEN TRACK & FIELD ATHLETES
Black American women in Olympic track & field, 93n843

WOMEN TRAVELERS
Wayward women: a gd to women travellers, 91n454

WOMEN VOLUNTEERS IN SOCIAL SERVICE
History of American women's voluntary orgs, 1810-1960, 90n848

WOMEN'S HEALTH SERVICES
Abstracts of active projects FY 1990, 91n1671
Directory of women's health care centers, 90n1616
Maternal & child health legislation: 1991, 93n594
Reaching out, 91n1649

WOMEN'S LIBERATION MOVEMENT. See FEMINISM

WOMEN'S PERIODICALS
American women's mags, 90n880
Sources on the hist of women's mags, 1792-1960, 92n861

WOMEN'S RIGHTS
American women's mags, 90n880

WOMEN'S STUDIES
Canadian women's movement, 1960-90, 94n966
Directory of women's studies programs & lib resources, 91n927
Feminism & women's issues, 92n859
Sources: an annot bibliog of women's issues, 92n856
WAVE: women's audio-visuals in English, 94n954
WIP: a dir of work-in-progress & recent pubs, 93n924
Women of color & S women annual suppl, 1991/92, 94n955
Women, race, & ethnicity, 93n931
Women's studies ency, 90n872
Women's studies ency, v.2, 92n863
Women's studies in India, 94n953
Women's studies index 1989, 92n869
Women's studies research hndbk, 3d ed, 92n864

WOOD
Concise ency of wood & wood-based materials, 91n1495
Encyclopedia of wood, 90n1465

WOOD PRODUCTS
Directory of the wood products industry, 1993, 94n1616

WOODWIND INSTRUMENTS
Woodwind music of black composers, 91n1276

WOODWORK
Encyclopedia of wood joints, 94n1030
Home building & woodworking in colonial America, 93n1612
Woodworker's dict, 92n1630

WOODWORKING TOOLS
Dictionary of woodworking tools c.1700-1970, rev ed, 91n1637
Illustrated ency of woodworking handtools instruments & devices, rev ed, 93n1610

WOODY PLANTS
Seeds of woody plants in N America, rev ed, 93n1521
Weeds of the woods, 93n1515

WOOLF, VIRGINIA
Concordance to the novels of Virginia Woolf, 92n1216

WORDS, NEW
Facts on File dict of new words, 90n1003
Family words, 90n1009
Fifty yrs among the new words, 93n1064
Futurespeak, 92n1145
New new words dict, rev ed, 90n1004
Oxford dict of new words, 93n1065
Third Barnhart dict of new English, 91n1059
Trash cash, fizzbos, & flatliners, 94n1095

WORK
Sociology of work, 91n244

WORK EXPERIENCE. See APPRENTICES

WORKING CLASS. See LABOR & LABORING CLASSES

WORLD BANK
World Bank depository lib program dir of libs, 90n626
World Bank group, 92n191
World Bank group dir, Sept 1990, 91n220

WORLD CUP (SOCCER)
World Cup 1930-90, 92n801

WORLD HEALTH
ACCIS gd to UN info sources on health, 94n1811

WORLD HISTORY. See also GEOGRAPHY
Atlas of 20th century world hist, 92n497
Children's atlas of world hist, 90n527
Chronicle of the world, 91n499
Encyclopedia of the First World, 91n85
Europa world yr bk 1989, 90n91
Great lives from hist: Renaissance to 1900 series, 91n549
Great lives from hist: 20th century series, 91n550
Guinness bk of records 1492, 93n558
Illustrated almanac of histl facts, 93n553

NBC News Rand McNally world news atlas, 1990 ed, 91n543
People in world hist, 1989 ed, 90n537
Power brokers, 90n481
Read more about it, v.3, 91n555
Times atlas of world hist, 4th ed, 94n530
World fact file, 92n83
World factbk 1991-92, 93n105
World hist for children & young adults, 93n561

WORLD HISTORY—CHRONOLOGY. *See* **CHRONOLOGY, HISTORICAL**

WORLD LITERATURE. *See* **LITERATURE**

WORLD POLITICS. *See also* **INTERNATIONAL RELATIONS**
Annual dir of world leaders 1988-89, 90n681
Annual register 1991, 93n725
Atlas of world affairs, 9th ed, 93n720
Atlas of world pol flashpoints, 94n794
Big Powers & the German question, 1941-90, 93n538
Chronology of conflict & resolution, 1945-85, 90n650
Countries of the world & their leaders yrbk 1989, 91n84
Countries of the world & their leaders yrbk 1993, 94n723
Current leaders of nations, 92n671
Dictionary of world pols, 92n673
Directory of world leaders & factbk, 1990 ed, 91n723
Europa world yr bk 1992, 94n82
Facts on File world pol almanac, 90n679
Facts on File world pol almanac, 2d ed, 93n719
Federal systems of the world, 93n726
Global/intl issues & problems, 90n685
Handbook of the nations, 10th ed, 92n676
Historic docs index, 1972-89, 92n702
Historic docs of 1990, 92n703
International armed conflict since 1945, 92n661
International dir of govt, 91n719
Names of countries & their capital cities, 93n104
New state of the world atlas, 4th ed, 93n475
Oxford companion to pols of the world, 94n717
Political hndbk of the world 1989, 91n722
Rand McNally world facts & maps, 90n424
Revolutionary & dissident movements, 3d ed, 93n728
Statesman's yr-bk histl companion, 90n709
Statesmen who changed the world, 94n716
Strategic atlas, rev. ed, 91n714
Strategic atlas, 3d ed, 94n712
World fact file, 92n83
World factbk 1991-92, 93n105
World news digest, v.1, no.2, 90n93
World tech policies, 94n1587
Worldwide govt dir 1990, 91n721
Worldwide govt dir 1992, 93n724

WORLD RECORDS
Book of women's firsts, 94n970
Guinness bk of records 1492, 93n558
Guinness bk of records 1991, 91n1337
Guinness bk of records 1993, 94n1401
Guinness bk of world records, 1990, 90n1308
Limca bk of records 1991, 93n1310
Number 1 in the USA, 2d ed, 92n1330

WORLD SERIES (BASEBALL)
Forgotten championships, 90n768

WORLD WAR, 1914-1918
American field serv archives of WW I, 1914-17, 90n657
Chronicle of the 1st World War, v.1, 92n504
Chronicle of the 1st World War, v.2, 93n551
Great battles of WW I, 90n658
Pivotal conflict: a comprehensive chronology of the 1st world war, 1914-19, 93n552
Women in the 1st & 2d world wars, 90n871
World War I source bk, 94n540

WORLD WAR, 1939-1945
Battles & battlescenes of WW II, 90n655
Battles of Coral Sea & Midway, 1942, 93n695

Canada's army in WW II, 94n702
Central Pacific campaign, 1943-44, 91n677
Chronological atlas of WW II, 90n646
Chronology & index of the 2d World War, 1938-45, 91n552
Dictionary of the 2d World War, 91n554
Encyclopedia of the 2d World War, 90n653
France under the German occupation, 1940-44, 92n491
Investigations of the attack on Pearl Harbor, 91n510
Japanese naval aces & fighter units in WW II, 91n511
Month-by-month atlas of WW II, 91n544
Nazi-retro film, 93n1362
Normandy campaign, 1944, 94n531
Novels of WW II: an annot bibliog, 94n1205
Novels of WW II: an annot bibliog of WW II fiction, 91n1131
Oral hist of contemporary Jewry, 91n408
Pearl Harbor, 1941, 93n696
Subject bibliog of the 2d World War, & aftermath, 91n547
War against Japan, 1941-45, 91n486
Women in the 1st & 2d world wars, 90n871
World in turmoil, 93n550
World War II: America at war 1941-45, 93n556
World War II at sea, 91n699

WOUNDS & INJURIES
Orthopedic & trauma surgery, 90n1665

WRESTLING
Encyclopedia of American wrestling, 91n840
Wrestling college & univ dir, 2d ed, 94n862

WRITERS' UNION OF CANADA
Who's who in the Writers' Union of Canada, 4th ed, 94n998

WRITING CENTERS
AWP official gd to writing programs, 6th ed, 94n993

WYOMING
Wyoming birds, 92n1562

XENOPHON
Bibliography of eds, translations, & commentary on Xenophon's Socratic writings, 90n1373

XERISCAPING
Shade & color with water-conserving plants, 93n1520

YALE UNIVERSITY LIBRARY
Guide to Yale Univ Lib Holocaust video testimonies, 91n521

YEARBOOKS
College media dir 1989, 90n891
World Book yr bk 1989, 90n55

YEATS, W. B. (WILLIAM BUTLER)
W. B. Yeats: a census of the mss, 92n1238
W. B. Yeats: a classified bibliog of criticism, 2d ed, 92n1217

YIDDISH LANGUAGE
Joys of Yinglish, 90n1062

YIDDISH LANGUAGE—DICTIONARIES—ENGLISH
English-Yiddish, Yiddish-English dict, 93n1105
Harduf's transliterated Yiddish-English dict, 4th v., 94n1137
Transliterated English-Yiddish, Yiddish-English dict, 93n1106

YOGA
Encyclopedic dict of yoga, 91n1405

YOUNG ADULT FICTION
Fiction index for readers 10 to 16, 94n1196
Fiction sequels for readers 10 to 16, 92n1115
Portraying persons with disabilities: an annot bibliog of fiction, 3d ed, 93n1132
Supernatural fiction for teens, 2d ed, 93n1156
Twins in children's & adolescent lit, 94n1183

YOUNG ADULT FILMS
Best videos for children & young adults, 92n617

YOUNG ADULT LITERATURE. See also CHILDREN'S LITERATURE
Adoption lit for children & young adults, 93n868
Author profile collection, 93n1138
Authors & artists for young adults, v.1, 90n1091
Authors & artists for young adults, v.2, 90n1092
Authors & artists for young adults, v.6, 92n1126
Award-winning bks for children & young adults, 91n1110
Best bks for sr high readers, 92n1117
Biographical index to children's & young adult authors & illustrators, 93n1144
Books by African-American authors & illustrators for children & young adults, 92n1122
Books for the teen age 1990, 91n362
Books for you, 11th ed, 94n1165
Characters from young adult lit, 93n1143
Fantasy lit for children & young adults, 3d ed, 90n1083
From page to screen, 93n1359
High interest easy reading, 6th ed, 91n366
Indian subcontinent in lit for children & young adults, 93n1126
Juniorplots 4, 94n1192
Literature for young people on war & peace, 90n1081
Masterplots 2: juvenile & young adult fiction series, 92n1128
Olderr's young adult fiction index 1988, 90n1097
100 world-class thin bks, 94n1164
Our family, our friends, our world, 93n1127
Portraying persons with disabilities: an annot bibliog of nonfiction, 2d ed, 93n1124
Read for your life, 94n383
Rip-roaring reads for reluctant teen readers, 94n1182
Seniorplots, 90n1093
Soviet Union in lit, 92n1229
Speaking for ourselves, 91n1118
Speaking for ourselves, too, 94n1186
Teens' favorite bks, 94n1175
University pr bks for public & secondary school libs 1991, 93n664
War & peace lit for children & young adults, 94n1185
Writers for young adults, 3d ed, 90n1098
Young adult 1991 annual bklist, 93n1136
Young adult reader's adviser, 93n1137
Young people's bks in series, 93n1133
Young reader's companion, 94n1189

YOUNG ADULT LITERATURE—BIBLIOGRAPHY—BEST BOOKS
Award-winning bks for children & young adults 1990-91, 94n1166
Children's bk awards intl, 94n1195

YOUNG ADULT LITERATURE, SPANISH
Books in Spanish for children & young adults, series 5, 90n1085
Books in Spanish for children & young adults, series 6, 94n1180

YOUNG ADULTS—BOOKS & READING
Behind the covers, v.2, 90n1087
Storytelling for young adults, 92n626

YOUNG, LESTER
You got to be original, man!, 91n1315

YOUTH
Contemporary Canadian childhood & youth, 94n924
Directory of American youth orgs 1990-91, 91n895
History of Canadian childhood & youth, 94n925
Substance abuse, 90n1650

YOUTH HOSTELS
International youth hostel hndbk 1991-92, v.1, 92n436
International youth hostel hndbk 1991-92, v.2, 92n437

YOUTH PERIODICALS
Magazines for young people, 2d ed, 93n84

YUCATAN PENINSULA
Archaeological gd to Mexico's Yucatan peninsula, 94n481

YUGOSLAV LITERATURE
First suppl to a comp bibliog of Yugoslav lit in English 1981-85, 90n1212
Second suppl to a comp bibliog of Yugoslav lit in English 1986-90, 93n1234

YUGOSLAVIA
Marshal Tito: a bibliog, 91n537
Yugoslav linguistics in English 1900-80, 92n1008
Yugoslavia: a comprehensive English-lang bibliog, 94n139

ZAIRE
Adventuring in E Africa, 91n465
Historical dict of Zaire, 90n114

ZEBROWSKI, GEORGE
Work of George Zebrowski, 2d ed, 92n1185

ZIMBABWE
Historical dict of Zimbabwe, 2d ed, 92n91

ZIONISM
Palestine question, 92n726
Soviet pubns on Judaism, Zionism, & the state of Israel 1984-88, 91n407

ZIP CODE
Instant natl locator gd, 93n955
Rand McNally zip code atlas & market planner, 2d ed, 91n147

ZOO ANIMALS
Where the animals are, 94n1688
Zoo animals, 91n1554

ZOOGEOGRAPHY
Children's animal atlas, 93n1531

ZOOLOGY
Animal life, 94n1685
Concise Oxford dict of zoology, 93n1529
Field gd to wildlife in Tex. & the Southwest, 90n1525
Illustrated ency of wildlife, 92n1559
Key works to the fauna & flora of the British Isles & NW Europe, 5th ed, 90n1495
Marshall Cavendish intl wildlife ency, 90n1515
Marshall Cavendish intl wildlife ency, rev ed, 91n1555
Spectrum guides: African wildlife safaris, 90n1527
Wild animals of W Canada, 93n1533